Chambers Dictionary of the Unexplained

Editor

Una McGovern

Chambers

CHAMBERS
An imprint of Chambers Harrap Publishers Ltd
7 Hopetoun Crescent
Edinburgh
EH7 4AY

First published by Chambers Harrap Publishers Ltd 2007

A CIP catalogue record for this book is available from the British Library.

ISBN-13: 978 0550 10215 7 (hardback edition)
ISBN-13: 978 0550 10395 6 (laminated cased cover edition)

Designed and typeset by Chambers Harrap Publishers Ltd, Edinburgh
Printed and bound in Singapore by Tien Wah Press

Contributors

Editor
Una McGovern

Specialist Consultant
Bob Rickard

Contributors
David V Barrett
Lorna Gilmour
David Hambling
Simon Hill
Michael Munro
Alan Murdie
Jenny Randles
Bob Rickard
Gordon Rutter
Dr Karl P N Shuker

Specialist Panel Contributors
David V Barrett (Cults, New Religious Movements and Alternative Religions; Heretical Sects;
Religion; Secret Societies)
Paul Devereux (Earth Mysteries; Megaliths)
David Hambling (Fringe Science)
Peter Lamont (Parapsychology)
Steve Moore (Friday the 13th)
Alan Murdie (Ghosts)
Jenny Randles (Ufology)
Bob Rickard (Chance and Coincidence; Forteanism; Hoaxes and Hoaxers; Scepticism)
Dr Karl P N Shuker (Cryptozoology)

Publishing Manager
Camilla Rockwood

Proofreaders
Jennifer Speake
Wendy Toole

Picture Research
Una McGovern

Prepress Controller
Becky Pickard

Preface

Depending upon which opinion poll you take, modern belief in UFOs, ghosts, psychic powers, astrology, luck, fairies, Atlantis and life after death – to name a few of the more popular subjects – has never been stronger. I am often asked if, generally, interest in the paranormal and the 'unexplained' is increasing; this is difficult to assess as a proper study has yet to be done. What we can say, with some certainty, is that personal and public discussion – augmented by media coverage, entertainment shows, book sales and the Internet – is at an unprecedented level of openness, where, previously, such interests were preferably private or the province of dedicated groups. Few have the time or opportunity to research in the depth and breadth necessary to answer their questions, or even to put them in context. Also, the more aware people are of these subjects, the more they are likely to be interested in historical precedent, inter-connections, current research and attempts at explanation. We hope that this dictionary will give them some help.

Given the extent to which the paranormal, in one form or another, pervades modern life the world over – as it has done throughout human history – what are we to make of its extensive and unseen influence on our personal and social lives? Inevitably, in such a wide-ranging forum, the variety and quality of information spans a full spectrum, from deeply personal (but ultimately unverifiable) experiences to the most rigorous of scholarly research papers. Fully represented, too, is the range of positions, from the hostile sceptic to the credulous believer.

Most of our subjects are not science – yet; though some subjects respond more to a scientific approach than others, and the proponents of some anomalous subjects, seeking respectability or scientific approval, try very hard to couch their data in scientific terms. This 'pseudo-science' is rarely successful if the underlying material cannot withstand critical examination. However, it is not helpful to lump this rich mix of subjects, opinions and data together and

dismiss it as time-wasting nonsense, as some hostile sceptics do. Nor can they all be the product of wilful attempts to deceive and defraud. Yet we must always be aware of the possibility of misidentification and misinterpretation in observational data, and of delusion and pious fraud in its interpretation.

I used the word 'yet' above because there are things incorporated into modern science, medicine and engineering that were once regarded (often by the best minds of the day) as something only uneducated peasants would believe in. One only has to think of Galileo's heliocentric heresy, of meteorites (officially rejected by the French Academy of Sciences in 1790 and not accepted until 1840), of Wegener's theory of continental drift (never accepted in his lifetime), of the ridicule heaped upon Edison's first light bulbs, of Pasteur's theory of germs, of Logie Baird (the inventor of television) who was judged 'a swindler' at first, of the gorilla (known since Roman times but only accepted in 1847), of ball lightning (a well-observed physical phenomenon, the nature of which is still in dispute), and of countless modern pharmaceuticals that once were known only to tribal healers. This brief list could be expanded, but it serves to illustrate two important points: firstly, that scientific knowledge grows by assimilating data it once excluded; and secondly, the value of the study of anomalies themselves.

But – when faced with such a vast and undisciplined subject field, with so many 'equal and opposite' experts – how is the ordinary person to distinguish what is real and lasting from what is misleading or wrong? Two and a half millennia ago, Gautama Buddha answered this dilemma by encouraging a true spirit of inquiry. The villagers of Kalama complained to him of their confusion at the endless procession of mystics, gurus and teachers through their village, each with a seemingly different message. The Buddha replied that doubt was the proper response, and that it is wise to make a proper examination before committing to any belief. As paraphrased from the Pali *Kalama Sutta*, he advised: 'Do not be led by what you are told. Do not be led by whatever has been handed down from past generations. Do not be led by hearsay or common opinion. Do not be led by what the scriptures say. Do not be led by mere logic. Do not be led by mere deduction or inference. Do not be led by considering only outward appearance. Do not be led by preconceived notions. Do not be led by what seems acceptable or believable. Do not be led by what your teacher tells you is so.'

Today the paranormal field is replete with its own self-professed 'experts', and I find Buddha's answer to be wholly appropriate and sensible when facing the bewildering range of opinions, conundrums and complexities of the 'paranormal'. My own mentor Charles Fort expressed the same advice: question everything, including authority. Test the data and opinions of others as far as you can, selecting what seems trustworthy and durable. This is pretty much the approach approved by science. Children's minds can be inoculated against all sorts of bunkum, nonsense and superstition if they are taught, as early as practical, to think for themselves, clearly, critically and decisively. Even so, caution must be married to enthusiasm, and curiosity about this wonderful universe in which we exist creatively encouraged. A true sceptic is never afraid to say: 'I don't know.' To which Fort would add: 'But I'll find out.'

Bob Rickard

Introduction

The areas of human experience that might loosely be categorized as 'the unexplained' have always exerted a widespread fascination. Indeed, the development of our understanding of the universe could be described as a series of attempts to 'explain the unexplained'. However, despite several centuries of rational, empirical scientific endeavour, there is still a vast (and growing) number of occurrences and beliefs that have been neither satisfactorily explained, nor satisfactorily explained away.

In this book we have gathered together information relating to a wide range of subjects that sit on the edge of, or even wholly outside, the widely accepted beliefs about the nature of the world in which we live. Our aim in doing this has been to provide a comprehensive, reliable general reference work, a first port of call for anyone with an interest in any of the areas of what might be described as the paranormal, supernatural or simply 'the strange' that could reasonably be expected to be the subject of enquiry. In doing so, we have attempted to set a new standard in an area that is often characterized by bias – siding with neither the credulous believer nor the hardline sceptic. The book gives balanced and authoritative accounts of the facts and opinions relating to individual cases and subject areas within such fields as cryptozoology, earth mysteries, fringe science, the occult, parapsychology, ghosts, ufology and witchcraft; and includes concise summaries of current thought provided by respected researchers.

The space limitations inherent in any attempt to cover such a range of potential material within a single volume have, inevitably, led to difficult decisions. There are, no doubt, countless alternative views as to where the lines could, and should, have been drawn. To ensure that the book remained useful, and easily useable, cases and whole subject areas have had to be omitted, complex subjects have had to be simplified and a certain amount of authority assumed in order to impose a unity of presentation upon such a diverse family of entries. However, every attempt has been made to ensure that the content has been carefully distilled so that compromises have not been made at the expense of essential information.

The dictionary format has been employed, with over 1,250 alphabetically ordered entries covering subjects, concepts, individual cases, occurrences and specialist terms. Each entry is comprehensively cross-referenced, allowing the reader to move easily to related entries to gain a wider understanding. The main text is also interspersed with 24 essay-style panels, giving a thorough overview of significant subject areas, and 30 panels giving entertaining and informative accounts of some of the more intriguing cases.

We hope that this book will serve both the general reader and the more serious student as a trustworthy and useful guide, entertaining and informing in equal measure.

Panels

ABCs *see* ALIEN BIG CATS

abductee *see* ALIEN ABDUCTION

abduction *See* ALIEN ABDUCTION

abominable snowman *See* YETI

acoustic archaeology *see* ARCHAEOACOUSTICS

acronymics
The practice of forming magical or spiritually significant words from the initials of a series of words, often used by kabbalists.

Acronyms, or words formed from the first letters of a series of words, have been widely used in Hebrew since at least the Middle Ages, and acronymics is a prominent feature of kabbalism. Important rabbinical writers were often referred to by acronyms of their names, especially in the Middle Ages, so that *Rabbi Moses ben Nahman* becomes *Ramban*. Jewish scholars teach that the Bible is not meant to be read purely at a surface level, but that there are four levels of meaning to every line: *pshat*, the most basic interpretation of the text; *remez*, a second layer of deeper textual meaning; *drash*, a textual analysis in which analogies and links to various aspects of life can be found; and *sod*, the deepest level of meaning, which contains the Bible's greatest secrets. The study of the 'hints' given in the Bible as hidden allusions and word associations is known as *remazim*, and acronyms are a constant feature of this approach to Torah interpretation. Indeed, the first letters of the names of these four levels of study – P, R, D and S – with the addition of vowel sounds give an acronym, the Hebrew word *pardes*, or paradise; thus, the key to paradise is seen to be the deep study of the Torah on all four levels.

Kabbalists in particular believed that God had encoded secret messages in the Torah, and a fundamental part of KABBALAH is therefore the esoteric study of holy texts. As well as the calculation of the numerical value of words known as GEMATRIA, various forms of wordplay including the formation and interpretation of acronyms are used to reveal the subtle secrets contained in a text. Sometimes the first and last letters of words in a phrase or sentence are combined to create new words or phrases in a special type of acronym formation called notarikon; words and phrases may also be formed by a systematic substitution of letters known as temura, or by reading only letters at a given interval, such as every 50th letter. This type of wordplay is often used in magic to find WORDS OF POWER which can be used for TALISMANS, and to hide secrets inside seemingly innocuous texts.

acupressure
The application of pressure on specific points on the body in order to relieve pain or treat various conditions.

Acupressure is one of the oldest healing traditions in the world, and references to this ancient technique are found in Chinese medical texts dating back as far as 3000 BC. Like ACUPUNCTURE, which it predates, acupressure works on the principle that the body requires a balance of YIN and YANG energy to function properly. An imbalance of yin and yang in some part of the body leads to an excess, deficiency or blockage of the UNIVERSAL LIFE FORCE known as QI which flows through the body, manifesting as physical or emotional symptoms which ultimately lead to illness. The qi flows along channels called MERIDIANS, and the twelve main meridians are connected to specific bodily organs and functions. The complex network which the meridians form throughout the body is thought to pass close to the surface of the skin at hundreds of points, and by manipulating the appropriate 'acupoints' by pressure or massage, the practitioner seeks to remove blockages, correct areas of excess or insufficient qi, and restore the balance and flow of energy.

The tip of the index or middle finger, or the thumb, is used to apply even pressure to the acupoint, usually in the direction of the flow of the meridian. Small, rotating movements are sometimes employed to stimulate the flow of energy and improve the circulation of blood and lymph fluids. Small wooden sticks with rounded ends may also be used for single acupoints, or rollers may be used to apply pressure to several points at once, such as on the back.

Unlike acupuncture, which requires a trained practitioner, acupressure has always been widely used in China as a self-help and first-aid technique by lay people, as well as a complementary therapy when offered by professional physicians. For example, arthritic pain in the elbow or shoulder is said to be alleviated by bending the arm, palm down, and pressing a spot on the inside crease of the elbow with the fingers of the other hand, and acupressure wristbands are commercially available which it is claimed can relieve motion sickness and nausea. See also REFLEXOLOGY; SHIATSU.

acupuncture

The insertion of needles into the skin at specific points in order to relieve pain or treat various conditions; originally Chinese, acupuncture is now used in many countries as a complementary therapy.

Acupuncture, the name of which derives from the Latin *acus*, meaning needle, and *pungere*, to prick, is one of the main branches of CHINESE MEDICINE. This therapeutic technique involves the insertion of needles into the skin at specific points, known as acupoints, in order to relieve pain, alleviate symptoms, or treat certain conditions.

Acupuncture is based on the theory that the body requires a balance of YIN and YANG energy to function properly. An imbalance of yin and yang in some part of the body leads to an excess, deficiency or blockage of the UNIVERSAL LIFE FORCE known as QI which circulates in the body, resulting in physical or emotional symptoms which eventually lead to illness. Qi is believed to circulate through channels called MERIDIANS, with the twelve main meridians having branches connected to various bodily organs and functions. These channels form a network of circuits which run through the body, connecting all its parts.

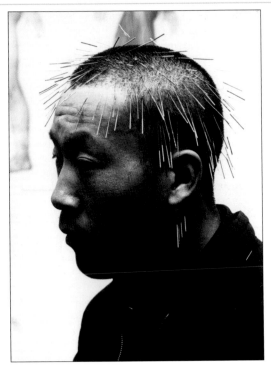

A patient receiving acupuncture at the Tseng I Yen Hospital of Traditional Medicine in Beijing.
(© TopFoto)

Qi moves through the meridians along both internal and external pathways; the meridians enter the body organs and cavities via the internal pathways, while the external pathways are where the meridians pass close to the surface of the skin. There are believed to be hundreds of specific points, called in Chinese *hsueh* ('cave' or 'hollow'), along these external pathways, which allow access to the internal organ systems, and needles are inserted into these acupoints to unblock, strengthen or reduce the flow of qi as required to restore balance.

In ancient times, the needles were made of stone, and later of bronze, silver and gold. In modern acupuncture, sterilized, disposable steel needles of a very fine diameter are generally used, with the upper part wound with bronze wire to strengthen the needle and form a handle. Sometimes moxibustion is also employed; here, heat is applied to the acupoint either by directly burning a powdered herb on it, or warming the needle by burning the herb on the end. Some practitioners place the needles at or near the affected site, while others determine the appropriate points for acupuncture by closely questioning the patient, checking various pulse aspects on each wrist, and other methods; traditional acupuncture uses a combination of both.

The practice of acupuncture in China goes back thousands of years. Centuries ago, it spread from China throughout the East, becoming an important feature of the traditional Korean and Japanese medicine systems. It had always been used in rural Chinese communities, but from the mid-17th century its practice declined as Western ideas increasingly influenced the East. However, with the establishment of the People's Republic of China in 1949, and the Cultural Revolution of 1966–76, there was a national resurgence of interest in traditional Chinese medicine techniques such as acupuncture, and its practice became widespread once more. In the East today, it is generally used in a hospital-based context, side by side with Western medical systems.

Acupuncture first appeared in the West in the 1950s, when it was studied by practitioners already involved in other branches of natural medicine, such as naturopathy, HOMEOPATHY and osteopathy. It is now commonly offered as a complementary therapy, and a treatment may also include AROMATHERAPY. Medical legislation on the practice of acupuncture in the West varies from country to country and state to state; in some places, it can be performed without any specific training, in others acupuncturists are required to work alongside a qualified doctor, and in other places, such as Australia, only state-registered acupuncturists are permitted to practise. Claims have been made for acupuncture's effectiveness in the treatment of disorders such as respiratory conditions, osteoarthritis, gastrointestinal problems, and addiction problems such as smoking, but it is still the subject of controversy in the Western medical world, and studies continue into its physiological and clinical value. See also ACUPRESSURE; REFLEXOLOGY; SHIATSU.

Adamski, George (1891–1965)

The first man to claim he had repeated encounters with both UFOs and their alien occupants; considered the leader of the contactee movement that was prominent during the 1950s.

George Adamski was born in Poland, but emigrated with his parents to New York State before the age of two. Following a succession of manual jobs, he started work in a café near the slopes of Mount Palomar in California, home of an important astronomical observatory. He had received a strict religious upbringing and developed many spiritual interests – in 1934 he established a minor OCCULT group with the grand name of The Royal Order of Tibet, leading to his involvement in lectures on local radio. He gained the nickname 'Professor', a title that was reinforced by his building a crude telescope which he used to watch the stars from a position near the observatory.

During the late 1940s and early 1950s, Adamski reported a number of UFO encounters. In 1946 (some months before the term FLYING SAUCER was invented and the first reports of the modern UFO phenomenon began to appear in the media) he claimed to have witnessed a huge alien craft while observing a meteor shower. The following year, again while SKYWATCHING, he reportedly saw 184 strange lights fly across the sky in quick succession, in what appeared to be squadron formations.

Adamski's real notoriety began on 20 November 1952, when he and six like-minded colleagues went looking for UFOs in the desert. On seeing a silvery, cigar-shaped UFO, Adamski announced that aliens were seeking him out for contact. He ordered his companions to drive him to a remote spot near the small town of Desert Center, California, before retiring to observe from a distance. They witnessed only a little of what happened next, but Adamski claimed that a small saucer-shaped craft landed and a handsome, blond, humanoid figure emerged. Through sign language and telepathy, this being explained that he was from Venus, and that the EXTRATERRESTRIAL presence on earth was peaceful – although the aliens were apparently afraid of the nuclear weapons that mankind had created.

Adamski recounted this story in a small pamphlet that was picked up by Irish writer Desmond Leslie, who included it in his 1953 book *Flying Saucers Have Landed*. The extraordinary tale helped make the book an international bestseller, ensuring that 'Professor' Adamski could publish several sequels over the next four years, reporting many further incidents of contact with alien beings. The adventures he described included travelling to see trees and rivers in space and to meet beings living on Mars, Venus and the Moon. These stories captured the attention of a population that was becoming excited by the dawn of the space age, and was, as yet, unsure whether claims such as Adamski's might be vindicated by science. Adamski gave lectures in many countries, met Queen Juliana of the Netherlands and claimed to have been granted a private audience with Pope John XXIII (although the Vatican subsequently denied this).

The media were largely sceptical – even hostile – but many of those critical of Adamski's claims nevertheless considered him to be a charming man. The science journalist Robert Chapman, who met Adamski during his UK lecture tour, described him as 'so damnably normal … He believed that he had made contact with a man from Venus, and he did not see why anyone should disbelieve him.'

Once the space programme was established, the

impossibility of Adamski's description of life on the planets of our solar system was soon exposed, and the CONTACTEE movement rapidly waned. The UFO COMMUNITY had, by and large, distanced itself from his stories, particularly as the photographs of the spacecraft that he had supposedly witnessed appeared to be crude and unconvincing fakes. He was further discredited by the discovery that in 1949 he had penned a novel, *Pioneers of Space*, which featured imaginary trips to other planets and employed similar ideas to those included in his later accounts of 'real' alien contact.

Adamski's celebrity greatly outweighed his influence on the serious investigation of the UFO phenomenon. While many people regard him as a harmless eccentric, whose enjoyable yarns caught the mood of the day, others feel that he was a key reason why science and the press adopted a negative attitude towards modern UFO investigation right from the start.

aerial phantoms
Apparitions that appear in the sky, often taken to have a symbolic or prophetic meaning.
Many cultures hold a belief in APPARITIONS appearing in the sky, usually as signs or portents. Some interpret these aerial phantoms as manifestations of gods, ANGELS or important human personages elevated to spiritual form. The archetypal aerial phantom in European mythology is the WILD HUNT of Odin. Norse tradition held that the god Odin rode across the sky on a phantom horse, Slepinir, followed by a pack of spectral hounds, chasing lost souls. The influence of Christianity changed the leader of the hunt to THE DEVIL snatching up the souls of sinners and unbaptized babies. In later stories the leader of the hunt changed to historical or quasi-historical figures such as Barbarossa or KING ARTHUR. Still later versions transform the hunt into a PHANTOM COACH. Underlying the belief in such appearances is the magical notion of correspondences and the idea that the heavenly realm may mirror upheavals upon earth.

Accounts of aerial phantoms enjoyed a particular vogue in the 16th and 17th centuries. The German writer Ludwig Lavatar, in *Of Ghosts and Spirits that Walk by Night* (1579), wrote:

> Before alterations and changes of kingdoms and in time of warres, seditions and other dangerous seasons, there most commonly happen very strange things in the aire … swords, speares and such like innumerable; there are heard in aire or upon earth whole armies of men, encountering together, and when one part is forced to flye,

there is heard horrible cries, and great clattering of armour.

In England at around this time, numerous accounts of galloping horses, strange emblems, dragons and SPECTRAL ARMIES appearing in the skies were circulated in pamphlets, particularly during periods of national crisis such as the English Civil War. A pamphlet held in the Ashmolean Museum, Oxford, contains a typically bizarre example of such a report. In its description of the vision of two country women who witnessed an aerial battle and angels on 16 April 1651, the angels are said to be 'of a blueish colour having faces … like owls'. A decade earlier, the Battle of Edgehill (1642) was said to have been re-enacted in the skies on successive Christmas Eves, with witnesses recognizing deceased soldiers. These events were allegedly investigated by a Royal Commission under the instructions of Charles I, but modern scholarship has found no corroboration for this. Reports found in pamphlet literature must be approached with caution. Even attempts to reinterpret them as misperceptions of naturally occurring phenomena (such as lightning or meteors) might themselves attribute a greater level of veracity to the testimony than it perhaps deserves, since the authors regularly recycled entirely hearsay stories, embellishing them for their own religious, political or financial reasons.

Expanding scientific knowledge of the universe led to fewer accounts of aerial phantoms from the 18th century onwards, with the exception of a brief revival during World War I with the ANGELS OF MONS. Perhaps the only classic cases of any significance recorded in the 20th century are the reports of MARIAN APPARITIONS at FÁTIMA in 1917 and at Zedoun, Egypt, in 1968. However, it is arguable that elements of UFOLOGY such as modern FLYING SAUCER accounts represent a new evolution of the tradition. See also CRISIS APPARITIONS; RE-ENACTMENT GHOSTS.

aerial phenomena
A term widely used in the early days of UFO study to describe unexplained observations in the sky.
The first UFO investigations were conducted by the military, and were initially aimed at logging reports of potential enemy aircraft or missile launches. The investigators used terms appropriate to their area of interest, such as GHOST ROCKETS, to describe what was observed.

Once the media became aware of the number of reports being made, rather more dramatic phrases were invented – notably FLYING SAUCERS. This term was soon associated with the theory that alien spacecraft were visiting the earth. Indeed, by the late 1950s the names 'flying saucers' and 'alien craft' were becoming interchangeable.

Researchers who considered that they were carrying out a more serious (and open-minded) investigation of the phenomenon wanted to avoid such colourful terminology. During the early 1950s the term 'aerial phenomena' began to be used in an attempt to describe unusual sightings without necessarily implying an alien origin. It was quickly adopted by the civilian UFO organizations such as the NATIONAL INVESTIGATIONS COMMITTEE ON AERIAL PHENOMENA (NICAP).

Use of 'aerial phenomena' has declined in popularity, having been replaced in most circumstances by the acronym 'UFO'. However, it continues to be used by some researchers, who feel that it is a more objective term.

aeroplanes, phantom *see* PHANTOM
AEROPLANES

Aetherius Society
A religious movement founded in 1955, dedicated to world peace and enlightenment; its founder claimed to have channelled communications mediumistically from advanced extraterrestrial beings.

The Aetherius Society is an international organization which mixes YOGA, THEOSOPHY and, most controversially, a form of spiritualism said to involve the yogic channelling of advanced extraterrestrial beings. The Society was founded in London by Dr George King in 1955. King had become interested in spirituality at an early age, first exploring orthodox Christianity and later, psychic phenomena and yoga. In 1954, he claimed to have been contacted telepathically by an alien intelligence using the pseudonym Aetherius, which represented what it called an interplanetary parliament. This being was said to have told King that Jesus, Buddha, Krishna and other religious leaders were of extraterrestrial origin, and had come to earth to help mankind; they were ASCENDED MASTERS (or Cosmic Masters) who made up the higher order of a great brotherhood, and King had been chosen by them to be a spiritual prophet – 'the Voice of the Interplanetary Parliament on Earth'. King then said that he was contacted a week later by a well-known Indian yogi who helped him to further develop his abilities in order to continue his mission, and to receive what he called Cosmic Transmissions. He founded the Aetherius Society a year after this, to act as a vehicle through which these Cosmic Transmissions could be disseminated to the rest of humanity.

Between 1954 and his death in 1997, King claimed to have received, after entering what he called a 'Positive Yogic Samadhic Trance', over 600

Members of the Aetherius Society direct prayer energy towards world peace. (© TopFoto)

such transmissions, all of which were meticulously recorded, and which form the basis of the Society's beliefs. Central to this belief system are the importance of yoga, MEDITATION, and MANTRAS; the laws of KARMA and REINCARNATION; the essential similarity in nature between the teachings of all major religions, and the necessity for all religious people to co-operate together for the good of mankind; and above all, an emphasis on service. The Society also believes that prayer can be stored up, as in a battery, and that this accumulated prayer energy may be kept until needed and then directed anywhere on the planet in times of crisis. They claim that such 'Cosmic Missions' have helped to alleviate and even avert some major disasters.

afterlife
The continuation of some form of existence, usually spiritual, after the death of the body; a belief in life after death is fundamental to many religions, although ideas as to its nature vary greatly.

Most cultures, both past and present, subscribe to a belief in some kind of afterlife. The idea that a form of existence, usually spiritual, continues after the death of the body predates recorded history, and is fundamental to many religions and belief systems. However, ideas about what happens to the SOUL, or spiritual part of the individual, after death vary greatly from religion to religion. Many testimonies as to the reality of an afterlife have been advanced throughout the ages; some people claim to have died for a short time and then been sent back to this life after NEAR-DEATH EXPERIENCES, which are frequently characterized by the person's seeing a long tunnel with a light at the end and being met by their departed loved ones before being instructed to return to life. Others claim to have visited the afterlife while unconscious, in OUT-OF-BODY EXPERIENCES, and some say they can remember past lives or have seen VISIONS of the afterlife. Many people believe it is possible to communicate with THE DEAD through SPIRITUALISM, and there are countless stories of the recently dead appearing to friends and family to tell them that they are well and happy in another world.

Most cultures have some concept of a land of the dead, which is located either in the sky, under the earth, across a body of water or in the West, and the afterlife is typically regarded as a time when people will be rewarded or punished according to how they lived their lives on earth. This idea of the afterlife was also found in ancient Greek and Roman religions, and various Asian belief systems, and is generally restricted to humans; animals are not held responsible for their actions. The belief in the afterlife determines many of the customs associated with death and burial, which are designed to help the soul attain eternal bliss. For example, the ancient Egyptian BOOK OF THE DEAD describes the many hymns and rituals to be performed for the dead. It also provides the spells, charms, passwords, magical numbers and formulas necessary to guide the deceased though the various trials they would encounter before reaching the Underworld. In ancient Egypt, food, drink and money were also provided for the dead person's journey to the afterlife. Many tribal societies include sacrifices to the dead as part of their funeral rites; in Hinduism, cremation is thought to be a means of releasing the spirit for REINCARNATION, while other cultures, such as those of the Native Americans, believe that the spirit cannot attain peace in the afterlife if the body is destroyed or dismembered.

Several belief systems, particularly Hinduism, Buddhism, and WICCA, believe that after death, the soul is reincarnated in a series of lives, either human or animal, and that events in an individual's current life are the consequences of the KARMA generated by their actions in past lives; the ultimate goal is to escape the cycle of reincarnation altogether and achieve union with the Infinite. Some neopagans believe that, on death, the energy of the soul reintegrates with the continuum of the UNIVERSAL LIFE FORCE and is recycled into other living things as they come into existence.

Fundamental to both Christianity and Islam is the belief that on the Day of Judgement, everyone will be called upon to answer for their actions during their earthly life, and will receive the eternal reward of a place in Heaven or eternal punishment in Hell. The Catholic Church also teaches that there is a third, intermediate destination for the souls of the dead, known as Purgatory, where those souls not condemned to Hell but not yet fit for Heaven are cleansed and purified, and their imperfections burned away.

agency
The active force, entity or process (human or otherwise) through which a paranormal event is brought about.
In the field of PARAPSYCHOLOGY the word 'agent' is used specifically to refer to a person who apparently produces, or is attempting to produce, a paranormal event. The effects are brought about through their 'agency'. For example, in experiments to investigate TELEPATHY, the agent is the person who attempts to transmit information to another individual (known as the 'percipient'), and in experiments investigating PSYCHOKINESIS, the agent is the individual attempting to influence the outcome of the experiment by, for example, levitating an object or bending a piece of metal using only the power of their mind.

The word 'agency' can also be more generally applied to phenomena occurring in SPIRITUALISM, in POLTERGEIST cases and in other areas of the paranormal – the person, or other entity, through which the effects are thought to be produced generally being called the agent (although the words are interchangeable to some extent in common usage, so they may also be referred to as the agency).

In the case of poltergeist phenomena, if they cannot easily be explained by simple fraud or natural causes, the question arises as to their origin. Many poltergeists appear to show signs of a limited intelligence, and so it is contended that they must either involve a living, human agent or a discarnate agent such as a SPIRIT. The majority of parapsychologists who accept the reality of poltergeist effects consider them to be examples of RECURRENT SPONTANEOUS PSYCHOKINESIS – originating in the unconscious mind of a living human agent. However, a minority entertain the hypothesis that they occur through the agency of a discarnate entity (for example, the spirit of a deceased person or even a non-human entity) – a view shared by many spiritualists and spiritists. A survey of 500 poltergeist cases conducted in 1979 by British psychical researchers Alan Gauld and Tony Cornell suggested that up to 25 per cent of poltergeist cases might be long-term, place-centred phenomena, rather than person-centred phenomena, giving support to the notion that (at least in these instances) they are not due to the agency of a living human.

agent *see* AGENCY

Age of Aquarius
An astrological age that will supposedly bring with it a period of enlightenment, accomplishment and peace.
In ASTROLOGY the period of human history is made up of ages lasting approximately 2,000 years. Each

age is named after the ZODIAC constellation in which the sun appears at the VERNAL EQUINOX and derives its dominant qualities from those associated with its sign. It is generally agreed (particularly among those astrologers who base their calculations on modern astronomical measurements) that we are currently in the Age of PISCES, with the Age of AQUARIUS to begin some time around the year 2600. However, there are ESOTERIC astrologers who disagree significantly with this view – some even argue that the transition has already occurred. The HERMETIC ORDER OF THE GOLDEN DAWN calculated that the Age of Aquarius would begin in 2160.

In addition to the effect during their age, zodiac signs are described as having an 'Orb of Influence' which reaches backwards into the age before. Many astrologers refer to the current period as the 'dawning of the Age of Aquarius', a view which (combined with certain conjunctions that occurred in the 1960s) led to the title 'Age of Aquarius' being associated with the movement that is now more usually referred to as 'NEW AGE'.

agogwe
A short hairy bipedal humanoid entity reported from Tanzania, with counterparts on record elsewhere in tropical Africa

Tanzanian tribes have long spoken of a rarely seen but remarkable forest-dwelling humanoid entity known as the agogwe, which walks upright on its hind legs, lacks a tail, and resembles a short man, roughly 1.2–1.5 metres (4–5 feet) tall, but is covered in brown or dark red fur. It is even claimed that such creatures sometimes barter with the local tribes. Nor are they unique to Tanzania. Very similar (if sometimes even shorter) entities have also been reported from such localities as the Democratic Republic of Congo (formerly Zaire), where they are known as the kakundakari, from Senegal (fating'ho), from southern Africa (tokoloshe), and the Ivory Coast (séhité). Indeed, an alleged séhité was shot and killed in 1947 by an elephant hunter, but its carcase was not made available for identification and study. Moreover, in 1957 a nearly dead kakundakari was allegedly captured, caged and exhibited to numerous people in a village near the Lugulu River.

Some of these may well be nothing more than mythical beings analogous to the LITTLE PEOPLE of European folklore, or be based upon confused descriptions of pygmies. However, veteran cryptozoologist Dr BERNARD HEUVELMANS conceded that certain examples, in particular the agogwe, may constitute relict populations of the earliest type of hominid, the gracile australopithecine (officially believed to have existed 4.4–1.4 million years ago),

nowadays confined to dense forested regions little explored by science and largely unfrequented by modern-day humans.

Agrippa von Nettesheim, Henricus Cornelius (1486–1535)
German occult scholar, astrologer and philosopher.

Heinrich Cornelius was born in Cologne in 1486. His life was characterized by his wide travels around Germany, Italy and France, and by his pursuit of various professions – he was at different times an ambassador, a soldier, a physician and a lecturer, as well as an occult scholar and writer. When still young, he was said to have gained a reputation in his native town for refusing to speak anything but Latin; certainly, after the fashion of the day, he adopted the Latin form of his name, Henricus Cornelius, although later he often referred to himself as Cornelius Agrippa, the name by which he is best known today. Between 1506 and 1510 he acted as a diplomatic agent for Maximilian I in Paris and London, but only a year or two later he was serving as a soldier in Italy, and by 1515 he was lecturing in Pavia, and became a doctor of both law and medicine. In 1518 he was back in Germany,

German occult scholar, astrologer and philosopher Henricus Cornelius Agrippa von Nettesheim. An engraving from *Bibliotheca Chalcographica* (1650).
(© Mary Evans Picture Library)

acting as town orator at Metz, but after successfully defending a woman accused of WITCHCRAFT, he incurred the hostility of the Inquisition, and had to leave. He then served as doctor and astrologer to Louise of Savoy, the Queen Mother of France, in Lyons, and as historian to Margaret of Austria in Antwerp, but neither position brought him wealth.

By his early twenties, he was skilled in ALCHEMY, and while studying at the University of Paris, he is reputed to have organized a secret society – a brotherhood of students interested in alchemy and MAGIC. His major work, a three-volume treatise on magic called *De occulta philosophia* ('On Occult Philosophy'), was completed in 1510, when he was only 23, but was not published until 1533, in an enlarged edition. In this influential work, he combined magic, ASTROLOGY, THEURGY and medicine, and united the streams of classical Neoplatonism, Hermetic philosophy, the Jewish KABBALAH and Christianity. He claimed that everything which existed had a spiritual component, which was part of a universal soul, and that this spiritual element showed itself in the magical properties of herbs, metals, stones, animal, and all other phenomena of nature. He suggested a system of the universe in which everything was part of a great spiritual whole which was God, and that magic was a means of understanding this system. It remains one of the leading texts of Western esoteric thought.

He continued to be absorbed in the question of how to achieve spiritual union with the Godhead throughout his life, and in his later, sceptical work *De incertitudine et vanitate atque atrium* ('On the Vanity and Uncertainty of the Arts and Sciences'), published in 1526, he contrasted the disillusion which he said artistic and scientific knowledge ultimately brought, with the spiritual strength that was gained through the only sure thing on which mankind could depend: the divinely revealed work of God.

ahool

A giant bat reportedly heard and occasionally also seen as it flies overhead in the remote valleys of Java.

Many of the native people of western Java in South East Asia believe in the existence of an enormous bat that they call the ahool – a rendition of the distinctive cry that it gives voice to when flying through secluded river valleys at night. According to their descriptions, the body of the ahool is as large as a one-year-old child's, it has a gigantic 3.6-metre (almost 12-foot) wingspan, its face resembles that of a monkey, its feet seem to point backwards on the rare occasions when it has been observed crouching on the ground (a familiar if odd-sounding characteristic of many bats), and it feeds primarily upon large fishes that it snatches from beneath stones on river beds.

Some eyewitness accounts of this creature have been obtained from experienced local hunters, who are familiar with all of Java's animals, and are therefore unlikely to mistake some well-known beast for a giant bat.

Nor is the ahool a peculiarly Javan anomaly. A similar animal has also been reported from Cameroon in western Africa, where it is known as the olitiau. One of these was encountered in 1932 by two American naturalists, Ivan Sanderson and Gerald Russell, when it flew directly at them as they were wading down a mountain stream. As far as they could tell, it was coal-black in colour, with a monkey-like face and jaws filled with large white teeth, and a wingspan of approximately 3.6 metres (almost 12 feet).

The largest bat presently known by scientists to be living today is a species of New Guinea fruit bat with a wingspan of 1.6 metres (5 feet 3 inches). Consequently, if the ahool and olitiau are eventually discovered, they will each more than double the known record.

air

One of the four elements believed in ancient and medieval cosmology to be the fundamental components of all things; of prime importance in magic and the occult.

In ancient and medieval philosophy and alchemy, all things were believed to be composed of a blend of four classical ELEMENTS: FIRE, WATER, EARTH and air. These four elements are central to magical and occult thought. Air is seen as the realm of the mind and the intellect, communication, and psychic powers – with thought being the first step toward creation – and represents the conception of new ideas and knowledge. The power of air may be called on for assistance in spells or rituals involving travel, DIVINATION and learning. It is associated with the east, the season of Spring, childhood, dawn, and the colour yellow, and is thought to be a masculine element, since it is dry, expansive and active. Air governs the zodiacal signs of GEMINI, LIBRA and AQUARIUS, and is connected with the planets Mercury and Uranus. In the TAROT, it is represented by the suit of swords (see SWORDS, SUIT OF). In the casting of a MAGIC CIRCLE, it is frequently symbolized in physical form by incense, and is associated with the magical tools of incense, sound and breath, the ritual knife or 'athame', the sword, and the censer. Its position in the five-pointed star or PENTAGRAM is the upper left point. The four fluids known as humours, which were once popularly believed to permeate the human body and determine the temperament, were each associated with an element, and air was associated with the humour of blood. The element of air is said to be governed by the archangel Raphael, and its specific animating spirit or ELEMENTAL is the sylph. Air is the element of hills, plains, mountain peaks, wind and breath.

aircraft, black *see* BLACK AIRCRAFT

airships
The interpretation often applied to sightings of UFOs in the late 19th and early 20th centuries.
UFO sightings are not a modern phenomenon. Records of sightings of unexplained objects in the sky exist in the archives of many major civilizations, dating back more than 2,500 years. Frequently such objects were described in terms then familiar to the local population, such as blazing shields or glowing arrows.

During the US WAVES of 1896 and 1897, and those in Europe and New Zealand between 1909 and 1914, most reported objects were described as resembling dirigibles or airships. At this time, airships were still revolutionary technology – the first powered airship flight took place in 1852, but even in 1896 airships did not make journeys of any distance. However, popular writers such as Jules Verne sometimes anticipated the possibilities of science and included airships in their fictional works, so many people who would never have seen one were aware of their existence in an exaggerated form.

One of the first documented cases of an unexplained airship sighting predates the late 19th-century US wave. The *Sante Fe Daily New Mexican* reported on 29 March 1880 that a group of witnesses had observed an airship over Galisteo Junction (later renamed Lamy). According to these witnesses, the airship carried a number of humanoid passengers conversing in a strange language and acting as if drunk. Several items were tossed overboard, including some pages of 'oriental' writing. Two days later a stranger allegedly arrived in town and purchased the items, explaining that he wished to return them to their owner who had now flown in the craft to New York. Nobody now knows if this piece of journalism was meant to be taken seriously, but it is interesting to note that mystery visitors who take away key evidence are often reported in modern UFO cases, under the name of MEN IN BLACK.

Hundreds of airship stories followed, with the majority coming from the American Midwest in late 1896 and early 1897. Some were clearly jokes, others were admitted to be hoaxes and, following modern evaluation, some reports are now thought to be misperceptions of astronomical bodies. The most popular theory in the contemporary press was that the craft were the product of mysterious inventors who would soon reveal their amazing technology; yet it wasn't until 1912, in Europe, that the first German-built Zeppelins were successfully flown in the manner described by many of the earlier witnesses.

In the years leading up to World War I, and particularly on 14 October 1912, a new burst of airship sightings over Sheerness in Kent caused much concern to the British government, and the sightings were the subject of parliamentary debate. Further sightings occurred over locations that were considered strategically important, such as the ports of Liverpool (25 January 1913) and Hull (25 February 1913), fuelling fears of an imminent German invasion. Only after the end of World War I did it become clear that German Zeppelins would have been unable to reach Britain at the time of the reports – that feat was not achieved until 1915.

Many of the British reports were of little more than bright lights in the sky, which were interpreted as the searchlights of an unseen airship. Even then, just as today, sceptics argued for a simple explanation. On 26 February 1913, the day after multiple reports of airship sightings across the country, the *Nottingham Daily Express* reported:

> Venus is now particularly bright, and suddenly appearing and disappearing behind wind-blown clouds, she gives the illusion desired.

Many modern UFO investigators conclude that similar theories could be used to explain more recent sightings of airship-like craft.

Akasha
In Hinduism, the primary principle of nature from which the other four principles – earth, air, fire and water – were created; a unifying energy or spiritual substance present in every living being, thought to contain a record of all that has ever happened and all future possibilities.
Akasha is the Sanskrit word for ether, sky or space. According to ancient Indian tradition, the universe is made up of two fundamental properties: motion, and the space through which this motion takes place. This space is called the Akasha. In Hinduism, the Akasha is one of the *Panchambhutha*, or five elements, and the other four elements of EARTH, AIR, FIRE and WATER are said to have been created from this primary principle of nature. In NEOPAGANISM and WICCA, the Akasha is the unifying energy which is present in all living beings, and in the four ELEMENTS; also known as Spirit, it is represented on the PENTAGRAM by the single, uppermost point.

The Akasha is believed to be eternal and all-pervading, and to be made up of infinite dimensions which comprise all possibilities of movement, both physical and spiritual. This mystical substance, sometimes referred to as 'soniferous ether', is thought to contain a record of everything which has ever happened, and everything which may come to pass in the future; all events and memories concerning human consciousness, in all realities, are said to have been stored in this 'astral light', in a kind of spiritual library known as the AKASHIC RECORDS, since the dawn of time. Many people believe that those with special psychic powers, or those in the appropriate state of consciousness, can tap into the Akasha and access these occult records, and it is claimed that such paranormal phenomena as CLAIRVOYANCE, spiritual insight and prophecy are made possible by this means. The Hindu *Vedas*, and the language of Sanskrit itself, are said to have been extracted from the Akasha.

Akashic records

A collection of mystical knowledge said to be stored in the ether; it is believed to contain every event, thought, action and feeling which ever has or ever will occur, and to be accessible through techniques such as meditation.

According to ancient Indian tradition, the universe is made up of two fundamental properties: motion, and the space through which this motion takes place, known as the AKASHA. This subtle substance, sometimes described as 'astral light' or 'soniferous ether', is believed to contain a record of every event, thought, action and feeling which has occurred since the beginning of our planet; it is also thought to be made up of infinite dimensions, and to contain all possible future realities. The concept of a collection of mystical knowledge stored in a non-physical plane of existence has a long history, appearing in belief systems all over the world, with the ancient Egyptians, Greeks, Persians, Tibetans, Indians, Chinese, Mayans, Christians and DRUIDS all laying claim to its use. There are believed to be various 'cosmic libraries' of knowledge, relating to the earth's human, animal, plant and mineral life, but most writings on what are usually referred to as the Akashic records refer to those in the area of human experience.

Although the idea of the Akashic records is universal, the term itself, and the concept of an etheric library, originated in the 19th century with the THEOSOPHICAL SOCIETY. In THEOSOPHY, and many NEW AGE belief systems, it is held that every event, thought and feeling experienced by every individual in all possible realities is recorded on the Akasha. Each human being thus adds to the Akashic records, which contain the entire history of every soul since the dawn of creation and connect us all to one another. The Akashic records have been compared by some writers to a cosmic consciousness, and are variously referred to as the Hall of All Knowledge, the Hall of Records, the Cosmic Mind, the Universal Mind, the Collective Unconscious, and the Collective Subconscious. Therefore every individual can, in theory, access all the knowledge in the universe, past and future, by tapping into the Akashic records. Various techniques, such as yogic breathing, MEDITATION, visualization, and trance states may be used to attain the necessary focused, preconscious state. Some practitioners claim that an individual's full birth name and birth date act like a fingerprint which is embedded and encoded in the Akasha, and that using this information, they can access and read a person's Akashic record in order to give them advice on their soul's mission, purpose and journey in this lifetime.

A number of highly influential figures in theosophy and ANTHROPOSOPHY claim to have consciously accessed and used the Akashic records, the most notable being DION FORTUNE, Annie Besant and the American mystic EDGAR CAYCE, who attributed the accuracy of his psychic readings to his ability to read the Akashic records of his subjects. RUDOLF STEINER, the founder of anthroposophy, claimed that he had gained his own knowledge of the occult, and of the entire history of the evolution of man and the world, by accessing the Akashic records. MADAME BLAVATSKY, founder of the Theosophical Society, held that they contain not only the history of every soul, but also every archetypal symbol and myth which has ever influenced human behaviour, and are thus not just a record of the past and of possible futures, but a powerful stimulus to human creativity and dreams.

Albertus Magnus, St, Graf von Bollstädt (c.1200–1280)

German philosopher, theologian and alchemist, often described as the most influential scientist of the Middle Ages.

Born in Lauingen, Swabia, Albert of Cologne was the eldest son of the Count of Bollstädt. He was educated in the liberal arts at Padua University, and became a Dominican monk in 1223. From 1228 to 1245, he taught at convents in Hildesheim, Freiburg, Ratisbon, Strasbourg and Cologne, and then moved to Paris, where he received a doctorate in theology. In 1254 he was elected as Provincial of the Dominican order in Germany, an office from which he resigned three years later in order to devote himself to study and teaching. He was made Bishop of Regensburg in 1260, but resigned in 1262, and spent the rest of his life preaching in Bavaria and its surrounding districts. He died in 1280, and was beatified in 1622, canonized as St Albert the Great in 1931, and in 1941 was declared patron saint of all who cultivate the natural sciences; his feast day is celebrated on 15 November.

His fame is due in part to the fact that he was the forerunner, guide and teacher of St Thomas Aquinas, but Albert of Cologne was known as Albertus Magnus even during his own lifetime because of his prolific scientific writings and his great influence on the study of philosophy and theology. During his time in Paris, he began work on a monumental project – the gathering together of all knowledge as understood in his time. This encyclopedic compilation, which included his works *Physica*, *Summa theologiae* and *De natura locorum*, would take him some 20 years to complete. It contained scientific treatises on alchemy, astronomy, mathematics, geography, physiology, economics, logic, rhetoric, ethics, politics, phrenology, metaphysics and all branches of natural science, justly earning him the title of *Doctor Universalis* or 'Universal Doctor'.

In his writings, Albertus Magnus stressed the importance of experiment and investigation, and made a clear distinction between knowledge received through faith, and that acquired by study, philosophical inquiry and scientific observation. In his belief that theology and science, far from being irreconcilably opposed, were in fact simply different aspects of a harmonious whole, he proved that the Church was not against the study of the natural world, and thus, through his writings and lectures, he helped to establish the study of nature as a legitimate science. Such was his interest in the experimental sciences that some considered him to be as much an alchemist (see ALCHEMY) as a theologian, and a number of legends attribute to him the powers of a magician or sorcerer. Among the claims made on his behalf are the discovery of the PHILOSOPHER'S STONE, the creation of automata that were able to speak and the ability to affect the weather – which he supposedly used to allow a meal with William II, Count of Holland, to take place outdoors on New Year's Day 1242. However, he himself expressed contempt for MAGIC and never laid claim to any supernatural powers.

alchemy

An esoteric philosophical system which was one of the precursors of modern science. It was principally (although not solely) concerned with turning base metals into gold and discovering an 'elixir of life'.

The word 'alchemy' entered the English language in the late medieval period as a borrowing from Arabic, via French. Its ultimate origin was a Greek term meaning the TRANSMUTATION of metals and, indeed, this is the sphere of activity that it is most commonly associated with – although alchemists were responsible for a wide range of more mundane (but highly important) developments in the area that would later be known as chemistry.

An illustration of 'Heat and Humidity from the Sun and the Moon', from the 15th-century *Discourse on Alchemy*.
(© Gianni Dagli Orti/Corbis)

In the pre-Christian era forms of alchemy arose in various parts of the world (including Greece and China), not necessarily connected with or borrowing from one another. In medieval Europe alchemy developed mainly from the translation of texts originally produced in the Arabic world. It was a discipline which combined practices that are not significantly different to the modern scientific method with the mystical and esoteric (including such areas of study as ASTROLOGY, the KABBALAH and THEURGY) – although to suggest that this was in any way unusual in the Middle Ages would be misleading. In the West, it was very much associated with Hermeticism (see HERMETICA) and later with the development of Rosicrucianism (see ROSICRUCIANS).

It is, of course, not difficult to see how the idea of the instant wealth that could be created by turning ordinary metals into gold would exert a powerful grip on the human imagination. It was believed that the transmutation would be achieved by means of a substance known to alchemists as the PHILOSOPHER'S STONE, which they believed was already in existence and awaited their discovery. This mysterious material was reputed to possess not only the power of transmutation, but also the ability to cure illness by its touch, and it was in an attempt to discover this substance that most alchemists conducted their experiments and researches. It was believed that an

ELIXIR OF LIFE could be prepared from it, which would act as a kind of universal panacea and could be used to prolong the lifespan of ordinary mortals.

Among renowned devotees of alchemy were the mathematician Dr JOHN DEE, one-time astrologer to Queen Elizabeth I, who claimed to own a CRYSTAL BALL that enabled him to communicate with ANGELS; the German physician PARACELSUS, who was chiefly interested in its possible medical uses, but who also coined the term 'alkahest' for the universal solvent which was another of the alchemists' goals; and ISAAC NEWTON, who reputedly devoted more time to the study of alchemy than to the study of physics. Possibly the most famous alchemist was the German philosopher and cleric ALBERTUS MAGNUS, who was reputed to have actually discovered the philosopher's stone.

The most famous appearance of alchemy in literature is undoubtedly in Ben Jonson's play *The Alchemist* (1610), a comedy in which the protagonist is a hoaxer exploiting the greedy and gullible in their desire for instant riches and long life. This reflected the growing body of opinion to the effect that alchemy was no more than a wild goose chase.

After the Renaissance, the growing emphasis on the developing scientific method tended to discredit the more mystical and indemonstrable elements of alchemy. However, much of the alchemists' work involved perfectly valid chemistry, and indeed laid the groundwork for the subsequent development of that science. Belief in some of the more esoteric, symbolic aspects of alchemy persists, and their influence may still be seen in some NEW AGE practices.

Alexander technique

A form of therapy which is designed to improve posture and eliminate dysfunctional patterns of movement which can lead to pain or disease.

The Alexander technique is a method of consciously re-educating the body to break harmful habits of movement and posture which can lead to pain and disease if left unchecked. It was developed in the late 19th century by an Australian Shakespearean actor, F Matthias Alexander, who noticed that when he prepared to recite in public he tended to stiffen his body unnecessarily and to contract his head and neck muscles. At first, he found it almost impossible to inhibit these contractions, but he persevered. After ten years of research and practice, he had formulated a complete system designed to adjust and correct habitual misaligned body posture in order to relieve muscle tension and allow greater ease and efficiency of movement. The basic discovery Alexander made was what he called the 'primary control mechanism', whose principle was that the head, neck and spine,

when in a properly balanced dynamic relationship, control the balance and co-ordination of the entire body.

By working one to one with a private Alexander technique teacher, a student is taught to become aware of their own movement patterns in everyday activities such as sitting, standing, walking, bending and lifting, to identify and correct deeply ingrained bad postural habits, and to use their bodies in the easiest and most balanced way possible. The technique is taught in many areas of the performing arts and in sports training, where it is said to help eliminate performance anxiety. It is also used as a remedial method to manage pain, aid recovery and avoid repetitive strain injury. It is said to bring an increased awareness of the connection between body and mind, and to be particularly effective in treating stress, fatigue, insomnia, neck and back pain, chronic muscle tension and digestive problems, as well as improving balance and ease of movement.

alien abduction

The alleged kidnapping of human subjects by the extraterrestrial occupants of UFOs.

One of the earliest claimants of abduction by aliens was ANTONIO VILLAS BOAS in 1957, and the first classic US alien abduction case was that of BETTY AND BARNEY HILL in 1961, although neither was made public until 1965. Both were studied extensively by medical doctors and shared similar features – features which cropped up regularly in subsequent reports:

The alleged abductees claimed that after first seeing a UFO, they then experienced a peculiar state of consciousness, sudden transfer into a strange room inside the landed UFO and finally contact with the alien occupants. Both cases included reports of intimate medical tests being carried out on the subjects by the crafts' occupants, and the extraction of sperm from the men involved. The full stories of the events on each occasion grew out of what were initially only experiences involving UFO sightings and MISSING TIME.

In the years that followed, reports of an altered state of awareness of time, referred to as the OZ FACTOR, led UFO researchers to examine otherwise ordinary UFO sightings more deeply. It became common for regression hypnosis to be used as a method for supposedly recovering a subject's lost memories from this missing time. In the USA a steady stream of newly discovered alien abduction cases entered the records by way of this technique, recourse to which was often prompted by a conscious memory that involved neither aliens nor abduction. Inevitably it became the subject of debate as to whether the hypnosis was

A depiction of Betty and Barney Hill's encounter with a UFO, prior to their alleged alien abduction. Taken from Hilary Evans, *UFOs, Greatest Mystery* (1979).
(© Mary Evans Picture Library)

revealing hidden memories or stimulating fantasies, and most of these cases remain highly controversial.

By 2006 approximately 6,000 abduction cases had been documented, although only about one-fifth of these were in any significant detail or involved any medical follow-up. An estimated 60 per cent of known cases are from the USA. Within Europe, Britain has the highest level of alien abduction reports, while France and Germany have very few. Even in Britain the level of cases per head of population is far less than that found in the USA. One factor in this difference could be the ban on the use of regression hypnosis in cases examined by the BRITISH UFO RESEARCH ASSOCIATION, which was implemented in 1989.

While some researchers accept the possibility that alien abduction cases really do involve alien visitations (and that humans are being used as the subjects for alien genetic engineering projects), there are a number of rather less literal theories to explain the reports. Several elements of the alleged incidents indicate that the subjects were not fully conscious during their experiences. Keith Basterfield, an Australian researcher, has noted the similarities between alien abductions and cases of 'false awakenings', where a witness experiences a vivid dream as a waking reality while totally unaware that they remain asleep. Susan Blackmore, a British psychologist, has found similarities in alien abduction cases and OUT-OF-BODY EXPERIENCES, and argues that the physical sensations reported by alleged abductees may well be those of muscle restraint (as experienced in SLEEP PARALYSIS).

The paucity of independent witnesses in these cases, and the absence of physical evidence (samples of non-terrestrial DNA, for example), has led many scientists and UFO researchers to doubt their physical reality. However, some do accept that the experiences may have an as yet not fully explained vivid subjective reality for the people involved.

alien autopsy

A procedure claimed to have been carried out in secret on the bodies of aliens recovered from the remains of UFO crashes.

There have been a number of reported sightings of UFOs crashing, leaving the crew dead or severely injured in the wreckage (including the likely hoax at AURORA, TEXAS, in 1897) – although only a handful of these cases are taken seriously by the majority of ufologists. Most of the reports come from the USA, with isolated examples from Russia and other parts of Europe, and they are generally characterized by the alleged involvement of covert government teams. If the claims are taken to be true, they would suggest that approximately 20 alien bodies have been recovered since 1947.

The US UFO researcher Len Stringfield specialized in collating the evidence from sites where alien bodies were allegedly recovered. He met a number of witnesses, including military personnel, who claimed that they had seen alien bodies before they were taken from the wreckage or after they were transported to Wright Patterson Air Force Base in Dayton, Ohio (see HANGAR 18). Stringfield also interviewed a number of military doctors who claimed to have had access to autopsy reports on these EXTRATERRESTRIALS. Quoting from an 'anatomical study' of such a body, Stringfield reported that one (anonymous) doctor had found that the beings were:

> … four feet three and three-eighth inches [tall] … The head was pear shaped in appearance and oversized by human standards … The eyes were Mongoloid [and were] recessed into the head. There seemed to be no visible eye-lids … The skin seemed greyish in colour and seemed mobile when moved.

Very few of these direct accounts are supported by any hard evidence. The statements made to Stringfield were off the record and the subjects remained anonymous – it was claimed that it would put their life at risk if their identity were exposed. However, Stringfield did find a considerable degree of consistency in the physical descriptions of aliens at different 'crash sites'.

One similar British case featured a military reservist who claimed he had been given a top-secret autopsy report by a worried superior officer. This witness said he would hand the files over to UFO researchers Peter Hough and Jenny Randles at a clandestine meeting. However, the file vanished before the meeting could take place and he only provided an account of the 200-page autopsy report, written by a mysterious Dr Frederick Hauser, to support the credibility of his story. The alien body was said to be:

> … smaller than average size and completely bald, with no eyebrows or eyelashes. No body hair at all. The nose was the most unusual feature, very flush into the face – almost not there.

One of the most remarkable claims concerning alien bodies was made by the Harvard physicist Dr Robert Sarbacher. During World War II he acted as science consultant to the US Navy, and following the war he became an engineering and missile technology specialist. In an interview with a Canadian military officer, while liaising on an intergovernmental project in September 1950, Sarbacher (who was then attached to the Pentagon) said that he had seen files relating to UFO crashes. He also said that the matter was the most highly classified in the USA at that time. Years later, when retired and close to death, he agreed to a written interview with UFO researcher William Steinman. On 29 November 1983 he repeated the claim that he had seen the files and had discussed the findings with the scientists involved, but said that he had been too busy to attend the secret meetings himself, despite being invited to do so. He said of the UFO crashes that:

> [the] people operating these machines were … of very light weight, sufficient to withstand the tremendous deceleration and acceleration associated with their machinery. I remember in talking with some of the people at the office that I got the impression these 'aliens' were constructed like certain insects we have observed on earth.

No solid evidence of aliens or reliable photographs of alien bodies are known to exist, although it was claimed in 1995 that the SANTILLI FILM showed an alien autopsy being carried out on a body recovered from the infamous ROSWELL crash.

alien big cats

Mysterious feline cryptids, variously likened to black panthers, pumas, lynxes and other large non-native cats. Sightings of alien big cats are reported regularly from the UK and elsewhere.

There were spasmodic reports of alien big cats, or ABCs for short, in the UK long before the 1960s, but this was the decade when they first attracted headline media coverage, courtesy of the Surrey Puma. That was the name given in newspaper stories to a very large tawny feline CRYPTID, most often likened to a puma, that was frequently observed in several regions in and around Surrey but never caught. A photo alleged to be of this creature was taken at Worplesdon in August 1966, but the felid depicted looked more like a large domestic cat than a puma. By the 1970s, however, puma sightings were being claimed throughout the UK, with numbers having risen dramatically by the late 1970s. There were also reports of powerful, ebony-furred, pantheresque ABCs.

It has been noted that in 1976 the Dangerous Wild Animals Act came into being, which required anyone keeping a big cat in captivity to purchase a licence and provide suitable caging facilities. This not inconsiderable added expense is nowadays thought by many cryptozoologists to have led private owners of such animals to release their exotic pets deliberately into the wild, perhaps explaining why sightings of sizeable feline creatures escalated in the following years.

The next major ABC case in Britain began in April 1983 on Exmoor, in south-west England. A number of sheep were found killed at Drewstone Farm, and several people reported seeing a large, all-black panther-like creature in the area. The animal soon became known as the Beast of Exmoor. In addition, there were reports of a brown puma-like beast in the area, and some people claimed to have seen a lynx-like cat with tufted ears and a short tail – leading investigators to consider the prospect that more than one species of big non-native cat was stalking the moorlands, and not only on Exmoor but also on Devon's Dartmoor (where a Dartmoor Beast had been reported). In May 1983, the army was brought in to seek out the Exmoor Beast – or Beasts – but failed to do so, even though sheep-killings continued. Yet although decidedly feline cryptids were often spied here, they were never seen actually killing sheep, or even eating the flesh from sheep carcases. Consequently, some ABC seekers, including Devon-based naturalist Trevor Beer, suggested it was possible that stray dogs were the real sheep killers, and not the ABCs after all.

Also during the 1980s some strange, gracile black cats, much smaller than a panther but with very prominent fangs, were captured in the Scottish Highlands, especially in the vicinity of the village of Kellas. This mysterious feline form was dubbed the Kellas cat by the cryptozoologist Dr Karl Shuker, who correctly predicted that it would prove merely to be an unusual crossbreed of a domestic cat and a Scottish wildcat.

The principal ABC of the 1990s was the Beast of Bodmin, a panther-like creature seen and even videoed stalking this famous Cornish moor, and blamed for a number of livestock kills. However, when government officials from the Ministry of Agriculture, Fisheries and Food were sent to investigate, and succeeded in measuring the background features visible in one video of the alleged Beast, they were able to confirm that the cat in that video was much smaller than it had seemed, and was far more likely to have been a hefty black domestic moggie than any panther.

Nevertheless, the sightings and photos of ABCs recorded all over the UK continue unabatedly to the present day, and to add substance to investigators' claims of their reality, some actual ABC bodies have turned up from time to time. Most of these have been shot or found dead, but a few have been captured alive – including a bona fide puma caught and caged at Cannich, Scotland. This became known as the Cannich Puma, and was captured in October 1980 by a farmer whose reports of a puma stalking his livestock had gone unheeded by the authorities. Other non-native cats procured in Britain during the last few decades include a black panther cub, an escapee clouded leopard, at least three Asian jungle cats, several Asian leopard cats and a lioness found dead in a Lancashire lake during 1980. More recently, an adult lynx that had been shot just outside Norwich by a gamekeeper back in 1991, but whose existence had remained unpublicized since then, belatedly made the headlines in March 2006 after a police report of the case was released following a freedom of information request made by a local newspaper.

What is particularly interesting about the ABC phenomenon, but is not widely realized, is that it is not confined to the UK. Corresponding reports of panther-like and puma-like cats in particular, and even the occasional maned leonine version, are frequently reported in many countries on the European mainland, from all over the USA and Canada, and also in Australia and New Zealand. True, the puma is native to North America, but many puma sightings have emerged from the eastern USA where this species has been extinct for many decades. It would seem that wherever exotic big cats are being maintained in captivity, especially as pets by private individuals, escapes and/or deliberate releases are occurring, and the creatures are surviving in the wild.

Indeed, for most cryptozoologists nowadays, the mystery of ABCs is no longer whether or not they are there but whether they are actually breeding. Quite a few reports in recent years from the UK, for instance, speak of sightings of a big cat with one or more smaller cub-like cats, or the discovery of tracks in the snow which show a set of large tracks accompanied by a set of smaller ones. If it is ever established that ABCs are mating and rearing young, the whole issue of ABCs in the UK will take on a more serious aspect.

aliens
Beings that are not from earth.

There are an estimated 12,000 reported claims to have seen an alien on record with UFO research groups – although surveys suggest that most witnesses never make their claims public. A Roper Poll survey of 5,947 people in the USA in 1992 indicated that up to 1.5 per cent of the population think that they have seen an alien. In the UK this percentage would equate to nearly one million people. However, British UFO groups have fewer than 1,000 such cases on file.

One of the first documented cases appeared in the US newspaper the *Stockton Evening Mail* on 27 November 1896. As with all such reports during the WAVE of AIRSHIP sightings, it is hard to judge its veracity. However, the witness was said to be Colonel H Shaw, who was riding with a companion near Lodi, California, when their horses reared up at the sight of some tall, lithe figures in the evening gloom. Shaw said that:

> Their faces and heads were without hair, the ears were very small and the nose had the appearance of polished ivory, while their eyes were large and lustrous … They tried to lift me, probably with the intention of carrying me away.

Although there are minor differences in each case, the aliens described in most documented reports fall into one of six broad types.

The first type are 'little people', very similar to the FAIRIES and ELVES of folklore. Said to be very like humans in appearance but only 60–90 centimetres (2–3 feet) tall, they represented almost a third of all sightings during the 1950s, but are now rarely reported.

Another folklore-related type is that of 'GOBLINS and DWARFS'. Often described as hairy and aggressive, they were seen in South America during the 1950s but are again now rarely reported. They have only ever represented a very small percentage of all alien sightings.

GREYS are the type of alien described in two-thirds of contemporary reports. Up to 120 centimetres (4 feet) tall with egg-shaped heads, large eyes, spindly bodies and greyish coloration, they made up fewer than one in ten sightings until the 1980s.

Another type now disappearing from modern reports is the once common NORDIC. These tall, blond figures, of Scandinavian appearance, are sometimes likened to wise magicians, Greek gods or clever scientists. Although they represented about a fifth of all sightings up to the 1970s, they are now confined to a few cases from Europe.

Other reports are more difficult to categorize, but many fall loosely within the last two types – APPARITIONS or projections akin to GHOSTS, and those that feature entities who are very human in appearance with, perhaps, their only alien feature being their 'space-age' clothing. See also CULTURAL TRACKING.

alignments *see* LEYS

alignments, planetary *see* ASTROLOGY

alignments, stone *see* STONE ROWS

Allagash, Maine

An alien abduction case from the USA in 1976, involving multiple witnesses and apparently dramatic physical effects.

This report of an ALIEN ABDUCTION from the Allagash River in Maine, USA, in 1976 stands out because it involved four subjects and claims that they suffered lasting physical symptoms. It was explored in great depth by a UFO investigator called Raymond Fowler. The story was related as follows.

On 26 August 1976, Chuck Rak, Charlie Foltz and twins Jack and Jim Weiner, all in their twenties, were on a camping trip together. That night they were fishing by canoe when Rak had a strange sensation of being watched. As he shouted to the others a large oval object rose from some trees behind them, with rippling paths of coloured energy travelling through it. This peculiar effect was later described as resembling a pan of hot sauce coming to the boil.

The men tried to get a better view by shining a torch towards the hovering object, at which point it appeared to head in their direction, projecting a searchlight beam onto the water. In panic the four men attempted to paddle away but the craft and its beam of light arrived directly above them. As the beam engulfed the canoe they felt strange sensations; time began to drain away and they did not recover consciousness for an unknown period.

Rak remembered staring upwards at the UFO as the other men leapt into the water. Foltz had no

memory of the time between this and his wading to the shore, with the UFO now departing. The twins both experienced a 'jump' from staring at the light to being on shore, without being able to recall getting there. It was only after the group returned to camp that they found the previously blazing fire now reduced to embers, indicating that hours had passed in what seemed to be just minutes.

All the witnesses went through physical and emotional trauma afterwards, but Jim Weiner suffered the most. His doctor diagnosed post-traumatic epilepsy and had to treat him for strange sensations in his genitals, feelings that he was floating out of his body and the repeated observation of APPARITIONS in his bedroom.

Fowler supervised regression hypnosis sessions with all four witnesses during the three-year period following the alleged incident. They then described a mutually consistent set of stories, which involved them being floated into a room where they saw small beings with large heads, pointed chins and huge, dark eyes. Samples of sperm, other bodily fluids and skin were extracted from them before they were returned to the canoe in a dazed state.

Allende letters

Letters that were sent to a US UFO author in 1955. They contained the claim that there had been a top-secret US Navy experiment involving the use of extraordinary technology and gave rise to the legend of the Philadelphia Experiment.

Morris K Jessup was a successful author in the early days of US UFO research. His book, *The Case for the UFO* (1955), was one of the first to promote the theory that aliens had visited the earth in the distant past (see ANCIENT ASTRONAUTS). Jessup was also the first writer to use the newly coined term 'UFO' in the title of a book.

The Case for the UFO achieved lasting fame because of two rambling letters sent to the author shortly after publication, from a man calling himself Carlos Allende. Both had a Pennsylvania postmark. They professed knowledge of an unreported US Navy experiment from 1943, during which a ship had become invisible and was transported instantly through many miles with devastating effects on some of the crew.

At the time Jessup seems to have paid little heed to this story and he did not try to trace the writer or research the alleged events. However, a year later he was invited to the Office of Naval Research (ONR) in Washington, DC, where he met with some officers who presented him with a copy of his own book. This copy had supposedly been sent to their head, Admiral Furth, and carried numerous marginal notes in the form of a three-way commentary between people who identified themselves only as A, B and Jemi. They had analysed what Jessup wrote, passed comments on alien technology and referred to the naval experiment mentioned in the Allende Letters. Jessup thought that the person who appeared as 'A' in the annotations seemed to be Carlos Allende.

Following this meeting, the naval officers paid for a new limited edition of Jessup's book – complete with all the annotations and with Allende's earlier letters as an appendix. Although the ONR later made it clear that this was merely a personal act on the part of a group of its officers, Jessup concluded that there had to be some substance to the story for them to go to such expense.

In April 1959, not long after the special edition of his book was published, Jessup committed suicide.

From these scraps the story known as the PHILADELPHIA EXPERIMENT has grown.

Allende did briefly reappear long after Jessup's death, confessing to UFO researchers that he had produced both the letters and the annotated book. He described these as 'the crazyest [sic] pack of lies I ever wrote'. He claimed that he had done it to deter scientists from attempting research of the kind that he had fabricated.

Soon afterwards he surfaced again to recant this confession but, in the meantime, he had been traced – his real name was Carl Allen. His family described him as a lover of practical jokes.

All-Hallows Eve *see* HALLOWE'EN

alligators in sewers
A well-known urban legend (attaching particularly to the city of New York) which may actually have some basis in fact.
One of the more popular URBAN LEGENDS revolves around the assertion that there are alligators living in the sewers under the streets of New York. The source of these alligators is usually supposed to be New York residents bringing back baby alligators from holidays in Florida and then flushing them down the toilet when they become too unwieldy. These discarded pets then continue to live and breed in the sewer system and are sometimes even said to have lost their eyesight and colouring through living in constant darkness. This version of the story may stem from a fanciful tale told by a retired sewer worker, which appeared in a book called *The World Beneath the City* (1959), written by Robert Daley. However, it is generally accepted that (among the many other practical difficulties) it is extremely unlikely that an alligator would be able to survive the winter temperatures in New York.

Despite this, there is a suggestion that the story

may have at least some earlier basis in fact. A claim that an alligator had been captured in a manhole near the Harlem River appeared in the *New York Times* on 10 February 1935, although there was no implication that the animal had been living in the sewer system – it was decided that it was probably there because 'a steamer from the mysterious Everglades, or thereabouts, had been passing 123rd Street, and the alligator had fallen overboard'. Over the years there have been numerous other reports of sightings, usually in lakes or rivers rather than sewers.

Perhaps more interestingly, the long-standing legend appeared to have become fact (see OSTENTION) when in June 2001 there were a number of sightings of a small alligator in the Harlem Meer in Central Park. This time the animal was eventually captured – a spectacled caiman that was 60 centimetres (2 feet) long, and was, indeed, believed to have been an abandoned pet. See also OUT-OF-PLACE ANIMALS.

almas
A hairy man-beast reported from Mongolia's Altai Mountains and other mountain ranges in Asia, said to resemble Neanderthal man.
Known in Mongolia's Altai Mountains as the almas ('wild man'), as the kaptar or almasty (both names translating as 'forest man') in the Caucasus Mountains, the chuchunaa ('outcast') in Siberia's Verkhoyansk Range, the dev ('demon') or nasnas ('wild man') in Iran, and the bar-manu ('big hairy one') in Pakistan, to mention just some of its local names and provenances, this wide-ranging Asian MAN-BEAST is one of the most 'human' of all such CRYPTIDS in overall appearance, except for its very hairy skin.

Approximately 1.5–1.8 metres (5–6 feet) tall, the adult almas is said to be covered in curly reddish-brown hair (except on its face and hands) that is 15 centimetres (6 inches) long. It is described as having prominent eyebrow ridges, protruding jaws but no chin, a short squat neck, long fingers and short thumbs, dark skin, short legs, broad feet, clearly delineated fingernails and toenails rather than claws, and no tail. It walks with legs spread apart – especially through snow – and with knees bent, and is said to generally inhabit the most remote peaks and caves in the mountain ranges in which it has been reported.

The most popular identity proposed for the almas is a relict version of Neanderthal man, as suggested by anthropologists Dr Myra Shackley and Dr Marie-Jeanne Koffmann, but if so it is a more primitive form than the fossil equivalent known to palaeontologists, and may even be the latter's direct ancestor. Alternatively, as suggested by US cryptozoologist Loren Coleman among others, it could be a living version of *Homo erectus*. A controversial ice-preserved hairy man-beast resembling an almas, dubbed the Minnesota iceman, was exhibited in a number of US sideshows and fairs during the 1960s by Frank Hansen. During mid-December 1968, it was closely examined by cryptozoologists Dr BERNARD HEUVELMANS and Ivan T Sanderson. Both believed the exhibit to be genuine (though today it is widely dismissed as a hoax and its whereabouts are no longer known), suggesting that it probably originated in Vietnam (where creatures of this nature have often been reported from the dense jungles) and may have been smuggled into the USA in a body bag during the Vietnam War. Heuvelmans was sufficiently impressed to christen its species *Homo pongoides* in 1969.

altered states of consciousness
Conditions in which an individual undergoes a range of unusual sensations and experiences that are now usually explained as being due to physical changes in the normal operation of the brain.

In the broadest sense the phrase 'altered states of consciousness' can be understood to refer to any level of consciousness that is different from those recognized as normal – that is, on a continuum with 'awake' at one end and 'asleep' at the other. They are subjective states – although they are usually associated with particular types of brain activity, the activity does not, in itself, constitute an altered state of consciousness. They are characterized by a loss of the sense of SELF and a loss of the sense of association of that self with the physical body, and can be brought about through the use of PSYCHEDELIC DRUGS, HYPNOSIS, MEDITATION, illness (delirium), sensory deprivation and trauma, among other things – although the question of whether the states induced in all of these cases (particularly hypnosis) are truly altered states of consciousness is a matter of debate.

As a term, altered states of consciousness was first proposed by the US writer Carlos Castaneda, in his descriptions of his involvement in Native American shamanic practices, to refer to states that had been deliberately and (usually) temporarily induced. They are often described as forming part of such things as OUT-OF-BODY EXPERIENCES, ASTRAL TRAVEL, CHANNELLING and various ECSTATIC PHENOMENA. However, the sceptic might contend that these experiences are merely illusions or HALLUCINATIONS brought about wholly through physical changes in the brain.

Alternative Medicine *see panel p19*

alternative religions *see CULTS, NEW*
RELIGIOUS MOVEMENTS AND ALTERNATIVE RELIGIONS

Alternative 3 *see panel p21*

American Society for Psychical Research
The oldest psychical research organization in the USA.

The American Society for Psychical Research (ASPR) was formed in Boston in 1885, making it the oldest psychical research organization in the USA. Since its inception the ASPR has used scientific methodology to investigate alleged PARANORMAL and PSYCHIC claims.

After a period as a branch of the British-based SOCIETY FOR PSYCHICAL RESEARCH the ASPR became independent in 1905. It opened a headquarters in New York, with an extensive library and archive. In 1907 the ASPR started to publish the *Journal of the American Society for Psychical Research*, which is still published quarterly. The society managed to recover from an internal split in the 1920s and has continued to maintain its strong scientific credentials ever since – despite its somewhat embarrassing involvement in number of cases over the years that were initially identified as genuine and then subsequently exposed as fraudulent.

The ASPR has an international membership and over the years a number of prominent scientists and psychologists have been actively involved with the society. The ASPR still funds research programmes into many areas of PARAPSYCHOLOGY and acts as a repository of knowledge and past research. A regular newsletter is produced, and all members are free to use the society's meeting rooms and resources.

Amityville
Famous alleged haunting in Amityville, USA, which led to a bestselling book and numerous films.

The house at 112 Ocean Avenue, Amityville, Long Island, New York, first acquired its gruesome reputation in November 1974 when a 23-year-old man called Ronnie Defeo shot and killed his parents and four siblings there. A year later the property was bought by George and Kathleen Lutz at a very cheap price and they moved into the house in December 1975 with their three young children. After only 28 days the family left the property, claiming to the media that they could no longer endure the bizarre and terrifying experiences they had suffered there: APPARITIONS of a talking pig; menacing figures in hoods; sinister voices; infestations by flies; sounds of a marching band; putrid smells and green slime running down the walls. Family members allegedly underwent physical and behavioural changes and visitors to the house were also affected – Father Ralph Pecoraro (a local priest) reportedly suffered a

Alternative Medicine

'Alternative medicine' is an umbrella term applied to a wide range of therapeutic or preventive healthcare practices which do not follow accepted or conventional medical methods. The phrase 'alternative medicine' is itself a controversial one; some people regard it as a misnomer and hold that it is modern Western medical techniques which are the 'alternative', since many of the systems and techniques termed 'alternative' predate those of conventional medicine by hundreds or even thousands of years. Alternative medicine's detractors, on the other hand, argue that as its various techniques have not been scientifically proven to work, they cannot truly be designated as legitimate 'alternatives' to conventional medicine.

Most alternative therapies, however diverse, tend to agree on and operate along certain common principles. Many share the belief that the body has a natural ability to heal itself, and that wherever possible, the aim should be to facilitate these natural healing powers, with an emphasis on the patient's taking responsibility for their own health and being actively involved in the healing process. They also generally adopt a holistic view of health (see HOLISTIC MEDICINE) in which the mind, body and spirit are regarded as an integrated whole, and all must be taken into account when diagnosing the ailment and prescribing its treatment. Alternative medicine often focuses on addressing the root cause of the patient's problem, rather than the obvious and immediate symptoms, which are seen as an expression of the body's attempts to cure its own imbalance – the main goal being the preservation of health and the prevention of illness, rather than its cure. Underpinning many alternative therapies is the belief that there is a natural ENERGY which pervades the universe and all living things in it, including humans. This energy, variously known as QI, prana or UNIVERSAL LIFE FORCE, is believed in traditional CHINESE MEDICINE to flow through the body along channels known as MERIDIANS, and in traditional Indian medicine, or AYURVEDA, to be concentrated in energy centres known as CHAKRAS; it not only sustains the physical body but is linked to a higher being or infinite source, and when it flows freely, it brings optimal health and vitality.

Some alternative therapies, such as chiropractic, osteopathy and massage, work directly on the body by manipulating it physically, or, as in ALEXANDER TECHNIQUE, by improving the posture. Others, such as PSYCHIC HEALING or FAITH HEALING, include spiritual or metaphysical elements. Some, like herbalism, HOMEOPATHY, Bach Flower Remedies® (see BACH, EDWARD) and AROMATHERAPY, use substances found in nature (plants, herbs and OILS) applied either externally or internally. Others, like MEDITATION, guided imagery, visualization, hypnotherapy and BIOFEEDBACK, are designed to enhance the mind's ability to affect the body, while energy therapies, or biofield therapies, such as QIGONG, REIKI, SHIATSU, THERAPEUTIC TOUCH, ACUPUNCTURE and ACUPRESSURE, seek to restore the balance of the complementary principles known as YIN and YANG, or the flow of energy where this has become blocked or disrupted, in the body. However, many practices, such as YOGA and T'AI CHI, fall into more than one category, since they treat both body and mind together, and may also include a spiritual dimension.

Some techniques of Chinese medicine, such as acupressure, acupuncture and qigong, have been used for thousands of years in the East, and Ayurveda has a 6,000-year history, while traditional healing methods based on nature, such as herbalism and hydrotherapy, have been used in Western Europe for some 3,000 years. Hippocrates, regarded as the father of Western medicine, taught doctors to observe their patients' life circumstances and emotional states as well as their physical conditions, and Socrates said, 'Curing the soul; that is the first thing.' Medicine in the West has throughout history followed two major paths: that of the professional trained physician, who belonged to and ministered chiefly to the upper classes, and that of the folk healer, wise woman or 'cunning man', who lived among, and was consulted by, the peasant and working classes. During the Middle Ages, folk medicine suffered at the hands of the Church-led drive against WITCHCRAFT and went underground to an extent from the 14th to the 17th century.

However, the use of herbs for healing was continued by the medieval monasteries which provided medical care for secular patients as well as for their monks and nuns.

Conventional Western medicine, as we know it, is only about 200 years old. Influenced by the dualistic philosophical beliefs of René Descartes (1596–1650), who regarded the mind and body as entirely separate, and by the principles of Sir Isaac Newton (1642–1727), who viewed the human body mechanistically as a series of parts, 19th-century doctors began to focus on 'fixing the broken machine' by treating physical symptoms in isolation with drugs and surgery, employing the same remedies for everyone and concentrating on individual organs and systems rather than the person as a whole. The discovery of bacteria and viruses led to an assumption that these were the sole causes of illness, and in the 20th century, especially in the decades following World War II, the dramatic successes achieved through medical breakthroughs such as the discovery of antibiotics, the development of increasingly sophisticated methods of vaccination, and the introduction of organ transplants and open-heart surgery, strengthened the belief that there was a pharmacological or surgical cure for most illnesses, and that the 'non-scientific' healing methods of earlier times or non-Western cultures were little more than quackery. However, throughout this period, alternative medicine refused to go away, and new techniques continued to be added; homeopathy, founded at the beginning of the 19th century by the German physician and chemist Samuel Hahnemann; osteopathy and chiropractic, developed at the end of the 19th century; and in the 20th century, aromatherapy, REFLEXOLOGY, RADIONICS, medical dowsing or RADIESTHESIA, and various energy therapies such as CRYSTAL and colour therapy.

During the latter part of the 20th century, there was a dramatic reversal in the Western attitude to alternative medicine. Some people have become disillusioned with or distrustful of conventional medicine, with what they consider to be its reliance on drugs and invasive surgery. The growing movement toward a more natural way of living has caused more and more patients to turn to alternative therapies, particularly in the light of studies within the mainstream medical community which suggest that there are links between illness and nutritional, emotional and lifestyle factors. The rise of the NEW AGE movement, with its eclectic interest in a variety of beliefs and practices, also contributed significantly to the revival of interest in Eastern and ancient therapies in the late 1980s.

Alternative medicine's critics contend that its perceived benefits are due to the PLACEBO EFFECT, that its effectiveness has not been scientifically proven and (perhaps most importantly) that it lacks proper regulation. However, the renewed interest in these therapies has led to a growing trend among Western doctors to recommend some of them in conjunction with, rather than in place of, standard medical practices. According to recent surveys, one in five people in the United Kingdom has tried at least one form of complementary therapy, with one in ten GPs having actively recommended and provided it, while 36 per cent of adults in the USA have used some form of CAM (the commonly used abbreviation for 'Complementary and Alternative Medicine'), mainly in conjunction with conventional medicine. Recent years have seen the emergence of integrated medicine (known as 'integrative medicine' in the USA) – that is, the selective incorporation of CAM and orthodox medical methods in a comprehensive treatment programme, with doctors either acquiring training in CAM methods themselves, or bringing licensed and registered CAM practitioners into medical centres. It is becoming increasingly common for doctors to suggest CAM in cases of chronic illness where conventional medicine can offer only management of the condition, not a cure. In the UK, the theory of a number of forms of alternative medicine is taught in several medical schools, to give GPs an understanding of the various techniques and enable them to communicate with alternative practitioners, and an increasing number of US medical colleges now offer courses in alternative medicine.

A major criticism over the years has been that the term 'alternative medicine' is open to abuse, with there being little control over who can describe themselves as an alternative therapist, no matter how bizarre the treatments they offer. Even within the established disciplines, people could set themselves up as practitioners having had little or no training. Some steps have now been taken toward much stricter regulation. In 1991, the US National Institutes of Health established the Office of Alternative and Complementary Medicine to examine the merits of various techniques. The biggest CAM professions in the UK are currently herbalism, osteopathy, homeopathy, aromatherapy, acupuncture and chiropractic, and these are monitored by the British Register of Complementary Practitioners.

Lorna Gilmour

Alternative 3

On 20 June 1977, a television programme entitled *Alternative 3*, produced by the British company Anglia TV, was broadcast simultaneously in the UK and a number of other countries. The programme took the form of a documentary, supposedly part of a series called 'Science Report'. It was presented by the well-known newsreader Tim Brinton, who started the show by explaining that the producers had originally set out to make a documentary about the 'brain drain', investigating the phenomenon of British scientists moving abroad in search of better pay. However, in doing so, they had inadvertently stumbled upon something far more sinister.

The story that unfolded was one of conspiracy at the highest level among the governments of the world, all related in the style of an investigative documentary, with a convincing presenter and dramatic footage from what were supposedly secretly recorded interviews. It had apparently come to light during the research for the original programme that a number of British scientists had not simply moved to another country – they had completely disappeared. As the evidence was pieced together, it became clear that they were being taken as part of a plan known as 'Alternative 3', formulated as the only solution to the inevitable environmental disaster that was looming on Earth as a result of pollution and overpopulation.

Alternative 3 was a plan to establish a colony on Mars, consisting of an elite group of humans, who would survive the disaster on Earth. It had been agreed upon when Alternatives 1 and 2 were dismissed. This secret had been unearthed through interviews with scientists and others involved in the space programme which revealed that, through joint US and Soviet collaboration, a landing on Mars had been made in 1961. The space flights shown to the public, and the evidence produced to

show that Mars could not sustain life, were merely a smokescreen. The programme ended with a secret videotape obtained by the production team. This showed the first Mars landing – including a fleeting glimpse of something moving on the ground below the craft.

There were a number of clues as to the real nature of the programme; it was originally intended for broadcast on 1 April 1977, but was delayed because of industrial action (the final screen before the credits still showed the original date); the interviews were far too slick to be real (including one with an entirely fictional US astronaut); and the actors were clearly listed in the final credits. However, Anglia TV was flooded with phone calls from viewers asking if the story was true – a reaction reminiscent of that following the famous Orson Welles WAR OF THE WORLDS radio broadcast. The media frenzy and speculation that immediately followed the show was revived the next year with the publication of the Leslie Watkins novel *Alternative 3*, purporting to tell the full story behind the TV programme and, rather provocatively, categorized as 'World Affairs/Speculation' by the publisher.

Despite clear statements from Anglia TV to the effect that the story was a hoax (let alone the fact that this becomes fairly obvious to the viewer within minutes of the TV programme's starting), the idea that it might be at least partly based on truth proved very attractive. Alternative 3 remains the subject of lively debate among those who believe that there are dark conspiracies at the highest level. To some, the programme itself is part of the web of misinformation put out by the governments of the world; a highly unlikely story, clearly a spoof, intended to distract attention from the disturbing truth that the project is already well under way.

debilitating illness after a disembodied voice ordered him to 'get out' while he was blessing the house with holy water.

In 1977 *The Amityville Horror: A True Story*, by Jay Anson, was published by Prentice Hall, ostensibly as a non-fiction book. It rapidly became a bestseller, eventually selling over six million copies, although scrutiny of the 'non-fiction' text revealed numerous factual errors and the inclusion of material drawn from the author's own imagination (with the implicit approval of the Lutzes who were part-credited with authorship in the early editions).

The credibility of *The Amityville Horror* was further damaged when, in 1979, Ronnie Defeo's attorney, William Webber, claimed that he had had the idea of the hoax haunting. When the Lutzes proceeded with the plan on their own he sued for a share of the royalties. The Lutzes countersued, still claiming that the haunting had really occurred. The trial judge, Jack Weinstein, stated for the record that 'the evidence shows fairly clearly that the Lutzes during this entire period were considering and acting with the thought of having a book published'. Further litigation followed – the subsequent purchasers of

A haunting legend in the making – the Defeo house in Amityville, following the shootings which took place there in 1974. (© Bettmann/Corbis)

the house (tiring of constant sightseers) sued Anson, the Lutzes and Prentice Hall and received an out-of-court settlement; Father Ralph Pecoraro also sued the Lutzes for invasion of privacy and distortion of his role and again received an out-of-court settlement. The story, however, continued to gain fame through film treatments such as *The Amityville Horror* (1979), *Amityville II: The Possession* (1982), *Amityville 3-D* (1983) and *The Amityville Horror* (2005) – a remake of the original film.

Subsequent occupiers have not reported any psychic manifestations, only disturbances from curiosity-seekers drawn to the house because of its reputation.

amulets

Objects that are thought to be magically empowered and are carried or worn to ward off evil or disease.

Amulets have been used since ancient times for the purpose of magically warding off harmful or negative influences, and were especially common in ancient Greece, Rome and Egypt. The word 'amulet' comes from Latin, and is applied to any object, either natural or manufactured, which is worn or carried to protect the bearer. An amulet may be a gem, a stone, a piece of jewellery, a small figure or symbol of a deity, part of an animal, or even a word written on a piece of paper. Unlike a TALISMAN, which is often designed to attract positive energies, the amulet's function is usually to deflect negative ones, such as evil or disease. The object is ritually charged to store and radiate protective energy, and in some traditions an amulet is used for short-term purposes, with the protective

charge being designed to function for anything from a few hours to a few days; the maximum time for which the amulet can be empowered is believed to be from one moon cycle to the next. After that, the amulet must be either re-charged, or disposed of ritually, usually by burial.

In ancient Egypt, amulets to protect children were common, and consisted of a metal cylinder containing a roll of parchment bearing a text in which three deities promised to protect the child. The ANKH was another popular Egyptian amulet, as was the figure of the scarab god, Khepri. The Jewish tradition of making amulets has been consistent for thousands of years, and the most famous of these is the Mezuzah, which contains sentences from the Scriptures; during the Middle Ages, Jewish amulets (usually made of metal discs or written on paper) were thought to be so effective that Christians bought and used them. Since medieval times, the five-pointed star or PENTAGRAM has been a commonly-used amulet in the West, and MAGIC SQUARES have been popular amulets since ancient times. Certain runes were used as protective amulets by the ancient Scandinavians and Anglo-Saxons, and are now enjoying a revival among neopagans; a number of peoples also use tattoos for this purpose.

Anastasia (1901–?1918)

Russian duchess reputed to have survived the execution of her family.

The Grand Duchess Anastasia Nikolayevna Romanov was the youngest daughter of Nicholas II (1868–1918), the last Tsar of Russia. When, in July 1918, the Russian Imperial family were executed by their Bolshevik captors at Yekaterinburg, it was rumoured that Anastasia had somehow survived.

In subsequent years, several women claimed to be Anastasia, the most persistent and successful being 'Anna Anderson'. She had tried to drown herself in Berlin in 1920, only to be rescued and committed to a mental asylum. It was there that she first identified herself as Anastasia.

Her cause was taken up by various Russian exiles who worked over a period of decades to have her formally accepted as the heir to the Imperial throne. These supporters had various motives, ranging from a romantic desire for a Romanov restoration to a simple greed for the riches believed to have been smuggled out of Russia by the Tsar before his death.

Romanov relatives were divided by the case, some believing in its legitimacy and others maintaining that Anderson had been carefully coached in her apparent knowledge of life in the Imperial family.

Although Anna Anderson died in America in 1984, interest in her claims was revived when the Russian government revealed in 1992 that the bodies of the executed Romanovs had been discovered. Two bodies were missing, one of them apparently being that of Anastasia.

DNA testing carried out on samples of Anderson's body tissue seemed to rule out any relationship with the Romanovs. However, the methods and results have been attacked as inaccurate and many continue to believe that Anastasia did indeed end her life as an American housewife.

Anna Anderson, who maintained to the end that she was the Grand Duchess Anastasia. (© TopFoto/AP)

ancient astronauts

A name given to hypothetical beings from outer space who it is suggested visited the earth and interacted with ancient peoples.

The theory that ancient astronauts visited the earth in our distant past is widely attributed to German writer ERICH VON DÄNIKEN. He has certainly popularized the idea, but he was not the first writer to develop the concept.

Several UFO writers during the 1950s (such as Desmond Leslie, the man who brought contactee GEORGE ADAMSKI to public attention) recognized that there were stories in ancient texts that could potentially be interpreted as UFO sightings. Examples included the fiery cloud seen in the sky by Ezekiel and a number of other dramatic visions in the Old Testament.

From 1960 onwards the British scholar Raymond Drake wrote several books known as the *Gods and Spacemen* series. The books contained analyses of the records of a number of ancient civilizations, including the Greeks and Romans. Many reports of what could be described as UFOs were uncovered, using words that were relevant to the time and place in question. These reports were of 'UFOs' in the strict sense, but may often describe phenomena (such as meteors, comets and atmospheric mirages) that have since become well understood.

Ancient astronaut researchers have been intrigued by the occasional discovery of artefacts that can be reliably dated back to civilizations believed not to possess such advanced technology. Examples include the PHAISTOS DISC, the unusually accurate Piri Re'is map (featuring a perspective suggesting an aerial viewpoint long before the discovery of flight) and the extraordinary NAZCA LINES in Peru. However, other scholars point out that it is easy to underestimate the capabilities of our ancestors – suggesting, for example, that balloons may have been used for mapping many centuries before the technique was rediscovered in Europe.

Details of one of the most intriguing cases which seemed to support the ancient astronauts thesis were published in 1976 by Robert Temple. He discovered that the Dogon tribe in Africa appeared to have possessed detailed knowledge relating to the bright star Sirius, including the existence and orbits of its companion stars, long before modern astronomers. The Dogon had a series of myths built around Sirius that included the appearance of beings from the sky who had taught them knowledge of the heavens. Sceptics have countered that the first contact with the tribe by European missionaries was made after scientists had gathered some knowledge about Sirius. It was, therefore, possible that influence from

Western culture had caused the folk stories to be partly adapted.

ancient structures
Structures erected by ancient cultures, the exact purpose of which is often obscure.
In various sites around the world ancient structures are still visible today which were built by the people of cultures that are now long dead, often for reasons that remain largely unexplained.

Among the oldest man-made constructions in the world are the great STONE CIRCLES found in the British Isles and Europe, especially that of STONEHENGE, the building of which is thought to have begun around 3100 BC. The complex of STANDING STONES and DOLMENS at CARNAC in Brittany is believed to mark the oldest continuously inhabited site in Europe. Various theories are advanced as to the reasons behind the erection of these structures, which must have entailed colossal effort on the part of the technology-poor peoples responsible. Dolmens have been explained as ceremonial tombs, with many grave sites having been excavated beneath them. Stone circles are often interpreted as giant astronomical observatories or calendars to chronicle the changing seasons or mark important days in the year. However, the fact that the surviving remains of these structures often represent only a small part of the original means that their true purposes can only be guessed at.

The PYRAMIDS of Egypt were, of course, built as royal tombs, beginning with that of Zoser at Saqqara (c.2700 BC), but mysteries remain as to the exact methods of their construction and the significance of their alignment with points of the compass or celestial bodies. Similar questions apply to the pyramid-shaped stone temples built in Central America (beginning c.1500 BC).

On the island of Crete, the Minoan culture which dominated Bronze Age Greece has left behind ruins of many extensive and once-magnificent palaces, notably those of Phaestos and Knossos. These contain many courtyards and rooms which seem to have been designed for use in religious observances about which little is known. It is believed that the complexity of the ruins of Knossos gave rise to the traditional stories of the labyrinth of King Minos, the Minotaur imprisoned within it and the escape from it of the legendary Greek hero Theseus.

In North America, in the south-west of what is now the USA, the Native American culture known as the Basket Weavers built large round underground chambers known as kivas (beginning c.700) which were entered through a hole in the roof. Excavation of the remains of these structures leads archaeologists to assume that they were for communal use, probably for religious or ceremonial purposes. The same peoples later built the impressive cliffside Anasazi dwellings.

ancient surgery
Surgery carried out in ancient times.
We tend to think of the practice of surgery as being relatively recent, going back perhaps no more than two centuries, but evidence exists to show that surgical techniques have been used for thousands of years.

The technique known as trepanation involves drilling into the skull of a living person and removing a circular piece of it. Excavations of grave sites in several parts of the world, from Europe to Africa and Asia to South America, have discovered skulls with neat holes cut in them, some dating back as far as 8000 BC. It is thought that these primitive operations would have been carried out to relieve headaches, excess pressure, or even forms of mental illness. The early surgeons would probably have seen what they were doing in terms of releasing evil spirits that had possessed the patient's brain. The fact that at least some of those operated on survived is shown by skulls where signs of healing can be detected.

From papyrus records it has been shown that the ancient Egyptians were familiar with the theory of trepanation as well as other surgical techniques, but there is little evidence of any of these being used in practice. Various mummies reveal that Egyptian doctors were certainly able to perform cosmetic reconstruction on the faces and bodies of the dead.

The ancient Greeks are known to have used surgery on those wounded in battle. Accounts exist of such operations as the successful removal of an arrow from the eye of Philip of Macedon (382–336 BC). The life of his son, Alexander the Great (356–323 BC), was saved when his physician Kritodemos removed an arrow that had penetrated through his chest and into his lung. Throughout the centuries, the Hippocratic oath has bound doctors to a code of medical ethics first enunciated by the Greek physician Hippocrates (c.460–377/359 BC).

When the army of Alexander the Great swept into India, among the Indian cultural influences they encountered is thought to have been a much more sophisticated art of medicine. The *Sushruta Samhita* is a body of ancient Indian writings on Ayurvedic medicine (see AYURVEDA), concentrating on surgery. It is believed to have been written by Sushruta, a legendary scholar, over 3,000 years ago and contains many descriptions of surgical techniques as well as the instruments used to carry them out. At the time of writing a common punishment for criminals was amputation of the nose, and accordingly one of the operations described is a form of rhinoplasty (or nose reconstruction) which shows an understanding of skin-grafting procedures that the Western world would not appreciate for centuries.

The Romans valued the medical knowledge and skill of the Greeks, and in the ruins of a Greek surgeon's house in Pompeii a range of metal surgical instruments was found, some of which are clearly recognizable from their modern equivalents. Another Greek physician, Claudius Galenus, known as Galen (c.130–c.201 AD), was a keen anatomist who served several Roman emperors and was regarded as the standard authority on medicine until the Renaissance.

Andean wolf

A canine cryptid from South America known only from a single controversial pelt and one skull.

In 1929, renowned animal dealer Lorenz Hagenbeck spotted a very unusual animal pelt at a market in Buenos Aires, Argentina. It reminded him of the pelt of the maned wolf, which is a long-legged, large-eared, flame-furred species of South American wild dog, but the pelt's fur – though similarly maned – was darker, thicker and longer, and the ears were smaller. Hagenbeck was so mystified by this pelt that he purchased it and brought it to the attention of noted German zoologist Dr Ingo Krumbiegel. He too was perplexed by it, as he had not seen anything else even remotely similar. However, he did have a large canine skull, derived from the Andes, that had also been puzzling him, and which, after close comparative study, he believed might belong to the same species as the pelt. Indeed, his studies concluded that skull and pelt might have derived from a hitherto-unknown species of wild dog closely related to the maned wolf but adapted for a more montane existence – hence the smaller ears and thicker coat (both of which would conserve heat better than the plains-dwelling maned wolf's equivalents).

After learning from Hagenbeck that he had seen three other pelts of this same distinctive type during his visit to Buenos Aires, Krumbiegel felt able to dismiss the worrying possibility that the purchased pelt was nothing more than the skin of a one-off domestic dog hybrid, and he formally described its originator as a new species, which became known as the Andean wolf (*Dasycyon hagenbecki*). However, no further specimen of it has ever been forthcoming, and subsequent analyses of its fur have indicated that Hagenbeck's mystery pelt, preserved at Munich's Zoological State Museum, may be nothing more than that of a sheepdog after all. Nevertheless, it has never been subjected to a full DNA analysis, so until such a study is conducted the Andean wolf is destined to remain a cryptozoological enigma.

angel hair

Clusters of web-like material that mysteriously fall from the sky.

Various people in different countries have reported the falling from the sky of clusters of fine filaments, usually compared to fine string or cobwebs, often covering large areas of ground. This material is said to quickly disappear, particularly if touched.

Different explanations have been put forward, linking such falls to the frozen contrails of jet aircraft, to the activities of UFOs, to secret military experiments with radar-cloaking material, or simply to the effects of long-term air pollution. One interesting idea is that angel hair is actually silk spun by so-called ballooning spiders. After hatching, these arachnids disperse themselves by spinning out silken threads into the air until enough is released to catch the prevailing wind, which then carries them (and their silk) through the air for distances varying from a matter of metres to several kilometres. It is said that Charles Darwin noted the arrival of such spiders while on a ship far off the South American coast.

However, no individual explanation of these gossamer-like falls has been able to account for all such phenomena, especially since the unfortunate tendency of the material to disappear soon after landing has made collection and analysis problematic, to say the least. See also FALLS.

angels

Spiritual beings generally believed to be messengers from God.

In the Bible, God speaks to humankind in various direct and indirect ways, but the idea of the divine messengers known as angels (from the Greek *angelos*, messenger) appears from the very beginning of the Old Testament. Angels are present in the Garden of Eden, and bring insight to Abraham, Jacob, Moses and others. In the New Testament it is the angel Gabriel who announces to Mary that she will bear the son of God. Angels are also mentioned in Jewish and Muslim holy scripture.

In Christianity, angels are believed to form a hierarchy in heaven, consisting of three orders. The first order is subdivided into seraphim (highest of the nine ranks or choirs), cherubim and thrones; the second into dominions, virtues and powers; the third into principalities, archangels and angels. The seven archangels include Gabriel, Michael, Raphael and Uriel. Even the DEVIL is often portrayed as being a FALLEN ANGEL, Lucifer, cast out of heaven for rebelling against God. In all cases angels are traditionally depicted in art as having a human form, with the addition of great feathered wings.

In the Jewish mystical KABBALAH, each of the

ten SEPHIROTH, or Divine emanations of the TREE OF LIFE, is associated with an archangel. Angels are also mentioned in Muslim holy scripture – the four archangels of Islam are Azrael, Israfil, Gabriel and Michael.

Perhaps the most significant modern example of supposed angelic intervention in human affairs is the legend of the ANGELS OF MONS. In 1914, in the early stages of World War I, when the British Expeditionary Force was being driven back by the Germans, a belief arose that when a successful stand was taken at Mons the British forces were assisted by St George and a host of angels.

The belief that every human soul has a guardian angel is not a specific article of Christian faith, but it is an idea that has shown great persistence. Even in the early 21st century, many believe that they are protected by an angel on whom they can call for help in times of need. In the philosophical system of ALEISTER CROWLEY, the divine element of the individual self is conceived of and externalized as the Holy Guardian Angel who can guide the believer's path through life. A poll conducted in the 1990s apparently showed that two-thirds of the US population believed in angels and nearly half believed they had a guardian angel.

In the Bible angels are often terrifying beings who express the wrath of God, and it was an Angel of Death who killed the firstborn sons of the Egyptian oppressors of the Jews. Nowadays, however, the word is almost exclusively synonymous with benevolence. A memorable and lasting angelic manifestation is provided by Anthony Gormley's giant statue *The Angel of the North* (1998), near Gateshead in England, which seems to welcome all of the people of the north-east into the protection of its huge outstretched wings.

angels, fallen
Angels cast out from Heaven as a punishment for disobeying or rebelling against God. The chief fallen angel is Lucifer, who became Satan after his fall from grace.
According to the Christian, Islamic and Jewish traditions, a number of angels were cast out from Heaven as a punishment for disobeying or rebelling against God. Although fallen angels are rarely mentioned in biblical scripture, there are a number of different beliefs as to how they misused the free will granted to them and incurred God's wrath. According to some sources, when God created Man, he called on the angelic hosts to bow before his creation, and LUCIFER, the proudest and most exalted of the angels, refused to abase himself in this way. The Koran relates a similar story in which Azazel, the chief of all the DJINN, refused to bow before Adam, and was transformed into the archdemon Iblis and banished from Heaven. In the Christian tradition it is generally believed that Lucifer

became overambitious and sought to raise himself to the same level as God, or to overthrow him. One-third of the heavenly host sided with Lucifer in the ensuing war against God and those angels who remained faithful to him. When Lucifer and his army were defeated, they were cast out of Heaven.

Another reason for the fall from grace of some angels is given in the apocryphal Book of Enoch, which tells of an order of angels called the Watchers, or Grigori. The Watchers fell in love with the daughters of men and took wives among them, creating hybrid offspring known as the Nephilim. They began to reveal to man certain sciences forbidden by God, such as ASTROLOGY, DIVINATION and MAGIC, and God punished their betrayal by expelling them from heaven.

Some believe that the fallen angels will roam the earth, attempting to corrupt mankind and opposing all that is holy, until Judgement Day (see DOOMSDAY CULTS), when they will be banished to Hell for eternity.

Angels of Mons
Aerial phantoms that allegedly appeared in support of Allied forces during World War I.
Following the Battle of Mons in August 1914, rumours spread that ghostly knights had appeared on the battlefield in support of the retreating French and British soldiers and that these APPARITIONS had counter-attacked the approaching German army. Later versions of what became known as the Angels of Mons legend had the Allies assisted by angels, St Michael, Joan of Arc or St George. Many now believe that these rumours stemmed from a short story – *The Bowmen* by journalist Arthur Machen – in which spectral English archers from the Battle of Agincourt join British soldiers in resisting a German advance. First published in the *London Evening News* on 14 September 1914, the story circulated widely – first among civilians in Britain and then across the Channel to soldiers in France. In his autobiography, *Goodbye To All That* (1929), Robert Graves recalls hearing the claims of the Angels of Mons while serving on the Western Front but notes that he never met any first-hand witnesses. For his part, Machen fervently denied there was any truth in his story, but it continued to be retold as truth (and with embellishments) throughout the war and after, suiting the patriotic public mood.

Contemporary testimony from soldiers present at Mons fails to corroborate anything resembling the apparitions. Although numerous service personnel and their relatives reported psychic experiences during World War I, these were primarily PREMONITIONS, CRISIS APPARITIONS or 'ordinary' GHOSTS. However, the

The cover of Arthur Machen's *The Bowmen, and other Legends of War*, the title story of which is often cited as the origin of the legend of the Angels of Mons.
(© Mary Evans Picture Library)

tale of the Angels of Mons may be seen as a rare 20th-century equivalent of the AERIAL PHANTOMS reported at times of national crisis in earlier centuries.

animal disturbance
The alleged effect on nearby animals that is often reported with UFO sightings.

There are hundreds of cases on record in which it has been reported that animals have reacted to the presence of a UFO. Human witnesses often say that animals appear to be aware of something well before they notice anything unusual themselves – the whole experience having begun with this strange or out-of-character behaviour on the part of their pet.

In the 1970s, the diplomat and UFO researcher Gordon Creighton published a study of over 200 animal disturbance cases in the publication *Flying Saucer Review*. The total number of reports has more than quadrupled since. Approximately half of these cases feature dogs – there are three times as many dogs mentioned as any other animal. This may be

partly explained by the prominence of dogs as pets, although the records would suggest that domestic cats are over fifty times less likely to react to the presence of a UFO.

Animal disturbance cases are of particular interest to UFO researchers because they sidestep two of the common criticisms levelled against reports of human-only sightings – that is, that the report is a fabrication, or that the witness has interpreted their experience in an extraterrestrial context because of their familiarity with the popular media coverage of UFOs.

The fact that some animals apparently respond in this way has led to suggestions that UFOs may emit something to which animals are more sensitive than humans – sound, microwave energy and ionized particles have all been proposed. This is similar to the suggestions that have arisen out of the observation that the behaviour of some animals changes immediately prior to an EARTHQUAKE or tremor.

animal ghosts
Ghosts that appear in the form of an animal.

Stories of animal ghosts are found throughout the world, often linked with specific religious and magical traditions. Although tales of animal ghosts are widespread, they have been little studied as a specific category by psychical researchers, largely because sightings of animal ghosts are relatively rare. The whole area is complicated by the existence of accounts of supernatural animals, such as BLACK DOGS and other bizarre creatures which, although they might be considered to fall within the province of CRYPTOZOOLOGY, sometimes exhibit ghost-like behaviour and lack of physical form. Furthermore, in some traditions the ghost may appear as an animal but be regarded by witnesses as the transmogrified spirit of a deceased human.

One popular study, *Animal Ghosts* (1913) by Elliot O'Donnell, dutifully records stories of phantom dogs, cats, horses, rabbits, wolves, bears and birds together with legends of more exotic creatures such as phantom tigers, but the majority of accounts are at best folkloric. Outside the realm of folklore, a nationwide survey of hauntings in Great Britain conducted between 1967 and 1973 by the *Journal of Paraphysics* revealed that animal ghosts accounted for an average of 2–5 per cent of all reported APPARITIONS annually, and there is no reason to believe this statistic has changed. Generally, in Western cultural tradition, only domestic animals such as dogs, cats and horses are said to appear as ghosts. The implication may be that some kind of emotional association with humans is necessary for an animal to manifest as a ghost, or it might simply be that it would be difficult to distinguish between sightings of physical or discarnate wild animals. See also GHOST DOGS.

animal magnetism

A proposed force or ethereal medium existing within human and animal bodies that could supposedly be employed for therapeutic purposes.

FRANZ ANTON MESMER used the term animal magnetism to describe a type of magnetic force that he believed existed in the body. This could be used to affect the flow of magnetic fluids (which came to be known as 'mesmeric fluids') within the body for the purpose of curing illnesses. The process came to be known as MESMERISM. Similar study (or the supposed use) of the interaction between electromagnetism and living things has also variously been known as 'psycodunamy', 'electropsychology' and 'electrobiology'. The phrase 'animal magnetism' is now popularly used, without the overtones of mesmerism, to describe someone's charismatic or sexual appeal.

animal psi

The suggested potential existence of psychic abilities in some animals.

Animal psi (often abbreviated to 'anpsi') describes the range of abilities, including EXTRASENSORY PERCEPTION, PRECOGNITION and TELEPATHY, that some people have ascribed to animals in the light of stories of feats that cannot apparently be explained by normal means. Such feats include the ability of a pet to find and be reunited with its owner over incredible distances; the apparent ability of a pet to know when its owner has suffered harm or has died, even when separated from them; an animal's apparent reaction to danger before it is upon them; an animal's supposed reactions to the presence of UFOS (see ANIMAL DISTURBANCE) or GHOSTS; and claims that animals can sense the presence of as-yet-undiscovered illnesses in their owners.

Sceptics would argue that, even if it is accepted that these things occur, they can be explained: we already know that many animals have vastly superior sensory abilities to our own; they may react to subtle signals of which we are not aware; humans have a tendency to anthropomorphize and misinterpret the behaviour of their pets; some events may occur simply by chance; or our observations may be subject to such things as cognitive bias (see CHANCE AND COINCIDENCE).

There has been little research of a scientific nature in this area. However, a classic example that is used to argue for the existence of animal psi is the fact that some dogs appear to know when their owners are about to arrive home, even if this is not at a regular time. Research into this area has been carried out by

'The Magic Finger', a satire on animal magnetism from c.1795. (© Mary Evans Picture Library)

(among others) the controversial biologist RUPERT SHELDRAKE. Sheldrake used a dog called Jaytee who reputedly reacted to the exact moment that his owner left work by running to the front window of the house – a feat that had been reproduced for various television programmes. Although Sheldrake's findings appeared to support the truth of the phenomenon, subsequent investigations carried out by Dr Richard Wiseman and Matthew Smith indicated that the dog in question made frequent trips to the front window during the day, often in reaction to obvious events in the street – so the appearance of psychic ability was nothing more than an effect of selective observation.

There are inherent difficulties in establishing in detail the exact sensory and cognitive processes underlying particular animal behaviour and so, at present, claimed examples of psi-driven behaviour on the part of animals remain at best anecdotal. However, as animals are less likely than humans to be involved in deliberate fraud and trickery, they may ultimately prove to be better subjects for future research.

animals, mystery *see* CRYPTOZOOLOGY

animism

The belief that every object contains a spirit or soul.

The word animism is derived from the Latin word *animus*, meaning 'spirit' or 'soul'. Its basic principle may be stated simply as 'everything is alive' or 'everything has a soul'. Animism is one of man's oldest beliefs, with origins probably dating back to the Palaeolithic age; animistic beliefs are still widespread today among native cultures, and some modern neopagans also describe their belief system as animist, with THE GODDESS and HORNED GOD who make up everything that exists, while pantheists similarly equate 'God' with 'existence'.

The concept of animism was first developed by the British anthropologist Sir Edward B Tylor in the late 19th century. In his book *Primitive Culture* (1871), Tylor defined animism as a general belief in spiritual beings, and considered it to be 'a minimum definition of religion', stating that all religions, from the simplest to the most complex, had in common some kind of animistic basis. He suggested that primitive man's belief in the existence of a human spirit evolved from his attempt to explain the causes of sleep, dreams and death, and that he then projected this idea of a spirit on to the natural world around him. The notions that humans possess souls, that these souls have an existence outside of the body before and after death, and that animals, plants, places and natural phenomena also possess or are an expression of spirits, are central to animism.

In the animistic worldviews of many hunter-gatherer cultures, humans are regarded as a part of nature, neither superior to nor separate from it, but on a level equal to animals, plants and natural forces. It is therefore considered essential to survival to treat the spirits of the natural world with respect, carrying out rituals or sacrifices to appease them or ensure their favour in providing food, shelter and fertility, and to ward off evil. Although specific beliefs of animism may vary, there are considerable similarities between the characteristics of the gods and goddesses worshipped in different animistic societies, and in the rituals they practise. These rituals are often performed by shamans or priests, who are believed to possess greater spiritual powers than ordinary humans, and who commune with the spirit world by means of visions, trances, dance and the use of sacred tools. A deep respect for animal, plant and tree spirits, and a strong sense of connection to and reverence for the spirits of ancestors, are also characteristic of animistic cultures, while some do not make a distinction between animate and inanimate objects, attributing spirits even to geographic features, everyday objects and manufactured items.

ankh

An ancient Egyptian symbol consisting of a T-shaped cross with a looped top, which represents life.

The ancient Egyptian symbol of the ankh, which consists of a T-shaped cross with a looped top arm, appears frequently in Egyptian tomb paintings and other art. Egyptians carried the ankh as an AMULET during life, and were buried with it to ensure their continuing existence in the afterlife. As a hieroglyph, the ankh is used to represent the words for both 'life' and 'hand mirror', and Egyptian mirrors were often made in the shape of an ankh; the ankh hieroglyph also forms part of the hieroglyphs of words such as 'health' and 'happiness'. It symbolizes the life principle, and since it resembles a key, it is sometimes called the Key of Life. Gods and goddesses are often depicted holding it, either by the loop, or bearing one in each hand, crossed over the breast. In Egyptian tomb paintings, the deity is shown using it to confer the gift of life on the dead person's mummy, and in other Egyptian art the god or goddess touches a person with it to denote conception. It was also known as the Key of the Nile, since it was thought to symbolize the mystic union of Isis and Osiris which was believed to initiate the annual flooding of the river on which life in Egypt depended.

There is much debate among Egyptologists as to what the ankh was intended to represent. Some see it as a stylized womb, and others as a sandal strap with the loop going round the ankle (in ancient Egyptian, the word for 'sandal thong' and the word for 'life' were homophones). To some it is a representation of the human genitalia, the loop symbolizing the vagina and the T-shaped cross the phallus, while to others it symbolizes the sunrise, the loop depicting the sun coming up over the horizon, which is represented by the crossbar. Because of the ankh's importance to Egyptians, it was adopted by the early Christian church in Egypt, and although the cross became the dominant symbol of Christianity, the ankh, also known as the *crux ansata*, was retained, especially on Christian TALISMANS, until well into medieval times. It is still worn today and used in popular culture as a symbol of arcane life-forces and spiritual magic.

anomalies

Events or things that deviate from the norm, the expected or the standard.

Anomalies have always played a role in man's understanding of the universe and his existence in it, because they give us a measure of the 'other'. Our view of the world has evolved out of the search for knowledge, reliable methods of prediction, and the formalization of this knowledge in laws and formulas. Generally, anomalies occur at the point where the familiar is disrupted by the unfamiliar. We take comfort in the known and tend to fear the unknown as capricious and unpredictable. If we believe in a natural order or a divine justice, an unexpected event may seem unsettling and even unjust.

To traditional cultures, the natural order governing both individual lives and the nation at large was summarized in the dictum 'As above, so below.' Anomalies – 'perturbations of the natural order' – became important as signs of cosmological imbalance, possibly of conduct that had offended the gods. Until more recent times, provincial officials, both religious and secular, in most cultures (but especially in ancient Babylon, Rome and China), were duty bound to file reports to central government on any unexpected event – quakes, monstrous births, excessive storms, unusual animal behaviour, etc – in case they were indications of divine displeasure. Christian priests and vicars often reported to their bishops, for similar reasons; Norway's Bishop Pontoppidan, in the mid-18th century, took the reports about SEA SERPENTS in the northern Atlantic as signs that the biblical Leviathan was abroad.

To some extent the history of modern science has been one of coming to terms with anomalies. At first, to the superstitious, anomalies were signs, PORTENTS, prodigies and monsters (from the Latin *monstrum*, to show or to warn) to be feared and shunned or argued over scholastically. In the great period of scientific growth, from the Enlightenment to the Victorian period, science's confidence in its ability to account for natural and observed phenomena ran high. Phenomena, observations and data that contradicted its laws or which threatened to upset the authority, dogma or status quo of science, tended to be ignored, suppressed, discredited or explained away. A famous example, attributed to the French academician Antoine Lavoisier (1743–94), enshrines the contemporary attitude to a report of a meteorite falling to earth: 'There are no stones in the sky, therefore no stones can fall from the sky.' In this case, the first-hand observation of the fall was an anomaly.

CHARLES FORT was one of the first modern thinkers to challenge the orthodox view that anomalies did not matter, arguing that anomalies – especially in the sciences or observations of natural phenomena – are often the first sign that perhaps we don't understand as much as we think we do. Anticipating Thomas Kuhn's theories about the nature of scientific revolutions, Fort observed that the progress of science is not a steady, cumulative acquisition of knowledge but often a vicious struggle between competing overviews. Fort called these overviews 'Dominants', but Kuhn's word 'paradigm' is more commonly used today. Kuhn defined a paradigm as 'an implicit body of theoretical and methodological belief that permits selection, evaluation, and criticism'.

William R Corliss has defined anomalies as 'observations that do not yield to mainstream explanations [or which] go beyond the reach of present scientific explanation'. He wrote that:

> Anomalousness is often in the eye of the beholder. It depends how well one is satisfied with those explanations based on currently accepted paradigms.

Kuhn noted that new science 'emerges only with difficulty, manifested by resistance, against a background provided by expectation'. Today's anomalists agree that anomalies can only be measured against the baseline of well-established theories: that is, relative to the current paradigm. The problem here, says Corliss, is that that baseline is constantly shifting. To paraphrase Charles Fort: an anomaly is only relative to something else which, itself, can only be defined relatively. See also ANOMALISTICS; FORTEANA.

anomalistics

An attempt to scientifically systematize the study of anomalous phenomena.

The term 'anomalistics' is thought to have been coined in 1973 by US anthropologist Roger W Wescott (1923–2000) in a paper in which he referred to the emerging interdisciplinary study of scientific anomalies, characterized by two central features. Firstly, and in contrast to FORTEANISM, it is scientific, concerned only with empirical evidence and avoiding discussion of metaphysical, theological or SUPERNATURAL issues. In the words of US sociologist Marcello Truzzi (1935–2003), who founded the Center for Scientific Anomalies Research:

> [While anomalistics] recognizes that unexplained phenomena exist, it does not presume these are unexplainable … it insists on the testability of claims (including both verifiability and falsifiability), seeks parsimonious explanations, places the burden of proof on the claimant, and expects evidence of a claim to be commensurate with its degree of extraordinariness (anomalousness).

According to Wescott, the second important characteristic of anomalistics is that it is interdisciplinary. An anomaly, when investigated, may reveal information that overhauls the current explanation that it violates, or it may reveal different relationships between existing fields; eg some phenomena of PARAPSYCHOLOGY, which grew out of the psychological investigation of PSI and ESP, may turn out to be more properly the domain of quantum physics; some UFO phenomena may involve neurophysiology, or seismology, not astronomy or meteorology; and some aspects of TELEPATHY research are purely statistical. In any case the anomaly can be said to point to an improved science – what CHARLES FORT called a 'more inclusive' science – one which explains more than it did before the anomaly. The new information may also precipitate a whole new area of knowledge.

Those who take this approach, wrote Truzzi, are 'anomalists'. Anomalists, like forteans, 'search for patterns in the acceptance and rejection of new scientific ideas' and this necessarily cuts across scientific disciplines, involving the history, sociology, psychology and philosophy of science. Truzzi, Wescott and others have been at pains to distance anomalists from other proponents of anomalies – particularly forteans, occultists, ufologists, cryptozoologists, etc – by their intention to work within the existing framework of scientific adjudication.

Writing in the *Bulletin* of the Research Institute of Anomalous Phenomena (RIAP), founded in Kharkiv, Ukraine, in 1992, Dr Vladimir Rubtsov, contradicting Truzzi somewhat, declared that 'anomalistics cannot be called a scientific discipline [or] even an interdisciplinary area of scientific research' because it lacks 'common methodological standards'. Apart from a small number of vigorous organizations – including the SOCIETY FOR PSYCHICAL RESEARCH, the SOCIETY FOR SCIENTIFIC EXPLORATION, the PRINCETON ENGINEERING ANOMALIES RESEARCH and the SOCIETY FOR INTERDISCIPLINARY STUDIES – the field has been left open to Truzzi's non-anomalists, including those he branded mystery-mongers and scoffers. Nevertheless, the body of work built up by fortean researchers, associations, periodicals and data accumulations, argues Dr Rubtsov, constitutes a valid and substantial 'anomalistic community' which has evolved out of the work of Charles Fort to provide a valuable critique of the scientific world-view.

William R Corliss, compiler of the *Sourcebook Project* volumes (see ANOMALIES), comments (in *Science Frontiers*, 1994):

> My view is that anomaly research, while not science *per se*, has the potential to destabilize paradigms and accelerate scientific change. Anomalies reveal nature as it really is: complex, chaotic, possibly even unplumbable. Anomalies also encourage the framing of rogue paradigms, such as [RUPERT SHELDRAKE's] 'morphic resonance' and the steady-state universe. Anomaly research

also transcends scientific currency by celebrating bizarre and incongruous facets of nature, such as coincidence and seriality.

This accords with Truzzi's view:

> While recognizing that a legitimate anomaly may constitute a crisis for conventional theories in science, anomalistics also sees them as an opportunity for progressive change in science.

Far from being anti-science, this provocative value of anomalies, relative to the main body of knowledge was recognized by William James in these words:

> Round about the accredited and orderly facts of every science, there ever floats a sort of dust-cloud of exceptional observations, of occurrences minute and irregular and seldom met with, which it always proves more easy to ignore than to attend to … Anyone will renovate his science who will steadily look after the irregular phenomena, and when the science is renewed, its new formulas often have more of the voice of the exception in them than of what were supposed to be the rules.

anpsi *see* ANIMAL PSI

anthroposophy

A human-based spiritual doctrine founded by Austrian social philosopher Rudolph Steiner, in which the aim is to nurture the life of the soul in the individual and in society.

Anthroposophy means, literally, 'human wisdom' or 'knowledge of the nature of man' (from Greek *anthrōpos*, man, and *sophiā*, knowledge). Its founder, Austrian social philosopher RUDOLPH STEINER, had originally been a member of the THEOSOPHICAL SOCIETY, and was the president of its German section, but after a difference of opinion with the Society's leader, Steiner left in 1912 to set up his own group, the Anthroposophical Society. Anthroposophy differs from theosophy in its emphasis on the importance of Western esoteric thought, rather than Eastern systems such as Hinduism and Buddhism, and although it views Christ and his mission on earth somewhat differently from mainstream Christianity, it nevertheless stresses their importance. Steiner, who sometimes also referred to it as 'Spiritual Science', described anthroposophy as a path of knowledge whose purpose was 'to guide the spiritual in the human being to the spiritual in the universe'.

The basis for anthroposophy is contained in Steiner's seminal work *The Philosophy of Freedom*

(1894), and his doctoral thesis *Truth and Science* (1891). Anthroposophy views human beings as consisting of three intimately connected parts: the physical body, the soul and the spirit. It also holds the view that four subtle bodies make up the human being: the physical body, the etheric body, the astral body, and the ego. The aim of anthroposophy is for one to become 'more human', by learning to be more conscious and deliberate about one's targets and deeds, and its adherents believe that one can reach higher levels of consciousness through meditation, observation and openness, in a lifelong quest for knowledge and spiritual development. According to anthroposophy, a real spiritual world exists, out of which the material world has gradually condensed and evolved, and this spiritual world can be accessed and researched, under the right circumstances, through direct experience, by those who practise rigorous self-discipline; Steiner's writings describe many exercises to help achieve this.

The practical application of the principles of anthroposophy have led to a number of social and scientific innovations: the introduction of a system of biodynamic agriculture, in which only organic materials are used for fertilization; the founding of a medical movement which gives particular importance to homeopathy, and which now has its own hospitals and medical universities; and a worldwide group of centres (Camphill Villages) dedicated to community-building for people with developmental or learning disabilities. But the most significant influence of anthroposophy is probably in the field of education, with Steiner or Waldorf Schools, which are now found in many countries, and which are based on Steiner's holistic educational theories. With a goal of educating the 'whole child', Steiner schools place great importance on balancing the child's natural stages of development with creativity and academic excellence, and there is a strong emphasis on the arts, social skills and spiritual values.

antigravity

A theoretical force that acts in the opposite direction to gravity, which might be harnessed to drive spaceships or other craft.

In his book *The First Men In The Moon* (1901), H G Wells invented an imaginary material called Cavorite, which could shield objects from the effects of gravity. The science involved was impossible, but ever since then there has been speculation on whether there might really be a way of nullifying gravity.

A possible route to antigravity might be offered by a Grand Unified Theory, one which unites the four fundamental forces of the universe (gravity, electromagnetic, strong nuclear and weak nuclear) in a single force. Einstein did not succeed in producing a Grand Unified Theory, and progress in this area has been slow. However, if completed such a theory might offer the possibility of controlling gravity by electromagnetic means, a field known as electrogravitics.

There was much excitement in the early 1990s when Russian scientist Eugene Podkletnov reported that he had found a way of blocking gravity using spinning superconductors. However, there were some irregularities in his work, and nobody has replicated his results. After some work based on Podkletnov's ideas, NASA's Breakthrough Propulsion Physics Laboratory has now abandoned this line of research. It is thought that the magnetic fields involved may have been affecting the measuring equipment rather than gravity itself.

In amateur science circles, a great deal of attention has been given to 'lifters', simple devices that generate a force from coils of wire. However, the force is caused by the acceleration of ions and has nothing to do with antigravity.

There is some serious academic work on antigravity, and many believe that our current theory of gravity can be improved. In particular, observations of the rate of expansion of the universe and the progress of NASA's Pioneer 10 and 11 probes suggest that as well as the pull of gravity there may be an additional force providing a push. However, work on actual antigravity drives remains in the realms of FRINGE SCIENCE.

ape men *see* MAN-BEASTS

aphrodisiacs

Foods or drugs credited with the effect of arousing sexual desire or causing someone to fall in love.

Historically, a wide range of plants, animals and even human or animal body parts were believed to have aphrodisiac properties because of their shape, ability to produce heat or association with sexual reproduction. Among the foods still popularly believed to have aphrodisiac properties are oysters and asparagus – the latter falling into a group of plants that were believed to derive their powers from their phallic shape.

WITCHES have long been credited with the power of producing love potions containing aphrodisiacs which, when administered, could cause someone to fall in love, even against their will. Indeed, such practices were outlawed in Britain under the various witchcraft Acts of the 16th and 17th centuries.

Aphrodisiacs, or love potions, would take one of two basic forms – they would either be administered to the intended victim, who would fall in love with the first person they saw, or (after the incorporation of hair or nail clippings from the target) they would be taken by the protagonist who would then be able to summon their intended prey. See also MAGIC, LOVE.

apocalypse
A Christian or Jewish text which claims to contain a disclosure or revelation of hidden things or of the future, made by God to a chosen prophet, and often describing the end of the world and the Last Judgement.

The Greek word for 'an uncovering' has given us the term 'apocalypse', which refers to a type of Jewish or Christian literature relating a disclosure or revelation given by God to a chosen prophet, and often describing the end of the world.

From the 2nd century AD onward, the term 'apocalypse' has been used to refer to a number of books which share several characteristic features. They are usually written in the first person, and claim to be a revelation of mysteries, in particular God's purpose for humanity; the disclosure is made through a dream or vision, and God usually speaks not directly to the prophet, but through ANGELS who act as the visionary's guide. They sometimes describe the deeds and nature of angels and evil spirits, and often include an account of the end of the world, the Last Judgement, the messianic age, Heaven and Hell, and are characterized by fantastic imagery and mystical symbolism.

Apocalyptic literature was much in vogue among the Jews of the first centuries before and after Christ, but the first real example of a Hebrew apocalypse text is the Old Testament Book of Daniel. Another is the Book of Enoch. Among Christian Gnostic writings there are five separate apocalypses: the First Apocalypse of James, which is said to contain the secret teachings of Christ to his brother, James the Just; the Second Apocalypse of James; the Apocalypse of Adam; the Apocalypse of Paul, an account of the apostle's ascent into Heaven; and the Gnostic Apocalypse of Peter, which is part of the New Testament Apocrypha, and records a vision of the apostle in which he speaks with Christ in the spirit.

The most well-known Christian apocalypse text is the last book of the New Testament, the Book of Revelation, also known as the Revelation of St John, with its allegorical description of the Four Horsemen of the Apocalypse, the Whore of Babylon, and the Great Beast (see BEAST, THE GREAT).

apotheosis
The elevation of a person to the rank of a god after their death.

Known as either apotheosis or deification, the elevation of a person to the rank of a god after their death is closely related to the ancestor worship found in a number of ancient cultures. The Egyptian pharaohs, who were already regarded as divine beings while alive, were believed to complete their apotheosis upon death. The custom of according divine status to a deceased person is, however, most commonly associated with the later Roman Empire. This Roman tradition began with the Senate's deification of Julius Caesar after his assassination in 44 BC. In AD 14 the Emperor Augustus was similarly honoured, as were many future emperors.

The apotheosis of a recently deceased emperor by his successor was a predominantly political act, but it was readily accepted in many parts of the empire; in a culture where it was the custom for children to worship the spirits of their fathers, it was natural that the emperor, who in life had been considered the father of the empire, should be accorded divine honours. However, this honour was not granted automatically; hated rulers, such as Caligula and Nero, were not made gods. Other members of the imperial family, such as Augustus' wife Livia, were also sometimes granted divine status after death.

The Roman process of apotheosis involved a ritual in which a waxen image of the deceased emperor was created, richly dressed and sitting in state, and after a given period, was ceremonially burned. The whole notion was parodied by the 1st century Roman writer Seneca in his satirical work *Apocolocyntosis divi Claudii* ('The Pumpkinification of the Emperor Claudius'), in which he described the Emperor Claudius being transformed after death, not into a god, but into a pumpkin.

apotropaics
Objects or practices which are believed to have the power to turn away evil.

The word 'apotropaic' comes from the Greek *apo*, meaning from, and *tropē*, meaning turning, and is used to refer to any object or practice believed to have the power to turn away evil, in particular the EVIL EYE. Under the heading of apotropaic magic comes any ritual or custom intended to ward off malign influences or bad luck – from an elaborate ceremony to a simple knocking on wood or crossing of fingers, or the carrying of an AMULET, CHARM or TALISMAN. One of the oldest and most universal apotropaics is the representation of an eye; in the Middle East, a ball or disc painted with a blue circle enclosing a black circle representing the evil eye is used to return the malevolent gaze to its source, and the Middle Eastern amulet known as the Hand of Fatima sometimes incorporates a blue eye for the same purpose. Large eyes are also painted on the prows of Mediterranean boats to protect them from the evil eye, and Greek drinking vessels dating back to the 6th century BC often had an exaggerated eye painted on them.

The doorways and windows of buildings were

The prow of this Maltese fishing vessel is decorated with an apotropaic, to return the malevolent gaze of the evil eye. (© Paul Thompson; Eye Ubiquitous/Corbis)

believed to be especially vulnerable to admitting evil, so important buildings such as churches and castles often have gargoyles, grotesque faces and other apotropaic figures carved around these openings to frighten away evil spirits. The faces carved on pumpkin and turnip lanterns at HALLOWE'EN have a similar function, since on that night evil spirits are thought to be abroad. Mirrors and other reflective objects are also believed to deflect the evil eye, and HORSESHOES are still hung up to ward off malevolent spirits. In vampire fiction, the word 'apotropaic' is sometimes used to refer to items such as garlic and crucifixes, which are said to repel or destroy vampires.

apparitions
Visual appearances of people, animals or objects that are not materially present.
Apparitions have been reported around the world for thousands of years. Every culture appears to have a belief both in the survival of the dead and in appearances of the deceased to the living. However, apparitions should not automatically be equated with the SPIRITS of the dead since they can include the forms of still-living people (see GHOSTS OF THE LIVING) and animals and also of inanimate objects or scenery. Apparitions are usually of short duration and are characterized by an ability to appear and disappear without explanation. They are generally visible to only a limited number of people and rarely leave any physical traces. Apparitions may

sometimes be interpreted as relating to past, present or future occurrences. It has been noted that not all people report seeing them (even in instances where others do), suggesting that there may be a subjective element to the process – ranging from some form of EXTRASENSORY PERCEPTION, through to non-paranormal processes such as HALLUCINATION or misperception caused by expectation – although it is often claimed that certain mammals, particularly dogs, CATS and horses, also appear to react to their appearance.

The most extensive collection of apparition reports was undertaken by the SOCIETY FOR PSYCHICAL RESEARCH (SPR) in its *Census of Hallucinations* in 1894. Collectors were sent out to obtain answers to the following question (among others):

> Have you ever, when believing yourself to be completely awake, had a vivid impression of seeing or being touched by a living being or inanimate object, or of hearing a voice; which impression, so far as you could discover, was not due to any external physical cause?

Of the 17,000 answers received, 2,272 were in the affirmative – although it is important to note that the question does not express, or invite, any opinion as to the source of the perception. Of those who had experienced impressions, 32 per cent reported seeing the form of a living person, 14 per cent had seen those of dead persons and 33 per cent persons who remained unidentified. Most were remarkably normal in appearance, although occasionally figures were partly formed or luminous. Extrapolating from the figures obtained from the census as a whole, one in six people in England believed in the existence of GHOSTS while one in fourteen believed they had seen one. The findings of the SPR surveys indicated that 'apparitions' were primarily a hallucinatory phenomenon, but with the curious elements that they could sometimes be seen by more than one percipient on the same occasion, or seen by different people on separate occasions. Much thought was given to the idea that the experience of seeing a ghost could be (at least partly) to do with some form of TELEPATHY between the living.

Surveys in the 20th century have tended to confirm these patterns. Again, the types of apparitions reported were remarkably mundane in appearance. In some cases the apparition was described as appearing to have a purpose (to impart information, to give a warning or to say farewell) but in the majority of cases it appeared to have no discernable motive or meaning.

Classifying apparitional reports is difficult because of the complexity and variety of the experiences described. In addition to apparitions of human beings, the following categories can be listed:

Animal apparitions – either real or symbolic animals (see ANIMAL GHOSTS).

Religious apparitions – appearances of deities or religious persons such as Christ, the Virgin Mary (see MARIAN APPARITIONS), individual saints, or religious symbols or emblems (eg crosses, flaming hearts).

Humanoid – apparitions with a superficial resemblance to a human being but incorporating features suggesting such things as a supernatural entity (for example, an ANGEL or FAIRY), a hybrid terrestrial species or an EXTRATERRESTRIAL form of life.

Inanimate objects or transport – including vehicles such as ships, cars or planes (see GHOST SHIPS; PHANTOM AEROPLANES).

Scenic apparitions – phantom scenery, such as buildings and gardens that do not exist, or wholesale re-enactments of scenes such as battles (see SPECTRAL ARMIES).

Occasionally apparitions also feature in POLTERGEIST cases but this is very much the exception rather than the rule.

There are many competing theories as to the causes of apparitions and what they may represent. The most detailed theory was that offered by G N M Tyrell (1879–1953) who proposed, in his book *Apparitions* (1942), that the subconscious mind receives PSYCHIC impressions and acts as 'stage carpenter' by creating an apparitional figure in the form of a visual hallucination. Alternatively, it has been suggested by others that apparitional experiences involve interaction between the mind and a 'deeper level of reality'. However, it is equally possible that the range of reports loosely grouped together as 'sightings of apparitions' may be brought about through a number of different mechanisms – including (and some might say limited to) a number of processes recognized by mainstream psychology. However, such things as COLLECTIVE APPARITIONS present more of a difficulty for those who wish to explain them away in entirely 'non-paranormal' terms – and the fact that there is still a huge amount that we do not understand about human perception, and the processing of sensory information, will ensure that the debate remains alive for some time to come.

apparitions, collective *see* COLLECTIVE APPARITIONS

apparitions, crisis *see* CRISIS APPARITIONS

apparitions, Marian *see* MARIAN APPARITIONS

apparitions, recurrent *see* RECURRENT APPARITIONS

appearances

An appearance is the sudden arrival of someone or something, at a place where they were not present (or had not been seen) before.

As used in discussions of FORTEANA, the term 'appearances' applies not to the way something looks but to the phenomenon of sudden arrival (or the noticing) of a person, animal or object that is 'out of place' or which was not present (or not noticed) a few moments before. It is the opposite of the phenomenon of DISAPPEARANCES and both might indicate the beginning and ending of a TELEPORTATION transaction. This hypothetical process may manifest differently in different sub-categories of phenomena.

CHARLES FORT wondered whether teleportation might play a part in explaining some of the peculiar characteristics of FALLS – ie objects or creatures falling under unusual circumstances. He suggested that if teleportation existed, it could show up in data of fishes, frogs or stones, etc, disappearing from wherever they were plentiful to materialize at an 'appearing point' in the air from which they are seen to fall. Almost any object or substance may be teleported in this way, so the hypothesis can be extended to account for the appearance of, for example, persistent stains or the flow of blood-like liquids on bleeding images (see IMAGES, BLEEDING).

Such a theory would certainly account for reports of stones falling from beneath the ceilings inside rooms or the way falling frogs seem to fall in defined areas instead of being scattered by the WHIRLWINDS as envisaged in the standard explanation. There are several cases in the POLTERGEIST literature of investigators – having been pelted with stones – picking up one or two, marking them and throwing them back in the direction of their trajectory, only to be surprised by the re-appearance of the marked stones in another volley. When objects appear during poltergeist disturbances or during the SÉANCES of physical mediums (see MEDIUMS, PHYSICAL) they are usually termed APPORTS.

Perhaps the largest category of appearances concerns the origin of OUT-OF-PLACE ANIMALS – especially those like ALIEN BIG CATS – which are 'alien' to the local ecology and landscape. Usually, the first we hear of them is a local news report of their sudden appearance, ie they are sighted where they have not been seen before. Very few cryptozoologists (see CRYPTOZOOLOGY) believe teleportation is involved, but they don't discount it either, even though experience shows that more conventional explanations for the animals' presence are probable.

Appearances of humans under mysterious circumstances are very rare and the few accounts very subjective. KASPAR HAUSER – the enigmatic boy found near Nuremberg in 1828 – is often described as a mysteriously appearing person but there is no suggestion here of teleportation, only of abandonment. In his case, all authorities agree he was probably raised locally, but no one knows where or by whom.

The most unusual class of appearances consists of objects or creatures that are sometimes found inside seemingly solid material. Examples would include a toad found entombed in a cavity in a rock or anachronistic artefacts found in geological strata laid down millennia earlier (see ENTOMBMENT). In the face of any convincing explanation for these ANOMALIES, some FORTEANS have suggested, half in jest, that they might result from a hypothetical malfunction of the hypothetical teleporting force.

apport

The supposed transport or sudden appearance of material objects without the involvement of a material agency.

The appearance of an apport (meaning 'to bring', from Latin, via French) is an example of a MATERIALIZATION, although the implication is usually that the object has been brought from somewhere else. The word was originally used in connection with SÉANCES. When apports appeared at spiritualist séances they were said to have been physically manifested by SPIRITS and were offered as proof of the reality of spirit communication. The word 'apport' is also sometimes used to refer to the unseen movement or sudden appearance of objects in POLTERGEIST cases.

One of the earliest records of the appearance of an apport comes from a séance in Paris in 1819. During the séance a dove was reportedly seen flying around with a package in its beak. The package was then deposited on the table, and upon inspection it was found to contain pieces of paper with small fragments of bone and the names of saints. One of the most famous producers of apports was the 19th-century MEDIUM Agnes Guppy. Mrs Guppy was renowned for the variety of objects that 'materialized' on her séance table – flowers, plants and food were all known to appear – although sceptics suggested that it might just be possible that these were hidden in advance in the medium's ample petticoats. Mrs Guppy's best-known feat occurred at a séance conducted in London by fellow mediums Frank Herne and Charles Williams. At this séance, someone apparently jokingly requested that Mrs Guppy be made to appear. After much debate as to whether this would be possible, in view of her size, there was a great thump on the table to the accompaniment of screams. A light was struck, and there was Mrs Guppy. One witness said, 'She was not by any means dressed for an excursion, as she was without shoes, and had a memorandum book in one hand and a pen in the other. The last word inscribed in her book was "onions", the ink of which was wet.' While many believed that Mrs Guppy had truly been transported across London, the less-exciting possibility that she had been hidden in the room all along has also been suggested.

Sceptics point to the fact that apports can be easily explained as examples of sleight of hand and misdirection. Some former séance leaders have confessed that even sleight of hand was not always required – the simple throwing of objects into the air was often enough to convince the unwary that an apport had taken place. See also TELEPORTATION.

April Fool's Day

1 April, the day on which tricks and practical jokes are traditionally played on people.

Although 1 April, known as April Fool's Day or All Fools' Day, is universally linked with hoaxes and practical jokes, the most popular theory about its origin is that it came about as a result of a serious historical event – the introduction of a new calendar. Many ancient cultures traditionally celebrated New

The 'spaghetti harvest' as it appeared on the BBC's *Panorama* programme on 1 April 1957. (© BBC/Corbis)

Year's Day on 1 April, since this date closely followed the spring equinox on 20 or 21 March. In medieval times, much of Europe celebrated the beginning of the New Year on 25 March, the Feast of the Annunciation, and the festivities went on for eight days, culminating on 1 April. However, in 1582, Pope Gregory XIII introduced a new calendar, known as the Gregorian calendar, to replace the existing Julian calendar. In the Gregorian system, New Year's Day was moved to 1 January. The reformed calendar met with considerable resistance at first; although France adopted it in 1582, Scotland continued to celebrate New Year's Day on 1 April until 1660, while Germany, Denmark and Norway held out against it until 1700, and England only accepted it officially in 1752.

After the introduction of the new calendar in France, people began to make fun of those who persisted in celebrating New Year's Day on 1 April because they either had not yet heard of the change or stubbornly refused to adopt it; pranks and practical jokes were played on these people, who according to some writers were referred to as '*poissons d'Avril*' or 'April fish', perhaps after the newly hatched and very easily caught fish abundant in French waters in April. Over time this evolved into a general tradition of

playing tricks on people and sending them on fool's errands on 1 April. By the 18th century this practice had reached England and Scotland.

But there are other theories as to the origins of April Fool's Day. According to some anthropologists and cultural historians, the celebration has its roots in older festivals marking the Spring Equinox, such as the Feast of Fools, which was celebrated in the Middle Ages, mostly in France, and which ultimately evolved from the Roman winter festival of the Saturnalia. In Spring, the weather is changeable, as if playing tricks on man, and Spring festivals traditionally reflected this capriciousness; they often involved temporary reversals of the normal social order, and riotous celebrations governed by a Lord of Misrule.

There are a number of superstitions and beliefs connected to April Fool's Day. The most well-known one is that any joke or trick must be played before noon; after that, it is said to rebound on the trickster. Anyone who takes an April Fool's Day joke in bad part is thought to risk bad luck, while a more optimistic belief holds that if a trick is played on a man by a pretty girl, he will be compensated later by her marrying him. Getting married on 1 April is not recommended to men, however, because it is believed that a man who marries on this date will be ruled by his wife from that day on. It is also said that children born on April Fool's Day will enjoy good luck in most respects, but will be disastrously unlucky gamblers.

April Fool's Day jokes are traditionally played on individuals, but in modern times the mass media have become increasingly involved in the trickery. Perhaps the most famous April Fool's Day joke carried out on television was the BBC's 1957 *Panorama* documentary item about the Swiss Spaghetti Harvest, which showed farmers harvesting their crop of spaghetti from trees.

Aquarius

In astrology, the eleventh sign of the zodiac, between Capricorn and Pisces.

In Western ASTROLOGY, Aquarius is the sign of the ZODIAC for those who are born between 21 January and 19 February. The symbol for Aquarius is the Water Bearer, and the sign is ruled by the planets Saturn and Uranus. Aquarians are said to be patient, idealistic and intuitive, although they may seem emotionally distant. Aquarius is believed to be an air sign, having an affinity with the element AIR.

Aradia, or the Gospel of the Witches

A book by Charles Godfrey Leland, first published in 1899, which purportedly contains details of surviving Italian witchcraft practice obtained from a primary source. The book exerted a strong influence on the early development of modern Wicca and neopaganism.

The US folklorist Charles Godfrey Leland (1825–1903) had a particular interest in the traditions of the Tuscan region of Italy, and *Aradia* was just one of a number of books that this led to. While carrying out his research he apparently met an Italian woman called Maddalena, from whom he obtained much assistance. He claimed that she had direct knowledge of folk beliefs, traditions and WITCHCRAFT rituals – the implication being that she herself was a practising WITCH. Leland explains in the appendix to *Aradia* that in 1886 he became aware of an Italian manuscript referred to as the *Vangelo* (or 'Gospel'), 'setting forth the doctrines of Italian witchcraft'. He asked Maddalena to obtain it for him, but she did not immediately do so, eventually providing it to him orally and in her own handwritten notes in 1897. What is claimed to be an English translation of this text forms the core of *Aradia*, with the remainder being composed of other information that Leland felt was relevant. It is a matter for debate among historians and folklorists how much of the book is a true account of witchcraft, as traditionally practised in Tuscany, and to what extent his source material was adapted (or even fabricated) to support his own views on the oppression and persecution of

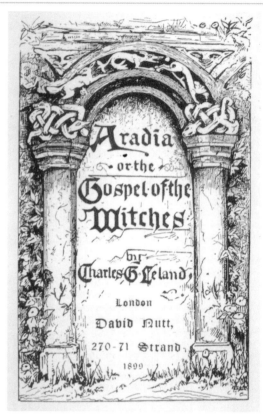

The original title page of Charles Godfrey Leland's *Aradia, or the Gospel of the Witches*. (© Mary Evans Picture Library)

witches by the Church. Neither the original Italian text from Maddelena, nor Maddelena herself, were ever produced.

Aradia contains spells, rituals and stories together with legends relating to the birth of witchcraft. The legends contain elements from both the pre-Christian Roman tradition and Roman Catholicism. The central characters are the goddess Diana, the Queen of the Witches, and her daughter Aradia who is sent to teach witchcraft on earth. In the preface, Leland summarizes the contents as follows:

> For brief explanation I may say that witch craft is known to its votaries as *la vecchia religione*, or the old religion, of which Diana is the Goddess, her daughter *Aradia* (or Herodias) the female Messiah, and that this little work sets forth how the latter was born, came down to earth, established witches and witchcraft, and then returned to heaven. With it are given the ceremonies and invocations or incantations to be addressed to *Diana* and *Aradia*, the exorcism of Cain, and the spells of the holy-stone, rue, and verbena, constituting, as

the text declares, the regular church-service, so to speak, which is to be chanted or pronounced at the witch-meetings. There are also included the very curious incantations or benedictions of the honey, meal, and salt, or cakes of the witch-supper, which is curiously classical, and evidently a relic of the Roman Mysteries.

Although its veracity has been called into question, the book's influence on modern WICCA and NEOPAGANISM cannot be denied. It was particularly popular in the early stages of the revival because it appeared to support the idea that the modern witchcraft practice was, in fact, a continuation of traditional belief. Extracts from the speeches by the goddess Aradia, taken from Leland's book, appear in the texts used in some Wiccan rituals, and in many forms of modern witchcraft practice Aradia is applied to THE GODDESS, moon goddess or Queen of the Witches.

arcana

The two main parts into which the traditional tarot deck is divided.

The traditional TAROT deck is made up of 78 cards, which are divided into two main groups – the trump cards, also known as the major or greater arcana, and the suit cards, also called the minor or lesser arcana (*arcana* is a Latin word meaning 'secrets' or 'mysteries').

The 22 cards in the major arcana, numbered from 0 to 21, feature highly allegorical, archetypal images such as The Fool, The Magician, The Hanged Man and The Devil, each of which is believed to symbolize a quality, a state of consciousness, a fundamental characteristic or a key stage in the life of the person for whom the reading is being done. Some tarot commentators liken the major arcana to a spiritual map presented as the story of an innocent (The Fool), who must go through the experiences symbolized by the other major arcana cards on his journey to enlightenment.

The 56 cards in the minor arcana are divided into four suits: the suit of cups (see CUPS, SUIT OF) or chalices, the suit of pentacles (see PENTACLES, SUIT OF) or coins, the suit of swords (see SWORDS, SUIT OF), and the suit of wands (see WANDS, SUIT OF), also known as batons, rods or sceptres. Each suit consists of numbered 'pip' cards going from one to ten, plus four court cards – the Page, the Knight, the King and the Queen. The minor arcana therefore resembles a deck of modern playing cards, with the suit of cups corresponding to that of hearts, pentacles corresponding to diamonds, swords corresponding to spades and wands corresponding to clubs. The cards of the minor arcana are seen as representing the more mundane and superficial aspects of and

occurrences in the subject's life, along with his or her reactions to these. However, in a standard tarot reading, the distinctions between the major and minor arcana usually become blurred as the cards are considered together to create a seamless, overall picture of the subject's situation and the influences over it.

archaeoacoustics

The study of the acoustic qualities of prehistoric constructions.

Among the theories developed to explain the siting and layout of prehistoric buildings is the idea that they may have been designed to have particular acoustic qualities. In the United Kingdom, research into the great megalithic STONE CIRCLES of STONEHENGE and AVEBURY has shown that sound is reflected from the standing stones in patterns that some would argue are probably no more accidental than their alignment with astronomical phenomena. Similarly, the passage tomb at Newgrange in Northern Ireland has been the subject of experiments into the reverberation of sound within its domed chamber, leading some to suggest that its distinctive decoration of concentric rings may even be an attempt to depict the patterns made in smoke by the reflected sound waves during periods of chanting.

In the Americas, it is claimed that the sound of a handclap made in front of the Mayan temple at Chichen Itzá will be reflected from the building to sound like the chirp of the holy quetzal bird. The ritual chambers of the Anasazi cliffside dwellings of New Mexico are also believed to have been constructed to reflect and amplify sound.

One area of research into this phenomenon involves experiments, at various locations, to establish whether the sound reflections and reverberations would have been likely to have had a mental, or even physical, effect on people if the initial sounds were produced by human voices – whether speaking, chanting or singing. This would support the theory that the effects were deliberately engineered to serve some social or spiritual purpose.

archetypes

One of the inherited mental images which make up the collective unconscious, postulated by the Swiss psychiatrist Carl Jung.

The Swiss psychiatrist CARL GUSTAV JUNG introduced several pioneering and highly influential psychological concepts, one of the most significant of which was the 'archetype'. Jung was fascinated by the recurrence of certain stories and symbols throughout the myths and legends of all ages and cultures, and he came to the conclusion that mankind shares a universal and underlying COLLECTIVE UNCONSCIOUS, which is biologically inherited rather than being grounded in experience This collective unconscious is made up of archetypes which give rise to these recurring, symbolic themes. These primal images appear in dreams, mythology and folk tales all over the world, and Jung believed this was because we all inherit the same forms, which are at the roots of our PSYCHES. These forms shape our perceptions of the world, with each of us attaching our own meanings and associations to them according to how we experience our lives, and projecting these interpretations into the outside world. He regarded these archetypes themselves as neither good nor bad, and saw them as having no form of their own, but acting solely as organizing principles for all we think, say and do.

Jung held that there was no fixed number or list of archetypes, but that they overlapped and changed into one another as required by the individual. However, he did identify several specific forms of archetype. The most important is the Self, which is the ultimate unity and perfection of the personality. There are also the Shadow – the 'dark side' of the ego, instinctive, irrational and sometimes appearing to be evil, which originates from our pre-human, animal ancestry, when our only concerns were survival and reproduction; the Persona – the public image we present to the outside world; the Anima – the female aspect present in the collective unconscious of all men, which may be summed up as all the unconscious female psychological qualities possessed by the male; and the male equivalent in the female collective unconscious, the Animus. Jung held that we are often attracted to members of the opposite sex whom we unconsciously perceive as corresponding to our Animus or Anima archetype.

Jungian psychology describes many archetypal symbols of the unconscious, the best known of which are the Father, often symbolized in DREAMS, MYTHOLOGY and FOLKLORE as a guide or authority figure; the Mother, manifesting either as the Good Mother, often represented as a benevolent fairy or female spirit, or the Terrible Mother, who may appear in fairy tales as the wicked stepmother; the Child, for example the Christ Child celebrated at Christmas; the Hero, who represents the ego and is often engaged in battling the Shadow, in the form of a dragon or other monster (as in many Greek, Norse and Celtic myths); the Wise Old Man, who reveals to the Hero the nature of the collective unconscious (for example, MERLIN); and the Trickster, often represented by a clown, magician or animal, such as the Norse god Loki, the Coyote in Native American lore, and Br'er Rabbit, whose origins can be traced back to the trickster hare figure prominent in the storytelling traditions of Central and Southern Africa.

Jung felt that the ultimate goal of psychology was the reconciliation and harmonization of the individual with these archetypal forces, and that the world of archetypes could only be revealed through an examination and understanding of the human psyche by means of the study of dreams, art, mythology, world religions, philosophy and occultism.

Area 51

The code name for a top-secret facility located at Groom Lake in the Nevada desert where it is reputed that alien technology has been stored and analysed.

In 1989 a man claiming to be a physicist called Robert Lazar told an amazing story on KLAS TV, a local station in Las Vegas. He claimed to have worked at a location called Area 51, part of a vast facility around 145 kilometres (90 miles) to the north. He said that while he was there he had worked on extraordinary disc-shaped craft, with incredible flight capabilities, that used technology well beyond current human knowledge. He believed that this involved anti-matter propulsion. Although their true origin had been kept from him, the craft he saw appeared to have been designed for pilots of smaller-than-human stature. His research had supposedly been part of a programme based in this highly restricted facility, the intention of which was to study (and to develop technology from) these craft.

Attempts were made to verify Lazar's story but it proved difficult. His former universities, including the prestigious Massachusetts Institute of Technology, denied any knowledge of him. Lazar argued that his background was being manipulated in order to protect this remarkable secret.

Others have since appeared with stories about the base – some including the presence of alien bodies and even live aliens. No clear chain of evidence has yet verified any of these claims. However, the base has attracted widespread media interest – featuring in TV shows and hit films such as *Independence Day* (1996). Bus-loads of sightseers are regularly taken from Las Vegas to the site, overlooking a large dry lake in the Groom Mountains, and UFO spotters have often reported sightings in the area of fast-moving lights that seem to behave strangely – some even stopping dead in mid-flight. Restrictions on access to the perimeter of the base were tightened in the late 1980s and early 1990s, with an exclusion zone of several miles being enforced – the creation of a new 8-kilometre (5-mile) runway was one reason cited for this. The facility opened in July 1955, at first being referred to as 'The Ranch' by its staff. The location takes advantage of the flat terrain and the security offered by the desert and the encircling mountains, although the US government remain reticent when discussing its intended purpose. The title 'Area 51' was allocated by the Atomic Energy Commission in 1958, but this was discontinued in the 1970s. However, the association with UFOs has ensured that the name persists.

Groom Lake Air Force Base has been used during the development of a number of highly secret aircraft – from the U-2 spy plane in the 1950s, through to the F-117 stealth fighter and the B-2 stealth bomber. Modern research projects are said to include small prototype aircraft employing experimental methods of propulsion. See also BLACK AIRCRAFT.

Aries

In astrology, the first sign of the zodiac, between Pisces and Taurus.

In Western ASTROLOGY, Aries is the sign of the ZODIAC for those who are born between 21 March and 20 April. The symbol for Aries is the ram, and the sign is ruled by Mars. It is taken to be an assertive sign (the ram is a symbol of aggression and Mars is associated with war and willpower), and Arians are said to be ambitious and uncompromising. Aries is believed to be a fire sign, having an affinity with the element FIRE.

armies, spectral *see* SPECTRAL ARMIES

Arnold, Kenneth (1915–84)

The US businessman and private pilot credited with reporting the pivotal UFO sighting that captured the popular imagination. He became the first private UFO investigator.

Kenneth Arnold had led an undistinguished life until the afternoon of 24 June 1947. On that date his life changed and a new phenomenon was born – a whole genre of TV programmes, books and films would not have been the same without him.

Arnold had his own fire equipment company in Boise, Idaho, and was an experienced pilot. He flew all over the north-western states of the USA selling and installing his safety devices. On the afternoon in question he left Chehalis, Washington, at 2pm for the relatively short hop to Yakima. On the way he chose to make a short detour to circle Mount Rainier, part of the snow-capped volcanic mountain chain where a military transport plane had recently crashed. Arnold was a member of the aerial search and rescue team and was attracted by the $5,000 reward for locating the crash site.

As he flew over Mineral, Washington, flying at around 2,800 metres (9,200 feet), a bright flash illuminated his canopy, but he could not find the cause. Then there was a second flash and he realized that it came from the bright sun reflecting off an

The US businessman Kenneth Arnold posing with the private aircraft from which he made his famous 'flying saucer' sighting in 1947. (© Mary Evans Picture Library)

object in the far distance. The object was one of a group of crescent-shaped aircraft moving at huge speed, in echelon formation, between Mount Adams and Mount Rainier. As he later reported:

> They didn't fly like any aircraft I had seen before. In the first place, their echelon formation was backward from that practised by our Air Force … their flight was like speed boats on rough water or similar to the tail of a Chinese kite that I once saw blowing in the wind.

Arnold landed at Yakima where he reported his encounter to ground staff. Then he flew on to Pendleton, Oregon, where he was greeted by a large crowd who had come to watch an air show, but who were now aware of his sighting. By the next day the sighting was reported all over the USA, and owing to a journalist's misunderstanding, the term FLYING SAUCERS was born.

Many possible explanations have been offered for this key sighting (including birds in flight, missiles, snow flurries and reflections on the aircraft canopy), although Arnold was not convinced by any of them. The US Air Force investigator DR J ALLEN HYNEK established that the UFO formation could not have been around 160 kilometres (100 miles) away, as Arnold had estimated – the objects would not have been visible to the naked eye unless they were much closer, so they must also have been moving at a far more modest velocity than originally suggested.

Having no satisfactory explanation for his own sighting, Arnold took it upon himself to travel to see many of the other people who reported UFO sightings in the wake of his own. In the process he became the world's first independent UFO investigator.

In 1952 Arnold co-authored a book with journalist Ray Palmer, entitled *The Coming of the Saucers*, which gave an account of his activities during and after this sighting. He was aware of the role that he had played in creating the modern UFO phenomenon, and he never lost his interest in the subject. Indeed he personally claimed to have a dozen more sightings, including one over Idaho Falls, Ohio, in 1966, during which he captured a glowing cylinder shape on cine film. However, after the 1950s he tended to remain out of the public eye, making a rare appearance at an international UFO conference in Chicago in 1977, which was staged to commemorate the 30th anniversary of his own sighting. He died in January 1984.

In the words of the FBI agent who reported on Arnold's original sighting:

> It is the personal opinion of the interviewer that he actually saw what he states he saw in the attached report.

aromatherapy
The therapeutic use of volatile plant oils known as essential oils, which are either inhaled or applied to the skin to alter mood or treat certain conditions.

Almost every ancient civilization recognized the therapeutic value of scent. Fragrant OILS were used for spiritual purification in many cultures, the Egyptians used aromatic oils and plants in their embalming process, and throughout the East, perfumes were prized not only for cosmetic purposes but for their medicinal effects. The therapeutic use of oils had largely been forgotten in the West until the 1920s, when a French cosmetic chemist, René Maurice Gattefossé, found that lavender oil seemed to help a burn on his arm to heal. Intrigued, he began to study in depth the effects of volatile plant oils, or essential oils, and discovered that as well as having its own characteristic aroma, each oil seemed to have specific therapeutic properties. He believed that some affected the mood, and were soothing and relaxing, or stimulating and invigorating, while some enhanced concentration. Others had antiseptic, antibacterial or anti-inflammatory properties. Gattefossé coined the French term *aromatherapie* to describe this new field.

The essential oils used in aromatherapy are obtained by distillation or cold pressing. When inhaled, aromatherapy oils are said to work by stimulating the pituitary gland and hypothalamus, and through them, the central nervous system. The oils may be burned in an oil burner; placed on a light bulb or a radiator to be released into the atmosphere by the action of heat; diluted in water and pumped into the air with a diffuser; or a few drops may be added to a warm bath. Applied to the skin, as in aromatherapy massage, the oils are usually diluted with a carrier oil such as almond oil to prevent irritation. Aromatherapy is often used in combination with massage therapy and ACUPUNCTURE, and it is one of the fastest-growing fields in alternative and complementary medicine, being used largely to treat stress and insomnia, as well as for pain relief and the treatment of wounds, especially burns.

Art of Memory
Also called 'Theatre of Memory', a mnemonic technique associated with Renaissance philosophers.

The Art of Memory, or Theatre of Memory or Memory Palace, were mnemonic systems revived and developed by several of the Hermetic philosophers of the Renaissance. They are aids to memory that work through the association of thoughts with images and particularly with places. In her classic work *The Art of Memory* (1966), Dame Frances Yates explored the origins of systematized memory techniques in ancient Greece and then Rome, and the development of symbolic imagery in medieval times.

The Spanish-born mystic Ramon Lull (c.1235–1315) devised an influential memory system known as the Lullian Art, using three moving concentric circles each inscribed with the nine letters B–K, each letter referring to a name or attribute of God, and triangular relationships between the many combinations.

Perhaps the clearest examples of late medieval pictorial imagery are the depiction of the four Virtues of Prudence, Justice, Fortitude and Temperance, and the illustrations of the *Trionfi* or *Triumphs* of Petrarch (1304–74). The *Trionfi* may be a possible origin of the early TAROT cards, which first appeared in northern Italy in the late 14th or early 15th century; the tarot pack itself can be seen as an esoteric Memory Theatre, the cards representing characters and situations.

The classic Theatre of Memory was designed and apparently built in wood by Giulio Camillo (1480–1544), who drew together the kabbalistic Hermetic philosophy of Pico della Mirondola and the Art of Memory. Looking up from the stage to the auditorium of a theatre, there are seven steps representing the planetary gods, divided by seven gangways; on each gangway are seven decorated gates, each one depicting symbolical images of the whole of creation. The user of the theatre, whether it be physical or imaginary, puts each thing to be remembered in a drawer or box under the relevant images. It is a system of memory places.

In the Renaissance the Art of Memory was certainly associated with heterodox beliefs. Its greatest proponent, Giordano Bruno (1548–1600), was burned at the stake in Rome after being invited to Italy in 1591 to teach the Art to 'a Venetian gentleman'. Bruno published several major books on memory, first of all greatly developing the Lullian Art into a hugely complicated system of four circles, or memory wheels, each divided into thirty segments, each subdivided into five, making 150 images on each wheel. On the central wheel are astrological images; on the next, plants, animals, birds, stones and metals; on the third, adjectives (knotty, formless, famous, etc); and on the outermost wheel, 150 mythological inventors of everything from agriculture to surgery to the flute to writing – aspects of human civilization and culture.

In his final work, Bruno describes a memory system which is more architectural, with 24 memory rooms, each containing nine memory places; in addition there are 15 fields, each divided into nine places; and 30 cubicles. Within these can be found all human knowledge. A similar system was devised by Tommaso Campanella (1568–1639) in *The City of the Sun*. This is a short piece of utopian writing, but Campanella himself said that his circular city – with a temple at its centre and images on its walls – could be used as a memory system. Robert Fludd (1574–1637) returned to Giulio Camillo's concept of a Theatre of Memory, but turned it around: instead of the auditorium being the framework for positioning details to be remembered, Fludd made symbolic use of the theatre stage, with doors and columns as the memory places.

Today's stage magicians use similar mnemonic techniques to aid their feats of memory (see also MAGIC, STAGE).

Arthur, King *see* KING ARTHUR

Arthurian legend *see* KING ARTHUR

Ascended Masters
In certain religious movements, the spiritually enlightened entities on whose teachings the religion is based.
Ascended Masters are broadly the same as SECRET CHIEFS, but while Secret Chiefs are the claimed authority behind magical orders such as the HERMETIC ORDER OF THE GOLDEN DAWN, Ascended Masters

(sometimes called the Great White Brotherhood) are the claimed authority behind a number of esoteric religious movements. These include THEOSOPHY and its offshoots, in particular the ALICE BAILEY-inspired movements. The Ascended Masters sometimes include revered figures from the mainstream religions, such as Krishna, the Buddha and Jesus. In the teachings of the AETHERIUS SOCIETY, for example, the Ascended or 'Cosmic' Masters include Jesus and Buddha (said to come from Venus) and Krishna (from Saturn). After the death of that movement's founder, George King, in 1997, it was announced that he himself had been an avatar of one of the Masters.

Similarly, following the death in 1973 of Mark Prophet, founder of the CHURCH UNIVERSAL AND TRIUMPHANT (CUT), it had been declared that he was the Ascended Master Lanello. CUT, like the other I AM MOVEMENTS, lays its greatest emphasis on the Ascended Masters Jesus and SAINT GERMAIN. Two others who feature widely in these and similar movements are Koot Hoomi (or Kuthumi) and El Morya, both first identified by MADAME BLAVATSKY, founder of the THEOSOPHICAL SOCIETY, in the late 19th century. BENJAMIN CREME'S Maitreya is also an Ascended Master, perhaps the most senior of the Masters, because he seems to be filling the roles of the returning Christ, the Jewish Messiah, the Muslim imam Mahdi and the Hindu Krishna, as well as the Buddhist Maitreya. Sometimes Ascended Masters are referred to as Mahatmas; they could also be seen as a concept similar to Buddhist Bodhisattvas – people who have achieved enlightenment but postpone entry into nirvana in order to help others on their own spiritual paths.

Some movements such as CUT have 'Messengers' who receive teachings from the Ascended Masters; other movements have 'Living Masters'. For example, in Eckankar, a modern offshoot of the SANT MAT group of religions, the current Living Master is Harold Klemp. He succeeded Darwin Gross who in turn succeeded the religion's founder, Paul Twitchell, who claimed to be the 971st Living Master.

ASPR *see* AMERICAN SOCIETY FOR PSYCHICAL RESEARCH

ASSAP *see* ASSOCIATION FOR THE SCIENTIFIC STUDY OF ANOMALOUS PHENOMENA

Association for the Scientific Study of Anomalous Phenomena
A British society investigating anomalous phenomena.
The Association for the Scientific Study of Anomalous

Phenomena (ASSAP) was founded in 1981 by a number of members of the SOCIETY FOR PSYCHICAL RESEARCH (SPR), who wanted to pursue investigations outside the SPR's remit; ie the many cases of psychical phenomena that involve anomalous phenomena from other fields, including for example 'UFO witnesses [who] often have psychic experiences both before and after their encounter'. ASSAP is a registered charity which undertakes educational activities as well as research, investigations and lectures. It publishes a newsletter and a journal (*Anomaly*), and runs an accredited training programme for field investigators.

ASSAP's emphasis on interdisciplinary investigations that comply with scientific standards of evidence-gathering demonstrates its ANOMALISTIC intent. However, unlike the more overtly scientific anomalists – such as the SOCIETY FOR SCIENTIFIC EXPLORATION and the SOCIETY FOR INTERDISCIPLINARY STUDIES – ASSAP maintains a watching brief for paranormal and psychical phenomena, which it categorizes under four main headings: psychic phenomena (eg TELEPATHY, GHOSTS, PREMONITIONS); UFOs; EARTH MYSTERIES (eg alignments of ancient monuments); and FORTEANA (odd occurrences like FALLS of fish, OUT-OF-PLACE ANIMALS). Recent investigations have included vigils in allegedly haunted locations, experiments in mentally influencing objects (TELEKINESIS), REMOTE VIEWING, hypnotic regression, and analysis of photographs said to show GHOST LIGHTS or UFOs.

astral body
The name given to the proposed spirit form which, within some mystical and religious traditions, is said to be a projection of our living bodies.
The astral body is said to be a SPIRIT form of our living bodies. As a spirit form it does not consist of physical matter and so the material world offers no boundaries to it. The astral body is said by believers to leave our body naturally during sleep and at times of extreme stress. Some spiritualists claim to be able to control their astral bodies – allowing them to roam free in the ASTRAL PLANE under their conscious control (see ASTRAL PROJECTION).

Historically the astral body has been equated with the SOUL by some, and 19th- and 20th-century theosophists (see THEOSOPHY) held that the astral body was the emotional side of a living being. As the human body was made of matter and was physical, so the astral body was made of emotions and was non-corporeal. The terms astral body and ASTRAL DOUBLE are often used interchangeably.

astral double
The astral double is supposedly the form that travels away from the physical body during astral projection.
An astral double is often described as being an exact duplicate of a human being, but one that is not usually encountered on the normal plane of existence. During ASTRAL PROJECTION an exact double of someone is pushed by them into another 'dimension' (the ASTRAL PLANE) – this astral double is supposedly connected to the physical body by what is described as a thin, silver cord which apparently acts as a safety line.

In some movements, such as THEOSOPHY, 'astral double' is used to describe the SPIRIT form of a deceased person, and this can appear after death. Deprived of the life force of the physical body, the astral double gradually dissipates and vanishes forever. In parts of India it is said that an astral double of this type can feed on the life force of the living and remain as a kind of psychic vampire.

The terms ASTRAL BODY and astral double are often used interchangeably.

astral plane
The name given in some belief systems to another realm of existence which is sometimes described as being just beyond the physical world.
In some esoteric and religious traditions the astral plane (sometimes called the world of emotion or illusion) is supposedly where the ASTRAL BODY travels to when we sleep or when the body repairs itself after extreme trauma. It is said to parallel the real world but, because of its nature, there can be no direct, physical evidence of its existence. Many believers claim to be able to visit it at will through MEDITATION or lucid dreaming.

A similar concept appears in some Hindu teachings where there is a realm to which the SOUL goes immediately upon death, prior to REINCARNATION or movement on to a higher form of consciousness.

The astral plane is said to allow the ASTRAL BODY and the ASTRAL DOUBLE to travel to new areas and to view things that the normal, conscious body cannot experience. See also ASTRAL PROJECTION; ASTRAL TRAVELLING.

astral projection
A system of movement of the spirit outside of the body that forms part of some mystical and religious belief systems.
Astral projection (sometimes just referred to as 'projection') might be described as a form of OUT-OF-BODY EXPERIENCE or a proposed explanation for such experiences. During astral projection it is said that the ASTRAL DOUBLE leaves the physical host and is taken to the ASTRAL PLANE, from which it is then free to travel anywhere. The astral double is often described as remaining connected to the physical body by a silver cord.

Astral projection can supposedly be achieved at will by adepts through means such as lucid dreaming, MEDITATION or the use of PSYCHEDELIC DRUGS. See also ASTRAL TRAVELLING.

astral travelling

A form of movement of the astral body independent of a physical body that forms a part some belief systems.

Astral travel is described by believers as the unfettered movement of a spirit form of our bodies. This travel takes place in a non-physical realm called the ASTRAL PLANE which cannot normally be experienced. The ASTRAL BODY (not the ASTRAL DOUBLE) is released into the astral plane where it can travel and interact with other beings. Astral travel differs from ASTRAL PROJECTION in that the astral body has to make its own way back to the physical body – in astral projection the astral double remains connected to the physical body by what might be described as a form of 'safety cord'. However, the terms astral projection and astral travelling are now frequently treated as interchangeable.

astrology

The study of the supposed influence of the movements and positions of the sun, moon and planets on human and terrestrial affairs.

The word astrology comes from the Greek *astron*, meaning star, and *logos*, meaning discourse. There are a number of different systems of astrology, but they all share the common belief that there is a connection between the relative positions and alignments of celestial bodies such as the sun, moon and planets, and events on earth.

The Western tradition of astrology is thought to have had its origins in Mesopotamia during the second millennium BC. Observers noticed that the various patterns of the stars regularly occurred in the sky at the same time each year, and coincided with annual events such as the coming of spring, seasonal changes and the migration of birds. From this they reasoned that these phenomena must be linked in some way, and in time, evolved complex systems of DIVINATION based on the principle that the movements and positions of various heavenly bodies, as well as the constellations, were reflected in the human sphere, and could be read by those who were skilled in their interpretation. The ancient Babylonians and Assyrians developed astrology to the status of a science, and after the overthrow of the Assyro-Babylonian Empire, the priests of those regions moved to Greece, bringing with them their astrological teachings. Astrology soon became a key element of Greek religious worship, and permeated the whole Greek philosophical view of nature.

By Roman times the status of astrology had become less secure, but despite repeated attempts to suppress it, it remained popular in the Roman Empire.

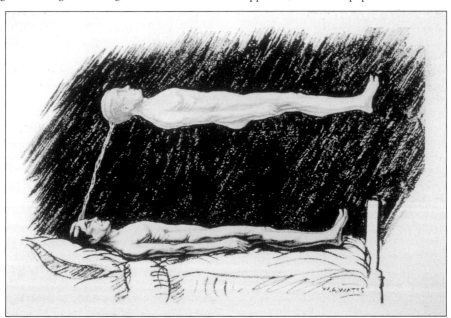

The astral body floating above the physical body, connected by a silver cord – from *The Projection of the Astral Body* (1929) by Sylvan Muldoon and Hereward Carrington. (© Mary Evans Picture Library)

However, the Christian Church strongly opposed astrology, and with the ascendancy of Christianity and the overthrow of the old Roman Empire, it lost its influence and reputation, disappearing for centuries from the Christian parts of Western Europe. But the Renaissance, with its revival of classical learning, brought many ancient Greek and Latin works to the attention of scholars once more, and among these texts were astrological teachings. Thus began a second period of prosperity for astrology. Emperors and popes employed their own court astrologers, and in medieval Europe, these were consulted before an ambassador was received in audience, and before important political or military decisions were made. Catherine de Medici made astrology popular in France, and her court astrologer was the famous occultist Michel de Notredame (NOSTRADAMUS).

From the very start, astrology and astronomy were closely linked, since astrologers had to study the movements and alignments of the stars and other heavenly bodies in order to interpret them, and every professional astronomer was also an astrologer. The Renaissance view was that astronomical research and knowledge were only profitable because they contributed to the development of astrology, and many prominent figures in the history of Western astronomy, such as Tycho Brahe, Johannes Kepler and even Galileo, supported themselves by acting as astrologers for wealthy patrons.

In Western astrology, the sky, as viewed from the earth, is traditionally seen as an imaginary band (the ZODIAC) divided into twelve segments of 30 degrees, each of which is named after a nearby constellation of stars. As the earth orbits the sun, the sun appears to pass through each of these 30-degree segments in turn, completing its journey through all twelve in the course of a year. The most common use of astrology is in the HOROSCOPE, also known as the natal chart or birth chart: a map of the heavens at the time of a person's birth, by which an astrologer predicts the events of a person's life.

Other traditions of astrology developed independently from that of the West, including Chinese, Jyotish (Vedic or Hindu), and Kabbalistic astrology. Chinese astrology has, in recent years, begun to enjoy widespread popularity in the West as well as the East. The Chinese zodiac is based on a twelve-year cycle, each year being symbolized by a different animal; in order, these are the Mouse or Rat, Ox, Tiger, Rabbit, Dragon, Snake, Horse, Sheep or Goat, Monkey, Rooster, Dog, and Pig or Boar. Each animal is believed to impart distinctive characteristics to a person born in its year, and is even thought, by some, to determine the degree of success and happiness they will enjoy throughout their lives.

Atlantis
A legendary vanished island in the Atlantic Ocean.

The legendary lost island of Atlantis is mentioned by the Greek philosopher Plato (c.428–c.348 BC) in two short pieces: the *Timaeus* and the *Critias*. In these works Plato describes a civilization that was already ancient at the time of his writing, a powerful and almost ideal kingdom ruling an empire that extended into the Mediterranean from its island home in the Atlantic Ocean. According to Plato, Atlantis was at war with Athens when it was rocked by earthquakes and floods before being entirely swallowed up by the sea.

Plato discusses the structure and layout, as well as the political and social organization of Atlantis in some detail but is more vague about its precise location. This has led many scholars to believe that it was imaginary and that the philosopher was merely using a convenient fiction, based perhaps on myths brought to Greece from Egypt, to make points about the ideal form of government. However, many believe in the reality of Atlantis and have suggested various possible locations for the vanished civilization. Candidates include the Greek city of Helike (known to have been destroyed by earthquake and tidal wave in 373 BC), the Caribbean and Polynesia. One of the more popular theories connects the story with the Bronze Age civilization of Minoan Crete which was largely destroyed by ash and tidal waves generated by the massive volcanic explosion of the island of Thera c.1500 BC.

There are those who believe that the concept of Atlantis really concerns an EXTRATERRESTRIAL race who colonized the earth thousands of years ago but established their civilization in the deepest parts of the sea. According to this theory, Atlanteans still operate from undersea bases and this explains the numerous reports over the years of unidentified metallic craft that can move at great speed both beneath the water and in the air. The existence in many parts of the world of structures that have been identified as UNDERWATER RUINS has fuelled speculation that these may be remnants of Atlantis. The Bimini Road, a linear stone formation in the Caribbean off the island of Bimini, has been particularly identified with the story since the American psychic EDGAR CAYCE prophesied that Atlantis would be discovered in that very location.

MADAME BLAVATSKY believed that Atlantis was peopled by the inhabitants of the (similarly lost) continent of LEMURIA, and, at around the same time, the US politician and writer Ignatius Donnelly did much to revive interest in Atlantis with the publication of his *Atlantis, The Antediluvian World* (1882). He believed that Atlantis had disappeared below the Atlantic 12,000 years earlier. The Scottish poet, anthropologist and occultist Lewis Spence also wrote on the subject in a series of books beginning with *The Problem of Atlantis* (1924), claiming to find evidence for its existence and cataclysmic destruction in the myths of Native American cultures. In any case, the idea of Atlantis exercises an enduring grip on popular imagination and continues to turn up in many places, from the novels of Jules Verne to the children's animated films of Disney.

auditory hallucinations

The phenomenon of experiencing the sensation of hearing sounds where there is no identifiable external cause.

Many individuals report experiencing sounds which have no apparent external cause. These may include such things as voices, breathing sounds, and the sounds of animals, birds or music. How such experiences come about is not entirely agreed upon, and to dismiss them as 'imaginary' is to fail to address the complexity of the mechanisms involved (paranormal or otherwise). In some cases, it is widely accepted that the sounds are wholly generated by the brain of the person, even though they may be believed by them to be external in origin – such as is the case in some psychological disorders or where the subject is using some form of HALLUCINOGEN. However, it is important to note that such voices or sounds can also occasionally occur in people who are not suffering from any condition that would usually be identified as a mental or physical illness. It has even been observed by some that there are cases where hearing such voices and sounds appears to be linked with creativity, leading to the suggestion that they may serve some perfectly ordinary functional purpose.

How such experiences are interpreted is often determined by the culture in which the individual lives. By some people they may be considered to be the voices of (or signals from) gods or SPIRITS, or to be other messages with a PSYCHIC or supernatural origin. To psychical researchers certain auditory hallucinations may even be evidence for the existence of EXTRASENSORY PERCEPTION, it being postulated that they arise from the exercise of a PSI faculty or power, leading to the generation of an auditory hallucination which is perceived by the conscious mind. However, the use of the phrase 'auditory hallucination' now usually carries with it the implication that the sound experiences are generated only through a process in the brain, and when the phrase is used by sceptics it is often taken by them to embody a complete and internally consistent alternative to a paranormal explanation.

augury

The art or practice of interpreting signs and omens, such as the flight or cries of birds, to gain knowledge of secrets or to predict the future.

The form of DIVINATION known as augury was central to life in ancient Rome. The augur was a priest or official whose main role was to interpret the will of the gods, as communicated principally through the movement and behaviour of birds (the word 'augur' probably derives from the Latin *avis*, meaning a bird). The omens revealed to the augur by his observations of birds were known as auspices (from Latin *avis*, a bird, and *specere*, to observe), and the ceremony of the augur's 'taking the auspices' was performed before every major public event; no important decision would be made without this guidance. Of particular import were the flight of eagles and vultures, the call of crows, the hoot of owls and the cry of ravens, while the number of birds seen, the direction of their flight, and whether or not they shed feathers as they flew were all highly significant. The augur also interpreted the meaning of thunder and lightning, believed to be a direct communication from the god Jupiter, and eclipses. Signs which manifested on the augur's east side were thought to denote a favourable outcome, while those on his west were held to be ill-omened.

Aum Shinrikyo

A Japanese sect which killed twelve people with sarin gas on the Tokyo underground system in 1995.

Aum Shinrikyo is known in the West for its sarin attack on the Tokyo underground – a rare case of a new religious movement being violent to outsiders. But this attack was the culmination of a series of killings.

Aum Shinrikyo, meaning 'Supreme Truth Society', was founded in 1987 by Shoko Asahara (born Chizuo Matsumoto in 1955). Its beliefs originally stemmed from a school of Buddhism, blended with a strong emphasis on yoga and a focus on Shiva, the Hindu god of destruction. As it developed it took on elements of apocalyptic Christianity – especially from the book of Revelation – as well as the prophecies of NOSTRADAMUS. The initial aim of Aum Shinrikyo was to avoid the forthcoming apocalypse by the members achieving enlightenment and changing negative energy into positive energy.

The movement was in conflict with society from early on. Its attempts to become legally registered as a religion were opposed, largely by the families of its members; Aum Shinrikyo taught that members must sever all ties with their families. Eventually the group gained legal status in 1989, but at the expense of much bad publicity. In the same year a young lawyer who had been hired to investigate the movement, Sakamato Tsutsumi, disappeared with his wife and small child; their bodies were found six years later.

The almost-blind guru Shoko Asahara had political ambitions, and 25 candidates of his Supreme Truth Party stood in the Japanese elections in 1990 but all of them lost. This very public humiliation triggered changes in the beliefs and activities of the movement. The apocalypse was now inevitable; Aum Shinrikyo must defend itself. It built nuclear fallout shelters, and became even more isolated from the outside world. It also began to develop chemical weapons.

In June 1994 the nerve gas sarin was released in the city of Matsumoto near the homes of three judges involved in cases against Aum Shinrikyo. Seven people died and hundreds, including the judges, were injured. In March 1995 ten members of the movement released sarin gas on the Tokyo subway. Twelve died and thousands were injured. Asahara and other senior members of the religion were found guilty of murder, kidnapping and other crimes. Asahara was sentenced to death by a Japanese court in 2004, although in 2006 psychiatric reports and appeals were ongoing.

In 2000 Aum Shinrikyo changed its name to Aleph and publicly dissociated itself from Asahara as a leader or guru, although members said that they would still follow his teachings.

auras

A field of energy said to be produced by and to surround all living beings. It can allegedly be sensed or seen by people with paranormal abilities.

The word aura is originally Greek, and means 'breath' or 'breeze'. The aura, also referred to as the auric field or auric haze, is usually defined as a field of energy which surrounds the body of a living being, and some psychics claim to be able to perceive it, either by sensing it psychically, or by actually seeing it as a luminous glow around the physical body.

The aura is generally described as being shaped like an egg, and to extend for some distance beyond the body, although this distance can vary from person to person and may depend on their emotional or physical state. It is said to consist of between seven and twelve layers, of which most psychics see only the three closest to the physical body – those which relate to the mind, emotions and health. The outer layers are believed to be connected with the soul and spirit. The innermost layer of the aura, closest to the skin, is usually referred to as the etheric aura, and is seen as a pale, narrow band that outlines the body. It is thought to expand when a person is sleeping, recharging itself

like a battery, and to contract close to the body when the person wakes.

The aura is usually seen as having a number of colours, which reflect the spiritual, emotional and physical state of a person, and are therefore constantly changing; the aura's colour spectrum varies according to changes in the subject's health or mood, although one colour frequently predominates. The interpretation of these colours varies greatly between practitioners, although in some systems an aura which is characteristically red is thought to indicate passion and will, and a mainly yellow one optimism, while a chiefly blue aura shows a quiet and calm personality. Some people use aura-reading as a diagnostic tool, since the aura is said to show the presence of a disease before the onset of physical symptoms.

In 1908, Dr WALTER J KILNER claimed to have invented a method for viewing the human aura using coloured screens made of thin, flat glass cells containing dyes in an alcohol solution. In another technique, known as KIRLIAN PHOTOGRAPHY, an image of the aura is said to be captured by placing an object on a photographic plate, and subjecting it to a high voltage field. Computer software is now available which it is claimed can photograph the aura and provide the subject with an interpretation of its shape, colours and features.

Many occultists believe that the HALOES traditionally depicted around the heads of Christian saints are examples of auras.

auric fields *see* AURAS

auric hazes *see* AURAS

Aurora, Texas

Site of one of the first documented reports of a crashed UFO on 17 April 1897. The case, which inspired the low-budget film Aurora Encounter *(1985), is widely regarded as a hoax.*

During 1896 and 1897 the American West was awash with stories describing mystery AIRSHIPS floating in the sky. This was the first significant burst of localized UFO activity of the kind that is today described as a WAVE.

The Aurora incident was reported at a time when the newspapers were filled with sensational stories – a few seemingly genuine reports were mixed with extraordinary accounts, each story seeking to outdo the last published tale. The only contemporary source for this case was the edition of the *Dallas Morning News* published two days after the events were alleged to have occurred. There is no evidence that any other newspaper followed it up, nor did the *News* publish follow-up articles. The case is also not featured in a local history of the area, which was written only ten years later.

According to the press report, the airship struck a windmill on the outskirts of Aurora and crashed. A badly mutilated alien body was found in the wreckage and interred in the local cemetery by the townsfolk. This alien theme was relatively unusual for an airship story, and is one reason why it attracted the interest of UFO investigators when it resurfaced in 1966, during a reassessment of the press coverage of the 19th-century wave.

DR J ALLEN HYNEK, science consultant to the US Air Force, set an investigation in motion. It revealed no unaccounted-for graves and no recollections among elderly locals that the events had really happened. In 1973 two nonagenarian residents did claim a vague memory of the story, but could not prove that it had actually occurred. Local authorities made it clear that they would not allow the graveyard to be dug up without convincing evidence that the story was anything more than a short-lived joke. At the time of the alleged incident, the small community of Aurora had been in decline after being bypassed by the trans-continental railways, and some felt that this story might have been an aborted attempt to revive interest in the town.

Aurora Borealis

Dramatic light effects seen in the sky at high latitudes in the northern hemisphere.

Also known as the Northern Lights, the Aurora Borealis is an atmospheric phenomenon characterized by vast trembling streamers or curtains of light. In simple terms, the aurora is an electromagnetic effect generated by electrons colliding with atoms in the upper atmosphere, driven by the combined effect of solar radiation and the earth's magnetic field. However, the scientific model is incomplete and has had to be developed greatly in recent years to accommodate new observations. Various colours are seen in the display, mainly red, blue, green and violet, with red being dominant. Sometimes the colours combine to give white light. The effect grows stronger the closer the observer is to the Pole and the further away they are from the light pollution of large cities.

The rhythmic movement of the light effects led observers in the distant past to attribute the phenomenon to the dancing of spirits in the sky, and this is reflected in the traditional Scottish name, 'the merry dancers'. In other societies the aurora was thought variously to be caused by the actions of gods or the reflections from heavenly shoals of herring, or (inspired by the predominance of red) to presage bloodshed and war.

In some folklore traditions it is believed that the lights are accompanied by sound, which takes the form of a continuous crackling or hissing. Even now there are many anecdotal reports of this phenomenon. However, it has not been successfully recorded and there is no widely accepted scientific theory for the mechanism by which such sounds might be produced (see also ELECTROPHONICS).

There is an equivalent phenomenon in the southern hemisphere, called the Aurora Australis.

A spectacular display of the Aurora Borealis, as seen in the sky above the Canadian town of Churchill, Manitoba. (© TopFoto/Imageworks)

auto-Ganzfeld experiments *see*

GANZFELD EXPERIMENTS

automatic art

The production of a piece of artwork without the person who is making it being aware of what is being produced.

Automatic art is a form of AUTOMATISM and is related to AUTOMATIC SPEECH and AUTOMATIC WRITING. It is often, but not always, produced by PSYCHICS at SÉANCES, who will produce works of art (of varying quality) while purportedly in the control of SPIRITS. The psychic (or MEDIUM) is said to be CHANNELLING the artistic ability of whoever is controlling them.

Frequently automatic art is produced by scribbling at great speed on a sheet of paper, often with the pen or pencil remaining in constant contact with the sheet. Once the work has been finished, if the process has been successful, it should be found to be a recognizable picture. Mediums often claim that the automatic art that they produce is in the style of a particular dead artist.

automatic speech

Speech which apparently comes from an individual but over which they seemingly have no control.

Automatic speech, like AUTOMATIC WRITING and AUTOMATIC ART, is a form of AUTOMATISM. As such it is alleged that the apparent originator of the speech has no control over the words that are being spoken; they are instead merely a conduit for communication from SPIRITS or other beings. The process is usually carried out by a MEDIUM who enters a trance, during which the speech is channelled (see CHANNELLING and TRANCE, MEDIUMISTIC).

In its modern form, the origin of automatic speech can be traced back to the spiritualists of the 19th century. However, much earlier examples can be found in the stories of ecstatics speaking in tongues reported in the Christian Bible. See also ECSTATIC PHENOMENA; XENOGLOSSY.

automatic writing

The production of written material, supposedly without the conscious control of the person who is writing it down.

Automatic writing is a form of AUTOMATISM like AUTOMATIC SPEECH and AUTOMATIC DRAWING. To produce it, a pen or pencil is held over a piece of paper and (if the process has been successful) it will begin to write, apparently without the conscious control of the person holding it. It is normally carried out by a MEDIUM, who may enter a trance – the pen or pencil is then supposedly being directed by SPIRITS.

Using this technique mediums have supposedly produced written material from once living individuals, such as new works from Beethoven, for example, or new creeds on how to live life by Jesus Christ (see *A COURSE IN MIRACLES*). One medium in the late 19th century even produced complex documents describing life on Mars. They were written in Martian which, fortunately, bore a striking resemblance to the medium's native French. See also CHANNELLING.

automatism

Behaviour on the part of an individual that occurs without their apparent intervention or conscious control.

Within the realms of SPIRITUALISM and other spiritual belief systems, automatism is behaviour that is supposedly born out of an individual's ability to receive and channel messages from SPIRITS, without their being aware of what is happening. The most frequently encountered forms of automatism are AUTOMATIC WRITING, AUTOMATIC SPEECH and AUTOMATIC ART.

The term 'automatism' (or, more commonly, 'automatic behaviour') is also used to describe the spontaneous production of verbal or motor behaviour without conscious self-control, which is associated with some medical conditions and with SLEEPWALKING. See also MEDIUM; CHANNELLING.

autumnal equinox

The day in the autumn when the sun is above the horizon for the same period as it is below the horizon. It is of importance in both ancient and modern pagan spiritual practice.

The autumnal equinox, which generally falls on 21 September in the northern hemisphere, is one of the four minor SABBATS recognized and celebrated as a festival by many modern pagans (see PAGANISM) and practitioners of WITCHCRAFT.

Known among other things as Mabon, the second harvest, cornucopia or the winter finding, the modern observance of the festival often combines elements from a variety of historical traditions including giving thanks for the harvest and offering libations to trees. It is a point at which the transition from summer into winter is recognized, and a time of balance between dark and light, which many Wiccans understand to be the time when THE GODDESS is changing from mother to crone. See also BELTANE; IMBOLC; LUGHNASADH; SAMHAIN; SUMMER SOLSTICE; VERNAL EQUINOX; WICCA; WINTER SOLSTICE.

Avebury

A large Neolithic stone circle in Wiltshire.

The village of Avebury in Wiltshire is the site of a Neolithic stone circle, even larger than STONEHENGE. A huge circular ditch encloses the main ring of individual standing stones, which measures almost 1.6 kilometres (1 mile) in circumference, with some of the stones almost 5 metres (16 feet) high. Two smaller rings, which are much less complete than the main ring, are enclosed within this. Two curving lines of stones, known as avenues, lead away from the circle, but so many stones are now missing that their exact significance remains unclear. It is thought that one of them connected the site with another nearby hilltop stone circle known as The Sanctuary. It is believed that building began c.2800 BC, using stones quarried from the nearby Avebury Hills, and continued over the next 500 years.

Various theories have been put forward as to the purposes of this ancient complex of stones. Some believe that the two inner circles were used as temples, and both of them had a central standing stone. The larger of these, which was known as The Obelisk until its destruction in the 18th century, is believed to have been erected to cast a shadow (in much the same way as the gnomon of a sundial) which could be interpreted as marking the changing seasons. Similarly, 'The Cove', a group of three stones (two of which remain) at the centre of the other inner circle, is thought to have been aligned with the position of sunrise at midsummer.

The relatively close proximity of other significant Neolithic remains, such as at SILBURY HILL and The Sanctuary, suggest that Avebury may have been part of a large area of interconnected sites with particular religious significance. It has been discovered relatively recently that some of the stones have faces carved into them but it is not known whether the builders or subsequent inhabitants are responsible for these.

In modern times, the stones were 'discovered' by John Aubrey (1626–97), the English antiquary, biographer and folklorist, who assumed that the structures must be connected with ancient druidic worship. He was supported in this theory by the antiquary William Stukeley (1687–1765), whose accounts of his researches at Avebury also record his dismay at the removal of stones by local farmers. Stukeley also suggested that the two avenues of stones represented a great serpent passing through the circles.

Several of the largest stones have been given names in local folklore, including the Swindon Stone, and the Devil's Chair, which has a hollow in which one can sit.

Avrocar

An experimental craft built in an attempt to reproduce the vertical take-off and landing claimed in reports of UFO sightings.

In 1953 the Canadian arm of aviation designers

The Avrocar, a terrestrial 'flying saucer' developed with sponsorship from the US Army and Air Force during the 1950s. (© Bettmann/Corbis)

A V Roe & Company (Avro Aircraft) employed British engineer John Frost to develop a vertical take-off and landing aircraft. Receiving government funding and code-named Project Y, the enterprise aimed to produce a jet capable of reaching speeds of around 2,400kph (1,500mph).

In 1954 Avro obtained a contract to continue this work for the US Army. Their remit now was to design a craft that would be capable of duplicating some of the behaviour of FLYING SAUCERS, as reported in the sightings then on record.

Frost employed a phenomenon known as the Coanda effect (discovered in 1910 by the French–Romanian scientist Henri-Marie Coanda). Coanda observed that a flow of gas or liquid will change direction to follow the line of a suitably positioned curved surface, being 'pulled' towards it and, as a result, producing a pull on the surface in the opposite direction. In this instance, it was intended that by directing air over the upper surface of the aircraft the required lift could be produced, even while the aircraft was horizontally stationary.

The design chosen for the prototype, which was called the Avrocar, took the form of a flattened saucer, 5.5 metres (18 feet) in diameter. The pilot sat in the centre while three gas turbine engines on the base were used to provide the necessary airflow. However, it proved very difficult to achieve the precision required.

Test flights were held in 1960, but these proved disastrous. Pilots found that the craft became impossible to control as soon as it was airborne. Consequently, it never achieved a height of more than a few feet or sustained flight for longer than a few moments. The $10-million project was closed down in 1961. One of the two prototypes was moved to the US Army Transport Museum in Virginia, where it remains as a monument to a failed dream.

However, this was not the end of the story. In April 2005 the British engineer Geoff Hatton managed to overcome many of the difficulties with the original design, and successfully flew a new prototype saucer called GSF7. This was an unmanned vehicle just one-fifth of the size of the Avrocar, but was otherwise similar, and again utilized the Coanda effect. It had been designed in a factory shed in Cambridgeshire, with the aid of a £250,000 grant from the British government. Both US and British military sources immediately entered into talks about developing the GSF7 as an unmanned reconnaissance vehicle.

Ayurveda

A traditional system of holistic Indian medicine which aims to bring about a healthy mind, body and spirit by balancing the body's energies through detoxification, diet, yoga, meditation and herbal preparations.

Ayurveda is the traditional system of medicine in India, where it is believed to have been practised for over 5,000 years. Its name comes from the Sanskrit words *ayu*, meaning life, and *veda*, meaning knowledge, and it is based on a HOLISTIC approach with roots in the Vedic culture. Ayurvedic medicine seeks to restore a harmonious flow of UNIVERSAL LIFE FORCE in the individual to bring about self-healing, good health and longevity, and has been adopted by Hindu, Buddhist and other Eastern religious groups; it is becoming prominent in India as an alternative to Western medicine, and is also gaining popularity in the West.

Ayurveda is based on the principle that all living beings have a universal life force called prana, which is centred in the human body in energy centres called CHAKRAS, and that a harmonious and balanced flow of prana is needed for a healthy mind, body and spirit. According to Ayurveda, the body functions through the interaction of three systems: the *doshas*, or vital energies; the *dhatus*, or body tissues; and the *malas*, or waste products. The doshas control the creation of tissues and the removal of waste products, and are responsible for all physiological and psychological functions. There are three doshas, known by the Sanskrit names *Vata*, *Pitta* and *Kapha*.

The Vata dosha is the most important, since it moves and drives the entire body. It is composed of the elements of air and space, and if it becomes imbalanced, it causes an imbalance in the other two doshas; a Vata imbalance is usually thought to be the first cause of disease. The Pitta dosha, composed of fire and water, governs the digestion, hunger and thirst, and mental activity, while the heaviest dosha, Kapha, composed of earth and water, gives the body its strength and stability. All three doshas are thought to be present in every part of the body, but each individual has a unique natural ratio of the three. However, the doshas are affected by habit, diet and lifestyle, which can deplete or increase them and cause an imbalance. The Ayurvedic practitioner therefore first classifies a patient by their body type as having a given proportion of each dosha in their healthy state, then diagnoses their imbalance by examining the whole person and questioning them extensively about their habits, lifestyle and emotions. Based on this diagnosis, an individualized course of treatment is then prescribed to restore the balance of doshas which is appropriate for that particular person. This treatment involves an exercise programme such as YOGA, a diet supplemented by herbal preparations, and often breathing and meditation exercises, massage and AROMATHERAPY.

azoth

A mysterious principle thought by alchemists to exist in all physical matter; also used as another name for mercury, for a universal remedy and for the philosopher's stone.

Alchemists believed that all physical matter was made up of three symbolic chemical substances – SALT (which corresponded to the element of EARTH), SULPHUR (which corresponded to FIRE) and MERCURY (corresponding to both AIR and WATER) – each of which had itself a threefold nature, since it contained the other two to some extent, so that the symbolic substance of salt also contained sulphur and mercury, but had salt predominating, and so on. The physical matter made up of these substances was believed to be held together by a fourth substance, called azoth, a mysterious universal principle which was sometimes referred to as 'the measureless spirit of life' or, by transcendentalists, as 'the astral light', and which has been interpreted by some scholars as being electricity or magnetism.

Azoth was also a name given by alchemists to mercury when considered as the first principle of all the metals, existing in and extractable from each one. The word is usually believed to come from the Arabic for 'mercury', although it has also been said to have been formed from the initial letter of the English, Greek and Hebrew alphabets (A), followed by the final letter of the English alphabet (Z), the Greek alphabet (Omega), and the Hebrew alphabet (Tau), thereby standing for 'alpha and omega' or the beginning and end of all things. It was, in addition, used to refer to the universal quicksilver remedy theorized by PARACELSUS, which contained the virtues of all other medicines; hence, it was also used as another name for the PHILOSOPHER'S STONE.

Baba Yaga

A hag fairy in Slavonic folklore, who eats human flesh and lives in the forest in a hut on chicken's legs.

Baba Yaga is a fearsome, cannibalistic character in Slavonic folklore. Sometimes described as a witch or ogress, she lives in the forest in a hut which moves around on chicken's legs and is fenced by the bones of her human victims. This gruesome fence is topped by human skulls whose blazing eye sockets light up the darkness. The hut can see with its windows and speak with its door, whose keyhole is a mouth filled with sharp teeth. It usually spins around on its chicken legs, screeching as it revolves, or stands with its back to visitors, and will only stop, with much creaking and groaning, if a secret incantation is spoken. Then it will lower itself down to face the visitor and fling its door open with a crash. Although Baba Yaga is usually depicted as a terrifying old crone, she has no power over the pure of heart, and will sometimes help them in her capacity as a wise woman by giving advice and magical gifts. However, she is likely to devour with her stone teeth those who come to her unprepared or with unclean spirits.

Baba Yaga flies about the skies in a huge mortar, steering herself with a pestle held in her right hand and obliterating all traces of her passage with a broom made of silver birch held in her left hand. She is often accompanied on her flights by a host of shrieking spirits. Her nose is so long that when she sleeps on her back on top of her ancient brick oven, it scrapes the roof of her hut, and despite her voracious appetite for human flesh, she remains as thin as a skeleton, so that in Russia she is also known as *Baba Yaga Kostianaya Noga*, or 'Grandmother Bonyshanks'. She controls the elements and can call up storms, and when she appears, she brings with her a wild wind. She is also the guardian of the FOUNTAIN OF YOUTH. Baba Yaga has three faithful servants: a White Horseman, a Red Horseman and a Black Horseman, who represent the bright dawn, the red sun and the dark midnight; in some stories she is also served by three bodiless pairs of hands which appear out of thin air to do her bidding.

She is thought by some to be a dark goddess who symbolizes the death of the ego which is needed to achieve wisdom and, through this death, rebirth to a new life.

Bach Flower Therapy *see* BACH, EDWARD

Bach, Edward (1886–1936)

English physician, bacteriologist and homeopath; he developed the 38 Bach Flower Remedies®, which are said to restore emotional balance by counteracting negative states of mind.

Edward Bach was born in 1886, and grew up in Birmingham. He studied medicine at University College Hospital in London, and obtained a Diploma in Public Health at Cambridge in 1901. In 1913, he became House Surgeon and casualty medical officer at University College Hospital, and during World War I was in charge of 400 beds. During this period, he became dissatisfied with the way in which doctors were expected to focus on the disease and not the patient, and began to spend time at his patients' bedsides allowing them to talk. This led him to believe that the real cause of many of their illnesses was worry, and he observed the effects of stress and trauma on their potential recovery.

He became a highly successful bacteriologist, studied HOMEOPATHY, and had a lucrative practice in Harley Street. He went to work at the London

Edward Bach, the English physician who was the pioneer of flower remedies. (© Mary Evans Picture Library)

the one which alleviated the state. He then prepared 'mother tinctures' of each flower remedy by exposing the flower buds to the sun in a bowl of spring water for several hours and then preserving the resulting liquid with brandy. This mother tincture was then greatly diluted to produce a solution which was taken as drops under the tongue. Each flower remedy might be taken alone or in combination with others, and was developed for the treatment of emotional and spiritual conditions such as depression, anxiety, insomnia and stress. Bach believed that each flower embodied a certain 'soul quality' which corresponded to a similar quality in humans, and that where this quality had become unbalanced in a person, the flower remedy's harmonious frequency could re-establish balance and harmony in the person's soul. Thus, aspen, which related to the soul quality of fearlessness, could be used to treat someone in a negative aspen state, in which they were subject to constant needless anxieties and fears, and beech, which related to sympathy and tolerance, could be used for a person who was narrow-minded and intolerant.

The Bach Centre continues to make and distribute mother tinctures for the 38 flower remedies according to the detailed instructions left behind by Bach; the best-known of these is Rescue Remedy, a pre-blended combination of Rock Rose, Impatiens, Clematis, Star of Bethlehem and Cherry Plum, which is used to relieve acute stress and panic attacks, particularly in emergencies.

Homeopathic Hospital, where he developed seven homeopathically prepared bacterial remedies which came to be known as the Bach nosodes. Their value was instantly recognized by like-minded practitioners; they were widely adopted by homeopaths throughout North America and Europe, and are now firmly established as homeopathic remedies. However, Bach felt he could develop remedies which would act with greater depth and harmony than these seven nosodes. Strongly influenced by the vitalist healing tradition, which emphasizes the importance of nature cures and herbal medicine, he gave up his Harley Street practice in 1930 at the age of 43, and devoted himself to the search for a simpler, more natural healing technique.

He went to live in Wales and began to research and prepare herbal remedies, then in 1934 he moved to Mount Vernon in Oxfordshire and set up the Dr Edward Bach Centre, where he lived and worked until his death.

Between 1928 and 1936, he discovered and designed a total of 38 flower remedies to counteract various negative states of mind which could lead to illness, and to restore the patient's emotional balance. He claimed that he personally experienced each negative emotional state which he sought to cure, and then tried various plants and flowers until he found

Bailey, Alice (1880–1949)

A mystical writer and teacher who was influential on the later New Age movement.

Born in Manchester, Alice Bailey did evangelistic work with the British Army in India, where she met her first husband, Walter Evans. They moved to the USA, where he became an Episcopalian minister, but the marriage was not successful. She encountered the teachings of MADAME BLAVATSKY, joined the THEOSOPHICAL SOCIETY in California, and met and later married Foster Bailey, the US secretary of the Society. Although a mystical Christ remained central to her beliefs, she turned her back on mainstream Christianity.

Alice Bailey claimed to be in contact with several ASCENDED MASTERS, including Koot Hoomi and Djwhal Khul, and began transcribing their messages into a number of books (24 by the end of her life). She fell out with Madame Blavatsky's successor in the Theosophical Society, ANNIE BESANT (who saw Alice Bailey as a threat to her own position), and Alice and her husband left the Society.

In 1922 the Baileys set up the Lucis Trust to publish Alice's books, including the influential *A*

Treatise on Cosmic Fire, and in 1923 they established the Arcane School to teach their growing number of followers. Their teachings were broadly theosophical, with an emphasis on the coming Maitreya (see BENJAMIN CREME). After Alice's death Foster Bailey continued to lead the Arcane School until his own death in 1977. The movement split into a number of offshoots, and through these Alice Bailey's teachings became extremely influential on the early NEW AGE movement.

In 1945 Alice Bailey wrote the Great Invocation, which is spoken as a world prayer by groups of people of many varieties of faith:

> From the point of Light within the Mind of God
> Let light stream forth into the minds of men.
> Let Light descend on Earth.
>
> From the point of Love within the Heart of God
> Let love stream forth into the hearts of men.
> May Christ return to Earth.
>
> From the centre where the Will of God is known
> Let purpose guide the little wills of men –
> The purpose which the Masters know and serve.
>
> From the centre which we call the race of men
> Let the Plan of Love and Light work out
> And may it seal the door where evil dwells.
>
> Let Light and Love and Power restore the Plan
>   on Earth.

A recently adapted version from the Lucis Trust has changed 'minds of men' etc to 'human minds' etc, and 'Christ' to 'the Coming One' to make the prayer more inclusive.

Baker, Rachel *see* SLEEPING PREACHER, THE

Ballard, Guy W(arren) (1878–1939)
Founder of the I AM Religious Activity and the Saint Germain Foundation.
In 1929 or 1930 (accounts vary) Guy W Ballard, having studied occult and theosophical writings, went on a walking holiday on Mount Shasta in California to seek out a supposed esoteric Brotherhood of Mount Shasta. While hiking there he claimed to have met the COMTE DE SAINT GERMAIN – an 18th-century alchemist whom many esoteric movements recognize as an ASCENDED MASTER.

Ballard claimed that Saint Germain told him that he had been scouring Europe for centuries for someone to whom he could impart the Great Laws of Life; finding no one suitable, he was now looking in

the USA. Ballard and his wife Edna claimed that they had regular meetings with Saint Germain, and set up the Saint Germain Press to publish their books on what became the I AM teachings as revealed to them by the Comte: *Unveiled Mysteries* (1934) and *The Magic Presence* (1935) under the pseudonym Godfre Ray King, and *I AM Adorations and Affirmations* (1936).

As the only 'Accredited Messengers' of the Ascended Masters, Guy and Edna Ballard and their son Don toured the USA in the 1930s, giving workshops and lectures on their teachings. By the time of Ballard's death in 1939 they were claiming a million students. Don left the movement in 1957 while Edna continued to run it until her own death in 1971.

See also I AM MOVEMENT; CHURCH UNIVERSAL AND TRIUMPHANT.

Ballechin House
A property in Perthshire, Scotland, that was the subject of a controversial haunting in the 19th century. It was once dubbed 'the most haunted house in Scotland'.
The alleged haunting of Ballechin House in Perthshire, Scotland was investigated by members of the SOCIETY FOR PSYCHICAL RESEARCH in 1897. Many ghostly phenomena were said to occur at the house – particularly strange noises, an APPARITION of a nun, and an apparition of a spectral dog – leading to the property being dubbed 'the most haunted house in Scotland' (a title later adapted for BORLEY RECTORY in England).

The Society for Psychical Research (SPR) took out a tenancy on the isolated building (a method later employed by Harry Price at Borley Rectory), and a team of investigators stayed at the property over a period of several months. Attempts at SÉANCE communication were undertaken and vigils were conducted in the hope of experiencing manifestations. However, adverse publicity followed in *The Times* in June 1897, when it was alleged that members of the SPR had not disclosed their intentions to the property's owners when taking on the lease – the owners maintained that they had been deceived. Further criticism of the approach of one of the leading investigators, Ada Goodrich-Freer, followed, leading to the investigation's being prematurely abandoned – members of the SPR tactfully avoided discussion of the case thereafter.

Goodrich-Freer went on to write a detailed book on the case, in conjunction with the Marquess of Bute, entitled *The Alleged Haunting of B----- House* (published in 1899, with an updated edition appearing the following year). Although no serious allegations of fraud were made concerning Ballechin, many of the accounts in the book were considered dubious – for example, the strange noises were dismissed as the product of minor earth tremors, in what is a seismically active area. Appreciation of the book was also handicapped by the lengths taken in the text to preserve the anonymity of witnesses. Apart from a nursery block, Ballechin House was entirely demolished in the 20th century. However, the case may well merit re-assessment.

Ballester-Olmos, Vicente-Juan (1948–   )

One of the leading scientific figures in European UFO research and a prolific case investigator and writer on Spanish UFOs.

Born in Valencia, Ballester-Olmos graduated from university with degrees in both engineering and computing, and has worked in an analytical capacity for the Ford Motor company. In 1971 he came to prominence as a UFO researcher when he co-authored a study of CLOSE ENCOUNTER cases with DR JACQUES VALLÉE. He has since published numerous papers, given lectures on his findings all over the world and written several further books.

He now acts as a consultant to the scientific UFO group, CUFOS, who have published many of his papers. These include the 1976 analysis of 200 major cases from Spain and Portugal where UFOs were reported to have landed, and often to have left behind physical evidence amenable to investigation.

During the 1990s he made in-depth studies of official files released by the Spanish government. Among them were a number of cases where military aircraft intercepted strange lights, or where civilian aircraft came in dangerously close proximity to UFOs.

Ballester-Olmos has stated that he believes there is evidence that UFO cases do possess a physical component and that they cannot entirely be explained in terms of known natural phenomena.

ball lightning

A moving ball of light seen during thunderstorms.

There have been many accounts throughout the ages of the mysterious phenomenon known as ball lightning. In general terms this is taken to mean the appearance, during a storm of thunder and lightning, of a roughly spherical glowing body of light. There are various descriptions, with quite a range of colours, durations, behaviour and eventual disappearance ascribed to the phenomenon, but what they have in common is that the light is ball-like and it moves, sometimes in the air, sometimes near the ground. The ball of light is said to be visible in daylight and photographs have been taken which, it is claimed, show ball lightning.

Ball lightning has been described as entering buildings, often appearing to be attracted to metal objects, and there is even a report from the 1960s of ball lightning appearing inside a passenger jet and rolling down the aisle. Some argue that sightings of ball lightning are responsible for many reports of UFOs. It has even been claimed that the movement of ball lightning on the ground is the true explanation of CROP CIRCLES. Could being struck by ball lightning be the true cause of the phenomenon known as SPONTANEOUS HUMAN COMBUSTION? Some theorists think so.

Scientific opinion is divided as to whether ball lightning really exists, although some claim to have created similar, if smaller-scale, effects in laboratory conditions. Various explanations of ball lightning have been suggested. One theory is that it is a form of plasma. Another that it is electrically charged (or superheated) gas or air. Others believe that ball lightning is a form of radiation or microwave energy. Some scientists say that it results from silica in the soil being vaporized by a conventional lightning strike, with the resultant gas condensing into floating dust which continues to oxidize.

Some witnesses maintain that ball lightning is hot and destructive and can kill whatever it comes into contact with, but others report no sensation of heat and no damage to anything at all, whether living or inanimate. The fact that descriptions vary so widely would seem to suggest that ball lightning may be merely a 'catch-all' category for several very different types of phenomenon. See also BLACK DOG OF BUNGAY.

Bamberg witches

Those who suffered at the hands of the prince-bishop of Bamberg, Germany, in the 17th century, during some of the most horrific witch trials in recorded history.

Gottfried Johann Georg II Fuchs von Dornheim, who ruled Bamberg from 1623 to 1633, was reputedly responsible for the execution of an estimated 600 people for practising WITCHCRAFT. The period of persecution had begun with his predecessor but reached its peak under von Dornheim, who, with the assistance of Suffragan Bishop Friedrich Förner, built an organization dedicated to finding WITCHES, extracting confessions and carrying out executions.

This reign of terror was conducted with little regard for legal procedure. Accusations were not made public, the accused were not allowed legal representation and trials were merely a formality. Those who were convicted had their estates seized by von Dornheim – a powerful incentive for him to discover more witches, which produced such a flow of suspects that a new prison was built specifically to house them. Torture was used extensively to extract confessions. Subjected to methods such as whipping, burning with feathers dipped in sulphur, immersion in baths containing lime, thumbscrews and worse, people readily admitted to such unlikely acts as participating in witches' SABBATS and sexual intercourse with the DEVIL.

Those who objected to the process (including the vice-chancellor of Bamberg, Dr Georg Hahn) were themselves tried and executed. The Emperor Ferdinand eventually took action in 1630 to ensure that proper legal procedures were followed (this did not mean an end to torture, however) but the trials did not come to an end until Bishop Förner died in 1631, closely followed by von Dornheim in 1633.

Von Dornheim was only one of the many people involved in bloodthirsty campaigns of this kind in Germany during the 16th and 17th centuries. However, the widely held belief that the total number of executions was in the tens or even hundreds of thousands may be something of an exaggeration.

Bandi of Cesena, Countess

An Italian woman whose death was reputedly caused by spontaneous human combustion.

According to an account first published in Italy in 1731, the 62-year-old Countess Bandi of Cesena burned to death in her bedroom. When her maid went to wake her in the morning she discovered a heap of ashes on the floor which, apart from three fingers, her stockinged legs and part of her head, was all that remained of the Countess. This is believed to be one of the earliest recorded instances of SPONTANEOUS HUMAN COMBUSTION.

In some reports it was said that the remains of her head were found between her legs, and this was taken as indicating that her body had been so quickly consumed that her head must have suddenly fallen to the ground. However, other interpretations found nothing remarkable about the position of the head.

The room was said to have been full of soot, but none of the furniture or other contents seemed to have been damaged by the fire. The bed-sheets appeared to have been turned down, as if the occupant had got out of bed during the night for some reason.

The ashes of the Countess were described as greasy to the touch, and a sticky odoriferous moisture was seen to be trickling down the windows of the room. Ash was found to have covered an oil lamp, which lay on the floor with no oil left in it, and a pair of candles on a table still had their wicks but had lost all of their tallow.

The case became more widely known when the English writer Charles Dickens (1812–70) referred to it in his preface to the 1853 edition of *Bleak House*. Dickens had been criticized for describing, in the serial publication of his novel, the death by apparent spontaneous combustion of one of his characters, the alcoholic rag and bottle dealer Krook. To defend himself against complaints that such a thing could never happen in real life, Dickens advanced the case of the Countess, citing the account of it published in 1731 by an Italian clergyman.

At the time it was thought that a lightning strike could have caused the death of the Countess. Another theory was that the house may have been built over an old sulphur mine, from which highly flammable fumes could have escaped. Some suggest that it seems more likely that the unfortunate lady had been taken ill during the night and getting out of bed, perhaps to summon help, simply collapsed on the floor. Her nightclothes caught fire from the oil lamp and this led to her body being burned while she was in a state of unconsciousness or even already dead from a heart attack or stroke.

banshee

In Irish and Scottish folklore, a female spirit who wails and shrieks before a death in the family to which she is attached.

The word banshee comes from the Irish *bean sidhe*, meaning 'woman of the fairies' or 'woman of the mounds'. The banshee is a ghostly white lady whose cry foretells death. According to tradition, a banshee only wails for members of certain old Irish and Scottish families, and once a banshee has attached herself to a family, she is even said to follow them abroad if they emigrate. When several banshees wail together, it foretells the death of someone very great or holy.

The banshee is sometimes thought to be the spirit of a woman who has died in childbirth, although in some places she is said to be the ghost of a dead friend or family member. She may appear in one of three guises – as a young woman, a stately matron, or an old hag; these forms represent the triple aspects of the Morrigan, the Celtic goddess of war and death with whom the banshee is associated. To see the banshee portends the death of the one who sees her. In the Scottish Highlands, the banshee is known as the Bean-Nighe, and it is said that she can be seen washing the winding sheet or bloodstained clothes of the doomed person; in some stories, the Scottish banshee is described as having only one nostril, one long front tooth, and pendulous breasts.

The banshee's cry is variously described as being so piercing that it can shatter glass; as a thin sound somewhere between the wail of a woman and the screech of an owl; and as a cross between the shriek of a wild goose, the howl of a wolf and the cry of an abandoned child. However, when she loves those whom she calls to death, it is said that her song may be a low, soft chant which reassures the dying person and comforts the survivors.

Baphomet

An idol said to have been worshipped by the Knights Templar in the 14th century; usually represented as having a goat's head, it has been widely adopted as a Satanic symbol.

Opinions regarding the origin and nature of Baphomet vary from scholar to scholar, but the first accounts of this idol come from the confessions of the KNIGHTS TEMPLAR during their heresy trials in the 14th century. The Templars were accused of worshipping Baphomet, and under torture, a small number of them admitted the charge. However, their descriptions of the idol vary widely: some said it was a human skull, others the head of a goat; it was also described as an image made of wood or metal, or a painting. The name Baphomet is thought by many to be a corruption of the word Mahomet (Muhammad), although some have suggested that it is a combination of two Greek words, *baphe* and *metis*, meaning 'absorption of knowledge'.

Since then, occultists have put forward the theory that the Templars' idol was derived from the nature

The Baphomet of Mendes, as drawn by French occult author Éliphas Lévi. (© Mary Evans Picture Library)

god, Pan. The best-known representation of Baphomet is by the 19th-century writer and occultist ÉLIPHAS LÉVI. This drawing, titled *The Baphomet of Mendes*, shows a figure with a human trunk, female breasts, a caduceus in its midriff, human arms and hands, cloven hooves, wings and a goat's head. Between its horns is a torch, and it has a pentagram on its forehead. The body is said to symbolize the burden of matter from which arose the repentance for sin, and the hands point to two crescent moons, one white and one black, symbolizing good and evil. The caduceus suggests the male phallus, and the female breasts denote maternity, toil and redemption. The torch is thought to represent the divine intellect, and the pentagram, with its single point uppermost, human intelligence.

ALEISTER CROWLEY took the magical name of 'Baphomet' during his time in the ORDO TEMPLI ORIENTIS, and in the 1960s Baphomet was adopted as the insignia of the CHURCH OF SATAN – in their Sigil of Baphomet, a goat's head is shown inside an inverted PENTAGRAM, enclosed in an outer circle around which five Hebrew letters spell out the name 'Leviathan'.

barghest *see* BLACK DOGS

batons, suit of *see* WANDS, SUIT OF

Bay Area remote-viewing experiments

CIA-funded research into remote viewing.

For the US government the study of REMOTE VIEWING began with an eight-month pilot in the Bay Area of San Francisco, using local targets. Conducted by Harold Puthoff and Russell Targ at Stanford Research Institute in 1972 –3, and funded by the CIA (apparently in response to similar research allegedly being carried out in the Soviet Union), the experiments started after New York-based artist Ingo Swann demonstrated an apparent ability to be able to tell what was inside sealed boxes. A subject, known as the 'outbounder', would be sent to an external location in the Bay Area and the remote viewer would have to describe where the person was. Impressed with the initial results, the government funded further research (see PROJECT STARGATE) before finally terminating the programme, amid concerns over its effectiveness, in the mid-1990s.

Beast of Bodmin *see* ALIEN BIG CATS

Beast, the Great

The beast mentioned in the Book of Revelation, whose number is 666; a name adopted by English occultist Aleister Crowley.

The Bible's Book of Revelation refers to a beast whose

number is given as 666, and which is identified with the Antichrist:

> And I stood upon the sand of the sea, and saw a beast rise up out of the sea, having seven heads and ten horns, and upon his horns ten crowns, and upon his heads the name of blasphemy. And the beast which I saw was like unto a leopard, and his feet were as the feet of a bear, and his mouth as the mouth of a lion: and the dragon gave him his power, and his seat, and great authority.

When the notorious English occultist ALEISTER CROWLEY was a child, his behaviour caused his devoutly religious mother to chastise him by calling him 'the Beast'. Later, Crowley, who also liked to refer to himself as 'the wickedest man alive', provoked Christians by adopting the Greek name *To Mega Therion*, and its translation, 'the Great Beast', and believed that his magical system was destined to destroy Christianity.

bed of nails

A board studded with nails on which fakirs lie.

A bed of nails is a rectangular wooden board with a large number of nails mounted on it so that their points protrude upwards. It is so called because a person lies down at full length on it, seeming to avoid being injured by some inexplicable means.

This is a feat originally associated with Indian ascetics, known as FAKIRS, undertaken to show the dominance of mind over body. Conjurers also performed it and it became part of the repertoire of 'magicians' all over the world, who would often elaborate on it by applying weights, or another board of nails, on top of the body.

The reason that the nails do not puncture the person's skin is that their weight is evenly distributed over the nails. The same principle applies when, as in magic stunts, another nailed board is placed on top of the person and struck with a heavy blow. Most of the force is absorbed by the board itself, with the rest being evenly distributed over all of the nails that are actually in contact with the person's body. If, for example, the person put all of their weight on a hand or any other small area of their body they would certainly risk injury.

behavioural medicine

A branch of medicine which focuses on the use of psychological means to help the patient make the lifestyle and behavioural changes believed necessary to influence their physical symptoms, prevent disease and promote health.

Behavioural medicine is an interdisciplinary field of

An Indian fakir photographed relaxing on a bed of nails.
(© TopFoto/Fortean)

medicine which provides a whole-person perspective. It is based on the belief that psychological, social, environmental, employment, educational and even spiritual problems can affect a patient's physical health, and that conversely, having a chronic or terminal illness can affect the patient's psychological condition, damaging their sense of self, their relationships, and their ability to function socially and at work. This branch of medicine applies the principles of behavioural therapy in order to diagnose, prevent and treat medical disorders, to rehabilitate the patient and to promote wellbeing. The practitioner observes and analyses the patient's behaviour, diagnoses unproductive or detrimental ways in which they deal with life situations, and discusses with them the various methods by which they can systematically learn new patterns of behaviour and modify their lifestyle in order to influence their physical symptoms and improve their health. The emphasis is on the patient's active participation in the treatment, and on their being provided with the appropriate knowledge to make an informed decision as to which methods will work best for them.

Also known as health psychology, behavioural medicine uses a blend of cognitive therapy and prescription medicine in conjunction with the practitioner's knowledge of the patient's physical and psychological condition and circumstances. Among the methods which may be used are BIOFEEDBACK, relaxation training and HYPNOSIS, and behavioural therapy techniques such as aversion therapy, desensitisation and role-playing. Diet, exercise, medication, psychotherapy, and complementary therapies such as AROMATHERAPY and YOGA may also be part of the treatment, as well as crisis counselling, grief therapy, and couple and family counselling. Using this set of tools, the practitioner seeks to manage specific clinical problems and situations and to help the patient to make the lifestyle and behavioural changes necessary to improve their condition. Behavioural medicine is often used to assist in stress prevention and reduction, smoking cessation, weight loss, the control of alcohol or substance addiction and the treatment of eating disorders.

The Belgian Wave *see panel p62*

believer effect
The apparent influence of the belief of an observer on the outcome of experiments in parapsychology.
Some parapsychologists have observed that in some instances the results of an experiment can appear to be influenced by the attitudes of those involved – in particular, positive results are more likely to be obtained if the person carrying out the experiment believes in the reality of the paranormal phenomenon under investigation. This is not to say that the experimenter is cheating and consciously altering the results, and those who argue for the believer effect claim that it is an example of PSYCHIC ability in itself.

However, sceptics would argue that there are other factors at work which affect the validity of the results (see EXPERIMENTER EFFECT). They are also particularly suspicious when it is seen in the negative – for example, when a psychic or MEDIUM claims that they cannot perform because there is an unbeliever present.

bells
Instruments used for protection against evil spirits in many religious, spiritual and magical traditions.
The use of bells for protection against evil spirits is a common feature of folkloric and religious systems throughout the world. The robes worn by ancient Hebrew priests were fringed with golden bells, and bells figure prominently in the costumes and paraphernalia of the SHAMANS, MEDICINE MEN and spiritual leaders of many cultures. In many belief systems bells serve not only as protection but also to clear the air and signal a change in consciousness – for example, bells are frequently used in FENG SHUI for protection and prosperity, and to revitalize a space by generating positive QI energy with each new ring.

In the folklore of Britain and the rest of Europe domestic animals and children were considered vulnerable to attack by WITCHES or other malevolent forces, and so were protected by an AMULET in the form of a small bell worn around the neck. It is possible that the bells held by Morris dancers were originally intended to frighten away evil spirits (as are the clashing sticks and fluttering handkerchiefs used in the dance). The ringing of church bells was once believed to help disperse storms and ward off lightning – before the nature of electricity was understood, people believed that lightning bolts, which were naturally attracted to the church towers as the highest structures in the area, were thrown by the DEVIL. The custom of ringing the 'passing bell' when someone was dying was also intended to scare away any evil spirits who might try to harm or steal the departing soul, while wedding bells were believed to drive away spirits envious of the couple's happiness. The bell is also a vital tool in the Christian rite of EXORCISM, and bells may also sometimes be rung at HALLOWE'EN.

FAIRIES were also said to find the ringing of church bells unbearable, and according to Teutonic legend, the DWARFS and TROLLS were driven out of Germany and Scandinavia by their sound. However, the 'seelie court' – the body of benevolent and graceful fairies in Celtic lore – were famous for the tinkling bells which adorned their garments and the bridles of their horses, and were thought to repel their malignant counterparts in the 'unseelie court'.

Bells are, of course, also used as warning devices, and there are many stories of bells ringing spontaneously as an omen of impending doom. In a number of legends, the warning comes from ghostly bells. In Cornwall, the Seven Stones Rocks to the west of Land's End are believed by some to be the remains of a great city which once stood in the now-submerged land of Lyonesse (sometimes associated with stories of KING ARTHUR), and local fisherman's legend has it that, on stormy nights, the church bells of the city can be heard ringing below the sea. In a further Cornish legend, three bells ordered for a local church in the Middle Ages by William, Lord of Bottreaux Castle in Boscastle, to ward off the plague, were lost when the ship carrying them sank in the bay within sight of the church tower for which they were intended; when a storm sweeps the bay, their ghostly peal can supposedly still be heard.

Bell Witch
A 19th-century poltergeist case from Tennessee, USA, characterized by claims of extremely aggressive behaviour on the part of the entity involved.
There are several versions of the story of the Bell Witch POLTERGEIST which afflicted John Bell, his wife and their eight children at a farm near Adams, Tennessee, in 1817. The main details of the occurrences were

The Belgian Wave

In a single day, on 29 November 1989, the Belgian UFO group SOBEPS (Société Belge d'Étude des Phénomènes Spatiaux) received 120 reports of UFO sightings – mostly from the vicinity of Liège and Eupen. This was just the beginning of what became one of the most famous European UFO WAVES, with many further sightings occurring over the next few weeks. The sightings were widely reported in the media, attracting attention across Europe and in the USA – especially when suspicions arose that the Americans might be conducting test flights of their then top-secret stealth aircraft.

The early sightings, on 29 November and the following days, varied greatly. Some involved rotating globes of light sweeping across a low cloud base. Such phenomena are now readily identified as laser searchlight displays promoting outdoor events. However, in Europe in 1989, they were still new, and undoubtedly thought mysterious by most people who observed them. These displays can be seen from around 50 kilometres (30 miles) away and still occasionally generate UFO reports today.

More interestingly, a large number of the reports (especially those from the first night) described a huge dark triangle the size of a football pitch. This had bright lights on each edge and a red fuzzy glow in the middle. According to some, it moved at very slow speed, making a faint humming noise. Witnesses included police officers who pulled in to the roadside to watch as the object flew over. Many observers were convinced that this was an enormous and very unusual aircraft – hence the concern that US stealth aircraft might have been operating in Belgian air space.

The diplomatic consequences of this wave were considerable. Several government agencies on both sides of the Atlantic filed reports. Some of these have now been released following the implementation of various freedom of information laws. One memo from the US Air Force headquarters in Europe, to Washington, DC, said:

> [There were] a large number of reported sightings, particularly in Nov 89 in the Liège area … the Belgian Air Force and MoD are taking the issue seriously. Belgian Air Force experts have not been able to explain the phenomena either.

Analysis clearly ruled out the possibility of stealth test flights – the F-117 aircraft were not like the objects reported and no such missions had been authorized.

Mystified, the Belgian authorities agreed to work with SOBEPS to try to resolve the issue by organizing a joint SKYWATCH. Over the Easter weekend in March 1990, SOBEPS was allowed to set up a monitor station at Bierset Airport near Liège and to post a team of investigators around the region, linked by mobile phone. The Belgian Air Force put two fighter jets on standby, one equipped with sophisticated cameras. This was an unprecedented joint operation, backed by a media campaign to get the public to report their sightings.

Sadly the wave was effectively over by the time of this experiment and few reports came in over that weekend. However, at about midnight on 31 March police officers near Wavre, around 60 kilometres (40 miles) west of Bierset, reported lights in the sky. From the description and long duration of the sighting, it is very likely that these were just stars seen through the icy atmosphere. However, the fighter planes were scrambled. As one F-16 jet closed in, its radar system locked on to something and there were also some ground radar reports of unknown targets. It seemed as if the project might be successful and that the cause of the UFO wave might have been discovered.

Unfortunately, subsequent analysis revealed little correlation between the radar targets and the star-like lights seen by the police. Neither F-16 pilot saw the lights or anything to match the brief radar target. The ground radar images had features often associated with spurious targets known as 'angels' – false signals caused by particular atmospheric conditions.

As for the football-field-sized object? This echoed sightings with identical features reported across central and eastern England just a year earlier. These earlier sightings had provoked questions in the House of Commons, where it became clear that witnesses also suspected they had seen US stealth aircraft. Although the cause of these sightings was never officially explained, some investigators believe that witnesses saw a midair refuelling exercise involving NATO aircraft practising for long-range bombing missions to the Middle East. The huge, slow-moving, low-altitude craft was, in fact, many aircraft strung with bright anti-collision lights, taking on fuel from a huge tanker plane. The array was very large but at great height, causing the movement to appear slow and the sound to be muted. A similar explanation may also account for the Belgian wave.

allegedly recorded in the diary of one of the sons, Richard Williams Bell.

The case is considered dubious, partly because of the extreme and long-running nature of the disturbances. The forms taken by the manifestations varied widely. Strange APPARITIONS were supposedly witnessed, followed by alarming noises. The poltergeist was also said to have launched violent attacks upon 12-year-old Betsy Bell who was slapped, pinched and later harassed to the point where she broke off an engagement with a local man of whom the poltergeist apparently disapproved. The poltergeist acquired a voice and delighted in cursing and shouting abuse. The voice claimed variously to be a DEMON or the SPIRITS of deceased persons, and allegedly uttered prophecies. It finally adopted the persona of Kate Betts, a woman who was living locally and was known to have a grudge against John Bell. It was thereafter referred to as 'Kate'. Physical phenomena were supposedly witnessed by amateur exorcists (see EXORCISM) and by sightseers who were drawn to the property – among them General Andrew Jackson.

The disturbances continued for three years during which the poltergeist persecuted several, but not all, of the members of the family. John Bell was a particular target, to the point that his health failed – when this happened the poltergeist still cursed him continuously as he lay sick in bed. On the morning of 19 December 1820 John Bell was found lying in a stupor and a strange bottle was found in his medicine cabinet. Its contents were tested upon a cat, which went into convulsions and died, whereupon 'Kate' declared she had poisoned John Bell. As he lay dying she sang rowdy songs in triumph.

After the death of John Bell the disturbances declined in severity, and 'Kate' declared she would depart and return in seven years' time to wreak further havoc. Seven years later the manifestations were limited to noises and the disturbance of bedclothes, but 'Kate' was said to have visited John Bell Jnr and pledged a further return in 107 years. No phenomena were experienced by descendants of the Bell family when the supposed return date was finally reached in 1935.

Various theories have been advanced as to the source of the Bell Witch poltergeist phenomena (in addition to the possibilities of exaggeration, hoax and deliberate acts on the part of one or more of the family members). Psychoanalyst Nandor Fodor suggested that it arose from the subconscious minds of one or more of the Bell daughters, with its behaviour being shaped by repressed conflicts within the family (see RECURRENT SPONTANEOUS PSYCHOKINESIS). Another theory, containing a popular theme in interpretations of US haunting cases, was put forward by Troy Taylor who suggested in *Season of the Witch* (1999) that a disturbed Native American burial mound in the area might be a factor.

Belmez faces
Mysterious images of faces which appeared in the fabric of a Spanish house in the 1970s.

In early 1971, mysterious marks resembling human faces appeared on the cement floor of the house of a lady named Maria Gomez Pereira in Belmez, Spain. The case received international publicity and many people, including a number of parapsychologists (see PARAPSYCHOLOGY), visited the house. To some the faces were evidence of SPIRIT manifestations on the part of deceased occupiers of the house or persons buried on the site. Consideration was also given to the possibility that they were created by the mind of Maria Pereira through PSYCHOKINESIS, the expressions on the faces being an external pictorial expression of her inner moods.

The case stimulated much debate, with some people claiming that the faces constituted a 'permanent PARANORMAL object' – a physical item which could be

A 'permanent paranormal object'? One of the famous facial images from the cement floor of a house in Belmez, Spain. (© Mary Evans Picture Library)

used to refute the arguments of sceptics. To others the faces were simply faked. Separate studies conducted by Spanish researchers J J Alonso and Manuel Martin Serrano reached diametrically opposed conclusions. Alonso considered that there was potentially a paranormal origin for some of the faces, while Serrano concluded they must all be forgeries. Both studies have been criticized and, regrettably, laboratory tests performed on some of the faces in 1975 and 1976 also proved less than satisfactory, failing even to determine the chemical composition of the markings with complete certainty.

The story of the faces of Belmez surfaced sporadically over the next 25 years but gradually faded from public attention. In October 2004 the house was reported to be empty and up for sale, the mystery still unsolved. See also IMAGES, SPONTANEOUS.

Beltane

One of the four major sabbats, celebrated from 30 April to 1 May in many forms of ancient and modern pagan spiritual practice.

The name 'Beltane' is derived from a pre-Christian celebration within the Celtic calendar. The festival coincides with the beginning of the warmer summer months – a time of birth, fertility and life. It has traditionally been celebrated in both Celtic and non-Celtic pagan cultures by the lighting of fires and other fertility-related rituals such as maypole-dancing.

The festival was adopted by the Christian Church in Britain as Roodmas, and in Germany as WALPURGISNACHT. See also AUTUMNAL EQUINOX; IMBOLC; LUGHNASADH; SABBATS; SAMHAIN; SUMMER SOLSTICE; VERNAL EQUINOX; WINTER SOLSTICE.

Bentwaters Air Force Base

Bentwaters was a Ministry of Defence base in Suffolk, England, leased for 40 years to the US Air Force in fulfilment of NATO obligations. It was the location of two of the most significant UFO events in the UK.

Bentwaters, and its smaller satellite base Woodbridge, are set in the pine woods of Rendlesham Forest (see RENDLESHAM FOREST INCIDENT) close to the east coast. This was the frontline of expected aerial invasion during World War II, and the early development and testing of radar was carried out nearby, heightening the sensitivity of the location. Long after the war there was much local suspicion about secret experiments. Fishermen and lighthouse keepers reported green glows in the sky and under the water, and reports of electrical disturbances were common. It is reputed that the infamous 'Over the Horizon' radar experiments (involving massive beams of energy fired into the upper atmosphere) were carried out in the area during the 1960s and 1970s.

The bases were leased to the US forces from the 1950s. During the 1980s, while the attention of peace campaigners was focused on bases such as Greenham Common, a covert US nuclear defence operation was set up at Bentwaters. This came to an end with the end of the Cold War, although rather bizarrely, in 2005, the base became the scene of an elaborate television hoax. A group of volunteers were flown there in the belief that they were going to a space centre in Russia to receive training that would culminate in a space flight. They were eventually duped into believing that they were in orbit, while in reality they were within a sophisticated ground-based simulator.

In 1980 Bentwaters was central to one of the most famous British UFO cases, the Rendlesham incident. By that time it had already been involved in the only British encounter studied by DR E U CONDON as part of the COLORADO UNIVERSITY STUDY of the 1960s.

The earlier incident came to light when an officer stationed at Bentwaters contacted the Colorado scientists assuming that they already knew of the case, because the US government had publicly insisted that all of its files had been handed over to the project. When the US files were later released (British records had apparently been 'routinely' destroyed in 1961), they confirmed that late on the night of 13 August 1956 fast-moving radar targets were tracked by the US Air Force stations at Lakenheath and Bentwaters and by the RAF unit at Neatishead, coming inland from over the North Sea. Ground observers at Bentwaters spotted a fuzzy glow overhead, and a US Air Force transport plane was able to see the UFO below them, meaning that it was flying at less than 1,800 metres (6,000 feet).

According to the US Air Force records, two RAF Venom fighters were sent toward the target. The pilot of one reported a radar lock and visual sighting, before being pursued in a cat-and-mouse chase across the darkened skies. The Colorado project radar expert, Dr Gordon Thayer, was so impressed by this case that he said in the final study:

> This is the most puzzling and unusual case in the radar/visual files. The apparently rational, intelligent behaviour of the UFO suggests a mechanical device of unknown origin as the most probable explanation of this sighting.

Now alerted to the case, British UFO researchers entered the fray. In 1978 Squadron Leader Freddie Wimbledon came forward to say that he scrambled the fighter jets and believed that visual contact with an object had been established. This UFO had been in front of the jet before vanishing and instantly reappearing behind. One RAF pilot had given the call sign 'Judy' to confirm radar lock-on with the target.

In January 1996 British UFO researcher Jenny Randles searched newly released government UFO files for a BBC documentary. Although the log books from their flights remained secured, Randles traced and interviewed the navigators from both Venom fighters. One did have a radar lock on a target but there was no visual contact. As Wimbledon reported, they kept trying to close on the object, which was almost stationary at 1,200 metres (4,000 feet), but every time they approached it, it reappeared behind them. This was put down to the effect of rapidly passing a slow-moving object, and not taken as evidence for intelligent behaviour. They were surprised that their sighting was considered a major UFO case – they felt that the most likely explanation was that it was a stray weather balloon. However, they did recall that radar controllers on the ground claimed to have seen targets moving at vast speeds, and in an extraordinary fashion, earlier in the night.

Beringer, Dr Johann *see* LYING STONES

Bermuda Triangle
An area in the Atlantic where ships and aircraft are alleged to have disappeared.

In the 20th century a belief arose that the roughly triangular area of the Atlantic bounded by Bermuda, Florida and Puerto Rico was a region in which ships and aircraft mysteriously vanished. Central to this legend was the unexplained disappearance of Flight 19 in this area on 5 December 1945. Later known as the 'Lost Patrol', Flight 19 consisted of five US Navy bombers and their 14 crew who set off on a training flight from the airbase at Fort Lauderdale but failed to return. The name Bermuda Triangle was first applied to the area in an article in *Argosy*, a magazine specializing in fiction, in a 1964 article by Vincent Gaddis ('The Deadly Bermuda Triangle'). However, it was not until the publication in 1974 of *The Bermuda Triangle* by Charles Berlitz (1914–2003) that the term became very widely known. In his book, Berlitz recounted not only the Flight 19 case but many other strange disappearances of ships and aircraft.

In 1975 a sceptical reply to Berlitz was published by Lawrence Kusche, *The Bermuda Triangle Mystery: Solved*, in which the author claimed that many of the cases cited by Berlitz were inaccurately reported. Some described incidents that had taken place in areas other than the Bermuda Triangle; some turned out to have explanations and outcomes that Berlitz chose to ignore; some 'incidents' had simply not happened at all. However, the idea was too deeply rooted in the popular imagination to be so easily discounted and various explanations were suggested, including ALIEN

ABDUCTION, freak waves and giant bubbles of methane gas rising from the ocean floor to sink ships and disable aircraft instruments. Several Hollywood movies were made, notably *The Bermuda Triangle* (1979), either recounting the story of the missing aviators or simply using the Triangle as a handy plot device.

The Flight 19 case is not considered a mystery by the US Navy, which cites radio messages from the flight commander reporting that his compasses were malfunctioning and that he was, in fact, lost. The Navy believes that the aircraft ran out of fuel and were forced to ditch in the open ocean at a location that it was impossible to pinpoint. Believers in the mystery point to the fact that an aircraft sent to search for the missing flight was also lost, but the official explanation blames an exploding fuel tank for the plane's loss. The failure of the aircraft compasses might also possibly be due to this being an area of natural MAGNETIC ANOMALIES, where compasses point to true north rather than magnetic north. Unless a pilot was aware of this and could compensate for it, extreme navigational errors would inevitably result.

However, while the Bermuda Triangle is an area of the Atlantic that is subject to heavy nautical and aerial traffic, the US Coast Guard maintains that the rate of accidents within it is no higher than in any other comparably busy region. Similarly, the nautical insurance specialists Lloyd's of London do not consider the area to be so hazardous as to warrant special consideration.

Bernadette of Lourdes, St (1844–79)
French nun and visionary.

Marie Bernarde Soubirous was the daughter of a miller and was born in LOURDES in the Department of Hautes Pyrénées, France. When she was 14 she claimed to have received a series of 18 VISIONS of the Virgin Mary at the Massabielle Rock, although no one else saw or heard what she witnessed. In 1866 she became a nun, joining the Sisters of Charity, and she spent the rest of her life in retirement at their convent in Nevers.

After her death (from asthma or tuberculosis), the grotto where her visions took place became the most visited place of pilgrimage in the Christian faith, and thousands of people suffering from various illnesses claim to have been miraculously cured by visiting the site or using the water from its nearby spring.

In 1909, as part of the beatification process, her coffin was opened and her body was found to be incorrupt. The body was exhumed again in 1919 and 1925, on each occasion being observed to be intact, and it remains on view in a glass coffin in a shrine at Nevers.

She was beatified in 1925 and canonized in 1933. See also MARIAN APPARITIONS; INCORRUPTIBILITY.

bibliomancy

Divination by opening a book at random and interpreting the passage which is revealed.

Bibliomancy, from the Greek words *biblion*, a book, and *manteia*, divination, is a form of divination in which a passage that is selected at random from a book is interpreted as being the answer to the seeker's question. The book used is frequently a sacred text, with the Bible being most commonly used among Christians, and the Koran in Muslim cultures, while in medieval Europe Virgil's *Aeneid* was a popular choice, and was known when used in this capacity as the *Sortes Virgilianae*.

The usual method involves balancing the book on its spine, and, with the eyes closed, letting it fall open at random. Then, with the eyes still closed, a finger is placed on the open page, and the passage or line thus indicated is read and its significance for the question being asked is determined. Sometimes, the book itself may also be selected at random from a library, and if a book should fall down from a shelf on its own, this is taken as a sign that it has been 'selected' for the purpose. Since a well-used book may tend to fall open more readily at the owner's favourite passages than elsewhere, some practitioners use another means of randomizing the page selection, such as DICE.

bigfin

An enigmatic squid larva that may explain the identity of a bizarre adult deep-sea squid that has been filmed but never captured for examination.

In 1991, three very strange larvae of a previously unknown species of squid were formally described by science, and informally dubbed 'bigfin', on account of their highly distinctive, noticeably large terminal fins. Ten years later, a report was published in the journal *Science* containing video stills of an amazing form of adult deep-sea squid that in recent years has been observed and videoed by submersibles in eight different locations around the globe, but which is dramatically different in appearance from any other type of adult squid on record. In particular, all ten of its arms are identical, whereas in all previously known squids two of the ten arms are much longer than the others. The mystery squid also holds its arms outwards in a strange, bent manner, making them appear to have elbows. Equally eye-catching is the pair of enormous wing-like terminal fins on its body, which flap vigorously when it swims rapidly. These fins have led scientists to speculate that the larva of this still-uncaptured adult squid type is none other than the bigfin, but until a specimen is finally procured and studied this possibility remains untested.

bigfoot

A very large, bipedal man-beast, which is North America's most famous cryptid.

Today, the bigfoot or sasquatch is the most famous North American CRYPTID, yet until as recently as 1967, this MAN-BEAST had attracted minimal attention outside that continent. It came to prominence through the claims of ranchers Roger Patterson and Bob Gimlin. According to their reports, they were riding through Bluff Creek, California, on 20 October 1967, to look for a bigfoot that had allegedly been seen in the area, when Patterson saw a very large ape-like creature squatting by the river. He said that as he rode towards it the creature stood upright on its hind legs. He described it as covered in dark fur, with a conical head, and apparently female as it had breasts. Patterson said that the sight of the creature caused his horse to shy, and he was thrown to the ground. Nevertheless, holding the cine camera that he had brought with him, Patterson says he stumbled after the creature, filming it as it strode away on its hind legs across the clearing towards some trees. Momentarily, however, it paused and looked round at him before disappearing into the forest.

Other snippets of film and numerous still photographs purportedly depicting bigfoots have subsequently been publicized, but Patterson's film remains the most famous – and controversial – piece of evidence. Numerous experts have analysed it, but remain divided as to whether it depicts a genuine bigfoot. Those in favour have included the late Professor GROVER KRANTZ (the leading scientific believer in the reality of the bigfoot), veteran bigfoot investigator John Green and Russian anthropologist Dr Dmitri Bayanov. They consider the manner in which the filmed creature (nicknamed Patty, after Patterson) walked was fundamentally unlike the gait of a human, and that its muscle movements could not be successfully mimicked by a human. They estimated its height to have been around 2 metres (6.5 feet), and reasoned that it was far heavier than a human from the depth of the footprints it left behind. The opposing school of thought, championed by, among others, the late Mark Chorvinsky, an expert in special effects as well as a long-standing cryptozoological investigator, remains convinced that Patty was a man in a skilfully designed ape-man suit. Moreover, veteran Hollywood 'monster-maker' John Chambers was frequently named as a likely candidate to have produced such a suit, though he always strenuously denied this charge. Intriguingly, when John Green contacted the special effects department at Walt Disney Studios in 1969, they stated that they could not have created such an authentic-looking man-beast at that time.

Although it took the Patterson–Gimlin film to

The most convincing evidence for the existence of bigfoot, or an elaborate hoax? A frame from the cine film taken by Roger Patterson at Bluff Creek, California, in 1967. (© TopFoto/Fortean)

introduce the bigfoot to the world at large, reports and sightings of such creatures had long been documented within North America. The bigfoot has allegedly been seen throughout mainland Canada (where it is most commonly referred to as the sasquatch), and every mainland state of the USA, but most frequently in the continent's Pacific North-West region. As with other commonly reported cryptids, eyewitness descriptions of the bigfoot vary greatly. However, the 'classic' bigfoot stands 1.8–3 metres (around 6–10 feet) tall, is almost invariably bipedal, is ape-like in overall appearance, has no tail, is covered in shaggy black or auburn-brown hair – and like certain other man-beasts on record from around the world, it is often claimed to emit a foul stench. The bigfoot's head is said to be conical, and its face is ape-like, with a sloping brow, prominent eyebrow ridges, light-reflecting eyes, a broad flattened nose and a slit-like lipless mouth. Its neck is short and thick, its shoulders are huge, its chest is muscular and powerful, and its arms are very long, with paw-like hands that have hairless palms and thick fingers. Its legs are muscular and sturdy, and its feet are very large, leaving footprints that are 30–55 centimetres (1–1.8 feet) long and that reveal two pads beneath the first toe on each foot. Many

sceptics dismiss all bigfoot tracks as fake, and there have certainly been a number of crude attempts to produce hoax tracks. However, there are also some bigfoot tracks on record which are so detailed that the presence of dermatoglyphs (fingerprints) can be discerned, which Krantz claimed would be impossible to hoax convincingly.

A particularly enigmatic piece of bigfoot evidence is the Skookum cast. In September 1999, a team of investigators from the Bigfoot Field Researchers Organization travelled to Skookum Meadow in south-western Washington, where bigfoot reports had previously emerged. They set food baits of fruit in mud wallows, daubed trees with gorilla scent, and played the cry of an alleged bigfoot (which was apparently answered, but the caller was not spied). On 22 September, they discovered that some of the food had gone, but although no footprints had been left behind, they did discover that in one of the mud wallows there appeared to be a deep impression left behind by some animal having rested there. After photographing it, the team made what is now referred to as the 'Skookum cast' of the impression, which shows the outline of a large humanoid creature's left arm, hip, thigh, testicles, buttocks, ankles and heels. As with the Patterson–Gimlin film, opinions as to the impression's authenticity are deeply split, though anthropologists such as Dr Jeffrey Meldrum and Professor Krantz were particularly impressed with the details of heel, sole and dermatoglyph presence that were visible.

Other physical evidence obtained in recent years includes hair samples that, when analysed via detailed trichological and DNA studies, have proven to be of primate origin yet recognizably different from the hair of any known primate species; and recordings of alleged bigfoot cries whose acoustics, though primate-like, could not have been produced by a human larynx. Faecal droppings said to be from bigfoots have occasionally been obtained too, but none has been submitted so far for detailed DNA analysis, which might well determine the zoological nature of their originator.

Assuming that the bigfoot does exist, and is not something as mundane as a bear that has been misinterpreted by witnesses, the most popular cryptozoological identity for it is a surviving species of *Gigantopithecus*. This was a giant ape that was 3 metres (around 10 feet) tall and officially died out around 100,000 years ago. It is also popularly said to be the true identity of the Tibetan dzu-teh or giant yeti (see YETI), to which the bigfoot bears a strong resemblance, according to eyewitness testimonies. However, *Gigantopithecus* fossils are known only from Asia – none has ever been obtained anywhere in the New World. Nevertheless, while this ape was known to be still alive in Asia, a land bridge across what is now the Bering Strait connected far-eastern Asia to northern North America. Many mammalian species entered North America across this land bridge, explaining why the mammalian faunas of Eurasia and North America contain so many shared species. Consequently, it is possible that *Gigantopithecus* also made the journey via this land link into the New World. An alternative identity that has been proposed is *Paranthropus* – an early species of hominid – but as this is currently known exclusively from African fossils, its existence in modern-day North America would be even more difficult to explain.

bilocation
The act of appearing in two different places simultaneously.

The ability to appear in two different places at the same time is a phenomenon that has been reported throughout history by holy men, sages and saints and is also described as occurring in cases involving GHOSTS OF THE LIVING. Examples from the Christian tradition include St Ambrose of Milan (c.339–397 AD), St Anthony of Padua (1195–1231) and ST PIO OF PIETRELCINA (1887–1968).

According to one OCCULT theory, the effect is caused by the separation of ASTRAL BODY, or etheric body, from the physical. In cases of so-called CRISIS APPARITIONS, TELEPATHY is also offered as an explanation. The phenomenon is also linked with the folkloric concept of the DOPPELGÄNGER which is sometimes said to presage the death of the individual concerned. See also DOUBLES.

Binah
In the kabbalah, the sephirah or emanation of God known as Understanding, which is assigned the number 3 and represents the powers of reasoning and analysis.

Binah is the third of the ten SEPHIROTH, or Divine emanations, in the KABBALAH. It is called Understanding, and denotes the powers of deductive and inductive reasoning and the ability to analyse and explain concepts, the second power of the conscious intellect within creation. It is assigned the number 3. It emanates from CHOKMAH, with which it has a polarized relationship, and is seen as taking the raw force of Chokmah and channelling it into various forms of creation; it represents the powers of archetypal femaleness. On the kabbalistic TREE OF LIFE, it is positioned directly opposite Chokmah and below and to the left of KETHER, and completes the highest triangle formed by the sephiroth, the Supernal Triangle, which it makes up with Kether and Chokmah. It is also the highest sphere on the left-hand axis, the Pillar of Severity. It is usually given four paths on the Tree of Life, to Kether, Chokmah, TIPHARETH and GEBURAH, which it is directly above. It is associated with the Divine name *Jehovah Elohim*, the archangel Tzaphkiel, the angelic order of the Aralim, and the planetary force of Saturn. In the TAROT, Binah corresponds to the four threes, and in the tarot Tree of Life spread, the card in the Binah position usually represents a person's restrictions, and leads to a consideration of how they can overcome these. In some kabbalistic systems it is attributed with the magical image of a mature woman, and is represented by the symbols of the Yoni and a cup or chalice. It is often connected with the Anja or 'third eye' CHAKRA. The word Binah in kabbalistic GEMATRIA gives the number 67, which, when united with the number of its polar opposite, Chokmah, gives 140, the sum of all the squares of the numbers from 1 to 7. Binah is sometimes also referred to as The Supernal Mother, Ama the Dark Sterile Mother, Aima the Bright Fertile Mother and Marah the Great Sea.

bioenergetics
A physical and psychological therapy which is based on the principle that the body and mind function in an identical way, and what happens in one is reflected in the other. Repressed emotions and traumas are thought to cause chronic muscular tension and blockages in the flow of energy through the body, and various techniques are therefore used to release the unresolved emotional blocks which the body expresses as physical tension.

Bioenergetics, also known as bioenergetic analysis, is a body-oriented form of psychotherapy developed and refined from REICHIAN THERAPY by Reich's pupil, Dr Alexander Lowen. It is based on the theory that the mind and body are functionally identical; what happens in the mind is reflected in the body, and vice versa. The body's cells are believed to record emotional reactions, and a repressed trauma or emotional conflict in the mind is expressed by the body as chronic muscular tension, which can lead to blockages in the body's life energy, known as bioenergy. A range of techniques is therefore used to help the individual to become aware of these tensions in the body and to release them, thereby removing the unresolved emotional blocks. Direct bodywork, such as movement, breathwork and various forms of massage are used to address the physical aspects of the patient's condition, while psychotherapy explores their emotional conflicts and the impact of these on the individual's history. Emotional release exercises such as beating a pile of mattresses with a tennis racket or the fists, or lying on the back kicking and screaming, are also sometimes employed. By a combination of physical and psychological techniques, it is believed that the person works to resolve their emotional issues, using the body to heal the mind and vice versa.

The term 'bioenergetics' is also sometimes used in a more general sense to refer collectively to a number of Western BODYWORK techniques which are based on the principle that a vital force circulates through and surrounds the body, and that the free and balanced flow of this energy is necessary for the wellbeing of the mind, body and spirit.

biofeedback

A technique for learning to control autonomic body functions, usually in response to monitoring by electronic instruments such as an electrocardiograph.
At a very basic level, something as simple as weighing oneself and deciding on the basis of the reading to take more exercise to reduce one's weight could be described as biofeedback. However, the word is generally used to describe methods of controlling what are generally automatic processes such as the heartbeat, blood pressure and muscle tension.

The study of biofeedback as a scientific discipline dates back to the 1960s. Dr Neal Miller at Yale University discovered that, through the use of electric shocks to the pleasure centres of their brains, rats could be trained to regulate a number of bodily functions, including their heart rate, the control of which was previously regarded as being carried out wholly by the autonomic nervous system.

In training someone to use some forms of biofeedback, their physiological processes are monitored, for example, their brain waves are monitored by an electroencephalograph, and their heart functions by an electrocardiograph. The subject is then taught relaxation and breathing techniques. They can then see what the relaxation does to their physiological processes by, for example, watching a graph of their heart rate, and from this learn how to control these processes.

Other forms of biofeedback, such as that successfully used with patients who wish to control their incontinence, will involve visualization and physical exercises, with regular biofeedback from physical examinations. Although biofeedback has been shown to teach patients to use relaxation and thought to control certain bodily processes, its use remains controversial.

It is also claimed that biofeedback can be employed as a method for rapidly attaining a highly relaxed state to enter into an ALTERED STATE OF CONSCIOUSNESS. Some mystics, particularly in India, appear to be able to use an internal system of biofeedback to regulate their breathing and heart rate to allow them to undergo feats of endurance, such as being buried alive for long periods.

bio-PK

The production of effects in living plants or animals through the use of psychic abilities.
Bio-PK (short for bio-PSYCHOKINESIS) describes the hypothetical ability or process that is at work in examples of DIRECT MENTAL INTERACTION WITH LIVING SYSTEMS. Its exponents include URI GELLER, who has claimed to be able to make seeds sprout using only the power of his mind – in demonstrations he empties a packet of seeds into his hand and, after concentrating on the seeds, he opens his hand to reveal that some of the seeds have sprouted. PSYCHIC HEALING is another example of the alleged use of bio-PK.

black, men in *see* MEN IN BLACK

black aircraft

Secret aeroplanes incorporating new technology. They are often associated with UFOs and some believe alien technology is involved in their creation.
New military aircraft have always been protected by a degree of secrecy to prevent enemies from gaining useful information. However, in modern times aircraft have been developed whose very existence has not been admitted, in particular at the secret US facility at Groom Lake in Nevada known as AREA 51. Since the 1950s this base has been used for testing top-secret aircraft with extraordinary capabilities, including the U-2 spy plane, the SR-71 Blackbird and the F-117 stealth fighter.

In many instances black aircraft have been reported as UFOS – the CIA estimated that up to half of the UFO sightings reported in the USA in the 1960s were caused by classified aircraft. The U-2 spy plane which flew at extreme altitude was initially silver, and its dazzling appearance in sunlight may have looked like a ball or disc of light to observers below. The Blackbird was the fastest aircraft ever built, and before it was declassified there was no earthly explanation for mysterious craft which appeared on radar screens moving at Mach 3. The stealth fighter caused similar confusion, as it can retract communications gear and disappear from radar at will.

In 1992, *Aviation Week* magazine published a report suggesting that the B-2 stealth bomber incorporated an ANTIGRAVITY drive. According to one version of this story, the B-2 is a spacecraft capable of operating outside the earth's atmosphere. The alleged disclosure was apparently made because some scientists involved in the project felt that the US government should not keep the technology secret but should share it with the world.

The 'black' budget is now estimated at some $30

billion a year, enough to buy dozens of exotic aircraft. No new operational black aircraft have been revealed since the B-2 in 1988, leading to much speculation as to what has been developed in the last decades. Some have suggested that small triangular UFOs seen in Belgium in 1989 and pursued by Belgian jets were US black aircraft, testing their ability to penetrate air defences (see BELGIAN WAVE). Another wave of UFO sightings in Iran in 2005 may well have been caused by unmanned US aircraft.

Black aircraft using plasma aerodynamics, a technique to reduce drag and decrease the radar signature of aircraft, may also be responsible for sightings of glowing UFOs at night. There are no 'white world' aircraft using this technology but there has been considerable research by the military.

Many rumours surrounding black aircraft claim that they are the result of 'reverse engineering' crashed ALIEN spacecraft, and this is why exotic technology such as antigravity drives are kept secret.

Since the 1990s there have been many sightings, particularly in the USA, of large silent UFOs known as black triangles. These are widely thought to be a new type of black aircraft, but debate continues as to whether they are powered by antigravity devices or are simply highly technological airships.

black arts

The use of magic with the intention of harming or destroying others, or for personal gain.

Among occultists, MAGIC is not generally considered to be in itself either good or evil, but a force which may be employed for positive or negative ends according to the intent of the magician. Some believe that a magician may summon DEMONS and still remain a 'white' magician as long as their purpose for doing so is benevolent; in occult lore, white magic (see MAGIC, WHITE) is concerned with expanding consciousness and contributing to the common good, while the sum of all knowledge about spells, magic and rituals which are used with the deliberate intent of harming, terrorizing, or controlling others, or of selfishly gaining power for its own sake, is referred to as the black arts. The image of the black arts practitioner as a magician who has sold his soul to or made an unholy pact with the DEVIL or other forces of evil is largely a creation of popular culture, but the concept of dark magic has been with us since ancient times.

The word 'necromancy' is often used synonymously with black magic, but strictly speaking, NECROMANCY is only one of the forms of magic commonly associated with the black arts, and is defined as divination by calling up and questioning the spirits of the dead (from the Greek *necros*, dead and *manteia*, divination). The term 'black art' is, in fact, thought by some to have originated from a confusion of this word's etymology with the Latin word *niger*, black, as is suggested by the alternative and archaic form *nigromancy*. Another black art, Goetic magic, is said to involve the evocation and binding of demons or evil spirits to the service of the magician.

There are many references to necromancy in the Bible. The Book of Deuteronomy explicitly warns the Israelites against the Canaanite practice of divination from the dead, and in the Book of Samuel, King Saul asks the Witch of Endor to invoke the spirit of the dead prophet Samuel. Muslims believe in magic, but forbid the practice of *Siher*, which translates as 'sorcery' or 'black magic'. A passage in the *Qu'ran* tells of how two ANGELS taught sorcery to mankind in order to test their obedience in refraining from using this forbidden knowledge:

> And they learn that which harmeth them and profiteth them not. And surely they do know that he who trafficketh therein will have no (happy) portion in the Hereafter; and surely evil is the price for which they sell their souls, if they but knew.

Hinduism, unlike most other religions, has sacred texts which pertain to both white and black magic. The *Atharva Veda* describes mantras which can be used either for good or for bad purposes, offering, for example, both charms against various illnesses, and curses to deprive an enemy of his strength.

The most famous symbol of magic is the PENTAGRAM, or five-pointed star, within a circle. The five points are taken to represent the four elements of earth, air, fire and water, and that which ties them together, spirit. When shown with one point at the top and two at the bottom, the pentagram symbolizes spirit balancing the other elements, and thus, cosmic and spiritual order. Inverted so that it has two points at the top and a single point at the bottom, it represents chaos, and the overthrow and perversion of the natural order, and is associated with black magic (see MAGIC, BLACK). Black magic, as an art, is said by some to derive its power from the channelling of chaotic force, while white magic seeks equilibrium and balance. See also OCCULT.

black book

A book containing a collection of spells, rites or other knowledge specifically relating to black magic or Satanism.

A number of books of magical knowledge, known as GRIMOIRES, were written between the late medieval period and the 18th century. These contained information such as astrological correspondences, lists of angels and demons, and directions on casting spells and summoning spirits. The word grimoire is nowadays used in a general sense to denote any book containing a personal collection of spells and other magical information, but a grimoire of knowledge relating specifically to black magic is often known as a 'black book'. A number of historical and contemporary magic texts are referred to by this title, and they are also commonly featured in popular culture, the most famous of fictional black books being THE NECRONOMICON. This book of black magic was a recurring theme in the Cthulhu Mythos created by the US horror writer H P LOVECRAFT, and although Lovecraft insisted the book was purely an invention on his part, it inspired a number of texts claiming to be the 'real' *Necronomicon*, reputed to be the blackest of all 'black books'.

In the modern Satanic tradition, each Master or Mistress responsible for a Satanic temple or group is appointed as custodian of the temple's or group's copy of the Black Book of Satan, which contains the basic Satanic rituals and instructions on ceremonial magic (see MAGIC, CEREMONIAL) in general. See also SATANISM.

The Black Dog of Bungay *see panel p72*

Black Dogs

Large black spectral dogs said to haunt places such as crossroads and churchyards; legends of black dogs are common all over the British Isles, with each area calling the apparition by a different name.

Many places in the British Isles have traditions of spectral Black Dogs, known by a variety of local names. In East Anglia, the Black Dog is known as Black Shuck or Old Shuck; in Lancashire, there are tales of the Bogey Beast, also known as Trash or Skriker; in Yorkshire it is called the Barghest or Padfoot; in Somerset, the Gurt (Great) Dog; in Ireland, the Pooka; on the Isle of Man, the Mauthe Dog; in Wales, the Gwyllgi ('dogs of the dusk'); and in Cumbria, the Cappel or Cappelthwaite. Black Dogs have a number of characteristics that set them apart from the phantoms of domestic dogs (see GHOST DOGS) and from normal domestic animals. These include their great size (they are frequently described as being as big as a calf), and their eyes, which are large and luminous, often described as blazing red saucers.

The Black Dog is often described as walking through solid objects, and its appearance is frequently said to be accompanied by lightning, or a fire or explosion; it may vanish or fade gradually from view, or disappear with a bang or flash, if the person who sees it lets their gaze wander, or tries to touch it. It is usually seen at night. It leaves no tracks, and makes no sound as it walks. Occasionally it is described as having the head or limbs of another animal or a human being, or to be headless, and although it is generally reported to be black and shaggy, there have been a few reported sightings in which it is white or (particularly in Scotland) green. In some stories Black Dogs have supposedly left physical traces in the form of burns or scratches on places or people, most famously at the churches of Blythburgh and Bungay in Suffolk during a thunderstorm in August 1577 (see BLACK DOG OF BUNGAY).

The appearance of a Black Dog is often interpreted as an omen of impending death or disaster for the person witnessing it – although in some areas, such as Essex, they traditionally have a protective function. Stories of such creatures have been told in one form or another for centuries, both in ballad and pamphlet form and in oral tradition. While in some legends the Black Dog is a manifestation of the DEVIL (leading to another popular name for the phenomenon, 'Devil Dog') or the transmogrified spirit of a wicked human being, the majority of Black Dog apparitions have no such accompanying legend to 'explain' their appearance. It is possible that the name of Shuck by which the Black Dog is generally known in East Anglia is derived from *scucca*, the Anglo-Saxon world for demon.

Legends of a ghostly black dog at Cromer in Norfolk are said to have provided the inspiration for SIR ARTHUR CONAN DOYLE's *The Hound of the Baskervilles* – although Dartmoor in Devon, the setting for the story, also has its own rich tradition of demonic dog folklore.

Perhaps surprisingly, there is a considerable amount of 20th-century testimony for the appearance of Black Dogs at different locations, although these more recent appearances have been somewhat less dramatic then those in earlier stories. Country roads, churchyards, ancient monuments and parish and county boundaries have historically been the favourite haunts of Black Dogs, with their appearance being celebrated in some local place names (eg Black Dog Lane, Uplyme on the Devon/Dorset border; Dogland and Shuckmoor in Coventry, Warwickshire). Black Dogs are rarely reported inside or close to buildings and a study conducted in the 1970s by a Lowestoft-based researcher called Ivan Bunn suggested that Black Dogs have an affinity for bodies of water such as rivers, streams and the sea. It has been suggested that Black Dogs are gradually being superseded by sightings of ALIEN BIG CATS.

The Black Dog of Bungay

On 4 August 1577 the townsfolk of Bungay in Suffolk reportedly witnessed a terrifying attack by a spectral BLACK DOG. The story has since become one of the best-known black dog incidents, achieving the status of a local legend.

According to a pamphlet apparently written soon after the event by Abraham Fleming, the attack occurred some time after 9am. While the parishioners cowered in the church praying for salvation, a violent thunderstorm raged outside. Suddenly, a fearsome-looking black dog burst into the church, lit by flashes of fire. It ran among the congregation, causing fear and panic, and as it passed between two people kneeling at prayer, it:

> ... wrung the necks of them bothe at one instant clene backward, in so much that even at a moment where they kneeled, they strangely died ...

And a third man whom it touched was so severely burned that:

> ... therewith all he was presently drawn togither and shrunk up, as it were a peece of lether scorched in a hot fire; or as the mouth of a purse or bag, drawen togither with string. The man albeit hee was in so strange a taking, dyed not, but as it is thought is yet alive: whiche thing is mervelous in the eyes of men, and offereth much matter of amasing the minde ...

Fleming says that the church tower was struck by lightning and the church clock was broken, although no physical traces of such damage remain. Also, a further attack is said to have occurred later the same day at the church in Blythburgh, just a few miles away. This time two men and a boy were killed and a number of others blasted by the hound. Again, the church tower was struck by lightning (collapsing through the roof). Scorch marks were reputedly left on the church door which can still be seen to this day.

There is no official record of the Bungay attack by a black dog. However, the storm appears in the parish records (and in other accounts of the period) and the churchwarden's account book mentions that two people were killed. The fact that both of these attacks were said to have taken place amid severe thunderstorms has led to the suggestion that a manifestation of BALL LIGHTNING is at the root of the tale – a theory supported by the fact that one person was burned and scorch marks were left on the second church's door. The remainder of the story could be put down to the overactive imagination of a superstitious congregation.

It may also be relevant that Abraham Fleming is known to have been a Puritan propagandist. He is believed to have lived in London and may never have even visited Bungay. Fleming (or his source) may simply have been exploiting the story of the damage caused by the storm, along with a long-standing local belief in a spectral black dog known as Black Shuck, to produce a terrifying image to reinforce the message of repentance. Indeed, in some versions of the legend it is stated that the visit was from the DEVIL himself.

The story of the Black Dog of Bungay is now regarded with some affection in the town, and a black dog appears on its coat of arms. The legend is also kept alive in names such as the Black Dog Marathon and the Black Dog Running Club, and by the local football team, who are known as the Black Dogs.

The title page of Abraham Fleming's pamphlet on the Black Dog of Bungay, the 'horrible shaped thing' that reportedly terrorized the congregations of two Suffolk churches in 1577. (© TopFoto/Fortean)

Black Elk (1863–1950)

Famous Oglala Sioux medicine man.

Black Elk (Ekhaka Sapa in his native Lakota tongue) was born into the Oglala sub-tribe of the Lakota Sioux and was a cousin of Crazy Horse. In his book *Black Elk Speaks: Being the Life Story of a Holy Man of the Oglala Sioux* (written with John G Neihardt and published in 1932), he relates that during his childhood he heard the voices of the Grandfathers (the spiritual powers of the World) and experienced many visions. Foremost among these was his 'great vision', when he claims the Grandfathers warned him that times of great trouble were ahead and in which the Sioux nation was symbolized by a sacred hoop that lay broken. He was told that he had been given the sacred hoop and the sacred stick of his people, and that he should plant the stick within the hoop to make it grow into a flowering tree. The vision culminated with an image of the whole world:

> Then I was standing on the highest mountain of them all, and round about beneath me was the whole hoop of the world. And while I stood there I saw more than I can tell and I understood more than I saw; for I was seeing in a sacred manner the shapes of all things in the spirit, and the shape of all shapes as they must live together like one being. And I saw that the sacred hoop of my people was one of many hoops that made one circle, wide as daylight and as starlight, and in the center grew one mighty flowering tree to shelter all the children of one mother and one father. And I saw that it was holy.

Following his great vision, Black Elk became withdrawn, and continued to experience further visions, allegedly including one of the Battle of Little Big Horn the day before it occurred. He was revered among his people as a holy man and healer.

In 1886 he joined Buffalo Bill Cody's Wild West Show, believing that seeing and understanding the world of the white man would help him to carry out the task handed to him by the Grandfathers. After travelling in Europe (including giving a performance for Queen Victoria in 1887), he returned to the USA and joined the GHOST DANCE movement, which came to an end following the massacre at Wounded Knee on 29 December 1890. Black Elk was sent to live on the Pine Ridge Reservation in South Dakota. Following the death of his wife in 1903 he was baptized as a Catholic (taking the name Nicholas Black Elk), seeing no contradiction in holding both Christian and traditional Native American beliefs.

In the early 1930s, Black Elk related his story (via the interpretation of his son Benjamin Black Elk) to the writer John G Neihardt. This was published as *Black Elk Speaks* (1932). He gave a sacred pipe to Neihardt, the secrets of which he later told to Joseph Epes Brown, who published them in his book *The Sacred Pipe: Black Elk's Account of the Seven Rites of the Oglala Sioux* (1953). See also CALUMET.

black magic *see* MAGIC, BLACK

black mass

A ceremony said to be celebrated by witches and Devil-worshippers as a parody of the Catholic Mass; a similar ritual performed by various modern Satanic groups.

The belief that WITCHES and Devil-worshippers celebrated the black mass as a parody of the Roman Catholic Mass goes back to the Middle Ages. In the 14th century, the KNIGHTS TEMPLAR were accused of heresies which included holding black masses, and during the WITCH TRIALS of those times, people charged with WITCHCRAFT were accused of participating in such ceremonies. There is no reliable first-hand description of what happened during these black masses, or concrete proof that they actually took place at all, since confessions regarding them were usually extracted under torture or the threat of torture. However, according to most accounts, the main objective was the profanation of the Host. Sources disagree on the nature of this profanation; some claim that pieces of flesh or blackened slices of rotten turnip were used in place of the Host, but most believe that real consecrated bread was used.

Other practices said to be included in the black mass were the inversion of the cross, spitting or stepping on the cross, the use of black candles instead of white, ritual sacrifices of both animals and children, the use of a naked woman's body as an altar, and the substitution of blood or urine for communion wine. As part of the ceremony, witches were said to perform the *OSCULUM INFAME*, or 'kiss of shame', in which they kissed the Devil's backside in ritual greeting, and the black mass was popularly believed to culminate in a sexual orgy. The black mass was believed to be presided over by a defrocked priest dressed in black or dark red vestments embroidered with inverted crosses, a goat's head, or other OCCULT symbols. A form of the black mass called the Mass of Saint-Secaire, in which the Catholic Mass was recited backward by a renegade priest, was said to have originated in Gascony in the Middle Ages. Its purpose was to curse an enemy with a slow illness which would eventually kill him, and there are several accounts of its having been performed.

While it is doubtful that any of the people accused of witchcraft in the Middle Ages participated in black masses, the idea of these rituals continued to be linked with witches' SABBATS for centuries. It is known, however, that between the 15th and 17th centuries, black masses became popular and fashionable among the nobility, the most notorious case being that of the French baron Gilles de Rais, who was executed in 1440 after being convicted of torturing and murdering a large number of children, apparently as human sacrifices in black masses which he held to gain riches and power.

The various HELLFIRE CLUBS which were popular in the 18th century were said to perform regular black masses, although it is likely that more time was spent in drinking and debauchery than in worshipping Satan. In modern times, most neopagan witches neither worship nor believe in the Devil, and the black mass has no association with modern witchcraft. Modern Satanic groups such as the CHURCH OF SATAN conduct various forms of ritual which they refer to as black masses, but these bear no resemblance to the sensationalist idea of the black mass – with sacrificial victims, blasphemous ceremonies and PACTS with the Devil – which survives in popular horror films and fiction.

Black Monk
Archetypal form of hooded apparition.
Hooded APPARITIONS falling within the type generally described as 'Black Monk' appear in reports from locations throughout Britain. They are also a common feature of numerous folk stories and legends: a hooded figure with a skeletal face is said to haunt Beacon Hill at Woodhouse Eaves in Leicestershire; a monk in black was said to walk the route of a secret tunnel at Binham in Norfolk; and a black monk apparition known as the 'Goblin Friar' was said to act as harbinger of disaster to the Byron family at Newstead Abbey in Nottinghamshire – the poet Lord Byron referred to the spectre in his poem *Don Juan* (1819–24), and was even said to have seen it himself before his ill-fated marriage to Anne Millbanke in 1816. Many more examples could also be listed.

Originally it was considered that such apparitions were simply the GHOSTS of deceased monks, who in their lives had been attached to one of the many monastic sites that existed in England and Wales until the Reformation. This view has now been challenged by the idea that, in at least some cases, the Black Monk figure is better understood as an archetypal figure linked with particular landscapes. If so, the Black Monk may have more in common with other symbolic apparitions such as the WHITE LADY and the BLACK DOG rather than resulting from manifestations connected with deceased individuals. There are also rare examples of hooded forms connected with POLTERGEIST outbreaks, notably the so-called 'Black Monk of Pontefract' case in 1966, in which the well-witnessed disturbances were attributed to the ghost of a monk from a Cluniac monastery who was supposedly executed in the reign of Henry VIII (although this theory was rejected by Colin Wilson who reviewed the case in 1980).

Although the Black Monk is a common ghost motif in Britain, it is much rarer in other European countries, particularly in those that didn't embrace Protestantism and remained mainly Catholic. It is also known in Latin American countries but does not appear in folklore or reports of hauntings from the USA.

Black Shuck *see* BLACK DOGS

Blake, William (1757–1827)
English poet, painter, engraver, and visionary mystic.
William Blake was born in London in 1757. The son of an Irish hosier, he received little formal education, but was apprenticed at the age of 14 to the engraver James Basire. In 1779 he went to study art at the Royal Academy School, going on to illustrate and print many books of his own poems. In these 'illuminated books', the text was interwoven with imaginative designs; Blake engraved the words and pictures on copper plates, and his wife, Catherine, who assisted him in his work, coloured and bound the books. The most notable of these were *Songs of Innocence* (1789), its sequel *Songs of Experience* (1794) which included his famous poem *The Tyger*, prophetic works such as *The Book of Thel* (1789) and *The Marriage of Heaven and Hell* (1793), and *Jerusalem* (1804–1820). Perhaps his finest artistic work is to be seen in the 21 *Illustrations to the Book of Job* (1826), which is unrivalled in modern religious art for its visionary power and imaginative force. When he died, he was working on a set of illustrations for Dante's *Divina Commedia*.

Blake saw his poetry and his art as being inseparable, unified aspects of his lifelong spiritual endeavours. The Bible had a profound influence on the young Blake, and would remain a powerful source of inspiration all his life. He claimed to have experienced VISIONS from an early age, the first taking place around the age of eight, when he saw a tree filled with ANGELS. On another occasion, watching haymakers at work, he saw angelic figures walking among them, and he also said that he had seen and conversed with the angel Gabriel, and the Virgin Mary. During his apprenticeship with Basire, he was sent to copy images from Gothic churches in London, and while in Westminster Abbey, he is said to have seen a vision of a great procession of monks and priests.

Blake abhorred slavery and was a firm believer in racial and sexual equality, and many of his poems express his notion of universal humanity, and his concern with the struggle of the soul to liberate its natural energies from reason and organized religion. In *Songs of Experience*, he distinguished between the Old Testament God, whose restrictions he rejected, and the New Testament God of Jesus Christ, whom he regarded as a positive influence. A follower of Unitarian philosophy, Blake is said to have been the Chosen Chief of the Ancient Druid Order from 1799 to 1827, and he is recognized as a saint in the Ecclesiastica Gnostica Catholica, the ecclesiastical arm of the international fraternal order of the ORDO TEMPLI ORIENTIS.

During his lifetime Blake's work went largely unrecognized, and he remained close to poverty, but he was upheld by his faith in the unseen, and his belief that he was guided by visitations from the spiritual world; his life in his realm of visions caused some of his contemporaries to regard him as a harmless lunatic, and his wife once remarked, 'I have very little of Mr Blake's company. He is always in Paradise.' He influenced the Pre-Raphaelites and W B Yeats, and in the 1960s his works were acclaimed by the Underground movement. After his death in 1827 he was buried in an unmarked grave in Bunhill Fields, London, but later, a memorial was erected for him and Catherine.

Madame Blavatsky, founder of the Theosophical Society, photographed in 1889. (© Mary Evans Picture Library)

Blavatsky, Madame Helena Petrovna (1831–91)

Russian-born US writer and co-founder of the Theosophical Society.

The woman who came to be known as Madame Blavatsky was born Helena Petrovna Hahn in Yekaterinoslav, Russia (now Dnipopetrovsk, Ukraine) in 1831. As a child she was surrounded by servants who still believed in many of the superstitions of old Russia, and who encouraged her to believe she had supernatural powers. She married General Nikifor Blavatsky when she was 17, but is said to have abandoned him within a few months of their marriage. Between 1848 and 1858 she travelled widely, and claimed to have entered Tibet to study for two years with the ASCENDED MASTERS, or Mahatmas, in particular the Masters Morya and Koot Hoomi, who she said were the keepers of a mysterious ancient wisdom. In 1871, she travelled to Cairo in Egypt, where she formed the Société Spirite (with Emma Cutting) to explore occult phenomena. This society closed amid accusations of fraudulent activities, and Blavatsky emigrated to New York in 1873.

There, her apparent psychic abilities impressed a number of people, and throughout her career she continued to claim the ability to perform paranormal feats such as CLAIRVOYANCE, LEVITATION, TELEPATHY and MATERIALIZATION. She married her second husband in 1875, but left him, too, within months, and soon after her divorce in 1878 she became a naturalized US citizen. In 1875 she founded the THEOSOPHICAL SOCIETY with the lawyer, writer and journalist Henry Steel Olcott and the attorney William Quan Judge, among others. The society was a modern-day Gnostic movement which took its inspiration from Hinduism and Buddhism, and did much to spread Eastern religious, philosophical, and OCCULT concepts throughout the Western world.

Blavatsky published her first major book, *Isis Unveiled*, in 1877, and her magnum opus, *The Secret Doctrine*, in 1888. She wrote that the chief aim of THEOSOPHY was to reconcile all religions, sects and nations under a common system of ethics, based on eternal verities, and while she did not reject religions, she believed that each had both an exoteric tradition, which was unique to that religion, and also an esoteric tradition, which was common to all religions; what she claimed to be passing on was the Secret Wisdom of these shared esoteric doctrines. This ancient wisdom was an eclectic combination of

Hindu, Egyptian, Gnostic, and other scriptures and teachings, along with Neoplatonism and stories such as the ATLANTIS myth.

In 1882, the headquarters of the Theosophical Society moved to Adyar, near Madras in India. Blavatsky spent time there before returning to Europe in 1885. She died in 1891, and her body was cremated; one-third of her ashes remained in Europe, one-third was sent to the USA and one-third was scattered in the River Ganges in India. Theosophists annually commemorate her death on 8 May as White Lotus Day.

See also LEFT-HAND PATH.

bleeding images *see* IMAGES, BLEEDING

Bloxham tapes
A series of recorded interviews purporting to offer proof of the reality of reincarnation.
The Bloxham tapes were first brought to the attention of the public in a 1976 BBC television documentary entitled *The Bloxham Tapes*. This was followed, in the same year, by the inevitable tie-in book by the programme's producer, Jeffrey Iverson – *More Lives Than One? The Incredible Evidence of the Bloxham Tapes*.

Cardiff-based hypnotherapist Arnall Bloxham spent 20 years hypnotizing and regressing over 400 men and women (see HYPNOSIS and MEMORIES, RECOVERED). He claimed that recordings from these sessions offered definite proof of REINCARNATION, and some of his best cases were investigated in the television documentary and subsequent book.

Jane Evans, while visiting Bloxham for relief from rheumatism, apparently gave detailed descriptions of six former lives under hypnosis. These included a Roman housewife (Livonia), a Jew from the York Massacres of the 12th century (Rebecca), a medieval servant to a French prince (Alison), a Maid of Honour to Catherine of Aragon (Anna), a servant in the early 18th century (Ann Tasker) and a 19th-century American nun (Sister Grace). Many of the facts that Evans gave were immediately verifiable, although they were also relatively easy to ascertain from a number of history books. As Rebecca, Evans claimed to have met her death in the cellar of a church in York. For the filming of the BBC documentary, a York church was used, which may have been the one referred to by Rebecca. When the church was located it was found to have no cellar. However, six months later restoration work uncovered a cellar. Unfortunately this was only one of three possible churches uncovered by the BBC, and it was used for filming simply because it was the easiest to gain permission to shoot in. Further evidence against the claims included the

fact that the former personifications of Evans seemed to have forgotten some rather important facts, for example Alison knew nothing of her master Jacques Couer's wife or five children – although she was well aware of the layout of the house. Similar facts and gaps appeared throughout all of the accounts. In the case of Alison, many aspects of her master's life can be found in a 1948 novel – *The Money Man* by Thomas Costain in which, for reasons of dramatic artistry, the family of Couer had been written out. Couer's house is also one of the most photographed houses in France and many books have carried pictures of it.

In the case of Evans and the other participants in Bloxham's work, verifiable facts could easily have been read prior to the hypnotic regressions. How much of this apparent 'memory recall' was brought about by leading questions, or through their merely remembering previously read novels, is unclear, but no evidence was found to indicate that Bloxham or any of the participants deliberately engaged in fraud.

blue tiger of Fujian
An ethereal yet allegedly real, but still-uncaptured, strain of mutant tiger from Fujian Province, China.
In September 1910, while hunting in south-eastern China's Fukien (now Fujian) Province, US missionary Harry R Caldwell was watching a goat when one of his native helpers directed his attention towards something else, moving nearby. Caldwell claimed that at first he thought it was another native, dressed in the blue garment worn by many in that region, but when he peered more closely he realized that he was looking at the chest and belly of a very large tiger. However, this was no ordinary tiger, because its black-striped fur was not orange-brown in colour as in normal specimens, but was instead a shade of blue.

Caldwell said he decided to shoot this creature, in order to prove that it really did exist, but the tiger was watching two children gathering vegetation in a ravine nearby, and he knew that if he tried to shoot it from where he was sitting he might injure the children. He moved a little to alter the direction of his shot, but the tiger disappeared into the forest and was not seen by him again. Nevertheless, he learnt that blue tigers had been spied several times before in that area, and others have reportedly been seen since, but none has ever been shot or captured, though a few blue hairs have been collected.

Although a blue tiger may seem impossible, in reality it is quite easily explained. Such tigers would almost certainly possess two mutant gene forms that in combination are responsible for the smoky blue-mauve fur coloration (termed 'blue dilution') characterizing the Maltese breed of domestic cat (as well as a few freak specimens of blue lynx and blue bobcat obtained over the years). Indian white tigers are well known nowadays, and a black tiger was born at an Oklahoma zoo during the 1970s. So it is not inconceivable that one day a Fujian blue tiger will be captured.

Boas, Antonio Villas (1934–92)
The subject of an early alien abduction case, who claimed to have provided genetic samples for the purpose of fathering an alien baby.
In October 1957 Antonio Villas Boas was a 23-year-old farmer working a modest ranch with his family near São Francisco de Sales in Brazil. Although often described as uneducated, he was actually taking a correspondence course and subsequently qualified as a lawyer.

At a time when elsewhere the Soviet Union was set to stun the world by launching the first Sputniks into orbit, strange lights were seen over the ranch, reaching a climax on 15 October. Boas claimed that he was alone on his tractor when a luminous, egg-shaped craft appeared in the sky and landed nearby. As this happened the tractor lights and engine failed – making this the first of many ALIEN ABDUCTION cases that began with a CAR STOP.

Boas said he leapt from the tractor but, before he could escape, he was grabbed by four beings. They appeared human-like but were only just over 150 centimetres (5 feet) tall. They wore grey coveralls and all that he could see of their faces was their prominent blue eyes. The entities took the terrified young man into a brightly lit room inside the craft and extracted blood samples from his chin. They then left him alone as a gas with a suffocating smell poured from the wall, causing him to vomit.

The aliens returned, exchanging barking sounds with one another as they stripped him naked and sponged him down. Then, to his astonishment, they left again and a naked woman with long fair hair entered the room. She had white skin, large blue slanted eyes and a peculiar V shape to her head, making the chin seem prominent. Another curious feature was that her pubic and underarm hair was blood red.

The woman encouraged Boas to have intercourse, and he did not fight. At the conclusion, she pointed to the sky, rubbed her midriff and left the hapless victim in no doubt that she would have his baby when back in space.

After being allowed to dress, Boas was shown around the UFO and was then returned to his tractor. He discovered that he had been missing for more than four hours. Suffering from some ill effects, including headaches and excessive tiredness, he was directed by a local journalist to Dr Olavo Fontes, a medical doctor who was also a UFO investigator. Fontes found evidence of mild radiation sickness and was impressed by the witness. In his report on the case he wrote:

> Right from the outset it was obvious he presented no psychopathic traits. Calm, talking freely, revealing no nervous tics or signs of emotional instability, all his reactions to the questions put to him were perfectly normal.

Fontes obtained a signed declaration on 22 February 1958, although the case was not made public until 1965, by which time the BETTY AND BARNEY HILL case had occurred in the USA. The independent appearance of the Boas and Hill abduction cases, without any significant chance of collusion, is seen as one of the more powerful arguments in favour of alien abduction.

Boas died in 1992, maintaining the veracity of his story to the end.

bodhisattva
In Buddhism, a person who is worthy of nirvana but who chooses to postpone their entry into it and remain in the world in order to help other sentient beings to achieve enlightenment.
The word 'bodhisattva' comes from the Sanskrit *bodhi*, meaning 'awakening' or 'enlightenment', and *sattva*, 'a sentient being'. In Theravada Buddhism, the term is used exclusively as a title of historical Buddhas, such as Shakyamuni (Gautama Buddha), before they attained Buddhahood. However, the Buddhist movement known as the Mahayana school, which developed in the 1st century AD, taught that Buddhahood could be attained without necessarily leaving the world, and used the term 'bohdisattva' in the sense most widely known today, to refer to a person who, out of compassion, has taken a vow to attain spiritual enlightenment not for themselves, but for the sake of all sentient beings. Such a person aims to discover the source of Ultimate Truth, or NIRVANA, but having done so, chooses to postpone their own entry into nirvana and Buddhahood until all sentient beings have been rescued from the wheel of rebirth and suffering, thus guiding others to the full enlightenment of a Buddha while remaining in the world themselves.

A person on the path of the bodhisattva seeks to develop *bodhicitta*, or 'mind of enlightenment', by cultivating the virtues known as the *pāramitās*, or 'Six Perfections': generosity, morality or ethics, patience, energy or effort, concentration, and wisdom, which is seen as the sum of the other five.

Two of the most important bodhisattvas in

Mahayana Buddhism are sometimes referred to as 'celestial bodhisattvas', and are considered to be almost Buddhas in their spiritual attainments. Avalokiteshvara is known to the Tibetan Buddhists as Chenrezi, in China as Kuan Yin and in Japan as Kannon, or the Buddha of Compassion. Manjushri, who is prominent in Buddhist TANTRA, is closely associated with wisdom and learning.

The place of a bodhisattva's earthly deeds is known as *bodhimandala*, and may be a site of pilgrimages and have temples or monasteries built there. The most famous such site is the bodhi tree under which Gautama Buddha is said to have achieved enlightenment.

Bodin, Jean (c.1530–1596)

French political philosopher and professor of law who wrote a number of books on the subject of witchcraft.

Born and educated in Angers, Jean Bodin is described by some as the father of political science. He is particularly known for his theories relating to sovereignty as laid out in *Les Six Livres de la République* (1576, *The Six Bookes of a Commonweale*, 1606).

However, he also dealt with the subject of WITCHCRAFT, expounding some extreme views in his 1580 treatise *Démonomanie des sorciers* ('Demonomania of Sorcerers'). The book was adopted as a guide by many of those involved in finding and trying WITCHES, although his other books were condemned by THE INQUISITION because it was held that they demonstrated sympathy for Calvinism.

Bodin established the idea that a witch was someone who had entered into a pact with the DEVIL; he clearly described the diabolical acts that witches carried out and argued for a much stricter approach to trying them. He believed that proving involvement in witchcraft was more difficult than proving involvement in other crimes, so it was desirable to seek conviction on the basis of secret accusations (indeed, these were to be actively encouraged); the testimony of children; and confessions extracted under torture. He felt that those who failed to treat people accused of witchcraft harshly enough would be 'abandoned by God to the mercy of the witches', and much of his treatise was taken up with descriptions of the methods of torture and execution that should be applied. He personally sat as a judge in a number of witchcraft trials and offered the view that any judge who failed to convict (and execute) following an accusation should themselves be executed.

Rather than being simply a crazed and bloodthirsty call-to-arms, Bodin's theories appear to have been born out of a conviction that, through their pacts with the Devil – and the powers to cause harm that this gave them – witches were an extremely dangerous and pernicious threat to Christian society. However, although his books were by no means universally popular, they did provide respectable academic justification for barbaric acts of persecution, often carried out for highly dubious reasons. See also WITCHFINDER; WITCH TRIALS.

body-snatching *see* RESURRECTION MEN

bodywork

The collective term for a number of alternative therapies which involve manipulation of the body and/or its energy field to bring about physical and emotional wellbeing.

Bodywork is the collective term for a wide range of alternative therapies whose aim is to improve the functioning of the body and to facilitate its natural healing response, principally by balancing the vital energy which is believed to permeate and surround it. Some forms involve direct work on the body's energy flow, while others operate through physical techniques such as massage, exercise, breathing, movement and posture, but all are designed to promote relaxation and emotional wellbeing as well as physical health.

Many bodywork techniques are based on the assumption of a vital force which circulates through the body and forms an energy field around it. When this vital force becomes blocked or sluggish in its flow, it is thought to cause symptoms which can lead to illness, and a wide range of bodywork therapies are designed to manipulate the energy flow in order to correct blockages and imbalances and restore the body's natural self-healing capacity. Some, such as ACUPRESSURE, SHIATSU and REFLEXOLOGY, are based on the principles of CHINESE MEDICINE, and in these the practitioner aims to correct the flow of energy (or QI) by the application of pressure (or, in ACUPUNCTURE, the insertion of needles) at certain points where the MERIDIANS along which it flows are believed to come close to the surface of the skin. Other forms of energy-rebalancing bodywork include REIKI, a Japanese technique in which UNIVERSAL LIFE FORCE is believed to be activated and to flow into the practitioner, who sends it through their hands into the energy field of the patient. It is then set to work in healing the patient's mind, body and spirit, and is said to be so powerful that it can flow through the air and clothing, so that no physical contact is needed. In a similar method called THERAPEUTIC TOUCH or touch-free massage, the healer claims to manipulate a person's energy field by passing their hands over the person's body and feeling compassion for them.

In other types of bodywork, such as T'AI CHI, QIGONG and YOGA, slow, choreographed exercises or postures are performed while breathing slowly and deeply and visualizing the movement of qi or life force through the body. These systems are designed not only to improve flexibility, balance and physical wellbeing, but to facilitate a harmonious flow of energy and enable the individual to integrate mind and body.

The term 'bodywork' is also often used to include Western therapies such as Swedish massage, osteopathy and chiropractic, which focus on physical manipulation and structural realignment, and ALEXANDER TECHNIQUE, which is based on posture and movement awareness, and seeks to correct unhealthy movement patterns.

Claims have been made for the effectiveness of the various techniques in helping conditions ranging from labour pain and premenstrual syndrome, to back pain, high blood pressure, asthma, eating disorders and migraines.

bogeyman
A frightening being often used to scare children.
The bogeyman, also known as the boogeyman, is a monster who is often used to frighten children into obedience. Parents may tell unruly offspring that the bogeyman preys on children who misbehave, and is waiting to pounce on them unless they mend their ways. However, he is powerless in daylight hours. He is generally described as being black, but apart from this, he has no specific appearance, and thus can take on the form of a child's worst fears in order to terrify them. He may hide in a child's bedroom cupboard or under their bed, or be lurking in any scary shadow, and if you look through a keyhole, you may be quick enough to catch sight of the bogeyman's eye looking back at you.

The origins of the word are uncertain. It first appeared in the English language in the 19th century as a term for the DEVIL, although 'bogey' is probably derived from the Middle English *bugge*, which may come from the Welsh *bwg*, meaning a hobgoblin. Similar shadowy figures of terror are spoken of in many countries. In Italy, naughty children are warned of *l'uomo nero* (the black man), who is described as a tall man wearing a heavy black coat and a black hood or hat which hides his face. Spanish parents threaten their children with *El Coco*, or *El Cuco*, a shapeless figure or hairy monster which eats children who misbehave when they are told to go to bed. The Romanian equivalent of the Bogeyman is known as *bau-bau*.

boggart
A usually malicious and destructive hobgoblin of the folklore of Northern England, which frequently attaches himself to a specific household.
The boggart of Northern England is a cousin of the friendly BROWNIE, and frequently attaches himself to a household as the brownie does; however, although the boggart can occasionally be helpful, he is usually ill-tempered, mischievous and destructive, behaving in the manner of a POLTERGEIST. Some people believe that a boggart is in fact a brownie who has been soured by neglect or ill-treatment. The presence of a boggart in a house is detectable by the unusual number of small accidents and strange noises which take place after dark. He likes to eat wood, and can consume an entire house as efficiently as a host of termites. He will rearrange furniture, blow out candles, throw crockery around, rap on windows and slam doors, and it is especially fond of tormenting children by pinching them, taking their food from them, and almost smothering them as they sleep. In some areas the boggart is also called the Padfoot, and is said to enjoy frightening travellers as well as disrupting households. In his natural state he is usually described as being dark and hairy with long yellow teeth, and is said to dress in tattered garments, but he may also assume the form of a white cow or horse, or a black dog. It is said that he should never be named, because this will only increase his destructiveness and malice. Once he has attached himself to a household, there is no way to appease or escape him, and even if the family tries to shake him off by moving house, he is likely to accompany them, hiding in a crock or butter churn. His name probably comes from Middle English *bugge*, which in turn is thought to derive from the Welsh *bwg*, meaning a hobgoblin.

bogle
A mischievous hobgoblin of the folklore of the Scottish Borders, Northern England, and Lincolnshire.
The bogle is a mischievous hobgoblin native to the Scottish Borders, the North of England, and Lincolnshire, and is a close relation of the BOGGART. He is seldom seen, but is described as having a dark, unpleasant appearance, and his presence may cause a sense of dread. Bogles were greatly feared by the fenmen of East Anglia, who circled their houses at dusk carrying lights and chanting protective charms to ward them off, and smeared blood on their doorsteps to scare them away. The bogles of the Scottish Borders are said to be virtuous creatures, and in general, bogles are considered to be the least harmful of their kind, and tend to target evildoers – thieves, cheats, liars and murderers – on behalf of their victims, rather than harming the innocent. One story tells of a bogle who punished a man who had stolen candles from a poor widow neighbour. The man saw a dark figure in his garden one night and attempted to shoot it with his gun. The next night he was working in an outhouse when the same figure appeared in the doorway and

said, 'I'm neither bone nor flesh nor blood, thou canst not harm me. Give back the candles, but I must take something from thee.' The man returned the candles, but the bogle plucked out one of his eyelashes and vanished. The man's eye twitched forever after.

In common with the boggart and BOGEYMAN, the bogle's name probably comes from Middle English *bugge*, which in turn is thought to derive from the Welsh *bwg*, meaning a hobgoblin.

Böhme, Jakob (1575–1624)
German writer and mystic.
Born near Görlitz in central Germany in 1575, Jacob Böhme was the son of poor peasants and received only an elementary education. He was brought up as a Lutheran and worked as a shoemaker in Görlitz, but had mystical experiences throughout his youth, and in 1600 he claimed to have had a vision in which the spiritual structure of the universe was revealed to him, along with the relationship between good and evil. At first he kept quiet about his spiritual revelations, but in 1610 he had another vision which prompted him to write an unfinished treatise, *Aurora*, in 1612. The manuscript of this treatise was circulated until it came to the attention of Gregorius Richter, the chief pastor of Görlitz, who declared it heretical and threatened Böhme with exile if he continued to propagate such writings. Banned from 1618 onward from circulating his works, Böhme returned to his profession of shoemaking for several years, but was persuaded by his friends and patrons to begin writing again. He produced a large body of work, handwritten copies of which were circulated in secret, and developed a following throughout Europe. When his first printed book, *The Way to Christ*, was published in 1623, it created a scandal which resulted in his exile to Dresden in the last year of his life. It was not until 1730 that his full writings were printed, including his major works *De Signatura Rerum* ('On the Signification of Things') and *Misterium Magnum* ('The Great Mystery').

Böhme was persecuted because of the Gnostic elements in his writings, which were influenced by Neoplatonist and alchemical thinkers such as JOHANNES ECKHART and PARACELSUS. He believed that everything exists and is intelligible only through its opposite. Thus, he claimed that evil was a necessary element of goodness, and that without evil, the will would become inert, making spiritual progress impossible. He considered that both good and evil emanated from God; the existence of both kept the cosmos in balance, but good tended to orientate it toward God. Lucifer, too, combined the qualities of both good and evil, but had freely chosen darkness over light, thus unbalancing the world. The chief subject of Böhme's writing was the nature of sin, evil and redemption, and he described the

Fall as having been a necessary stage in the evolution of the universe; Man had to freely choose to fall from grace so that creation could evolve to a new state of redemption which would be more perfect than its original state of innocence, and allow God to interact with a creation which was at once part of, and distinct from, his own self. In this way, he could achieve a new self-awareness.

Böhme's suggestion that God would have been incomplete without the Creation, and his emphasis on the importance of faith and self-awareness rather than on dogma and scripture, were incompatible with Lutheran teachings, and although his seminal writings were often paradoxical and even confused, they greatly influenced many later anti-authoritarian mystical movements, such as the Religious Society of Friends, the Philadelphians and the THEOSOPHICAL SOCIETY, as well as the work of writers like Goethe and major figures in philosophy, particularly the German Romantics G W F Hegel and Friedrich Schelling. The psychologist CARL JUNG also makes a number of references to Böhme in his works.

Boleskine House *see* CROWLEY, ALEISTER

Bonnybridge
A Scottish town which attracted media attention in 1992 following a series of UFO sightings. It has been referred to as the 'world's most UFO-haunted location'.
Bonnybridge is a small town near Falkirk, at the heart of what became known as a WINDOW AREA. Considerably more UFO sightings per head of population have been reported from this region than would be expected.

The only major case to have occurred in the area before 1992 was the LIVINGSTON INCIDENT, involving a UFO landing and the physical assault of a forester. This episode created headlines in 1979, and later inspired the local council to erect a plaque where the incident took place, creating a small tourist attraction and ensuring a footnote in UFO folklore. The council in Bonnybridge also adopted a positive approach to the many reported sightings. This undoubtedly helped to ensure that locals were more willing to make their accounts public.

The wave began in November 1992 when a Bonnybridge council member, Billy Buchanan, received a late-night call from a local businessman, who was distressed after seeing a strange object in the sky. He hoped that, as his representative, Buchanan might be able to get to the bottom of the events. Buchanan used the media to ask for further witnesses, and dozens of statements came from locals describing sightings over the past few months or years.

Earlier that autumn, there had been some debate

Councillor Billy Buchanan, who campaigned for Bonnybridge to be twinned with the town of Roswell, New Mexico, following its own wave of UFO sightings in 1992. (© McPherson, Colin/Corbis Sygma)

in the Scottish media as to whether the country was a prime location for UFO sightings. This, together with the arrival of official support in the form of a local councillor, encouraged witnesses to step forward. Buchanan called town meetings, wrote to Westminster asking for a government investigation and assisted local UFO groups to set up telephone hotlines to collect new reports of sightings. As the story gathered momentum Bonnybridge became famous. Within a year, some 800 sightings had been documented from the towns and villages in the area.

The local media were not slow to capitalize on the celebrity. Stories about potential overseas investment, talk of plans to set up a UFO theme park, and calls to twin Bonnybridge with the New Mexico town of ROSWELL all appeared.

Among the interesting cases to emerge was an alleged CLOSE ENCOUNTER late one night in August 1992. Two young men in a car near the Harperrig Reservoir in the Pentland Hills said that they rounded a bend to find a domed object in front of them. In a UFO report form the driver wrote:

> When I saw the object I got such a fright that
> I pushed down hard on the accelerator ... (we)

drove underneath the object (and) can't remember anything else.

The car drove straight through a curtain of black mist suspended beneath the object, and the two occupants suffered a loss of awareness and a sense of temporal and spatial distortion (see OZ FACTOR). When they recovered, the UFO had gone and the car was intact and still on the road.

Most UFO investigators agree that the Bonnybridge area has generated some intriguing reports of sightings. However, the unusually high percentage of recorded UFO incidents may have much to do with the manner in which making such reports became socially acceptable after 1992.

Book of Changes *see I CHING*

Book of the Dead
One of several collections of texts in various cultures which are intended to prepare and guide the recently deceased in their passage through the afterlife; the best known of these are the Egyptian Book of the Dead and the Tibetan Book of the Dead.

The concept that the dead require specific incantations, spells and rituals to prepare and guide them through the AFTERLIFE has been shared by a number of belief systems throughout the centuries, and collections of texts detailing these rituals and spells are known to have existed in Aztec and Mayan cultures, and in early Christianity. But the best-known bodies of such material, generally known as 'Books of the Dead', are the two which set out the Egyptian and Tibetan rituals for those who have recently died.

The ancient Egyptian funerary texts which detailed the hymns and rituals to be performed for the dead, and instructions for the spirit's behaviour in the afterlife, are thought to have been written by many different scribes between around 2400 BC and 1500 BC. They were a collection of spells, charms, passwords, magical numbers and formulas intended to guide the deceased though the various trials they would encounter before reaching the Underworld. Knowledge of the correct spells was thought essential for happiness after death, and copies of all or parts of these texts were carved on pyramids, written on papyrus scrolls and placed with the body inside the sarcophagus, inscribed on mummy cases, and included on AMULETS buried with the dead person. Different spells were held to be required depending on the prominence and social status of the deceased, and the texts were often individualized to the dead person, so no two collections are the same. But most were illustrated with depictions of the tests awaiting the deceased, and their ancient Egyptian name translates as *The Book of Going Forth By Day*. Since the texts were said to have been originally transcribed by the Egyptian god Thoth, they are also sometimes known as *The Book of Thoth*.

The name 'Book of the Dead' was coined by the German Egyptologist Karl Richard Lepsius, who published a selection from these Egyptian funerary texts in 1842. But the best-known version of the *Egyptian Book of the Dead* is the one discovered in 1888 by Dr E A Wallis Budge. Written around 1500 BC for Ani, the Royal Scribe of Thebes, it was found in an 18th-Dynasty tomb near Luxor, and is the largest, most perfectly preserved, and best-illuminated of the surviving Egyptian papyri.

The *Tibetan Book of the Dead* was the title given to the Tibetan funerary text, the *Bardo Thodol*, by the editor of its first English translation, W Y Evans-Wentz. Its name literally means 'liberation through hearing in the intermediary stage', and its authorship is traditionally ascribed to the legendary 8th-century sage, Padma Sambhava, although many scholars believe it is the work of a number of authors over several generations.

The text is intended as a guide for the dead during the intermediate stages between death and rebirth known as *bardos*. It is believed that as soon as physical death takes place, the spirit goes into a trance state during which it is disoriented and the person is not aware that they have died. This period is called the First Bardo. Toward the end of this time, the person is thought to see a brilliant light, and if they can embrace it without fear, they will be freed from the cycle of rebirth. However, most people flee from it, and thus enter the Second Bardo, in which all their deeds and thoughts in this life pass before them. In the Third Bardo, the person assesses what they have seen and makes resolutions for their achievements in their next incarnation. The *Bardo Thodol* is therefore recited by lamas over a dying or recently deceased person, or sometimes over an effigy of them, to enable them to recognize the nature of their state and either escape rebirth altogether, or achieve a calm and successful passage to their next life.

Booth, David *see* CINCINNATI PREMONITION

Borley Rectory *see panel p84*

Brahan Seer

Kenneth Mackenzie, also called Coinneach Odhar, a legendary seer said to have lived in the Scottish Highlands in the 17th century.

Most of what we know about Kenneth Mackenzie, also called Coinneach Odhar, but better known as the Brahan Seer, comes from the Gaelic oral tradition; in a generally well-documented century, there is very little direct evidence of his existence. He is reputed to have been born some time around the beginning of the 17th century at Baile-na-Cille on the Isle of Lewis. Nothing is recorded of his early life, but as a teenager he is said to have obtained the gift of SECOND SIGHT through a mysterious touchstone. In one version of the story, he was given this stone by his mother, who was guided to it by the ghost of a Norwegian princess, and in another version, he found the stone after falling asleep on a heath. All the accounts agree that after gaining possession of the stone, Coinneach's reputation as a SEER began to spread far and wide. He moved to the Brahan estate of the third Earl of Seaforth in Ross-shire, where he worked as a labourer, but he was much sought after by the local gentry for his psychic abilities.

His prophecies deal mostly with Scotland; his believers claim that some have come true already, while the fulfilment of others is still awaited. He is said to have foreseen events such as the coming of mechanization and industrialization, and his mention of 'black bridleless horses' is often interpreted as being a reference to the advent of railways. Some say that he also predicted the Highland Clearances, the building of the Caledonian Canal and, a hundred years before it took place, the Battle of Culloden. He made several prophecies regarding the River Ness, including one that when a ninth bridge crossed the river, there would be fire, flood and calamity; the ninth bridge over the river was built in 1987, and within a few years of its completion, the Piper Alpha oil rig in the North Sea exploded, a passenger plane crashed in flames on Lockerbie and the rail bridge across the River Ness was washed away when the river flooded. Another prophecy he made concerns the Eagle Stone at Strathpeffer, which was allegedly put up by the Munro clan after a battle with the Mackenzies. He said that if this stone fell over three times, Loch Ussie would flood the valley below. It has already fallen twice, and is now firmly concreted in place to ensure its stability!

The Brahan Seer's most famous prediction is the one which was said to have cost him his life. Isabella, the wife of the third Earl of Seaforth, was anxious because her husband had not yet returned from a trip to France, and consulted Coinneach. He assured her that her husband was safe and well, but she pressed him for more details, and he eventually informed her that the Earl was enjoying the company of another woman over in France. Isabella furiously accused Coinneach of lying to destroy her husband's reputation, and had him arrested, convicted of WITCHCRAFT and sentenced to death. Before his execution, he was said to have thrown his seer's stone into Loch Ussie, declaring that it would one day be found in the belly of a fish, whereupon his prophetic gift would pass to its finder. He then made one final prediction – the downfall of the Seaforth clan. He prophesied death and destruction for the family, the loss of property and the end of the clan's line. It was said that all of his predictions for the clan came true, and the last Lord Seaforth died in 1815, after which the title became extinct. A small memorial stone at Chanonry Point marks the site where Coinneach was said to have been put to death.

brainwashing
The use of coercive persuasion to forcibly alter an individual's beliefs and behaviour.
Brainwashing is a term that can be understood at many different levels – indeed it is generally considered to be too vague to be used by psychologists. In general use it can be taken to mean something as simple as persuasion via propaganda or advertising. However, when the term first appeared in the US during the 1950s, it was used to describe extreme processes that it was alleged were carried out by the communists on foreign prisoners. When used in this context, the implication was that it referred to a process whereby an individual's beliefs and ideals could be 'removed' in some way and permanently replaced. This was supposed to be achieved through a process of constant reinforcement, repetition and reward combined with techniques such as sensory deprivation and torture.

However, although there is no doubt that extreme forms of coercive persuasion do produce psychological effects (as do more subtle ones), whether any techniques exist that could produce the kind of extreme and permanent effect implied by the term 'brainwashing' is a highly controversial question.

There have been claims over the years that 'brainwashing' techniques have been used by some alternative religious groups (see CULTS) – techniques through which previous friendships are supposedly destroyed and individuals are shown that only their new friends and the group have their best interests at heart. However, it has generally been shown that little more than ordinary persuasion or indoctrination is employed by religious movements. 'Deprogramming' was a process invented by anti-cultists who believed that it was a way of undoing the 'brainwashing' that they thought had been carried out. Unfortunately, as well as being based upon a misguided assumption, the methods used were themselves as brutal as those that they attributed to the cult members.

A classic fictional depiction of brainwashing is seen in the Richard Condon novel *The Manchurian Candidate* (1959, with film adaptations in 1962 and 2004), in which a captured soldier's beliefs and personality are broken down so that he can be used as an assassination 'tool' by a communist regime. Most psychologists would now agree that such an exaggerated version of the power of 'coercive persuasion' belongs wholly in the realms of fiction. See also MIND CONTROL and MANCHURIAN CANDIDATE.

Branch Davidians
The millennialist sect made famous by the siege and fire at Waco, Texas, in 1993.
The Branch Davidians descend from an offshoot of the Seventh-day Adventist Church. Victor Houteff (1886–1955), a Bulgarian immigrant to the USA, was expelled from the Seventh-day Adventist Church for his radical teachings on the biblical books of Daniel and Revelation. With perhaps a dozen families, he set up a splinter movement called the Shepherd's Rod. In 1935 they established a small community of about 65 people at Mount Carmel, near Waco, Texas, and in 1942 changed their name to the Davidian Seventh-day Adventists, emphasizing the restoration of the Old Testament king David's kingdom. Their aim was to build up to 144,000 true Christians in readiness for the Second Coming, by converting Seventh-day Adventists back to what they saw as the truth.

Borley Rectory

The notorious Borley Rectory in Essex, known as 'the most haunted house in England', was the scene of unrivalled paranormal activity between its construction in 1863 and its destruction by fire in February 1939. Five successive rectors and their families claimed to have experienced a wide range of GHOST and POLTERGEIST phenomena in and around the Rectory, along with locals, visitors and investigators attracted to site. It has been claimed that in excess of 200 people witnessed strange events in and around the rectory over the years.

Ghostly phenomena reported at Borley Rectory included the frequent APPARITION of a nun, a PHANTOM COACH and horses in the grounds, a headless man and a spectral cat. The sounds of footsteps, galloping horses and DISEMBODIED VOICES were also heard, and numerous poltergeist incidents were apparently witnessed. The majority of the poltergeist activity occurred between 1927 and 1935, and was said to include bell-ringing, the movement and breakage of objects, APPORTS which included bottles and religious medals, and pencilled wall writings calling for 'help', 'light', 'mass' and 'prayers'.

The fame achieved by Borley Rectory largely stems from two bestselling books – *The Most Haunted House in England* (1940) and *The End of Borley Rectory* (1946), both written by the flamboyant PSYCHICAL RESEARCHer Harry Price. Price investigated the case for nearly 20 years, following national publicity in the *Daily Mirror* newspaper in 1929 – although his relationship with the various occupants of the rectory was not always good. Price rented the house in 1937 and, in a year-long effort at experimental investigation, moved in teams of observers recruited through *The Times*. SÉANCES were also held, including one in 1937 when the participants supposedly communicated with someone called 'Marie Lairre'. It was claimed that she was a nun, murdered at Borley on 17 May 1667, and that her remains lay buried under the building.

Following the end of the Price tenancy in 1938, the rectory was sold to a Captain Gregson. On 11 February 1939 the building was destroyed by fire, exactly eleven months after a séance prediction that a ghost calling itself Sunex Amures would burn it down. The fire was supposedly caused by a paraffin lamp falling over. There were suspicions of deliberate arson by Gregson, although the insurance claim was ultimately settled.

In 1943 the cellar floor of the ruined rectory was excavated and a jaw bone, supposedly that of the ghostly nun or even 'Marie Lairre', was discovered; this was buried at Liston Churchyard in 1945. The remains of the rectory were demolished in 1944. Further digging occurred on the site in 1954 and 1955, organized by Philip Paul – but nothing was revealed beyond the remains of a 17th-century wall suggesting an earlier building had once stood there.

Houteff was succeeded as leader by his wife Florence, who said the Second Coming would occur on 22 April 1959. When this did not happen, the movement splintered into several different groups, one of them led by Benjamin Roden who told his followers to 'Get off the dead Rod and move on to a living Branch' (meaning Christ), and named his group the Branch Davidians. They took over the Mount Carmel settlement in 1965. Roden died in 1978, and was succeeded by his wife Lois. Their son George claimed to be the Messiah, but fell out with many members including his own mother.

In 1981 Vernon Howell (1959–93) joined the Branch Davidians, and by 1983 Lois Roden was allowing him to teach his own message, recognizing him as the next prophet of the group. This led to confrontation with George Roden, and when Lois died in 1986, George Roden forced Howell and his followers out of the community at gunpoint. In 1987, trying to establish his own leadership, Roden said he would raise a 20-years-dead member back to life.

Howell tipped off the police, and confronted Roden himself. After a gun battle, Roden was imprisoned and Howell was freed – and free to take over the leadership.

Howell moved his followers back to Mount Carmel, and in 1990 changed his name legally to David Koresh: David for the Old Testament king, and Koresh as a variant of the name Cyrus (after the Persian king). Koresh chose to take the names of kings because kings are anointed, and the Aramaic and Hebrew for 'anointed one' is 'messiah'. Koresh saw himself as not just a messiah figure, but as the Lamb of Revelation 5, who would open the seven seals and interpret the scroll (Revelation 5:2). By doing this he would hasten Christ's return. Despite popular accounts, however, he did not claim to be God.

As a prophetic leader Koresh took on two controversial roles. In Bible study sessions that often lasted for many hours he expounded on the seven seals, saying that he had the power to open the

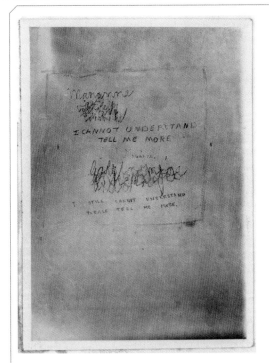

Attempted correspondence with 'ghostly' graffiti on a wall at Borley Rectory, 'the most haunted house in England', photographed in 1931.
(© Mary Evans Picture Library)

With no physical remains of the rectory left to investigate, researchers turned to re-examining the testimony and background of the original witnesses. A sceptical tone was set in the *Haunting of Borley Rectory* (1956) by E J Dingwall, K Goldney and T Hall. The book was severely critical of Price, his methods and his treatment of incidents at the rectory. Particularly damning was the discovery that a photograph published in *Life* magazine of a brick apparently hovering in midair on the rectory site was a hoax, set up as the building was being demolished. This had been passed off by Price as a genuine manifestation. Since then attention has focused on the lives of some of Borley Rectory's colourful inhabitants, and the question of to what extent phenomena were helped along by trickery and self-deception. Elaborate theories have been debated back and forth in books and articles on the case. Some maintain that the haunting has now transferred to the nearby church, but the existence of a large crypt prone to flooding, which was found beneath the building in 1988, may account for many of the strange noises that have been heard there.

Assessing the truth about Borley is difficult amid the wealth of claims and counterclaims. Any final verdict necessarily rests upon the view taken as to the reliability of human testimony. Nonetheless, an arguable case can be made for Borley being haunted both before and after the periods in which Price was involved.

seventh (Revelation 8:1). He also taught that the new generation of God's children should come from his own seed. Having married the 14-year-old daughter of a senior Church elder in 1984, Koresh now began sexual relationships with many of the women in his Church.

These two aspects of Koresh's leadership, messianic and sexual, eventually led to the downfall of the movement. Believing that Christ's return would be in the USA, not Israel, and so expecting the tribulations of the End Times to be violent confrontations, the Church began to stockpile not just food but weapons; Koresh was actually a registered arms dealer. On 28 February 1993 agents from the Bureau of Alcohol, Tobacco and Firearms (BATF) raided Mount Carmel to investigate possible firearms violations. The raid was influenced by hysterical reports of a 'suicide cult' from anti-cultists, fuelled by accusations from discontented ex-members who were offended by Koresh's sexual practices. (Ex-members' accusations of child abuse had already been investigated but not

confirmed.) The BATF chose to raid the compound rather than arrest Koresh when he was away from it.

It is unclear who fired the first shots in the BATF raid, but in the ensuing shoot-out four BATF officers were killed. Six Branch Davidians died and many more were injured, including Koresh, who was shot in the wrist and the waist. The FBI then put Mount Carmel under siege, a situation that ensued for 51 days (although several Branch Davidians did leave the compound during this time). Koresh made tape recordings of his teachings and agreed to surrender if they were broadcast – they were, but Koresh still refused to surrender (saying he had received a message from God telling him to wait). In addition to ongoing negotiations, the FBI cut off electricity to the compound and used bright lights, massively amplified music and helicopter fly-bys to deny sleep to those inside.

Sociologists of religion with a specialist knowledge of millennialist movements offered to help in the negotiations; the FBI allegedly refused their offers.

Dr Phillip Arnold, a Sabbatarian academic who understood the background and the detail of Koresh's millennialist teachings, later wrote:

> I implored the FBI to listen to David Koresh: 'I can help you interpret what he's saying so we can resolve this crisis peacefully,' I told them ... But the FBI expressed no real interest in what I was saying to them.

On 14 April Koresh told the FBI that he would surrender when he had completed a manuscript describing the seven seals. Arnold claims that Koresh was writing this late into the night of 18 April, and planned to surrender the following day. But on the morning of 19 April the FBI attacked, punching holes through the walls of the compound with tanks, and flooding it with tear gas. By around noon, three fires were reported in various parts of the compound. Fire-fighting efforts began at around 12.40pm but the compound rapidly became engulfed in flames. Around 80 Branch Davidians, including Koresh and a number of children, died.

Today, a small chapel has been built on the site of Mount Carmel, with memorial trees commemorating those who died there. Several different Branch Davidian factions still exist, some followers of Koresh, others not.

Despite official US government enquiries clearing the authorities of any blame, there is still a strong and widespread belief that the FBI and the BATF were at least partially culpable.

British UFO Research Association

The best-known amateur UFO investigation group in Britain and one of the oldest in the world.

Britain adopted freelance UFO investigation slightly later than the USA, but by the mid-1950s there were local organizations in major cities such as Manchester, where the Direct Investigation Group into Aerial Phenomena (DIGAP) had been operating since 1953. Its capital-city equivalent, the London UFO Research Organisation (LUFORO), arrived in 1959 and soon approached DIGAP and a few other small teams with the aim of creating a united national association. The result was the British UFO Research Association (BUFORA), officially formed in 1962 (although not incorporated under that name until two years later).

BUFORA produced a magazine, began a national sightings investigation programme and staged monthly lectures by leading researchers and authors.

BUFORA adopted a conservative approach to investigation, seeking explanations for sightings wherever possible, and pioneered the schooling of its investigation team with the aid of a postal training course and written examination. In 1981 it also produced a code of practice governing the ethical behaviour of its members when dealing with witnesses. This was followed in 1989 by an unprecedented ban on the (by then widespread) use of regression hypnosis for exploring ALIEN ABDUCTION cases (see MEMORIES, RECOVERED).

During the 1980s BUFORA ran a number of major conferences at prestigious venues, which included presentations by some of the best-known scientists involved in UFO research, including DR J ALLEN HYNEK. It also took the lead in the study of CROP CIRCLES, producing the world's first publication on the subject, *Mystery of the Circles*, in 1986, and holding the first open symposium to debate the issue in the same year. This was several years before the subject attracted major international attention. BUFORA took the stance that crop circle cases could be best explained either as HOAXES or as an effect of wind-generated atmospheric phenomena, rather than by resorting to explanations involving aliens or anything similarly exotic.

In common with most UFO groups around the world, BUFORA experienced a decline in membership following the rise of the Internet in the 1990s. By 2006 BUFORA had drastically scaled down its public events but, unlike many UFO groups, has survived into the 21st century by evolving into a web-based information network, with a database of over 10,000 British sightings.

Brocken spectre *see* SPECTRE

Brodgar, Ring of

A megalithic stone circle in Orkney

The Ring of Brodgar is a circle of standing stones in the parish of Stenness in Orkney. Situated on a narrow strip of flat land between two lochs, it dates from the late Neolithic or early Bronze Age, between 2500 and 2000 BC. Of the original 60 stones, 27 remain standing and the circle is surrounded by a ditch. It is the third-largest STONE CIRCLE in the British Isles, being approximately the same size as the inner ring at AVEBURY.

It has been suggested that this construction, like many such stone circles, is a kind of giant astronomical observatory, built so as to align with movements of the sun or moon. In fact, the supposed traditional name for the circle is the 'Temple of the Sun', but this was probably invented by antiquarians guessing at its purpose. Brodgar itself is a Norse name, deriving according to some sources from words meaning 'earth-bridge'. About a mile away is a smaller stone circle, the Stones of Stenness, and it is possible that the two sites were connected in some kind of ritual use.

Some of the stones have carvings on them, but these are Norse runes dating from a much later era than that of the original builders. According to local legend, the megaliths are the figures of giants who came out to dance one night and, too caught up in their dancing to notice the break of day, were turned to stone by the rising sun.

Brooklyn Bridge

Regarded as the most remarkable alien abduction case on record. This incident in central Manhattan featured multiple independent witnesses viewing the scene from different perspectives.

A New York resident, Linda Napolitano, contacted local artist and ALIEN ABDUCTION specialist BUDD HOPKINS in 1989. Hopkins spent several months investigating her story, alongside dozens of other similar cases from around the world.

Napolitano reported to Hopkins that in the early hours of 30 November 1989 she had been taken from her bedroom in a high-rise apartment block by the occupants of a UFO and abducted. Her family slept, oblivious to her ordeal, as she was probed by a number of small beings with oversized heads (see GREYS).

Hopkins used regression hypnosis in an attempt to obtain a better picture of what happened (see MEMORIES, RECOVERED). Napolitano described how she was floated from her bed through the open window high above the streets, with the aliens floating in midair alongside her. She was led inside the UFO in a semi-conscious state. However, apart from this dramatic description of the kidnapping, the remainder of the abduction account was similar to hundreds of others then on file.

One year into the investigation Hopkins received a series of letters and taped statements from two men, identified only as Richard and Dan, who professed to have witnessed an extraordinary event. Hopkins had not yet made the Napolitano case public but he recognized that these new claims appeared to be an account of seeing the abduction from the highway below. Further, these witnesses said they were bodyguards, working for the CIA, who had been escorting a world-renowned statesman at the time. Their charge had also seen a woman being floated out of her high-rise window, into a hovering UFO, in the company of 'ugly' little creatures.

Battling secrecy and a reluctance to talk on the part of these men, Hopkins could only slowly piece their story together. It was to be some years before the supposed identity of the statesman was revealed – he was eventually told that it was Javier Perez de Cuellar, former Secretary-General of the United Nations. Hopkins did receive an unsigned letter purporting to confirm this, on UN paper, but only of the type that could be bought at the gift shop in the UN building. He eventually met de Cuellar at Chicago O'Hare airport in 1993, in a brief session set up by a mutual contact. When asked about the story de Cuellar said that he did not recall anything like it, but, when pressed, thought that a bodyguard might once have seen a strange light.

Other witnesses have since come forward

The Brooklyn Bridge, New York, scene of the alleged alien abduction incident that some researchers call the 'case of the century'. (© Alan Schein Photography/Corbis)

– including a driver on the Brooklyn Bridge (from which the Napolitano apartment can be seen). They claim that they saw the abduction take place, but did not report it at the time because they assumed it was a scene being shot for a science-fiction film.

Sceptics pointed out that although the *New York Post* newspaper had a very busy loading dock looking directly out onto the apartment block, no one had reported seeing anything. In response to this, in 2003, Linda Napolitano claimed that she had been contacted by a newspaper employee who had witnessed the events.

This case may stand or fall on whether a figure as influential as de Cuellar was or was not involved. It remains at present a rare example of an alien abduction claim that is possibly supported by independent witnesses. See also CAHILL, KELLY.

broomsticks

In the popular 'storybook' image of witchcraft, broomsticks were the means witches employed to achieve magical flight.

Records of WITCH TRIALS from the 15th century onwards show that magical FLIGHT has long been associated with witchcraft. Among the other diabolical acts of which they were accused, WITCHES were commonly believed to fly to their SABBATS. Originally, broomsticks were only one of the many means by which this was supposedly achieved – animals, sticks, shovels and DEMONS were among the other vehicles thought to be employed.

It has been suggested that the idea that witches could fly in this way may have its origins in the memory of pre-Christian fertility rites, in which participants would dance and jump while riding broomsticks (or other stick-handled tools) as though they were hobby-horses. Indeed, the hobby-horse rituals which survive in some areas to this day may be a continuation of such customs.

There are also a number of theories as to why the association with broomsticks has persisted. In folklore, broomsticks are often credited with other mystical powers, especially relating to fertility and marriage – jumping over a broomstick was a well-known wedding custom which survived until fairly recently in many areas, particularly in Wales. Also, the broomstick is a traditional symbol of womanhood. Persistence in the belief that witches fly on broomsticks could simply be down to the fact that broomsticks were associated with, and commonly employed by, women, and that in popular folk tales witches are usually women. See also FLYING OINTMENT.

brownies

Good-natured and benevolent fairies who attach themselves to a particular household and perform domestic tasks at night.

The brownie is a benevolent fairy found in folklore from the Scottish Highlands and Islands to the English Midlands, and most commonly in the Scottish Borders. Brownies become attached to a particular household and help out by doing odd jobs around the house or farm, cleaning, tidying up, sweeping the floors, and so on. In addition to helping with domestic chores, they will protect the home, chasing away malicious spirits who seek to harm the family. They can go about during the day but prefer not to do so. They are skilled at hiding and can vanish at will, so they are seldom seen, but they are usually described as being about 90 centimetres (3 feet) tall with shaggy brown hair, and as either naked, dressed in rags, or clad in a brown hood and mantle, from which they get their name. They are ugly creatures, having flat faces, huge eyes and tiny nostrils, although their features vary from place to place; the brownies of the Scottish lowlands are said to have no noses, only nostril holes, or else a huge nose but no mouth, while in Aberdeenshire they have no separate fingers and toes. They are usually solitary, but in the Scottish Highlands are sometimes reported as appearing in groups.

Brownies are attracted to humans who show kindness to all living creatures, but hate misers, cheat and liars. They will often become personally attached to one member of a household and will strive to please them. However, they are easily offended. A brownie who feels slighted will not generally leave a household, but will become spiteful and destructive instead of helpful, turning into a BOGGART. Their help should never be taken for granted, but there is a strict taboo against any attempt to repay them directly for their kindness. They appreciate rewards in the form of cakes and bowls of cream, but these should not be specifically offered to the brownie; instead, etiquette demands that the food and drink be simply left out within the brownie's reach, so that he can come across them as if by accident. But one sure way to make a brownie leave a household he has favoured with his presence is to give him clothes; he will depart at once, mortally offended.

If a brownie becomes attached to a family, he may accompany them even if they move house or go abroad; in Canada and the USA there are stories of brownies who are presumed to have travelled there with their immigrant families. See also FAIRIES.

Brown Lady of Raynham Hall

A female apparition said to haunt Raynham Hall in Norfolk, England; the Brown Lady was made famous by a 'ghost photograph'.

The Brown Lady is the name given to a female APPARITION said to have haunted Raynham Hall in Norfolk, which was for many generations the home of the Townsend family. The name of the apparition refers to the brown brocade dress which she is said to have worn. It has been claimed that the Brown Lady was the GHOST of Dorothy Walpole, sister of the first British prime minister Sir Robert Walpole, as Dorothy died of smallpox at Raynham Hall in 1729. The apparition was frequently reported at the Hall in the 19th and early 20th centuries.

In September 1936 two photographers, Indira Shira and Captain Provand, working on a commission for *Country Life* magazine, took a picture of a glowing figure descending a staircase at the Hall. This was immediately held to be an image of the Brown Lady and has been widely considered one of the best GHOST PHOTOGRAPHS ever taken. On investigation no evidence of deliberate trickery was found and researchers who interviewed Shira and Provand considered them truthful, Provand being a sceptic who was at a loss to explain how the image had appeared. In 1937 C V C Herbert investigated the photograph for the SOCIETY FOR PSYCHICAL RESEARCH. Herbert suspected camera malfunction, but found it curious that this should occur at the same moment one of the photographers believed he saw the ghost. While some still champion the picture as a genuine example of a ghost photograph, others now believe that although there is little to suggest deliberate fraud, close scrutiny of the full photograph presents evidence of double exposure.

BUFORA *see* BRITISH UFO RESEARCH ASSOCIATION

Bungay, Black Dog of *see* BLACK DOG OF BUNGAY, THE

bunyip

A semi-legendary Australian water monster.

The bunyip is one of Australia's best-known legendary creatures, but it is also cryptozoological, because some reports seem to describe a genuine but scientifically undocumented species. Familiar to the indigenous Aboriginal people as well as to Western settlers there, the bunyip is most commonly described as being a black, shaggy-furred, dog-headed aquatic beast, but certain observers state that its neck is long and hairy and its head resembles a kangaroo's. This dichotomy

Possibly the most famous ghost photograph ever taken; first published in *Country Life* magazine on 26 December 1936. It shows what appears to be a phantom figure descending a staircase at Raynham Hall, Norfolk.
(© Mary Evans Picture Library)

of description has led some cryptozoologists to believe that there could be two quite separate kinds of bunyip, with the former possibly allied to seals and the latter more akin to the long-necked LAKE MONSTERS and SEA SERPENTS reported elsewhere in the world. Australian zoologists Dr Michael Archer and Dr Tim Flannery consider it possible that reports of bunyips may derive from Aboriginal legends of certain now-vanished giant marsupials known as diprotodonts, which may well have been amphibious in nature, but this explanation may not resolve modern-day bunyip sightings, which have been reported by Westerners as well as by Aboriginal eyewitnesses.

buru

A swamp-dwelling cryptid from a remote upland valley in northern Assam, India.

The Apa Tani Valley, in northern Assam, India, was once believed to harbour in its swamps a very large aquatic CRYPTID known to the local tribe as the buru. According to their accounts, it was almost entirely water-dwelling, but would sometimes raise its head above the water surface and emit a loud bellow. Morphologically, it was elongate, and measured 3.5–4 metres (11.5–13 feet) long, including a head that was 50 centimetres (1.5 feet) long and terminated in a very large snout. Its tail was 1.5 metres (5 feet) long and was rounded, tapering and fringed. Its skin was like that of a scaleless fish, and its four sturdy limbs were clawed. In colour it was blue with white blotches. Sadly, the Apa Tani Valley natives stated that they had exterminated the buru here long ago, but they also claimed that it still existed in a second valley, called Rilo. In 1948, an expedition sponsored by London's *Daily Mail* newspaper searched unsuccessfully for the buru in Rilo. However, the expedition obtained sufficient anecdotal evidence to suggest that the local people believed that it had once existed here, and if that was the case, it had only died out quite recently.

Traditionally, cryptozoologists had deemed the buru to be some kind of reptile, possibly a crocodile or large monitor lizard. In 1991, however, English cryptozoologist Dr Karl Shuker published a detailed re-examination of the buru, revealing that it compared much more closely to an extra-large lungfish.

Bux, Kuda (1906–81)

Indian mystic and magician.

Kuda Bux was the name adopted by the Indian mystic and magician Khudah Bukhsh. In his native India he studied the performances of FAKIRS and was one of the most well-known exponents in the West of their fire-walking demonstrations (see FIRE IMMUNITY). In 1935 he performed this feat while being observed by a team of scientists from the University of London Council for Psychical Research, who were able to verify that no protective lotions had been applied to his bare feet. He repeated his walk over the hot coals when asked to do so by a photographer.

Calling himself 'The Man with X-Ray Eyes', he famously demonstrated his power to see when his eyes were covered. He would go to great lengths to convince all onlookers that he really couldn't see, covering his eyes with pads of soft dough, followed by a blindfold, then swathing his whole head in lengths of cloth. He would then carry out various stunts to show that he was miraculously still able to see, identifying the colour of balloons shown to him, threading a needle and reading messages written by audience members on a blackboard. In 1945, he rode a bicycle on the busy streets of New York City while 'blinded' in his usual fashion, successfully navigating through the traffic of Times Square. According to Bux, his normal vision was poor and he could actually see better when using his 'X-Ray vision'.

Bux claimed that this extraordinary power was

Kuda Bux reads the newspaper using his famous 'blindfold vision'. (© Mary Evans Picture Library)

simply the product of intense concentration and that anyone who learned his techniques of focusing the mind could achieve comparable results. The same concentration, he said, had allowed him to heal himself after his back had been broken and medical science had apparently given him up as a lost cause.

At the height of his fame in the 1950s Bux had his own show on US television, *Kuda Bux, Hindu Mystic*, in which he regularly demonstrated his blindfold vision as well as his mind-reading abilities.

While Bux's fire-walking was absolutely genuine, we know now that many people can perform this if their concentration and willpower are strong enough and they move quickly and confidently. As to his 'X-Ray vision' claims, sceptics have always contended that his elaborate head-coverings were in fact very carefully arranged so as to leave him a narrow, disguised line of sight – probably along the side of his nose. Tellingly, many stage magicians claimed to be able to replicate his methods and some even incorporated a 'Kuda Bux act' in their own stage performances.

Whatever the truth of his claims, Kuda Bux eventually suffered a gradual diminution in his sight, caused by glaucoma. See also EXTRA-RETINAL VISION; MAGIC, STAGE.

cabala *see* KABBALAH

cabbala *see* KABBALAH

Cabrera, Dr Javier *see* ICA STONES

Cadborosaurus *see* CADDY

Caddy

The name given to a sea serpent said to live in Cadboro Bay, Canada.

Many freshwater cryptids have morphological marine counterparts (and vice versa), so Ogopogo of Canada's LAKE OKANAGAN is by no means unique in having a very similar-looking marine equivalent. This latter CRYPTID has the equally colloquial and memorable name of Caddy – after Cadboro Bay, where it has often been reported, frequenting the Straits of Georgia that separate Vancouver Island and mainland British Columbia. Known to the Native American people in this area as the hiachuckaluck, Caddy has allegedly been sighted on many occasions, often by multiple eyewitnesses, and reports have markedly increased in recent years.

Observers claim that Caddy measures anything from 4.9 to 30.5 metres (16 to 100 feet) in total length, and possesses an exceedingly elongate blackish-brown body capable of forming humps or even vertical loops. The head is said to be distinctly camel-like, with a downturned muzzle and a pair of discernable ears or horns. The neck is 1 metre (3 feet) long and may have a mane, and this SEA SERPENT also has a pair of front flippers, a flattened fluked tail that might result from fused rear flippers, and what could be a series of serrations or even short spines running down the centre of its back. When it moves, its body throws itself into a series of vertically undulating humps or loops – as observed from aboard a boat by Osmond Fergusson and his partner on 26 June 1897, when they encountered a Caddy near the Charlotte Islands. They claimed it was around 7.6 metres (25 feet) long and that it raised the front section of its body – estimated at 1.8 metres (6 feet) long – above the surface of the water, reminding the two sailors of a cobra. They could also see the remainder of its body, stretched out horizontally just below the water surface, and terminating in a fluked tail that gently wafted from side to side.

A more recently reported sighting was made on 14 June 1993 by two pilots who were practising landing a Cessna float plane at Saanich Inlet. Prior to landing the plane, the pilots claim they spotted a pair of Caddy cryptids, each exposing a couple of body loops above the water surface. When they tried to land the aeroplane, the two Caddies sped away through the water, throwing their bodies into tall vertical greyish-green loops as they moved.

There has also been one alleged Caddy carcase. In 1937, a sperm whale was split open at Naden Harbor whaling station, and a curious dead animal was found in its gut. Measuring 3.1–3.7 metres (10–12 feet) long, it was badly mangled and partly decomposed, but certain features could be discerned – such as the large, decidedly camel- or sheep-like face; three sinuous body coils just behind its neck; the remains of what appeared to be front flippers; and other remains of an apparently fluked tail. Photos of this extraordinary beast were taken and preserved – unlike the carcase itself, which was discarded after having been placed on display at the Harbor.

Firmly believing this enigmatic carcase to be

the remains of a juvenile Caddy, in 1995 veteran Caddy investigator Ed Bousfield joined forces with oceanographer and keen amateur cryptozoology enthusiast Professor Paul Le Blond to publish a formal scientific paper describing the carcase as a hitherto-unknown species, which they dubbed *Cadborosaurus willsi*. They deemed it likeliest that Caddy is a species of reptile, possibly an evolved plesiosaur. However, most cryptozoologists favour a mammalian identity, particularly an evolved zeuglodont (as also favoured for Ogopogo), which would explain how it can undulate vertically (reptiles cannot do this). As for the Naden Harbor carcase specifically, non-cryptozoological identities include a dead whale foetus or even a decaying basking shark. Whatever is at their source, the frequency of modern-day sightings bodes well for this cryptid's formal exposure occurring in the not-too-distant future.

Cagliostro, Alessandro di *see* EGYPTIAN
RITE FREEMASONRY

Cahill, Kelly (1966–)
A rare example of an alien abduction case with multiple, independent witnesses.
On the night of 7 August 1993, Kelly Cahill and her husband Andrew had been to see friends in the Dandenong mountains near Melbourne. They claimed that while returning home in the early hours of the morning, they came face to face with a dark, round object on a quiet road between Belgrave and Fountain Gate. It had glassy 'windows' in the side, behind which there appeared to be some shadowy figures. No sooner had the couple reacted to its presence than the object seemed to have vanished. Kelly said to Andrew, 'Weren't we just about to see a UFO?' to which his confused reply was, 'We must have turned a corner.' Kelly felt unwell, so they drove home, noticing when they arrived that it had taken an hour longer than expected.

Over the next few days Kelly's health deteriorated. She had a strange scar on her navel, her period came on much too early and she felt debilitated. By the end of the month she was in hospital, where a uterine infection was diagnosed. Doctors suggested that the most likely cause was a miscarriage, although tests established that this was not the case.

While driving near the same spot on 1 October 1993, Kelly reportedly had a flashback in which she recalled the full details of what had happened two months before. Now she remembered rounding a bend and seeing a large object with orange lights beside the road. On getting out of the car the Cahills had seen tall, dark entities floating towards them.

Their only visible features were glowing red eyes. Using telepathy, the aliens had assured the couple that they would come to no harm, but Andrew was not convinced and began screaming at them. Kelly then felt herself pushed backwards by a sudden force, triggering her feeling of nausea. When the couple recovered composure they were both back in the car and the UFO had gone.

The most significant part of Kelly Cahill's fuller recollection of the incident was that they had not been alone during the alien contact. Another car, containing a man and two women, had been stopped on the road nearby. These people would have witnessed the whole thing. Kelly was able to describe the car and its passengers to UFO researcher BILL CHALKER, who enlisted the help of colleague John Auchettl to begin a search.

Auchettl was able to locate the car in the local area. It had contained a married couple, identified as Jan and Bill, and their friend, a nurse called Glenda. They confirmed that something strange had happened to them on the road that night, but they had chosen not to report it because they felt that nobody would believe them. They had no idea that the Cahills had also been present – their car was obviously out of view. Jan and Glenda described being taken into the UFO by tall beings and receiving a medical probe that left them with vaginal swelling and red marks on their thighs.

Jan and Glenda later underwent regression hypnosis (see MEMORIES, RECOVERED). Following this, they claimed to recall that there had been a third car, containing a single male occupant. It was ahead of them and would not have been visible from the Cahills' position. This additional witness was tracked down in 1997. The driver only had a limited memory of the events but did confirm seeing the UFO.

Many Australian UFO researchers consider this case to be one of the most significant on record because the original story appears to have been verified by the testimony of independent witnesses, lending credence to the claim that ALIEN ABDUCTIONS occur. See also BROOKLYN BRIDGE.

cairns
Stone mounds covering prehistoric burial sites.
A cairn (derived from a Gaelic word) is a man-made pile of stones built up to mark something, such as the site of an important event, a pathway or a boundary. In archaeology the term is specifically applied to the large mounds of stones covering various types of prehistoric tombs. They were probably first used to protect recently buried bodies from being dug up by wolves or other scavengers, but the more elaborate and extensive cairns covering some ancient graves suggest

that they came to acquire ceremonial or symbolic value and were associated with the power and status of the person interred beneath.

An unexcavated cairn simply looks like a low grassy mound, but what lies beneath is often a fairly sophisticated tomb. The dating of bones found in these burial places has shown that many cairns were in use over periods of hundreds of years and it may be that they were often revisited rather than being simply closed up and abandoned after an interment. Auchenlaich Cairn, near Callander in Scotland, is a fine example of a chambered cairn, that is, one containing separate burial 'rooms' or chambers. It is the longest megalithic cairn in Britain.

Callanish standing stones

A megalithic stone circle on the Isle of Lewis.

At Callanish (in Gaelic, Calanais) on the Isle of Lewis there is a remarkable complex of prehistoric MEGALITHS. There are several STONE CIRCLES as well as individual MENHIRS, but the most important is the great circle popularly known as the 'Stonehenge of the North'. Unlike many such constructions, the layout is not a simple circle but rather a cruciform shape with a circle at the centre, almost like a Celtic cross. Around 50 stones are to be seen, in four avenues, meeting at the central circle of 13 stones, in the middle of which is a single, taller monolith. A CAIRN tomb has been excavated at the centre but this is of later date than the standing stones themselves, which are thought to have been erected before 2000 BC. The stones are made of Lewisian gneiss and were covered by peat until they were excavated in the mid-19th century.

Like many stone circles, Callanish is believed to have been built along astronomical lines, and its western row points towards sunset at the equinoxes. More importantly, it is suggested that Callanish is the site mentioned by the ancient Greek historian Diodorus Siculus, who described an island of hyperboreans where, every 19 years, the moon came very close to earth. Modern research shows that, at Callanish, the moon can be observed rising briefly before immediately setting (a phenomenon called a 'lunar standstill') at certain times of the year every 18.5 years.

Local folklore has it that the stones are the petrified forms of giants who plotted to resist the encroachment of Christianity.

calumet

The sacred pipe traditionally used by plains and western Native Americans.

The word calumet comes from the French word *chalumet*, meaning a reed. It was used by white settlers to describe the sacred pipes (sometimes also

The remarkable standing stones at Callanish on the Isle of Lewis, a location from which a periodic 'lunar standstill' can be observed. (© TopFoto)

known as ceremonial pipes or peace pipes) of the Native Americans.

The calumet, in which tobacco is smoked, is employed in various religious and social ceremonies, with the construction and decoration often reflecting the pipe's purpose. The smoking of the calumet can be used as a means of seeing visions and of achieving communion with the spirit world.

There are many different myths surrounding the origin of the calumet, one of the best known being that of the Oglala Sioux (see BLACK ELK). In this version the pipe was the first of seven gifts given by White Buffalo Calf Woman, a representative of the Great Spirit. The other six were rites in which it was to be used – these included the Sweat Lodge, SUN DANCE and VISION QUEST. The bowl, stem and carvings and the feathers attached to the pipe represent earth, plants, animals and birds – so to pray with the pipe means to pray with and for everything. The sacred bundle containing what is said to be this original pipe, known as the 'Calf Pipe', is still kept on the Cheanne River reservation in South Dakota.

Cancer

In astrology, the fourth sign of the zodiac, between Gemini and Leo.

In Western ASTROLOGY, Cancer is the sign of the ZODIAC for those who are born between 22 June and 23 July. The symbol for Cancer is the crab, and the sign is ruled by the moon. Cancerians are said to be sensitive (and at times oversensitive), with a good sense of humour. Cancer is believed to be a water sign, having an affinity with the element WATER.

Candomblé

A Brazilian religion combining African beliefs and Roman Catholicism.

Broadly speaking, Candomblé is the Brazilian equivalent of the Caribbean religion SANTERÍA and the Haitian religion VOUDUN. It is sometimes called Macumba, but this term was not coined by Afro-Brazilians.

Candomblé is a syncretic religion (see SYNCRETISM), merging the half-remembered tribal beliefs of West African slaves, brought to Brazil between the early 16th and late 19th centuries, with Roman Catholic imagery – particularly of saints, and SPIRITISM. It is usually classified as a mediumistic religion. Although originating with the African population of Brazil, from the 1960s it began to become popular among middle-class white Brazilians.

There is no central organization in Candomblé. Priests are members of local 'families' led by a 'mother-of-saint', or *ialorixá*, and are associated with 'houses' (small temples). The rituals involve sacred music and dance – the spirit MEDIUMS, usually dressed in white, dancing in a circle to the rhythm of drums. Animal sacrifice often forms part of the ritual, and the ceremonies usually end with a banquet.

Other Afro-Brazilian religions closely related to Candomblé, in different areas of Brazil, include Umbanda, Xangu, Tambor de Mina and Batuque. Most of these believe that there are no evil spirits, but that some spirits misbehave and need to be educated. A 'darker' version of the religion, Quimbanda, draws its power from these misbehaving spirits.

Cannich Puma *see* ALIEN BIG CATS

Capricorn

In astrology, the tenth sign of the zodiac, between Sagittarius and Aquarius.

In Western ASTROLOGY, Capricorn is the sign of the ZODIAC for those who are born between 23 December and 20 January. The symbol for Capricorn is the goat, and the sign is ruled by Saturn. Capricornians are said to be steady, persistent and self-disciplined, although they can seem self-centred. Capricorn is believed to be an earth sign, having an affinity with the element EARTH.

card-guessing experiments

Experiments which use picture cards to research the possible existence of psychic abilities.

The most common form of card-guessing experiment involves two participants. One person looks at a card and concentrates on it, attempting to 'send' the information, while the other tries to receive this information using TELEPATHY. Where CLAIRVOYANCE, or general EXTRASENSORY PERCEPTION, is being tested, the participant guesses cards which have not been viewed by anyone else (for example, by guessing the order of the cards in a shuffled pack). Initially cards were shuffled by hand, later by machine, and in some tests the images of cards are now randomly generated by computer. The success of a card-guessing experiment is gauged by how the results differ from those that would be expected through chance alone.

A normal pack of playing cards can be used, in which case, if a full deck is used, it would be expected that a person would get one in fifty-two guesses correct by chance alone. Tests using playing cards were carried out as early as 1884 by the French Nobel Prize-winning physiologist Charles Richet. In 1930, ZENER CARDS were first used to test psychic ability by J B RHINE and his colleague Karl Zener at Duke University in North Carolina. Zener cards feature only five different designs (a circle, a cross, wavy lines, a square and a star), so the chances of guessing the correct card are one in five. Experiments of this type, where the number of possible 'targets' is restricted, are known as FORCED-CHOICE EXPERIMENTS.

Normally a person is tested a number of times to gain a statistically valid score. If the experiment is carried out carefully enough, the higher the score is, the more it tends to indicate that some form of psychic ability is at work. In his card-guessing experiments using Zener cards, Rhine found that participants often scored well above the 20 per cent hit-rate that one would expect by chance. However, critics maintain that there was too much potential for fraud in his experiments, including the way in which the cards were shuffled, the fact that participants could pick up clues from the body language of the person they were working with, and even that in some lighting conditions the design would show through the back of the card. Rhine made many further experiments, with a variety of procedures in place to avoid any fraud on the part of the participants or unconscious influence on the part of the testers, and continued to receive scores above chance.

Whether any valid test results have ever been

Mr J. G. Pratt (left), as he handled the cards in long-distance B.T. clairvoyance with Mr Hubert Pearce (right) as percipient (E.S.P.). Distance, 100 yards and 250 yards. The card, kept face down, lying on the book, is the one 'exposed' at the moment.

Participants in card-guessing experiments at Duke University, as featured in J B Rhine's *Extra-Sensory Perception* (1934). (© Mary Evans Picture Library)

obtained which clearly prove the existence of psychic abilities is still hotly debated. See also GANZFELD EXPERIMENTS; PARAPSYCHOLOGY; REMOTE VIEWING.

cards

A set of small, usually rectangular pieces of cardboard with figures or symbols, used for playing games, and for fortune-telling or divination.

Throughout history, cards have been used for two main purposes – playing games, and DIVINATION or CARTOMANCY. Some historians believe that playing cards were brought back to Europe from Palestine by the Crusaders in the second half of the 14th century. Islamic playing cards had four suit emblems (polo-sticks, cups, swords and coins), and these are thought to have inspired the four suits (clubs, hearts, spades and diamonds) originating in France around 1480, which still make up the 52 cards in the modern playing card deck.

The TAROT deck, now mainly employed for divination and other occult purposes, was originally used in the game of Tarocchi, an ancestor of bridge. The traditional tarot deck is made up of 78 cards divided into two main groups – the 22 trump cards of the major ARCANA, with their highly allegorical images, and the 56 numbered 'pip' cards of the minor arcana, which are grouped into four suits of 14 cards – the suit of cups (corresponding to hearts in the playing card deck, see CUPS, SUIT OF), suit of pentacles (corresponding to diamonds, see

PENTACLES, SUIT OF), suit of swords (corresponding to spades, see SWORDS, SUIT OF) and suit of wands (corresponding to clubs, see WANDS, SUIT OF). Although it was once thought that playing cards were descended from the tarot, historians now believe that both types of deck originated at around the same time, and both began to be used for divination in the 16th century, although by the end of the 18th century the tarot had come to be used almost exclusively for this purpose. There are many different layouts, or spreads, available to the tarot reader, each designed to answer different kinds of question, and these are easily adapted for cartomancy with ordinary playing cards; however, some practitioners believe that cards used for playing games should not also be used for divination, and vice versa. Tarot cards are sometimes used for spells as well as divination.

Each card has a specific meaning, although this is affected by the other cards which come up in the reading. A typical interpretation of the cards might be: King of Hearts (or Cups in the tarot) signifies a fair-haired man who is affectionate, generous and impulsive; Seven of Hearts (or Cups) denotes an unreliable person, or a promise broken by a friend; Four of Spades (or Swords in tarot) represents jealousy, sickness or business troubles; Ace of Diamonds (or Pentacles in tarot) symbolizes money, a valuable gift or important news; and Nine of Clubs (or Wands in tarot) means a new romance or a quarrel.

Because of their use in both gambling and

fortune-telling, playing cards have for centuries been condemned by some as 'the Devil's Picture Book', and are the subject of a number of superstitions. It is though unlucky for those in dangerous occupations, for example miners and sailors, to take a pack of cards to work, and it is also unlucky to throw a pack away; they must be burned, but not before they have been replaced with a new pack. Thieves are also advised not to steal a pack of cards, as it will bring them bad luck. In gambling, it is believed that anyone who receives the Four of Clubs on the first deal will have bad hands for the rest of the play, and the Dead Man's Hand, aces over eights, which was said to have been held by Wild Bill Hickok when he was killed, is an extremely unlucky hand.

At one time, parapsychologists also used playing cards to conduct EXTRASENSORY PERCEPTION tests, but later a special set of cards known as ZENER CARDS was developed specifically for this purpose. See also CARD-GUESSING EXPERIMENTS.

cargo cults

Late 19th- and 20th-century religious activity on the islands of the south-west Pacific.

Cargo CULTS were first described by Western observers in Melanesia and the South Pacific in the late 19th century – although they particularly came to prominence during and shortly after World War II, when the Allied forces used islands in the area as air bases.

It is widely believed that the native islanders saw the power and wealth of the Europeans and Americans coming to the islands (as manifested in boats, aeroplanes and cargo) and wanted to draw this power and wealth to themselves. Not fully understanding the real processes by which these items were manufactured and then brought to the islands, they built facsimiles of airstrips, aeroplanes, radio sets, etc, out of wood and straw in acts of sympathetic magic (see MAGIC, SYMPATHETIC), with the aim of summoning the goods and money, or 'cargo', to themselves.

Although this was how the religious activity was seen, the beliefs behind it were rather more complex. The islanders of Papua New Guinea and elsewhere believed that their ancestors were going to return, in planes and ships, and bring wealth. More importantly, they would be ushering in a new age. This was equivalent to beliefs elsewhere relating to the Christian MILLENNIUM, so the movement can loosely be described as 'millennial' (see DOOMSDAY CULTS). In preparation for the return of their ancestors, the islanders' spiritual leaders preached the need for moral reform.

Carnac

A huge complex of megalithic structures near Carnac in Brittany, France.

The area near to the town of Carnac in southern Brittany is home to one of the most important megalithic sites in Europe. Thousands of individual standing stones have been used to create an extraordinary complex of STONE ROWS, cromlechs (stone circles attached to dolmens) and DOLMENS. The site also contains tumuli (see TUMULUS) under which passage graves have been discovered and excavated.

The stone alignments appear in three major groupings: the Alignments of Kerlescan, with 555 stones in thirteen rows, the Alignments of Kermario, with 1029 stones in ten rows, and, largest of all, the Alignments of Menec, with 1169 stones in eleven rows. The Kercado dolmen is a particularly fine example and is rare in that it still stands under its original CAIRN. The Tumulus of Saint Michel is a huge mound constructed of earth heaped above a dolmen and at least two further burial chambers. There are also several large MENHIRS, notably the Manio Giant which is around 5.5 metres (over 18 feet) high.

It is believed to be the oldest continuously inhabited site in the Europe, dating back to at least 5700 BC, which means it is older than STONEHENGE, Knossos or the Egyptian PYRAMIDS. Nothing much is known about the people who created and inhabited the site. Findings from graves suggest that they were short, in both stature and lifespan. Whoever they were, their culture was an enduring one – it has been shown that some of the monuments at Carnac differ in age by as much as 5,000 years.

While the dolmens and tumuli had obvious purposes as burial sites, opinions differ on the intentions behind the construction of the stone circles and alignments. Some argue that these constructions had astronomical uses, whether as calendars of the seasons or for observing and marking the passage of celestial bodies across the heavens. Others maintain that their purposes were more likely to be symbolic, marking the territory of the local people or demonstrating their power and sophistication. Perhaps adding another monolith to an existing alignment was a regular event, helping to strengthen the bonds of the community by the immense co-operative labour that would be needed. Many stones have been moved or taken away completely over the generations, and it is probable that the remains of prehistoric Carnac, impressive as they are, bear little resemblance to the appearance of the site at its zenith. For this reason, much of the thinking about the meaning and purpose of the megaliths can only be speculative.

Carnarvon, George Edward Stanhope Molyneux Herbert, 5th Earl of (1866–1923)

English amateur Egyptologist.

Lord Carnarvon is best known as the amateur Egyptologist who sponsored the excavations at Thebes carried out by HOWARD CARTER. He was the son of the Conservative colonial secretary Henry Carnarvon (1831–90). The fact that he died soon after the discovery of the tomb of Tutankhamen added weight to belief in the curse of Tutankhamen (see TUTANKHAMEN, CURSE OF).

Carnarvon was a wealthy man who owned racehorses and personally raced motor cars until a driving accident in 1901 left him with lasting injuries. Such was his weakened state that he was advised to avoid the damp English winters. It was for this reason that he first visited Egypt in 1903, where he became interested in Egyptology.

His personal wealth allowed him to sponsor the excavations of Howard Carter from 1907, and together they were responsible for several important finds, including the tomb of Queen Hatshepsut (c.1540–c.1481 BC), and Carnarvon built up an impressive collection of Egyptian artefacts. However, it was the finding of the tomb of Tutankhamen that brought both men lasting fame.

In the popular imagination, Carnarvon's death shortly after the opening of this tomb seemed to confirm the idea that its desecrators would be cursed. However, this ignores his age and his already poor state of health (the chief reason for his presence in Egypt in the first place). The cause of his death was more prosaic: infection from a mosquito bite weakened him until he contracted the pneumonia that proved fatal. However, those who prefer to believe in the curse of Tutankhamen continue to consider him its first victim.

car stops

UFO sightings during which a motor vehicle suffers electrical interference, often resulting in total immobilization until the UFO has disappeared.

Car stops are a recurring theme in UFO reports and are often claimed to occur at the start of ALIEN ABDUCTION incidents. They tend to follow the same basic pattern in that they happen late at night, on isolated roads. Most cases involve cars, but motorcycles, trucks, buses, tractors and even aircraft have been reported to suffer electrical interference to some degree. In a few reports where diesel engines are involved, the claim has been that the electrical systems were affected but the engine did not fail. Batteries on all vehicles tend to be drained of charge after the sighting.

The following story is a typical example of a car stop incident:

Brian Grimshawe and Jeff Farmer claimed that they were driving through the deserted streets of Nelson, Lancashire, in the early hours of 9 March 1977, when a large cigar-shaped craft came from the sky above Pendle Hill (a place notorious for its past associations with WITCHCRAFT). It dropped to hover above their car, glowing orange from the base like the embers of a coal fire. At this point the car engine and lights faltered and then failed, leaving them stranded. They got out and tried to escape, but felt a strange sensation pushing down on them, their skins tingling as if inside an electrical field. They managed to get back into the car, the UFO drifted away and the car returned to life on its own. Both men were left with physical symptoms, including pounding headaches, and Grimshawe suffered from watering eyes that persisted for several days.

During the COLORADO UNIVERSITY STUDY in 1968, tests were carried out to ascertain the electromagnetic field strength required to stop a car engine. It was found to be of a level so high that it would leave a lasting, measurable trace in the metal bodywork of a vehicle. No such telltale signs have ever been recorded following a reported car stop incident.

In the 1970s the BRITISH UFO RESEARCH ASSOCIATION compiled a detailed catalogue of over 300 car stop cases and CUFOS later expanded upon this. Over 1,000 cases are now on record, although car stop reports have become less common since the 1980s. It has also been observed that there are few reports of car stops prior to 1951, when the popular science fiction film *The Day the Earth Stood Still* featured aliens who impeded electrical power, including car engines, as a warning to earth. This might suggest that CULTURAL TRACKING is at work.

Carter, Howard (1874–1939)

English Egyptologist who discovered the tomb of Tutankhamen.

Howard Carter was the son of an artist and was trained in drawing and painting. He became involved in Egyptology from 1891, when he began working as a draughtsman on the archaeological survey headed by Flinders Petrie (1853–1942). Under Petrie he was involved in several important discoveries.

Between 1899 and 1905 Carter held the post of inspector-general of the Egyptian antiquities department. From 1907 he was able to carry out his own excavations with the sponsorship of Lord CARNARVON. He discovered and excavated several notable tombs, including those of Queen Hatshepsut (c.1540–c.1481 BC) and Thutmose IV (fl.1400–1390 BC), but it is the discovery of the largely intact

Howard Carter examining the sarcophagus of Tutankhamen in 1922. Although there were claims that a curse brought about the deaths of others involved in the expedition, Carter lived for a further 16 years. (© TopFoto)

tomb of Tutankhamen in 1922 for which he is best known.

Carter spent the rest of his life excavating this tomb and photographing and cataloguing its contents, the richness and variety of which were of immense value to the study of Egyptology. Despite the supposed curse of Tutankhamen (see TUTANKHAMEN, CURSE OF), Carter, the man who actually opened the tomb and might have been supposed to have borne the full weight of its protective maleficence, survived Lord Carnarvon by 16 years, dying in England at the age of 65.

cartomancy
Divination or fortune-telling by means of cards.
Fortune-telling by means of a deck of cards, known as cartomancy (from Late Latin *carta*, a card, and Greek *manteiā*, divination), has a history as old as playing cards themselves, and can be traced back as far as 14th-century Europe. Although a standard deck of playing cards can be used for cartomancy, many practitioners disapprove of this practice, holding that cards used for playing games should not also be used for divination – a belief which has given rise to the large numbers of decks designed specifically for divination, the best known of which is the TAROT deck, in all its forms.

Whichever kind of deck is used, there are many different layouts, or spreads, available to the cartomancer, each designed to answer different kinds of question. Some spreads are used to address specific

issues, such as relationships or work. Although each card has a specific meaning, this is influenced by the other cards in the reading. A single card may be drawn from the deck to give guidance just for that day; a three-card spread may be chosen to represent the past, present and future in a given situation; ten cards may be laid out in the most famous of all tarot spreads, the Celtic Cross, which goes into considerable depth and helps the subject to understand the factors influencing their situation, and how they can shape this situation and its future; and as many as 30 cards, or even the whole deck, may be used in an even more complex reading which covers the subject's whole life.

Cash–Landrum
A report of a UFO close encounter from the USA which is one of the few instances where it is claimed that the trauma caused was so great that it eventually cost the primary witness her life.
Late in the evening of 29 December 1980, restaurant owner Betty Cash set off with staff member Vickie Landrum and Vickie's grandson Colby to sample the menu at a competitor's restaurant in Dayton, Texas.

They later reported that while they were driving through a pine wood near Huffman at about 9pm, a fiery object descended suddenly to treetop height and hovered over the road ahead, blocking their path. Betty stopped the car and all three got out to look at what they described as an incredible diamond-shaped mass, spurting flame. The heat was apparently so intense that they had to shield their faces.

Colby became distressed, so he and his grandmother returned to the shelter of the car, leaving Betty to stare in awe at the object. A few moments later 23 Chinook helicopters arrived, and seemed to shepherd the UFO away across the forest. Betty returned to the car and drove the Landrums home, before returning to her own house.

On arriving home all three of the people involved were taken very ill. Colby suffered a severe sunburn-like rash and eye irritation. His grandmother's eyes also became sore and large tufts of her hair fell out over the next few days. Both were nauseous and tired. Betty was affected even more severely. Within hours she was suffering from a pounding headache, nausea, diarrhoea, vomiting and swollen eyes. By 3 January she was slipping in and out of consciousness and was rushed to hospital in Houston. Over the next two months she spent several weeks in intensive care and her hair fell out to such an extent that she was noticeably bald by the spring. She went on to develop multiple cancers, requiring several operations, including a mastectomy, and was hospitalized on 25 occasions over the next decade.

John Schuessler, a NASA scientist and UFO investigator pressed for a government enquiry, suggesting that the Chinook helicopters must have come from an official source. He found other witnesses to the flight of these aircraft, but the government continued to deny any knowledge of the incident. The case was finally rejected by the courts in August 1986 on the grounds that the US government had no device like the one reported, so could not be held responsible for whatever might have happened. This was taken by some UFO researchers (possibly slightly disingenuously) to be tantamount to an official admission that the object was a UFO.

Betty Cash died in 1998 on the anniversary of the alleged incident. See also CLOSE ENCOUNTERS.

catalepsy
A trancelike state of incapacity and bodily rigidity.
Catalepsy is a state in which a person appears to lose consciousness for a long period of time, usually with rigidity of the muscles. The whole body becomes rigid, with the limbs becoming fixed in their positions, even if these are abnormal or seem to be strained, and they return to these positions if they are moved by someone else.

A person in a cataleptic state is completely unresponsive to outward stimuli, and their bodily functions, such as breathing or heartbeat, slow down markedly.

As far as medicine is concerned, various causes for catalepsy have been identified. These include sudden shock or severe emotional trauma. It has

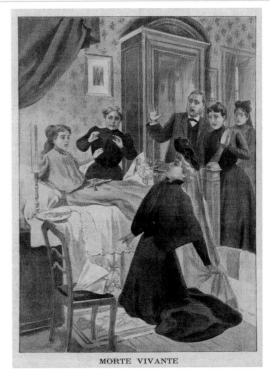

MORTE VIVANTE

A catalepsy sufferer from Argentat, France, who has been presumed dead for 14 hours, 'comes back to life'. From *Le Petit Journal* (13 April 1902). (© Mary Evans Picture Library)

also been associated with depression, epilepsy and schizophrenia.

In the past, and more recently in primitive societies, the failure to recognize and understand catalepsy led to people suffering from this to be thought of as dead. The fact that they would sometimes recover and seem to be miraculously restored is thought to explain the idea of people rising from the dead, whether as GHOSTS or vampires, and to be behind the ZOMBIE myth of the Caribbean. In the New Testament, one of the miracles performed by Jesus Christ was to resurrect Lazarus, who was said to have been dead for four days. Some say that this could be explained by Lazarus not having actually died but having been in a cataleptic state.

It has been suggested that some individuals who were believed to undergo religious ecstasy may in fact have been suffering from catalepsy. The fact that sufferers have been shown to experience HALLUCINATIONS while in a cataleptic state could be said to account for the religious visions experienced by some mystics. In some faiths, a cataleptic state is thought to be achieved by ascetics engaging in prolonged periods of deep meditation.

Many of the symptoms of catalepsy can be reproduced in people by the use of HYPNOSIS, including apparent rigidity of the body. This is often exploited by stage hypnotists, who suspend or balance their subjects between very narrow supports. A hypnotized person may be made to keep unnaturally still, often in awkward or difficult bodily positions, and may be convinced by their hypnotist that they cannot open their eyes or move their limbs voluntarily. The identification of catalepsy in a limb, ie when a limb is moved by the hypnotist and it remains rigidly in the new position, is often used as a test of whether or not a person has been successfully hypnotized.

cats

Cats have historically been associated with luck, magic and witchcraft.

In world folklore a vast range of (often contradictory) beliefs and superstitions have attached to cats. Although, along with dogs, they have long since been domesticated and have lived alongside humans, their independent behaviour, nocturnal habits and often apparently cruel behaviour when hunting have attracted suspicion.

The Egyptians considered cats sacred. They appear in Egyptian art and some Egyptian gods are depicted as cat-headed. The cat was particularly associated with the goddess Bast, the goddess of fertility and marriage, an association that was mirrored elsewhere in the practice of burying a cat in a field as a fertility CHARM.

In later times the cat has been associated with good and bad luck in equal measure, black cats especially so. To have a black cat cross your path was said by some to be bad luck, but to others seeing a black cat, or owning a black cat charm, was said to be good luck. Cats were also sometimes credited with the power of affecting the weather, perhaps leading to the somewhat ambivalent relationship between cats and sailors. In some areas a stray black cat onboard ship was considered unlucky, but in others, a black cat would be taken on board as a good luck charm. Throwing a cat overboard to drown was believed to bring on a storm – in 1590 the NORTH BERWICK WITCHES were accused of raising a storm in an attempt to drown JAMES VI (James I of England) by baptizing a cat and then throwing it into the sea.

In modern times, cats have become as important a part of the popular image of WITCHES and WITCHCRAFT as pointed hats, CAULDRONS and BROOMSTICKS, although their position as the primary animal companion of witches only really dates back to the 19th century. Cats were originally only one of the many animals associated with witches and in earlier folklore a witch was as likely to keep a hare, crow, owl or toad. However, cats did appear regularly in the anti-witchcraft propaganda of the Middle Ages. It was often claimed that a cat belonging to an accused witch was her FAMILIAR, assisting her in carrying out her evil work, and some witches were even accused of being able to assume the shape of a cat themselves. When Elizabeth Francis was convicted of witchcraft in Chelmsford in 1556, she confessed to keeping a cat called Sathan, that she said had been passed down to her and that she in turn had passed on. The cat would perform tasks for her, for which it would be rewarded with her blood.

Although the majority of the superstitions relating to cats have almost died out, there is still a belief among some people that they are particularly sensitive to the presence of GHOSTS and other paranormal phenomena.

cattle mutilation

Mysterious livestock mutilations, predominantly of cattle but also of other animals, that often involve surgical wounds and have been associated with UFO sightings.

UFOS and their occupants have been reportedly interested in cattle for more than a century. On 19 April 1897, during the AIRSHIP wave across the American Midwest, a farmer called Alex Hamilton told the *Yates Center Farmers Advocate* that a strange ship descended over his Kansas farm and threw a rope around a frightened calf, lifting it skywards and flying away. Its butchered remains were apparently found nearby the next day. However, Hamilton admitted two weeks later that this was a hoax, citing a local liars club as the reason for the tale.

UFO author John Keel (see MOTHMAN) was the first to publicize modern mutilation cases, when they were reported to him by witnesses in the Ohio Valley during 1966 and 1967. He said that he personally studied the bodies of several horses and cows that had been killed with skilled surgical cuts to the throat, the blood seeming to have been drained and removed from the site. The number of reports has escalated ever since.

These gruesome acts are particularly common in the American Midwest, but there have been localized WAVES in South America, in Puerto Rico and to a lesser degree in the UK. Links with UFO sightings are only sporadic, with mysterious lights or unidentified dark helicopters also sometimes featuring in the testimony of witnesses. However, in most cases the animals are simply discovered in a mutilated state, with local vets arguing against predator attack on the basis of the precision of the cuts and the missing blood. In Puerto Rico, where dead livestock has been reported as sucked dry of blood, the blame has been put upon a CRYPTID known as CHUPACABRAS ('goatsucker').

Opinion is divided as to the cause of these cases. Some researchers think that the same entities who seek body fluids during ALIEN ABDUCTIONS may be taking animal medical samples to further their research into earthly species. Others favour the possibility that the mutilations have a human origin – some claiming that they are the acts of members of Satanic cults (see SATANISM).

TV documentary maker Linda Moulton Howe has investigated the phenomenon in detail, seeking clear evidence for the association of mutilations with UFOs. She has found some circumstantial links, but UFO researchers remain undecided as to whether this phenomenon falls within their field.

cauldrons

Large cooking pots that have historically had mystical and religious significance in many cultures.

The cauldron, usually in the form of an iron pot, was an important part of early religious and magical ceremonies – probably because it would have played a central role in the cooking of food for feasts. Examples of cauldrons decorated with religious symbols have appeared among archaeological finds throughout Europe.

During the Middle Ages cauldrons became particularly associated with the practice of WITCHCRAFT and SORCERY. WITCHES were said to use them for concocting magic potions and were believed to take them to their SABBATS, where they would dance around them. These beliefs probably had their basis in their earlier religious and ceremonial use among the Celts and other pre-Christian peoples.

Cayce, Edgar (1877–1945)

US psychic who claimed to channel answers to questions on a wide variety of topics while in a self-induced trance state; he was best known for his psychic medical diagnoses and readings of the past lives of his subjects.

Edgar Cayce was born into a farming family in 1877, near Kentucky. He was said to have discovered his psychic powers by accident in 1901 when, at the age of 24, he suffered a form of throat paralysis which caused him to lose his voice. Having tried various treatments without success, Cayce agreed to consult a local hypnotist, but insisted on putting himself under hypnosis. While in a trance state, he described the condition of his vocal cords, and detailed a remedy – that the hypnotist should suggest to him the increase of blood circulation to the afflicted area. According to Cayce, when he came out of the trance, he had regained his voice, and after several follow-up sessions, the cure was found to be permanent.

Word soon spread about Cayce's abilities, and he was bombarded with requests from other people

to diagnose and prescribe for them in the same way. Although at first reluctant, he eventually agreed. On his business card, Cayce described himself as a 'psychic diagnostician', and the vast majority of what came to be called his 'readings' dealt with the maintenance of health and the treatment of illnesses. He also claimed that he used astral projection, and could make prophecies, contact the dead as a MEDIUM, and see AURAS.

Cayce seldom met the subjects of his readings; most of them lived hundreds of miles away and made their requests by letter. He claimed that he only needed to know their names, addresses and where they would be when he made the reading. He would lie on a couch and enter a self-induced trance state – a method which earned him the nickname of 'the sleeping prophet' – and he would then be asked the subject's question, and his answers would be noted. He gave over 14,000 readings between 1901 and 1944, most of these from 1925 onward, with his wife Gertrude asking the questions and his lifelong secretary, Gladys Davis, taking down his answers in shorthand. Cayce claimed not to remember what he had said while in the trances, but described his work as Christian service, being a devout and lifelong member of the Disciples of Christ. The cures he prescribed after his diagnoses included remedies such as poultices, osteopathy and massage, and recommendations on exercise and diet, such as the avoidance of red meat, white bread, fried foods and all alcohol apart from red wine. He is thus often regarded as a practitioner of HOLISTIC MEDICINE, and a naturopath.

Later, the scope of Cayce's readings expanded, and he also became known for his life readings, in which he described the subject's present physical, emotional and mental condition in terms of their past lives; for his business readings, in which he gave advice on subjects such as business partners and the stock market; for his dream readings, in which he interpreted his subjects' dreams; and for his mental and spiritual readings, in which he focused on what the subject could do to attain a better mental or spiritual state. At one point, Cayce was asked during a reading where he got his information, and he replied that he received it from two sources; the first was the subject's own unconscious or subconscious, and the second was the universal memory of nature known as the AKASHIC RECORDS, which he claimed to be able to access in his trance state.

In 1944 he suffered a stroke from which he never recovered, and he died in 1945. Since his death, the many transcripts of his readings have been held by the Association for Enlightenment and Research, which Cayce founded in 1931, and some dozen biographies and over 300 books have been written based on his work. Although he lived before the advent of the NEW AGE movement, he remains a major influence on its teachings. See also ATLANTIS; SEER.

cellular memory
The idea that memories, likes and interests may somehow be stored at a cellular level throughout the body.
There have been a number of anecdotal accounts suggesting that organ transplant patients have inherited characteristics or even memories from the organ donor. Stories have included cases such as that of a recipient of a transplanted heart who developed a previously unknown craving for beer (the favourite drink of her donor), and a case in which the recipient supposedly identified the donor's murderer. The theory of cellular memory was developed as a possible explanation for these tales. Although some small studies have been carried out, there has been no significant scientific investigation of the phenomenon and the concept is widely dismissed by the scientific community.

Center for UFO Studies *see* CUFOS

cerealogy *see* CEREOLOGY

ceremonial magic *see* MAGIC, CEREMONIAL

cereology
The study of crop circles.
Cereology is the name given to the study of CROP CIRCLES – the collection of examples, the investigation of their nature, the comparison of various types and the generation of theories as to their cause and purpose. The word is interchangeable with 'cerealogy' – the former being derived from the name of the Roman corn goddess, Ceres, and the latter derived in a slightly more light-hearted way from the word 'cereal' (which, of course, also has Ceres as its root).

The study of crop circles reached its peak during the late 1980s and early 1990s, but suffered a severe blow when hoaxers (such as DOUG AND DAVE) demonstrated how they could produce them – until then, there had been a wide range of popular theories, ranging from the action of fungi on the growing plants, through meteorological phenomena (such as the postulated PLASMA VORTEX) to the intervention of EXTRATERRESTRIALS. However, there is still a hard core of cereologists who maintain that hoaxing cannot account for all of the examples on record.

Cerne Abbas Giant
The giant figure of a man cut into a chalk hillside in Dorset.
Near Cerne Abbas in Dorset a figure of a man appears on a hillside, marked out by cutting through the grass and soil to expose the white chalk beneath. The man is of gigantic proportions, around 55 metres (180 feet) tall, brandishes a huge club 36.5 metres (120 feet) long, and is shown in a state of sexual arousal.

Different theories exist as to who created this image and why. The fact that such a striking and obvious landmark is not mentioned in any documents before the 17th century leads many to believe that it cannot have existed before then. They explain its creation as either a caricature lampooning Oliver Cromwell put there by the anti-Parliamentarian landowner, or as a kind of joke perpetrated by monks from a local religious house.

However, many landmarks and monuments that are known to be ancient go unmentioned in written records and those who argue for the figure's antiquity

An aerial view of the 55-metre-tall Cerne Abbas Giant, cut into a chalk hillside in Dorset. (© TopFoto/Fortean)

point out that an Iron Age earthwork has been found very close to the figure's head. A popular explanation is that the giant represents Hercules, who is often depicted in classical art as carrying a club, and that worship of the demigod came to the area along with the Romans, perhaps linking neatly with that of a local Celtic deity.

The giant's obvious virility led local people to ascribe fertility powers to it and local women hoping to conceive would spend the night there. It is a commonly believed myth that the scandalized Victorians covered up the offending member, and study has shown that the phallus has been cut to different lengths at different times, but the giant is now maintained in its full glory by the National Trust.

ceromancy
Divination by interpreting the shapes formed by melted wax.

Ceromancy (from the Greek *kēros*, wax, and *manteiā*, divination) is an ancient practice which some people believe originated in Russia in pre-Christian times. A question is asked and the patterns formed by melted candle wax are studied and interpreted as the answer. In one method, a taper candle is allowed to burn all the way down, and once the drippings have formed, they are examined for shapes which suggest a symbol to the observer. This method can also be used for a question with a yes/no answer; it is thought that if the wax drips mostly down the right side of the candle, the answer is yes, and if down the left, no. If it drips equally down both sides, or not at all, the question cannot be answered at that time and should be asked again later. In another method, the questioner holds a candle over a bowl of cold water which has first been stirred in a clockwise direction, and allows the wax from the candle to drip into the water while they think of their question. If the symbol formed by the wax breaks apart after forming, its meaning is modified. In either method, different colours of candle are traditionally used, depending on the subject of the question; for example, a red candle is thought to be best for questions about love and relationships, and a green candle for questions concerning money or work.

Some typical symbols and their interpretations are:

  a circle: reconciliation
  a cup: a bitter quarrel with a friend
  a feather: the solving of a problem
  a tree: a good time for new undertakings.

chakras
Energy centres believed to be situated at various points in the human body, which act as gateways through which universal life force can enter and leave the body. There are seven major chakras and many other minor chakras.

For thousands of years, the concept of UNIVERSAL LIFE FORCE or vital energy has been recognized in many cultures, along with the notion that a subtle energy surrounds and pervades the physical body, integrating the mind, body and spirit. In the Hindu belief system, the body is said to have seven major energy centres, often described as rotating or vibrating, which are called chakras (from the Sanskrit word for 'spinning wheel'), and these are seen as gateways through which this vital energy, known as prana, both enters and leaves the body. The earliest known mention of chakras is in the later Upanishads, although other Eastern traditions, such as CHINESE MEDICINE and Tibetan Buddhism, also have a similar concept.

The most well-known concept of chakras in the West is derived from the Tantric Shakta theory, which describes seven major chakras, although there are also said to be many smaller ones. These seven main chakras are vertically aligned up the centre of the body, from the base of the pelvis to the top of the head. Each chakra is said to vibrate or rotate at a different frequency, the highest at the fastest speed and the lowest at the slowest; each has its own individual characteristics and functions, and corresponds to a particular organ and body structure, to one of the endocrine glands, and to a colour of the spectrum. Each is also believed to be the centre of a particular mental, emotional or spiritual aspect, and through the network of the chakras, the mind, body and spirit are thought to interact as a holistic system.

The lowest chakra, the root chakra, is situated at the base of the spine, and its colour is red. It is the centre of physical vitality and the survival instinct, and corresponds to the adrenal glands and to the kidneys, bladder and spine. The next is the sexual or navel chakra, located slightly below the navel. Its colour is orange, and it is the centre of sexual energy and self-worth. Its gland is the gonads and it corresponds to the reproductive organs and legs. The third is the solar plexus chakra, and its colour is yellow. This is slightly above the navel, and is the centre of personal power, ego and passions. It corresponds to the pancreas, and to the stomach, liver and gall-bladder. Next is the heart chakra; its colour is green and it is the centre of unconditional affection, compassion, love and spiritual growth. It corresponds to the heart, liver, lungs and circulatory system. The fifth chakra is the throat chakra; it is blue and is the centre of communication, self-expression and creativity. It

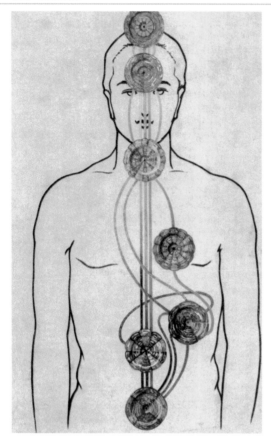

A diagram of the seven chakras, from Charles Leadbeater's *The Chakras* (1927). (© Mary Evans Picture Library)

gemstones in a colour corresponding to the affected chakra are also sometimes placed there to counteract energy blockages and imbalances.

chalices, suit of *see* CUPS, SUIT OF

Chalker, Bill (1952–)

Possibly the most celebrated UFO researcher in the southern hemisphere, Chalker has spent four decades collating alleged physical UFO evidence in Australia.

Bill Chalker studied mathematics and chemistry at the University of New England in New South Wales and has worked as an industrial chemist, bringing his expertise to bear on a wide range of UFO sightings where physical traces have reportedly been left behind. He has established a worldwide reputation through his lectures and papers for CUFOS and has written several books assessing the history of UFO cases in Australia. His research has included the so-called 'saucer nests' found in reed beds in Queensland from 1966 (similar in nature to the CROP CIRCLES popularized a decade later in the UK) which were matted circular patterns that had been connected with reports of objects seen rising from the location.

Chalker was also involved in the investigation of one of the oldest cases in the Australian archives. On 25 July 1868, according to words in his notebook, Frederick Birmingham of Parramatta Park, New South Wales, had a 'visionary' experience in his cottage, from which he saw a huge ark-like craft that:

> … moved through the air in a zig-zag fashion …
> [a voice then explained] that [it] is a machine to go through the air. Do you wish to enter upon it?

Birmingham reports entering a strange room and seeing a human 'spirit' who had papers filled with mathematical formulae that he was told he must learn. He then found himself coming round, his head filled with these strange images.

Chalker traced the notebook back to 1940 (before the birth of the modern UFO phenomenon) and found evidence for its having been handed down through several generations prior to that. The house really existed, as did the witness – he established that Birmingham was an engineer who lived in Parramatta between 1868 and 1873.

In 1982 Bill Chalker became the first UFO researcher to be offered direct access to government UFO records. At the onset of the Australian Freedom of Information Act he was invited to Canberra and allowed to scan the thousands of files from the Royal Australian Air Force, who had investigated official sighting reports since the 1950s. Chalker was encouraged by the Australian government to report

corresponds to the throat, upper lungs and digestive tract. The sixth is the third eye chakra, situated in the middle of the forehead, just above the eyebrows. It is purple, and is the centre of the will, intellect and spiritual awakening. Its gland is the pituitary, and it corresponds to the spine, lower brain, face and eyes. The highest chakra is the crown chakra, located at the top of the head. It is golden-white, and is the centre of spiritual enlightenment and the highest level of consciousness. It corresponds to the pineal gland and to the upper brain.

The chakras are said to regulate the energy system, and when they are in balance, they maintain a healthy mind, body and spirit. It is believed that if one chakra does not function correctly, it adversely affects the others, as well as the organs which it serves; the body's energy intake is unbalanced, and illness, physical or otherwise, may be the result. Various methods are used to re-balance the chakras and allow the body to return to normal, such as massage, breathing exercises, and YOGA techniques. CRYSTALS or on his findings to the UFO community in an attempt to deter an anticipated flood of requests from other enthusiasts. Although he found no dramatic proof in these records, there were many puzzling cases, and some hints that there had been co-operation with the CIA in America.

chalk figures
Giant figures created on hillsides by cutting away turf to reveal the chalk beneath.
In the south of England several hillsides are adorned by giant figures, mostly those of horses, 'drawn' by cutting lines through the turf to expose the chalk underneath. Famous examples include the CERNE ABBAS GIANT in Dorset and the UFFINGTON WHITE HORSE in Oxfordshire. Various claims are made as to the age of many of these chalk or hill figures. While the Uffington White Horse is now generally accepted as belonging to the Bronze Age (although it was traditionally believed to have been executed to commemorate Alfred the Great's victory over the Danes at nearby Edington), some argue that the Cerne Abbas Giant is only a few hundred years old.

Certainly, the cutting of chalk figures as some form of commemoration is a long-established activity, perhaps because it is relatively easy to perform and the contrast of the white figures against the green turf is a striking one, although one which requires maintenance. In the 19th century particularly there seems to have been something of a craze among southern English landowners, especially in Wiltshire, for the cutting of white horses, such as those at Alton Barnes and Broad Town. During World War I soldiers exercising on Salisbury Plain often carved their regimental badges into the turf and as recently as 1999 a white horse was created at Devizes to mark the millennium.

Some of the figures that we see now have been radically changed in the years since they were first documented: at Westbury White Horse in Wiltshire, the realistic 'modern' horse was cut in 1778, replacing an earlier design; it was reshaped again in 1873, and in the 20th century the horse was concreted and painted white to reduce the maintenance required.

As far as genuinely ancient chalk figures are concerned, there are various theories about their meaning. Some suggest that they represent local gods, the horse in particular being sacred to Celtic peoples, and played some part in religious observances. The fact that they are often best observed from the air lends credence to the idea that they were intended to be seen by heavenly eyes. Another explanation is that they are symbols of the tribes that created them and are a means of asserting ownership of areas of land.

In later times, many chalk figures were maintained by local people ('scouring' the chalk areas to keep them white and trimming back encroaching grass) long after their origins were forgotten. Some, particularly the Cerne Abbas Giant, became associated with fertility rites and traditional folk beliefs. On the other hand, some chalk figures whose existence was recorded in documents were allowed to become overgrown and lost.

Champ *see* LAKE CHAMPLAIN MONSTER

Chance and Coincidence *see panel p106*

changeling
In folklore, a fairy baby substituted for a kidnapped human child.
One of the oldest traditions of European fairy lore is the tendency for fairies to steal human babies and leave a substitute in their place. Various tales suggest that many fairy children die before they are born, and that those which do survive are often feeble, stunted or deformed. A healthy human baby may be stolen to reinforce the fairy stock and revive their dwindling race, and the sickly fairy baby, called a changeling, is left in its place. Babies most at risk are those who have not yet been christened, and whose parents have not taken adequate precautions, such as leaving something made of iron, for example a set of tongs or a knife, in the cradle – an infallible protection against fairies, who cannot bear iron. The changeling is usually identifiable by its ill temper, ugliness and voracious appetite; no matter how much it is fed, it always wants more, but remains scrawny and weak. It may have some physical deformity, such as a crooked back, and will grow a full set of teeth long before a human child would, by its first birthday or even earlier. Alternatively, the fairies may leave a piece of wood called a 'stock', shaped roughly like a child and endowed with the appearance of life, or an ancient and wizened fairy of no further use to its tribe, who prefers a cosseted life being fed by its human 'mother'.

If the changeling can be made to reveal its true nature in time, the fairies must return the human child unharmed. In some tales, a baby that was suspected of being a changeling would be deliberately tortured so that its fairy parents would take it back; one popular method was to place it on a shovel and hold it over a fire. If the changeling was an old fairy, he might be tricked into revealing his true age by various ploys, the favourite being to boil water in eggshells so that he would say something like, 'I have lived many hundreds of years, but I have never seen brewing in an eggshell before!' When a changeling has

Chance and Coincidence

Chance and coincidence are quite different things, although the usages of the words sometimes overlap.

A 'chance' tends to mean both the *possibility* of something happening and the *probability* or likelihood of it happening, depending on context.

A 'coincidence' is, simply, two or more things happening at the same locality in time or space. Sometimes, in human perception, a coincidence may seem more than a mere chance happening because it acquires a specific meaning for the observer, and it may play a significant role in conditioning the further perception of more events which confirm the pattern or meaning. An example of this is given in an Episcopalian bishop's very personal account of his psychical experiences: in *On the other Side* (1970), Bishop James A Pike tells how the suicide, in 1966, of his son Jim affected him deeply. He became a supporter of SPIRITUALISM and, for a while, became convinced Jim was trying to communicate with him from the AFTERLIFE. On separate occasions, he found an open book, two postcards and a bent safety pin, each open at an angle that corresponded to the time of his son's death.

Another well-known example, from Swiss psychologist CARL JUNG, underlines the sense of 'meaningfulness'. A woman patient told him of a dream in which she was given a golden scarab. As she described it, Jung heard a tapping at the window behind him and saw an insect outside, knocking against the glass. He opened the window and caught the creature as it flew in. To his great surprise he found it was a scarab-like beetle – a rose-chafer (*Cetonia aurata*) – 'which contrary to its usual habits had evidently felt an urge to get into a dark room at this particular moment'. This incident happened early in Jung's career, probably in the 1920s, and led to a successful analysis of the dream and help for the patient. He included it in the first publication, in 1951, of his theory of coincidences, *Synchronicity: An Acausal Connecting Principle*.

The more meaningful a coincidence, the rarer it is deemed by those it influences. Sceptics, such as members of the 'humanist' school of the US organization COMMITTEE FOR THE SCIENTIFIC INVESTIGATION OF CLAIMS OF THE PARANORMAL (CSICOP), would have us believe that the number of events that are happening at any given moment, from the simple and minute to the most complex and universal, is so vast that the probability of some of them being 'coincidences' is itself very large. Dr Robert Carroll's *Skeptical Dictionary* presents a statistical argument for this so-called 'law of very large numbers'. For example, 'at a typical football game with 50,000 fans, most fans are likely to share their birthday with about 135 others in attendance'. Even more impressive is the statement that, 'In a random selection of twenty-three persons there is a 50 per cent chance that at least two of them celebrate the same birthdate'. These sceptics use the same logic to dismiss a range of paranormal topics, including precognitive DREAMS ('with over 6 billion people on earth having an average of 250 dream themes each per night there should be about 1.5 million people a day who have dreams that seem clairvoyant' – for example, that correspond with a plane crash the next day); claims that certain NUMBERS encapsulate or encode messages or relate to specific events or conspiracies; and the notorious 'talk-of-the-devil' effect that most of us are familiar with.

Sceptics have sought further explanations for 'meaningful coincidences' in a number of psychological theories. 'Confirmation bias' refers to selective perception, whereby things are only noticed because they conform to, or accord with, one's belief or preoccupation. Those that don't are ignored, so each successive positive occurrence reinforces the belief. Belief in lucky numbers tends to work like this. When US author Alan Vaughn was working on his 1979 book *Incredible Coincidences*, he wrote, 'The more I focused on SYNCHRONICITY, the more it began happening.' This effect is quite familiar to most writer-researchers and is referred to as 'the library angel'.

Two more psychological terms that may be applied to the perceptions of 'meaningful coincidences' seem to overlap. Perceptions of significant connections between spontaneous and seemingly unrelated phenomena have been called 'apophenia'. In the

A contemporary illustration of the French astronomer Camille Flammarion in his study, from the journal *Science Illustré* (January 1894). (© Mary Evans Picture Library)

example given above, it is entirely possible that Bishop Pike was rendered susceptible to apophenia by his grief – but this does not detract from fact that, for him, such coincidences were full of personal meaning. 'Pareidolia' describes the condition in which perceptions involving vague stimuli can be overlaid with distinct meaning or details because of suggestion or beliefs. Pareidolia is frequently described as an ILLUSION or misperception in the psychological literature because the percipient is reading more into the perception than it originally provides; for example, it is employed deliberately during the Roschach 'ink blot' test to assess an individual's powers of association. Some CSICOP sceptics have seriously maintained that many of the topics of FORTEANA (including sightings such as those of UFOs, Elvis, BIGFOOT, MARIAN APPARITIONS, the MARTIAN FACE and the figure of Jesus in a mould stain, and messages such as those discerned when music is played backwards) can all be explained by pareidolia.

Nevertheless, impressive coincidences happen that seem to defy the narrow materialist view of some sceptics. The chances (odds) of being hit by a meteorite are said to be billions to one (calculations are varied and arbitrary) – but reports of 'close shaves' or non-lethal hits may be reported several times a year. Sometimes the odds can seem incredible, as in an example provided by the French astronomer Camille Flammarion. He had been working on a chapter on the force of winds for his great work *L'Atmosphere* (1888), when a gust of wind carried his papers out of the window and beyond recovery. A few days later, he received the proof of that chapter from the publisher, with the missing section intact and in situ. On inquiry, he learned that the messenger from the publisher had been walking down a street when the 'miniature whirlwind' deposited the recently abducted papers at his feet. He had picked them up under the impression that he had dropped them.

Such improbable events also happen in everyday lives. In 1967, an Essex police station was given a new telephone number. Peter Moscardi, who was stationed there, gave the number to a friend, but inadvertently got it wrong. Several days later, while patrolling an industrial estate, he found the door to a factory open and a light on. As he investigated the empty building, an office phone rang. He answered it and found it was his friend wanting to speak to him. Examining the phone, he found it had the number he had given to his friend, not the correct number for the police station. Later he learned that the factory manager had forgotten that night to lock up the building, something that had never happened before.

The puzzle underlying coincidences interested the US philosopher CHARLES FORT, who wrote:

> My liveliest interest is not so much in things, as in the relation of things. I have spent much time thinking about the alleged pseudo-relations that are called coincidences. What if some of them should not be coincidences?

Fort was referring to his own theory of Continuity in which all things are connected or continuous, only seeming to be separate to our limited senses. This would imply that the seemingly unconnected items gained their meaningful associations through being simultaneous projections or manifestations of an 'underlying oneness', rather than through the meaning read into their coincidence by the observer. Fort's notion of 'connectedness', or Continuity, was similar to (but less tied to individual perception than) the position of Carl Jung, who was quite clear that meaningful coincidences sprang from a common ground that he called the COLLECTIVE UNCONSCIOUS. To some extent, Fort believed that all events and things are 'coincidences', but in his view, each of them is an expression of an intermediate position between two or more opposing absolutes (see FORTEANISM). Another theory of coincidences, which was very similar to Jung's, was put forward by the Austrian biologist Paul Kammerer, who labelled it 'seriality'. From a study of his own 'coincidence diaries', he wrote, 'Seriality is ubiquitous and continuous in life, nature and cosmos' – coincidentally, in 1919, the same year that Fort was writing.

Bob Rickard

been forced to reveal its fairy nature, it will disappear up the chimney, cursing, and the real baby will be restored, being found at the door, in its cradle or at the nearest fairy mound. See also FAIRIES.

channelling

The process whereby a spirit apparently communicates through a human medium.

Channelling involves a person (usually described as a MEDIUM) being willingly possessed by a SPIRIT, and allowing the spirit to communicate through them. Channelling was popular within the SPIRITUALISM movement in the Victorian era. This alleged phenomenon came to modern prominence in 1963 when Jane Roberts claimed to have been possessed by a spirit called Seth and dictated a book to her husband, Robert Butts, supposedly under its guidance. In 1970 they published *The Seth Material*, which popularized this form of spirit communication. With the death of Jane Roberts in 1984, Seth apparently started to speak through Jean Loomis. Other celebrated channelled spirits include John (co-creator of the world with God), Ramtha (a 35,000-year-old Cro-Magnon warrior), Buddha, Vishnu, Jesus Christ (see *A COURSE IN MIRACLES*) and Mark Twain. All are apparently interested in the welfare of humans and generally preach that love and understanding is the way forward.

HARRY HOUDINI spent much of his later life debunking PSYCHICS and channellers. Houdini believed that channellers employed standard stage magicians' techniques such as cold reading (giving out general statements and then adapting the next piece based on the reaction of the audience member) or hot reading (gaining knowledge of the person who is having the reading carried out, without their knowledge).

Practices that might be described as channelling also form a part of many religious belief systems. It can be seen as essentially a similar phenomenon to benign POSSESSION. See also AUTOMATISM.

chaos magic *see* MAGIC, CHAOS

Charbel Makhlouf, St (1828–98)

Lebanese Christian saint to whom miracles are attributed.

Joseph Zaroun Makhlouf was born in Lebanon, the son of a mule driver. He was a pious youth, but it was not until he was 23 that he joined a Baladite monastery. He assumed the name of Charbel, a 2nd-century Christian martyr.

In imitation of the desert fathers he admired, he lived as a hermit for the last 23 years of his life, gaining a reputation for holiness and healing, and was said to levitate while praying; he was known as 'the hermit of Lebanon'. After his death several MIRACLES were attributed to him, among which was the emergence in 1927, and again in 1950, of bloody sweat from his body, which was collected and used in miraculous cures. A nun suffering from a crippling intestinal disorder was said to have been cured by the act of praying at his graveside.

His tomb soon became a place of pilgrimage. The grave has been opened several times and each time his body was said to have remained incorrupt (see INCORRUPTIBILITY).

In 1965 he was beatified by Pope Paul VI, who subsequently canonized him in 1977.

Chariots of the Gods *see* DÄNIKEN, ERICH VON

charms

A magical spell chanted or recited, or an amulet or talisman magically empowered by such a spell.

Throughout history, people in every culture have sought to protect themselves from danger or to gain some control over their lives or those of others by supernatural means, and charms have been used for a wide range of magical purposes since ancient times. Strictly speaking, a charm is a magic spell chanted or recited to bring about a desired effect; the word comes from the French *charme*, from the Latin *carmen*, a song. However, 'charm' has also over time come to be used to refer to an object which has been magically empowered by such a spell, for example an AMULET or TALISMAN. A spoken charm may consist of a word, phrase, formula or prayer, is usually short, and frequently in rhyme, since this makes it easier to remember, and often includes a mention of the spell's purpose; in WICCA, it is traditionally repeated three, seven or nine times, three being the most usual number – once to declare the intent of the magic and summon the required spiritual assistance, once to banish any unwanted energies, and once to magically charge the physical object or the person for whom the charm is being performed, and to seal the spell. The words of the charm, as well as being spoken, may be written or inscribed on paper, parchment, wood or other material and worn as an amulet, and can be repeated regularly over the charmed object to strengthen its influence and the magical intent.

Charms may be used for protection against evil, for health, to gain money, luck or love, to ensure fertility or potency, to gain power over an enemy or curse them, and in agricultural communities, to protect crops and livestock, or to get rid of pests. Practitioners of magic frequently recite charms when gathering herbs for sacred or medicinal purposes, or consecrating ritual objects. Once a charm is no longer required, it should be ritually burned or buried, not simply thrown away.

One of the best-known charms, which survives to this day as a catchphrase of stage magicians and conjurers, is the word *abracadabra*. Thought to date back to 2nd-century Rome, the word was historically used as a healing charm; it was written on a piece of paper or parchment or inscribed on a metal amulet in a series of decreasing lines, with one letter being removed from the beginning on each line, and it was believed that as the word decreased, so would the illness.

Cheese Well

A spring on the hillside at Minchmuir in Peeblesshire, Scotland, at which passers-by traditionally leave an offering of cheese for the fairies.

There are a number of sites all over Britain which it is considered unlucky to pass without performing some ceremony or making an offering to appease the FAIRIES who live there. In folklore, fairies are believed to have a special fondness for dairy products such as cream and cheese, and on the hillside at Minchmuir in Peeblesshire, there is a small freshwater spring known as the Cheese Well, where passers-by traditionally leave offerings of cheese to ensure the goodwill of the fairies. This site was once located on an ancient drove road between Traquair and Selkirk, and as such, would have formerly enjoyed more frequent traffic than it does now; it may have been a pagan shrine in ancient days, whose original function was forgotten but which retained enough mystery to have become the focus of local superstition. In the 1960s, two stones were placed beside the well, one shaped like an old gravestone and inscribed 'Cheese Well', and the other shaped like a kite and inscribed with a thistle. The Cheese Well fairies are mentioned by Sir Walter Scott in his *Minstrelsy of the Scottish Border* (1802–3).

Cheiro (1866–1936)

Pseudonym of the Irish palmist and clairvoyant William John Warner, better known as Count Louis Hamon, one of the most famous and colourful occult figures of the early 20th century.

Born in or near Dublin, Ireland, in 1866, William John Warner claimed to be the son of a Greek nobleman, Count William de Hamon, and to have been kidnapped as a child by Gypsies who wished to exploit his clairvoyant gifts. No evidence exists to support his story, but after moving to England, where according to one account he worked for a while as a stage hand, he established himself in London and embarked on what was to become a

highly successful career as a psychic. He adopted the professional pseudonym of Cheiro, from the Greek word *kheir*, meaning hand, and using a combination of ASTROLOGY, NUMEROLOGY and, in particular, character analysis and predictive PALMISTRY – all of which he said he had studied in India – he operated for many years from an exclusive address in London's West End. His dazzling list of clients came from all over Europe and America, and included such celebrities as Mark Twain, Sarah Bernhardt, Oscar Wilde, Thomas Edison, William Gladstone, Mata Hari and the Prince of Wales. He toured the major cities of the world, lecturing, and wrote a number of books, two of which continue to be used by modern palmists: *Language of the Hand* and *Palmistry for All*; in 1925 he also wrote *Cheiro's World Predictions*. He is said to have successfully predicted many world events, such as the dates of both Queen Victoria's and King Edward VII's deaths, the fate of the tsar of Russia and his family, the date and manner of death of England's Lord Kitchener, the Boer War and the abdication of the then Prince of Wales, later King Edward VIII, so that he could marry for love.

In 1930 Cheiro moved to the USA, settling in Hollywood, where he continued to see as many as 20 clients a day. Under another name, he is also, in his Hollywood years, said to have written screenplays for a time. He died in 1936, but his legacy is still acknowledged by palmists today.

Chesed

In the kabbalah, the sephirah or emanation of God known as Mercy or Love, which is assigned the number 4; it represents God's infinite mercy in pouring his energy into creation.

Chesed, also known as Gedulah, is the fourth of the ten SEPHIROTH, or Divine emanations, in the KABBALAH. It is called Mercy or Love, and is the first of the emotive attributes of the sephiroth. It emanates from BINAH, and represents God's infinite mercy in pouring his energy into creation. From it proceed all the spiritual virtues. It is assigned the number 4. On the kabbalistic TREE OF LIFE, it is positioned directly below CHOKMAH, directly opposite GEBURAH, with which it has a polarized relationship, and directly above NETZACH. Chesed is the first point on the middle triangle on the Tree of Life, the Moral or Ethical Triangle, which it forms with Geburah and TIPHARETH, and it is also the second sphere on the right-hand axis, the Pillar of Mercy, to which it gives its name. It is the sphere of archetypal ideas, and is usually given four paths on the Tree of Life, to Chokmah, Geburah, Tiphareth and Netzach. It is associated with the Divine name *El*, meaning 'Lord', the archangel Tzadkiel, the angelic order of the Chasmalim, and the planetary force of Jupiter. In the TAROT, Chesed corresponds to the four fours, and in the tarot Tree of Life spread, the card in the Chesed position usually represents worldly gains, and sometimes also the ways in which these gains will affect the person. In some kabbalistic systems it is attributed with the magical image of a crowned and throned king, and is represented by various symbols, such as a tetrahedron, an orb, a wand, a pyramid, a sceptre or a crook. It is often connected with the heart CHAKRA. The word Chesed in kabbalistic GEMATRIA gives the number 72, or 2×6^2, which represents perfect love and harmony within creation; THE ZOHAR speaks of 72 'bridges' of love (corresponding to the 72 hidden names of God) which connect all of created reality in perfect harmony. Chesed is sometimes also referred to as Majesty or Magnificence.

chi *see* QI

ch'i kung *see* QIGONG

Chinese medicine
A complete medical system with its origins in the traditions of ancient China and other Eastern countries, which focuses on the maintenance of health by a balancing of the body's energies, and uses such techniques as acupuncture, exercise, diet programmes and Chinese herbal remedies.

The full name for Chinese medicine is traditional Chinese medicine, often abbreviated to TCM. This is a range of medical practices which has developed over nearly 5,000 years in China, and which is still an integral part of the healthcare system in mainland China and Taiwan today. It has its origins in several related healing traditions not only in China, but also in Japan, Korea and parts of South East Asia. Unlike the indigenous medical practices of most other parts of the world, Chinese medicine has not been supplanted by Western medical practices, but is used side by side with Western techniques; the term is often used to refer specifically to a standardized set of theories and practices introduced to China under the government of Mao, when, in response to the health needs of the country's huge population, the Chinese communist government adopted a programme to integrate rural Chinese medicine into their Western-type modern hospitals.

The oldest known medical text is believed to be the *Huang Di Nei Jing Su Wen*, or *The Yellow Emperor's Classic of Chinese Medicine*, which is thought to date back to the final centuries BC, but remains the most influential work on Chinese medicine. Chinese

Herbal remedies being prepared in a traditional Chinese pharmacy. (© Bob Krist/Corbis)

medicine was developed as a non-invasive form of therapy, and is mainly rooted in the ancient belief system of TAOISM. The focus of Chinese medicine is on the maintenance of health and the prevention of illness, rather than on the treatment of symptoms and diseases. The system encompasses physical, emotional and psychological healing as well as preventive health care, and is based on the Confucian-Taoist theory that all things, including human beings, must be in balance, and that the body is a universe in miniature, with a set of integrated systems which work to maintain wellbeing. The body is believed to require a balance of YIN and YANG energy in order to function properly; if these are in balance, the body has a natural ability to resist and recover from disease. An imbalance of yin and yang in some part of the body leads to an excess, deficiency or blockage of the UNIVERSAL LIFE FORCE known as QI, which is thought to circulate in the body along channels known as MERIDIANS, and a disruption in the flow of qi results in physical or emotional symptoms which ultimately lead to illness. Health is therefore best maintained by identifying an imbalance and correcting it before it becomes an illness, and various conditions are treated by regulating and rebalancing the flow of qi, rather than by addressing only the symptoms.

Chinese medicine is said to rest on five pillars: ACUPUNCTURE; diet and nutrition – certain foods are considered to be predominantly either yin or yang, so that a person diagnosed as having too much yin may be prescribed yang foods to restore their yin-yang balance; exercise programmes such as T'AI CHI or QIGONG, stress reduction and lifestyle counselling; massage, which is designed to relax and heal the body and release toxins from the tissues; and traditional Chinese herbal remedies, although these are avoided if possible, since the emphasis is on helping the body to restore its self-healing function rather than interfering with it. In a typical consultation, the practitioner will question the patient in detail about all aspects of their health, family history, lifestyle and diet, emotional state, and work and home environment, and will also analyse their pulse closely, examine the colour and condition of their tongue and palpate parts of their body, particularly the acupuncture points. The imbalance is then diagnosed, and treatment prescribed.

Chinese medicine is said to be most effective in treating conditions such as lower back pain, muscular pain and cramps, headaches (including migraine), nausea, withdrawal symptoms during recovery from addiction, and paralysis. It is fast gaining popularity in the West as an alternative medicine, and the potential value of its traditional herbal remedies is now being investigated by Western pharmaceutical companies.

Chingle Hall

Reputed to be the oldest brick house in Britain, Chingle Hall in Cheshire attracted the epithet 'most haunted house in England' during the 1990s.

The manor house of Chingle Hall in Cheshire was one of a number of sites promoted as the most haunted house in England during the 1990s. Said to date back to 1260, the house is reputedly haunted by a phantom monk (see BLACK MONK), unusual temperature variations and unexplained footsteps. There are many stories of investigators hearing strange noises in the hall, or experiencing camera malfunctions or equipment breakdowns while carrying out their work. In recent years some owners have sought to make money from the reputation of the house by charging individuals and groups to spend a night there, and charity events have also taken place at the house. See also BORLEY RECTORY; HAUNTINGS.

chirognomy

The reading of a person's character by inspecting the size, shape and appearance of their hands.

PALMISTRY is divided into three main subsets: CHIROMANCY, which involves studying the lines and markings on a person's hands; dermatoglyphics, the study and interpretation of the fingerprints; and chirognomy (from the Greek *cheir*, hand, and *gnōmē*, understanding) or chirology, in which a person's character is read from the size, shape and appearance of the hands and fingers.

Palmists divide hand shapes into several basic types, each of which is considered to indicate particular character traits. One popular system classifies the hand into seven types: Elementary, Square, Spatulate, Philosophic, Conic, Psychic and Mixed. In traditional Chinese palmistry there are five hand types that correspond to the five elements of water, fire, wood, earth and metal. The simplest classification reflects the four elemental categories used in western astrology, EARTH, AIR, FIRE and WATER:

A hand with a square palm and short fingers is linked with the earth element, and the astrological signs of TAURUS, VIRGO and CAPRICORN. People with this hand shape are thought to be practical, hard-working, honest and down-to-earth.

A hand with a long palm and short fingers is linked with the element of fire, and the signs of LEO, ARIES and SAGITTARIUS, and the qualities of energy, restlessness and intuition.

A hand with a long palm and long fingers is associated with the element of water, and the signs of CANCER, SCORPIO and PISCES, and a person with this hand shape is thought to be sensitive, emotional and imaginative.

A hand with a square palm and long fingers is

linked with the air element, and the signs of GEMINI, LIBRA and AQUARIUS, and indicates a person who is intellectual, clever and forward-thinking.

The shape of the thumb and fingers of each hand are often read separately.

chirology *see* CHIROGNOMY

chiromancy

The reading of a person's future by inspecting and interpreting the lines, marks and bumps on their hands.
PALMISTRY is divided into three main subsets: CHIROGNOMY or chirology, in which a person's character is read from the size, shape and general appearance of their hands; dermatoglyphics, the study and interpretation of the fingerprints; and chiromancy (from the Greek *cheir*, hand, and *manteiã*, divination), in which the person's future is read by studying the lines and markings on their palms.

The hand with which the subject writes is known as the dominant hand, and the other as the destiny hand. The lines on the dominant hand are thought to represent the person's conscious self, and to reflect the changes in behaviour, attitude, lifestyle and experiences they have undergone. This is believed to be the reason why the lines on the dominant hand change much more during the course of life than those on the destiny hand, which is thought to reflect the person's potential at birth, their subconscious self, and their future. Both hands are therefore studied in order to get a reading of the whole person and their destiny.

The lines in the hand can be divided into three main groups: major lines, minor lines and personal lines. The major lines are the best known, and consist of the Life line, which indicates not the length of the subject's life, as is popularly believed, but their vitality, enthusiasm for life and state of health; the Head line, which relates to the subject's mental capacity and intellect; and the Heart line, which reveals a person's way of relating to others, their sensitivity and their emotions. Most hands contain all three major lines, but sometimes the Head and Heart lines are combined in a single line, known as the Simian line, which is thought to indicate that the subject's emotional and mental functions do not operate separately, and that, as a result, the person has an intense temperament.

The minor lines run vertically on the hand, and some hands may have more minor lines than others. Each minor line is named after the planet which is believed to rule the finger under which the line terminates, and the presence or absence of a minor line, and the way it appears, is taken as an indication of a different characteristic. For instance, a hand which shows the Line of Apollo (a minor line running under the ring finger) is believed to signify artistic talent.

The personal lines are very specific to the individual; some have names and fit into categories, while others are unique to that hand, and are only generally interpreted by someone who claims to be a highly skilled reader.

Also considered to be of importance are the mounts of the hand – the raised pads at the base of each finger and situated around the palm. The hand has seven mounts: the Mounts of Jupiter, Saturn, Apollo, Mercury, the Moon, Venus and Mars. Each has its own interpretation, according to its shape; for example, the Mount of Jupiter at the base of the first finger, when well developed, is believed to reveal an ambitious nature. See also PALMISTRY.

Chokmah

In the kabbalah, the sephirah or emanation of God known as Wisdom, which is assigned the number 2 and represents intuitive awareness and truth.
Chokmah is the second of the ten SEPHIROTH, or Divine emanations, in the KABBALAH. It is called Wisdom, and denotes intuitive awareness and truth, the first power of the conscious intellect within creation. It is assigned the number 2. It represents the archetypal powers of maleness. On the kabbalistic TREE OF LIFE, it is the first intermediate step between KETHER and the rest of the sephiroth; it emanates from Kether and is positioned beneath and to the right of it, and is the second point of the highest triangle formed by the sephiroth, the Supernal Triangle, which it makes up with Kether and BINAH. It is also is the highest sphere on the right-hand axis, the Pillar of Mercy. It is in a polarized relationship with Binah, and is usually given four paths on the Tree of Life, to Kether, Binah, CHESED and TIPHARETH. It is associated with the Divine name *Jehovah* or *Jah*, the archangel Ratziel, the angelic order of the Auphanim and the planetary force of the ZODIAC. In the TAROT, Chokmah corresponds to the four twos, and in the tarot Tree of Life spread, the card in the Chokmah position usually represents the creative intelligence and the way in which a person moves toward their goal of highest development. In some kabbalistic systems it is attributed with the magical image of a bearded male figure, and is represented by several symbols: a phallus, a standing stone and a straight line. It is often connected with the Anja or 'third eye' CHAKRA. The word Chokmah in kabbalistic GEMATRIA gives the number 73. Chokmah is sometimes also referred to as The Supernal Father, The Power of Yetzirah, Ab or Abba, Tetragrammaton or the Yod of Tetragrammaton.

Christian Science

A metaphysical religious system based on spiritual healing through prayer, founded by Mary Baker Eddy in 1866.

Christian Science was founded in 1866 by MARY BAKER EDDY, who claimed to have been miraculously cured of a severe injury after reading and pondering the meaning of the New Testament passage in which Christ heals a man afflicted by palsy. Believing that she had been healed by the same method used by Christ, she embarked on a study of the Bible, and developed her discoveries into the spiritual and metaphysical healing system which she called Christian Science. She began to teach her healing method, and in 1875 published *Science and Health With Key to the Scriptures*, which remains the primary text of Christian Science. In 1879 she founded the Church of Christ, Scientist, in Boston; Christian Scientists are usually, but not always, members of this Church.

Christian Science teaches that the material world is an illusion caused by our misperception of the true and wholly perfect spiritual world, and that man is an expression of a perfect, good and loving God, in whom illness cannot exist. Illness in man is therefore also regarded as an illusion, caused by faulty beliefs, fear, ignorance or sin, which, by PRAYER, can be replaced with true spiritual ideas – substituting trust in an all-loving God for fear, an understanding of one's identity as a reflection of God for ignorance, and abandoning sin. According to Christian Science, suffering only occurs for as long as it is believed that the illness is real, but by the re-orientation of thought, that is, by prayer, it is possible to reach the understanding that the apparent illness is not real, thereby robbing it of its power and eliminating it. Christian Scientists believe that Christ healed by this method of 'spiritualization of thought', and that the Christian faith requires demonstration in healing; their aim is therefore to reinstate the element of healing by prayer which they believe has been lost since early Christianity. By a scientific study of the Bible, particularly Christ's works and words, they claim that one can learn to heal, and that this healing is a natural result of drawing nearer to God.

Christ in the Snow

A photograph showing an image of Christ which has appeared, with varying accounts of how it came to be taken, in a number of reports over many decades.

Since the early 20th century, the same image of Christ in the pose of the Sacred Heart (right hand raised, left hand clutching his robe) has appeared in magazines and newspapers and on the Internet. Each time it is accompanied by a story relating how it was accidentally taken or spontaneously appeared on the camera film.

The photograph has attracted the title 'Christ in the Snow' because more recent versions of the story generally claim that the image appeared when a photograph was being taken of a snow scene. It is suggested that this is due to the fact that the picture has now been copied so many times that the loss of detail makes it appear to comprise white areas of melting snow and black areas of exposed earth.

The origin of the photograph is not certain. It has been attributed to a Mrs Mildred Swanson of Seattle, USA, who was trying to photograph her daughter in 1920, when the camera shutter clicked by itself. A later version of this same story gives the date as 1937 and the location as Winnipeg, Canada. It has also been claimed that it was taken in the trenches in France during World War I. On 10 October 1958 a copy of the picture appeared in the British newspaper the *Sunday People* with the explanation that it had been taken from an aeroplane flying over the Alps.

Although in each case the pictures can clearly be shown to be copies derived from a much clearer original (albeit of mysterious provenance), versions of the picture can still regularly be seen for sale on the Internet. See also IMAGES, SPONTANEOUS.

Chronovisor

A machine purported to have been made by Italian priest Father Pellegrino Ernetti which enabled its operator to view events from the past.

Father Ernetti (1925–94) was an Italian Benedictine monk and a great scholar who, among other things, was an expert in archaic music, held a degree in quantum and subatomic physics and was in great demand as an exorcist. However, in the mid-1950s, Father Ernetti claimed he had produced a machine, which he called the Chronovisor, that could, perhaps, best be described as a 'time camera'.

The Chronovisor was never displayed to the public and no photographs or plans have ever been seen. Ernetti's own account of the full details of his machine's invention and use was only made public in 1993 in a book by the French Jesuit priest Father François Brune, *En Direct de l'Au-Delà* ('Live from the Hereafter', written with Rémy Chauvin). It was said to have consisted of a number of antennae which had direction-finding and recording apparatus attached to them. It could supposedly be tuned in to a particular person, time or place. Ernetti claimed that the Chronovisor was the result of research carried out by him and a group of twelve anonymous scientists, letting slip that two of these were the physicist Enrico Fermi and the rocket scientist Werner von Braun.

After a number of tests, including supposedly using the machine to watch speeches by Mussolini, Napoleon and Cicero, Ernetti attracted public attention by claiming that he had used the Chronovisor to watch the lost Quintus Ennius tragedy *Thyestes* being performed in Rome in 169 BC. Further than this, as proof, he produced a manuscript of the lost play, which he said he had transcribed from these sessions. This text was discredited many years later by US classicist Katherine Owen Eldred, who pointed out a number of inconsistencies, such as the overuse of certain words implying a limited Latin vocabulary on the part of its author, and the use of anachronistic language.

Ernetti's most extravagant and controversial claim, however, was that he had tuned in to, and witnessed, the crucifixion of Christ. On 2 May 1972 a photograph of the face of the dying Christ, purportedly taken with the aid of the Chronovisor, was published in the Italian newspaper *Domenica del Corriere*. Shortly after publication, it was pointed out that the picture was an exact mirror image of a close-up photograph of a wooden crucifix available for sale in the gift shop of the Sanctuary of Merciful Love at Collevalenza (near Perugia). This inevitably brought with it a certain amount of ridicule and opened up a debate as to whether the Chronovisor story was a PIOUS FRAUD concocted by Ernetti or whether he was simply a victim of a minor fabrication which grew out of control. Indeed, there is a disputed claim that on his deathbed he admitted that, although he had worked on the Chronovisor for many years, it had never worked.

Despite the convincing challenges to Ernetti's controversial claims, there are still many people who believe that some form of time machine was produced – pointing out that, as an accomplished academic, he had no reason to fabricate such a wild story and suggesting that he was prevented from defending himself adequately during his lifetime. Some allege that his machine is still secretly in the possession of the Vatican where, depending on their point of view, it is being held for either benevolent or sinister reasons.

Chupacabras *see panel p116*

Church and School of Wicca
The oldest federally recognized church of witchcraft in the USA.
The Church and School of Wicca was founded in 1968 by Gavin and Yvonne Frost. The school was founded alongside the church to offer correspondence courses on WITCHCRAFT and a wide range of other related subjects. The Frosts worked extensively in the early years to gain federal recognition of witchcraft as a religion, finally achieving this in 1972. In the 1980s they went on to establish that WICCA was a religion

equal to any other, meaning that, among other things, individual Wiccan churches do not have to disclose financial information to the IRS.

Gavin Frost came from a Welsh family and many of the church's beliefs are drawn from the Welsh Celtic tradition. The beliefs and practices of the church were outlined in a controversial book entitled *The Witch's Bible* (1972, since updated and re-issued as *The Good Witch's Bible*). They do not place the same emphasis on nature worship and on worshiping THE GODDESS as many other neopagans – indeed, although the Frosts consider themselves to be WITCHES they do not consider themselves to be pagans. The church's ethical position is summarized in their version of the Wiccan Rede (essentially the rule that governs their behaviour):

> If it harm none, do what you will.

In addition to this there are four other basic tenets of the church, summarized as: The Law of Attraction, Harmony and Serenity, Power through Knowledge, and Progressive Reincarnation. Members of the church observe the four major and the four minor SABBATS.

The Church has attracted a certain amount of controversy over the years and, in particular, they have been criticized by some for appearing to advocate practices that could be considered paedophilic and incestuous. See also NEOPAGANISM; PAGANISM.

Churchill, Sir Winston Leonard Spencer (1874–1965)
British Prime Minister during World War II, widely believed to be the original driving force behind government UFO investigation in the UK.
After reported sightings of AIRSHIPS over Kent in October 1912, the then admiral of the fleet, Winston Churchill, told the British parliament that the craft being seen were definitely not of British origin and they constituted a risk of invasion from Germany. The investigation that followed was effectively the first ever government UFO study, although the UFO phenomenon in its modern guise would not appear for a further three decades.

Forty years later, while Churchill was serving his final term as prime minister, strange lights in the sky were making the headlines again – this time they were sighted over Washington, DC (see WASHINGTON DC WAVE). Files released by the Public Record Office in Kew show that on 28 July 1952 Churchill wrote to his Secretary of State for Air (Lord Cherwell) asking:

> What does all this stuff about FLYING SAUCERS amount to? What can it mean? What is the truth? Let me have a report at your convenience.

Chupacabras (The 'Goatsucker')

Originally spelt without the 's' but nowadays most commonly spelt with it, the chupacabras ('goatsucker') is little short of a cryptozoological phenomenon, let alone a mere enigma. Whereas many of this scientific field's major subjects have long been reported and discussed, sometimes for centuries, the chupacabras was largely unknown until as recently as the mid-1990s, yet today it is one of the most publicized CRYPTIDs of all time.

Back in the 1970s, cases of livestock-killing and mutilation featuring carcases sucked dry of blood had spasmodically been reported from Puerto Rico, alongside accounts of a bizarre unidentified bipedal creature. However, it wasn't until the 1990s, when several more such cases hit the news there, that the chupacabras suddenly became an internationally known mystery beast – due in no small way to extensive Internet coverage and interest. Reports involving mysterious bloodsucking livestock assailants had previously been recorded from many disparate regions of the world, but nothing matching the truly extraordinary appearance claimed for the chupacabras had ever been documented before.

According to a sizeable number of eyewitness accounts, this grotesque creature is apparently bipedal (but also capable of climbing trees), stands 1–1.5 metres (3–5 feet) tall and superficially resembles a hairy grey kangaroo in overall shape and form. No kangaroo known to science, however, shares any of the chupacabras's more exotic attributes. These include its webbed arms with three-clawed hands, a series of sharp glowing spikes running from the top of its head down the full length of its back, in some reports a

A drawing of the mysterious chupacabras, based on the testimony of some of those who claim to have seen the creature. (© TopFoto/Fortean)

pair of wings, plus a distinctly round head, huge black almond-shaped eyes that lack eyelids and sometimes glow bright red, an eerie-looking lipless mouth, two bare holes in the sides of its head in place of ears and two more above its mouth in place of nostrils, and very large pointed teeth. It has also been described as having the ability to change colour like a chameleon (its normal coloration is grey with darker blotches), and, strangest of all, it has often been reported that it can induce nausea or intense dizziness in eyewitnesses simply by rocking its head from side to side and hissing as it gazes at them.

Over the years, several alleged chupacabras corpses have been reported, together with photos, but none has yet stood up to formal scientific scrutiny. Not surprisingly, the chupacabras has attracted a singularly varied range of proposed identities. These include an escaped monkey, some form of UFO-originating EXTRATERRESTRIAL being (inspired by its superficial similarity to the famous 'GREY' category of ALIEN), an elusive real-life version of the supposedly mythical merfolk (exemplified by MERMAIDS and tritons), and even a grotesque mutant creature created in top-secret laboratory research that has absconded from its place of creation. However, any identity needs to take into account that within a couple of years of reports emerging from Puerto Rico in the mid-1990s, comparable sightings were also being recorded in Mexico and the USA. Intriguingly, however, these have largely been confined to Hispanic communities, rather than spreading throughout the USA, which has led investigators to conclude that the chupacabras is as much a cultural as a cryptozoological phenomenon.

Ralph Noyes, a civil servant working for Cherwell at the time, later reported that Churchill was told that a 'full intelligence study' had been carried out the previous year and had concluded that 'all the incidents reported could be explained'. The explanations included astronomical bodies, birds, balloons, optical illusions and hoaxes. It was added that, thanks to the special relationship, British intelligence had been assured that studies carried out in the USA in 1949 had established much the same thing.

Shortly after this, in September 1952, a number of UFO sightings occurred during Operation Mainbrace, a NATO exercise carried out on the east coast of England. These included a daylight encounter above a Yorkshire RAF base on 19 September, during which a Meteor jet was apparently chased, and a report of a silvery disc hovering above a US aircraft carrier the following day. According to Noyes, and Edward J Ruppelt (who was head of the US Air Force UFO project), these events resulted in co-operation over UFO investigations between British and US intelligence staff.

On 16 December 1952 strict orders were issued to senior RAF personnel, ordering them to file future reports only with an intelligence task force set up at the Air Ministry in London. It made it clear that military witnesses should be prevented from talking openly, because 'the public attach more credence to reports by RAF personnel' and so 'it is essential that the information should be examined at the Air Ministry and that its release should be controlled officially.' This was the starting point of what UFO researchers saw as a government cover-up, believing that the most important sightings were being suppressed.

From the official memos, which were released 40 years later, the origin of this policy can be traced back to Winston Churchill.

Church of All Worlds

An important neopagan religious movement and the first such group to be officially recognized as a church in the United States.

The Church of All Worlds evolved out of an earlier organization called 'Atl', formed by a group of friends at Westminster College in Fulton, Missouri, in the early 1960s. Under the leadership of Tim Zell (now Oberon Zell-Ravenheart) it was incorporated in 1968, making it the first neopagan organization to be officially recognized in the USA.

Zell and his friends were inspired by the 1961 Robert A Heinlein novel *Stranger in a Strange Land*. The structure of the church, particularly the way that it is built around small groups called 'Nests', and many of the rituals (such as the sacred rite of 'Watersharing') are based on ideas taken from the 'Church of All Worlds' which was founded by the central character in the novel. From the very beginning the church's dogma has been that there is no dogma.

As the Church evolved during the early 1970s it began to place a greater emphasis on nature and ecology, applying the word 'pagan' to nature lovers in general rather than imbuing it with any particular religious connotations. The current stated mission of the church is:

> ... to evolve a network of information, mythology and experience that provides a context and stimulus for re-awakening Gaia, and re-uniting her children through tribal community dedicated to responsible stewardship and evolving consciousness.

The Church brings together many elements from a diverse range of neopagan practices. They recognize a pantheon of deities, including the Earth Mother Goddess and, in common with many other neopagan and Wiccan groups, the Church celebrates the eight SABBATS.

The church suffered a decline in membership during the 1980s but was resurrected and grew again in the early 1990s. Since then there have been a number of leadership changes and, after the mass resignation of the board of directors in 2004, it has recently been revived again with Oberon Zell-Ravenheart at the helm. See also NEOPAGANISM; WICCA.

Church of Satan

An organization formed in 1966, which promotes Satanism as defined by its founder, Anton LaVey, in his Satanic Bible.

There are a number of comparatively high-profile organizations which promote Satanism, the best known of these being the Church of Satan. It was officially established in San Francisco on WALPURGISNACHT (30 April) 1966, by ANTON LAVEY, who was the Church's High Priest until his death in 1997.

LaVey criticized many religions, particularly Christianity and the Eastern mystical traditions, believing they forced unnatural laws on humans and caused them unnecessary guilt and remorse. He founded the Church of Satan to meet what he perceived as the need for a religion which celebrated the individual as a carnal being with desires which were meant to be fulfilled, and created a belief system which mixed a hedonistic philosophy with magical rituals. The Church received nationwide attention in 1967 when LaVey officiated at the first Satanic wedding, following it in the same year with a Satanic funeral service for a Church of Satan member, and the Satanic baptism of LaVey's three-year-old daughter.

Anton LaVey, founder of the controversial Church of Satan, carries out the Satanic baptism of his daughter in May 1967. (© Bettmann/Corbis)

The Church of Satan's principles are based on LaVey's *The Satanic Bible* (1969), *The Satanic Witch* (1970) and *The Satanic Rituals* (1972). These hold that human emotions such as greed, lust and hatred are natural instincts which should be indulged rather than denied. But, despite its name, *The Satanic Bible* does not promote the worship of Satan, or indeed a belief in his existence as a supernatural being. Instead, it regards Satan as a pre-Christian principle representing the carnal, earthly and mundane aspects of life – a force of nature, not a living, quasi-divine entity – and uses him as a symbol of defiance and rebellion against a conformist, God-fearing society. LaVey's Nine Satanic Statements form the core of the Church's beliefs, and include the promotion of vengeance rather than forgiveness, indulgence rather than abstinence, and vital existence instead of what it calls 'spiritual pipe dreams'. The Church also teaches that heaven and hell do not exist, and it does not worship any living deity; its emphasis is on the power and authority of the individual, who it holds to be fully responsible for his or her own life and destiny, and one of its claims is that each person can be their own god. Its list of 'sins' includes stupidity, pretentiousness, self-deceit, herd conformity, lack of perspective and counterproductive pride.

As the Church treats membership details as confidential, its exact numbers are not known, although these are thought to have declined since LaVey's death in 1997. However, many famous people have at one time or another been associated with the Church of Satan, including the singer Marilyn Manson. Its central office is now situated in the Hell's Kitchen neighbourhood of New York City, although it continues to be a highly decentralized organization, with each Satanist being expected to follow his or her own path. Local Church of Satan groups are usually known as grottos. See also BAPHOMET.

Church Universal and Triumphant
The best known of the 'ancient wisdom' movements in the USA.

The Church Universal and Triumphant (CUT) was founded in 1958 by Mark L Prophet (1919–73) as the Summit Lighthouse. Prophet had been a member of an offshoot of the I AM Activity called the Bridge to Freedom (founded in 1951 by Geraldine Innocente). He claimed to receive teachings from ASCENDED MASTERS and set up this new I AM MOVEMENT with himself as the 'Messenger'.

In 1961 Prophet met Elizabeth Clare Wulf (1939–); they married in 1963. Trained by Prophet and (allegedly) by the Ascended Master El Morya, she too became a Messenger. They published the dictations they received from Ascended Masters in a periodical, *The Pearls of Wisdom*. In 1962 they set up the Keepers of the Flame, an inner circle of committed believers, and in 1971 established Summit University to train followers. They had four children, one of whom, Erin, was trained to become a future Messenger, though she and the other children have now left the Church.

In 1973 Mark Prophet died suddenly of a stroke, leaving Elizabeth Clare Prophet as the sole Messenger. The following year she set up the Church Universal and Triumphant 'to meet the deeper spiritual needs of those who wanted to apply the teachings of the Ascended Masters'. Mark became acknowledged as the Ascended Master Lanello. The Summit Lighthouse became effectively the publishing wing of the religion. Since Mark's death Elizabeth and Mark/Lanello have published over 75 books of the teachings of the Ascended Masters, with a wider readership than the membership of the Church.

The teachings of CUT are eclectic. At their heart they stem from GUY BALLARD's I AM Religious Activity, with considerable elements of THEOSOPHY, Hinduism, Buddhism, KABBALAH and mystical Christianity. CUT teaches the Gnostic belief that there is a spark of the divine flame within each of us. The aim is to achieve oneness with God. Those spiritually enlightened ones who have ascended back to God can assist humanity; they are the Ascended Masters. Like other groups in the I AM movement, CUT teaches the use of affirmations – affirming the member's relationship with God – and decrees using the name of God in statements of power, eg 'I AM a being of violet fire, I AM the purity God desires'.

CUT received a great deal of adverse publicity in the 1990s. Elizabeth's fourth husband, Ed Francis (by whom she had a fifth child at the age of 55), was jailed for buying guns under a false name in 1989. In 1990 Elizabeth Clare Prophet seemed to say that the USA was about to suffer a nuclear attack. Hundreds of members moved into underground shelters at the movement's headquarters on the Royal Teton Ranch in Montana, next door to the famous Yellowstone National Park; some had sold their own homes to do so. When the prophesied attack failed to happen the Church lost about half its membership, including some very senior members.

Just as CUT is an offshoot of an offshoot of the I AM Activity, there have been several offshoots from CUT. In 1995 two former CUT members, Monroe and Caroline Shearer, set up the Temple of the Presence with themselves as the Messengers. They were thus ideally placed to attract members who left CUT when, in the late 1990s, Elizabeth Clare Prophet announced that she had Alzheimer's disease and stepped down from active leadership of her Church, which is now run by a board of directors. As her illness progressed, leaving CUT without a functioning Messenger, more former CUT members set themselves up as Messengers – a total of eight by 2006.

Cincinnati premonition

A classic case which is cited as an example of a premonition, in this instance in the form of a precognitive dream.

In 1979 David Booth, an office worker in Cincinnati, had the same DREAM ten nights in a row. In his dream Booth would see an American Airlines jet take off from an airport, then crash and burst into flames. On 22 May, spurred by the apparent reality of his dreams, Booth contacted the Federal Aviation Authority (FAA). The FAA apparently took his dreams seriously and attempted to identify the type of plane (possibly a 727 or DC-10 from Booth's descriptions) and which flight it was. Booth awoke from his last dream on 25 May. Later that day American Airlines Flight 191, a DC-10 leaving from Chicago's O'Hare International Airport, lost one of its engines on take-off. The plane flipped over on its back and burst into flames, exactly as predicted by Booth. A total of 273 people were killed in the disaster.

Those who doubt whether this was a 'real' premonition point to the fact that airlines and related organizations must receive calls of this type regularly, and that at some point a 'premonition' will come true.

In 2003 David Booth had what he believed to be a second premonition, in which a large object from space descends towards the south pole and an enormous explosion takes place in western USA. See also PREMONITIONS.

circles

The circle is a universal symbol of unity and wholeness in magic and religion.

The circle, a closed plane curve every point of which is equidistant from the centre, is one of the oldest and most universal SYMBOLS of MAGIC and RELIGION, and has appeared in one form or another in almost every belief system since ancient times. It represents unity, wholeness and infinity. To earth-centred religions throughout history, and to neopagans, it symbolizes the feminine principle, the cosmos and Mother Earth. In Hinduism and Buddhism, a circle with a dot in the centre represents the merging of male and female forces, with the dot, known as a bindu, symbolizing the male principle. In Native American traditions the circle is quartered by a cross and is known as a MEDICINE WHEEL, with the four equal lines of the cross extending from the centre of the circle to the cardinal points of North, East, South and West. This quartered circle plays a central role in major spiritual rituals, and is sometimes known as the sacred hoop. A variation of this shape is also seen in the Christian Celtic cross. The ancient symbol of a snake or dragon swallowing its own tail, thus creating an unbroken circle, is associated with Gnostic traditions, medieval ALCHEMY, and Hermetic magical traditions, and represents eternity and the cyclical nature of all things.

The circle is the most ancient form of sacred space, and prehistoric STONE CIRCLES and HENGES, most commonly found in the British Isles, are thought to have been constructed for ritual purposes. Walking in a circle around an object, person or place in a religious ceremony, as an act of reverence, or as part of a magical ritual, is known as circumambulation, and this practice is found all over the world, particularly in ceremonies of birth, death and marriage. Whatever the religion or purpose of the circumambulation, it is nearly always performed in a clockwise direction – that is, in the same direction as the sun. The casting of a MAGIC CIRCLE within which to perform rituals or do any kind of magical work is a central feature of NEOPAGANISM, WICCA, and Western ceremonial magic (see MAGIC, CEREMONIAL).

The spiritual significance of the circle is still recognized today in the circle dance, a revival of perhaps the oldest known dance form, which is found in cultures all over the world, including those of ancient Greece, Africa, Eastern Europe, North

America and South America. Performed in a circle without partners, contemporary circle dances became popular among alternative, feminist and NEW AGE groups from the 1980s onward. While some are performed just for fun, others, known as Sacred Dance, have a symbolic spiritual element derived from various traditions, and the dance is performed around a small altar of flowers or some other object.

cities, lost *see* LOST CITIES

clairaudience
The claimed ability to hear things which normal humans cannot.
Clairaudience (from the French for 'clear hearing') could be described as a form of EXTRASENSORY PERCEPTION, as it purportedly involves 'hearing' sounds that others cannot – suggesting that the sound experience in the percipient's brain originates other than through the normal physical process. Clairaudience is sometimes talked about as a form of CLAIRVOYANCE (which involves seeing) but strictly speaking they are not the same thing. However, for obvious reasons, they are often described as being experienced together.

Clairaudience is one of a range of phenomena that it is claimed are experienced by some PSYCHICS or MEDIUMS at a SÉANCE, through which they pass on messages that are allegedly from SPIRITS of the dead. Watching people who claim to have this ability is indeed like watching a conversation of which one is aware of only one side.

clairsentience
The claimed ability to receive information about people or objects just by touching them.
Clairsentience (from the French for 'clear feeling') might be described as the ability to receive information through a PSYCHIC sense of touch. Merely by holding an object or by touching a person, a clairsentient claims to be able to gain and relate information about their history. A clairsentient claims also to be able to tell details about previous owners of any objects held and some, but not all, claim to be able to see the future for a person or object by touch. See also EXTRASENSORY PERCEPTION.

clairvoyance
Strictly, the claimed ability to see things which are not normally visible. However, the term is more generally used to include any form of discerning information that is beyond the normal range of sense or perception.
Clairvoyance (from the French for 'clear seeing') has long been claimed as a technique for gaining

information other than via the normal senses. As such, the word describes a form of EXTRASENSORY PERCEPTION. It is a skill claimed by many MEDIUMS, PSYCHICS and other individuals who might simply refer to themselves as 'clairvoyants', and is an ability that is often claimed to be employed during a SÉANCE (in which instance the information is supposedly obtained from SPIRITS of the dead). REMOTE VIEWING also falls into the general category of clairvoyance.

Clairvoyance is a skill that has also historically been associated with many religious and magical practices, in which the source of the information is usually understood to be SPIRITS, GODS or other supernatural beings. See also CLAIRAUDIENCE.

close encounters
A term used to describe the quality of a UFO sighting, commonly, but not exclusively, based on the proximity of the UFO to the witness.
The phrase 'close encounter' is now widely familiar, following its extensive use by UFO researchers and, in particular, its adoption by director Steven Spielberg for his film CLOSE ENCOUNTERS OF THE THIRD KIND.

The concept was first proposed by astrophysicist and retired US Air Force consultant, DR J ALLEN HYNEK, in his book, *The UFO Experience* (1972). He sought to classify the data that was in the 13,000 case files at his disposal and, more specifically, to identify those cases that might offer more useful evidence for proper analysis.

A close encounter of the first kind was defined by him as a sighting made at close range. Inevitably there have been arguments as to how 'close' it should be.

For a close encounter of the second kind tangible, physical evidence must be left behind after the incident – for example, landing traces. Such cases are more amenable to investigation and offer the possibility of collecting scientific data.

In Hynek's definition, a close encounter of the third kind requires the involvement of 'animated creatures' (what might be more popularly described as ALIENS or EXTRATERRESTRIALS) associated with the UFO.

The Hynek system was widely adopted by UFO researchers once it started to be applied by CUFOS, the organization that he founded in 1973. During the 1980s some attempts were made to modify its application – including a suggestion that physical evidence should be required for all close encounters and that none should be dependent only on the subjective estimation of distance. The term close encounter of the fourth kind is now sometimes used to describe ALIEN ABDUCTIONS, or any case where the aliens reportedly interact with the witness in some way.

Close Encounters of the Third Kind

A Steven Spielberg film from 1977, featuring UFOs as its central theme. The film was a box-office success and is widely considered to be a classic.

Steven Spielberg was a relatively new director in 1975 when he experienced great success with *Jaws*, his film about a killer shark. To follow this he decided to produce the first serious drama about UFOs – a subject that had fascinated him since childhood.

Spielberg worked with leading UFO researcher, DR J ALLEN HYNEK. The title comes from the case classification system in Hynek's book, *The UFO Experience* (see CLOSE ENCOUNTERS). The final film was based around a fictional story about government scientists struggling to unravel alien contact, and included UFO incidents that were mostly based on real reported cases. This built towards a special effects extravaganza featuring an alien landing that avoided 'space invasion' clichés and emphasized the magic and mystery that is often reported to accompany allegedly real sightings.

The ALIENS created by Spielberg are of the type known as GREYS, but were more childlike than those that featured in many subsequent UFO movies. It has been suggested that CULTURAL TRACKING was at work in many UFO cases after the movie, with sceptics arguing that the massive success of this film caused people to report sightings that mirrored Spielberg's version of the phenomenon. However, Spielberg had set out to represent the phenomenon as it was already being reported at the time, and by the late 1970s ALIEN ABDUCTION reports were already becoming more common.

Spielberg modelled the scientist at the head of the alien contact project on DR JACQUES VALLÉE, who had also assisted in the production. Vallée had been coaxed to the USA by Hynek to help him form an 'invisible college' of academic UFO researchers. This is why the leader of the US government UFO team in the film is a Frenchman who seems to support the PSYCHOSOCIAL HYPOTHESIS.

Hynek appears briefly as himself during the movie's climax, fulfilling his dream of meeting aliens. He reported that this contact went even further in shots left on the cutting-room floor, in which the aliens stroked the distinguished UFO expert's beard!

coaches, phantom *see* PHANTOM COACHES

Cock Lane ghost

Famous 18th-century poltergeist case in London which became a euphemism for fraud.

The Cock Lane ghost was supposedly active between 1762 and 1764 at a tiny house in Smithfield, London, which was occupied by a family named Parsons. Strange knocks were heard in a small room occupied by 12-year-old Elizabeth Parsons and, by means of questions and rapped answers, a form of crude communication was established with the alleged entity. The ghost apparently identified itself as the SPIRIT of a woman named Frances Lynes who claimed to have been poisoned by her lover. The culprit was identified by the ghost as William Kent, a stockbroker and former tenant of the house with whom Elizabeth's father had an on-going dispute over money.

The ghost was given the nickname 'Scratching Fanny', and sightseers flocked to the house, Dr Samuel Johnson among them. Suspicions soon grew

A still from *Close Encounters of the Third Kind* (1977). This hugely successful film featured fictional aliens of a type that became known as 'greys'. (© Columbia Pictures/Album/AKG)

that the Cock Lane ghost was a fraud. It was noticed that when Elizabeth was restrained the knocks would cease. Also, when the spirit promised to make raps in the vault of a local church where Frances Lynes was buried, nothing was forthcoming.

Amid growing public hysteria, William Kent issued proceedings through the Guildhall Court to restrain the slanders on his character. A number of individuals were convicted, including some who had helped publicize the communications. Elizabeth's father was sentenced to the pillory and imprisonment.

The story was satirized in a print by Hogarth, and for many years the phrase 'Cock Lane ghost' became a euphemism for deception and credulity in cases of alleged paranormal phenomena. However, the possibility that at least some of the claims were genuine has not been wholly discounted.

coffee grounds, divination by *see*

TASSEOGRAPHY

coincidence *see* CHANCE AND COINCIDENCE

coins, suit of *see* PENTACLES, SUIT OF

cold fusion
A hypothetical method of achieving nuclear fusion without an initial input of energy.
Nuclear fusion is the creation of a new atomic nucleus by the merging of two lighter ones, resulting in a release of energy. The process is 'cleaner' than nuclear fission, and the most suitable element to use as a starting point, hydrogen, is the most abundant element in the universe. However, the reaction involves heating the materials used to extremely high temperatures so, currently, the cost, and the side effects of creating the conditions for the reaction to take place within a nuclear reactor, negate any benefits. Cold fusion is the term used for a hypothetical method of accomplishing nuclear fusion, and thereby generating energy, without having to heat the materials to these high temperatures.

Various scientists have conducted experiments and carried out research in this field, but an effective method of producing cold fusion has yet to be found. In 1989, the research chemists Stanley Pons and Martin Fleischmann claimed to have achieved cold fusion while carrying out research at the University of Utah in Salt Lake City, using heavy water (containing deuterium, an isotope of hydrogen). However, doubts arose about this method when scientists around the world tried to duplicate their experiments and failed. Pons and Fleischmann were largely discredited in the ensuing controversy.

It was argued that cold fusion was still potentially possible, but involved processes that the current levels of knowledge in chemistry and physics were unable to fully understand, let alone succeed in replicating in a laboratory. Many of those who were convinced of this were driven by the desire to discover what was sometimes derided as a kind of scientific 'holy grail': a form of energy generation that would not only be cheap but almost infinite (see FREE ENERGY).

Some scientists remain convinced that nuclear fusion reactions can be stimulated at room temperature, and envisage benefits such as individual homes being able to generate their own electricity and heating. Cold fusion technology could also be used to power motor vehicles. The most important implication of this would be the ending of mankind's current dependence on fossil fuels and the introduction of a 'clean' form of energy generation, as it is thought that cold fusion would produce relatively little waste.

The cold fusion controversy, like many others, has attracted conspiracy theorists. In this case, they believe that potential breakthroughs in the field are suppressed or discredited by the scientific establishment, backed by oil companies and oil-rich countries who would have most to lose if such a cheap energy source were to be discovered and made practicable.

An International Conference on Cold Fusion (ICCF) was set up in 1990, but in the early 21st century a shift in the focus of research away from cold fusion towards other nuclear effects, such as the release of energy in the form of heat through nuclear transmutations, led to it being replaced by the International Conference on Condensed Matter Nuclear Science.

Within the scientific mainstream there is still a belief that cold fusion is theoretically possible but that it is unlikely to be achieved in practice. Research into cold fusion continues, however, in several countries around the world.

collective apparitions
The name given to apparitions that are perceived simultaneously by two or more people.
The majority of GHOSTS and APPARITIONS are reported by single witnesses. Nonetheless, a significant number of cases involve apparitions that are perceived simultaneously by two or more witnesses, apparently either seeing the same thing or sharing the same hallucination. At least two hundred well-attested examples had been accumulated by the societies for PSYCHICAL RESEARCH in Great Britain and the USA by 1940, and this figure has continued to increase in the years since.

In such cases the shared nature of the perception has been taken by some to be evidence of the occurrence of a paranormal event – either that there must have been an entity external to the brains of the observers, or that some form of TELEPATHY must have taken place between them. Sceptics would contend that the 'entity' could still quite easily have been something mundane that was misperceived by all of the observers or that their interpretations of their experience may have been (consciously or subconsciously) shaped by their subsequent communication with the others involved.

collective unconscious
A phrase coined by the psychologist Carl Jung as a name for a part of the unconscious that he believed was shared by all humans.
According to CARL JUNG, the collective unconscious is the part of each person's mind which contains ARCHETYPES which we have apparently not learned from experience and which form an instinctual part of the mind of all humans – in effect we are all born with these basic mental 'forms'. In his later works, Jung used the term 'objective psyche' to describe this concept.

Some people who accept Jung's basic model dismiss the 'innateness' of the forms that make up the collective unconscious, arguing that there are very basic experiences that are common throughout all human life and, as all human brains work in a similar way, we all construct a similar set of forms upon which our unconscious is built.

The already slightly mystical concept of the collective unconscious has been taken further elsewhere, with some people claiming that it is a result of a primal form of TELEPATHY, through which we all share these archetypal forms.

Colorado University study
A US government-funded UFO investigation project from the 1960s, during which scientists were given access to official records.
In March 1966 a committee chaired by optical scientist, Dr Brian O'Brien, published a review of the US Air Force UFO investigation team, PROJECT BLUE BOOK. Until then UFO reports had been subject to military analysis, but the Air Force had long wished to rid themselves of what they regarded as an unwelcome headache. In the review it was proposed that, as any defence threat seemed to be minimal, a number of universities should be approached to take over the role of assessing UFO data.

The US government decided to offer a contract to a single university to review the official records and to assess future policy. However, most of the prestigious academic institutes (including Massachusetts Institute of Technology and Harvard) declined to touch the

'poisoned chalice' – as the subject of UFOs was considered to be by academics. On 6 October 1966, the University of Colorado agreed to run a short study, funded by the taxpayer at $313,000. The period of the project was then extended to 31 October 1968 and the total cost increased to over half a million dollars. Evidence suggests that the university thought at the time that they were the first choice.

DR E U CONDON, a physics professor, was placed in charge. The project co-ordinator at the university was graduate school administrator, Robert Low, and the mathematician and psychologist, Dr David Saunders, became full-time case investigator. It was decided that no scientists with any prior association with UFOs would be invited to assist the team of specialists, beyond being asked to make suggestions. In practice this probably meant that they made some basic mistakes that might have been avoided.

From the start there was much debate over what questions the team should try to answer – the arguments continued until it was almost time to write the final report. When cases such as the BENTWATERS episode were looked at it became clear that not all government UFO records had been made available from the outset, despite Pentagon assurances. Only a few contemporary cases from 1967 were followed up. Of the old cases that were studied, many baffled the research team and featured in the final report alongside comments to the effect that the probability was high that a genuine UFO had been seen.

In its final months the project went into disarray when a controversial memo came to light. It had been written by Low during the period when the university had been discussing taking on the project, and it contained the following words:

> [The study] would be conducted almost exclusively by non-believers [who] could and probably would add an impressive body of evidence that there is no reality to the observations. The trick would be, I think, to describe the project so that, to the public, it would appear a totally objective study ...

The recriminations over what some of the scientists felt was evidence for bias led to those who dissented being fired. Some of these, led by Saunders, wrote their own alternative (and far more positive) final report.

The Colorado study itself was published in early 1969, attracting a great deal of publicity. Most reviewers only read its conclusion, which stated that no evidence had been found that UFOs were alien in origin. It was recommended that the US government close down its US Air Force investigation project, which they did later that year. However, with the passing of the Freedom of Information Bill in 1976 it became clear that, despite this very public closure, covert analysis of cases with potential security implications (such as the later BELGIAN WAVE) would continue.

comets

A comet is a type of heavenly body to which many interpretations and theories have attached throughout history.

A comet is a body of rock and ice moving through space that periodically passes close to the earth on its eccentric orbit around the sun. In earlier times the appearance of a comet in the night sky was often taken as an evil OMEN. This was perhaps because, unlike the familiar charted stars and planets, a comet's appearance was unpredictable and its movements erratic, leading to its being interpreted as a frightening disturbance in the natural course of events. It was an obvious step to conclude that a comet was a kind of heavenly message that mankind dare not ignore.

This association between comets and disaster is seen in many cultures. The ancient Romans, for example, believed that a fiery comet appeared after the assassination of Julius Caesar. A comet was said to have appeared to the Jews before their unsuccessful revolt against Rome that led to the destruction of Jerusalem in AD 70. In South America, the Incas observed a comet before the arrival of their conqueror Pizarro in 1531. One of the most famous comets, Halley's Comet, was believed to presage the Norman Conquest in 1066 and is thought to be depicted in the Bayeux Tapestry. It was also associated with the outbreak of the Black Death in the 14th century. Legend has it that Pope Calixtus III later identified the comet as an instrument of the Devil and formally excommunicated it in 1456.

However, the association of comets with disasters is not just a phenomenon of the distant past. When the earth passed through the tail of Halley's Comet in 1910, newspaper reports spread a fear that poisonous substances contained within it would kill millions of people. An example of a more extreme reaction to the approach of a comet occurred in 1997, when one photograph of Hale Bopp appeared to show a small dot near to it. This prompted a claim that a spaceship containing ALIENS was hiding behind the comet – an occurrence that was supposedly taken as a sign by members of the ill-fated HEAVEN'S GATE movement that the time was right for their mass suicide.

In the early 1980s, the British astronomer Fred Hoyle offered the theory that evolution on earth was driven by the periodic arrival of viruses transported by comets. This formed part of his overall criticism of the

The title page of a pamphlet from 1680. At that time sightings of comets were still often considered to be ill omens, presaging disaster. (© TopFoto/HIP)

mainstream explanation of the origins of life and the process of evolution. Although this was the subject of much derision within the scientific community at the time, the idea that there could be EXTRATERRESTRIAL life in the form of micro-organisms existing in comets and other bodies in space has not been universally dismissed.

Committee for the Scientific Investigation of Claims of the Paranormal

An organization dedicated to the 'critical investigation of paranormal and fringe-science claims'.

The Committee for the Scientific Investigation of Claims of the Paranormal (CSICOP) was founded in the USA at the 1976 convention of the American Humanist Association. Founding members include Carl Sagan, Isaac Asimov, JAMES RANDI and Paul Kurtz, who is the current chairman. CSICOP's stated aims include encouraging 'research by objective and impartial inquiry in areas where it is needed', and they approach all claims of the paranormal from what they describe as the scientific point of view. A number of other groups throughout the world are formal associates of CSICOP and they carry out investigations on its behalf. In 1981, CSICOP adopted a policy of not directly carrying out research, although many of the individual members are active in this field. This policy change was a direct result of some of the findings of one of their own investigations, which appeared to uphold the idea that astrological signs controlled the success of athletes. The findings themselves were not the problem, rather the allegations that attempts had been made by some members of CSICOP to hide their own project's results. A number of members left as a result of this affair.

As well as being an umbrella organization for sceptics, CSICOP is actively involved in encouraging a general scientific literacy in the population as a whole, with a view to helping people to see nonsensical claims for what they are.

CSICOP has its headquarters in New York and it is currently attempting to set up a large centre in Los Angeles. It publishes a bimonthly magazine, the *Skeptical Inquirer*, and is associated with the Council for Secular Humanism and the Centre for Inquiry.

Critics of CSICOP have accused its members of arrogance and of having closed minds; in particular it has been claimed that CSICOP is already convinced that paranormal phenomena do not exist before it starts any investigation, and that any amount of evidence would be regarded as insufficient.

James Randi is one of the highest-profile members of the organization, and he is often cited in the debunking of claims of the paranormal. Randi also runs the James Randi Educational Foundation which has similar aims to CSICOP. See also SCEPTICISM.

Condon, Dr E(dward) U(hler) (1902–74)

A leading academic physicist who led the only ever major, taxpayer-funded UFO investigation at the request of the US government.

Dr Edward U Condon was a distinguished physicist who taught at Princeton before World War II and was co-opted onto the top-secret Manhattan Project, which produced the first atom bombs. After the war he was appointed director of the National Bureau of Standards, before becoming a physics professor at the University of Colorado at the age of 61.

While at the university he was persuaded to take on a government-funded UFO project (see COLORADO UNIVERSITY STUDY). He led the project from its inception in 1966, until the publication of the final

Dr E U Condon seen talking to Connie Menger, wife of the 'contactee' Howard Menger who claimed he made contact with aliens in New Jersey in 1956. (© TopFoto/ Fortean)

report in 1969, stressing his strongly sceptical position throughout. A few weeks after it began he told a press conference:

> It is my inclination right now to recommend that the government get out of this business. My attitude right now is that there is nothing to it. But I am not supposed to reach a conclusion for another year.

His bias was perhaps further evidenced by the way he pronounced 'UFOs', as 'oofoes' (to rhyme with 'goofoes'). In setting his criteria for choosing cases he ignored advice from DR J ALLEN HYNEK, who thought the study should focus on those that were unsolved. He set out specifically to disprove that UFOs were alien spaceships, rather than to explore whether reported sightings had a broader potential to add to scientific knowledge.

Condon's only major input into the project (a summary conclusion of what he thought it had discovered) was placed at the beginning of the final report. Many journalists only read this – ignoring the 900 pages of data that followed. In his piece he suggested that children who included UFO data in school projects should lose marks. Later he went further, saying that writers and publishers of such 'pseudo-science' should be publicly horsewhipped.

Shortly after the report's publication the American Association for the Advancement of Science (AAAS) arranged a conference on the subject of UFOs. Condon attempted to stop the event, unsuccessfully appealing for intervention from his personal friend, Vice-President Spiro Agnew. The conference went ahead and resulted in a highly influential book, *UFOs: A Scientific Debate*, co-edited by participants Carl Sagan and Thornton Page. The debate also secured the retention of government UFO records that might otherwise have been destroyed in the wake of Condon's report.

confabulation

The conscious or unconscious invention of past experiences.

Confabulation is a term used in psychiatry to describe the invention of experiences, either consciously or unconsciously, to replace gaps in the memory.

It has been argued that confabulation is the true source of the memories claimed by many people who say they have experienced ALIEN ABDUCTION. When the person involved has suffered a period of amnesia, or simply cannot remember what happened to them on a particular occasion, some say that confabulation comes to their rescue (perhaps encouraged by the leading questions asked by an investigator), supplying 'memories' that they then convince themselves are true.

A similar process of confabulation is said to account for the false memories (see MEMORY, FALSE) 'recalled' by people under HYPNOSIS or during psychotherapy, in which they suddenly uncover supposedly repressed memories (see MEMORIES, REPRESSED) of usually traumatic experiences, such as sexual abuse in their childhood.

Confabulation is recognized as a characteristic symptom of various forms of dementia, in particular, in the condition known as Korsakoff's psychosis, which involves damage to an area of the brain (usually through alcoholism) causing absolute loss of recent memory. Sufferers are sometimes observed to replace these lost memories with imaginary ones rather than endure the insecurity and doubt of remembering nothing.

See also MEMORIES, RECOVERED.

conjuration

The summoning of a spirit for a predetermined purpose by means of a magical charm or ritual.

Conjuration is the magical act of summoning a spirit for a predetermined purpose by means of a charm or ritual. The spirit of a herb which is being used for magic may be conjured to release the herb's positive energy, or a benevolent house spirit may be conjured to enter and protect a home. NECROMANCY is the conjuration of the spirits of the dead for DIVINATION purposes. There are many rituals and ceremonies (see MAGIC, CEREMONIAL) for conjuring the spirits of ANGELS or DEMONS. Such a conjuration may be preceded by a ritual of purification of mind, body and spirit to attract the desired entity or to protect the magician, who may also wear special clothes or TALISMANS. A MAGIC CIRCLE or magic symbols may be drawn on the floor, specific incenses may be burned, and the ritual may be timed so that it is performed at the most propitious hour of the day or night for the purpose, or with the most favourable planetary aspects. The words recited to summon the spirit may be a few simple sentences, or a long and complex text, depending on the nature and aim of the conjuration.

consciousness, altered states of *see*

ALTERED STATES OF CONSCIOUSNESS

contactees

The collective title by which those involved in the first major 'alien contact' claims in the early 1950s became known. Unlike the later 'abduction' cases, their stories featured voluntary journeys inside UFOs and friendly contact with their occupants.

The best-known member of the contactee movement was GEORGE ADAMSKI. His tales about meeting friendly ALIENS, and the dubious photographs he produced as evidence, captured the imagination of a society fascinated by the developing space race.

During the mid-1950s, dozens of people came forward with similar claims – mostly (but not exclusively) in the USA. These included meetings with the residents of Mars, Venus and Saturn, and often involved entities that were said to look so much like us that they could be passed in the street without attracting attention. Many of these stories were hard to take seriously. For instance, the alien Val Thor, whom Frank Stranges claimed to have met inside the Pentagon in Washington, DC, had supposedly come from Venus to meet officials from the government in secret congress.

The contactee movement often combined UFO stories with religious mysticism – a notable example of this is the AETHERIUS SOCIETY, which survives to this day. It was also common for the aliens' messages to humankind to be of an anti-nuclear and ecological nature, suggesting the possibility that some contactees may have been using the new UFO craze as a medium through which they could disseminate messages of their own.

It appears from documents released later under the FREEDOM OF INFORMATION ACT that the contactees were of interest to the US intelligence agencies. After the WASHINGTON DC WAVE of 1952 it was feared that mass UFO sightings might clog reporting channels, aiding a Communist invasion. A CIA panel sought ways to defuse public interest in UFOs, even considering employing cartoonists to belittle the subject. The records show that they were pleased by the somewhat fortunate coincidental arrival of the contactees, whose bizarre stories helped them greatly in their task.

Although they were not taken seriously by many early UFO researchers, in more recent times some have suggested that the contactees' claims may warrant more careful treatment – especially where they included elements that also appeared in the ALIEN ABDUCTION cases that came later.

contagious magic *see* MAGIC, CONTAGIOUS

contemporary legends *see* URBAN LEGENDS

continents, lost *see* LOST CONTINENTS

Cook, Florence (1856–1904)

A 19th-century medium famous for apparently being able to produce full-body materializations of her spirit guide, Katie King.

Florence Cook began her career as a medium in her early teens by conducting SÉANCES for the amusement of her family and friends. With the support of a wealthy patron, she went on to perform for a great many sitters over a number of years. Initially she specialized in making faces appear at an opening in a cabinet in which she was tied up, although it was pointed out by some people at the time that the faces all bore a remarkable similarity to her own.

In 1872, she is said to have materialized a full-body SPIRIT for the first time. The full-form figure she materialized was called Katie King – supposedly the daughter of John King, a popular 'spirit control' (that it was also claimed was the spirit of the pirate Henry Morgan) apparently manifested during many séances since the 1850s. After this initial appearance Cook continued to materialize King at séances for the public, and she was investigated thoroughly by the scientist Sir William Crookes (along with DANIEL DUNGLAS HOME and Kate Fox – see FOX SISTERS).

Manifestations of Katie King were carried out in poor lighting – the spirits apparently preferred this. Florence Cook would be tied up in a spirit cabinet (just a large box to hide her from sight) and eventually, after sufficient time had passed for Cook to 'build up her PSYCHIC energies' (or, as some more cynical

The medium Florence Cook lies in a trance while an alleged spirit form manifests behind her. The photograph was taken during a séance at the home of the scientist William Crookes in 1874. (© Mary Evans Picture Library)

people might suggest, free herself from the ropes and get changed into her Katie King costume), the spirit of Katie King would walk out of the cabinet. King would walk around talking to participants in the séance and allowing them to touch her. Eventually after this display King would return to the cabinet, wherein Cook would be found still bound. Over the course of his investigations Crookes produced many photographs of King and of Cook, confirming to many people the similarities between the facial features of the two. Photographs purported to be of the pair together show signs of double exposure or reflections in mirrors or do not clearly show both faces – one of them usually being covered by what was said to be ECTOPLASM.

In 1875, Katie King apparently announced that she would be leaving Florence Cook and that her time on earth was nearing an end. However, Cook returned to the world of the séance in 1880, with a new spirit named Marie. During one sitting a member of the séance noticed that Marie appeared to be wearing a corset under her spirit garb. He grabbed hold of her and opened the door to Cook's cabinet, to find it empty. He was in fact holding onto the struggling figure of Florence Cook. After this her séances dropped off in frequency and she eventually retired to Monmouthshire to live out the last of her days. Katie King, however, apparently continued to put in appearances at séances – initially in the United States, but more recently in Rome in 1974.

corpse candle *see* WILL-O'-THE-WISP

corpse light *see* WILL-O'-THE-WISP

cosmic joker
A name given to the source of bizarre incidents and strange coincidences in our lives, humorously implying that they are due to the acts of a supernatural prankster.
CHARLES FORT has been credited with coining the phrase 'cosmic joker' but, while there is no findable instance of him using that phrase, the idea of a divine prankster is one he repeatedly uses in his four books. Certainly, many people have felt, at one time or another, that their lives are the playthings of cosmic forces and this has been reflected in many different cultures, from the impulsive antics of the gods of ancient Greece to the Hindu notions of *Maya* (that this world of sensory experiences is an illusion) and *Leela* ('the playful nature of Supreme Consciousness').

A divine joker is a convenient and often funny way to account for life's absurdities. For most people, this 'playfulness' is evident, most days, in the kind of coincidences (see CHANCE AND COINCIDENCE) that are memorable for involving some meaningful association – for example the Canada goose that crashed through the window of a home in Derby while the occupant was listening to a recording of Frankie Lane singing 'Cry of the Wild Goose'; or the murder in October 1678 of English magistrate Sir Edmund Berry Godfrey, for which three men – Robert Green, Henry Berry and Lawrence Hill – were hanged on Greenberry Hill the following year.

Most cultures have featured a semi-divine character that folklorists and anthropologists call a 'Trickster'. He can be malicious or humorous, clever or idiotic, but can also take an instructive role, challenging the laws or rules of gods and nature, partly on behalf of humans and partly because he can. The Norse Loki, the Greek Prometheus, the Native American Coyote and Raven, the Chinese Han Shan, and even Brer Rabbit and Bugs Bunny are all examples. The modern word 'contrarian' was derived from a translation of

Heyoka, the name of the Lakota Trickster, who did everything backwards.

The chief difficulty for sceptics (see SCEPTICISM) is the inherent improbability of a SUPERNATURAL entity who has the power to manipulate matter, time and space but wastes it on trivia. Is it credible, they ask (somewhat rhetorically), that a divine being would write his name (and badly, at that) inside an aubergine? Or impress the image of a saint on a cinnamon bun? (See HOLY VEGETABLES; IMAGES, SPONTANEOUS.) The same critique may be applied to the puzzle of inappropriate and appropriate accidents and deaths; for example, a blasphemer struck by lightning; a convention of health and safety experts laid low with mass food poisoning; or religious pilgrims killed in a coach accident on the way home.

There is a dark side to the Joker. Victims of unusual accidents, especially a series of them, may come to believe they are cursed, victimized or 'toyed with'. This question tormented US forest ranger ROY SULLIVAN who, against all odds, was struck by lightning seven times, eventually shooting himself in despair in 1983. The feeling is intensified by depression and paranoia. In 1969, yachtsman Donald Crowhurst fell into a severe depression during a round-the-world attempt. He wrote in his log:

> … the explanation of our troubles is that cosmic beings are playing games with us … according to one simple rule, the apes were not allowed to know anything of gods.

A few days later Crowhurst drowned himself. Similar cynicism, but born of disillusionment rather than madness, has driven nearly every major conspiracy theory.

A practical alternative to the helplessness felt by Crowhurst and millions of others is provided by the argument that such events are nothing to do with superhuman but arbitrary, vindictive, cruel beings with wicked senses of humour and everything to do with our perception of the world around us. Humans, it seems, are hard-wired to detect patterns: what US psychologist Jule Eisenbud called, 'subtle ordering tendencies or dispositions hidden in the very warp and woof of the universe'. This view, and that of the German philosopher Schopenhauer, whose notion of the 'subjective connection' underlying physical causality influenced CARL JUNG's theory of SYNCHRONICITY, suggests that the real significance of coincidences is relative only to each observer. In fact most of the adjectives that can be applied to the cosmic joker – by turns boundlessly creative, magnificent, audacious, frivolous, capricious, terrifying, awe-inspiring, perceptively appropriate, tireless and omnipresent – can be applied just as well to the subconscious and COLLECTIVE UNCONSCIOUS minds.

Of all the philosophies, Buddhist mysticism comes closest to providing insights into the cosmic joker phenomenon. In *The Chinese Mind* (1967), E R Hughes characterizes the Zen (Japanese) and Chan (Chinese) schools of Buddhism as 'consciously and deliberately paradoxical, even with the intention of causing laughter, to make evident the incongruities of the human situation'. It is a view enshrined in FORTEANISM, which takes a rather surrealist view of phenomena and their associations. For example, the US astronomer J Allen Hynek, once characterized modern CONTACTEE ufology, with its parade of absurd entities and their often outrageous behaviour, impossible craft, preposterous names and 'magical' tricks as 'both shocking and paradoxical'.

This affinity is not altogether frivolous. Zen masters have always taught by exploiting the metaphysical tension of contradiction and absurdity. Its purpose is to create a parallel between the moment we 'get' a joke and the 'sudden awakening' of enlightenment. Laughter is often an explosive accompaniment to both. *Koan*s – the paradoxical teaching riddles of Zen – then, have much in common with anomalous phenomena, in that both challenge our presumptions and expectations, bringing us face to face with the mystery of our existence. In Jungian theory, confrontations with the paranormal are equivalent to confrontations with the unconscious. Perhaps the message of the cosmic joker is that laughter is the best antidote to fear of the unknown. 'The world is indeed comic', wrote the master of horror tales H P LOVECRAFT, 'but the joke is on mankind.'

Some forteans claim that Fort functioned as a kind of Trickster for pompous, authoritarian, dogmatic science. The observation was best expressed by Enid Elsford in her book *The Fool: His Social and Literary History* (1935):

> The Fool does not lead a revolt against the Law; he lures us into a region of the spirit where … the writ does not run.

cosmogony
A theory or belief about how the universe came into being, usually a mytho-religious story which describes its origins as a deliberate act of creation by a supreme being.

The word 'cosmogony', in its broadest sense, can refer to scientific or philosophical theories regarding the origin and development of the universe, such as its evolution from primeval gases or the random movement of atoms. However, the term is usually applied to the wide diversity of mytho-religious stories which explain the beginnings of the universe, as found in many cultures, both ancient and contemporary. Many cosmogonies describe the universe as being deliberately created by SUPREME BEINGS, and may share several common motifs, such as the separation of the sky, earth and waters from a primordial chaos; mother and father gods; land emerging from an infinite and timeless ocean; or one or several gods fashioning elements of the universe from themselves or from pre-existing material. Others, such as the cosmogonies of Judaism, Islam and Christianity, describe the creation of the material of the universe by the supreme being *ex nihilo*, that is, from nothingness or void.

Some ancient and indigenous cultures have diverse mythologies and, as a result, may subscribe to several CREATION MYTHS without attempting to reconcile the contradictions between them; for example, in some Australian aboriginal traditions, earth was created by one of the gods of Dreamtime, while in others, specific creatures are said to have been created by particular gods or spirit ancestors. Mythical and religious cosmogonies may express what are perceived to be truths at a symbolic level, rather than being intended as a literal account of the origins of the universe.

Cottingley fairies
Probably the most famous 'fairy story' of the 20th century, involving two young cousins who claimed to have taken photographs of fairies in Cottingley, near Bradford, between 1917 and 1920.

In the first two decades of the 20th century there was a trend, among those with an interest in magic and the supernatural, for claiming contact with the fairy realm. So it is perhaps not surprising that the case of the Cottingley fairies, which began in 1917, caused such excitement and controversy.

Two young cousins, 16-year-old Elsie Wright and 9-year-old Frances Griffiths, claimed to have taken two photographs showing fairies in a glen just behind their home in Cottingley, near Bradford. Elsie took a photograph of Frances in July 1917, and when her father developed the plate, it showed diminutive figures which Elsie said were FAIRIES. A month later, Frances took a photograph of Elsie, apparently with a gnome about 30 centimetres (12 inches) tall. Elsie's father, suspecting a trick, refused to lend the girls his camera again, and he and his wife searched the house and riverbank for scraps of paper as evidence that the fairy figures had been cut out of books, but found nothing. The girls maintained the photographs were real, and in the summer of 1919, Elsie's mother, Polly Wright, who was interested in the OCCULT, attended a meeting of the THEOSOPHICAL SOCIETY in Bradford at which there was a lecture on the subject of fairies. Polly

One of the famous Cottingley photographs, apparently showing Frances Griffiths surrounded by a group of dancing fairies. (© TopFoto/Fortean)

mentioned that her daughter and niece had taken two photographs which appeared to prove the existence of fairies, and the two rough prints were circulated among the Theosophical Society, eventually coming to the notice of leading theosophist Edward Gardner in 1920.

It happened that the writer Sir ARTHUR CONAN DOYLE, who was a spiritualist, had been commissioned to write an article on fairies for the Christmas 1920 edition of the *Strand Magazine*. While collecting material for it that June, he heard about the two prints and contacted Gardner to borrow copies of them. Not quite sure what to make of the photographs, he showed them to Sir Oliver Lodge, a pioneer in PSYCHICAL RESEARCH, who thought them fakes. Conan Doyle then sent Gardner to Cottingley; he reported that the Wrights seemed honest, and he left cameras and photographic plates with the girls, who took three more photographs that year.

Interestingly, no one asked to examine the two original photographs; only the prints were analysed, and the retouched and enhanced prints which appeared in the *Strand Magazine* are the versions which are most commonly seen today. In these, the fairies actually look more like paper cut-outs than they

did in the originals. Nevertheless, Harold Snelling, a contemporary expert in fake photography, said the figures were not made of paper or fabric, nor had they been painted onto a photographic background, and when the article was published in December 1920, it caused much controversy. Most people who saw the pictures were sceptical, and Elsie's father could not understand why so many people were fooled by them, although his wife was convinced of their authenticity. Some people pointed out that Elsie was a very good artist, and that, having worked for a photographer for a while, she would have been knowledgeable about photography. They also said it was suspicious that no third party had ever been present when the pictures were taken. But neither the believers nor the disbelievers could prove the case either way.

It was not until 1981, when Elsie and Frances were interviewed for a magazine article, that they finally admitted the photographs had been faked; Elsie had copied the fairy images from illustrations by Arthur Shepperson in a book called *Princess Mary's Gift Book* (1914), and the cut-out figures had been fixed with hatpins. Their prank had got out of hand, and they had had to stick to their story. However, Frances said that the final picture they had taken had been genuine, and both maintained to the end that they had really seen fairies, but had initially been unable to photograph them.

Two films, both released in 1997, were based on the Cottingley fairies case: *Fairy Tale: A True Story* and *Photographing Fairies*.

Coué, Émile (1857–1926)

A French pharmacist and hypnotist who developed a 'self-improvement' system based on autosuggestion.

As a pharmacist in Troyes from 1882, Émile Coué took up the study of psychotherapy. He developed a method of healing and self-improvement based on 'autosuggestion', a system involving constant repetition and affirmation which is sometimes described as a form of self-HYPNOSIS. The technique came to be known as Couéism or the Coué method.

The method apparently developed from a test Coué carried out when dispensing medicines. He would praise the efficacy of the medicine to some patients and simply hand the medicine over to others without passing comment. Where all other factors were the same, he claimed that those who had heard his praise of the medicine showed greater or faster improvement than those who had not. In 1913, Coué founded the Lorraine Society of Applied Psychology and in 1920 he published *Self Mastery Through Conscious Autosuggestion*, which outlined his system. The technique involves training the mind by the frequent repetition of short fixed phrases, such as the now well-known mantra, 'Day by day, in every way, I am getting better and better.'

Couéism *see* COUÉ, ÉMILE

Council of Nine *see* NINE, THE (COUNCIL OF)

Course in Miracles, A

A book that was allegedly dictated by Jesus to Helen Schucman.

From 1965 to 1972 the New York City-based psychologist Helen Schucman claimed she had had a series of symbolic DREAMS. Urged to write down the content of these by her colleague, William Thetford, Schucman apparently found that when she started to do so the dreams changed and took the form of a subconscious dictation of text. When Schucman started to write, the fully fledged text appeared in her mind, with the first words being:

> This is a course in miracles. Please take notes.

Schucman would take notes and dictate text; Thetford would then put these two sources together and type up the result. When Thetford died in early 1972 his place was taken by Kenneth and Gloria Wapnick. Later, in 1983, the Wapnicks also started the Foundation for A Course in Miracles, an organization designed to spread the word and sell the book.

The book, which has sold over one and a half million copies in 15 languages since its publication in 1976, consists of three parts. The largest section is the text itself; this is then followed by a manual for students and finally a manual for teachers. Written in the first person, it claims to be the words of Jesus Christ and the central message is essentially one of forgiveness, which will in turn lead to a greater openness to love, and to love itself.

Schucman and associates edited the book from 1973 to 1975, removing material regarded as too personal and rearranging certain sections. Several different versions of *A Course in Miracles* exist with only minor differences between them. The names of those responsible for the book do not appear on the cover as they believe it should stand on its own merits, and Schucman and her collaborators wish to avoid a cult following, preferring people to listen to their own 'inner teacher'. The Foundation offers a number of courses and there are over 2,000 self-help groups for those having difficulty following their inner teacher.

A Course in Miracles is an example of a book which has apparently been produced by CHANNELLING.

couvade

Symbolic or sympathetic pregnancy in males.

In some cultures, it is the custom for an expectant father to behave, and be treated by others, as if it is he who is going to give birth to the child. This behaviour has been noted in such widely distant and disparate societies as those of China, Papua New Guinea, Native American peoples and the Basques of southern France and northern Spain.

Common features include the man taking to his bed and complaining loudly of the pangs of childbirth. Various suggestions have been put forward to explain this behaviour. It is thought that it affirms the father's bond with both the mother and the child, asserting his paternity and giving him a role to play rather than merely looking on and waiting anxiously. Another idea is that the man's counterfeit pregnancy is meant to draw the attention of evil spirits away from the actual child that is being born.

As well as this symbolic male 'pregnancy', the term 'couvade' is also applied to sympathetic pregnancy in males, which is a recognized psychosomatic medical condition. In this case, expectant fathers may complain of symptoms that seem to mimic those of a pregnant woman, such as nausea, indigestion, head and back pain and mood swings. It is thought that these effects arise from strong empathy with the pregnant partner, and particularly anxiety about the rigour and danger of childbearing, or even from male jealousy of a woman's power to bring a new life into the world.

covens

Groups or gatherings of witches, traditionally numbering 13.

It is unclear whether the idea that WITCHES historically formed small groups or covens (and more particularly that these always contained 13 people) was ever more than superstition or an invention of those who persecuted witches during the Middle Ages.

The word itself is probably derived from the same root as 'convene' and 'convent' and may not have always been associated solely with WITCHCRAFT; for example, the word 'covent' appears in the works of Chaucer in relation to a meeting of 13 people; the archaic word 'covin' was used to mean an agreement or conspiracy; and in Scotland guests at large houses would be met beneath a 'covin-tree'.

During the Middle Ages many witches were forced to confess to membership of groups that were alleged to meet at SABBATS to cavort and to work their unholy magic. The Scottish witch ISOBEL GOWDIE was said to have confessed to membership of a coven of 13 witches during her trial in 1662.

Whatever the historical basis for the tradition, many modern witches do organize themselves into covens. Although GERALD GARDNER believed that 13

(six couples and a leader) was the ideal number of members, the size of modern covens varies. They are often led by a female member who takes on the role of high priestess, representing THE GODDESS, and meet together at monthly ESBATS. However, as modern witchcraft and neopagan practice is extremely fluid and diverse, the exact organization and activities of an individual coven are down to its founder and members. See also NEOPAGANISM.

cover-up, governmental *see*

GOVERNMENTAL COVER-UP

Coyne, Captain Lawrence J

The US serviceman who led the mission that resulted in one of the most interesting midair UFO encounters on record.

October 1973 saw a major UFO WAVE in the USA. On the night of 18 October an Army Reserve Huey UH-1 helicopter was returning from Columbus, Ohio, to its home base of Cleveland. On board was a four-man crew – Captain Lawrence J Coyne, the pilot Lieutenant Arigo Jezzi and two other reservists, John Healey and Robert Yanacsek.

They reported that at 11pm, as they cruised at an altitude of around 1,100 metres (3,700 feet), first Healey and then Yanacsek spotted a red light, without navigation beacons. It flew past, behind and then kept pace with the Huey. As Coyne turned to see it, it appeared to be heading towards them, forcing him

Members of the North Berwick coven are shown drinking, listening to the Devil as he preaches and working at the cauldron to raise a storm.
(©TopFoto/Fortean)

to take over the controls from Jezzi. Coyne contacted the nearest jet interceptor base (at Mansfield) to see if they had a high-performance aircraft in their vicinity. However, as he put the helicopter into a steady descent all contact with the base was lost.

According to their reports, the light appeared to be accelerating towards them at an incredible pace. Believing they were at risk of an imminent collision, Coyne made a rapid descent, noting that they were soon only around 200 metres (650 feet) above the ground and descending at around 600 metres (2,000 feet) per minute. The light had now expanded and was filled the entire windscreen area of the UH-1. They could see a cigar shape, with a slight raised dome on top, but without wings or markings. A green spotlight beam swept from side to side, in a downward arc, passing through the helicopter windscreen. By now the UFO was directly overhead and stopped dead, hovering there for at least ten seconds. As the four men watched in disbelief, the strange craft sped away towards the north-west and made an extremely sharp 45 degree turn before vanishing.

Still in shock, Coyne discovered that they were now climbing at around 300 metres (1,000 feet) per minute, and had already reached around 1000 metres (3,500 feet) – although the controls were still set for a descent. He had to reverse the usual pattern of the settings before he could level off the flight.

Jennie Zeidman investigated the incident on behalf of the UFO group CUFOS. Several ground observers were found who reported seeing both the helicopter and the UFO. A mother and her four teenage children, who were driving near Charles Mill Reservoir at the time, said they had witnessed the coming together of the two craft and had seen the green beam shining on the Huey as it began its rapid ascent.

Sceptic PHILIP J KLASS proposed that the incident was due to the misperception of a bright meteor, and that the sudden ascent was due to an instinctive response on the part of Coyne to the aircraft's over-rapid descent. All four crew disputed this, and the witnesses on the ground claimed to have observed the UFO for much longer than would have been possible had it been a meteor.

creationism
The belief that the universe and everything in it were created directly by a supreme being or deity. The term is most often used of the belief held by some Christians that creation occurred literally as described in the Old Testament book of Genesis, a belief which is in direct conflict with the theory of evolution.
Creationism is the belief that the universe and everything in it are the result of a deliberate act of creation by SUPREME BEINGS or a deity who either brought it into being out of nothing (*ex nihilo*) by an act of free will, or from parts of itself, or from pre-existing chaotic material. Although the idea that the universe was created by a supreme being or beings appears in the CREATION MYTHS of almost all cultures throughout history, the term 'creationism' is most often used to refer to the belief held by some Christians that creation occurred literally as described in the Old Testament book of Genesis. The description found in Genesis is regarded as a factual account of events; as the word of God, this account is taken to be infallibly true, and since scientific theories on the origin of the universe, such as the Big Bang, are incompatible with this account, they are rejected as false. Creationism has become particularly associated with beliefs which conflict with Charles Darwin's theory of evolution, and with the creation–evolution controversy which is most prevalent in the USA. Scientific evolutionary theories about the origin of the physical universe, the geological history of the earth and the origin of life are disputed by those who hold a literal creation view, and the suggestion that humans descended from 'lesser creatures' is particularly unacceptable to strict creationists.

Throughout the medieval period, the biblical account of creation was unquestioned by Christians. During the Renaissance and the Enlightenment, the traditional biblical COSMOGONY was challenged by scientific and philosophical movements in Europe and America, and the 18th and 19th centuries saw naturalists questioning the literal interpretation of Genesis as being in conflict with their empirical observations of natural history. By the late 19th century, the term 'creationism' had come into common use to refer to those who held to the traditional belief in the literal truth of the biblical story. The creation–evolution controversy became most prominent in the 20th century with regard to the area of public education; in 1925, in Tennessee, after the state had passed a law banning the teaching of theories of human origins that were seen to conflict with the biblical account, a biology teacher called John Scopes was convicted for teaching Darwin's theory of evolution, although his conviction was later overturned. Since the 1960s, creationists have insisted that as much time be given in schools to the teaching of creationism as to evolution in science classes, since they hold that both theories should be treated as equally valid 'faith positions'.

While liberal theologists believe that Genesis is a poetic work and not to be taken literally, literal creationists object that adopting such a view calls into question the historicity of all the events in the Bible. However, some creationists have developed a number of ways of interpreting the events as described in the Bible in an attempt to reconcile them with scientific evidence. 'Young-Earth' creationism holds that the earth was created by God several thousand years ago, and that God only made the earth appear much older; fossils are sometimes seen as having been put in the earth by God to test man's faith. 'Day-age' creationism takes the view that the 'six days' of Genesis do not refer to six 24-hour days, but to millions of years of time. 'Progressive' creationism suggests that species have changed or evolved, but in a process guided continuously by God, rather than by natural selection. The idea that evolution did take place, but as a tool used by God, is also held by proponents of theistic evolution, also known as evolutionary creation, in which the scriptural account of creation is seen as a metaphor. These last two positions are developments of the philosophical argument known as 'intelligent design', which has become very popular in recent years, particularly in the USA. Proponents of intelligent design would argue that Darwinism or evolutionary theory cannot adequately explain the vast complexity exhibited by life on earth. As a theory in itself, intelligent design is ostensibly independent of any claims as to the nature of the guiding force; however, in practice its most vociferous supporters are also creationists.

Creation science, or the attempt to use science to support the creationist worldview, as put forward by the Creation Research Society, is dismissed by most of the scientific community as a pseudoscience, but according to a 2001 Gallup poll, an estimated 72 per cent of Americans believe in some form of creationism.

creation myths
Mytho-religious stories which explain the beginning of the universe, earth, life and humanity, usually as a deliberate act of creation by a supreme being or beings.
The term 'creation myth' is usually applied to a mytho-religious story which explains the beginning of humanity, life, the earth and the universe as being the result of a deliberate act of creation by SUPREME BEINGS or being. A number of people object to the use of the expression 'creation myth' with reference to creation stories which are still believed in today, since the word 'myth' suggests fictional ideas; several religious groups have, controversially, claimed that their accounts of creation should be taught alongside, or even instead of, scientific theories of evolution, and some creationists believe that all life on earth was created already fully speciated as the organisms which exist today. However, it may be argued that creation myths are not intended as literal descriptions of actual events, but are meant to express deeper truths in a symbolic way.

Creation myths vary widely from age to age and culture to culture, but many share similar motifs, such as the emergence of the components of the universe and the world from a primordial chaos; the theme of birth; the separation of mother and father figures; the emergence of land from an infinite and eternal ocean, or of a supreme being's retrieval from beneath this ocean of earth or mud which becomes land (known as 'diver myths'); or the fashioning by a supreme being of the universe either from his or her own body, from pre-existing chaotic material, or, as in the Christian, Judaic and Islamic religions, out of nothing at all (*ex nihilo*).

In the ancient Babylonian creation myth, the god Marduk destroys the monster Tiamat and cuts her body into two halves, which become the earth and the sky, and later also kills her husband, Kingu, using his blood to create mankind. The Bantu story of the creation tells of how the earth originally consisted of just water and darkness, until its ruler, the white giant Mbombo, vomited up the sun, moon and stars, and later trees, animals and people. According to the Maori creation myth, the Sky Father Ranginui and the Earth Mother Papatuanuku were joined in a tight embrace and gave rise to many children, who existed in the darkness between them. However, the children, wishing to live in the light, separated their parents, who grieve for one another to this day. The Norse god Odin and his brothers were said to have created the nine worlds of the universe from the body of the giant Ymir, whose flesh was used to create the earth, his blood the sea, his skull Heaven, and his eyebrows Midgeard, where humans could live; the first humans, Ask and Embla, were created from logs.

In TAOISM, the Tao is the ultimate force behind creation. With the Tao, nothingness is thought to have given rise to existence, existence to YIN and YANG, and from yin and yang, all things came into being. In Hinduism, the existence of the universe is believed to be governed by the Trimurti, or threefold interaction, of Brahma the Creator, Vishnu the Sustainer and Shiva the Destroyer; nature and all of God's creations are seen as manifestations of Him. In Islam, all creation is attributed to Allah, who is clearly identified in the Koran as the 'first cause'. Similarly, in Judaism and Christianity, God is believed to have created order, the universe and all humanity by commanding them into existence, making man in His image in the form of the first humans, Adam and Eve, to be caretakers of the world. See also COSMOGONY; CREATIONISM.

Creme, Benjamin (1922–   )

The prophet of Maitreya.

Benjamin Creme was born in Glasgow in 1922. An accomplished artist, he has also studied esoteric philosophy, including the teachings of ALICE BAILEY's Arcane School, which in turn was based on THEOSOPHY. Through his reading he became aware of the ASCENDED MASTERS – one of whom (he claims) contacted him in 1959, informing him that 'Maitreya', or 'the World Teacher', would return in 20 years. In 1974, Creme made this information public, lecturing around the world from 1975 onwards.

The Maitreya has been a concept in most schools of Buddhism for centuries, as the bodhisattva or enlightened being for the future, the one who would some day return to earth. In Creme's teaching, the Maitreya is the most senior of the Ascended Masters of the Great White Brotherhood. He is Jesus, returning in his Second Coming; he is the Messiah of Judaism; he is the Mahdi of some branches of Islam; he is Krishna; he is the one to unite all people of all religions.

Creme claims that the Maitreya is already among us. He announced in 1982 that the Maitreya was living anonymously in the Asian community of the East End of London, but at a well-publicized gathering of 22 journalists in July 1985, Maitreya failed to appear as promised. Through his organization Share International, Creme provides lists of Maitreya's appearances around the world, including photographs of his first acknowledged appearance at a healing meeting in Nairobi, Kenya, in 1988. Share International does note that 'he always looks different, depending on the circumstances and the person he appears to', but claims that in each instance Maitreya first creates magnetized, healing waters.

Maitreya's message is straightforward: 'Share and save the world … Take your brother's need as the measure for your action and solve the problems of the world.'

Cremo, Michael (1948–   )

An author who challenges scientific orthodoxy in archaeology.

Michael Cremo is a US-born writer who maintains that mankind is much older than current scientific orthodoxy would have us believe. Particularly in his book *Forbidden Archeology* (co-written with R L Thompson, 1993), he points to the discovery of fossils and man-made artefacts that appear to disprove accepted theories of when and where humankind appeared on earth. These include humanoid bones found in a Pennsylvania coal

The controversial writer Michael Cremo photographed at the *Fortean Times* 'UnConvention' in 1999.
(© TopFoto)

seam that has been dated as 286 million years old, as well as a 5-million-year-old skull found in Italy.

Cremo contends that discoveries like these have been sidelined or completely ignored by the archaeological establishment simply because their existence does not fit in with accepted theories. He describes himself as a Vedic archaeologist, which essentially means that he follows the Vedic scriptures of India in claiming that man has been on earth for 'tens of millions of years'. His ideas have inevitably led him into conflict with the Darwinian theory of evolution, attracting the support of creationists, and given succour to those who believe in lost civilizations in human history.

Cremo's critics, however, accuse him of ignoring scientific methodology and of taking at face value findings which have been inaccurately or even fraudulently arrived at. In effect, he has had an element of his own criticism of scientific orthodoxy turned back against him: that he accepts what suits his theories and disregards anything that does not.

crisis apparitions

Ghosts of living individuals seen elsewhere at the moment of their death or when they are suffering a trauma.

The term 'crisis apparition' appears to have been coined by researcher D J West in 1946 when he was examining some sixty years of testimony accumulated by the SOCIETY FOR PSYCHICAL RESEARCH. In such cases the APPARITION of a person who is dying or suffering a trauma is seen or sensed by a relative or friend many miles away. Hundreds of such cases were collected by members of the Society and published in a two-volume work entitled *Phantasms of the Living* (Edmond Gurney, Frederic Myers and Frank Podmore, 1886). The 19th-century reports often contained symbolic elements – such as water dripping from the body of an apparition representing a person who had drowned at sea. Of the cases recorded in *Phantasms of the Living* many involved family relationships and in nearly a third of cases the death would be classed as sudden. Reports of crisis apparitions are now markedly rarer than in the 19th century – the apparitions have generally been replaced by stories of dreams or vague feelings of unease at the time of the death of a friend or relative.

Croglin Grange vampire

One of the best-known reports of a vampire in Britain, an account of which was published by Augustus Hare in 1872.

The story of the Croglin Grange vampire is one of the most famous, allegedly factual, accounts of a vampire attack taking place in Britain. It was first published in 1872 in *Memorials of a Quiet Life* by the English writer and raconteur Augustus Hare (1834–1903), who claimed to have recorded it as it was related to him by a man called Captain Fisher.

The story goes that Croglin Grange, a large single-storey house in Cumberland, Cumbria, had been owned by the Fisher family for many centuries, and that in the early 19th century, they had moved out and put the house up for let. It was taken by two brothers and a sister – Michael, Edward and Amelia Cranswell. One summer night, Amelia went to bed, but was unable to sleep because of the heat. Looking out of her bedroom window, she became aware of two points of light in the darkness of the churchyard that lay beyond the wall around the grounds of the house. As she watched, they began to move, gliding over the wall and across the lawn towards her, and she saw that they were surrounded by a dark form. She heard a rustling outside, then a brown face with flaming eyes looked in at her, and a bony hand first scratched on the window, then began to unpick the lead from around the windowpanes. One of the panes fell in, and the hand slipped in and opened the latch. Then the creature climbed into the room, grasped Amelia by the hair, pulled her head back and bit her on the neck. Her scream brought her brothers to her rescue, but by the time they arrived to find her bleeding profusely from a gash in her neck, her attacker had escaped across the lawn, over the wall and into the churchyard. Amelia survived her wound, and once she was well enough, her brothers took her to Switzerland to help her to recover from her ordeal.

The three returned to Croglin Grange that autumn, and the winter passed peacefully enough, although Amelia took care to close the shutters on her windows, and her brothers moved into a room directly across from hers, with loaded pistols ready. In the following March, Amelia was woken one night by a scratching sound, and saw the same hideous face as before looking in at her over the top pane of the window, which the shutters did not cover. She screamed, and her brothers rushed in and managed to shoot the creature in the leg, but it once more escaped into the churchyard, seeming to disappear into a vault. The next morning, Michael and Edward summoned the other tenants of the Grange, and opened the vault. They found it full of coffins which had been broken open, and their hideously mangled contents were scattered across the floor. One coffin lay intact, but with its lid lying loosely on top. When this was removed, there lay the brown, shrivelled, but whole body of the creature they had seen the night before, the fresh wound of a pistol-shot in its leg. Realizing they were dealing with a vampire, they did the only thing they could, and burned it.

For a long time, Hare's story was discounted by many as simply the tallest of many tall tales in his memoirs. There is no record of a building called Croglin Grange, although there is a Croglin Low Hall. A churchyard is situated in the area, but it is about a mile away from Croglin Low Hall, and it has no vault matching the one described in Hare's account. But recent research suggests that the story is in fact much older than he reported it to be; one of his critics, F Clive Ross, visited the area and was told by the locals that Hare had got some of his facts wrong – the story, they said, had taken place in the 1680s, not the 19th century. Furthermore, a chapel and vault located much closer to the house were said to have been demolished in Cromwell's day, and a second storey is said to have been added to the building after that. So the description of the house and the churchyard matches a 17th-century setting, rather than a 19th-century one.

See also VAMPIRISM.

Croiset, Gerard (1909–80)

A Dutch clairvoyant who became famous as a psychic detective, involved in helping the police of a number of countries.

Gerard Croiset is said to have exhibited clairvoyant (see CLAIRVOYANCE) abilities from the age of six. He is known to have become involved in SPIRITUALISM in 1935, and to have worked as a psychometrist (see PSYCHOMETRY), claiming to be able to gain information about people by holding items which either belonged to them, or were connected with them in some way. He also claimed to be able to heal people through the LAYING-ON OF HANDS.

Shortly after World War II, Croiset attended a lecture on PARAPSYCHOLOGY and afterwards volunteered to have his psychic abilities tested at the University of Utrecht. His abilities were said to be good, and Croiset became involved in police work; initially he was consulted by the Dutch police in a number of missing-person cases. His involvement with the police led to a great deal of publicity and a number of anecdotal examples of his successes. Eventually his help was sought by police forces from a number of other countries but, during the 1960s and 1970s, he was involved in a series of high-profile failures and his fame waned.

It is true that Croiset did appear to achieve some measure of success during his career, but some have argued that, in view of the great number of cases he was involved in overall, his successes could be put down to pure chance.

crop circles

Mysterious flattened circular areas in growing cereal crops.

In southern England in the late 1970s and early 1980s farmers were baffled by the overnight appearance of strange circular patterns in their fields of standing cereal crops. The patterns were created by flattening stalks, but the force or forces that produced this effect were a mystery.

Initially the patterns were generally simple and based upon circles; however, as the phenomenon developed, the patterns became increasingly complex and sophisticated, with interlinked circles of varying sizes, swirling patterns, and symmetrical designs of geometric precision. Various explanations have been suggested.

One theory is that the circles are entirely natural, having been caused by the effect of fungi or infection on the growing crops, causing the stalks to weaken and bend. The patterns are, therefore, produced

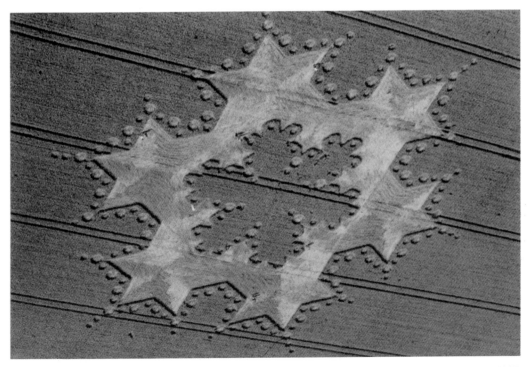

An incredibly complex crop circle which appeared in a field of wheat near Alton Barnes, Wiltshire, on 8 August 1997. It measured 71 metres (234 feet) across, and included 192 small circles around the edges of its snowflake design.
(© Mary Evans Picture Library)

completely by chance. Another explanation is that localized meteorological effects are to blame, such as freak tornado-like winds, BALL LIGHTNING or the hypothetical PLASMA VORTEX. However, the complexity and precision of many of the patterns tend to count against these explanations – certainly for all occurrences of the phenomenon.

Others have suggested that the circular patterns are caused by EXTRATERRESTRIAL action, whether accidentally, marking the places where the aliens' spacecraft have landed and taken off, or deliberately, as some kind of as-yet unexplained messages to humankind. Satellites originating on earth have also been blamed, with conspiracy theorists suggesting that the military is secretly testing a microwave beam weapon on empty fields.

Many people now believe that crop circles are nothing more than elaborate hoaxes, which have fooled a public all too ready to believe in aliens and conspiracies. Indeed, in 1991, two Englishmen (see DOUG AND DAVE) famously confessed to having created crop circles since 1978, and various methods of producing patterns have been demonstrated. There is no doubt that hoaxers have been shown to have been involved in some circles, but many people hold that this does not adequately explain all of the recorded occurrences. The fact that crop circles have appeared in many parts of the world, including some relatively remote areas, is cited as evidence against the hoax theory. There is also at least one historical precedent for the phenomenon – a case known as the MOWING DEVIL, dating from the 17th century.

Some crop circle researchers, know as cereologists (see CEREOLOGY), claim to have detected strange electromagnetic fields within certain circles, causing radio interference and the malfunction of mobile phones (see ELECTROMAGNETIC PHENOMENA). This leads them to conclude that some electromagnetic force is responsible for the circles. However, this is not necessarily extraterrestrial in origin, but could be a product of unexplained anomalies in the earth's magnetic field. They also claim that seeds taken from affected crops are seen to have undergone mutation and that their subsequent growth is faster and stronger than unaffected seeds from the same field.

While films have been made of people setting out to create crop circles, and do-it-yourself instructions are available on the Internet, it remains true that many circles have not been 'claimed' by hoaxers or anyone else and, in the absence of reliable witnesses to their appearance, their origins remain unexplained. There are also occasionally examples which are so large, complex and accurately produced that the suggestion that they could have been produced in a single night, unobserved, seems unbelievable. For example, a formation that appeared at Milk Hill, near Alton Barnes, Wiltshire, in 2001, was nearly 300 metres (980 feet) across and contained 409 separate circles in a precise pattern of arms spiralling outwards from a central point.

cropwatchers
People who watch over growing cereal crops to detect crop circle formation or follow up reports of new circle formations.

With CROP CIRCLES continuing to appear in cereal fields in various parts of the world, people known as cropwatchers, or sometimes just 'croppies', still continue to keep a night-time lookout at likely sites during the growing season. The terms do not necessarily imply any element of wider (or even scientific) study of the phenomenon, as is the case with the associated terms 'cereologist' or 'cerealogist' (see CEREOLOGY).

There are various types of cropwatcher. Some are simply farmers, or their family members or employees, anxious to prevent what they see as vandalism by hoaxers bent on creating their own crop circles. Others are more interested in the crop circle phenomenon itself, some from the point of view of gathering evidence that all such circles are man-made, and some taking the opposite tack and seeking proof that hitherto-unexplained forces are at work. Some merely depend on using powerful lights to reveal any goings-on, but others are more high-tech and come equipped with infrared cameras and night-vision goggles.

While the activities of cropwatchers have resulted in the exposure of some hoaxes, little reliable evidence for any other form of circle creation has been assembled. However, there have been some intriguing stories of the undetected appearance of circles in close proximity to cropwatches while they were in progress. (See also CEREOLOGY)

cross correspondence
A proposed way to test the truth of mediumistic messages.

In the early part of the 20th century a particular series of tests were carried out in an attempt to prove or disprove the reality of the 'communications' conducted by MEDIUMS. The theory was that, if the information a medium communicates is true, then potentially any medium could, independently, communicate the same information. This agreement was described as 'cross correspondence' and, assuming of course that there was no normal means by which the parties could have gained access to the same information, examples of such agreement would be taken as confirmation of the mediums' claims.

From 1901 to 1930 a series of apparent cross correspondences between several mediums who utilized AUTOMATIC WRITING were investigated. A simple cross correspondence would involve the same words or phrase being produced, a complex cross correspondence would contain messages which would need to be interpreted, and finally, an ideal cross correspondence would involve incomplete messages which would have to be put together like a puzzle (part of the final complete message coming from each medium and, in itself, being meaningless). Some claimed these cross correspondences were indeed caused by several mediums communicating with the same SPIRIT; others claimed that this was actually evidence of TELEPATHY. Many cases were studied extensively by the SOCIETY FOR PSYCHICAL RESEARCH, which tended towards the communication with the dead hypothesis. However, despite some claims that it had produced strong evidence, the study of cross correspondences has fallen out of favour.

crossroads

The folkloric belief that crossroads are particularly haunted by supernatural entities.

In European folklore crossroads are reputed to have a peculiar attraction for GHOSTS and other supernatural entities, a notion perpetuated in the 20th century through the prolific writings of Elliot O'Donnell (1872–1965). Although road ghosts (see HAUNTED HIGHWAYS) are regularly reported, there is little to suggest that crossroads are actually more prone to generating such reports than other locations.

In England the uncanny reputation of crossroads was undoubtedly fuelled by their choice, until the early 19th century, as the burial place for those who had committed suicide. This was possibly due to a folk belief that the four roads would confuse any restless SPIRIT that had thwarted other traditional precautions (such as the driving of a stake through the body in order to bind it to the spot). In a Christian society the shape of the cross might also have been thought to neutralize harmful influences.

Crossroad burials were condemned in Parliament in 1813 and rendered superfluous in 1821 by an Act requiring all churchyards to have a section of unconsecrated ground reserved for the bodies of suicides. Nonetheless the uncanny reputation of crossroads is also found in many other European cultures, including the mythology of ancient Greece in which crossroads were sacred to Hecate, the goddess of WITCHES. It is also noticeable that ghost lore worldwide often invests meeting points and various kinds of man-made or natural boundaries with supernatural significance.

crowing crested cobra

An alleged African snake said to crow like a cockerel and to have a comb and wattles.

With few exceptions – the major ones being the loud grunt of the bull snake and the miaowing yowl of the Bornean cave racer – snakes are not known for their vocal capabilities, which is one reason why a serpentine CRYPTID from Africa known as the crowing crested cobra is so distinctive. As its name suggests, the male of this unidentified snake, measuring up to 6 metres (almost 20 feet) long and buffish-brown or greyish-black in colour, is said by those who claim to have encountered it to give voice to a very loud crowing cry, like that of a cockerel. This strange creature is also claimed to bear a bright-red comb on top of its head (but projecting forwards rather than backwards, as those of cockerels do), and also (in the male, but not in the female) a pair of red facial wattles.

Reports of this snake range from Natal in the south of the continent to Victoria Nyanza in east Central Africa, and also to Lake Tanganyika, Zambia and the Indian Ocean. Not surprisingly, it has acquired many local names, most memorable of which is *inkhomi* ('the killer') in Chi-ngoni and Chi-nkhonde, on account of its supposedly venomous bite and ferocious, highly aggressive temperament.

A reptile with a comb and wattles, and which crows like a cockerel, is immediately reminiscent of the legendary monster the cockatrice, but African native tribes and Westerners who say they have seen it claim that the crowing crested cobra is real. One of the most interesting reports came from John Knott, who claimed to have run over a crowing crested cobra while driving one evening at the end of May 1959 in what was then Southern Rhodesia (now Zimbabwe). He claims to have inspected the snake, and described it as jet-black, measuring around 2 metres (6.5 feet) long, and bearing a perfectly symmetrical crest on its head, capable of being raised via five internal prop-like structures. The snake was mortally wounded, and Knott did not attempt to retain its body.

Conversely, what he believed to be the bony skeleton of the comb and part of the neck (containing several vertebrae) from another such snake was retained for some time by Dr J O Shircore of Karonga, Nyasaland (now Malawi), who in 1944 published a very detailed description of it in the journal *African Affairs*. The present-day locality of this specimen, however, is unknown. The most popular explanation for crowing crested cobras is that they are nothing more than black mambas that have incompletely shed their skin, leaving pieces of unshed skin adhering to their head, resembling a crest. Certainly, some very large, ostensibly crested snakes that have been caught and examined have been found to be old mambas adorned in this manner. However, the symmetrical, prop-supported crest reported by Knott, and the even more precise crest documented by Shircore, cannot be explained away like this, suggesting that there may genuinely be some basis in fact for the elusive crowing crested cobra.

Crowley, Aleister (1875–1947)

English writer and magician, the most notorious occultist of his generation.

Born Edward Alexander Crowley in Leamington Spa, Warwickshire, he was raised by strict Christian parents. Crowley was first called 'the Beast' by his mother, a member of the Plymouth Brethren sect, for what she perceived to be his ungodly behaviour. While an undergraduate at Cambridge, Crowley became a published poet and skilled mountaineer and developed his interests in the occult. In 1898 he joined the London chapter of the occult society the HERMETIC ORDER OF THE GOLDEN DAWN and rose rapidly through the hierarchy. He left Cambridge without a degree, and moved to London, calling himself Count Vladimir. Crowley clashed with MACGREGOR MATHERS, one of the founders of the society, and the two allegedly fought, using astral demons. Crowley was expelled from the Golden Dawn and became interested in Eastern mysticism. He lived for a time at Boleskine House, near Loch Ness in Scotland, where he allegedly celebrated the BLACK MASS, summoned DEMONS and took part in sexual orgies.

Crowley married his first wife, Rose Kelly, in 1903, but continued to take mistresses, whom he called 'scarlet women'. In 1904, while the couple were in Egypt, Kelly claimed to have received astral communications from the Egyptian god Horus. Crowley performed an invocation and a voice which identified itself as Aiwass, whom Crowley took to be his true self, began to speak. Aiwass spoke on three consecutive days, and dictated *The Book of the Law*. Central to this, one of Crowley's most important works, is the Law of THELEMA: 'Do what thou wilt shall be the whole of the law.' Kelly gave birth to a daughter, Lola Zaza, but during a trip to Vietnam Crowley left them and the child died of typhoid. Crowley blamed Kelly and her alcoholism for the death, and Kelly was left mentally unstable.

Crowley continued his exploration of the occult, taking the poet Victor Neuberg as a lover and assistant. He became involved in the esoteric ORDO TEMPLI ORIENTIS, a group associated with the teaching of sex magic (see MAGIC, SEX). During World War I Crowley lived in the USA, writing anti-British propaganda. In 1920 he settled in Sicily and with a group of disciples, including his new mistress, Leah Hirsig, he founded the Sacred Abbey of the Thelemic Mysteries. Rumours

'The Great Beast', Aleister Crowley – once described in the British press as the 'wickedest man in the world'.
(© Mary Evans Picture Library)

of orgies, drugs and magical ceremonies involving the ritual sacrifice of animals soon circulated. A young disciple died, and the British media subsequently dubbed Crowley 'the wickedest man in the world'. In 1923 Mussolini expelled Crowley from Italy. Crowley married his second wife, Maria Ferrari de Miramar, in 1929.

Crowley continued to publish his writings, but his final years were spent in poverty. A chronic heroin addict, he died in a boarding house in Hastings.

A great mystique arose around Crowley and his practices of sex magic and sacrifice. Crowley himself believed he was the reincarnation of such occultists as Pope Alexander VI, Cagliostro and ÉLIPHAS LÉVI. He proclaimed himself to be 'the Great Beast' and 'the beast 666' (see BEAST, THE GREAT), and many linked the madness and deaths of those around him to his occult practices.

cryptid

The official term for all cryptozoological animals

Although the term 'cryptozoology' was first coined as far back as the 1950s to describe the scientific study of animals whose existence or identity is still unrecognized by science, for the next three decades there was no corresponding official term for such creatures themselves. Instead, a variety of loose, generalized terms were used, such as 'mystery animal', 'undiscovered animal', 'unidentified animal', 'unknown animal' (as used by BERNARD HEUVELMANS in the title of his pioneering cryptozoological book, *On the Track of Unknown Animals*), and even 'monster'. In the summer 1983 issue of the *ISC* [International Society of Cryptozoology] *Newsletter*, however, John E Wall proposed that the term 'cryptid' ('hidden animal') should be used for this purpose – this was swiftly accepted and is now in regular use.

cryptomnesia

The concept that memories can be 'hidden' in the mind in such a way that they cannot be consciously accessed.

Swiss psychologist Théodore Flournoy (1854–1920) coined the word 'cryptomnesia' to describe the (now controversial) idea of 'hidden memory' or 'concealed recollection'. The supposed hidden memories referred to cannot be consciously recalled, although some people believe that they can be recovered through processes such as HYPNOSIS (see MEMORIES, RECOVERED).

It is claimed that these hidden memories may be evidence for a number of paranormal phenomena, particularly REINCARNATION (see PAST-LIFE REGRESSION). However, in the case of the supposed reincarnation of BRIDEY MURPHY, many of the events recalled under regression hypnosis were found to relate to tales that Virginia Tighe had heard as a child from an Irish neighbour so, even if the memories were 'hidden', they had quite possibly come from a mundane source. Some people have also suggested cryptomnesia as an alternative mechanism for the phenomena produced during such things as AUTOMATIC WRITING and the apparent CHANNELLING of spirits. It also forms the basis of a proposed explanation for DÉJÀ VU – that experiencing a particular object or sensation can trigger the partial recall of a hidden memory bringing about the sensation of prior knowledge even though there is no conscious memory of the prior experience. See also MEMORIES, REPRESSED; MEMORY, FALSE.

Cryptozoology *see panel p142*

crystal balls

A globe of rock-crystal or glass, stared into in order to obtain visual images, or as a means of divination.

The practice of gazing into a crystal ball to obtain visions or OCCULT knowledge, known as SCRYING, has a long history. The Druid Merlin is said to have used a crystal ball to see into the future, and Queen Elizabeth I's court astrologer and personal adviser, JOHN DEE, was probably the best-known practitioner of this ancient art.

Pure rock crystal has always been believed to attract

The US psychic and astrologer Jeane Dixon claimed that she successfully employed a number of methods of divination, including gazing into a crystal ball.
(© Bettmann/Corbis)

and concentrate occult virtues, so this is thought to be the best constituent for a crystal ball. Since rock crystals seldom exceed one inch in thickness, balls made from rock crystal tend not to exceed an inch in diameter, but the absence of flaws in the ball is considered to be more important than its size. The next best alternative is thought to be a sphere made of high-quality glass.

Crystal-gazing is said to best done in near or total darkness, to minimize the possibility of distracting reflections. A candle may be used for illumination, preferably placed behind the scryer so that it is not reflected in the ball. The gaze should be focused, not on the surface of the ball, but in its centre, as if the ball is a window on the astral world. Practitioners claim that after a while, milky clouds spread out from the centre of the ball, and these then lift to reveal images, which must be observed with an 'absent mind', since the moment the scryers focus their critical faculties on the image, it will disappear.

Some scryers recommend that the crystal ball should be 'activated' by treating it like a living thing, for example, by speaking to it, giving it a personal name and handling it often. Others believe a crystal ball's effectiveness is improved by charging it once a month in the light of the full moon.

Cryptozoology

The term 'cryptozoology' is derived from the Greek roots *kryptos* ('hidden'), *zoon* ('animal') and *logos* ('discourse' or 'study'), and therefore translates literally as 'the study of hidden animals'. It is generally defined as the study of unexpected animals whose existence or identity is currently undetermined by science. This definition emphasizes the crucial fact that such animals are unknown only to scientists; almost invariably, they are familiar creatures to the people who share their native domain (and hence are said to be 'ethnoknown' – a term coined in print by cryptozoologist Richard Greenwell in 1985). It also underlines that, to be classed as cryptozoological, such animals need to be unexpected in some way, eg relatively large and inhabiting a locality where scientists would not expect them to be; otherwise, any undiscovered animal, including the tiniest insect or least significant worm, could be considered cryptozoological.

Veteran Belgian cryptozoologist Dr BERNARD HEUVELMANS, popularly dubbed 'The Father of Cryptozoology', frequently claimed that he was the person responsible for coining this term, during the 1950s, but so too did leading American cryptozoologist Ivan T Sanderson (1911–73). Moreover, Sanderson's claim was even acknowledged by Heuvelmans himself, so it is likely that it was coined independently by these researchers. It first appeared in print in 1959, when Lucien Blancou, Chief Game Inspector of the French Overseas Territories, who had reported a number of African mystery beasts in various publications, dedicated his latest book, *Géographie cynégétique du Monde*, to 'Bernard Heuvelmans, *maître de la cryptozoologie*' ('master of cryptozoology'). In 1983, Manitoba resident John E Wall coined the companion term CRYPTID, referring to any creature classed as a cryptozoological animal. Until then, such creatures had been referred to by a plethora of loose, generalized terms, such as 'mystery animal', 'hidden animal', 'unknown animal', 'undiscovered animal' or 'unidentified animal'.

What precisely constitutes a cryptid has engendered much controversy, even among cryptozoologists, with some investigators expanding its definition to include exotic OUT-OF PLACE ANIMALS and even paranormal entities. Consequently, in 1985, Richard Greenwell of the International Society of Cryptozoology published a formal classification system for cryptozoology in the Society's refereed scientific journal, *Cryptozoology*. He proposed and defined a series of seven cryptid categories. These are as follows:

Category I: Cryptids constituting aberrant individuals, ie individuals of known species or subspecies whose form, size or colouration is unusual or unique. Such cryptids include giant-sized anacondas, Sri Lankan horned jackals and the BLUE TIGER OF FUJIAN.

Category II: Cryptids constituting known species or subspecies in geographical areas in which they are currently unrecognized by science as naturally existing, because there is no conclusive evidence, as yet, to confirm this unexpected zoogeographical distribution. The leopard *Panthera pardus* as reported in Bali is an example of this category of cryptid. Conversely, ALIEN BIG CATS are not, because these are merely escapee or deliberately released exotic, non-native individuals (ie their occurrence in, for instance, the United Kingdom is not an example of natural zoogeographical distribution).

Category III: Cryptids constituting presumably living species or subspecies that are known only from incomplete specimens, and do not represent fossil forms – as with the Florida GIANT OCTOPUS from 1896.

Category IV: Cryptids constituting known species or subspecies that officially became extinct in historical times, but which may have survived into more recent times than originally believed – or may even still survive today and thus await rediscovery. The THYLACINE and the dwarf upland moa (see MOA, LIVING) are good examples of such cryptids.

Category V: Cryptids constituting species or subspecies currently known to science only from fossils, but which may have survived into historical times – or may even still exist today and thus await discovery in the living state. Cryptids deemed likely by cryptozoologists to be living plesiosaurs, zeuglodonts or dinosaurs (see MOKELE-MBEMBE), for example, fall into this category. Several noteworthy precedents are already known, such as the coelacanth and the Chacoan peccary.

Category VI: Cryptids constituting new species or subspecies of already-known animal groups (eg new species or subspecies of cat, whale or monitor lizard) but for which no physical evidence currently exists. These include such cryptids as the AHOOL and the RHINOCEROS DOLPHIN.

Category VII: Cryptids constituting new species or subspecies of animal whose existence is currently unknown not only to scientists but also to native people sharing their domain – ie they are ethnounknown instead of ethnoknown. An excellent precedent for this category of cryptid is the megamouth shark *Megachasma pelagios*, whose existence remained wholly unknown, not only to science but also to local fishermen, until a specimen was accidentally caught by a research vessel off the Hawaiian island of Oahu in 1976.

Technically, as conceded by Greenwell, Categories I and VII are only semi-cryptozoological, as cryptozoology in its strictest sense does not deal with freak individuals (Category I) or with mystery beasts that are not ethnoknown (Category VII).

Although Greenwell's classification system was an admirable attempt to introduce a degree of order and categorization to the diverse array of cryptids on file, it is ultimately unsatisfactory for the simple reason that, by definition, the zoological identity of any given cryptid remains undetermined until the moment that conclusive physical evidence for its existence is obtained – whereupon it is no longer a cryptid but an officially recognized, classifiable animal. Consequently, as frequently happens, especially when a particular case attracts attention from several different cryptozoologists, more than one identity may be proposed for a cryptid – which means that it could conceivably be placed into more than one of Greenwell's categories.

A good example of this futility in attempting to pigeon-hole cryptids into specific categories is the North American THUNDERBIRD. As discussed in detail by British zoologist and cryptozoologist Dr Karl Shuker in *In Search of Prehistoric Survivors* (1995), a number of different identities are on offer for this cryptid. It may, for instance, be a surviving species of prehistoric condor-related vulture known as a teratorn (which therefore places it in Category V of Greenwell's classification system), or it could be an unknown species of eagle (placing it in Category VI) or possibly a population of Andean condors well outside this species' recognized zoogeographical

distribution (Category II). It may even be based upon freak, extra-large individuals of a known species of North American vulture (Category I). In short, any attempt to categorize cryptids taxonomically can only be speculative at best, and, at worst, a needless detraction from the cryptids themselves.

Whereas the investigation of many famous unexplained phenomena as discrete subjects set apart from mainstream studies date back to the earliest ages of human enquiry, as with GHOSTS, EXTRASENSORY PERCEPTION and unexplained AERIAL PHENOMENA, for instance, cryptozoology is something of an anomaly, because there was no need for its delineation from mainstream zoology as a separate field of study until as recently as the 20th century. This is because there was once (and still is even today, for that matter) so much virgin, unexplored territory in the more remote, exotic regions of the globe that zoologists had no doubt whatsoever that major new animal species still awaited discovery. Consequently, every report of an ostensibly new, unclassified species attracted serious attention from the scientific community. This open-minded trend continued until the early 1800s, when a number of leading figures in the international zoological community began to cast doubt on the prospect of further such discoveries being made, believing instead that the world was now too well explored for any significant new animals to remain concealed.

Prominent among these sceptics was Baron Georges Cuvier, an eminent French zoologist, who, in 1812, boldly, but also (as it soon transpired) rashly, proclaimed: 'There is little hope of discovering new species of large quadrupeds.' A mere seven years later, he was startled to receive a communication from a colleague concerning a spectacular new mammal freshly discovered in Asia. It was a very novel species of tapir, a trunked hoofed mammal related to horses and rhinoceroses which was previously only known to occur in the New World. Moreover, unlike the American species, which are all uniformly dark, the newly revealed Asian tapir was instantly distinguished by its showy saddle of white colouration across its back and flanks. Although hitherto undescribed by science, it was well known to the local people, setting a precedent for future cryptozoological discoveries. So too was another previously unsuspected species of tapir, the pinchaque or mountain tapir of South America's high Andes, formally documented scientifically in 1835. During the remainder of the 19th century all manner of other dramatic new species were exposed, including the lowland gorilla, pygmy hippopotamus, Himalayan takin, Père David's deer, lesser panda and giant panda, Grant's gazelle, gerenuk and Grévy's zebra.

Nevertheless, the dark shadow of scepticism that had been cast by Cuvier and a number of other influential but highly sceptical zoologists, including Sir Richard Owen and Rudolf Virchow, lingered on. Indeed, such was the extent to which it blighted scientific enthusiasm for new finds that even the discovery in 1901 of the Congolese okapi, an incongruous short-necked forest-dwelling giraffe with zebra-striped haunches, which created a scientific sensation worldwide, was nonetheless deemed to be surely the last great zoological find. Of course, it was not – just as the Asian tapir was only the first of many remarkable new animals to be unveiled in the 19th century, so too was the okapi merely the herald of a new wave of extraordinary new creatures that would be discovered and documented in the 20th century. Indeed, more than 300 major new animals were revealed during the 1900s, including the rediscovery of a number of spectacular creatures hitherto assumed to have died out long ago.

In 1993, the first book ever devoted solely to such creatures was produced – *The Lost Ark: New and Rediscovered Animals of the 20th Century* (republished in 2002 as *The New Zoo*), written by Dr Karl Shuker. The book has become the standard work on the subject, and contains every major animal to have been discovered or rediscovered between 1900 and 1999. In addition to the okapi, these include the gigantic but gentle mountain gorilla (discovered in 1902), the equally sizeable giant forest hog (1904), the resurrected lobe-finned coelacanth (1938) that belongs to an ancient lineage of fishes formerly believed to have died out at least 64 million years ago, large spectacular birds such as the Congo peacock (1936) and Vo Quy's pheasant (1964), the once-mythical king cheetah (1926) that is now known to be a rare striped variety of the normal spotted cheetah, the megamouth shark (1976), a pig-like mammal called the Chacoan peccary (1974) hitherto believed to have died out during the Ice Ages, several different species of beaked whale, the formidable Komodo dragon (1912) that constitutes the world's largest lizard, the Cambodian wild ox or kouprey (1937), the Queen of Sheba's gazelle (1985), the amazing saola or Vu Quang ox (1992), the giant muntjac deer (1994) and a great many more.

Yet despite such discoveries as these turning up on a regular basis during the 1900s, zoological scepticism concerning new animals still awaiting scientific detection paradoxically remained rife throughout much of that century, with each new find being dismissed as a mere exception, an anomaly, not likely to be repeated – until the next time. Meanwhile, however, a new generation of more open-minded zoologists was also springing forth, encouraged by such

finds to investigate and document reports of additional mystery beasts. The first true cryptozoology book was published in 1950, and was entitled *Von Neuen und Unentdeckten Tierarten* ('Of New and Undiscovered Animals'), written by German zoologist Dr Ingo Krumbiegel. This was followed five years later by Dr Bernard Heuvelmans' major two-volume study *Sur La Piste des Bêtes Ignorées*, which was translated into English in 1958 as the single-volume tome *On the Track of Unknown Animals*. This comprehensive work introduced a host of previously obscure mystery beasts to a worldwide readership, containing exhaustively researched investigation and documentation of such nowadays-familiar cryptids as the YETI, QUEENSLAND TIGER, NANDI BEAR, WAITOREKE, mokele-mbembe, TATZELWORM, MINHOCÃO, ORANG PENDEK, KONGAMATO, NUNDA, LOYS'S APE, TRATRATRATRA and numerous others. It also inspired the foundation of a new zoological discipline, cryptozoology, concentrating exclusively upon the investigation of creatures still apparently unknown to science through field searches and bibliographical research.

During the decades that followed, numerous additional publications appeared, dealing with a vast range of mystery beasts, and many expeditions sought these beasts in their native terrain. In January 1982, the first scientific society devoted to cryptozoology, the International Society of Cryptozoology, was founded in Tucson, Arizona, with Heuvelmans as its president, Greenwell as its secretary and publications editor and a distinguished panel of leading zoologists with cryptozoological interests as its board of directors. After decades in the wilderness, cryptozoology, and the beasts that its supporters sought, had finally become respectable.

None of the principal cryptids discussed half a century ago in Heuvelmans' book has so far been discovered – although not all of them have attracted major searches. However, the cryptozoological principle of listening to native testimony, and pursuing the leads offered by it, has yielded some other, no less exciting, finds – including a number of sizeable new mammals in Vietnam and South America. Even in modern times, the potential for discovering spectacular new species is still present. The 21st century has already seen expeditions in search of such diverse cryptids as the mokele-mbembe, the orang pendek, several different LAKE MONSTERS and the MONGOLIAN DEATH WORM, to name just a few. After almost 200 years, it would appear that the sceptical influence of Cuvier and others is finally receding, and cryptozoology continues to gain acceptance as a valid and worthwhile discipline within the mainstream scientific community.

Dr Karl P N Shuker

crystals

Thought to possess mystical properties and healing qualities, crystals have been used for thousands of years in medicine and as talismans and divination tools.

Crystals are solid minerals which have formed in a regular geometric shape. They include precious gemstones such as diamonds, sapphires and emeralds, semiprecious stones such as amethyst, aquamarine and topaz, and other stones such as quartz, jasper, fluorite and agate.

Crystals have fascinated mankind from the earliest times, and for many centuries some people have believed that they possess magical powers and particularly healing properties. The earliest records of crystal healing come from ancient Egypt, where crystals have been found in tombs and temples. Crystal healing is also recorded in writings of the Hindu AYURVEDA, and in texts on CHINESE MEDICINE. Greek mythology contains numerous references to the magical powers of certain stones, and the ancient Roman naturalist Pliny recorded in detail the properties of various crystals. In the Middle Ages, crystals were often ground into powders to be mixed with water and taken medicinally, while many cultures throughout history, such as the Native Americans, have used crystals in healing and spiritual ceremonies, and have carried them as TALISMANS or AMULETS.

Crystal healing works on the theory that all living organisms, and also all minerals, have an electromagnetic energy field, and that the particles which make up these energy fields vibrate constantly. Crystals also vibrate, each at their own speed, and when brought into contact with a person, a crystal is believed to start resonating with the person's individual frequency and to interact with their body as part of a single, unified energy system, thus increasing the body's energy. It has also been suggested that the crystal resonates with the frequency of the body's healthy cells and brings the abnormally high or low frequency of unhealthy cells into line with that of the healthy ones, in a process known as entrainment. Quartz in particular is thought to have healing and balancing properties.

Nowadays, crystals are also commonly used in the belief that they can rebalance and tune the CHAKRAS (which are thought to be part of the body's vibrational energy system). Here, crystals with colours that correspond to those attributed to the seven main chakras are placed on them in order to improve and regulate the flow of UNIVERSAL LIFE FORCE. Thus, clear quartz may be used for the crown chakra; amethyst for the third eye chakra; aquamarine for the throat chakra; rose quartz for the heart chakra; citrine for the solar plexus chakra; carnelian for the navel chakra; and smoky quartz for the base chakra. Some crystals are thought to transform energies, while others are said to absorb or transmit them. Uncut crystals are believed to contain more energy than polished stones.

Individual crystals are also used, worn or carried for their specific qualities; for example, blue agate is said to strengthen bone and tissue, eliminate impurities, allow a person to dispel anger and negativity, and to bring hidden talents to the surface. Placed in the home or office, some believe that amethyst or quartz crystals may be used as protection against electron radiation from televisions and computer screens, to relieve stress from the environment or to improve creativity. Crystals can also be used as PENDULUMS for DOWSING, and CRYSTAL BALLS have for centuries been used as a means of DIVINATION.

Many people who use crystals believe that they should be cleansed before use in such a way that they clear away undesirable or inappropriate energy patterns and attune their energies with those of the user. They may be washed in sea salt and rinsed in clear water; placed in a bowl of water and bathed in the light of the full moon, then left to absorb the sun's rays (often performed as a monthly ritual); placed on a cluster of crystals; returned to the earth for two or three days; or purified in the smoke of burning sage. Although the use of crystals remains popular, particularly since its resurgence in the 1980s, there is no scientific evidence that they have any healing properties.

CSICOP *see* COMMITTEE FOR THE SCIENTIFIC INVESTIGATION OF CLAIMS OF THE PARANORMAL

CUFOS

The first independent UFO investigation group to be founded wholly by scientists.

DR J ALLEN HYNEK had served as the UFO consultant to the US Air Force from the inception of its official study programme until its closure. In 1969, freed from the constraints imposed on him during this period, he brought together a number of like-minded colleagues (including JACQUES VALLÉE) to form what they described as an 'invisible college'. Their aim was to apply scientific methods to research selected UFO cases.

In 1972 Hynek outlined his philosophy in his book *The UFO Experience*, and the following year he decided to create a UFO investigation team that adopted the same principles. The Center for UFO Studies (CUFOS) was created in Evanston, Illinois, with the assistance of a local businessman, Sherman J Larsen. Among the early officers in this team were Allan Hendry, who later produced a manual for UFO investigation, *The UFO Handbook*, in 1979, and Dr

David Saunders, who had been the chief investigator with the COLORADO UNIVERSITY STUDY.

CUFOS produced a publication, entitled *International UFO*, which kept the wider membership up to date with its research. This was accompanied annually by a more ambitious, refereed publication, the *Journal of UFO Studies*, containing scientific papers which included thorough appraisals of key cases.

Following Hynek's death in 1986, CUFOS was renamed the 'J Allen Hynek Center for UFO Studies' in his honour, although it is still widely known by the original abbreviation. Its database was also expanded by taking over the case files from another UFO group, the NATIONAL INVESTIGATIONS COMMITTEE ON AERIAL PHENOMENA (NICAP).

Just before his death, Hynek named sociologist Mark Rodeghier as his successor in the post of scientific director. Western Michigan University Natural Sciences Professor Michael Swords took on the duty of continuing the *Journal of UFO Studies*, taking it through a period which saw new approaches to the UFO phenomenon (including such things as the comparative analysis of ALIEN ABDUCTION cases by the folklorist Dr Thomas Bullard). *International UFO Reporter* was revived under the editorship of the author Jerome Clark, with a team of international correspondents (including BILL CHALKER).

As it has with most UFO groups, the 21st century has brought with it a reduction in public profile for CUFOS, and a move away from traditional publication methods. However, CUFOS still continues to operate as a scientifically orientated UFO investigation team in line with the principles of its founder.

cults, doomsday *see* DOOMSDAY CULTS

Cults, New Religious Movements and Alternative Religions *see panel p147*

cultural tracking
The manner in which the features of UFO sighting reports appear to follow cultural trends.

The UFO phenomenon in its modern form only really began to be widely discussed after the KENNETH ARNOLD case in 1947. Before this there were many recorded incidents, dating back over hundreds (if not thousands) of years, that could certainly be described as 'UFO' sightings in the strictest sense. However, at the time, they were described in terms of concepts that were familiar to the witnesses – so the ancient Romans saw blazing shields and World War II pilots interpreted their sightings as unusual enemy craft,

weapons or ghost aeroplanes (see also FOO FIGHTERS). The AIRSHIPS wave of 1896 is also a good example of this phenomenon.

It has been popular with some people to reinterpret these stories in terms of the current cultural paradigm, where the abbreviation 'UFO' carries with it connotations of spaceships and ALIENS. Ironically, this act in itself may simply be a continuation of the same phenomenon. Having recognized the way that descriptions of unidentified objects in the sky have changed over time, it may be prudent to look again at the fact that the period during which UFOs have been seen and reported as alien spaceships is almost exactly contemporaneous with a period of culture commonly referred to as the 'space age'.

'Cultural tracking' is the title given to this phenomenon. In 1947, the media misinterpreted Arnold's description of the UFOs he claimed to have seen and reported the craft as saucer-shaped (even though Arnold said they were crescent-shaped). Soon afterwards thousands of people claimed to have seen 'FLYING SAUCERS', the obvious conclusion being that (whether their stories were fabrications or otherwise) people had become conditioned into thinking that UFOs should be saucer-shaped.

The effect of cultural tracking can also be seen as the types of aliens described by alleged witnesses have changed over the years. For example, until the 1960s, NORDICS were commonly reported, but these now seem to have left the popular imagination. In the last 30 or so years GREYS have appeared in numerous films and books, including *CLOSE ENCOUNTERS OF THE THIRD KIND* (1977) and Whitley Strieber's *Communion* (1987). They have become the standard alien that witnesses expect to see, and now appear in two-thirds of contemporary reports.

Recognition of the fact that cultural tracking takes place has led researchers to reach varying conclusions. It is widely accepted that it tends to suggest that not all UFO sighting claims should simply be taken at face value. The phenomenon was of interest to psychologists as far back as 1959, when CARL JUNG formulated his PSYCHOSOCIAL HYPOTHESIS. More recently, psychologists have noted that in the process of perceiving new things we seem to apply images already stored in our brains – possibly leading us to see something wholly unfamiliar only in terms of things that we already recognize.

Although it must be accepted that at least some reports are completely fictitious, and that they reflect current trends for this simple reason, it may also be the case that witnesses' reports of real sightings are shaped by the (conscious or unconscious) application of images and expectations that they already carry with them.

Cults, New Religious Movements and Alternative Religions

In its most basic sense, the word 'cult' (from the Latin *colere*, 'to worship') describes admiration, devotion or concentration of time and attention on a particular person, place or idea.

In ancient Greece and Rome there were various mystery cults devoted to, among others, Mithras, Dionysus, Isis and Osiris, Cybele and Attis, Demeter and Persephone (the ELEUSINIAN MYSTERIES) and Orpheus (the Orphic movement). These were respected initiatory religious movements, to which many thousands of people at all levels of society belonged. Later, with the coming of Christianity to Europe, it began to be used to describe particular devotions within the Catholic Church – such as the cults of Mary and other individual saints, or the cults of LOURDES, MEDJUGORJE and similar places of pilgrimage.

In recent times, the word 'cult' has also been applied to new groups that are different from their religious surroundings – distinguishing them from 'sects', which are splinter movements of an existing religion or denomination. It is also now popularly used outside the context of religious worship – for example, people often talk about cult books and cult TV series.

However, particularly at the hands of the media, the religion-related usage of 'cult' has developed strongly pejorative connotations. Its application to a group has come to imply that they are a dangerous small religion, with an unscrupulous leader, that brainwashes its recruits – taking their money and separating them from their family in the process. This pejorative use of the word has become so widespread that many sociologists of religion now prefer to use the terms 'new religious movement' (NRM) or 'alternative religion'.

In the 1960s and 1970s, alternative religions were very much part of the counter-culture. Young people were challenging not only their parents' music and lifestyle but also their moral strictures and their religious beliefs. They questioned everything, and they looked for answers. Some found their answers in drugs, some in sexual experimentation, some in feminism, some in radical politics – and some in religion.

From Britain, the Beatles followed the MAHARISHI MAHESH YOGI to India, and many followed the Beatles. In the USA, ironically as part of a deal to get South-East Asian support for the war in Vietnam, immigration controls on Asians were relaxed in 1965 – and among those now free to enter the USA were a number of gurus. Over the next few years, among others, BHAGWAN SHREE RAJNEESH introduced the Rajneesh Movement (now called Osho International), the teenage Maharaji introduced the Divine Light Mission (now called Elan Vital), Swami Prabhupada introduced the International Society for Krishna Consciousness (ISKCON, or the Hare Krishna movement) and Sun Myung Moon introduced the Unification Church (commonly called the Moonies).

Alongside these Eastern imports to both the USA and Britain, and to a lesser extent continental Europe, were numerous 'homegrown' movements – some Christian, some neopagan, some NEW AGE and some to do with personal development or self-help. There were the Children of God (now called the Family), the Jesus Army and the Boston (or London, or other cities) Church of Christ; there were groups devoted to WICCA, Druidry, HEATHENRY and SHAMANISM; there were any number of offshoots of THEOSOPHY, including the CHURCH UNIVERSAL AND TRIUMPHANT, and 'FLYING SAUCER cults' including the AETHERIUS SOCIETY, the RAELIAN MOVEMENT, UNARIUS and others; and there were the Church of SCIENTOLOGY, *est*, NEUROLINGUISTIC PROGRAMMING and many others. In the Sixties, if you thought it was 'square' to go to your parents' church, then it was 'cool' to join any of these.

Suddenly new religious movements were everywhere, and growing rapidly. As with other organizations, NRMs like to grow and spread. This rapid growth carried its own risks. As the new religions grew in numbers they opened new 'branches', whether they were ashrams, churches or missions. Each of these needed someone to take on the role of administrative and spiritual leader. However, unlike established religions, or business corporations, that have access to trained and experienced people for such eventualities (for example a bishop will have trained and spent years as a priest, and the manager of a newly opened branch of a bank will have risen through the company ranks), some NRMs grew so rapidly that there weren't enough trained and experienced people to fill the positions. It was possible that someone in his early twenties (most were male), who might only have been a member of the movement for six or eight months, might find himself in charge of an ashram, church or mission, responsible not only for running it but for the spiritual leadership and teaching of the members under him – and for spreading the word and recruiting new members. Untrained, untested, young and immature leaders might not be very good at the job, and there was a risk that some of the young leaders were in a position to pocket the money that their followers were raising, and use it to buy drugs or live a comfortable lifestyle, or that they were able to take advantage of the teenagers who looked up to them.

There was a further problem in the many Eastern new religions. Most of these came from a centuries-old spiritual background where a guru's disciples followed his every word. They gave him unquestioning obedience; that was part of their spiritual discipline. In Western terms they were like monks obeying their abbot and the strict rule of their order. This traditional guru–disciple relationship clashed with Western culture and expectations; and even though new young members might have accepted it in the flush of conversion, their parents were less sanguine.

In fact it was a Christian group, the Children of God, who were the first to trigger action by concerned parents. They took the biblical instruction to forsake their father and mother for Jesus' name's sake (Matthew 19:29; cf Matthew 10:37) literally. In 1972, some of their parents in the USA set up FREECOG to work to free their (adult) children from the movement; over the next few years this became the Citizens Freedom Foundation, and later the Cult Awareness Network.

In the 1970s, some extreme anti-cultists promoted 'deprogramming'. Young adult members of new religions were kidnapped from their movements, forcibly imprisoned and subjected to substantial psychological pressure to give up their beliefs and rejoin 'normal' society. Needless to say this was not only illegal, it was also morally reprehensible – deprogrammers who accused cults of BRAINWASHING their members were themselves trying to 're-brainwash' them. In addition to this, it remains a highly controversial question within the academic community as to whether 'brainwashing'

(certainly in the strong sense in which it is popularly understood) has ever been carried out by religious groups and, more importantly, whether such a process is even possible. Certainly, people can be persuaded to join movements and accept beliefs; this is how all conversions occur. And certainly it can be shown that many people joining new religions in the 1960s and 1970s were not in full possession of the facts about what they were joining; they were not necessarily deliberately tricked, but they might not have joined so enthusiastically had they known in advance the commitments they would be expected to make.

Studies have also shown that the majority of people who join new religions leave them within a few months or a year, and that the majority of those are quite happy with their experience. Some people have drawn comparisons between membership of religious groups and love relationships. The conversion experience has been described as akin to falling in love – there may be doubts before committing, but once they join, members (especially younger members) are often starry-eyed and hugely enthusiastic in the early days. This initial enthusiasm can wane, sometimes rapidly, sometimes slowly, and many people try several religions during their lives, possibly eventually settling in one. The circumstances surrounding a member's departure from a religion can often leave them feeling betrayed, angry and bitter – some argue that this is the main source of the 'cult victims' who regularly appear in the press.

There are a number of organizations that can be described as 'anti-cult' or 'counter-cult' – the latter are generally Christian organizations who oppose 'sects' and 'cults' on a doctrinal basis. Both offer help and advice to members of new religious movements (particularly those wishing to leave) and to their families. In general they take a negative attitude towards alternative religions, looking for the features that might identify them as 'cults' in the pejorative sense, and they have occasionally been accused of provided misleading information to the sensation-hungry media. The former anti-cult organization, Cult Awareness Network, was bankrupted in a legal case in 1996. Its name and assets were bought and are now being used by a group which includes Scientologists – leading some to challenge its claim that it is now in a position to provide neutral assistance and information.

In contrast to these groups, there are a number of organizations set up by scholars, mainly sociologists of religion, to provide balanced and accurate factual information on NRMs – both positive and negative. These include Inform (Britain), the Institute for the Study of American Religion (USA), Cesnur (Italy) and Ontario Consultants on Religious Tolerance (Canada).

There have certainly been cases over the years of alternative religious (and non-religious) movements abusing their members in ways associated with the pejorative usage of the word 'cult'. Anti-cultists claim that these abuses are the norm; others argue they are the exception, and that anti-cult scare stories are as inflated as the membership often claimed by movements (for example, the Church of Scientology regularly claims to have eight million members worldwide, but as this figure includes every person who has taken an auditing session over more than half a century, more realistic external estimates put the total at perhaps 700,000, of whom maybe a tenth are active).

Some movements are economical with the truth about themselves in other ways, covering up past misdeeds, rewriting their history or their founder's biography. In some cases this is little more than dubious PR, but in other cases it might go beyond that. Some groups have also gained a reputation for taking heavy-handed legal action against former members and others who publish criticisms of them. But most studies show that the majority of so-called 'cults' are no more abusive, deceptive or dangerous than mainstream religions. It was said by Leo Pfeffer, an ardent campaigner for religious tolerance, that '... if you believe in it, it is a religion or perhaps "the" religion; and if you do not care one way or another about it, it is a sect, but if you fear and hate it, it is a cult'.

David V Barrett

cups

Vessels for holding water or other liquid, used as ritual tools in Wiccan and neopagan traditions and in ceremonial magic.

The cup, or chalice, is an important ritual tool in WICCA, NEOPAGANISM and ceremonial magic (see MAGIC, CEREMONIAL). It is traditionally made of silver, or sometimes of pewter or crystal, and symbolizes the element of WATER, and all that this element signifies – intuition, emotional power, mutability and love. The cup is placed in the west of the altar during rituals, the west being the direction associated with the element of water. In some pagan traditions, the altar will have two cups on it, one, filled with water, to represent the element itself, and the other, filled with wine, mead or some other drink; most Wiccan rites end with a small celebration in which cakes and wine are blessed and shared by the participants, and the second cup is used for this purpose.

Since the cup is considered to be a feminine tool which represents the womb, it is also sometimes used in male/female sacred rites along with the ritual knife or 'athame', which is lowered into the chalice to symbolize the union between the God and THE GODDESS. The cup can also be filled with water and used for SCRYING. The cup's importance as a magical symbol can also be seen in the TAROT (see CUPS, SUIT OF).

cups, suit of

One of the four suits into which the cards of the tarot's minor arcana are divided.

The suit of cups in the TAROT is also known as the suit of chalices. It contains fourteen cards: numbered 'pip' cards going from one to ten, plus four 'court' cards – the Page, the Knight, the King and the Queen. Some people believe that the four suit emblems may originally have symbolized the four main social classes in medieval Europe, with the cups representing the priesthood, who used chalices in the mass. Astrologically, this suit is associated with the element of WATER, and the three water signs, PISCES, CANCER and SCORPIO. Corresponding to the suit of hearts in a modern deck of playing cards, the suit of cups is identified principally with the emotional aspects of life, feelings and sensations, the subjective world of inner experiences, imagination and the creative arts. General characteristics of the suit are said to include self-awareness, increased sensitivity and vulnerability. See also PENTACLES, SUIT OF; SWORDS, SUIT OF; WANDS, SUIT OF.

The King of Cups, as represented in the Grimaud version of the Tarot of Marseille by Paul Marteau. (© Mary Evans Picture Library)

Curé of Ars (1786–1859)

French Catholic priest and saint.

Jean Marie Baptiste Vianney was the son of a farmer. He wished to become a priest but he was not academically gifted, and his lack of progress led to his dismissal from the seminary. Not until the age of 29 was he able to be ordained.

He was assigned to the small, run-down village of Ars-en-Dombes near Lyon, but he soon became famous for his preaching and people travelled from all over the region (and later, from all France) to hear him. He was much revered as a spiritual counsellor and thousands came to have him hear their confessions.

His life was one of austerity, sleeping and eating little, and he claimed to be tormented by evil spirits during the night. Supernatural knowledge of the past and future were attributed to him as well as powers of healing.

When his body was exhumed as part of the beatification process it was found not to have decomposed (see INCORRUPTIBILITY). Nowadays, over 500,000 people visit Ars each year, where his incorrupt body is on view.

He was beatified by Pope Pius X in 1905. Pius XI canonized him in 1925, and then in 1929 declared him patron saint of parish priests.

He is known as St John Vianney, or more simply as the Curé of Ars.

Curran, Pearl *see* WORTH, PATIENCE

curses
The deliberate use of magic to cause evil or harm.
Curses, or the deliberate use of magic to inflict evil or harm, are a universal feature of the religion and folklore of almost every culture. A person who wishes to curse another usually invokes some supernatural force, such as a god, angel or demon, by a spell or ritual, and directs their harmful intent toward the victim to bring about their illness, loss, bad luck or death. In ancient Rome, spells which were in effect a prayer to a god to bring evil on a victim were frequently inscribed on tablets and left with sacrifices at the god's shrine.

Curses are sometimes referred to as baneful magic or black magic (see MAGIC, BLACK), and it is believed that once performed, a curse cannot be withdrawn, although there are various means by which a cursed person may be able to negate or break the curse. A curse may be laid on a home, treasure or grave as protection against trespassers or thieves who will suffer its dire consequences, and the tomb of TUTANKHAMEN was said to have been protected by such a curse. The HOPE DIAMOND is also said to be cursed and to have brought illness, misfortune and death to its owners throughout history. There are also legends of entire families being under a curse, so that generation after generation is plagued by its effects, or the family dies out due to childlessness or the untimely death of its heirs.

The best-known method of cursing an individual is the use of an effigy, as was believed to have been practised by witches in Europe in medieval and Renaissance times: a wax representation of the victim, known as a poppet, was melted or stuck with pins, knives or thorns, and the evil inflicted on the image of the person was thought to have a direct effect on the victim themselves. The use of EFFIGIES to curse a victim is also known to have been practised in ancient India, Persia, Egypt and Africa. Like AMULETS and TALISMANS, curses have been made and sold by practitioners of magic throughout the centuries. A curse made by someone on their deathbed is also believed to have special force, since all the dying person's remaining energy is invested in it.

Some magicians believe that the victim should be made aware that they have been cursed, so that their own fear will lend extra power to the curse. Others believe that they should be kept in ignorance so that they will not seek help from another magician to break the curse, or attempt to propitiate the evil force in some way. There are as many methods of breaking a curse as there are of casting one, and it is believed that a curse cast using the power of a specific element, such as water, is best lifted by means of a spell which invokes the power of the same element. Cursing someone also carries potential danger for the one who casts the curse; it is thought that if the curse is too powerful for the magician who casts it, it may come down on him as well as or instead of on his intended victim, and that to be guilty of the same behaviour for which he is cursing his victim may also cause the curse to rebound on him.

In most neopagan and Wiccan traditions, it is considered unethical and against the laws of the Craft to curse others, and it is believed that the curse will return to the curser threefold in what is referred to as the Law of Return. This belief is echoed in the proverb 'Curses, like chickens, always come home to roost'.

cyclic ghosts
Ghosts that are said to manifest repeatedly on a particular date or anniversary.
In popular tradition the GHOSTS of the dead are prone to manifest regularly on specific dates, usually the anniversary of the date on which their life ended. This is generally an annual cycle, but occasionally longer periods are claimed (eg 6, 20 or 50 years). An extensive list of examples could be compiled. For instance: Queen Anne Boleyn is said to appear at Blickling Hall in Norfolk, on 19 May, the anniversary of her execution; a ghostly monk named Rahere is said to appear at St Bartholemew's Church in Smithfield, London, on 1 July; on 27 July a ghostly glow is said to be seen at Killicrankie in Perthshire on the anniversary of a battle; on 28 July a phantom nun is said to walk at BORLEY RECTORY in Essex; and on 2 August the ghost of King William Rufus is said to materialize by the Rufus Stone in the New Forest, Hampshire. Many SPECTRES are said to venture forth on HALLOWE'EN, but this date is soundly beaten by Christmas Eve, on which ghosts are said to appear at over 150 different locations throughout the British Isles.

Despite the proliferation of such stories, there is little reliable evidence to suggest that ghosts follow annual anniversary cycles or come to order. GHOST HUNTING vigils organized for the specified date are notoriously disappointing for participants, and detailed research often fails to reveal any historical basis for such legends. There is no doubt that many famous anniversary ghosts (particularly those associated with the Norfolk and Suffolk Broads – see GHOSTS OF THE BROADS) are pure invention. Problems might also be posed by the switch from the Julian to the Gregorian calendar in 1752. This would have required many alleged anniversary ghosts to accommodate an artificial shift of 11 days into their cycle.

Nonetheless, there are indications of shorter cyclic periods at work with some better-attested ghosts.

Occupants of haunted houses may note that their ghosts are more active at certain times of the day or week. Ghosts are rarely seen at breakfast time but the frequency of sightings seems to increase as the day progresses, with a peak after midnight and into the early hours of the morning. These features may simply point to the fact that the human mind is more receptive to PSYCHIC impressions at certain periods than at others. Subconscious expectation or other purely psychological factors may also play a crucial part. Another popular, and slightly more esoteric, suggestion is that reports of manifestations are more prevalent at the time of the waning moon. However, any firm connection with the lunar cycle has yet to be demonstrated.

D

dactyliomancy

Divination using a finger-ring.

In dactyliomancy (from the Greek *dactylios*, a finger-ring, and *manteiā*, divination), a finger-ring is used to obtain the answer to a question. Several methods may be employed. The ring can be dropped into a bowl of water, where the position it ends up in determines the response to the question; the bowl used is sometimes specially marked for this purpose. Suspended on a hair or thread, the ring can be used like a PENDULUM, perhaps being held over a OUIJA BOARD or a circular table with letters arranged around its circumference, and allowed to swing freely until it points at letters to spell out a message. The ring can also be dangled inside or within swinging distance of a goblet or glass, the number of times it then clinks against the side being interpreted according to a previously determined code such as once for 'yes' and twice for 'no'. In the Middle Ages, rings engraved with the names of the Three Wise Men (Caspar, Melchior and Balthasar) were often used for this form of divination, but wedding rings, especially those that include the inscription 'Love and Obey', have for centuries been the tool of choice for dactyliomancy – although it is said that the divination is rendered null and void if the bride whose ring is being used crosses her fingers!

daemon

A spirit in Classical mythology which held a place intermediate between gods and men, and which often protected and guided humans or watched over specific places.

The spelling 'daemon', or 'daimon', is used specifically to distinguish a group of spirits in Classical mythology from the Judeo-Christian concept of the DEMON. The Greek translation of the Septuagint Bible (made for the Greek-speaking Jews of Alexandria), and the use of the word *daemon* in the New Testament's original Greek text, had caused it to be used by Judeo-Christians with the same sense as 'demon' by the early 2nd century AD. But while the word 'demon' usually refers to a malignant spirit which can possess humans, the daemon of ancient Greece and Rome was thought to hold a position intermediate between gods and men; the Greek word *daimōn*, usually interpreted as meaning 'gifted with knowledge of the future', 'divine power' or 'spirit', was Latinized as *daemon*, and translated as the Latin *genius*. The word did not necessarily denote an evil spirit; the daemon was sometimes an inferior divinity, and sometimes the ghost of a dead hero. Daemons were usually invisible, but it was believed that some acted as personal attendants to higher deities, and these were represented as having a particular form and a specific name. Others were thought to preside over specific districts, towns or nations.

Around the 5th century BC, the concept of the personal daemon emerged. The Greeks believed that Zeus assigned a daemon to each human at birth, and these attended, protected and guided their human charges, dying with them. The most famous of these was the 'good genius' of Socrates, a small daemon who was said to have advised him against bad decisions, but who never commanded or compelled him to obey; Socrates also claimed that its predictions were more accurate than those made using any form of DIVINATION. The Hellenistic Greeks divided daemons into two categories: eudaemons, agathodaemons or calodaemons, who resembled guardian ANGELS and watched over mortals to protect them, and cacodaemons, who led men astray and tried to bring them to evil.

Damanhur, Federation of

A New Age community in Italy, with a spectacular underground temple.

The Federation of Damanhur, a spiritual community near Turin, in the foothills of the Alps in northern Italy, was founded in 1975 by Oberto Airaudi (1950–). What immediately separates it from other spiritual communities is its spectacular underground temple, carved out of the solid rock of a mountain by the members.

Until 1992, the Temples of Humankind, containing miles of corridors and halls on six levels, richly decorated with paintings and sculptures, were unknown to outsiders. Then a senior ex-member revealed their existence, and the community fell foul of the local authorities, who said the temples had been built without planning permission and must be demolished. But over the next few years Damanhur won a number of court cases allowing not only the temples' continued existence but their continued expansion, and they are now open to the public and have become a major tourist attraction.

The Federation of Damanhur has around a thousand members living in the area in 44 communities, with other supporters living nearby. It has been described as a social experiment rather than a religious movement, though it is based on esoteric NEW AGE beliefs. The movement describes its temples as 'the visible and tangible example of architectural esoteric thought; built, lived in and used' and 'a three-dimensional book that can be read by those with the knowledge to read it, just like the Pyramids and the Gothic Cathedrals'. The aims of the community are:

> … the freedom and re-awakening of the Human Being as a divine, spiritual and material principle; the creation of a self-sustaining model of life based on ethical principles of good communal living and love; harmonic integration and co-operation with all the Forces linked to the evolution of Humankind.

The movement has been criticized by the Roman Catholic Church in Italy for its beliefs; it has also been attacked for its policy of short-term contract marriages between its members, though most of these appear to be renewed. They have also been noted for their 'time travel experiments' – effectively spiritual or religious experiences involving travel in and of consciousness, akin to shamanic travel (see OUT-OF-BODY EXPERIENCES; SHAMANIC VISUALIZATION). As noted on their website:

> For over thirty years the Damanhur community in Italy has used the lost science of Astral Travel to chart the vast energetic flows of power that run through our planet. Their techniques for accomplishing focused intentional out of body experiences (OBEs) have been documented in numerous magazines and books.

An Egyptian-influenced hallway in the Federation of Damanhur's Temples of Humankind. (© Floris Leeuwenberg/The Cover Story/Corbis)

Däniken, Erich von (1935–)

A hugely successful author who popularized the idea that aliens visited the earth in the distant past leaving behind archaeological evidence of their interaction with ancient human cultures.

Erich von Däniken was born in Switzerland and, after working in the hotel trade for a number of years, he began writing in 1959, developing an interest in the frequent references to contact with sky gods and similar intelligent beings that appear in the texts of some ancient civilizations. The contemporary academic position was that these textual and pictorial portrayals were either allegorical or represented wise men dressed in ceremonial costume. Von Däniken suggested that they might be literal descriptions of ALIEN beings with whom there had been contact.

Although von Däniken was not the originator of this ANCIENT ASTRONAUTS hypothesis he became its most prolific spokesperson. In 1968 he published his first book, *Chariots of the Gods?*, which became a worldwide bestseller. In the next decade he sold 40 million copies of this book, and a string of sequels, in which he discussed evidence gathered from around the world. He included details of various anomalous artefacts that had been found by archaeologists – for example, an item found in Persia which appeared to be a battery, dating from centuries before its modern invention. Sceptics point out that throughout history there have been instances where technology has arisen out of accidental discoveries, long before human science was able to explain the processes involved. Even if we accept von Däniken's interpretation of the purpose of the items, they could simply be examples of technology that was accidentally discovered and then later abandoned or forgotten until reproduced in the modern era.

Von Däniken's worldwide public profile diminished during the 1980s. However he remained a popular lecturer and media figure in German-speaking countries, and published further books in the late 1990s. See also NAZCA LINES.

daoine sidhe

In Irish folklore, the remains of the divine fairy race of Ireland, the Tuatha de Danaan, who were forced to take refuge in the hills after the country was conquered by the Milesians, and dwindled into the diminutive 'Little People'.

Irish folklore tells of a once divine fairy race, the Tuatha de Danaan, who were as tall as humans, if not taller. They lived in Ireland until the coming of the Gaelic Milesians, the fifth and last Celtic people to invade and settle in the country, and those who chose to remain in Ireland were forced to take refuge in the hills and mountains; 'daoine sidhe' means literally 'people of the mounds'. They developed the art of invisibility, and since that time, cannot be seen by mortals unless they choose to show themselves, or the mortal either possesses SECOND SIGHT or smears a magical ointment on his or her eyes. The one exception is Midsummer Night, when ordinary people may catch a glimpse of them.

As time went on, they dwindled in size and became a diminutive race, which caused them to be known by another name: the 'daoine beaga' or 'Little People'. They are ruled by King Finvarra (Finbheara), high king of the Irish fairies, and his beautiful wife, Oonagh, who hold court beneath the fairy hill of Knockma in Connaught. They enjoy the field sport of hurling, and also chess; many a mortal man has bet and lost all his possessions playing chess against Finvarra, who has never been beaten. The 'daoine sidhe' are merry, but mischievous, and sometimes cruel to humans, so they must be dealt with carefully. They also love to hunt, and when they ride abroad on their snow-white horses, only the tinkling sound of their harnesses betrays their presence.

Dartmoor Beast *see* ALIEN BIG CATS

David-Néel, Alexandra (1868–1969)

French traveller, writer, oriental scholar and authority on Tibetan Buddhism.

Born Louise Eugenie Alexandrine Marie David in Paris in 1868, Alexandra David-Néel had, by the age of 18, already visited England, Switzerland and Spain on her own, and was studying in MADAME BLAVATSKY'S THEOSOPHICAL SOCIETY. In 1891, aged 23, she travelled through Ceylon and India, and at Adyar, near Madras, she joined the theosophists under Annie Besant, and studied Sanskrit. In 1904, she married railroad engineer Philippe Néel. By 1911 she had returned to India, and in 1912 she visited the Dalai Lama twice in exile at Darjeeling, an unprecedented act for a European woman at that time. After being invited to the royal monastery of Sikkim, she spent 1914–16 studying Tibetan Buddhism in a high mountain cave with a religious hermit called Aphur Yongden; he became her lifelong travelling companion, and she later adopted him. In 1916, they went illegally to Shigatse in Tibet to meet the Panchen Lama, and were expelled from the country, travelling to Japan and then crossing China from east to west before settling to study for three years at the monastery of Kumbum. Between 1921 and 1924, disguised as a Tibetan pilgrim, she made a journey to Lhasa, the capital of Tibet – a city forbidden to foreigners – the first European woman ever to do so. In 1927, she published an account of this adventure in *My Journey to Lhasa*, which became a worldwide bestseller.

Returning to France in 1925, she settled in Digne, Provence, and in 1928 built a 'fortress of meditation' called Samten-Dzong, and embarked on a series of lecture tours. In 1937, at the age of 70, she went back to China, where she worked and studied until she was forced by the Japanese advance of 1944 to go back to France. She then retired from her travels, but continued to write and study until her death in 1969 at the age of 100. In 1973, her ashes were scattered with those of Yongden over the waters of the Ganges at Varanasi (Benares).

A renowned authority on Tibetan Buddhism, David-Néel was said, during her time at the Tibetan monastery in Kumbum, to have succeeded in creating a thought-form known as a *kulpa* – a phantom produced by intensely focused thought and the repetition of mystical rites. She wrote over 30 books about Eastern religion, philosophy and her travels, and her works influenced the beat writers Jack Kerouac and Allen Ginsberg and the philosopher Alan Watts.

Da Vinci Code, The

Controversial bestselling novel which has helped to promote interest in theories concerning the Holy Grail legend and the role of Mary Magdalene in the history of Christianity.

In 2003, the US author Dan Brown published *The Da Vinci Code*, a sequel to his 2000 novel *Angels and Demons*. The story combines the popular literary genres of detective fiction, thriller and conspiracy theory, and was an instant worldwide bestseller. It has now been translated into around 44 languages, and a film adaptation was released in 2006. Part of the advertising campaign for the novel was a competition – the book itself included four codes, and the reader who solved all four would win a trip to Paris. In fact, several thousand people solved the codes, so the winner was drawn from a list of these at random.

The novel begins with the murder of the curator of the Louvre Museum in Paris, on whose naked body have been left several cryptic messages. The solving of the mystery requires the interpretation of these messages, together with others supposedly hidden inside Leonardo da Vinci's paintings *Mona Lisa* and *The Last Supper*, and a number of other anagrams and puzzles. The solution is found to be connected with the possible location of the HOLY GRAIL, a secret which has been preserved for 2,000 years by a mysterious society called the Priory of Sion, along with the KNIGHTS TEMPLAR and the Catholic organization Opus Dei. A key element of the story is the premise that the figure seated at the right hand of Jesus in *The Last Supper* is not John the Apostle, but Mary Magdalene, who, according to the novel, was Jesus'

wife, and was pregnant with his child at the time of the Crucifixion. The absence of a chalice in the painting is seen as proof that Leonardo was a member of the Priory of Sion, and that by deliberately leaving it out, he was indicating that the 'Holy Grail' was not, as the Church has led us to believe, an actual chalice used by Jesus at the Last Supper, but was instead a symbolic reference to Mary Magdalene, the bearer of Christ's bloodline. The Grail relics, traced in the novel to a possible location in a secret crypt beneath ROSLYN CHAPEL, near Edinburgh, are in fact Mary Magdalene's bones and documents testifying to this bloodline. The Grail-keepers have been guarding the secret of Christ's descendants to this day.

The novel's popularity helped to spur a widespread interest in theories concerning the Holy Grail and the role of Mary Magdalene in the history of Christianity, but many Christians hold these theories to be heretical, since they question the entire legitimacy of Christian history. It is influenced by several other works, in particular the 1982 book *The Holy Blood and the Holy Grail*, by Michael Baigent, Richard Leigh and Henry Lincoln, which is actually mentioned in the novel. Because it claims to contain elements of historical truth within its fictional narrative, many of its readers have mistakenly accepted it as being factually correct throughout (a mistake which has had positive benefits for the tourist industries of Paris and Edinburgh). These historical claims, together with the author's tendency to treat what are just (often controversial) opinions within unresolved debates as fact, have attracted a great deal of criticism from historians. However, many historians have actually benefited indirectly from this by taking the opportunity to write one of the growing number of books published with the sole purpose of pointing out the novel's historical inaccuracies and false assumptions.

daylight disc

The name given by Dr J Allen Hynek to a UFO with a structured shape and good definition, seen while strongly illuminated.

When creating his own classifications system, DR J ALLEN HYNEK wanted a term to describe cases that were more than just LIGHTS IN THE SKY but were not in any way CLOSE ENCOUNTERS. Hynek felt that clear sightings of this type were of greater potential scientific value, although such cases represent less than one in ten of all UFO reports.

The term 'daylight disc' was applied to sightings of UFOs with any form of structured shape, not just discs. In formulating his terminology, Hynek drew upon and adapted that used in the established US military studies, where disc-like objects had been commonplace in the early reports.

While the phrases 'close encounters' and 'lights in the sky' remain in frequent use, the term 'daylight disc' is possibly the least used of the original Hynek classification system.

dead, the

Those who have died; the spirits of the dead are thought in many belief systems to continue on another plane of existence and to possess supernatural knowledge or power.

In most cultures, the bodies of those who have died are given some form of ritual disposal before the onset of significant decay, usually either by cremation, or by interment in a grave, barrow or mound, sarcophagus, crypt, mausoleum or pyramid. Sometimes the burial ritual includes measures to slow down the process of physical decay, as in the ancient Egyptian practice of MUMMIFICATION or embalming. In Tibet, 'sky burial' involves placing the body of the dead person on high ground or on a mountain so that it can be disposed of by birds of prey – seen as carriers of the soul to heaven. Many funerary customs are based on a belief that the spirit continues to exist in some form of AFTERLIFE, and are intended to help the dead person to move on to the next plane or the next incarnation, or to attain heavenly bliss.

A number of cultures subscribe to some form of ancestor worship. In China, the deeds and memories of departed relatives are honoured and offerings made to them, and in VOUDUN, the spirits of the dead are also revered. In many traditions the spirits of those who have 'passed over' are believed to possess supernatural knowledge and power.

The idea that the spirits of the dead can return to earth as ghosts, especially if they died violently and seek revenge, or have unfinished business, is found in almost all cultures and ages. In earlier times, NECROMANCY, or the practice of seeking to conjure the spirits of the dead as a form of DIVINATION, was regarded as a BLACK ART, but the 19th century saw the rise of the religious movement of SPIRITUALISM, which is founded on the belief that the spirits of the dead exist on a higher spiritual plane than humans, and can be contacted by MEDIUMS in order to provide guidance on both worldly and spiritual matters. See also DEATH.

Dean device

A device that was purported to offer a futuristic form of propulsion for spacecraft.

In standard rocket engines the mass of the rocket is accelerated in one direction as a reaction to the ejection of a mass in the opposite direction (as described in Newton's laws of motion). In the 1950s an American inventor called Norman L Dean claimed to have invented a mechanical device that could transform energy into linear acceleration, without using this effect. He called this a 'reactionless drive', but it was soon labelled the Dean device (or Dean drive) and this is the name by which it continues to be known.

The possibilities of such a drive were of great interest particularly to the US space programme. Space rockets were dependent on massive engines designed to generate the reaction necessary to rise beyond earth's gravity, and if the Dean device worked it could make space travel a real possibility – the spacecraft involved could be smaller and lighter, with no need for rocket engines or large quantities of fuel.

Dean was rather secretive about his device, fearful that his idea would be stolen, and showed it to few people. Some claimed to have seen a model of it set in motion as it rested on some bathroom scales. Apparently the operation of the machine led to a decrease in its own weight as registered by the scales.

Among others, the US armed forces were interested in the device but Dean refused to demonstrate it without being paid large sums of money beforehand. He is also said to have requested a Nobel Prize in advance. Unsurprisingly, no one was prepared to grant Dean what he wanted. He did register a patent for his invention but it has been claimed that the version described in the patent simply did not work.

death

The cessation of physical life, considered by many to be the greatest human mystery.

Because of its finality, and the mystery of what, if anything, lies beyond it, death has always been invested with great ritual significance throughout the ages. Many religions and belief systems subscribe to the idea of an AFTERLIFE, with the soul continuing in some form after death. Spiritualists claim to be able to communicate with the DEAD, while many people believe they have memories of past lives (see REINCARNATION), and the idea that people can return to the earthly plane after death as GHOSTS is found in almost every culture.

Death, as a personified mythological figure, has been a feature of storytelling and popular culture since the earliest times, and the traditional Western image of Death, known as the GRIM REAPER, is that of a skeletal figure in black robes who holds a scythe. The late medieval allegory of the Dance of Death, also known as *La Danse Macabre* or *Totentanz*, depicted this figure leading a row of dead people of all ranks and occupations to the grave, a reminder of the universality and inevitability of death, the transitory nature of life and the vanity of earthly glory.

See also NEAR-DEATH EXPERIENCE.

death bird

An unidentified species of Ethiopian bat greatly feared by the local people who claim that it drinks the blood of sleeping humans.

Only three species of blood-drinking bat are known to science – the vampire bats, all of which are endemic to the New World. However, in his book *Dead Men Do Tell Tales* (1943), traveller Byron de Prorok claimed that a comparable creature, whose identity remains unknown to science, also exists in Ethiopia, where it is referred to as the death bird. While residing in the Ethiopian province of Walaga during the 1930s, he was told of the remote Devil's Cave inhabited by these greatly feared creatures, and when he investigated this locality and entered the cave he startled a great flock of bats – with wingspans of 60–90 centimetres (2–3 feet) – which flew over his head and deposited a shower of droppings over him.

De Prorok did not collect a bat specimen but he did visit a nearby camp where local goatherds lived, and was shocked to see that they were virtually skeletal and that their arms bore wounds reputedly made by these bats when they bit into the goatherds' flesh as they slept. In particular, he was shown one man, swathed in blood-soaked rags and near to death, whose skin was pale from blood loss and liberally scored with wounds. As an alternative to the theory that the death bird is responsible, it is possible that living in close proximity to this bat-infested cave, the goatherds had contracted a parasite-borne disease, caused by lice or ticks dropped from bats flying overhead.

Dee, John (1527–1608)

The greatest scientific and occult mind of the Elizabethan era.

Born in London, John Dee was a mathematician, an astronomer, a cartographer, a prolific author, a magician, an alchemist, a Hermetic philosopher, a major influence on the ROSICRUCIANS, probably a spy and Queen Elizabeth I's astrologer – he chose the day of her coronation.

Whatever follies he was perhaps led into by Edward Kelley in his later life (see below), there is no doubt that Dee was one of the greatest scholars of his day. His library in his home at Mortlake, London, was the largest in England, with some 3,000 books. Dame Frances Yates argued convincingly in *The Rosicrucian Enlightenment* (1972) that his writings and philosophy lay behind the Rosicrucian Manifestos (1614–16).

It is unfortunate that Dee is perhaps best known today for his work with Edward Kelley (1555–97), whom he met in 1582. Kelley claimed to be able to contact angels through a SCRYING glass, which Dee himself was unable to do. Kelley communicated with the angels in their own language, which he

The 16th-century British scientist and occultist John Dee, pictured with his scrying glass, as Edward Kelley looks on. (© Mary Evans Picture Library)

called Enochian. He also had a red powder or elixir, the PHILOSOPHER'S STONE, which he claimed would enable him to transmute base metals into gold – the dream of alchemists through the ages. Whether Kelley himself believed any of this, or whether he cynically set out to deceive Dee from the start, is a matter for debate. But Dee, in his late fifties, appears to have been convinced of Kelley's genuineness, even when, in 1587, Kelley said the angels had told him they should hold all things in common, including their wives. (Jane Dee was young and reportedly very attractive – and not pleased at the arrangement.)

From 1583 to 1589 Dee and Kelley lived in Prague and Trebon, seeking the financial patronage of assorted mid-European noblemen and kings, and eventually finding it from the Bohemian Count Vilem Rosenberg. In 1589, Dee left Kelley to his alchemical research and returned with his family to England, to find that many of his books and precious alchemical instruments had been stolen or destroyed. Queen Elizabeth I gave him a position as Warden of Christ's College, Manchester, but his occult reputation lost him the respect of the fellows. Dee returned to Mortlake in 1605 in poor health and increasing poverty, which King James I (see JAMES VI AND I) would not alleviate. The greatest scholar of his age ended his days scratching a living as a common fortune-teller.

deification *see* APOTHEOSIS

deities

Gods and goddesses; supernatural beings, usually powerful, who are or have been worshipped or honoured throughout the ages in the religions and belief systems of nearly every culture.

Throughout history, humans in nearly every age

and culture have believed in the existence of deities – divine, supernatural beings, usually immortal and powerful, who are to be respected, worshipped, petitioned or propitiated according to circumstances and the nature of the god or goddess. In some belief systems, these beings are all-powerful, the creators of earth or the universe, controlling and overseeing all aspects of human existence, capable of performing MIRACLES, the ultimate judges of human fate, apportioning rewards or punishments in this life or in the AFTERLIFE. In many cultures, especially ancient and indigenous ones, natural phenomena such as storms and floods may be attributed to the agency of gods and goddesses, while others do not ascribe power as such to their deities, but simply regard them as commanding worship and reverence. Some deities are said to be able to assume a variety of forms, especially human or animal; ancient Egyptian deities were sometimes portrayed symbolically in art as having human bodies with animal heads, for example Anubis, the jackal-headed god of the dead. Other deities are described as being invisible to humans, unless they choose to manifest themselves either in visible form or through the effects of their powers. They are often said to dwell in some inaccessible place such as a high mountain, or an otherworldly realm such as Heaven, Hell, an Underworld or a celestial sphere, and are usually, but not always, worshipped or venerated in a place or building set aside exclusively for this purpose, such as a shrine, altar or temple.

Some belief systems, such as Islam, Judaism and Christianity, are monotheistic, and assert a single and unique deity, although they acknowledge the existence of other supernatural beings, such as ANGELS and DEMONS or devils, in addition to this supreme God. Others are dualistic, holding that there are two deities, one representing Good and one Evil, who are in eternal opposition to one another. A large number of religions and mythologies, both ancient and contemporary, are polytheistic, and subscribe to a pantheon of gods and goddesses, who are commonly described as having personalities, intellects and emotions like humans; in such belief systems, each deity is often regarded as controlling or personifying an element, natural phenomenon or feature, quality, art or other aspect of the world or universe as experienced by man. Thus, a specific deity would be prayed or sacrificed to, depending on the nature of the petition; for example, the ancient Romans sought the help of Mars, the god of war, for victory in battle. Many polytheistic pantheons feature a lunar and solar deity, and a god or goddess of death, who is often regarded as being of great importance in the religion. Some also include domestic deities who protect the individual household and its members, and are worshipped at home rather than in a temple, being treated as members of the family and given offerings of food and drink. The best known of these are the *lares* and *penates* worshipped by the ancient Romans, although the ancient Egyptians and some Chinese traditions also feature household gods and goddesses.

In some cultures, such as that of ancient Egypt, the distinction between deities and humans was blurred, with royal houses claiming divine ancestry, while in the later Roman empire, many emperors were accorded the status of gods after their deaths through APOTHEOSIS.

déjà vu

The illusion of having already experienced something that is really being experienced for the first time.

Déjà vu (from the French, 'already seen') is a sensation that, according to some studies, has been experienced by approximately 70 per cent of the population. When it occurs the sensation is often extremely strong – a situation or experience will feel very familiar, despite the rational understanding that it cannot have occurred before.

The sensation can be so strong and compelling that it has led people to cite it as evidence of PRECOGNITION, precognitive DREAMS or EXTRASENSORY PERCEPTION. Some have even made the stronger assertion that it is caused by subconscious memories of events that have occurred in a previous life (see REINCARNATION), although the counter argument to this is that the feeling of remembered detail could not arise out of an experience from the distant past, when the surroundings would have been significantly different.

Scientific theories for the cause of déjà vu come at the problem from two basic directions.

One set of theories (versions of which were originally suggested in the late 19th century) revolve around an anomaly occurring in the brain wholly within the present. A number of different mechanisms have been suggested whereby the brain could potentially receive the sensory message from the same stimulus from two different (internal) sources a split second apart. A variation on this has arisen out of the observation that there is a strong association between sensations of déjà vu and temporal lobe epilepsy. This has led to the suggestion that it may be caused by an anomalous electrical discharge in the brain which caused the false impression of memory.

The second set of theories is based upon the conflation of a real, existing memory of something different with the current stimulus. The feeling of déjà vu arises out of the association between the immediate sensations produced by the current experience and the sensations produced by the earlier experience which can no longer be remembered (or at least consciously identified as the source).

delayed death touch

A martial arts technique in which it is claimed that a blow to a specific vital point on an opponent's body can cause death at a later time.

In the martial arts world, there is much debate over the legendary 'delayed death touch', a blow to one of several places on the body which it is said will cause death at a later time – anything up to ten days after the technique has been employed. A number of contemporary martial arts masters claim to be able to teach the secret of the delayed death touch, although orthodox medicine tends to regard it as an URBAN LEGEND, and the idea is viewed with extreme scepticism by many members of the martial arts community.

Those who believe it to be a reality claim that there are certain vital points on the body, for example on the back of the head, or on the forehead or chest, a blow to which may either be fatal on impact, or which can result in death anything from three to ten days later. A 13th-century Chinese manuscript called the *Xi Yuan Lu*, which was translated into English in 1874, includes charts which are believed to show these vital points. Several books published in the early 1900s also discuss the use of vital point techniques.

The martial art of Dim Mak, sometimes known as 'Chinese death striking', is most closely associated with the delayed death touch. It claims to use an applied knowledge of ACUPUNCTURE points and energy MERIDIANS to identify the points on the body which, if struck, can induce unconsciousness or illness, or cause instant or delayed death. A blow to these points is said to stop the flow of QI through the body and affect the nervous and cardiovascular systems, sometimes fatally. However, since most martial arts practitioners are rarely in a situation where the use of such allegedly deadly techniques would be permissible, hard evidence for the authenticity of the delayed death touch is not forthcoming. Nevertheless, the concept has been popularized in films, and one of the various rumours surrounding the death of the martial arts actor Bruce Lee in 1973 was that he had been killed by such a technique.

Delphic oracle *see* ORACLE OF DELPHI, THE

dematerialization

The apparent unexplained disappearance of an object – usually used for situations where this is supposedly brought about by psychic means.

A dematerialization, or 'deport', is the opposite of a MATERIALIZATION (or APPORT) – it is the paranormal disappearance of a material object. Dematerializations of objects can reputedly occur during séances, and there have also been claims that parts of mediums have dematerialized. However, sceptics would point out that similar 'disappearances' can appear to occur in simple conjuring tricks.

demonology

The study and classification of demons, an occult science practised chiefly from the Middle Ages until around the 18th century; a book dealing with demonology.

The belief in the existence of DEMONS, and the attempt to classify and study them, has been universal to almost all cultures since ancient times. Accounts of demons are found in ancient Egyptian texts, as well as Assyrian, Babylonian, Iranian and Jewish writings. According to Christian mythology, demons were those ANGELS who chose the path of EVIL, and after man's fall from grace, were permitted by God to tempt humans to sin. While some demons are free to propagate evil in the world, others are, in Scripture, said to be restrained in a type of spiritual prison, bound by 'chains of darkness'.

The study of demons in the Christian tradition goes back to medieval times, and their classification and hierarchy has been the focus of much discussion among experts in theology and the occult over the centuries, with many books being written on the subject, each borrowing from its predecessors and from earlier systems of Jewish and Greek demonology. While some of these books purported to be written in the service of Christianity, many more were intended for practitioners of ritual magic who wished to harness the supernatural powers of demons, and the 13th-century German philosopher ALBERTUS MAGNUS warned of the dangers of this science:

> It is taught by the demons, it teaches about the demons, and it leads to the demons.

Lists of demons appear in some of the darker GRIMOIRES written between the late Middle Ages and the 18th century, notably *The Lesser Key of Solomon*, a collection of writings on the ritual EVOCATION of spirits. The first tract in this work, *The Goetia*, consists of a descriptive list of the 72 demons which were said to have been bound by King Solomon. Some demonologies list the multiple names of demons, such as Beelzebub, the Lord of the Flies; Asmodeus, the Destroyer; and Abbadon, the Prince of War. Others ascribe a specific sin or vice to them, such as Beelzebub (Pride), Asmodeus (Avarice or Luxury) and Astaroth (Vanity and Sloth). The number of demons varies from source to source; for instance, one writer tells of 111 legions of 666 demons ruled by 72 princes, while another gives 6 legions each with 66 cohorts divided into 666 companies of 6666 individuals. Various elaborate hierarchies are also put forward, reflecting the feudal systems of the time; in the 13th-century grimoire of Pope Honorius, for example, the Principal Infernal Spirits are listed as Lucifer (Emperor), Beelzebub (Prince), and Astaroth (Grand Duke), with below these, a rank of Superior Spirits followed by one of Subordinate Spirits. In 1467, Alphonse of Spina listed ten species of demons, including POLTERGEISTS, who created mischief; incubi and succubi, who incited lust and perversion; FAMILIARS, who assisted witches; and demons whose sole task it was to 'assail the saintly'.

Many demonologies included descriptions of demons, along with their habits, and the specific forms which demons of rank assumed when they appeared, by which they could be recognized. Those who wished to make use of the powers of darkness were advised to call on specific demons for specific tasks, according to their particular qualities. During the height of the European witch hunts of the 16th and 17th centuries, demonology reached its peak. The medieval grimoires were elaborated on, and King James VI and I published his own treatise, *Daemonologie*. The study of demonology continued until around the beginning of the 18th century, but fell into disuse as a learned discipline after that, although it continues to be an important aspect of many occult traditions. See also INCUBUS; SUCCUBUS.

demons

In religion, folklore and mythology, spirits which are generally described as malevolent and as having the ability to possess the bodies of humans and to tempt them to do evil.

The idea of demons is as old as religion itself, and appears in many beliefs and cultures. The spelling 'demon' is generally used to distinguish the malevolent spirits of Judeo-Christianity from the DAEMONS of classical mythology, who were not necessarily evil and were often well disposed toward humans. Outside the Judeo-Christian tradition, a demon was viewed as a kind of elemental spirit that could be conjured and commanded by MAGIC. In Jewish rabbinical literature, demons were generally workers of harm who caused diseases by entering the body of a person, and some sources refer to their having a king, called Asmodeus or Samael, and a queen, Lilith. However, DEMONOLOGY, the study of demons, was not an essential feature of Jewish theology.

According to Christian mythology, when God created the ANGELS, he offered them the choice between following him, or being cast apart from him and choosing the path of EVIL. The angels who chose

evil became the pre-human spirit entities known as demons, and after man's fall from grace, they, along with SATAN, were permitted by God to tempt humans to sin. However, the names ascribed to many of these demons, as found in late medieval GRIMOIRES, include those of Semitic, Near Eastern and other pre-Christian gods, making it clear that from the early Church's point of view, all pagan idols were considered demons. Some medieval demonologies suggested a hierarchy of demons similar to that of angels, with each demon having a specific sin associated with it – Asmodeus with avarice, Beelzebub with pride and so on. In some present-day cultures, demons are still feared, largely due to their alleged power to possess humans and to cause illness, and they remain an important concept in many modern religions and occult traditions. In the gospels of the New Testament, Jesus is described as casting out demons from afflicted people, and the Roman Catholic Church teaches that demons are real, and that they can be cast out by the formal rite of EXORCISM. See also DJINN.

deosil

The word used to describe circular movement in witch-craft and magical practice that goes with the direction of the movement of the sun around the sky.

The word 'deosil' comes from the Irish Gaelic *deiseal*, meaning 'turning to the right'. Circular movement in this direction, the same direction in which the sun moves around the sky in the northern hemisphere (also known as 'sunwise'), is associated with good luck and is believed to produce positive magic.

Deosil dances are performed when casting positive SPELLS or when taking part in rituals and SABBAT celebrations. Movement in the opposite direction is referred to as WIDDERSHINS.

dervishes, whirling

Members of a Sufi Muslim order who seek to attain religious ecstasy by performing a whirling dance.

The Sufi tradition in Islam is noted for its distinctive practices, and the best known of these in the West is the spinning dance of the Turkish Mevlevi Order popularly known as the whirling dervishes. The term 'dervish' comes from a Persian word meaning literally 'poor man or beggar', and members of the various Muslim dervish fraternities profess poverty and lead an austere life. The Mevlevi Order was founded in 1273 in Konya, Asia Minor, by the followers of the dervish Jalal al-Din Muhammad Rumi, also known as Mavlana, after his death, and most of the whirling dervishes of Turkey belong to this order. The whirling dervishes practise the remembrance of Allah, known as *dhikr*, in the form of a dance called the *sema*, which represents

A 16th-century painting depicting whirling dervishes.
(© Archivo Iconografico, S.A./Corbis)

the mystical journey of man's spiritual ascent to perfection. According to one legend, the dance was inspired when Rumi began to spin in harmony with the music of the craftsmen's hammers while in the goldsmith area of Konya.

The dervishes wear tall, conical felt hats which represent the tombs of their egos, white robes which symbolize the shrouds of their egos and black cloaks which are discarded at the start of the ritual to symbolize their liberation from the attachments of the world. They then form a circle around their guide or master, known as the *shaykh*, who acts as their link with Allah, and spin with the right hand held palm upward to receive the blessings of Allah and the left hand held palm downward to transfer them to earth. By this spinning the dervishes seek to empty themselves of distracting thoughts and achieve a trance state leading to a religious ecstasy called *fana*, in which they are not aware of the world around them and attain a spiritual connection with Allah. It is also believed that the dance simulates the orbit of the planets around the sun.

As well as being a religious practice, whirling dervish dances are now also a tourist attraction in Turkey, and are performed annually at the Mevlana Festival near the Mevlevi Museum in Konya on the anniversary of Rumi's death. See also ECSTATIC PHENOMENA; SUFISM.

Desmond, Countess of (d. early 17th century)

Katherine Fitzgerald, long-lived Irish noblewoman.
When Katherine Fitzgerald, Countess of Desmond, died in the early 17th century, she was reputed to be around 140 years old. She is referred to by Francis Bacon (1561–1626) in his *Natural History* (1627):

> They tell a tale of the old Countess of Desmond who lived till she was seven score years old, that she did dentire [grow teeth] twice or thrice; casting her old teeth, and others coming in their place.

She is also mentioned by Sir Walter Raleigh (1552–1618) in his *History of the World* (1614):

> I myself knew the old Countess of Desmond, of Inchiquin, in Munster, who lived in the year 1589, and many years since, who was married in Edward the Fourth's time [died 1483], and held her jointure from all the Earls of Desmond since then; and that this is true all the noblemen and gentlemen in Munster can witness.

In an age when the average life expectancy must have been less than a quarter of her supposed span, this was remarkable longevity indeed. She was reputed to have danced with Richard III (died 1485) and found him handsome. Towards the end of her life, she was even said to have travelled to London to appeal for financial aid from the Crown to alleviate the poverty in which she found herself. Another tradition is that she would have lived even longer had she not climbed into a tree to gather nuts (or in some versions, cherries) and fallen from it, suffering injuries that led to her much-deferred demise. As noted in *The Dublin Review* (February 1862):

> The extent of her longevity, which was the original source of her celebrity, has been stretched to various limits, and is still undetermined.

See also EXTREME LONGEVITY.

Devil, the

The personification of evil and opponent of God in the Christian tradition, also referred to as Satan or Lucifer.
The Devil is the name given in the Christian tradition to the supernatural entity who, in most Western religions, is regarded as the personification of EVIL. He is the archfiend SATAN, who was created as the most radiant of all the angels, LUCIFER, but whose pride caused him to rebel against God and to be expelled

from Heaven. Now the opponent and enemy of God, he constantly attempts to corrupt humans and lead them to sin so that they, too, might be condemned with him to the eternal punishment of Hell. The word 'Devil' comes from the Greek *diabolos*, meaning 'accuser' or 'slanderer', and when not used as a proper name, it refers to one of the many subordinate evil spirits or DEMONS of Jewish and Christian belief who, as followers of Satan, were cast out of Heaven with him. In the New Testament book of Revelation, he is referred to thus:

> And that great dragon was cast out, that old serpent, who is called the devil and Satan, who seduceth the whole world; and he was cast unto the earth, and his angels were thrown down with him.

The Devil is mentioned in many passages of both the Old and New Testaments, but no full account of him is given in any one place; some people claim that the serpent who tempted Adam and Eve in the Garden of Eden, as related in the book of Genesis, was the Devil in disguise. In both Christian and Islamic scriptures, the Devil and Satan are at times identified as the same entity, but at also appear elsewhere as separate figures. In the Koran, the Devil is named Iblis, and is the chief of all the evil DJINN, or Shaitan. He was expelled from Allah's grace when he refused, in his pride, to pay homage to Adam, believing himself to be his superior, and thereafter dedicated himself to tempting mankind to sin. He is depicted in the Koran not as Allah's adversary, but as one of His creations, and his power is limited to the ability to put evil suggestions to men in the hope that they will act upon them.

The people of medieval Europe lived in fear of the Devil's power and evil intent, but in many folk tales, he is, paradoxically, often treated with good-natured mockery, and is portrayed as an ogre-like trickster who can be easily and humorously outwitted, and who is mischievous rather than evil. This view of the Devil, as well as the popular depiction of him as a black or red man with horns, a pointed tail and cloven hoofs, strongly resembles that of the pre-Christian nature god of Central and Eastern Europe, a half-human and half-goat figure who resembled Pan and was regarded as both malicious and beneficent. Some suggest that this shows that the pagan deity was not fully absorbed into the Christian mythos as Satan, despite the Church's attempts to demonize him as such. In older representations, the Devil is often shown as a grotesque monster with attributes of animals such as snakes, dogs and scorpions.

It is considered unlucky to call the Devil by name, so over the centuries, he has come to be referred to by a wide range of nicknames and euphemisms, some of them almost affectionate, such as the Dark One, the Prince of Darkness, the Angel of the Abyss, the Enemy, the Evil One, Old Nick, Old Clootie, Old Bendy and Old Scratch. He is also commonly referred to by a variety of other names, such as Leviathan, Asmodai, Beelzebub, Belial and Mephistopheles, although in Christian demonology, these are in fact the names of specific demons, and not alternative names for the Devil.

devil dogs *see* BLACK DOGS

Devil's Footprints
An intriguing 19th-century case from Devon involving the appearance of a set of mysterious 'footprints' in the snow that reportedly stretched in an unbroken line across several parishes.

On the morning of 8 February 1855 the residents of parishes in south Devon between Topsham and Totnes awoke to discover a line of what appeared to be footprints, in the fresh snow, following a continuous meandering course for what was claimed to be a distance of over 100 miles (160 kilometres). The tracks were thought to have appeared some time in the early hours, as the last snow had fallen at around midnight.

On 16 February *The Times* reported that:

> The track appeared more like that of a biped than a quadruped, and the steps were generally eight inches in advance of each other. The impressions of the feet closely resembled that of a donkey's shoe, and measured from an inch and a half to (in some instances) two and a half inches across. Here and there it appeared as if cloven, but in the generality of the steps the shoe was continuous, and, from the snow in the centre remaining entire, merely showing the outer crest of the foot, it must have been convex.

There were reports that the tracks appeared to have been made by something that could travel over rooftops, through or over walls and through narrow drainpipes. The tracks were said to stop on one side of the Exe estuary only to continue again on the other side. At certain points in the journey the tracks appeared to go up to, and then away from, the doors of houses.

The incident certainly caused something of a stir at the time. The newspaper coverage brought forth more claims and a number of theories as to the cause. The scientific community made suggestions ranging from escaped kangaroos to a hot air balloon trailing a rope or chain. However, most of these seem to be almost as far-fetched as the idea amongst some of the more superstitious locals that the footprints were evidence of a visit from THE DEVIL.

The story has gained something of the status of a local legend and it is now very difficult to ascertain whether many of the claims attaching to it have any basis in truth – it is likely that even the original reports were greatly exaggerated. However, to this day, no widely accepted solution to the mystery has ever been provided.

Devil's mark

A mark on the skin, insensitive to pain, considered to be proof that an accused person had entered a covenant with the Devil.

In medieval times it was believed that the DEVIL always permanently marked his initiates, either by branding them, licking them or raking his claw across their flesh. Devil's marks were not always clearly visible, but through the process of pricking, the naked body of an accused witch would be searched with a sharp implement until an insensitive area was found, which was then taken as proof that the Devil had marked that person as one of his own. See also WITCH'S MARK; DEVIL'S PACT.

Devil's pact

A pact made with the Devil, traditionally a contract signed in the person's own blood, in which wealth, success, talent or knowledge are usually granted in return for the person's soul.

The idea that a person can enter into a binding contract with the DEVIL for wealth, success, talent or knowledge is a very old one. The contract is usually said to be written and signed with the person's blood, and the price demanded by the Devil, after an agreed period, is traditionally the person's soul, although it was also believed that some people made diabolic pacts not for material gain or power, but simply to acknowledge Satan as their master.

The earliest written account of a person making a diabolic pact comes from the 4th century, and tells of a young man, Proterius of Caesarea, who agreed to renounce Christ in return for the favour of a beautiful woman he desired; his soul was said to have been saved by the prayers of St Basil. There are also several versions of the legend of the 6th-century cleric, St Theophilus of Adana, who made a pact with the Devil to gain the ecclesiastical position of bishop in return for his renunciation of Christ and the Virgin Mary. Years later, fearful for his soul, he repented and prayed to the Virgin Mary for forgiveness, and after he had prayed and fasted for 40 days, she is said to have appeared to him and promised to intercede for him with God, eventually obtaining his absolution. Theophilus was said to have died peacefully shortly afterwards, filled with joy and relief that his soul had been saved. This story was popular in the Middle Ages and is believed by some to have been the inspiration for the FAUST legend.

There are said to be several ways of making a pact with the Devil. One is to go to church early on a Sunday morning, accompanied by others who

The Devil requires newcomers to the sabbat to enter into a pact with him. From the *Compendium Maleficarum* (1626) by Francesco Maria Guazzo.
(© Mary Evans Picture Library)

have also made such a pact, renounce God and the Church, pay homage to the Devil, declare one's desire to trade one's soul for favours from the Evil One and sign a contract in blood drawn from one's left arm. Another is to take a piece of virgin parchment – that is, parchment which is made from the first calf a cow bears, and which has never been written on – and write in one's own blood a promise to repay the Devil after an agreed period of time for whatever he grants. The document is then held in the hand while the person stands inside a MAGIC CIRCLE and invokes the Great Demon, to whom the pact is thrown without the person's leaving the circle. Verbal pacts could also be made, and according to some witch trials, the DEVIL'S MARK was physical evidence of these. During the witch trials of the 12th to 18th centuries, it was commonly believed that all witches had made a pact with the Devil, and by 1398, 'contracts' made with Satan were being used in courts as evidence.

Although Faust loses his soul after making his devil's pact, in many folk tales the hero tricks the Devil by finding a loophole in the contract, and escapes the consequences of the pact. Many writers state that the soul can repent at any time by an act of will, and that true repentance renders the pact null and void, regardless of its terms. It is said that a pact with the Devil can be broken if the person renounces the contract, destroys all items connected with the black arts, burns the contract and makes restitution for any harm they have done.

It was also believed that musicians sometimes sold their souls to the Devil in exchange for expertise and fame. The 19th-century virtuoso violinist Niccolo Paganini was reputed to have made such a bargain, a myth which he encouraged and may have started himself. More recently, the celebrated 1930s blues musician Robert Johnson was said to have sold his soul to the Devil in return for his talent.

diabolic pact *see* DEVIL'S PACT

Dianetics
A psychotherapeutic technique developed by L Ron Hubbard.
Dianetics is a psychotherapeutic technique for personal development developed by science fiction writer L RON HUBBARD. In April 1950, *Astounding Science Fiction* magazine ran Hubbard's 40-page article 'Dianetics: The Evolution of a Science'; his book *Dianetics: The Modern Science of Mental Health* was published the following month.

The central idea of Dianetics is that the unconscious or 'reactive' mind stores the trauma of every unpleasant incident in our lives (and our past lives) in the form of 'engrams' (recorded mental images). Engrams hold us back in life by causing us unnecessary distress and psychological harm. The aim of Dianetics is to help individuals rid themselves of all the engrams and 'go Clear'. The 'pre-Clear' holds two tin cans connected to a device called the E-Meter, which measures skin resistance and conductivity in the same way as a polygraph or lie detector, while being asked questions by an 'auditor'. After perhaps many months of auditing sessions the pre-Clear erases the reactive mind and goes Clear. A 1967 definition of Clear says:

> It erases the Reactive Mind, overcoming the barriers to spiritual independence and serenity. It totally removes the cause of counter-efforts to one's happiness, awareness, goals and abilities.

Early claims that the Clear would have remarkable powers of memory recall, greatly increased intelligence and better health, eyesight and hearing were later to be played down. As SCIENTOLOGY developed, going Clear, while still important, became an early stage in a long 'spiritual career path' called 'The Bridge to Total Freedom'.

dice
Small cubes with the faces usually numbered from one to six, used in games of chance and as a means of divination.
The word 'dice' is the plural form of the singular 'die', which derives from Old French *de* (plural *dez*), from Latin *datus*, meaning 'given or cast'. Dice probably evolved from knucklebones, an origin which is still reflected today in the colloquial term 'bones' for dice. Standard dice are six-sided cubes with each face having a number of dots ranging from 1 to 6, and the pairs of numbers on opposing faces always totalling 7: 1 and 6, 2 and 5, 3 and 4. These are thrown to provide supposedly uniformly distributed random numbers, hence their use for gambling and games of chance.

Dice have also long been used for DIVINATION. Specialized sets of dice may be employed for this purpose; astrological dice consist of three 12-sided dice based on the concepts of Western ASTROLOGY, and rune dice, with RUNES instead of numbers on the faces, are also used. A pair of standard, six-numbered dice can also be used for fortune-telling purposes, and divination by dice is sometimes known as cleromancy or astragalomancy. This practice was common in Egypt as far back as 2000 BC, and also in ancient Rome, where the god Mercury was regarded as the patron of this type of divination. The Tibetans also used dice in this way, in a practice they called Sho-Mo, and the Hindu divination technique of Ramala uses dice very similar to standard spotted ones, except that these are spun on a rod. This practice is also associated with present-day Roma.

The simplest method of dice divination commonly used is to draw a circle, usually around 30 centimetres (12 inches) in diameter, lay it flat and, thinking of a question, roll two or three dice into the circle. Any which roll outside the circle do not count. If all the dice fall outside the circle, the questioner should roll them all again. The number of spots on the upward faces of the dice inside the circle are then added up, and their meaning interpreted. For example, in one system, one spot means 'yes', two spots mean 'no', three spots mean 'take care', and four spots mean 'be wise'. It is traditionally believed that the prediction will come true within nine days of casting the dice.

Because dice are a kind of RANDOM NUMBER GENERATOR, they have also lent themselves to various experiments in PSYCHIC research. The dice are mainly used to test for two kinds of psychic ability: CLAIRVOYANCE, in which the subject can predict in advance the number or numbers that will come up before the dice are thrown; or PSYCHOKINESIS, in which the subject actually influences the outcome of the throw. The most famous of these experiments began in 1934, when J B RHINE, a US parapsychologist at Duke University in North Carolina, conducted experiments to try to determine whether it was possible to influence the falling dice to roll to certain numbers or combinations. The dice were placed in cups before being shaken and thrown, so that the subjects could not influence the throw. First, one die was thrown, and the subject was asked to will it to fall with a given face upwards. Since there was a 1 in 6 probability of the subject's desired number coming up simply by chance, any result higher than one correct out of six was considered significant. The same procedure was then used for two and three dice. By the end of 1941, Rhine had conducted a total of 651,216 experimental dice throws, and he felt that the results pointed towards some kind of genuine psychic phenomenon. Many other similar experiments followed, but the scientific community in general holds the results of such trials to be inconclusive.

dingonek
An amphibious walrus-like cryptid with scales, indigenous to Kenya.
The walrus-like water beast known to the Wa-Ndorobo tribe as the dingonek is one of tropical Africa's most extraordinary CRYPTIDS. Its most famous reported Western eyewitness was an explorer called John Alfred Jordan, who claimed that in 1907 he spied and unsuccessfully shot at one in the River Maggori (Migori), which runs into Lake Victoria.

He described it as being 4.6–5.5 metres (15–18 feet) long, covered in scales, with a spotted back as wide as a male hippo's, hippo-sized footprints, long claws, a broad tail and a massive head whose jaws sported a pair of projecting walrus-like upper tusks. If the scales were merely clumps of wet fur, as some cryptozoologists have suggested, then the dingonek is probably mammalian and bears a close resemblance to similar mystery beasts reported elsewhere in Africa, such as the mourou n'gou ('water leopard') in the Central African Republic, the coje ya menia ('water lion') in Angola and the simba ya mail ('water lion') in the Democratic Congo (formerly Zaire). Intriguingly, there is an ancient cave painting at Brackfontein Ridge in South Africa's Orange Free State that depicts a still-unidentified creature bearing a strong resemblance to a walrus, including its long downward-curving tusks, lengthy elongated body and paddle-like limbs. Moreover, unlike a true walrus but like the mystery beasts noted here, it also possesses a long tail.

direct mental interaction with living systems
An area of parapsychological study involved with the investigation of the possible ability to influence living things using the power of the mind alone.
Study of direct mental interaction with living systems (DMILS) is a relatively recent field of research within PARAPSYCHOLOGY, dating essentially from the time of the Cold War and particularly the work of the psychologist Dr William G Braud at the Mind Science Foundation in San Antonio, Texas, in the late 1970s. It is a slightly wider term than BIO-PK although research into bio-PK still forms the core of work in this area. Research in this field has included studies of NINA KULAGINA, who could allegedly influence, and ultimately stop, the beating of a frog heart *in vitro*, and successes have been claimed elsewhere in this field for everything from keeping human red blood cells alive in hostile environments (see DISTANT-INFLUENCE EXPERIMENTS), through to making goats faint merely by staring at them and concentrating. RUPERT SHELDRAKE's staring experiments are also a classic example of research in this area.

One of the more bizarre claims relating to the use of bio-PK is the allegation that part of the CIA's involvement in parapsychological research (see BAY AREA REMOTE-VIEWING EXPERIMENTS and PROJECT STARGATE) included the training of individuals as psychic assassins who would be able to kill people at a distance through the power of thought. However, to date, no one has claimed to have successfully assassinated a person using this technique. See also PARAPSYCHOLOGY.

direct voice medium *see* MEDIUM, DIRECT VOICE

directions, four

The four cardinal directions, north, east, south and west; in a number of belief systems, particularly Western ceremonial magic, Wicca and neopaganism, each direction is associated with an element, and its power is called upon during rituals.

In a number of belief systems, the four cardinal directions, north, east, south and west, are associated with the four ELEMENTS, and are believed to symbolize different energies and forces. Western ceremonial magic, WICCA and NEOPAGANISM focus strongly on the power of the four directions and their elements, which are honoured and invoked during the casting of a MAGIC CIRCLE and represented on the altar and at each corner of the circle.

Each magical tradition has its own set of associations, so elemental and directional correspondences and colours may vary from one tradition to the next. But in general, the north is associated with the element of EARTH and is represented in physical form on the altar and in the magic circle by salt, crystals, soil or stones. It is often assigned the colour green, or, in some traditions, black, and is represented by the ritual tool of the pentacle. The east is associated with the element of AIR and is represented by incense; it is assigned the colour yellow in many traditions, and its ritual tool is the ceremonial knife or SWORD, or the censer. The south is the direction associated with FIRE, and is represented by a candle. Its colour is usually red, and its ritual tool is the WAND. The west, the direction of the element WATER, may be represented by a bowl of water, or sea shells; its colour is usually blue, and it is associated with the ritual tool of the CUP, bowl or chalice.

Especially in ceremonial magic, the magic circle is divided into the four directions, or four quarters, known as the Watchtowers. Since each direction represents an element, the specific ELEMENTAL associated with that direction may be invoked to lend the element's protection and particular qualities to the magical work. But each direction is also believed to be protected by a higher spiritual being or essence which controls and directs the elemental powers, and these higher beings are sometimes referred to and invoked as the Kings, the Devas, the Guardians or the Lords of the Watchtowers. Ceremonial magicians may invoke archangels as the Lords of the Watchtowers; Uriel is often seen as the guardian of the north, Raphael of the east, Michael of the south and Gabriel of the west.

disappearances

A disappearance is a sudden vanishing of someone or something.

As used in discussions of FORTEANA, the term 'disappearances' applies to the phenomenon of sudden vanishings of people, animals or objects (or the realization that they are no longer present). It is the opposite of the phenomenon of APPEARANCES and both might indicate the beginning and ending of a hypothetical TELEPORTATION transaction. This hypothetical process may manifest differently in different sub-categories of phenomena.

There are very few unequivocal observations of disappearances for the obvious reason; while appearances and disappearances can both happen unexpectedly, at least things that appear are available for study. Objects supposedly teleported, or moved by POLTERGEISTS, are only referred to as APPORTS if or when they reappear in the same place or at another location. Stories about animals that disappear are more prevalent in folklore, in which they are often regarded as supernatural creatures such as BLACK DOGS.

Uncovering the truth about well-known cases is time-consuming and can sometimes raise more questions that it answers. An example is the alleged disappearance of David Lang, in September 1880, a story that is entrenched in forteana and UFOLOGY and which has been researched by many diligent forteans and historians. Variations of the same story sometimes substitute other names for David Lang: eg Oliver Larch, Orion Williamson and Charles Ashmore. Lang, who farmed near Gallatin, Tennessee, is said to have vanished while crossing a field in full view of five people. Researchers found no record of a David Lang or his family in Gallatin. The earliest account is by writer Stuart Palmer, published in 1953. However, it was later proved that Palmer had forged documents in support of his account. The story is also credited to a contemporary character called Joe Mulhatten, famous for winning 'liar's contests' for tall stories. When researchers pointed out the similarity between Palmer's account of Lang and two short stories by US writer Ambrose Bierce (1842–c.1914) – 'The Difficulty of Crossing a Field' and 'Charles Ashmore's Trail' – both published in 1909, Palmer's proponents suggested that Bierce may have heard the story from Mulhatten. This was patently untrue as the names Orion Williamson and Charles Ashmore are the protagonists of Bierce's stories. It was far more likely that Palmer's re-telling was inspired by Bierce's fiction and cleverly exploited the real existence of Mulhatten. Despite this detailed exposé, the various versions of the Lang story have been copied endlessly in the fortean literature without correction or qualification.

Ambrose Bierce, whose fictional stories possibly inspired a purportedly true tale of a mysterious disappearance – a fate which ironically befell Bierce several years later.
(© TopFoto)

Curiously, Bierce himself famously disappeared; he was last seen in Chihuahua, Mexico, at the end of 1913, having joined Pancho Villa's army as an observer.

However, there is a considerable body of literature on larger-scale disappearances. Perhaps it is not surprising that many of these are connected with tempestuous storms and dangerous seas. For example, the FLANNAN ISLES MYSTERY, when three lighthousekeepers vanished from a remote island off the west coast of Scotland; the more famous disappearance of the entire crew of the *MARY CELESTE*; and the loss of Flight 19, a group of five US Navy planes off the coast of Florida in December 1945, which was inevitably blamed on the BERMUDA TRIANGLE.

Despite the many real-life vanishings for mundane reasons, hoaxes and legends, there are still cases of genuine mystery, largely because of a lack of real evidence one way or another. For example, what happened to the first British colony in America, established in 1587, on Roanoke Island, in what is now North Carolina? When their re-supply ship returned from England in 1590, three years later, there was no sign of more than a hundred men, women and children that had been left there. It is thought likely that, facing starvation if they stayed put, they integrated with native tribes and moved

away with them. Similarly, the disappearance of a small battalion of the Royal Norfolk Regiment in August 1915, fighting at GALLIPOLI during World War I, left wild speculation behind it. The men were last seen advancing into fog behind enemy lines, but this entered the mythology of UFOS as an ALIEN ABDUCTION. Military historians believe the group got lost and were massacred, but have not been able to establish it as fact.

Many historical vanishings have been retold in films, and although some would dispute whether it is actually based on fact, the haunting and evocative *Picnic at Hanging Rock* (1975) is one of the most popular. It is based on the alleged disappearance of a party of schoolgirls who never returned from an outing to the HANGING ROCK reserve in Australia's Victoria state on 14 February 1900. Each year on Valentine's Day the film is shown at the picnic grounds after dusk.

discarnate entity

An entity with mental attributes which exists independently of a physical body.

The concept of independent non-material beings possessing mental attributes is found in all societies. Often termed SPIRITS, they are considered to exist within the material body during life and to be capable of maintaining an independent existence after the death of the physical body. This surviving, non-material portion of an individual is considered to retain mental attributes including intention, emotion, memory and a degree of personality and self-awareness.

Discarnate entities are believed to be capable of interacting with living humans and are often proposed as the explanation for many PSYCHIC phenomena including GHOSTS, POLTERGEISTS, POSSESSION states and many spiritualist manifestations – the 'discarnate entity theory'. They also form a part of many religious and occult traditions and in some belief systems spirits are joined by various other classes of non-human discarnate entities such as ANGELS, DEMONS and ELEMENTALS.

From a materialist perspective, there are major scientific and philosophical objections to the idea of discarnate entities, not least the question of how mental processes of any sort could be maintained in the complete absence of a body, brain or nervous system. Even as an explanation for many psychic phenomena, the concept of the discarnate entity runs into problems. For example, at SÉANCES, discarnate entities are deemed capable of responding to verbal questions from sitters. But by what mechanism could a discarnate being actually hear such questions being put, and, indeed, if there is a non-physical mechanism through which it receives the question, why must the questions be spoken aloud at all? There is also the general question of how a discarnate entity would interact with the physical world to produce raps, APPARITIONS or other physical phenomena.

However, many people would also argue that the materialist model of human consciousness offered by mainstream science is still incomplete, and so the possibility of forms of consciousness existing outside the living human brain cannot be unreservedly dismissed. It must also be said that many traditions do not recognize firm distinctions between material and discarnate forms of existence, and accept both as aspects of a single spiritual reality. Even some of the theories of modern physics ultimately challenge the simplistic, commonsense concept of the solid, material world – leaving scope for forms of non-physical or even (as yet uncomprehended) physical existence to be postulated.

disembodied voices

Anomalous voices which occur without identifiable physical cause.

Human-sounding voices lacking any identifiable physical cause are a class of spontaneous manifestation common in PSYCHIC literature. They are reported at HAUNTED HOUSES and other locations, during SÉANCE communications and in the form of anomalous recordings obtained on magnetic tape, where they are known as ELECTRONIC VOICE PHENOMENA (EVP).

In HAUNTINGS, disembodied voices are often reported as appearing to re-enact past events. Typical is the 1888 account of a Mrs Gilby who heard a voice declare 'Oh do forgive me' three times in her bedroom in a rented house in Brighton, accompanied by unexplained sounds including human sobs and cries. She was apparently neither the first nor the last occupant to experience strange sounds in the house, and the occurrences eventually drove her and her children from the property. The SOCIETY FOR PSYCHICAL RESEARCH collected reports of strange noises from five other sets of residents but at no point did any entity attempt to communicate, suggesting to them that it was an echo of a past tragedy in the house.

In other cases, disembodied voices seem to be directed at living human persons. Such voices may enter into apparent communication, give warnings, guidance or commands or impart information. As with AUDITORY HALLUCINATIONS (the category that some would argue many apparent disembodied voice manifestations fall into), such voices may be interpreted in many ways – as messages from SPIRITS, ANGELS, DEMONS or even EXTRATERRESTRIAL beings for example. Alternatively, it has been proposed that such voices may represent examples of TELEPATHY or

psychic projections from the subconscious minds of living persons.

distant-influence experiments

Experiments which investigate the apparent use of psychic abilities to produce effects at a distance from the agent.

Distant-influence experiments examine the possibility that the human mind is able to exert an influence at a distance. In general terms, any effect that is brought about without physical contact is an example of 'distant influence'.

An example of experimentation in this area is that carried out by the US psychologist Dr William G Braud, who (among many other things) carried out an extensive study of a form of PSYCHIC HEALING. In order to rule out the PLACEBO EFFECT (which was claimed to have affected results when human patients knew that they were part of such a test), Braud conducted an experiment involving 32 subjects, all of whom attempted to exert an influence on human red blood cells from a distance (see DIRECT MENTAL INTERACTION WITH LIVING SYSTEMS and BIO-PK). The red blood cells were placed in a solution which would normally destroy the cells (by haemolysis – literally a bursting of the cells). The results were published in 1985, and the containers that were concentrated upon apparently showed a greater amount of cell survival than those left to fend for themselves in control tubes. See also PSYCHOKINESIS; PARAPSYCHOLOGY.

divination

The art or practice of seeking to learn the future, or unknown things, by supernatural means.

Since the earliest stages of civilization, humans have used many different means of divination in an attempt to seek information or help in their lives. The word 'divination' derives from the Latin *divinus*, from *divus*, *dues*, a god, reflecting the belief in many cultures that divination revealed the will of the gods. For this reason, it was traditionally performed by a specially trained individual, such as a priest, SHAMAN, MEDICINE MAN or WITCH DOCTOR. The ancient Romans favoured AUGURY, the Egyptians and Hebrews SCRYING, the Druids both scrying and the reading of sacrificial animals' entrails, while the Greeks had an ORACLE through which the gods were believed to speak directly. But almost everything imaginable has at one time or another been used as a tool for divination; candle wax (CEROMANCY), books opened at random (BIBLIOMANCY), water (HYDROMANCY), stones (LITHOMANCY), PENDULUMS, mirrors, lamps, ink, the shape of clouds, and cards (CARTOMANCY). Divination is usually used for prediction of the future, and is still frequently practised. Most modern practitioners

Two people from Mali, West Africa, employing a form of divination which involves the interpretation of animal prints left in the sand. (© Charles & Josette Lenars/Corbis)

believe that the use of divination does not interfere with free will, since everyone has the freedom to make their own decisions, but that divination is a tool which helps them to make better choices.

divination using ink *see* INK, DIVINATION USING

diviners' bones

A set of bones or other small objects, cast as a means of divination in a number of shamanic cultures, most notably those of South Africa.

The use of a set of bones or other small objects as a means of DIVINATION is an ancient practice found in a number of shamanic cultures, but is most commonly associated with the tribal diviner-healers of South Africa. Although this practice is usually referred to as 'throwing the bones', and actual bones are frequently used, the 'bones' may also be stones, shell, beads or engraved pieces of wood or ivory, which have been gathered together over time. The actual number of bones may vary from as few as 4 to 14 or more. It is believed that the ancestor spirits communicate messages through the bones, and the reading is usually preceded by some form of ritual purification and ceremonial offerings to ensure the blessings of the spirits. The diviner then blows on the bones to imbue them symbolically with the spirit of the person seeking the answer, and throws them onto a special mat or into a circle which has been drawn or marked off for this purpose, and the way the bones fall, and the configurations in which they land in relation to one another, are interpreted, either to read a person's

future, or to diagnose a physical or spiritual ailment and to divine a remedy.

divining rods *see* DOWSING RODS

Dixon, Jeane (1918–97)

A famous US psychic and astrologer.

Jeane Dixon was a US astrologer who claimed she could foretell the future – an ability she attributed to God. She was catapulted to fame following what appeared to be an accurate prediction of the assassination of John F Kennedy. In 1956, writing in *Parade Magazine* about the forthcoming 1960 US presidential elections, she said that they would be:

> … dominated by labor and won by a Democrat … (who will be) assassinated or die in office though not necessarily in his first term.

A 1965 biography of Dixon by RUTH MONTGOMERY related the story and tied it in to the death of Kennedy in 1963. The public took Dixon to their hearts, as did a number of US politicians. President Richard Nixon called her 'the SOOTHSAYER' and apparently put defence plans in place based on her prediction of a terrorist attack. Dixon was also claimed to be one of several advisers to Nancy Reagan during Ronald Reagan's time in office.

Dixon claimed that she also accurately predicted the assassination of Martin Luther King, Jnr, as well as a number of other influential events, and foresaw the death of the actress Carole Lombard and advised her not to fly (Lombard was subsequently killed in a plane crash). The mathematician John Paulos noted that, although some of Dixon's predictions did appear to be correct, she had many more failures. However, it was the hits rather than the failures that people remembered – Paulos named this the 'Jeane Dixon effect' (see also CHANCE AND COINCIDENCE).

Dixon is said to have used various methods of DIVINATION, including a CRYSTAL BALL, ASTROLOGY and NUMEROLOGY. She also had VISIONS, and would sometimes simply 'sense' that certain things were going to happen. She wrote a popular syndicated HOROSCOPES column for many years.

Among her less-remembered predictions, Dixon suggested that World War III would begin in 1958, that the first man on the moon would be from the Soviet Union and that there would be peace on earth by the year 2000.

djinn

Supernatural beings of Arabic folklore and Islamic tradition, spirits of fire whose favourite abode is the desert.

The Arabic spirits of fire known as djinn, jinn or genies are frequently mentioned in the Koran, where they are said to have been created by God from smokeless fire long before He created Adam from the earth. They are described as spiritual beings somewhere between humans and angels; they have great magical powers, and live for a very long time – although they can be killed – but they mate, raise families and live in communities as humans do. The djinn, like mankind, were given free will by God, and may choose to be good or evil; the prophet Muhammad was said to have come as a prophet to both man and djinn, and djinn will be held accountable at the Last Judgement.

Djinn, being composed of fire, have no physical bodies, but they are consummate shape-shifters, and can appear as humans, monsters, black cats, black dogs or snakes. In their human form, they are recognizable by their flaming eyes, which are set vertically in their heads, not horizontally like a human's. They are divided into many different classes, and the chief of all the djinn is Iblis, also known as Azazel, who is synonymous with the DEVIL in Islam; it is said that for every human who is born, an evil djinni is also born, whose sole purpose is to tempt his human 'twin' to do evil. According to Persian myth, the land of the djinn is called Jinnistan, and its capital is the City of Jewels. However, their favourite abode is the desert, and they may also take up residence in wells, rivers, ruins, ovens and market places. For this reason, before pouring water on the ground, letting a bucket down into a well or getting into a bath, an Arab will ask the djinni's permission, and anyone journeying through the Arabian Desert should call out to the area's local djinni and ask leave to pass through its territory; if the answer is a sudden whirling pillar of sand, it is best to turn back at once.

Djinn are wonderful metalworkers, and their fabulous rings play a prominent role in many tales. Djinn may be helpful household guardians, or annoying pranksters – spilling milk, pushing people downstairs or making them yawn uncontrollably. But they can also be powerfully malicious, causing sandstorms, waterspouts, epidemics, insanity and death. Since they are invisible, and as numerous as grains of sand, it is wise to assume they are always present and listening, and to take care when discussing them – especially as they are said to be able to understand every language. However, there are numerous forms of protection against evil djinn: they hate iron, steel, silver, pins, needles and salt, and they cannot bear loud noises or strong odours, the smell of tar being particularly repugnant to them. Unless the protective word *bismillah* '(in the name of Allah') is spoken before eating, a djinni may enter someone's food and be ingested along with it. Once a djinni is inside a person, it must be expelled before it drives them insane, and salt and tar can be used to drive them out. One odd superstition states that if a human unknowingly eats djinn excrement, his intelligence will soar, giving rise to the proverbial expression 'He has eaten djinn dung!', used to refer to a very bright child.

In Arabian folk tales, the djinn sometimes appear as supernatural helpers, and can be commanded with TALISMANS and magic words. They can also be bound magically to an object such as the famous MAGIC LAMP of Aladdin to grant wishes or tell the future, and King Solomon is said to have possessed a magic ring with which he called up djinn to help his armies in battle.

DMILS *see* DIRECT MENTAL INTERACTION WITH LIVING SYSTEMS

dobhar-chú

A savage otter-like lake monster from Ireland, depicted on the gravestone of an alleged victim.

Conwall (Congbháil) cemetery in the town of Drummans (Drumáin), forming part of the approach to the Valley of Glenade in Ireland's County Sligo, contains a grave of considerable cryptozoological interest. The grave is that of Grace Connolly, who was allegedly killed one morning in September 1722 by a very large and savage otter-like LAKE MONSTER known as the dobhar-chú ('water hound') or master otter. According to local lore, it had emerged from Glenade Lake while Grace was nearby, and fiercely attacked her. Her husband, Terence, later found her dead, bloodstained body at the lakeside, with the dobhar-chú lying across her. Enraged, he shot the beast dead, but before it died the creature let out a shrill scream and moments later a second dobhar-chú rose up from the lake's depths and chased after Terence, who fled on horseback. Finally, however, Terence succeeded in stabbing the second dobhar-chú to death – and depicted on Grace's tombstone is the act of the dobhar-chú being mortally stabbed in the chest by Terence, with its head thrown backwards in its death throes.

This tombstone portrays the dobhar-chú as being decidedly canine in overall form (thus explaining its Gaelic name's derivation), with long limbs, muscular haunches, deep chest and a long tufted tail, but combined with these features are others that are undeniably otter-like, such as its tiny ears, very large paws, short head and fairly long heavy neck – hence 'master otter'. Collectively, they yield an animal unlike anything known to contemporary zoology. Intriguingly, however, cryptozoology can offer a more recent reported sighting of a similar creature.

On 1 May 1968, John Cooney and Michael McNulty claim they saw an extremely strange creature run across the road just in front of their vehicle and vanish into some undergrowth, as they were driving home past Sraheens Lough – a lake on Achill Island, off the western coast of County Mayo. They later described this animal as having four well-developed legs on which it rocked from side to side as it ran, a long sturdy tail, small head and lengthy neck. Shiny dark-brown in colour, it measured 2.4–3.0 metres (around 7–10 feet) in total length. During the next few weeks, several similar reports were made in this vicinity by others. Could this CRYPTID have been a dobhar-chú?

There have been many claims of lake monsters inhabiting various of Ireland's loughs, but as many of these bodies of water are very small, sceptics have dismissed such a possibility by claiming that the loughs could not sustain such creatures. If, however, they have the ability to move from one lough to another, rather than residing permanently in any single body of water, lough size would not be a problem – and perhaps that is what the Sraheens Lough creature was doing when sighted. The nature of its zoological identity, meanwhile, and that of Glenade Lake's morphologically reminiscent dobhar-chú remain a complete mystery.

dolls *see* EFFIGIES

dolmen
A megalithic structure consisting of a flat stone on top of two or more standing stones.
'Dolmen' is the name given to the type of prehistoric megalithic structure, common in the British Isles and France, consisting of a relatively flat stone supported

Lanyon Quoit, near Penzance, Cornwall – an impressive dolmen through which it was apparently once possible to ride a horse. (© TopFoto/HIP)

on two other STANDING STONES. The word seems to be of Celtic origin (probably coming from the Breton *dol* or *taol* meaning 'table' and *men* meaning 'stone' or from the Cornish *tōlmen* meaning 'hole of stone') and is first recorded in English in the 19th century. Dolmens are sometimes also referred to as 'quoits'.

It is thought that dolmens are the remains of tombs, and many grave sites have been found beneath them. When they were built they would probably have been topped by a CAIRN of stones and perhaps a mound of earth, but in many cases these have disappeared, exposing the giant stones. Many fine examples of dolmens can be found at CARNAC in Brittany.

In British folklore they were traditionally known as devil's or fairies' tables, while their enormous size gave rise to legends that they were built by giants.

doomsday cults
Movements which include a forecast of the (sometimes imminent) end of the world among their beliefs.
According to some interpreters of ancient Mayan carvings, the world will come to an end in 2012.

However, this is just the latest in a long line of such claims – believers have been foretelling the End of the World for centuries (see APOCALYPSE).

Messianic Jews at the time of Jesus, and for two centuries before, expected God to save them from their oppressive conquerors by sending an anointed priest-king, a Messiah (a godly man, but *not* a God-man), instigating a MILLENNIUM of peace and justice. Once this belief had been adapted into Christian terms, Christians from the New Testament writers onwards have predicted Christ's imminent return.

In the 2nd century AD, Montanists, followers of a prophet called Montanus, expected the New Jerusalem to descend from the skies onto the Phrygian plains. In the 6th century Bishop Gregory of Tours set the date for Christ's Second Coming to some time between 799 and 806. The popular belief that large numbers of people expected Christ to return in the year 1000 is incorrect; the majority of people didn't even know that it was the year 1000. But Joachim of Fiore (1135–1202) and his followers expected the Antichrist to appear around 1260, closely followed by Christ.

Stepping on some centuries, the mathematician John Napier (1550–1617), who devised logarithms and an early slide rule, performed calculations using the many apocalyptic passages in the Bible and forecast that the Last Judgement would be in 1688 (going by Revelation) or 1700 (going by Daniel). He is not thought to have had much of a following, but other millennial prophets in the 17th and 18th centuries did. Around the time of the English Civil War social unrest went hand in hand with prophecies of the End Times: not just the Diggers and the Ranters, but the Muggletonians and the Fifth Monarchy Men believed that a social utopia was just around the corner with the New Age of Christ's reign on earth. Joanna Southcott (1750–1814) is famous for supposedly being pregnant with the new ruler of the world at the age of 64, but when she died and was cut open the Christ-child was gone. The Panacea Society still keep 'Joanna Southcott's box', which is supposed to contain her prophecies and the key to world peace and is to be opened by 24 bishops of the Church of England 'in a time of grave National Emergency'.

An American Baptist minister, William Miller, attracted thousands of followers with his belief that Christ would return in 1843. When nothing happened he examined his calculations, admitted he had made a mistake and said that Christ would return on 22 October 1844. What became known as the Great Disappointment eventually gave birth to the Seventh-day Adventist movement, whose offshoots include the ill-fated BRANCH DAVIDIANS and the Worldwide Church of God.

In Britain the Catholic Apostolic Church preached that Christ would return between 1838 and 1855; they were so sure of this that they created twelve apostles in 1835, but made no provision for appointing new ones when, inevitably, they died. The last apostle died in 1901 and the last priest in 1970, by which time the Church had been absorbed into the Church of England.

Several so-called HERETICAL SECTS of Christianity preach a doomsday message, including the Mormons, Jehovah's Witnesses and Christadelphians. Time is running out for the famous slogan of the Jehovah's Witnesses, first used in 1920: 'Millions now living will never die.' Jehovah's Witnesses, like all those who put a date on the prophecies, have had to live with the failure of events to corroborate beliefs; Christ was supposed to return in 1874, then 1914, then 1925, and then 1975. The 1975 date was also the preferred one of the Worldwide Church of God (WCG), which even had a booklet entitled *1975 in Prophecy*. The WCG's many offshoot Churches still preach that Christ's return is imminent, but having been embarrassed by 1975 few of them now put a date on it.

It is not just heterodox Christian sects that eagerly await the End Times; millions of evangelical Christians, especially in the USA, take the *Left Behind* series of novels (1995 onwards) by Tim LaHaye and Jerry B Jenkins as fictionalized fact. Ronald Reagan was reportedly so impressed with Hal Lindsay's book *The Late Great Planet Earth* (1971) that when he became president he invited Lindsay to speak on 'theological' plans for a nuclear war to chief planners in the Pentagon.

Many others outside Christianity also make the mistake of setting specific dates for future events. Nostradamus 'experts' regularly make fools of themselves – having claimed, among other things, that King Charles III would be crowned in 1992, that a massive earthquake would hit California in 1993, that aliens would be televised in 1998 and that man would land on Mars in 2000.

Ruth Norman, leader of the UFO movement UNARIUS, said that aliens would openly come to earth in 1974, then 1975, then 1976, then 2001 – by which time she could no longer be embarrassed by her failed prophecy. She was following in the footsteps of a small UFO group near Chicago, which expected a spaceship to land in the early 1950s. It was infiltrated by sociologists including Leo Festinger who wrote about the aftermath in *When Prophecy Fails* (1956) and came up with the concept of 'cognitive dissonance', when expectations and reality are out of step. Festinger was actually pre-empted by an Edwardian writer, Edward Miller, who wrote in

1908 that the Catholic Apostolic Church 'are forced by the stern logic of life to turn their backs upon their past history, and to make their doctrines square with facts when facts absolutely refuse to square with doctrines'. But many doomsday-prophets just set a new date ...

The phrase 'doomsday cults' (often adapted to 'destructive doomsday cults' for the sake of clarity) is now sometimes also used to describe groups (or 'CULTS') whose members exhibit a strong intensity in their following, and have caused, or are considered likely to cause, the death of their members or members of the general public. Groups of this type are extremely rare, but would include such organizations as the Branch Davidians, HEAVEN'S GATE and AUM SHINRIKYO.

doomsday sects *see* DOOMSDAY CULTS

doorway amnesia
The term used to describe the phenomenon whereby those involved in the majority of alien abduction claims fail to remember the moment of supposed entry into the UFO.
Dr Thomas Bullard, a folklore professor and specialist in the collection of abduction reports, studied over 500 ALIEN ABDUCTION cases and discovered that doorway amnesia was almost universal. Only a handful of witnesses could describe the transfer to the place where the heart of the abduction story then took place. Indeed, it was often just inferred that this location was inside the UFO.

Experiments were conducted in Britain for an abduction conference to be staged at Massachusetts Institute of Technology in Cambridge, Massachusetts, in June 1992. These revealed that when asked to describe an imaginary abduction, the point of entry into the UFO tended to be one of the key dramatic moments – just as most science-fiction films featuring alien kidnap will recreate that moment. In fact, the people involved in the experiment included the entry into the UFO 20 times more often than those who claim to have been involved in real abduction cases.

Some people have suggested that this phenomenon indicates that real abductions must be being recalled, because a dream, vision or fabrication would be likely to include the entry into the UFO. The subject may not be conscious while being taken into the UFO – often, in their initial report, the last memory that they have prior to the missing time is of being overcome by a bright light. However, sceptics would point out that as the memories from the missing time in many of these cases have been 'recovered' through the use of hypnotic regression, the doorway amnesia phenomenon could equally be a product of this controversial process. See TIME, MISSING.

doppelgänger
A term which comes from Germanic folklore and refers to an apparitional double of a still living person.
The term 'doppelgänger' is a German word meaning 'double-goer'. The best-known story from German literature is that of the 18th-century poet and dramatist Johann Goethe who is said to have met his own double while out riding one day. His double was wearing a grey suit with gold embroidery, which Goethe did not then possess. It did not foretell his death, rather it seemed to be a representation of his future state – some eight years later Goethe found himself riding at the same spot wearing identical clothing.

Some authorities restrict the term doppelgänger to those cases where the double is seen only by the person of whom it is an image, and usually only where it is in close proximity. In folklore, seeing one's doppelgänger is sometimes (but not always)

Arthur Rackham's illustration of the character Mr Wilson meeting his doppelgänger, from Edgar Allan Poe's *Tales of Mystery* ... (1935 edition). (© Mary Evans Picture Library)

considered to be an omen of death. The category would appear to merge with other classes of apparitional DOUBLES, GHOSTS OF THE LIVING and the phenomenon of BILOCATION. However, on the strict understanding of the term given above, it may well be difficult ever to establish that doppelgängers are a genuine paranormal phenomenon. In addition to the problem of corroborating the testimony of witnesses, it is also the case that people with a number of conditions, including epilepsy, migraines and certain neurological disorders, sometimes report encounters with a hallucinatory second self, appearing either whole or in part, among their symptoms. See also FETCH.

doubles

Apparitions of a living person which are exact duplicates.

'Doubles' is the term used for GHOSTS OF THE LIVING where the phantom 'copy' is perceived to be exactly the same as the original – even to the point of being dressed like them. Traditionally such doubles were considered to be an outward manifestation of the idea that each human individual possesses a non-physical component in the form of a SPIRIT or SOUL, or what some occultists might call an etheric or ASTRAL BODY. In Scotland such doubles were known as 'co-walkers', and in *The Secret Commonwealth* (1691), Rev Robert Kirk describes them as being 'in every way like the Man, as a Twin brother and companion, haunting him as a shadow, both before and after the original is dead'.

Stories of apparitional doubles were common during the 19th century. In 1810 Sir Robert Peel believed he saw his friend Lord Byron walking in a London street. Later he saw him again while in the company of the poet's brother, who also agreed that it was him. In fact Byron was in Turkey at the time. The most celebrated case from the period is that of a 32-year-old French school teacher named Amelie Saegee, who taught in Latvia, and was reputedly seen as a double by pupils on a number of occasions. Such stories continued to be popular through to the 1890s. Examples were discussed at length in the spiritualist magazine *Borderland*, whose editor, W T Stead, claimed to have witnessed a number of doubles himself.

There also exists a collection of (mostly 19th-century) cases suggesting that individuals may be able to project themselves in the form of an APPARITION visible to others (see ASTRAL PROJECTION). However, as with CRISIS APPARITIONS, such cases have declined in the 20th century – some might contend that this is due to lack of experimentation. See also DOPPELGÄNGER; BILOCATION.

Doug and Dave

A partnership involved in faking crop circles.

In 1991 Doug Bower and Dave Chorley, from Southampton, publicly claimed that they had been responsible for the CROP CIRCLES appearing in southern England, having begun their hoaxing activities in 1978. They claimed that until then any crop circles discovered had been caused by wind damage effects. Their motivation was apparently partly simple fun (both men were amateur artists) and partly to make fun of those who believe in EXTRATERRESTRIALS and other mysterious forces. Doug Bower subsequently took part in a demonstration on BBC Television's *Country File* in 1999, aiming to reconstruct a typical night's work creating a circle. The results of this attempt could not be claimed as impressive and led those who believed that crop circles were not man-made to dismiss the exercise as yet another hoax, designed to obfuscate the true origin of these formations.

It was pointed out that many of the more complex patterns found could not have been created in a single night by only two individuals using primitive implements such as wooden boards. The sheer number of examples, and the wide area over which they appeared (and still do appear), also means that Doug and Dave's confession, even if it is accepted, is definitely not, in itself, an adequate explanation for the phenomenon as a whole.

dowsing

The use of a tool such as a pendulum or dowsing rods in an attempt to locate underground water, metal or lost objects.

Dowsing is a technique which has been used for thousands of years in an attempt to locate underground water, metals, oil and artefacts, as well as lost objects and even people. Dowsers appear engraved on ancient Egyptian stonework, and on a statue of Chinese emperor dating from around 2200 BC, and the biblical story of Moses producing water from a rock, in the book of Exodus, is often cited as the first written reference to dowsing. Dowsing was used in the Middle Ages to try to locate coal deposits, and in 1556, Agricola described mining dowsers searching for metals with forked twigs. Interest in this practice enjoyed a revival in Victorian times, and today, dowsing is sometimes attempted in archaeological and geological work, and by utility companies to locate damaged pipes and cables.

The traditional tools used for dowsing are DOWSING RODS and PENDULUMS, but a 'bobber' – a single flexible rod, wand or wire – is also sometimes used. The dowser may physically walk around the search area with the dowsing tool, or may dowse

Jack Timms dowsing with an assistant at Sendford-on-Thames in 1937. Timms was said to have found over 1,000 hidden water supplies using a dowsing rod.
(© Mary Evans Picture Library)

'remotely' using the technique of MAP DOWSING, but whichever method or tool is used, the principle is the same: the tool is supposed to indicate the location of the object in question by moving, and its movements become more pronounced with increased proximity to the target. Dowsing with rods is sometimes known as rhabdomancy.

There are several theories as to how dowsing might work, although there is no scientific evidence that it actually does. The most popular theory is that the tool has no powers of its own, but is a means of accessing the dowser's subconscious sensitivity to the object's electromagnetic field, which produces tiny, involuntary muscle movements in the dowser that are amplified by the tool into a visible movement. A further theory suggests that dowsers actually possess some form of psychic ability, which guides them to their hidden target. However, there is some experimental evidence to suggest that dowsers may use environmental clues to subconsciously guess the correct location of the object in question, as in some scientific tests, dowsers have been unable to find the target object at a success rate above chance when all the environmental clues have been removed. See also THE DOWSING DETECTIVE.

The Dowsing Detective *see panel p177*

dowsing rods
A forked twig or pair of metal rods used to attempt to detect the presence of water or metals underground, or to locate lost objects.
The tools most often used in DOWSING are PENDULUMS and dowsing rods. The traditional dowsing rod, also known as a divining rod, is a forked wooden stick, and certain woods, such as willow, ash, rowan and especially hazel, are said to give the best results. The dowser holds the forked end of the rod with one fork in each hand, and the palms turned upward, and walks around the area being searched until the rod trembles and dips down, which should occur at the spot where the object is located. Another popular form of dowsing tool is a pair of L-shaped metal rods, one of which is held in each hand. The rods are said to either cross each other or move apart when the dowser is close to the target, or one or both may spin in a clockwise or anticlockwise direction. Most rods of this kind feature tubes round the parts which are held in the hands, so that the rods can move more freely.

Doyle, Sir Arthur Conan (1859–1930)
Famous Scottish author who was greatly interested in all aspects of the paranormal.
Sir Arthur Conan Doyle is best known as a writer, particularly for his creation of the detective Sherlock Holmes, but he was also a committed spiritualist and defender of many paranormal claims – to the extent that when Margaret Fox, of the FOX SISTERS, confessed that their SÉANCES were faked, he stated that there was nothing they could say that would change his opinion of the reality of the spiritual world. He was a close friend of HARRY HOUDINI, despite their polar views on the subject of SPIRITUALISM – Houdini was a confirmed sceptic. In *The Edge of the Unknown* (1930), Conan Doyle states his belief that Houdini had PSYCHIC powers but would simply not admit it.

In 1917, Elise Wright and her cousin Frances Griffiths claimed to have photographed FAIRIES in Cottingley Glen in Yorkshire, and in 1920 they repeated the feat. Without visiting the location, or meeting the girls concerned, Conan Doyle wrote two articles in the *Strand Magazine* and a book entitled *The Coming of the Fairies* (1922). It has since been admitted that (at least most of) the photographs were faked and, ironically, the original illustrations, which were copied to make the cardboard cut-outs, came from a book that also included a short story by Conan Doyle (see COTTINGLEY FAIRIES).

Conan Doyle's wife Jean was said to be an accomplished MEDIUM, and she conducted a séance

The Dowsing Detective

In 1692, city officials in Lyon, France, were trying to solve a brutal murder case, after the bodies of a wine merchant and his wife were found in their cellar, apparently killed by burglars. Desperate officials called in a young man called Jacques Aymar-Vernay, from the province of Dauphiné, who had already gained a reputation locally for being able to find anything by means of DOWSING with a forked stick. At the age of 18, Aymar (as he was known) was reputed to have successfully used this method to locate the body of a woman, who had been killed and hidden in a wine barrel – his DOWSING ROD had then identified her husband as the murderer. The man had confessed at once.

It is said that on visiting the crime scene in Lyon, Aymar used his stick to find the murder weapon – a billhook – and correctly located the spot in the cellar where the bodies had lain. Then, accompanied by a crowd of onlookers, he proceeded to follow the trail of the killers, his forked stick twisting in his hands every time he crossed the suspects' path of flight. He led the officers through the streets, across the river and south along the Rhône valley for over 240 kilometres (150 miles) to the prison at Beaucaire, where he used the rod to select a prisoner from a line-up. The man, a young hunchback who had only been brought in to jail earlier that day for a petty offence, was taken back to Lyon where he eventually confessed to assisting the two murderers who had done the deed. The search for these criminals resumed, and Aymar traced them as far as the port town of Toulon,

where he claimed that the killers had embarked on a ship bound for the Italian port of Genoa. The search had to be abandoned, since the officers had no jurisdiction outside France. However, Aymar's reputation was made, and he was subsequently called upon to use his gifts to solve a number of other cases.

The use of dowsing to identify criminals provoked controversy; some people believed it had associations with WITCHCRAFT, and others were concerned that innocent men might be convicted on the basis of what they considered to be an unjust process. The press became involved in the debate, and finally Aymar was called back to Lyon for several public tests of his abilities. The Prince de Condé then brought him to Paris to be tested by members of the Academy of Sciences. Six holes were dug in a courtyard – four were filled with different metals, one with gravel and one left empty. The holes were then covered up and all traces of their locations removed, and Aymar was asked to dowse for the holes containing the metals. He failed dismally, finding only the empty hole and the hole with the gravel, having wrongly identified them both as containing metal. It was also said that he had failed to trace the murderer of an archer-sentry who had been killed by a swordsman only a few days before.

Aymar's popularity went into decline after this, although he continued to practise. Despite his failures, he is still the first person officially recognized as having successfully tracked down criminals by means of dowsing.

---

for Houdini in which his mother was supposedly called from the spirit world. Conan Doyle took Houdini's mood afterwards to be one of shock at having his beliefs torn apart – it was in fact fury at his great friend. Houdini had not wanted the séance to take place and, when it did, he was angered by the use of his mother – she communicated in perfect English using Christian imagery, neither of which would be likely for a Hungarian Jew.

Conan Doyle's interest in spiritualism had been greatly increased by the death of his son in World War I, and in his later years it took on the form of an evangelical crusade. It has been observed that Conan Doyle, famous for creating the ultimate investigator, could be quite 'unobjective' when confronted with disagreeable evidence himself.

Dracula

The most famous vampire in literature, created by the Irish writer Bram Stoker in his 1897 novel of the same name. Although the book was only a modest success in Stoker's own lifetime, after his death it went on to inspire a huge body of literature, film, drama and academic study, and sparked off an enduring popular interest in the subject of vampires.

When the Irish writer Bram Stoker published his novel *Dracula* in 1897, he created a central character that remains the most famous vampire in literature. Stoker began this hugely influential work of Gothic horror in 1890, setting three of its chapters in Whitby, England, where he spent a summer holiday that year. He conducted much of his meticulous background research for the novel in Whitby Library, and consulted at least 32 sources for information on

Eastern European history, geography and folklore on VAMPIRISM. He had initially planned to set Dracula's castle in Austria, but changed its location to Transylvania. In the course of his reading, he came across the name Vlad Draculea, a name used for the 15th-century Wallachian prince Vlad III, also known as *Vlad Tepes* ('Vlad the Impaler' in Romanian), and adopted the name 'Dracula' for his character in place of his first choice, 'Count Wampyr'. While Stoker certainly based the name of his vampire on this historical figure, most Dracula scholars now agree that this is probably the only real connection the fictional Dracula has with Vlad III. Stoker published the novel in 1897 under the title *Dracula* (rather than his original title, *The Un-Dead*) to mixed reviews, and while it never brought him much financial success in his lifetime, it was still in print when he died in 1912.

The story is told mostly in the first person by several of its main characters, in the form of letters and diary entries, although we never hear from Dracula himself. Jonathan Harker, an English solicitor, is sent to Count Dracula's castle on the border of Transylvania, with contracts for the Count's purchase of the ruined Carfax Abbey in London. Soon Harker becomes a prisoner in the castle, but gradually realizing Dracula's true nature, he manages to escape. Meanwhile, his fiancée, Mina Murray, and her friend, Lucy Westenra, are on holiday in Whitby, when a Russian ship, the *Demeter*, crashes into the harbour in the middle of a terrible storm, and a huge wolf – Dracula in one of his shape-shifting forms – jumps from the ship and runs off. Everyone on the ship is dead, and its cargo is made up of boxes of Transylvanian soil.

Lucy begins to sleepwalk, and, following her one night, Mina sees her being attacked by a dark figure with red eyes. When Lucy starts to waste away, one of her suitors, Dr John Seward, calls in his old teacher, Professor Abraham Van Helsing, who realizes the nature of her illness. Despite blood transfusions, Lucy dies, but comes back as a vampire, and the men have to drive a stake through her heart, stuff her mouth with garlic and decapitate her to free her of the vampire's curse. They find Dracula's boxes of Transylvanian earth in Carfax Abbey. Meanwhile, Dracula attacks Mina, and the men put consecrated wafers in the boxes to prevent the vampire from resting in his native soil. He flees to his home country, but is tracked by Mina, who now has a psychic connection with him, and he and his three brides are killed.

Like any novelist, Stoker embroidered on his research, and some of the vampire characteristics he incorporates in his story appear nowhere in recorded Eastern European folklore. The necessity for the vampire to sleep in his own native earth, his inability to cross running water and the fact that he casts neither a shadow nor a reflection in a mirror are all Stoker's own inventions. On the other hand, a few now very popular myths about vampires are absent from Stoker's story. Although vampires are nocturnal, traditional folklore does not hold that sunlight is fatal to them, and in the novel, Dracula can move about during the day, although with reduced powers, and is not harmed by bright sunlight; this piece of vampire lore was only introduced with the first film based on the book, *Nosferatu* (1922). Dracula is also killed with a knife, not a stake. The book might have slipped into obscurity, like much of Stoker's work, if it had not captured the imagination of stage and film producers who saw its potential. A 1924 stage adaptation by Hamilton Deane romanticized the Count and gave him his now famous red-lined black cape, and the Hungarian actor Bela Lugosi took the role in the Broadway production before being cast as Dracula in Tod Browning's 1931 adaptation for Universal Films. This was the first official film version of the book; *Nosferatu* (1922) was clearly based on the novel, and Stoker's estate successfully sued for copyright infringement. Since then, Dracula has appeared in over 130 films – more than any other fictional character apart from Sherlock Holmes.

Dracula has inspired many literary tributes and parodies, and has been the inspiration of many vampire characters.

dragon

One of the most familiar of all mythological beasts, which might have been inspired by real-life animals encountered by early humans.

Described and feared by human cultures worldwide from the earliest times, the dragon exists in a vast range of forms and abodes in myth and legend.

The classical Western dragon is a malevolent fire-breathing monster encased in an armour of shimmering scales, borne upon four powerful limbs with talon-equipped feet, and sporting a pair of huge leathery wings, plus a long tail tipped with a poisonous barb or arrow-headed sting. Such was the monster reputedly faced by St George, believed to have been a martyr in Palestine, probably before the time of Constantine.

According to a familiar version of the legend (of which there are countless variations), the dragon inhabited a lake near Sylene in Libya, and threatened to lay waste to the town unless it was fed daily with a female virgin. Learning of Sylene's plight, George arrived to do battle with the monster, on the day that the king's daughter was due to be sacrificed. Dispatching the dragon after a furious confrontation, George saved the princess's life. Although it is unclear why this Middle Eastern figure became the patron saint of England, in later versions the location of this battle was transplanted to England – the two most popular sites are Brinsop in Herefordshire, and a flat-topped hill near Oxfordshire's famous UFFINGTON WHITE HORSE.

Most British dragons, however, are of the worm variety – lacking wings and legs, with lengthy, elongate bodies, and emitting poisonous vapours rather than fire. Probably the most famous British dragon legend is that of the Lambton worm of north-eastern England, which began as a small newt-like beast thrown into a well by the heir of Lambton Castle during the 14th century, but grew so large that it eventually left the well, wrapped itself around a nearby hill and began devouring the local farmers' livestock to sustain its immense bulk. After inflicting a reign of tyranny that desecrated the entire region, the beast was finally slain by its discoverer, the heir of Lambton, recently returned home from the Crusades, who wore a special suit of armour bearing numerous sharp spikes that fatally severed the worm into numerous segments when it attempted to crush its assailant in its coils.

Other tales of Western dragons include the two-legged, winged wyvern; the lindorm (a wingless wyvern); the guivre (a limbless, wingless dragon resembling a monstrous snake); and the amphiptere (a legless winged dragon). Even more bizarre than these was the tarasque. Originating in Asia Minor and said to be the offspring of a famous biblical monster called the leviathan, it was claimed that it was an extraordinary six-legged lion-headed dragon with a shell of spikes upon its back. Migrating westward, it eventually reached Provence, where it terrorized travellers along or upon the River Rhône – until St Martha tamed it by sprinkling it with holy water.

Equally strange was the shaggy beast or peluda, a water dragon of French lore from the Middle Ages. Allegedly a survivor of the Great Flood, this long-necked monster had a green furry body bristling with poisonous quills, turtle-like feet and a serpent's head. It frequented the banks of the River Huisne, from where it made many forays into the surrounding countryside to kill not only the local livestock but also any maidens or children that it could find – until it was eventually slain by a valiant swordsman who sliced its tail in half, killing it instantly.

Our erstwhile belief in Western dragons was probably inspired at least in part by encounters with real animals, such as huge monitor lizards or gigantic pythons, or even with the fossilised remains of dinosaurs and winged pterosaurs. In his book *The Dragons of Eden* (1977), Cornell University scientist Professor Carl Sagan contemplated a still closer link between fictional dragons and factual giant reptiles – speculating that perhaps some prehistoric reptiles survived into more recent times than currently accepted by science, and that mankind's myths and legends of dragons may stem from ancient, inherited memories of our long-distant ancestors' encounters with living dinosaurs.

Oriental dragons are very different from the dragons of the West. Oriental mythology includes many kinds of dragons, and collectively they influence and control every aspect of nature and the affairs of mankind. In stark contrast to their Western counterparts, Oriental dragons are exceedingly wise, are capable of flying without the aid of wings and (aside from spasmodic outbursts of anger) they appear relatively benevolent in their interactions with humanity. They are also revered – to the extent that many of the East's most ancient and august human lineages claim direct descent from a dragon.

Dragon Project Trust

An organization set up to investigate energies at prehistoric sites.

It has long been part of folklore that prehistoric sites and associated phenomena such as LEYS seem to have unusual forms of energy or other forces connected with them. In 1977, the English writer and researcher Paul Devereux founded the Dragon Project Trust (DPT) with the aim of investigating various sites to establish whether or not there was any substance to these ideas.

Using volunteers from a range of disciplines as well as ordinary members of the public, the DPT monitored many sites in Britain and Europe with various types of equipment over a period of years. They claimed to have detected ANOMALIES in magnetic fields and unusual radiation levels at various sites, and in some cases ultrasonic and infrared effects, while at others nothing of the kind was found. The DPT claimed to have established that all megalithic STONE CIRCLES in the British Isles were built close to geological fault lines. Such sites were also linked to reports of the phenomenon known as EARTH LIGHTS.

An important conclusion reached by the DPT was that some of the effects reportedly experienced by visitors to many ancient sites were more likely to be mental reactions to the atmosphere or physical location encountered there. This was one of the reasons why much of this monitoring was discontinued in 1990 in favour of a more psychically attuned approach. Throughout the ages, people have claimed to have experienced VISIONS or acquired the power of prophecy at ancient sacred locations. Perhaps there was something about these places that acted directly on the human imagination. It was decided to investigate the DREAMS of people sleeping at particular prehistoric sites, with a view to establishing a link between these places and the unconscious mind. Could such sites retain a kind of ancestral memory that could be tapped into by a dreaming modern mind?

The dreamers at these sites were watched over by companions with instructions to wake them if they detected the rapid eye movement that normally accompanies dreaming. The companion would then take down details of what had been dreamt for later analysis and comparison. While some dreams appeared to have similarities or resonances with others, so far the results from this programme seem to have been largely inconclusive. The 'dreamwork programme' was discontinued in 2003, although further analysis remains to be done on the data collected. See also EARTH MYSTERIES.

Drawing Down the Moon
A ritual which is important in some forms of modern witchcraft practice.

The ritual of Drawing Down the Moon is said to involve the transformation of the high priestess of a COVEN into THE GODDESS. During the ritual the high priestess usually enters a trance and, with the assistance of the high priest, the spirit of the Goddess is 'drawn down' into her.

Those that follow the Gardnerian tradition (see GERALD GARDNER) may recite the 'Charge of the Goddess' as part of the process. The version produced by Gardner (and later adapted by one of his students, Doreen Valiente) drew heavily on one which appears in *ARADIA, OR THE GOSPEL OF THE WITCHES* by Charles Godfrey Leland, who claimed that it formed part of a Tuscan witchcraft tradition which had survived since before the Middle Ages.

dreams
Experiences of images, sounds, sensations and emotions that are not directly due to external stimuli. They normally occur during sleep and are not apparently the subject of conscious control.

There are a wide range of conflicting scientific theories as to how and why dreams occur and, for this reason, there is no universally accepted definition of what constitutes a dream – some admit such concepts as 'waking dreams' (which are often offered as an explanation for paranormal experiences; see DREAMS, WAKING), 'daydreams' and other dream-like experiences into the general category of dreams.

Within the scientific community, dreams are regarded as a normal brain activity which (in very loose and general terms) involves the processing of ordinary sensory information that has previously been received. It used to be believed that they

occurred only during phases of sleep known as 'rapid eye movement' (REM) sleep – this phase of sleep can be distinguished visually by an external observer due to the obvious movement of the eyeball beneath the eyelid. However, recent research and opinion suggests that the simple fact that dreams are more clearly remembered by subjects when they are woken from REM sleep (as opposed to deep sleep) does not necessarily mean that they are entirely restricted to these phases. Dreams are still the subject of extensive and on-going scientific research.

Two particularly interesting areas of dream research are 'lucid dreams' (in which the dreamer is aware that they are dreaming and can often exercise an element of control over the dream) and 'false awakenings' (in which the dreamer experiences the sensation of waking up and going about normal routines while they are actually still asleep).

Historically, dreams have been interpreted in a number of different ways and they continue to be the subject of a wide range of paranormal claims. They have been regarded in cultures throughout the world as experiences that result from one of several variations on the theme of the SOUL, SPIRIT or ASTRAL BODY leaving the physical body during sleep to enter another world or realm. Conversely, they are sometimes used by those who believe that they are a 'normal' phenomenon as a counter argument to paranormal explanations for such things as OUT-OF-BODY EXPERIENCES.

Perhaps the most widely held paranormal belief relating to dreams is the idea that people can experience 'precognitive dreams' (see PRECOGNITION). Throughout history, dreams have been strongly associated with predicting the future, as illustrated by the Old Testament story of Joseph interpreting Pharaoh's dream, and the argument over the value of dreams between Chauntecleer the cock and his hen-consort Pertelote in Chaucer's *Nun's Priest's Tale*. The CINCINNATI PREMONITION is a modern example of what is alleged to be an accurate precognitive dream. The standard sceptics' answer to such claims is that, with so many dreams being experienced on a daily basis, there is a strong statistical likelihood that at least some of them will resemble actual future events. See also WAKING IMPRESSIONS.

dreams, waking
Periods when the mind enters a dreamlike state but which is not accompanied by the physical condition of sleep.

DREAMS are generally associated with sleep, particularly phases of sleep known as REM (rapid eye movement) sleep – although this strict connection is now questioned. However, some experts believe that the brain states required for dream activity can even occasionally occur during periods when we are apparently awake, especially when we are exceptionally tired or even suffering from sleep deprivation. In such states a person may see or hear things which might be described as visual or auditory HALLUCINATIONS. This is related to the phenomenon of SLEEP PARALYSIS, in which people in the process of waking up go through dreamlike experiences.

The condition of narcolepsy, in which a person suffers short attacks of irresistible drowsiness at any time of day, has also been blamed for producing hallucinations. Narcoleptics are often described as experiencing periods of consciousness that are midway between sleeping and waking, and in which their perceived environment appears dreamlike and what are essentially 'waking dreams' are accepted as reality.

The term 'waking dream' is sometimes also applied to the states of trance attained through deep meditation or religious devotion (see ECSTATIC PHENOMENA), as well as the hallucinatory conditions resulting from the use of PSYCHEDELIC DRUGS. Writers and other artists have traditionally tried to achieve this kind of state of mind when looking for inspiration and have then sought, often in vain, to reproduce the images they have seen.

Whatever factors produce the waking dream, such states of consciousness are often postulated as the reason for reports of such seemingly supernatural phenomena as VISIONS of gods, SAINTS or other spiritual beings, as well as sightings of UFOS and EXTRATERRESTRIAL encounters. The argument is that the people involved may have simply been experiencing dream images shaped by their own beliefs, wishes or fears – it is also suggested that this could account for the fact that the 'visions' are often not shared by others in the same location as the one experiencing them. Accounts of ALIEN ABDUCTIONS often contain periods within them in which the memory of the 'victim' has a gap or a phase that is not remembered as clearly as others (see TIME, MISSING) – these are often attributed to their being under the influence of some kind of hypnosis or alien-administered drug. It may be argued that these 'blanks' are also typical of dreams, in which levels of sleep can vary and recollection is often patchy. The counter argument is that, even if the waking dream theory is shown to adequately explain some occurrences, it cannot, in itself, fully explain shared encounters (although these are admittedly rare).

drugs, psychedelic *see* PSYCHEDELIC DRUGS

Druids

An order of priests in pre-Christian Gaul, Britain and Ireland, who appear in Welsh and Irish legend as prophets and sorcerers; one of several modern movements seeking to revive this ancient tradition.

Scholars often compare the priestly order known as the Druids, who wielded great spiritual, social and political power in pre-Christian Gaul, Britain and Ireland, to the shamans or holy men of other non-literate tribal cultures. The Druids were highly respected philosopher-priests who played an important role in ancient Celtic society prior to the Roman conquest, since they not only presided over the religious rituals and ceremonies, which centred on the worship of a pantheon of nature deities, but also acted as judges in cases involving both individuals and tribes, were responsible for the education of the young and preserved the history and intellectual life of the community.

According to Julius Caesar, whose *Gallic Wars* provides us with much of what we know about the ancient Druids, they were organized into brotherhoods which transcended tribal divisions, and they thus unified the Celtic tribes and were at the heart of their rebellions against Rome. The Romans therefore saw them as a threat which must be removed, and set about destroying them; in c.60 AD, they were said to have slaughtered an entire college of Druids on an island now known as Anglesey in Wales, and the subsequent Romanization and Christianization of the British and Gaulish tribes effectively wiped out Druidism. Since the Druids passed down their knowledge from master to student in an oral tradition, rather than writing their wisdom down, this meant that their lore was effectively lost, and the only writings which remained on them were those of the Greeks and Romans, who regarded them as enemies and barbarians; it is possible, therefore, that some of the more negative claims in these accounts, such as that the Druids performed human sacrifices, were propaganda rather than historical fact. After the Roman conquest, Druidic knowledge was only preserved in Irish and Welsh folklore and mythology, as set down by Christian monks in the Dark Ages, and the practices of witches and 'cunning men'.

In the late 18th and 19th centuries, archaeological discoveries, combined with the Romantic Movement, sparked off a renewed interest in the Druids, and England and Wales saw a Druid revival, inspired by the works of writers such as John Aubrey (1626–97) and William Stukeley (1687–1765). In 1781, the Ancient Order of Druids was founded in London, and other Druid revival organizations followed, although most of these were based not on pagan spirituality, but focused more on values such as brotherhood and civic and national pride. However, in the 20th century, a group of students in Minnesota formed an organization called the Reformed Druids of North America (RDNA), and although it was begun as a joke, it nevertheless spread, and eventually one of its members, Isaac Bonewits, founded a group called *Ár nDraíocht Féin* (A Druid Fellowship), which was based specifically on the revival of the ancient Druid practices, as far as these could be pieced together from the study of Celtic myths, the pagan practices of other parts of Europe, the folk practices of the British Isles and archaeological evidence.

It is known that the ancient Druids venerated trees, wells and rivers, as well as the Celtic gods and goddesses, and that they believed in the immortality of the soul, which passed to a non-judgemental Underworld after death. Their order consisted of three categories: the Bards, poet-musicians who memorized the Celtic myths and the history of their people and performed them as poems and songs; the Ovates, or SEERS, PSYCHICS and visionaries who practised DIVINATION and other forms of MAGIC; and the Druids, keepers of the wisdom, law and lore of the Celts, who presided over the rituals and religious ceremonies thought to have been chiefly performed in sacred oak groves. These categories are still preserved in many modern Druid orders, who refer to their communities as 'groves'.

Drummer of Tedworth

A famous 17th-century English poltergeist case.

The 17th-century case of the Demon Drummer of Tedworth (now Tidworth) in Wiltshire is one of the more convincing early modern POLTERGEIST accounts.

The occurrences began in March 1661 at the house of John Mompesson, a local magistrate, who had recently tried an itinerant conjurer named William Drury. A drum possessed by Drury was confiscated and, on being banished from the area, he supposedly uttered CURSES against Mompesson and his household. Soon after this, Mompesson's house was disturbed by rapping and booming sounds followed by a range of other phenomena that would now be recognized as typical of alleged poltergeist cases. Objects were moved, children were pestered and levitated from their beds and unexplained animal noises were heard in the house. A DISEMBODIED VOICE was reportedly heard crying 'a witch, a witch' over a hundred times and the raps and knocks became particularly intense, with drumming sounds continuing for days on end. There were also a number of other bizarre incidents, such as the coins in the pockets of a visitor to the house being turned black.

The disturbances at the house lasted more than a year and were investigated by the royal chaplain Joseph Glanvil, who visited the house and heard the

An illustration depicting the Drummer of Tedworth, from Joseph Glanvill's *Saducismus Triumphatus* (first published in 1681). (© TopFoto)

noises for himself. Glanvil also traced other witnesses and described the events in his book *Saducismus Triumphatus* (1681), which is now hailed as a classic of early PSYCHICAL RESEARCH. The phenomena were attributed at the time to sorcery on the part of Drury, who was duly tried as a WITCH and transported. According to later tales, the penal ship carrying him abroad was supposedly disturbed by storms conjured by him in further acts of WITCHCRAFT.

Many modern psychical researchers cite the Drummer of Tedworth as a classic poltergeist case because the phenomena occurred in the presence of young children approaching puberty (a common theme in more recent cases). There have also been a number of other theories based on the suggestions that Drury was of Roma ancestry, or possibly even a Siberian shaman, who possessed knowledge of how to induce fits and trance states by way of ritual drumming.

dryads

A wood nymph which is bound to the tree in or near which it dwells, most commonly found in Greek and Celtic mythology.

The word 'dryad' in Greek mythology was originally used to refer specifically to a wood nymph of the oak tree (the Greek word *drys* means oak), but the term eventually came to be used of all tree nymphs. Dryads are seldom seen, except as patches of light in the trees, but they may take a physical form like that of a human or elf. According to some writers, their hair and complexion change with the seasons, so that in spring they are green, in autumn, brown, and in winter, white. Being nymphs, they are all female, and are said to sing beautifully. In the Greek tradition, they are the companions of Artemis, goddess of the moon and of the hunt, and sometimes, of Dionysus, god of wine. Each dryad is born with a certain tree, to which she is bound; if the tree is injured, the dryad feels the injury, and if the tree dies, so does its dryad. Therefore, although usually playful and non-violent, they will defend their trees and forests with force, and will punish any careless mortal who harms them.

In Celtic lore, dryads have more freedom of movement than their Greek counterparts, and can move from tree to tree and dwell in any of the thirteen Celtic sacred trees (birch, rowan, ash, alder, willow, hawthorn, oak, holly, hazel, vine, ivy, reed and elder) but prefer willow trees above all others. Willows inhabited by dryads are said to walk about at night in search of new places to put down their roots. The dryads are said to have given the secrets of DIVINATION and tree magic to the DRUIDS, and are sometimes called *sidhe Draoi* (fairy Druids).

duah *see* ROPEN

Duncan, Helen (1897–1956)

The last person to be tried in Britain under the Witchcraft Act.

Helen Duncan was born in Callander, Stirlingshire, and went on to become a famous spiritualist and MEDIUM. She conducted SÉANCES throughout Britain, at which it was claimed that she could cause the spirits of the dead to materialize in the form of ECTOPLASM that issued from her mouth. These spirits would supposedly take solid, human form so that they could be talked to and even touched.

She gathered a large following of supporters, although in 1931 she was denounced as a fraud by the London Spiritual Alliance. She was also found guilty of trickery in 1934 when one of the participants at a séance in Edinburgh grabbed the 'ectoplasm' – only to find that it was a stockinet undervest.

However, the incidents for which she is most famous occurred during World War II, when she was living in Portsmouth (an important naval base at the time). She first came to the attention of the authorities when, during a séance in 1941, she apparently spoke with a dead sailor, who informed her that his ship, HMS *Barham*, had sunk in the Mediterranean. News of the sinking had not yet been released by the government and, indeed, it was not released until several months later.

In 1944, she and three members of the audience were arrested during another séance in Portsmouth. They were initially charged with vagrancy and, unusually, refused bail. However, after consideration was given briefly to the charge of conspiracy, she was eventually brought to trial at the Old Bailey under the Witchcraft Act of 1735. Under the terms of the act she was accused of exercising or using 'human conjuration that through the agency of Helen Duncan spirits of deceased dead persons should appear to be present'. In addition to this, she was also charged, under the terms of the Larceny Act, with taking money under the false pretence that she could produce these spirits. Although this appeared to put her in something of a difficult position, it should be noted that the Witchcraft Act did, in fact, also cover fraudulent acts.

The trial became something of a farce, with numerous witnesses coming forward to testify to the truth of her powers, drawing the attention of the national newspapers. At one point, the defence suggested that she should be allowed to give a demonstration of her gifts from the dock – an offer that was eventually declined by the prosecution. Helen Duncan was finally found guilty of contravening the Witchcraft Act, found not guilty of all other charges and sentenced to nine months in prison.

Many of her spiritualist supporters alleged that the intelligence services had engineered the trial to ensure that she did not represent a threat to national security – particularly when it came to light later that the D-Day landings were being planned at the time.

The general uproar following the trial, both from her supporters and the legal establishment, led to the abolition of the Witchcraft Act in 1951 (to be replaced by the Fraudulent Mediums Act) and to the recognition of SPIRITUALISM as a religion in 1954. It is said that this was partly due to WINSTON CHURCHILL, who was known to be sympathetic to the spiritualist cause and was said to have visited Helen Duncan in prison.

Having apparently promised on her release that she would conduct no further séances, Helen Duncan was arrested again at a séance in Nottingham in 1956. She was found to have severe burns to her stomach – caused, her supporters said, by the ectoplasm re-entering her body too quickly during the arrest. Whatever the truth of the matter, she was admitted to hospital and died five weeks later.

dwarfs

A race of beings in Scandinavian and Germanic folk-lore, who are small, squat and usually bearded; they live either inside mountains or underground, and are highly skilled miners, metalworkers and makers of jewellery.
According to Icelandic myth, when the gods created the world from the dismembered parts of the giant Ymir, maggots fell from his decaying flesh, and the gods granted them human appearance and intelligence. These creatures became the dwarfs (from Old Norse *dvergr*, Old English *dweorg*). They are all small, with large heads and gnarled faces, and their skin, hair and eyes tend to be in earthy colours. They are hot-tempered and quick to take offence, but once their trust has been gained, they are loyal friends. There are several types of dwarf: Black Dwarfs, who dress in black and are ugly and unfriendly to humans; Brown Dwarfs, who dress in brown and are good-natured and smaller than the other two types; and White Dwarfs, who dress in white and are the most friendly of the dwarfs, sometimes rewarding humans for good deeds. All types of dwarf move easily through the earth, are strong, wise and long-lived and are highly skilled miners and metalworkers, makers of weapons, armour and wonderful jewellery; in Norse mythology, they crafted several magical objects for the gods, including Odin's spear and Freyja's necklace. They live either inside mountains or underground, so are seldom seen by humans, and they build their cities in vast caves and tunnel systems deep inside the earth, in a region known by the North Germans and Scandinavians as the Nibelungen. Mountain-dwelling dwarfs are usually thought to be more benevolent than those who live in mines. All dwarfs avoid sunlight, because if they are caught above ground at daybreak, they will be trapped and unable to re-enter their homes until nightfall. It is said by some that there are no female dwarfs, and new dwarfs have to be sculpted from stone.

The traditional plural form of 'dwarf' is 'dwarfs', but since J R R Tolkien used 'dwarves' as his plural in *Lord of the Rings*, this form has also come to be accepted as valid.

Earhart, Amelia Mary (1897–1937)

US aviator who disappeared on a round-the-world flight.

Amelia Earhart achieved fame by becoming the first woman to fly across the Atlantic, first as a passenger in 1928, then as a solo pilot in 1932. In 1935, she also made the first solo flight from Hawaii to California. As an inspiring and engaging celebrity, she made use of her fame to advance the cause of feminism as well as to argue on behalf of commercial aviation.

Eager to establish further flying records, she decided to attempt a round-the-world flight, setting off with her navigator, Fred Noonan, from Miami in 1937. After arriving at Lae, New Guinea, Earhart took off on another leg of the journey, aiming to land at a small island, Howland Island, in the mid-Pacific. The aircraft was in radio contact with a US ship throughout the flight but Earhart's communications grew more and more faint until they stopped altogether.

The US authorities immediately initiated an extensive air and sea search, but after finding nothing, abandoned the attempt after two weeks. No trace of the aircraft or its crew has ever been found on land or beneath the sea, despite several private expeditions, including one as recently as 2004.

Various theories have been advanced to account for Earhart's disappearance, including the idea that she was captured by the then-expansionist Japanese and executed as a spy. There have also been unconfirmed sightings of Earhart, and there are those that believe she continued her life anonymously on a South Pacific island. However, the most likely explanation is that, owing to navigational error and changing weather conditions, her plane simply ran out of fuel and crashed into the Pacific, a mere pinprick in that vast ocean.

Amelia Earhart photographed in 1932 after becoming the first woman to fly solo across the Atlantic. She disappeared five years later while attempting a round-the-world flight. (© Mary Evans Picture Library)

earth

One of the four elements believed in ancient and medieval cosmology to be the fundamental components of all things; of prime importance in magic and the occult.

In ancient and medieval philosophy and alchemy, all things were believed to be composed of a blend of four classical ELEMENTS: AIR, WATER, FIRE and earth. These four elements are central to magical and occult thought. Earth is seen as the realm of the body, solidity, permanence, stability and security. The power of earth may be called on for assistance in spells or rituals involving physical healing, career matters, prosperity, abundance, fertility and the breaking of bad habits; it governs tree, knot and crystal magic. It is associated with the north, the season of Winter, old age, midnight and the colour green, and is thought to be a feminine element, since it is warm, passive and dry. Earth governs the zodiacal signs of TAURUS, VIRGO and CAPRICORN, and is connected with the planets Venus and Jupiter. In the TAROT, it is represented by the suit of pentacles or coins (see PENTACLES, SUIT OF). In the casting of a MAGIC CIRCLE, it is frequently symbolized in physical form by salt or a bowl of earth, and is associated with the magical tools of crystals, powders, salts and sands, and the cauldron and the pentacle. Its position in the five-pointed star or PENTAGRAM is the lower left point. The four fluids known as humours, which were once popularly believed to permeate the human body and determine the temperament, were each associated with an element, and earth was associated with the humour of black bile. The element of earth is said to be governed by the archangel Uriel, and its specific animating spirit or ELEMENTAL is the gnome. Earth is the element of soil, plants, animals, mountains, forests, caves and gardens.

earth hound

A little-known but grotesque cryptid from Scotland.

With published references concerning its nefarious activities dating back to the 1800s, the earth hound or 'yard pig' is one of the more grotesque CRYPTIDS reported in Great Britain. This macabre creature is said to inhabit graveyards (especially any near water) in Banffshire, north-eastern Scotland, where it allegedly burrows among corpses and devours them. According to the description of one eyewitness, a gardener who claimed he had accidentally dug an earth hound out of its nest and killed it, its fur is brown like a rat's but its tail is bushier, and its head is long like a dog's and also canine in shape. Other alleged eyewitnesses have stated that it is roughly the size of a ferret, with a fairly short tail, mole-like feet, prominent pig-like nostrils and tusk-like teeth. Very rarely seen even in the 1800s, today the earth hound seems to have vanished, though it is still referred to locally, and its zoological identity remains a mystery.

earth lights

Mysterious displays of light seen in particular areas.

In many parts of the world there have long been descriptions of mysterious lights seen at night in particular places. These lights can be small or large, stationary or mobile, taking a particular form or changing in shape, and can appear in various colours. The thing that they have in common is that they are seen relatively close to the ground rather than in the sky.

In folklore the lights were often attributed to supernatural or magical phenomena such as ghostly SPIRITS, the breath of DRAGONS, SORCERERS in flight or dancing FAIRIES and they were given names like 'spooklights', 'min-min' (in Australia) or 'the Devil's Bonfires' (Derbyshire). The term 'earth lights' was introduced by the British author and researcher Paul Devereux in the 1980s – it reflects the theory that the lights are the result of processes within the ground.

Many observers had noticed that EARTHQUAKES were sometimes preceded or followed by this kind of anomalous light display, and some suggested that the lights were caused by the earthquakes. This led many people to look for links between earthquakes and reports of UFO sightings. However, others argued that the lights were seen in places where earthquakes were rare. It was in the 1960s that studies of the phenomena began to link them with the presence of geological fault lines and anomalies in the earth's magnetic field. Tectonic strain (the constant subterranean pressure produced by the earth's tectonic plates shifting against one another) coinciding with areas of marked faulting and certain mineral deposits was identified as the cause of earth lights, which are essentially generated through the release of electrons from the earth into the air.

One such area was HESSDALEN in Norway, for example, where mysterious lights had been seen for generations, often accompanied by subterranean rumbling. A study beginning there in the 1980s produced significant photographs of the light phenomena.

Sceptics claim that many sightings of earth lights are in fact simply effects created by the headlights of unseen distant vehicles or (particularly in hot regions) by light being reflected from another area, along similar lines to the well-known mirages in deserts. However, those who argue against this explanation point out that earth lights have been seen in some places for many years, long before the invention of electric light, and that there have been cases where no potential source of reflected light could be identified. See also ELECTROMAGNETIC PHENOMENA.

Earth Mysteries *see panel p187*

Earth Mysteries

The term 'earth mysteries' covers a wide area of interest in antiquity, ranging from the simple fascination that ancient sacred places can provoke in us to the supposed re-discovery of the knowledge of the ancients. Such a broad-spectrum curiosity is at least three centuries old, but the expression 'earth mysteries' itself was coined in 1974, when it appeared as a headline in *The Whole Earth Catalog*. The associated article dealt with what was then a fresh wave of modern attention to the ancient past. In the media this was largely due to the books of ERICH VON DÄNIKEN and other 'ANCIENT ASTRONAUT' and 'Atlantean' writers. In more serious circles it was occasioned by the advent of revolutionary archaeological techniques, such as radiocarbon dating, that showed Stone Age monuments to be older than had previously been suspected, together with a new understanding of ancient astronomy revealing hitherto under-acknowledged intellectual achievements in the distant past. Earth mysteries, then, is a portmanteau term for a topic area.

Over the decades, acts in the earth mysteries circus have included the following.
- LEYS (or 'ley lines'): supposed alignments of ancient sites, originally described by Alfred Watkins.
- Ancient astronomy ('archaeoastronomy'): the orientation of monuments to heavenly bodies, particularly sun and moon.
- PSYCHIC ARCHAEOLOGY: the use of apparent parapsychological techniques at monumental sites. The use of psychometrists (MEDIUMS claiming the ability to pick up information by psychic means from objects and places) at ancient sites was very popular in the 1930s.
- DOWSING: typically employing a rod or PENDULUM, this was traditionally used for finding water or metal ore, but used in earth mysteries contexts for detecting supposed 'energy lines'.
- Speculations about major lost civilizations, whether Atlantean or derived from EXTRATERRESTRIAL visitors.
- Claims about unusual energies or forces being present at ancient sites, and the occurrence of unexplained AERIAL PHENOMENA such as 'EARTH LIGHTS', accounts of which feature in folklore associated with ancient monuments.
- Studies of ground markings like the NAZCA LINES of Peru and effigy mounds such as those in northern Midwest USA, and other kinds of ground images (known as 'geoglyphs').
- The folklore of ancient places, and landscape-based mythology.
- The beliefs and ritual practices of ancient, traditional indigenous peoples.
- Ancient metrology and the geometry and ratios inherent in temple architecture or Stone Age monument groundplans.
- Traditional geomantic and spiritual systems such as Chinese FENG SHUI, landscape divination, Old European locational, metrological or calendrical traditions, or shamanic religions worldwide.
- The positioning of monuments in the landscape.
- Effects of sacred and venerated places on mind and body.

And more besides. The earlier writings of John Michell (especially his *The View Over Atlantis*, 1969, and later editions) and Janet and Colin Bord (notably their *Mysterious Britain*, 1972) gave the whole messy subject area a vague impression of coherence, a valiant effort continued by them and other authors on and off for over 30 years.

Various topics within the earth mysteries spectrum have risen or fallen in popularity over the years. Perhaps the best intellectual barometer has been the matter of leys. These were first understood as being old straight tracks by the British inventor, businessman and pioneer photographer, Alfred Watkins, in 1921 (his key work was *The Old Straight Track*, 1925). He believed that vestiges of them survived mainly as alignments of various kinds of ancient sites, and it was these lines he dubbed 'leys'. Over time this modest observation became endowed with fantastic accretions, so that by the 1960s leys had become 'ley lines', variously interpreted as being lines of occult force (initiated in the 1936 novel *The Goat-Foot God*, by DION FORTUNE), magnetic lines in the ground facilitating the trajectories of

UFOS (initiated in the 1961 pamphlet *Skyways and Landmarks*, by Tony Wedd) or dowsable lines of unspecified energies (initiated in the 1939 pamphlet *Mysteries of Ancient Man*, by Arthur Lawton, and reprised many times in subsequent decades). The latter is the popular understanding of the term even today. Much written and said about leys was hearsay, and most people were unaware that that there had never been such an archaeological entity as a 'ley line'. In the 1970s, there was intense debate about the statistics associated with drawing straight lines on maps linking points representing ancient sites, much of which was conducted in the pages of *The Ley Hunter* magazine (published 1969–98). From the late 1980s onwards some 'ley hunters' began researching actual, archaeological linear features, such as the pre-Columbian straight landscape lines in the Americas (like the Nazca lines) which ethnographical and archaeological evidence indicates were spiritual geographies related to shamanism. The research-based ley hunters also became aware of linear features like Neolithic cursuses (mysterious earthen avenues sometimes running for kilometres across country) in Britain, and Bronze Age STONE ROWS (see also MEGALITHS) in Britain and continental Europe. They further discovered that in medieval Europe there were specialized routes (both actual, visible paths and 'virtual' ways, ie geographically located routes but invisible, existing only in folklore) apparently relating to an archaic agrarian shamanism and spirit lore that probably had its roots in prehistory.

Although some viewed this progress into authentic research as exciting, many could not stomach it and what was understood holistically as earth mysteries began to fragment into separate areas in the popular culture from the 1980s onwards. These can be summarized as: (i) various forms of NEOPAGANISM; (ii) NEW AGE notions relating to 'energies' and 'Earth CHAKRAS'; (iii) a new wave of so-called 'alternative history' books hinting at the existence of great global civilizations before the dawn of known human history – a marginally up-market reprise of the von Däniken phenomenon; (iv) 'Modern Antiquarianism', a term coined by the musician Julian Cope and made popular by dint of his following in rock music circles, which probably most closely approximates the old earth mysteries holism – though many of its adherents are generally unaware of its history; (v) CROP CIRCLE mania, a now-waning insistence that the earth art appearing primarily in British crop fields is of non-human origin, and (vi) a stubborn rump of traditional, Alfred Watkins-style, ley hunting.

The research-based work deriving from the initial earth mysteries impetus also continues in various forms. One of these involves field and literature research akin to the relatively recently created archaeological sub-discipline of 'cognitive archaeology', in which the placing of ancient sacred monuments and their relationships with their surrounding landscapes are studied as nearly as possible as if through the eyes of prehistoric people. This branch of archaeology, which took form in the early 1990s, displays many attributes of the interdisciplinary ways of perceiving and thinking about monuments pioneered by some of the early earth mysteries adherents.

Another area of enquiry emerging from the earth mysteries matrix focuses on the spirit roads and death routes of Europe referred to above. This involves study of prehistoric funerary landscapes, including medieval corpse ways, which seem to carry earlier ideas about spirit ways through the landscape. In Holland, these features were called 'Doodwegen', meaning 'death roads', or 'Spokenwegen', meaning 'spook' or 'ghost roads'. In Britain, even church paths (surviving examples of which can still be walked) carried spirit significance in the folk mind, as Shakespeare reveals in *A Midsummer Night's Dream*, when he has Puck say in his penultimate speech:

> Now it is that time of night,
> That the graves all gaping wide,
> Every one lets forth his sprite,
> In the church-way paths to glide.

Many of the virtual spirit ways of Old Europe, and even some of the physical routes, were dead straight, just like Watkins' 'leys'.

As far as earth energy research goes, little now happens outside of unsubstantiated (and often contradictory) New Age dowsing claims about 'energy lines'. In the late 1970s, the Dragon Project (see DRAGON PROJECT TRUST) was set up to test if energy claims at sacred sites could be instrumentally measured. It did find unexpected magnetic and radiation properties at some monuments, primarily resulting from the use of energetic rocks such as granite by the megalith builders. Anomalous ultrasound behaviour was also noted – high-frequency sound beyond human hearing, such as that produced by dolphins and bats. Some of these results were detailed in *Places of Power* (1990/2000) by Paul Devereux. The Dragon Project continues its work today, but it now analyses human response, such as dreaming, at Stone Age monumental sites.

Another newly designated area of archaeology is 'ARCHAEOACOUSTICS', the investigation of sound at ancient sites. Numbered among its pioneers are individuals who were very much involved in early earth mysteries activities. Their work is already showing that resonant acoustic frequencies in Neolithic chambered tombs can produce dramatic effects on brain function, and that certain rocky outcrops on the Preseli hills in Wales, where the STONEHENGE bluestones originated, have ringing, naturally musical qualities.

So the best aspects of the earth mysteries' interdisciplinary spirit survive and thrive in real research contexts, promising yet further discoveries about the ancient past. Unfortunately, where it is used at all, the label is also still applied without discernment to the popular, New Age residues resulting from the late 20th-century fragmentation of the topic area, and thus old fantasies will continue to be recycled and early, naïve notions remain unrepaired.

Paul Devereux

earthquakes

Shakings of the earth caused by movements in the earth's crust.

Throughout the ages, earthquakes have been seen as a terrifying and destructive force. The ancient Greeks believed they were caused by giants imprisoned under the earth by Zeus, while other cultures ascribed them to the movements of a giant animal, such as an elephant or a tortoise, on which the world rests.

Modern science has established that most earthquakes are caused by movements in the earth's crust, which is made up of rigid tectonic plates that can shift in relation to one another. When such a shifting occurs great stress is built up until it is suddenly released. Some earthquakes are caused by volcanic activity, which again leads to the build-up and release of stresses in the earth. Earthquakes happen somewhere on the planet every day, but while we tend to think of them as dramatic events, most are so minor that they are only detected by special monitoring instruments (seismometers).

However, when a major earthquake occurs, the damage caused to buildings and the loss of life can be terrible indeed. Perhaps the worst earthquake in history devastated the Chinese province of Shensi in 1556, resulting in an estimated 800,000 deaths. In 1755, over 70,000 people died when an earthquake all but destroyed the Portuguese city of Lisbon. San Francisco suffered great damage in the very powerful quake of 1906.

Various effects can accompany earthquakes, including more minor tremors either before the main earthquake (foreshocks) or following it (aftershocks). Landslides can be triggered, and the surface of the earth can be liquefied due to the release of underground water. The most terrifying consequence is undoubtedly the tsunami, which is an enormous sea wave or series of waves generated by an undersea earthquake. The destruction caused when such a wave reaches inhabited land can be dreadful. The most recent example of this is the earthquake that took place in the Indian Ocean in 2004, causing a tsunami that devastated coastal regions throughout South-East Asia.

Another phenomenon accompanying some earthquakes is that known as 'earthquake lights' or 'quake lights'. Accounts of strange lights appearing before or during earthquakes go back as far as the ancient Greeks but scientists have always been sceptical of their reality. However, photographs proving their existence were taken in Japan in the 1960s. These light effects vary in colour, duration and intensity and have been compared to the auroras (see AURORA BOREALIS), 'tongues of fire', or glowing balls of light. Particularly dramatic light displays were documented during the 1995 earthquake in Kobe, Japan. Various explanations have been put forward, including the ignition of underground gases or the ionizing piezoelectric effect of rock surfaces grinding against one another, but no completely satisfactory theory has been developed. However, the fact that these lights are often seen to precede a tremor means that many seismologists continue to study the phenomenon in the hope that this may lead to a means of predicting future earthquakes. See also EARTH LIGHTS; ELECTROMAGNETIC PHENOMENA.

earthworks

Ancient fortifications made by digging ditches and heaping up earth.

Earthworks are the most ancient surviving form of structure built by human beings, and examples are found in many parts of the world. The basic method remained the same, whether prehistoric people were constructing religious sites such as HENGES, burial mounds or fortifications: a mixture of earth and stones was dug up to form a ditch and then heaped up to create a bank or mound.

The British Isles contain many impressive examples, including the great mound and ditch at SILBURY HILL and the fortress known as Maiden Castle in Dorset. The latter is an Iron Age site at Fordington Hill, near Dorchester, covering an area of 120 acres. It is thought that a Neolithic barrow was first built there c.3000 BC and then later adapted into a fort by the digging of further ditches and building of earth ramparts. It survived as a sizeable settlement until, after being stormed by the Romans in AD 43, it was finally abandoned c.70 AD. The Badbury Rings in Dorset is another fine instance of an Iron Age hill fort, with three concentric ditches and ramparts. The nearby Neolithic barrows suggest that, like Maiden Castle, its occupancy stretches back even further in time.

In North America, substantial prehistoric earthworks have been found, the largest of which are those at Poverty Point in Louisiana, dated c.1800 BC. This settlement was so large in scale (including a main system of concentric semicircles almost 1.6 kilometres (1 mile) wide) that it was difficult to appreciate at ground level. Only with the advent of aerial photography was its complexity revealed. Even earlier are earthworks at Watson Break, also in Louisiana, which were constructed c.3300 BC. Little is known about the cultures that produced these constructions, but their discovery opened up a tremendously important new chapter in the study of pre-Columbian America.

Some earthworks were built as boundaries

rather than fortifications or settlements, and in Britain this continued into Anglo-Saxon times. Offa's Dyke, a ditch and bank running for some 240 kilometres (150 miles), was built by the Mercian king Offa c.785 to mark his border with the Welsh. This took the place of Wat's Dyke, an earthwork built further east for the same purpose about 80 years before.

The reason for building such earthworks as boundaries and defensive sites is clear enough, but we can only guess at the purpose of many prehistoric constructions – it is generally contended that they had some kind of ritual or religious significance. Whatever the nature, or assumed purpose, of individual earthworks is, their common factor is the phenomenal amount of vision, planning and communal work required in building them. Such efforts can only be justified by a shared belief in the importance of what was being built. The fact that these cultures with comparatively low levels of technology were able to create monuments that endure to this day, and still have the power to impress us with their very scale, remains astonishing.

east *see* DIRECTIONS, FOUR

Easter Island statues
Enigmatic giant stone heads on Easter Island in the South Pacific.

In 1722, the Dutch navigator Jakob Roggeveen (1659–1729) discovered an island in the South Pacific which, as it was Easter Day, he named Easter Island. It was inhabited by a Polynesian people who called themselves the Rapanui. The ancestors of these people had erected a remarkable series of giant stone statues known as *moai*.

While many of the statues take the form of giant heads, a large number also have complete torsos which have sometimes been buried by the natural movement of soil. The number of statues has been estimated at between 800 and 1000, with many unfinished examples still lying in the quarry where they all seem to have been carved. They vary widely in size, from around 180 centimetres (6 feet) tall to an enormous 20-metre (65-foot) specimen that was never completely carved out of its native rock – a volcanic tuff that is relatively easily worked.

Some of the statues were decorated with eyes made from coral and many were surmounted by a circular ornament made from scoria, a different variety of lava from that used to form the main figures. The

Some of the mysterious giant statues, or *moai*, on Easter Island. (© TopFoto)

significance of these 'topknots' is uncertain, with some theories describing them as hats or headdresses, others as stylized hair, but most agreeing that they indicated higher status of some kind.

It is thought that the figures represent gods or sacred chiefs and that they were erected in places that had religious significance. It is difficult to be certain as much of the native culture and tradition was lost when Easter Island was repeatedly raided by slavers in the 19th century, greatly depopulating the island. Many statues appear to have been toppled by the natives, perhaps as a consequence of disputes and rivalries between chiefs or religious leaders.

How the statues were moved from the quarry when finished cannot be known for certain. It is thought that a system of ropes and rollers would have been used but that this became less possible as the islanders gradually stripped the island of its trees. Local legend has it that the finished statues simply walked to their appointed destinations.

The island's culture was undoubtedly shaped by its isolation – Chile is over 4,000 kilometres (2,500 miles) away to the east; Tahiti 3,200 kilometres (2,000 miles) to the west – and tablets have been found there inscribed in a script that has never been satisfactorily deciphered. However, it has been shown that the statues are not unique but have resemblances to figures carved by the Polynesian people of the Marquesas Islands.

Eckhart, Johannes (c.1260–1327)

German theologian and philosopher, regarded as the first of the great speculative mystics and the founder of mysticism in Germany.

Johannes Eckhart, also known as Meister Eckhart, was born around 1260 in Hochheim, near Gotha, in Germany. He entered the Dominican Order, and in 1300 he went to Paris to lecture and take his academic degrees; the title 'Meister', by which he is often known, refers to the academic title he received there. He held a series of offices in his order, becoming the Dominican vicar for Thuringia, vicar-general of Bohemia and Dominican provincial in Saxony, where he was distinguished for his practical reforms and power in preaching. He preached and taught in Strasbourg, Frankfurt, Cologne and Paris from 1311 onwards. He wrote both in Latin, in his tractates for the learned clergy, and, more famously, in the German vernacular, in his sermons to the people. His independent thinking caused him to arrive at views that were not in harmony with the traditional teachings of the Church, resulting in his being charged with heresy by the Archbishop of Cologne in 1325. He appealed against these charges, apparently making a conditional recantation in which

he professed to disavow anything in his writings which could be proved to be erroneous, but the charges were upheld, and Eckhart died in 1329, just before Pope John XXII issued a papal bull condemning many of his propositions as heretical.

In his writings, Eckhard communicated his burning sense of God's nearness to humanity, and the individual soul's need to be united with God. From his works, it is clear that he was highly learned in the philosophy of his time, and was a Neoplatonist. His method of expression is brief and simple, yet abstract, and his writings on metaphysics and spiritual philosophy draw extensively on mythic imagery and symbolism. His manner of thinking is clear, calm and logical, and in his theories, the element of mystical speculation becomes for the first time of prime importance; he was the first thinker who attempted to give such a basis to religious doctrines with complete freedom and logical consistency, and was thus the first of the great speculative mystics. From his influence there rose a popular mystical movement in 14th-century Germany.

But he wrote his sermons for the ordinary people in German, and it is in his German works that his greatest significance lies, because in them he was striving to impart spiritual truths, not to the privileged and learned few, but to everyone. He thus broke the narrow bonds of medieval scholasticism and became the forerunner of a new understanding of Christianity, making the Church doctrines and dogmas and their importance intelligible to the many. He taught that man's greatest need is for his soul to be united with God, and that, for this, it is necessary to have both an understanding of God and his relation to the world, and a knowledge of the soul and its nature; such knowledge, he said, is given in the traditional faith of the Church, but anyone who wishes for salvation must arrive at it through their own understanding, and seek the divine spark for themselves.

For centuries none of Johannes Eckhart's writings was known, except for a number of his German sermons, but in the 19th century a considerable body of further manuscript material in Latin was discovered. His extant Latin writings appear to be part of a very large work, the *Opus Tripartitum*. See also MYSTIC; MYSTICISM.

eclipses

The masking of a heavenly body by another passing between it and an observer.

There are various types of eclipse. When the moon passes between the sun and the earth this is known as a solar eclipse. A lunar eclipse occurs when the earth passes between the sun and the moon. When the eclipsed body seems to be completely hidden this is called a total eclipse. Partial eclipses are, however, more common. An annular eclipse occurs when an outer ring of the eclipsed body remains visible.

Throughout the centuries, and in many countries around the world, eclipses have been interpreted as bad OMENS. The loss of the light from sun or moon could have been terrifying to peoples with no sophisticated grasp of astronomy and no knowledge that the effect was transitory. Some people have suggested that in the past, an eclipse may have been interpreted as the end of the world. Some cultures chose to explain the phenomenon by saying that the heavenly body was being eaten by a monster and would carry out rituals to drive the beast away.

Various phenomena can be experienced by people from within an area affected during a solar eclipse. Observers report that as the moon begins to pass across the sun there is a strange sensation of a distinct change in the atmosphere. Animals begin to behave as if it were evening, and day-opening flowers close up. As the darkness increases the ambient temperature falls. Where the remaining light of the sun passes through narrow spaces, as, for example, between the leaves of a tree, images of the now crescent-shaped sun will be projected onto surfaces below. Bands of shadows appear on the ground. The sun's corona, or outer atmosphere, becomes visible as a brilliant ring around the black disc of the moon. Bright spots, like a string of beads, appear in the final few seconds before total eclipse. These are in effect the last glimpses of the sun's corona, broken up by the mountainous surface of the moon. They were first documented by the English astronomer Francis Baily (1774–1844) in 1836 and were named 'Baily's beads' in his honour. Elsewhere in the sky some of the brighter stars and planets, particularly Venus, become visible, and solar flares may be seen projecting from the obscured sun.

A lunar eclipse is less spectacular, but one striking effect is a change in the moon's colour, caused by the refraction of light through dust particles.

As mankind's knowledge of astronomy grew, so did understanding of the causes and cyclic nature of eclipses, with the results that the phenomena became predictable. It is said that the explorer Christopher Columbus (1451–1506) used his knowledge of an imminent lunar eclipse to awe an uncooperative native tribe while stranded in Jamaica in 1503. Whether or not this actually happened, it was certainly an idea that was seized on by writers of fiction and often turns up as a plot device.

eco-paganism

An area of modern pagan practice that brings together pagan spirituality and environmental activism.

Eco-paganism is a term used to describe an eclectic mixture of people and beliefs. In general terms it brings together neopagan religious beliefs, rituals and magic with campaigning and action against damage to the earth and the natural environment.

As with all areas of PAGANISM, eco-pagans do not follow one particular set of practices, and there is no universally accepted set of rules and teachings. There are, however, associations and groups such as the Dragon Network, founded in 1990 and based in London, which is a decentralized network of people who practise 'ecomagic' as part of their practical involvement in conservation work and environmental campaigns.

Eco-paganism has arisen in the period since the 1960s, partly through practising pagans moving towards environmental activism as an outward expression of their belief in the sanctity of nature, and partly through environmentalists recognizing or developing a spiritual side to their work. An early proponent of this mixture of spiritual practice and environmental awareness was Oberon Zell-Ravenheart, founder of the CHURCH OF ALL WORLDS, who offered his version of 'deep ecology' (which is similar to James Lovelock's GAIA HYPOTHESIS) in 1970. However, eco-paganism really entered the public imagination during the direct action protests against road building in Britain during the 1990s. See also NEOPAGANISM.

ecstatic phenomena

The variety of phenomena that may be experienced by an individual while in a state of religious ecstasy or trance.

The phenomenon of being carried beyond ordinary, everyday experience into an intense spiritual state (usually characterized by a physical state described as 'trance') is an ancient one, and is common to almost all religions. It is known as ecstasy, from the Greek word *ekstasis* meaning 'to cause to stand outside'; in the ecstatic trance, the individual's SPIRIT or SELF is (literally or metaphorically) taken 'outside their body'.

An individual undergoing an ecstatic religious experience is conscious of a dramatic expansion in awareness of the spiritual, and concentrates their will totally upon it; their external awareness is greatly reduced, and in a complete state of ecstasy, they are usually unaware of their physical condition or surroundings. Religious ecstasy is often accompanied by VISIONS and emotional euphoria, and there are many accounts of such experiences continuing for several days, or recurring many times during a person's lifetime. Another type of ecstatic phenomenon is glossolalia, or speaking in tongues (see XENOGLOSSY) – the uttering of language-like but unintelligible sounds.

A trance state may be induced by a number of means, such as prayer, meditation, fasting, dance, the adoption of certain body postures or sweating. Self-flagellation was commonly practised by monastic orders in earlier times, and drumming and rattling have been used in shamanic traditions (see SHAMANISM) all over the world for centuries. It is known that a persistent beat can induce physical changes within the brain, resulting in what might be described as an altered state of consciousness, and shamans in cultures throughout the world use this phenomenon to induce trance states for spiritual or healing purposes. Some shamans or holy men also use drugs such as PEYOTE, SOMA or cannabis (see PSYCHEDELIC DRUGS).

A type of YOGA known as Kriya yoga includes techniques for achieving the ecstatic state of Samadhi, its practitioners claiming that there are various stages of ecstasy, the highest being Nirvikalpa Samadhi. In Buddhism, there are said to be eight stages of ecstatic trance which can ultimately lead to enlightenment; to reach even the first stage, which is said to be characterized by the student's perception of a bright light enveloping them, takes years of sustained meditation.

In monotheistic religions, such as Judaism and Christianity, ecstasy is usually associated with the experience of communion and oneness with God, and is the primary means by which biblical prophetic visions and revelations were said to be received. Many Christian saints are said to have been granted religious ecstasies, perhaps the most famous being St Teresa of Avila, a 16th-century ascetic Carmelite nun who described experiencing a number of visions during a long period of illness, including one in which Christ became present to her in physical form, which started on St Peter's Day, 1559, and lasted for over two years.

ectoplasm

Ectoplasm is a hypothetical substance of which it is suggested materializations of spirits within the physical world are constituted.

The word 'ectoplasm' comes from the Greek *ektos*, meaning 'outside', and *plasma*, meaning 'something moulded'. It is the hypothetical substance which allows ghosts to materialize and interact with the world of the living. An early name for this material was 'teleplasmic mass' – 'ectoplasm' was coined in the latter part of the 19th century by either the German doctor Albert Freiherr von Schrenck-Notzing or the Nobel Prize-winning French physiologist Charles Richet.

During 19th- and early 20th-century SÉANCES, ectoplasm (which was generally white) regularly appeared from every orifice of many physical

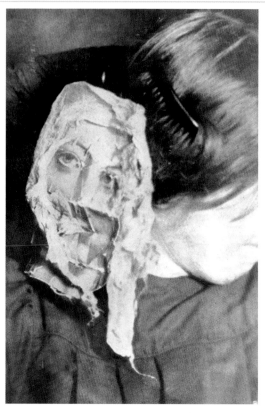

A medium manifesting a face during a séance in 1912. It was claimed that the spirit image was formed from ectoplasm which had been exuded from her ear.
(© TopFoto/Fortean)

mediums (see MEDIUM, PHYSICAL), and was taken by many spiritualists as proof of the existence of spirits. MATERIALIZATIONS took many forms – ranging from amorphous blobs and strings through to hands and eventually full figures with faces. It was believed that the spirits could mould the ectoplasm as it emanated from the body of the medium. Some of the ectoplasm glowed in the dark, and one investigator who attended a séance found that after being tapped by an ectoplasmic hand he had a spot on his arm which continued to glow some 20 minutes later.

Spiritualism and photography achieved prominence at a similar time, and many new photographic techniques were employed in an attempt to photograph ectoplasm and thus prove (or disprove) its existence (see SPIRIT PHOTOGRAPHY). Many photographs of ectoplasm were taken and hailed by some spiritualists as proof positive of the existence of the spirit world. However, it has been suggested that many mediums were unaware of the capabilities of the cameras that were used, as the ectoplasm in photographs showed more clearly than it did in the darkened séance room, and many of these photographs appear preposterous, with the ectoplasmic spirit looking very similar to various man-made concoctions – often cardboard and muslin.

From the 1930s, scientific investigations into ectoplasm meant mediums were thoroughly searched to ensure that no material had been secreted about their person prior to the séance. To reduce embarrassment, a séance garment was invented which covered everything except the head of the medium. However, this did not help when ectoplasm was fraudulently produced via regurgitation or with the aid of an accomplice in the séance room. From around the same time as these investigations, the appearance of ectoplasm at séances became less and less frequent.

Eddy, Mary Baker (1821–1910)
US founder of the Christian Science Church.
Born Mary Morse Baker on a farm in Bow, New Hampshire, in 1821, Mary Baker Eddy suffered from poor health throughout most of her childhood and youth. She married George Glover in 1843, but was widowed within a year, and her second marriage in 1853, to Daniel Paterson, ended in divorce. In an attempt to improve her chronic ill-health, she experimented with a number of alternative therapies, especially HOMEOPATHY, and developed a strong interest in the idea of FAITH HEALING. In the 1860s, she received treatment from Phineas P Quimby, who practised a form of medicine-free mental healing which he called 'The Science of Health and Happiness'. Later, Quimby's influence on Eddy's system of CHRISTIAN SCIENCE would become a subject of much dispute, but although Eddy respected her one-time healer, she eventually disclaimed his technique as being based on MESMERISM rather than spiritual belief.

In 1866, after a severe injury received from a fall, Eddy was not expected to recover. But, according to her own account, she turned to the Bible, studying in particular the New Testament passage describing Christ's healing of the man sick from palsy. Eddy claimed that she felt God's presence strongly, rose from her sick-bed, and recovered. Believing that she had been cured by the same method used by Christ, she embarked on a three-year study of the Bible in a search for an understanding of the relationship between mind and body, and the Bible's promises of spiritual healing. She developed a spiritual and metaphysical system based on Christ's healing works which she called Christian Science.

Eddy strove to restore the emphasis on healing which she felt had been lost to Christianity since its earliest times, and began to heal others, and to teach her method. In 1875, she published her discoveries and beliefs in *Science and Health with Key to the Scriptures*, which became the main text for Christian Science.

In 1877, she married for the third time, to an active Christian Scientist called Asa Gilbert Eddy, and in 1879, she founded the Church of Christ, Scientist, in Boston, with the purpose of 'commemorating the word and works of our Master', acting as its chief pastor for ten years. The Church attracted a large number of followers, many of whom claimed to have found healing there. The movement went from strength to strength, with its power being based on the healing work done by both Eddy and the thousands of students whom she taught between 1883 and 1889 at the Massachusetts Metaphysical College (which she had established in Boston in 1881). In 1883, she founded the Church's official monthly publication, *The Christian Science Journal*. As pastor emeritus of the Mother Church in Boston, and head of all other branches of the Church, Eddy continued to exert a strong influence on it even in her later years. In 1908, at the age of 87, she founded the daily newspaper, *The Christian Science Monitor*, and she also established the weekly religious periodical *The Christian Science Sentinel* and the *Herald of Christian Science*.

Mary Baker Eddy died in 1910, and in 1995 she was inducted into the US National Women's Hall of Fame.

Edinburgh's vaults
Supposedly haunted underground passageways and chambers in Edinburgh that were chosen for experiments in 2003.
The South Bridge Vaults in Edinburgh were selected in 2003 for a series of experiments, conducted by Dr Richard Wiseman of the University of Hertford, to record the reactions of people in supposedly haunted places. The vaults are one of a number of locations that are reputed to be haunted, in a city which claims a high spectral population. Celebrated GHOSTS above and below the city are said to include Major Weir who was a 17th-century WITCH, a phantom monk, a sad-looking beggar, a woman in 18th-century costume and an invisible entity dubbed 'the McKenzie poltergeist' at the Greyfriars cemetery. These and other stories have featured in numerous ghost tours conducted around the city since 1985 – with particularly spine-chilling manifestations being associated with the vaults beneath the city. Built in the late 18th century, the vaults are said to be haunted by a boy who pulls at clothing and by a 'Mr Boots' who pushes people and whispers obscenities.

Some 250 volunteers took part in the tests,

and the results were published in May 2003 in the *British Journal of Psychology*. The findings suggested that a substantial number of people were prone to interpret areas with naturally occurring cold spots, poor lighting or strong magnetic fields as haunted locations. Some participants reported strong feelings of anxiety but little was recorded in the way of visual APPARITIONS. Similar experiments were also conducted at HAMPTON COURT PALACE. Wiseman postulated that ghost experiences might be a form of warning triggered by a person's subconscious mind in response to claustrophobic situations or to slight sensory perceptions which indicate a possible danger. Added to the effects of suggestion, this theory may explain the many complaints of distressing sensations and hysteria experienced by visitors in a vault in the Greyfriars cemetery since the end of the 1990s.

While it confirms that people may feel uneasy in spooky locations, the theory fails to address the fact that reported ghost encounters are more likely to occur in mundane settings (such as ordinary houses or offices) than in romantic and dramatic locations (such as stately homes or castle dungeons). Furthermore, in accounts of apparitions (for example, the MORTON GHOST) they usually appear when least expected and not when observers are agitated.

effigies
Models, likenesses or images of humans.

The use of effigies has been important throughout history in magical practices from around the world. They are central to much image magic, wherein it is believed by some that acts can be carried out upon the representation of an individual to bring about real effects in a chosen target – much like the popular belief in the use of 'voodoo' dolls (see MAGIC, IMAGE).

In medieval WITCHCRAFT practice in Europe, effigies were often figures specially made of clay or wax (and sometimes referred to as 'poppets'), although some WITCHES would use any representation of the human form such as a rag doll or carved wooden figure. In some versions of the practice, it was important that the effigy included something real from the intended target, such as hair and fingernail clippings.

Damaging or destroying effigies is a practice that also appears outside the realms of magic and witchcraft, although usually simply to symbolize a desire to be rid of a political figure rather than through any belief that it is possible to bring about real harm. Pictures or effigies are often burned during demonstrations, and in Britain effigies of the conspirator Guy Fawkes are still burnt every 5 November.

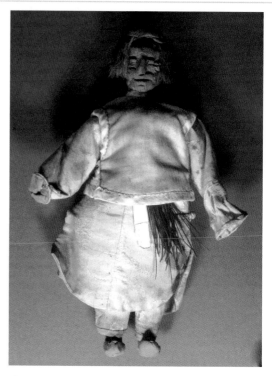

A witch's 'poppet', an effigy employed in the practice of image magic. (© TopFoto/Fortean)

Egyptian Rite Freemasonry
A form of Freemasonry founded in the late 18th century by Alessandro di Cagliostro and based on the ancient Egyptian mysteries.

Egyptian Rite Freemasonry was founded by Count Alessandro di Cagliostro (1743–95), a traveller, adventurer and occultist of the late 18th century. Most writers agree that this name was an alias, and that his real name was Giuseppe Balsamo. Born of a poor family in Palermo, Sicily, he was said to have learnt a little chemistry and medicine at a monastery in Caltagirone, and subsequently travelled around Europe with his wife, selling an 'ELIXIR OF LIFE'. While in London, Cagliostro was initiated into FREEMASONRY. He claimed that as a youth he had travelled to Egypt, where the temple priests had taken him through palaces never shown to strangers, and passed on ancient esoteric knowledge to him; whether or not this was true, shortly after becoming a Freemason, Cagliostro founded Egyptian Rite Freemasonry in The Hague, the Netherlands. This new order was based on the ancient Egyptian mysteries and incorporated many doctrines which can be found in the *Egyptian Book of the Dead* and other documents of a similar origin. Cagliostro also adopted his own secret sign – a serpent with its tail in its mouth, an ancient Egyptian symbol. The aim of Egyptian Rite

Freemasonry was said to be the moral and spiritual reform of mankind, and it was open to both sexes, initiating men and women in separate lodges, with the female lodge headed by Cagliostro's wife, Serafina.

Under Cagliostro's charismatic leadership, Egyptian Rite Freemasonry flourished, attracting members from the highest ranks of society and gaining him entrée to the best social circles in Europe. He persuaded many people to invest in his new form of Freemasonry, and his fame grew as he travelled throughout Russia, Germany and France to promote it. However, while in Rome in 1789, he was arrested by the Inquisition for peddling Freemasonry, and was sentenced to death, although the Pope commuted this sentence to life imprisonment. He died in prison in 1795.

Although Cagliostro's form of Freemasonry cannot be said to have survived him, it nevertheless had an influence on later organizations. During the late 1780s and 1790s, modern Egyptology was enjoying a boom as Napoleon extended the French empire into Egypt and brought treasures and artefacts back to Europe. The exoticism of all things Egyptian, and the inevitable interest in the long-lost secrets of ancient Egypt, ensured that other styles of Freemasonry based on Egyptian mysteries would soon follow. Two such were the Oriental Rite of Mizraim and the Ancient and Primitive Rite of Memphis, which were combined at the close of the 19th century, and are still practised today.

eight

The eighth whole number, represented by the digit 8; considered significant in numerology.

Eight is the eighth whole number. It is thought to be the number of new beginnings, and in the Jewish faith, baby boys are circumcised on the eighth day after they are born. The number represents hard work and lessons learned through experience, personal power, and materialism. In the minor ARCANA of the TAROT, the eights represent material success, rewards for effort, movement and justice. In the major arcana, 8 is the number associated with the Strength card. In Hebrew GEMATRIA, 8 corresponds to the Hebrew letter Chet, and in the KABBALAH, it is the number assigned to the sephirah HOD. In NUMEROLOGY, it is considered to be a YIN number; it is the numerical value of the letters H, Q and Z, and a person with 8 in their numerological profile is believed to be a natural leader, relentlessly dedicated to work and possessing the ability to solve problems. However, an eight personality also has the potential for great reversals in fortune in their pursuit of material rewards, and may be dominant and controlling.

In the Chinese culture, 8 is thought to be a lucky number because it sounds the same as the Chinese word meaning 'to grow or thrive'. See also ONE; TWO; THREE; FOUR; FIVE; SIX; SEVEN; NINE; TEN; ELEVEN; TWELVE.

electrical storms *see* THUNDERSTORMS

electric people

People who seem to have an affinity with electricity.

Most of us will, at one time or another, have experienced the brief 'electric shock' of static electricity being discharged when we touch something such as the handle of the door of a room or car. However, for many people the effects of their interaction with electricity seem to be much more striking and fundamental.

Many people around the world have reported the phenomenon of electric street lights turning off as they pass them in sequence. Others claim that their very presence in a building can trigger fire and burglar alarm systems, while some seem to cause light bulbs to blow or computers to crash when they sit down to work at them. Some people claim to be unable to wear an electronic wristwatch without it being sent haywire or stopping altogether.

In most cases this is an unconscious and non-deliberate effect, but some claim to be able to exercise different degrees of control over this apparent 'power', turning lights and other electric devices on and off at will or even consciously suppressing the effect altogether.

Among those who have investigated this kind of phenomenon many suggest that it is caused by a build-up of static electricity in the body being discharged when the person comes into contact with, or even into the close vicinity of, electrical equipment. Others have attributed the effect to a personal electric or electromagnetic field.

As electroencephalographs show, the brain and nervous system work on tiny electric impulses, and it has been suggested that these contribute to generating an electric field which is emitted by and surrounds the individual. This field, it is claimed, can interfere with the corresponding electric field of electrical equipment, causing devices to switch on and off or malfunction, in much the same way as a powerful electromagnetic source or lightning strike can disrupt the functioning of navigational compasses or other electrical devices. The fact that only some people have this property is explained by the claim that such fields vary in strength from person to person, just as one individual may have a more powerful sense of smell or possess a greater artistic talent than another.

This personal electric field seems to increase in intensity when the individual is under stress or experiencing any kind of intense emotion, and many people reporting such an effect say that it is more common or more marked when they are distressed or angry.

Some have linked this phenomenon with PSYCHOKINESIS or other apparent extrasensory powers, while others have detected only passive effects. In most cases it seems not to have any harmful consequences for the individual demonstrating it. It has to be said that mainstream scientific opinion remains highly sceptical about the very existence of 'electric people'.

electromagnetic phenomena
Strange effects associated with the earth's magnetic field.
There are accounts of various mysterious effects of light and magnetism going back over centuries. Modern science, however, now categorizes these as electromagnetic phenomena.

This category includes such phenomena as EARTH LIGHTS, earthquake lights (see EARTHQUAKES) and MAGNETIC ANOMALIES. Earth lights have been associated with geological fault lines and the movement of the tectonic plates in the earth's crust. Similarly, earthquake lights are usually seen before or after an earthquake and are often considered to be a forewarning of a tremor. These lights, it is now believed, may well account for some sightings of UFOS.

Magnetic anomalies occur at places where there are marked differences in the composition of the earth's crust, with more magnetic substances being concentrated in particular spots. These are known to play havoc with sea or aerial navigation, especially through their interference with the normal working of compasses.

Instances of localized disruption of electrical equipment in particular places, such as the seemingly automatic switching on and off of lighting or the failure of sound-recording devices to function, have been reported for almost a century. Various explanations have been suggested, from POLTERGEIST activity to the intervention of EXTRATERRESTRIALS. However, many scientists believe that there are 'electromagnetic hotspots' all over the world where the fluctuating electromagnetic energy of the earth can produce surges of power strong enough to affect any electronic device in the area.

Some of the effects of electromagnetism on human beings are only beginning to be understood by science, such as the postulated connection between living close to power lines or telephone masts and certain mental or physical effects in the human body, and there is much to be discovered in this field. See also ELECTROSENSITIVITY.

electronic random number generator *see* RANDOM NUMBER GENERATOR

electronic voice phenomena
Apparently mysterious voices captured using electronic audio equipment.
Electronic voice phenomena (EVP) are voices that appear on audio recording media (originally tape), for which there is no known source and which some claim to be voices from the spirit world.

In the 1920s, Thomas Edison suggested in an interview for *Scientific American* that it might be possible to construct a machine that could record the voices of the spirit world. Little was done in this field until 1959 when the Latvian-born Swedish singer, painter and film producer Friedrich Jurgenson made a recording of nocturnal bird song. When he played the tape back he heard what he believed to be a Norwegian voice discussing the nocturnal habits of birds, when no one had been present. At the time, Jurgenson believed he had inadvertently picked up on a radio broadcast, but several weeks later he

Latvian psychologist Konstantin Raudive with the apparatus he used to record electronic voice phenomena. (© TopFoto/Fortean)

believed he had recorded the DISEMBODIED VOICE of his dead mother speaking directly to him. Jurgenson went on to make hundreds of recordings, and in 1964 published his findings in *Voices from the Universe*. The Latvian psychologist Konstantin Raudive heard of this work, and he too began recording 'spirit' voices. He did much to popularize this area and for a time EVP were known as 'Raudive voices'.

Recordings are made either by simply allowing audio equipment to record, or by recording a radio which has been detuned, in other words when it is picking up only static or white noise. Such recordings are then listened to carefully, often at different speeds, until the 'voices' are picked up. Thousands of alleged voices have been recorded in experiments in Europe and the USA over the last four decades. The voices are difficult to hear and interpret and even the language being spoken is in doubt in many cases. Messages are frequently short, nonsensical or banal in content, though occasionally researchers have reported receiving lucid and coherent statements in response to spoken questions.

Sceptics maintain that the voices can be explained without recourse to the paranormal: they could represent interference from various radio sources, previously recorded material not fully erased from the tape or simply the desire of the listener to hear voices when none are there.

The term Instrumental Transcommunication (ITC) has been coined to cover all forms of attempted electronic communication with the dead. See also SPIRICOM.

electrophonics
The sensation of hearing sounds arising from electromagnetic energy.

Witness reports of meteors throughout the centuries have often included descriptions of the noises they made, such as hissing or crackling. Both the Bible and the English astronomer Edmund Halley (1656–1742) noted examples of this. However, the fact that the meteors were presumably too far away from the earth to make sounds audible to those on the ground, as well as the failure of other witnesses to hear the sounds, led many to conclude that this was an imaginary or purely psychological phenomenon.

However, when in 1979 the passing of a large meteor over Australia led to several similar accounts of accompanying noises, the Australian physicist John Keay studied the phenomenon. He developed the theory that that the sounds were produced by an electromagnetic effect on the human body of very low frequency electrical signals generated by the meteor's trail. According to this theory, the signals are converted to physical noise by any of a range of naturally transducing materials, such as metal foil, thin wire or even pine needles. This would explain why other nearby witnesses did not hear the sounds: it was a question of relative proximity to a transducer.

The theory would also cover similar sounds experienced near other sources of electromagnetic radiation such as lightning strikes, auroras (see AURORA BOREALIS) and EARTHQUAKES. Sceptics, however, believe that the levels of radiation involved are too low to bring about this phenomenon and wonder why the same effect is not produced by low-frequency radio transmitters. For them, a psychological explanation is more likely.

electrosensitivity
The theory that certain people are hypersensitive to electromagnetism.

An increasing minority of people complaining of a variety of illnesses are blaming their conditions on electrosensitivity, a heightened sensitivity to electromagnetic fields. A range of symptoms, from headaches, dizziness and flu-like feelings to skin allergies, irregular heartbeats and depression, are being attributed to proximity to computer screens, telephone masts, mobile phones and electricity pylons, all of which produce non-ionizing radiation. Some people claim to be affected by the ordinary electrical wiring within their homes.

As with other medical conditions such as allergies, some individuals seem to be more sensitive to this kind of radiation and are thus more often and more adversely affected by it. It has been linked to the fact that the human body depends for many of its functions on electromagnetic impulses carrying messages along the neural network to and from the brain. It is claimed that the fields produced by electrical equipment interfere with the normal working of the body's natural electromagnetic system.

This condition has long been recognized in some countries, such as Sweden, where the Swedish Association for the ElectroSensitive (FEB) was founded in 1987 and the condition was recognized by the government as a legitimate physical impairment in 2000. Sufferers from electrosensitivity in Sweden are given state support in reducing exposure to the effect in their homes through such measures as covering walls with aluminium foil, replacing standard wiring with specially insulated cables and replacing electric cookers with gas ones.

In other countries, such as the United Kingdom, the condition is not generally acknowledged by the medical profession, and it is claimed that GPs are not prepared for diagnosing or treating it. It has been recognized, however, by the British Health Protection Agency as worthy of further investigation to establish whether or not it truly exists.

Some parapsychologists have noted links between electrosensitivity and apparent psychic abilities, such as CLAIRVOYANCE, EXTRASENSORY PERCEPTION, TELEPATHY and MIND-READING, leading them to suggest that the body's natural electromagnetism is involved in all of these areas. Conspiracy theorists point to the increasing prevalence of electrosensitive reactions as evidence of mass brainwashing programmes, to which only the more sensitive among us are attuned. Surprisingly enough, however, evidence for this theory is not immediately forthcoming.

elemental

A spirit composed entirely of a single element – fire, water, earth or air – and which dwells within the spirit realm of this element. The term is also sometimes used loosely of any nature spirit.

Scientists of ancient Greece believed that all things were composed of a combination of four ELEMENTS – fire, water, earth and air. Following this theory, Neoplatonists of the 3rd century AD divided all nature spirits into four classes, each associated with one of the elements, so that MERMAIDS and naiads were classed as water elementals, satyrs and DRYADS were classed as earth elementals, and so on, and the word 'elemental' is still sometimes used in this looser sense. But the 16th-century alchemist PARACELSUS formulated the concept of elementals as being spirits composed entirely of a single element, and which dwell in the spirit realm of that element. He gave these elementals the names by which they are still known today: gnomes (earth elementals), sylphs (air elementals), undines (water elementals) and SALAMANDERS (fire elementals). According to Paracelsus, sylphs and undines are usually well disposed toward humans, but gnomes are generally malicious, and salamanders, being made of fire, are too dangerous to approach directly. Elementals are said to occupy a position somewhere between humans and ANGELS; they have no souls, but they possess free will, and can choose to do evil or good.

Elementals were believed to be able to change their size or appearance at will. Gnomes are said to usually appear to humans as small, dwarf-like creatures, and their ruler is called Gob or Ghom. Sylphs are said to live on high mountain tops, and often assume human form, but only for brief periods, and are usually seen with wings. Their ruler is called Paralda. Undines are also said to assume human form and size, except for those which live in smaller streams and ponds, and are ruled by Necksa. Salamanders are said to often appear as flaming balls or small lizard-like creatures nestling in the heart of a fire, and are ruled by a magnificent fiery creature called Djin. Books on ALCHEMY and SORCERY written in the Middle Ages and the Renaissance contain many references to them, and give details on how to summon them for assistance in magic.

elements

The elements are the archetypal substances – usually fire, air, earth and water – believed in ancient and medieval cosmology to be the fundamental components of all things; of prime importance in magic and the occult.

Many ancient philosophies explained the patterns in nature by conceiving of a set of archetypal elements of which all things were believed to be composed. Most cosmologies speak of four or five elements: in the Chinese system, these elements are fire, water, earth, metal and wood; in Hinduism, earth, air, fire, water and space; and in Japanese philosophy, earth, air, fire, water and void. The classical Western elements are EARTH, AIR, FIRE and WATER, and the existence of these four fundamental principles of matter seems to have been first suggested by the Greek philosopher Empedocles in the 5th century BC. Aristotle further developed the theory of the elements, and proposed a fifth element which he called ether, a heavenly substance also known as the quintessence. The Aristotelian theory of the classical elements was a prominent part of the medieval worldview, and was further refined in the Renaissance by the 16th-century alchemist PARACELSUS; it remained the basis for Western thinking about the natural world until the rise of chemistry in the 18th century.

Each of the four physical elements is also believed to contain a spiritual essence which can be worked with in magic; the fifth element, ether or spirit, is thought to transcend yet be a part of all the other elements, and the magical symbol of the five-pointed star or PENTAGRAM represents these five elements in balance. ASTROLOGY has incorporated the concept of the four classical elements since ancient times, and each element is seen as ruling three signs of the zodiac; similarly, the four suits of the TAROT correspond to the four elements. The four fluids known as humours, which were once popularly believed to permeate the human body and determine the temperament, were also each associated with an element.

In Western magical systems such as WICCA, the four elements are called upon when performing rituals or spells, and their energies are invited to enter the working area and offer their unique qualities to the project. When a MAGIC CIRCLE is cast to create sacred space and form a barrier against any unwanted influences outside the circle, the four elements are called on to protect the circle, and are frequently represented in physical form at each of the four cardinal points associated with them; earth in the north may be symbolized by a rock, salt or a bowl of soil, air in the east by incense, fire in the south by a candle and water in the west by a bowl of water. Paracelsus also defined each element as having its specific animating spirit, known as an ELEMENTAL, which may sometimes be called on for assistance in working magic.

Eleusinian mysteries

The religious ceremonies of the goddess Demeter celebrated at Eleusis in Greece.

The sanctuary of Demeter, the ancient Greek goddess of crops and fruit, at the town of Eleusis in Attica (absorbed as a district of Athens by the 7th century BC), was famous as the centre of annual religious rites celebrated in her honour. These secret ceremonies, or mysteries, drew believers from throughout the Hellenic world, and to accommodate them the sanctuary was enlarged over the centuries to become the largest public building of its time.

It is known that the purpose of the ceremonies, which took place over several days and nights, was to ensure a happy AFTERLIFE for the celebrants and that they involved such activities as participating in religious processions and dramas, ritual uttering of obscenities, animal sacrifice and ritual purification by bathing in the sea. However, initiates were forbidden ever to speak of the most important elements of the rites, and these remain mysterious.

The main procession took initiates from Athens to Eleusis, some 22.5 kilometres (14 miles). At a point along the way they would be subjected to ritual abuse and the shouting of obscenities, perhaps as a symbolic humbling exercise. It was in the sanctuary at Eleusis that the secret rites were carried out. It has been suggested that these involved taking part in some kind of re-enactment of the myths surrounding Demeter and her daughter Persephone, who became queen of the Underworld and symbolized death and rebirth, and the display of secret holy objects, but nothing is known for certain. Special ritual drinks were involved in the rites and it may be that these contained HALLUCINOGENS that would allow initiates to achieve a particularly receptive state of mind, but, again, no definitive information exists.

Towards the end of the festival there would be a night-long celebration with dancing and feasting, followed by the sacrifice of a bull. The end of the ceremonies was signalled by the pouring of libations to honour the dead.

The cult exerted a powerful hold on the Greeks and lasted well over a thousand years. The Romans, who identified Demeter with their corn goddess Ceres, honoured the tradition of the mysteries when they became the dominant power in the Mediterranean.

A 19th-century book illustration depicting the Eleusinian mysteries. (© Stapleton Collection/Corbis)

Emperors made the journey to take part in the rites, and some conserved and embellished the sanctuary. However, in the 4th century AD the Christian Emperor Theodosius (c.347–395) finally banned the mysteries along with all other pagan practices. The mysteries continued to fascinate throughout the ages and various writers attempted to investigate and elucidate them, including the English occultist ALEISTER CROWLEY.

eleven

The eleventh whole number, represented by the digits 11; considered significant in numerology.

Eleven is the eleventh whole number. It is a higher octave of the number 2 and is considered to be highly significant in NUMEROLOGY because it is a master number – a double-digit number in which the first and second digits are the same. People who have a master number such as 11, 22 or 33 in their numerological profile are thought to be old souls who carry much wisdom and spiritual knowledge which they have learned from previous lifetimes, and are believed to have come back in this incarnation to perform some service to humankind. Where 11 appears in a person's numerological profile, although it is reduced to the single root number of 2 by adding its first and second digits together, it is therefore also considered separately as a master number. It is thought to indicate a path of spiritual awareness, and is the most intuitive of all the numbers; it represents illumination, psychic awareness and idealism. However, the spiritual potential of an eleven personality often goes unfulfilled, because the influence of 11's root number, 2, is thought to bring the possibility of inner conflict, and an 11 may walk a fine line between greatness and self-destruction; balance is required for the sensitive and often impractical 11 to find their place in a negative and materialistic world. An eleven personality is full of nervous energy and often experiences intense emotions, but has the potential to be a great spiritual teacher if he or she can learn to draw on their intuitive abilities to find their own spiritual truths, and bring their insights to others. See also ONE; TWO; THREE; FOUR; FIVE; SIX; SEVEN; EIGHT; NINE; TEN; TWELVE.

elixir of life

A fabled potion which is believed to give its drinker eternal life or eternal youth.

The elixir of life is a legendary potion which is said to give whoever drinks it eternal life or eternal youth. Throughout the centuries, the Magnum Opus or 'Great Work' of countless practitioners of ALCHEMY was the quest for the PHILOSOPHER'S STONE, not only because the stone was said to have the power to turn base metals into gold, but also because it was thought that it could be used to make the elixir of life. Alchemists also believed that the elixir could be used to create life, as well as to preserve and prolong it. The 2nd-century AD Chinese alchemist Wei Boyang's principal work, *Ts'an T'ung Ch'i* or 'The Convergence of the Three', which is believed to be the earliest known full alchemical text, is largely devoted to a description of the materials and procedures required to produce elixirs of long life and immortality, and there are said to be a thousand known names for these Chinese elixirs, such as 'Grand Concord Dragon Elixir' and 'Roseate Cloud Elixir of the Grand Immortal'. The Elizabethan alchemist Edward Kelley claimed to have discovered the philosopher's stone and to have succeeded in making the elixir of life.

elves

A race of supernatural beings in Germanic and Norse folklore. In Britain, over the centuries, they came to be almost synonymous with the diminutive fairies of native British folklore, until J R R Tolkien's depiction of them in Lord of the Rings *helped to restore a concept of them which was much closer to the original Germanic one.*

Elves were originally described in Germanic and Norse folklore as being semi-divine creatures, gods of nature and fertility, who were of human stature. The word 'elf' comes from Old Norse *alfr*, via Anglo-Saxon *aelf*. The Scandinavian elves were divided into light elves and dark elves, the light elves being benevolent and the dark elves, who were said to live underground, being malevolent; in this tradition, the dark elves appear to be synonymous with DWARFS. Scandinavian elf women are generally portrayed as being beautiful, but in some traditions they may have some deformity which gives away their true nature, such as a cow's tail or a hollow back. Elves are very quick to retaliate if offended or angered, and are credited with blighting livestock and causing nightmares, skin rashes or sudden paralysis; 'elf-stroke', the original and full form of the word 'stroke', shows how this affliction was once blamed on the malice of elves.

By the 8th century, stories about elves had started appearing in Britain, where they were initially portrayed much like their Germanic and Norse counterparts. The word was also sometimes applied to mischievous woodland spirits such as PUCK and Robin Goodfellow, and to small fairy boys. However, in England the word 'elf' gradually became interchangeable with the fairy of native British folklore, although in Scotland, the word 'elf' still tended to denote a being of human size. Shakespeare apparently made no distinction between elves and fairies, and his influence helped to distance elves further from their mythic origins, so that by the time of the English folk tales of the early modern period, they had been reduced to the status of small, mischievous nature spirits. However, the English philologist and writer J R R Tolkien did much to resurrect the concept of elves as a race of human-sized, semi-divine beings with his portrayal of them in his enormously successful *The Lord of the Rings* (3 volumes, 1954–5). See also FAIRIES.

Emdrive

A revolutionary new space drive invented by Roger Shawyer. Critics claim it cannot work because it violates our current understanding of the laws of physics.

The name Emdrive comes from 'electromagnetic drive'. It is essentially a tapering tube filled with microwaves, a form of electromagnetic radiation. According to Shawyer's theory, the microwaves will exert slightly more pressure on the narrow end of the tube than the broad end, leading to a small net thrust. A large Emdrive could be used to drive a spacecraft – given a suitable power source it could accelerate almost indefinitely. This would make travel within the solar system far faster than at present. An Emdrive using superconducting magnets as the microwave source could be more powerful than a jet engine, providing silent, clean air travel without pollution.

Roger Shawyer's credentials are good. He previously worked with the European Space Agency, and his financial backing has come from the British government in the form of grants from the Department of Trade and Industry. However, his physics are controversial. The device is impossible according to Newtonian physics but, at close to the speed of light, Einstein's relativity takes over. According to Shawyer's theory, this makes it possible for the tapering tube to act as a waveguide, effectively accelerating the microwaves in one direction and slowing them in the other so there is some net force. Scientists have dismissed the theory but none has actually demonstrated any flaws in Shawyer's physics.

Shawyer's experimental Emdrive does appear to produce a small amount of thrust which validates his theory. However, because the theory has not been accepted by other physicists it is considered FRINGE SCIENCE and Shawyer has had difficulty attracting further funding.

emela-ntouka

A ferocious swamp-dwelling cryptid reported in the Republic of Congo.

The dinosaurian MOKELE-MBEMBE may well be the most famous Congolese CRYPTID, but it is not the only one. Sharing the latter's inaccessible swamp-dwelling habitat in the Republic of Congo are several other mystifying creatures still awaiting formal acceptance and identification by science, of which perhaps the most extraordinary is the emela-ntouka ('killer of elephants'). According to the local pygmies, this is a truly ferocious beast, reddish-brown in colour, hairless and almost as large as an elephant itself. It has massive legs, and is able to submerge itself completely underwater. If an elephant attempts to cross a swamp or lake containing this formidable beast, the emela-ntouka will attack it savagely, disembowelling the elephant with the long, sharp, ivory-like horn mounted on the emela-ntouka's snout. It does not devour the elephant afterwards, however, as it is strictly herbivorous.

In the past, some cryptozoologists have attempted to identify the emela-ntouka as an unknown type of aquatic, swamp-dwelling rhinoceros. However, whereas the horn of all other modern-day rhinos is formed of compressed hair, the emela-ntouka's is said to be solid ivory, just like the tusks of elephants. Also, it is described as having a very long, heavy tail, which is very different from the short, inconspicuous tail of all known living rhinos. During the 1980s, veteran cryptozoologist Professor Roy Mackal led two separate expeditions to the Congo's Likouala swamplands in search of the mokele-mbembe, and while there he collected several reports and descriptions of the emela-ntouka too. These led him to speculate whether this remarkable beast could conceivably be an undiscovered, modern-day descendant of the ceratopsian dinosaurs, exemplified by such famous

prehistoric stalwarts as *Triceratops* and *Styracosaurus*. Also, the one-horned *Monoclonius* would have borne a very close resemblance to the emela-ntouka, right down to the latter's long, heavy tail and its horn of bone, not compressed hair. The only major difference is that whereas ceratopsians were known for the large bony frill protecting their neck, no such structure has been reported for the emela-ntouka.

It has also been noted that reports of creatures very like the emela-ntouka have emerged from outside the Congo too. Zambia's Lake Bangweulu is reportedly home to the single-horned chipekwe ('monster'), with similar creatures also reported from Lake Mweru, Lake Tanganyika and the Kafue swamps. The Democratic Republic of Congo (formerly Zaire) also has its own counterpart, dubbed the irizima, and there are even reports from as far west as Liberia. In 2004, a French mokele-mbembe seeker called Michel Ballot photographed a wooden sculpture of an emela-ntouka-type beast while visiting a village in northern Cameroon, which depicts an animal with an elephantine body, single horn and long, hefty tail, as well as a pair of small frilly ears not previously alluded to in accounts of this cryptid.

energy

An invisible force which is believed to surround and permeate all things and to be the source of life. The basis of many alternative therapies is that physical, mental and spiritual health require a free and balanced flow of energy in the body. Practitioners of magic also believe that this energy, which is thought to connect all things in the universe, can be raised and focused for magical use.

The unifying principle behind almost all branches of ALTERNATIVE MEDICINE is the metaphysical concept of an invisible, vital force which surrounds and permeates all living things. This force, often referred to as the UNIVERSAL LIFE FORCE, is called prana in Indian philosophy, QI in Chinese medicine and ki in Japanese. In the West, it is also known as bioenergy. Most alternative therapies are based on the belief that this energy flows around the body along paths known as MERIDIANS, or is controlled by energy centres called CHAKRAS, and that it also extends beyond the body in an energy field called the AURA. Illnesses of all kinds are identified as being the manifestations of disrupted energy flow, and a wide range of therapies such as ACUPUNCTURE, QIGONG, REIKI, SHIATSU, THERAPEUTIC TOUCH and YOGA are said to manipulate the energy flow in order to correct blockages and imbalances and restore the body's natural self-healing capacity.

In many cultures, energy is also linked to MAGIC and the PARANORMAL. In Hinduism, prana is believed to be the source of magical power, and it is popularly believed that qi, controlled by a master, can be used to perform feats of supernatural power. Throughout the centuries, magicians and occultists have believed that energy abounds in the universe, and makes up everything in it. All things which exist are therefore connected to all others, and in order to perform an act of magic, the magician raises energy from within himself, focuses it on his magical intent and directs it out into the universe, using the interconnectedness of all things through this universal energy to bring about the desired change.

The energy generated during sexual intercourse is also sometimes harnessed and directed towards a spiritual or magical goal. One of the oldest forms of sex magic is Tantric sex, an advanced form of spiritual communion in which sexual energy is used as a vehicle by which practitioners can merge with the Divine and achieve profound spiritual experiences (see MAGIC, SEX). In the West, the practice of using the energy released in sexual orgasm for magical purposes is mainly associated with occult traditions like WITCHCRAFT, WICCA, and PAGANISM, and is said by many to be the most powerful of all magical techniques.

One yogic tradition is that a dormant energy known as KUNDALINI rests at the base of the spine. By a system of movements, breath control and meditation, it is believed that this energy can be awakened and directed up through the chakras, activating each one as it passes through it until it reaches the crown chakra to bring spiritual enlightenment. The energy raised in this way may also be used for healing purposes.

The Enfield Poltergeist *see panel p206*

Enochian magic *see* MAGIC, ENOCHIAN

entombment
The apparent entombment in rock or wood of living animals.
Insects and other animals trapped in amber thousands of years ago have long provided scientists with insights into evolutionary history. Outside fiction, these long-dead creatures can never be brought to life. However, there have been numerous stories throughout history of the accidental discovery of living animals that seem to have survived being encased in rock, to be released only when the rocks are broken open.

In 1761, an account appeared in the *Annual Register*, attributed to Ambroise Paré, surgeon to Henry III of France in the 16th century, describing the appearance of a large living toad in the middle of a stone that had been broken open by a labourer. There seemed to be no opening in the cavity for the creature to have entered it, and the labourer claimed to have come across examples of the phenomenon before.

A similar instance was reported in England in 1865, in this case the live toad being released from a block of limestone quarried over 6 metres (around 20 feet) below ground level. As in many such cases, the cavity in which the animal was found was no larger than its body.

Other small animals, such as lizards, have also reportedly been found in similar circumstances, and in some cases the place of 'entombment' is a living tree. Perhaps the most fantastic of these accounts is that maintaining that in 1856 French workers digging a railway tunnel liberated a living pterodactyl from Jurassic-era limestone.

In 1975, American builders in Texas claimed that they found a living turtle inside concrete that had been poured in the previous year. They said that the creature must have been trapped inside the material as it solidified because it left the impression of its form behind when it was set free.

Many of these stories are no doubt hoaxes, some of which will have arisen from making a mistake as to where the creature in question really came from. Was it actually *inside* the split stone or was it merely underneath it when it was broken? In many cases, however, the cavity in which the animal appeared to be trapped is described as being exactly tailored to its size, showing the 'imprint' of its body on the surrounding material. This would suggest that the rock material had actually formed around the creature while still in an incompletely solid state. With some rocks being millions of years old, how could this be possible?

According to current scientific thinking, it would be inconceivable for an animal to be somehow sealed alive into such an airless enclosed space and survive for any great length of time. Also, if it had been trapped in a cramped space with no room to move, how would it be able, as so many accounts relate, to begin to move around in a free and lively way when released? Had it been born there, perhaps from a fertilized egg that had slid into a minute crack in the stone, it would still have been totally cut off from any form of food.

Could it be possible that such animals have undergone a form of hibernation, or SUSPENDED ANIMATION, lasting for a period of many years? If any of these accounts is true, there seems to be no other obvious explanation. However, conclusive evidence for an actual occurrence is still required.

epicentre
The person or object upon which paranormal phenomena are centred, particularly in poltergeist cases.
In the majority of POLTERGEIST cases a living human individual (usually a person under stress), rather than a place, seems to be the focus for disturbances (see

HAUNTED PEOPLE). For example, in the case of the Miami poltergeist in 1967, the US researcher William Roll concluded that the epicentre of the disturbances in a warehouse was a 19-year-old Cuban refugee named Julio who was working as a shipping clerk. After studying the flight paths of displaced objects, Roll tentatively suggested that the force moved in an anti-clockwise direction around the focus. The phenomena may even follow the individual from place to place. For example, in *Apparitions* (1942), G N Tyrrell cites the case of an English cook who seemed to be accompanied by crashing sounds in successive homes.

In other cases the epicentre may be an object with alleged supernatural significance, but reliable evidence for such effects is scarce. See also AGENCY.

Epworth Parsonage poltergeist

A well-attested 18th-century poltergeist which afflicted the family of John Wesley, the founder of Methodism.

The mysterious noises at Epworth Parsonage, Lincolnshire, the home of the Wesley family, occurred during December 1716 and January 1717. The events were recorded in family letters and in the diary of Rev Samuel Wesley, John Wesley's father. There were a number of extraordinary noises, including numerous raps, rumblings, vibrations and groans and a noise 'like a nightgown sweeping along the ground'. The knocks interrupted family prayers, and it is recorded that these included prayers for the King. Animal APPARITIONS were also apparently witnessed.

The sceptical writer Trevor Hall proposed that the disturbances were caused by a servant prankster who was never detected – but this theory is hard to reconcile with an account by Jack Wesley who recorded that the noises '… very often seemed in the air in the middle of a room, nor could they [the household] ever make such themselves by any contrivance'. The phenomena were variously attributed to SPIRITS or WITCHCRAFT, and the entity was dubbed 'Old Jeffrey'. Samuel Wesley rebuffed suggestions that the family should flee the house, and his judgement proved to have been sound when the phenomena ceased within two months. Sacheverell Sitwell noted in his book *Poltergeists* (1940) that a number of classic POLTERGEISTS were given names which were variants of Jeff or Jeffrey (see also GEF THE TALKING MONGOOSE) and suggested that the case encouraged a tradition of poltergeists in non-conformist Christian households.

equinox *see* AUTUMNAL EQUINOX; VERNAL EQUINOX

Ernetti, Father Pellegrino *see*

CHRONOVISOR

esbats

The name given to the regular meetings of witches in some modern witchcraft traditions.

In most modern COVENS, esbats usually occur 13 times a year at each full moon, although they may be more regular – sometimes even weekly. The term is usually only used formally, with the meetings more commonly referred to as 'circles'. These meetings are now distinct from the SABBAT celebrations.

The term 'esbat' only appears to have come to be used in this way during the 20th century – historically all witches' gatherings were referred to as sabbats. It may come originally from an old French word meaning a frolic or romp, and it has been suggested that its modern usage stems from the British anthropologist Margaret Murray who misinterpreted its derogatory use in records from the Middle Ages.

escapology

The practice of escaping from constraints or confinement.

The art of escapology as entertainment seems to have had its origins on the French stage in the late 18th century with simple demonstrations of people freeing themselves from handcuffs, ropes, chains and other forms of restraint. Later theatrical performers would

The escapologist Harry Houdini, locked in a crate, is lowered into the water at the Battery in New York on 15 July 1914. (© Bettmann/Corbis)

The Enfield Poltergeist

What is probably the best-known British POLTERGEIST event took place in a semi-detached council house in Enfield, North London, in 1977 and 1978. Its fame stems mostly from the fact that, as the following bizarre events unfolded, they were covered in great detail by the media.

The occupants of the house were the Harper family – Mrs Harper (a divorcée in her forties), her two sons and her two daughters. The occurrences that were to turn into an ordeal lasting some 14 months started on 31 August 1977, when the younger daughter, Janet, and her brother, Pete, told their mother that their beds had been shaken and furniture had moved by itself. Mrs Harper later saw for herself the movement of a heavy dresser, which then stubbornly refused to be replaced in its original position. The Harpers went to their neighbours for help, and the police were called – one of the officers later offering a statement to the effect that they had heard a strange knocking sound and witnessed the mysterious movement of a chair.

The phenomena continued – furniture slid around the floors, knocks came from the walls and toys flew through the air. The Harpers and their neighbours turned unsuccessfully to the local vicar, MEDIUMS, the council and again to the police. Finally they contacted the tabloid newspaper the *Daily Mail*. Despite being assaulted by flying marbles, a reporter and photographer from the newspaper spent several days covering the story, which eventually made the front page (under the title 'The House of Strange Happenings') on 10 September. One of the *Daily Mail* reporters contacted the SOCIETY FOR PSYCHICAL RESEARCH on the family's behalf. Investigators Maurice Grosse and Guy Lyon Playfair reported witnessing many of the unusual occurrences first hand (recording over 400 in total), although unexplained malfunctions in their hi-tech equipment interfered with their results and prevented them obtaining any conclusive photographs.

It became clear from the investigation that this was very much a 'classic' poltergeist case in that the events appeared to be centred on an adolescent girl, in this case Janet (aged 11) and to a lesser extent her older sister Rose (aged 13). A wide range of phenomena were recorded, including knocking sounds (with which the investigators were able to establish a form of communication, by asking questions and receiving a set number of knocks for yes or no), moving objects, flying objects, spontaneous fires, falls of coins, flows of water, electrical disturbances affecting recording equipment and a force which could throw the girls from their beds. *Daily Mail* photographer Graham Morris did manage to achieve some success in capturing these goings-on, including a famous sequence of frames showing the bedclothes apparently being pulled by unseen hands from one of the girl's beds as she lay beneath them.

As the investigation progressed an entity (or entities) apparently manifested itself (or themselves) in the form of a deep, gruff voice which appeared to emanate from Janet. Opinion was divided among the investigators (including a ventriloquist called in by the *Daily Mail*) as to how the voice was produced and as to whether Janet was producing it deliberately. It seems likely that the voice came from a part of the larynx known as the false vocal folds. However, if this was the case, how an adolescent girl could sustain the voice for hours on end (when it would normally hurt after just a few seconds) remains something of a mystery.

allow themselves to be bound in order to suggest that they could not have carried out 'magical' effects that they would later produce, while in fact they would have been working with hands freed by their own efforts.

However, it was only with the earlier 20th century and the career of HARRY HOUDINI that escapology achieved its greatest popularity, with exponents staging escapes from ever more elaborate, seemingly infallible and even life-threatening methods of confinement. These included metal cages, straitjackets, wooden barrels and tanks of water in which the already-bound escapologist was submerged.

What exactly goes on in a feat of escapology?

Some examples are not true escapes at all but illusions, tricks in which the performer is never really restrained in the first place but relies on convincing the audience otherwise. Some types of handcuffs or locks are specially made to spring open when force is applied in a particular way known only to the escapologist. Sometimes a member of the audience is asked to verify that the bonds used are in fact secure and this person is actually a planted accomplice.

However, when a true escape is made there are several methods that are most commonly used. These include the swallowing and later regurgitation of small keys (to padlocks or handcuffs, for example) or

Investigator Maurice Grosse with a collection of the objects involved in the Enfield poltergeist case.
(© TopFoto/Fortean)

The voice regularly used obscene language and on at least one occasion implied that it belonged to a deceased local resident.

The occurrence of the phenomena, whether hoaxed by the children (as they certainly were on occasion later in the investigation) or of supernatural origin, seemed to be exacerbated by the tension within the family. This was added to greatly by the constant intrusive presence of the investigators and the intense media interest (the case was even reported on by the prime-time BBC programme *Nationwide*). They reached a peak at around the time of Janet's first period, on the first day of which she was reportedly seen flying round her bedroom by several passers-by in the street outside. She also claimed to have been through the wall to the house next door (where one of her books was later found by the neighbour).

The poltergeist activity, and the media interest, gradually waned over the months that followed. The true cause of the occurrences remains a matter for debate.

the concealment about the person of a picklock or a shim (a thin slip of metal used to open locks or manipulate catches).

Some escapologists develop the bodily flexibility and strength of an acrobat or gymnast, exploiting this to manipulate themselves out of bonds that would successfully immobilize the average person.

Before being fastened into a straitjacket or tied with ropes, a skilled performer will use the technique of expanding the chest and shoulders as far as possible to ensure that unsuspected 'wriggle room' will be left for him or her to take advantage of. Some exponents, among whom was Houdini, use the ability to temporarily dislocate joints such as the shoulders to allow them to slip out of confinement.

Escapology continues to be a popular form of entertainment, whether on stage or on television, and, just as with magic, part of the pleasure for the audience lies in trying to detect exactly how the 'impossible' feat is performed.

esoteric

Historically, 'esoteric' was used to describe knowledge that was secret and taught only to a select few, but it has now taken on a wider meaning.

The word 'esoteric' comes from the Greek *esōterikos*,

from *esōtero*, the comparative form of *esō*, meaning 'within'. It was originally used to mean knowledge that was 'inner'. When the word entered the English language in the early 18th century it loosely retained this meaning, and was applied to secret societies such as FREEMASONRY. However, its use has since developed to include any knowledge relating to the OCCULT, or anything that is mysterious or difficult to understand.

This wider usage has resulted in a number of other related words entering the language. Among these are 'esotericism' which describes the holding or learning of esoteric knowledge and beliefs, and 'esoterica', a collective word for elements of esoteric knowledge, writings, occurrences and artefacts. 'Esoteric studies' is the academic field devoted to the study of esoteric groups and organizations. See also ALCHEMY; ASTROLOGY; GNOSTICISM; MAGIC; MYSTICISM; ROSICRUCIANS; SECRET SOCIETIES.

ESP *see* EXTRASENSORY PERCEPTION

ESP, super- *see* SUPER-ESP

Estimate of the Situation report
A top-secret memo written by US Air Force officers in the early days of UFO study.
PROJECT SIGN was the first and shortest lived of the US Air Force UFO projects. It covered some dramatic cases during 1948, including an encounter in the early hours of 24 July 1948, when Clarence Chiles and John Whitted, the pilot and co-pilot of an Eastern Airlines DC-3 flying over Montgomery, Alabama, were buzzed by a fast-moving object. The pilots argued that this was definitely a strange craft, bullet-shaped with windows and a phosphorous glow, which they described as a 'Flash Gordon rocket ship'.
DR J ALLEN HYNEK, recently appointed as scientific consultant to the US Air Force, suggested that this was a bright meteor known as a bolide, but the crew would not accept this theory.

The staff of Project Sign were split in their opinion of this case, but there was a powerful faction of officers who saw it as proof that the EXTRATERRESTRIAL HYPOTHESIS must be correct. Only days after the sighting occurred, Captain Robert Sneider wrote an 'Estimate of Situation' report, giving an assessment of where the UFO project stood after six months of investigation.

Captain EDWARD J RUPPELT claims to have read the report in about 1952 when he took on the leadership of the longer-running PROJECT BLUE BOOK. In *The Report on UFOs* (1956), describing his time at Project Blue Book, he wrote:

In intelligence, if you have something to say about some vital problem you write a report that is known as an estimate of situation. A few days after the DC-3 was buzzed the people at ATIC decided that the time had arrived to make an estimate. The situation was the UFOs; the estimate was that they were interplanetary.

The report went to the chief of air staff, General Hoyt S Vandenburg, but he summarily rejected it, arguing that it was based on eyewitness testimony and not on any physical evidence. Vandenburg then declassified the file and immediately destroyed all known copies. It is likely that it was considered politically unwise for the public to know that its Air Force was taking seriously the idea that alien spaceships were visiting the earth.

Despite regular requests from ufologists (even invoking the FREEDOM OF INFORMATION ACT), the file has never been released.

ET *see* EXTRATERRESTRIAL

ETH *see* EXTRATERRESTRIAL HYPOTHESIS

ETI *see* EXTRATERRESTRIAL INTELLIGENCE

evil
That which is considered morally wrong or bad, intrinsically corrupt or wicked. In many religions, absolute evil is personified as an entity, such as Satan in the Judeo-Christian tradition, who is in eternal opposition to the Creator or deity of good.
The term 'evil' generally refers to that which is considered morally wrong or harmful, intrinsically corrupt or wicked. Most cultures use the word to describe actions, ideas and thoughts which bring about affliction or destruction, but there are many different opinions as to what constitutes evil. Some philosophers, such as Plato, reject the notion of evil altogether, and claim that what we describe as 'evil' is merely ignorance. Others, such as Kant, hold that the only true evil is an evil will, and that there are no evil people, only evil acts. Some people believe that evil requires an intent to do harm, and argue that a morally wrong act done for altruistic motives, that is, for the greater good, should not be described as evil, since the end justifies the means. Moral absolutism views good and evil as fixed concepts established by a deity or other authority, while moral relativism holds that standards of good and evil not fixed, but the products of culture, custom and prejudice.

Those who subscribe to the notion of evil tend to regard it as the deliberate deviation from a code of laws or a moral standard. In a religious context, this code is usually imposed by a deity, and the concept of absolute evil often leads to a belief in a figure such as SATAN or THE DEVIL, who personifies the eternal principle of evil and is in opposition to God or the Creator, constantly challenging his will and tempting man to perform evil acts. Some religions, such as Zoroastrianism, see the world as a battleground between the deity of good and that of evil, while in others, especially Judaism and Christianity, evil is linked to the concept of sin and the wilful breaking of God's commandments.

evil eye

The belief that some people have the power to cause harm by a glance or look.

The belief that some people can cause harm by a malevolent gaze is a very common one, which is found in the folklore of many countries. The oldest references to it appear in Babylonian texts of around 3000 BC, and it is mentioned in both the Old and New Testaments. In some cultures, it is thought that the evil eye, as this harmful gaze is known, is used deliberately to inflict injury, but in others, it is thought to be involuntary; anyone who has unusual eyes, for example someone with a squint, or a person with blue eyes in a district where this colour is rare, might be thought to possess the evil eye simply because they are different. Belief in the evil eye is strongest in the Middle East, Asia and Europe, particularly the Mediterranean, and is also found in Mexico and Central America. It is also a feature of Islamic folk mythology and Jewish folklore. The deliberate use of the evil eye is sometimes known as FASCINATION or overlooking, and all kinds of harm, from bad luck, poverty or the loss of a lover, to injury, illness or death have been ascribed to its use. In the Middle Ages, WITCHES were said to be able to put the evil eye on anyone who crossed them, and many innocent people were accused of witchcraft by those who had suffered misfortune and wanted someone to blame.

A number of measures may be taken to ward off the evil eye, which is known in France as *mauvais oeil*, in Italy as *mal occhio* and in Germany as *boser Blick*. Since envy is thought to be the most common cause of the evil eye, it is wise not to appear enviable, so boasting about one's possessions or family should be avoided; many cultures therefore protect the most vulnerable targets, their cattle, wives and children, by speaking of them disparagingly, and in the Middle East children are rarely praised in public, while in many Asian cultures, compliments are not welcomed, since they lay the object of the compliment open to envy. The tradition of the bridal veil may have its origins in a desire to shield the bride from ill luck inflicted by

an envious gaze. In Scotland and Ireland, a red ribbon may be tied to a new baby's crib, or attached to a young child's clothing, to protect it from the evil eye, and this custom is also found in India. In Jewish folklore, the gaze is known as *ayin harah*, and if someone or something is unwisely praised out loud, or someone's good luck is spoken of, the Yiddish phrase '*Keyn ayin harah!*' ('No evil eye!') is traditionally uttered to ward off an envious jinx.

Spitting, a universal good luck measure, may be employed to avert the evil eye. This practice was common among the ancient Greeks and Romans, who also used AMULETS in the form of phallic symbols. Sexual gestures are similarly used for protection; a fist with the index finger and little finger extended upward, or with the thumb held tightly between the index finger and middle finger, are both considered effective. In Brazil, amulets in these forms are still carried. In the Middle East, a ball or disc painted with a blue circle enclosing a black circle representing the evil eye is used to return the malevolent gaze back to the supposed sorcerer, and the Middle Eastern amulet known as the Hand of Fatima sometimes incorporates a blue eye for the same purpose. Large eyes are also painted on the prows of Mediterranean boats to protect them from the evil eye.

evocation

The magical act of calling forth spirits to do the will of the magician or to provide information; also, the calling forth of positive energy from within the self for magical purposes.

The term evocation, from the Latin *ēvocāre*, meaning 'to call out', has two distinct magical senses. In ceremonial magic, it usually refers to the calling forth of spirits to do the bidding of the magician, or to provide information (see MAGIC, CEREMONIAL). The evocation of spirits is an important element of most of the world's magical traditions, and many GRIMOIRES of the Western magical tradition contain details of demons and other spirits, with rituals and ceremonies to evoke these beings. Such evocations are usually preceded by a ritual purification of the mind, body and spirit to attract the desired entity and protect the participants, and are performed within a MAGIC CIRCLE. Forceful evocation, that is, against the spirit's will, is sometimes referred to as CONJURATION, and the evocation of the spirits of the dead for purposes of DIVINATION is known as NECROMANCY. The spirit may be evoked into a medium such as a pillar of smoke, a crystal ball or a human volunteer who allows himself or herself to be possessed by the spirit. In most magical systems, the spirit is believed to remain close to the place where it has been evoked. Evocation is also used to refer to the creation of an artificial ELEMENTAL TO accomplish a magical task. In this case, the magician is said to summon the being up from within himself or herself, and to externalize it.

The second sense of evocation is used mainly in WICCA, and is defined as the drawing out of positive energy from within the self for magical purposes.

Those who have written on the subject of evocation include AGRIPPA VON NETTESHEIM, ALEISTER CROWLEY, ISRAEL REGARDIE and Peter Carroll.

EVP *see* ELECTRONIC VOICE PHENOMENA

Exmoor Beast *see* ALIEN BIG CATS

exorcism

The performance of a ritual, usually by a priest or other religious authority, to drive out a spirit or demon believed to have possessed a person or place.

The concept of POSSESSION by a ghost or evil spirit which enters and takes control of a person or place is an ancient and widespread one, as is exorcism – the ritualized driving out of this entity. This ancient practice is still part of the belief systems of many religions, although its use by most religious groups has diminished in the last two centuries or so, largely due to the decrease in superstition which followed the age of the Enlightenment, and our greater understanding of psychology; many people who would in earlier centuries have been thought to be possessed are nowadays recognized as suffering from mental illness.

In most religions, the expulsion of the spirit or demon is carried out in a ceremonial rite performed by a professional. Prayers, religious symbols and set formulas are often employed, as is the invocation of a benign supernatural power to assist in the expulsion of the spirit. Since, in many traditions, the knowledge and use of a demon or spirit's name is believed to confer power over it, it is often regarded as of prime importance for the exorcist to find out the spirit's name and address it by this name. The spirit's response to the exorcism is often described as violent, with the possessed person writhing, vomiting or screaming abuse, and the victim may die before the exorcism is completed. The spirit may also leave the victim only to possess the exorcist.

The possessing spirit is often, but not always, a demon. In Judaism, it is believed that the restless spirit of a person who died before they had fulfilled some function in their lifetime may possess a living person. This spirit, known as a *dybbuk*, must be exorcized by a rabbi. Similarly, in Hinduism, the ghosts of people who have died an untimely death may possess a living person; the exorcist enlists the help of his own tutelary deity and performs rituals, seeking to coax the ghost out of the possessed victim. The victim is then required to make an offering to the ghost, as well as to the exorcist and his deity.

In some traditions, the possessed person is first put on a diet which excludes the demonic entity's favourite foods of eggs and meat, and then given a protective mantra to recite. If the demon is willing to negotiate with the exorcist, it may demand a sacrifice of meat or the provision of an animal which it can possess instead of the victim. If the possession is believed to be the result of a malicious spell, the exorcism may also involve the sending back of the demon to the person whose ill will invoked it. In Arabic folklore and Islamic tradition, fire spirits known as DJINN are believed to possess those who do not hold true to God, but may be exorcized by the use of tar and salt (both of which are repugnant to djinn), the repetition of sacred words and written charms. Exorcism as a cure for illnesses thought to be caused by evil spirits is still common in many tribal cultures.

The Christian New Testament describes Jesus as performing exorcisms and as giving this power to his disciples; possession and exorcism have thus been part of the Christian belief system since its earliest beginnings, and exorcism is still a recognized practice in Eastern Orthodox, Roman Catholic and some Protestant traditions. In the Catholic Church, exorcism may only be performed by an ordained priest with the express permission of the local bishop, and only after the possibility of mental illness has been ruled out. The Catholic rite of exorcism is set out in the *Rituale Romanum*, and makes use of prayers, blessings, invocations, salt, wine to represent the blood of Christ, holy water and sometimes, RELICS of the saints. It also traditionally involves the symbolic use of a bell, book and candle. In Protestantism, exorcism is recognized but is less formalized than the Catholic rite, and in many denominations is performed very sparingly, while some hold that all Christians, not just ordained clergy, have the power to perform exorcisms.

There was an explosion of popular interest in exorcism after the 1973 release of the film *THE EXORCIST*. However, there have been a number of cases in which attempted exorcisms, especially by improperly trained individuals, have resulted in injury or death for the 'possessed' person, and the death in 1976 of a German student, Annelise Michel, during an exorcism inspired the 2005 film *The Exorcism of Emily Rose*.

Exorcist, The

A 1973 film directed by William Friedkin with screenplay by William Peter Blatty, who based it on his 1971 novel of the same name. The novel was based on an allegedly true story of an exorcism, and tells the story of the demonic possession of a 12-year-old girl and the exorcism of this demon by two priests. The film's graphic special effects, and the obscene and blasphemous nature of its key scenes, caused it to be banned from video release in the UK until 1998.

William Peter Blatty's 1971 novel *The Exorcist* was based on the allegedly true story of an exorcism which took place in 1949, in Maryland, US, where a minister claimed to have exorcized a demonic spirit from a 13-year-old boy in an ordeal lasting almost two months. In Blatty's novel, the child possessed is a 12-year-old girl. Blatty adapted his book into the screenplay of a 1973 film, also called *The Exorcist*, which was directed by William Friedkin.

The film opens in the Middle East, with an elderly priest, Father Lankester Merrin (Max von Sydow), whose discovery of a statue of a Babylonian demon, later identified as Pazuzu, appears to release some evil force. Meanwhile, in Georgetown, Washington, an actress, Chris MacNeil (Ellen Burstyn), becomes concerned by the sudden and inexplicable illness of her 12-year-old daughter, Regan (Linda Blair). As Regan undergoes increasingly horrific physical and behavioural changes, a battery of medical and psychological tests proves useless in determining the cause, and her mother finally turns to religion, consulting a Catholic priest, Father Damien Karras (Jason Miller), who is experiencing a crisis of faith after

the death of his mother. Convinced that Regan is the victim of demonic possession and not illness, Karras obtains permission to assist Merrin, an experienced exorcist, in performing a lengthy exorcism which tests both men physically and spiritually. Before the exorcism can be completed, Merrin, who has a serious heart condition, dies, and Karras goads the demon into leaving Regan's body and taking him instead. He then plummets down a flight of steps and dies.

The film was a huge international success, and received ten Academy Award nominations, of which it won two. It also won four Golden Globe awards. However, it provoked great controversy; audiences were horrified by the disturbing depiction of Regan's possession, which included graphic special effects of projectile vomiting, the 360-degree rotation of her head, a scene in which she masturbates with a crucifix and her use of obscenities and blasphemies delivered in a deep, rasping voice (provided by actress Mercedes McCambridge). Some people were so traumatized, or nauseated, that they fled the cinemas, while others became convinced, after seeing the film, that they too were possessed, and there was a huge surge of popular interest in exorcism after its release.

Two sequels followed the original film's release: *The Exorcist II: The Heretic* (1977) and *The Exorcist III: Legion* (1990), which was written and directed by Blatty and based on *Legion*, his 1983 sequel to the novel *The Exorcist*. In a 1990 parody, *Repossessed*, Linda Blair lampooned her role in the 1973 film, and in 2004, two versions of a 'prequel' were released: *Exorcist: The Beginning*, and *Dominion: Prequel to The Exorcist*.

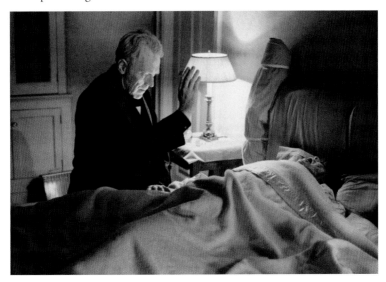

A still from the controversial film, *The Exorcist* (1973), in which an exorcism is seen being performed by a Catholic priest. (© Bettmann/Corbis)

Rumours that *The Exorcist* was a cursed film began while it was still in production, and sensational stories of accidents and tragedies befalling a number of people involved in its creation are still circulated to this day, although some dismiss these as a promotional ploy.

experimenter effect

The effect on the results of an experiment of the expectations of the experimenter.

Science by definition relies on experiment and observation, both conducted with objectivity and strict attention to accuracy. Error is always possible in any scientific field, but sometimes the results of an experiment may be called into question on the grounds that they have been affected by what the person carrying out the experiment expected to happen. This is known as the experimenter effect and it has been identified as playing a part in psychology in general and PARAPSYCHOLOGY in particular.

One of the ways in which results of experiments can be validated is for the original experiment to be replicated by someone else. Obviously, if a second independent experiment produces similar findings this will tend to confirm the original results. One of the difficulties with experiments in parapsychology, such as trials of EXTRASENSORY PERCEPTION, is that spectacular results can be obtained by one experimenter while another investigation produces an outcome that is far less convincing.

One theory used to explain this is that when experiments are carried out by someone who already believes in the existence of the phenomenon being studied, the experimenter will seize on results that confirm his or her assumptions, playing down any findings that contradict the desired outcome. When dealing with human subjects, the experimenter may, whether consciously or unconsciously, suggest the answers that are sought.

This can be done in the way that a question is phrased, the tone of voice used, the way in which particular answers are received or even the body language of the questioner. People who are not actively hostile to the experimenter will unconsciously tend to give them what they seem to want to hear.

It is argued that a person who is deeply sceptical about the subject of an experiment will unintentionally communicate this to the subjects and thus tend to discourage any demonstration of the phenomenon concerned. The argument is sometimes taken further, suggesting that there are people who possess an inherent sympathy with parapsychological effects and will consequently encourage favourable results.

According to this argument, people who have no instinctive sympathy with parapsychology will never be able to reproduce the results obtained by an experimenter who has. While there may be truth in this suggestion, it inevitably detracts from the status of parapsychology as a true science. If the experimental side of the discipline is so greatly influenced by the experimenter effect, it invites the criticism that, even if no dishonesty is involved, there can be no absolute objectivity.

experiments

Procedures employing objective and systematic scientific methodology to investigate an idea or observed phenomenon.

In the fields of PARAPSYCHOLOGY and the general investigation of the PARANORMAL, experiments are employed as a way of attempting to establish, to the general satisfaction of the scientific community and the population as a whole, first whether a particular phenomenon exists at all, and second whether it can only have been brought about by paranormal means. In the classical version, 'good science' involves the production of theories and hypotheses which have a predictive nature; the predictions are then tested by carrying out experiments to see if the experience fits the theory. If a significant number of results are as the theory would predict, and none of the results contradicts the theory, then the theory is considered to be sound. In practice, this is a slightly idealized version of the conduct of science, and a number of people have argued that in reality, things are somewhat different (for example, see FORTEANISM).

CARD-GUESSING EXPERIMENTS are a classic example of the type of experiment employed – in this instance to investigate claims relating to forms of EXTRASENSORY PERCEPTION such as TELEPATHY and CLAIRVOYANCE. Attempts are made to exclude all normal means of ascertaining what is shown on a succession of cards, and the number of accurate 'guesses' is compared with the statistically calculated expected outcome based on chance alone. The GANZFELD EXPERIMENT is a more sophisticated development, and differs particularly in that it is a FREE-RESPONSE EXPERIMENT as opposed to a FORCED-CHOICE EXPERIMENT. There are also a wide range of experiments to test claims of PSYCHOKINESIS, carried out under the general heading of DISTANT-INFLUENCE EXPERIMENTS, and the concept of REMOTE VIEWING was tested over a number of years in a US Government-funded project (see BAY AREA REMOTE-VIEWING EXPERIMENTS). Over the years, the results obtained by those who believe in the existence of paranormal phenomena have tended to be more positive than those obtained by sceptics. Both groups would disagree as to whether this was due to the BELIEVER EFFECT or the EXPERIMENTER EFFECT.

The claims investigated by parapsychologists are often extraordinary, and fall outside the set of beliefs that are generally accepted within the scientific mainstream. For this reason their experimental evidence needs to be particularly convincing, and their experimental design and their analysis of results are often subject to intense scrutiny and criticism from sceptics. The JAMES RANDI Educational Foundation has famously offered one million dollars to 'anyone who can show, under proper observing conditions, evidence of any paranormal, supernatural, or occult power or event' – an offer to which a number of other strict conditions are attached. Randi was also involved in organizing PROJECT ALPHA, designed to shown how easy it can be to fool researchers who are attempting to prove a pet theory. However, some people argue that sceptics such as Randi have already decided that there is no such thing as a paranormal event and would not accept *any* evidence that appeared to indicate the contrary.

Many famous PSYCHICS, clairvoyants and other claimants of paranormal powers have been the subject of experiments – FLORENCE COOK, URI GELLER and EUSAPIA PALLADINO among them – and there are still a number of organizations dedicated to research in this area, such as the COMMITTEE FOR THE SCIENTIFIC INVESTIGATION OF CLAIMS OF THE PARANORMAL, as well as institutions dedicated to research in the area of parapsychology, such as the RHINE RESEARCH CENTER and ARTHUR KOESTLER's legacy, the Koestler Parapsychology Unit at Edinburgh University.

However, on the evidence so far, if psychic powers and abilities do exist, then they seem to be at best very weak, or very rare. Although a large number of experiments have been carried out, and some have appeared to produce evidence which is statistically significant, so far no incontrovertible proof has been forthcoming.

extra-retinal vision

The claimed ability to see without using the eyes.
The phrase 'extra-retinal vision', also sometimes referred to as 'eyeless sight', describes instances where an individual appears to be getting information, without using their eyes, that would normally require (and would ordinarily be possible through) the use of normal sight – as contrasted with CLAIRVOYANCE which describes a wider form of EXTRASENSORY PERCEPTION.

Supposed examples of extra-retinal vision take two basic forms – those where the subject has to be in contact with the item they are 'seeing' (sometimes known as 'paroptic vision' or 'dermo-optical perception') and those where they do not. There are a number of tales on record, stretching from the 17th century to the present day, which claim to give examples of the former. These often involve people who are said to be able to identify colours by touch

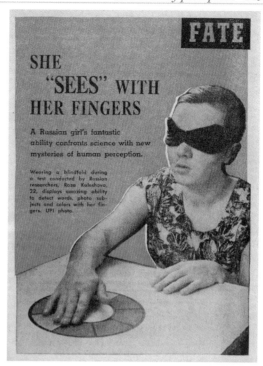

Roza Kuleshova, a Russian psychic who could allegedly 'see' colours using only her fingers – from the cover of *Fate* magazine (July 1963). (© Mary Evans Picture Library)

alone, or people who are able to read normal books using their fingertips (one of the many talents ascribed to MOLLIE FANCHER). Similar stories still regularly appear. There are also many supposed examples which fall into the latter category, involving people who claim to still be able to see when blindfolded, without using the sense of touch (the Indian mystic KUDA BUX, for instance).

While many of the claims of extra-retinal vision are hoaxes, some people have suggested that others are not, and that the apparent phenomenon of 'seeing' colours by touch can be explained by differences in the heat absorption properties of different colours, and that an enhanced sense of touch is being employed. Some have even claimed that it is evidence for the presence of light-sensitive cells in the skin. Others point out that many stage magicians incorporate blindfolded reading or even car driving into their acts and suggest that such people may be able to offer a more convincing explanation.

extrasensory perception

The claimed ability to obtain information without using the known senses.
Although the general concept of extrasensory

perception (ESP) has existed in various forms for millennia, our modern understanding of this theoretical phenomenon stems from the work of J B RHINE at Duke University in North Carolina in the 1930s, since when it has been one of the main areas of study within PARAPSYCHOLOGY. Rhine carried out a range of EXPERIMENTS to investigate ESP, which he understood particularly to include TELEPATHY, PRECOGNITION and CLAIRVOYANCE. He studied these extensively, notably through the use of CARD-GUESSING EXPERIMENTS with a specially designed set of cards called ZENER CARDS. Other means that have been employed since include the GANZFELD EXPERIMENT and RANDOM NUMBER GENERATORS.

A vast range of claimed abilities fall within the general category of ESP, although most are variations on the three main themes of telepathy, precognition and clairvoyance – being either different names for the same thing or differing in the explanation given for how the same effect is achieved. An extended list might include such PSYCHIC phenomena as SECOND SIGHT, REMOTE VIEWING, PSYCHOMETRY, the reading of AURAS, some forms of DIVINATION and various SÉANCE phenomena.

While some apparent evidence in favour of the existence of ESP has been produced over the years, sceptics argue that it all involves flawed experimental procedure, is the result of the misinterpretation of data or is simply fraudulent. The debate is on-going.

extraterrestrial

A word meaning simply 'other than from the earth' which is used in ufology to mean a being that is not from earth or is from another planet.

The existence of extraterrestrial entities has been a source of speculation ever since mankind discovered that earth was just one planet among many. Some of the earliest science-fiction stories and films featured imaginary journeys to the moon and creative descriptions and images of the beings that might live there.

Until the 1960s, when spacecraft photographed planets such as Mars and Venus from orbit, it was still widely thought possible that other planets in our solar system might be able to sustain life. It was only as the evidence against this possibility mounted that the hope that we might soon discover alien beings in our own solar system began to disappear. However, this coincided with advances in technology which allowed the detection of planets around stars other than our own sun. As the next nearest star is more than four light years from us (our own sun being just eight light minutes away), the distances involved make these possible worlds safe subjects for renewed speculation.

Scientists can now use computer modelling to predict the likely environments on newly discovered planets and to suggest the forms that living organisms would have to take to be able to exist there. So far there is little correlation between the features of these hypothetical entities and the descriptions of those involved in reports of UFO encounters. See also ALIENS.

extraterrestrial hypothesis

The theory that UFOs are alien spacecraft, flown by extraterrestrials visiting earth. It is often abbreviated to ETH.

The term 'UFOs' is now commonly taken to be synonymous with 'alien spacecraft'. To say that you believe in UFOs is usually understood to mean that you accept that aliens from another planet visit the earth.

In fact, there are dozens of proposed explanations for unsolved UFO cases, ranging from as yet unexplained (or simply misidentified) natural phenomena, through to time-travelling humans from our own future. The ETH has gained popularity because the media often present UFO stories only in this context.

The principal reason that the ETH seems attractive is that it neatly ties up with the descriptions given of sightings and CLOSE ENCOUNTERS. However, the often absurd catalogue of home planets and personal names said to have been provided by aliens can appear to owe more to science fiction than to astronomical fact. Indeed, the existence of CULTURAL TRACKING in accounts of UFO claims is a reason for caution – the popularity of the ETH may be in some ways responsible for generating the 'evidence' which supports it. In the 1950s, the visitors told us that they were Martians, coming to warn against our use of atom bombs, but, by the turn of the millennium, they were more likely to talk about ecology or genetic engineering, and to describe their home world as being far away across the galaxy.

Some scientists would agree that there is a strong statistical chance that EXTRATERRESTRIAL INTELLIGENCE exists. However, this is not the hard evidence that is required to support the ETH as a proposed explanation for some UFO reports. There are interconnected threads running through some UFO cases that might suggest that there is more than just imagination at work. However, there is almost no solid evidence for the ETH, and certainly none that would not be disputed. No known alien DNA samples or manufactured materials that are not found on earth have ever been collected. There are no universally accepted photographs of landed UFOs clearly indicating them to be spacecraft of non-terrestrial design, nor any close-up shots of their alien crew. On the other hand there are photographs, spectrum analyses, radar tracks and other evidence of the kind collected by the researchers at HESSDALEN. However, these only support the existence of an as yet unexplained phenomenon, which could potentially turn out to be of natural, earthly origin. They don't, in themselves, necessarily lead to the conclusion that the phenomenon is due to the activities of alien beings.

For fifty years, UFO researchers have been waiting for the definitive case that will persuade the world that aliens are here. It has still not arrived. Some contend that there is already proof but that it is the subject of a GOVERNMENTAL COVER-UP. Others counter that when humans visited the moon they left many telltale signs of their visit. If aliens were regularly flying to earth we could reasonably expect that some indisputable traces would have been left behind.

extraterrestrial intelligence
The term used to describe intelligent life which may exist on planets other than our own.
The existence of planets circling stars other than the sun is now proven. However, scientists have been searching, without success, for signs of extraterrestrial intelligence since the 1930s (see SEARCH FOR EXTRATERRESTRIAL INTELLIGENCE). The existence of intelligent life on other planets is, of course, central to the EXTRATERRESTRIAL HYPOTHESIS. For now, in the absence of any clear evidence, its existence remains a matter for theoretical debate.

This has not stopped informed speculation as to the possible forms that intelligent life on other worlds

might take. By observing the way that life on earth evolves to cope with its environment (particularly looking at the differences and parallels displayed by life that evolved in a level of isolation in Australia and that elsewhere on earth), exobiologists have used computer modelling to suggest hypothetical life-forms to match the environmental conditions thought to exist on some of the planets discovered so far. Their suggestions have included giant whale-like beasts floating in the sky and walking forests of intelligent vegetation. However, until we can send craft to investigate these other worlds, or make contact in some other way, such activities are little more than entertaining guesswork.

Dr Paul Davies, a mathematical physicist who has worked in this area, says:

> Unfortunately, until we contact a form of life from off the earth we will not know which parts of our lives are unique to us and which parts are universal in the truest sense of the word. But I tend to think that we are not that special.

extreme longevity
The phenomenon of living much longer than the average lifespan.
Throughout human history there have been reports of human beings living for much longer than most people. Sometimes these claims can be seen to be mythical, concerned with establishing the pedigree of individuals considered important to a people's history; in primitive societies, where age was often linked to

Jeanne Calment, officially recognized as the world's longest living person, photographed enjoying her daily cigarette on her 117th birthday. She died in 1997, aged 122. (© Jean Pierre Fizet/Sygma/Corbis)

wisdom or authority, claiming long life was a means of reinforcing an elder's credentials. As an example of this, in the Old Testament the Hebrew patriarch Methuselah is said to have attained 969 years of age.

Legends abounded in many cultures of a FOUNTAIN OF YOUTH, drinking from which would either maintain life or restore an elderly person to youth and strength. As late as the 16th century, the Spanish explorer Juan Ponce de León (1460–1521) vainly searched the Caribbean and Florida for a reputed fountain of perpetual youth.

Some myths of longevity assigned a life-extending power to a particular place. For example, the Himalayan pass of Shangri-la imagined in the novel *Lost Horizon* (1933) by English writer James Hilton (1900–54), quickly became proverbial as an earthly paradise where life was prolonged.

In the Caucasus under the Soviets, living to pass the age of 100 was promoted as being typical, but this is now generally dismissed as being mere Cold War propaganda. The Japanese island of Okinawa, however, does appear to have a far higher than average proportion of centenarians per head of population than most parts of the world, but the reasons for this are as yet unexplained.

In the British Isles, there have been several famous examples of extreme longevity, including the COUNTESS OF DESMOND and Thomas Parr, who, when he died in London in 1635, was reputed to have been 152 years old. It has to be borne in mind, however, that these examples pre-date a truly reliable register of births and deaths, and, essentially, a person's claim to great age (for whatever reason) could neither be proved nor disproved.

One attestable British case is that of Charlotte Hughes (1877–1993). The officially recognized world record, however, is 122 years of age, a span achieved by the Frenchwoman Jeanne Calment (1875–1997). The oldest-living man whose dates are generally accepted as valid was Christian Mortensen, who was born in Denmark in 1882 and died in the USA in 1998.

Why do some individuals attain extreme old age while others do not? Genetic factors are undoubtedly crucial. Types of diet and lifestyles can also be seen to play a part, with moderation and generally taking care of one's health being important. The precise and proportionate effects of such factors are still largely the subject of debate in various scientific fields.

There is no doubt that extreme longevity is becoming less uncommon than in previous centuries, and most countries in the developed world are home to an aging population. In the 21st century research into the processes involved in aging leads many to believe that anti-aging treatments may well be achievable.

eyeless sight *see* EXTRA-RETINAL VISION

fairies

Magical beings, generally of diminutive human form, common in British and European folklore.

The word 'fairy', also spelt 'faery' or 'faerie', is a late derivation of *fay*, which comes via the Old French *feie*, from Latin *fata*, meaning 'the Fates'. Originally 'fairy' (fay-erie) meant 'a state of enchantment', and it was only later that it came to be used for the creatures who caused this enchantment. The term is now broadly used to refer to any supernatural being of human form (and usually diminutive size) which is capable of performing magic.

Stories about fairies tend to be more common in Asian and European cultures than elsewhere in the world, and some folklorists have suggested that, within these cultures, they are all that remains of an earlier belief in ANIMISM or that they are a development of beliefs originally relating to the spirits of the dead. In more recent folklore, fairies have become romanticized and are seldom seen as harmful, but in older times, they were considered dangerous creatures to be avoided, and placated if encountered. Medieval romances developed the idea of a court of fairies ruled by a king and queen, who liked to ride out in formal processions, especially on May Eve and Midsummer Night, and there has for a long time been a distinction between this aristocratic body of generally benevolent fairies – often known as the trooping fairies, or the seelie (blessed) court – and the malevolent solitary fairies, sometimes identified with the souls of the damned, who are known as the unseelie (unblessed) court.

The realm of the fairies supposedly impinges on that of humans, but it is rarely glimpsed. Fairies are often said to live underground, in hills or mounds, to be able to make themselves invisible and to be fiercely protective of their privacy. In British and European folkloric traditions, there are a vast range of common SUPERSTITIONS and beliefs relating to them.

Anyone who has dealings with fairies must tread very carefully, as they are quick to take offence and will avenge any insult. It is considered unlucky to name them, or even to use the word 'fairy' – either because to do so might summon them, or because they dislike being called fairies. Instead, they should be referred to euphemistically by a term like the GOOD FOLK, the Good Neighbours, the LITTLE PEOPLE or the Gentry. Fairies hate pretentiousness and meanness, but love simple, sincere and generous humans, and will always reward kindness shown to them. They sometimes borrow implements or grain, but will usually return anything they borrow with interest. However, you should never thank them for any gift directly, but should show your gratitude by praising the gift. Care must also be taken if you wish to make them a present in return; clothes should never be offered, and you must never return more than they have given or lent to you. Nor should anyone who has been favoured by the fairies ever mention what has been done for them.

Fairies sometimes steal food from humans, and can extract all the essential goodness from it while leaving its outer form. They love milk and cheese, and any milk which is spilt should be left as their share. Their own food is dangerous to humans; any mortal who eats fairy food can never return to the land of the living, and if he does, he will pine away with the longing to get back to fairyland. Fairy music is unbearably sweet and melancholy, and will haunt any human who hears it till the day he dies; *The Londonderry Air* is said to be of fairy origin. They like to dance in FAIRY RINGS, sometimes enticing humans to join them. Fairies are skilled in weaving and spinning, and are said, like humans, to domesticate and breed animals, and they love horses. They hate salt, iron or smoke, so these may be used as protection against them. Fairies sometimes mate and have children with humans, and the offspring from such unions will often have SECOND SIGHT or great musical ability. Fairies will sometimes abduct a human midwife to assist in fairy childbirth, rewarding her richly for her help. They will also sometimes kidnap a human baby and leave a CHANGELING in its place. See also CHEESE WELL.

fairy light *see* WILL-O'-THE-WISP

fairy ring

A circle of mushrooms or toadstools growing on grass, or a circular patch of brighter, taller grass, popularly thought to mark a site where fairies have danced in a circle.

Three types of fairy ring are common in Britain, Europe and North America. The first is a circle of mushrooms or toadstools; the second is a round patch of grass which is lusher and taller than that surrounding it; and the third is a patch of poorly growing grass, or even bare earth, in a circular pattern.

In folklore, fairies love to dance, and it is said that where they have danced on grass in a magic circle, they cause a fairy ring to grow. If a human comes across a fairy revel and is lured to join in, he will become invisible outside the circle, and cannot get out of it unless his friends outside it form a human chain and pull him out, and he may be forced to dance until he collapses and dies from exhaustion. Or he may find that during one evening spent in the fairy ring, many years have passed in the human world, and all his family and friends are long gone. If someone jumps into an empty fairy ring, it is thought that he will die young – although in certain areas it is considered to bring good luck, and some believe it is a marker of hidden treasure. A glove tossed into the ring is said to make it safe to enter. A young woman collecting dew to wash her face on May Day morning should avoid any she finds inside a fairy ring, since, instead of making it more beautiful, it will transform her face into that of a crone.

Fairy rings are now known to be caused by a number of fungi, particularly the edible *Marasmius oreades*, although they may also be formed by various species of poisonous toadstools. They are also known as fairy dances, fairy courts, fairy walks, fairy grounds or hag tracks.

fairy tree

A tree associated with or thought to be sacred to fairies.

FAIRIES are closely connected with all trees, but in most Western European traditions the trees thought to be especially sacred to fairies are the hawthorn, hazel, willow, elder, holly, birch, oak, ash, elm, apple and rowan. Most closely associated with fairies is the hawthorn, especially a solitary hawthorn which grows near a fairy mound, or a group of three or more hawthorns growing in a ring. It is said that good fairies find shelter from evil spirits under the elder tree, and a grafted apple tree or 'imp-tree' is believed to be under fairy influence; anyone who falls asleep beneath it may find themselves carried off by the Little People. Where the three fairy trees oak, ash and hawthorn grow together, their magic is particularly strong, and a twig taken from each and bound together with a red thread is thought to be a powerful protection against spirits of the night. Fairies are fiercely protective of their trees and will defend them from human attack, and folklore is full of cautionary tales in which a heavy price is paid by a mortal who cuts down a fairy tree. See also LATOON FAIRY TREE.

faith healing

A form of healing in which solely spiritual means, such as prayer to a divine being or the laying of hands on the sick person, are used to treat an illness.

Throughout history, mankind has had a belief in the beneficial effects of prayer and the LAYING-ON OF HANDS on those afflicted by illness. Until relatively recently, medicine and religion were so intertwined that often the same individual was both healer and priest for the community, and in those cultures which still believe that diseases are caused by evil spirits, the anger of the gods or the work of a sorcerer, it is the priest, SHAMAN, MEDICINE MAN or other spiritual figure who is called on to heal the sick person. Some healers use touch, putting their hands directly onto the affected person or on their energy field, while others perform sacrifices, rituals, incantations or EXORCISMS to appease the gods or drive out the evil spirits. In the West, too, this fusion of religion and medicine still existed until the end of the Middle Ages; the first Western hospitals were monasteries founded by physicians who were usually monks. The idea of faith healing is referred to in both the Old and New Testaments in the Bible, and in the New Testament Epistle of James, the faithful are told that to be healed, those who are sick should:

> Call upon the elders of the church to pray over [them] and anoint [them] with OIL in the name of the Lord.

Nowadays, 'faith healing', also known as spiritual healing or divine healing, is often used to refer specifically to the Christian belief in the power of the Holy Spirit to effect cures by channelling healing energy from God through a minister or other healer, although the term is generally used by those outside the faith movement, rather than by its members. Some Christian religious groups believe in faith healing as the sole remedy for all illnesses, and this can cause ethical problems for medical professionals where the parents or partners of patients refuse conventional medical care on their behalf. A common feature of many modern American evangelical television programmes is the healing of afflicted people who are brought up on stage and struck on the head by the preacher; the spirit of God is thus said to enter the sick person in a procedure known as 'being slain in the spirit', miraculously healing them. Faith healing is open to abuse by fraudulent practitioners, and many of the negative connotations which are sometimes attached to faith healing are due to cases such as that of the 1980s faith healer and televangelist Peter Popoff, who was publicly exposed as a fraud by the noted sceptic JAMES RANDI and TV host Johnny Carson.

Critics claim that faith healing has not been proven to be scientifically effective, because its advocates only cite anecdotal evidence for its success, and ignore all of the cases where it was unsuccessful. They also say that many of the people who are allegedly cured by faith healers are later found to be still sick. Doctors often hold that any success in faith healing is due to the placebo effect, or to spontaneous remission. However, research has shown that religious practices such as worship attendance, meditation and prayer have significant implications for health; they tend to promote a more positive outlook, and by bringing about what is known as a 'relaxation response', they contribute to a less stressful and therefore healthier life, and people who practise their religion have often been found to recover from illness more quickly than others. It is not scientifically known how belief in a higher power can have a healing effect, but there are those who believe that it does.

See also LAYING-ON OF HANDS; PSYCHIC HEALING; PSYCHIC SURGERY.

fakir

A member of a mendicant Sufi order, or an ascetic Hindu holy man; also, an itinerant Indian conjuror.
The word 'fakir' comes from the Arabic *faqīr*, meaning 'poor', and strictly speaking, refers to a religious mendicant who has rejected worldly possessions. In its original sense, it was applied to an initiate of a Muslim Sufi order, but the term has been extended in Western usage to refer also to an ascetic Indian holy man or

sadhu. In addition, however, it has come to be used of the itinerant Indian conjurors who travel from village to village, often with an assistant, performing 'miracles' such as walking on hot coals, lying on BEDS OF NAILS and piercing their faces with long needles, without suffering any harm. Some such performers claim not to need food and to be able to 'live on air', to have been buried alive for months or to have the power to levitate, and the most famous feat popularly associated with the Indian fakir is the legendary INDIAN ROPE TRICK. See also PAIN ENDURANCE; SUFISM.

fallen angel *see* ANGELS, FALLEN

falls

Unexplained instances of strange things falling from the sky.
Human history is full of instances of things that appeared strange and inexplicable to our ancestors coming to be understood as science advances. However, one phenomenon that has been reported for centuries and still resists explanation is that of weird objects falling from the sky, also known as 'mystery rains'.

One of the more common themes in this is that of falling fish or other aquatic animals. Many cases are on record, including a shower of sprats landing on the Norfolk seaside town of Great Yarmouth in 2002, a rain of frogs in Llanddewi, Wales, in 1996, and another in Croydon, London, in 1998. The usual explanation of such occurrences is that the creatures were sucked up into the air by a localized whirlwind or waterspout to be deposited elsewhere. This theory is given credence by the fact that reports also exist of ponds and their contents disappearing overnight or lakes being suddenly empty of fish.

However, not all falls are as easy to account for. In *Mysterious Worlds* (1980), Arthur C Clarke (1917–) gives an account of hundreds of hazelnuts falling from the sky in Bristol in 1977. Puzzling enough in itself, the event was made even more mysterious by the fact that it occurred in spring, when no nuts would be in season. Similarly baffling was the experience claimed by one W G Grottendieck in Sumatra in 1903 of small hot stones raining down in his bedroom during the night, without appearing to damage his roof and seeming to fall at a much slower speed than would be expected.

Also common are falls of ice, not as mundane hail or sleet but as often dangerously large lumps. One modern-day explanation attributes this phenomenon to water, or waste, falling from jet aircraft flying so high that any liquid leaving them must freeze in the atmosphere. However, many accounts of ice falls pre-date the invention of the aircraft, including a block of ice about 6 metres (20 feet) in diameter, estimated at half a ton in weight, that dropped on a farm in the Scottish Highlands in 1849. This ice was reportedly perfectly clear, but other falling chunks have been described as being milky, of various colours and containing rocky debris. Such large pieces of ice cannot be attributed to weather conditions, nor could they be debris from a comet as they would not survive as ice long enough to hit the earth.

Other strange falls include a red rain that fell in 2001 on Kerala in India. The liquid was analysed and found to contain fungal spores. While this accounted for the unusual colour, it didn't explain how the spores came to be there. In various states of the USA showers of corn husks or kernels have been reported in places where no such crops were being farmed nearby. Stories of showers of stones peppering the roofs of isolated houses with no apparent culprit to be found are not uncommon and many of these have been attributed to the activity of POLTERGEISTS.

The suggested explanations for this range of phenomena, from freak weather to a kind of volcanic activity hitherto unknown to science, are really only in the realm of conjecture and a convincing theory remains to be found. See also ANGEL HAIR.

false memory *see* MEMORY, FALSE

Falun Gong

A Chinese meditation movement persecuted by the Chinese government.

Falun Gong (also known as Falun Dafa) is a spiritual movement based on meditation, originating in China and brought to worldwide prominence by the Chinese government's attempted suppression of it. It has been claimed that there are tens of millions of practitioners worldwide.

The aim of practising Falun Gong (meaning 'the Practice of the Wheel of the Dharma') is partly for self-healing, but mainly to aid the practitioners in their journey towards enlightenment. The movement was founded in 1992 by Li Hongzhi (disputably born in either 1951 or 1952), and contains elements from Buddhism and TAOISM. It teaches QIGONG, a form of meditation through slow-motion exercises similar in some ways to T'AI CHI. With ACUPUNCTURE, massage and herbal medicine, qigong is one of the four pillars of Chinese traditional medicine.

Initially the Chinese government praised Falun Gong because it was thought to be so effective that it was reducing the country's expensive health-care burden. But in 1999 Falun Gong was criticized as 'feudalistic superstition' by a physicist on Beijing television, and was not allowed its legal right of reply. This prompted the peaceful protest in Tiananmen

Falun Gong members meditate near the United Nations headquarters in New York. Peaceful protests have taken place worldwide to publicize the Chinese government's treatment of Falun Gong practitioners. (© Reuters/Corbis)

Square when between 10,000 and 15,000 practitioners simply stood or sat quietly for twelve hours.

As thousands of people had appeared at the protest without prior warning, the government perceived this as a public-order issue and a threat to state control. It cracked down, banning what it called 'heretic cult organizations' and criminalizing the practice of Falun Gong. Since then many practitioners have been arrested, imprisoned and sent to mental hospitals for 're-education'. There are many reports of torture, and some of death in custody. The Chinese government's treatment of Falun Gong practitioners has become a major human rights issue.

familiars

The animal companions of witches, believed in medieval times to be demons in animal form.

As with much of the surviving folklore relating to British and European WITCHCRAFT, the popular conception of the WITCH's familiar dates back to the persecution of witches during the Middle Ages.

Familiars, which were also sometimes referred to as imps, usually took the form of an animal such as a CAT, crow, toad or hare, but were also occasionally recorded as being in the shape of more fantastic creatures or even as human in appearance. It was also commonly believed that they could take more than one form. Familiars would carry out evil tasks for their master, or assist them in working their magic, for which they would be rewarded with drops of their master's blood, sucking this from a point on their body specifically for this purpose (see also WITCH'S MARK).

Most of the historical information relating to familiars comes from the wild accusations made by witch hunters and from unreliable confessions extracted under torture during WITCH TRIALS. During the questioning of an alleged witch it was common for the interrogators to watch to see if her familiars came to her aid. MATTHEW HOPKINS claimed to have witnessed the appearance of five unearthly familiars belonging to the witch Elizabeth Clark. These familiars included Vinegar Tom, who was:

> ... like a longlegg'd greyhound, with a head like an ox, with a long tail and broad eyes, who when this discoverer spoke to, and bade him go to the place provided for him and his Angels, immediately transformed himself into the shape of a child of four years old without a head, and gave half a dozen turns about the house, and vanished at the door.

The idea of spirit helpers (either good or bad) in animal form also appears in a number of other magical traditions around the world.

Fancher, Mollie (1848–1916)

Known as 'The Brooklyn Enigma' or the 'Fasting Girl', Mollie Fancher apparently ate very little for 50 years and some claim that she channelled five different personalities.

Mollie Fancher led a relatively uneventful life until she was removed from her school, the Brooklyn Heights Seminary, in 1864. Fancher was suffering from dyspepsia – extreme indigestion – as well as probable anorexia and fainting spells. After a prescribed cure of rest was unsuccessful a doctor recommended the opposite – exercise. During this course of exercise Fancher was thrown from a horse, breaking two ribs and striking her head in the process. In June 1865, after her convalescence, Mollie suffered a second, and more serious accident, when her dress was caught on the streetcar she was alighting from and she was dragged along for a considerable distance.

After a brief spell when she was not bedridden in late 1865, Fancher spent the rest of her life in bed. Over the following years Fancher suffered from a wide range of maladies. She experienced her first trance in 1866, and is said, in that year, to have fallen into a trance that lasted nine years – this being the period in which she became most famed for extraordinary feats. Although she was almost completely immobilized, Fancher is said to have written 6,500 letters, prepared a great deal of worsted, carried out fine embroidery, fashioned delicate wax flowers and kept a diary.

In 1875, Mollie lapsed into a coma lasting a month and upon awakening she had amnesia of all the events of the preceding nine years. Fancher now showed apparent psychic abilities including CHANNELLING

five personalities – Sunbeam, Idol, Rosebud, Pearl and Ruby. It was also reported that Fancher ate almost nothing and went for periods of three months without the need to use any toilet facilities, and that she was clairvoyant and clairaudient (see CLAIRVOYANCE; CLAIRAUDIENCE) and possessed EXTRA-RETINAL VISION.

Mollie Fancher was investigated by spiritualists and doctors alike, and the reports polarized popular feeling. Some felt she was faking, some that she was a miracle worker. Noted showman P T Barnum attempted to pay her to appear as one of his attractions, such was her fame.

She was said to have been visited by over 100,000 people, curious to see the famous Fasting Girl.

fascination

The action of harming or controlling another person by means of a spell, usually cast by gazing at them; another name for the evil eye.

The belief in the EVIL EYE is almost universal, being found in most cultures, both past and present. In ancient Roman times, it was commonly thought that one person could harm or control another by means of a spell cast by gazing at them, and this power, or the spell itself, was called *fascinum*, from Latin *fascinare*, meaning 'to enchant'. The Romans employed a number of methods to avert this evil eye, one of which was the wearing of an AMULET shaped like a phallus, and this protective amulet was also known as a *fascinum*.

In the English language, the word 'fascination' was used synonymously with 'evil eye' until the 17th century. In occultism, it is still used in its older sense, to refer to the casting of a spell on a person by looking at them, or to the spell itself. In a non-magical use, the word nowadays, like 'enchantment', simply denotes a compelling interest or attraction, with no negative or occult connotations.

Fate and Luck *see panel p222*

Fátima

Site in Portugal of Marian visions.

In 1917 at Fátima, a rural village in Portugal, three young shepherds called Lucia dos Santos (aged 10), Francisco (9) and Jacinta Marto (7) reported experiencing a series of VISIONS over a period of six months. They described seeing ANGELS but most of the apparitions involved the Virgin Mary who enjoined the children to urge the world to repent and focus upon herself as the way to God (see MARIAN APPARITIONS).

Although the visions had ceased, believers had already begun to travel to the spot, and on 13

Fate and Luck

Throughout the ages human beings have struggled to find explanations as to why certain events happen and others do not. Probably one of the first lessons learned by intelligent humankind was that an outcome which has been planned, worked for or simply devoutly wished for will not necessarily come about in the desired way. People, seeing themselves as subject to a higher force than their own efforts, tended to ascribe this overruling power to a deity or group of deities, often visualizing mortals as helpless playthings of capricious gods who assigned blessings or grief merely according to their whims. While this line of thought is one of the roots of religious belief, it also gave rise to the concepts of fate and luck. Fate (from the Latin *fatum*, a prediction) is conceived as inevitable destiny, a path in life that cannot be changed by men or gods, while luck is not so predetermined.

In ancient Greek mythology, fate was personified in the form of three sister goddesses, the Moirai (known later to the Romans as the Parcae) who controlled the life of every individual in the form of a thread. Clotho was the goddess who spun the thread of life from her distaff; her sister Lachesis would measure the length of the thread and decide its final extent; the third sister, Atropos, would cut the thread, thus bringing the mortal life to an end. No argument from either mortals or immortals could alter the goddesses' decisions. The Greeks believed that fate was thus ordained by implacable forces outside man's control. A person's destiny was unalterable, no matter how they might try to sway the gods by devotion, sacrifices or pleading, and no matter how they sought to lead their lives, whether in exemplary morality and good deeds or in self-serving wickedness.

This idea of inexorable fate being governed by three goddesses was echoed later in Norse mythology and religious belief, in which the three fatal sisters were known as the Norns, individually Urd, Verdande and Skuld. Like their Classical counterparts these deities spun the thread of life, measured and then severed it.

Given that a person's fate was unavoidable, it was an obvious step to seek to know in advance what that fate might be. This gave rise to various forms of PROPHECY and DIVINATION, such as ASTROLOGY, the consultation of ORACLES and SHAMANS, the casting of lots or runes, the examination of the entrails of sacrificed beasts, NUMEROLOGY, BIBLIOMANCY and NECROMANCY. In China, the *I CHING* evolved from a simple casting of bones into a sophisticated set of symbols and interpretations. The fundamental idea was that if one's fate could be known beforehand, then one's life could be lived in such a way as to make the most of the span of time that was definitely allotted.

With the coming of Christianity, the capriciousness of the deities was replaced among the faithful by the idea of a loving and forgiving God. Sinners could be redeemed from their apparent fate of damnation by genuine repentance, and those who lived a blameless life could expect Heaven as their reward rather than an unforeseen and possibly dreadful destiny. To a Christian the concept of the all-powerful nature of fate was deprived of meaning. However, the idea of all things having being decided in advance resurfaced in the doctrine of predestination, which held that God had decreed all events from the beginning of time. In some strands of Christian theology, notably Calvinism, this led to the belief that whether or not a person would be among the saved (the elect) or the damned at the Day of Judgement was already laid down before they were even born, no matter the manner in which they lived out the intervening years. Some have detected in this resonances of the pagan belief in inexorable fate, arguing that this reflects a fundamental part of the human make-up. Aside from religion, in philosophy there are various forms of determinism, essentially holding that there is no such thing as free will and that every event springs from a direct and identifiable cause.

Certainly, at a less philosophical level, many of us, no matter what our religious beliefs, pay lip service to the idea of fate. We glibly speak of things that, with hindsight, seem to have been inevitable as being 'fated to happen' and describe people who have found their perfect partner in life as being 'meant for each other'. Many greet the ups and downs of everyday life with resignation and acceptance that what is meant to happen will happen, and we call this fatalism. A widespread contemporary adherence to the concept of fate is found among those who consult fortune-tellers or scan their daily HOROSCOPES in the belief, however light-heartedly they would refer to the practice, that their future has already been decided and that foreknowledge of it is the best we can hope for.

The concept of luck is quite distinct from that of fate, in that luck is not predetermined or inexorable but may be gained or lost, whether by cultivating it or being subject to the vagaries of fortune. There are similarities between the two, however, such as that luck is also often given the blame (or the credit) when the results of human actions appear to be unconnected with the efforts or worthiness of those carrying them out. Another quality that luck shares with fate is found in the ancient belief that it is arbitrary, and in many cultures luck was also personified as a capricious deity.

The ancient Romans believed in a goddess Fortuna, who was responsible for the blessings or misfortunes that happened to each individual. She was often portrayed as holding a wheel, known as the wheel of fortune, which symbolized change and mutability; one day a person might be enjoying good luck and riding high on the wheel, the next an arbitrary turn of the wheel might bring that person low. People could fall foul of Fortuna, whether or not they felt they deserved it, and it was to this that many would ascribe their disappointments and setbacks in everyday life. Fortuna was sometimes shown as being blindfolded, and this gave rise to the ascription of random events to 'blind chance'. This female personification is one that persists to this day, with common references to Lady Luck.

The ancients thought that they could affect their own luck by wooing the goddess Fortuna with sacrifices, ritual practices and entreaties, and elements of this attitude persisted into the Christian era in the form of various SUPERSTITIONS; for example, we talk about keeping our fingers crossed when we wish for a favourable result in any activity whose outcome is uncertain. Indeed, even the physical gesture of crossing the fingers is not uncommon, and it is a highly visible part of the 'corporate identity' of the British National Lottery.

Some people believe that luck may be attracted or conserved by the possession of a TALISMAN or 'lucky CHARM'. These might include such things as a stone with a hole made naturally in it by the action of water, a horseshoe, a preserved rabbit's foot or an old and treasured coin. Sportsmen often believe

that a particular pair of boots, jersey or other piece of equipment will bring them luck, and some even have rituals that they must perform before taking the field.

Conversely, in many cultures it is believed that bad luck can be wished upon another person by the use of CURSES or the EVIL EYE. The accidental breaking of a mirror proverbially results in seven years' bad luck, and in the theatrical world it is considered unlucky to speak aloud the name of Shakespeare's *Macbeth*, with 'The Scottish Play' being the approved and safe substitute title. Some people are believed to bring bad luck and are stigmatized as JINXES. The idea of a 'Jonah', a bringer of bad luck (especially on a ship), goes back to the Old Testament account of Jonah and the whale.

Many people, particularly gamblers, believe in lucky numbers. Punters will play the same lottery numbers again and again in the face of continued lack of success, or bet on a horse in a race according to the number assigned to it rather than putting their faith in the wisdom to be accrued through a study of form. Odd numbers have been considered particularly lucky ever since human beings began to count, especially THREE and SEVEN. Other numbers are generally believed to be unlucky, especially THIRTEEN.

Not everyone is content to remain passive in the face of the vagaries of luck. There are always those who are convinced that 'fortune favours the brave' – an echo of wooing the goddess Fortuna – or that 'you make your own luck'.

The fact that, despite the rationalist arguments that underpin modern science, the concept of luck remains deeply buried in even the 21st-century psyche is continually revealed by our attitudes and everyday turns of phrase. A repeated action can always be done 'once more for luck'. Who has not attributed a rival's success to sheer good luck rather than excellence (especially when a novice competitor has 'beginner's luck'), mournfully greeted an unwelcome event as 'just my luck' or crowed over 'a stroke of luck'? We commiserate with unfortunate friends using such expressions as 'tough luck' or 'your luck was out' and wish them future success with 'good luck' or 'best of luck'. We hope that they will have a 'change of luck' or be blessed by 'the luck of the Irish'. The idea of luck seems to be born out of an instinctive need, within even the most coldly rational or unspiritual of us, to acknowledge the influence of undefinable forces beyond human control.

Michael Munro

The three young shepherds, Jacinta, Francisco and Lucia, who reportedly saw a series of visions of the Virgin Mary at Fátima, Portugal, in 1917.
(© Mary Evans Picture Library)

September 1917 many among a huge crowd claimed to have witnessed the sun moving suddenly and unnaturally. Some even described it as having danced. Others, however, failed to see anything extraordinary taking place. This phenomenon was taken by the faithful as divine conformation of the visions experienced by the children, while sceptics attributed it to MASS HYSTERIA or even the appearance of an EXTRATERRESTRIAL spacecraft.

The children said they had been entrusted with three secrets: the first was a vision of hell and the eternal punishment that awaited for unrepentant sinners; the second was a prediction of another world war that would follow the one currently raging unless mankind repented; the third secret was not revealed at the time but written down from the children's accounts and kept hidden away from the public in the Vatican.

After a period of investigation, the Roman Catholic Church declared that the visions were worthy of belief in 1930, and the site has become a place of pilgrimage for millions of Catholics from around the world.

The third secret entrusted to the children was revealed by the Vatican in 2000, although some Catholics maintain that this revelation was incomplete and that more knowledge (of presumably momentous significance) remains to be disclosed. It concerned a vision of a bishop dressed in white being cut down by a hail of bullets while making his way to the Cross. The Vatican claimed that the vision related to the attempted assassination by a gunman of Pope John Paul II in St Peter's Square in 1981, on an anniversary of one of the original visions. The Pope himself believed that the Madonna of Fátima saved his life by ensuring that he was not fatally wounded, and he ordered that one of the bullets fired at him should be placed in the crown of the statue of the Virgin at Fátima.

When he visited the shrine in 2000, John Paul II beatified Francisco and Jacinta, who had died in the influenza epidemic that swept Europe after World War I. Lucia became a nun at the age of 18 and in 1929 she claimed to have had another vision of the Virgin, who commanded her to work for the consecration of Russia. She continued to urge the Church to carry this out until her death in 2005.

Faust

The protagonist of a popular German tale in which a scholar makes a pact with the Devil; based on a historical 16th-century figure, the legend has inspired many fictional, operatic and musical works and films.

The historical character on whom the popular German legend of Doctor Faustus was based was Georg (or Johannes) Faust, a magician and alchemist from Heidelberg who travelled widely, performed apparently magical feats and died under mysterious circumstances some time around 1540. The idea of DEVIL'S PACTS was a common one in the mid-16th to mid-17th centuries, and Faust was widely believed to have sold his soul to the Devil for knowledge and power. Many features of stories originally told of earlier magicians, such as PARACELSUS and Simon Magus, became added to the lore surrounding Faust, and he quickly became the archetypal man who sells his soul to the Devil. In Faust's legend, the ambitious scholar, in his quest for forbidden knowledge, rejects the legitimate forms of learning and resorts to black magic. He summons a demon, usually identified as MEPHISTOPHELES, through whom he enters into a pact with the Devil, promising his soul in return for an agreed period during which he will be granted power, knowledge, youth and physical gratification. At the end of this period, payment is claimed by the Devil, and Faust is dragged down to Hell. In Polish folklore, a tale which appears to have originated around the same time as that of the historical Faust, tells of Pan Twardowski, a physician who makes a similar bargain and comes to the same end.

Faust's legend grew, and his exploits allegedly included such feats as the production of a bunch of grapes from across the world in the middle of winter, and the summoning of various spirits – most famously that of Helen of Troy. For a long time, popular interest focused on his reputation as a wonder-worker, rather than on his ultimate fate, and the numerous stories which grew around him were assembled after his death into a 'biography', a small chapbook published in Frankfurt in 1587. This *Historia von Dr Iohan Fausten* portrayed Faust as a 'damnable' rogue who was said to have enjoyed an allotted period of 24 years filled with luxury, excess and perversion, to have become the most famous astrologer of his day with predictions which never failed and to have astonished his contemporaries with his knowledge. The book was translated into English and was an instant success. The English playwright Christopher Marlowe used this English translation as the basis for his 1604 play *The Tragical History of Doctor Faustus*, although it is likely that his work was also influenced by stories of two other historical occultists, CORNELIUS AGRIPPA and Dr JOHN DEE. Marlowe portrays Faust as a highly intelligent man and invites us to pity him as a victim of his own intellect and pride. Later, the 19th-century German writer Goethe was inspired by Marlowe's drama to produce his own, definitive classical work on the legend, a two-part play *Faust*, in which Faust is ultimately redeemed.

The Faust story has been retold and alluded to in many other works of fiction, in opera and music, in films and in forms of popular culture such as video and computer games, graphic novels, manga and anime. In modern times, the adjective 'Faustian' is often used figuratively to denote any act in which hubris leads a person to their doom.

fay

An older form of the word 'fairy'; it was originally used as a noun to refer to the creatures themselves, but when 'fairy' replaced it as their name, the word became an adjective with several meanings such as 'enchanted', 'fairy-like' and 'doomed'.

The word 'fay', also spelled 'fee' or 'fey', comes via the Old French *feie*, from Latin *fata*, meaning 'the Fates'. Originally 'fairy' (fay-erie) meant 'a state of enchantment', but it came to be used for the creatures who caused this enchantment, replacing 'fay'. The word 'fay' remained in the language, however, evolving into an adjective with a number of meanings. Initially it stayed close to its roots, and was used to mean enchanted or fairy-like, but it gradually developed several extended senses: possessing an otherworldly quality; having the

ability to see into the future; slightly crazed (as people who had had contact with the fairy world were sometimes believed to be); and, especially in Scotland, doomed to die a violent death, thought to be indicated by unnaturally high spirits. It is also often used nowadays of someone who is pretentiously whimsical or eccentric.

fee *see* FAY

feng shui

The ancient Chinese art of placement, design and the arrangement of space to achieve harmony within an environment so as to create a free flow of energy or qi; this is believed to result in good health, prosperity and happiness.

'Feng shui' is the Chinese for 'wind' and 'water', and is the ancient Chinese art of balancing energies by using placement, design and the arrangement of space in order to integrate people, buildings and the landscape into one harmonious whole. It is based on the theory that the space people live and work in is inextricably connected to their health, vitality and prosperity, and that only when a balance and harmony of YIN and YANG are achieved between people and their environment can the energy known as QI flow freely, bringing good health, prosperity and happiness. In Chinese culture, feng shui is taken so seriously that the construction of new buildings and alterations to existing ones are undertaken only once a feng shui expert has been consulted, and correcting inauspicious feng shui is considered as much of a healing process as are the various aspects of CHINESE MEDICINE.

The practice of feng shui is thought to be over 3000 years old, and has its origins in TAOISM. It encompasses the design and layout of cities and villages, homes and public buildings, and also the construction of graves, although the feng shui rules for the houses of the dead, or 'yin houses', are different from those applied to buildings intended for the living. When Christian missionaries went to China in the 19th century, they erroneously translated feng shui as 'geomancy', but feng shui and GEOMANCY have very different means and aims. Traditional feng shui uses a compass called a *luopan*, along with a comprehensive series of calculations, including astrological ones. The traditional schools can be divided into two broad groups: *San He* (Three Harmonies), which emphasizes the effect of surrounding land forms, and *San Yuan* (Three Cycles), which focuses more on the factor of time. There are also now a number of NEW AGE versions, such as Pyramid Feng Shui, which do not share the long history of the traditional schools, and which typically use intuitive methods and concepts

A feng shui compass, or *luopan*, as used by many traditional feng shui masters. (© TopFoto)

from the spiritualist movement of the 19th century, along with modern interior design. The Black Hat Sect version of feng shui began in Hong Kong in the 1960s; unlike traditional feng shui, which sees the objects within a building as being of less significance than the position and environment of the building itself, Black Hat feng shui places great importance on the arrangement of objects within a building or room.

One of the easiest ways to determine the feng shui of an environment is by using a *Pa Kua*, an octagonal map or grid which contains symbols from the ancient I CHING oracle. These symbols relate to all the areas or aspects of life. They are divided into categories such as fame, relationships and marriage, helpful people and travel, children and creativity, health and wealth. The *Pa Kua* is placed over the land, building, room or area to show negative or missing spaces, or inauspicious situations. For example, if the grid shows that the bathroom in a house is in the 'wealth' area, it is thought that any money coming into the house will be lost quickly, as if going 'down the drain'. Remedies are prescribed to counteract this bad feng shui, such as putting a round-leaved plant in the bathroom, hanging a crystal or wind chime up in it, or using the wealth colours blue and green. Trees, plants, flowers, crystals, mirrors, colours and sounds, and water features such as fountains, are used to create the required type of qi for every situation.

Feng shui is increasingly being used by Western companies in their attempts to improve business, and by homeowners during the planning and construction of their houses, or as an element of interior design; architects and landscape designers all round the world are now often asked to incorporate feng shui principles in their designs.

fetch

A form of apparitional double of a person that is said to be seen when they are close to death.

In Celtic folklore, it is believed that the phantom DOUBLE of a person may be seen when they are near to death. Such a belief is a variation of the German concept of the DOPPELGÄNGER, and some have suggested that it may have arisen from early reports of CRISIS APPARITIONS.

The antiquarian John Aubrey recorded a number of accounts of fetches in his work *Miscellanies* (1696), including cases of individuals who met their spectral doubles in the grounds of Holland House, London, shortly before their lives ended. Aubrey also recounted the case of a Sir William Napier who experienced a vision of his own corpse lying upon a bed at an inn while he was on a journey to Berkshire. Although he was in seeming good health, he died within a few days of arriving at his destination.

However, a fetch may not always be a harbinger of death – according to Irish tradition much depends on the time of day the fetch is seen. If it is witnessed early in the morning it is considered to foretell a long life.

fey *see* FAY

fire

One of the four elements believed in ancient and medieval cosmology to be the fundamental components of all things; of prime importance in magic and the occult.

In ancient and medieval philosophy and alchemy, all things were believed to be composed of a blend of four classical ELEMENTS: AIR, WATER, EARTH and fire. These four elements are central to magical and occult thought. Fire is seen as the realm of the will, change and passion, and is the force which keeps us focused on our goals and helps us to overcome obstacles. The power of fire may be called on for assistance in spells or rituals involving protection, courage, competitions and sex; it governs all candle magic. It is associated with the south, the season of Summer, young adulthood, noon and the colour red, and is thought to be a masculine element, since it is active, hot and dry. Fire governs the zodiacal signs of ARIES, LEO and SAGITTARIUS, and is connected with the Sun and the planet Mars. In the TAROT, it is represented by the suit of wands (see WANDS, SUIT OF). In the casting of a MAGIC CIRCLE, it is frequently symbolized in physical form by a candle, and is associated with the magical tools of the WAND, which conducts and aims the will of the magician to the goal, the censer and the ritual knife or 'athame'. Its position in the five-pointed star or PENTAGRAM is the lower right point. The four fluids known as humours, which were once popularly believed to permeate the human body and determine the temperament, were each associated with an element, and earth was associated with the humour of yellow bile. Fire is said to be governed by the archangel Michael, and its specific animating spirit or ELEMENTAL is the SALAMANDER. Fire is the element of the sun, lightning, fires, volcanoes and all forms of light.

fireballs

Particularly bright meteors.

The International Astronomical Union defines a fireball as a meteor brighter than magnitude –4, which in lay terms means one as bright as the planet Venus in the night sky. Essentially, a fireball is caused by the entry into the earth's atmosphere of a larger-than-usual object, anything from a few centimetres in size. They generally have a long glowing tail and observers have occasionally reported hearing a roaring sound to accompany their flight. They are both rare and unpredictable and never fail to have a striking effect on those lucky enough to see one.

An unusually well-documented incident took place at Peekskill, a suburban town in New York State, on 9 October 1992. The fireball was observed by many people attending an evening football game, and several of them recorded the event in photographs and video footage. A large rocky fragment was later found to have landed on a parked car.

In earlier times, fireballs were variously interpreted as stars falling to earth, expressions of the anger of gods or the travelling of the SPIRITS of the dead. In many cultures they were taken as evil OMENS. In more recent years they have generated UFO reports or sparked claims that the military are testing 'Star Wars' weaponry in space.

fire genii *see* FIRESTARTERS

fire-handling *see* FIRE IMMUNITY

fire immunity

The apparent ability of some humans to resist fire and extreme heat.

Fire immunity has been linked with religious and magical practice for millennia. For example, in the Old Testament of the Bible, Shadrach, Meshach and Abednigo are thrown into a fiery furnace by Nebuchadnezzar, King of Babylon (died 562 BC) for refusing to worship another god than their own. Miraculously, they survive unharmed. Less extreme examples, such as fire-walking and fire-handling, are more common. Fire-walking in particular has been a part of religious ceremonies (particularly for

A fire-walker crosses burning coals during a ceremony in a rural Sri Lankan village. (© TopFoto)

purification or initiation) in various cultures around the world, from the Brahmins of India to Native North Americans.

Various explanations are given for this ability. For the religious it is simply a matter of faith – the successful handling of fire demonstrating deep spirituality or protection by a deity.

Others cite it as an example of the power of MIND OVER MATTER, or suggest that practitioners enter a state of ecstasy or trance, enabling them to experience no pain in circumstances where it would normally be unbearable (see PAIN ENDURANCE). The Sufi Muslim ascetics (see SUFISM), known as dervishes (see DERVISHES, WHIRLING) have been known to swallow hot coals or handle hot iron without apparent damage while in a state of religious ecstasy.

A number of more straightforward physical explanations have also been offered. These are based around the fact that the body is not a good conductor of heat, and that, as long as the contact is brief enough, there is actually very little risk of burning. The risk is reduced further if the skin is wet, or where the hot object is of a substance which is itself a poor conductor of heat, or is a very small object or is of a substance with a very low specific heat capacity. Snuffing out a candle with your fingers and contact with the sparks from a sparkler are often cited as examples. In the case of fire-walking, it has also been suggested that the layer of ashes that usually covers the coals acts as insulation, keeping the surface temperature below that necessary to instantly burn human skin.

Some contend that there have been demonstrations of fire immunity where the time of contact between the skin and the hot object has been for too long a period of time for these explanations to be sufficient. For example, the Scottish spiritualist DANIEL DUNGLAS HOME was said to have been able to handle hot coals and even lie down upon a 'bed' of them without being harmed. However, very impressive feats of apparent fire immunity can also be performed by conjurors and illusionists, and fire-handling and 'fire eating' (or 'fire breathing') are all popular forms of entertainment. In the late 20th century, fire-walking was even adopted as an activity at corporate bonding sessions used by businesses to motivate employees and encourage team-building.

Extreme resistance to burning (even attempts at cremation after death) is usually called INCOMBUSTIBILITY.

firestarters

People with the ability to start spontaneous fires around them without any apparent means of ignition.

The term 'firestarter' is used to describe someone who apparently has the power to produce spontaneous fires. CHARLES FORT used the alternative description 'fire genii' when reporting on the phenomenon in his writings. In a similar way to POLTERGEIST cases (which are often associated with teenage girls), the majority of firestarting cases involve children or teenagers. Famous cases include that of Lily White from Antigua, as reported in the *New York Times* in August 1929. It was alleged that she could cause her clothes and bed sheets to catch fire and burn while she remained unharmed.

A popular theory is that the fires are caused through some form of unconscious PSYCHOKINESIS. However, despite most cases involving witnesses who claim that the firestarter could not have started the fires by normal means, the official explanation tends to be that they are simply starting the fires themselves without being observed.

fire-walking *see* FIRE IMMUNITY

fish, falls of *see* FALLS

five

The fifth whole number, represented by the digit 5; considered significant in numerology.

Five is the fifth whole number. There are five senses,

and 5 is thus connected with the idea of sensuality and pleasure. It is also seen as the number of grace. In the minor ARCANA of the TAROT, the fives represent loss and conflict. In the major arcana, 5 is the number associated with the Hierophant card. In Hebrew GEMATRIA, 5 corresponds to the Hebrew letter He, and in the KABBALAH, it is the number assigned to the sephirah GEBURAH. In NUMEROLOGY, it is considered to be a YANG number; it is the numerical value of the letters E, N and W, and a person with 5 in their numerological profile is believed to be unorthodox, freedom-seeking and adventurous, rebelling against the status quo. They are curious, impulsive, sensual and resourceful, and crave change and variety. A five personality may also display the more negative traits of being unwilling to take responsibility or to make commitments, and a tendency toward overindulgence.

Five has always held strong mystical associations, and is much revered in magical traditions as a number signifying spiritual communication and completion. The PENTAGRAM or five-pointed star is a powerful magical symbol which is said to link the human body to the heavens, and can be taken as representing the whole person, as made up by the four limbs and the head. See also ONE; TWO; THREE; FOUR; SIX; SEVEN; EIGHT; NINE; TEN; ELEVEN; TWELVE.

Flannan Isles mystery

The strange disappearance of three lighthousemen from the Flannan lighthouse in December 1900.

On 26 December 1900, the lighthouse tender *Hesperus* arrived on a routine visit at Eileen Mor, the largest of the Flannan Isles, a remote group of islands off the west coast of Scotland. However, when it arrived, the lighthouse was found to be deserted.

A telegram sent by the master of the *Hesperus*, taken from the records of the Northern Lighthouse Board, reads:

> A dreadful accident has happened at Flannans. The three Keepers, Ducat, Marshall and the occasional have disappeared from the island. On our arrival there this afternoon no sign of life was to be seen on the Island. Fired a rocket but, as no response was made, managed to land Moore, who went up to the Station but found no Keepers there. The clocks were stopped and other signs indicated that the accident must have happened about a week ago. Poor fellows they must been blown over the cliffs or drowned trying to secure a crane or something like that.

The conclusion in the reports of the time was that the keepers had left the lighthouse buildings for some reason during bad weather and been swept out to sea by an unexpected wave. However, there were some intriguing circumstances surrounding the disappearance which, fuelled by press speculation and the Wilfrid William Gibson poem 'Flannan Isle', have continued to keep the mystery alive in the public imagination. The fact that the iron railings around the west landing and the crane platform were displaced and twisted, as noted in Superintendent Muirhead's report following the incident, led to suggestions of the involvement of some 'unearthly' force. It was also noted by Mr Moore that the coat of one of the keepers remained inside, although the oilskins and sea boots of the other two keepers were missing. The very fact that all three must have left the building together has also been taken to be unusual – normal practice would require one keeper to remain inside to tend the light at all times.

As with that other famous maritime disappearance, the MARY CELESTE, some accounts state that a half-eaten meal was discovered on the table. In the Gibson poem, the discovery is related as follows:

Yet, as we crowded through the door,
We only saw a table, spread
For dinner, meat and cheese and bread;
But all untouch'd; and no one there:
As though, when they sat down to eat,
Ere they could even taste,
Alarm had come; and they in haste
Had risen and left the bread and meat:
For at the table-head a chair
Lay tumbled on the floor.

This certainly doesn't agree with the eye-witness reports. It was partly from the discovery that (among other morning work) the meal things had been cleared away, that the time of the incident was placed in the afternoon of 15 December 1900, the day on which the last entry appeared on the slate (where notes were made before being transferred to the log). Indeed, everything was found to be in order at the lighthouse buildings, even to the extent that the gate had been secured. This in itself might be considered odd if the loss of all three keepers was due to a situation, occurring during a severe storm, which induced such a state of panic that one of those involved did not have time to put on his oilskins.

Suggested explanations over the years have included insanity on the part of the keepers, an attack by a SEA SERPENT, THE DEVIL and the inevitable ALIEN ABDUCTION. However, it seems likely that this was simply a tragic accident behind which were left too few clues for certainty.

flight

An important part of various forms of mystical and spiritual belief.

Flight, whether actual, in spirit or in the mind, is a recurring theme in many religious and magical traditions throughout the world. For example, it appears among the miracles attributed to Christian SAINTS, the feats performed by spiritualist MEDIUMS and in the East in the form of YOGIC FLYING.

Historically, in the West, flight has particularly been associated with WITCHCRAFT, where it is also sometimes referred to as 'transvection'. WITCHES were popularly believed to be able to fly, usually by using BROOMSTICKS or other means, possibly with the assistance of FLYING OINTMENTS. However, even during the Middle Ages, this belief was not universally held. The Christian Church originally denied that witches could actually fly, stating that they simply imagined that they could – a position consistent with the idea that flying ointments had a hallucinogenic effect which induced the sensation of flying. Later on, as the persecution of witches gained momentum, the belief in real, corporeal flight became more widely accepted – amongst other things, it appears amongst the accusations levelled at witches in the MALLEUS MALEFICARUM. See also LEVITATION.

Flight 19 *see* BERMUDA TRIANGLE

flows

Paranormal manifestations in the form of mysterious flows of water and other liquids.

The idea of supernaturally induced flows of blood or water is a popular motif in folklore and fiction. It also arises in accounts of miracles associated with images of the Virgin Mary and many Christian saints, particularly in Catholic countries (see IMAGES, BLEEDING).

In Great Britain, many ancient houses display supposedly indelible stains purported to have arisen from murders in the past, and certain stones, grave markers and relics are said to bleed on the anniversary of heinous crimes. For example, the tombstone of Richard Smith reputedly murdered at Hinckley, Leicestershire, in 1726, is said to become wet with blood on the anniversary of his death each year on 12 April, and the SCREAMING SKULL of Bettiscombe, Dorset, is said to have sweated blood before World War I. However, reliable testimony for flows of blood in haunted houses is scant – such stories seem to be confined to folklore and horror fiction.

There is better attested evidence of the mysterious appearance of water and other liquids in POLTERGEIST cases. Flows of water and paraffin oil were reported during a poltergeist outbreak at Swanton Novers Rectory in Norfolk in 1919, where the disturbances appeared to be linked to a teenage serving maid. In 1963, flows and pools of water appeared without explanation in a family home in Somerset during a poltergeist case that was investigated by Tony Cornell for the SOCIETY FOR PSYCHICAL RESEARCH. Pools of water were also reported during the ENFIELD POLTERGEIST case.

Flying Dutchman

A legendary ghost ship which inspired an opera by Wagner.

According to popular legend, the *Flying Dutchman* is a ship that was doomed to sail the oceans of the world for eternity because of crimes committed by its captain. Several versions of the story are known. In one version, popularized by Richard Wagner in the opera *Der Fliegender Holländer* in 1843, the vessel was captained by a man named Hendrik Vanderdecken who cursed God and was condemned to sail the seas until doomsday.

The waters around the Cape of Good Hope have long been associated with alleged sightings of the *Flying Dutchman*, but another version of the story places the vessel in the northern seas. In this version, the captain was a nobleman, by the name of Falkenburg, who murdered his brother and his bride in a fit of jealous passion. As a consequence he was condemned to sail the northern oceans in a GHOST SHIP in which evil spirits play dice for his soul. According to Sir Walter Scott, a sighting of the *Flying Dutchman* is a portent of death and disaster for those sailors who witness it. The legend of the *Flying Dutchman* was the subject of a popular stage show involving the use of magic lanterns in England in the 1820s and also inspired the story *The Phantom Ship* (1839) by Captain Marryat.

It has been claimed that as a young naval rating in 1880, the future King George V witnessed an APPARITION of the *Flying Dutchman*, while aboard the flagship *Inconstant*, off the coast of Australia. However, careful scrutiny of relevant diary entries reveals that the alleged experience was actually that of thirteen other seamen, who reported seeing:

> A strange red light as of a phantom ship all aglow, on the midst of which light the masts, spars and sails of a brig 200 yards distant stood out in strong relief as she came up on the port bow.

The vision may have been a mirage, an optical illusion, an effect involving phosphorescence or even an effect created by a magic lantern. Nonetheless, it was taken seriously as an omen of death, and the sailor who first sighted the phantom reportedly died shortly afterwards in an accident.

flying ointment

A concoction believed to be used by witches to help them to achieve magical flight.

During the Middle Ages, it was widely believed that witches smeared their bodies, and sometimes their BROOMSTICKS or other items, with magical ointments to enable them to fly to their SABBATS.

It was commonly claimed that these ointments were

THE FLYING DUTCHMAN.

ENGRAVED BY E. H. DEL'ORME.

An artist's rendition of a sighting of the ghostly *Flying Dutchman*, published in *Century* magazine (July 1894). (© Mary Evans Picture Library)

based on the boiled fat of human babies. From the lists of other ingredients that are alleged to have been included in flying ointments, such as hemlock, deadly nightshade, henbane and mandrake, it is clear that if such ointments were used they would probably have had a toxic or hallucinogenic effect that may have brought about the sensation of FLIGHT. The use of drugs to induce trance-like states, during which there may be an experience akin to flying, is widespread in magical and shamanic belief systems throughout the world – it is possible that the myth of corporeal flight on the part of witches arose out of this practice.

flying saucers

A phrase in widespread use as a synonym for UFO. Its use was born out of a misunderstanding and has significantly altered the public perception of the UFO phenomenon.

Until 1947, UFO sightings were described using a wide range of different terms. In Victorian times, there were AIRSHIPS; in 1946, there were GHOST ROCKETS; and the first sightings reported to US military units during the WAVE in the summer of 1947 were called flying discs – a term that persisted in government documents well into the 1950s.

However, none of these captured the public imagination in the way that the highly charged phrase 'flying saucer' did. It became so widely accepted that it appeared in the title of Hollywood films for decades and remains in widespread use even in the 21st century.

Nevertheless, the phrase stems from a misunderstanding. The day after KENNETH ARNOLD's alleged UFO sighting over Mount Rainier in June 1947 he gave an interview to the *East Oregonian* newspaper in Pendleton. Reporter Bill Bequette filed a wire report that was picked up all across the USA. But the media misinterpreted what Arnold meant when he described nine objects as flying 'like a saucer would if you skipped it across water'. Arnold intended this to reflect their motion – he actually described the objects as being crescent-shaped. Bequette stated in his report that the craft were 'saucer-like' and this was picked up by other reporters as if it related to the shape of Arnold's objects and not their movement. Within hours, headline writers were calling them 'flying saucers'.

In the wake of Arnold's sighting dozens of other people described seeing saucer-shaped craft, often flying in formation, something that was only common in those early days (see CULTURAL TRACKING).

Arnold often tried to correct the misinterpretation but it made little difference. The idea that ALIENS were coming to earth in saucer-shaped craft became the dominant version of the phenomenon, and persists even today in science-fiction stories and artwork.

flying triangles

One of the most common modern types of UFO, resembling a large triangular aircraft. They have been reported in large numbers from the late 1970s onward.

During October 1978, there were reported sightings of a large triangular craft moving slowly and silently through the night across the East Midlands of

Publicity for the 1956 film *Earth vs. The Flying Saucers* – an example from the hugely popular 'flying saucer' genre, which can ultimately be traced back to a simple misquotation. (© Corbis)

England. Some of the witnesses likened what they saw to a Vulcan bomber – a huge triangular plane then still in use by the RAF. The only notable difference was that a Vulcan can be heard from miles away and couldn't be described as silent. Other small WAVES followed across the UK.

UFO researchers suspected that the cause might be a new kind of terrestrial aircraft, probably of military origin, and suspicion fell on the Aurora (Stealth) fighter that the US Air Force were rumoured to be testing. Its existence was steadfastly denied in 1978, even when a model kit was put on sale. When the Aurora was finally revealed to the public it was admitted that this fighter had been on test flights over the UK during the late 1970s. A similar explanation was later suggested for the large flying triangles seen during the BELGIAN WAVE.

Reports of flying triangle sightings have continued to be made, and the type is now seen more frequently than the traditional FLYING SAUCER. In 1996, UFO researcher Victor Kean set up a database to help analyse these reports. He found that British cases focused on certain locations, including the East Anglian coast, and often occurred near to power stations. This may support the view that they are linked to spy planes. French Minister of Defence Robert Galley (who formed the UFO sightings team GEPAN) reported on his retirement that his government had caught such a triangular stealth jet taking photographs above a nuclear power plant. This was denied by the nation that had flown it across French airspace, but the French were then able to produce the photographs that the plane had taken.

foaflore *see* URBAN LEGENDS

foaftale *see* URBAN LEGENDS

Folklore *see panel p233*

foo fighters
Strange aerial lights seen by pilots during World War II.
During World War II, Allied aircrews reported encounters with mysterious balls of light during the course of combat missions over both Europe and the Pacific. The luminous forms would apparently fly near to, or with, their aircraft and then manoeuvre suddenly away. The phenomena were dubbed 'foo fighters' after a catchphrase belonging to a 1940s cartoon character: 'Where there's foo there's fire'.

Speculation was rife – a popular concern was that foo fighters were a secret weapon deployed by the Axis powers. However, the lights did not fire upon, attack or otherwise interfere with Allied aircraft.

Alternative theories included balloons, artillery flak or ST ELMO'S FIRE but, as a contemporary commentator remarked, 'no explanation stood up' and they remain an unsolved mystery of World War II. The Nazi secret weapon theory still circulates, but ufologists cite them as pre-1947 examples of UFOs. An alternative suggestion is that foo fighters were an unrecognized electromagnetic effect generated by the intense use of military radar during war time.

footprints *see* DEVIL'S FOOTPRINTS

forced-choice experiments
Experiments in parapsychology using a limited number of possible choices or 'targets'.
Forced-choice experiments are regularly used in PARAPSYCHOLOGY, particularly for the investigation of EXTRASENSORY PERCEPTION. CARD-GUESSING EXPERIMENTS are a classic example. With a standard deck of cards the subject can only chose from one of 52 possible options when attempting to 'guess' what is shown on the target card. The use of ZENER CARDS reduces the possibilities even further, as they employ only five different designs. One distinct advantage of forced-choice experiments, as opposed to a FREE-RESPONSE EXPERIMENTS, is that the statistical analysis of the results is relatively straightforward. For example, with Zener cards it would be expected that, through chance alone, an average hit rate of 20 per cent (ie one in five cards guessed correctly) should be achieved – so any result that was consistently higher than this would indicate that something more than pure guesswork was involved.

foreign accent syndrome
A condition in which a person loses their native accent.
A relatively small number of people who have suffered a stroke, or some other form of injury to the brain, have found that when they regain the power of speech they seem to be speaking in a foreign accent rather than in their previous, native one. Enough examples of this phenomenon have been documented to allow the condition to be labelled as 'foreign accent syndrome'.

The condition seems to have been first observed in Norway in 1941. A young woman who suffered head injuries in an air raid was found to have severe problems in recovering her ability to speak. When she eventually regained her voice, people hearing her speak believed that she had developed a German accent. As Norway and Germany were at war at the time, the unfortunate woman was ostracized by her community.

In a more recent example from the USA, a female

Folklore

Although most of us can easily name several stories, customs, songs or superstitions that we would describe as items of folklore, it is a term that is notoriously difficult to pin down to a definition that would be accepted by all the people with an interest in the field. Folklore is generally considered to consist mainly of oral tradition (at least historically) and to be characterized by repetition leading to a constant, dynamic variation. This could be further developed by recognizing that in pre-literate societies and groups, folk tales, rhymes, songs, SUPERSTITIONS and sayings were (and still are) used as a way to pass on customs, skills, knowledge and warnings from one generation to the next, helping to underpin and preserve value systems and a sense of identity. However, to restrict a definition to this would ignore the fact that in all of these forms there is also an element of pure entertainment.

The boundaries between the figurative narratives that form much of what would be described as folklore and those that might be described as myths or legends are, at the very least, blurred. In general terms, 'folklore' is usually reserved for those that do not form part of a religious belief system (as is usually the case with MYTHOLOGY) or that are not intended (at least partly) to describe real historical events or characters (as with LEGEND). However, in practice, it is extremely difficult to separate the three, and 'folklore' is often used as a catch-all term. Within the academic study of folklore, the working definitions employed have tended to become very wide in recent years – for example, after tackling the question, the US folklorist Dan Ben-Amos settled on 'artistic communication in small groups'.

In 1812, the first volume of *Grimm's Fairy Tales* by the German philologist brothers Jacob and Wilhelm Grimm was published, a work which drew heavily on the folklore and traditional tales of central Europe. The work of the Grimms inspired many other collectors to write down vast quantities of folklore, preserving it before it was lost through the industrialization and urbanization of Western society – although, ironically, some might say that in doing so they fixed stories in one particular form, containing much of their own interpretation, so that they effectively ceased to be folklore.

The word 'folklore' was coined by the English antiquary W J Thoms in 1846, as an alternative name for what had generally been described until then as 'popular antiquities'. The dramatic rise in academic interest in folklore during the 19th century was due in part to the rise of romantic nationalism throughout Europe, which encouraged interest in popular stories and traditions as a means to establish or reinforce national identities. This was paralleled within the Romantic literary movement, which drew on folklore, particularly fairy tales, as one of its sources of inspiration – as can be seen in poems such as Shelley's 'Queen Mab' (1813) or Keats' 'Eve of St Agnes' (1820). Much of the poetry of Sir Walter Scott grew out of his extensive knowledge of traditional ballads and stories, and the same source informed many of his novels.

It has been observed that the words 'folklore' and 'folk' (in a similar way to 'mythology') are often used in a dismissive, or even pejorative, sense. The use of the word 'folklore' can sometimes imply that something represents a childish or inferior mode of belief, because it does not correspond with the current mainstream view – for example, much of what is now described as folklore in the West may stem from, or contain remnants of, pre-Christian religious belief. Similar examples can be found where 'folk' is applied to practices, remedies and stories that do not correspond with the current mainstream views in science, medicine and the study of history. Before the arrival of widespread literacy, everyday knowledge was often transmitted and preserved through such media as nursery rhymes, proverbs and other sayings. These could cover a wide range of topics including, amongst other things, food and drink, travel, work, relationships and the art of WEATHER FORECASTING.

However, many traditional stories are clearly fictional and employ characters that are archetypal. Stories about wicked step-parents, mysterious strangers or WITCHES were wholly fictional, but may have acted as cautionary tales, giving warnings against the many types of folly to which human beings are prone, or containing other kinds of life lessons. Others gave homely explanations for seemingly mysterious phenomena in everyday life, such as the MAN IN THE MOON.

A common characteristic of many strains of folklore is the suggestion (possibly sometimes believed, possibly sometimes only figurative) that there are other worlds that exist in parallel to our own and occasionally interact with it – whether at certain 'magical' times of the year or at the behest of their strange inhabitants. All around the world, everyday events that seem to be unexplained have been attributed to the activities of mysterious non-human (but often human-like) creatures. These beings are often described as being of smaller than human stature but endowed with magical powers, and are known by a variety of names, including BROWNIES, ELVES, DJINN, FAIRIES, LITTLE PEOPLE and LEPRECHAUNS. They may be helpful or troublesome, kindly or malevolent, but generally tend to treat human beings as an inferior race to be instructed like children or made the subject of cruel tricks – such as the secret replacement of human babies with feeble fairy CHANGELINGS. These other-worldly beings may also be of a more directly terrifying aspect, and take the form of GHOSTS or SPIRITS – such as the BANSHEE, BLACK DOGS or the wild huntsman known in parts of England as HERNE THE HUNTER.

Many people tend to think of folklore as something that belongs to the distant past, which has decreasing relevance to the world of today and is the province of historians, anthropologists and storytellers. However, folklore is still very much alive in the modern world. Indeed, new folk tales and beliefs are being created and spread far more quickly than ever before – oral repetition having been joined by the mass media, the photocopier and the Internet. In the modern world, cunning or foolish peasants, vain or cruel kings and wicked stepmothers have given way to ALIEN ABDUCTIONS, web wizards, PHANTOM HITCH-HIKERS and disappearing mothers-in-law.

Perhaps the best-known current form of folklore is the genre usually described as URBAN LEGENDS. Like traditional stories, these contemporary folk tales were largely spread by word of mouth until the arrival of the Internet allowed them to be disseminated worldwide with extreme rapidity. Such stories exhibit an important feature of folk tales in that they mutate and grow in the telling, allowing the narrator to add or subtract details according to their local relevance or the expectations of the audience.

Similar to these are the conspiracy theories and other stories that spring up alongside the 'accepted' versions of events – such as the supposed non-accidental death of Diana, Princess of Wales or the belief that man has never really landed on the moon. In the popular imagination, certain real people have undergone a transformation into larger-than-life, almost mythical, figures, not so very long after their (real or assumed) deaths. Examples include ELVIS PRESLEY, who continues to be sighted by the faithful in the most unlikely of places despite having died in 1977, the famously elusive LORD LUCAN or the tragically romantic Russian Grand Duchess ANASTASIA. Places and inanimate objects have also undergone a similar process – such as the famous BERMUDA TRIANGLE, HANGING ROCK in Australia, the HOPE DIAMOND with its legendary curse and the ill-fated *TITANIC*.

It could be argued that folklore is still as important as it ever was, reflecting the real hopes, fears, interests, prejudices and beliefs of the population – as contrasted with the 'official' wisdom of policymakers and academics. Perhaps what the stories of modern folklore have in common with their historical counterparts is that they stem from a desire for the romantic rather than the prosaic. They can be seen, in an increasingly secular society, as fulfilling a deep-seated need to believe in something that transcends the banality of everyday life.

Simon Hill and Michael Munro

stroke victim born and raised until her sixties in the state of Indiana was described in 2003 as speaking in a British accent, and at a higher pitch than before her illness, despite never having been to the United Kingdom.

Similarly, another American woman, this time a native of Missouri, found that on recovering from a stroke she seemed to be speaking not in her normal accent but in that of a non-native speaker of English, perhaps of a Spanish or Brazilian person.

When cases of this type were first observed, many doctors believed that the cause must be a psychiatric rather than a medical one, thus adding to the distress of the sufferers who now had to fear for their sanity as well as their physical health. However, with more examples of the phenomenon to study, medical opinion now generally favours a form of brain damage as the real explanation of the condition.

It seems that even slight damage, such as is caused by a stroke, to the part of the brain from which speech is controlled can affect a person's ability to speak. However, the idea that the native accent has been replaced by a foreign one is misleading.

Damage to the network of nerves within the brain that allow us to form and pronounce words may produce changes in the victim's speech patterns, such as pitch and the respective lengths of syllables, as well as impairing their ability to physically reproduce the sounds involved in forming words. Victims report the frustration of knowing the words they want to say but being unable to articulate them. They may also seem to struggle to find the right word, or mispronounce the ones that they use.

This can have the effect of making it sound as if they are speaking with the accent of someone who has learnt English in another part of the world or as a second language. Part of this is conditioned by the hearer, of course, and what may sound to an American like a British accent may well not be recognized as such, at least consistently, by a native of the United Kingdom.

Many doctors, however, believe that the condition need not be permanent and that sufferers may regain their previous accent as their general recovery progresses.

foretelling
The art or practice of prophesying an event or outcome before it happens.

Throughout human history, people have tried to use supernatural means of foretelling or prophesying what the future holds. In ancient Rome, no major decision was taken before a priest had performed the ritual of 'taking the auspices' to determine the outcome of the undertaking, and a similar role has been played for thousands of years by the priests, SHAMANS, WITCH DOCTORS and MEDICINE MEN of ancient and indigenous cultures. There have always been people who have claimed to be able to foretell natural disasters or major world events, often by means of DREAMS or VISIONS experienced beforehand, and there are a wide range of tools available to the individual who aims to see what the future holds, with ASTROLOGY, TAROT cards, RUNES and the *I CHING* being the most popular. See also DIVINATION.

Fort, Charles Hoy (1874–1932)
The US philosopher who pioneered the collection and study of reports of anomalies.

Charles Fort, after whom the subject of FORTEANA was named, has been called one of the USA's most important modern philosophers. He developed a philosophy that was both critical of and satirized authoritarianism in both science and religion. Fort was sceptical about many scientific explanations, observing how some scientists argued according to their own beliefs rather than the rules of evidence and then relied on their authority to convince others. Any data that threatened to contradict them was ignored, suppressed, discredited or explained away. He coined the term TELEPORTATION and was perhaps the first to speculate that mysterious lights seen in the sky might be craft from outer space (see UFOS).

Fort spent years in the New York Public Library and the British Museum Library, reading widely in the scientific literature and making thousands of notes on reported ANOMALIES in the science journals, periodicals and newspapers published between 1800 and 1932. His evidence and commentaries fill four books: *The Book of the Damned* (1919), *New Lands* (1923), *Lo!* (1931) and *Wild Talents* (1932).

Fort was born into a fairly prosperous family of Dutch immigrants who owned a wholesale grocery business in Albany, New York State. He was the eldest of three brothers. Although the young Fort was intelligent, curious and witty, he did not do well in at school, preferring to devote his time to reading and his passion for natural history. Beatings by his tyrannical father helped set him against authority and dogma, as he states in his autobiography *Many Parts* (unpublished). Leaving home at the age of 18, he worked as a reporter in New York City before hitch-hiking through Europe 'to put some capital into the bank of experience'. In 1896, aged 22, he contracted malaria in South Africa and returned to New York where, in October that year, he married Anna Filan (or Filing), an English servant girl in his father's house. Fort and Anna were devoted to each other and lived in great poverty in a succession of tiny apartments in the Bronx and Hell's Kitchen quarters

Charles Fort, the US philosopher and famous collector of anomalies. (© TopFoto/Fortean)

of New York City. Odd jobs and infrequent sales of his short stories barely kept them alive as he worked at the library during the day and wrote up his notes into the night. In 1916, at the age of 42, Fort received a modest inheritance from an uncle; it was enough to allow him to concentrate on writing.

Between 1910 and 1918, Fort worked on two experimental manuscripts – called *X* and *Y* – both arguing that a hidden civilization – one on Mars and the other at the South Pole – affected our own. Theodore Dreiser (1871–1945) was editing *Smith's Magazine* when he first met Fort in 1905. He had bought a few of his humorous stories and recalled of *X*: 'It was so strange, so forceful, so beautiful that … it was certainly one of the greatest books I have ever read in my life.' Fort replied: 'You have at least one thing to be thankful for – I might have begun with 'A'.' Fort set about revising *X* and *Y*, collating them with new material into a single book he called *The Book of the Damned*, which Dreiser used his influence to bring to publication in 1919.

On rare occasions, Fort's concentration was quickly soured by doubt, plunging him into a depression. Twice, he burned his current collection of tens of thousands of notes because 'they were not what I wanted'. Then, undaunted and driven by his curiosity, he would begin again his exhaustive reading and note-taking, but in a new direction. *New Lands*, his second book, which focuses more on astronomical anomalies, was published in 1921.

That same year, Fort moved to London. From lodgings close to the British Museum and its library, he undertook his 'grand tour' of the Museum's holdings several times, widening his horizons to new subjects and correlations at every pass. In this period, he speculated on the inevitability of space travel. He wrote to newspapers about the colonization of space, comparing its pioneers to the wagon trains that opened up the American West, and even spoke on the subject at Hyde Park Corner.

When he returned to New York in 1929, Fort struck up an acquaintance with an ebullient young novelist, Tiffany Thayer, who went on to edit the collected volume of Fort's four books. Were it not for his wife's insistence that he accompany her to the cinema most evenings, Fort had no social life. His only other visitor was Dreiser, who called Fort 'the Hermit of the Bronx'. They would talk into the night, surrounded by Fort's collection of curiosities and the great wall of shoe boxes in which his myriad notes roosted.

In 1931, on the day of the publication of Fort's third book, *Lo!* – which introduced the idea of teleportation – Thayer and Aaron Sussman, a young advertising executive, formed the FORTEAN SOCIETY in his honour. Typically, Fort said he wanted nothing to do with it, warning against the institutionalization of his philosophy.

There are very few descriptions of Fort. He was a complex and private man, dedicated to his work. In his exuberant introduction to the 1941 edition of the *Collected Books*, Thayer describes Fort as a jolly giant with 'the most magnificent sense of humour'. However, Thayer's Fort, 'roaring at his subject' and 'packing a belly laugh in either typewriter hand', is at odds with the 'shy and introverted' hermit seen by others, including Fort's oldest friend Theodore Dreiser, who likened him to Oliver Hardy: 'that unctuous, ingratiating mood, those unwieldy, deferential, twittery mannerisms were Fort's.' One of Dreiser's friends said of Fort, 'there was something fascinating about him; he seemed utterly alive, carefree and all-knowing as he talked.' To Aaron Sussman, Fort was 'a gentle man, inveterately polite, very tender toward Anna'. With his deep voice and booming laugh, he gave Sussman the impression of 'a great mind that had withdrawn from the world'.

Fort was growing progressively blind. No sooner had his fourth and last book – *Wild Talents*, concerning the anomalous abilities of human beings – been proofed than he was admitted to New York's Royal

Hospital, suffering from 'unspecified weakness'. The next day, 3 May 1932, he died, aged 58, apparently of leukaemia. He took notes almost to the end – the last said, simply, 'Difficulty shaving. Gaunt places in face.'

Fort's complex philosophy – FORTEANISM – has inspired a diverse group of disciples, who are by their nature individualists and contrarians, each with their own interpretation of FORTEANA, with little allegiance to any form of orthodoxy. The term 'fortean' was first used by the playwright Ben Hecht in a review of *The Book of the Damned* for the *Chicago Daily News* in 1919: 'I am the first disciple of Charles Fort … Henceforth, I am a Fortean'.

forteana

A collective noun for a wide range of subjects dealing with reports and analysis of strange experiences and anomalous phenomena.

Strictly, forteana refers to the range of ANOMALIES and strange observations considered by CHARLES FORT in his four books – *The Book of the Damned* (1919), *New Lands* (1923), *Lo!* (1931) and *Wild Talents* (1932). Since his death in 1932, the use of the word has been extended to refer more generally to the whole spectrum of ANOMALIES, PARANORMAL phenomena and even SUPERNATURAL topics. The essential characteristic of the fortean approach is the sense of structure imparted to seemingly diverse phenomena and the connections between them, and a theory that the advance of scientific understanding is tied to its being 'more inclusive', ie absorbing, explaining or accounting for more of the anomalies that it, at one time, rejected (see FORTEANISM).

Fort spent nearly 35 years in the great libraries of New York and London, reading voraciously and taking notes on anomalies that caught his interest. To make the task more manageable, he imposed an arbitrary starting date of 1800. It is sometimes said of him, wrongly, that he obtained all his data from popular sources; on the contrary, he gave considerable attention to scientific books and periodicals, which, in the early 19th century, seemed content to include reports of anomalies of all kinds. Fort noted a change in attitude, which gradually hardened between 1860 and 1890, in which first-hand accounts, usually from amateur scientists and others, became rarer as science publishing became more 'professional' and research oriented. Not unreasonably, anyone who had witnessed something unusual began to eschew *Nature*, the *Report of the British Association* and even *Scientific American*, to write to newspapers and 'hobbyist' publications such as the *Gentleman's Magazine*, *English Mechanic* and *Monthly Weather Review*. Today, reports of forteana are mainly picked up from newspapers and, to paraphrase Fort's *caveat*, they should only be accepted temporarily (if at all) until they can be verified by further investigations.

Charles Fort collected data on a great many of the subjects listed in this dictionary – too many to list here. What is important, and what has earned him a place as one of the 20th-century's important thinkers, is his discourse on a number of novel areas of research that bridged the divide between FOLKLORE and science. These include TELEPORTATION; enigmatic APPEARANCES or DISAPPEARANCES of people (eg KASPAR HAUSER or the crew of the *MARY CELESTE*); POLTERGEIST phenomena associated with adolescents; PSYCHICAL phenomena associated with religious movements; fire-proneness, FIRE IMMUNITY and SPONTANEOUS COMBUSTION of humans; archaeological 'erratics' (eg anomalous artefacts found embedded in ancient strata); FALLS of creatures, ice, stones, organic matter and manna; the possibility of space travel and EXTRATERRESTRIALS; PARAPSYCHOLOGY; conspiracies; CRYPTOZOOLOGY; and significant conjunctions of natural phenomena (eg correlations between odd rains, METEORITES and EARTHQUAKES).

Two important conditions apply to forteana. First, that some forms of phenomena can diminish, as though 'going out of fashion'; examples include toads embedded in stones (see ENTOMBMENT), and sightings of SEA SERPENTS. The second corollary is that new and unexpected forms of phenomena can arise. Since his death in 1932, the following topics have been regarded as fortean: BIGFOOT and other man-like creatures; encounters with FAIRIES and LITTLE PEOPLE; ALIEN ABDUCTIONS; sightings of OUT-OF-PLACE ANIMALS; suicide and end-of-the-world cults (see DOOMSDAY CULTS); CROP CIRCLES; ANTIGRAVITY; LEVITATION; false memory recovery (see MEMORY, FALSE) and the 'SATANIC RITUAL ABUSE' scares; historical revisionism; LOST CONTINENTS; LEYS and other 'EARTH MYSTERIES' – to name some of the most prominent.

Today, the collection of reports of forteana remains a relatively unorganized activity, although the nascent Charles Fort Institute has long-term plans to establish a web-based archive of indexed forteana. Most topics mentioned in this reference work have their 'activists', collecting news-clippings, photographs, publications of all sorts, audio and video recordings and ephemera in their field of interest. Those specifically tending the garden of forteana are few indeed, but two are worthy of mention. The first is Mr X (which is his legal name), who is diligently checking every datum referenced by Fort for the corrected, online version of Fort's four books and other writings that he maintains.

The other is the encyclopedist William R Corliss, whose labour of love is his *Catalog of Anomalies*, a 35-volume project to publish 'some 50,000 items gleaned from a 30-year survey of about 16,000 volumes of science journals and magazines from 1820 to date'. This actually exceeds Charles Fort's own collections in quantity of data but complements them in timeframe; at one point Fort had 40,000 notes collected over nearly 40 years from journals, papers and books published between 1800 and 1930. Corliss describes his *Catalogs* as:

> … a massive hoard of scientific enigmas, paradoxes, and esoterica, assembled bit by bit from 427+ volumes of *Nature*, 304+ volumes of *Science*, and long library shelves of other journals. I believe my collection is unique. It transcends modern computerized data bases in its very wide time frame and its focus on the anomalous and curious.

Forteanism *see panel p239*

Fortean Society

The original Fortean Society was founded in New York, on 26 January 1931, to honour the work of Charles Fort.

CHARLES FORT'S novelist friend Tiffany Thayer announced the formation of the Fortean Society (FS) on the day of the publication of Fort's third book, *Lo!* in January 1931. It was enthusiastically supported by many leading US writers, artists, publishers and critics, including Ben Hecht, Maynard Shipley, Buckminster Fuller and Vincent Gaddis, and young science-fiction writers such as Edmund Hamilton, Eric Frank Russell and James Blish.

In 1935 – three years after Fort's death – Thayer declared that the FS would publish a magazine called *The Fortean*. In the event, the first issue did not appear until September 1937 and was called the *Fortean Society Magazine*. With its eleventh issue (Winter 1944–45), Thayer again changed its name – to *Doubt*, thought to better encapsulate the essence of Fort's philosophy.

Despite its eclectic and celebrity membership, the FS was dominated by Thayer, who ran it largely as a 'one man show'. His witty and acerbic rants championed cranks and the oddest theories (such as HOLLOW EARTH and SEA SERPENTS), simply because they angered more orthodox opinions. Thayer has been described as a 'contrarian', joyously opposing nearly every form of authoritarianism (from fluoridation of drinking water to the opposition by scientists to reports of FLYING SAUCERS).

Fort himself, famously, refused to be a part of the FS, largely on the grounds that it would attract those crusading against science for the wrong reasons. He was also a shy man and was horrified at the idea of being a figurehead. He wrote to Theodore Dreiser: 'I wouldn't join it, any more than I'd be an Elk.' Dreiser too, felt that Thayer's motives were both opportunistic and personal, and never forgave Thayer for 'seizing' Fort's notes for his personal use.

Nevertheless, *Doubt* became a repository of fortean commentary on the modern world largely because Thayer encouraged members to send in news from all over the world, continuing to record fortean phenomena after Fort's death in 1932. Thayer should also be remembered for rescuing Fort's collections of notes, which he began publishing in their original form. *Doubt* was published with decreasing frequency until the last one appeared in the spring of 1959. Four months later Thayer died and, to all intents, the Fortean Society died with him. However, old members in New York and California continued with their infrequent chapter meetings.

Seven years lapsed between the demise of the Thayer-centric Fortean Society and the formation of the INTERNATIONAL FORTEAN ORGANIZATION (INFO) and the SOCIETY FOR THE INVESTIGATION OF THE UNEXPLAINED (SITU). Both of these played a vital role in encouraging a new generation of young forteans. Today, there are thriving local fortean groups in London, New York, Dublin, Edinburgh and the Isle of Wight, among many other places. Forteans have also colonized the Internet.

Fort's work is continued today in various ways: through magazines such as *FORTEAN TIMES*; and through organizations such as INFO, the Society for Scientific Exploration (SSE), the ASSOCIATION FOR THE SCIENTIFIC STUDY OF ANOMALOUS PHENOMENA (ASSAP) and the nascent Charles Fort Institute, a long-term working party planning a web-based archive. Fort, a SCEPTIC himself, would appreciate the work of such sceptical organizations the COMMITTEE FOR THE SCIENTIFIC INVESTIGATION OF CLAIMS OF THE PARANORMAL (CSICOP).

Fortean Times

A British monthly magazine of news, reviews and esearch on strange phenomena and experiences, inspired by the writings of Charles Fort, published continuously since 1973.

Fortean Times: The Journal of Strange Phenomena (FT) was founded in November 1973 by Bob Rickard. It began life as a 'sporadical' typewritten fanzine called *The News* (after Samuel Butler's *News from Nowhere*), aided by the *I CHING* scholar Steve Moore, cartoonist Hunt Emerson and also by Ion Will. In June 1976, on a suggestion by Paul Willis (one of the founders of the INTERNATIONAL FORTEAN ORGANIZATION), the title was changed to *Fortean Times*.

In 1978, Rickard was joined by Paul Sieveking

Forteanism

The word 'forteanism' is used to describe the philosophy derived by CHARLES FORT from his study of anomalous phenomena. Charles Fort never pretended to be a scientist and would have been the first to agree that 'forteanism' is not science. His was a philosophical critique of, and commentary on, scientific method as practised between 1800 and 1931, and its attitude towards ANOMALIES. Typical targets were the scornful opinions of famous scientists who held that such things as BALL LIGHTNING, FALLS of frogs or METEORITES were folk myths at best – for example, the French chemist Antoine Lavoisier reported in 1772 that 'There are no stones in the sky, therefore stones cannot fall from the sky.' Beyond 1931, the mounting work on quantum physics and the implications of Heisenberg's 'uncertainty principle' changed the nature of the primary sciences and the philosophy of science. Consequently, some of Fort's criticisms of contemporary science and scientists have lost their relevance, but only because they, and some of the anomalies he spotlighted, have now been drawn into the mainstream.

It is still very much the case that, as the US philosopher Thomas Kuhn (1922–96) observed, modern scientific research tends to be heavily politicized and practical, concerned more with 'normalizing' data than paying attention to anomalies. However, in recent years, some open-ended research has begun to reflect a scientific worldview that differs enormously from that to which Fort was reacting. The encyclopedist William R Corliss summarized this sea-change: 'The entire outlook of science [now] is in flux. The words "chaos" and "complexity" are the current buzz words. They betoken the formal recognition by science that nature is frequently unpredictable, complex, nonlinear, and out-of-equilibrium.' In this context, as US sociologist Marcello Truzzi acknowledged in 1979, 'anomalies are viewed not as nuisances but as welcome discoveries that may lead to the expansion of our scientific understanding.' This is what Fort anticipated and what he meant by a more 'inclusive science'.

Many of Fort's ideas have been shown to correspond with concepts that appear within more widely recognized philosophies – eg his 'Dominants' resemble the 'paradigms' of Kuhn and psychologist Carl Jung's 'ARCHETYPES'; his 'extremes' echo the 'Ideals' of PLATO; his 'Continuity' has echoes in TAOISM; and his use of a doctrine of correspondences (as in the association between the 'Local' and the 'Universal') echo aspects of Jewish mysticism. Some forteans believe that he spontaneously discovered and applied such insights during his meditations on the data he had gathered on anomalies.

Criticism of 'forteanism', among both forteans *and* their detractors, is muddied by different interpretations of the word; some use it to mean a credulous opposite to SCEPTICISM, while others argue that it is the very epitome of scepticism. Some forteans have restricted their interpretation of forteanism not to Fort's metaphysical ideas but to the core subjects from which his examples were drawn (see FORTEANA). Other forteans think his importance lies more in his synthesis of a number of new topics: these include UFOS; TELEPORTATION; falls of creatures and objects; the possibility of space travel and ALIEN visitors to Earth; controlled PSYCHICAL abilities; the connection between POLTERGEIST phenomena and human AGENCY; and unexpected associations between seemingly unconnected phenomena.

Among the declared opposition to forteanism is an unfounded prejudice based largely on misunderstanding and bigotry. Because of his unusual subject matter and because initial reviews of *The Book of the Damned* (1919) wrongly labelled Fort 'the arch-enemy of science', many critics of Fort in the field of science and scepticism never bothered to investigate further. In fact Fort wrote with compassion for the very human predicament of hide-bound scientists facing the threat of the new.

Fort saw 'belief' as an all-round hindrance to proper investigation, and especially to the understanding of anomalies. Pre-disposing beliefs were evident in many of the scientific statements (such as Lavoisier's) that he analysed – the stronger the belief, the less it was able to adapt to new or 'more nearly true' knowledge.

His practical advice – 'to substitute acceptance for belief' until better data comes along – is as applicable to scientific investigation as it is to general living.

In all this, Fort sought a middle ground, side-stepping the pressure to adopt one position or another. He can be characterized as an *agnostic* (one who admits to uncertainty of knowledge) and a *zetetic* (one who proceeds by inquiry); only thus could he develop the detachment to collect data with the impartiality he demanded of himself. The charge that Fort made no attempt to validate his sources is also wrong; his books contain many references to his correspondence with witnesses and 'experts' to determine first-hand details and solicit opinions. This practice is deemed necessary by any serious fortean investigator today as a complement to archival work. Despite his alarms at the evils of 'categorizing', Fort, himself, found it necessary to devise a complex card-file system filling dozens of shoeboxes to manage his tens of thousands of notes, arranged under 1,300 headings. Today's forteans have the benefit of computer databases.

Some scientists object to Fort's 'presumption' on two grounds. First, Fort was an 'outsider' daring to comment on issues they feel should be left to scientists. Second, he did not write in the language of science at all; his was a unique style, by turns poetic and grand, full of satire and irony, and he had a tendency to anthropomorphize the forces and events of nature, attributing to them the dynamism of human emotions and motives. 'Maybe I am a pioneer of a new kind of writing,' he once mused, 'that instead of heroes and villains, will have floods and bugs and stars and earthquakes for its characters and motifs.' Some objectors to Fort characterize him as 'believing' his own use of humour and poetic metaphors (eg intergalactic predators or a stationary region above the earth which collects all things that vanish or are whisked away by winds). To Fort, they were simply rhetorical devices; a counterpoint to dogmatic pedagogy. By deliberately deriving absurd examples from the same data as 'official' explanations, he could demonstrate the weakness of some arguments.

It is difficult to encapsulate the essence of forteanism; however, the following, seemingly disparate, elements are all integral to it. Until recently, forteanism has not attracted the scholastic attention received by more central philosophies of science and therefore it has not yet generated a significant school of criticism itself. The growing body of accumulated data on scientific and other anomalies equates to what Kuhn calls 'a pre-scientific morass'; much of it also awaits a thorough scientific deconstruction. Fort's own philosophy – which evolved through his four main books (published 1919–32) – is summarized in a series of statements presented in chapters 1 and 3 of *Book of the Damned*; most of the rest of his work can be considered as the working out of examples.

According to Fort, the attitudes and explanations of an age are shaped by its 'Dominants' (resembling Kuhn's 'paradigms'). In a previous age, Religion and Faith were the Dominants; in our intermediate age, Science and Reason are the emerging Dominants. Ideological conflicts arise as the Old Dominant is replaced with the New. Science, under the Old Dominant, tended to conform to that Dominant, behaving like an institutionalized religion, with much of its discourse couched in semi-religious language. Inevitably, some of its scientists behaved like a priesthood, closing ranks to defend against threats to its authority, especially from a new theory, observation or data that challenged the prevailing dogma and found it wanting. Under this regime anomalies were 'explained away' rather than 'explained' (ie argued from the evidence).

Facts may be 'objective', but they remain open to personal and sociological interpretations. In his metaphysics, all qualities will be complete at their extremes and arbitrary in the intermediate state. For example, a hand, 'thought of only as a hand', can seem beautiful; but found on a battlefield, obviously a part and not a whole, it is not beautiful. Thus, he noted, 'every attempt to achieve beauty is an attempt to give to the local the attribute of the universal.'

Fort characterized his anomalous data as 'the Damned' – damned because it was rejected by scientific orthodoxy, cast out beyond the pale of acceptability and excluded from scientific consideration. In this he again anticipated the opinion of Thomas Kuhn, that progress in science is not always a dignified progression but often a series of vicious skirmishes between the proponents of the new and the defenders of the old. 'Science has done its utmost to prevent whatever science has done,' said Fort. This was inevitable, he suggested, as science, like existence itself, behaved like a living organism; it would resist the new at first, data or ideas would emerge from the conflict which were 'more nearly true' than their predecessors, and science would then absorb them and adapt accordingly.

Fort observed that rigorous experiment – one of the pillars of the 'scientific method' – was, in essence, an attempt to define and separate the phenomenal, to isolate the local from the influence of the rest of the universe. While necessary for the practice of science, it created a situation that was, philosophically, artificial and arbitrary and went contrary to the perceived continuity of phenomena. Fort proposed that all phenomena (objects, emotions, perceptions, qualities, etc) were continuous through their shared co-existence between opposing extremes (hot–cold, positive–negative, up–down, beneficial–harmful, etc). Most perceived phenomena were like 'coral islands in a dark blue sea', apparently separate, yet rooted in 'an underlying oneness' that provided continuity and transition. US mathematician Martin Gardner, in his *Fads and Fallacies in the Name of Science* (1952), summarized Fort's argument:

> Because everything is continuous with everything else, it is impossible to draw a line between truth and fiction. If science tries to accept red things and exclude yellow, then where will it put orange? Similarly, nothing is 'included' by science which does not contain error, nor is there anything 'damned' by science which does not contain some truth.

In terms of 'scientific rhetoric', said Fort, this manifested in the absurdity of 'circular reasoning'. Among his many examples are fossils that are dated by the strata they are found in and strata dated by the fossils found in them (this was before the advent of carbon-dating methods); and Newton's law of motion relating to change in the direction of a moving body, which he summarizes as: 'if something is changed, it is changed as much as it is changed.' Again: 'The

fittest survive … There is no way of determining fitness except in that a thing does survive. [Therefore] Darwinism [says] that survivors survive.' Fort would have agreed with Karl Popper that 'Every scientific statement must remain tentative forever. It may be corroborated, but every corroboration is relative to other statements which are, again, tentative.' As Fort put it, 'There never was an explanation that didn't itself have to be explained.'

In Fort's state of Continuity, phenomenal events occur as nexuses between multiple extremes and are indistinguishable at their merging points. 'All phenomena,' he wrote, 'are approximations … between realness and unrealness.' These 'extremes' – which he also called 'absolutes' – are quite unknowable for any entity whose perceptions and existence lie in the intermediate realm, as do ours; all we can hope to do is to approximate more closely to an extreme. By 'real' Fort meant 'that which does not merge away into something else, and that which is not partly something else'. He declared, 'We are not realists. We are not idealists. We are intermediatists.'

Bob Rickard

and together, with the advent of desk-top publishing, they gradually increased the magazine's quality and circulation. From the start, FT cultivated a world-wide network of 'clipsters' who regularly sent in packets of stories clipped from local newspapers; these would form the basis of summary news reports filling at least a third of each issue, creating a unique 'journal of record' covering more than three decades. Over the years the magazine has featured articles by most of the field's leading writers and researchers.

Rickard retired in 2002, having served 29 years as editor, but remains a regular contributor. FT has published selections of its news reports and a scholarly journal *Fortean Studies* (seven volumes). It also organizes an annual conference (the UnConvention).

The FT editorial team has remained committed to Fort's philosophy of open inquiry, challenging authority and proof, while making the subject matter accessible for the general reader as well as its loyal fortean congregation. Their 'mission statement' declares:

> We are struck by the cultural connotations of our subject matter – its subversiveness, surrealism and iconoclasm – and enjoy experimenting with new ways of presenting it in words, graphics and humour.

Fortune, Dion (1890–1946)

Leading English occultist and author, founder of the Society of the Inner Light. Her books greatly influenced modern witchcraft and neopaganism.

Dion Fortune was born Violet Mary Firth in 1890, in Llandudno, North Wales. In her early twenties, she suffered a nervous breakdown which she attributed to a vindictive psychic attack by a boss who disliked her, and who had knowledge of yogic and hypnotic techniques. This experience sparked off her interest in the workings of the human mind, and she studied both Freudian and Jungian psychology, becoming a lay psychotherapist during World War I. However, she felt neither system adequately addressed the complexities and subtleties of the mind, and she began to study the OCCULT. In 1919, she joined the Alpha and Omega Lodge of the Stella Matutina, an outer order of the HERMETIC ORDER OF THE GOLDEN DAWN, and shortly after that, the Christian Mystic Lodge of the THEOSOPHICAL SOCIETY, of which she soon became president. During this time, she developed her talents as a natural MEDIUM – talents which she claimed she had first demonstrated in her teens.

Under the name Dion Fortune, which was taken from her family motto, *Deo Non Fortuna* ('by God, not luck'), she began to write articles and short stories which explored various aspects of MAGIC and MYSTICISM. Some of her writings were criticized by her fellow Golden Dawn members, who felt that she was betraying the secrets of their order, and she left to found her own order, the Fraternity of the Inner Light (later renamed the Society of the Inner Light), which was originally part of the Golden Dawn, but later separated from it. It was at first based in Glastonbury, but soon afterwards also had headquarters in London, and it quickly became a highly respected initiatory school whose influence continues to be felt in the Western magical tradition. Fortune claimed to be able to operate consciously on the etheric and astral planes, and to project her consciousness at will. She also said she was in direct contact with perfected beings known as ASCENDED MASTERS who guided her work. An adept in ceremonial magic (see MAGIC, CEREMONIAL), she was one of the first occult authors to approach magic from a psychological angle. Her work as a psychotherapist brought her into contact with many people whom she identified as being the victims of PSYCHIC ATTACK. She deduced that hostile psychic energy could emanate from certain people, either deliberately or unwittingly, and that it was possible to protect oneself against such attacks; she published *Psychic Self-Defence* in 1930.

During the 1930s, she wrote several novels containing much allegedly practical occult detail and pagan rituals; the most notable of these were *The Goat-Foot God* (1936), *The Sea Priestess* (1938) and *Moon Magic* (completed after her death, reportedly by Fortune dictating through a medium, and published in 1956). Her best-known non-fiction works are *The Mystical Qabalah* (1936), a discussion of the Western magical tradition and of how the KABBALAH is used by modern students of the Mysteries, and *The Cosmic Doctrine* (first printed privately in 1949), a highly abstract text intended as a summation of her basic teachings on mysticism.

During World War II, Fortune was said to have organized a project called 'The Magical Battle of Britain', in which she and other British magicians aimed to contribute to the war effort on a magical level.

fortune-telling

The foretelling of a person's future by reading their palms, gazing into a crystal ball, or by other supernatural means.

Fortune-telling is the FORETELLING of an individual's future by apparently mystical or supernatural means, and is usually performed on a commercial basis. The most popular methods used by fortune-tellers are ASTROLOGY, TAROT cards, a CRYSTAL BALL or PALMISTRY. The use of cards, crystal balls and palmistry are popularly associated in the West with

Two women visit a Roma fortune-teller in Blackpool in July 1955. (© Hulton-Deutsch Collection/Corbis)

the Roma, who have a long tradition of professional fortune-telling.

The typical topics which a fortune-teller predicts are the subject's future romantic and financial prospects, and whether they will have children. In contemporary Western culture, statistics show that more women than men consult fortune-tellers, and this is reflected in the large number of advertisements for commercial fortune-telling services which appear in magazines whose target readership is predominantly female. Throughout the 1990s, psychics offering consultancies over the telephone became very popular, and many websites on the Internet now offer online fortune-telling. See also DIVINATION.

Foundation for Research on the Nature of Man *see* RHINE RESEARCH CENTER

foundling
An infant child of unknown parents, found and brought up by strangers; foundlings are a frequent theme in mythology and folklore.
The foundling, an infant child abandoned by its parents and then rescued and brought up by others, is a widespread theme in mythology and folklore. In Greek myth, the child is often the illegitimate result of a liaison between a god and a woman or nymph, or the son of a ruler who orders his own child to be killed because a prophecy has been made that the son will grow up to overthrow or kill the father. The child is usually saved because the person sent to dispose of it cannot bring themselves to kill it; instead, they either give it to someone else to bring up, or merely abandon it to be found by humans or animals who then care for the child.

In the Bible, the infant Moses is placed in a basket and abandoned to the River Nile, but is rescued and brought up by Pharaoh's daughter. In Greek myth, the infant Oedipus is left by his father to die of exposure after it is prophesied that he will kill his father and marry his mother, but is instead given to the King and Queen of Corinth and brought up as their own son. Paris, the son of King Priam of Troy, is abandoned and suckled by a she-bear. Pelius and Neleus, the twin sons of Poseidon, are abandoned by their mother and are found and brought up by horse-herders. Romulus, the legendary founder of Rome, is said to have been suckled by a she-wolf and fed by woodpeckers, along with his twin brother Remus. In other mythical traditions, the Babylonian queen Semiramis was, according to legend, abandoned and raised by doves; the Celtic warrior Oisin was suckled by a hind; and the Celtic bard, Taliesin, was put in a leather sack and abandoned to the river by his mother, but was found by a poor fisherman who raised him as his own. In the late medieval French romance of *Valentine and Orson*, infant twin brothers are lost in the forest; Valentine is quickly found and rescued, but Orson is brought up by a she-bear. Even in the 20th century the motif remains popular; Pecos Bill, the legendary cowboy hero of the American Southwest, is said to have been rescued and brought up by coyotes after falling out of a wagon as a baby, while Mowgli in Kipling's *The Jungle Book* is raised by wolves, and Edgar Rice Burroughs' Tarzan by apes.

There are also genuine, well-documented accounts of foundling children being brought up by wild animals, particularly wolves. The most famous case of 'feral children' is that of Kamala and Amala, two sisters who were found to be living with a family of wolves in Midnapore, India, in 1920 by the Rev J A L Singh. Aged about nine and two years at the time of their capture, the girls ran around on all fours, fighting for food with the domestic dogs and going off to hunt for fresh meat whenever they could. Attempts were made to rehabilitate them, but Amala fell ill and died about a year after her capture, and Kamala died at the age of 17.

Fountain of Youth

A legendary spring whose water has the power to restore health and youth or to confer immortality.

The legend of a spring which can restore health and youth, and even give immortality to the drinker, appears in various mythologies. In the Hindu fable of Cyavana, an elderly priest reveals religious secrets to two demigods in exchange for rejuvenation in the Fountain of Youth, and the theme of this miraculous water source is expanded on in a number of ancient Hebrew, Greek and Roman writings. In Celtic folklore, it is said to be situated in the magical otherworld of Tir Na Nog. The Fountain of Youth is also mentioned in the 3rd century in *The Alexander Romance*, in which Alexander the Great is described as crossing the Land of Darkness in search of it. Arabic versions of this work were very popular in Spain during and after the period of Moorish rule, and the Spanish explorers who went to the New World would have been familiar with the legend. When they arrived in the Americas, they heard native stories of a Fountain of Youth which was said to be located in the mythical land of Bimini, somewhere north of present-day Cuba, and these tales also reached Europeans in the Caribbean. Adventurers therefore sought the legendary spring. One Spanish explorer, Juan Ponce de León, was said to have heard tales of the fountain from the natives of Puerto Rico when he conquered the island, and to have gone in search of it. It is unlikely that this was the motive for his explorations, especially as his name was not associated with the legend until after his death, but there is no doubt that whatever he had been looking for, he discovered Florida in 1513, and ever since, some of the most persistent myths associated with the state relate to its being the location of the Fountain of Youth.

four

The fourth whole number, represented by the digit 4; considered significant in numerology.

Four is the fourth whole number, and the first composite number – that is, the first number which can be produced by multiplying two numbers other than itself and 1. In geometry, 4 represents the third dimension, which allows solids to exist, and the simplest geometrical solid, a tetrahedron, has four sides. Thus, 4 is the number of creation, and denotes solid matter in general and the earth in particular, with its four cardinal points of north, south, east and west. There are four seasons, four classical ELEMENTS (earth, air, fire and water) and four aspects of the self (physical, mental, spiritual and emotional). In the minor ARCANA of the TAROT, the fours represent form, structure and order. In the major arcana, 4 is the number associated with the Emperor card. In Hebrew GEMATRIA, 4 corresponds to the Hebrew letter Dalet, and in the KABBALAH, it is the number assigned to the sephirah CHESED. In NUMEROLOGY, it is considered to be a YIN number. It is the numerical value of the letters D, M and V, and a person with 4 in their numerological profile is believed to be serious, cautious, disciplined, reliable and practical; it is the most solid and stable of the numbers. A four personality may also display the more negative traits of dullness, inflexibility and a need to be in control.

In Judaism, 4 is a highly significant number because the Tetragrammaton, the true name of God which is considered so holy that speaking it is forbidden, consists of four letters. In the Chinese culture, 4 is thought to be unlucky because the word 'four' sounds like the Chinese word for 'death'. See also ONE; TWO; THREE; FIVE; SIX; SEVEN; EIGHT; NINE; TEN; ELEVEN; TWELVE.

fox fire *see* WILL-O'-THE-WISP

The Fox Sisters *see panel p245*

Francis of Assisi, St (c.1181–1226)

Italian founder of the Franciscan Order.

St Francis of Assisi was born in Assisi, Umbria, and was baptized Giovanni di Pietro di Bernardone, although he later came to be known as Francesco. The son of a wealthy cloth merchant, he enjoyed drinking and street brawling in the company of other rich young men. However, in 1201 he joined a military expedition against Perugia, and was captured, spending a year as a prisoner of war. During this time, his thoughts turned toward spiritual matters, and after a pilgrimage to Rome in 1205, where he begged at church doors for the poor, he had a mystical experience in which an icon of Christ spoke to him and told him to repair the wayside chapel of St Damian's in Assisi. He then devoted himself to caring for the poor and sick, renounced his father and his patrimony, and restored several ruined churches.

By 1209 he had a brotherhood of eleven, and was granted permission by Pope Innocent III to establish a new religious order which he called the Friars Minor, later to be known as the Franciscans. In 1212, he also founded the order of Franciscan nuns now known as the Poor Clares. In 1224, he was said to have received, while praying, a vision of a fiery angel on a cross, who pierced his hands, feet and chest in imitation of the wounds of Jesus – the first historical account of STIGMATA – and he was canonized by Pope Gregory IX in 1228, two years after his death. Because of the many stories of his love of and compassion towards animals, he was

The Fox Sisters

In 1848, the Fox family were living in a small house in Hydesville, New York. The house already had a reputation for being haunted when they moved there, and in March of that year the family reported hearing strange noises and rapping sounds during the night. It was claimed by their mother that, on the night of 31 March, the two youngest daughters, Margaret (Margaretta, 1836–93) and Kate (Catherine, 1838–92), began communicating with whatever was causing these noises by use of a code – this was apparently started by Kate issuing the challenge 'Mr Splitfoot, do as I do' and clapping her hands. Margaret followed suit and over time, in front of various neighbours, the family proceeded to ask questions, which were correctly answered with rapping noises. The daughters eventually claimed that they had established that the entity was the SPIRIT of a pedlar called Charles B Rosma, who had been murdered and buried in the cellar of the house some years earlier.

The girls were sent away to Rochester. Kate went to stay with her elder sister, Leah, and Margaret was sent to her brother's home – but apparently the noises followed them. Stories of their abilities soon spread and they started to hold public demonstrations, initially at private SÉANCES but then in music halls and theatres. Leah Fox took on the job of managing her two younger sisters in their capacity as public MEDIUMS. They eventually moved in high circles on both sides of the Atlantic, greatly impressing, among others, the scientist William Crookes. While others had claimed to be able to contact the dead, the Fox sisters were the first to claim a direct two-way communication with the 'other side'. Communication with spirits took the world by storm, and the modern SPIRITUALISM movement was born as a direct result.

However, by 1888 alcoholism was taking its toll on both Kate and Margaret, leading them into difficulties in their relationships with their older sister and other members of the spiritualist community. Leah had given up managing her two younger sisters, and embarked on her own career as a medium. While the two sisters were at this low ebb, a reporter offered $1,500 to Margaret and Kate for an exposé of their methods. On the night of 21 October 1888 Margaret performed at the New York Academy of Music, with Kate in the audience. Margaret showed how a simple cracking of the joints of her toes could produce a sound loud enough to be heard throughout the whole theatre. This had been put forward as a possible explanation for the rapping sounds in 1851 but no one had been able to prove it until this admission was made. In 1889, Margaret retracted her confession and returned to the world of the séance. Kate had never stopped performing, although she had been badly affected by her sister's confession. Both Kate and Margaret died within a few years and were buried in paupers' graves.

The Fox sisters apparently demonstrate their powers by causing a table to levitate. From Louis Figuier, *Mystères de la Science* (c.1850). (© Mary Evans Picture Library)

In 1904, the house where it all began was taken down and moved from Hydesville to be reconstructed in Lily Dale, a spiritualist community in New York State. During the move a skeleton was discovered buried in the basement, apparently substantiating the sisters' original claims. However, no record of a missing person named Charles B Rosma has ever been found.

made patron saint of animals as well as of merchants, and in 1980 he was also designated patron saint of ecology. His feast day is 4 October.

Frankenstein

The hero of Mary Shelley's novel, who creates an animate being like a man.

In 1818, the English writer Mary Wollstonecraft Shelley (1797–1851) published her novel *Frankenstein, or the Modern Prometheus*. In this Gothic romance, the eponymous hero is a student of natural philosophy who creates an animate being assembled from parts of corpses and brings it to life by electricity.

The creature, while unnaturally strong, is repulsive to look at and cannot establish any sympathetic contact with human beings. Frankenstein creates a mate for it but destroys the female creature in remorse. The original monster then kills its creator's bride and brings about the death of Frankenstein himself.

A major theme of the book is the arrogance of a human being daring to usurp the place of God in creating life. The reference to Prometheus in the subtitle underlines this by recalling the Greek myth in which Prometheus steals fire from the gods in order to give it to mankind and suffers their eternal punishment for it.

In the 20th century, several films were made based on both Mary Shelley's novel as well as specially written stories featuring the monster. This helped to generate confusion in which the name 'Frankenstein' is often popularly applied to the creature itself.

The details of the particular kind of science that Frankenstein uses to create his monster are never made very clear, but one of the sources of inspiration for the novel was the relatively new science of galvanism. Luigi Galvani (1737–98) was an Italian physiologist who discovered 'animal electricity' after observing convulsive movements produced in dead frogs when they were part of a circuit involving metals. He wrongly believed that the current was produced by the dead creatures' nerves and muscles, but his ideas (possibly through the scientific interests of her husband, the poet Shelley) undoubtedly influenced Mary Shelley's concept of reanimating dead flesh by the application of electric charge.

Mary Shelley would also have been aware of medical experiments on corpses in which electric current would be used to make their limbs twitch or even make their eyes open in a semblance of being restored to life. Her circle, which also included the poet Byron, often debated the existence of a 'spark of life', and whether this could be identified and isolated from its receptacle, the human body.

The frontispiece from Mary Shelley's *Frankenstein, or the Modern Prometheus*. (© Mary Evans Picture Library)

The creation of artificial life was an idea much explored in the 18th century. The French engineer and inventor Jacques de Vaucanson (1709–82) was inspired by medical science to try to construct a 'living anatomy', a type of automaton that would allow the study of anatomy through movement rather than on a corpse. He created a wooden figure of a flute player that contained a mechanism allowing it to 'play' a number of tunes, as well as a duck that could flap its wings, swim, quack and swallow food.

Another of Vaucanson's projects (one which he did not live to carry out) was to build:

> … an automaton's face which would closely imitate the animal processes by its movements: blood circulation, breathing, digestion, the set of muscles, tendons, nerves …

Mary Shelley's novel is often regarded as part of the horror genre, but it is equally possible to place it in the category of science fiction.

Frazer, Sir James George (1854–1941)

Scottish social anthropologist, classicist and folklorist: author of The Golden Bough: A Study in Comparative Religion.

James George Frazer was born in Glasgow in 1854, and studied at the University of Glasgow and Trinity College, Cambridge, where he became a Classics Fellow for the rest of his life. His interest in social anthropology was sparked off by reading E B Tylor's *Primitive Culture* (1871), and anthropology, myth and religion became the main focus of his studies.

All his knowledge of primitive societies was second-hand; Frazer did not travel himself, but sent questionnaires out to missionaries and imperial officials working in primitive cultures all over the world.

Frazer was the first to detail the relations between myths and rituals, and in the first edition of his major work, *The Golden Bough: A Study in Comparative Religion*, published in 1890 in two volumes, he traced the evolution of human behaviour, ancient and primitive myth, magic, religion, ritual and taboo. He argued that throughout human history, a belief in magic was followed by religion, which in turn was followed in the West by science, and that customs and myths from the first stage persisted into the later stages, frequently reinterpreted according to the current mode of thinking. He drew parallels between early Christianity and the symbolic cycle of life, death and rebirth which he saw in the myths of all cultures; later anthropologists criticized his theories, and fieldwork has shown many of them to be invalid, but *The Golden Bough* had a great impact on early 20th-century thinking and influenced not only academics, but artists and writers, most notably T S Eliot, D H Lawrence, W B Yeats and James Joyce, and is still regarded as a rich source of ethnographic and mythological information. It was expanded and republished in twelve volumes in 1911–15, and an abridged single-volume edition was published in 1922. Frazer was knighted in 1914 and continued to teach at Cambridge until 1922, remaining there until he died in 1941.

freak shows

Fairground sideshows and circus acts featuring people and animals with apparently abnormal features or strange abilities, often accompanied by inflated claims and improbable stories.

Records of freak shows date back to at least the 16th century in Europe, but they were at their most popular in the USA from the late 19th to the mid-20th century.

The English poet William Wordsworth (1770–1850) describes a freak show at Bartholomew Fair in London in *The Prelude*:

> All moveables of wonder, from all parts,
> Are here—Albinos, painted Indians, Dwarfs,
> The Horse of knowledge, and the learned Pig,
> The Stone-eater, the man that swallows fire …
> … All out-o'-the-way, far-fetched, perverted things,
> All freaks of nature, all Promethean thoughts
> Of man, his dulness, madness, and their feats
> All jumbled up together, to compose
> A Parliament of Monsters.

Freak shows were often sideshows at travelling fairs or circuses, and among the typical exhibits were the 'bearded lady', exceptionally small or tall individuals, two-headed animals, deformed fetuses, 'double-jointed' people, conjoined twins and people with facial or bodily deformities. Many of the exhibits were simply hoaxes, exploiting public credulity, and some featured people who were simply rather odd-looking and had used make-up and costumes to emphasize their distinctiveness.

Their appeal, especially in an age before television or other forms of mass entertainment, was to provide a glimpse of the strange and outlandish, and often to offer the all-too-human thrill of simultaneous fascination and repulsion.

Exploitation was certainly involved on the part of those who ran the freak shows, with some claiming to 'own' their charges, having paid sums of money for sole control of them; some managers were kinder than others. Some of the people who appeared as exhibits achieved a measure of fame, such as Charles Sherwood Stratton (1838–83), the US showman who, as 'General Tom Thumb', toured with the circus impresario P T Barnum throughout the USA and Europe.

While modern medical science is able to explain the appearance of many of the individuals involved in freak shows, at the time they were often considered to be inexplicable 'wonders'. A large proportion of these people (and animals) were simply suffering from various forms of congenital genetic abnormality, such as being born without limbs, malformation of the skull or other parts of the anatomy or hermaphroditism. Others may have contracted disfiguring diseases such as elephantiasis, which causes excessive growth of skin and connective tissue and was responsible for the 'giant' legs and feet of some individuals.

Joseph Carey Merrick (1862–90), who developed grotesque enlargement of the head and irregular skin and bone growths, became famous in an English freak show as the 'Elephant Man'. He is now thought to have been suffering from the rare Proteus syndrome.

Public attitudes towards freak shows changed during the 20th century – a desire to understand, treat or protect replacing the passive acceptance of the exploitation involved. Most people would now baulk at the use of the term 'freaks' in this context. However, the term 'freak show' continues to be used in circus publicity, usually in a non-exploitative context, to describe shows involving feats of PAIN ENDURANCE, FIRE IMMUNITY, all-over tattooing, extreme body piercing and other such acts.

free energy

Any means of extracting power directly from the environment without the need for fuel by utilizing novel physical principles.

Although many types of power generation, such as solar or wave power, might be called free energy, the term is generally applied to FRINGE SCIENCE inventions. There are several different types, which involve either electrical forces, quantum vacuum fluctuations ('Zero Point Energy') or other less well-accepted physical principles. NIKOLA TESLA, whose involvement in electrical power generation gives him a degree of credibility, is often cited as the source of these inventions. Free energy enthusiasts also tend to be believers in COLD FUSION, ANTIGRAVITY and similar areas.

Free energy is often described as a modern version of PERPETUAL MOTION, and in many cases this is true (see WATER, CAR RUNNING ON). Sometimes free energy projects are outright scams and an attempt to persuade gullible investors to hand over cash; in other instances there seems to be a degree of self-deception by the inventors themselves.

In some cases free energy involves a genuine attempt to harness novel physics. The appearance of the entire universe out of nothing in the Big Bang shows the potential of Zero Point Energy which arises from quantum fluctuations. Unfortunately attempts to harness this for practical purposes are likely to fail; according to Nobel Prize winner Steven Weinberg, the total amount of energy contained in a volume the size of the earth is only equal to a gallon of petrol.

Freedom of Information Acts

Parliamentary acts that allow the public freedom of access to government records. They have become more common in recent years, allowing UFO researchers to obtain previously secret information relating to the military investigation of UFO reports.

The US public knew from the late 1940s that US Air Force intelligence officers collected and studied the details of UFO sightings. The team was known colloquially as 'Project Saucer', but their official title was subject to secrecy, as were their findings.

The amount of information released to the public was also heavily controlled elsewhere; for example, in the UK, such information fell within the scope of the Official Secrets Act. Regular protests were made by UFO researchers but it was only in the wake of the COLORADO UNIVERSITY STUDY in 1969 that these gathered momentum. The general public mood was also changing and a Freedom of Information (FoI) Act became law in the USA in 1976.

Many other countries around the world responded similarly, although it took another three decades for a similar act to be passed in Britain. The passing of these acts caused UFO researchers to swamp government offices with requests for their files, often in hope that these would prove that there had been a GOVERNMENTAL COVER-UP.

In the USA, requests for UFO files outstripped all other types of freedom of information applications. Thousands of documents were released – including those held by US Air Force agencies, intelligence bodies such as the CIA and investigation bureaux like the FBI. Other more secret bodies were also found to possess files on UFOs, notably the National Security Agency, a satellite and electronic monitoring spy team. However, access to countless files was denied on the grounds that this would compromise national security.

A few countries learnt from the American experience and agreed to work with respected UFO researchers in an attempt to reduce the tide of requests. BILL CHALKER in Australia was given access to the air force files and encouraged to publish them. In the UK, many files were placed in the Public Records Office years before the official act that would have forced their release.

These official UFO records all follow much the same pattern. Investigations into UFO sightings were limited and did not always solve cases, and staff opinion was often split. However, the majority view was usually that UFO sightings were misperceptions and offered no hard evidence for an alien presence.

Perhaps the biggest surprise was the extent to which intelligence agencies became involved, especially during the Cold War. In particular, the CIA seemed to fear the strategic use of UFO sightings by enemy powers and even considered ways to deter UFO reporting. Other agencies engaged high-level scientists to consider the evidence in secret.

Many UFO researchers continue to think that there are countless hidden files, possibly in the hands of ultra-secret organizations not subject to legislation on disclosure. There is some possible evidence for that suspicion. In 1969, when the US Air Force closed its official UFO investigation team, the memo presaging

Friday the 13th

The belief in many parts of the Western world that Friday the 13th is the unluckiest day in the calendar is probably the most widespread of all superstitions. Children born on Friday the 13th are said to be unlucky and short-lived, while if a funeral procession passes a person on this day, they are likely to be condemned to death. There are numerous other superstitions relating to the date – for example, it is unlucky to be married on the day or to cut your hair or go out at night. More generally, Friday the 13th is just assumed to be unlucky for almost everything, and believers in the tradition often spend the day at home, rather than risk an expedition. It has been estimated that as many as 8 per cent of Americans actually suffer from a fear of Friday the 13th, technically known as *paraskevidekatriaphobia*.

The superstition is often said to have ancient origins, and a number of theories have been proposed to explain it. The most common comes from the Christian tradition, and combines the separate fears that both Fridays and the number THIRTEEN are unlucky. Friday is the day on which Jesus was crucified, and some theologians have suggested that Adam and Eve ate the forbidden fruit on a Friday. Friday was also considered a bad day to start any new undertaking and, in the medieval Christian tradition, may have been considered unlucky because it was the Muslim Sabbath. Added to this, there were thirteen people at the Last Supper (Jesus and his twelve disciples), and Judas Iscariot is said to have either been the thirteenth to arrive at the feast, or the first leave it, on his way to betray Jesus. However, thirteen was considered unlucky before this by the Romans, for whom twelve was a number of completeness (as, for instance, there being twelve months in a complete year, twelve signs of the ZODIAC, and so on). Thirteen was one beyond this, and thus beyond the pale. Thirteen is also the traditional number of members of a COVEN: sometimes said to be twelve WITCHES and SATAN.

A feminist hypothesis is that the lunar year (considered more 'female' than the usual solar calendar) contains thirteen months, while, throughout Europe, Friday is named after a goddess (Venus in the Latin countries, Freyja or Frigg in the Germanic ones). The idea that Friday the 13th is unlucky is thus considered to be a patriarchal invention.

Another theory relates the belief to the KNIGHTS TEMPLAR, the chivalrous order suppressed by King Philip IV of France from 1307 on charges of heresy and homosexuality – although the true motive was almost certainly to impound the order's wealth. A series of well-coordinated raids was carried out at dawn on Friday, 13 October, resulting in a large number of arrests and eventual executions, including that of the Templars' Grand Master, Jacques de Molay, since when the day has been considered unlucky.

Unfortunately for theories such as these, there appears to be no evidence that Friday the 13th (as a particular combination of day of the week and date of the month) was believed to be unlucky before the end of the 19th century. As late as the 1898 edition of E Cobham Brewer's immense *Dictionary of Phrase & Fable*, there are separate entries for Friday as unlucky and thirteen as unlucky, but nothing about the combination of the two.

Recent research by Nathaniel Lachenmeyer has shown that while the separate superstitions were strong in the 19th century, the combination of the two only really began to affect public consciousness from 1907 onwards. In that year, the Boston financier Thomas W Lawson published his novel *Friday, the Thirteenth*, a mixture of romantic love-story and polemic against the stock market, which cemented the connection between day and date by using the title phrase as both the opening and closing words of the story. Thanks to Lawson's massive self-promotion, the book sold 60,000 copies in its first month and was even filmed in 1916 as a feature-length silent movie. The novel is almost entirely forgotten today, while the film no longer exists, but it appears that Lawson's book is the primary origin of the modern fear of the date. That being the case, the fact that Philip IV moved against the Templars on Friday the 13th, while true, starts to look coincidental, with only retrospective significance.

By the 1930s, Friday the 13th had become the USA's most popular superstition, and has remained strongly associated with the stock market, a notion that would undoubtedly have delighted Lawson. Share-trading tends to drop on Friday the 13th, and if the date occurs in October, the markets can become particularly nervous. The day is also bad for business generally: the Stress Management Center and Phobia Institute in Asheville, North Carolina, estimates that in the USA between 800 and 900 million dollars' worth of business are lost on Friday the 13th because people refuse to travel or go to work.

As a matter of course, there are between one and three occurrences of Friday the 13th every year, and another layer of belief has been added to the original; that is, that years with three occurrences are particularly unlucky. It also turns out that, under the Gregorian calendar in use today, the 13th day of the month is statistically slightly more likely (by a vanishingly small amount) to fall on a Friday.

Sometimes, the superstition is combined with others, such as that it is bad luck to meet a black cat. On Thursday, 12 October 1939 the town of French Lick, Indiana, passed a law, beginning at midnight and running throughout the following day, to the effect that all black cats should be belled so the population could avoid them. Off and on, the law remained in force for the ill-omened Fridays until 1942.

Surprisingly, there is some evidence to suggest that Friday the 13th can actually be unlucky. An article called 'Is Friday the 13th bad for your health?' appeared in the *British Medical Journal* in 1993. This compared traffic volumes and hospital admissions for transport accidents on Friday the 13th with those for the preceding Friday. The results showed that, while the numbers of shoppers weren't significantly different on the two days, there were far fewer vehicles on the road on the 13th than on the 6th. At the same time, a far greater number of people were taken to hospital after traffic accidents on the 13th than on the 6th. Both results can probably be explained by public fears about the 13th: fewer people are prepared to drive on that day because it's considered unlucky, while those who do are probably more nervous than usual, and thus more prone to getting involved in accidents. Such an explanation is supported by recent research

A calendar showing Friday the 13th, commonly believed to be the unluckiest combination of day and date. (© Bettmann/Corbis)

carried out by the psychologist Professor Richard Wiseman, who surveyed 4,000 people and found that people who generally considered themselves unlucky in their daily lives were far more likely to believe in bad-luck superstitions, such as Friday the 13th, than those who thought themselves lucky.

Of course, Friday the 13th is not considered unlucky by everyone. In Greece and the Spanish-speaking world, Tuesday the 13th is the day that brings bad luck. Also, the North American biker community seems to embrace Friday the 13th and its evil connotations, rather than fearing it. Since 1981, motorbike enthusiasts and vendors have gathered every Friday the 13th in Port Dover, Ontario, Canada, and by 2004 the event had grown so large that an estimated 100,000 people attended, with rock bands, a bike show and other attractions.

The date has also been used as a title for the popular series of *Friday the 13th* horror films, although these fall more into the 'slasher' or serial killer genre, rather than concentrating on the reputation of the day concerned. In the story, the central character, Jason Vorhees, usually seen wearing an ice-hockey goalkeeper's mask and carrying a machete, was, however, born on Friday the 13th. The series began in 1980, and Jason has so far slaughtered his way through eleven films, his victims being mostly teenagers and college students.

The main reason for the survival of the superstition into the 21st century is, perhaps, the attention of the mass media, ever hungry for material. Topical newspaper, magazine or television features frequently appear when the 13th day of the month falls on a Friday and, whether they provide examples of apparent bad luck, examine the origin of the belief or take an anti-superstition stance, they continue to keep the idea in the public consciousness.

However, if you still can't be persuaded that the superstition is unfounded, you could try any one of a number of folk remedies for avoiding bad luck on the day – such as standing on your head and eating a piece of gristle …

Steve Moore

this was interesting. It was only released thanks to the Freedom of Information Act, and is dated 20 October 1969. Brigadier General C H Bolender notes that: 'reports of unidentified flying objects which could affect national security' were never part of the publicly disclosed system now being closed. So these cases would 'continue to be handled through the standard Air Force procedures designed for this purpose'.

Freemasonry

The institutions, rites and practices of the freemasons, members of a secret male fraternity.

Freemasonry is the term used to refer to the institutions, rites and practices of the Fraternity of Free and Accepted Masons, widely known as Freemasons, or Masons. The oldest-known branch of this worldwide organization, the Grand Lodge of England, dates back to 1717, with a Continental branch, the Grand Orient de France, being founded in 1728.

The historical origins of Freemasonry are a subject of much speculation and debate, with some claiming that it is directly descended from the KNIGHTS TEMPLAR, and others that it was an offshoot of the ancient mystery religions of the Egyptians and Babylonians (see also EGYPTIAN RITE FREEMASONRY). But the most commonly held view is that it was an institutional outgrowth of the medieval guildsmen and craftsmen called masons, who formed primitive trade unions known as lodges, for their mutual protection. It is widely believed in OCCULT circles that these men, who travelled throughout Europe building the great cathedrals, incorporated ESOTERIC knowledge into the sacred architecture of these cathedrals. As the lodges gradually opened up to admit people from other professions and walks of life, it is said that their purpose changed, and the various grades which workers had originally gone through in learning their craft were replaced by degrees of advancement in esoteric knowledge, eventually resulting in the form of Freemasonry practised today. Modern Freemasonry is sometime referred to as 'speculative' Masonry, because it speculates on the true meanings behind the original symbolism employed by the earlier form, known as 'operative' Masonry.

Whatever its real origins, Freemasonry relies heavily on architectural and geometrical symbolism, with one of its prime symbols being the square and compasses, tools of the stonemason's trade, arranged to form a quadrilateral; the square is often said to represent matter, and the compasses spirit or mind. Sometimes in the space between these, a blazing star or other symbol of light is incorporated to represent truth or knowledge. Alternatively, a letter G may be used to represent God, and/or Geometry, and the Supreme Being, or God, is sometimes referred to in Masonic ritual as the Grand Geometer, or Great Architect of the Universe.

There is no central Masonic authority; instead, there are independent jurisdictions, which normally correspond to a single country, although their territory may be bigger or smaller than this – for example, in North America, each state and province has its own jurisdiction. The ruling authority of the jurisdiction is usually called a Grand Lodge or Grand Orient, and the smaller geographical areas in the jurisdiction each have their own Lodge, which meets in a building known as a temple or Masonic centre, each Lodge being governed by a Worshipful Master or Right Worshipful Master.

Freemasonry upholds the principles of brotherly love, faith and charity, and accepts members from almost every religion, including Christianity, Judaism, Hinduism and Buddhism. Although most branches require that candidates must profess their belief in a Supreme Being, this phrase is often given a very broad interpretation, and a principle of non-dogmatism and tolerance is stressed. Freemasons are taught moral lessons through rituals, and members progress through 'degrees', the three initial ones being Entered Apprentice, Fellow Craft and Master Mason. However, the organization continues to be open only to men.

Freemasonry is often called a secret society, but the level of secrecy about its membership and practices varies widely around the world. However, precise details about the rituals are not made public, and Freemasons have a system of secret modes of recognition – the best known being the secret grip used in handshakes. This secrecy, combined with speculation as to the exact nature and level of commitment that members make to the organization and each other, has led to a great deal of suspicion over the years – particularly the suggestion that it can affect the partiality of members who hold high positions in the public services. Freemasons would counter that the organization is committed to community and charity work and that the meetings are simply a social outlet.

One of the most famous Freemasons in history was Mozart, whose opera *The Magic Flute* makes extensive used of Masonic symbolism. See also SECRET SOCIETIES.

Freemasonry, Egyptian Rite *see*

EGYPTIAN RITE FREEMASONRY

free-response experiments

Experiments in parapsychology in which the subject is not restricted to a limited number of options when responding to a question or describing a 'target'.

Free-response experiments are used in PARA-PSYCHOLOGY or investigations into EXTRASENSORY PERCEPTION. In contrast to FORCED-CHOICE EXPERIMENTS, they do not involve a limited number of choices for the subject.

In their simplest form, free-response experiments might involve someone describing an unknown object in another room, describing what a participant elsewhere has drawn or attempting to guess what another participant is thinking (with suitable checks and controls in place). GANZFELD EXPERIMENTS employ sensory-deprivation techniques to develop these basic themes. Experiments with REMOTE VIEWING also generally take the form of free-response experiments. One type of experiment used involves one participant being sent to a location, the choice of which is effectively unlimited, while another is asked to describe where they are.

Although the statistical analysis of the results of free-response experiments is more difficult, individuals who can consistently describe or name a target with accuracy in such experiments should offer extremely convincing evidence because, if the experiment is well designed, they should have no possible starting point from which they can make an educated guess. However, in reality, the results can often be vague and open to interpretation.

Freud, Sigmund (1856–1939)

Austrian neurologist, founder of psychoanalysis.

Sigmund Freud was an Austrian neurologist who is regarded as the founder of psychoanalysis. One of his major contributions to the science was his theory of the unconscious. While many medical practitioners before Freud considered mental illness to be an inexplicable affliction, Freud was convinced that it must have an identifiable cause. In his search for this he came to the conclusion that beneath the conscious mind there must be a level of unconscious mental activity which influenced our behaviour without our being aware of it.

He divided this unconscious mind into three parts: the id, the ego and the superego. The first of these he described as a mass of primitive energy out of which arose impulses towards the gratification of desires (such as for food or sex), the avoidance of pain and the death wish. While the id was not constrained by logic or sympathy for others, it did impart a vital psychic energy.

Freud saw the ego as the embodiment of the self, which, while fairly rational, was continually at the mercy of the id. The superego was defined as an overriding force acting to inhibit the ego from being too greatly influenced by the primitive impulses of the id.

When it came to matters of the OCCULT, Freud's attitude is probably best described as ambivalent. The occult seems to have held an attraction for him, particularly in the areas of TELEPATHY and the SPIRIT world. At times he seems to have believed in such things and at others dismissed them as being, like organized religion, merely illusory ways of satisfying a primitive need in the human psyche, the products of psychological processes rather than objective realities. He voiced disappointment when his former protégé the Swiss psychiatrist CARL JUNG became deeply interested in the occult, especially ASTROLOGY and the TAROT. However, in personal life he seems to have been rather a superstitious man.

Another of Freud's particular areas of interest was that of 'suppressed memories'. He believed that many forms of neurosis or mental illness were caused by the unconscious suppression of unpleasant memories or sexual desires. By uncovering these, Freud thought that the neuroses they generated would be cured.

At first he sought to unlock these memories using HYPNOSIS, by means of which the patient would be brought into a state of suggestibility in which they would allow suppressed memories to be revealed. He later abandoned hypnosis for the technique of conversational 'free association', often described by contemporaries as the 'talking cure'.

Critics of Freud have asserted that there is little scientific evidence to back up his theories, and that his triple division of the unconscious was no more than arbitrary. His belief in the recovering of suppressed memories has also been attacked as having given rise to the acceptance of 'false memories', retrieved through hypnosis or psychoanalysis, as real, leading in particular to false accusations of sexual abuse in childhood. Many such 'memories' later came to be interpreted as the products of CONFABULATION. See also MEMORIES, REPRESSED; MEMORY, FALSE.

Friday the 13th *see panel p249*

Fringe Science *see panel p253*

frogs *see* FALLS

funerals, phantom *see* PHANTOM FUNERALS

Fringe Science

Fringe science is scientific investigation which takes place outside the scope of orthodox, mainstream science. Its practitioners maintain that they are scientists and that they follow the accepted protocols of good science. Critics maintain that they are deluded or actually fraudulent, that they produce 'bad science' and that their results have no value.

The boundaries between the fringe and the mainstream are not always clear-cut, as there is considerable movement over time. It can also be difficult for non-scientists to distinguish between fringe and mainstream science because some advanced concepts in the mainstream are so outlandish. Quantum physicists are happy to talk about negative energy, objects being in two places at once and how observation affects phenomena, all of which seem just as unreasonable to the layman as PERPETUAL MOTION. While the converting of matter to huge amounts of energy is an accepted fact, as demonstrated by the atomic bomb, extracting FREE ENERGY from thin air is automatically classed as a fringe science topic because it violates the law of conservation of energy.

The philosophy of science – as the rational basis underpinning what can be considered scientific – advanced considerably during the 20th century. One of the key aspects of good science is 'repeatability' which means it can be verified by other researchers. Cases where the EXPERIMENTER EFFECT comes into play and results cannot be replicated will lead to doubts over the original data. A second criterion for good science, put forward by the philosopher Karl Popper, is 'falsifiability', which dictates that a scientific theory must be capable of being disproved. This is a problem for UFOLOGY, for example, as a theory such as 'UFOs come from outer space' cannot be falsified; simply collecting cases where UFOs are of terrestrial origin will never show that all are, so the statement as it stands cannot be considered to constitute a scientific theory.

Even in the hard sciences such as physics, human factors can come into play when determining whether an activity is respectable or fringe. The physicist Max Planck noted that the ingrained resistance to novel ideas was often so great that:

> A new scientific truth does not triumph by convincing its opponents and making them see the light, but rather because its opponents eventually die, and a new generation grows up that is familiar with it.

Many vicious struggles have taken place when fringe scientists have attempted to get their work accepted into the mainstream (see GOLEM SCIENCE). While in medicine there is a thriving 'alternative' culture which is happy to declare itself outside of the realm of orthodox Western medical understanding (see ALTERNATIVE MEDICINE), in science the mainstream reigns supreme. Those outside it have little influence in academia, industry or commerce, and this makes it risky for a scientist to put forward a new theory which is outside the bounds of orthodoxy. Acceptance of a radical new theory means fame, funding and a place in the textbooks, but rejection can mean the loss of position, ridicule and a twilight existence beyond the pale. Some notable cases of exile into the fringe were the COLD FUSION researchers Pons and Fleischmann, and Alton Harp whose theories on QUASARS have been rejected.

Sometimes highly respected scientists can be carried away by enthusiasm and lapse into VOODOO SCIENCE. Perhaps the most famous outcast to the fringe was NIKOLA TESLA, but many other scientists move in this direction later in life, including astronomer Fred Hoyle, whose theory of the cometary origin of new viruses is ridiculed by many.

Occasionally a whole area of what was previously considered science falls into disrepute. PHRENOLOGY and PHYSIOGNOMY, both respectable Victorian techniques for reading character from outward signs, have now been discredited. The racial science of eugenics, which classifies people or races as inferior or superior, is also considered fringe science, its fall accelerated by its association with the Nazis and their brutal 'final solution'. HOLLOW EARTH THEORY WAS once fairly mainstream and attracted some eminent scientists, but with the increase in knowledge about our planet it now has no more credibility than the idea of a flat earth. ASTROLOGY, which in ancient times was ranked alongside astronomy, has been relegated to the role of popular entertainment, having failed to keep up with evolving scientific principles.

There is also some occasional traffic in the other direction, as fringe science enters the mainstream. CHARLES FORT called data 'damned' when it was rejected by scientists because it clashed with their theories (he notably applied this to accounts of FALLS of fish or other curious objects – see FORTEANISM). When such damned data turns up in front of scientists or is recreated in the laboratory it may be reassessed and absorbed into respectable science. Cases of phenomena coming in from the fringe include GIANT WAVES which are now accepted as real, having been captured on satellite radar images. The unexplained whispering sound produced by the AURORA BOREALIS, once said to be the voices of the dead, and the hissing of METEORITES are both now known to be the result of ELECTROPHONIC effects. Some early observers thought that fire-walkers who walked across pits filled with red-hot coals were using some kind of trickery, or that they possessed paranormal powers. Closer investigation has found that it is the predictable, if surprising, consequence of the low thermal conductivity of the coals and falls within the bounds of accepted science.

Although scientists do not know exactly what causes BALL LIGHTNING it is no longer dismissed as a fantasy but is the topic of mainstream research. Previously anyone working in this field would have been considered fringe. Similarly, there is a growing body of scientific evidence for the existence of EARTH LIGHTS associated with EARTHQUAKES, and these are being studied as possible predictors of imminent quakes.

Some fringe science grows up around 'damned' data and strange phenomena. CROP CIRCLES are considered by most to be the product of hoaxers like DOUG AND DAVE, but some CROP WATCHERS have attempted to come up with scientific explanations for these phenomena. This area of study is sometimes called CEREOLOGY. They have suggested that the mysterious patterns may have been created by VORTICES, ball lightning, miniature WHIRLWINDS, PLASMA VORTICES or other previously unknown meteorological effects. The process of explaining an observed unknown phenomenon by invoking a second unknown one is sometimes termed 'ignotum per ignotius' – 'the obscure from the more obscure'. Unless the explanation can be made with reference to known science, it has little likelihood of being accepted. A

philosophical principle called 'Occam's Razor' is often invoked. The basis of this is that unknowns should not be multiplied, and no theory should invent more new phenomena than strictly necessary.

SPONTANEOUS HUMAN COMBUSTION is a fringe topic with a long history (see COUNTESS BANDI OF CASENA). Attempts to explain it in terms of known science, notably the wick effect, have brought more serious scientific scrutiny and it is no longer dismissed out of hand.

Psychology is an area where fringe and mainstream often overlap. The reputation of SIGMUND FREUD has long been falling, and some question whether his work can be considered scientific at all. WILHELM REICH's work took him from orthodox psychoanalysis to the depths of the fringe science, when the Food and Drug Administration declared his apparatus for accumulating psychic 'orgone energy' a fraud and ordered it to be destroyed. More recently there have been doubts over the validity of recovered memories, and whether psychologists may accidentally plant false memories, which have undermined much of the basis of such work (see MEMORIES, RECOVERED; MEMORY, FALSE). HYPNOSIS, once considered a reliable means of extracting information which has been forgotten by the conscious mind, is no longer accepted in courts of law. NEUROLINGUISTIC PROGRAMMING presents itself as being scientific and is popular but it has little recognition among psychologists. Technology for MIND CONTROL, such as the CIA's MKULTRA programme, enjoyed a brief vogue and, although it still has some credibility in Russia, is not now taken seriously in the West.

Some other areas of psychology that would once have been described as fringe science are now making progress towards scientific orthodoxy, partly through the use of tools which were not previously available. Functional magnetic resonance imaging (FMRI) of the brain has been used to locate the physical activity that might be described as corresponding with the SELF, and there has been a steady stream of new discoveries. Observing the physical processes at the heart of phenomena such as SLEEP PARALYSIS and HYPNAGOGIC and HYPNOPOMPIC states is very helpful in developing our understanding of why these states occur and what their effects are. Psychologists are also using similar tools to investigate the PLACEBO EFFECT, and this may help distinguish in future between remedies with a chemical action and those which work purely through suggestion.

Backyard inventors constitute a small but vocal group in fringe science. These are people firmly outside the scientific establishment who believe that they have made important discoveries which have been missed by the mainstream. There are a profusion of such inventors in the realms of perpetual motion, free energy (see also WATER, CARS RUNNING ON) and TIME TRAVEL. Fringe science inventions for space travel include the DEAN DEVICE, EMDRIVE and various ANTIGRAVITY contraptions. Needless to say, they invariably struggle for acceptance in the mainstream, but there are a vast number of books and websites dedicated to their work. Some of these are also linked to conspiracy theories suggesting that their inventions are being deliberately suppressed by powerful interest groups. So far the inventors have failed to rock the foundations of science. However, it would be wrong – indeed unscientific – to assume that this could never happen.

As fringe scientists often point out, some of the most brilliant science of the 20th century came from outside academia – from a young patent clerk called Albert Einstein.

David Hambling

Gaia hypothesis

The theory that the planet earth is a living organism.

The idea of 'Mother Earth' is one that has appeared in the mythology of many cultures throughout the ages and around the world. The ancient Greeks personified the earth as the goddess Gaia (or Gaea) and it is from here that the Gaia hypothesis takes its name.

According to this theory, the whole planet is a living organism which maintains the conditions necessary to support all living things and thereby ensures its own continuing existence. The theory was first set out by the English chemist James Lovelock (1919–) in the 1970s, particularly in his book *Gaia: a new look at life on Earth* (1979). Lovelock perceived the planet as a single complex entity comprising the soil, the oceans and the atmosphere, which regulates itself to achieve a state of homeostasis or stability. It is a system in which energy derived from the sun is used by biological, chemical, geological and physical elements in maintaining a natural balance.

Lovelock compared the earth to a human body, with the atmosphere corresponding to the lungs, the oceans and rivers to the blood, the land to the bones, and the living organisms to the senses. He called the study of the earth from this point of view 'geophysiology'. His theory described the earth as evolving as an organism through the ages. While some exponents of the Gaia theory suggest that the earth, as a living being, consciously makes changes that will be of benefit to itself, Lovelock describes the process as evolutionary and automatic rather than being the result of any form of intention or planning.

The planet acts to recycle matter and energy through various biochemical processes, such as the carbon cycle, the nitrogen cycle and the sulphur cycle, and the agents used to perform this recycling are the earth's living organisms, which consume and excrete, transform and transport material. Humankind is simply one of the types of living organism involved in these processes. Through these processes conditions necessary for life are maintained, such as the composition of the earth's atmosphere and the salinity of its oceans.

According to the Gaia hypothesis, the self-regulating aspect of the earth's existence will take account of the activities of human beings, compensating for negative influences such as destruction of rainforest and pollution. A logical deduction from this is that if mankind threatens to destabilize the earth's balance radically then conditions on earth will evolve to a point where human life is no longer viable and the human race will become extinct just like the dinosaurs or any other lost species.

Scientific opinion remains divided on the validity of the Gaia hypothesis, particularly because it is impossible to subject it to the tests that other scientific theories normally undergo to prove their validity. The majority of scientists accept that the interaction between living organisms and the non-living elements of the earth affect the natural processes that the planet undergoes, especially in terms of climate. In addition, the theory has contributed to thinking on ecology and the idea of the earth as an ecosystem. However, the concept of the planet existing as a single self-sustaining entity remains no more than a metaphor to many.

The idea that life influences planetary processes (ie has a substantial effect on abiotic processes) has become known as the 'weak Gaia hypothesis' (or the 'influential Gaia hypothesis'). This hypothesis is generally supported by scientists today and, in fact, is probably most responsible for stimulating continued research on Gaia. Even the most conservative scientists agree that research on the way in which living organisms interact with non-living processes may yield useful information. Much of our modern-day climate research is based, to some degree, on this idea.

As a result of defining a weak Gaia hypothesis, the original Gaia hypothesis (ie that life controls planetary processes) became known as the 'strong Gaia hypothesis' (or 'optimizing Gaia hypothesis'). Few scientists are willing to support this. See also PLANETARY CONSCIOUSNESS.

Gallipoli
Site of the alleged disappearance of a battalion of the Royal Norfolk Regiment during World War I.

A major but ultimately unsuccessful Allied campaign of World War I was fought on the Gallipoli Peninsula in Turkey. Its aim was to secure passage of the Dardanelles for Allied shipping, aid Russia and possibly even remove Turkey from the war. After a promising start, with amphibious landings of thousands of troops in April 1915, the campaign soon degenerated into the kind of trench warfare and stalemate that characterized the Western Front in Europe.

One of the elements of the British Army sent to Gallipoli was E Company of the 5th Territorial Battalion of the Royal Norfolk Regiment. Like many bodies of soldiers raised to fight in the Great War, this battalion differed from regular army units in being composed exclusively of men of the same occupation or from the same area, in this case all employees on the royal estate at Sandringham. For this reason they were known unofficially as the King's Own Sandringhams.

In their very first engagement, on 12 August 1915, the Sandringhams went forward to attack the Turkish lines. Moving resolutely under artillery and machine-gun fire into a wooded area, they disappeared into the smoke and confusion of battle and were never seen again. Not a single man returned to the Allied lines.

Their families were simply notified that the men were missing in action; not even King George V (1865–1936) himself could find out any more information. Enquiries made through the Red Cross to discover if any of them were in Turkish prisoner-of-war camps drew a blank. It was as if they had vanished from the face of the earth.

The mystery took on a romantic tinge when in 1965 a New Zealand veteran of Gallipoli, supported by a few others, claimed to have witnessed oddly shaped clouds hovering at a low level over the area where the Sandringhams were making their attack. According to this account, the company advanced into one of these clouds and did not re-emerge. The cloud then rose up into the sky. In the popular imagination, the brave Sandringhams had been carried bodily out of the blood and mire of battle and up to heaven. An alternative theory was that the oddly shaped cloud was in fact a UFO, and this was a case of ALIEN ABDUCTION. However, military historians believe that the group became lost and were massacred – while this has not been thoroughly established as fact, it is taken by many to be, although tragic, the most likely explanation.

Ganzfeld experiment
An experiment employing sensory deprivation which is used by parapsychologists to test for ESP abilities, particularly telepathy.

Ganzfeld (from the German for 'whole field' or 'total field') experiments were devised by parapsychologists (see PARAPSYCHOLOGY) during the 1970s. They were developed in response to a theory that PSI signals are around us all of the time but are 'masked' by the constant brain activity and reception of ordinary sensory data that characterizes the normal conscious state.

In the standard version of the experiment, the subject who is to receive information (the 'percipient' or 'receiver') is placed in a room on their own and cut off from external stimuli. Their eyes are covered with half ping-pong balls (upon which red light is shone to give a uniform colour field) and they are played white noise through headphones. Relaxation techniques may also be employed. This is all intended to cut out external and internal distractions, helping the subject to concentrate on accessing a 'target' by PSYCHIC means – this usually involves attempting to receive information transmitted by another subject (the 'agent' or 'sender'), in a similar soundproof room elsewhere. A target is chosen (for example a picture, word or film clip) and the agent attempts to transmit this by means of TELEPATHY. As they do so, the percipient talks about the images that are coming into their head. At the conclusion of the experiment the percipient is presented with the actual target and three other randomly selected alternatives and asked to choose which they think was being transmitted to them.

Several statistical analyses of all known Ganzfeld experiments (a meta-analysis) between 1974 and 1981 showed a success rate of 38 per cent, when 25 per cent would be expected if only chance were at work. However, many sceptics pointed out that there were a number of flaws in the experimental procedures which might have introduced bias. Several refinements were added, the main one being the introduction of the 'auto-Ganzfeld' procedure. The auto-Ganzfeld experiment employs automated

A subject undergoes sensory deprivation in a Ganzfeld experiment, used to test for extrasensory perception.
(© TopFoto/Fortean)

selection of the target, which is then displayed to the sender (as opposed to the sender choosing it themselves). At the end of the experiment the receiver is shown four images and asked to rank on a 40-point scale the correspondence between these and the images they were 'receiving' during the experiment. Auto-Ganzfeld targets are also shown on a screen so they are not handled by the sender, removing the possibility of 'handling clues' (creases or thumbprints on pictures, for example). Increased soundproofing, stricter isolation and a much larger pool of targets were also introduced, and stage magicians were invited to help design the experimental procedure in an attempt to reduce deliberate instances of fraud.

A meta-analysis carried out for experiments between 1983 and 1989 showed a success rate of 34 per cent, still significantly above expectation. However, Ganzfeld experiments remain controversial. The various meta-analyses have been criticized for including data from experiments that were not peer reviewed, or did not involve rigorous enough controls. It has also been argued that deviation from chance (which has already been shown to be partly dependent on experimental procedure) is not, in itself, evidence of psi.

Garabandal *see* MARIAN APPARITIONS

Gardner, Gerald (1884–1964)

British occultist, writer and amateur archaeologist who was the initiator of the dominant tradition within the practice of modern witchcraft.

Gerald Gardner was born near Liverpool, into a wealthy family of Scottish descent that had made its money in the timber trade. Among his claims to a family history of WITCHCRAFT was that the family tree could be traced back to Grissell Gairdner, who was burned as a WITCH in Newburgh in Scotland in 1610. Gardner suffered from asthma as a child and, in an effort to alleviate his condition, he spent much of his young life travelling with his nursemaid in warmer climes on the continent of Europe and in Asia, eventually settling in South-East Asia, where he worked first in the rubber trade and later as a civil servant. While in the Far East, he became interested in the local spiritual practices and ritual weapons – writing what is still an important book on the latter subject, *Keris and Other Malay Weapons*, on his return to England in 1936.

However, it is for his activities following his retirement in 1936 that Gardner is most famous. In the years immediately prior to World War II he lived in Christchurch on the edge of the New Forest, during which time he became involved with a ROSICRUCIAN group known as the Fellowship of Crotona. It was through the fellowship that he came to be introduced to another group of people who claimed to be hereditary witches, practitioners of a form of witchcraft that had apparently been in continuous existence in the New Forest since before the Middle Ages (a similar claim to that made in Charles Godfrey Leland's book *ARADIA, OR THE GOSPEL OF THE WITCHES*). He was initiated into their COVEN in 1939 and it was this association that helped to support his belief (which was shared by a number of other historians and anthropologists at the time, notably Margaret Murray) that there was a surviving tradition of witchcraft which had its roots in ancient pagan religious practices (see PAGANISM). Shortly after the war he was also made an honorary member of the ORDO TEMPLI ORIENTIS by ALEISTER CROWLEY.

It is not clear to what extent each of his various occult connections influenced Gardner's later works. However, in 1949 he published a novel, *High Magic's Aid*, which purportedly contained details of many of the rituals he had learned from the New Forest coven. Following the repeal of the Witchcraft Act in 1951 (see HELEN DUNCAN) Gardner left the New Forest coven to found his own, the rituals of which were originally a mixture of those from his previous coven, his own work and borrowings from Aleister Crowley (among others). In 1953 he initiated Doreen Valiente into his coven, and for a number of years they worked together to produce the texts that formed the basis of what came to be known as the 'Gardnerian tradition'. During this time, Gardner also published two non-fiction books on the subject of witchcraft – *Witchcraft Today* (1954) and *The Meaning of Witchcraft* (1959). In these books, Gardner referred to what he claimed was the ancient religion which underlies neopagan witchcraft variously as 'the Craft' or 'Wica' (which subsequently came to be spelt 'WICCA').

Gardner's influence remains extremely important within modern witchcraft, and he is considered to be the father of NEOPAGANISM. However, many academics would now question the veracity of his claims that there is a direct and continuous link between ancient pagan religious practices and the modern practice of Wicca.

Gate of Horn, the

One of the two gates (the other being the Gate of Ivory) that the god of dreams passed through when visiting a dreamer.

In ancient Greek philosophy, DREAMS were considered important. It was believed that a dream was a visit to the dreamer made by Oneiros, god of dreams and son of Nyx ('night'). However, it was believed that there were two types of dream: those that had significance (whether for the dreamer or others), and those that had no significance. It depended on which of the two Gates of Sleep Oneiros had passed through. Dreams that contained truth came to the dreamer through the Gate of Horn (literally a gate made of horn), and dreams that were delusory came through the Gate of Ivory (a gate made of ivory).

In the *Odyssey* Homer describes Penelope, the long-suffering wife of Odysseus, as asking to have a dream interpreted. As she believes the dream to presage her husband's return, she expresses the hope that it came through the Gate of Horn.

It has been suggested that the origin of this idea hinges on word associations in Greek, in which the word for ivory (*elephas*) resembles a verb (*elephairomai*) which means, essentially, to delude with false hope. Similarly, the Greek word for horn (*keras*) is linked to *karanoo*, meaning 'accomplish'.

Gate of Ivory, the *see* GATE OF HORN, THE

Geburah

In the kabbalah, the sephirah or emanation of God known as Judgement or Severity, which is assigned the number 5; it represents the aspect of God that allows death and suffering in the world.

Geburah, or Gevurah, is the fifth of the ten SEPHIROTH, or Divine emanations, in the KABBALAH. It is called Judgement or Severity, and is the second of the emotive attributes of the sephiroth. It represents the aspect of God which allows death and suffering in the world. Geburah is associated with the ability to make hard decisions, and the power to restrain one's innate urge to bestow goodness on others where the recipient is undeserving. It is the force which measures and assesses the worthiness of creation. It is assigned the number 5. On the kabbalistic TREE OF LIFE, it is positioned directly below BINAH, directly opposite CHESED, with which it has a polarized relationship, and directly above HOD. Chesed and Geburah act together to create an inner balance in the soul's approach to the outside world. Geburah is the second point on the middle triangle on the Tree of Life, the Moral or Ethical Triangle, which it forms with Chesed and TIPHARETH, and it is also the second sphere on the left-hand axis, the Pillar of Severity, to which it gives its name. It is usually given four paths on the Tree of Life, to Binah, Chesed, Tiphareth and Hod. It is associated with the Divine name *Gebor Ilohim*, meaning 'God of Battles', the archangel Khamael, the angelic order of the Seraphim, and the planetary force of Mars. In the TAROT, Geburah corresponds to the four fives, and in the tarot Tree of Life spread, the card in the Geburah position usually represents life's painful realities and difficulties. In some kabbalistic systems the magical image of a mighty warrior in a chariot is attributed to it, and it is represented by various symbols: a pentagon, a five-petalled rose, a sword, a spear, a scourge and a chain. It is often connected with the heart CHAKRA. The word 'Geburah' in kabbalistic GEMATRIA gives the number 216, which is 3×72, the number of its polar opposite, Chesed; each of God's 72 hidden names has three letters, making a total of 216. Geburah is sometimes also referred to as Pachad (Fear) or Din (Justice).

Gef the Talking Mongoose

Bizarre early 20th-century poltergeist case from the Isle of Man.

Possibly the strangest British POLTERGEIST case of the 20th century allegedly occurred between 1932 and 1936 at a farm called Cashen's Gap on the Isle of Man. The farm was occupied by a Mr and Mrs Irving and their teenage daughter Voirrey. What took the case far beyond a conventional poltergeist outbreak was that the family claimed the manifestations to be the work of a talking mongoose named Gef which lived on their farm. Gef was allegedly capable of conducting lengthy conversations with the family on a range of subjects but was rarely seen. The story was investigated by English ghost hunter Harry Price, and a Captain

Uri Geller, the famous self-proclaimed psychic, poses with his Cadillac, which is decorated with over 5,000 pieces of bent cutlery. (© TopFoto/UPP)

MacDonald who attended the farm on behalf of Price heard a strange whistling sound that lasted for 20 seconds and was attributed to Gef. Predictably such an extraordinary story caused a sensation and generated much ridicule in the media of the day. There was little independent evidence from outside the family of the phenomena and a fuzzy photograph supposedly showing Gef failed to convince.

Together with G S Lambert, Price later devoted a remarkably low-key book to the case, *The Haunting of Cashen's Gap* (1936). As well as giving an account of the alleged manifestations, Lambert and Price considered the possibility of conscious and unconscious ventriloquism or mediumship on the part of members of the family, ultimately concluding that the case involved 'a voice and little else'. Most poltergeist researchers have preferred to shut their eyes to the story altogether, an exception being Sacheverell Sitwell who, in his book *Poltergeists* (1940), pointed to parallels with 17th- and 18th-century WITCHCRAFT cases including the DRUMMER OF TEDWORTH. The case was also examined by the US psychoanalyst Nandor Fodor who put a Freudian interpretation on events, spawning even more extraordinary speculation. The most fantastic theory which emerged was that the mongoose was a phallic symbol psychically projected

from the unconscious mind of Voirrey Irving in an attempt to express the sexual feelings that she had stifled in an authoritarian family environment. The Irvings later sold Cashen's Gap and moved away. In 1947, a later owner of Cashen's Gap farm claimed to have shot a real mongoose on the land.

Geller, Uri (1946–)

Probably the most famous self-proclaimed psychic, particularly noted for his 'spoon-bending' performances.
Uri Geller was born in Israel in 1946. In the early 1970s, after military service and an early career as a nightclub entertainer, he achieved great fame throughout the world for his METAL-BENDING skills (usually demonstrated using spoons and forks) which were said to be carried out using only the power of the mind – an example of PSYCHOKINESIS. He offered the explanation that his powers had been given to him by a race of ALIENS when he was five years old – with the result that later, when he was eating a bowl of soup, the spoon he was using mysteriously bent in his hand. A number of television appearances, and some apparently successful demonstrations under controlled conditions, cemented his reputation. The most significant favourable reports came from investigations carried out by Hal Puthoff and Russell

Targ at the Stanford Research Institute in California – but those involved in similar tests at London University expressed the opinion that some of Puthoff and Targ's controls had been too lax.

Geller now claims he makes most of his money by DOWSING to assist a range of companies in prospecting for oil and minerals. He also claims that the FBI, CIA and numerous police forces have used his services at one time or another. Over the years he has written two novels and has produced a range of self-help books and materials to enable people to develop their own PSYCHIC powers. He has also kept himself in the public eye by coming forward on a number of occasions to claim responsibility for well-publicized events – for example, it was apparently his mind that stopped the Great Clock at Westminster (popularly known as 'Big Ben') in 1991; and he ensured that England beat Scotland in a football match in 1996 by making the ball wobble at the critical moment when a penalty was being taken. However, some people have since observed that, if Geller is able to affect football matches in this way, it was rather unfortunate that Exeter City were relegated the season after he became their honorary co-chairman in 2002.

Many people still accept Geller's claims uncritically, whereas others maintain that he is nothing more than a stage magician (see MAGIC, STAGE). The famous sceptic JAMES RANDI (the most prominent member of the COMMITTEE FOR THE SCIENTIFIC INVESTIGATION OF CLAIMS OF THE PARANORMAL) has written several books (for example, *The Truth About Uri Geller*, 1982) which purport to demonstrate how anyone can emulate Geller's feats. Geller has so far declined to take up Randi's much publicized challenge, in which a million dollars is to be paid to anyone who (in accordance with a strict set of rules) can demonstrate a paranormal event.

Geller is not able to perform with 100 per cent success, and has had some spectacular and very public failures. However, in common with many other people who claim PSI abilities, he suggests that such failures are due to the presence of those who doubt his powers (see the BELIEVER EFFECT). Sceptics counter that he is simply unable to perform if the precautions against trickery are too rigorous. Although he still has many followers, his public performances are now primarily limited to occasional appearances on television chat shows and promotional tours for his books.

gematria

A system of replacing letters, usually of the Hebrew alphabet, with a numerical equivalent based on where the letters fall in the alphabet, in order to discover hidden truths and links between words or passages in scripture which have the same numerical value.

Gematria is a system in which letters are replaced with numerical equivalents, based on where each letter falls in the alphabet. This is done in order to calculate the numerical value of words, or even entire phrases or sentences, as it is believed that by doing so hidden truths may be discovered; the basic theory of gematria is that words or passages with the same numerical value share the same qualities and are therefore linked in some way.

The word 'gematria' comes from the Rabbinical Hebrew *gēmatriyā*, from Greek *geōmetriā*, meaning 'geometry', and the practice is also known by the Greek name of *isopsephia*. Although gematria was not originally a Jewish invention, it was the medieval kabbalists (see KABBALAH) who studied this system and fully developed it, and nowadays the term is generally used to refer to a means of interpreting the Torah. The first practitioners of gematria were thought to be the Mesopotamians; according to legend, the Babylonian king Sargon II of the 8th century BC built the perimeter wall of his palace to be exactly 16,283 cubits long, because that was the numerical equivalent of his own name. The ancient Greeks also used gematria, and many Greek temples were said to have been built so that their design reflected the numerical value of the Greek letters which made up the names of the deities to which the temples were dedicated.

The study of gematria in connection with the Hebrew alphabet was first introduced around the 2nd century, when Jewish scholars began to see that connections between words and ideas in the Torah might be determined from the relationships between their numerical values; they believed that since the world was created through God's 'speech', each Hebrew letter had its own divine significance, and thus, the mystical nature of names could be determined, and relationships perceived between them and passages in scripture. They therefore added up the numerical equivalences of words or phrases and interpreted them in terms of other words or phrases with the same numerical value. In this way, they used gematria to provide links between concepts and scripture, on which they could then meditate to gain spiritual insights.

The medieval kabbalists did much to develop the concept of gematria into various complex systems – one kabbalistic tract lists 72 different methods – and it is with the kabbalah that gematria is most commonly associated today. The method of gematria most familiar to modern Jews is the 'absolute value' system. In this, the first ten letters of the Hebrew alphabet are assigned the numbers 1 to 10. The eleventh letter is given the numerical value of 20, the twelfth letter 30, and so on. In the 'ordinal value' system, the first ten letters are given the numbers 1 to 10 as before, but then the numbering continues sequentially, so that the eleventh letter is given the number 11, the twelfth 12, and so on. In a third method, known as the 'reduced value' system, the first nine letters are numbered 1 to 9, but with the tenth letter, the numbering starts again at 1, the eleventh letter is numbered 2, and so on, with the numbering going back to 1 after every ninth letter. The 'integral reduced value' method reduces the total numerical value of the entire word to a single digit; if the word's sum exceeds nine, the integer values of its total are added repeatedly until they produce a single figure, so that any word, however many letters it has, ends up with a numerical equivalence between 1 and 9.

The basic methods described above are collectively called 'revealed gematria', and such methods were occasionally used in the Talmud and have been elaborated on by post-Talmudic commentators. But kabbalistic texts such as THE ZOHAR focus on a highly esoteric branch of gematria, known as 'mystical gematria'. This system recognizes the correspondences between the ten SEPHIROTH and the 22 letters of the Hebrew alphabet, and the 22 paths between the sephiroth on the kabbalistic TREE OF LIFE are each associated with a Hebrew letter. Gematria is also used to determine the power of the names of angels and other spirits for use as WORDS OF POWER in magic, or on TALISMANS, and some modern occultists also apply the system to the TAROT, associating each card in the major ARCANA with a Hebrew letter. See also NUMEROLOGY.

Gemini

In astrology, the third sign of the zodiac, between Taurus and Cancer.

In Western ASTROLOGY, Taurus is the sign of the ZODIAC for those who are born between 21 May and 21 June. The symbol for Gemini is the twins, after the constellation containing the two bright stars Castor and Pollux, and the sign is ruled by Mercury. Geminians are said to be outgoing and inquisitive, although they can also be inconsistent (and 'two-faced'). Gemini is believed to be an air sign, having an affinity with the element AIR.

genie *see* DJINN

genital retraction syndrome *see* PENIS PANIC

geomancy

Divination by the interpretation of shapes formed when a handful of earth is thrown down onto a surface, or the pattern formed by dots or lines drawn at random.

Geomancy, from Greek *gē*, meaning earth, and *manteiā*, meaning divination, is an earth-based form of divination found all over the world. In its simplest form, as practised in Africa, a handful of earth is tossed into the air, and the patterns in which the soil lands are noted and interpreted. Sand, seeds or small pebbles may also be used. But the most popular form is that in which lines or dots are drawn on the ground at random while the diviner thinks of a question, and their configurations, shapes and positions are then read according to a method which is partly intuitive, and partly based on a system similar to the interpretation of the hexagrams in the *I CHING*. This type of geomancy was one of the most popular forms of divination in the Middle Ages. Nowadays, a paper and pen or pencil are more likely to be used than the ground itself, but the principles remain the same. The word geomancy is also often used of the Chinese practice of FENG SHUI, and in the 19th century was erroneously given as a direct translation of this Chinese phrase.

Georgia Wonder

The name given to a number of women from Georgia, USA, during the 19th century who could perform apparent feats of prodigious strength.

Lulu Hurst (1869–1950), from Polk County, Georgia was the original 'Georgia Wonder'. In 1883, aged 14, she showed that by the merest touch of her hand she could stop strong men moving objects such as canes or chairs. The reverse was also true – a strong man attempting to hold a walking stick motionless would be unable to do so when she laid her hand on it. These displays proved extremely popular and Hurst developed a successful vaudeville act that made her one of the most famous women in North America. A number of other women from Georgia also came forward with similar abilities – notably Annie Abbot, the 'Georgia Magnet', who produced feats of IMMOVABILITY and could apparently resist being lifted from the floor.

By 1885 the many imitators had saturated the market and Lulu's career was over. In 1897 she published an autobiography in which she explained that her methods evolved out of an understanding of forces and motion, the location of the centre of gravity in an object and the use of suggestion. These principles continue to be employed in a number of stage magic acts today.

GEPAN

A team of French scientists brought together to become the first, full-time government-funded UFO research unit in the world.

In March 1974 the French Minister of Defence, Robert Galley, acknowledged during an appearance on national radio that UFOs were known to be real, and that the public would be concerned by some of the data in his government's files – an astonishing admission from a major Western power.

On 1 May 1977, a research team was set up at the French Space Agency in Toulouse. It was given the name GEPAN, from *Groupe d'Etude des Phénomène Aérospatiaux Non-identifiés* (Study Group into Unidentified Aerospatial Phenomena). The astronomers Dr Claude Poher and Dr Pierre Guerin were placed in charge, and they were given a government budget to study 'high strangeness' cases – following a strategy at least partly based on the COLORADO UNIVERSITY STUDY, the outcome of which had impressed them.

At first GEPAN was publicly accountable. Its key personnel were allowed to attend UFO conferences to present their findings, and papers produced by them appeared in major UFO journals, including Britain's quaintly named but respected *Flying Saucer Review*. Their reports indicated that GEPAN had a strong structure, which included a team of laboratories on standby to investigate physical evidence, and trained police officers who would make initial case appraisals before picking the best quality reports for investigation.

In 1978 GEPAN investigated 354 cases, and by 1985 it had studied more than 1,600. LIGHTS IN THE SKY made up only a few of these, the selection process ensuring that a much greater percentage were CLOSE ENCOUNTERS. They claimed that one-quarter of the cases they investigated remained unexplained and they also went on to say that they had found that cases were more likely to fall within the unexplained category if they occurred when the clarity of the atmosphere was good. This, they said, supported the existence of a real UFO phenomenon, as opposed to the possibility that all reports were due to misperceptions.

From 1980 GEPAN received increased government funding but was made less accountable. Scientific advisers to President Mitterrand told GEPAN that 'great vigilance' was needed as to what it was allowed to say concerning its discoveries. Its in-depth case histories ceased to be released soon after an impressive case on 9 January 1981, in which a small UFO was reported to have been seen to land on a terraced slope at Trans-en-Provence. A circle had been left on the ground (allegedly by the UFO), and this was subjected to extensive chemical analysis by Michael Bounais at the National Institute for Agronomy Research. The GEPAN report found changes in the chlorophyll content of the plants and Bounais suggested that the most likely cause was a strong electro-magnetic field. GEPAN concluded:

We cannot give any precise or specific interpretation for this remarkable set of results … But we can state that there is nevertheless confirmation from them that a very significant incident took place on this spot.

The organization went through a series of personnel changes and was replaced by the outwardly non-UFO-specific organization SEPRA, *Service d'Expertise des Phénomènes de Rentrées Atmosphériques* ('Atmospheric Re-entry Phenomena Expertise Department') in 1988, which finally closed in 2004. However, the study of the UFO phenomenon, or, more specifically, the study of 'PAN' – *Phénomène Aérospatial Non-identifié* ('Unidentified Aerial Phenomena'), was revived by the French government under the name GEIPAN, *Groupe d'Études et d'Informations sur les Phénomènes Aérospatiaux Non-identifies*, in 2006.

Gévaudan beast

A mysterious canine cryptid to which a number of gruesome murders were attributed in France during the 1760s.

During the 1760s the district of Gévaudan (in Lozère, south-western France) experienced what might be described as a reign of terror – apparently at the hands of a mysterious, rapacious creature dubbed the Gévaudan beast. The beast was blamed for many horrific murders, mostly featuring women and children, in which the victims' throats were savagely torn out. Those few who claimed to have seen this monster described it as a huge black wolf-like creature and, in September 1765, Antoine de Beauterne (the personal gun-carrier of France's King Louis XV) tracked and shot dead an animal fitting the description. Initially, this seemed to put an end to the matter – however, the killings soon recommenced.

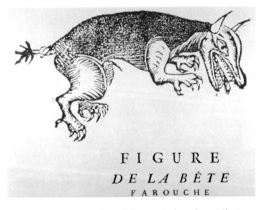

A woodcut illustration of the mysterious beast that terrorized the French district of Gévaudan in the 1760s.
(© TopFoto)

On 19 June 1767, a second giant reddish-black lupine beast was shot at Mount Chauvet – this time by Jean Chastel. Finally the killings (now totalling 100 in all) came to an end. However, the real nature of the Gévaudan beast is still debated. Some researchers have noted that there were rumours that an escaped hyena may have been responsible – indeed, it has been claimed that a stuffed animal, said to be Chastel's creature, which was exhibited for a time at the Muséum d'Histoire Naturelle in Paris, was in fact a striped hyena. Others have proposed that human serial killers played a major part, their heinous crimes concealed behind a smokescreen created by the fear of man-eating wolves. There have even been suggestions that a murderous werewolf (see LYCANTHROPY) was the true culprit. It is unlikely that the real killer will ever be identified.

Ghost Dance

A 19th-century plains and western Native American religious movement.

The Ghost Dance movement arose in the late 1880s at a time when the plains Native Americans were being persecuted by the US government. It took its name from the dance performed by its adherents; a dance which had its roots in a long-standing Native American tradition. This tradition held that the world would come to and end and be reborn, with the dead returning to live side by side with the living. The dance was performed to help this return of the dead.

This tradition evolved, specifically through the teachings of the Paiute holy man Tavibo and his son Wovoka, to a belief that the culture of the white man would come to an end and that this would herald a return to the old ways. The movement encouraged Native Americans to purge themselves of the evil ways of the white man (particularly the drinking of alcohol) and to engage in ceremonial preparation, including dancing the Ghost Dance.

Participants in the dance would purify themselves in a sweat lodge, then paint themselves with red pigment and dress in a sacred white costume adorned with feathers and decorated with pictures representing their visions. Among the Lakota Sioux tribes, it was even believed that this costume would protect them from the bullets of the white man. The dance involved standing in a circle around a tree (or representation of a tree) while looking towards the sun and shuffling in an anticlockwise direction to the accompaniment of chanting. The dance would sometimes last for several days, culminating in the dancers falling to the ground and experiencing visions of the new world to come.

The Ghost Dance movement, although essentially peaceful, instilled a fear of hostility in the white settlers of the plains and prompted a violent reaction from the government. The movement came to an end with the massacre at Wounded Knee in 1890. See also BLACK ELK.

ghost dogs

Spectral manifestations in the form of a dog.

Accounts of ghost dogs take three forms: apparitions of domestic animals; manifestations of symbolic canine creatures; and members of phantom hunting packs in folklore. Among apparitional reports of domestic dogs, one of the best known was the experience of British ghost hunter Andrew Green (1927–2004), who claimed to have seen a black terrier in a locked bedroom in the house of a relative in Sidmouth, Devon, in 1951. A number of previous occupants of the room had also reported seeing a similar dog over the previous twelve months. Green subsequently traced the couple who had previously lived in the property and had owned a much-loved dog which strongly resembled the apparition. When the dog was accidentally killed by a car they had been so traumatized by its loss that they had sold their home and moved away. Such instances raise the question as to whether the apparition arises from the death of the dog itself or represents a visual form created by the minds of human owners. More rarely, ghost dogs have also been reported as a form of CRISIS APPARITION. In 1904 the writer Rider Haggard apparently experienced a waking nightmare of his dog being killed, the same night as his dog was fatally wounded by a train on a Norfolk railway line, prompting extensive correspondence in *The Times* on the topic.

Symbolic ghost dogs have a supernatural significance (eg a portent of death or disaster) and frequently possess a variety of striking visual characteristics which distinguish them from domestic canines. Such dogs are often of immense size with black shaggy coats (see BLACK DOGS) but may also be white, as with the phantom dog reputedly seen at Mistley in Essex before major floods in 1953. However, reliable testimony is lacking for some of the more bizarre visual features recounted in ghost dog traditions such as large, saucer-like eyes, luminous features, discharges of fire and the dog appearing headless. More fantastic still may be the incorporation of human features or elements from other species. An oft-quoted example is the Cambridgeshire tradition of the 'Shug-Monkey', a dog with the face of an ape said to prowl the lanes of the village of West Wratting. First recorded by folklorists in the 1950s, the story is dubious even as folklore, but parallels may be drawn with stories of dog-headed men and the tales of werewolves and LYNCATHROPY that flourished in Europe during medieval times.

The existence of the third category of ghost dogs (see HELLHOUNDS), perhaps fortunately, seems to be confined to folklore – there are virtually no reports outside established tradition.

ghost hunting
Organized investigations of alleged ghostly manifestations.

Although previous centuries saw occasional localized attempts at the investigation of GHOSTS and POLTERGEISTS, the first 'scientific' investigations of HAUNTINGS did not take place until the latter half of the 19th century. Prior to the 1870s, ghost hunting was largely indistinguishable from the efforts of the necromancer (see NECROMANCY) or the spiritualist (see SPIRITUALISM) whereby spirits were summoned to a specific place (for example, the SÉANCE room), rather than being the subject of an active search at a specific location, typically a HAUNTED HOUSE. Greater ease of travel and communication made practical ghost hunting an option for psychic researchers from the end of the 19th century, although many claims of success must be treated with suspicion. From the early 20th century there were increasing efforts to deploy instrumentation at allegedly haunted houses, notably by Harry Price (1881–1948) at BORLEY RECTORY, where teams of observers hoped to record ghostly phenomena. However, such efforts still often degenerated into attempts to contact the dead by way of séances and scientific ghost hunting languished after Price's death.

The growth in the availability and affordability of audio and video recording equipment in the 1970s and the publication in 1973 of a popular guide to ghost hunting by Andrew Green (1927–2004) revived interest in technical approaches to investigating hauntings. However, the results of equipment-based ghost hunting have been disappointing, although some apparent success has been achieved in poltergeist cases (see ROSENHEIM POLTERGEIST). Most investigations yield little more than evidence of natural causes behind the 'ghostly' phenomena, or subjective impressions from participants; some would hold that the study of haunted sites is handicapped by a lack of any common agreement as to the nature of manifestations and whether they occur on an objective or subjective level. A further problem is that virtually all ghost hunting is conducted at an amateur level without any shared consensus as to the approach to be taken and frequently without any critical perspective. Although a minority of ghost hunters seek to conduct research by reference to scientific standards, they are greatly outnumbered by those who either see ghost hunting simply as fun or as an exercise in confirming existing spiritualist beliefs.

ghost lights
Unexplained lights attributed to a supernatural force or presence.

Ghost lights are a cross-cultural paranormal manifestation, with anthropological studies revealing remarkable convergences in respect of their supposed nature and behaviour. Both indigenous and developed societies provide numerous reports of their appearance. Ghost lights are often centred on particular places, particularly rural, undeveloped or wild areas. In many Old and New World traditions ghost lights are the SPIRITS of the dead, while cultures ranging from the

The 'ghost-hunting' kit used by English psychic researcher Harry Price. (© Mary Evans Picture Library)

Guissi of Kenya to the Hispanic population of New Mexico in the USA explain ghost lights as manifestations of WITCHES or non-human spirit entities. Ghost lights may be considered to be good or evil OMENS. They are also said to be a sign of buried treasure in widely separated traditions, ranging from Romania in Eastern Europe to Colombia in South America.

In reports, ghost lights are regularly described as resembling a torch or lantern. They are usually spherical in appearance, but can be other shapes, and may even alter their shape as they are observed. Some may be the size of basketballs and many commentators place them within the wider, general category of UFOs. Ghost lights may react to sound and light and on occasion seem to respond to the presence of observers. In some cases ghost lights may only be seen from certain angles and perspectives, may appear to be highly manoeuvrable and may emit sounds.

In the USA, ghost lights are often known as 'spook lights' and are said to frequent cemeteries and lonely roads. The most celebrated examples are at Marfa, Texas, reported since 1886, and the Hornet Spook Light, near Joplin, Missouri, which was investigated by the University of Michigan in 1942 and US Army Corps of Engineering in 1946. Neither investigation was able to find an explanation. In 1982 ghost hunter Dale Kaczmarek succeeded in photographing the Hornet Spook Light, but its cause remains a mystery.

Notable British examples of ghost lights include the 1904–5 outbreak at Barmouth in Wales, which was linked with a religious revival, and strange luminous forms seen in Norfolk in 1924–5 which were implausibly ascribed to a luminous owl – an avian wonder which has never been reported before or since. The St Bride's Bay area of Wales, the Oban area in Scotland, and in England, Hexworthy on Dartmoor and Castlerigg in Cumbria have generated well-attested examples of anomalous lights over the years. GLASTONBURY TOR in Somerset has also apparently been a long-standing centre of light activity.

Ghost lights may also be accompanied by APPARITIONS, such as that experienced by a doctor at Broadford on the Isle of Skye c.1950, who reported seeing a globe of light followed immediately by a vision of a cloaked woman holding an infant. At Anolaima in Colombia in July 1969 over 20 witnesses saw a strange light come close to a farm, and one witness, 54-year-old Arcesio Bermudez, reported seeing what appeared to be the figure of a small man within the light. Unfortunately, Bermudez died soon afterwards, his sudden decline and sickness being ascribed to his venturing too close to the light. However, stories of such fatalities are very much the exception.

There is little doubt as to the existence of ghost lights in at least some form, with the most convincing evidence coming from a remote valley at HESSDALEN in Norway where anomalous lights have been tracked on scientific instruments and regularly filmed since 1984. A long-standing theory to explain some ghost lights is that they are caused by spontaneous combustion of marsh gas in swampy or low lying areas arising from putrefying organic matter (see WILL-O'-THE-WISP). However, very little scientific work has been done on the chemistry of the processes involved. In the 20th century, the phenomena have been linked with fault lines in the earth's crust (leading to Paul Devereux's EARTH LIGHTS hypothesis) or with anomalous weather (see, for example, BALL LIGHTNING) – although the fact that some reportedly appear to interact with observers remains puzzling.

The term 'ghost lights' can also be used to refer to a seemingly separate person-centred PSYCHIC phenomenon. A number of 19th-century mediums, such as DANIEL DUNGLAS HOME and EUSAPIA PALLADINO, were reportedly able to produce strange lights; the phenomenon has also been associated with SAINTS and MYSTICS as well as with stories of HAUNTED HOUSES and POLTERGEISTS. Unexplained lights have also been reported as a form of death-bed apparition. What connection, if any, such reports have with those of ghost lights seen in the open remains a matter of speculation.

ghost photographs
Photographs which allegedly show images of ghosts.
Photography has often been regarded as more of a hindrance then a help in attempts to prove the existence of ghosts. In the 19th-century heyday of SPIRITUALISM, some of the images published by séance-room photographers were taken up by the enthusiastic as proof of genuine mediumistic talents. However, it is hard today to see how anyone was ever deceived by such crude pictures, including clear cases of 'spirits' that were actually all-too-physical human hoaxers wrapped in linen. Since the 1930s, the emphasis has shifted away from such SPIRIT PHOTOGRAPHY, towards attempts to capture photographs of ghost at haunted locations (particularly HAUNTED HOUSES). With few exceptions, the results have been disappointing, a large number of purported images of ghosts being identified as deliberate hoaxes, accidental double exposures, flaws on the film or simple misperceptions of natural objects. A few cases, such as the famous photograph of the BROWN LADY OF RAYNHAM HALL, and a small number of images collected by the SOCIETY FOR PSYCHICAL RESEARCH, are generally held to be interesting. However, such examples are few and far between.

Since the advent of digital photography in the

1990s the idea that strange images, particularly ORBS, represent evidence for ghosts has become widespread. However, there is ample evidence to show that identical photographic anomalies can be produced simply through the presence of dust particles or moisture droplets in the air; so their appearance in allegedly haunted locations – which are often dusty and damp buildings – is really no mystery at all. Odd effects can also be generated by mundane household electrical equipment, such as the infrared emission of television remote controls.

Nonetheless, some doubt remains about the persistent appearance of fogging and mist effects on a number of photographs taken in haunted houses. Electromagnetic anomalies are often reported at such locations and it is postulated that these may be recorded as blurry images on photographs. An alternative theory, representing something of a halfway house, is the idea that these images represent a signature effect of a haunting presence. If so, they are indicative of the presence of an apparition but do not constitute a picture of the ghost itself.

Certainly, the idea that ghosts may be recorded on film continues to have a strong emotional appeal for many, particularly the recently bereaved. The attraction is obvious since ghost photographs seemingly provide tangible proof for the existence of an AFTERLIFE. In the 21st century, the Society for Psychical Research still receives a regular supply of photographs from puzzled members of the public. It is noticeable that in nearly all such cases neither the photographer, nor any other person nearby, reports seeing anything unusual at the time the picture was taken – the 'ghost' only appears when the film has been developed. Frequently, the interpretation of the photographic anomaly as a ghost appears to be a subjective perception, brought to the image by a viewer who is often hoping for a confirmation of personal beliefs.

Over 140 years after the first claims that images of apparitions had been captured on film, the question of whether photography can ever provide evidence of the existence of ghosts remains unresolved.

ghost rockets
Fast-moving missiles of which there were reportedly almost 1,000 sightings in the skies over Scandinavia during the summer of 1946. They were officially investigated because of the fear that they were secret weapons being tested by the Soviet Union.

The first sighting in the WAVE of so-called 'ghost rockets' came from the north of Finland on 26 February 1946, when a number of reports of unusual meteor activity were made. The sightings spread into Sweden, and in September 1946 an analysis of 996 reports was conducted.

One of the best examples came from a meteorologist in Stockholm who was, by chance, using a telescope when one of the objects flew overhead. He described it as:

> … at least 90 feet long. The body was torpedo-shaped and shining like metal. It had a tapered tail that spewed glowing blue and green smoke and a series of fireballs.

The press applied the term 'ghost rocket' to the phenomenon and printed many reports, until ordered to refrain from doing so by the Allied authorities. In 1944 Germany had tested the first advanced 'V' weapons over Scandinavia, before they were eventually launched against London. Now the fear was that the Soviet Union had captured German scientists and was attempting to develop the V weapons into long-range missiles, particularly because they had taken Peenemunde (the base where the V weapon technology was developed) in the final weeks of World War II.

The only known photograph of a ghost rocket was taken on 9 July 1946 and depicts a teardrop-shaped glow falling almost vertically through the air. It was concluded that this was a bolide, or bright meteor. In the final report the Swedish defence authorities felt that 80 per cent of the sightings could probably be explained in a similar way, and that the wave of sightings had been fuelled by the media speculation.

In 1983 Scandinavian UFO researchers Clas Svahn and Anders Liljegren obtained access to the declassified files on the Swedish study. This showed that the investigation actually ended in December 1946, without reaching any definite conclusion. The report noted that:

> Despite the extensive effort which has been carried out with all available means, there is no actual proof that a test of rocket projectiles has taken place over Sweden.

However, they added that not all reports could be put down to 'celestial phenomena' or 'public imagination', leaving their 'UFO' status open.

Ghosts *see panel p268*

ghosts, animal *see* ANIMAL GHOSTS

ghosts, cyclic *see* CYCLIC GHOSTS

ghosts, re-enactment *see* RE-ENACTMENT GHOSTS

Ghosts

The term 'ghost' has been used popularly for centuries, but defies precise definition. Broadly speaking, it encompasses alleged manifestations believed to arise from a human being or animal, once living and now deceased. Ghosts typically involve the sighting of APPARITIONS, but a range of other phenomena are taken as indications of their presence (see HAUNTINGS). Traditional beliefs regarding ghosts have invariably viewed them as manifestations of SPIRITS or DISCARNATE ENTITIES, which may occur only once or reoccur over a lengthy period of time at a particular location. Attitudes to the reality of ghosts remain ultimately governed by personal belief, such as the question of life after death.

It has been said that every culture in human history has held some form of belief in ghosts and the possibility that the dead can return to the world of the living; this is a cultural constant, drawing its strength in part from continuing human experience. Numerous examples of ghost beliefs are found among indigenous cultures in North and South America, Africa, Asia, Australasia and the Pacific. Such beliefs also seem to have flourished in prehistoric Europe, where bodies might be weighed down with stones or pierced with stakes to prevent spirits from 'walking'. The classical cultures of ancient Greece and Rome held that the ghosts of those who died by violence returned to prowl the battlefield or house where their bones had been deposited, and would continue to do so until they received proper funerary rites. Homer describes Hades as full of shadowy ghosts, crying, gibbering and calling for libations of freshly spilled human blood; and in Virgil's *Aeneid*, those who venture into the underworld – ferried across the river Styx in Charon's boat – find the souls of the dead swarming around them.

Both the Old and New Testaments include direct and indirect mention of spirits and ghosts. The First Book of Samuel includes the story of the witch of Endor, who conjures a spirit for Saul. In the New Testament, when Jesus walks upon the water, the disciples mistake him for a ghost (Matthew 14: 26). St Paul's second letter to the Corinthians lists the ability to identify good and bad spirits as a gift of the Holy Spirit. However, both Judaism and Christianity have historically stood against traditions of divination by spirits (see NECROMANCY). For example, the early Christian writer Tertullian, in condemning TABLE-TURNING, referred to:

> … magicians [who] call ghosts and departed souls from the shades below, and by their infernal charms represent an infinite number of delusions … they perform all this by the assistance of angels and spirits, by which they are to make stools and tables prophesy.

Spiritual interpretations of ghosts have endured into the modern era, with ghost stories tending to reflect the prevailing religious attitudes of their historical period. In the Middle Ages ghosts were often described as REVENANTS, delivering requests and complex messages (particularly regarding the fate of the SOUL of the deceased) to the living. During the 16th and early 17th centuries the meaning and nature of ghosts was the subject of controversy between Catholic and Protestant theologians, the former seeing apparitions as evidence of souls in Purgatory while the latter interpreted them as tricks played by THE DEVIL. However, in later years ghost stories were recounted as a rebuttal of atheist doctrines, or for propaganda purposes – particularly in the case of dramatic AERIAL PHANTOMS.

From an evidential viewpoint, the more interesting accounts appear from around 1650 onwards in the form of direct witness testimony, rather than through a filter of preconceived religious doctrine. From the end of the 17th century, limited steps were taken to try to corroborate the authenticity of the reports of ghostly phenomena, as with Joseph Glanvil's study of the DRUMMER OF TEDWORTH. Even in such early accounts of alleged ghost experiences we can see patterns that persist to this day, particularly in cases of POLTERGEIST disturbance. The rise of SPIRITUALISM in the mid-19th century stimulated a Victorian interest in ghosts, but was largely independent of ghost experiences; spiritualism concentrated on deliberate attempts at communicating with the dead, while ghost experiences tend to involve spontaneous and uninvited appearances, generally lacking any specific message or meaning. Indeed, the last 150 years have shown that ghosts continue to be reported even by people who reject the idea of any post-mortem 'survival'.

The significance of ghosts in many forms of spiritual belief is matched by their popularity as a cultural theme. They are frequently used in literature and drama as symbols of emotional states, as representations of loss and grief occasioned through death or simply as entertaining subject matter. Shakespeare, Jonson and Dickens, to name but a few, all used ghosts as characters. Ghost fiction itself is still a popular genre, although some would say that its heyday was 100 years ago, in the era of M R JAMES. Many writers have been interested in both fictitious and allegedly true stories; fictitious stories are often presented as fact, and elements of 'real-life' reports of ghosts have been woven into fiction. Behind the rich literature of ghosts is an even greater body of popular folklore. Generations of people have expressed a belief in ghosts in many forms – in Britain alone, this body of traditional and popular lore is so enormous that no complete catalogue of it has ever been made (or is probably even worth attempting). Folkloric apparitions tend to be dramatic but are now rarely reported, although popular examples such as a WHITE LADY, BLACK MONK and BLACK DOG do still sometimes occur in modern accounts. Others, such as PHANTOM HITCH-HIKERS, appear to have been adapted from older themes, but are now popular in URBAN LEGENDS. Published collections of 'true' ghost stories have been in vogue since the Victorian era, and it has been estimated that Great Britain has at least 10,000 reputedly haunted sites (see HAUNTED HOUSES).

The earliest 'scientific' attempts at studying ghosts were made in the late 19th century, contemporary with investigations into the phenomena of spiritualism. Scientific investigation in this area does not attempt to discover whether ghosts exist; instead, it starts with the question asked by English psychical researcher G N M Tyrrell in 1942: 'Do people experience apparitions?' The answer is that they undoubtedly do – the issue to be determined is what these experiences represent. It has long been recognized that the brain may generate HALLUCINATIONS as a result of a variety of causes, and that many reports of ghosts are illusory, a misinterpretation of natural phenomena, or the result of imagination, wishful thinking or hoaxes.

One of the difficulties of studying ghosts is the fact that they are not seen by everyone, and even when they are seen it is usually only by one person at a time (although a number of multi-witness cases do exist). Such experiences are usually fleeting and, as with DREAMS, are not capable of independent corroboration. As a result, researchers have only 'ghost experiences' rather than actual ghosts to study, and the testimony is vulnerable to the usual human fallibilities. This aspect alone has provided sufficient excuse for most psychologists and scientists to ignore the entire area. With a few recent exceptions, such as the 2003 mass observation study in EDINBURGH'S VAULTS, the study of ghost experiences has remained a field for psychical researchers and parapsychologists (see PARAPSYCHOLOGY).

Most psychical researchers are prepared to entertain the possibility that ghosts form part of a wider category of personal PSI experiences. Accordingly, ghosts now take their place alongside EXTRASENSORY PERCEPTION, PSYCHOKINESIS or PRECOGNITION, TELEPATHY and a range of other phenomena occurring outside laboratory and experimental conditions. Certainly, much of the material gathered by psychical researchers suggests that the simple and direct interpretation of ghosts as manifestations of spirits of the deceased is outmoded. Studies conducted by the SOCIETY FOR PSYCHICAL RESEARCH, including *Phantasms of the Living* (1886) and its major *Census of Hallucinations* (1894), indicated that GHOSTS OF THE LIVING might be encountered more frequently than those of the dead. A substantial number of apparitions recorded in these studies related to appearances of individuals at the moment of death or trauma; these CRISIS APPARITIONS gave rise to speculation that telepathy might be a factor.

The results of GHOST HUNTING efforts over the years have generally been inconclusive, and a number of investigations have been blighted with controversy, particularly that at BORLEY RECTORY. A further handicap to such research is that there are no common protocols as to how investigations should be conducted, or even agreement on the nature of the phenomena being sought and to what extent (if at all) they are independent of the human brain. Attempts at photographing ghosts have been disappointing (see GHOST PHOTOGRAPHY), suggesting that they are largely a hallucinatory phenomenon, although some success has been claimed in recording poltergeist manifestations such as the ROSENHEIM POLTERGEIST. Success has also been claimed in experiments in creating ghosts (see the PHILIP EXPERIMENT), though there have been few attempts at replication.

No single theory appears to adequately explain all aspects of reported ghost phenomena. After centuries of belief and more than a hundred years of scientific study, ghosts still remain a mystery – further progress is only likely to occur when the intricacies of human perception, consciousness and the operation of the brain are better understood.

Alan Murdie

ghosts, theatre *see* THEATRE GHOSTS

ghost ships

Ships and sailing craft that have taken spectral form.
Ghostly boats and ships are known in the lore of many seafaring societies, ranging from paddle-propelled canoes in tribal cultures to apparitions of much larger vessels in European societies. A number of mythologies feature phantom ships as the means by which souls of the dead are conveyed to the AFTERLIFE. Legends of phantom ships occur in the folklore of Great Britain (particularly around the Cornish coast) and many other parts of Europe, including France (particularly Brittany), Norway, Denmark, Germany and Iceland. Ghost ships have also proved a popular theme in poetry, such as Coleridge's 'The Rime of the Ancient Mariner'.

A spectre ship was said to haunt Cap d'Espoir in the Gulf of St Lawrence, off Canada. It was supposedly an English flagship wrecked in the reign of Queen Anne. Sightings of the ghost ship were described by the Rev Thistleton Dyer in *The Ghost World* (1893):

> … crowded with soldiers, lights are seen, and on the bowsprit stands an officer, pointing to the shore with one hand, while a woman is on the other … [The] lights suddenly go out, a scream is heard, and the ill-fated vessel sinks.

But by the time it was described in print there had been no reported sightings for many years.

In February 1998 watchers hoping to see the ghost ship *The Lady Lovibond* near Deal, Kent, were disappointed when the vessel failed to materialize. Supposedly wrecked on the Goodwin Sands on 13 February 1748, the ship was said to appear at 50-year intervals, with sightings being claimed in 1898 and 1948. However, subsequent research failed to reveal any official record of a ship called *The Lady Lovibond*, let alone ghostly re-appearances every 50 years.

One of the few plausible sightings of a ghostly vessel was made off Cape Town in 1923, and recorded by Sir Ernest Bennett in his classic collection *Apparitions and Haunted Houses* (1938). The witnesses were four members of the crew of the SS *Barrabool*, which was en route between Australia and London. Late one night they saw a luminous but apparently derelict ship. The vessel was estimated as being around 3–5 kilometres (2–3 miles) away and was spotted through a telescope and binoculars. Travelling on a course towards the *Barrabool*, it vanished when it was less than a kilometre away. Sir Ernest Bennett received two first-hand accounts of the sighting and noted that 'many legends were current of a phantom ship in these waters', a reference to the legend of the *FLYING DUTCHMAN*.

Although in vogue in the 19th century, stories of ghost or phantom ships seem to have undergone a dramatic decline following the development of steam- and oil-powered ocean-going vessels. Although oceans are now busier than ever and vessels continue to be lost, no cases of modern ships returning as ghosts are known.

Ghosts of the Broads

Tongue-in-cheek book about ghosts allegedly haunting the waterways of Norfolk and Suffolk
In 1931, Harley Street doctor and yachting enthusiast Charles Sampson (1881–1941) penned a short book called *Ghosts of the Broads*. Nearly all of the stories featured in the book purported to be examples of CYCLIC GHOSTS manifesting on certain days and nights of the year on the waterways and lakes that make up the Norfolk and Suffolk broads. Far removed from the shadowy forms and footsteps familiar in modern ghost stories, the apparitions were often highly dramatic and involved in wholesale re-enactments of scenes from the past, including transformations of entire landscapes. Showing a predilection for phantom skeletons, ships and manifestations of the DEVIL, many of the apparitions had been supposedly witnessed by people of authority and eminence and further documented in a variety of sources. Sampson also claimed to have personally encountered a number of the ghosts by either accident or design.

Despite a sardonic style and the highly improbable nature of many of the ghosts, Sampson's stories were often accepted as genuine accounts by gullible holidaymakers and some ghost-book authors in later years. Reprinted with staged photographs in 1973, *Ghosts of the Broads* went through a number of editions in the next 15 years, ensuring an even wider circulation of the tales. Research undertaken by Mike Burgess of Lowestoft in 1982 for the magazine *Lantern* revealed that none of the alleged witnesses ever existed. Furthermore, with a couple of possible exceptions there was not even a folkloric basis for any of the stories, since many of Sampson's source materials were pure invention too.

ghosts of the living

'Ghosts' which appear to be of living persons rather than the deceased.
One of the conclusions drawn from the *Census of Hallucinations* conducted by the SOCIETY FOR PSYCHICAL RESEARCH in 1894 (see APPARITIONS) was that many reported ghosts were actually those of living people, rather than the deceased. Numerous examples can be found in psychic literature. In 1922, Lady Troubridge reported seeing the ghost of a living acquaintance she was due to meet later the

same day, and the apparitional form of Anglican envoy Terry Waite was reported by a visitor to Canterbury Cathedral in 1987, at the time he was being held as a hostage in Lebanon. One British ghost researcher, Andrew Green (1927–2004), considered that as many as 40 per cent of reported apparitions represented ghosts of the living. Ghosts of the living occur in reports of CRISIS APPARITIONS, but in many instances appear only to represent the last moments of that person's life, being seen close to the time of their death.

Sceptics would claim that reports of ghosts of the living simply represent misperceptions on the part of the observer. See also BILOCATION; DOPPELGÄNGER.

Ghostwatch

Controversial BBC television drama that took the form of a 'live' broadcast. It was aired on 31 October 1992 and involved an investigation of a family tormented by a poltergeist. It was inspired by the case of the Enfield poltergeist.

Broadcast on HALLOWE'EN 1992, the BBC drama *Ghostwatch* took the form of a 'live' televised investigation into a haunted house in north London. The play featured well-known BBC presenters appearing as themselves, seemingly reporting in real time from the haunted house and linking up to veteran chat-show host Michael Parkinson in a broadcasting studio. In reality, the programme was pre-recorded and all participants were following a fictional script. Punctuated with apparently real telephone calls from concerned viewers, the play culminated in the eruption of ghostly forces, firstly within the house and then spreading to devastate the television studio. *Ghostwatch* ended with Parkinson grunting incoherently at the camera, supposedly possessed by an entity from the house.

While many members of the audience realized that they were watching a drama, others were convinced that it was real. The BBC phone lines were jammed by angry viewers claiming that they and their children had been truly frightened by the 'irresponsible' programme. Headlines in British newspapers on the following day included 'TV Spoof Spooks Viewers' (*Sunday Mirror*) and 'Parky Panned for Halloween Fright' (*News of the World*). On 8 November the *Mail on Sunday* claimed that the programme had caused the suicide of a young man (although the programme was not mentioned by the coroner). The BBC immediately tried to distance itself from the programme.

It has been noted that the POLTERGEIST case in the programme bears many similarities to that of the ENFIELD POLTERGEIST.

giant octopus

There is controversial physical evidence that may support the prospect that colossal octopuses far bigger than any recognized by science do exist.

On 30 November 1896, the remains of a huge sea creature, with an estimated weight of 5–7 tonnes, were discovered on a beach at St Augustine, Florida. From the description (including photos that seemed to show the stumps of five huge tentacles and one detached tentacle) and samples of its tissues sent to him shortly afterwards, the marine biologist Addison E Verrill of Yale University identified the creature as an immense octopus, and estimated that its tentacles had probably measured up to 9 metres (29.5 feet) in length. If true, this meant that they had been more than three times as long as those of the world's largest known octopus.

Verrill believed the St Augustine creature represented a hitherto undiscovered species, which he duly named *Octopus giganteus*. However, many other scientists were reluctant to believe that a species of octopus of such enormous size could exist unknown to science. Eventually, even Verrill changed his mind, stating that he had been mistaken and that the carcase was most probably that of a sperm whale (tentacle stumps and detached tentacle notwithstanding).

Some tissue samples from the creature's remains were preserved and retained in the Smithsonian Institution, but otherwise this strange episode was forgotten for many years – until, in 1963, the samples were analysed histologically by Dr Joseph Gennaro, a Florida University biologist. He concluded that they were definitely not from any type of whale, and that their microscopical structure most closely compared with the structure of octopus tissue.

In 1986 Professor Roy Mackal, a Chicago University biochemist, undertook amino acid analyses on sample tissues from the St Augustine beast. He suggested that the samples' chemical content differed very noticeably from that of whales, and even that of squids. Mackal shares Gennaro's opinion that the beast was truly a giant octopus and that Verrill's initial identification had been correct after all.

Conversely, electron microscope and biochemical studies conducted in 1994 by a Maryland University team claimed that the chemical composition of the samples' collagen (a principal constituent of connective tissue) was apparently mammalian, thereby ruling out an octopus identity and supporting that of a sperm whale.

However, as Gennaro subsequently pointed out, the samples have been stored in an unidentified preservative fluid for so long that it is likely they have become too contaminated and distorted for any conclusive determination of their originator's

The remains discovered on a Florida beach in 1896, said to be those of a giant octopus. (© TopFoto)

taxonomic identity to be possible. In contrast, numerous eyewitness accounts of enormous octopuses, notably from waters off the Bahamas, Bermuda and Kiribati, indicate that such creatures may exist.

giants
Mythical human beings of huge size.
The folklore of most cultures around the world contains references to mythical giant human beings.

In Greek mythology they were considered to be the sons of Gaia (the earth-goddess) and Uranus (the sky-god), and were so strong that only a god could kill one of them. They were said to have waged a war against the Olympian gods (the gigantomachy) but on being defeated were buried beneath Mount Etna. The Cyclops were a race of one-eyed giants, one of whom, according to Homer, fell foul of Odysseus, illustrating a common quality often ascribed to giants: that of being rather dim-witted.

The existence of large-scale prehistoric constructions all over the world, such as STONEHENGE or the 'Cyclopean' masonry of ancient Greece, gave rise to the common idea that they must have been built by giants. Similarly, giants are traditionally given credit for constructing natural formations like the volcanic Giant's Causeway in Northern Ireland.

In many cases this type of belief reflects the widespread idea that humankind has undergone a process of degeneration from prodigious ancestors.

The Bible, for example, includes a reference to the mighty predecessors of ordinary men:

> There were giants in the earth in those days.
> (Genesis 6:4)

Another biblical reference is to Goliath, the champion of the Philistines, 'whose height was six cubits and a span' (approximately 3.4 metres or 11 feet). This daunting and seemingly invincible enemy is, of course, killed by David with the help of the Lord and a slingshot.

Perhaps the most famous giants in British mythology are Gog and Magog, the last two survivors of a giant race said to have been defeated by the legendary King Brutus. They were taken prisoner and made to work as porters, and their images were often commemorated in buildings, represented as massive figures bearing the weight of great lintels on their shoulders.

Giants also feature in folk tales, such as 'Jack and the Beanstalk' and 'Jack the Giant-killer', and one was immortalized by the Irish writer Oscar Wilde (1854–1900) in his children's fairy story 'The Selfish Giant' (1888).

Do giants exist in reality? Throughout the ages there have been reports of taller-than-average human beings, usually men, but substantiating such claims has always been difficult. However, there are some giants whose existence can be proven. Among these is Charles O'Brien, or Byrne, (1761–83), known as the Irish Giant, whose height was 2.5 metres (8 feet 4 inches) and whose skeleton is preserved in the Royal College of Surgeons in London.

In the USA, Robert Pershing Wadlow (1918–40) of Illinois topped 1.8 metres (6 feet) by the age of 10, and eventually grew to a height of 2.7 metres (8 feet 11 inches), making him the world's tallest recorded person, a record still unsurpassed.

The woman documented as the world's tallest was Zeng Jinlian, of China (1964–82), who measured almost 2.5 metres (8 feet 2 inches).

In many cases of modern giantism it is known that the condition is caused by the excessive production of growth hormone by an overactive pituitary gland. It is possible to treat this problem medically, but basketball teams might be denied many a star player if this remedy were universally applied.

giant squid

Former cryptid thought to be the inspiration for the fabled kraken.

For centuries, sailors reported encounters with a terrifying tentacled sea monster known as the kraken. It was said to attack their ships, wrapping its suckered tentacles around hapless seamen and hauling them to their deaths in the waters below. It was said that before it attacked it could be mistaken for a floating island. Not surprisingly, zoologists denounced such lurid tales and the kraken itself as sheer fantasy – until some remains from a specimen remarkably similar to this supposedly non-existent monster were washed ashore near Albaek, Denmark, in 1853. These were formally documented two years later by Danish naturalist Japetus Streenstrup – a hitherto-undescribed, gigantic species of squid finally gained full scientific recognition. Since then, many dead or dying specimens of this species, the giant squid *Architeuthis dux*, have been recorded, including a number that were subsequently rescued, examined and preserved, but the biggest-ever specimen remains a truly immense 2-tonne individual stranded in Newfoundland's Thimble Tickle Bay on 2 November 1878. From tail to beak, it measured 6.1 metres (20 feet), and the longest of its ten tentacles measured 10.7 metres (35 feet), yielding a total length of 16.8 metres (55 feet). It is possible that even bigger specimens of the giant squid still await discovery.

Yet although a giant squid was no longer a CRYPTID, for well over a century afterwards it nonetheless remained uniquely elusive, inasmuch as no living specimen was captured or even filmed in its natural habitat. However, in 2002, marine biologist Dr Steve O'Shea announced that a team of scientific researchers led by him had recently captured seven juvenile giant squids off the coast of New Zealand. Far from being the enormous creatures that giant squids become as they mature, these youngsters were only 9–13 millimetres (around 0.5 inches) long, but they were genuine giant squids, and were filmed in captivity. Sadly, they died not long after having been captured. Two and a half years later, however, another giant squid milestone took place with the first-ever filming of a live, healthy adult giant squid. It measured 8 metres (26 feet) long, and was discovered off Japan's Ogasawara Islands.

While it is not thought possible that a giant squid could wreck a ship or drown a sailor, it is now generally believed that genuine sightings of this creature were the inspiration for the kraken fables of the past. See also SEA SERPENTS.

giant waves

Sailors have reported encounters with giant waves since ancient times. These were originally dismissed as tall stories, but recent satellite studies have confirmed that the waves are real.

It is extremely difficult to estimate the size of waves, and in rough seas waves often appear bigger than their actual size. A Victorian scientist calculated that any wave greater than 18 metres (60 feet) high would collapse under its own weight, and it was generally thought that the giant waves described by sailors could not be real. Tsunamis or tidal waves which are caused by earthquakes are no more than a few feet high in deep water, only reaching larger size as they approach land. The giant waves that the Victorians dismissed were clearly in another category entirely.

Some instances of giant waves were recorded by reliable observers, and meteorologists were forced to reconsider whether some of the reports were accurate. In 1861 the bell of the Bishop Lighthouse in the Scilly Isles was broken by a wave which reached more than 30 metres (100 feet) above sea level, and a wave of 34 metres (112 feet) was measured from the USS *Ramapo* in 1934.

Giant waves were then considered to be freak occurrences that would only come about once in a thousand years or more at any given spot. However, a detailed satellite survey carried out by the EU-funded MaxWave programme which started in 2000 found this was not the case. In 30,000 images the researchers found ten waves with a height in excess of 24 metres (80 feet), making them far more common than anyone had previously thought.

Further scientific work modelling the waves revealed that they can be created when smaller waves combine to form a larger one. Research continues on identifying the geographical areas where these combinations are likely to occur and the weather conditions that produce them.

Giant waves are now believed to have sunk some 22 supercarriers – ships more than 200 metres (650 feet) long – between 1969 and 1994. They are no longer regarded as mythical but are treated as a real threat to shipping.

Gimlin, Bob *see* BIGFOOT

Glastonbury Tor

A teardrop-shaped hill situated at Glastonbury in Somerset, England, which has for thousands of years been regarded as a place of great magical power; it is associated both with the legend of King Arthur and with Gwyn ap Nudd, King of the Fairies, and is identified with the mystical Isle of Avalon.

Glastonbury Tor has for thousands of years been regarded as a place of great magical power. Situated at Glastonbury in Somerset, the Tor (a local word of Celtic origin, meaning 'conical hill') is strikingly located in the middle of a plain called the Summerland Meadows, which is recovered fenland. Neolithic flint tools have been found on the site, and the remains of a lake village show that there was a Celtic settlement there some time between 300 BC and 200 BC, while Roman remains and earthworks provide evidence of later occupation. Stones from a 5th-century building, thought to have been a monks' retreat or a fort, were used to build the 12th-century Church of St Michael on the Tor; in 1275 this church was demolished by an earthquake, and although it was rebuilt, all that now remains of it is its tower, which has been restored in recent times and is the only standing architectural feature of the Tor. The church's stones were then used to build an abbey on its site in the 1360s, but this, too, was destroyed, as part of the Dissolution of the Monasteries in 1539, when the last abbot of Glastonbury was hanged there.

The Tor was once known by the Celtic name of *Ynis Witrin*, or 'Isle of Glass'; it is thought that thousands of years ago the plain was flooded, and the hill was one of only a few islands left unsubmerged, remaining for centuries afterwards an islet which became a peninsula at low tide. The Tor's slopes appear to be fairly regularly terraced, and some believe their formation to be the remains of an ancient, possibly Neolithic, sacred spiral maze or labyrinth – a ceremonial way dedicated to THE GODDESS. Indeed, it has been suggested that the Tor itself is a representation of the Goddess's body.

Glastonbury Tor has, for centuries, been the focus of legends and folklore which all point to its being a site at which the veil between this

Glastonbury Tor in Somerset, England, long held to be a place of great magic and mystery. (© TopFoto/Fortean)

world and the next is thin. The Tor has long been associated with Gwyn ap Nudd, first Lord of the Underworld and King of the Fairies, and is widely believed to be the entrance to Avalon or Annwn, the land of the FAIRIES. It is also said to have been one of the strongholds of the legendary Celtic hero, KING ARTHUR, and on Christmas Eve, Arthur's ghost is believed to lead a spectral procession of knights along a ley (see LEYS) which links Cadbury to Glastonbury. According to one story, the young Arthur visited Avalon and was given a cauldron of rebirth and power; after being mortally wounded, he was taken to the Isle in a sacred boat, and he is rumoured to be buried on the site of the abbey, where he awaits the time when he will rise again as 'the Once and Future King' to aid Britain in its time of greatest need.

The Tor is also reputed to be the hiding place chosen by JOSEPH OF ARIMATHEA for the HOLY GRAIL, which he is said to have buried near the Chalice Well, a natural spring at the Tor's foot. Another claim relates to the GLASTONBURY ZODIAC, a giant astrological zodiac believed by some to have been carved into the land around Glastonbury. According to legend, the Tor once boasted a stone circle like that at STONEHENGE, and recent archaeological work has led to the discovery of foundations of what appears to be an ancient stone circle temple. The Tor is also believed to be a highly powerful energy centre and the converging point of a number of geomagnetic power lines; there have been many reports of sightings of strange balls of light in the area and, in recent years, of UFOs.

Glastonbury Zodiac

A vast physical representation of the zodiac in the countryside around Glastonbury.

In 1927 the English artist Katherine Maltwood (1878–1961) claimed to have discovered that a system of landmarks and prehistoric earthworks around Glastonbury could be interpreted as a gigantic zodiacal chart imprinted on the landscape. Having been asked to illustrate a book on the HOLY GRAIL, she found that places mentioned as being in the Vale of Avalon (which some associate with the Glastonbury area) could be identified on a map and that the figures representing the signs of the ZODIAC were then revealed. The makers of this zodiac, which Maltwood believed dated from c.2700 BC, dug earthworks in such a way that they incorporated natural features such as rivers, hills (including Glastonbury Tor) and roads to form images of the signs of the zodiac, which cover a circular area some 16 kilometres (10 miles) in diameter.

Maltwood linked this to the Round Table of KING ARTHUR, who had long been associated with Glastonbury, as well as to the Grail legends, believing that initiates had both kept the secret of the zodiac and maintained the earthworks over the centuries of the Christian era. Sceptics, however, question whether the ancient culture that is supposed to have created the earthworks involved would have had the same idea of the zodiac as that which came down to us via the Greeks and Romans.

globsters

Huge amorphous blobs of tissue that are occasionally washed ashore from the sea, the biological nature of which has long perplexed cryptozoologists.

Like several other useful and apposite cryptozoological terms (see CRYPTOZOOLOGY), 'globster' (an apparent portmanteau word combining 'glob' and 'monster') was coined by American cryptozoologist Ivan T Sanderson. Globsters are huge amorphous, but often noticeably hirsute, masses of biological tissue that are occasionally discovered washed ashore. Their identity has proven particularly mystifying and controversial, and all manner of suggestions have been proffered – including decomposed blobs of connective tissue or blubber from whales, the carcases of colossal octopuses, the earthly remains of ALIEN skyborne entities and the dead bodies of bizarre deep-sea life forms currently unknown to science.

Probably the most famous globster was also the earliest to receive scientific attention – Florida's St Augustine globster, washed up in 1896. However, there have been many later, but no less intriguing examples. Take, for instance, the massive 4-tonne carcase, measuring over 6 metres (19.7 feet) long, which drifted ashore on Tasmania's Four Mile Beach in 1998. Covered in hair-like fibres, with several sturdy tentacle-resembling projections around its edge, but lacking any recognizable head or sensory organs or an internal skeleton, this bizarre object piqued the curiosity of local observers, who were wholly unable to offer any suggestion as to what it might be. Wildlife officials suggested that it was probably just a lump of decomposing whale blubber – however, explaining how whale blubber could look like a beached octopus was not so easy.

Tasmania is not entirely unused to globsters – in 1960, a very sizeable rubbery-textured example, with a distinctive pleated perimeter and a hump that was 1.2 metres (4 feet) high, washed up at Sandy Cape. It was this example that inspired Sanderson to coin the term. Measuring 6 metres (19.7 feet) long, 5.5 metres (18 feet) wide, and estimated to weigh anything between 5 and 10 tonnes, it seemed to possess a series of gill-like slits around its edge, and was covered in greasy hair-like strands. However, it took more than a year for zoologists to become aware of this globster's existence and, although samples were finally taken for analysis, the subsequent report's description suggested a very different specimen from the original one. Some cryptozoologists concluded that the investigators had actually examined a totally separate, much smaller globster than the Sandy Cape specimen.

Globsters have been recorded from all over the world, including New Zealand, Bermuda, Scotland's Outer Hebrides, South Africa, Newfoundland, Greenland and the coasts of South America. It was a Chilean specimen that finally yielded the long-awaited solution to the mystery. On 23 June 2003, a massive example, grey and pink in colour with a gelatinous consistency and a leathery texture (causing it to be memorably likened in some news reports to a squashed elephant), was discovered beached at Los Muermos in southern Chile. If nothing else, it was undeniably of elephantine proportions. Approximately 1 tonne in weight, it measured 12 metres (39 feet) long, 5.5 metres (18 feet) across, and 1 metre (around 3 feet) at its highest point, and bore more than a passing resemblance to a gargantuan octopus.

As advances in genetic analysis techniques had by then attained a level that would enable the secret of this globster's identity to be unlocked, plans were made to send tissue samples to several laboratories around the world for DNA analysis. However, before this could even begin, a discovery was made within the globster's bulky mass that ended speculation as to what it was – or had been. Dr Sergio Letelier from Santiago's Museum of Natural History and a colleague, Dr Jose Yanez, announced on 11 July that they had discovered within the globster a spermaceti organ – a unique structure that contains a milky fluid and is found only inside the head of sperm whales. This identity was independently confirmed in 2004 following protein and genetic analyses of further tissue samples that had been taken.

Yet how could the remains of a sperm whale take on the guise of a giant octopus? The answer is a fascinating metamorphosis later described by Letelier, Yanez and fellow globster researcher Dr Steven M Carr. The British cryptozoologist Dr Karl Shuker dubbed this the 'quasi-octopus effect' (in line with the 'pseudoplesiosaur effect' that transforms a dead basking shark into what appears to be a plesiosaurian SEA SERPENT carcase). Shuker described the process in an article that appeared in the *FORTEAN TIMES* in 2003:

> After a whale dies, its body can float for months, decomposing, until eventually its heavy backbone and skull dissociate from their encompassing skin-sac of rotting blubber, and sink to the sea bottom, leaving behind a thick gelatinous matrix of collagen – the tough protein found in skin and connective tissue. It is this mass of collagen that washes ashore, as a globster. Furthermore, if a few of the whale's ribs remain within the collagen matrix, and any 'fingers' of fibrous flesh are attached to them, these resemble tentacles. And if the whale is a sperm whale, the spermaceti organ gives the resulting globster a bulky shape reminiscent of an octopus.

The mystery of the globsters was a mystery no more – although, having said that, there is at least one Greenland globster on record that has been categorically shown to be the grossly decomposed remains of a basking shark; and the globster that started it all – the St Augustine specimen from 1896 – has been the subject of biochemical tests that seem to show that it does possess octopus traits. By and large, however, if a stranded mass of flesh looks like a globster, and feels like a globster, the chances are that it is indeed … a whale!

glossolalia *see* XENOGLOSSY

Gnosticism

A group of religious systems active in the first few centuries AD around the Mediterranean and in central Asia. The beliefs of the various Gnostic groups, such as their doctrine of salvation by mystical knowledge rather than by faith and works, differed from mainstream Christian thought in several important respects and led them to be regarded as heretical by the orthodox Christian Church.

The origins and history of Gnosticism are still obscure in many respects, and subject to much debate. The complex and varied group of religious movements known collectively as Gnosticism flourished until around the 5th century. Most active in the 1st and 2nd centuries AD around the Mediterranean and extending as far as central Asia, its teachings had been declared heretical by the mainstream Christian Church by the 2nd century.

The various initiatory religions, sects and knowledge schools which come under the general heading of Gnosticism are thought to have at least some roots in Jewish and pagan thought, and typically advocate the pursuit of MYSTICISM, and a doctrine of salvation by direct knowledge and experience of the Divine, rather than by faith and works. They also commonly include the concept of a remote, supreme and unknowable Godhead who is distinct from the creator god of the universe. They believe that Christ's purpose in coming to earth was to teach mankind how to achieve the special knowledge, or *gnosis*, which will allow us to recover our awareness of the divine origins of humanity, to transcend our gross physical existence, and to return to the *pleroma*, or 'region of light' which is the fullness of God's powers and the centre of divine life.

Gnostic traditions tend to fall into one of two categories: the 'Eastern' or 'Persian' school, which views creation as the dualistic result of a mythological interaction between the realms of light and darkness; and the 'Syrian' or 'Egyptian' school, which regards creation as the consequence of a series of emanations from the supreme Godhead. In the latter, this remote primal source, sometimes referred to as *the Monad*, or *The One*, is believed to have given off a series of emanations, or *aeons*, which usually come as male and female pairs, known as *syzygies*. When the final and lowest emanation of the Godhead, often named as *Sophia*, came into being without her partner aeon, the result was the *Demiurge*, an inferior god depicted in some Gnostic systems as malign, and sometimes identified with the Jehovah of the Old Testament, who created the material universe. Thus the material world is, in many Gnostic traditions, regarded as a corruption of the spirit, an evil, flawed and constricting prison deliberately created to keep man trapped in the physical realm. The Monad therefore emanated two saviour aeons, Christ and the Holy Spirit, to rescue man from the Demiurge, and Christ came to earth to teach man how to redeem his spirit from matter by attaining the knowledge which comes from a direct personal experience of the Divine. In most Gnostic systems, this mystical knowledge is seen as sufficient cause for salvation.

Some Gnostic groups also promoted Docetism, the belief that Christ was a pure spirit and did not come to earth in a physical body, and that his physical appearance and apparent sufferings on the cross were thus an illusion.

Until recently, much of our knowledge about Gnosticism was 'second-hand', coming as it did from critiques of it written by orthodox Christians. However, in 1945, a number of Gnostic scriptures (written in Coptic) were discovered in Nag Hammadi, in Upper Egypt; this made a modern study of actual Gnostic texts possible, and did much to clarify ideas about Gnosticism. The 20th century saw a renewed interest in Gnostic ideas, and several modern spiritual movements influenced by these ancient beliefs have developed, some of which refer to themselves as 'Gnostic'.

goatsucker *see* CHUPACABRAS

goblin
A general term for a small, dark, ugly and mischievous or evil fairy.

In Western folklore, the word 'goblin' is used to refer to any small, dark and ugly fairy of a mischievous or evil disposition. It comes from the Old French *gobelin*, which probably derived from the Greek *kobālos*, meaning a mischievous spirit, and the term includes BOGGARTS, bogies and BOGLES, among others. They are said to live underground, especially in churchyards, or between the roots of ancient trees, and are most likely to be seen at HALLOWE'EN. Some people claim that the race of goblins originated from a cleft in the Spanish Pyrenees, and from there spread all over Europe. Goblins are most common in English and French folklore, and are usually portrayed as diminutive and grotesque figures who visit human dwellings, usually in order to wreak havoc there at night, knocking on doors and walls, breaking crockery, moving furniture around and banging on pots and pans. Folk tales generally hold that it is wise to leave some food and milk out for them at night to gain their goodwill. They are usually merely playful, but like most FAIRIES, can be malicious and harmful if crossed. A smile from a goblin can turn milk sour and curdle the blood, and its laugh makes the fruit fall off the trees. HOBGOBLINS, however, are a much friendlier and more benevolent type of goblin.

Goddess, the
One of the two primary deities (or aspects of the supreme deity) in neopagan witchcraft, the worship of whom is based on earlier pagan beliefs which possibly survived in some form in the witchcraft practice of the Middle Ages.

Variously referred to as the Great Goddess, the Mother Goddess, the Moon Goddess, Diana, Aradia, the Great Mother and many other names, the Goddess is central to the practise of WITCHCRAFT. The Goddess is understood in many ways – as an embodiment of the female principle, the creative force and of nature itself – and is associated particularly with the MOON. Most pagan traditions (see NEOPAGANISM) recognize both a female and a male element within nature and the divine, although they are often characterized by their concentration upon the female, in some cases almost to the exclusion of the male, usually represented by the HORNED GOD.

Some have tried to argue that the modern worship of the Goddess is a continuation of a tradition that can be observed in cultures throughout history. Certainly, there have been numerous figures found by archaeologists, dating back thousands of years, that could be interpreted as relating to a female deity, or mother goddess. Some might argue that this worship of the female principle is present even in modern Christian practice in the form of the veneration of the Virgin Mary. However, in general, modern pagans tend to draw their inspiration from aspects of the pre-Christian religious traditions of the Greeks, the Romans, the Celts and other European peoples – all of whom had goddesses associated with fertility, nature and the moon.

Although, as with the practice of neopagan witchcraft in general, there have been many claims that the modern worship of the Goddess is a continuation of a surviving tradition (famously those of Charles Godfrey Leland relating to the worship of Diana, a goddess of Roman origin – see *ARADIA, OR THE GOSPEL OF THE WITCHES*), much of the modern concentration upon, and interpretation of, the concept of the Goddess stems from the work of GERALD GARDNER.

Godfrey, Alan (1947–)
An English police officer who claimed he had been abducted from his patrol car by aliens in what is often considered to be the most significant case of its type to occur in the UK.

On the afternoon of 11 June 1980, Alan Godfrey, a police officer from Todmorden in West Yorkshire, was called to the coal yard of the local railway station. He found the body of a man called Zigmund Adamski on top of a tall slippery pile of slack, in full view of passing trains. Adamski had vanished five days earlier while on a five-minute walk to the corner shop. The dead man had a burn on his head and neck, the cause of which was never identified. After five months and several hearings the inquest was adjourned without resolution, the coroner describing the case as a mysterious puzzle. Godfrey (who, coincidentally, was born in the same week in June 1947 that the KENNETH ARNOLD sighting triggered the modern interest in the

The alleged alien abductee Alan Godfrey describes his experiences at a seminar in May 1982. (©TopFoto/Fortean)

UFO phenomenon) was apparently unaware of the significance carried by the name Adamski within UFO circles (see GEORGE ADAMSKI).

Later the same year, on 29 November, Godfrey was on duty during the early hours of the morning. At just after 5am, with his shift coming to an end, he drove onto Burnley Road to look out for some cows that had been reported straying into a small housing estate. The weather had been wet, but the rain had just stopped. Instead of finding the cows, he was apparently confronted by an object that looked like a huge spinning top hovering over the road ahead. As he propped up a sketch pad on the windscreen of the car, and began to draw the object, he was overcome by a blinding light.

Godfrey said that he came to his senses, still in the vehicle, but a few hundred yards down the road on the outskirts of the town. He had no recollection of getting there. On returning to the spot where he had seen the object he found a dried circle on the road surface. He also discovered on his arrival back at the police station that approximately 15 minutes of time had 'disappeared' (see TIME, MISSING).

In 1981 Godfrey underwent regression hypnosis at the hands of two different psychiatrists, who had not previously been involved in potential UFO cases. During these sessions he was allegedly able to recall the details of what had occurred after the light beam struck (see MEMORY, RECOVERED). He had apparently felt himself floating and then found himself inside a strange room in the company of a tall, bearded figure who called himself 'Yosef'. There were also other entities present. He described these, with fear in his voice:

Them are horrible ... I don't want to talk about them ... They're small ... About, like a five-year-old lad. They have heads like a lamp ...

Yosef had then taken Godfrey to a flat table and made him lie down. The recollection continued:

There's a light above my head. I'm confused. There is a lot of machinery in here. Ow! There is a pain in my head.

Much more information trickled out in later sessions – some involving medical tests that had supposedly been conducted by small robot figures under the guidance of Yosef. Many of the details are similar to those found in other ALIEN ABDUCTION cases. However, there were also some strange anomalies – for example, the inside of the room often sounded more like the inside of a house, complete with carpets, and the 'aliens' apparently had a big dog with them!

Although Godfrey himself has expressed doubts as to the status of the details 'recovered' under hypnosis, he stood firmly by the story of his UFO encounter, despite much harassment and ridicule.

gods

Superhuman or supernatural beings, worshipped in various cultures and belief systems throughout history as creators of the universe, personifications of natural forces, or controllers of specific aspects of human existence.

Since the dawn of history, man's attempts to understand the world and to come to terms with his own existence have given rise to the belief in gods. These supernatural beings, immortal and powerful, are often held to be the creators of the universe, and are perceived and worshipped differently in every culture and belief system. Monotheistic religions, such as Christianity, Judaism and Islam, assert that there is a single and unique God, while many ancient religions, such as those of Babylon, Egypt, Greece, Rome and Scandinavia, were polytheistic, with a pantheon of gods and goddesses who personified various natural forces or controlled specific aspects of human life, and who were usually described as having a human appearance and human attributes and personalities. A number of indigenous belief systems, which are typically shamanic, revere totemic nature spirits and ancestral entities; these are generally regarded as an aggregate of various spiritual forces rather than a personified single God, although most African traditions, while acknowledging the influence and importance of these spirits, also worship a supreme God who operates on the highest level. The many gods worshipped in Hinduism, the three supreme of which are Brahma, Vishnu and Shiva, are generally understood by believers to be symbols of a single, ultimate reality. See also DEITIES.

gold

A yellow-coloured precious metal which has been thought throughout history to possess various spiritual and magical properties.

Gold is the most malleable and ductile metal known, and while pure gold is too soft for everyday use, it readily forms alloys with other metals, and is used to make jewellery and coins. However, as well as being prized for its value, gold has throughout history been thought to possess magical, spiritual and even medicinal properties. Gold has been linked to religion since ancient times, and icons and sacred objects made from gold are found in almost every culture in the world. There are many myths regarding its origin; in ancient Egypt it was held sacred and was thought to be the flesh of the gods, while the Hindus called it 'the mineral light', supposing it to be a form of congealed sunlight buried underground. Gold is associated with the notion of IMMORTALITY because it is not tarnished, dimmed or corroded by rust, water or the action of the soil, and although fire can melt it, it does not impair its lustre. Its impervious nature has therefore made it a powerful symbol of purity, wholeness and eternity, especially in the Orient and in ancient Egypt, where the honoured dead were encased in gold caskets in the belief that the 'immortal' metal would confer its qualities to them. Gold is also the traditional material used for wedding rings, symbolizing the hope that, like gold, the marriage will be long-lasting and unaffected by the passage of time. When worn as jewellery, gold is thought to draw the light of the sun

to the wearer, bringing them vitality and confidence, and is said to help stabilize and energize the magical properties of any gemstones worn with it. It has also been traditionally used as a form of medication in China, India and Europe, in the belief that it can pass on its qualities of wholeness and incorruptibility by SYMPATHETIC MAGIC.

Gold has throughout the ages been equated with the sun because of its colour and brightness, and the alchemical and astrological symbol for gold is the same as that for the sun: a circle with a point at its centre. Gold was of particular importance to medieval alchemists (see ALCHEMY). They believed that all physical substances could be divided, via alchemical processes, into the 'three principles' of which they were ultimately composed – SALT, SULPHUR and MERCURY. Also known as the *tria prima*, these three principles were thought to be present in all base matter, and were said to be in perfect balance in gold. The transmuting of base metals into gold was one of goals of some alchemists, and to this end they sought the PHILOSOPHER'S STONE, which was believed to have the power to bring about this transformation. Some alchemists, such as Nicolas Flamel, working in 15th-century France, claimed that the stone was itself a refined form of gold brought to the highest state of purity and perfection.

Golden Dawn *see* HERMETIC ORDER OF THE GOLDEN DAWN

golem

In Jewish folklore, a figure of a human being brought to life by supernatural means.

The word 'golem' comes from the Yiddish *goylem* and Hebrew *gōlem*, meaning a shapeless thing or an incomplete substance, and the earliest stories of golems date back to early Judaism. In Jewish folklore, a golem is a figure of a human being made from mud or clay and brought to life by being inscribed with a magic or religious Hebrew WORD OF POWER. For example, the name of God, or the word *Emet* ('truth') might be written on its forehead, or on a clay tablet or slip of paper placed under its tongue. Only those who were very holy and close to God could aspire to his power of creating life. The mystic way to create a golem is outlined in the *Sefer Yetzirah*, the Book of Creation, which is generally grouped with kabbalistic texts (see KABBALAH). The golem was created as a servant, and while it was not very intelligent, it could perform simple tasks, although it could not speak and could gradually become more clumsy and dangerous. The possession of a golem servant was the ultimate mark of wisdom and holiness, and many tales of golems are associated with prominent rabbis throughout the Middle Ages. The most famous story is that of the Golem of Prague; it tells of the 16th-century Rabbi Loeb, who in 1580 was said to have created a golem to defend the Prague ghetto from anti-Semitic attacks. However, as the golem grew bigger, it became more violent and became a danger to everyone. The rabbi was promised that if he would destroy the golem, the violence against the Jews would stop, so he agreed, deactivating the golem by recalling the magical words with which he had brought it to life. Paul Wegener's expressionistic 1920 silent film, released in the USA as *The Golem* and now considered a classic, was based on this story.

golem science

The idea that science is not as pure as it is represented to be, but contains human flaws.

Scientific endeavour is sometimes assumed to be a completely objective process free from bias, with results that are handed down as though on tablets of stone. This view is often assisted by the media suggesting that scientists are superhuman beings with access to secrets which are beyond lesser mortals. However, the truth is rather different.

One recent way of expressing this is the term 'golem science', coined by scientist and sociologist Trevor Pinch and sociologist Harry Collins. Golem science compares science to the GOLEM: a foolish and imperfect being which, without sufficient control, can become clumsy and dangerous. In particular, sociological studies of how discoveries are made show that the outcome of an experiment is rarely as clear and unambiguous as researchers might suggest. The two processes of observation and prediction are not as distinct as they should be, and scientists, like everyone else, are likely to find excuses for discarding failures and overstating their successes. This means that researchers' pet theories might thrive, while anything which challenges them might be ignored.

If science were a purely objective activity, then investigating the unexplained would be a fairly simple matter. But since the very existence of GHOSTS or POLTERGEISTS or PREMONITIONS would challenge the beliefs of established scientists, such phenomena are likely to be derided and left to FRINGE SCIENCE at best.

Good Folk

One of the many euphemistic terms used to refer to fairies in order to avoid the bad luck caused by naming them directly.

In folklore, it is considered very unlucky to refer to the FAIRIES directly, since to use their name might summon them. Some people also believe that they do not like being referred to as fairies. Either way, in folk tales it is generally thought to be safer not to use the word 'fairy', so instead, a wide range of euphemistic phrases are employed when speaking of this otherworldly race. One such term is the Good Folk. Other commonly used variations of this are the Good People and the Good Neighbours. See also LITTLE PEOPLE.

governmental cover-up

Alleged attempts by government agencies to suppress information relating to UFOs, forming part of a systematic process that UFO enthusiasts claim has existed since the earliest days of the phenomenon.

The first claims of a governmental cover-up appeared in January 1950, in an article entitled 'Flying Saucers are Real' (see FLYING SAUCERS), published by retired US Marine Major, DONALD KEYHOE.

Keyhoe said that he had used his relationship with former colleagues to access information relating to cases that were being investigated on behalf of the government. Some of those involved had apparently been persuaded that UFOs were of alien origin. The investigations had resulted in the publication of the sceptical ESTIMATE OF THE SITUATION REPORT. Those who favoured the 'ALIENS' theory were reassigned, and a few of these allegedly chose to leak information.

The numerous UFO groups that sprang up across the USA adopted the view that the government had been convinced that UFOs were alien in origin, and that the secrecy was possibly due to the fact that they now held physical proof. Rumours of crashed spaceships and recovered alien bodies spread.

Documents released in recent years under various FREEDOM OF INFORMATION ACTS show that there were suspicions at the time that aliens might be involved, although there was no proof. UFO reporting channels were monitored, secret agencies did have a role in manipulating public opinion, and the investigation teams working for the US Air Force had found that decisions were taken well above their heads. Likewise in the UK, in January 1953, the British government imposed restrictions on RAF personnel preventing them from making any sightings public in order to keep potentially important cases from the media. They also expressed approval at successes in hiding the most puzzling cases. To this extent, a genuine governmental cover-up did exist, but it is not clear exactly what was being covered up, or why.

Released files indicate that the governments of many countries remained in as much doubt over the nature of UFOs as most experienced enthusiasts. The reasons behind the cover-up probably had more to do with natural bureaucratic secrecy, protection of intelligence-gathering techniques and other intriguing possibilities – the uncertainty surrounding UFO sightings could, for example, be a useful smokescreen for the testing of secret aircraft (see BLACK AIRCRAFT).

Gowdie, Isobel (d.c.1662)

A Scottish woman who, in 1662, voluntarily confessed to practising witchcraft.

Although Isobel Gowdie has become known as possibly the most famous Scottish WITCH, it is extremely debatable whether there was any truth at all in her 'confession'. On four occasions in the spring of 1662 Gowdie voluntarily confessed to WITCHCRAFT. She claimed that her involvement had started 15 years previously when she had met with THE DEVIL in the form of a man in grey near her home in Auldearn near Nairn in the Scottish Highlands. He had baptized her as a witch, in the local kirk, using blood he had sucked from her (leaving her with a DEVIL'S MARK), and giving her the name Janet. She claimed that she had belonged to a COVEN, numbering 13 (in agreement with the folkloric belief) and that she and her companions were able to transform themselves into animals, giving the following example of the spell used to change herself into a hare:

> I shall go into a hare,
> With sorrow and sych and meickle care;
> And I shall go in the Devil's name,
> Ay while I come home again.

She said that she and her companions met regularly at SABBATS, flying there on straws or beanstalks to cavort and take part in sexual orgies with DEMONS and the Devil (from which occasions she apparently derived great pleasure). Their list of crimes seemed to include all of the misdeeds that witches had routinely been accused of during the Middle Ages, including storm-raising (see WEATHER MAGIC), making farmland sterile using a miniature plough drawn by toads, destroying crops using the corpses of unbaptized children, shooting 'elf arrows' made by FAIRIES (from whom they had learnt much of their witchcraft) and injuring or killing through the use of IMAGE MAGIC. All of this had taken place without arousing the slightest suspicion among the local community – Gowdie had apparently even fooled her husband by placing a BROOMSTICK in her place in the bed when she left at night to indulge in this outrageous behaviour.

What drove her to voluntarily make such a dangerous confession, which almost certainly led to her execution and to those of a number of others (although there is no surviving record of the executions actually taking place), is not known – suggestions range from mental illness or boredom leading to a desire for attention, through to a malicious attempt to bring suffering upon those she implicated or even the unlikely possibility that there was some truth in the claims and that the confession was born out of remorse. However, if nothing else, the confession gives a unique and detailed insight into the folkloric beliefs relating to witchcraft in Scotland at the time.

grail *see* HOLY GRAIL

Great Beast *see* BEAST, THE GREAT

Great Pyramid

The largest of the Egyptian pyramids, built by Cheops.

The Great Pyramid at Giza was built by Cheops (or Khufu), the 26th-century BC king of Memphis. It is the largest of the PYRAMIDS of Egypt and one of the legendary Seven Wonders of the World.

The statistics of its dimensions alone reveal it to be a colossal feat of engineering. It occupies an area of 5.3 hectares (13 acres) and its original height has been calculated at 147 metres (481 feet) – its apex is missing and it has been suggested that it was never actually completed. It is square in cross-section at every level and the length of the base of each side is 229 metres (751 feet). It is constructed of limestone blocks, over two million of them, each weighing more than two tonnes. Even more massive are the blocks used to form the ceiling of the 'King's Chamber', each of which weighs more than nine tonnes. Originally, it was covered in a smooth casing of stone but this has been lost over the centuries, particularly since earthquakes in the 14th century dislodged much of it. Local Arabs are said to have pillaged the stones for use in building their own mosques and palaces. For thousands of years it was the highest construction in the world, until the builders of the 19th century began to outstrip it.

No one can be certain as to how it was built, but most theories involve the construction of an enormous ramp of bricks and earth, which may have been lubricated with water, to allow the enormous blocks to be hauled or pushed into position. One theory suggests that hoists using counterbalancing baskets of sand may have been employed. It has been estimated that the construction of the pyramid would have taken at least 20 years, even given a massive force of labour. The precision of the building is remarkable, with less than 0.1 per cent of error in the alignment of the sides, and the fitting together of the blocks is extremely tight.

Why was the Great Pyramid built? The generally accepted explanation is that it was designed as the tomb of Cheops. This has led to the naming of the various chambers within the structure. The King's Chamber is the largest of these and contains a red granite structure identified as a sarcophagus. A smaller chamber has been labelled the Queen's Chamber although it contains no similar structure. Scientists have studied the pyramid throughout the ages (Sir Isaac Newton thought that finding its dimensions would allow him to calculate the ancient Egyptian cubit) and various surprising discoveries have been made. The siting of the building has been shown to suggest a deliberate alignment of its four sides with the cardinal points of the compass. It has also been argued that the various passages inside it are aligned with the stars of the constellation of Orion. It is claimed that the pyramid's proportions give it unexplained qualities. In particular, some say that objects placed inside a scale model of it will be physically affected, with food being preserved and dull razors becoming sharp.

Some theorize that the Great Pyramid was not built as a tomb at all but as a kind of ideal structure in which now-unknown religious or cult observances would be carried out. Others believe that it is an elaborate astronomical observatory, aligned with significant points in the heavens, or a giant sundial whose shadow indicates the solstices and equinoxes. Yet others maintain that there must be further undiscovered chambers within the structure that will one day provide the key to its proper purpose.

Greatrakes, Valentine *see panel p283*

Green Man

A pagan representation of a vegetation spirit consisting of a man's head surrounded by or sprouting living foliage, found carved in medieval churches all over Europe, and particularly in Britain.

Although he is almost certainly a pre-Christian icon, the Green Man can be seen in the stonework, wood carvings, stained glass and even illuminated manuscripts of countless medieval churches and cathedrals all over Europe, and especially in Britain. He is a vegetation spirit who represents the raw, primal force of nature, and as an embodiment of the life force which renews the world in spring, he is still associated with spring festivals today. He may appear in one of three main forms: as a human head surrounded by foliage; as a head surrounded by but also partly made up of leaves; or as a head surrounded by and made up of foliage but also with living vegetation and branches growing out of its mouth. Very little is known for certain about his origins. When most of Britain was covered with forest, there were many legends of forest fairies called Green Men, spirits with human forms who cared for the trees and dressed in scanty outfits made of leaves. Other stories told of wild men who lived in the forest and were sometimes referred to as WOODWUSES. Either of these may have given rise to the image of the Green Man. It has also been suggested that he may be a representation of some ancient god, or a relic of ancient European tree worship.

There has been much discussion as to why the Green Man appears so frequently in the decorations of churches and chapels, but the most probable explanation is that when Christianity replaced paganism as the dominant religion in Europe, the Church incorporated a degree of pagan symbolism into the fabric of its places of worship to appeal to the local community and bring a touch of the familiar to their new religion, particularly when the churches were built on old pagan sites.

The name 'Green Man' appears to have been coined by a scholar called Lady Raglan in 1939, in an article she wrote for the *Folklore Journal* called 'The Green Man in Church Architecture'. He is also known as the Foliate Head, Green Jack, Green George and Jack-in-the-Green; in France, he is *Tête de feuilles* ('head of leaves') and in Germany, *Blattmaske* ('leaf mask'). The Green Knight in the medieval poem *Gawain and the Green Knight* may be a chivalric incarnation of the Green Man; he belongs to a pre-Christian world which is initially seen as antagonistic to Christianity, but eventually becomes harmonious with it. A representation of the Green Man seems to have survived in the character of Jack-in-the-Green who still appears as part of the May Day revels in certain British villages and towns; this is a young man or boy who dances at the head of the procession encased in a costume consisting of a tall wooden frame entirely covered in greenery, flowers and ribbons. The Green Man also appears on many pub signs all over Britain, and is a popular image with modern Wiccans (see WICCA) and other neopagans (see NEOPAGANISM), since he depicts an earth-centred concept of male spirituality.

Gregory XVII (1946–2005)

Clemente Domínguez y Gomez, a Spanish heretic who proclaimed himself Pope Gregory XVII in 1978 after claiming to have received visions of the Virgin Mary and Jesus.

Clemente Domínguez y Gomez was born in Seville, Spain. In 1978 he became closely associated with the Palmar de Troya movement, a breakaway group of the Catholic Church. The Palmarian Catholic Church had its origins in an apparition of the Virgin Mary which was said to have been seen in the Seville village of El Palmar de Troya in 1968. From 1969 onward, Domínguez claimed to experience VISIONS of the Virgin himself, in

Valentine Greatrakes (1629–83)

The Irish faith healer Valentine Greatrakes was born in Affane, County Waterford. From 1649 to 1656 he was a lieutenant in the Parliamentary New Model Army in Ireland, but when it was disbanded in 1656, he became a county magistrate. In 1662, he claimed to have been informed by a 'mysterious impulse' that he had the gift of curing the KING'S EVIL (a scrofulous disease), but kept the knowledge to himself for a time. However, when his wife suggested he try out his powers on a local boy called William Maher, who was suffering from the disease, he apparently did so successfully. His fame as a healer spread, and for the next three years he concentrated on the healing of scrofula, but in 1665 he also began to use his powers for other ailments, such as the ague, epilepsy, ulcers and lameness, and many patients came to him from England as well as Ireland.

Greatrakes attributed his healing powers to God, and was said to have always used the form of words: 'God Almighty heal thee for His mercy's sake'; if the patient claimed to have been helped or cured, Greatrakes told them to give the praise to God. However, he was summoned before an ecclesiastical court in Lismore to explain his activities, and was ordered to stop healing. He ignored the order. He was said to take no fees, and to have refused to take cases that were clearly incurable. He became popularly known as 'the stroker' or 'the touch doctor' from the method he employed, in which he stroked the afflicted person's body, allegedly drawing the illness out from it as if by a magnet.

In 1661, Greatrakes was asked to examine Florence Newton, to help determine whether she was a WITCH. In 1665, he was invited to Ragley in England to try his healing powers on Anne,

The true and truely Pourtraicture of Valentine Greatrakes Esq of Affane in y.º County of Waterford in y.º Kingdome of Ireland famous for curing severall Deseases and distempers by the stroak of his Hand only.

The Irish faith healer Valentine Greatrakes, who claimed he was able to heal the sick by stroking them. (© Mary Evans Picture Library)

Viscountess Conway, who suffered from chronic headaches. The Conways' acquaintances included some of England's most noted physicists, philosophers and scientists, and a distinguished group came to watch the attempted healing. Although it was a failure, Greatrakes was asked to stay at Ragley for a number of weeks, during which time he was said to have performed several successful cures. Many of the leading intellectuals of the day attested to these cures, and he was championed by luminaries such as the philosopher and theologian Henry More, and the scientists Robert Boyle and John Wilkins. From Ragley, he was then invited to visit King Charles II at Whitehall, and when he arrived in London he was besieged by crowds and was said to have healed many people. Although the demonstration he attempted before the King and his court was a failure, his techniques were widely imitated, and some of his followers concluded that his healing force was due not to faith alone, but to faith augmented by a kind of magnetism. He returned to Ireland five months later, and resumed his duties as a Justice of the Peace and a country squire.

Both his supporters and detractors published a number of pamphlets regarding his healing, one critic referring to him as a 'miracle-monger' who tried to cure an ague by the use of 'that hobgoblin word, *Abrodacara*', while another contemporary account described him as affirming that all diseases were caused by evil spirits, and boasting that he was well acquainted with their demonic ways. In 1666, Greatrakes published an account of his life and work entitled *A Brief Account of Mr Valentine Greatrakes and Divers of the Strange Cures by Him Lately Performed*, in the form of a letter addressed to Robert Boyle. He died in 1683 and was buried beside his father at Affane.

which she condemned heresy and the reform of the Catholic Church which was under way at that time. His followers alleged that Domínguez possessed the STIGMATA, the wounds of Christ's crucifixion, on his hands, and also, more rarely for stigmatics, a cross-shaped wound on his forehead. However, the Catholic Church questioned the legitimacy of both the visions and the stigmata, and regarded the beliefs of the Palmarians as heretical.

In 1975, Domínguez founded his own religious order, the Carmelites of the Holy Face, saying that he was acting under instructions from the Virgin. Blinded in a car accident in 1976, he claimed to experience further visions after he lost his sight, including several in which Jesus, along with St Peter and St Paul, told him he was to be the next pope. Therefore, when Pope Paul died in 1978, Domínguez declared his own papacy and took the name Gregory XVII, being crowned by four of his newly created College of Cardinals. As 'the Pope', he canonized Generalissimo Franco and Christopher Columbus as saints. However, he was regarded as an antipope by the mainstream Catholic Church, which held that his papacy was in no way valid, and it was first John Paul and then John Paul II who were accepted by the Church as the legitimate popes during his time. He died in El Palmar de Troya in 2005.

greys
The alien entity 'type' which appears most often in modern reports of UFO encounters.

Modern ALIEN ABDUCTION cases almost invariably involve descriptions of ALIENS that fall into the general category known as 'greys'. The following typical description comes from a woman from Nebraska called Jennie. She was supposedly taken from her bedroom late at night by a being calling himself 'the explorer'. Although the incident had apparently happened when she was a teenager in 1955, she did not 'remember' the details until she was placed under HYPNOSIS in 1984, by which time other reports of greys already existed (see MEMORY, RECOVERED). She said that the entity was:

> … tinier than four feet, but bigger than three. I don't think that he has hair. The head is shaped like an egg. The face is waxy – real pale, pinkish, greyish … The nose is just a tiny bump. The mouth is a slit. The eyes are long slits with nobody home.

During the 1950s, when this abduction reputedly occurred, fewer than 3 per cent of all reported alien sightings involved this type of entity. The first

An artist's impression of a 'grey', the most commonly reported alien type of recent years. (© TopFoto/Fortean)

accounts which included them arrived in 1965 and by the late 1970s, by which time the use of hypnosis was widespread, they had become more common – although they were still far from dominant outside the USA.

The real turning point came in the spring of 1987 when the US novelist, Whitley Strieber, told his story of meetings with similar beings in his book, *Communion*. The book became an international bestseller, and was turned into a film backed by a massive promotional campaign, central to which was the eerie facial image of a grey. This fixed a particular version of the alien abduction phenomenon in the global consciousness. Although numbers of grey sightings had gradually been increasing until that point, the vast majority of cases that came afterwards now involved them, including those in countries where they had previously been unknown.

UFO researchers are divided as to what this means. Some feel that this process is a clear example of CULTURAL TRACKING. Others claim that the publicity merely opened up the 'locked doors' in many people's minds, behind which REPRESSED MEMORIES of hidden encounters lay dormant.

Griffiths, Frances *see* COTTINGLEY FAIRIES

grimoire

A book of spells; specifically, one of several books of magical knowledge written between the late medieval period and the 18th century.

In its more general sense, the word 'grimoire' is used to refer to any book containing a personal collection of spells, rites, recipes or other magical information. But it is more specifically applied to one of the books of magical knowledge written between the late medieval period and the 18th century, which contained astrological correspondences, lists of angels and demons, and directions on casting spells and charms, summoning spirits and making talismans. Notable historic grimoires include *The Book of the Sacred Magic of Abramelin the Mage* (apparently translated by MACGREGOR MATHERS from a 15th-century French manuscript) and *The Greater Key of Solomon* (which is attributed to King Solomon, and of which MacGregor Mathers again provided a translation). In the late 19th century, several of these historic texts were reclaimed by magical organizations such as the HERMETIC ORDER OF THE GOLDEN DAWN and the ORDO TEMPLI ORIENTIS. The word itself comes from the Old French *gramaire*, and shares the same root – the Greek *gramma*, meaning a letter – as the word 'grammar'. See also *NECRONOMICON, THE*.

Grim Reaper

A personification of death as a dark or skeletal figure in a monk's robe, usually carrying a scythe and sometimes also an hourglass.

The personification of death exists in the mythology of almost every culture and religion. In the West, Death is seen as one of the four horsemen of the Apocalypse. Since medieval times Death has been portrayed in European-based folklore as a male figure who usually carries a scythe (to symbolize his task of harvesting the souls of the recently dead), and sometimes also bears an hourglass (to remind us of the inexorable passage of time and the fact that death must come to us all). He appears as one of the cards of the MAJOR ARCANA in the TAROT. He is often shown as a skeletal being, and especially in later times is depicted as wearing a black monk's robe. Sometimes he has no discernible features, with a black void instead of a face and no visible extremities. This figure is known as the Grim Reaper, and his function is that of a 'psychopomp' – a spirit whose task it is to conduct the souls of those who have recently died into the AFTERLIFE. Since he is believed to be present at the point of death to assist the dying person with the transition to the other side, it is perhaps not surprising that many seriously ill hospital patients have claimed that they have seen an apparition of the Grim Reaper standing at the foot of their bed. In most accounts, his appearance causes a sudden drop in temperature in the room; he rarely speaks, and glides rather than walks, but he fades away if the patient decides it is not yet time for them to go with him. However, few people who have had NEAR-DEATH EXPERIENCES claim to have seen the Grim Reaper, and many of the recorded sightings of this apparition do not in fact result in the death of the observer or of a close friend or relative; instead, his alleged manifestations have sometimes been interpreted as a warning of imminent danger. The Grim Reaper has become an iconic figure in literature, art and popular culture, and nowadays is sometimes portrayed as a somewhat sympathetic character.

Groom Lake Air Force Base *see* AREA 51

Guadaloupe *see* MARIAN APPARITIONS

guardian spirit

A spiritual protector or guide, the idea of which features in many religious belief systems, spiritualism and some areas of New Age thought.

In numerous cultures individuals are said to be protected by guardian SPIRITS. In many cases, such as in some Native American spiritual belief systems, these take the form of an animal spirit and the person is sometimes said to be imbued with some of the powers and qualities of the animal in question. In some systems it is believed that all people are protected in this manner, whereas in others it is only the holy or wise people, or the tribal shaman (see SHAMANISM). In some interpretations of Christian teaching people are believed to have a 'guardian spirit' in the form of an ANGEL – belief in guardian angels is particularly popular in the USA. In SPIRITUALISM and many New Age belief systems a guardian spirit might be variously understood to be a spirit helper who brings messages from the spirit realm, an assistant on visits to the ASTRAL PLANE or a guide who helps with an individual's spiritual development.

Gulf Breeze

An affair based around one of the most spectacular series of UFO photographs taken by a single witness over a short period of time.

UFOs have been captured on camera since the 19th century, but few cases have been as controversial as that which came to be known as the Gulf Breeze affair. It began in mid-November 1987, when the local newspaper in the small Florida town of Gulf Breeze received a visit from Ed Walters, a successful

A display of Ed Walters' Gulf Breeze UFO photographs at the 1988 Mutual UFO Network symposium. (© TopFoto/Fortean)

businessman, who brought them a collection of photographs that were apparently taken by an anonymous local man on the night of 11 November. It soon emerged that the photographer was Walters himself, and this initial story was followed by further claims of encounters and more photographs over the next few weeks.

The pictures were taken on a Polaroid camera and show an object with a slightly reflective appearance and an apparent structure, topped by a shape with windows or portholes around the edge. Walters told of repeated encounters with these craft above his home, saying that beams of light sometimes came from them and that strange odours were also noticeable when they appeared. Walters had apparently seen ALIENS (but had no photographs of these) and he also claimed to have 'seen' various curious messages and images in his mind.

By early 1988 the story had become a sensation in UFO circles – some researchers were convinced that this was the definitive proof that they had been waiting for, and others were worried by the way in which it differed from previous photographic cases. It was also observed that repetitive photographs, taken during alleged ongoing alien contact, had only previously featured among the claims of the CONTACTEES of the 1950s – this 'evidence' was usually later found to be suspect.

Researchers who considered Walters to be sincere handed him a special stereoscopic camera, so that he could obtain high-quality images from which size and distance could be measured. Although he did provide some further pictures, they were not the same type as those taken before and they seemed to show a smaller object.

In 1990 Ed Walters published a book about his photographs, *The Gulf Breeze Sightings*, in which some leading UFO researchers lent their backing to his story. He followed this in 1994 with a sequel which included details of ALIEN ABDUCTION activity in the town. Several other local people took photographs during this short WAVE and by 1992 there were regular skywatches (see SKYWATCHING) in the area of the Pensacola Bay Bridge, during which floating lights were often seen and filmed. However, suspicions arose that some of these floating lights were simply home-made hot-air balloons, launched to tease the watching crowds – possibly by servicemen from a local base.

After Walters moved from the house where his encounters had taken place, what appeared to be a drawing of a model UFO was found inside – however, he remained adamant that his story was genuine and claimed that this sketch was planted by someone attempting to discredit him. UFO researchers continue to discuss this highly publicized case.

Gurdjieff, Georgei Ivanovich (c.1865–1949)

Armenian thinker who taught that man lives his life in a form of sleep, and that in order to achieve higher levels of consciousness, we must learn to develop a full awareness of ourselves in our daily lives..

Georgei Ivanovich Gurdjieff was born in Alexandropol, Armenia, to Greek–Armenian parents. He grew up in the Caucasus among multicultural traditions, both ancient and modern, and in his youth he studied medicine, science and religion, but felt these disciplines did not answer his questions about the essential nature of humanity. He embarked on a lifelong search for the knowledge which he suspected was rooted in ancient traditions, and which might shed light on man's existence. He travelled widely through the Middle East, Africa, India and central Asia, visiting almost inaccessible centres of learning, temples and monasteries, and learning about the rituals of dance and music of many central Asian countries. He returned to Russia around 1910 and practised as a healer in St Petersburg between 1910 and 1917, bringing with him a distinctive and contemporary teaching which was based in the spiritual traditions of both East and West.

During the Russian Revolution, Gurdjieff and a group of his closest students made their way to Western Europe, and in 1922 he moved to Fontainebleau near Paris, where he set up the Institute for the Harmonious Development of Man, to train what he called 'helper-instructors' to practise and disseminate his teachings. He continued to teach in Paris and New York until his death in 1949. In 1924 Gurdjieff almost died in a car crash, and after he had recovered, he began writing the three books which were published after his death: *Beelzebub's Tales to His Grandson*, *Meetings with Remarkable Men* and *Life Is Real Only Then, When 'I Am'*; these came to be known collectively as *All or Everything*.

Some of those who had contact with Gurdjieff regarded him as a 'Master'. He once described his work by saying, 'I teach people how to listen to themselves.' He believed that man lives his life in a kind of sleep, but that higher levels of consciousness are possible if we can become fully aware of ourselves in our everyday lives. The goal of the development of consciousness was to create a new 'centre' within oneself, from which one could 'self-observe' objectively and honestly; this consciousness, which he referred to as 'self-remembering', brought its possessor self-unification, an ever-increasing effectiveness in all

pursuits and freedom from illusion. Without such consciousness, man was condemned to 'automatic' or 'accidental' living, in which life happened to him instead of his being able to take control of life. To be fully 'present' required that a person work on themselves over time, initially with the guidance of a helper-instructor who had trained in the practice of Gurdjieff's teaching either directly under him or under one of his pupils.

Many accounts have been written of Gurdjieff, and his teachings are best known through the work of his pupils, such as P D Ouspensky's *In Search of the Miraculous* (1949). His teachings are continued to this day by various groups, some under the auspices of the Gurdjieff Foundation in New York, London and Paris.

gyromancy
Divination by walking in a circle and then falling from giddiness.

Unlike some other forms of divination, gyromancy, from the Greek *gyros*, a circle or ring, and *manteiā*, divination, is seldom practised in modern times. A person walks round and round, usually inside a circle around whose circumference letters are placed, until he or she falls down from dizziness. The letter on which they fall is noted, and the procedure repeated until a message has been spelled out, on the same principle as an OUIJA BOARD. In a simpler version of this technique, it is the position in which the diviner falls that is interpreted as predicting the outcome of an event. The purpose of the repeated circling is said to be to exclude the interference of the person's will and to ensure that their fall is genuine chance, but it may also be, in some cases, done to induce a prophetic state of delirium or trance.

H

hairy hands

A local tradition of disembodied phantom hands being held responsible for traffic accidents on a stretch of road on Dartmoor, Devon.

In 1921 an article in the *Daily Mail* purportedly told the story of a series of bizarre incidents on a lonely road across Dartmoor, Devon. Apparently, a medical officer from Dartmoor prison was riding on a motorbike, with his two children in a sidecar, along the road between Two Bridges and Postbridge, when the motorbike suddenly went out of control. The children managed to jump clear before the machine crashed, killing the doctor. Some weeks later another motorcyclist travelling the road was involved in a crash at the same spot but survived. He claimed that seconds before the crash he felt rough, hairy hands trying to wrench away control of the handlebars of his machine and force him from the road. A third story told of a coach driver also feeling invisible hands pulling at the steering wheel of his vehicle as he passed near the spot. Three years later a self-proclaimed psychic who was staying in a caravan near to the road reputedly saw a pair of disembodied hairy hands climbing up the window pane – they apparently vanished when she uttered a prayer.

No further encounters seem to have been reported in the press, but the story was promoted in the region for many years by Graham Danton, a West Country broadcaster. As late as 1974 the author Marc Alexander heard stories in the area that the 'hairy hands' (as the phenomenon was dubbed) were still being blamed for inexplicable accidents on the road.

Hallowe'en

A festival celebrated on 31 October which has its roots in the Celtic celebrations associated with the end of summer.

The modern celebration of Hallowe'en is generally considered to represent a partial survival of the pagan observance of the festival known to the Irish and Scots Celts as SAMHAIN. It is primarily a feature of western cultures, particularly where there has been some British or Irish influence, although it has become more widespread through the effects of the spread of US popular culture.

Samhain, occurring on 1 November in the Roman calendar, was the festival of the harvest and the end of summer. It also marked the beginning of winter, a time associated with death. Throughout Europe there were also a number of similar celebrations at this time of the year. As with many other earlier pagan celebrations, these were 'Christianized', becoming All Saints Day or All Hallows, and so the night before became All Hallows Eve or Hallowe'en.

The modern symbolism surrounding Hallowe'en has developed from the folkloric belief that the SPIRITS of the dead were particularly active at this time of the year, mixed with other aspects of the celebration of autumn and harvest. Pumpkin lanterns (or jack-o'-lanterns) are a US development of the earlier British and Irish traditions of carving lanterns with faces out of root vegetables. These may have originally been intended to frighten away evil spirits. Trick or treating, involving children going from door to door in disguise asking for treats, is an activity that arose in the USA during the 20th century. It may have developed from the much older Scottish and Irish tradition of 'guising', where groups of children travelled from house to

Carved Hallowe'en pumpkins, which some believe were originally intended to frighten away evil spirits. (© Franz-Marc Frei/Corbis)

house performing party pieces in exchange for nuts, fruit or even money.

hallucinations

The perception of things that are not objectively real.

A hallucination (from a Greek term meaning 'to wander in the mind') is technically defined as a sensory perception that has no external cause. That is, it represents the perception by any of the senses of something that does not exist outside the mind of the person experiencing it.

Hallucinations can be perceived by each of the senses individually or in combination: sight (visual hallucinations), hearing (AUDITORY HALLUCINATIONS), smell (olfactory hallucinations), taste (gustatory hallucinations) and touch (tactile hallucinations). In addition, hallucinations can affect the judgement of size (dimensional hallucinations).

Some of the most common types of hallucination occur when a person is in a HYPNAGOGIC or HYPNOPOMPIC STATE, that is, in the process either of falling asleep or of waking up.

In the 19th century many psychologists thought that hallucinations could be explained as a kind of acting out of suppressed desires or fantasies. Later psychological theories concentrated more on defects or malfunctions in the brain as being the source.

Hallucinations can be the product of extremes in human activity or experience. For example, it is argued that it is a relatively normal part of the grieving process for a recently bereaved person to see, or hear the voice of, a lost loved one. Exhaustion or sleep deprivation can also produce hallucinations, such as those experienced by hostages or prisoners being kept awake as a form of torture, or the mirages seen by travellers who become lost and suffer from lack of food or water.

Other common causes include illnesses that affect the brain. For example, there are certain conditions in which people report 'hearing voices' – this is sometimes explained as part of the process of the mind trying to make sense of mental disorder. People suffering from fever, migraine attacks, epilepsy, sleep disorders or post-traumatic stress disorder are also often prone to hallucination. Another type of hallucination well known to the medical community is that of the 'phantom limb'; that is, when a person who has had a limb amputated believes that they can feel the sensations in it as if it were still present.

Drugs are another cause of hallucinations, especially HALLUCINOGENS such as LSD, mescaline (see PEYOTE) or the stronger varieties of cannabis. The use of psychedelic drugs is known to produce 'flashbacks' in which people seem to re-experience events from previous periods in their lives. Many 19th-century writers and other artists used opiates to inspire visual images and ideas. The English poet Samuel Taylor Coleridge (1772–1834) famously composed his 'Kubla Khan' while in a dreamlike state induced by laudanum. The tactile hallucination described as a feeling of 'ants crawling on the skin' is one of the relatively common side effects of certain medicines or their over-use.

Whatever the particular cause, it is often argued by sceptics that those who claim to have seen ANGELS, EXTRATERRESTRIALS or FLYING SAUCERS, heard the voices of deities or had supernatural visions such as of the Virgin Mary (see MARIAN APPARITIONS) have actually experienced hallucinations – although this proposed explanation becomes less satisfactory in situations where there are apparently a number of witnesses.

hallucinations, auditory *see* AUDITORY HALLUCINATIONS

hallucinogens
Drugs that produce hallucinatory sensations.
Plants prized for their hallucinogenic properties are believed to be among the oldest form of drugs used by humankind. There are various plants and fungi that contain chemicals able to produce HALLUCINATIONS in people who consume them. Among these are ergot, the ayahuasca vine of South America, the PEYOTE cactus, from which mescal is derived, the seeds of the morning glory flower, which contain lysergic acid, and 'magic mushrooms', which contain psilocybin.

Such plants have been used in rituals, divination, communication with spirits and healing by priests of many ancient cultures, including the Egyptians, ancient Greeks (such as in the ELEUSINIAN MYSTERIES), Aztecs and Mayas. Hallucinogens have also been a feature of the shamanic rituals of Asian and North American cultures, for example in 'spirit flying' in which the SHAMAN appears to travel great distances mentally, and they are still in use among certain peoples.

In the medicine of the modern world, chemical derivatives of such plants were used to create drugs that were later exploited for recreational use, such as LSD and ecstasy.

haloes
A ring of light shown around the head of a holy or enlightened person in religious iconography.
The halo, or nimbus, a ring of light shown around the head of a holy or enlightened person, is most commonly associated with Christian and Buddhist iconography, but its use can be traced back to ancient Egyptian art, in which deities are represented with what appears to be a small sun on their heads to symbolize spiritual light. Haloes are also found in pre-Christian Greek and Roman art, where in addition to indicating divine influence, they are shown around the head of a person of power, majesty, prominence or genius; from about AD 100, Roman coins included a halo around the head of the Emperor. Even during the Christian period, haloes were still used in depictions of famous people as well as those who were holy or sanctified, until around 1600, when Pope Urban III forbade their use in images of anyone who was not

at least beatified, and the halo came to represent the light of divine grace suffusing the soul.

In Christian iconography, it was formerly traditional to use a round halo to represent a saint, a halo with a cross inside it to denote Jesus, a triangular halo to signify the Holy Trinity and a square halo to indicate a particularly saintly living person. During the Renaissance, the depiction of the halo altered. Originally, the glow of sanctity emanating from the head was drawn as a circle, but in the Renaissance, perspective in art became more important, and as a result the halo's representation changed from a circle of light surrounding the head to a golden ring which floated above it, shown in correct perspective. This form of the halo continues to be used in popular images of Christ, the Virgin Mary, saints and angels to this day.

The halo has also been widely used in Buddhist iconography since at least the 1st century AD; it is thought that Buddhist art was influenced by the Greek artists who came to India with Alexander the Great. The Buddha, and Buddhist saints, are shown with a circular halo which is thought to symbolize the enlightened one's consciousness as radiating beyond their physical body, and to serve as a reminder of their transcendence of the body.

Haloes as they appear in art and iconography have been interpreted as symbolic representations of the AURA, or the crown CHAKRA.

Hamon, Count Louis *see* CHEIRO

Hampton Court Palace
A palace built by Henry VIII which has a century-old tradition of ghosts and hauntings.
Hampton Court is reputedly Britain's most haunted royal palace. Stories of hauntings have been in circulation since 1894 when *Cassell's Family Magazine* published a letter from a resident telling of 'loud screams at dead of night' in the Long Gallery. Among those alleged to have heard the screams were a Lady Westlake and a Mrs Cavendish Boyle. The cries were attributed to the ghost of Catherine Howard running along the gallery, and were said to be most regularly heard at around the anniversary of her execution, on 4 November. For many years a staged photograph purporting to show this ghost was sold at the Palace as a souvenir.

Another alleged apparition associated with the anniversary of a death is that of Jane Seymour, who reputedly walks near the building in October. Yet another ghost associated with the Palace is that of Sibell Penn, nurse to the future Edward VI. She is said to have haunted certain apartments following the disturbance of her tomb in nearby Hampton

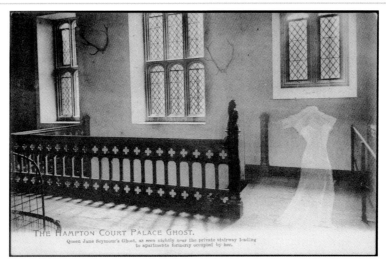

In this old postcard, Hampton Court Palace shows how proud it is of its ghostly reputation. Note the image of an 'apparition' in the bottom-right corner. (© Mary Evans Picture Library)

Church in 1829, making her presence felt through the sound of a spinning wheel. Other less specific ghostly occurrences that have been reported include disembodied sighs and mutterings, and the sensation of being touched.

Such stories have been endlessly repeated in popular ghost books, although it is many years since the ghost of Catherine Howard has been heard. However, there is no doubt that many staff and visitors continue to report strange experiences in the Long Gallery and elsewhere in the Palace. Official interest has led to a log of phenomena being maintained by curators since 1999.

In 2003 Hampton Court Palace was selected along with EDINBURGH'S VAULTS for mass experiments in the psychology of ghost experiences conducted by Dr Richard Wiseman. In the same year it was revealed that a ghost had apparently been caught on film by CCTV cameras at the Palace. Apparently, on three successive days in October, an alarm signalled that a set of fire doors had been opened. CCTV footage of the first and last occasions simply showed the doors swinging open, but on the second occasion, a 'ghostly' figure was recorded closing them. Some claimed that the film showed a ghost of Henry VIII, others that the figure (apparently wearing a hood and a long cloak) looked more like the GRIM REAPER. It has also been suggested that the figure was simply a (slightly oddly dressed) member of the public, helpfully shutting the doors, or a costumed guide.

In total there are believed to be legends relating to 30 separate ghosts at Hampton Court Palace.

Hangar 18

A top-secret building which is alleged to exist inside Wright Patterson Air Force Base, to which it is claimed that the US government has taken the wreckage of crashed UFOs.

Wright Field, later Wright Patterson Air Force Base, in Dayton, Ohio, was home to the US Air Force intelligence unit charged with the investigation of UFOs from January 1948. DR J ALLEN HYNEK, who was a young astronomer based locally at the time, became the project's scientific adviser.

The base was primarily used as a centre for administrative work, and it was there that the records of officially reported UFO cases were collated. However, it went on to develop a reputation, largely based on rumour, as a site used to store the debris from alleged UFO crashes – notably the July 1947 incident at ROSWELL. When, many years later, a FREEDOM OF INFORMATION ACT resulted in the release of documentation relating to these events, it became clear from a memo dated 8 July 1947 that the initial plan had indeed been to take the Roswell debris to Wright Field. However, the fact that en route the remains were identified as those of a weather balloon may have changed this. There are some witnesses who claim that the remains were still taken to Dayton – which would not have been that unlikely as foreign aircraft parts recovered from air crashes were studied at the base for intelligence purposes.

In UFO lore the building housing the UFO wreckage at Wright Patterson was called Hangar 18. It was supposedly under heavy guard and, over the years, a few anonymous sources have approached

UFO researchers with further allegations that alien bodies were placed there before being transferred to more secure facilities in AREA 51. In 1980 a film called *Hangar 18*, a fictional tale about the capture of a crashed UFO and the subsequent GOVERNMENTAL COVER-UP, further confused the chain of evidence by implying that a greater level of certainty lay behind the alleged existence of this location. There is, however, no documentary evidence to support the claim that the mysterious Hangar 18 was ever home to UFO wreckage.

Hanging Rock
Geological formation in Australia associated with a mysterious disappearance.

Hanging Rock is the popular name for an unusual geological formation, also known as Mount Diogenes, in a rural area of Victoria, Australia. It is an example of a volcanic plug, a mass of solidified lava blocking the vent of an extinct volcano.

In 1967 the Australian writer Joan Lindsay (1896–1984) published a novel telling the story of a group of schoolgirls taken by their boarding-school teachers for a picnic at the rock on 14 February 1900. Several of the girls and one accompanying teacher apparently vanish in mysterious circumstances and are never seen again. One girl from this group is later found in a dishevelled and disturbed state, entirely unable to give a coherent account of what happened to her companions. The novel ends tantalizingly with no explanation offered for the disappearance.

The novel was popular in Australia but was not widely known elsewhere until it was made into a film in 1975 by the Australian director Peter Weir. The film was a great international success, establishing Weir's reputation and bearing the allusive style and atmosphere of mystery that were to become recognized as his hallmarks. The film's publicity claimed that it was based on a true story, leading to a widely held belief that it portrayed actual events.

While the novel was grounded in the author's own experience, describing locations that she knew well, Lindsay never explicitly claimed that the story was anything other than a product of her imagination – although (as with the film) there was an implication that the story was based on real-life events. Those who believe the story to be entirely fictional have pointed out that, in the story, St Valentine's Day falls on a Saturday, although, in reality, 14 February 1900 was a Wednesday. Also, while such an event, if true, would have been certain to become a news item, researchers have combed Australian newspaper archives in vain for any mention of an unexplained disappearance at Hanging Rock at around that time. However, this has not stopped speculation as to what might have caused

the DISAPPEARANCES, and in 1980 Yvonne Rousseau's *The Murders at Hanging Rock* was published, offering several hypothetical explanations for the mystery. Again, this added to the general perception that book and film were based in fact.

In the original manuscript of her novel, Lindsay apparently included a final chapter in which she hinted that the victims of the disappearance had entered a 'time warp'. However, her publisher advised her to drop this chapter in favour of leaving the reader with an entirely unexplained mystery.

Harmonic Convergence
A spiritual event which took place on 17 August 1987, when New Age groups gathered at various sacred and mystical sites all over the world to usher in the new era of global peace and harmony which it was believed would begin on this propitious astrological date.

On 17 August 1987, a loosely organized spiritual event called the Harmonic Convergence took place. All over the world, NEW AGE groups gathered at 'focus locations' – sacred and mystical sites such as STONEHENGE, Mount Shasta and Creston, Colorado – to greet the new era of global peace and harmony which believers thought this astrologically propitious date would herald. The event was intended to be a worldwide awakening to love and unity through divine transformation, and was initiated by José Arguelles, whose research into Mayan Toltec calendars and interpretation of Mayan cosmology had led him to identify this date as the end of 22 cycles, each lasting 52 years. According to Mayan prophecies, the end of these 22 cycles would signal a turning point in the earth's collective KARMA, with a major energy shift powerful enough to change the global perspective from one of conflict to one of harmony and co-operation. Arguelles also claimed that the earth would, at this crucial date, slip out of its 'time beam' and be in danger of spinning off into space, and could only be made to keep its proper alignment by the concerted psychic efforts of human mediators working together. A great increase in UFO sightings was also expected at this time.

The 22 cycles, totalling 1,144 years, consisted of the 13 'heaven' cycles of the plumed serpent god, Quetzalcoatl, which in the Mayan calendar began in the year 843 and ended in 1519, followed by 9 'hell' cycles, which according to the Mayan prophecies would end in 1987, marking the inauguration of a new era of love and peace. Some claimed that the Harmonic Convergence would also begin the final 26-year countdown to the end of the traditional Mayan Long Count, which it was believed would take place in 2012, and would signal the 'end of history' and the beginning of a new 5,200-year cycle.

haunted highways

A belief that man-made roads and tracks may be haunted by apparitions.

In many folk tales, GHOSTS and supernatural entities are encountered by travellers during the course of their journey, and there are many stories of haunted roads and highways throughout Europe, the USA and other parts of the world. Some researchers believe that such stories ultimately derive from even earlier traditions of sacred roads and spirit paths in the landscape, dating back to prehistory.

Whatever the background, there is no doubt as to the continuing appeal of road ghosts, with one of the most popular modern folk tales being that of the PHANTOM HITCH-HIKER – typically, a young female hitch-hiker who mysteriously vanishes part way through a journey. Other reports of what are termed SPECTRAL PEDESTRIANS include apparitions seen crossing or standing in the road. Numerous examples have been collected since the end of the 19th century. Sometimes the figure is said to be immediately recognizable as an apparition because of its unusual movement or appearance – such as seeming to float above the level of the road – while in other cases people believe they have seen a spectral pedestrian when someone they take to be a living person suddenly vanishes. There are many cases of motorists reporting apparent collisions with such figures only to discover no physical traces of any person on the road. A strong symbolic or archetypal element attaches to many road ghosts, lonely highways frequently providing the backdrop for encounters with either a WHITE LADY, BLACK DOGS or phantom monks (see BLACK MONK). More rarely cases of auditory ghost experiences are associated with highways, particularly the sound of galloping horses when this would seem to be impossible.

Haunted highways have also been the setting for alleged encounters with apparitional vehicles. In the past, some people believed that they witnessed PHANTOM COACHES, but in more recent times tales are reported of spectral cyclists and ghostly motor vehicles.

The vast majority of apparitional experiences on haunted highways take place on quiet and empty roads, usually at night, a pattern also found with PHANTOM FUNERALS in Scottish and Celtic tradition. It may simply be that when travelling at night, the combination of darkness, isolation, tiredness and monotonous visual stimuli generates HALLUCINATIONS; alternatively, some have suggested that the same factors may encourage the brain to enter into a relaxed state, making it more receptive to psychic impressions – and able to see ghosts.

haunted houses

Domestic dwellings that are allegedly subject to hauntings; haunted houses are recorded in many cultures.

Stories of haunted houses are known throughout the world and have been in circulation since ancient times. In tradition, haunted houses are properties to which the spirits of former inhabitants return; to psychical researchers they are dwellings where psychical phenomena occur spontaneously over a period of time, the precise mechanism behind this being unclear.

One of the earliest recorded stories of a haunted house is found in one of the letters of Pliny the Younger, written in around AD 90. It concerns a house in Athens abandoned by its inhabitants because of the disturbance caused there by the ghost of a filthy old man with a flowing beard and rattling chains. Following this, the house was rented by a philosopher named Athenodorus who, on seeing the ghost for himself, followed it to a spot in a courtyard where it vanished. The ground there was subsequently dug up – revealing the bones of a man. After these bones were given a religious burial the ghost appeared no more. Stories in which the dead return to haunt their former abodes to secure proper funeral rites can be found in many cultures and countries – including China, ancient Egypt and South America – spread over many centuries. The idea that the ghostly phenomena found in haunted houses are caused by unquiet spirits remains strongly in vogue today, despite the alternative theories that have been postulated from the 19th century onwards (see HAUNTINGS).

The first attempt to study haunted houses in a 'scientific' manner was made by the 'Committee on Haunted Houses', as established by the SOCIETY FOR PSYCHICAL RESEARCH at its foundation in 1882. The Committee immediately found itself overwhelmed with material, declaring, 'Our labours in this direction have been fruitful beyond our expectation.' Seeking to separate haunted houses from other types of ghostly phenomena, another contemporary researcher, Ada Goodrich Freer, declared in 1894:

> What we have to deal with here are those houses which are, with more or less frequency, habitually visited by phantasms commonly supposed to be those of former inhabitants.

From the outset, the 'scientific' researchers of the 19th century claimed that the manifestations described in haunted houses indicated a place-centred form of haunting, with successive living occupants experiencing paranormal phenomena suggestive of the continuing presence of a deceased individual or

The ghosts of both a lady in a green cloak and a medieval knight are said to haunt Bamburgh Castle, one of Britain's many 'haunted houses'. (© Adam Woolfitt/Corbis)

individuals. Often these dead individuals had a habitual or emotional association with the property, but in many other cases no clear link could be established.

Classic phenomena reported by those who have either lived in or visited what they believe to be a haunted house include visual APPARITIONS, the sensation of there being 'a presence', feelings of being touched, unexplained noises (particularly footsteps), temperature variations, unusual smells, and the unexplained movement of objects. Domestic pets, such as cats and dogs, are often said to display unusual reactions inside haunted houses, and anomalous electrical activity of various sorts is also frequently reported. With the exception of the disruption of electrical devices such as televisions or tape recorders, and the fogging or misting of photographs, these patterns are consistent in reports since the 19th century. In a number of cases the reported phenomena resemble those in POLTERGEIST cases, but classically poltergeists seem to be focused on a particular person, rather than a place.

The literature of haunted houses is vast and it is often claimed that Great Britain has more haunted houses than anywhere else in the world. Such assertions remain unprovable, but it seems certain that the UK has recorded and preserved more stories than any other nation. Classic Victorian collections include the research of Mrs Catherine Crowe in *The Night Side of Nature* (1848), and John Ingram's two-volume work, *The Haunted Homes and Family Traditions of Great Britain* (1884). The latter concentrates upon stately homes, castles and manor houses and set the pattern

for popular collections of 'true' ghost stories which continues to this day. Houses which are famously reputed to be haunted include Bamburgh Castle in Northumberland, Bettiscombe Manor in Dorset (see SCREAMING SKULLS), Burton Agnes Hall in Yorkshire, Corby Castle in Cumbria, Felbrigg Hall in Norfolk, Himpton Ampner Manor House in Hampshire, Newstead Abbey in Nottinghamshire (see BLACK MONK), Peele Castle on the Isle of Man and Sawston Hall in Cambridgeshire. Most royal residences are reputedly haunted, including Buckingham Palace, Glamis Castle in Scotland, HAMPTON COURT PALACE in Surrey, St James's Palace in London, Sandringham in Norfolk and Windsor Castle in Berkshire, and virtually every historic ruin in Great Britain has a ghost story associated with it, particularly monastic remains. Such locations inevitably provide a more interesting and impressive background than more humble residences, as well as fitting the dramatic demands of a popular ghost story.

However, from the end of the 19th century reports were being made of hauntings at middle- and working-class dwellings, the latter apparently being more prone to poltergeist outbreaks than visual apparitions. The 19th and early 20th centuries also saw a preponderance of alleged hauntings at rural rectories and parsonages, such as BORLEY RECTORY in Essex, but this category seems to have declined in recent decades. From the mid-20th century onwards there are numerous reports of haunted council houses as well as many other types of building, and it would seem that today any house may be haunted, no matter how grand or small.

haunted people

People believed to be haunted by ghosts or other supernatural entities.

The folklore of many nations avers that GHOSTS can attach themselves to the living. Sometimes the attachment is affectionate (for example, deceased relatives who protect children) but, more often, the returning presence will be the victim of a crime, wrong or broken promise perpetrated by the living person. A classic example is the 17th-century story of Caisho Burroughs recorded by John Aubrey in *Miscellanies* (1696). Caisho Burroughs was a handsome man who took the virginity of a passionate Italian gentlewoman who had fallen in love with him. The lady swore him to secrecy but after her death he boasted of the affair to acquaintances at a tavern. Almost immediately, her ghost appeared before him, though she was unseen by others. Thereafter she made regular appearances to him, always preceded by a sense of chilliness, with her last appearance being on the same morning Burroughs was killed in a duel.

Many religious traditions also countenance the possibility of SPIRITS or DEMONS possessing or harassing the living, sometimes displaying violence (see INVISIBLE ASSAILANTS). Such ideas were mostly replaced in the 20th century by theories which attributed such POLTERGEIST phenomena to an effect of the mind of a living person, rather than to a DISCARNATE ENTITY. In 1928 the German researcher A F Von Schrenk-Notzing wrote:

> So, we see that these phenomena take the place of neurosis. Sensations of guilt, sadistic inclinations, an attitude of enmity and malice toward the environment, all these come to a reality, through the phenomena, in other words through paranormal and unconscious channels.

The idea that poltergeist phenomena are generated by the unconscious mind of individuals, particularly those under stress, was taken up by the American psychoanalyst and psychical researcher Nandor Fodor. It has become widely accepted among parapsychologists (see PARAPSYCHOLOGY) in the decades since. PSYCHICAL RESEARCH has thus embraced the idea of haunted individuals – but as examples of manifestations of RECURRENT SPONTANEOUS PSYCHOKINESIS rather than some form of external entity.

However, not all researchers believe that the unconscious mind is at the root of every poltergeist outbreak. The methodology for making such assessments has been severely criticized, and there are examples of cases which (if the truth of the reports is accepted) appear to stretch the theory to its limit.

These include cases in which the poltergeist apparently inflicts suffering and harm on its human focus, and cases of alleged POSSESSION; although whether the claims that EXORCISM has been successful in some of these cases support a spiritual explanation, or simply offer evidence for the power of suggestion, is a matter of opinion.

hauntings

Place-, person- or object-centred spontaneous paranormal phenomena – the word is popularly understood to relate to cases where the events are said to be caused by discarnate, supernatural entities.

Although in some cases the phenomena may seem to be focused upon a particular individual (see HAUNTED PEOPLE) or even an object, the term 'haunting' is most often used for those that are place-centred. The popular view is that hauntings involve the GHOSTS of the dead. The phenomena may include visual apparitions, the sensation of a presence, anomalous noises (particularly footsteps), temperature variations, smells, object movements, doors opening and closing by themselves, electrical anomalies and strange reactions on the part of domestic animals. In certain cases, manifestations reported in HAUNTED HOUSES are reminiscent of POLTERGEISTS; they can also resemble certain alleged SÉANCE room phenomena although they seemingly occur without the deliberate involvement of any identifiable MEDIUM. However, attempts to record haunting activity with automated equipment have been largely disappointing – one of the (less cynical) suggestions to explain this being that hauntings may always require the presence of living persons to occur.

Interestingly, the 20th century saw a marked expansion in the types of premises that featured in reports of hauntings. They are apparently no longer confined to ancient castles, ruined abbeys or stately homes and have now been reported in a wide variety of domestic, commercial and industrial buildings – including offices, power stations and factories – as well as in the open air.

Theories relating to the nature of hauntings have been discussed for centuries and can be divided into naturalistic and spiritual (or PSYCHIC). Naturalistic theories include explanations based around human frailties including fraud, wishful thinking, mental illness and misperception of normal phenomena, and there is no doubt that these certainly account for many claims. More complex 'geophysical' theories, particularly those proposed by Guy Lambert (1878–1973) of the SOCIETY FOR PSYCHICAL RESEARCH in the 1950s and 1960s, suggest that hauntings arise from vibrations set up by tides and underground water. Other advanced seismic theories contend that electromagnetic energy released from tectonic plates may be responsible for some reports – an idea suggested primarily by the Canadian researchers Michael Persinger and R A Cameron. Such discharges, it is proposed, might affect the temporal lobes of the brain, causing HALLUCINATIONS. Man-made electromagnetic radiation and infra-sound have also been offered as potential causes.

Spiritual and psychic explanations are equally varied. Until the end of the 19th century hauntings were predominantly seen as spiritual phenomena, arising from manifestations of unquiet SPIRITS or even diabolical forces. The unquiet spirit hypothesis remains a popular theory even in the 21st century. However, a number of other psychic theories have been proposed.

From the 1890s it was accepted by many psychical researchers (see PSYCHICAL RESEARCH) that visual APPARITIONS were essentially hallucinatory in nature and a number of theories about hauntings reflect this. G N M Tyrell was one of a number of researchers who proposed that TELEPATHY plays a major part in their creation. Such theories maintain that apparitions are perceptual ideas, transmitted through telepathy from living minds, and perhaps also from those of the deceased who may survive as DISCARNATE ENTITIES. Other theories see thoughts as capable of independent existence and capable of leaving traces or imprinting themselves either upon the environment (see STONE TAPE THEORY) or upon a postulated 'psychic ether' which permeates all matter. Other psychic theories include those based around interactions with other dimensions, or a 'level of reality' beyond the material world – however, on our present understanding of the nature of the universe such ideas can at best only be described as speculative.

Currently, no one theory is adequately able to account for all of the phenomena reported in connection with hauntings, particularly those involving object movements and the disturbance of the physical environment. Certainly, the psychic theories will require further understanding (and of course indisputable proof) of PSYCHOKINESIS, poltergeist phenomena and mediumship before they can be developed to provide a satisfactory explanation of the mechanism by which hauntings occur.

One final common claim in relation to hauntings is the observation that they appear to become milder and fade away with time – suggesting that whatever energy sustains them may gradually dissipate. It has even been postulated by some researchers that ghosts may have a 'life' of about 400 years; relatively few visible apparitions seem to date from before this period, so far as any historical origin can be identified – although phantom monks and nuns seem to be an exception to this rule. Reports of Roman ghosts are exceedingly rare, and the ghostly horseman allegedly witnessed by Dr R C C Clay (who, conveniently, was an archaeologist) at Bottlebush Down in Dorset in 1927 is the only known example of a Bronze Age ghost in the British Isles. Whatever lies behind hauntings, it would seem that even ghosts are not immortal.

Hauser, Kaspar (c.1812–1833)
A German foundling, apparently a 'wild boy'.
Kaspar Hauser came to public attention as a strange youth found wandering in the marketplace of Nuremberg, Germany, in May 1828.

Witnesses estimated his age as around 16, but his behaviour was that of a much younger child and he could give no explanation of his origins or of how he had come to be there. Later, he told a story of having lived in a hole in the ground, completely isolated from the world apart from a mysterious man who looked after his needs but had eventually abandoned him in the marketplace.

He seemed to be completely unused to human contact and walked with the unsteady gait of a toddler. While he was able to speak and understand German, his vocabulary and grasp of grammar were childish. He was carrying two letters, one purportedly written by his mother, saying that his name was Kaspar and explaining that he was the illegitimate son of a cavalry officer. The writer claimed to be too poor to care for him and asked for him to be taken in by a peasant family until he was old enough to join the cavalry like his father. The other letter, from the family who had raised the baby, asked that he be enrolled in a cavalry regiment. It was later argued that both documents were forgeries.

Hauser would eat only bread and water at first, claiming that these had been his only form of nourishment throughout his life. However, he did not exhibit the effects of the malnutrition he would undoubtedly have suffered if this had been the case.

Rumours about his origins soon spread, one of the most persistent being that he was a scion of a noble family. In particular, it was claimed that he was the son of Karl, Grand Duke of Baden (1786–1818), whose title had passed to an uncle after he had died without a living son. The theory was that a dying baby boy had been substituted for Kaspar, thus cheating him of his inheritance. Presumably those responsible lacked the hardness of heart to murder the boy. On the other hand, many believed Hauser to be a fake.

The youth's story became famous throughout Europe and he was looked after and studied by various eminent men. He was educated and gradually brought to be more at home in society but never lost an air of strangeness and other-worldly innocence.

His senses were said to be more acute than normal, especially his sense of smell and his eyesight, which allegedly allowed him to see in the dark.

In 1829 he was the victim of a knife attack by a hooded man which left him with a serious head wound. While some accused him of having inflicted the injury on himself, others took the incident as proof that vested interests were concerned with having Hauser put out of the way or frightened into silence.

Whatever the truth of the first incident, four years later Hauser was fatally stabbed by an unidentified assailant, dying after three days in which he was often accused of having attempted suicide. Hauser died insisting that he had not harmed himself.

The story was brought to a wider audience in 1974 when the German director and screenwriter Werner Herzog (1942–   ) filmed it as *The Enigma of Kaspar Hauser*.

In 2002 DNA-matching tests were carried out on samples from Hauser's clothing and from the royal family of Baden. The results appeared to show that the boy was indeed related to them. However, the truth behind his short and sad existence remains a mystery.

headless horseman

A decapitated phantom known in folklore and common in popular ghost fiction.

The ghostly motif of a headless rider upon a phantom horse is a popular and widespread one. Early instances arise in German and Scandinavian folklore and are linked with the Norse legend of the WILD HUNT. Although examples of headless horsemen are also known in British and Irish folklore, such as the Headless Rider of Castle Sheela, Ireland, there are fewer examples in folklore (taken to refer to oral tradition rather than imaginative literature) than might be supposed.

Accounts of apparently real-life sightings of headless horsemen are certainly few and far between, although apparitions of a ghostly decapitated horseman are occasionally linked with a historic incident. Legends of a headless horseman at Temple Bridge, Icklingham, Suffolk, were linked to the Peasant's Revolt of 1381, when the clergyman John de Cambridge was beheaded there by Wat Tyler's mob.

Headless horsemen are most often found in fiction, with perhaps the best known appearing in Washington Irving's story 'The Legend of Sleepy Hollow' (1820), and the novel *The Headless Horseman* (1869) by Captain Mayne Reid.

Latin American ghost tradition also contains an archetypal horse-riding phantom who is sometimes considered to be headless, the 'jinete negro' or 'black rider'.

healing *see* FAITH HEALING; LAYING-ON OF HANDS; PSYCHIC HEALING; PSYCHIC SURGERY

healing magic *see* MAGIC, HEALING

Heathenry

A recreation of the Old Norse and Germanic religious beliefs and practices.

Also known as Odinism, Asatru and the Northern Tradition, among other names, Heathenry is the modern resurgence of the Old Norse and Germanic religious beliefs. It is related to but distinct from modern PAGANISM. The word Heathen is generally thought to mean 'of the heath', just as pagan means 'of the country', in both cases distinguishing the polytheistic 'folk' religion of the ordinary country people from the monotheistic Christianity which was imported to northern Europe during the Dark Ages.

The main reason that the terms 'Heathenry' and the 'Northern Tradition' tend to be preferred to other names is that the alternatives are thought to be too deity-specific. Followers of Odinism respect the whole pantheon, and often have allegiance to other gods as well as Odin. Followers of Asatru (the religion of the Asa or Aesir) will also acknowledge the other family of gods in Norse mythology, the Vanir; in fact, there is a linked religious tradition called Vanatru.

There is a distinction between retro-Heathens, who attempt to recreate the old beliefs and practices as closely as possible, and neo-Heathens who, like neopagans (see NEOPAGANISM), adapt the old beliefs for today's world. But all Heathens root their beliefs in Norse, Germanic and Anglo-Saxon mythology, as expressed in the *Eddas* or their German equivalent, the *Niebelengenlied*.

Heathens are strongly environmentalist, lay a great deal of stress on the family, and have a strong ethical code, with an emphasis on 'honour, courage, truth, loyalty, self-discipline, hospitality, industriousness, independence and endurance'.

There are numerous Heathen organizations in Britain, Germany, Scandinavia and the USA, including the Troth (formerly the Ring of Troth), the Odinic Rite, Odinshof and, since 2004, the Association of Polytheist Traditions. Members include a number of academics and authors of both non-fiction and fiction.

A few Heathen groups, particularly in Germany and the USA, are politically far right, even neo-Nazi or white-supremacist. The majority, however, are not, and dissociate themselves firmly from such extreme groups.

Heaven's Gate

A UFO religious group whose members committed suicide in 1997.

In March 1997, 39 members of a small religious group committed suicide. Outside academia Heaven's Gate were almost completely unknown, but unusually, they had been studied by one sociologist of religion almost since their beginning, so a great deal is known about their history and their beliefs.

The group, which went under several names in its 22-year life, was founded in 1975 by Marshall Herff Applewhite (1931–97) and Bonnie Nettles (1927–85); at different times they were known as 'The Two', or Bo and Peep, or Do and Ti. They were not sexual partners; Applewhite was homosexual, and also, along with several of the other male members, had voluntarily been castrated. Over the years perhaps 1,000 people were associated with the group, although at its highest its membership was only around 200. By 1997 membership had dwindled to very few more than those who died.

The beliefs of Heaven's Gate were a complex

Marshall Herff Applewhite and Bonnie Nettles (known variously as 'The Two', 'Bo and Peep', and 'Do and Ti'), founders of the UFO religious group Heaven's Gate.
(© Bettmann/Corbis)

mixture of NEW AGE ideas, THEOSOPHY and science fiction, with a strong emphasis on UFOs. Like some other religious groups, they believed that they were divine spirits trapped within the physical shell of their human bodies. Applewhite wrote:

> The final act of metamorphosis or separation from the human kingdom is the 'disconnect' or separation from the human physical container or body in order to be released from the human environment.

In March 1997 the comet Hale-Bopp became visible from the Earth. One photograph of the approaching comet seemed to show a small dot following behind it. A well-known practitioner of so-called 'remote viewing' studied the dot and claimed on a radio show that it was a spaceship. This was the sign that Heaven's Gate had been waiting for, in order to 'disconnect ... from the human physical container'. The members of the group believed that the spaceship would take them on to the next level of their existence.

Those who died were mainly in their forties, and were the core of the group who had remained with the movement since the beginning, while other members had joined and left over the years. Shortly before they committed suicide they made a video in which they explained what they were about to do and why. It seems that all of them were happy to 'disconnect'; there appears to have been no hint of coercion or of possible 'suicide/murder' as with the Peoples Temple at Jonestown in 1978, the BRANCH DAVIDIANS at Waco in 1993 and the Order of the Solar Temple in 1994.

hellfire clubs

A number of exclusive clubs popular among rich and privileged young men of the 18th century, the most famous of which was founded by Sir Francis Dashwood in 1746; such clubs were notoriously rumoured to indulge in orgiastic behaviour and Satanic worship.

In the 18th century, a number of social organizations provided the elite of British society with pleasures, many of which violated the moral standards of the time. The members of these clubs were usually young rakes and bucks whose activities consisted of heavy drinking, public brawling, practical jokes, vandalism and whoring. It was highly fashionable for young upper-class men to belong to such clubs, but several organizations were said to have gone a stage further and added Satanic orgies to their curriculum. Such organizations popularly called themselves 'Hellfire Clubs' and the most prominent of these were the Dublin Hellfire Club, and the English club founded by Sir Francis Dashwood. Neither was the first such organization; in 1721, before either was founded, a

Royal Edict had been passed, condemning gatherings of this kind. But they were the two best-known of the various 'Hellfire Clubs' of the 18th century.

The Dublin Hellfire Club, which formed in 1735, usually met in the Eagle Tavern on Cork Hill. As well as indulging in drinking, gambling and debauchery, its members liked to promote the idea that they held Satanic rituals. The Dublin Hellfire Club continued till about 1741, but tales of demonic appearances, BLACK MASSES and sacrifices have been associated with its venue ever since. Another Hellfire Club existed in Limerick around the same time, and Dublin saw a second Hellfire Club in the 1780s. However, despite the reputation they cultivated, the members of the Irish Hellfire Clubs seem to have spent most of their time drinking and fighting duels, rather than worshipping SATAN.

The most famous Hellfire Club, founded and run by Sir Francis Dashwood, never actually called itself by that name. It held its first meetings in the public house, the George and Vulture, in Lombard Street, London, in 1746, to celebrate an earlier organization called the Hellfire Club which had gathered there in the 1720s. Dashwood's club appears to have been more exclusive and better organized than its Irish counterparts, and at first its membership was restricted to twelve, although it soon grew. The original twelve members included Dashwood himself, who was an MP, the artist William Hogarth and the politician John Wilkes. Although not a member, Benjamin Franklin also attended meetings. The group variously called itself the Brotherhood of St Francis of Wycombe, the Order of Knights of West Wycombe, and the Monks of Medmenham. They addressed one another as 'brothers', called Dashwood 'abbot', and referred to their female guests as 'nuns'. The club's motto was *Fay ce que vouldras* ('Do what thou wilt'), which was later adopted by ALEISTER CROWLEY.

In 1749, the George and Vulture burned down, possibly as a result of one of the club's meetings. Dashwood then built a temple in the grounds of his West Wycombe home, and had a network of caves excavated under West Wycombe Hill, which are said to have been used for wild parties. He also acquired the ruins of Medmenham Abbey in 1755. He had it rebuilt in the style of the Gothic revival, for the use of the club, but by 1762, factions and political rivalries had caused it to disband. There are varied accounts of their orgiastic practices and Satanic rites, but no club records were kept, so nothing is known for sure. However, since Dashwood and some of the other members had powerful political enemies, it may be that the accounts of their exploits were considerably exaggerated to blacken their names, and that many of the wilder stories owed more to popular fantasy than

to fact; while some of the club's members probably did indulge in pseudo-Satanic rites as a prelude to their orgies, most of them appear to have been, in the words of one of their order, content to be 'happy disciples of Venus and Bacchus who got together occasionally to celebrate women and wine'.

Hell Hole *see* SIBERIAN HELL HOLE

hellhounds

Ghostly dogs that hunt in a pack, often linked with the Devil.

Stories of packs of hellhounds feature particularly in the folklore of the west and north of England. Some commentators have linked these stories with Norse legends of Odin and the WILD HUNT; these were later Christianized, with the huntsman becoming THE DEVIL on a quest to snatch up the souls of sinners and unbaptized children. Later traditions replace the Devil with the spirit of a human being of ill repute and transform the dogs into a supernatural menace to the life of anyone unfortunate enough to encounter them. In many stories their barks and howls alone are considered fatal or at the very least an OMEN of impending death. Hellhounds are known as the Devil's Dandy Dogs in Cornwall, as the Wish or Yeth Hounds in Devon, Cwn Annwn in Wales, the Hooters in Warwickshire and the Gabriel Ratchetts in Lancashire. On Dartmoor, the leader of the hellhounds is said to be Sir Francis Drake – it is locally rumoured that he dabbled in BLACK MAGIC. In other local traditions the identity of the pack-master becomes an unpopular local member of the aristocracy or judiciary as with Colonel Sidney, an 18th-century squire at Ranworth, Norfolk, or Judge Sir John Popham (1531–1607) at Wellington, Somerset.

henges

A prehistoric enclosed circular or oval area.

'Henge' is the name given to two types of prehistoric construction. The first is a circular or oval plateau enclosed by an earthen bank and an internal ditch; some of these contain a burial chamber. It seems that the material excavated to make the ditch was usually used to form the outer bank. Sometimes a second encircling ditch is found, and occasionally there is no ditch at all. The second type of henge is again a circular or oval plateau, but in this case surrounded by a construction of large standing stones, such as at STONEHENGE or AVEBURY, or wooden posts, such as at WOODHENGE. Each type had at least one formal entrance leading to the central enclosure. The word itself is a back-formation from Stonehenge, which literally means 'stone gallows'.

The purpose of henges is still a matter of conjecture, but it is assumed that they had some sort of religious or ritual function. The fact that the ditch is always inside the bank would indicate that they were certainly not intended as fortified sites. Some henges are believed to have been built with a deliberate alignment of the axis (and the entrance) towards a particular point of the compass or the position of sunrise or sunset on important days. However, many do not fit into this category and it is thought local geographical conditions often determined the siting. See also MEGALITHS.

hepatoscopy

Divination by inspecting the livers of animals.

Hepatoscopy, or 'liver-gazing' (from the Greek *hēpar, hēpatos*, liver, and *skopeein*, to view), was a form of divination believed to have originated with the ancient Etruscans. The Babylonians also practised it, as did the Romans. The liver was thought to be the source of blood, and hence, the basis of life, and the livers of sacrificial animals (usually sheep) were studied and interpreted by a specially trained priest, known to the Romans as the haruspex, to learn the will of the gods. Each region of the liver was thought to represent a particular deity, and the markings in each zone were of great significance. An Etruscan bronze sculpture of a sheep's liver, with the areas assigned to the various gods marked on it, was discovered in 1877 near Piacenta in Northern Italy.

Heretical Sects *see panel p301*

Hermetica

A body of esoteric literature whose authorship is ascribed to Hermes Trismegistus, a priest and teacher deified by the Egyptians as the god Thoth, although the texts are generally believed to have been produced by a number of individuals between the 2nd and 3rd centuries AD. Most of the books in this extensive corpus have been lost, but a few of the texts survived and were rediscovered during the Renaissance; since then, they have been a major influence on the development of Western occultism and magic.

Hermes Trismegistus, or 'thrice-great Hermes', was the name given to a legendary priest, teacher, prophet and scribe deified by the Egyptians as the god Thoth and also identified with Hermes, the Greek god of science and wisdom. He was said to have introduced ALCHEMY to Egypt, and an extensive body of esoteric writings in various languages such as Syriac, Arabic, Armenian, Coptic and Byzantine Greek, collectively known as the Hermetica, was ascribed to him.

Most of these Hermetic books were lost, but a number of Greek texts survived, and Byzantine copies of them were rediscovered and popularized in Italy during the Renaissance after being translated into Latin by Marsilio Ficino as *De potestate et sapientia Dei*. At that time, the texts were believed to be copies of much older Egyptian works, but in 1614 the classical scholar Isaac Casaubon's analysis of their language proved that some of them, in particular those which dealt with philosophy, contained vocabulary which was too modern to have such an ancient origin, and these texts, which came to be known as the *Corpus Hermeticum*, are generally thought to have been composed between the 2nd and 3rd centuries AD, by a number of individuals or small groups of people as part of the rebirth of syncretistic and intellectualized pagan thought which was taking place at this time. The wide-ranging subject matter of the *Corpus Hermeticum* includes alchemy, MAGIC, ASTROLOGY, Platonism (see PLATO), Stoicism and Gnostic (see GNOSTICISM) thought. It is presented mainly as dialogue, a favourite form for didactic material in Greek antiquity, in which Hermes Trismegistus instructs one of three pupils – Tat, Asclepius or Ammon – on points of hidden wisdom. In 1650, John Everard translated Ficino's Latin version into English as *The Divine Pymander in XVII Books*.

While the most well-known of the texts of the *Corpus Hermeticum* were written by Greek speakers under Roman rule, the Hermetic genre continued after the fall of the Roman Empire. The most famous example of later Hermetic literature is the Emerald Tablet. This short and cryptic work is the most influential text in alchemy, and was said to have been found in the tomb of Hermes Trismegistus, clutched in the dead sage's mummified hands. It was regarded by European alchemists as the foundation of their art, and in its dozen or so verses it is said to contain the sum of all knowledge; the famous occult maxim 'As above, so below' is a paraphrase of one of these verses.

Hermetic literature was a seminal force in Renaissance thought and culture, and hermeticism, the study and practice of occult philosophy and magic based on these writings, was profoundly influential in the development of the Western magical tradition. It was revived in the 19th century by occultists such as ÉLIPHAS LÉVI and groups like the HERMETIC ORDER OF THE GOLDEN DAWN, and neopagan witchcraft is full of rituals and symbolism derived from Hermetic texts.

Heretical Sects

The words 'heresy' and 'heretic' come from the Greek *hairesis*, meaning 'choice'. A heretic is someone who chooses to believe something different from the prevailing orthodox, mainstream, established doctrine. It is defined by the ruling orthodoxy, a word that literally means 'straight opinion' (ie 'correct' opinion), as 'heterodoxy' means 'other or different opinions'. The word 'sect', which is often used pejoratively to mean a troublesome or even dangerous religious group, actually simply means a group which has split away from a parent body; Christianity was originally a Jewish sect, before its beliefs changed so markedly that it became a completely new religion.

The early centuries of Christianity were characterized by a multiplicity of beliefs and practices. Even in the period described in the Acts of the Apostles there were huge differences between the Jerusalem Church, led by James, who were (in simple terms) messianic Jews, and the largely Gentile Church scattered around the northern Mediterranean, founded, taught and led by Paul (who had never met Jesus). After the Roman destruction of the temple in Jerusalem and the routing of the Jews in AD 70, the Pauline version of Christianity quickly gained the ascendancy.

But as the Church had no local bishops and no central authority, the way that Christianity was practised, and the details of what Christians actually believed, varied from place to place. This was not acceptable to Irenaeus (c.130–200 AD), a Greek bishop in Gaul, who wrote the five-volume *Against Heresies*, and insisted that only one version of Christianity could be right, making all the others wrong. Christianity's distinctive intolerance of heterodox belief (compared, for example, with Hinduism's and Buddhism's acceptance of the validity of very different 'schools') began at this stage.

Despite Irenaeus, over the next few centuries different bishops in different places often had very different ideas about core Christian beliefs. How much was Jesus God, and how much was he man? Was he equal to the Father, or subordinate to him? Was the Holy Spirit a he or an it? Eventually the concept of the Trinity was developed: that there is one God in three distinct beings ('hypostases'). The wording of the Nicene Creed (from the Council of Constantinople in AD 381, not from the Council of Nicaea in AD 325) gives a flavour of the complications involved in defining the exact relationship between the various persons of the Godhead: Jesus is 'very God of very God, begotten, not made, being of one substance with the Father, by Whom all things were made'. But this is nothing compared to the convolutions of the Athanasian Creed:

> Such as the Father is, such is the Son, and such is the Holy Spirit.
> The Father uncreated, the Son uncreated, and the Holy Spirit uncreated.
> The Father incomprehensible, the Son incomprehensible, and the Holy Spirit incomprehensible.
> The Father eternal, the Son eternal, and the Holy Spirit eternal.
> And yet they are not three eternals but one eternal.
> As also there are not three uncreated nor three incomprehensible, but one uncreated and one incomprehensible.
> So likewise the Father is almighty, the Son almighty, and the Holy Spirit almighty.
> And yet they are not three almighties, but one almighty.

A creed (from the Latin *credo*, meaning 'I believe') is a formulaic statement of correct beliefs. The Athanasian Creed begins by saying that unless one keeps the faith defined within it 'whole and undefiled' then 'without doubt he shall perish everlastingly'. Council after council of the Early Church put out statements condemning one heresy after another.

GNOSTICISM was the great heresy for several centuries, and attracted many; even the great theologian of the Early Church, Saint Augustine, was a Manichean for some years. Gnosticism resurfaced as Bogomilism in Bulgaria, Bosnia and Hungary in the 10th to 12th centuries and most famously as Catharism in 12th- and 13th-century southern France.

Most of the variant beliefs in the Early Church concerned the nature of God. Arianism was the very widespread belief that although Jesus was God, he was subordinate to the Father because he had not always existed. Monarchianism (or Sabellianism) was the belief that there is only one God, not three, or even three-in-one, therefore Jesus and the Father were the same being – and therefore the Father suffered on the cross. Nestorianism argued that there was a clear distinction between God the Word and Jesus the man. Apollinarianism said that although Jesus was the Word in a human body, he did not have a human mind or soul.

There were many more. In each case the followers of the belief sincerely thought that they were following the truth, and that their opponents were wrong; no one defines himself as a heretic. In each case one group of bishops argued with another group of bishops – one side won and defined orthodoxy, the other side lost and were defined as heretics. Each council clarified and corrected the rulings of previous councils, and so Christian beliefs slowly and tortuously evolved. In terms of what later became the definitive version of Christian theology, many of the Church Fathers, including Origen and Augustine, actually held heretical beliefs.

Over the centuries Christianity split into three major denominational groups: first Roman Catholicism and the Eastern Orthodox Church, then Protestantism. With a few minor exceptions, these all held to the rulings of the early Church councils. Although some Evangelical Protestant books on heresies include Roman Catholicism, and at least one Roman Catholic book on heresies includes Protestantism, generally these main groups accept each other as Christian. But in the last few centuries a number of Christian sects have sprung up which are not accepted by mainstream Christianity – largely because they hold different beliefs as to the nature of God.

Earliest, dating from the 16th century, and most obviously, Unitarianism specifically denies the Trinity: it believes that the Father is God, Jesus was a man, and the Holy Spirit is God's influence. It has two other major differences from mainstream Christianity: it has no creed, and it welcomes religious pluralism. Unitarianism has these two characteristics in common with another early dissenting Church, the Society of Friends (or Quakers), founded in Britain around 1650.

Several millennialist sects, which believe in the imminent return of Jesus to reign for a MILLENNIUM on Earth, are also classed by mainstream Christianity as heretical, though not for their millennial beliefs, which tend to be little different from those of Evangelical Christian groups, but rather because of their unorthodox beliefs about the nature of God. Jehovah's Witnesses, for example, have a belief similar to Arianism, that Jesus is the first of God's creations, and so is inferior to God; the Holy Spirit is not part of the Trinity, but simply God-in-action. Christadelphians believe much the same about the Holy Spirit – that the Holy Spirit is the power and influence of God – but they see Jesus as literally the son of God and not God himself. The Church of Jesus Christ of Latter-day Saints (the Mormon Church) believes that the Godhead is made up of three quite distinct persons, the father and son being flesh-and-blood physical, and the Holy Spirit being a personage of spirit.

Although they often are, Seventh-day Adventists object to being classed with such heterodox movements because, they say, the majority of their beliefs are either the same as those of mainstream Christian Churches, or within the 'acceptable' bounds of denominational difference. For example, they believe in the orthodox Trinity, and the full divinity and humanity of Jesus.

Within mainstream Christianity today there are several movements which, to many traditional mainstream Christians, might appear sectarian, and possibly heretical. There are extreme charismatic groups which not only have speaking in tongues ('glossolalia') and prophecy but also the 'Toronto Blessing', with believers being 'slain in the Spirit', falling down laughing or crying or barking like a dog at the touch of a preacher. And although healing has always (at least theoretically) been part of Christian belief, if not practice, it is now often accompanied by the violent casting out of demons, especially in independent black Pentecostal churches.

It has been suggested that the dispute within the Anglican Communion over gay clergy, and the Christian Churches' perceived over-reaction to the novel *THE DA VINCI CODE*, show that in the 21st century conventional Christianity has still not come to terms with heresy.

David V Barrett

Hermetic Order of the Golden Dawn

An occult society founded in 1888, which incorporated elements of Rosicrucianism, Freemasonry and the kabbalah, and focused on both practical and ritual magic; although short-lived, it was probably the most influential Western magical order of modern times.

Originally titled the Fraternity of the Esoteric Order of the Golden Dawn, the occult society better known as the Hermetic Order of the Golden Dawn was founded in 1888 by three members of a group called the Societas Rosicruciana – Dr William R Woodman, Dr Wynn Westcott, and MACGREGOR MATHERS. The founders compiled and developed a system of philosophy, rituals, magical incantations and symbols that incorporated elements from the KABBALAH, Rosicrucianism (see ROSICRUCIANS) and FREEMASONRY, as well as material from the Egyptian BOOK OF THE DEAD. Its concepts and works were also influenced by THEOSOPHY, ÉLIPHAS LÉVI, and late medieval GRIMOIRES. The stated purpose of the Order was to test, purify and exalt the spiritual nature of the individual, and to further what it called 'the Great Work', which was to obtain control of the nature and power of one's being. The Outer Order of the Golden Dawn was controlled by an Inner Order of which only Westcott, Woodman and Mathers were members and the self-appointed chiefs. Mathers claimed to receive his orders and teachings from a third order of superhuman adepts called the SECRET CHIEFS, thought to be entities of the astral plane. The structured hierarchy was based upon the TREE OF LIFE of the kabbalah, with ten grades corresponding to the Tree of Life's ten SEPHIROTH. The Order taught three magical systems: the Key of Solomon, Abramelin, and Enochian. It also gave instruction in astral travel, SCRYING, ALCHEMY, the TAROT, and ASTROLOGY.

Commonly referred to as the Golden Dawn, this organization was probably the single greatest influence on 20th-century occultism. In it, most of the concepts of magic and ritual that have since become core elements of WICCA, THELEMA, Western Mystery Schools and other forms of magical spirituality were first formulated. From its very beginnings, it wrapped itself in a cloak of manufactured legend and secrecy; members took an oath not to publicly reveal its teachings, on pain of being struck down by spirits. It attracted a membership which included a number of prominent poets and artists, notably the authors Algernon Blackwood and W B Yeats, who in later life stated that all of his work derived from his study and practice of magic. One of its most revolutionary aspects was the admittance of women to its ranks, unlike Masonic and Rosicrucian lodges, which were exclusively male.

Its Outer Order focused on practical magic, while its Inner Order, which was also the organization's repository of Rosicrucian knowledge, dedicated itself to experimental ritual magic (see MAGIC, RITUAL). In 1891, Westcott founded the Westcott Hermetic Library as an alchemical resource for its members. One of its best-known and lasting legacies is the Golden Dawn Tarot, designed by Mathers.

When Woodman died in 1891, he was not replaced within the organization. Westcott resigned to protect his position as the London coroner, leaving Mathers in effective control of the Order. ALEISTER CROWLEY joined the society in 1898, quickly rising through its ranks, but then he and Mathers fell out; the antagonism between them is said to have led to their engaging in a psychic war which went on for years. In any event, both were eventually expelled from the Order, which subsequently fragmented, with various members claiming leadership. Some members left to form a society which retained the name of the Golden Dawn, but was more focused on mysticism than magic, and this underwent further splits; the followers of Mathers founded one spin-off organization, the Alpha et Omega Temple, and another main splinter group was called the Stella Matutina. Today, numerous societies exist which claim heirdom to the Golden Dawn tradition. Although it only lasted 15 years, it remains one of the most influential Western magical orders of modern times.

Herne the Hunter

In folklore, a spectral huntsman wearing a pair of stag's antlers, who is said to haunt Windsor Great Park. According to legend, he appears when the monarch is about to die or at other times of national crisis.

The first recorded reference to Herne the Hunter, a ghostly figure wearing a pair of stag's horns who is said to haunt Windsor Great Park, is from around 1597, in Shakespeare's play *The Merry Wives of Windsor*:

> Sometime a keeper here in Windsor Forest,
> Doth all the winter-time, at still midnight,
> Walk round about an oak, with great ragg'd horns …
> You have heard of such a spirit, and well you know
> The superstitious idle-headed eld
> Receiv'd, and did deliver to our age,
> This tale of Herne the Hunter for a truth.

There are several versions of the legend of Herne the Hunter, but the traditional story is that he was one of many huntsmen employed by King Richard II on the Windsor Castle estate. During a hunting party,

Herne saved the King's life when he was attacked by a wounded stag, but in doing so was mortally injured himself. A local wizard called Philip Urwick appeared from nowhere and offered to help, and he ordered that the dead stag's antlers should be removed and placed on Herne's head. He then took Herne to his hut and tended him for a month, and when he was restored to health, Herne returned to court and the King made him his favourite, giving him magnificent gifts such as a gold chain. But Herne's fellow foresters, jealous at his rise, went to Urwick and persuaded him to use his powers to remove Herne's hunting skills. He did so, and the King was forced to dismiss Herne from his service. In one version of the story, Herne's rivals also framed him for poaching. In shame and despair, Herne hanged himself from an oak tree in the forest, and the tree was blasted by lightning during a terrible thunderstorm.

Herne's rivals were at first delighted, but soon they too lost their hunting abilities, and consulting Urwick, they were told that they would have to appeal to Herne's spirit for mercy. They went to the oak and called on him, and he appeared, wearing his antlers, and ordered them to bring the royal horses and hounds to him and ride out to hunt with him the next night, and every night following. They obeyed, and soon the deer herds were depleted and the King demanded to know the cause. The huntsmen confessed their story. That night, Richard walked through the park, and Herne's spirit appeared and told him that the huntsmen who had brought about his death must be hanged from his oak. After this was done, the deer returned to the park as if by magic, and Herne never appeared again during Richard's reign, until the King's murder. Every winter, he is said to ride out at midnight on a black horse, accompanied by fierce hunting dogs and a horned owl, carrying a hunting horn and his golden chain, and still wearing his antlers. The hanged huntsmen are compelled to ride with him for all eternity, and he leads a wild hunt through the forest at the midwinter solstice, collecting damned souls to join with him. He is said to appear at the tree now known as Herne's Oak whenever the monarch behaves unjustly, or is about to die, or when the nation is in danger, and is said to have been sighted before such historic events as the execution of Charles I in 1649, the eve of both World Wars in 1914 and 1939, the abdication of Edward VIII in 1936, and George VI's death in 1952. It is generally believed that the Herne's Oak of Shakespeare's time was felled by accident in 1796, and that replacements have been planted on or around the original site since then.

Some people have suggested that certain motifs in the story – the wearing of stag's horns, the significance of the oak tree and the reference to the Wild Hunt – are echoes of much older myths of a HORNED GOD, as worshipped in Britain in pagan times, and that these elements, retained as a distant folk memory, were combined with a local ghost story to create a legend that has become part of British folkore.

Hessdalen

A remote region of Norway where numerous anomalous lights and sounds were recorded during the 1980s, inspiring the first co-ordinated scientific UFO hunt.

The mountainous Hessdalen Valley is 118 kilometres (73 miles) south of the Swedish city of Trondheim. It suffers exceptionally harsh winters and has a very isolated population, numbering just a few hundred, all of whom are inherently experienced in their observation and understanding of the natural world.

In November 1981 a number of locals started seeing yellowish-white bullet-shaped lights and small red dots in the sky. Most of them appeared at night, but a few were seen during the day. They moved low on the horizon and over the hills. Others reported hearing rumbling noises below the ground, passing over great distances. There had only been sporadic reports of this type prior to 1981, but the regular sightings continued until 1986, when they faded away, to be followed by only a few reoccurrences in the years since.

The study of UFOs is often criticized as a discipline for the lack of any solid proof of anything strange. Recognizing the unique opportunity that these recurring sightings presented, a team of researchers put together Project Hessdalen in an attempt to capture valuable evidence. The team included a number of Scandinavian UFO researchers and the English researcher Paul Devereux, who had investigated ELECTROMAGNETIC PHENOMENA associated with EARTHQUAKES and tremors. The project received support from several University departments in Oslo and Bergen which lent equipment to the researchers.

In January and February 1984 observations were carried out using seismographs, infrared viewers, radar, magnetographs and specially equipped cameras that allowed for spectrum analysis. The team saw many lights during the weeks that they camped out in the valley, and on three occasions they were able to follow them simultaneously on their radar screens. A laser beam was flashed skywards by the team towards one light – which appeared to react by repeatedly altering its pattern of flashes coincident with the beam. Magnetic changes were recorded during many of the sightings and several photographs were taken. One radar specialist who studied the evidence collected by the expedition argued that the images were caused either by a solid object or by something that was

Project Hessdalen's observation post in 1984; the investigators witnessed numerous lights and took a number of intriguing photographs. (© Mary Evans Picture Library)

strongly ionized. A further expedition was mounted a year later, with DR J ALLEN HYNEK as a participant. However, by then the sightings had become few in number and the trip was mostly unsuccessful.

Opinions as to the nature of the Hessdalen lights vary. Devereux argued that they were geophysical phenomena linked to the local rocks and fault lines (see EARTH LIGHTS). Some of the other team members also agreed that although they were very unusual, the phenomena were probably of natural, earthly origin. Others, however, were persuaded that the apparently intelligent reaction occasionally displayed by the lights means that there was something more to this case.

Heuvelmans, Bernard (1916–2001)

Pioneering figure in cryptozoology, the author of several classic books on this subject, who became known as the 'Father of Cryptozoology'.

Born in Le Havre, France, Bernard Heuvelmans was introduced to the subject of mystery animals at an early age by his father, who had amassed a noteworthy collection of data on such animals – data that was later incorporated into his son's own, much more sizeable archive. Heuvelmans was also interested in science fiction novels, such as SIR ARTHUR CONAN DOYLE's *The Lost World* (1912), which contains all manner of surviving dinosaurs and ape-men.

In 1939, Heuvelmans obtained his PhD in zoology from the Free University in Brussels. Shortly afterwards, he joined the French army, was captured in Belgium by the Germans during World War II,

and was interned as a prisoner of war, escaping four times. Following the war, his skill as a jazz performer sustained him financially until, after reading an article on putative living dinosaurs by US mystery beast investigator Ivan T Sanderson (1911–73), his enthusiasm for this subject was revived. Steadily compiling a huge archive of published articles and reports, books and correspondence from fellow investigators and scientists worldwide, he set about researching and writing what became recognized as the standard work on the subject – *Sur la Piste des Bêtes Ignorées*, published in two volumes in 1955, and translated into English as the single volume *On the Track of Unknown Animals* in 1958. He also popularized the term 'CRYPTOZOOLOGY' for the scientific study of animals still awaiting formal description or recognition, and subsequently became known as the 'Father of Cryptozoology'.

Although Heuvelmans's work attracted a degree of cynicism from some zoologists, it was so rigorously analytical and comprehensively researched that it also received more than sufficient praise and interest from others to encourage him to continue writing on this subject, and several other books (as well as many articles) followed in due course. These dealt with GIANT OCTOPUSES and GIANT SQUIDS, SEA SERPENTS, the highly controversial Minnesota iceman (which he and Sanderson had personally examined, concluding that it was a preserved recently killed specimen of a Neanderthal-like human, which they christened *Homo pongoides*), living dinosaurs of Africa and MAN-BEASTS of Africa. Although best known for his cryptozoological writings, Heuvelmans wrote and edited many mainstream zoological publications too, as well as certain more esoteric works, such as those dealing with reincarnation and the history of jazz.

In 1982, Heuvelmans was elected President of the newly established INTERNATIONAL SOCIETY OF CRYPTOZOOLOGY, based in Tucson, Arizona. And in 1984, he announced that he was planning to write a monumental 20-volume cryptozoological encyclopedia, entitled *The Unknown Animals of the World*. Sadly, however, owing to a complex series of problems associated with this major work, the series never materialized, but in 1995 a revised edition of *On the Track of Unknown Animals* appeared, followed several years later by the long-awaited first English edition of his book on the giant octopus.

By the late 1990s, Heuvelmans's deteriorating health had brought his writing career to an end, and in 1999 he donated his entire cryptozoological archive to the Museum of Zoology in Lausanne, Switzerland. He died in 2001, but the passionate interest in cryptozoology that his books generated in many of his readers lives on in countless modern-day cryptozoologists, seeking those elusive CRYPTIDS that may still await discovery in the more remote regions of the world.

hexagram
A symmetrical six-pointed star formed by two overlapping equilateral triangles; a powerful symbol in alchemy and ceremonial magic, it has also been widely accepted as the emblem of Judaism since the 19th century.

The hexagram, also known as the sexagram and the magician's or sorcerer's star, is one of the oldest and most universal of spiritual symbols. It is a six-pointed star formed by two overlapping equilateral triangles, one pointing upward and the other downward, the intersection of which forms a regular hexagon. The earliest examples of the hexagram date back to around 700 BC, and according to some legends, King Solomon used it to exorcize negativity; in RITUAL MAGIC it is therefore known as the Seal of Solomon, and represents Divine Union. For many centuries it was revered in India as a symbol of the perpetual sexual union between the goddess Kali and the god Shiva which represented unity and harmony, and which was believed to maintain life in the universe. Later, it was adopted by medieval alchemists who saw it as uniting the alchemical symbol of fire (an upward-pointing triangle) with that of water (a downward-pointing triangle); it was thus used by them to refer to alcohol, which they believed was water infused with heat, but it was also seen as a symbol representing all four ELEMENTS, along with the fifth element, Spirit or

'quintessence'. The hexagram is often used in MAGIC to invoke all four elements and Spirit, and to invoke the powers of six of the seven classical 'planets' – Saturn, Venus, Mercury, Mars, the Moon and Jupiter – and medieval GRIMOIRES included a number of spells and seals which used it. In the KABBALAH, the hexagon formed in the centre of the figure when the six points are connected represents the sephirah TIPHARETH.

Interlaced patterns which can be drawn in a single, unbroken line are used by magicians for protection, since it is believed that such figures do not allow unwelcome spirits access, and the PENTAGRAM is the most popular symbol for this purpose. However, unlike the pentagram, the traditional hexagram is not formed from a single unbroken line, and so a version was devised by the HERMETIC ORDER OF THE GOLDEN DAWN which could be drawn in one continuous movement. This is sometimes known as the Unicursal Hexagram, or the Magic Hexagram.

Since the 19th century, the traditional hexagram has also been widely accepted as the emblem of Judaism. It appears on the coat of arms of the State of Israel, and is referred to as the Star of David or the Star of Zion.

hidden memory *see* CRYPTOMNESIA

high magic *see* MAGIC, HIGH

Hill, Betty (1919–2004) and Barney (1922–69)
The first classic alien abduction case reported in the USA, which could be seen as the prototype for hundreds of similar reports that have since followed.

Betty and Barney Hill were a mixed-race couple from Portsmouth, New Hampshire, who were both active in the civil rights movement and the New England church, and enjoyed a very good reputation in their local community. Betty was a social worker and Barney worked for the postal service and, at the time that they made the following incredible claim, they were in their early middle age.

Their story began late on 19 September 1961 when they were driving home after a short visit to Canada. As midnight approached they say they were crossing the White Mountains with little other traffic for company when they became intrigued by a white light that appeared to have been following them for some distance. As they neared North Woodstock Barney decided to stop the car and investigate the source of the light. With binoculars in hand Barney stared at what seemed to be a pancake-shaped craft with a large picture window, behind which several humanoid figures were moving.

Betty and Barney Hill photographed in 1967 with a book which
described their alien abduction claims. (© Bettmann/Corbis)

Back at the car Betty was becoming increasingly
worried and started shouting to her husband to
return. He did, crying out that 'they' were trying
to capture him, and the couple rapidly drove away.
Shortly afterwards, near Indian Head, the car seemed
to shake with a strange beeping noise and the Hills
began to feel odd sensations (akin to those sometimes
described as the OZ FACTOR). Their bodies were
tingling; they entered a dream-like state and lost
awareness of time and space. When they recovered
they were near Plymouth, 56 kilometres (35 miles)
further on – they later calculated that this part of the
journey had taken two hours longer than it should
have (see TIME, MISSING). On their arrival home they
both felt that something terrible had happened, but
could not recall anything specific. Barney apparently
spent some time staring at his genitals in a mirror
because the area felt very sore.

Five days later Betty wrote to the NATIONAL
INVESTIGATIONS COMMITTEE ON AERIAL PHENOMENA
(NICAP), after finding their address in a book at
the library. She suggested that she wished to find a

psychiatrist who could employ HYPNOSIS to try to fill
the gap in her memory – a technique she was aware
of through her work. This later led to the association
between ALIEN ABDUCTION cases and an investigation
method that was to become extremely widely
used, and also highly controversial (see MEMORIES,
RECOVERED).

Over the next few weeks, as Barney tried to forget
the incident, Betty was plagued by nightmares in
which she saw beings who were 1.5 metres (5 feet)
tall, with greyish skin tone and dark hair. They
seemed generally human in appearance. In the dreams
that Betty reported, the beings carried out a series of
medical tests on the couple, including one in which
a long needle was placed into Betty's abdomen – a
procedure that the entities told her was a pregnancy
test. NICAP sent a local astronomer, Walter Webb,
to investigate. NICAP filed their report but with
no history of previous ALIEN ABDUCTION reports to
refer to, they had no way to recognize the potential
significance of these after-effects.

A few months later Barney developed a growth

on his groin that had to be surgically removed. Despite Betty telling the doctor that she thought it was linked to their mountain adventure, they were advised against hypnosis. However, Betty's fears and nightmares would not go away and she eventually found her way to see Dr Benjamin Simon, a leading Boston psychiatrist. Over six months he conducted a series of sessions with both witnesses, apparently revealing that the dreams seemed to relate to the incident and the missing two hours. A few more details were added, including the taking of sperm samples from Barney. However, Simon rejected any connection with UFOs – he suggested that they might have seen a secret military aircraft and fantasized the rest. Eventually he concluded that they had been subject to a shared delusion, but he agreed that they were sincere and that they had clearly seen something that had frightened them.

While this case was being investigated a similar story told by ANTONIO VILLAS BOAS was being documented in South America. Neither case was made public until 1965, by which point they had both been fully recorded. The Hills' story only eventually found its way into a local newspaper after they spoke to their local church. The columnist John Fuller then took up their cause and wrote a book about their story. This text, *The Interrupted Journey*, was published in 1966 and was serialized in newspapers all over the world. Almost on its own, it created a pattern for the abduction phenomenon. In 1975 the book was made into a TV film, *The UFO Incident* – the first time a story based upon a purportedly real UFO encounter had been dramatized in this way, and a forerunner of later films such as *CLOSE ENCOUNTERS OF THE THIRD KIND*.

Barney died from a brain haemorrhage in 1969 at the age of 47. Betty went on to report many further UFO sightings. These were primarily LIGHTS IN THE SKY, and were rejected by many investigators who considered them to be simply aircraft or stars. She refused to accept much of the modern abduction lore, arguing that the beings she saw were not egg-headed GREYS.

hill figures *see* CHALK FIGURES

hitch-hikers, phantom *see* PHANTOM HITCH-HIKERS

Hoaxes and Hoaxers *see panel p309*

hobgoblin
In folklore, a small, dark and ugly fairy which is generally good-natured and well-disposed toward humans.

While GOBLINS are usually of an evil disposition, hobgoblins are much more good-natured and friendly spirits of the BROWNIE type. In folk tales, they are said to like to move into human houses to be near the warmth of the fire, and are ready to be helpful, doing domestic chores and often rewarding good children and punishing disobedient ones. They are fond of practical jokes, and like most FAIRIES, they are sensitive and must be treated with respect, since, if offended or angered, they can be troublesome houseguests. The 'hob' part of their name comes from the diminutive of the proper name Robin or Robert. They are said to be found most commonly throughout England and the Scottish lowlands. The Puritans took an unequivocally negative view of stories of hobgoblins, and used the word 'hobgoblin' to refer to satanic creatures; in John Bunyan's *Pilgrim's Progress* they are classed with 'foul fiends'. They are portrayed as small, dark and ugly, and either going naked or wearing ragged clothes.

Hod
In the kabbalah, the sephirah or emanation of God known as Splendour or Glory, which is assigned the number 8; it represents the lower channel through which God's judgement comes down to the world, and is associated with intellectuality, learning and the power to advance toward one's life goals.

Hod is the eighth of the ten SEPHIROTH, or Divine emanations, in the KABBALAH. It is called Splendour or Glory, and is the fifth of the emotive attributes of the sephiroth. Hod represents the lower channel through which God's judgement comes down to the world. It is assigned the number 8. On the kabbalistic TREE OF LIFE, it is positioned directly below GEBURAH, and directly opposite NETZACH, with which it has a polarized relationship, and is the third and lowest sphere of the left-hand axis, the Pillar of Severity. It is also the second point on the lowest of the three triangles formed by the sephiroth, the Astral or Psychological Triangle, which it makes up with Netzach and YESOD. It is given five paths on the Tree of Life – to Geburah, TIPHARETH, Netzach, Yesod and MALKUTH. Netzach and Hod achieve balance in Yesod, and taken together, these two sephiroth constitute the powers of Force and Form within the Astral Triangle; in *THE ZOHAR* they are referred to as 'the scales of justice'. Hod is associated with the power to continually advance toward one's life goals with the determination and perseverance born of deep inner commitment; it is said to be the sphere in which magicians mostly work, and to be linked

Hoaxes and Hoaxers

A hoax is an act deliberately intended to deceive or trick others. It is commonly said to be derived from the pseudo-Latin phrase *hocus pocus* meaning 'contemptuous nonsense', 'trickery' and also used an as impressive (but bogus) magical incantation. However, opinion then varies on the origin of this phrase; some believe it is a corruption of a phrase from the Latin Mass, *hoc est corpus* ('this is the body'); others, that it comes from an earlier pseudo-Latin chant used by conjurors in the 17th century, *Hax pax man Deus adimax*.

Many commonplace hoaxes are simple social play; for example, encouraging the belief in Father Christmas, or 'practical jokes' and APRIL FOOL'S DAY tricks. At the other extreme, they can be malicious and criminal, such as bogus 'anthrax' packets, and the infamous fake document known as the *PROTOCOLS OF THE LEARNED ELDERS OF ZION*, which pretended to expose a Jewish conspiracy aimed at global domination. Hoaxes come in as many forms as hoaxers have motives; while a 'confidence trick' of some sort is at the heart of most (a simple example would be a convincing drama or novel), not all of them are 'scams' (defrauding for monetary gain), while some are even perpetrated for understandable, if misguided, reasons (see PIOUS FRAUD). The following categories sample the sheer variety of hoaxes.

Scientists have been surprisingly susceptible to hoaxing – sometimes with very serious consequences. In 2005, Korean biologist Professor Hwang Woo-suk's claims to have cloned human stem cells from fertilized eggs raised hopes of new treatments and affected many stem cell research programmes. The geological dating of the entire Himalayan region is to be re-examined after India's leading palaeontologist, Professor Viswa Jit Gupta, was accused in 1987 of deliberately misidentifying fossils and of planting fossils (that he had bought in other countries) in Himalayan strata. For examples of other science-based hoaxes, see COLD FUSION; THE 1835 MOON HOAX; PERPETUAL MOTION.

There is no doubt that the infamous Piltdown Man skull was a hoax. Allegedly unearthed, piecemeal, in a gravel pit in Surrey, over several years, it was presented to the Royal Geographical Society in 1912 as the 'missing link' between modern man and his more ape-like forebears. It was finally exposed in 1953 as being composed of human, chimpanzee and orang-utan bones, but the debate over the identity of the hoaxer or hoaxers (with many names in the frame) has never been resolved definitively. For other antiquarian hoaxes, see ICA STONES; LYING STONES.

The 'softer' sciences – sociology, anthropology, psychology, etc – have fared no better. A prominent example is the British anthropologist and Egyptologist Margaret Murray, who had a significant influence on the growth of WICCA and neopagan religions in the early 20th century. Unfortunately, her ground-breaking book, *The Witch Cult in Western Europe* (1921), which proposed the idea of a pan-European pre-Christian religion featuring a HORNED GOD, was subsequently severely criticized for quoting historical sources selectively and out of context to support her theory.

In 1975, Robert Temple's *The Sirius Mystery* drew attention to the mysterious astronomical knowledge of the Dogon people of central Mali. Temple claimed that the Dogon knew of the star Sirius and its companion, Sirius B, and this knowledge was incorporated into their CREATION MYTHS and RITUALS. As Sirius B cannot be seen without a telescope, and as the Dogon had no telescopes, Temple – whose mentor, Arthur Young, believed in the extraterrestrial COUNCIL OF NINE – argued that the tribe had had contact either with an ancient civilization with advanced sciences, or with ALIENS. This idea became a cornerstone of 1970s UFOLOGY. Later scholars equated the Dogon star lore with that of European astronomy in the 1920s, suggesting that the tribe could have acquired it recently. Temple's information was based on the work of the eminent French ethnologist Marcel Griaule and his team, who studied the Dogon in the 1930s and 1940s. A 1991 expedition, led by German anthropologist Walter van Beek, spent a decade with the Dogon, and found their lore generally to be a chaos of individual interpretations.

In the 1960s, two other writers whose works were essentially hoaxes were also hugely influential, with international followings for their many books: naturalized American Carlos Castaneda and the 'possessed' Englishman T Lobsang Rampa. Castaneda claimed he had learnt shamanistic teachings on magic, drugs and mysticism during his apprenticeship to a Yaqui sorcerer, and wrote a series of books that allegedly described this training. In 1976, Richard de Mille – a psychology professor who knew both Castaneda and L RON HUBBARD – published a devastating exposé, *Castaneda's Journey: The Power and the Allegory*, accusing Castaneda of inventing much his work while he wrote his dissertation at the University of California, Los Angeles. Oddly, this has enhanced Castaneda's reputation among his followers as a 'Trickster' figure (see COSMIC JOKER). T Lobsang Rampa, similarly, is highly revered as the author of 20 books – beginning with *The Third Eye* (1956) – detailing his life as a Tibetan lama given psychic powers and sent to teach in the West after taking over the body of an Englishman who died falling from a tree. In 1958, a group of scholars of Tibetan Buddhism exposed Rampa as Cyril Henry Hoskins, who had always been interested in the OCCULT. Rampa's followers still say this does not invalidate his teaching.

The 'impostor' class of hoaxers is dominated by those who thrive on the sympathy they receive for their alleged suffering. Many pose as victims or survivors of newsworthy tragedies. In a bestselling 1995 memoir, *Fragments: Memories of a Wartime Childhood*, Binjamin Wilkomirski described growing up in a Jewish ghetto in Latvia and in the German-run concentration camps of Majdanek and Auschwitz. The convincing and moving story went on to win Jewish literature prizes in Britain, France and the USA. Eventually, it was discovered that Wilkomirski was actually born in Switzerland and raised from infancy by the middle-class Doessekker family in Zurich.

Many of those who pretend to have been assaulted, robbed or even kidnapped (faking their own disappearance for a few days) have low self-esteem and are motivated by an unhealthy desire for sympathy. This is demonstrated by those affected by 'Munchausen's syndrome' and 'Munchausen's by proxy', characterized by often convincing and detailed performances relating to claims that they or their children have a serious (or in some cases, fatal) illness. Some of these comments may apply to those who believe that they are victims of ALIEN ABDUCTION.

Of course there are also hoaxers who are inspired purely by criminal intent, seeking compensation that is not rightfully theirs. A significant form of 'bogus victim' claim since the late 1970s has been

that of surviving a so-called SATANIC RITUAL ABUSE cult. Canadian Michelle Smith set the pattern with her book, *Michelle Remembers* (1980). She claimed that she was sexually abused by her parents and neighbours (a charge they strongly deny) from an early age. Forcibly starved of food and sleep, she said she was subjected to 'Satanic rituals', such as being placed in an open grave with dead cats around her. The climax of her story is an 81-day ritual to summon Satan, whose attempt to possess Michelle was frustrated by the appearance of Jesus, his Mother and the archangel Michael. Her psychiatrist Dr Lawrence Pazder (whom she later married and who co-wrote the book) recovered her childhood memories through hypnotism (see MEMORIES, RECOVERED), EXORCISM and her conversion to Catholicism.

Michelle's case opened the floodgates for similar claims, each more fantastic than the last. During two decades of mounting hysteria, confused child welfare and social service teams, on the most dubious information, broke up families in the hope of rescuing children from similar fates. Since then judges, anthropologists, psychiatrists and forensic investigators have raised serious concerns that this was partly, or even wholly, an example of MASS HYSTERIA; they point to the lack of tangible evidence of large-scale Devil-worshipping, child-abusing cults and their alleged activities; the inept questioning of child informants; and the readiness of local teams to act on the unsupported fantasies of children.

Professional psychiatric institutions have condemned the controversial yet widespread radical practice of some psychotherapists of becoming personally involved in their clients' treatment. In particular, HYPNOSIS was employed to elicit 'hidden' or REPRESSED MEMORIES, especially those suggestive of past lives (see PAST-LIFE REGRESSION), life in the womb or lives on other planets. In their rush to mine their patients' latent memories of Satanic abuse, the psychotherapists involved had overlooked the lessons of such earlier cases as that of BRIDEY MURPHY, or the child accusers of witches at SALEM and elsewhere. The nature of FALSE MEMORIES is still the subject of debate; some long-forgotten memories (see CRYPTOMNESIA) may be distorted in the recollection.

The assertion that the term *hocus pocus* was a parody of a phrase from the Latin Mass itself points to a persistent belief that the rituals of the Christian Churches were all, historically, a monumental deceit. History affords us many examples of hoaxing in the area of religion, with fake prophets and fake 'Bibles' abounding, and, of course, fake 'confessions'. Among many examples are Leo Taxil's bogus books about Satanic FREEMASONRY and DEMONOLOGY. He confessed, in 1897, that they were intended to slander both the Freemasons (who had rejected him) and the Catholic church. Even the founding books and prophets of the major world religions have their critics, sceptics and accusers. The situation is exemplified when a schismatic sect adapts older traditions. For example, the *Urantia Book* is said to be a compilation of 196 dissertations, dictated by 'superhuman personalities' between 1928 and 1935, that range from the life of Jesus to life on other worlds; it is often cited as an early influence on the UFO CONTACTEE movement. An investigation by the COMMITTEE FOR THE SCIENTIFIC INVESTIGATION OF CLAIMS OF THE PARANORMAL sceptic Martin Gardner found it originated in a breakaway sect of Seventh-day Adventists, for whom it was 'channelled' by Wilfred Kellogg (of the cornflakes family) and 'edited' by the group's founder, William Sadler, a Chicago psychiatrist. See also: CHANNELLING; the *NECRONOMICON*.

Media hoaxing has been prevalent since the growth of newspapers in the 19th century, and television in the 20th. The 'liar's clubs' that flourished in the American Midwest in the 19th century are thought to be the origin of many of the dubious historical mysteries promulgated by lazy writers on paranormal subjects. Among the known hoaxes of this sort that forteans (see FORTEANA) have put in a great deal of time untangling are the DISAPPEARANCES of David Lang and others, and very probably the THUNDERBIRD (or at least the version based around the supposed shooting of a pterodactyl in Arizona in 1890). The Herculean labour of untangling the entrenched belief in such false and hoax stories seems never-ending: examples of 'mockumentaries' include *GHOSTWATCH*, and *ALTERNATIVE 3*, two dramas (by BBC and Anglia TV, respectively) which were taken for actual documentaries; and the UNICORN OF THE HARZ, a Swiss television and periodical hoax. For other hoaxes that exploited modern media, see AMITYVILLE; SIBERIAN HELL HOLE; PHILADELPHIA EXPERIMENT; *THE WAR OF THE WORLDS*.

Many modern hoaxes involve photographs. These can now be digitally manipulated so easily with computer software that sceptics (on all sides) no longer trust them without supporting evidence. This category includes countless photographs and video clips of FAIRIES, GHOSTS, ALIENS and UFOs, and the infamous SANTILLI FILM of an ALIEN AUTOPSY. The case of the editors at *Penthouse* magazine, serves as an illustration of how 'hoaxes' may arise inadvertently or from misunderstanding. In the late 1990s, the magazine was sent a set of photographs of dead aliens said to have been taken in China. Impressed, *Penthouse* reprinted them with cautious endorsements; however, research by the *FORTEAN TIMES* revealed that the 'aliens'

were, in fact, models at the International UFO Museum at ROSWELL, New Mexico. For other UFO-related hoaxes, see ALLENDE LETTERS; BILLY MEIER.

A modern development of media hoaxing is so-called 'viral hoaxing' – drumming up 'fan' interest by using the Internet's ability to propagate fantastic rumours, usually about some fortean phenomenon, ultimately for a commercial purpose. This first came to public attention in connexion with the hit 1999 movie *The Blair Witch Project*, which itself used the narrative device of a fake 'real' team investigating a fake legend. Several other successes have exploited the public's interest in CRYPTOZOOLOGY. Around 2000, Haxan, the company behind the *Blair Witch* film, tried the trick again, but for a television show, using a battered old sepia photograph; it appeared to show a group of soldiers from the American Civil War period, standing around the carcase of a pterodactyl they had shot down. The tsunami of Christmas 2004 inspired a video clip, circulated on the Internet, purporting to be a report from an Indian TV news station about the carcase of a giant sea monster thrown up by the tsunami onto a beach near Mahabalipurnam, in Tamil Nadu. The waves did indeed uncover the ruins of an ancient temple there, but the GLOBSTER had been generated by a computer to promote a computer game called *Shadow of the Colossus*. For other discussions of hoaxing in a paranormal context, see: CROP CIRCLES; DELAYED DEATH TOUCH; INDIAN ROPE TRICK; PSYCHIC SURGERY; HÉLÈNE SMITH; SPIRIT PHOTOGRAPHY; MARY TOFT.

As if the subject of hoaxing needed complicating further, it has an aspect that is rarely considered, but which appears throughout the history of paranormal phenomena, often with far-reaching influences – the 'pious fraud'. This term, often used by sceptics in a derogatory sense, is usually defined as someone who perpetrates a hoax, usually in a religious context, through genuine but misguided zeal. However, Robert T Carroll's *Skeptic's Dictionary* (2003) exemplifies the hostile sceptic's scorn for anything to do with MIRACLES, applying the term to 'all who lie about witnessing miracles'. By ruling out, *a priori*, any possibility of paranormal phenomena, the only view left to the sceptic is that they are all hoaxes. The book's entry on Lucia dos Santos, the central percipient of the series of MARIAN APPARITIONS at FÁTIMA, Portugal, says: 'To skeptics, Lucia is just another liar for Jesus, a pious fraud.' The *intention* to deceive is central to such cases and is sometimes difficult to resolve – for example, consider the two girls at the centre of the COTTINGLEY FAIRIES case. According to the record, they wanted to demonstrate to their father what they believed they saw in the fairy glen. When they replicated it with his camera, they did not intend to deceive him and were dismayed when the images gathered more and more notoriety and believers. In the end, they said, they dared not confess and make these gentlemen out to be fools.

Similarly, anthropologists have long reported on the tricks used by SHAMANS, WITCH DOCTORS and wise-folk (see WISDOM). According to the Harvard palaeoanthropologist William Howells, their purpose is an honest one – to reinforce the community's belief in their ability to help and intercede for them in their shared belief in a SPIRIT world. Of course, to a hostile sceptic, the shaman is a charlatan, his justification is bogus and the tricks nothing more than simple conjuring – but in the field, anthropologists report the unwavering belief in the underlying magic of the community and the shaman, who has no sense that he is deceiving people. Some communities, groups and religious movements are strongly held together by similar, uncritical participation in a collective belief. It is too simplistic to dismiss it lightly. Indeed, some would argue that many of the historical documents of Christianity and other religions, and many of the 'miracles' attributed to saints and others, fall into this category – they are well-intentioned but ultimately fraudulent assertions.

Pious frauds also fascinated two great scholars of mystical phenomena, Dr Eric Dingwall and Fr Herbert Thurston. Thurston, in his *Physical Phenomena of Mysticism* (1952), was prepared to consider that some of those who apparently experienced LEVITATION and STIGMATA in particular might be suffering from a mental disorder, and yet could still be considered pious – these phenomena being an earnest but unconscious participation in the suffering of Jesus. He lists, among many others, the Spanish nun Magdalena de la Cruz, who, in 1546, was found guilty by THE INQUISITION of pretending to sanctity and faking her stigmata, despite being revered by all who knew her. She condemned herself while seriously ill, in a belief that she was worthless and should be punished, not because there was evidence her phenomena were fake. In other cases, stigmatic wounds may have been cause psychosomatically during trance or vision states, in circumstances favourable to the idea that they were caused by divine intervention. For other cases of pious or unwitting fraud, see: CHRONOVISOR, THE.

Bob Rickard

with the power of prophecy. It is associated with the Divine name *Elohim Tzabaoth* (the God of Hosts), the archangel Michael, the angelic order of the Beni Elohim, and the planetary force of Mercury. In the TAROT, Hod corresponds to the four eights, and in the tarot Tree of Life spread, the card in the Hod position usually represents love or lust. In some kabbalistic systems it is linked with the magical image of a hermaphrodite, and is represented by the symbol of an apron. It is often connected with the solar plexus CHAKRA. The word Hod in kabbalistic GEMATRIA gives the number 15, which is the sum of all the numbers from 1 to 5; it expresses and reflects all five emotions of the heart, from CHESED to Hod.

hogboon

A mound-dwelling fairy in the folklore of Orkney, which often attaches itself to a nearby farm, protecting its livestock and acting as a guardian spirit of the household.

The hogboon, also known as the hogboy or hugboy, is an Orkney fairy something like a BROWNIE. Hogboons are said to be solitary creatures that live in burial chambers, or mounds – the word is a corruption of the Old Norse *haug-buinn*, meaning mound-dweller – and guard them from intruders. Every mound in Orkney is said to have its own hogboon, and if anyone disturbs the mound, perhaps thinking to find buried treasure there, the hogboon will appear in the form of a small grey man in tattered clothes, and attack the intruder. They attach themselves to nearby farms, acting as the guardian spirit of the household, protecting livestock and bringing the family good luck as long as they show their appreciation by sharing some of their produce with the hogboon. This is done by pouring ale or milk over the top of the hogboon's mound, or leaving food there. While generally benign, they are, like most fairy folk, thought to be very easily offended, and one Orkney story tells of an unfortunate family who took up residence in Hellihowe Farm but, being ignorant of hogboon lore, did not give him milk, ale or food. The hogboon then proceeded to avenge himself for their neglect by tormenting them with practical jokes. The family decided to cut their losses and move, and kept their plans secret so that the hogboon would not learn of them. On the day of the move, however, when a neighbour was bidding them farewell and congratulating them on their escape, the hogboon popped his head out of a butter churn and said with a grin that they had a fine day for moving house – proving that it is not so easy to shake off a fairy who has decided to make your life a misery.

The hogboon's origin can be traced back to the ancient beliefs of the Norsemen who settled in Orkney. They thought that after a person died, their spirit continued to live on or near their family farm. A large burial mound was built over the body of the founder of the estate, whose spirit was believed to remain in the mound, becoming the family's guardian. It has been suggested that when the Norsemen came to settle in Orkney, they built their homesteads close to the many conspicuous mounds all over the landscape in the hopes of thereby gaining the protection of the spirit that they believed lived within it. There are still houses and farms in Orkney which have been built and rebuilt in the same location near these mounds. See also HOUSEHOLD SPIRITS.

holistic medicine

A form of medicine that considers the whole person, physically and psychologically, rather than treating merely the diseased part or addressing the symptoms.

Holistic medicine, a term sometimes used interchangeably with ALTERNATIVE MEDICINE, refers to a philosophy of wellbeing which considers the physical, spiritual and mental aspects of life as being closely interconnected. It is based on the view that the whole person should be taken into account as regards health and illness, not just the physical body, and many aspects of holistic medicine focus on the body's natural ability to heal itself; holistic medicine is seen as boosting those abilities, rather than working against or overriding them by using drugs and invasive medical procedures.

Holistic medicine stresses prevention rather than cure, and to this end, its practitioners often encourage patients to adopt a less stressful lifestyle, modify their diet or exercise routine, or use medicines which boost the body's natural defence system. The focus is on the patient rather than the disease; a holistic diagnosis usually includes an analysis of the patient's whole lifestyle, and the physical, nutritional, social, environmental and spiritual elements of their life. The healer believes that many contributing factors may be involved in an illness, and that what may work for one person with a given condition will not necessarily be right for another. It is therefore the healer's task to determine the set of factors which are relevant to the individual. The aim is to identify the underlying cause of the disease rather than treat the symptoms alone, and illness is seen as a manifestation of a dysfunction in the whole person, rather than as an isolated event.

Complementary or alternative medicine is a typical feature of holistic treatment, which makes use of a wide variety of practices, such as ACUPUNCTURE, chiropractic, naturopathy, AROMATHERAPY, YOGA, HOMEOPATHY, REIKI and medical herbalism. Optimal health is regarded as more than simply the absence of sickness; it is seen as the conscious pursuit of the best possible physical, environmental, social, mental, emotional and spiritual state.

hollow earth theory

The idea that the earth is not solid but hollow.

The idea that the planet earth is not a solid mass but is hollow inside was first given scientific credence by the English astronomer Edmond Halley (1656–1742). Halley was interested in magnetic variations of the compass and he developed the theory that these could be accounted for by the existence of more than one magnetic field. He came to believe that there were several spheres, one inside another, that were filled with a luminous gas. Quantities of this gas escaping at the North Pole where the outer crust was thin were, he thought, the explanation of the AURORA BOREALIS.

The hollow earth theory was also supported by the American businessman John Symmes (1780–1829), who also believed that there were entrances to another world of the interior, thousands of miles wide, at each of the poles. He dreamed of mounting an expedition to explore the Arctic and discover the 'Symmes' Hole' there. This never happened, but some of those who took part in a US expedition to Antarctica (1838–42) were aware of the theory, though, of course, no such hole was found.

Other followers of the theory included Cyrus Read Teed (1839–1908), a US physician who believed not only that the earth was hollow but that the interior was populated and illuminated by its own sun. Teed went on to found his own religious cult, centred on belief in his theories.

When a frozen woolly mammoth was found in Siberia in 1846, believers in the hollow earth hypothesis took this as proof, arguing that the creature was not extinct in the centre of the Earth and had emerged from there only to freeze to death relatively recently.

The idea perhaps found its most lasting 19th-century exposition in the science fiction of the French novelist Jules Verne (1828–1905). In his *A Journey to the Centre of the Earth* (1872), he describes explorers descending inside a volcano to discover a prehistoric world, complete with dinosaurs, at the earth's core.

In the 20th century, the hollow earth theory became linked to belief in ALIENS, as the idea became popular that the centre of the earth was populated by extraterrestrials. These beings were said to emerge from the poles from time to time in spacecraft, thus providing an explanation for some sightings of UFOs. Some people apparently believe that the Nazis were aware of an entrance to the centre of the world at the South Pole and that Hitler and his immediate retinue escaped there at the end of World War II.

Aircraft flights over both poles, beginning with that of US admiral Richard Byrd (1888–1957) over the North Pole in 1926, and the photographic evidence they provided failed to convince believers that there were in fact no vast entrances to the hollow interior of our planet. The advent of space flight and the photographs of earth taken from space would also seem to add weight to the argument against the existence of such enormous holes in the earth's surface.

However, the hollow earth theory still has its adherents, and not only in the world of science fiction and fantasy.

Holy Grail

In Christian mythology, the dish or cup said to have been used by Jesus at the Last Supper, and in some accounts, to have been used by Joseph of Arimathea to catch the blood of Jesus as he hung on the cross. This legendary vessel featured prominently as the object of a quest by the knights of the Round Table in the medieval Arthurian romance cycle, and belief in its existence, and speculation as to its whereabouts, persist to this day.

The Holy Grail, also known as the Sangraal, is the legendary subject of several late medieval Arthurian romances. This dish or cup, which possessed magical powers such as the ability to heal all wounds, was said to have been used by Jesus at the Last Supper, and in some versions of the story, to have been used by Joseph of Arimathea to catch the blood of Jesus as he hung on the cross. The origin of the Grail legend is obscure, but it is thought that much of its setting and imagery draws from pagan Celtic mythology, which includes a number of stories featuring magical cauldrons which can restore life. The Grail romances started in the 12th century, in France ('the word 'grail' comes from the French *graal*), and were translated into other European languages.

A common theme in the Grail cycle is that it is a symbol of God's grace, which can only be attained by someone who is spiritually pure. In some accounts, the Grail was brought to GLASTONBURY TOR in Britain by JOSEPH OF ARIMATHEA, who established a dynasty of custodians to guard it, but it was lost because of their unworthiness. A number of Christian revisionists have claimed that the identification of the Grail of Joseph with the Holy Chalice used by Christ at the Last Supper is erroneous, but this remains historical practice.

Belief in the Grail's existence, and speculation as to its whereabouts, persist to this day. It is rumoured by some to have been brought to Britain and hidden by the KNIGHTS TEMPLAR, or to have been thrown into the Chalice Well at Glastonbury. Books such as *THE DA VINCI CODE* have also popularized the idea that the Grail is hidden in ROSLYN CHAPEL, in Scotland.

Holy Office, the *see* INQUISITION, THE

holy vegetables

Fruits and vegetables that, because of their shape, are interpreted as having magical or divine powers. The phrase is particularly applied to those which appear to contain written messages.

Deformations of fruit and vegetables often cause them to be shaped into bizarre forms, often loosely resembling faces and figures. Photographs of such occurrences have been sent in to newspapers and periodicals for more than a century. Mandrake roots have long been prized by WITCHES, apothecaries and alchemists for their curious resemblance to the human form, often with a recognizable head, trunk, arms and legs. Ginseng roots, like the mandrake, were also believed to derive some of their credited healing properties from their humanoid shape. Sometimes these roots are forked in a way which suggests rudimentary male and female or twin forms.

A more interesting category of 'holy vegetable' includes those in which signs or symbols are revealed when they are cut or sliced. For example, a popular form of DIVINATION (particularly among children in the Far East) involves thinking of a simple question when slicing off the end tip of a banana. In the cross-section, the central rows of seeds will show an 'N' for 'no' and a 'Y' for 'yes'. Stories regularly appear in the press of domestic discoveries of 'holy vegetables', usually in the form of an aubergine or tomato, with a wavy line formed by a line of pips, seeds or discoloration which, it is claimed, resembles the word 'Allah' in Arabic script. On closer examination, this likeness is never precise, being partly or wholly an approximation. Nevertheless, the families who make such discoveries feel particularly blessed.

Cut fruit and vegetables are not the only places such script appears – sometimes it seems that almost any wavy line will do! An aerial photo of the December 2004 tsunami breaking on a shore in Sri Lanka appears to spell out the word 'Allah'. A butterfly fish went one better – according to an illustration in J R Norman's *History of Fishes* (1931), its tail bears markings which resemble, in Arabic, the phrase 'There is no God but God' (see also CHANCE AND COINCIDENCE; IMAGES, SPONTANEOUS; SIMULACRA).

A third form of holy vegetable comprises those that grow in, or on, a holy site. However, while popular traditions often credit them with magical properties, priests are generally more sceptical – one rabbi ruled that there was no blessing to be obtained from eating the type of caper that grows out of the *Kotel* (the western wall of the Temple of Jerusalem) other than the blessings normally said over that type of vegetable before eating.

holy wells

Springs of fresh water flowing naturally from the earth, venerated as places of healing and visited by pilgrims.

In pagan Celtic times, wells were thought to be magical places associated with fertility and healing, and the cult of springs and wells is well documented throughout the Celtic world, especially in Wales, Ireland and Scotland. Votive offerings of small statues or coins were originally made to the nature spirits or goddesses who presided over them, but in later times the offerings were more likely to be pins (especially in Wales) or small pieces of rag tied to the branches of a tree growing near the well (especially in Scotland, Cornwall and Ireland). The belief was that by the time the rag had rotted, the prayed-for healing would have taken place – a form of SYMPATHETIC MAGIC. To this day, many 'rag trees' or 'clootie trees' are still found near holy wells. People also sometimes requested the cursing of their enemies at sacred wells, and dreaming at them was a popular form of DIVINATION.

With the coming of Christianity, the early Church Christianized the pagan spirits by rededicating the sacred wells to local saints and adopting them as holy places. Between the 7th and 9th centuries, many wells had Christian legends attached to them to account for their origins; for example, the Well of St Kenelm in the Clent Hills is said to have sprung from the ground where the young king's murdered body fell, and the waters of St Ludgvan's Well in Cornwall appeared when the saint prayed for a wonder which would help him convert the heathen locals. Gwynllyw's Well in Glamorgan and Illtud's Well on the Gower Peninsula both sprang forth when their respective saints struck the ground with their staffs. The many wells sacred to the goddess Brigit were rededicated to St Brigid or the Virgin Mary, as is seen in the number of well locations called Bridewell or Ladywell. However, the pagan origins of these 'Christian' holy wells may still be detected in the fact that three visits to or three circuits of the well, usually in a clockwise direction (that is, in the direction the sun travels), were often prescribed. Visiting Madron Well in Penwith, Cornwall, on the first three Sundays in May was believed to cure rickets. The Holy Pool of St Fillan in Perthshire, was thought to provide a cure for insanity if the patient was led three times round the pool, in the name of the Father, the Son, and the Holy Ghost, and then immersed in the name of the Holy Trinity. The continued practice of leaving votive offerings at holy wells also points to their pre-Christian origins.

Once a sacred well had been 'sanctified', it became a place of pilgrimage associated with the cult of the local saint, and its waters were believed to bring about MIRACLE CURES. Some wells were associated with a particular illness. The most common ailments said to be healed at holy wells were eye problems, infertility, rickets, polio and whooping cough, and less commonly lameness, insanity, skin diseases and leprosy. Perhaps the most famous healing well in Britain is ST WINEFRIDE'S WELL at Holywell in North Wales, known as 'the Welsh Lourdes', which in the Middle Ages was one of the most important pilgrimage centres in the country, and continues to be visited by thousands of people every year.

Of the hundreds of holy wells situated throughout England, many are now neglected and overgrown. A much higher proportion of the holy wells of Scotland, Wales and particularly Ireland are still venerated and visited to this day, with over 220 surviving in County Clare alone. Holy wells nearly always have to be visited on their particular saint's day, or on significant dates such as Easter Sunday or Whit Sunday, and in Ireland, pilgrimages to holy wells are an important part of the Christian calendar.

Home, Daniel Dunglas *see panel p317*

homeopathic magic *see* MAGIC, HOMEOPATHIC

homeopathy
A holistic form of medicine which aims to help the body to heal itself by administering very small doses of substances which in larger doses would produce the relevant symptoms in a healthy person; it is based on the theory that 'like cures like'.

Homeopathy (from the Greek *omoios*, similar, and *pathos*, feeling) is a holistic therapeutic system based on what is referred to as the Law of Similars. It operates on the theory that very small doses of a substance which would produce a given symptom in a healthy person can be used to cure the same symptom in a sick person, and that the substance which produces the symptoms which most closely resemble the illness in question is the one most likely to trigger a curative response. The principle of homeopathy is that every person's body has an ENERGY or vital force, and a self-healing mechanism. When the energy is disrupted or put out of balance, this results in the development of health problems, and homeopathy seeks to stimulate the body's natural self-healing capacity.

Homeopathy as we know it today is almost 200 years old. It was developed by the German physician and chemist Samuel Hahnemann at the beginning of the 19th century, and became popular, particularly in the USA, from around 1825, reaching its peak between 1865 and 1885. By the 1930s, its popularity had waned, partly because of advances in conventional medicine, but it enjoyed a revival in the 1970s, and the general rise in alternative medicine in the last few decades has brought it back into prominence.

In homeopathy, health is seen as a person's ability to adapt their equilibrium in response to external and internal changes, and illness as an imbalance of the vital force. The balance of energy requires adequate nutrition, exercise, rest, good hygiene and a healthy environment. The symptoms of illness are in fact the body's attempt to heal itself, so that, for example, a fever is the body's way of creating a physical environment which is not conducive to bacterial or viral growth. Working on this assumption, the homeopath seeks to help the body adapt to the illness by administering small doses of a substance which will stimulate the immune and defence responses. It is believed that this will lead to the spontaneous resolution of the symptoms, although these may get worse before they get better.

A homeopathic diagnosis is a holistic one in which the practitioner considers the whole person, including all aspects of their lifestyle and their mental and emotional state. The patient is closely questioned about subjective symptoms such as pain and fatigue, the location of the symptoms, whether certain factors – such as heat and cold or the time of day – affect the symptoms, whether they are sudden or gradual, and so on. After building up this composite picture of the person, as opposed to the disease, the homeopath may try several remedies, one at a time. These remedies are natural healing compounds which are prepared through a process of serial dilution. The compound is first left to dissolve in a mixture of water and alcohol to produce what is known as the mother tincture. One drop of this tincture is then mixed with ten drops of water and alcohol, and the same process repeated hundreds, and sometimes thousands, of times, until it has been diluted to the point where the chance that even one molecule of the original substance can still be found in the liquid is infinitesimally small. The more diluted the original substance, the more powerful a remedy it is believed to be. Belladonna is used for fevers; monkshood for colds and flu; and poison ivy for arthritis, sprains and strains. There are over 3,000 homeopathic remedies, which may be bought over the counter in most countries.

Homeopathy cannot cure illnesses resulting from structural conditions such as diabetes and cancer, but is sometimes used to relieve their symptoms. Research into homeopathy's effectiveness has produced contradictory results, and its critics claim that there is no evidence to prove that it works. See also ALTERNATIVE MEDICINE; HOLISTIC MEDICINE.

Daniel Dunglas Home (1833–86)

Daniel Dunglas Home (pronounced 'Hume') is renowned as possibly the greatest ever MEDIUM, and was the first person to whom the word PSYCHIC was applied. He is said to have exhibited a wide range of extraordinary powers – as well as simply conducting SÉANCES (apparently displaying the abilities of a DIRECT VOICE MEDIUM, a TRANCE MEDIUM, a PHYSICAL MEDIUM as well as CLAIRVOYANCE) Home could reputedly levitate (once allegedly flying out of one window and into another on the third floor), handle hot coals with impunity (see FIRE IMMUNITY) and elongate at will.

Born in what is now part of Edinburgh, Home claimed to be the illegitimate son of the 10th Earl of Home. Early documents list his name as 'Hume' and they also indicate that his middle name (sometimes quoted as being 'Douglas') was probably a later addition. By the age of 17 he was living with an aunt in the USA, when their house was beset by the kind of noises and POLTERGEIST events that also apparently infested the home of the FOX SISTERS. Fearing that he had called the devil upon them, Home's aunt threw him out of the house, and he spent the next 20 years travelling the USA and Europe, earning money (in the form of gifts) by performing at séances. Hume moved in exceedingly well-to-do circles, and could count many famous people among his acquaintances – William Makepeace Thackeray defended him and Mark Twain praised him, while Michael Faraday denounced him and George Eliot described him as 'an object of moral disgust'. In London the famous chemist Sir William Crookes (who also investigated FLORENCE COOK) declared that he was a genuine medium, and attested to his other paranormal skills.

One of the most famous effects in a Home séance was the apparent spirit playing of an accordion sealed in a metal framework. It was

An artist's impression of Daniel Dunglas Home levitating to the ceiling – a feat he apparently performed before a number of witnesses. (© Mary Evans Picture Library)

claimed many years after his death that a number of mini one-octave mouth organs had been discovered among his personal effects – the suggestion being that these had been employed as a means of faking the performance. Sceptics have also pointed out that he sported a rather large moustache which they suggest could potentially have been used to hide small objects to be produced later as APPORTS. However, no mouth organs have ever been produced in support of the former claim, and the latter, somewhat bizarre suggestion remains equally unproven.

In 1866 a Mrs Lyon adopted Home and gave him a very considerable sum of money. This money was eventually returned as the result of a court case in which it was successfully argued that he had obtained the money by adverse influence. It was alleged that Home had conducted a number of séances in which the spirits had told Mrs Lyon to adopt him and give him the money.

In 1871, shortly after his second marriage, Home retired from the public séance circuit, claiming that his powers were leaving him. In truth he had suffered from tuberculosis for most of his life and the disease was taking its toll. In 1877 he wrote a book called *Lights and Shadows of Spiritualism* in which he exposed the techniques of fraudulent mediums – he apparently had little time for many of his contemporaries.

Although Home exercised a great deal of control over the conditions in which he demonstrated his alleged abilities and, as such, is open to the challenge that he may well have employed misdirection, sleight-of-hand and a number of other STAGE MAGIC techniques, in an age characterized by charlatans and fraudulent mediums, he is notable for the fact that he was never convincingly exposed as a fake. See also SPIRITUALISM.

homunculus

A tiny man which, according to alchemists, could be produced artificially from human semen and endowed with magical powers to serve its creator.

The word 'homunculus' is Latin for 'little man', and the term appears to have been first used by the 16th-century alchemist PARACELSUS. Like Aristotle, Paracelsus believed that the central ingredient for the generation of offspring was the male semen, and that the mother contributed only the matter from which the young was made. He therefore reasoned that it should be possible to generate a little man artificially by cultivating human semen in a flask, keeping it warm, and providing it with nutrients as it developed. In his *De Rerum Natura*, he describes the process by which a homunculus may be created: semen is kept in decaying horse dung until it begins to live and move, after which it is fed with 'the arcanum of human blood' and kept in the dung for 40 weeks, until is has become a fully developed miniature man. It may then be educated to serve (as with the GOLEM of Jewish folklore) and protect its creator. Paracelsus claimed to have created such a creature, which was allegedly no more than 30 centimetres (12 inches) tall.

Other alchemists had different theories on the best way to create a homunculus; one involved mandrake. This plant was popularly believed to grow in ground where the semen of a hanged man had fallen (ejaculated in the final throes before death), possibly because the form of its root often roughly resembled the shape of a man. It was believed that after the root was picked it should be washed and 'fed' with milk and honey, or sometimes blood, until it developed into a homunculus. Another writer, Dr David Christianus, wrote in the 18th century of a method involving an egg. An egg laid by a black hen has a hole poked in the shell and a small amount of the white is replaced with human semen. The hole is then sealed with virgin parchment, and the egg buried in horse dung. In this method it was claimed that a tiny human would develop after 30 days, which would protect its creator if fed regularly.

It was believed that the homunculus was in every respect identical to a human, except that it did not possess a soul, and was endowed with magical powers and insights.

Hope Diamond

A blue Indian diamond which is said to be cursed.

The Hope Diamond is the world's largest blue diamond, currently in the possession of the Smithsonian Institution in Washington, DC. Apart from its size and beauty, it is famous for the legendary curse said to befall those who own it.

Socialite Evalyn Walsh McLean wearing the Hope Diamond on a necklace; some claim that the misfortunes in her life were consequences of the jewel's curse. (© Bettmann/Corbis)

The stone is believed to have originated in India, as part of a much larger diamond bought in the 17th century by the French traveller Jean Baptiste Tavernier (1605–89), who subsequently sold it to Louis XIV (1638–1715). As part of the French crown jewels, it became known as the 'French Blue' until it was stolen in 1792, during the French Revolution.

It reappeared as a smaller stone in England, and its owners included George IV (1762–1830). In 1839 it appeared in the catalogue of the collection of the banker Henry Philip Hope (d.1839), from whom it acquired its lasting name. The gem remained in the Hope family until it was sold in 1901 to pay off debts, eventually becoming the property of the French jeweller Pierre Cartier (1878–1965).

In 1911 Cartier sold the diamond to US socialite Mrs Evalyn Walsh McLean (1886–1947), who had it set in a necklace. Sold after her death, it was donated to the Smithsonian Institution in 1958 by New York diamond merchant Harry Winston (1896–1978).

The legend of a curse seems to derive from an article published in *The Times* in 1909 while the jewel was being sold at auction in Paris. The journalist related a history of untimely deaths suffered by people through whose hands the diamond had passed. According to this, the curse arose from the original diamond having been stolen from a Hindu temple, where it had formed one of the eyes of an idol of the god Siva.

The first victim was said to be Jean Baptiste Tavernier who, on another journey to India, was apparently torn to pieces by wild dogs. Among other unlucky owners were Louis XVI (1754–93) and his queen Marie Antoinette (1754–93) who were executed during the French Revolution. The last Sultan of Turkey, Abd-ul-Hamid II (1842–1918), was said to have owned the gem for a time before being deposed in 1909.

The legend grew in 1929 when the American actress and singer May Yohe (1869–1938), who was married to Lord Francis Hope, last of the Hopes to own the diamond, published her book *The Mystery of the Hope Diamond*. This volume recounted the well-known stories and added a few more, although some of the protagonists seem to be fictional.

Is there any truth in the notion of a curse? Much of the evidence does not stand up to scrutiny. It is unlikely that the diamond was ever the eye of an idol, being the wrong shape according to descriptions and sketches by Tavernier (who died, an old man, in his bed and not between the teeth of savage dogs). Any student of history could point out reasons for the fate of the French king and queen that are quite independent of their jewellery collection. The same is true of the Turkish Sultan, whose empire was on its last legs before backing the losing side in World War I finished it off.

As for Mrs Evalyn Walsh McLean, it has to be said that her life was afflicted with misfortunes. Her son was killed in a car accident while still a child, her estranged husband died an alcoholic in an asylum and her daughter succumbed to a drug overdose at the age of 25. However, hers is not the only family to find wealth no guarantee of happiness.

Hopkins, Budd (1931–)

The best-known US researcher into alien abduction cases and a famous supporter of the theory that they are genuinely due to visitors from another world.
Budd Hopkins was a celebrated part of the New York art scene before he became involved in research into ALIEN ABDUCTION cases. During the 1970s he worked on a number of cases from the eastern USA with a local psychiatrist, Dr Aphrodite Clamar, conducting HYPNOSIS on people who felt that they harboured REPRESSED MEMORIES following a UFO sighting.

From the first few dozen cases Hopkins believed that he recognized a pattern and identified the importance of MISSING TIME as a clue when seeking out further potential abductions. *Missing Time* became the title of his first book in 1981.

Throughout the 1980s Hopkins gave numerous presentations to the UFO COMMUNITY emphasizing his belief that witnesses blocked out the terrifying ordeal of an alien abduction by creating a cover story in their mind, and suggested that these cover stories might even be placed there by the ALIENS to hide the truth. In one example this had apparently involved the memory of seeing a large number of rabbits, when hypnosis uncovered the 'fact' that small alien creatures had been encountered.

In 1987, as the public profile of the alien abduction phenomenon increased following the release of the novelist Whitley Strieber's own story in his book *Communion*, Hopkins produced his second book, *Intruders*. This told the interwoven stories of a rural family who believed that they had undergone repeated abductions, which brought to the fore the theme of alien–human hybrid babies. These were seemingly the consequence of the alien medical experiments which were often reported during such cases. The book was made into a TV mini-series, ensuring that very few people were now unfamiliar with the kind of abduction reports that Hopkins was investigating.

His compassion for the witnesses' suffering, which he felt was due to a lack of public understanding, led Hopkins to launch the Intruders Foundation, dedicated to furthering study of the phenomenon, in 1989. His new fame brought witnesses to him from all over the world, leading, among other things, to his investigation of the BROOKLYN BRIDGE case, which became the subject of his third book, *Witnessed*, in 1996.

Hopkins, Matthew (d.1647)

The 17th-century English self-styled 'witchfinder-general' who has attained near legendary status as a merciless persecutor of suspected witches.
The WITCHFINDER Matthew Hopkins was a colourful figure who has attracted a vast amount of folklore and about whom many exaggerated claims have been made. His legend has been adapted into numerous books and films, which have all added to the muddying of the waters surrounding the real details of his life.

He was the son of a church minister, James Hopkins, and grew up in Wenham in Suffolk. Very little is known of his early life but it is thought that he worked for a lawyer in Ipswich for a time and that by 1644 he was at Manningtree in Essex. He was raised in a Puritan household and by 1645, when he came to prominence, he was living in an area containing a number of powerful Puritans. At the time, Puritans were already feeling disillusioned with what they felt was a lack of enthusiasm for prosecuting WITCHES in the country, and they were also concerned that the king was drawing the country back towards

Catholicism. Added to this was the political turmoil and fear brought about by the Civil War, which had started in 1642, creating fertile ground in which the righteous persecution of those who represented the forces of darkness could be pursued with a renewed vigour.

The stories of the WITCH TRIALS that followed were greatly exaggerated and adapted by the press of the time for their own political (or even purely sensationalist) ends – making it difficult to separate truth from fiction. However, even allowing for this, it is possible that this particular witchfinding craze, centred on East Anglia, resulted in as many as 300 trials and over 100 executions. Matthew Hopkins was just one of the many people involved, although he certainly pursued his job with enthusiasm and dedication.

Hopkins's campaign began in Manningtree in 1645 when he was appointed by two Puritan magistrates, Sir Harbottle Grimston and Sir Thomas Bowes, to accompany John Stearne to investigate an accusation of WITCHCRAFT made against a one-legged widow called Elizabeth Clarke. They watched Clarke for three days and nights (sleep deprivation being just one of the many dubious and brutal methods employed at a time when the political situation meant that the law against torture was often bent or even ignored), during which time she was allegedly visited by a series of bizarre demonic FAMILIARS. Hopkins and Stearne testified to her confession and to being given a list of other witches in the area by Clarke, going on to pursue these and other 'leads' and sending over 30 women for trial in Colchester, of whom 19 were hanged.

Stearne and Hopkins then separated in Suffolk, with Hopkins taking the east of the county and travelling over 480 kilometres (300 miles) with his company, extracting confessions and sending numerous accused witches to trial. However, as the jails were filled with suspects and the costs of the investigations and trials mounted, enthusiasm began to wane. During 1646 Hopkins and Stearne spread their wings and travelled through the counties to the west. However, despite some further successes, there was a rising tide of dissent, resulting in complaints about their methods being made to judges in Norwich in 1647. At about this time, Hopkins returned to Manningtree, where it is believed he died from consumption. In answer to claims that Hopkins had been tried and even executed for witchcraft himself, Stearne wrote in his memoir, *A Confirmation and Discovery of Witch Craft* (1648), that:

> I am certain (notwithstanding whatsoever hath been said of him) he died peacefully at Manningtree, after a long sicknesse of consumption …

Horned God

One of the two primary deities (or aspects of the supreme deity) in neopagan witchcraft, the worship of whom is based on earlier pagan beliefs.

The Horned God, also referred to variously as Cernunnos, Pan and HERNE THE HUNTER (among other things), embodies the male principle, balancing the female principle embodied by THE GODDESS. The Horned God is associated with the sun, hunting, forests and animals.

As with the Goddess, some neopagans (see NEOPAGANISM, WICCA) argue that the worship of the Horned God is simply a continuation of an ancient pagan practice which survived the WITCHCRAFT persecutions of the Middle Ages (during which time such pagan horned deities became associated with THE DEVIL). Whether this is true or not, there is certainly archaeological evidence to suggest that the worship of a half-man and half-animal horned deity was present in European cultures spanning thousands of years – two of the later notable examples being Pan, the Greek god of the woodlands, and Cernunnos, the Celtic god of fertility (of whom it has been suggested that the CERNE ABBAS GIANT is a representation).

horoscopes

Maps of the heavens at the hour or on the day of a person's birth.

The most common use of ASTROLOGY is in the horoscope, also known as the natal chart or birth chart. This is a two-dimensional, diagrammatic representation of the relative positions of the Sun, Moon and planets (Mercury, Venus, Mars, Jupiter, Saturn, Uranus, Neptune and Pluto) as seen at the precise time and place of a person's birth. The sign of the ZODIAC occupied by the Sun on the subject's date of birth is called the subject's birth sign or sun sign, but is often also, erroneously, referred to as their star sign. In addition to the sun sign and the positions of the planets, a detailed horoscope will also show features such as the position of the heavenly bodies relative to the constellations, and to the horizon, and each of these factors is then interpreted by the astrologer to build a picture of the subject's personality and characteristics, to evaluate their potential strengths and weaknesses, and to help them make personal decisions.

The word 'horoscope' (from the Greek *hōroskopos*, from *hōra*, an hour, and *skopeein*, to observe) is also now commonly associated with the predictions for each birth sign found in many magazines and newspapers.

horse eels

Serpent-like aquatic cryptids, combining an eel-like body with an equine head, reputedly inhabiting several loughs in Ireland.

On the evening of 18 May 1960, three priests from Dublin were in a rowing boat, fishing on the eastern side of Lough Ree, a lake in central Ireland. At about 9.30pm, Fathers Matthew Burke, Daniel Murray and Richard Quigley say they saw an extraordinary animal swimming through the water roughly 73 metres (240 feet) away, with a neck that was 0.45–0.6 metres (around 1.5–2 feet) long and a snake-like head, followed by a hump that was around the same length as the neck. It submerged twice during its 2–3-minute progression, and disappeared around 27.5 metres (90 feet) from the lough's north-eastern shore.

During the early evening of 22 February 1968, a similar creature was spied by Stephen Coyne, his wife and their five children, as they stood on the shore of Lough Nahooin in County Galway. They estimated it to be 3.7 metres (12 feet) long, and stated that it possessed a smooth black hairless skin of eel-like texture, a slender body raised into a couple of vertical humps as it lowered its horn-bearing horse-like head and neck beneath the water, and a briefly glimpsed tail.

Many other sightings like these have been reported from a number of loughs elsewhere in Ireland, and the locals refer to such creatures as horse eels. Their zoological identity, however, remains a mystery. Cryptozoologists have speculated that, should these creatures exist as they have been described, they may be surviving, evolved zeuglodonts – primitive, supposedly long-extinct whales that sported remarkably elongate, serpentine bodies, and which continuing evolution could have transformed into highly flexible forms. Alternatively, they could be some very unusual, specialized type of eel, capable like other eels of moving overland from one body of water to another, but also, uniquely for eels (and most other fishes), able to raise their head above their body when swimming. However, for now the Irish horse eel remains a creature of legend.

horseshoe

A U-shaped frame, usually made of iron, nailed to a horse's hoof to protect it from injury by wear and considered a symbol of good luck in many areas of the world, especially in Europe and North America.

The horseshoe, a U-shaped piece of forged iron nailed to the hoof of a horse to protect it against wear and tear, has long been seen as a symbol of good luck in many areas of the world, particularly in Europe and North America. It is also thought to be a powerful TALISMAN against evil FAIRIES; in folklore, anything made from iron is said to give protection against fairies, who cannot bear this metal, but horseshoes have the additional power of being made by blacksmiths, who are believed to be lucky because they work with magical iron and the element of fire. Horseshoes also carry the good luck associated with the number SEVEN, because they are traditionally attached with seven nails.

Horseshoes are even said to be an effective guard against THE DEVIL; according to one legend, in the 10th century St Dunstan nailed horseshoes to the Devil's cloven hoofs and extracted a promise from him that he would never enter a place which displayed a horseshoe on its door. The horseshoe should be nailed to the outside of the door to be most effective, and while in many parts of Europe it is hung on the door with the points facing downward, in most areas of Britain it is believed that the points should face upward to stop the good luck from falling out of it. In Pennsylvania, horseshoes are attached to the door with the ends pointing back in toward the house to channel the good luck into the building.

A horseshoe found on the road is thought to be particularly lucky, and the more nails it still has in it when it is found, the more luck it will bring. Sailors used to nail horseshoes to the masts of their ships to protect them, and it is still traditional in North America and many parts of Europe to present a bride with a good luck token in the shape of a horseshoe. A horseshoe hung up in a bedroom is also thought to keep nightmares away.

Some scholars have also suggested that the horseshoe is such a popular symbol of good luck because of its resemblance to the twin horns of the new moon, a shape echoed in ancient Aztec fertility symbols and found in other North American countries.

Houdini, Harry (1874–1926)

US magician and escape artist.

Harry Houdini was born as Erich Weiss in Budapest, Hungary. His family emigrated to the USA and he became a trapeze artist and magician, taking his stage name in honour of the French conjuror Robert Houdin (1805–71), whom he greatly admired.

However, it is as the world's greatest escapologist (see ESCAPOLOGY) that Houdini is celebrated. It seemed that no form of confinement could restrain him, and he successfully escaped from an ever more complicated and daunting series of restraints, including handcuffs, chains and shackles, and straitjackets. He made his feats even more impressive by performing some of them while hanging upside down or submerged in a tank of water and usually in full view of his audience,

While he is best remembered as an escapologist, Harry Houdini also included exposés of fraudulent mediums in his shows. (© Corbis)

unlike many of his competitors who often worked behind a curtain.

In January 1906 he astonished the USA by escaping from the condemned cell of the jail in Washington, DC. Six years later he escaped from a packing case dropped from a ship into the East River, New York City. His fame became international when he toured successfully in England, Germany, Russia and Australia. In later years he also appeared in a number of films, both as himself and playing fictional characters.

How was Houdini able to bring off these sensational stunts? In common with other escapologists, he was extremely fit and had a physique that was both lithe and powerful. He was adept at flexing his muscles to their greatest size and expanding his chest to its utmost extent before being tied up or shackled. This would allow him a measure of space in which to manoeuvre once he relaxed his body.

Houdini was also skilled in secreting various aids on his person, such as small keys (which he was able to swallow and regurgitate at will), picklocks and thin metal shims for manipulating locks or catches. He also had the ability to temporarily dislocate various joints of his body, especially the shoulders, in order to wriggle free, and trained himself to be able to open locks with his toes.

He became interested in SPIRITUALISM, especially after the death of his mother, but, incensed at the frauds being perpetrated on a public eager to believe, he spent much of his time exposing the tricks used by fake MEDIUMS. This made him enemies, including the Scottish writer SIR ARTHUR CONAN DOYLE, a convinced spiritualist with whom he had previously been on friendly terms. According to Houdini's wife, he told her that when he was dead, if there was an AFTERLIFE, he would find a way to communicate with her. After ten years without receiving any message from the beyond she apparently gave up waiting.

One of Houdini's stunts involved inviting people to punch him in the stomach. He would then betray no reaction to even the most powerful blow. When he died of peritonitis, it was popularly believed that this was caused by being struck in this way before he could properly tense his abdominal muscles. However, in the opinion of most doctors his appendix had ruptured without the need for outside trauma.

Houdini's fame was such that his name became proverbial throughout the English-speaking world for anyone who performed a remarkable feat of escape ('to do a Houdini').

household spirits

In folklore, benign spirits that are attached to a domestic dwelling; stories of household spirits are found in many cultures.

Although the idea of a HAUNTED HOUSE is a source of dread in many cultures, there also exist a number of folkloric beliefs in which the haunting entity is considered to be a benign presence. Such household spirits perform positive or protective functions for the occupants of the dwelling and help to bring them prosperity and wellbeing. In some instances such traditions are linked with a belief that the spirits of ancestors remain in a house to help future generations.

Indications from archaeology and folklore suggest that belief in household spirits was once widespread in Europe, including many parts of the British Isles. Household spirits often manifest as a benign type of POLTERGEIST, their presence detected by occasional noises, object movements, the performance of domestic chores and the delivery of gifts. When visible they are often said to resemble diminutive human figures, examples including Spanish and Latin American traditions of *duende* and the BROWNIES of British folklore.

Cultures as widely spread as Europe, the Far East,

Africa and the Pacific stress that household spirits can be temperamental on occasion and demand respect. Many household spirits are said to be obsessed by cleanliness and houses must be kept tidy if friendly terms are to be maintained. Often household spirits may be kept happy with offerings or token payments (particularly food and tobacco), by the performance of special rituals or the maintenance of domestic shrines.

A belief in benign household spirits has an undoubted appeal, and some people have suggested that modern HAUNTINGS that are attributed to the loving presence of a deceased relative represent a continuation of the tradition. See also HOGBOON.

Hubbard, L(afeyette) Ron(ald) (1911–86)

Science fiction writer, creator of Dianetics and founder of the Church of Scientology.

Born in Tilden, Nebraska, L Ron Hubbard grew up in Montana and Washington State. He became a prolific writer of adventure stories and science fiction in the 1930s and 1940s. Many of his stories featured the concept of supermen, people with advanced physical and mental powers. In 1950 he published an article, 'Dianetics: The Evolution of a Science' in *Astounding Science Fiction* magazine, followed by a book, *Dianetics: The Modern Science of Mental Health*. He developed the self-help psychotherapeutic ideas of DIANETICS into a wider spiritual philosophy, SCIENTOLOGY. The first Church of Scientology was founded in 1954.

As the founder of the religion, Hubbard is held in extremely high regard by his followers. His early life has been invested with a mythical quality by the Church of Scientology, emphasizing his talents as an author, adventurer, explorer and philosopher. It is therefore difficult to be certain of some of the factual details of his life, including even his educational qualifications, his naval career during World War II, his war injuries and his medals and decorations. The allegation that he was involved in ritual SEX MAGIC along with a member of the ORDO TEMPLI ORIENTIS in 1946 is countered by the Church's assertion that he was infiltrating them as an undercover agent for the US Navy. The oft-quoted claim by critics of Scientology that Hubbard once said 'The easiest way to make a lot of money is to found a new religion' is roundly dismissed by the Church, despite the evidence of people who claim to have heard him say it.

Hubbard remains a controversial figure, with critics continuing to vilify him long after his death and the Church of Scientology continuing to hold him in the very highest esteem, calling him 'mankind's greatest friend'. Scientologists are encouraged to buy his many books, both fiction and non-fiction. Every Scientology headquarters building keeps his office ready for his return, with sharpened pencils on his desk.

human magnets

People who appear to have the power to attract objects to them.

In 1881, the magazine *The Theosophist* published an article by MADAME BLAVATSKY entitled 'Nature's Human Magnets' in which the author described supposed magnetic conditions of the human body.

Among the phenomena she described was the story of a young Russian girl who was seemingly able to attract potatoes to her person at will, levitate iron bedsteads and cause water containers to overrun. Blavatsky attributed this apparent gift of PSYCHOKINESIS to 'vital magnetism', and went on to cite other cases, such as that of a ten-year-old American boy whose hands acted like magnets in attracting metal objects.

Blavatsky believed that the human body was filled with a mysterious magnetic force which was stronger in some individuals than in most of the population. This force could act to attract objects or to attract a person's limbs towards a strong magnetic source. Obviously, this theory would serve as an explanation for various unexplained phenomena such as some POLTERGEIST activity when connected with a particular individual.

This idea of magnetic power residing in the human body was exploited in the 19th century by people who described themselves as healers (even as 'human magnets') and who attempted to use magnetism to treat various physical disorders – from blindness to diabetes and cancer. The Austrian physician FRANZ MESMER invented a therapeutic process which was named after him as MESMERISM. He believed that he could effect cures through the use of his own ANIMAL MAGNETISM.

Believers in the power of healing using magnets claim that the human body has an internal magnetic field, just as the earth has, and it is disturbances in this magnetic field that are the true causes of illness.

Another theory holds that the cells of the body contain tiny magnetic particles and that the phenomenon known as a 'sense of direction' results from these particles being attracted to the magnetic north in the same way as a needle on a compass.

Some believe that this apparent ability is due to an electrical effect, with some individuals apparently being able to store static electricity in their bodies and subsequently discharge it, sometimes at will and sometimes involuntarily. This theory has been used to explain, among other things, the apparent METAL-BENDING abilities of people like URI GELLER.

The ability to attract objects to the body apparently by magnetism continued to be documented throughout the 20th century, and in the early 21st century the alternative name 'bioattraction' has begun to be applied by those investigating it.

Sceptics would argue that the demonstrations of this apparent ability involve the use of simple STAGE MAGIC techniques, as were employed in the displays of IMMOVABILITY and human magnetism produced by the GEORGIA WONDER and her imitators.

hummadruz

A mysterious humming, droning or buzzing sound.

For centuries various individuals have reported being aware of a mysterious humming, droning or buzzing sound without being able to identify its source, and this phenomenon has come to be known as hummadruz. The word itself seems to have been coined in the 19th century.

While modern-day accounts might be explained by reference to 'noise pollution', the humming of overhead electricity wires or the fact that true quiet is increasingly rare anywhere, many reports predate electricity. The famous English naturalist Gilbert White (1720–93) described it as a natural and not uncommon phenomenon, comparing it to the humming of a swarm of bees.

There are various common factors in many reports of this effect, especially that it happens on a calm, still day, most often in summer, and usually in open countryside. Some people experience a sound so loud that it is alarming (and some have claimed to have made audio recordings of it), while others describe it as a background noise that is far from disturbing.

Various attempts have been made to explain the phenomenon. Some have connected it with other EARTH MYSTERIES, such as LEYS or EARTH LIGHTS, claimed to be present in the same area. Others believe it is linked to low-level seismic activity or the otherwise imperceptible movement of tectonic plates in the earth's crust. Just as there are levels of ultra-frequency sound that can be heard by animals but not humans, it has been suggested that hummadruz is low-frequency infrasound, perhaps produced by even the slightest of winds, that only certain individuals can detect.

Humpty Doo poltergeist

A remarkable stone-throwing poltergeist case from Australia.

What became known as the 'Humpty Doo poltergeist' afflicted a house at Humpty Doo in the Northern Territory of Australia early in 1998. Occupied by two adult couples, a friend and a child, the house apparently suffered repeated bombardment by stones,

Paul Cropper, one of the researchers who investigated the Humpty Doo poltergeist, holds a handful of pebbles which had apparently fallen from the ceiling.
(© TopFoto/Fortean)

a classic feature of many POLTERGEIST cases, as well as other missiles. As with many similar outbreaks, pebbles were reported falling both outside and inside the property, often seeming to materialize out of thin air or teleport into the room. The stones matched those from a gravel driveway at the house, but even in the monsoon season those that fell were said to be completely dry when picked up. The whole household was also disturbed by strange messages that appeared on the walls and floors of the house, which purported to come from a friend who had been killed in a road accident. These messages were either scrawled in pen or carefully spelled out with Scrabble tiles or lines of pebbles.

At the request of the occupants, a series of blessings and EXORCISMS were conducted by religious ministers of different denominations. However, these seemed to exacerbate rather than reduce the phenomena. The case came to the attention of the local press, and Humpty Doo was soon famous. The 'hauntees' signed an exclusive contract with the television network, Channel 7, who sent a film crew that set up camp in the house for 24 days. The film crew were apparently convinced by the poltergeist phenomena that they witnessed, but in their time at the house they only succeeded in recording three object movements on film, the poltergeist seemingly being adept at avoiding their cameras. The final broadcast actually suggested that the poltergeist was a hoax.

Two psychic researchers, Paul Cropper and Tony Healy, who also stayed at the property were convinced that the case was genuine, having observed a number of inexplicable phenomena for themselves. While the Humpty Doo poltergeist resembled many other similar cases recorded around the world, one observation was considered unique. This was a strange black object seen flying up a driveway. Described as smaller than a fist, it left a trail of gravel behind it and was interpreted as 'a poltergeist re-loading' by Cropper and Healey.

Huna
A form of modern shamanism which is based on ancient Hawaiian teachings.
Huna is the name which Max Freedom Long (1890– 1971) gave to his version of the ancient Hawaiian spiritual shamanic tradition. While working in Hawaii as a schoolteacher, Long learned about Hawaiian spiritual healing and shamanic teachings from William Tufts Brigham, who had spent 40 years living in Hawaii and trying to discover the secrets of Hawaiian SPIRITUALISM; this was not an easy task, since it was passed on by word of mouth, and its few remaining practitioners were reluctant to discuss it with him. Long spent the next 40 years of his life studying and working with those teachings that had been discovered, and from them developed a modern system which he called 'Huna'; this term does not appear to have been used of the ancient esoteric tradition by those who practised it, and in Hawaiian, the word means simply 'hidden'. Long may have chosen it because it appears to be part of the Hawaiian word *kahuna*, which is often used to refer to a Hawaiian sorcerer. He founded the Huna Fellowship in 1945, and in 1948 he began to publish a series of books on Huna. Another practitioner of Huna, Serge Kahili King, also published books on Huna and established the One Order of Huna International in 1973. However, neither Long nor King were ethnic Hawaiians, and neither were they initiated by the *kahunas* into their lore, so many native Hawaiians and academic experts regard Huna as a NEW AGE system rather than a revival of the ancient traditions.

Long described Huna as a psycho-spiritual system which encompasses not only healing methods, but also magic. The understanding and application of the principles of Huna are believed by its practitioners to bring about healing and harmony through the power of the mind, and to integrate mind, body and spirit. Huna teaches the celebration of life on the physical plane, and aims to merge matter and spirit, rather than to seek to transcend this plane.

The seven principles of Huna are given as: The world is what you think it is; There are no limits and everything is possible; Energy flows where attention is directed; Now is the moment of power; To love is to be happy with; All power comes from within; and Effectiveness is the measure of truth.

The Huna view is that humans consist of three selves, and that the key to living a fulfilled life is in the integration of these three selves: the subconscious, or 'low self', known in Hawaiian as the *unihipili*; the conscious, or 'middle self', known as the *uhane*; and the spiritual or 'high self', known as the *aumakua*. It is believed that the high self expresses all the divine qualities, and can control anything on the physical plane, but is bound by the cosmic law that it will not intervene on this plane unless asked to do so. Connection with the high self occurs naturally during sleep, and it is thought to be part of a combined community of spirits. The UNIVERSAL LIFE FORCE involved in the practice of Huna healing and magic is known as mana, and the high self requires mana before it can manifest prayers. It receives this vital force from the middle and low selves, in which a charge of mana is accumulated by various methods, including physical exercise, posture, nutritious food, the use of affirmations spoken out loud, and most importantly, deep breathing. Before the accumulated mana is directed to the high self for use in prayer, all negative thought forms in the middle and low selves are removed in a process known as 'Clearing the Path'. The prayer is then created as a thought form, energized by the mana, and visualized as being manifested.

Hurst, Lulu *see* GEORGIA WONDER

hydromancy
Divination by water.
The word 'hydromancy', from the Greek *hydōr*, 'water', and *manteiā*, 'divination', covers a number of divination techniques using water. The colour of a body of water, or the movements or shapes observed in it, were sometimes taken to have a special significance, and this gave rise to a whole separate branch of divination based on fountains; in the 2nd century AD, the Greek travel writer Pausanias described a fountain dedicated to Ino, into which worshippers seeking an oracle would throw loaves. If the loaves sank, it indicated a favourable outcome, but if they were

washed up by the fountain, it signified bad luck. In the 17th century, water was used to identify whether an accused person was guilty of WITCHCRAFT or not – if, upon being thrown into a pond or river, they floated, this indicated their guilt, but if they drowned, they were innocent. Other uses of water for divination include throwing three pebbles into standing water and observing the circles they make; suspending a ring in a vessel of water and making a prediction from the number of times it strikes the sides; and speaking mysterious words over a glass of water and then watching its surface for spontaneous movement. A bowl of water may also be used for SCRYING.

Hynek, Dr J(osef) Allen (1910–86)

A celebrated US astronomer who is often credited with being the first scientist to take the subject of UFOs seriously. Popularly described as the father of the UFO movement.

Dr J Allen Hynek was an astronomer, working at the Ohio State University, when the US Air Force began its UFO investigation programme at nearby Wright Field in 1949. He accepted the post of scientific adviser to the project.

For 22 years Hynek worked for PROJECT BLUE BOOK on a part-time basis. Elsewhere, his science career progressed – he became the associate director of the Smithsonian Astrophysics Observatory in Massachusetts, where he led the US optical satellite tracking programme, and went on to the Northwestern University in Evanston, Illinois, a suburb of his native Chicago, where he ended his working life as an emeritus professor.

During his time with the US Air Force Hynek attempted to encourage a more scientific approach, particularly as he began to be persuaded by the evidence that something significant might underlie the unsolved cases. He was unaware of the true purpose of these projects, or of the role played in them by intelligence agencies. After one failed attempt to improve the standard of investigation, he was allegedly taken aside by a senior aide during a trip to the Pentagon and told that there were reasons why the government could not be seen to be taking UFOs more seriously. However, Hynek was then left with the following intriguing question: 'But, do you really think that we would be doing nothing?'

When the US Air Force UFO investigation came to an end in 1969, following the publication of the COLORADO UNIVERSITY STUDY report, Hynek took the opportunity presented by this freedom to write what became a hugely influential book on the subject of UFOs – *The UFO Experience: A scientific Inquiry* (1972). The book contained his classification system for UFO cases, including the now famous term CLOSE ENCOUNTERS. This excited the film-maker Steven Spielberg, who built his fictional drama, *CLOSE ENCOUNTERS OF THE THIRD KIND* (1976), around its themes. Hynek was an official consultant to the film, appeared in trailers explaining its title and even played a cameo role.

In 1973 Hynek launched CUFOS, the first UFO investigation team run by scientists, in an attempt to put into practice the principles that he tried to persuade the Air Force to adopt.

Right up until the end of his life Hynek travelled the world giving lectures and taking part in field research into promising cases, including the

US astronomer Dr J Allen Hynek presents a purported UFO photograph to a press conference in March 1966. (© Bettmann/Corbis)

HESSDALEN wave. However, he never found a solution to the UFO mystery, and he remained unconvinced that UFOs were, as he put it, 'the ALIEN equivalent of Apollo 11'. Toward the end of his life he seemed to favour a more subtle theory and, for example, suggested the possibility that ALIEN ABDUCTIONS might be visionary experiences.

Hynek had always joked that he was born with the appearance of Haley's Comet and expected to die when it returned. This proved to be correct, and his death in April 1986 was widely mourned within the UFO COMMUNITY.

hypnagogic state
The state of drowsiness preceding sleep.
The hypnagogic state is the name given to the transitional phase between being awake and falling asleep. It has been known for centuries that HALLUCINATIONS, or 'lucid DREAMS' can be experienced by people in this state. Hypnagogic imagery is the term used in behavioural science to describe this type of hallucination or fantasy.

While the hypnagogic state is a fairly normal experience, in the minds of some people it becomes associated with anomalous experiences. It has been suggested that this state is the 'trance' entered into by MEDIUMS, and that people who believe they have communicated with the dead, gone through OUT-OF-BODY EXPERIENCES, seen VISIONS of religious figures or DEMONS, or even encountered ALIENS have really been dreaming or hallucinating while in the hypnagogic state.

Another argument is that people in this state are tapping into the unconscious, in much the same way as when dreaming, and that hallucinations experienced have no deeper significance than the normal dreams that are mostly forgotten on awakening. Thinking along these lines, many artists and writers have sought to deliberately enter this state, believing that their imaginations will be set free and that they will remember and be able to use what they have dreamed. See also HYPNOPOMPIC STATE.

hypnopompic state
The state between sleeping and being awake.
The hypnopompic state is the term used for the transitional phase between being alseep and waking up: the counterpart of the HYPNAGOGIC STATE. Like the latter, it has long been known as a fruitful time for DREAMS, VISIONS or HALLUCINATIONS, which were labelled as hypnopompic imagery by F W H Myers (1843–1901), the English poet and essayist and a founder of the SOCIETY FOR PSYCHICAL RESEARCH. Myers defined hypnopompic imagery as:

> … pictures consisting generally in the persistence of some dream-image into the first moments of waking.

Again like the hypnagogic state, the hypnopompic state has been seen as responsible for experiences regarded as EXTRASENSORY PERCEPTION, religious VISIONS, ALIEN ABDUCTIONS and other anomalous and seemingly inexplicable phenomena.

hypnosis
A psychological condition, sometimes described as a 'sleep-like' state, which can apparently be deliberately induced in some people.
Hypnosis (from the Greek *hypno*, meaning 'sleep') can apparently be induced in some people using variations on a process involving intense concentration and extreme relaxation (see TRANCE, HYPNOTIC). Once in such a state, which some people refer to as an 'ALTERED STATE OF CONSCIOUSNESS' (although whether this is literally correct is a matter of argument), the subject can sometimes become highly suggestible and can apparently be induced to behave or even think in certain ways. However, there are wide variations in individuals' reactions to attempts to place them in a state of hypnosis, and to their responses once in such a condition.

Hypnotism is said to have originally developed from the techniques employed by FRANZ ANTON MESMER, although he believed that his method, known as MESMERISM, worked in a very different way to the modern understanding of hypnosis. It is also related to the processes employed in self-suggestion systems such as that of ÉMILE COUÉ, which are often described as self-hypnosis. Some people claim that a state of hypnosis can also be induced in animals, although the value of this is questionable – all that this seems to produce is temporary inactivity, and it is very difficult to ascertain whether this is the same condition that it is alleged to be produced in humans.

Hypnosis is widely employed as a popular form of entertainment, in which volunteers are placed into a hypnotic trance and are apparently then made to behave in a range of (often comical) ways that are contrary to their normal nature. There are also numerous examples of the apparent successful use of hypnosis as a therapeutic tool – it is employed as a means to increase the suggestibility of some patients so that their behaviour can be changed, with the effect that they lose weight or give up smoking, for example. It is even claimed that it can be used as a method of pain control, reducing the need for the use of pain-relieving drugs. However, those who practise such hypnotherapy do not usually claim that it is a complete treatment in itself, but rather that it is a tool to help a patient who already consciously wishes to attain the desired end result, or that it is a process that complements other forms of treatment. As with many other forms of ALTERNATIVE MEDICINE, hypnotherapy attracts the criticism that successes may well be due to the PLACEBO EFFECT.

One of the most controversial claims relating to hypnosis is that it can be used as a tool to recover so-called 'lost' or 'hidden' memories (see CRYPTOMNESIA and MEMORIES, RECOVERED). Indeed, although hypnotism has even been used as a method for apparently obtaining evidence in criminal cases, in the legal systems of many countries a witness's testimony is now inadmissible if they have only revealed it under hypnosis. Hypnosis has also been employed in this way to supposedly recover memories of child abuse, encounters with UFOS, ALIEN ABDUCTIONS and details of past lives (see PAST-LIFE REGRESSION). Many people counter such claims by pointing out that those who champion hypnosis hold that it increases the suggestibility of the subject, in which case they must accept that this greatly reduces the value of anything the subject says while in such a condition – particularly where leading questions are used, or the subject knows or can guess what the questioner wants to hear (see also MEMORY, FALSE). In a number of such cases it has also become patently clear that some of the details recalled come from information that the subject has encountered previously but may not consciously remember.

Hypnotism is commonly alleged to be used as a MIND CONTROL technique, and is said to be one of the methods employed in BRAINWASHING. Whether either of these is even possible (in the strong sense implied by the terms) remains a matter of debate, and there is certainly little evidence to suggest that hypnotism can be used to produce such dramatic effects.

Hypnosis has long been a controversial subject and many argue that a substantial amount of research is still required. Indeed, the question of whether it deserves to be recognized as a distinct mental state in its own right remains open, and some psychologists have even gone so far as to suggest that hypnosis is a purely social construct – in effect, everyone knows how someone in a trance is supposed to behave and so, at an unconscious level, they 'play along'. See also MASS HYPNOSIS.

hypnosis, mass *see* MASS HYPNOSIS

hypnotic suggestion
The 'implanting' of an idea into the mind of an individual while they are under hypnosis.
Some individuals can be induced into a state described as HYPNOSIS, in which they display changes in their behaviour and thinking, and experience sensations that are often cited as evidence of entry into an ALTERED STATE OF CONSCIOUSNESS – although whether this is really the case remains controversial.

The condition is often characterized by an increase in suggestibility – while in the state of hypnosis a person can often be instructed to perform a certain action at a particular time, usually in response to an appropriate cue. For example, in a show performed by a stage hypnotist the cue might be a particular piece of music, on hearing which the subject will begin to act in a pre-arranged strange or comical way. In therapeutic hypnosis it may be suggested to an individual that when a certain signal is given they will feel no pain, or that when a cigarette is placed in the mouth an unpleasant memory is recalled, ultimately leading to a cessation of smoking. There is evidence to show that such techniques can work for some people.

Fictional representations of hypnotic suggestion feature in the films of *The Manchurian Candidate* (1962 and 2004) in which a subject becomes an assassin upon hearing a trigger phrase. However, as with the controversial concept of BRAINWASHING, which is another theme of the films, there is no evidence to indicate that hypnotic suggestion can actually produce such a strong response.

hypnotic trance *see* TRANCE, HYPNOTIC

hysteria, mass *see* MASS HYSTERIA

I AM movement
*Organizations and beliefs originating from Guy
Ballard's teachings from the Ascended Masters.*
The I AM movement grew out of the teachings of GUY
W BALLARD, who claimed to have met SAINT GERMAIN
and to have been given, with his wife Edna, over
3,000 'discourses' from the ASCENDED MASTERS. It is
important to distinguish between the I AM Activity,
Ballard's own organization, and the wider I AM
movement which includes offshoot organizations.

The Ballards founded the I AM Religious Activity
in 1932. They toured the USA as the only 'Accredited
Messengers' of the Ascended Masters (also known as
the Great White Brotherhood), who are higher beings
who have advanced beyond the normal spiritual levels
of humanity. The Ascended Masters are common to
a wide range of religious movements, most of them
traceable back to THEOSOPHY, and including ALICE
BAILEY's Arcane School and the CHURCH UNIVERSAL
AND TRIUMPHANT.

The main teaching of the I AM movement is that
there is a spark of the Divine Flame of God, the I
AM presence, within each one of us. By tuning into
this through meditation and through 'affirmations'
and 'decrees' the believer can come to a state of
divine realization. Affirmations affirm the believer's
relationship with God and give thanks for future
blessings as if they have already occurred; decrees use
the name of God, I AM, to make statements of power
which are expected to come true. (The belief that
by verbally affirming healing the healing will occur
is taken from 'New Thought', a spiritual philosophy
similar to CHRISTIAN SCIENCE.) The Violet Consuming
Flame is the activity of the sacred fire or the divine
presence within us.

Among other beliefs the I AM Religious Activity

taught that the believer would have health and
youthfulness, so Guy Ballard's unexpected death in
1939 came as a shock to the organization. Many
members left, but Edna Ballard announced that Guy
Ballard had now become an Ascended Master, and she
led the group until her own death in 1971. Their son
Don, who had also been an Accredited Messenger,
left the organization in 1957; it has been run by a
Board of Directors, with no new Messengers, since
1971.

The parent organization of the I AM Religious
Activity is the Saint Germain Foundation, and its
books and magazines are published by the Saint
Germain Press. These include 19 volumes of 'The
Saint Germain Series' which contain 'the original
instruction from the Ascended Masters on the Eternal
Laws of Life'. Because of the success of offshoot I
AM organizations such as the Church Universal and
Triumphant, the Saint Germain Foundation has
trademarked many of the distinctive phrases of the I
AM Religious Activity. On its website it says that its
books, magazines, pictures and music:

> … carry the personal Radiation of the Ascended
> Masters who are working for the Illumination of
> mankind at this time. There are many imitations,
> however. *These and only these Books, Pictures and
> Music are charged with Their Ascended Master
> Consciousness, the Rays of Light and Love from
> Their Hearts and Their Ascended Master Feeling
> and Comprehension of the Victory of the Light.*

Many of the images of Saint Germain, Jesus and the
Violet Flame are very similar throughout the wider I
AM movement.

Although they have centres and members around

the world, both the I AM Religious Activity and the wider I AM movement are based in and very oriented towards the USA, and are very patriotic. The Ascended Master Saint Germain is said to have inspired the American Constitution and the Declaration of Independence.

In 1952 several senior members of the I AM Religious Activity split away to form the Bridge to Freedom, with Geraldine Innocente as the Messenger. In 1958 a number of members of this organization split away to found what would eventually become the largest and most influential I AM movement, the CHURCH UNIVERSAL AND TRIUMPHANT.

Ica stones

The alleged relics of an ancient civilization in Peru.

The Ica stones are a number of decorated rounded stones, amounting to around 15,000, collected by the Peruvian Dr Javier Cabrera (1924–2001). The stones are carved with a variety of stylized images of human beings and animals, including some which Cabrera claimed to show, among other things, men hunting dinosaurs, carrying out complicated medical procedures and observing the planets through telescopes.

The name comes from the village and river of Ica in a region of Peru to the north of the site of the NAZCA LINES. Cabrera claimed that he had been aware of the stones since his childhood as his father had found one in a field. However, the main body of stones was said to have been discovered in the 1960s in a cave which was only revealed when the Ica river flooded and washed away the earth covering

it. Inside this cave peasants apparently found an enormous cache of carved stones.

Cabrera maintained that the images on these stones represented a library of images left behind by a vanished civilization, one sophisticated enough, if the evidence of the carvings was to be believed, to carry out human organ transplants, blood transfusions and caesarean sections and to use ACUPUNCTURE as an anaesthetic. Even more controversial were those images that seemed to show human beings hunting or fighting dinosaurs. If these were authentic, then the scientific orthodoxy that had shown that dinosaurs were extinct long before *Homo sapiens* appeared would be called into question. According to Cabrera's interpretation, the stones were carved by a technologically superior race which had left the earth for another planet, probably harnessing the energy of a passing comet to accomplish this. Neatly enough, this tied in with the interpretation of the Nazca lines as a kind of landing zone for alien spacecraft.

However, sceptics soon began to cast doubt on the authenticity of the stones. Analysis showed that they were made of andesite, a very hard rock which was certainly in abundance locally. Despite Cabrera's claims that very sophisticated metal tools would have been needed to carve this highly resistant material, close examination established that the rock itself was not incised. The images were made by removing a layer of natural 'varnish' deposited on the stone by bacterial action.

Radiocarbon dating was useless in attempting to date the stones as they contain no organic material. Dating them by examining the strata in which they were found was impossible as no one

The controversial Ica stones, generally regarded to be the work of hoaxers, but held by some to be the relics of an ancient and sophisticated civilization.

(© Charles & Josette Lenars/Corbis)

was willing or able to identify the precise site of the cave that yielded them. When one of the 'finders' of the stones was threatened with prosecution for selling antiquities he admitted that he had made them himself, recanting later when the legal threat was lifted.

It was pointed out that a civilization technologically advanced enough to undertake space travel would surely have left a more sophisticated record of their achievements than a collection of pictures scratched on stones. Also, if they had co-existed with dinosaurs, they must have had more advanced means of killing them than the crude bladed weapons depicted. Those who do not accept the authenticity of the stones will do no more than admit that a few of them (the least controversial in content) have similarities to other pre-Columbian art. The majority, however, are considered to be the work of hoaxers attempting to profit from gullible relic hunters.

ice circles

Mysterious circles found in frozen ponds and rivers.

In various parts of the world, but most commonly in North America, northern Europe and Russia, people have discovered and photographed mysterious circle patterns that have appeared in frozen bodies of water overnight. Like CROP CIRCLES, these ice circles are usually perfectly geometrical in shape, but unlike crop circles, no more elaborate patterns or complex designs have been found. Again like crop circles, there is considerable variation in the size of the ice circles: some occur on thinner ice than others; some appear smooth and contained within the ice; others seem to have been scored into the surface with a sharp implement, leaving shards.

In the absence of skating FAIRIES, some link these formations with UFO activity, and speak of seeing strange glows in the sky or briefly glimpsed silvery craft hovering over the site. Unfortunately, no photographs have appeared to back up these claims. Sceptics point to circles that have obviously been scored into the surface and detect the hand of hoaxers, but in some cases these scored circles have appeared on ice too thin to support the weight of a person. It has been pointed out that in rivers, rotating ice sheets often form and freeze where the river turns, but this obviously fails to explain circles formed in still water.

ice falls *see* FALLS

I Ching

An ancient Chinese book thought to be some 3,000 years old. It consists of a series of 64 hexagrams (figures made up of six lines), and a text giving interpretations of these. Originally used as an oracle, the I Ching developed into a book of wisdom from which both the Confucian and Taoist philosophies drew inspiration, although it is still best known in the West as a form of divination.

The *I Ching* is thought to date back some 3,000 years. Its name, which is Mandarin for 'Book of Changes', refers to the constant change which Chinese philosophy holds to be the result of the interaction of the two complementary principles of the universe, YIN and YANG. In the West, the *I Ching* is in general regarded simply as a system of divination, but in the East, it is also seen as a book of wisdom which expresses the cosmology and philosophy of ancient China, and was an inspiration for both TAOISM and Confucianism.

The *I Ching* consists of 64 abstract line arrangements called hexagrams, and a text which gives an interpretation of these. Each hexagram has a name such as Initial Difficulties, Treading Wisely, Stagnation, Humility and The Restraining Force, and is understood to represent a state or process, and also possibly a change. The hexagrams are composed of six horizontal lines which are either unbroken (yang) or broken, with a gap in the middle (yin); there are 64 hexagrams because there are 64 possible combinations of six yin or yang lines. Each hexagram is seen as an upper and lower pair of three parallel lines, or trigrams, of which either no lines, one line, two lines, or all three lines may be broken, and the eight trigrams which in all their combinations make up the 64 hexagrams correspond to the powers of nature: *Ch'ien* (Heaven), *Chen* (Thunder), *K'an* (Water), *Ken* (Mountain), *K'un* (Earth), *Sun* (Wind), *Li* (Fire) and *Tui* (Lake). According to legend, the Chinese ruler Fu Hsi copied these trigrams from the back of a turtle. The oracular meanings of the hexagrams were said to have been divined by Chinese philosopher-priests, with their images and concepts taken partly from ancient oracles and partly from the mythology, history and poetry of earlier ages. The text of the *I Ching* is generally attributed to King Wen, founder of the Chou dynasty, and his son, the Duke of Chou, while the commentaries are ascribed to Confucius, who, when he was nearly 70, was reported to have said:

> If some years were added to my life, I would give fifty to the study of the *I Ching*, and I might then escape falling into great errors.

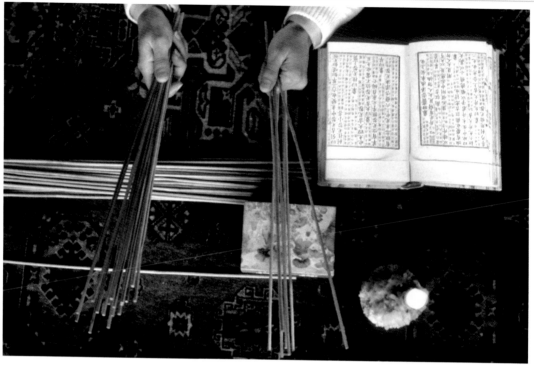

Consulting the Chinese divinatory text, the *I Ching*, using the traditional method of yarrow sticks.
(© TopFoto)

Unlike other types of ORACLE, the *I Ching* does not regard the past and future as fixed, but as dynamic, flowing and changeable. It therefore offers possibilities – 'If this is done, it may produce such-and-such a result' – rather than giving the questioner instructions. The 64 hexagrams between them symbolize all the states of change and flux which are caused in the universe by the interaction of yin and yang, and the texts interpret these changes as they are seen to apply to the question at the moment when the hexagram is cast.

A number of methods may be used to consult the *I Ching*. Traditionally, a bundle of 50 yarrow stalks is used, but pairs of DICE, or marbles or beads, can also be employed. However, the most commonly used method in the West involves three coins, which are tossed onto a flat surface six times in a row. 'Heads' are valued at 3, and 'tails' at 2, so that each throw of three coins may give a total of 6, 7, 8 or 9, which indicate respectively Old Yin (a yin line which changes to a yang one), Young Yang (which remains unchanged), Young Yin (unchanging) and Old Yang (a yang line changing to a yin one). The first throw gives the bottom line of the hexagram, the next the second line from the bottom, and so on. Any changing lines are significant. The first hexagram is interpreted using the text, and then the second one, which is derived

from the first plus its changing lines, is also read. The changing lines indicate specific attitudes or conditions inherent in the present situation, and are interpreted separately in addition to the overall hexagram, and the second hexagram, derived from the changing lines, indicates the direction of the transformation, and gives additional advice. See also DIVINATION.

identified flying object

The title given to the object involved in a UFO sighting when, after investigation, an acceptable explanation is found. It is usually abbreviated to IFO.

Although there is great disparity in the opinions of UFO researchers, the one aspect of the phenomenon upon which they agree is that the vast majority of reported UFO sightings are not actually of 'unidentifiable' objects – they are only 'unidentified' by the witness at the time of observation.

At least 90 per cent of reported sightings are ultimately explained and thus become identified flying objects (IFOs). Many researchers think that this figure may even be as high as 95 per cent. In fact, because no case can ever be proven to be irresolvable (it is always possible that future data and findings will present a solution), sceptics might contend that the remaining 5 per cent are merely unresolved IFOs.

Over 250 different IFO phenomena have been shown to have caused reports of UFO sightings. The most common are aircraft, stars and planets, weather balloons, atmospheric distortions (such as mirages), satellites and laser light shows. However, there are many more unusual things that occasionally cause UFO sightings – reports have been discovered to result from such things as bin bags blowing in the wind, swarms of insects, telegraph poles silhouetted against the moon and oddly shaped clouds.

A number of well-established UFO sightings have become IFOs when the final clues were discovered, sometimes several years after their occurrence. A major sighting from Oxfordshire in January 1973, which involved a number of witnesses and a cine film showing an orange ball of light crossing the daytime sky, was only solved two decades later when documents were released under the FREEDOM OF INFORMATION ACT. These showed that the ball was ejected aviation fuel, deliberately set ablaze by the crew of a stricken military jet.

However, there is some evidence to suggest that there is a significant difference between unsolved UFO cases and IFO cases. For example, a comparative study carried out in the USA by the Battelle Memorial Institute, on behalf of PROJECT BLUE BOOK, looked at a number of different parameters and concluded that it was statistically highly unlikely that the cases classified as 'unexplained' were of the same type as those classified as IFOs.

Illuminati

A name adopted by various philosophical or religious societies which claim enlightenment, and especially used to refer to an 18th-century group of German free-thinkers known as the Bavarian Illuminati. Since its abolition in the late 18th century, this organization has been the focus of numerous claims that it survives and continues to work towards a goal of world domination.
The word *illuminati*, which is Latin for 'the enlightened ones', was originally used by the Ante-Nicene clergy to refer to those who underwent Christian baptism, on the grounds that they then had an enlightened understanding. The name was subsequently adopted by a number of secret or mystical societies which claimed special enlightenment, such as the Alumbrados, a 16th-century Spanish sect, However, it is now most commonly associated with the Bavarian Illuminati, a short-lived movement of German republican free-thinkers that was founded in 1776 by ex-Jesuit Adam Weishaupt and Baron Adolph von Knigge.

Originally calling itself the Order of Perfectibilists, the group aimed to discuss and disseminate the radical philosophies of the day; to combat religious superstition and encourage rationalism; to increase morality and virtue and oppose evil; and thus to lay the foundations for the reformation of the world. While there is some dispute as to whether or not its members were principally Freemasons (see FREEMASONRY), or former Freemasons, it certainly incorporated or adapted much Masonic ritual, although its approach was of a rationalistic rather than an OCCULT nature. This offshoot of the European Enlightenment attracted a considerable membership, including literary men such as Goethe and Herder, and in its heyday it had branches in most countries on the continent of Europe. However, it soon became subject to internal splits and factions, and an edict issued by the Bavarian government in 1785 led to its abolition. It had officially ceased to exist by 1790.

However, it was not long before its opponents began to suggest that the organization had survived abolition and continued to operate in secret. In 1798 the British author John Robison and the French author Abbé Augustin Barruél both published works making these claims; Barruél stated that the French Revolution of 1789 had been engineered and controlled through the Jacobins by the Illuminati, and later theorists also claimed that they were responsible for the Russian Revolution in 1917. The movement has been the subject of various conspiracy theories alleging its ongoing influence on world affairs. Some say that the Illuminati are in league with the KNIGHTS TEMPLAR and the ROSICRUCIANS, and that their conspiracy leads back to the Vatican; some that the organization is much older than its Bavarian incarnation, and that it dates back to ancient Egyptian times, while others go further and claim that it is of EXTRATERRESTRIAL origin. The common theme which runs through all of these theories is that its aim is world domination. It is generally said to be working towards the replacement of all religions and nations with humanism and a single world power – employing such methods as blackmail, assassination, the control of banks, the infiltration of government, wars, revolution and even MIND CONTROL, in order to move its members into positions of power.

This notion of an all-powerful secret society controlling world affairs has captured the imagination of many writers, and has had a distinct influence on popular culture; a number of science fiction authors have used it as a theme, and Umberto Eco's novel *Foucault's Pendulum* (1988) includes references to the Illuminati, as does Dan Brown's 2000 novel *Angels and Demons*; several video and computer games are also based on storylines involving them, and the villains of the 2001 film *Lara Croft: Tomb Raider* are a group called the Illuminati, whose plan is to rule the world, and who claim to have existed for millennia for this purpose.

Although there is little or no reliable evidence

to support the claim that the Bavarian Illuminati survived after the end of the 18th century, one possible reason for the persistence of conspiracy theories about them may be the fact that a number of groups have used the name since then, many of which claim to be descended from the Bavarian Illuminati. See also SECRET SOCIETIES.

illusion

A false appearance or deceptive impression of reality, especially one performed for entertainment in conjuring or stage magic.

Illusion, or the deceptive impression of reality, may be caused in a number of ways. Optical illusions created by means such as the use of false perspective exploit the assumptions made by the visual system, and mirages are natural illusions caused by distortions in the atmosphere. But the most well-known type of illusions are those which have been performed for centuries to entertain and amaze as part of the art of conjuring or stage magic (see MAGIC, STAGE). The illusionist uses various techniques to give the audience the impression that they have seen something which is apparently impossible, although it is generally understood by all that the 'magic' has been accomplished by sleight of hand and trickery and not by any occult or supernatural means; the performer seeks to present an effect so skilfully that the audience cannot believe the evidence of their own eyes and cannot think how the illusion has been achieved.

Modern magicians do not usually claim to possess genuine spiritual or occult powers, but the techniques used by illusionists have, in the past, been exploited by those making such claims. However, some claim that the psychic URI GELLER, who became famous in the 1970s for his purported 'paranormal' powers, is an example of a modern-day illusionist claiming psychic powers. In the late 19th century, at the height of the vogue for SPIRITUALISM, many fraudulent MEDIUMS used the methods of conjuring and stage magic to perform illusions designed to convince those present at their SÉANCES that genuine supernatural events were taking place – such as apparitions of spirits, ghostly music, and objects moving without being touched. Since the séances were invariably held in darkened rooms, it was not difficult for a fake medium, often aided by an accomplice, to fool the participants, and in the last century or so, several professional magicians, most notably HARRY HOUDINI, Joseph Dunninger, and in modern times, JAMES RANDI, have devoted themselves to exposing phony mediums and fraudulent paranormal claims.

image magic *see* MAGIC, IMAGE

images

Representations which feature in a wide variety of paranormal and strange phenomena, from drawings and paintings, to sculpture, photographic oddities and the spontaneous natural images called 'simulacra'.

In the view of many archaic societies, making an image was a magical act. The old meaning of 'simulacrum' was a 'divine vessel', as though the making of one called down the SPIRIT of a supernatural being, or the essence of a divine force to inhabit it. Images were also possibly believed to be empowered in some way through being a likeness – for example, Neolithic hunters might paint an image of their quarry on rock and then stab it to evoke a successful hunt. In Greek legend, the gods were invoked to possess their images; they were regarded as actually present and their behaviour studied for DIVINATION. When Alexander marched towards Tyre (in the region of today's Lebanon), the Tyrians thought their patron god Apollo would desert them for the Macedonian conqueror, so they tied the wooden statue with ropes and nailed it to the floor.

Oscar Wilde's story of Dorian Grey explores the idea of the close association between a thing and its representation; as he defied the aging process, so his portrait grew older. This correspondence was especially important where the likeness, often a symbolic one, was intended to attract (SYMPATHETIC MAGIC) or ward off (prophylactic magic) and was the basis for AMULETS and CHARMS of all kinds (see MAGIC, IMAGE).

Paranormal phenomena involving images frequently occur in a religious context and include pictures, icons and statues said to bleed or weep (see IMAGES, BLEEDING, and IMAGES, WEEPING). There is considerable overlap in the ways that such exudations are reported and interpreted – for example, in the case of statues that supposedly 'weep' tears of blood. Other images are observed to move or grow extra parts. For example, in 1985, a group of people praying at the open-air shrine at Ballinspittal, Ireland, claimed they saw a statue of the Virgin Mary change position. Within weeks, dozens of similar observations were reported from other shines. The last few decades have seen an unprecedented rise in the number of reports of MARIAN APPARITIONS in Roman Catholic communities. Despite the growing number of incidents, and the widespread, ready belief in such 'miracles' by pious Catholics, the Vatican has been extremely cautious about endorsing any of them. Part of the problem for the authorities is that local groups quickly form around the phenomenon and experience further occurrences, soon finding themselves at odds with the local bishop on doctrinal matters – as happened at the major apparition shrines at MEDJUGORJE, Marpingen and elsewhere. To address the dilemma, the Congregation for the Doctrine of the Faith (formerly THE INQUISITION) announced, in 2003, a major review of the 25-year-old guidelines for local clergy in such matters.

Supernatural origins are claimed for especially revered images, possibly the most famous of which is the TURIN SHROUD. Again, in 1531, just ten years after Hernán Cortés's Conquistadors seized Mexico's Aztec capital, the Virgin Mary is said to have appeared to one of the first Aztec converts. She asked him to convey roses to the bishop in his cloak, and as he did so, a coloured image of the Virgin was revealed imprinted on its lining. Now known as the 'Virgin of Guadaloupe', this image has been adopted as a national symbol by Mexico.

There are dozens of photographs said to be portraits of Jesus (see CHRIST IN THE SNOW), Mary, the Buddha and even the Chinese goddess Kuan Yin. The photographers sometimes say a mysterious voice told them to take picture, or the camera 'went off by itself'. Many look dubious (see HOAXES AND HOAXERS) but are sincerely believed by their owners to be a class of MIRACLE. Some investigators have even suggested that the human mind might have the power to impress images onto receptive material, such as photographic film, as is the case in claimed examples of THOUGHTOGRAPHY. See also IMAGES, SPONTANEOUS; SIMULACRA; SPIRIT PHOTOGRAPHS.

images, bleeding
Apparently miraculous images that appear to 'bleed'.
In the classical Greek period, there were stories of sacred groves of trees which yielded wood for crafting divine effigies, which bled when attacked. While it may not be the origin of modern accounts of statues and pictures that bleed, it shows that the pious belief that sacred IMAGES may 'come alive' when a divine spirit inhabits them is quite ancient. That this tradition is persistent is demonstrated by the occasional historical example, such as the 'miraculous painting' of the Virgin Mary of Mantua, in Lombardy, Italy. According to legend, it was looted in the 17th century and hung on a tree for target practice. It is said that when a bullet rebounded off the icon, blood spurted from the damaged painting. It is now on display in the Church of Maria and St Anthony of Padua, in Prague, and supposedly still bleeds to this day.

Since the 1980s, there has been an unprecedented rise in the number of reports of bleeding images, nearly all of them in a Catholic context. A cursory listing includes incidents from the following countries,

The crying Virgin of Civitavecchia, a plaster statue of the Virgin Mary that is said to cry tears of blood.
(© Neri Grazia/Corbis Sygma)

many of which have apparently recurred for years: Australia (2004), Bolivia (1995), Canada (1984), Chile (1983), Ecuador (1990), France (1914, 1996), India (1998, 2003), Italy (1972, 1995), Korea (1989, 2005), Philippines (1989), Spain (1998), USA (1992, 2003, 2004) and Venezuela (2003). The phenomena exhibited include bleeding from the wounds of the crucifixion, sweating blood, a flow of tears of blood from the eyes (see also IMAGES, WEEPING) and, more rarely, bleeding from a Eucharistic host held by a statuette. Many of the images involved were bought on visits to SHRINES of earlier 'MIRACLES' or VISIONS, so there is also an element of 'transmission' in this phenomenon.

The majority of cases are never properly investigated. Of those that are, most are quickly unmasked as simple, if pious, frauds (see PIOUS FRAUD and HOAXES AND HOAXERS), and bishops have not shrunk from condemning them. A very few cases have been tentatively authenticated and hotly contested. One of the most famous of these, which illustrates the difficulties involved in investigation, occurred in the Italian port of Civitavecchia, in 1995. The small plaster statuette of the Virgin Mary had been bought at MEDJUGORJE (the MARIAN APPARITION site in Bosnia-Herzegovina) and installed in the garden of the Gregori family home. One day, blood-like tracks that streamed from its eyes were found. This was quickly proclaimed a 'miracle', and thousands came to see the 'tears of blood'. The local bishop, Girolamo Grillo, a renowned sceptic in matters of superstition, ordered an investigation by civil and forensic authorities. However, instead of revealing a hoax, as the bishop hoped, the study by the Institute for Forensic Medicine at the University of Rome established that the statue was solid and had no mechanism for delivering a fluid to the eyes, and that the red fluid was all or partly male human blood. A theological commission, set up to consider the implications of at least 60 eye-witness testimonies, judged that the male blood on the female statue indicated the unity of the Holy Mother and Son. During these investigations the statue was locked away in Bishop Grillo's possession and, he claims, it once cried tears of blood in his hands. Now convinced of its authenticity, he placed it on public display in Civitavecchia's Church of San Agostino. Since then, the numbers of MIRACLE CURES, conversions and pilgrims attributed to it have grown each year.

Almost immediately, one of Italy's largest consumer groups brought a formal complaint against 'unknown persons' under a 1930s law prohibiting fraudulent magicians and hoaxers, which was followed by allegations of fraud from other sources. In 2001, the ongoing inquiry by police and other authorities was hindered by the Gregori family's refusal to provide DNA samples. The case was eventually dismissed by a judge on the grounds of failure to come up with any evidence to support the allegations within a period of six years. Since then, the phenomenon seems to have received some unofficial approval from senior clergy.

Proper sceptical inquiry can also be fraught with conflicting ideologies. For example, in Cochambamba, Bolivia, a statue of the crucified Christ is believed by many to bleed from wounds, shed tears of blood and sweat blood. The phenomenon began in March 1995 and has apparently returned each Easter Holy Week since then. Later that year, film-maker Ron Tesoriero and Dr Ricardo Castanon twice took samples of the blood-like liquid for DNA analysis, at Gentest in the USA and at a state forensic laboratory in Australia. Both confirmed the presence of human female blood products. Michael Willesee, who included this account in the documentary he made for Fox, the US TV network (*Signs From God: Science Tests Faith*, first aired in the USA in July 1999), was not fazed by the discovery of female blood exuding from the statue of a male deity – the opposite of the situation at Civitavecchia. A born-again Catholic, Willesee

suggested that the blood was either the Virgin Mary's or, as Jesus had a single human parent, he somehow shared her female genetic make-up.

Inevitably, this creative interpretation failed to impress the CSICOP-school of sceptics (see COMMITTEE FOR THE SCIENTIFIC INVESTIGATION OF CLAIMS OF THE PARANORMAL) who commented on the documentary. Not only did they propose a number of ways in which statues and icons can, surreptitiously, be made to appear to weep or bleed, but they raised the suspicion that, as the owner of the statue was female, the blood might be hers. The doubts were not resolved because no proof was offered to support these claims. To complicate matters, the 'bleeding' statue of Cochambamba is also closely associated with two female 'mystics' – Catalina Rivas (who herself developed STIGMATA) and Nancy Fowler – who both claim to receive messages from Jesus and who both have their own devout followers.

The most bizarre claim in this category is the menstruating statue of the Hindu goddess Bhagawati, at a temple in Kerala, India. The temple is built on the site of a visit by the god Shiva, and his wife Parvati, to a local SAGE. During the visit, the goddess began to menstruate and, according to tradition, went into seclusion for three days. The statue of Bhagawati is made of iron and said to be a replica of an ancient one, lost in a fire. The statue wears a napkin which is periodically examined for signs of menstruation; if present, the statue is removed for a three-day cleansing ritual, following which it is reinstated in a grand ceremony.

images, spontaneous
Meaningful images which apparently appear without human intervention.

Human beings have an exceptional visual sense. Once the mind is engaged, the simple act of looking (ie merely directing the eyes towards something) becomes the immeasurably greater and more complex act of perception – involving consideration, deduction, extrapolation, memory, understanding, curiosity and especially imagination. The organizational processes the mind applies to our perceptions, particularly vision and hearing, allow us to quickly detect patterns in the sensory input. Among these processes are *apophenia* (perception of connections between seemingly unrelated data) and *pareidolia* (perceptions in which vague stimuli can be overlaid with distinct meaning or details). In effect, humans are predisposed to see meaningful images wherever they look (see also CHANCE AND COINCIDENCE).

Forms, figures and scenes occurring spontaneously through natural or accidental processes come under the general fortean (see CHARLES FORT) heading of SIMULACRA. Typical examples would include the shapes of animals in clouds, faces in the bark of trees or grain of wood, or abstract landscapes in rock formations or polished sections of stone (such as those Richard Shaver saw as signs of an ancient civilization inside the Earth – see SHAVER MYSTERY). Other such images, claimed by some to be divinely created, are called *acheiropoieta* (see TURIN SHROUD). There are no certain boundaries to these definitions. Many spontaneous images cross categories and are interpreted according to the opinions of the viewer – such as marks that resemble holy script or symbols (for examples, see HOLY VEGETABLES).

We might also include within the category of spontaneous images some of the photographs said to contain images of GHOSTS, SAINTS or Jesus and the Virgin Mary; these are often said to have occurred when the camera 'went off by itself' (see CHRIST IN THE SNOW).

More problematical cases involve religious images that are 'seen' to move, weep or bleed, because they usually occur within a fervent atmosphere of devotion and expectation (for examples, see IMAGES, BLEEDING and IMAGES, WEEPING).

images, weeping
Apparently miraculous images that appear to 'weep'.
While there has been an unprecedented rise in the number of reports of bleeding statues and pictures since the 1980s (see IMAGES, BLEEDING), reports of statues and pictures of Jesus and of his Mother weeping, oozing or sweating clear or oily liquids began increasing in the 1970s. A cursory listing includes incidents occurring in the following countries, many of which have supposedly recurred for years: Australia (1994, 2001, 2004), Bangladesh (2003), Benin (1997), Bolivia (1995), Canada (1984, 1985), Ecuador (2004), Haiti (1976), Ireland (1994, 1995), Italy (1485, 1947, 1953, 1972, 1975, 1987, 1992, 1994, 1995, 1997, 2003), Greece (1823), Japan (1973), Mexico (1992), Philippines (2003, 2004), Poland (1641), Puerto Rico (1994), Romania (2000, 2003), Russia (1998, 2005), Spain (1998), Syria (1977), Trinidad (1996), USA (1960, 1972, 1973, 1980, 1984, 1986, 1990, 1991, 1992, 1993, 1994, 1996, 1998, 1999, 2003, 2004) and Venezuela (2002, 2003).

The antiquity of this phenomenon is well established by relatively isolated events. From the time of the Middle Ages, accounts of pilgrimages to the Holy Land sometimes mentioned locations of weeping icons. The Madonna and Child icon of Marijapovch, in north-eastern Hungary, which has reportedly been weeping since 1715, is itself a copy of an earlier icon which apparently began weeping in

1696, and was appropriated by the Austrian emperor Leopold I. A similar weeping icon was venerated in the Slovakian village of Klokochovo, in 1670. Another typical example is the statue of the scourged Christ, once used during processions in Steingaden, Germany – until it was put away in 1735 because it appeared 'uncomfortably pitiful'. When it was found again in 1738, in a farmhouse, in Wies, it was said to be wet with tears. St Gregory of Tours (538–94) described the practice, by some religious communities, of using weeping statues to convert non-believers, but it is not clear whether these were examples of PIOUS FRAUD or supposedly authentic occurrences.

The overwhelming majority of weeping images are representations of the Virgin Mary and, like the bleeding images, have often been bought at the SHRINES of earlier miracles. The theological explanation for the phenomenon is that it represents Mary's desolation at the sins and sufferings of this world. Many are associated with the initial mystical experience of a nun or pilgrim – such as Sister Agnes Sasagawa at Akita, in Japan, who, in the throes of her own stigmatization (see STIGMATA), in July 1973, heard a voice from a wooden statuette of Mary. Like the statuette, Agnes bore a cross-shaped wound on one hand, from which blood flowed. In January 1975, the nature of the exudations changed; they became clear and more like tears or sweat, and continued like that for the next six years. Bishop Ito of Niigata ordered a sample of blood and tears from the statue to be sent to the faculty of Legal Medicine of the University of Akita for scientific analysis. They confirmed that the samples were of human origin but from three different blood groups – this was interpreted as a sign of the Holy Trinity being present, rather than indicating a hoax. In 1984, Bishop Ito declared the phenomenon to be 'of supernatural origin', and, in June 1988, Cardinal Ratzinger (then Prefect of the Congregation for the Doctrine of the Faith, later to become Pope Benedict XVI) judged the phenomenon at Akita 'reliable and worthy of belief'.

Some sceptics remain unconvinced. It is all too easy to fake the weeping or bleeding of a statue. A leading Italian sceptic, Dr Luigi Garlaschelli of Pavia University, has recreated one using 'a hollow statue made of a porous material … glazed or painted with some sort of impermeable coating'. The statue is filled with liquid which then seeps out through a tiny hole or scratch in the head. 'When I put it to the test, this trick proved to be very satisfactory, baffling all onlookers', he wrote.

This hypothesis accounts well for some cases, such as the plaster statuette of the Virgin Mary at the Inala Vietnamese Catholic Centre in Brisbane, Australia, which was said in May 2002 to be seeping a scented oil. The Archbishop of Brisbane, John Bathersby, convened a commission, headed by an agnostic chemistry professor, which subjected the statue to X-ray examination and the oil to gas chromatography and mass spectroscopy tests. They found the oil was similar to a commercial product, a red substance which was not blood, and that 'two small-diameter holes had been drilled through the statute through which liquids could have been injected'. The archbishop promptly declared that the exudations were 'not, within the proper meaning of the word, a miracle' and that the statue should be removed from public veneration, and ordered an inquiry into the funds and donations it had generated.

On the other hand, Dr Luigi Garlaschelli's hypothesis does not seem to explain the instances where statues involved are solid or non-porous, where the phenomenon persists over a long period or where the liquids contain identifiable human blood. It leaves many questions still unanswered. Parapsychologists and forteans (see PARAPSYCHOLOGY and CHARLES FORT) have speculated as to whether, if any authentic phenomena were proved to be involved, these cases might be related to those POLTERGEIST cases which are alleged to include mysterious FLOWS of liquids, TELEPORTATIONS of liquids and so-called 'persistent stains'.

An artist's impression of the alien encounter at Imjärvi, Finland, in 1970. (© Mary Evans Picture Library)

Imbolc
One of the four major sabbats of the modern pagan calendar, celebrated on 1 February and derived from the earlier pre-Christian Celtic festival associated with fertility and light.

The festival of Imbolc (also referred to as Imbolg or Oimelc) is traditionally associated with lengthening days, the coming of light and the pregnancy of livestock. The name itself is thought to come from the Gaelic for 'in the belly' (*imbolc*) or 'ewe's milk' (*oimelc*).

The festival was Christianized as St Brigid's Day (and, some argue, Candlemas) although Brigid is the name of the pre-Christian goddess of fire. See also AUTUMNAL EQUINOX; BELTANE; LUGHNASADH; PAGANISM; SABBATS; SAMHAIN; SUMMER SOLSTICE; VERNAL EQUINOX; WINTER SOLSTICE.

imitative magic *see* MAGIC, IMITATIVE

Imjärvi
One of the strangest UFO cases to have been recorded in Europe, which combined aspects of Nordic mythology with claims of contact with aliens.

On the bitterly cold day of 7 January 1970, local farmer Esko Viljo and forester Aarno Heinonen were taking advantage of the weather conditions on the tree-lined mountain slopes outside the village of Imjärvi in Finland. They later reported that as they skied beneath a beautiful starlit sky they heard a buzzing noise and stopped in a clearing to investigate its source.

They claim that the sound appeared to be coming from a ball of light, engulfed in a reddish-grey mist. As the ball descended to the ground the mist began to spread outwards, exposing a small disc-like object hovering just a few feet in the air. A beam of light then projected downwards from this craft with a small, goblin-like entity inside. The being was approximately 1 metre (3 feet) tall, with waxy features, and was wearing green clothing and gauntlets. The description given of this being resembled that of the TROLLS that form part of the local folklore. Sparks fell all around the creature from the base of the UFO towards the ground.

Viljo and Heinonen say that after they had stared at this remarkable sight for a few moments, the beam of light was retracted upwards into the craft, like a ladder being hauled in. This was followed by a silent flash of light that blew the mist apart and left the forest empty. When the two men recovered from the shock of these events Heinonen realized that the side of his body that had been facing the explosion was numb and tingling. He tried to walk forward but collapsed, one leg apparently paralysed. Viljo was forced to pick up his friend and help him back towards the village, leaving their expensive ski equipment on the slopes. By the time they arrived home their memory of the incident was becoming fuzzy and both were ill enough to require medical help.

Viljo found his skin turned red as if it was sunburnt and his face and eyes became swollen. Heinonen was even more seriously affected. The paralysis took several days to clear, during which time he suffered from acute migraine, nausea and badly discoloured urine. He went on to experience protracted urinary infections that lasted for several months, and was left in a psychological state that meant it was a number of years before he was passed fit to work again. Doctors who studied the men suspected they were suffering from radiation sickness, but no abnormal readings were taken from the site of the alleged incident.

Heinonen went on to recount increasingly bizarre memories of contacts with a tall, blonde female alien of the NORDIC type. He also claimed that three different types of being were visiting the earth, and that an IMPLANT had been placed in his head to help them talk to him – something which became a common feature of ALIEN ABDUCTION stories that followed in later years.

immortality

The state of living forever, usually thought to be an attribute of gods and goddesses, and of some other supernatural beings. The quest for immortality is a recurring theme in mythology and folklore, and most religious traditions express a belief in the immortality of the human soul.

The gods and goddesses of many polytheistic religions and mythologies are described as possessing immortality, and are not subject to death, illness or decay. This divine immortality is often conferred by a special food or drink reserved only for the gods: ambrosia in classical mythology, *amrita* in Hindu tradition, and the golden apples tended by Freya in Norse myths. Immortality is also attributed to some supernatural creatures, such as ELVES, in that they are not subject to old age and may effectively live for ever unless they are killed. The quest for physical immortality is a recurring theme in folklore and mythology; alchemists (see ALCHEMY) sought to discover the PHILOSOPHER'S STONE, which could be used to make an ELIXIR OF LIFE that would enable the drinker to live forever, and the legend of the FOUNTAIN OF YOUTH, a spring which can restore health and youth, and

give immortality to the drinker, appears in various mythologies. However, eternal life is not enough, as the Greek story of Eos, goddess of the dawn, demonstrates. Falling in love with a mortal prince called Tithonus, she asked Zeus to grant him eternal life so that they could be together forever, but she forgot to ask for eternal youth as well, and his immortality became a curse as he grew older and older, unable to die.

Most religious traditions express a belief in spiritual immortality, that is, that the human SOUL transcends physical death. In belief systems such as Hinduism and Buddhism, this immortal spirit is believed to be subject to a cycle of death and rebirth until it achieves union with Ultimate Reality. In other traditions, such as Christianity, Judaism and Islam, physical death is believed to be followed by a final judgement which determines the fate of the immortal soul for eternity. The Old Testament Book of Genesis tells how mankind possessed immortality until Adam and Eve ate from the Tree of Knowledge.

immortals

Beings who are not subject to death, usually gods or goddesses.

In many polytheistic religions and mythologies, the gods and goddesses are immortals, beings who are not subject to death, illness or decay. The pantheon of Greek and Roman deities preserved their immortality with ambrosia, the food or drink reserved for the gods, while in Norse mythology, it was Freya's golden apples which kept the gods eternally young. The Chinese believed that ordinary humans could, through study, learn the secrets of nature that would allow them to become immortal, and TAOISM usually recognizes and reveres eight such legendary figures, known as the Eight Immortals.

immovability

The apparent ability to resist being physically moved.

Some people claim to be able to make themselves immovable, harnessing some 'miraculous' power such as magnetism or electricity. This alleged ability has often been used in acts such as that of the GEORGIA WONDER. This rather slight young woman seemed able to defy the strength of several men attempting to push her along a stage or to lift her up when she was standing on a board.

In fact, as was later admitted by a number of its exponents, there was no MAGIC or mysterious power involved in these feats. They were actually tricks, depending on the performer's knowledge of the physical forces of action and reaction and balance and counterbalance. See also HUMAN MAGNETS.

immunity

An invulnerability to injury or harm apparently displayed by some people.

The human body, given the right conditions, seems to be capable of surprising degrees of immunity from pain or injury in circumstances where these might seem inevitable.

The trance-like state (see ALTERED STATES OF CONSCIOUSNESS and ECSTATIC PHENOMENA) entered into by some religious devotees is often suggested as a means by which this is possible.

However, although this might seem to offer a reasonable explanation for feats of PAIN ENDURANCE, it is not clear how it can account for all of the abilities that are sometimes demonstrated. For example, in Thailand, pilgrims at religious festivals use various sharp objects, such as swords, skewers and hooks, to pierce the skin of their faces. They often seem to shed little or no blood during these feats and recover afterwards with no lasting damage. Similarly, witnesses to the ecstatic states of ST BERNADETTE describe her fingers passing through the flames of burning candles with no sign of pain or burning.

One seemingly inexplicable modern case is that of the Dutchman Arnold Gerrit Henskes (1912–48), who, performing as a fakir under the name Mirin Dajo, repeatedly allowed assistants to transfix him with a rapier. No bleeding was seen to occur. Dajo submitted himself to X-ray examination, with the weapon still piercing his body, and this apparently showed that no trickery was involved. Dajo was a devotee of MEDITATION, and it has been suggested that he was able to induce a mental state in which he not only felt no pain, but was also able to exercise incredible control over the physical functioning of his body.

A legendary case of immunity was that of the Russian mystic RASPUTIN, who was said to have survived poisoning and shooting at the hands of his assassins before meeting death by drowning in the river into which they threw him. Modern forensic analysis, however, has shown that he was never poisoned and died of a gunshot wound to the head.

imp

A small demonic spirit, thought to be mischievous rather than genuinely evil.

An imp is a small demonic spirit. The name comes from the Anglo-Saxon *impe*, meaning a young shoot or sapling. Imping is an old agricultural term which refers to the technique of grafting, with the new bud being called an 'imp', so that in the supernatural sense, an imp is quite literally considered to be an 'offshoot' of Satan. Imps are the smallest and most minor of DEMONS in mythology and superstition. They are described as dark creatures who can assume different forms, and according to some accounts, they are so desperately lonely that they always go around in pairs or groups. In later folklore, the distinction between these demonic beings and other small mischievous spirits, such as GOBLINS and BOGLES, became blurred as Puritans and other religious groups came to regard all types of fairy as manifestations of SATAN. At the time of the WITCH TRIALS of the Middle Ages, many believed that witches kept imps, in animal form, as their FAMILIARS.

The most famous imp in British legend is probably the Lincoln Imp, a little demon who was said to have wreaked havoc in Lincoln Cathedral, dancing on the altar, tripping up the bishop, pushing over the dean and teasing the choir. The cathedral's guardian angels came to the rescue, turning the imp to stone and placing him high above the Angel Choir, at the top of one of the columns. His little figure, only about 30 centimetres (1 foot) high, still sits there with one leg across his knee, laughing wickedly, and is a great tourist attraction; it is considered something of a challenge to find him. He is regarded with great affection and has been adopted as the unofficial symbol of the city.

implants

Tiny objects that are sometimes said to have been placed inside the body of human captives during alleged encounters with aliens. There are about a hundred cases on record where such claims have been made.

A significant problem with ALIEN ABDUCTION cases is their lack of physical evidence. While witnesses often seem sincere in their belief that they have been subjected to medical tests by ALIENS, they are rarely able to offer any proof – other than their own recollection of the incident which has often been triggered by the highly controversial use of regression HYPNOSIS (see MEMORIES, RECOVERED).

In a few cases some witnesses have reported a belief that a small object was implanted into their body during the procedure on board the UFO. Their abductors may have told them about this – as in the IMJÄRVI case, where it was said to be a device to aid communication between the aliens and the witness. In other cases they may simply sense the presence of some foreign body under their skin. In some very rare instances it has been claimed that the implant was first recognized only when it emerged from the body accidentally – it is usually said to have been expelled via the nasal cavity.

Some of these small, fibrous objects that people have claimed are implants have been analysed, and they have almost invariably been found to possess terrestrial structure and DNA. In one case what was believed to be an implant, sneezed out by a witness who had claimed a history of alien contact, turned out to be a cotton fibre ball that had probably been accidentally ingested.

In 1996 the US TV science documentary programme, *Nova*, offered to make MRI scanner procedures available to test any 'abductees' who were certain that they had an implant inside their body. UFO researchers had previously been unable to convince doctors to use these expensive techniques to assist them in their search for evidence. The programme reported that no suitable candidate willing to submit to this test of their convictions had emerged.

More recently a few scans and X-rays have been carried out on people who have claimed contact with aliens, and some of these have been said to reveal shadowy objects. In some cases these shadowy objects have disappeared between one scan and the next, leading to the suspicion that the 'objects' were probably minor aberrations resulting from the equipment itself. No case has yet offered any proof that has been accepted by the wider scientific community.

incantations

An incantation is a set formula of words, often in rhyme, which is sung or spoken for the purposes of working magic.

An incantation is a set formula of words which is either spoken or sung for the purposes of performing magic. Incantations appear in all cultures and are usually an INVOCATION to a deity or supernatural spirit to elicit aid, protection or inspiration; they may also be a CHARM or SPELL to bless or heal, or to ward off evil spirits or influences. Incantations are frequently used as part of a magical ritual, and are repeated during the performance of the ritual, for example, while lighting candles, sprinkling waters or powders, or making and consecrating a TALISMAN or magical tool. They are usually in the form of a poem, since rhyme and rhythm are thought to have an effect on the unconscious mind; this also makes them easier to remember, which is believed to allow the magician to focus their concentration more fully on the magical intention and practical aspects of the work in hand. In incantations the magical intention of the ritual or spell is stated as briefly as possible. They are often formulaic in composition, use highly metaphorical language, and may contain nonsense words, strings of vowels, or other non-linguistic sounds. Most require some form of physical action on the part of the magician to bring about the intention expressed in the incantation.

incorruptibility

The absence of normal decay in a corpse, associated particularly with the bodies of saints.

Instances of the apparent absence of normal decay in the corpses of holy men and women, principally saints, have been attested throughout the history of the Christian religion, and, more recently, especially in the Roman Catholic Church.

At first, the discovery of this incorruptibility was accidental, as when a saint's remains were to be moved and were exhumed for that purpose. However, exhumation became part of the identification procedure followed by the Catholic Church in the process of canonization and there are several instances of the bodies of prospective saints being found to be without decay. Notable examples include ST BERNADETTE OF LOURDES, ST CHARBEL MAKHLOUF, ST ISIDORE and St John Vianney (the CURÉ OF ARS).

Witnesses of such exhumations often describe perceiving not a smell of putrefaction but a pleasant fragrance, known as the ODOUR OF SANCTITY, and this has been taken as alleged proof of sainthood.

However, while the incorruptibility of the bodies of certain saints has been well documented, the remains of other saints of comparable holiness have simply decomposed as might be expected. Also, there have been examples of the apparent natural preservation of the bodies of individuals known to be far from holy. This would suggest that saintliness and incorruptibility are not identical, and indeed, the Catholic Church does not say that these always go hand in hand but that incorruptibility is only an indication, not proof, of holiness.

The phenomenon is not restricted to Christianity: the undecayed remains of several especially devout monks are regarded as objects of reverence within the Buddhist faith. People of various religions assert that the effect occurs because the spiritual and physical aspects of a person become more entwined in the flesh when someone has led a pure and holy life.

Particularly for those without religious beliefs, is there a natural explanation for this? Some argue that the phenomenon may be explained by the physical conditions surrounding the original interment. If the corpse was placed in a dry, airtight coffin or other hermetically sealed container, oxygen, bacteria and the other usual natural agents of decomposition would be prevented from affecting the body. As evidence for this, it has been pointed out that some exhumed incorrupt bodies have been observed to start to decompose after they have been removed from their grave or coffin.

It also been shown that certain natural conditions will aid the preservation of a body: for example, certain types of earth, such as sandy soil or

The body of St Bernadette of Lourdes, apparently incorrupt over a hundred years after her death. (© TopFoto/Fortean)

the arid soil of hot climates such as Egypt, or the peat bogs of northern Europe. However, religious believers would maintain that such instances of natural preservation simply mimic the miraculous effects of incorruptibility, and the undecayed bodies of saints remain objects of veneration worldwide.

incubus

A demon said to assume a male body and have sexual intercourse with women as they sleep.

In DEMONOLOGY, an incubus (from Latin *incubus*, 'a nightmare', from *in*, meaning 'on', and *cubāre*, meaning 'to lie') is a demon that takes on male form and visits women as they sleep to have sexual intercourse with them and incite them to lust and perversion. The female equivalent of the incubus is the SUCCUBUS.

The depravity of witches who have had sex with incubi is discussed in the *MALLEUS MALEFICARUM*, where it is noted that:

> ... in times long past the Incubus devils used to infest women against their wills ... But the theory that modern witches are tainted with this sort of diabolic filthiness is not substantiated only in our opinion, since the expert testimony of the witches themselves has made all these things credible; and that they do not now, as in times past, subject themselves unwillingly, but willingly embrace this most foul and miserable servitude.

Incubi were said to be able to take on the form of a woman's husband or lover, but the sexual act was said to be unpleasant, with the incubus having a huge or ice-cold phallus. During the WITCH TRIALS of the Middle Ages, WITCHES were regularly accused of having had sex with incubi, and many alleged confessions admitted this. It was also commonly believed that an incubus could act as a witch's FAMILIAR.

Incubi were said to be particularly attracted to virgins, and many nuns claimed that demons tormented them as they slept. Incubi were also said to be able to impregnate women, using semen that they collected from men (as they had none of their own).

One famous incubus case noted in the *Malleus Maleficarum* and in Reginald Scot's *Discoverie of Witchcraft* (1584) involved the Bishop of Nazareth (either Sylvanus or Silvanus). This notable man was accused of appearing in a lady's bedchamber and making love to her – the Bishop was cleared when he explained that it had not been him but an incubus that had taken his form.

Indian rope trick

A magic trick, popularly believed to be performed by Indian fakirs.

In its classic form the Indian rope trick is performed in the following way:

An Indian FAKIR throws a rope straight up into the air. Instead of falling back down, the rope remains suspended in the air with no apparent means of support. A young boy is sent up the rope, and when he reaches the top he vanishes. The fakir then pulls a sword from his robes and climbs up after the boy and, upon reaching the top of the rope, he too vanishes. A shower of body parts then falls to the ground and the

It is popularly believed that the Indian rope trick is a magical feat performed by Indian fakirs. However, it has now been suggested that stories of the trick are based on a newspaper hoax. (© Mary Evans Picture Library)

fakir reappears at the top of the rope and lowers himself down. Once on the ground the fakir gathers up the body parts and places them in a basket which he covers with a blanket. After uttering a few magic words he removes the blanket to reveal the unharmed boy.

There are many minor variations to this basic form, and some parts are occasionally missed out when the story is related. Such a trick would be impressive enough today. However, the trick was originally reported to have been performed outside, in India, in the late 19th century.

Many people actually claimed to have seen the trick. All manner of explanations were offered, ranging from MASS HYPNOSIS to the use of twin boys, one being genuinely killed during the performance. Rewards were offered to anyone who could perform the trick – the MAGIC CIRCLE famously offered 500 guineas. The best response they received was a film showing a British magician pretending to be an Indian fakir. In the film the magician threw a rope into the air and it apparently remained erect at a height of about 3 metres (10 feet); his young son then climbed halfway up the rope, before safely coming back down. Other attempts at offering proof included films shown in reverse and still photographs of Indian pole balancers.

However, no one was able to come close to replicating the trick as set out in the rules that the Magic Circle provided.

In his 2004 book *The Rise of the Indian Rope Trick*, the magician, parapsychologist and author Peter Lamont demonstrated that the title 'Indian rope trick' was, in fact, originally applied to an entirely different act – a type of ESCAPOLOGY performed by Indian jugglers who came to the West in the mid-19th century. Sceptics at the time (such as JOHN NEVIL MASKELYNE) pointed out that it was an Indian rope trick of this type which lay behind the popular 'spirit cabinet' performances of many 'MEDIUMS'. The classic version of the Indian rope trick, and the investigations and theories that surrounded it, evolved out of exaggerated memories of several different tricks put together in people's minds to form a fantastic whole. Further, it seems to have actually first appeared in this form in a hoax story in the *Chicago Tribune* in 1890, the central character of which was a Fred S Ellmore – whose middle initial and surname put together give a clue as to the story's status.

inedia

The alleged ability to live without food indefinitely, or for extended periods of time.

While many religions have a long-established tradition of fasting as a spiritual practice for the purification of the body and mind, some people claim to have attained such a level of spirituality that they are able to survive without taking in any physical nourishment at all. This ability, known as inedia, has for centuries been attributed to various Hindu yogis, who maintain that we can derive all the nourishment we require from the UNIVERSAL LIFE FORCE known as *prana*; for this reason, some believers refer to the ability as 'pranic nourishment'. One contemporary Indian ascetic, Prahladbhai Jani, claims not to have eaten in 68 years. Buddha was also said to have meditated without food for a long period of time, while in the Bible Jesus survived in the wilderness without food for 40 days and nights.

The spiritual power of inedia, abstaining from all nourishment apart from Holy Communion for extended periods, has been attributed to various Christian saints throughout history: the 1st-century saint Alphais of Cudot; Helen Enselmini; Elisabeth the Good; Mary Ann de Paredes; Nicholas of Flue, 15th-century patron saint of Switzerland, who was said to have lived only on the Eucharist for 19 years; and Lydwina of Schiedam. The Bavarian stigmatic (see STIGMATA) Therese Neuman (1898–1962) similarly claimed to have been sustained 'by the Holy Breath alone' from 1923 until her death.

The practice is also known as breatharianism, and

some modern secular inediates, such as the Australian Ellen Grove, or Jasmuheen, claim not only to be able to survive on light or air alone, but offer courses on how to acquire this ability. There have been a number of documented cases in which people have apparently died as a result of attempting inedia.

INFO *see* INTERNATIONAL FORTEAN ORGANIZATION

initiation

A ceremony, ritual, test or period of instruction in which a new member is admitted to a group or is recognized as having passed from childhood or puberty to adulthood.

Initiation, the practice by which a person is admitted to a group by means of a ceremony, ritual, test or period of instruction, has been a central feature of practically all cultures throughout human history. The symbolic integration and acceptance of an individual into a religious or social group, often marking their transition from childhood or puberty to adulthood and their subsequent new status in the community, is found in many forms, and is an important and enduring feature of almost all societies.

The most traditional type of initiation is the rite of passage marking the transition from boyhood to manhood, which is typical of many tribal cultures. Such initiations share a number of common features: the initiate may have to undergo various ordeals to prove himself worthy of full adult status, for example a period of isolation in which he has to fend for himself, or to fast; he may be subjected to various tests of strength, skill or endurance; he may have to bear some form of mutilation or torture willingly and without complaint; or he may be ritually humiliated, perhaps by being jeered at by the women and children of the community. Once he has successfully passed all the required tests, he is instated as an adult member of the group, possibly taking an oath and having certain secrets revealed to him. In his new status, he is often required to cut himself off from non-initiated family members, such as his mother or younger siblings, to symbolize his death as a child and his rebirth as an adult.

It is less common for women to be granted positions of privilege and power in tribal societies, and female initiation ceremonies usually centre on the onset of menstruation, for example by a girl's entry into a menstrual hut at the commencement of her first period, and the presentation of new clothes on her emergence, to symbolize her new status as an adult woman capable of bearing children.

Initiation is also practised in many non-tribal religions as a symbol of an individual's acceptance as a full member of the religious group, again often at the point where they pass from childhood to adulthood.

The Christian rite of confirmation, the Jewish tradition of *Bar Mitzvah*, and the Muslim *Shahada*, which all usually take place around puberty or the mid-teens, mark a person's new status as an adult practitioner of the faith. Hindu boys are initiated in the *upanayama*, a ceremony in which they receive a 'sacred thread' which runs over the left shoulder and under the right, and after this ritual, they take on the full religious duties of their caste, and thereafter eat only with the men of the family.

Initiation is also a key element in the integration of an individual into a SECRET SOCIETY, such as FREEMASONRY, or a magical community, such as a Wiccan COVEN or other esoteric group. Secular forms of initiation, in which a person has to undergo some rite of passage in order to be accepted into a social group or trade, are also a commonly found feature of modern life; candidates for membership of college fraternities in the USA are often subjected to a ritual humiliation known as 'hazing', sailors still traditionally 'initiate' those on board ship who are crossing the equator for the first time by ducking them in sea water, and apprentices who begin to learn a trade run the risk of being sent by their more experienced workmates to fetch a joke item such as a left-handed monkey wrench.

ink, divination using

The practice of gazing into a bowl filled with ink in order to obtain visions or occult knowledge.

Since any kind of reflective surface lends itself to the divination technique of SCRYING, a bowl filled with ink is particularly suitable, and ink has been used as a scrying medium for centuries, either on its own or mixed with water. Gazing at the surface of the ink is believed to help the diviner to attain a meditative state in which visions may more readily be received, and in ancient times, spirits were also invoked as part of the process. The room is either kept dark, or illuminated softly, and the bowl positioned so that the ink surface does not show either shadows or clear reflections, since both are distracting. The scryer does not seek to see images or patterns in the ink itself, but to look through the depths of the ink as if through a clear pane of glass, and to use it as a window to the astral world.

Inquisition, the

The collective term for a number of historical Roman Catholic movements established from the 12th century onward to suppress heresy. The most notorious of these was the Spanish Inquisition, founded in Spain in 1487.

The Inquisition, or 'Holy Office', is the collective term for various Roman Catholic groups set up from the 12th century onward to suppress heresy. Until the Middle Ages, the Christian Church's response to

An illustration of the Inquisition depicting a judge accusing a young woman of witchcraft, as a torturer heats coals. (© Bettmann/Corbis)

heresy (ie beliefs contrary to its authorized teachings) was in general ad hoc, loosely organized and non-violent, consisting mainly of writings by the Church fathers against the heretical beliefs, and the occasional excommunication of heretics such as the Gnostics (see GNOSTICISM). However, by the 12th century the Catholic Church had become, unlike many other religions, a hierarchical organization with a central bureaucracy, and in 1184 it established the first of four major movements known as 'inquisitions'. These were intended to be permanent structures that would combat heresy by investigating suspected heretics and seeking, by various means, to induce them to recant their heretical beliefs.

The first inquisition, established by a papal bull in an attempt to combat the growing Catharist heresy in Southern France, was known as the Episcopal Inquisition. This had limited success, but in the 1230s a new Papal Inquisition was set up under Pope Gregory IX, administered by specially trained professionals recruited mainly from the Dominican order, who were noted for their history of anti-heresy and their skill in debate. This movement, also known as the Albigensian Inquisition, succeeded in eradicating the Cathars. Those accused of heresy were offered a month's grace in which to confess and recant, or be subjected to a secret trial. If, as was usually the case, they were then found guilty, their property was sequestered, and those who repented were likely to be sentenced to life imprisonment with salutary penance, while unrepentant heretics might face the death penalty.

Although the Church was theoretically against extreme measures to extract confessions, its inquisitors

were making use of torture by the mid-13th century. But it was the Spanish Inquisition, founded in 1478, which gained lasting notoriety for the zeal and cruelty with which it persecuted supposed heretics. This separate national institution was, to a large extent, under the control of the Spanish monarch, Ferdinand, but was endorsed by Pope Sixtus IV in 1483, and its first and most famous Grand Inquisitor, Tomas de Torquemada, was nominated by the king and confirmed by the Pope. The Spanish Inquisition was set up to root out and rid the country of *conversos*, Jews and Muslims who had been forced to convert to Christianity, but who it was believed secretly persisted in their old religions, thus undermining the church; however, St Ignatius of Loyola and St Teresa of Avila were also investigated for heresy by the Spanish Inquisition, and later, in the 16th century, it sought to deal with the 'heresy' of Protestantism in the same way as it had the converted Jews and Muslims. During this dark period in the history of the church, thousands of people in Spain were brought to trial and, by means of imprisonment and torture, made to confess to heresy and subjected to an elaborate ritual public penance called the *auto-da-fé*, or 'act of faith', involving a showy procession, mass and sermon, before being handed over to be burned at the stake. It has been suggested that around 2,000 people were executed in this way under Torquemada. A similar inquisition was set up by the king in Portugal in 1536. The Spanish Inquisition continued until 1834.

In 1542, Pope Paul III established the Roman Inquisition, whose task it was to maintain and defend the integrity of the faith and to examine and proscribe false doctrines. It was this body which tried Galileo in 1633 and banned all his works on grounds of heresy. In 1587 this was reorganized into the Congregation of the Roman and Universal Inquisition to supervise faith and morals in the Church, and after the Second Vatican Council, it was further reorganized to become the Congregation for the Doctrine of the Faith, which is still a powerful branch of the Catholic Church's hierarchy.

insensitivity

The absence of the normal physical response to pain.
Pain is a normal reaction of the human body to damage – in simple terms it alerts us to injury and encourages us to avoid it. While different people seem to be able to tolerate different levels of pain, complete insensitivity is neither natural nor desirable.

Many people, such as practitioners of MARTIAL ARTS FEATS, can apparently use mental discipline, and other techniques, to achieve impressive levels of PAIN ENDURANCE – however, these are methods of ignoring or temporarily blocking the normal pain response.

True insensitivity does exist, in the form of a condition known as 'Congenital Insensitivity to Pain'. Victims of this rare genetic disorder simply do not feel any pain at all, because of the malfunction of the nerves that should carry pain messages to the brain. Sufferers regularly incur injuries (particularly minor, self-inflicted damage such as biting the tongue) and tolerate illnesses that others would avoid or detect through feeling pain.

International Fortean Organization

An American fortean society founded in 1966 by two brothers from St Louis, Missouri, Ron and Paul Willis.
Paul Willis's interest in CHARLES FORT grew from his love of science fiction. Paul was active in the local science fiction group and, in the mid-1960s, published his own fanzine, called *Anubis*, with a focus on the writings of H P LOVECRAFT. When elder brother Ron Willis gained work as a psychologist in Washington, DC, Paul joined him, and together, they set up the International Fortean Organization (INFO). While Ron handled the administration, Paul began and edited their quarterly publication, *INFO Journal*, first published in Spring 1967.

The *INFO Journal* was the first truly fortean magazine since the demise of the old FORTEAN SOCIETY and its publication *Doubt*. Unlike the more commercial *Fate Magazine*, founded by Ray Palmer in 1948, *INFO Journal* was free to publish the most obscure material on almost every fortean topic for a small but appreciative readership. Its well-researched articles updated Charles Fort's case material and it also introduced a new level of scholarship with wit and erudition. Many of today's leading writers and

researchers acknowledge the importance of their early correspondence with the Willis brothers, who were unstinting in their encouragement of new talent.

When Ron died in 1975, Paul found it increasingly hard to cope with his loss and with keeping the society and journal going. In the summer of the following year, several of INFO's board members and contributors – including the astronomer John Carlson, ufologist Richard Hall and engineer Ray Manners, were concerned enough to help Paul Willis, taking over the society administration and publication when Paul moved to Tennessee. Carlson served as president until 1982, handing over to Manners who served until his death in 1996. INFO's current president, Phyllis Benjamin, has continued to hold the society's annual conference (FortFest) and the *Journal* was transformed into an online bulletin.

Paul's body was found under mysterious circumstances in October 1998; he had died in bed, in his rented attic, and lain undiscovered for at least 16 months.

International Society of Cryptozoology

A society formed to document and evaluate evidence of 'mystery animals'.
The International Society of Cryptozoology (ISC) was founded in 1982 to serve as a scholarly centre for documenting and evaluating evidence of 'hidden' or 'undescribed' animals (see CRYPTID; CRYPTOZOOLOGY). The official emblem of the society was the okapi, chosen because its story was typical of many cryptozoological animals; it had been well known to the local communities in its habitat long before it was discovered and described by science in 1901. The organization is now defunct.

The ISC was brought into existence in the correspondence between fortean (see CHARLES FORT) Jerome Clark; Dr George Zug (Smithsonian Institution); Dr Roy Mackal (University of Chicago); J Richard Greenwell (Office of Arid Lands Studies, University of Arizona, in Tucson) and Dr BERNARD HEUVELMANS, the world's foremost cryptozoologist. This came to fruition in January 1982 at a meeting hosted by Zug at the Smithsonian's National Museum of Natural History. Also in attendance were Forrest G Wood (Naval Ocean Systems Center), GROVER KRANTZ (Washington State University) and Joseph Gennaro (New York University). Other supportive cryptozoologists involved in the formation of the Society included Loren Coleman and John Green, who became Life and Honorary members. Heuvelmans was elected as the first President, and Greenwell as its Secretary and editor of its *Journal* and *Newsletter*; both held the positions until their deaths.

Bernard Heuvelmans, French cryptozoologist and first president of the International Society of Cryptozoology.
(© Mary Evans Picture Library)

What began with high hope and distinct promise ended, to the regret of many, in a financial fiasco. Greenwell applied the ISC's limited resources towards a series of private expeditions and field trips to more than 30 countries, sometimes with other ISC members, either to investigate sightings of 'undiscovered' creatures or to gather specimens. For example, they went to seek the MERMAID-like 'ri' in Papua New Guinea (which turned out to be a dugong); the ONZA in Mexico; and the YEREN in China. Many of these adventures have been wrongly called ISC expeditions. His famous search for the MOKELE-MBEMBE at Lake Tele, in the Congo, in 1980 and in 1981, with biologist Roy P Mackal of the University of Chicago, took place at least a year before the formation of the ISC. The other expeditions had to be self-financed and sponsored because of the lack of official ISC funds, a lack which led to the early demise of both the ISC's *Newsletter* and its *Journal*. The ISC never recovered from the destabilization of its 'cash flow' and ground to a halt, as an official body, with the death of its president, Heuvelmans (in 2001), followed by the death of its secretary, Greenwell (in 2005).

invisibility

A condition in which a solid, non-microscopic object or person has physical existence but has been rendered impossible to see.

The ability to move among our fellow human beings and carry out acts unseen has always had attractions. These have been reflected in myths and legends from around the world. In Greek mythology, Gyges, King of Lydia, possessed a brass ring that could render the wearer invisible, and the hero Perseus wore a helmet conferring invisibility in his quest to kill Medusa.

The gemstone known as heliotrope (now usually called bloodstone) was once popularly believed to have the power to render its possessor invisible, and magical cloaks, rings, amulets and potions with similar powers are sometimes to be found in folk tales.

The English writer H G Wells (1866–1946) produced a fictional account of invisibility in *The Invisible Man* (1897). In the story, a scientist succeeds in changing the refractive index of his body to that of air. Unable to reverse the process, the hero becomes insane and homicidal. Several films and television series have been made, loosely based on Wells's original idea, and the concept of invisibility has gone on to form a popular theme in science fiction and fantasy stories.

Probably the most famous modern claim that invisibility has been successfully induced is the unsubstantiated allegation that the US Navy engaged in a project, known as the PHILADELPHIA EXPERIMENT, in which degaussing technology was supposedly used to make a warship invisible. However, although there are many theoretical suggestions as to how invisibility might be achieved, for the time being 'real' invisibility or perfect transparency (in which an object does not reflect, refract or absorb light – rather than being simply obscured or camouflaged) remains firmly within the realm of science fiction.

invisible assailant

An invisible entity that can apparently inflict physical force or violence upon a victim.

Stories exist around the world of invisible assailants that can inflict physical harm on human beings. The lives of medieval saints often feature torments and temptations inflicted by demons and evil spirits and even into more recent periods certain religious figures, such as St John Vianney, the CURÉ OF ARS, claimed to be the victim of supernatural attacks.

However, stories of religious figures being persecuted by invisible assailants have declined, and in the 20th century were almost wholly replaced by examples featuring secular individuals. According to the popular mystery writer Frank Edwards, in August 1960 a South African police chief and three constables watched helplessly as 20-year-old Jimmy de Bruin was cut deeply on the legs by 'an invisible assailant with an equally insubstantial scalpel'. Other cases arise in the literature of POLTERGEIST phenomena: cuts and bites appeared on the skin of the young girls at the centre of the LAMB INN poltergeist case, and ELEONORE ZUGUN displayed scratches and weals on her face and body. In 1928 in Poona, India, a young boy apparently suffered poltergeist assaults in a case examined by the AMERICAN SOCIETY FOR PSYCHICAL RESEARCH. More recently, mysterious bruises, cuts and scratches have been claimed among parties of tourists and sightseers visiting a vault in the Greyfriars Churchyard in Edinburgh (see EDINBURGH'S VAULTS). And in Colombia in 1999, scratched messages threatening death were said to have appeared on the skin of a young woman as she was being interviewed by journalists from the newspaper *El Tiempo*.

While such instances may be labelled assault by an invisible assailant, it is by no means certain that an external agency is involved. Firstly, such claims of physical injury must be treated carefully, given the tendency of some psychologically vulnerable people towards self-harm, consciously or subconsciously, or the possibility that such 'paranormal' injuries are simply hoaxed. It has also been suggested that in some instances, marks have apparently been induced on the skin by suggestion alone. Cases of apparently spontaneous bodily damage are often comparable to examples of STIGMATA on the bodies of saints and mystics in the Christian tradition.

invocation

The act of calling upon a deity or spirit to be present so that its blessing or help can be obtained; a set formula of words used for this purpose.

Invocation is the action of invoking, or calling upon, a deity or supernatural spirit using a magical ritual or INCANTATION. The presence of the deity or spirit is requested so that its assistance or blessing may be sought, and the invocation is usually in the form of a poem or prayer. One of the best-known invocations is the Lord's Prayer in Christianity. In shamanistic religions, invocation specifically refers to the drawing of the spirit into the magician's body, rather than simply asking them to be present. Some belief systems make a distinction between invocation, the invitation or request for a spirit's presence, and EVOCATION, the compelling of its presence. Invocation is also used by some occultists to refer to the taking in of the desired qualities of the deity invoked, for example the powers of attraction of Aphrodite, and in such cases, the deity is believed to be either drawn into them as an external force, or called up from within the magician as an ARCHETYPE by establishing a conscious tie with the aspect of the god or goddess thought to exist in all of us. See also CONJURATION.

invulnerability

The property of being incapable of being hurt, granted or achieved by supernatural powers.

The power of invulnerability is a popular motif in mythology and legend. It is usually granted by a deity, or achieved through supernatural means. However, the invulnerable person frequently has one weak or unprotected spot, or their invulnerability is contingent on a specific condition, which ultimately brings about their downfall.

In Roman mythology, Turnus, a favourite of the goddess Juno, was granted invulnerability in battle by her, so long as he remained pure, steadfast and honourable. But when he killed the young prince Pallas in single combat and took his belt to wear as a trophy, Juno withdrew her protection and allowed him to be killed by Aeneas. In Greek mythology, the sorceress Medea fell in love with Jason, and anointed him with an unguent made from a herb on which some of the blood of Prometheus had fallen, rendering his body invulnerable to fire and weapons. However, Jason abandoned Medea, and many years later, sitting under the rotting hulk of his ship, the *Argos*, he was killed by a falling beam. The most famous story of invulnerability is that of the Greek warrior Achilles. The waters of the river Styx, which formed the boundary between the earth and Hades, the Underworld, were said to have the power to grant immortality, so his mother dipped him in them when he was a baby. The waters made his body invulnerable, except for the heel by which he had been held, and this was his only weak point. He was killed in the Trojan War when Paris shot a single arrow into the original 'Achilles' heel'.

In a similar story in Old Norse mythology, the hero Sigurd (who became Siegfried in German myth) achieved invulnerability when, after slaying the dragon Fafnir, he bathed in the dragon's blood. This blood touched all the parts of his body, but for one – a spot on his shoulder where a leaf had stuck, and through which he was later murdered in bed.

irkuiem

A huge unidentified bear reported from Kamchatka, Russia.

Since the 1980s, Russian scientists have become increasingly interested in reports of a gigantic type of bear reputedly inhabiting the remote Kamchatka Peninsula in far north-eastern Russia, and referred to by the local reindeer breeders as the irkuiem (sometimes spelled 'irquiem', and translating, bizarrely, from the local Chukotko-Kamchatkan dialect as 'trousers pulled down') or kainyn-kutkho ('god bear').

In 1986, an experienced hunter called Rodion Sivolobov sent details concerning this unidentified creature to the eminent Russian zoologist Dr Nikolaj Vereshchagin. During his investigations in Kamchatka, Sivolobov had been informed that the irkuiem was rare, but was nonetheless occasionally killed by the reindeer breeders, who stated that it was snow-white in colour, with a height reaching 1.5 metres (around 5 feet) at the withers, and a weight of up to 1.5 tonnes. A year later, Sivolobov succeeded in obtaining the skin of a supposed irkuiem. It resembles the pelt of a polar bear, but if this is really what it is, then the polar bear in question must have been truly enormous.

If not a polar bear, however, what could the irkuiem be? Dr Vereshchagin was sufficiently impressed by Sivolobov's information to speculate that it might be a surviving modern-day version of the short-faced bear *Arctodus simus*, widely believed to have become extinct around 12,000 years ago. Short-faced bears were huge animals, with a fairly squat body but long limbs, and with an unusually broad muzzle and face. Although they are presently known only from fossils found in the far north of North America, it is possible that short-faced bears could have migrated across the land bridge that, at the time of their existence, connected their American homeland with north-eastern Russia.

While this identity for the irkuiem may seem a rather bold one to put forward, Kamchatka is an inaccessible land rarely visited by scientists, so cryptozoologists concede that it is by no means impossible for this little-explored region to house large creatures still undiscovered by science.

iron

The most widely used of all the metals, thought to have special magical properties including protection against fairies and evil spirits.

Classical ALCHEMY traditionally recognized seven metals: LEAD, tin, GOLD, copper, MERCURY, silver and iron. Each of these seven metals was linked with one of the seven 'planets', and iron, used to make instruments of war, was associated with Mars. Iron was alchemically seen as being the metal with the strongest connection with the earth. It is also the only one of the seven metals which burns, and in some magical traditions, iron's ELEMENT is FIRE.

Historically, iron was used for protection against evil spirits, since it was believed to give out powerful vibrations that could repel DEMONS, FAIRIES, DJINN, and other creatures. In the Western magical tradition, magicians use an iron knife for banishing rituals. In India, iron arrowheads were driven into the ground at the head and foot of a dead body to prevent the spirit from trying to re-enter it. In ancient Rome, nails were

driven into house walls to protect the health of the inhabitants, especially during times of plague. The nailing of an iron HORSESHOE to the door of a house to keep away evil spirits is a centuries-old practice throughout Europe and North America. Similarly, in 16th- and 17th-century England, there was a custom of sealing a knife made from a single piece of iron into a wall near the door; several old English houses are also known to have had large iron slabs built into their thresholds for protection. Also, in European folklore, placing an implement made of iron in a baby's cradle was a traditional measure taken to prevent the baby being stolen and a CHANGELING left in its place.

Since demons and spirits were once thought to be the primary source of disease, iron has also been used throughout the ages as a cure, with an iron ring, amulet or bracelet being worn, or a piece of iron placed under a pillow, to ward off the spirit which caused the illness.

ISC *see* INTERNATIONAL SOCIETY OF CRYPTOZOOLOGY

Isidore, St (c.1070–1130)

Spanish saint whose body remained incorrupt.

St Isidore the Farmer (as he is known, to distinguish him from St Isidore of Seville) was born in Madrid. He worked as a farmer on the lands of a local nobleman. Deeply religious, he attended Mass daily and was said to communicate with ANGELS.

Isidore was criticized for spending time in church when he should have been working, but it was said that angels carried out his ploughing for him while he was at his devotions.

He is said to have lived a simple life, to have loved animals and to have given generously to the poor. He was originally buried in the churchyard of St Andrew's in Madrid, but when his body was being moved from its grave into a place of honour in the church itself, it was found to be incorrupt (see INCORRUPTIBILITY).

Isidore was canonized in 1622 by Pope Gregory XV and is the patron saint of Madrid as well as of farmers and peasants.

isnachi

A very large unidentified monkey reported from the jungles of Peru.

Peruvian zoologist Dr Peter Hocking has documented reports of several seemingly unknown species of mammal from the jungles of his native country, but one of the most remarkable is the isnachi ('strong man'). Muscular and powerful, it is said to have a black face, black or dark brown short fur, a baboon-like snout, barrel chest, long teeth and a thick tail that is around 15 centimetres (6 inches) long, and to be as big as a chimpanzee – much bigger than any known species of South American monkey living today. It is also said to be mostly arboreal, but will run on its hind legs if attacking.

The isnachi is actively avoided by its human neighbours on account of its aggressive reputation, and its strength is said to be readily demonstrated by its characteristic activity of ripping apart the tops of chonta palm trees in order to extract the tender vegetable matter inside – as no other animal in the region is strong enough to do this, the isnachi's presence in a given locality is thought to be confirmed by finding chontas damaged in such a manner. In 1985, an apparent isnachi was encountered and photographed by Ecuadorean botanist Benigno Malo on the Peru–Ecuador border, but the photograph has never been made public.

jackalope

A jackalope is a legendary cross between a jack rabbit and an antelope.

The legend of the jackalope (a creature with the body of a jack rabbit and the horns of a small antelope, that it is said can become extremely vicious if provoked) is believed to have been created in the small US town of Douglas, Wyoming. In the 1930s two residents of the town, Douglas and Ralph Herrick, started selling stuffed and mounted jackalope heads, apparently having returned from a hunting trip with a jack rabbit that they placed near some antlers in their taxidermy shop, thus finding the inspiration for this new creature.

Stories are told of jackalopes joining cowboys in their campfire songs (jackalopes are apparently good singers) and legend has it that the first Douglas jackalope was actually spotted in 1829. The town still issues hunting licences for jackalopes, 'despite rules specifying that the hunter cannot have an IQ higher than 72 and can hunt only between midnight and 2am each 31 June'. It is claimed that Ronald Reagan had a mounted jackalope head on his wall, which he joked about with journalists, saying that he had shot it himself.

However, the jackalope is not the only example of a horned hare. In Europe, there are tales of the German Wolpertinger, a hare with antlers, wings and fangs, and in 1918 a Swedish taxidermist created another winged hare called a skvader.

The jackalope, a famous hoax cryptid. (© Chase Swift/ Corbis)

jack o' lantern *see* WILL-O'-THE-WISP

Jainism

An ascetic Indian religion with elements similar to Hinduism and Buddhism, whose central doctrine is compassion toward all living beings.

Jainism, also traditionally known as Jain Dharma, is one of the three most ancient Indian religions still practised today. It is believed to have been founded at the same time as Hinduism, if not before. While it is nowadays a minority religion in modern India, most of its followers are still located there, although Jain communities are growing in the USA, Western Europe, Africa, the Far East and elsewhere.

Rather than subscribing to the idea of an all-powerful supreme creator or being, Jainism proposes an eternal universe which passes through an endless series of cycles divided into world ages, each of which lasts for thousands of years. It teaches that all living beings have an individual and immortal soul called a *jiva*, and that reality is made up of two eternal principles – *jiva* and *ajiva*, or matter and its manifestations of time and space. The universe consists of *jivas* suffering because they are trapped, through KARMA and the transmigration of souls, in *ajiva*, and the only way for a *jiva* to escape this suffering is to practise the teachings of Jainism constantly, so that it may ultimately attain *moksha*, also known as NIRVANA – thus escaping the cycle of death and rebirth.

Jains believe that the actual faith of Jainism is uncreated and eternal, and has been and will continue to be revealed through the successive ages of the world by enlightened beings called *Tirthankara*. A human who achieves spiritual enlightenment by adopting asceticism and following the principles of Jainism becomes a *Tirthankar*, or *Jina* ('conqueror') – the name Jainism is derived from the word *Jina* – and teaches the path of enlightenment to others. The religious teachings of the *Tirthankara* form the canon of Jainism, and these figures are revered in Jain temples. In each world age there are said always to be 24 *Tirthankara*, the 24th and last one of the present age being Mahavira (599–527 BC), who is considered to have been the founder of the present Jain community.

The aim of Jainism is to live, think and act in ways which honour and respect the spirit of all living beings, with the ultimate goal of attaining *moksha*. The Jain religious order, or *sangha*, consists of both monastic and lay members, the latter being known as *shravakas* or 'listeners'. Compassion for all fellow living beings is central to Jainism, and its followers are required to be vegetarian, while many are vegan, and some even wear masks to avoid the possibility of breathing in and thus killing tiny insects. Strict Jains do not eat, drink or travel after sunset, and rise before sunrise every day. The ethical code of Jainism is summarized in the Five Vows, which are followed by monastic and lay Jains alike: *ahimsa*, or 'non-violence'; *satya*, or 'truth'; *asteya*, or 'non-stealing'; *brahmacharya*, or 'chastity' (celibacy for monks and nuns, sex only within a marriage for lay Jains); and *aparigraha*, or 'non-possessiveness'. Jains also seek to practise forgiveness and to avoid harbouring harmful feelings toward others, and to follow the principle of *anekantavada*, which literally translates as 'the doctrine of non-onesidedness' – that is, that reality may be perceived as different when seen from different points of view, and that other views or beliefs should always be considered. Jain monastics practise strict asceticism with the goal of making this incarnation their last, while lay Jains strive to do good deeds in this life, thereby 'lightening' their burden of KARMA in the next one (see also REINCARNATION). Lay Jains are also required to follow a profession or job which does not break their vow of non-harm to themselves or others.

Jainism has significantly influenced Indian religion, thinking, art, literature, ethics and politics for over 2,000 years, and Mahatma Gandhi incorporated its peaceful, non-harming way of life as an integral part of his own philosophy.

James VI and I (1566–1625)

King of Scotland from 1567, as James VI, and of England from 1603, as James I; writer of works on political philosophy and author of Daemonologie, *a treatise against witchcraft.*

Born in 1566, James was the son of Mary, Queen of Scots, and Henry, Lord Darnley. When his mother was forced to abdicate in 1567, he was proclaimed King of Scotland as James VI, and brought up by several regents. After the execution of his mother in 1587, he married Princess Anne of Denmark by proxy in 1589, and in 1590 he brought her back to Scotland. On the death of Elizabeth I in 1603, he succeeded to the throne of England as James I. At first he was well received by his English subjects, but his favouritism brought him unpopularity.

James was also an author, publishing his first book in 1584. Most of his works were on theological subjects, and two were specifically concerned with the justification of the divine right of monarchs; *Basilikon Doron* was written for his eldest son, Prince Henry, and in *The True Law of Free Monarchies* he set out a simple explanation of his theories for the general public. He also wrote *Meditations on the Lord's Prayer*. He is possibly best known for his encouragement of and participation in the translation of the Bible into English in 1611, the result being known as the King James Bible.

However, another of his works achieved lasting fame for a different reason. In his younger days, James was a firm believer in the reality of WITCHCRAFT. Upon his marriage to Princess Anne of Denmark in 1589, his bride sailed for Scotland, but her ship was driven back by storms, which some people blamed on WITCHES in Copenhagen. James then sailed to Denmark himself, and it has been suggested that he absorbed there some of the continental ideas about witchcraft; when he and Anne sailed back to Scotland together in 1590, their ship again ran into storms at sea, which were subsequently blamed on a group of Scottish witches. James participated personally in some of their interrogations, and became convinced that they had tried to kill him, not only by raising storms during his voyage back to Scotland, but also by using wax images and poison. The case of the NORTH BERWICK WITCHES is still famous today, and a number of people were implicated, with an attempt being made at one point to accuse the King's own cousin, Francis, Earl of Bothwell, of involvement in the OCCULT plot.

Following this, James wrote *Daemonologie*, a tract on witchcraft and DEMONOLOGY, which was published in 1597. In it, he attempted to persuade sceptics of the power and danger of witchcraft, and to counter the works of rationalists like Reginald Scot, who argued against the belief in witchcraft and demonic magic. Subsequently, James strongly supported the trial and execution of witches in Scotland until his accession to the English throne in 1603. Thereafter, he seems to have become less active in this respect, and it appears that he took a more sceptical approach to witchcraft – in fact, he was strongly critical of judges and juries who employed poor legal practice in WITCH TRIALS, and actively overturned a number of convictions.

However, the King James Bible still included the translation of Exodus 22:18 as 'Thou shalt not suffer a witch to live.'

James, M(ontague) R(hodes) (1862–1936)

English writer and scholar.

The son of a clergyman, M R James spent much of his adult life at Cambridge – as a fellow, dean, tutor and ultimately Provost of King's College. Later he became Provost at Eton. James was a distinguished medieval scholar and author of what remains the leading study of the apocryphal books of the Bible. However, it is for his 30 short stories about ghosts that his name endures. Most were written between 1893 and 1911 and published as *Ghost Stories of an Antiquary* (1904) and *A Warning to the Curious* (1911). Their success results from the skilful creation of atmosphere, with James adopting a restrained, antiquarian tone

reflecting the scholarly world in which he spent his adult life. Many of his human characters are scholars and academics into whose dry, bookish lives James progressively introduces manifestations of malevolent and physically dangerous ghosts, with the reader being terrified by the use of suggestion rather than explicit horror. Classic stories include 'Oh, Whistle and I'll Come to You, My Lad', 'Count Magnus', 'Lost Hearts', 'The Treasure of Abbot Thomas' and 'Number 13'. These stories have remained in print for over a century, either as collections or in anthologies, and have frequently been adapted for radio, television and the theatre.

James stated openly that he sought to make his fictional ghosts consistent with the spectres of supernatural folklore and declared that he was prepared to accept the evidence for ghosts if it convinced him. He was willing to explain what he considered to be the rules of the genre to a wider audience and for his own part considered the 19th-century Irish writer Sheridan Le Fanu as the greatest exponent of the literary ghost story. James also took a scholarly interest in historic ghost stories, translating a number from medieval Latin manuscripts. Although he denied that his stories were based upon personal experience, it later emerged that the village of Great Livermere, Suffolk, in which James grew up, enjoyed a local reputation for being very haunted. This stimulated speculation that his interest in ghosts and his last story, 'A Vignette', had arisen from a childhood experience or nightmare.

Januarius, St (the blood miracle of)

Bishop of Beneventum (Benevento, Italy) and Christian martyr; associated with a blood miracle which is still performed in ceremonies at the Cathedral of Naples.

Januarius is believed to have been the bishop of Beneventum (the modern-day Benevento, near Naples) during the reign of the Emperor Diocletian. Very few details of his life are known. However, it would appear that he was executed, along with a number of other Christian clergy, in c.305 AD under the direction of Timotheus, the governor of Campania. In the version of his life story given in the present Roman Breviary, it is said that he and his companions were first thrown into a furnace, and when this failed to kill them they were exposed to wild beasts in the amphitheatre, again without any effect. Timotheus declared that this was due to magic and so ordered them to be beheaded.

The life story, and the claimed MIRACLES surrounding his eventual martyrdom, do not particularly set Januarius apart from other Christian saints from the early years of the church. His relics were moved to Naples in the 5th century and he was

Phials said to contain the miraculous blood of St Januarius are examined three times a year at the Cathedral of Naples. (© Neri Grazia/Corbis Sygma)

declared the patron saint of the city. In the 9th century they were stolen by a Lombard king and, after being lost for several centuries, they were eventually returned to Naples, where Charles II of Anjou had them placed in a silver reliquary in 1304. However, although a chronicle of Naples from 1382 (which mentions the cult surrounding St Januarius) makes no reference to a blood miracle, in 1389 the following entry appears in the diary of an anonymous Neapolitan:

> On the seventeenth day there was a great procession to mark the miracle wrought by our divine Lord with the blood of St Januarius. The blood, which is kept in a phial, turned into liquid just as if it had been in the living body of Januarius on that very day.

The two phials which purportedly contain the blood of St Januarius are sealed within a glass case and stored in a guarded vault. One phial contains only traces, while the other is half filled with a dark, opaque, solid mass. Three times during the year the case is removed for display to the public – on the Saturday before the first Sunday in May, on 19 September and on 16 December (the feast days of his translation and his martyrdom, and that honouring him as the patron saint of Naples). During the ceremony, the case containing the phials is regularly turned upside down to ascertain whether the blood has liquefied. Members of the congregation on these occasions pray for the miracle to occur and are usually rewarded after periods ranging from minutes to hours. It is also said

that the blood appears to boil within the container, grow paler in colour and increase in volume. If the blood fails to liquefy it is said to be an omen of bad fortune (an interpretation not supported by the modern Catholic Church).

The phenomenon has intrigued scientists since the early 19th century and many possible explanations have been offered. The contents of the phials have twice been subjected to spectroscopic analysis and, on both occasions the results indicated the possible presence of haemoglobin (although, by necessity, the tests were carried out through layers of medieval glass and, unusually on the second occasion, did not involve the use of a modern electronic spectrophotometer). However, a full and thorough scientific investigation has not been possible because the Catholic Church will not allow the sealed containers to be opened. Research has therefore been based around attempts to replicate the phenomenon.

One of the more convincing hypotheses centres around the suggestion that the 'blood' is a substance with a very low melting point which reacts to the slight warming when it is displayed (a theory perhaps supported by the fact that failures to liquefy occur more often during the December ceremonies). However, as the melting point would remain constant, this does not account for the fact that the miracle is performed at different ambient temperatures.

Another suggestion is that the blood is a substance that displays thixotropy – that is, it can become more fluid or even change from solid to liquid if it is shaken. The case for this explanation is supported by work carried out by Luigi Garlaschelli and others in the early 1990s in which they first replicated the behaviour and appearance of the blood with a gel containing iron hydroxide, and then demonstrated how it could have been made with equipment and materials available in the vicinity of Naples in the 14th century. However, this explanation cannot, in itself, account for the apparent inconsistency with which the phenomenon manifests. Without access to the contents of the phials, the scientific community cannot provide conclusive evidence for a non-supernatural mechanism through which the miracle occurs.

Jeanne d'Arc *see* JOAN OF ARC, ST

Jeffries, Anne (c.1626–c.1698)
A Cornish woman who, in 1645, claimed to have been spirited away by fairies and taken to Fairyland. On her return, she apparently possessed healing powers and the gift of clairvoyance.
The story of Anne Jeffries has passed into West Country legend. This Cornish woman was said to

have gone into service with a family living in St Teath at the age of 19. Intelligent but illiterate, Anne had always been fascinated by FAIRIES, and in her free time she often searched for them. In 1645, she fell into a fit, and was ill for some time afterward, but later, when she had recovered, she began to make prophecies, and apparently demonstrated healing powers. She said that while she was suffering from her fit, she had been taken to Fairyland, and that the fairies had given her these new powers.

According to Anne, she had been sitting knitting in the bower of the garden when she had heard tinkling sounds, rustling and laughter, and six beautiful little men dressed handsomely in green had appeared before her. They scrambled onto her lap and began to kiss and stroke her affectionately, much to her delight, and then one had put his hands over her eyes. She felt a sharp stinging and everything went dark. Then she was lifted into the air and carried away, and when she was set down again and her sight was restored, she found herself, dressed in magnificent clothes, in a wonderful land full of fairies who appeared to be human-sized. Her six companions were there, also now full-sized, and they continued to court her. She would have happily stayed there forever; she was particularly enamoured of their leader, and presently the two of them stole off together to make love. However, they were interrupted by her other suitors, who were accompanied by an angry crowd, and in the fight which ensued, her lover was struck down and fell wounded at her feet. The fairy who had blinded her once again put his hands over her eyes, and she felt herself being transported back to the bower, where she woke to find herself surrounded by anxious friends.

Although Anne never returned to Fairyland, she said the fairies were with her constantly, although only she could see them. Word of Anne's healing touch and her curative salves and medicines soon spread, and people came to seek her help. But although, after her fairy experience, Anne became very devout in her religion, her powers brought her to the attention of a local Justice of the Peace, John Tregeagle, who had her arrested and imprisoned first in Bodmin Jail, and later in the house of the Mayor of Bodmin, for six months. During this time, she was apparently not fed, but she did not complain and remained in good health until her release.

In 1696, while Anne was still alive, Moses Pitt, the son of her old master and mistress, sent a letter to the Bishop of Gloucester which gives an account of Anne's later life and his own early memories – he was still a child when Anne had come to work for his family. He recalled seeing her dancing in the orchard, and her telling him that she had been dancing with the fairies. She said they fed her fairy food, and Moses related how she had once given him a piece of fairy bread, and it had been the most delicious he had ever tasted.

While composing his letter, Moses Pitt sent an old friend of the family to speak to Anne, but, not wishing to repeat her experiences at John Tregeagle's hands or draw further attention to herself, Anne refused to say anything. She never took any payment for her alleged cures, and is thought to have died in 1698.

The Jersey Devil *see panel p356*

jinn *see* DJINN

jinxes
People, objects, occurrences or spells that bring bad luck.
The word 'jinx' is possibly derived from the name of a bird, the jynx (from Latin *iynx*), which was once used in magical rituals. Its modern usage first appeared in the USA, probably in the late 19th or early 20th century, although the word 'jyng', meaning a charm or spell, had been in use prior to this.

A jinx can take the form of a CURSE or SPELL, which brings bad luck and misfortune upon its chosen target. Indeed, it is still very common for someone who appears to suffer from bad luck to be described as jinxed – although this normally does not imply that the state has been brought about through magical means.

The word 'jinx' is also used to describe an individual who has gained a reputation for appearing to be at the centre of more than their fair share of accidents, unfortunate incidents and bad luck – often affecting those around them more than they affect themselves. Similar usage applies to situations where bad luck appears to be associated with the possession of a particular object (the opposite of a CHARM) or the occurrence of a particular event.

As with lucky charms and other SUPERSTITIONS, the idea that particular people, objects or occurrences can be jinxes is common in the world of sport. In the USA, there is a popular belief in the '*Sports Illustrated* cover jinx', based on the observation that there have been a number of people who have suffered injuries or other misfortunes shortly after appearing on the cover of the sports magazine *Sports Illustrated*. However, there have, of course, been many more people who have appeared on the cover and suffered no ill effects, and plenty of people who have suffered bad luck without ever appearing on the cover.

Many would argue that, in common with other beliefs relating to luck and chance, jinxes probably have more to do with the way that humans perceive,

The Jersey Devil

During January 1909, over a hundred people across southern New Jersey and eastern Pennsylvania in the USA claimed to have seen a bizarre winged creature, sometimes said to have horns, that became known as the Jersey devil. The name was 'borrowed' from a strange legend from two centuries earlier concerning the supposed birth to a New Jersey woman of a cursed child with a horse's head, bat-like wings, cloven hooves and a serpent for a tail. Nelson Evans and his wife, eyewitnesses of the 1909 Jersey devil, described a creature very similar to the original Jersey devil. In contrast, the creature reported by another 1909 eyewitness, postmaster E W Minster, who claimed to have spied it flying over the Delaware River on the morning of 1 January, was rather different. He said it resembled a large crane, but that it was glowing very brightly, bore a pair of curled horns on its ram-like head, sported two short forelegs and two longer hindlegs, had a pair of long thin wings, and flew with its lengthy, slender neck held outstretched. He also claimed that it gave out a terrifying cry that sounded like a combination of a squawk and a whistle.

Not long afterwards, reports emerged that a Jersey devil had been captured alive and was being exhibited at Philadelphia's Arch Street Museum. When curious visitors attended, however, they soon discovered that the animal in question was nothing more than an ordinary kangaroo decorated with bright green stripes, and bearing a pair of fake bronze-coloured wings strapped to its shoulders – in short, an amusing hoax. Indeed, most cryptozoologists now believe that the Jersey devil as a whole was a hoax, with perhaps a few reports of genuine but misidentified creatures, such as a crane or some other large long-legged bird (plus more than a dash of MASS HYSTERIA and URBAN LEGEND), mixed up in it.

An illustration of the Jersey Devil based on the testimony of those who claimed to have seen it, from the *Philadelphia Evening Bulletin*, January 1909.
(© TopFoto/ Fortean)

and then try to make sense of their perceptions, than with any objective quality of people or objects. See also CHANCE AND COINCIDENCE; FATE AND LUCK.

Joan of Arc, St (c.1412–1431)

French 15th-century patriot and martyr, who claimed to experience religious visions and hear voices and led the resistance to the English occupation of France. She was burned at the stake for heresy and sorcery in a politically motivated trial, but her case was reopened some 20 years after her death, and she was declared innocent. She was canonized as a saint in 1920.

Jeanne d'Arc, better known to history as Joan of Arc, was born in Domrémy, France. At the age of 13, she claimed to hear the voices of St Michael, St Catherine and St Margaret, accompanied by brilliant light, telling her to serve the dauphin and save France; the country was at that time undergoing one of the lowest points in its history, with much of its former territory under the domination of England and Burgundy during the Hundred Years' War. Despite her conviction, her attempts to join the French army were greeted with derision, but she persisted, and after her prophecy of defeat was fulfilled at the Battle of Herrings in 1429, the commander at Vaucouleurs gave her an escort to Chinon to see the dauphin. Although he was disguised among his courtiers, Joan at once identified him, an act which was taken as divine confirmation of his hitherto doubted legitimacy and claim to the throne. She was then subjected to a three-week examination by a group of theologians, after which she was allowed to join the army at Blois.

Apparently, in April 1429, wearing a suit of white armour and bearing her own standard, she entered Orleans with an advance guard and within just nine days saved the city. She captured several English forts and forced the English to raise their siege and, a month later, retire from their principal strongholds in the Loire. This victory earned her the name by which she came to be popularly known – the Maid of Orleans. Several more swift victories followed, in which almost every town the army passed through returned to French allegiance without resistance, and in June 1429 Joan succeeded in capturing Troyes after a four-day, almost bloodless siege. She and her 12,000-strong army then took the dauphin through English-held territory to be crowned Charles VII in Reims Cathedral.

Her mission to recapture Paris in August of that year failed. She set out in the spring of 1430 to relieve Compiègne from the Burgundians, but was captured and sold to the English by John of Luxembourg. She was then put on trial for heresy and sorcery by an ecclesiastical court of the Inquisition, but the trial was clearly motivated by political considerations rather than religious ones; it was held by the English regent, John, Duke of Bedford, who claimed the throne of France for his nephew, Henry VI, and wished to discredit Charles VII's claim. He was also eager to prove that Joan could not have won her victories over the English so easily but by WITCHCRAFT. Charles made no attempt to save Joan, and she was found guilty and sentenced to be burned at the stake. She recanted her heresy and might have escaped death, but she defiantly resumed her customary male attire, which was in violation of the Church rules and which she had promised to abandon, and abjured her recantation. She was then burned in the market place at Rouen, remaining faithful to her 'voices' to the end, and her ashes were thrown into the Seine. She was 19 years old.

Some 20 years later, Joan's aged mother, Isabelle, persuaded the authorities that the case should be reopened, and this was done at the request of the Inquisitor General, Jean Brehal. Her conviction trial was declared irregular on several counts, and in 1456 her original conviction was overturned and she was found innocent. Joan of Arc was one of the first people in history to be martyred for a Christian-inspired concept of nationalism, and is a powerful national symbol of France. In 1920, she was canonized as a saint by Pope Benedict XV. She is one of the most popular saints of the Roman Catholic Church, and is the second patron saint of France and the patron saint of soldiers. Her feast day is 30 May.

John Vianney, St *see* CURÉ OF ARS

Jones, Candy (1925–90)
Alleged victim of CIA mind control.

Candy Jones was born Jessica Wilcox in New Jersey in 1925. She rose to fame as a fashion model in the 1940s, becoming a popular pin-up among US servicemen during World War II. In later life she went on to run a modelling school.

In 1972 she married her second husband 'Long John' Nebel, a well-known New York radio show host who specialized in discussing the paranormal. Nebel soon began to notice abrupt and violent mood swings in his wife, during which she would exhibit an almost completely different, and unpleasant, personality. When questioned she claimed that she occasionally did work for the FBI, which involved absences about which she could not speak freely.

Intrigued, Nebel hypnotized her (see HYPNOSIS) and apparently brought to light an alternative personality called 'Arlene'. The process also allegedly resulted in the recovery of memories (see MEMORIES, RECOVERED) that convinced him that Candy had been involved in a MIND CONTROL programme run by the CIA. According to Nebel's analysis, Candy had been hypnotized by the CIA, and the personality of 'Arlene' had been created and groomed by the secret organization so that Candy could be used to carry out tasks of which she would later have no memory.

These claims and other material were published in a book by Donald Bain, *The Control of Candy Jones* (1976), but the story was not widely taken seriously. However, it subsequently emerged that the CIA had indeed conducted experiments into mind control, in a programme called MKULTRA, which began in the 1950s, leading some to consider the possibility that Nebel and Jones might be telling the truth.

It was officially denied that Candy Jones, or her alternative personality Arlene Grant, had been involved in any CIA activities. In addition, it emerged that Jones had had a rather disturbed childhood, in which she had suffered abuse, and to cope with this trauma she had invented an imaginary friend called Arlene.

The use of hypnotic regression is now highly controversial. It is widely recognized that many of the 'memories' recovered are actually false, and that they sometimes appear to be the product of CONFABULATION. It was suggested that when Jones's personality seemed to change under hypnosis, she was actually aping the behaviour of her cold and abusive mother.

No evidence for the claims of Nebel and Jones has ever been produced (other than the tapes made during hypnosis). However, their supporters would argue that this is to be expected in a case involving undercover government activities.

Joseph of Arimathea, St (1st century AD)

A wealthy Jew who, according to biblical lore, took Jesus's body down from the cross and laid it in the tomb he had prepared for himself. In medieval times he became connected with the Arthurian cycle as the first keeper of the Holy Grail, which he is said to have brought to Britain.

According to the New Testament gospels, a wealthy Jew called Joseph, who lived in the Judean city of Arimathea and may have been a member of the Sanhedrin, was a secret follower of Jesus. After the crucifixion, he went to Pontius Pilate and asked for Jesus's body; on being granted it, he purchased a fine linen cloth and wrapped the body in it, then placed it in a tomb which he had prepared for his own burial. Further details of his story appear in several New Testament apocrypha, such as the Acts of Pilate, known in medieval times as the Gospel of Nicodemus or the Narrative of Joseph; this book tells of how the Jewish elders, angered by Joseph's burial of Jesus's body, had him imprisoned, and of how he miraculously escaped and testified to the elders that Jesus had risen from the dead and ascended to Heaven. Christians often interpret Joseph's role as fulfilling Isaiah's prophecy that the grave of the Messiah would be 'with a rich man'.

During the Middle Ages, a series of legends came to be attached to Joseph, most of which first appear in Robert de Boron's epic romance of c.1200, *Joseph d'Arimathie*. Joseph is said to have been held in a Roman prison for twelve years, and while there, to have received the HOLY GRAIL from an apparition of Christ, becoming its first keeper; after his release he travelled to Britain, and hid the Grail near the Chalice Well at GLASTONBURY TOR. Later works also describe him as being a founder of Christianity in Britain, building the first church and converting the Britons even before the new religion had become established in Rome, and the legend of the Glastonbury Thorn tells of how he planted his hawthorn staff in the ground at Glastonbury where it flowered for many years afterward, every 5 January (the old Christmas Eve). According to some accounts, he was the uncle of Jesus's mother, Mary, and Jesus is even said to have visited Britain with him as a boy – a legend which inspired WILLIAM BLAKE's mystical hymn 'Jerusalem'.

Joseph of Arimathea is venerated as a saint by the Catholic and Eastern Orthodox Churches, and his feast day is 17 March in the West and 31 July in the East.

Jung, Carl Gustav (1875–1961)

Swiss psychiatrist and founder of analytical psychology; he introduced the concepts of the collective unconscious, synchronicity and archetypes, and inspired the New Age movement with his interest in occultism, Eastern religions, and mythology.

Carl Jung was born in Kesswil, Switzerland. He studied medicine there and then worked in a psychiatric clinic in Zurich (1900–9), being elected president of the International Psychoanalytical Association in 1910. He met SIGMUND FREUD in Vienna in 1907 and they worked together for some years, but Jung's independent research led him to disagree with Freud's insistence that all neuroses were of psychosexual origin, and they parted company in 1913.

From that time onward, Jung founded and developed a new school of analytical psychology, and introduced several pioneering and influential psychological concepts, the best known being the complex, the ARCHETYPE and the COLLECTIVE UNCONSCIOUS. His theory was that while the individual unconscious is organized by 'complexes' – ideas or impulses which have been repressed or forgotten, but which nevertheless continue to influence a person's behaviour – mankind also shares a 'collective unconscious' which is characterized by archetypes; all humans, he claimed, have common

The Swiss psychologist Carl Gustav Jung, photographed in 1940. (© Mary Evans Picture Library)

psychological predispositions which give rise to certain symbolic themes that exist across all cultures and times, and in all individuals, and together, these symbolic themes make up the 'archetypes' of the collective unconscious. He felt that the ultimate goal of psychology was the reconciliation and harmonization of the individual with these archetypal forces, and that the world of archetypes could only be revealed through an examination and understanding of the human psyche – not through experimental science, but by the exploration of dreams, art, mythology, world religions, philosophy and occultism. He therefore devoted himself to a lifelong study of these, travelling extensively through North Africa, New Mexico, Kenya and India. His later writings show a deep interest in the WESTERN MYSTERY TRADITION, esoteric Christianity and ALCHEMY.

Jung also introduced the new concept of SYNCHRONICITY, or 'meaningful coincidence'. He believed that many experiences perceived as coincidences were not in fact due to chance, but reflected the alignment of universal forces with the life experience of an individual – what he called an 'acausal principle' that connected events just as cause and effect do. He proposed that if a person could become intuitively aware of these forces, they could actually shape events around them by allowing their consciousness to communicate with the collective unconscious. The principle of synchronicity is at the heart of many techniques of DIVINATION, the idea being that the TAROT card or rune stone is not chosen by chance, but its selection is governed by the action of these universal forces at that particular moment to communicate information to the individual.

Jung held professorships at Zurich (1933–41) and Basle (1944–61), and published a number of works, including *The Psychology of the Unconscious* (1911–12), *On Psychic Energy* (1928), *Psychology and Religion* (1937), *Psychology and Alchemy* (1944) and *The Undiscovered Self* (1957).

Carl Jung's concept of the collective unconscious has had a deep and lasting influence, not only on psychology and psychotherapy, but on philosophy and the arts. His studies in occultism, world religions and mythology helped to inspire the NEW AGE movement, and he is regarded by many as the founder of a new humanism.

kabbalah

A Jewish mystical tradition based on an esoteric interpretation of the Old Testament and other texts, or a system which incorporates kabbalistic principles; any secret, occult or mystical doctrine.

The kabbalah, also spelled cabala, cabbala, kabala, kabbala and qabalah, is an ancient tradition of Jewish mysticism and occult knowledge. The word 'kabbalah', which means 'received doctrine', was first applied in the 11th century to secret, oral mystical teachings passed on from adepts to initiates, although it later came to be used of all Jewish mystical practices. One story claims that Moses received its teachings on Mount Sinai, another that God taught it to some of his angels, and that they passed it on to mankind after the Fall. However, it is generally agreed that the kabbalah originated around the 11th century as a development of earlier Jewish esoteric and occult traditions.

In the early Middle Ages there appeared the first of two mystical written texts which formed the cornerstone of kabbalistic philosophy – the *Sepher Yetzirah* or 'Book of Creation'. In this brief and cryptic work, which is thought to have been written some time between the 3rd and 6th centuries, the process of creation is described through the symbolism of letters and numbers; the anonymous author sets out a vivid and concise series of meditations on the Hebrew alphabet and details the 32 hidden paths by means of which God created the universe – the ten emanations of God known as the SEPHIROTH, and the 22 letters of the Hebrew alphabet.

The concepts of what came to be known as the Classical Kabbalah were developed extensively by Spanish Hebrews in the 13th century, and the second primary text of the kabbalah, THE ZOHAR or

'Book of Splendour', was published at this time. A Spanish Jew called Moses de Leon claimed to have discovered the text, which he attributed to the 2nd-century rabbi Shimon bar Yohai, and it was widely accepted throughout the Jewish world, although later a number of scholars asserted that it was written by de Leon himself. It elaborates on much of the material found in the *Sepher Yetzirah*, focusing primarily on the sephiroth. Medieval Jewish mystics created various visual structures of the sephiroth to show the relations between them, the most well-known of these being the TREE OF LIFE, which was a means of uniting the ten sephiroth and the 22 Hebrew letters. Medieval kabbalists speculated on 22 'pathways' between the ten sephiroth, with each pathway corresponding to a letter.

The expulsion of the Jews from Spain in 1492 helped to spread the Spanish kabbalah to the rest of Europe, and the German kabbalah, which began in the 16th century, emphasized the magical use of WORDS OF POWER and fuelled the development of kabbalistic techniques such as GEMATRIA, the study of the numerical values of letters and words. The kabbalah dwells deeply on the symbolism of the Hebrew alphabet; it teaches that every Hebrew letter, word and number contains a hidden meaning, and gives methods for interpreting these meanings. The Western or Christian kabbalah developed largely from the German kabbalah; medieval ceremonial magicians adopted the use of words of power, and in the late 15th and 16th centuries, Western kabbalists combined aspects of Christian theology and ALCHEMY with kabbalistic knowledge. In the 18th century there was an explosion of new interest in the kabbalah, and the late 19th and early 20th centuries saw a major development of the Western kabbalah by occultists such as ÉLIPHAS LÉVI and various Western magical traditions, particularly the HERMETIC ORDER OF THE GOLDEN DAWN. In the 1770s a link between the 22 letters of the Hebrew alphabet and the 22 cards of the major ARCANA in the TAROT was suggested by Antoine Court de Gébelin, and later, Éliphas Lévi set the tarot into a coherent kabbalistic system which was fully developed by the Hermetic Order of the Golden Dawn; although there is no historical evidence to support the claim that the tarot is based on the kabbalah, the connection between the two has since then formed the basis of the main symbolic interpretation of the tarot.

Kabbalah has been a fundamental element of Jewish thought and belief for centuries, and is now studied even in conservative rabbinical seminaries. In recent years, knowledge of the kabbalah has spread throughout the world. The controversial Kabbalah Centre, founded in Los Angeles in 1984, has sparked off a modern revival of interest in this esoteric tradition, and has gained many high-profile celebrity adherents. Reactions to this new development from organized Jewish groups has so far been almost universally negative, and the debate over the kabbalah's meaning and its intended audience continues to this day.

The term has also come to be used in a general sense to refer to any secret knowledge or mystic art.

kachina
Spirit beings who act as intermediaries between humans and the gods among the Pueblo people of the south-western USA.

The Hopi word 'kachina' refers to SPIRIT beings capable of influencing the natural world. They are associated with the ancestral dead and with duties such as bringing rain. In Hopi mythology they live in the San Francisco Mountains (which is also the location of the world of the dead) and their return from there to the people is symbolized in dances, where male dancers dress in masks and costumes, each designed to represent an individual kachina. The masked dancers take on the powers of the kachinas during the dance, and the masks must not be worn outside the ceremony. The kachinas are also represented by dolls which, unlike the masks, do not have any powers or sacred significance.

Another Pueblo people, the Zuñi, have a similar tradition. They refer to the kachinas as koko, and the otherworld in which they reside is at the bottom of the Lake of the Dead (Listening Spring Lake at the junction of the Little Colorado and Zuñi rivers).

Kaikoura
A case from New Zealand that became one of the most widely reported UFO incidents. It involved multiple witnesses, repeated encounters and film evidence, all apparently supported by radar observations.

In late 1978 a major WAVE of UFO sightings were reported across the southern hemisphere. The incidents included the globally reported disappearance of Australian pilot FREDERICK VALENTICH. There were also numerous reported sightings of strange lights in the foothills of the coastal mountains along New Zealand's South Island, accompanied by claims that sheep were being abducted in the Clarence and Kaikoura region.

At around midnight on 20 December 1978, Ian Offendell, a Warrant Officer at the nearby military base at Blenheim, spotted three strange lights drifting out to sea off the Kaikoura coast. He was so intrigued that he called the air traffic control tower in an attempt to identify them. Unable to account for the sightings, the base put a call through to the main radar centre at Wellington, around 130 kilometres (80 miles) away across the Cook Strait. Here, duty operator John Cordy confirmed that he and his colleague, Andy Heard, had also been watching something odd on their radar screens as they waited for an incoming commercial flight. Cordy said:

> We just sat there and watched them quietly because we had no aircraft to talk with and nobody we could ask to take a look. The blips were moving in a random fashion but purposeful. They were making little circles and going backwards and forwards.

The radar operators stayed in contact with Blenheim for an hour, during which time the radar targets appeared to correspond perfectly with the lights seen by the ground observers. At one point beams of light were seen to be projected onto the sea – local police contacted the base because they were receiving calls from householders who thought that these must be helicopters searching for something. All of those involved were agreed that although there should be no aircraft in the area at the time, there was definitely something flying around the coast that was visible to ground observers and to radar.

At 1.20am a Safe Air cargo plane took off from Blenheim to fly south to Christchurch with a consignment of newspapers. The pilot and first officer both reported seeing the lights, and the beams projected onto the sea, off Kaikoura. At the same

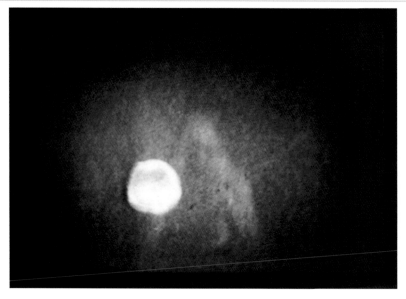

A still from the film taken by the Australian TV reporter Quentin Fogarty and his cameraman Dave Crockett, during the wave of UFO sightings at Kaikoura, New Zealand, in 1978. (© Mary Evans Picture Library)

time Cordy tracked the targets which appeared to be moving at 1,930 kph (1,200 mph). Throughout the night there were further such observations as this aircraft and a second Safe Air flight made more journeys across the region to deliver their cargos of newspapers. At one stage an object seemed to close in on a Safe Air plane, as if it were watching it closely. Another pilot reported seeing a trace on the aircraft radar screen that was made by an object moving so fast that it left a visible trail.

Members of the Wellington radar team were apparently so perturbed by these sightings that they dismantled their system between passing flights to verify that it was working properly – they did not want to put any lives at risk if their equipment was malfunctioning.

By chance the Australian TV reporter Quentin Fogarty was on holiday in New Zealand at the time and, with the interest stirred by the Valentich case still high back in Melbourne, he arranged to film interviews with the witnesses to take back with him. He was also invited to travel on board a Safe Air flight on the night of 30 December, to film background images with cameraman Dave Crockett. This flight produced a further series of sightings from the Clarence River area, and this time the UFOs were captured on film.

The footage was shown in TV news broadcasts around the world. However, it was fraught with

problems – apparently caused by the rocking motion of the cargo plane. Essentially, the film just shows lights jerking across the screen and fading in and out as attempts were made to focus on them. However, the footage still created a sensation – particularly because the stress being suffered by those on board the aircraft came across as very real. At one point Fogarty recorded live commentary, as the UFOs were flying below, using the words 'let's hope they're friendly' – which was to become the title of his subsequent book.

The Kaikoura case led to more suggested explanations for what had been seen than any other sighting in history. Over 20 different theories were proposed – ranging from the sublime (searchlights on squid fishing boats) to the ridiculous (moonlight reflecting off cabbage patches) – although most commentators based their opinions on the film footage only, rather than giving full consideration to the potentially more significant events that had occurred ten days earlier. One by one these suggested solutions were shown to be inadequate. A particularly popular theory was that the sightings had been of bright stars or planets (particularly Venus). However, although these bodies remained visible in the sky long after the initial sightings, the theory was weakened by the fact that there were no further reports, despite a constant lookout by Safe Air crews during January 1979.

karma

In Hinduism, Buddhism, Jainism and other predominantly Eastern belief systems, the law of cause and effect with regard to one's actions which is the driving force behind the belief in the cycle of reincarnation. Every action is thought to have an unavoidable consequence which will come to fruition either in this life or in a future one, and karma is the sum of all an individual has done or will do, which will affect their future incarnations.

The 'law of karma' is central to a number of Eastern belief systems, particularly Hinduism, Buddhism, JAINISM and Sikhism. 'Karma' is the Sanskrit word for 'action or deed', and karma may be described as the sum of all a person has done or will do, good or bad, with its inevitable consequences not only in this life, but also in future incarnations. This impartial principle is not seen as one of reward and punishment for good or bad deeds, but a strict law of cause and effect. Every thought, word or action results in karma which is accumulated and may come to fruition either in this life or in a future one. Man acts with free will and creates his own destiny. Karma is also seen as the force which traps an individual in the cycle of death and rebirth, or *samsara*, which always leads to suffering; the karma accumulated from one's actions in a previous life influences the conditions of one's next life, and only by freeing the spirit of karma altogether can the cycle be broken.

In Hinduism, karma functions predominantly as a means of explaining the problem of evil, and the inequalities and hardships encountered in this life, which are seen as being the result of actions in a previous life. All living creatures are held to be responsible for their own karma, since they act with free will. The law of karma determines whether a person is born in their next incarnation as a human, an animal or an insect, and, if they are reincarnated in human form, their status and situation. However, God, the ultimate dispenser of karma, may intervene and mitigate the natural consequences of this impersonal law. There are said to be three kinds of karma: *prarabdha* (karma to be experienced in the present lifetime), *sancita* (latent karma which has yet to come to fruition), and *sanciyama* (karma sown in the present lifetime, which will be reaped in a future incarnation). If an individual can attain *moksha*, or NIRVANA, they can be liberated from the karmic cycle; the latent karma is 'burned out', and while the present lifetime's karma still has to be worked through, no new karma is created, so that at death, the enlightened person has no karma remaining, and is thus freed from the cycle of *samsara* and will not be reincarnated.

In Sikhism, it is also believed that if, through grace, a person can live in complete obedience to God's commands, they will accumulate no more karma, so that once they have worked out their remaining karma, they will attain spiritual liberation and achieve union with God.

Unlike Hinduism, Buddhism does not subscribe to the idea of a supernatural Being who may intervene in the karmic process. The chief causes of karma in Buddhism are seen as *avijja*, or ignorance (of the true nature of reality), and *tanha*, or craving (after the objects of the senses and the mind).

In Jainism, karma is seen as a subtle form of matter which attaches itself to the spirit, or *jiva*, obscuring its innate faculties and weighing it down in the cycle of death and REINCARNATION. It is therefore to be treated like all other aspects of worldly existence, and dealt with by detachment from materialism, by the pursuit of an ascetic life. This is believed to prevent the further association of the spirit with karma, and speed up the decay of that karma which has been accumulated, so that the spirit can at last rise to the uppermost regions of the universe for eternity.

The concept of karma was popularized in the West largely through the work of the THEOSOPHICAL SOCIETY, and now also features in a number of Western esoteric belief systems, such as PAGANISM.

kawekaweau

A large lizard of Maori folklore that may hold the key to a unique and enigmatic museum exhibit.

According to the folklore of New Zealand's Maori people, the kawekaweau ('long tail') or kaweau is a large brown long-tailed lizard, with red longitudinal body stripes, that measures approximately 60 centimetres (2 feet) in total length. There are claims of kawekaweaus being killed by hunters as recently as the 1800s, including one in 1870 by a Urewera Maori chief in North Island's Waimana Valley. Yet zoologists had never been able to identify this creature with any known species of New Zealand lizard – until, that is, a remarkable museum exhibit on the other side of the world very belatedly received scientific attention.

For over a century, the Marseilles Natural History Museum had owned, and for quite a time publicly displayed, the stuffed specimen of a strange-looking long-tailed lizard, brown in colour with red longitudinal stripes, and measuring just over 60 centimetres (2 feet) long. Yet it was not until 1979, when examined by the museum's herpetology curator, Alain Delcourt, that it was realized that this specimen represented a totally unknown, hitherto-undescribed species. Studies revealed that it was a gecko, but far bigger than any previously known species, and in 1986 it was finally described scientifically, and named *Hoplodactylus delcourti* – the world's largest species of gecko.

Yet one major mystery remained – where had this specimen come from? There was no data concerning its provenance on file. However, various closely related (albeit much smaller) species exist in New Zealand, so scientists agree that this is the most likely origin of the Marseilles – and only known – specimen of Delcourt's giant gecko too, and that its species must have become extinct shortly after this specimen was collected. It seems likely, in view of the similarity between the two, that Delcourt's giant gecko is the lizard described in Maori folklore as the kawekaweau. During the 1990s, new reports of mystery lizards closely resembling Delcourt's giant gecko emerged from the east coast of New Zealand, lending hope to the possibility that this long-overlooked species – and, in turn, the kawekaweau – still exists after all.

Keel, John *see* MOTHMAN

Kelley, Edward *see* DEE, JOHN

Kether

In the kabbalah, the sephirah or emanation of God known as The Crown, which is assigned the number 1 and represents unity and perfection.

Kether is the first and highest of the ten SEPHIROTH, or Divine emanations, in the KABBALAH. It is called The Crown, and is regarded as the closest point to the consciousness of God, the uppermost aspect of his revealed self which can be contemplated by humans. It represents that which is above all else, unity and perfection, and corresponds to the 'superconscious' realm of experience. It is assigned the number 1. On the kabbalistic TREE OF LIFE, it is positioned as the highest point of the top triangle formed by the sephiroth, the Supernal Triangle, which it makes up with CHOKMAH and BINAH. It is also the highest sphere on the middle axis, the Pillar of Equilibrium. It is usually given three paths on the Tree of Life, to Chokmah, TIPHARETH and Binah, and is also linked to the lowest sephirah, MALKUTH. It is associated with the Divine name *Eheieh*, which means 'I am', the archangel Metatron, the angelic order of the Chaioth He Qadesh, or Seraphim, and the planetary force known as the Primum Mobile, the outermost sphere of heaven. In the TAROT, Kether corresponds to the four aces, and in the tarot Tree of Life spread, the card in the Kether position usually represents the highest spiritual development, the best qualities of a person and the way in which they attain these. In some kabbalistic systems its attributes include the magical image of an ancient bearded king, and it is represented by several symbols: a point, a point within a circle, and a swastika. It is often connected with the crown CHAKRA. The word 'Kether' in kabbalistic GEMATRIA gives the number 620; this is the full number of God's commandments to Israel, and the Torah text of the Ten Commandments has 620 letters. Later kabbalists also speak of the Kether sephirah as radiating 620 points of light. The often-debated 'hidden' eleventh sephirah, Daath, is held to be Kether viewed from a different aspect. Kether is sometimes also referred to as The Ancient of Days, The Primordial Point, The Most High, the Great Countenance, and The Lux Occulta.

Keyhoe, Donald (1897–1988)

The first private UFO investigator, author of the world's first UFO book and originator of the claim that the government was covering up the truth behind the mystery. Keyhoe was regarded as the leader of the modern UFO movement during its early years.

Donald Keyhoe was born in Iowa in June 1897 – just weeks after the AIRSHIP wave had struck the US Midwest, and 50 years to the very week before the KENNETH ARNOLD sighting gave birth to the modern UFO mystery. He graduated from the US Naval Academy in Annapolis, Maryland, and joined the US Marines, reaching the rank of Major before he retired.

Keyhoe became a writer during his convalescence after an air crash, producing many articles on military and aviation subjects for publications such as *Readers Digest* and *True*. In 1949 he was asked by the latter to investigate the UFO mystery, and was fortunate in that he approached his US Air Force contacts at a time when many of them had been angered by the rejection of the ESTIMATE OF THE SITUATION REPORT. As a result he was given many leads, and gained the impression that many of the people involved in the project had become convinced that UFOs were alien craft, only to be hastily transferred away from this work. This group were a disillusioned faction, but Keyhoe was left to conclude that their treatment indicated that there had been a GOVERNMENTAL COVER-UP of huge proportions. He set out to tell his readers this story – convinced that the Pentagon knew that ALIENS were visiting the Earth but could not tell the public.

The *True* article in 1950 was the most widely read in its history, and Keyhoe wasted no time in expanding it to produce the first ever book on the UFO phenomenon, *The Flying Saucers Are Real*, which was published in the spring of that same year. It sold half a million copies and cemented Keyhoe's position as the leader of the civilian UFO movement.

Several more books followed, mostly in the 1950s. His final book, *Aliens from Space*, appeared, after a lengthy gap, in 1973. Keyhoe's publications were packed with breathless presentations of cases

US UFO investigator Donald Keyhoe, with a copy of his book, *Flying Saucers from Outer Space* (1953).
(© Bettmann/Corbis)

that apparently supported his claims. The last also included various curious ideas, notably his suggestion that a decommissioned military base should be converted into a gigantic cosmic welcome mat to attract the aliens, so that their visit could be witnessed by the world.

In 1957 Keyhoe took charge of the NATIONAL INVESTIGATIONS COMMITTEE ON AERIAL PHENOMENA, a civilian body set up in an attempt to end the perceived cover-up conspiracy. However, membership declined rapidly at the end of the 1960s as UFO enthusiasts moved to less confrontational groups that shunned political campaigning and placed more emphasis on case investigation. Keyhoe died in 1988, having had only limited involvement in the field during the last two decades of his life.

Kibeho *see* MARIAN APPARITIONS

Kilner, Walter J(ohn) (1847–1920)
An English doctor who claimed to be able to diagnose disease in patients by viewing their 'aura'.
While working at St Thomas's Hospital in London in 1911, Walter J Kilner believed that he had developed equipment that enabled him to see coloured AURAS surrounding his patients. He used a blue dye called dicyanin, derived from coal tar, sandwiched between two pieces of glass. This 'Kilner screen' was later developed into a pair of goggles, known as 'Kilner goggles'.

Kilner claimed that the size, colour and intensity of a patient's aura would alter according to their health, and he was apparently able to use this observation to diagnose the presence of illness before the symptoms appeared. By experimenting he also found that using different screens of different colours he seemed to be able to see different parts of an aura. He went on to produce two books on the subject, *Human Atmosphere* in 1911 and *Human Aura* in 1920.

Kilner claimed that he learnt to see the auras without the aid of screens or goggles, although he continued to hold that they were a physical rather than supernatural phenomenon. It is now generally accepted that the 'auras' that can be seen by anyone using his equipment are indeed a physical phenomenon, but one that is wholly the result of an optical effect produced by the dye rather than a property of the body being observed. See also KIRLIAN PHOTOGRAPHY.

King Arthur
Semi-legendary 6th-century king of the Britons.
Enduring legends have ensured a place in British tradition for King Arthur, but was there ever such a person in reality, and how much of the legend is true?

If a historical Arthur existed, he was probably a war leader (not necessarily a king) of the British people who, both Romanized and Christian, resisted the encroachments of the pagan Saxons in the 6th century. He is supposed to have won a great victory at Mount Badon (c.518), to have met his death in a further battle at Camlan (c.539) and to have been buried at Glastonbury. In fact the sites of these battles have not been comprehensively identified and there is no firm evidence to connect Arthur with Glastonbury.

As far as historical chronicles are concerned, the first appearance of Arthur is in the *Historia Britonum* ascribed to the Welsh writer Nennius (fl.769). It might have been expected that he would merit a mention in the Anglo-Saxon Chronicles, which are usually dated to the reign of Alfred the Great (849–99), but no such personage is included.

It has been suggested that Arthur is based on a legendary Celtic hero, as shown by the widespread occurrence of traditional tales about him throughout the former Celtic strongholds, from Cornwall to Scotland and from Wales to Brittany.

Whether or not a real Arthur existed, it is the legend that has become more important, especially as it was elaborated at the hands of writers such as Geoffrey of Monmouth (c.1100–c.1154) and Sir Thomas Malory (d.1471). It is to these later authors that we owe the tradition of his being the son of a high king of Britain, Uther Pendragon, as well as the famous tales of Camelot, the Knights of the Round Table and their quest for the HOLY GRAIL, the magical sword Excalibur, Lancelot and Guinevere, and MERLIN. The post-medieval themes of chivalry and the purity of the knight would certainly not have made much sense to a war leader fighting for the survival of his people against the Saxons.

According to the stories, after a glorious career of winning battles and righting wrongs, Arthur was mortally wounded at the battle of Camlan by his nephew Mordred. From there he was carried to Avalon, whence in his people's hour of greatest need he will return to save them. Support for this notion is lent by the alleged inscription on his grave: *Hic iacet artorius rex quondam rexque futurus* ('Here lies Arthur, the once and future king'). However, the magnitude of the disaster awaiting the British people that would be severe enough to summon Arthur from his rest must be cataclysmic indeed, given that World War II was not enough to inspire his reappearance.

It is essentially impossible to say for sure whether or not there was a historical Arthur. The chronicles on which we depend for evidence were known to 'print the legend' as well as recount fact. Perhaps Arthur is really a composite figure made up of attributes of several real or legendary heroes and the battles and sites associated with his name belong to more than one individual.

king's evil

A former name for scrofula, a disease which it was once believed could be cured by the touch of the monarch.

Scrofula, also known as struma, is a form of tuberculosis characterized by a swelling of the lymphatic glands. In France and England it was once popularly thought to be curable by the touch of a monarch, and so was known as the king's evil. According to legend, the power of healing this disease was bestowed on French monarchs by Saint Remigius, who converted Clovis, King of the Franks, in the 6th century, and gave him the power to cure the disease. Later, all French kings were said to be given this healing touch on their coronation. Edward the Confessor was the first English king recorded as touching and healing scrofulous sores with his ring. The 'king's touch' was believed to be a manifestation of the divine right of the monarch, and the original Book of Common Prayer of the Anglican Church contained a ceremony for the procedure.

The custom of 'touching for the evil' came to be accompanied by great pomp and ritual in England, with many thousands of subjects assembling for the king's touch, and some English monarchs were credited with hundreds of cures; on Midsummer's Day

1633, Charles I was said to have healed 100 people in Holyrood Chapel, and the custom reached its zenith in England during the Restoration, when Charles II was reputed to have touched 90,000 scrofula victims between 1660 and 1682. King Henry IV of France was said to have touched and healed as many as 1,500 individuals at a time. By the 16th century, sufferers who had been touched were presented with a gold coin, usually an angel (named after the figure of the archangel Michael which appeared on it), which the king had also laid hands on. This coin was pierced so that it could be worn round the neck as a TALISMAN or CHARM to reinforce the cure. After production of the angel ceased in the mid-17th century, it was replaced by small medals of a similar design, produced specially for the purpose. Around the figure of the angel was an inscription which translated as 'to God alone the glory', a reminder that the ultimate source of the cure was not the monarch but God himself. One of the last people to be touched for the king's evil in England was Dr Samuel Johnson, who was touched as a sickly child by Queen Anne in 1711. The first Hanoverian monarch, George I, abandoned the practice, which he regarded as superstitious, but the custom persisted in France for another century, and was briefly revived by Charles X between 1824 and 1839.

Kirlian photography

A process by which it is allegedly possible to produce a photographic record of the 'aura' of a living thing.

In 1939 Russian scientist Semyon Davidovich Kirlian (1898–1978) discovered that objects placed on a photographic plate which was subjected to a high voltage field left behind an image which appeared to show some form of illuminated discharge surrounding them. Kirlian and his wife Valentina developed the idea that these images were records of the 'AURA' that surrounds all living things. They believed that this aura was a form of electromagnetic field that they called 'biological plasma' (now often referred to as 'bioplasma').

For Kirlian's method to work the object had to be in direct contact with the photographic plate, and this limited the size of the objects which could be photographed to ones such as leaves and fingertips. Kirlian apparently observed that the size and colour of the aura around the object appeared to be an indicator of health, and (in a similar way to WALTER J KILNER) he believed that his method might be used as a way to diagnose illness. The Kirlians also claimed that the longer an item had been dead, the weaker the image that was produced.

However, the biggest, and most controversial, apparent discovery that the Kirlians made is embodied in a famous photograph that they took of a

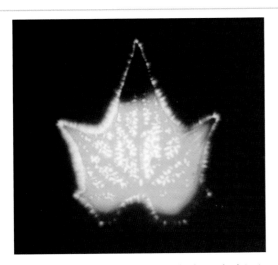

A Kirlian photograph which apparently shows the intact aura of a section of a leaf that has been removed.
(© Mary Evans Picture Library)

damaged leaf. In this image, although a section of the leaf had been removed, the full aura was still visible – suggesting that the bioplasma field could 'remember' its original shape.

In more recent times there have been claims that images produced from the fingers of PSYCHICS are more intense than those of 'ordinary' people, that psychiatric patients produce images showing broken auras and that a person's emotional state can affect the picture produced.

Sceptics argue that the effects can actually be explained quite easily. They suggest that the images are produced by a 'coronal discharge' – an electrical discharge brought on by the ionization of the air around the object, ultimately as a result of the charge applied to the photographic plate. It has been observed that levels of surface moisture, and the pressure applied to the plate, can affect the 'aura' recorded – this may explain the variations in the quality of the images more effectively than 'psychic energy', illness or how long something has been dead. Tests have also shown that pictures can be produced from objects that were never living, such as coins; and, most damningly, researchers have found that they cannot recreate the famous cut leaf picture if they cut the leaf and then place it on a new sheet of glass (rather than place it on a sheet of glass and then cut it) before the photograph is taken.

kiss of shame *see* OSCULUM INFAME

Klass, Philip J(ulian) (1919–2005)

A UFO sceptic who, for a period of five decades, was widely regarded as the most outspoken critic of the UFO movement.

Philip J Klass was born in Iowa and graduated from Iowa State University as an electrical engineer. However, he went on to specialize in writing articles on aviation and space technology, and in 1952 he became senior editor for the prestigious *Aviation Week and Space Technology* journal, based in Washington, DC. He remained with the magazine until his retirement in 1986.

Throughout his working career, and long into his retirement, Klass was determined to challenge what he perceived to be the pseudo-science that was rife within the UFO COMMUNITY. He fought bitter duels in the media and through private correspondence with many leading UFO researchers. In particular he was strongly dismissive of the EXTRATERRESTRIAL HYPOTHESIS – in fact, he was so certain of his position that for many years he offered to pay a large cash prize to anyone who could provide acceptable proof to the contrary. He never had to pay, although many UFO researchers countered that the conditions attached were so stringent that they could never have satisfied them.

Klass once caused some anger in the USA by implying a link between interest in UFOs and an unconscious furthering of the Communist cause, mirroring the CIA thinking which followed the WASHINGTON DC WAVE in 1952. His approach was disliked by a wide range of UFO researchers – even the moderate DR J ALLEN HYNEK declined open debates with him, and others refused to even appear on the same platform at conferences. However, he was more readily tolerated by the UFO community outside the USA, and he found some support among UFO researchers in Europe, where he lectured at both sceptics' and enthusiasts' events.

To help promote his arguments Klass became one of the founders of the COMMITTEE FOR THE SCIENTIFIC INVESTIGATION OF CLAIMS OF THE PARANORMAL (CSICOP), a group composed of magicians and scientists zealously determined to eradicate uncritical belief in strange phenomena. He also edited his own newsletter, the *SUN*, or *Skeptics UFO Newsletter*, in which he criticized numerous UFO cases.

Klass was the author of seven UFO books over a period of 34 years, and their titles, including *UFOs: The Public Deceived* (1983) and *UFO Abductions: A Dangerous Game* (1989), often demonstrated his passion. However, although he proposed that many cases were hoaxes (sometimes with good cause), he was also one of the first promoters of the theory that some UFO cases might involve strange (terrestrial) natural phenomena.

He put forward the ideas that plasma energy and BALL LIGHTNING might be potential causes of sightings, long before they became popular among sections of the UFO community. Such ideas have always been better supported outside the USA – possibly another reason why Klass had a happier relationship with UFO researchers outside his native land.

Even after ill health took him away from the public eye, Klass continued to argue his case on the Internet almost until his death in 2005.

Knights Templar
A religious and military order founded by Crusaders in c.1119 for the protection of the Holy Sepulchre and pilgrims visiting it; suppressed 1307–14.

The Knights Templar was the largest and most powerful of the Christian military orders. Founded in c.1119 in the aftermath of the 1096 Crusade, its purpose was to help the new Kingdom of Jerusalem to defend itself against its hostile Muslim neighbours, and to protect the large numbers of pilgrims who travelled to Jerusalem after its conquest by the Crusaders. Its members took a vow of poverty, and this vow was reflected in the Order's seal, which depicted two knights riding on one horse; the Order's full name was originally the Poor Knights (or Fellow Soldiers) of Christ and the Temple of Solomon, although it soon came to be referred to as the Order of the Knights Templar, or simply the Templars. The name derived from the temple, supposedly built by Solomon, near which in Jerusalem the Templars were assigned quarters.

They quickly became a powerful force in the international politics of the Crusades period, and were permitted by various Papal bulls to levy taxes and exact tithes in all the areas under their control, being officially exempted from having to answer to any authority except the Pope's.

Because they regularly transported money and goods between Europe and Palestine, the Knights Templar came to develop a highly efficient banking system, and became very successful investors and moneylenders. But it was this success, and their great power, which was probably the cause of their downfall. Having been refused a loan by the Order to finance his wars, King Philip IV of France waged a campaign to have them discredited and excommunicated so that he could get control of their wealth for himself, and in 1307, he had most or all of the Templars in France arrested. Interrogated under torture, some confessed to sacrilegious acts, and to the worship of a demonic figure known as BAPHOMET, and when their leaders denied these admissions, they were executed. A Papal inquiry into the practices of the Order followed, and by 1314, it had officially ceased to exist, its banking system broken up and its property either seized or turned over to the Hospitallers, a rival military order. As he burned at the stake, Jacque de Molay, the Grand Master of the Knights Templar, is said to have cursed both King Philip and the Pope, and when they both died within a few months of his execution, this added to the legends which later built up around the Order.

The Knights Templar figure strongly in the foundation and ritual of FREEMASONRY, and several self-styled orders have claimed to be descended from, or to be a revival of, the Templars. Conspiracy theorists have suggested that the motives for their suppression went far beyond simple jealousy of their wealth and power. Over the centuries, they have been surrounded by stories of secrets and mysteries, with some claiming that the Templars were the repository for secret knowledge which linked them to the ROSICRUCIANS, the Priory of Sion, the Gnostics (see GNOSTICISM), and lost relics and teachings of Jesus. The best-known of these theories is that the Templars found the HOLY GRAIL, and after their suppression, they took it to Scotland, where it was hidden somewhere in ROSLYN CHAPEL. Others say that they found the Ark of the Covenant, a chest containing sacred objects such as the stone tablets on which God inscribed the Ten Commandments. The mythos of the Knights Templar as the keepers and guardians of the Holy Grail has captured the imagination of writers and has had a number of influences on popular culture; it forms a central plot point in Umberto Eco's *Foucault's Pendulum* (1989) and, more recently, in Dan Brown's THE DA VINCI CODE, and also figures prominently in the storyline of the 1989 film *Indiana Jones and the Last Crusade*. See also FRIDAY THE 13TH.

Knock
An Irish village where people experienced visions of the Virgin Mary.

On 21 August 1879, at the village of Knock in County Mayo, Ireland, a group of people reported experiencing VISIONS of the Virgin Mary (see also MARIAN APPARITIONS).

In the apparition, 15 individuals of all ages, including men, women and children, reported seeing, outside the parish church, a beautiful woman wearing a crown topped by a golden rose and dressed in white, with her hands raised in an attitude of prayer. They identified her as the Virgin Mary. Also seen were St Joseph and St John the Evangelist, in the garments of a bishop, as well as an image of an altar surmounted by a lamb and a cross and surrounded by ANGELS. The figures appeared to be floating around 60 centimetres (2 feet) above the ground and were seen to move towards the witnesses and back again.

The vision was said to have lasted for two hours, and even people who were not close enough to the scene to experience it reported seeing the church bathed in an extraordinary bright light. While it rained continuously during the apparition, the witnesses found that the ground where the visions had appeared had remained dry.

As the news spread, people began to journey to the area and a series of miraculous cures were linked with a visit to the church at Knock. The Catholic Church investigated the phenomenon, interviewing those who had witnessed it and finding them to be trustworthy, but it was not until 1936 that the visions were officially accepted as divinely inspired and 'worthy of belief'.

In 1880 further apparitions were reported, but these were discounted as false. Clergymen pointed out that these were largely reported by individuals and not witnessed by groups the size of the one that had experienced the first vision. It was argued that people were now coming to Knock with the expectation of seeing something extraordinary and therefore an element of auto-suggestion, even of hysteria, was coming into play.

Knock soon became acknowledged as a Marian shrine and the thousands of pilgrims that it attracts annually led to the construction of a pilgrims' hostel and a centre for invalids as well as the opening nearby of an international airport in 1986. In 1979 Pope John Paul II celebrated Mass at Knock on the centenary of the apparition.

Whatever the truth of the apparition, it has been suggested by sceptics that the Church in Ireland exploited the phenomenon to distract the people's attention from ongoing Nationalist agitation.

knockers *see* MINES

Koestler, Arthur (1905–83)

A writer, polymath and political thinker whose legacy enabled the founding of one of the most famous parapsychology units in the world.

Arthur Koestler was born Kösztler Artúr in Budapest, in what was then Austria-Hungary and, after studying science and psychology at the University of Vienna, he travelled the world as a news correspondent. At the start of World War II he was working in France. After a very brief period in the French Foreign Legion, Koestler fled to England, where he served in the British Pioneer Corps until 1942, and was then employed at the BBC. In 1945 he took British citizenship. Throughout the war he campaigned vigorously to highlight the atrocities being carried out by the Nazi regime.

Koestler was a prolific writer and produced a number of autobiographical, political (he had once been a communist, but became disillusioned following the Stalinist purges in the Soviet Union), philosophical and historical works in a range of languages; he was awarded the CBE for his services to literature in 1970. In the last 30 years of his life he wrote a substantial amount of controversial, sceptical work on the practice of science. These writings were strongly coloured by his interest in MYSTICISM and the PARANORMAL – interests that had been strengthened by investigations that he had carried out into Japanese and Indian mysticism, and possibly by experiments with hallucinogens during the 1950s and 1960s (although he challenged the notion that drug-induced experiences had any religious or spiritual significance). He became convinced that the coincidence of certain rare events was so improbable that their occurrence was beyond mere chance, leading to the publication of his 1972 book, *The Roots of Coincidence*, in which he evaluated the work of Paul Kammerer (see CHANCE AND COINCIDENCE) and his theory of SYNCHRONICITY.

In 1983 Koestler and his third wife were discovered dead, apparently having entered into a suicide pact. He had been a lifelong believer in euthanasia and a prominent member of the voluntary euthanasia campaign group EXIT. However, although he was suffering from Parkinson's disease and leukaemia at the time of his death, his wife was apparently healthy, leading to suggestions that he had unfairly persuaded her to join him in taking her own life.

Koestler never claimed to be PSYCHIC, but he did claim to have had a number of paranormal experiences during his life, and had been particularly interested in the ideas of TELEPATHY and LEVITATION. He made provision in his will for a Chair of PARAPSYCHOLOGY to be set up within a British university. The Chair was awarded to University of Edinburgh in 1984, and the following year the position was instigated within the Psychology Department. The Koestler Parapsychology Unit continues to carry out research in a wide range of areas, although a bust of Koestler, formerly on display at the university, was removed amid protests relating to claims that Koestler's had been brutal in his treatment of women.

kongamato

An alleged modern-day pterodactyl inhabiting the dense swamplands of tropical Africa.

The close of the Cretaceous Period 64 million years ago not only marked the apparent extinction of the dinosaurs but also saw the demise of the last pterosaurs or flying reptiles, typified by the familiar pterodactyls. Yet if native descriptions of an undiscovered creature reputedly inhabiting Zimbabwe and Zambia in tropical Africa are to be believed, there may be at least one species of pterodactyl alive today.

Allegedly dwelling within dense, swampy forests, the CRYPTID in question is referred to by the native people here as the kongamato ('broken boats' – after its tendency to capsize boats by swooping down at them), and is strongly associated with disaster and death. They declare that it is most similar in overall appearance to a lizard with long slender jaws lined with short sharp teeth, but that it also possesses a pair of unfeathered, membranous wings, similar to a bat's but with a span of 1.2–2.1 metres (around 4–7 feet). This description, made by people who have no palaeontological knowledge, is very similar to that of a small pterodactyl.

While passing through what is now north-western Zambia during the early part of the 20th century, a western traveller named Frank Melland became very interested in kongamato reports, and asked the local people if they could identify the creature in a picture-book of animals that he was carrying with him. This book contained illustrations of prehistoric as well as modern animals. All of the native people to whom he showed the book pointed to the picture of the pterodactyl, insisting that this was the kongamato.

Alternatively, the kongamato may simply be a very large, possibly unknown species of bat. It could even be a purely mythical monster – many such fabulous animals exist in African legends and folklore. However, a number of supposedly mythical African animals, such as the okapi, giant forest hog and pygmy hippopotamus, have been ultimately confirmed as genuine creatures, so at present the kongamato's status remains undecided.

Koresh, David *see* BRANCH DAVIDIANS

Koro *see* PENIS PANIC

kraken *see* GIANT SQUID

Kramer, Heinrich *see* MALLEUS MALEFICARUM

Krantz, Grover (1931–2002)
US academic and renowned bigfoot investigator.
Born in Salt Lake City, Utah, Grover Krantz pursued an academic career in physical anthropology throughout his working life, obtaining his PhD in 1971 at the University of Minnesota, and lecturing in human evolution at Washington State University from 1968 until his retirement during the 1990s. In 1963, he developed an interest in America's most famous CRYPTID, the BIGFOOT or sasquatch, which he continued to pursue throughout his life. Krantz's

meticulous analysis of the Patterson–Gimlin film of an alleged bigfoot at Bluff Creek, California, convinced him that it was genuine. He eventually concluded that the bigfoot is a surviving species of *Gigantopithecus* – a giant ape known to have existed in Asia until at least as recently as 100,000 years ago, and which may conceivably have crossed the Bering land bridge formerly linking Asia to North America.

Although Krantz's abiding interest in the bigfoot controversy alienated him in certain academic quarters, his resolve to confirm this cryptid's existence remained undimmed throughout his working life. Ironically, it was this resolve that also alienated him from some fellow bigfoot investigators when he announced that he considered it necessary for a bigfoot to be killed in order to provide conclusive evidence of the reality of this species. In 1982, Krantz became a founding Board Member of the INTERNATIONAL SOCIETY OF CRYPTOZOOLOGY. He also published four books on the bigfoot, which remain the most scientific and detailed studies of this cryptid ever produced.

(Jiddu) Krishnamurti (1895–1986)
Indian spiritual teacher. Initially declared an incarnation of Maitreya, one of the five earthly buddhas, by the English theosophists Annie Besant and Charles W Leadbeater, he subsequently renounced his claims of divinity and spent the rest of his life travelling the world as an independent speaker.
Jiddu Krishnamurti was born in a small village in southern India. His father joined the THEOSOPHICAL SOCIETY in 1881, and in 1909 his family went to live at the society's headquarters in Adyar. There, he was discovered as a teenager by the English theosophist CHARLES W LEADBEATER, who declared him to be the 'World Teacher', the vehicle of Maitreya, one of the five earthly buddhas or BODHISATTVAS, who was believed to manifest himself in human form every 2,000 years. He was adopted by theosophist Annie Besant and brought to England to complete his education, and in 1911 he was made head of the Order of the Star in the East, which had been newly founded by Besant to support his divine destiny. However, in 1929 Krishnamurti abandoned the role which the theosophists had assigned to him – he renounced all claims to divinity, turned away all his followers and disbanded the Order.

Krishnamurti then spent the rest of his life – almost 60 years – travelling the world as an independent speaker. The aim of his teachings was to set people free from prejudice and dogma so that they might achieve harmony with themselves, nature and others. He maintained that only the transformation of the human psyche could bring about an end to the violence and suffering of the world, but that there

US bigfoot investigator Grover Krantz pictured with the cast of a mysterious giant footprint. (© TopFoto/Fortean)

was no 'path' to this transformation, and that it could not be learned from a guru; each individual had to transform themselves through self-knowledge. To this end, he established several schools where young people and adults could explore the possibility of becoming fully free and unprejudiced in daily living. In 1984, he was awarded the United Nations Peace Medal, and he died at the age of 91, in 1986. His supporters have transcribed and published many of his thousands of talks as educational and philosophical books.

Kulagina, Nina (1926–90)
An alleged powerful psychic from Russia investigated by the Soviet military.
Nina Kulagina was one of the mainstays of Soviet research into PSYCHIC abilities during the latter years of the Cold War. She was reportedly able to move a range of small objects using only the power of her mind (see PSYCHOKINESIS). It was even claimed that in one series of experiments she demonstrated control over a frog's heart suspended in a nutrient solution, and was able to slow it down, speed it up and ultimately stop it.

As a child Kulagina said that she could diagnose diseases simply by looking at a person, and found herself surrounded by the sort of occurrences normally associated with POLTERGEIST activity. She apparently learned to control her powers and, while recovering in hospital from a nervous breakdown in 1964, she amazed doctors with her apparent demonstrations of EXTRA-RETINAL VISION – one such example, displayed while she was sewing, involved her gathering new thread of the appropriate colour from her basket without looking. This led to her being investigated extensively, ultimately by the Soviet authorities.

Ill health, which was claimed to be a direct result of her using her psychic powers, meant that Kulagina only performed under controlled, laboratory conditions in front of a select few; she was apparently unable to give the sort of large-scale demonstrations typical of Western psychics, such as URI GELLER. The only evidence that was publicly disseminated, and leaked to the West, took the form of performances on film – leading to suggestions that it was nothing more than propaganda and deliberate misinformation. Even if this possibility is discounted, it has also been considered suspicious that she required an extended period of preparation before a demonstration, possibly allowing her scope to make arrangements to produce the effects fraudulently.

Kundalini

In yoga, the life force which is believed to rest at the base of the spine; by meditation it is said to be possible to release it and cause it to rise up through the chakras, activating each one as it does so, to achieve spiritual enlightenment and healing.

The concept of Kundalini comes from the philosophy of YOGA. Its name derives from a Sanskrit word meaning 'coiling like a snake' or 'serpent power'. The source text for the idea of Kundalini is the *Hatha Yoga Pradipika*, written by Swami Svatmarama some time between the 12th and 15th centuries. In Tantra yoga, Kundalini is an aspect of Shakti, the divine female energy and consort of Shiva, and is thus regarded as a type of deity. According to yogic tradition, Kundalini is seen as a serpent which rests in the back part of the root CHAKRA, at the base of the spine, coiled in three and a half turns around the sacrum. By a system of yogic movements, breathing techniques and MEDITATION known as Kundalini yoga, which places particular emphasis on the role of the spine and endocrine system, yogis believe that they can awaken Kundalini's dormant energy in a process known as Pranic Awakening; prana is the UNIVERSAL LIFE FORCE which resides in all of us, and by awakening Kundalini, an intensified form of prana known as pranotthana is said to be generated from the reservoir of subtle energy at the base of the spine.

Once awakened, Kundalini is thought to rise up from the root chakra through the spinal column, activating each chakra as it goes. The objective of Kundalini yoga is to raise its energy to the crown chakra, where as an aspect of Shakti, it will unite with the Shiva, or male polarity, bringing spiritual enlightenment. This energy can also be used for healing purposes, as in a branch of REIKI known as Kundalini reiki. It is believed that Kundalini rising can open new pathways in the nervous system, awaken

the abilities of CLAIRVOYANCE and CLAIRAUDIENCE, generate a feeling of oneness with the universe, and bring about a connection with a higher frequency of thought and consciousness.

The power of Kundalini is reputed to be enormous, often accompanied by VISIONS, shaking, ecstasy and sometimes pain. However, it is also said to be dangerous; yogis claim that the body must be adequately attuned and prepared for the experience of controlled Kundalini rising by yoga, and that premature or too sudden an awakening of this energy can lead to insanity or even death. When practised in a religious context, under the guidance of a reliable teacher and with thorough preparation beforehand, it is thought to be mostly beneficial. But with the increasing interest in Kundalini yoga techniques in the West since the 1970s and Kundalini's popularization by the NEW AGE movement, psychologists and physiologists have identified a condition known as Kundalini Syndrome in Westerners who have been involved in the prolonged and intensive practice of meditation and yoga techniques. This is said to cause an overload of the nervous system, destabilization and disorientation. Sufferers sometimes describe a feeling of energy travelling along the spine or up the body, and may be subject to tremors, involuntary body movement, headaches, gastrointestinal problems, mood swings or HALLUCINATIONS.

Although Kundalini is chiefly associated with Indian religions such as Hinduism, it appears to be a universal phenomenon dating back some 3,000 years; Kundalini-type experiences are mentioned in the esoteric teachings of the Sufis (see SUFISM), the ancient Egyptians, Tibetans and Chinese, and parallels may also be seen in ecstatic shamanic trance dancing and Islam's WHIRLING DERVISHES. While the Kundalini experience is usually initiated by meditation, a guru may also sometimes bring it about by touching the body or forehead of the subject in a practice called *shaktipat*, and it is also said to be induced by trauma or NEAR-DEATH EXPERIENCES.

Lake Champlain monster

Periscope-necked aquatic cryptid said to inhabit Lake Champlain, USA; popularly known as Champ, the monster is as famous in the USA as the Loch Ness monster is in Scotland.

The Lake Champlain monster, or 'Champ' for short, is a long-necked water monster traditionally claimed to inhabit the vast volume of freshwater constituting Lake Champlain in the USA. Sandwiched between New York and Vermont for much of its length, Lake Champlain is 175.5 kilometres (109 miles) long, 17.7 kilometres (11 miles) wide, and has a water surface area of 1,140.5 square kilometres (440 square miles). The earliest reports of a monster here date back to Native American lore, which tells of a huge horse-headed water beast known as the 'chaousarou'. In modern times, countless sightings have been reported, which collectively yield a Champ 'identikit image' of a LOCH NESS MONSTER-type creature with a long periscope-like neck, a horse-like eared (or horned) head and mane, one or more humps along its back, dark skin and a total length of 4.6–15.3 metres (15–50 feet).

However, Champ only attracted international interest during the 1960s, rather like the BIGFOOT, but since then – again like bigfoot – it has become one of the most famous mystery beasts in the world. This was due in no small way to Champ's answer to the Patterson–Gimlin bigfoot film – the famous film footage that was alleged to be evidence of a living bigfoot. In the case of Champ, the 'evidence' is in the form of a colour photograph taken by Sandra Mansi on 5 July 1977, in the vicinity of St Albans, Vermont. The photograph seems to show a long-necked water beast with a section of its back visible above the water surface, dark brown in colour and seemingly quite smooth in texture. The photograph

was taken at a range of 30–45.8 metres (98–150 feet). Mansi and her husband both estimated that the creature was 4.6–6.1 metres (15–20 feet) long, with its head and neck raised 1.8–2.5 metres (around 6–8 feet) above the surface of the water. The photograph was later examined by Professor Paul LeBlond, an expert in wave dynamics based at the University of British Columbia's Department of Oceanography. In 1982 he announced that the lower and upper limits for the length of the object at the water-line were 4.9–17.5 metres (16–57 feet) – and this is only for its photographed section; it does not include the body section remaining hidden beneath the water.

Lake Champlain is named after Samuel de Champlain, a European explorer who actually claimed to have sighted some monsters in its waters during July 1609. However, the beasts that he described were each only 1.5 metres (5 feet) long, as thick as his thigh, with a head as big as his two fists, a long snout and a double row of very sharp teeth – far removed from the Champ reported in more modern times, which resembles the extinct plesiosaur. De Champlain's monsters resemble the garpike – a very primitive, prehistoric-looking fish of similar size and appearance, known only from a few present-day species all endemic to bodies of fresh water in North America, with no living Old World species. Consequently, in de Champlain's eyes these unfamiliar but very striking creatures would have seemed like monsters. See also LAKE MONSTERS.

lake monsters

Aquatic cryptids of greatly varying form reported from numerous lakes around the world.

Cryptozoologists now believe that there are several wholly distinct species of SEA SERPENT, although there is little agreement as to the precise zoological identities of these CRYPTIDS. However, even their reported morphological diversity pales into insignificance when compared with the vast array of freshwater cryptids on record, especially so-called lake monsters, inhabiting large landlocked bodies of water around the world.

Intriguingly, quite a few apparent lake monsters – especially in temperate climes – seem to be freshwater equivalents of certain categories of sea serpent. Certainly, there are lake-dwelling cryptids whose descriptions correspond very closely indeed to the 'marine longneck', and others that correspond to the 'many-humped' sea serpent. Freshwater 'longnecks' include Scotland's LOCH NESS MONSTER, America's LAKE CHAMPLAIN MONSTER and Sweden's LAKE STORSJÖN MONSTER, whereas freshwater 'many-humped' cryptids include Canada's LAKE OKANAGAN MONSTER, Ireland's HORSE EELS and Norway's LAKE SELJORDSVATNET MONSTER. Indeed, if we take it that lake monsters and sea serpents do exist, the morphological correspondence between the lake monsters and their marine counterparts would suggest that they are descended from marine cryptids which long ago, during glacial times, entered sea-linked inland bodies of water but became trapped in them when lowering sea levels transformed these bodies into landlocked, steep-sided lakes. Also, some claim that many-humped aquatic cryptids are capable of at least limited movement overland from lake to lake, and from coastal waters into nearby lakes and back again.

These two categories of lake monster (especially the longneck version) are apparently not sighted randomly throughout the world, but, as noted by Dr BERNARD HEUVELMANS, are reported from bodies of fresh water within quite a specific isothermal zone, ie between 0°C and 20°C. Some suggest that in itself this offers noteworthy circumstantial evidence of their reality. As might also be expected, lake monsters reported from warmer, subtropical or tropical bodies of fresh water appear to be much more diverse, and vary greatly from one continent to another.

Perhaps the most famous lake monster in sub-Saharan Africa is the Congolese MOKELE-MBEMBE, said to resemble an elephant-sized sauropod dinosaur and to be capable of terrestrial movement – via its four sturdy legs – as well as aquatic activity. Similar cryptids have also been reported from Cameroon, Gabon, the Central African Republic and elsewhere. Very different are the superficially snake-like, crested 'lau' of the Upper Nile and Lake Victoria's 'lukwata', which are conceivably giant forms of catfish, their 'crests' being nothing more than an array of barbels around their mouth – a familiar catfish characteristic.

Ethiopia's Lake Tana lays claim to a heavy, sheep-sized cryptid known variously as the 'auli', 'aila', or 'ia-bahr-tedcha' ('water calf'), which might be a species of manatee. And an apparently bloodsucking, brain-eating mystery beast known as the 'mamba mutu' ('crocodile man'), that allegedly inhabits Lake Tanganyika, could conceivably be an extremely large, unknown species of flat-skulled otter, as proposed by zoologist Carlos Bonet.

No less intriguing is tropical Asia's complement of lake cryptids. The BURU, formerly reported from swampy lakes in Assam although now seemingly extinct, was most probably a giant species of lungfish, but a smaller, still-undescribed species may survive in Vietnam. Long-necked sauropod-like water beasts reminiscent of Africa's mokele-mbembe have been reported from the remote Malaysian lakes of Tasek Bera and Tasek Chini, though as their limbs have not been described they may conceivably be more plesiosaurian, with flippers, than dinosaurian. The monster of Java's Lake Patenggang has been variously likened to a dinosaur and a giant fish; and enormous red salmon-like fish have been reported on many occasions from China's Lake Hanas, and even viewed in July 1985 by a visiting biology professor with a team of students, who estimated that the biggest specimens were more than 9 metres (29.5 feet) long. Strangest of all, however, must surely be the surrealistic water cryptid of Lake Duobuzhe in Tibet. One such beast was supposedly killed in 1972 by some Chinese soldiers, and was said to have an ox-like body, hippo-like skin, turtle-like legs and a pair of short curly horns on its head.

For many years, one of Australia's most enigmatic water beasts was the 'migo', allegedly resembling a giant aquatic lizard and inhabiting Lake Dakataua on the island of New Britain in the Bismarck Archipelago, east of New Guinea. In 1994, however, after accompanying a Japanese team to New Britain, where they succeeded in filming a migo, US cryptozoologist Dr Roy Mackal announced that what was being witnessed was nothing more than three crocodiles engaged in a mating ritual. Also dethroned in this area of the world was the 'ri' of New Ireland, a supposedly MERMAID-like creature that was actually a dugong. Australia is apparently home to at least two species of BUNYIP, and New Guinea's Lake Sentani is known to contain an unidentified species of shark, though this is most probably the bull shark *Carcharhinus leucas*, which is confirmed from New Guinea's Lake Jamoer, as well as Central America's Lake Nicaragua.

South America's most famous lake monster is the so-called 'Patagonian plesiosaur', a swan-necked cryptid reported from Patagonia's White Lake that was unsuccessfully sought during the 1920s. No less mysterious is the 'sawtooth' dolphin not only seen but also filmed and photographed on two separate occasions during the mid-1990s by English writer-explorer Jeremy Wade in and near a lake beside a southern Brazilian tributary of the Amazon. Pink in colour, it resembled the bouto, a familiar species of South American river dolphin, except that instead of possessing a simple triangular dorsal fin, this mystery dolphin sported a precisely-notched version resembling the edge of a circular saw. As with Africa and Asia, South America has hosted reports of lake monsters resembling sauropod dinosaurs, as well as a water beast of Lake Titicaca said to be 3.7 metres (12 feet) long and variously likened to a seal or a manatee.

Perhaps the most extraordinary lake monster of all, however, was reported not from any remote tropical body of inland water but from a lake in Ireland. Lough Dubh is situated in County Galway. While schoolteacher Alphonsus Mullaney and his son were fishing at this lake in March 1962, they felt something tug at the end of their line. When they attempted to haul their catch out of the water their line snapped – which was apparently very fortunate, as they later described the creature 'that got away' as a monstrous beast as big as a cow, with a face like a hippopotamus but with a horn on its snout like a rhinoceros. After hearing their tale a number of locals returned to the scene to seek this beast, but nothing was found.

Whether an unknown species of aquatic rhinoceros remains reclusively ensconced in an Irish lake remains a matter for much conjecture, but what cannot be disputed is that a sizeable number of lakes around the world harbour animate mysteries, some of which may conceivably constitute zoological species still awaiting formal scientific identification and documentation.

Lake Okanagan monster

A lake monster said to inhabit Lake Okanagan, Canada; popularly known as Ogopogo, some believe that it may be a modern-day descendant of prehistoric serpent-like whales known as zeuglodonts.

One of the closest encounters with a freshwater CRYPTID reported in modern times took place one morning in mid-July 1974, when a Mrs B Clark was swimming in Lake Okanagan, a large body of freshwater in Canada's British Columbia. She later said that she was near a raft-like diving platform when something big and heavy bumped against her legs under the water. Frightened, she said that she dashed towards the raft, got on it and looked back into the water to see what had bumped into her. She claims that she then saw an extraordinary creature that looked and acted like a whale but was long, narrow and snake-like in shape, moving through the clear water via a series of vertical undulations that reminded her of the movements of a caterpillar. However, it had a whale-like tail. Clark estimated the creature's total length at 7.6–9.2 metres (around 25–30 feet), its width at 0.9–1.2 metres (around 3–4 feet), and stated that its body was hairless, smooth and dark grey in colour, with light stripes on its back and light round spots on its tail. She did not see its head, as the creature was swimming directly away from her throughout her sighting, at a speed she estimated at 4.8–8.1 kilometres per hour (3–5 miles per hour).

A model of Lake Okanagan's monster, 'Ogopogo', at Kelowna, British Columbia.
(© TopFoto/Fortean)

Once her 'sighting' became public, it was noted that only mammals undulate vertically when swimming – reptiles and fish undulate horizontally.

Clark believes that she witnessed the cryptid known locally as Ogopogo – the monster of Lake Okanagan. Over 200 relatively consistent sightings of a mysterious creature at this lake have been collected by Ogopogo's most diligent investigator, Arlene Gaal. Those that claim to have seen Ogopogo's head have variously described it as horse-like or sheep-like, bearing a pair of small ear-like or horn-like projections. The monster appears to have long been known to the local Native Americans, who call it 'naitaka' ('lake monster'); bizarrely, it owes its Western name, Ogopogo, to an English music-hall song from 1924 entitled 'The Ogo-Pogo', telling of a pixie-headed, banjo-playing monster from Hindustan. In addition to reported sightings, several photographs and video films of alleged Ogopogos have been made public, including a 90-second film clip obtained by a documentary team on 18 August 2002. This shows a dark hump passing through the water.

The most popular cryptozoological identity for Ogopogo and similar serpent-like water monsters is an evolved, modern-day zeuglodont species. Believed to have become extinct around 30 million years ago, zeuglodonts were remarkably elongate, open sea and coastal whales, totally unlike any species known to exist today. Traditionally, palaeontological reconstructions of these creatures portrayed them as exceedingly flexible beasts – genuine SEA SERPENTS, in fact. However, in recent times, this reconstruction has been replaced by one that depicts zeuglodonts with a very rigid, inflexible backbone incapable of yielding the vertical undulations so frequently reported for Ogopogo and similar cryptids. Yet if the latter creatures are indeed living zeuglodonts, this means that the zeuglodont lineage has undergone 30-odd million years of continued evolution since its most recent fossil species. This is more than enough time for evolution to have created a much more flexible zeuglodont backbone, as well as a neck capable of being raised vertically – and also for such animals to have invaded large bodies of fresh water, just as dolphins have invaded rivers in Asia and South America, yielding several unique freshwater species found nowhere else. However, the certain existence of monsters such as Ogopogo remains to be proved. See also LAKE MONSTERS.

Lake Seljordsvatnet monster

Dubbed Selma, this large lake monster, said to inhabit Norway's Lake Seljordsvatnet, has apparently been traced on sonar several times in recent years.

Claims of sightings of the monster of Lake Seljordsvatnet, in Norway's Telemark County, have been reported for over 250 years. In the earliest report, dating back to 1750, it was described as a 'sea horse' by local resident Gunleid Andersson-Verpe, who claimed that it attacked him and overturned his boat while he was rowing across the lake. A century later, a more detailed description of the monster (known locally as Selma) was provided by Captain Hans Klokkarstogo, who apparently spied it, as did several passengers, while taking his paddle-steamer across the lake. He stated that it had the head and mane of a horse, and a fish-like tail, with a very elongate serpentine body. Since then, reports of Selma have variously described it as hump-backed, crocodile-like, deer-headed, black in colour, having two front flippers and ranging in length from 4–53.5 metres (13–175.5 feet).

Not widely known outside Scandinavia until the 1970s, Selma's fame spread at that time owing to a series of intriguing sonar traces obtained below the lake's surface by an investigating team named GUST (Global Underwater Search Team), headed by Swedish cryptozoologist Jan-Ove Sundberg. On one occasion GUST's sonar equipment detected three very large submerged objects moving on parallel courses, just two days after recording one such object moving underwater to within 9 metres (29.5 feet) of their boat. In 2000, the sonar equipment of a new GUST expedition (led once more by Sundberg) detected two apparently animate objects each measuring over 18 metres (59 feet) long, swimming just above the bottom of the lake. GUST has also obtained some dim above-surface footage of an animal swimming at twilight towards the shore, plus a recording of a peculiar noise, recorded by sophisticated underwater hydrophones, that Sundberg likened to 'a cross between a snorting horse and an eating pig'. Many now accept that an animal species of unusual size does exist in Lake Seljordsvatnet, but its identity currently remains undetermined. See also LAKE MONSTERS.

Lake Storsjön monster

Sweden's long-necked 'water cow', noted for its enormous fin-like ears.

Known locally as Storsjöodjuret, this alleged denizen of Lake Storsjön in Jämtland County is Sweden's most famous CRYPTID, with reported sightings dating back to 1635. Cryptozoologist Ivan T Sanderson referred to it as a Swedish 'water cow', but, from the descriptions of those who believe they have seen it, its general form is more reminiscent of the LOCH NESS MONSTER and other long-necked LAKE MONSTERS than any bovine beast. It is described as being very large – up to 14 metres (46 feet) in length – with shiny greenish skin, a small horse-like head, very large eyes, a thin neck at least 3.1 metres (10 feet) long, two pairs of large flipper-like limbs, a powerful tail,

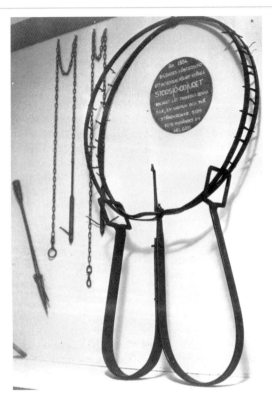

Some of the tools made by the people of the Swedish town of Östersund, which were used in an attempt to catch the Lake Storsjön monster.
(© TopFoto)

humps along its back and truly immense ears or ear-like fins. It is said that these ears or fins, resembling small snails, can be laid tight onto the neck, and have an estimated diameter of 1 metre (3 feet). This has led some cryptozoologists to suggest that it is more likely that they are actually just a portion of a much larger dorsal crest whose remaining sections are hidden beneath the water. According to eyewitnesses, this monster moves across the lake at great speed, creating a sizeable wake, and is able to make very sharp turns.

In 1894, an amusement park owner called Maria Helin attempted to snare the monster using a specially constructed cage. She was helped by various residents of Östersund, a town on the eastern shore of the lake, but the attempt did not meet with success. More than a century later, sightings continue to be reported. One typical encounter was reported by Elin and Cecilia Hemreus. They claim that on 8 August 1997 they saw a long-necked, horse-headed creature just 9 metres (29.5 feet) away from them – close enough for them to discern its black eyes and a single arched loop of its body, which bore large round scales like armour plates.

Lamb Inn

The location of an 18th-century case of a biting poltergeist in Bristol.

The alleged POLTERGEIST activity at the Lamb Inn, Lawfords-Gate, Bristol, started in November 1761 and lasted until December 1762, making it contemporaneous with the COCK LANE GHOST. Affecting a family named Giles, the phenomena were said to focus particularly on two young sisters, 13-year-old Molly and 8-year-old Dobby. The first incidents involved strange scratching and rapping sounds from the girls' bedrooms, followed by the mysterious movement of various objects. Many of the events described were what came to be thought of as 'routine' poltergeist disturbances, but a remarkable feature was a series of assaults upon the two girls. Both Molly and Dobby were said to suffer severely from pinches and bites from an unseen assailant. More seriously, pins were thrust into the girls by some undetected agency and they were repeatedly cut; on one occasion Molly received more than 40 cuts described as:

> … all about two inches and a half long, and about the thickness of a shilling deep; the skin not jagged, but smooth, as if cut with a penknife.

Events were investigated by a Mr Henry Durbin who later wrote a pamphlet on the case which was posthumously published in 1800. Durbin and other investigators made efforts to observe the phenomena under conditions which excluded fraud. On 30 January 1761, he witnessed a bite mark appear on Dobby's shoulder:

> I saw Dobby wiping her hands in a towel, while I was talking to her, she cried out [and] was bitten in the neck. I looked and saw the mark of teeth, about eighteen, and wet with spittle.

As with the Cock Lane ghost and the later ENFIELD POLTERGEIST, the poltergeist appeared to show signs of intelligence and was said to engage in communication with the family and investigators by means of scratching noises. The messages declared that the disturbances were the work of a WITCH. Eventually the family resorted to sympathetic magic (see MAGIC, SYMPATHETIC) and after following the advice of a 'cunning woman' the disturbances ceased. Although nearly 250 years old, the Lamb Inn case is considered by many modern researchers to be evidential because of the detail set down in the account by Durbin and the resemblance to other cases involving biting poltergeists, both historic and modern.

Lambton worm *see* DRAGON

Lammas *see* LUGHNASADH

lampadomancy

Divination by interpreting the movements of and shapes formed by the flame of a candle or oil lamp.

In lampadomancy (Greek *lampein*, to shine, and *manteiā*, divination), also sometimes called lychnomancy, the flame of a candle or oil lamp is stared at directly and its movements and shapes are interpreted. It is taken as a good sign if the flame has a single point, but bad luck if it has two points. A flame that bends is supposed to be an omen of illness, while sparks mean that news can be expected, and it is a very bad sign if the flame goes out altogether.

This form of divination was popular in ancient Egypt. In the ancient Egyptian method, the reading was said to have been performed at midday in a darkened room lit by a single stone lamp filled with 'oasis oil' – probably a kind of clear palm oil – but this lamp must not be red in colour, since red was the colour of Set, the god of evil, and might draw infernal demons. It was common for Egyptian lamp diviners to paint their eyes with magically powerful colours such as blue and green, and with herbal substances believed to facilitate the seeing of visions, like mugwort and vervain.

Other forms of lampadomancy involve holding a sheet of paper over the flame and reading the spots of carbon deposited on it, or using the lamp to attract spirits to the flames in the hope of consulting them on what the future holds.

landing traces

Physical evidence that has allegedly been left behind on some of the rare occasions when a UFO has reportedly been seen to land. Such traces offer the potential to determine whether a UFO sighting involved something that was physically real and even the chance to gain valuable clues as to its nature.

A farmer from Langenburg in Saskatchewan, Canada, reported that, while he was harvesting his crop of oilseed rape (known as canola in Canada) on the morning of 1 September 1974, he noticed five small grey domes hovering just over the field. As the domes climbed upwards, one after another, a mist or vapour poured from underneath them, the blast flattening the crop below. When the UFOs had gone the farmer found that the oilseed rape was 'swirled' into clockwise circles several feet across, with the strands matted together – outside the affected area it was still standing quite normally. The physical marks left behind were very much like the CROP CIRCLES that

received a great deal of attention across the Atlantic a decade later – however, the case illustrates a type of landing trace has long been connected with UFO CLOSE ENCOUNTERS all over the world.

Ted Phillips, a researcher for CUFOS (Center for UFO Studies), conducted a detailed investigation into this case. The following year he produced a catalogue of several hundred landing-trace reports and found that there were many similarities among the descriptions. Indeed, claims that 'swirled' patterns of this type have been left on the ground by a departing UFO are particularly common – they have reportedly been discovered in grass, ice fields and even dust. The British ALIEN ABDUCTION case involving ALAN GODFREY included a description of an almost identical effect on a wet road surface.

Physical traces of this type are particularly interesting because they provide strong evidence that something real has occurred at the location of an alleged sighting. However, even assuming that the possibility that they have been hoaxed can be eliminated, they are still not sufficient to conclusively establish the past presence of an ALIEN flying machine – for example, they could equally be due to one of a range of UNIDENTIFIED ATMOSPHERIC PHENOMENA or rare meteorological occurrences, such as WHIRLWINDS or the hypothetical PLASMA VORTEX.

There have been some attempts to obtain further data by carrying out a thorough analysis of the ground where the traces are left. These have particularly centred on establishing whether the area is displaying the lasting effects of exposure to intense radiation or strong electromagnetic fields. In one case from West Palm Beach, Florida, on 19 August 1952, a UFO reportedly hovered low above a scoutmaster and sent a beam of light down to the ground. When the plants in the area were sampled by members of the PROJECT BLUE BOOK team, they were found to have been burnt at the roots but not above the ground. The Air Force chemists involved in the research were bemused by this and suggested that they must have been subjected to an alternating magnetic field, which induced an electric current in the roots but not in the stems. A more recent study might also have considered microwave radiation as another potential cause of this effect.

Sightings supposedly supported by landing traces are relatively rare (less than one in 500 cases involve such claims), but they are of great interest to UFO researchers and are considered by most to be significant enough to warrant rapid investigation.

lands, lost *see* LOST LANDS

Lao Tzu (Laozi) (6th century BC)

Chinese philosopher and sage who was said to have lived in the 6th century BC; he is traditionally credited with writing the Tao Te Ching *and is regarded as the founder of Taoism.*

Lao Tzu, the Chinese philosopher and sage credited with the authorship of the TAO TE CHING and regarded as the founding father of TAOISM, is a legendary figure whose historical existence is much debated. According to tradition, he was born in 604 BC, in the Ku Prefecture of the Chinese state of Chu, and was appointed by King Wu as head librarian and archivist in the Imperial Library, where he immersed himself in the study of history, philosophy and literature, gaining much insight along the way. There, he was said to have met Confucius, who had gone to the library to study some scrolls, and over the next few months, they discussed social conduct and order, ethics and morality, and ritual and propriety – the cornerstones of Confucius's philosophy. Lao Tzu strongly opposed what he saw as hollow practices, and held that a person's conduct should be governed, not by rigid laws, as Confucius taught, but by instinct and conscience. The story goes that Confucius, awed by the older man's intellect, likened him to a mysterious dragon, and learnt much more from him than he did from the scrolls in the library.

Lao Tzu's wise counsel was said to have attracted many followers, but he refused to set his teachings down in writing, believing that once wisdom was written down, it was in danger of becoming dogma. He wished his philosophy to remain a natural way of life characterized by goodness, humility and serenity. However, when he was 80, it is said that he became disillusioned by the court and saddened that men were unwilling to follow the path of natural goodness which he wished to teach them, and he left his position as librarian and travelled west through Qin to go and live in the desert. At the westernmost gate of the Great Wall, he was said to have met a guard called Yin Xi, who persuaded him to record his teachings before he left, and he dictated them on his journey before disappearing into the desert without trace. Thus was written the *Tao Te Ching*, or 'The Way and Its Power', a small book which totalled a mere 5,000 characters, consisting of 81 sayings. Lao Tzu is said to have been searching for a way of life that would avoid the feudal warfare and conflicts which constantly disrupted society during his lifetime. The *Tao Te Ching* sets forth the seminal Taoist doctrine that living in accordance with nature and its laws is the way to truth and freedom. It teaches self-sufficiency, simplicity and detachment, and an instinctive unity with nature.

Scholars have debated the details of this traditional story of Lao Tzu's life. Some say that if he was a historical figure, it is more likely that he lived around the 4th century BC, during the Warring States periods, than the 6th century BC. Others hold that the *Tao Te Ching* was compiled some 300 years after Lao Tzu is credited with having written it, and that he was merely a fictitious character created by its real authors, to make its origins seem more mysterious and ancient. This theory dismisses the discussions he is said to have had with Confucius as an invention by Taoists attempting to give more weight to their school of philosophy. The name 'Lao Tzu' is an honorific title which translates as 'old master'; according to some sources, his real name may have been Li Er, while, in honour of his achievements during life, he was given the posthumous name Dān, meaning 'mysterious'. During the Li Tang dynasty, in order to establish Lao Tzu as an ancestor of the imperial family, he was also given the posthumous name of Emperor Xuanyuan, meaning 'profoundly elementary'. He became a culture hero and a popular deity in the Taoist religion's pantheon.

La Salette *see* MARIAN APPARITIONS

Latoon fairy tree

A lone hawthorn bush in Latoon, County Clare, Ireland, believed to have been a stopping-point on a fairy path; Eddie Lenihan, a traditional storyteller and folklorist, successfully headed a campaign to save it from being uprooted to make way for a bypass, but it was vandalized in 2003.

In Latoon near Newmarket-on-Fergus in County Clare, Ireland, there stands a lone hawthorn tree known as the Latoon fairy tree. According to Irish legend, lone hawthorns have a strong association with the LITTLE PEOPLE, and should not be destroyed for fear of incurring their wrath. The Latoon hawthorn was believed to be a marker and stopping-point for the FAIRIES of Munster on their way back from doing battle with the fairies of Connaught, and when in 2002 plans were announced for the Ennis bypass which would have involved the uprooting of the Latoon fairy tree, there was a public outcry, and Eddie Lenihan, a County Clare folklorist, author and traditional storyteller, successfully campaigned to save the tree, warning of the bad luck which would befall those who worked on and used the new road if the fairy tree was destroyed to make way for it. The town planners agreed to divert the road around the tree, and even built a wooden fence round it to protect it. The tree became a popular tourist attraction until, in the summer of 2003, it was vandalized with a chainsaw; all its branches were cut off and it was reduced to an almost bare stump. However, the tree subsequently began to grow new shoots, and it became apparent that it had managed to survive the attack. See also FAIRY TREE.

Laveau, Marie (c.1794–c.1881)
The feared and respected 'Voodoo Queen' of New Orleans.

Marie Laveau was famous in the 19th century as the 'Voodoo Queen' of New Orleans. It is almost impossible to say now which of the many accounts of her are true, which contain a grain of truth and which are completely fictional. One of many stories told about her is that she would dance with her snake, called Zombi, wrapped around her.

Born of a white father (possibly a wealthy plantation owner) and a black mother (possibly a slave), Marie Laveau was raised a Roman Catholic; she later became a VOUDUN priestess, but apparently saw no conflict between the two. Following her husband's disappearance and presumed death in 1820 she became a hairdresser to rich white women in New Orleans. Between her husband and her later lover she is said to have borne 15 children.

Partly through her upper-class hairdressing clientele and their servants, but also through a huge network of informants, Laveau knew much of what went on in New Orleans, including at the highest social and political levels. It is clear that much of her supposed magical power came from this knowledge. She was respected and feared throughout the city, and many came to her for charms and potions, or for other magical help.

Her most famous case, around 1830, was saving a young Creole man from being found guilty of murder. The man's father, although sceptical, approached Laveau for help. He had no money, but offered her his house if she could save his son. She apparently placed AMULETS around the courtroom (though she probably also intimidated a witness to give helpful evidence), and the young man was found not guilty and freed. His father kept to his word and gave Laveau his house.

Once she became the undisputed 'Voodoo Queen' of New Orleans she presided over the Voudun dances held each Sunday in Congo Square. She is also said to have run a high-class brothel for wealthy white men wanting sex with beautiful black or part-black women.

One of Laveau's children was a daughter, also called Marie, who bore an amazing likeness to her mother, and was also a Voudun priestess. This is undoubtedly the explanation for Laveau's supposed ability to be in two places at one time (BILOCATION), and for reports of Laveau still being seen walking the streets of New Orleans long after her death. It is also

The grave of New Orleans 'Voodoo Queen', Marie Laveau. Many pilgrims to the grave mark it with an X, and leave small offerings or coins. (© TopFoto/Fortean)

quite possible that many of the tales told about Marie Laveau, the mother, are actually about Marie Laveau, the daughter.

LaVey, Anton Szander (1930–97)
US writer, musician and founder and High Priest of the Church of Satan.

Anton Szander LaVey was born Howard Stanton Levey in Chicago, but spent most of his life in California. From an early age he read horror literature and science fiction pulp magazines, developing an interest in dark legends and historical characters such as Alessandro di Cagliostro (founder of EGYPTIAN RITE FREEMASONRY) and RASPUTIN. He dropped out of high school, and always claimed that he then spent some time working in circuses and carnivals. Apparently, it was seeing the same men watch the bawdy Saturday night shows and then attend church meetings the next morning that formed the basis of LaVey's cynical views on religion. He also worked as an organist in various bars and nightclubs, before moving back to San Francisco, where for a time he was a police photographer, and then, to avoid the draft during the Korean War, he enrolled as a criminology major at San Francisco College. These experiences gave him further, grim insights into human nature. In the 1950s, he worked as a 'psychic investigator' of crank calls referred to him by the police, and gained some local celebrity.

His studies of the OCCULT led LaVey to dismiss white magic (see MAGIC, WHITE) as sanctimonious, and he criticized many religions, especially Christianity and the Eastern Mystical Traditions, for forcing unnatural laws on humans and causing them unnecessary guilt and remorse. He stressed the need for a religion which celebrated the individual as a carnal being with desires which needed to be fulfilled. He began giving Friday night lectures on his research and his philosophy to a group of like-minded associates, which he called his 'Magic Circle', and it was suggested that he had the basis for a new religion. Accordingly, on WALPURGISNACHT (30 April) 1966, Lavey ritualistically shaved his head, declared the founding of the CHURCH OF SATAN, and proclaimed 1966 as 'the year One, Anno Satanas' – the first year of the Age of Satan. He claimed no supernatural inspiration for this new religion of Laveyan Satanism, but rather, synthesized his unique philosophy, based on his research and understanding of human nature, with principles of materialism and individualism. After he performed the first Satanic wedding in 1967, he and his church attracted a great deal of media attention, and he was dubbed 'the Black Pope'. He was the subject of many newspaper and magazine articles, and made appearances on television talk shows.

Lavey was also an accomplished musician, and he again brought his philosophy to the attention of the public with the release of an album called *The Satanic Mass* (1968). The cover artwork of the album featured a graphic he called the 'Sigil of BAPHOMET' – a goat's head inside an inverted pentagram, circled with the Hebrew word 'Leviathan'. This image has since become a symbol of SATANISM all over the world.

In 1969, LaVey published *The Satanic Bible*, which remains the chief source for the contemporary Satanist movement. In 1971, he followed this with *The Compleat Witch* (re-released as *The Satanic Witch* in 1989), a manual on the reading and manipulation of people, which brought together the teachings from his 'Witches' Workshops'. LaVey's other works include *The Satanic Rituals* (1972), a collection of rituals that he gathered from Satanic traditions in cultures all over the world.

Anton LaVey died on 29 October 1996, but in keeping with his lifelong showmanship, his family listed his death date as being two days later – on HALLOWE'EN.

laying-on of hands

A spiritual practice found throughout the world in various forms, especially in Christianity, where it is used as a symbolic and formal means of invoking the Holy Spirit to confer blessings or authority, and to heal; also applied to various secular types of energy healing which do not necessarily involve physical contact.

The spiritual or religious practice of the laying-on of hands is found in various forms all over the world, but it is most closely associated with the Christian Church, in which it is used as both a symbolic and a formal means of invoking the Holy Spirit for various purposes: the ordination of priests, ministers and other church officials, baptism and confirmation and healing.

The Christian tradition of healing by the laying-on of hands has its precedent in the various biblical accounts of Jesus placing his hands on sick people before healing them, and at his ascension, he told his disciples that, in his name, believers would be able to heal by laying their hands on afflicted people. In the New Testament, the laying-on of hands was associated with the receiving of the Holy Spirit, and it was a common practice in the early Church, and was considered a sacrament. Modern Christian healing services usually include prayer and the cleansing of the spirit to create a union with the Holy Spirit before the ritual laying-on of hands is performed, and many televangelists also claim to heal in this way.

The term is also used in a non-religious context to refer to various types of ALTERNATIVE MEDICINE known collectively as 'energy healing' or 'energy-balancing therapies', which may or may not involve physical contact. For example, in THERAPEUTIC TOUCH the healer is said to manipulate the energy field or AURA of patients without touching them, in order to correct blockages and imbalances in the body's energy flow. In REIKI the practitioner is similarly believed to tap into a universal source of energy which then flows from their hands into the subject's body, either by placing the hands on or over the body. See also FAITH HEALING.

lead

A heavy bluish-grey metal, thought to have certain magical properties; the oldest of the seven metals recognized in traditional alchemy.

Classical ALCHEMY traditionally recognized seven metals: tin, GOLD, copper, MERCURY, silver, IRON and lead. Each of these seven metals was linked with one of the seven 'planets', and lead was associated with Saturn. Lead was the first metal to be extracted from ores, and is seen as the first and oldest of the seven alchemical metals. Its magical ELEMENT is EARTH; it is considered to be the 'basest' of the base metals, and was usually the one chosen by the alchemists for attempts at TRANSMUTATION into gold. It has a long tradition of use in magic, and in ancient Greece and Rome, tablets of lead were ritually charged and then inscribed with WORDS OF POWER, usually in curses; it was believed that the lasting power of lead ensured that the negative spell would remain in effect for a long time. Lead is also known for its magically protective properties, and if placed near the entrance to a house, is believed to prevent negativity from gaining access. Lead is also used in a form of divination known as molybdomancy, in which molten lead is poured into water; the noises it makes are interpreted, as are the shapes the lead forms as it cools.

Leadbeater, Charles W(ebster) (1854–1934)

English theosophist, writer, alleged clairvoyant, leader of the Liberal Catholic Church and discoverer of the Indian spiritual teacher Krishnamurti.

Charles W Leadbeater was born in Cheshire in 1854 (although Leadbeater himself gave his birth date as 1847, genealogical research has confirmed that 1854 is the correct date). He was ordained as an Anglican priest in 1879 and in 1883 he joined the THEOSOPHICAL SOCIETY. With Annie Besant, MADAME BLAVATSKY's successor as leader, Leadbeater changed the emphasis of the group away from esoteric Buddhism towards esoteric Christianity.

Accused of pederasty, Leadbeater was defrocked as a priest in 1906; he also left the Theosophical Society, but rejoined in 1909. That year he discovered the 14-year-old KRISHNAMURTI, and announced that he would become the Maitreya, the long-awaited earthly buddha. It is widely believed that Leadbeater, as his mentor, wrote Krishnamurti's book, *At the Feet of the Master* (1910).

In 1915, Leadbeater moved to Australia where he met James Ingall Wedgwood, who ordained him as a priest and consecrated him as a bishop of the LIBERAL CATHOLIC CHURCH; he succeeded Wedgwood as Presiding Bishop of the Church in 1922. The Liberal Catholic Church, with its WANDERING BISHOPS, traditionalist rites and liberal theology, became significant in the 20th-century development of the WESTERN MYSTERY TRADITION.

Leadbeater claimed to be clairvoyant (see CLAIRVOYANCE) and was a prolific writer on this and many other topics; his published works include *Clairvoyance* (1899), *Occult Chemistry* (1908, with Annie Besant), *A Textbook of Theosophy* (1912) and *The Chakras* (1927).

Left-Hand Path

A religion or spiritual system characterized by a belief in free thought, a rejection of absolutism and moralism and the paramount importance of personal development and self-empowerment; often identified with Satanism and, erroneously, with occultism in general.

The origin of the term 'Left-Hand Path' as used in the West is uncertain, but it is thought to have been introduced by MADAME BLAVATSKY and the theosophists, who were influenced by Eastern traditions; Tantra, which has roots in both Hinduism and Buddhism, is often divided by its practitioners into two different paths, whose names translate as 'Right-Hand Path' and 'Left-Hand Path'. Blavatsky adopted the term 'Right-Hand Path' to denote the self-denying spiritual systems of which she approved, and 'Left-Hand Path' to describe those she considered 'immoral'. The exact meaning of the terms have varied over time, but the Left-Hand Path is now almost exclusively used by its self-proclaimed followers to denote a religion or spiritual system which is solitary, individualistic and personal, and which stresses self-development and self-empowerment; the most commonly listed features of the Left-Hand Path are an emphasis on free thought, rather than on the worship of deities, and the rejection of absolutism, dogma and strict moral codes. There is also a strong emphasis on personal belief, and Left-Hand Path systems in general do not claim to be the only valid religion, or the best one, or to actively seek new converts. All forms of SATANISM are usually considered to be Left-Hand Path, and the term is sometimes used loosely, and less accurately, to refer to any NEW AGE movement considered OCCULT.

legends

Traditional stories distinguished from myths or folk tales by the fact that they are attached to a historical event, person or place and are often claimed to be true (or are at least thought to contain an element of truth).

The word 'legend' (from the Latin *legenda*, meaning 'to be read') was originally used in connection with mottos or inscriptions, but it came to be understood more widely to mean a traditional story of a saint's life, and later, as a general description of stories lying somewhere between myths and folk tales. Legends are usually understood to be distinguished from MYTHOLOGY or FOLKLORE by the fact that they are connected to a historical event, person or place, are often told as true stories and are believed to contain a kernel of truth and to be based, however tenuously, on historical fact. However, there is often a blurring of the myth/folk tale/legend distinction, since some myths (such as those from ancient Greece) include references to historical figures and places like Achilles and Corinth, as well as to gods and mythological creatures. It could also be argued that all are examples of folklore.

Before the advent of the printing press, legends were often passed on orally, sometimes by professional storytellers. Some, such as the legends of KING ARTHUR and his knights, were handed down through poems and ballads. The earliest surviving complete epic poem written in English, the Anglo-Saxon story of the southern Swedish hero Beowulf, is dated at around AD 1000, but it is thought to have been originally composed some 300 years earlier. Although the poem is a work of fiction, which relates the hero's slaying of the monster Grendel and his mother and, later, a DRAGON, it also mentions a historic event – King Hygelac's raid on Frisia, which took place around AD 516 – and many scholars believe some other people and events in the legend were also real. Another legend which comes to us through ballads is that of Thomas the Rhymer (known as 'True Thomas' for his gift of PROPHECY), a 13th-century poet who was said to have been swept away by the Faerie Queen into fairyland, to be her lover for seven years.

Legends usually involve a heroic character, a fantastic place or a fabulous beast. The most famous British legendary character is King Arthur, whose historical basis is the subject of many theories. In medieval times, the Arthurian legend became entwined with another legend, that of the HOLY GRAIL, which became the object of a quest by Arthur's knights. The next most prominent British legendary hero is Robin Hood, although the only source for his historical existence is a ballad cycle thought to have begun in the 14th century, and he may be an entirely fictitious character. Other legendary characters are the BRAHAN SEER, FAUST, HERNE THE HUNTER and Roland, the 8th-century Frankish commander in Charlemagne's service, whose legendary status was established in an 11th-century poem called *The Song of Roland*.

Many cryptozoological creatures (see CRYPTOZOOLOGY), of which stories are told in relation to specific locations, might be regarded as legendary – the stories are offered as truth but, in the absence of indisputable evidence, they have something of the status of folklore. The story of the LOCH NESS MONSTER, which began with the tale of a sighting by St Columba in the 6th century, is a long-standing example. The same can also apply to places, such as ATLANTIS, the ancient island said by Plato to have been destroyed by a natural disaster 9,000 years before his time; El Dorado, a golden city believed to be located somewhere in South America, and which inspired many expeditions to find it (notably by Sir Walter Raleigh); and more recently, the BERMUDA TRIANGLE,

in which a number of ships and planes are said to have 'mysteriously' disappeared.

The enduring appeal of fantastic-but-allegedly-true stories is attested to by the popularity and pervasive nature of the modern URBAN LEGEND.

lemniscate

A symbol (∞) resembling a figure 8 laid on its side, used in mathematics to represent infinity and as an occult symbol of infinity or eternity.

In mathematics, the lemniscate (∞) is used as a symbol to denote infinity. The term itself was first used by the 17th-century Swiss mathematician Jacob Bernoulli, who described this shape as a 'lemniscus' (from the Greek *lemniskos*, meaning 'a ribbon'), but it was the English mathematician John Wallis who first used it as a mathematical symbol for infinity, in 1655.

However, the esoteric use of the symbol can be traced back to ancient times; similar figures have been found in Tibetan rock carvings, and it was described both by Plato and by St Thomas Aquinas, who used it to depict the circular movement of the ANGELS. It is also found in the divination tables of the Elizabethan magician and alchemist JOHN DEE. The symbol came to the West through Arabic numerals; in Indian religions, it stood for infinity and completeness, since it was made up of a clockwise and an anticlockwise circle, that is, a male, solar, right-handed one united with a female, lunar, left-handed one. Outside of mathematics, the lemniscate is seen most often in occult contexts. It is regarded as symbolizing the higher spiritual powers, eternal life, a harmonious interaction between the conscious and subconscious and dominion over the physical plane. The figure of the Magician, the first card in the major ARCANA of the TAROT, is often represented with a lemniscate above his head, or in the form of a wide-brimmed hat, to symbolize the balance of forces and the divine powers which he attempts to control. Another symbol of infinity, the ouroboros, a snake with its tail in its mouth, is sometimes shown looped into this shape.

Lemuria

Legendary lost land beneath the Indian Ocean.

In 1864, the British ornithologist Philip Sclater (1829–1913) published his theory that a stretch of land had at one time connected Madagascar with South-East Asia. In his opinion this would explain the existence of lemurs in both Madagascar and India but not in Africa. In honour of this humble mammal he named the lost land, which had presumably sunk beneath what is now the Indian Ocean, Lemuria.

The German biologist E H Haeckel (1834–1919) took this theory further, suggesting that the sunken land was where the human race had begun (the site of the Garden of Eden) and that its inundation would explain gaps in the fossil record of mankind.

Nineteenth-century occultists took up the idea of Lemuria and suggested that survivors of the original inhabitants still existed, possessed of superhuman qualities and living secretly in various parts of the world. The theosophist MADAME BLAVATSKY believed that ATLANTIS was peopled by inhabitants who succeeded those of Lemuria. Some people also used the name MU for Lemuria.

The study of plate tectonics, with its concept of the movement of continental plates, nowadays gives a more likely explanation for the widespread distribution of similar species than a legend of lost continents.

Leo

In astrology, the fifth sign of the zodiac, between Cancer and Virgo.

In Western ASTROLOGY, Leo is the sign of ZODIAC for those who are born between 24 July and 23 August. The symbol for Leo is the lion, and the sign is ruled by the sun. Leonians are said to be ambitious, energetic and courageous, although they can be arrogant. Leo is believed to be a fire sign, having an affinity with the element FIRE.

leprechaun

A small mischievous fairy of Irish folklore.

The most famous of the fairy folk in Irish folklore is the mischievous leprechaun. His name probably comes from the Middle Irish *luchorpan*, meaning 'little body'. Said to be shoemakers by trade, but only making footwear for other fairies, leprechauns never work on a pair of shoes – only on a single shoe. They are usually described as wearing a green jerkin with silver buttons, silver-buckled shoes and often a three-cornered hat, on which they sometimes turn upside down and spin. Leprechauns are thought to live under the roots of trees or in ruined castles. Every leprechaun has a pot of gold hidden somewhere, and if captured, can be forced to tell where it is buried or to grant his captor three wishes. They are said to be very solitary FAIRIES, only socializing with others of their kind at parties, when they get very drunk. They are also said to love to dance to Irish folk music, and if someone plays music to a leprechaun, he will not be able to stop dancing until the music stops, so tradition states that one way to gain power over him is to play music until he is so exhausted that he promises to do anything if you will only stop. Other traditional ways of capturing a leprechaun are to see him before he sees you or to catch his glance and outstare him. However, it is useless to try and grab him, because he will fade away at once, still there, but no longer visible. Even after being caught, the wily leprechaun may be able to trick his captor by distracting his attention and vanishing as soon as he takes his eyes off him. If he has been forced to grant three wishes, he may manage to lure an unwary human into making a fourth wish, whereupon he will lose all he has wished for. And in one story, a captured leprechaun who has to show a farmer where his pot of gold is buried still has the last laugh; the farmer marks the spot by tying a red ribbon round a ragwort plant growing there, but when he returns with a shovel, every ragwort plant in the field

A 'leprechaun crossing' sign at a viewpoint in Killarney National Park. (© Richard Cummins/Corbis)

has a red ribbon tied round it. Leprechauns are said to be quick-witted except when drunk, and to love riddles and word games.

Lethbridge, T(homas) C(harles) (1901–71)

English archaeologist, writer and psychic researcher, pioneer in the scientific study of dowsing.

T C Lethbridge was born in the West Country, of a well-to-do family. He was educated at Wellington College, and went up to Trinity College, Cambridge, at the age of 17. It was there that his lifelong interest in archaeological fieldwork was kindled. He went on numerous expeditions, including three to the Arctic, and between 1937 and 1954 he published a unique series of books based on the results of his explorations. At the same time he was becoming more and more interested in the archaeology of Anglo-Saxon England, and was eventually appointed as honorary Keeper of Anglo-Saxon antiquities at the Archaeological Museum in Cambridge. He led several excavations for the Cambridge Antiquarian Society and published several successful books on British history during this period.

However, Lethbridge never felt very much at home among the mainstream archaeological establishment, and, in 1948, he published *Merlin's Island*, a book aimed at a more popular audience, which was not well received by academic reviewers. But it was his book *Gogmagog: The Buried Gods*, published in 1957, which caused real controversy among Cambridge archaeologists; he claimed to have found the outline of a giant chalk figure of a woman on horseback on the Gogmagog Hills at Wandlebury, Cambridgeshire, and suggested that this depicted the Celtic goddess Matrona, and bore out the theory of a female-centred prehistoric religion. Both the methodology by which he claimed to have located the figure – he had simply walked round the site inserting metal spikes into the ground, and wherever the spike went deeper into the soil, he concluded that this was because it was part of the outline – and his interpretation of the results were criticized, and he retired to Devon, where he continued to write prolifically.

During the 1930s, while engaged in a search for Viking graves on the island of Lundy in the Bristol Channel, Lethbridge gave a demonstration of the ancient art of DOWSING with a PENDULUM, and he used it, allegedly with some success, to trace sub-surface seams of volcanic rock. Later, he claimed to have felt electric shocks from the stones of the Merry Maidens stone circle in Cornwall, and, again using a pendulum, said that he could trace lines of force in the ground. This led him to make the radical suggestion that stone circles acted as guidance beacons for

UFOs. Theories like this guaranteed his estrangement from mainstream academia, but Lethbridge was unconcerned; he presented his theories as ideas and possibilities, and left it to others to disprove them, believing strongly that dogma was the curse of all learning, and that one should always remain open to new ideas. He went on publishing on various topics in the field of psychic research until his death in 1971: he expanded his ideas about the female archetypal deity in *Witches: Investigating an Ancient Religion* (1962); in *Ghost and Ghoul* (1961) and *The Ghost and the Divining Rod* (1963), he put forward his theories that every inanimate object could store information about itself and its history, and that GHOSTS might be explained by the fact that events and atmospheres could, given the right conditions, record themselves on the ether, and that these recordings could replay to certain people under the appropriate circumstances; and in *A Step in the Dark* (1967), he dealt with various ideas about the AFTERLIFE.

Levelland, Texas

The location of an important UFO case from the 1950s which included multiple-witness sightings and reports of physical effects. Its timing was seen by some to be significant.

In early November 1957, there was a major WAVE of UFO sightings in the south-west USA. Probably the most spectacular occurred on the night of 2 November, centred on the town of Levelland, Texas.

A dozen witnesses from within a 16-kilometre (10-mile) radius of this small town claimed that, during a two-hour period either side of midnight, they had seen an egg-shaped object flying low over the country roads. Drivers left their cars to watch and some people had even fallen to the ground as the glowing mass flew over them with a rush of air. Among those who apparently encountered this phenomenon during its unusually protracted appearance were Sheriff Weir Clem and a deputy officer (who had been called out following the first sightings), and the local fire marshal.

The majority of the reports from car and truck drivers involved experiences of electrical interference, similar to those apparently occurring in other CAR STOP cases. However, it remains unheard of in UFO cases elsewhere for so many independent vehicles supposedly to be affected in this way. The extent of the effects varied, but often included the stopping of the engine and the loss of lights, and all of the vehicles worked normally when the UFO departed. A report of a sighting at Whitharral (a small town north of Levelland) included an interesting new feature – the UFO apparently pulsed from bright to extremely bright, causing the running of a car's engine to alter in a coincident cyclical fashion.

Two days after the incident, the US Air Force sent a PROJECT BLUE BOOK investigator to Levelland. He concluded that an electrical storm was to blame. Although there was apparently no lightning in the area that night, the official Project Blue Book line was that the sightings had been caused by BALL LIGHTNING. Physicists have since disputed that there is any evidence for ball lightning lasting as long as this (it usually lasts for a number of seconds, certainly not for as long as two hours), or of it having such a dramatic effect on car engines and lights. The project's own science consultant, DR J ALLEN HYNEK, even argued at the time that the theory did not work.

The incident was interpreted by some to be a demonstration of power by ALIENS – an idea that grew out of events which occurred the morning after the Levelland sightings. At dawn a UFO was seen near the disused bunkers at White Sands, New Mexico, where the world's first atomic explosions had been monitored twelve years earlier. At almost the same time, on the other side of the world in Maralinga, Australia, a UFO was seen hovering above the site of the most recent nuclear detonation, conducted by the British just a few weeks before; the witnesses were RAF personnel involved in cleaning up the site. Meanwhile, in the Soviet Union, the satellite Sputnik 2 was being launched, carrying the first living creature to be sent into space.

It has been suggested by some UFO enthusiasts that this juxtaposition of sightings, all occurring within the space of just a few hours, offers strong circumstantial evidence for the EXTRATERRESTRIAL HYPOTHESIS.

Lévi, Éliphas (1810–75)
French author on occultism and magic.
Éliphas Lévi was the pseudonym under which the 19th-century French author and occultist Alphonse Louis Constant wrote his influential works on magic. Born in Paris in 1810, Constant trained to be a priest, but left the seminary without being ordained. He later became a journalist, and his outspoken and radical political views and writings earned him several short prison sentences. In 1852, he met the Polish mathematician and occultist Hoene Wronski, under whose influence Constant's interest in the OCCULT blossomed.

Constant was convinced of the existence of a universal secret doctrine of MAGIC which had prevailed throughout history, and which he felt was evident all over the world. This belief led him to attempt a synthesis of all the different strains of Western magic and occult philosophies, and, in 1855, he published *Transcendental Magic: Its Doctrine and Ritual*. In it he brought together aspects of Western

magic, the KABBALAH and the TAROT; the importance he placed upon the kabbalah can be seen from the fact that Éliphas Lévi, the pseudonym under which he published this and all his subsequent works on magic, was his transliteration of the Hebraic form of his first two names, Alphonse Louis. Lévi was the first to note the apparent symbolic correlation between the 22 cards of the major ARCANA, and the kabbalistic TREE OF LIFE.

He enthusiastically advocated magic as a legitimate spiritual path, and suggested that it was not only compatible with both Christianity and science, but was actually capable of unifying them. He continued to write books on magic and give lessons in occult studies for the rest of his life, and what some would consider to be his best work was collected in the anthology *The Mysteries of Magic* (1886) by A E WAITE.

Lévi died in 1875; ALEISTER CROWLEY was born in the same year and would later claim to be the reincarnation of Lévi.

levitation
The lifting into the air of people or objects without any visible physical means.
Levitation is the lifting of people or objects into the air without any visible physical means being present. Some believe that it is a form of PSYCHOKINESIS, and it has been claimed as a power by spiritualists, FAKIRS and stage magicians. It is also found in various religious faiths around the world, including Christianity, Islam, Hinduism, Buddhism and shamanism. The magic carpet, which can carry people through the air, is a staple of fairy stories around the world.

Reports of instances of demonic POSSESSION often include details of the possessed person levitating or of objects being invisibly, and often violently, hurled around. Similar effects have been attributed to the activities of POLTERGEISTS.

According to the New Testament, the Samaritan sorcerer Simon Magus (1st century AD) was able to levitate or even fly through the air. This is treated as a manifestation of evil, unlike the levitation ascribed to later Christian saints. St Joseph of Cupertino (1603–63) was said to levitate when in a state of religious ecstasy, as were St Teresa of Avila (1515–82) and St Philip Neri (1515–95).

Whereas the levitation of saints is described as being a spontaneous and uncontrolled product of religious rapture, spiritualist MEDIUMS have often claimed the power of levitating themselves or objects, whether in a state of trance or fully conscious. The Scottish spiritualist DAVID DUNGLAS HOME was said to have levitated himself out of a building by one window and back in by another, although witnesses

St Joseph of Cupertino, who it was claimed could reach a state of religious ecstasy that enabled him to levitate.
(© TopFoto/Fortean)

to this act appear to disagree over what it was they actually saw.

Indian fakirs and Brahmins were said to practise levitation through the control of the UNIVERSAL LIFE FORCE, achieved by MEDITATION, fasting and techniques to control breathing. Many of the fakirs' feats were adopted for performance by magicians, and levitation became an important part of many stage acts.

Does levitation really exist? In religious contexts, obviously, belief in it is really a matter of faith. Religious ecstasy, HALLUCINATION, MASS HYPNOSIS or simply the will to witness the miraculous have been advanced as explanations of the phenomenon. As far as SPIRITUALISM or MAGIC is concerned, sceptics believe that it is always an illusion, relying on the suggestibility of the audience, or even a crude deception involving wires, powerful magnets and other hidden devices.

Nowadays, unlike in the past, conjurors are often persuaded to reveal the secrets behind levitation and other well-known feats of 'magic'. Street magicians are known to achieve an illusion of levitating themselves

a few inches into the air simply by carefully choosing the angle at which they are seen, which allows them to disguise the fact that the toes of one foot are still in contact with the ground.

The only form of levitation recognized by science involves the use of electromagnetic fields. The type of railway known as 'maglev' takes its name from magnetic levitation, in which the vehicle is suspended in the air above the track by means of a magnetic field, which in turn is powered by an energy source.

ley lines *see* EARTH MYSTERIES; LEYS

leys
Supposed alignments of ancient sites, originally described by the English antiquarian and photographer Alfred Watkins.
In 1921, the English antiquarian scholar and pioneer photographer Alfred Watkins (1855–1935) first lectured on his discovery of old straight tracks across Britain. He believed that vestiges of these tracks remained, primarily in the alignment of various ancient sites, including STONE CIRCLES, STANDING STONES, barrows, cairns and burial mounds. He called these lines 'leys'. The word derives from 'lea' meaning 'open country' or 'pasture'. *The Old Straight Track*, Watkins' key work on this subject, was published in 1925.

By the 1960s leys had become 'ley lines' (see EARTH MYSTERIES) and had been endowed with far greater significance than Watkins had recognized, including a popularly held belief that they are 'energy lines'.

Liberal Catholic Church
An esoteric Church linked to theosophical beliefs.
Despite its relatively small numbers, the lack of recognition of its legitimacy by the established Churches and its many schisms, the Liberal Catholic Church has had a significant influence on many of the organizations within the WESTERN MYSTERY TRADITION today.

The Liberal Catholic Church is one of many small denominations known as Independent (or Autocephalous – 'self-headed') Episcopal Churches. Its origins lie in the Old Catholic Church in Great Britain, founded in 1906 by Bishop Arnold Harris Mathew (1852–1919). Formerly a Roman Catholic priest, Mathew persuaded the Old Catholic Church of Utrecht, which had separated from the Roman Catholic Church in 1870 over the issue of papal infallibility, to consecrate him as a bishop, in order that he could begin an Old Catholic Church in Britain. He claimed that many Roman Catholic and Anglican clergy in Britain would want to join – however, in the end, very few did.

A few years later, Mathew decided to return to Roman Catholicism, but in 1914, before he left, he consecrated a bishop to take over his role in the Old Catholic Church. Although Bishop Frederick Samuel Willoughby was a theosophist, he too very shortly felt called to join Rome, but consecrated three new bishops in 1915 and 1916 before he left. One of these was James Ingall Wedgwood (1883–1951), who became the Presiding Bishop of what was a very small Church.

Bishop Wedgwood was significant for three things. First, realizing that the Church, albeit small, had now drifted theologically far away from its Old Catholic roots, he renamed it the Liberal Christian Church in 1917; this was changed to the Liberal Catholic Church in 1918. Second, Wedgwood, who had a background as a missionary priest in India, moved to Australia and began successfully recruiting members to his new Church, boosting its profile. And third, one of these was the leading theosophist CHARLES W LEADBEATER, whom he ordained and consecrated, and who became the second Presiding Bishop of the Liberal Catholic Church in 1922.

Since 1922, the Liberal Catholic Church has largely been associated with theosophical beliefs, if not always with the THEOSOPHICAL SOCIETY itself. Various other esoteric movements, such as some of the successors to the HERMETIC ORDER OF THE GOLDEN DAWN, have had Liberal Catholic clergy among their leaders. For people with esoteric Christian beliefs, the Liberal Catholic Church enables them to celebrate the Eucharist outside the mainstream Churches (see WANDERING BISHOPS).

The Church has suffered a number of schisms over the years, so that today there are several separate denominations called the Liberal Catholic Church. There have also been numerous offshoot Churches formed when bishops have fallen out with other bishops over theology, practices or personal differences and have left, taking a few priests and members with them. One of the main differences has been the link with theosophical beliefs; although many Liberal Catholics have esoteric beliefs, others have abandoned this path and returned to traditional (though non-papal) Catholic beliefs and practices. One such offshoot is the Open Episcopal Church, founded in 2000, which views itself as the legitimate successor to Mathew's Old Catholic Church in Britain.

Libra

In astrology, the seventh sign of the zodiac, between Virgo and Scorpio.

In Western ASTROLOGY, Libra is the sign of ZODIAC for those who are born between 24 September and 22 October. The symbol for Libra is the balance (a pair of scales), and the sign is ruled by Venus. Librans are said to be agreeable and artistic, although they can seem indecisive. Libra is believed to be an air sign, having an affinity with the element AIR.

life after death *see* AFTERLIFE; REINCARNATION

life review *see* NEAR-DEATH EXPERIENCE

light

An important feature of most reports of UFO sightings, which plays a significant part in their interpretation.

Over 90 per cent of reported UFOs are said to emit light. Commonly, the description is similar to that of navigation beacons on aircraft – which tends to indicate that such cases may well involve misperceptions of ordinary air traffic. Sceptics often argue that alien craft would hardly draw attention to themselves with flashing lights, unless they wanted to be noticed – in which case they would surely have clearly and conclusively revealed their presence by now. However, some UFO researchers counter that they may be attempting to disguise themselves by mimicking terrestrial aircraft.

Many reported UFOs are said to glow internally. The colour of the emitted light varies; but it is usually white, but reds and blues are also often described. There is some evidence to indicate that the colour may be dependent on the amount of moisture in the atmosphere, with reddish hues predominating when there is water vapour present, and blue tones when the air is dry. This supports theories based around the idea that some UFO sightings are the result of atmospheric processes.

In some cases it is claimed that exposure to the light emitted by UFOs has been accompanied by other physical effects – including reactions akin to sunburn in witnesses (see LOCH RAVEN, MARYLAND) or sudden temperature increases in metal objects such as wedding rings – leading to the suggestion that it is the visible portion of a broad-band radiation emission.

There are also a number of interesting cases which involve ultra-violet light – the emission of which has formed part of various claimed CLOSE ENCOUNTERS and ALIEN ABDUCTIONS. It is sometimes said to have an effect on the eyes of those involved, including temporary blindness and severe weeping.

It was particularly common in older cases for witnesses to describe a beam of light (often described as a 'ray' or 'energy beam') which appeared to be deliberately fired at them. In the VALENSOLE case (and a number of others) a strike by such a beam was said to have resulted in temporary muscle paralysis. See also AURAS; AURORA BOREALIS; EARTH LIGHTS; GHOST

LIGHTS; HALOES; LIGHT, SOLID; LIGHTS IN THE SKY; WHEELS OF LIGHT.

light, solid

A rarely reported phenomenon in which beams of light are said to behave as if they were solid, sometimes bending or even penetrating objects. It features in some UFO reports.

On the night of 15 June 1981, several people across the Rossendale Valley in Lancashire reported seeing a bright yellow oval drifting into the prevailing wind, before hovering above an artificial ski slope in Rawtenstall. Once there, it apparently sent a beam of light into deserted woodland below. But this beam had a most peculiar nature – the light appeared to unfurl from the UFO, forming a rigid structure that then descended as if it were a ladder.

Such beams of 'solid light' also appear in other UFO reports. They have even been said to pass through objects in their path and enter buildings when projected by an object hovering outside.

UFOs have also been reported to change the behaviour of light being emitted by ordinary sources in their immediate vicinity, apparently causing it to behave in ways that defy our current understanding of its nature. For example, Ron Sullivan, an Australian businessman, claimed that while he was driving near Burke's Flat on the evening of 4 April 1966, he encountered a glowing object next to the road. This swirling shape took the form of a phosphorescent cone of light with colours dancing around the edge, which slowly contracted into a single point and disappeared, apparently swallowing up all of the ambient light in its proximity. It even appeared to pull the headlamp beams sideways towards it – causing them to act as if they were solid by bending them to form an arc.

light, wheels of *see* WHEELS OF LIGHT

lightning *see* SULLIVAN, ROY; THUNDERSTORMS

lightning, ball *see* BALL LIGHTNING

lights in the sky

The term widely used by UFO researchers to describe the most common and basic type of UFO sighting, in which only sources of illumination are observed.

The phrase 'lights in the sky' (commonly abbreviated to LITS) is used by UFO researchers to mean any reported sighting during which lights are seen but nothing more substantial is witnessed. The overwhelming majority of nocturnal UFO sightings are of the LITS variety and, indeed, they represent approximately 90 per cent of all reported cases worldwide.

In 1972, the phrase was adopted by DR J ALLEN HYNEK to form part of his universal classification scheme for UFO sightings. To Hynek, who also used the (now less fashionable) term 'nocturnal lights', such sightings represented the simplest and scientifically least valuable category of report, and he encouraged a general approach in which little time and effort was wasted on pursuing them because it was considered highly likely that they would eventually be revealed as one of the many types of IDENTIFIED FLYING OBJECT.

Most modern UFO researchers concur that LITS cases have a high probability of being identified – with misperceptions of aircraft lights, meteors, stars or planets, laser searchlights and satellites being common causes of reports. Indeed, they are also sometimes referred to as 'low definition' cases, reflecting their modest scientific value. However, LITS, especially those seen in daylight, have featured in several important WAVES, such as that which occurred at HESSDALEN, where it was suggested that they were examples of a rare natural phenomenon. See also EARTH LIGHTS.

lithomancy

Divination using stones.

In lithomancy (from Greek *lithos*, stone, and *manteiā*, divination), coloured crystals or stones are used to obtain the answer to a question. There are several ways of doing this. One method involves illuminating the stones by the light of a single candle, and studying and interpreting the colour of the light reflected by them, so that, for example, a red reflection is thought to indicate love, marriage or a sexual relationship, and a green reflection success or money. A second method uses 13 smooth pebbles or crystals, cast in lots so that omens may be divined from the positions in which they land. The 13 stones are taken to represent the sun, the moon, Mars, Venus, Mercury, Jupiter, Saturn, the home, the love life, health matters, magic, fortune and news.

Another system uses eight tumbled stones of various colours, each of which is ascribed a meaning: a red stone, such as jasper; an orange one, such as carnelian; a yellow one, such as citrine; a green one, such as malachite; a blue one, such as sodalite; a purple one, such as amethyst; a white or clear one, such as quartz; and a black one, such as obsidian. If a simple yes/no answer is required, the red, green and white stones only are used. The white stone is laid down, and the diviner, holding the other two stones in one hand, thinks clearly of the question, and then tosses the stones. If the red stone lands nearer to the white one, the answer is taken to be no, and if the green one lands nearer, the answer is yes. To gain insight about a given situation or possible action, the black stone is set down as the central point, and the other stones are held while the situation or action is contemplated, then they are all thrown simultaneously. The three stones which land closest to the black one are read.

LITS *see* LIGHTS IN THE SKY

little green men

A colloquial term for the aliens that feature in reports of UFO encounters, often used humorously or dismissively.
The origin of the phrase 'little green men' is the subject of much debate within the UFO COMMUNITY. However, it certainly does not appear to be taken directly from actual modern reports of UFO sightings, in which green beings rarely feature. It may stem from older references to the LITTLE PEOPLE – stories of such entities are common to the folklore of cultures from all over the world. In European folklore, ELVES, GOBLINS and FAIRIES are often described as being small and dressed in green.

In fact, modern versions of folk tales have tended to over-emphasize the miniature stature of the Little People; those who claimed to have actually seen them often said that they were 60–90 centimetres (2–3 feet) in height – similar, in fact, to some of the common types of alien entity reported in modern UFO cases. DR JACQUES VALLÉE was one of the first UFO experts to draw this comparison and he suggested that there might be a connection between the two types of encounter. This observation has been further developed by others into a theory that they might all be examples of contact with a species that co-exists with us on earth, rather than involving visitors from another planet.

The phrase 'little green men' was commonly employed as a derogatory term for the unconvincing science fiction monsters encountered in the Hollywood B-movies of the 1950s. At the same time, little green caricature aliens began to appear in cartoons and comic books, and the term was extended to real-life UFO claims, especially by those seeking to ridicule those who made them.

Little People

One of the many euphemistic terms used to refer to fairies in order to avoid the bad luck caused by naming them directly.
In folklore, it is considered very unlucky to refer to the fairy folk directly, since to use their name might summon them. Also, some people believe that they do not like being referred to as FAIRIES. Either way, it is thought to be safer not to use the word 'fairy' when speaking of them, and instead, a wide range of euphemistic phrases such as the Little People or the Little Folk are employed. See also DAOINE SIDHE; GOOD FOLK.

The Livingston Incident *see panel p391*

Llandrillo

A Welsh village from which a number of strange lights were seen. These were accompanied by a sound akin to that of an explosion, leading to allegations that there had been a UFO crash.
On the night of 23 January 1974, the villagers of Llandrillo in North Wales were startled by a massive explosion and a deep rumbling sound. Houses shook for a period of a few seconds. Many people reported seeing bright lights moving very rapidly across the night sky. Subsequent events led many to suspect that this all of these phenomena had been caused by a UFO crashing on the nearby mountain, Cader Berwyn, around which strange lights were seen by several witnesses.

A local nurse hurried to the scene, fearing that an aircraft had crashed, but found no crash site or debris. What she did report seeing was a glowing sphere on the ground surrounded by other smaller lights. She estimated that this was some distance away, too far for her to reach on foot across the mountainside in the dark, and she returned to her home.

Rumours soon spread that not only had an extraterrestrial craft fallen to earth but that its ALIEN occupants had been taken away, some of them still alive, under a cloak of secrecy by the military. This led to the incident being referred to as the 'Welsh ROSWELL'. Some ufologists even claimed that the crash was no accident and that the craft had been brought down by an electromagnetic weapon that was being secretly tested.

However, other explanations for the events of that evening have been suggested. Astronomers at the time recorded a series of bolide meteors (see METEORITES) being sighted in the area. Bolides are often mistakenly reported as UFO sightings. The area was also known for earth tremors, being close to a fault line known as the Bala Fault (see EARTH LIGHTS). In addition, it was later discovered that a team of poachers using powerful lamps had been out on the mountain that night. They would not have been in any hurry to come forward and admit their activities to the police.

The rumours of retrieved extraterrestrials were fuelled some years later when a former member of the military 'confessed' to having seen skinny humanoid bodies being secretly loaded into a military vehicle. Certainly, the arrival of the police and military on the scene, warning people to stay away, might have also led some to conclude that something was being hushed up, although such procedures would be

The Livingston Incident

Early on the morning of 9 November 1979, forester Bob Taylor was with his dog in a woodland clearing at Dechmont Law near Livingston in the Scottish lowlands. He claims that what he encountered there on that damp autumnal morning transformed his life.

Taylor later reported that he saw a large domed object on the ground or hovering inches above it. He described this UFO as having a rim around the middle carrying objects that resembled arms. The metallic-coloured craft faded in and out of visibility (temporarily allowing views of the trees behind it each time it became invisible). As he stared in amazement Taylor says that he became aware of a 'sucking' noise. He then saw two objects, which seemed to have come from the UFO, that looked like round metal sea mines with spikes emerging from them. They floated towards him, bouncing on the wet soil as they did so and creating the sucking sounds. Within seconds he says that they had reached him and he felt a powerful tugging on his trouser legs. At the same moment there was a pungent smell and Taylor believes that he collapsed, unconscious, onto the ground.

A depiction of Bob Taylor's close encounter with a UFO near Livingston, Scotland, on 9 November 1979. (© Mary Evans Picture Library)

When Taylor recovered, an unknown time later, all the strange objects had disappeared. His dog was still nearby, running around barking furiously – Taylor later said that he believed that the dog had scared the UFO away. In his account of the incident, the woodsman attempted to stand but felt weak and nauseous. He dragged himself towards his vehicle, parked at the edge of the clearing. However, when he tried to drive away his co-ordination was so poor that he backed into a muddy ditch, leaving him with no alternative but to stumble through the forest on foot, heading towards his nearby home.

When Taylor arrived home his wife asked him if he had been assaulted. He could only mumble that something had 'gassed' him. She sent for his boss at the Livingston New Town Development Corporation, and a doctor and the police were also called. Taylor was suffering from cuts and a severe headache, and there were holes in his trousers. The police went to the clearing and roped it off for investigation – regarding the incident as an assault by persons unknown.

While Taylor was examined in hospital, the police carried out an investigation of the site. Some of the police finds have been taken as supporting Taylor's claims. There were marks on the ground where Taylor claimed the object had been, and about 40 small holes were found that perhaps coincided with the indents from the 'sea mines'. Taylor's vehicle was in the ditch where he had left it. Detective Sergeant Ian Wark admitted that at first he was sceptical but when no plant machinery was found that could have made the marks, he became persuaded that Taylor was sincere.

The forester's trousers were sent for forensic analysis and police expert Lester Knibb confirmed that the tears were consistent with the witness's story – that a mechanical force had created them. The police case was left open.

UFO researchers were impressed by Taylor's testimony, but the unusual nature of what he apparently experienced caused debate. Although there are a number of reported cases where a CLOSE ENCOUNTER is followed by a lack of physical co-ordination, this feature has led to speculation that there might be a physiological cause. Steuart Campbell, a sceptical UFO researcher, suggested that epilepsy could explain a number of aspects of the sighting, including the physical sensations. However, Taylor was never diagnosed as epileptic. Campbell also suggested that the UFO was a HALLUCINATION, although this would not explain the marks that the police found on the ground.

After the story was featured on British television, the New Town Development Corporation erected a plaque on the site. It disappeared not long afterwards.

See also BONNYBRIDGE.

standard in any situation where it is feared that there has been a plane crash. There has certainly been no official recognition that anything anomalous occurred that night.

The Loch Ness Monster *see panel p394*

Loch Raven, Maryland
The location of a classic UFO close encounter case that it was claimed involved physical effects which appeared to offer evidence that the UFO had emitted some form of radiation.

This case involved a classic CAR STOP incident and greatly puzzled those who investigated it, including the team from PROJECT BLUE BOOK. It occurred on 26 October 1958, by the Loch Raven Dam located just outside Baltimore in Maryland.

Two men claimed that while they were driving near the dam at about 9.30pm a large egg-shaped object loomed ahead of them, hovering just above the water. Puzzled by this, they tried to drive closer to investigate but, at this point, the car engine and lights failed as all electrical power appeared to drain away. The object then glowed very brightly, there was a flash of light, and air flooded over the faces of the witnesses, making them feel warm. At the same time a sound like a clap of thunder or dull explosion was heard. The UFO then climbed skywards at speed and vanished within seconds. During its acceleration the edges of the UFO had appeared 'fuzzy', as if surrounded by mist or vapour.

The two men called the police from the nearest phone, and officers were sent in a patrol car to interview them. Their faces were now burning, as if they were suffering from sunburn, and they attended a local hospital. The slight tingling sensation that they also reported quickly faded without further ill effect.

Several other witnesses in the area reported seeing a large oval object before and after the UFO had apparently appeared beside the dam. Also, occupants of a nearby restaurant confirmed that they heard the noise but had not gone outside to check on its cause, having thought that it might be thunder. However, an investigation into the local weather conditions at the time indicated that there had been no signs of storm activity in the area.

Many of the features of this case – notably the draining of electrical power, the sensation of heat, with apparent lasting effects on the witnesses' bodies, the explosive noise at the point of departure and the 'fuzzy' edges of the object – are consistent with many other reported car stop cases. This consistency might be seen either to give a real clue as to the nature of UFOs, and the radiation emitted by them, or to indicate that an awareness of the details presented in other cases conditions people's beliefs – leading to misperception, embellishment or even fabrication of some or all of the details.

London Monster
A case that revolved around allegations that a stalker was abroad in 18th-century London carrying out bizarre attacks on women; it is often cited as a historical example of mass hysteria.

Between 1788 and 1790 there were 30 recorded cases of attacks by a criminal that the press referred to as the London Monster. A man was said to stalk his female victims, shout obscenities at them and then slash or cut their dresses (and often their buttocks too) with a sharp blade. In some instances the attacker was said to force a small bunch of artificial flowers into the face of his victim, before completing his usual crimes. Hysteria grew, alongside sensationalist reporting in the press, and many women are said to have attempted to safeguard themselves from the monster's attentions by investing in brass or copper armour to protect their buttocks (for the wealthy) or cooking pots and 'cork rumps' (for the poor). Pickpockets are thought to have used the panic to their advantage, as to shout the word 'monster' distracted everyone's attention. Also, many men were said to have been attacked and falsely accused simply for looking 'suspicious'.

Law enforcement was, at this time, in its infancy, and the police force of the day, the Bow Street Runners, was unable to apprehend this confident criminal. A philanthropist called John Julius Angerstein offered a reward of £100 for information leading to the capture of the monster. Soon afterwards the Bow Street Runners were flooded with new allegations of attacks (with many women claiming to be the 'latest' victim) and with vigilantes who claimed that they had found the man. Eventually, one John Coleman accused an artificial-flower maker called Rhynwick Williams of stabbing his fiancée, Anne Porter. Porter is said to have fainted when confronted with Williams, and a number of other women agreed that he was the monster.

The trial of Williams was somewhat bizarre. The charge first brought against him was that of assault with the intention to deface someone's clothing, judged to be the most serious law on the statute books which fitted this unprecedented crime – this little-known charge related to a felony, whereas common assault was only judged as a misdemeanour. It was clear that the judges wanted the London Monster to receive the death penalty or transportation at the very least. Also, the main witnesses for the prosecution in the trial were Coleman and Porter, who still hoped to receive the £100 reward. Williams was granted a retrial, and in this instance was represented by an

Irish poet called Theophilus Swift. Swift attempted to discredit the prosecution (and their desire for the reward) but he handled the case badly and Williams was convicted – albeit for a misdemeanour this time, which carried the maximum penalty of six years' imprisonment. The attacks ceased.

It is impossible to know the truth behind the London Monster, and whether Rhynwick Williams was simply a scapegoat. It has been suggested that MASS HYSTERIA led women to fabricate monstrous attacks, or to believe that they had narrowly escaped an attack when they had not. Some have said that the monster was never anything more than a rumour, and certainly, as distressing as the attacks might sound, no grave injury was ever done.

London Underground ghosts

Ghostly apparitions reportedly seen on the London Underground.

A number of hauntings are associated with stations on the underground railway in London. Sightings have generally been reported by employees rather than passengers, and some are associated with stations that have long been closed, such as the British Museum station. These unused stations are often referred to as ghost stations.

The British Museum station, which was closed in 1933, was reputedly haunted by the ghost of an ancient Egyptian – sometimes described as complete with headdress and loincloth, and in other tales described as a mummy from the collection at the museum. It has also been claimed that when the station closed, a newspaper offered a reward to anyone willing to spend a night in the station – although as this newspaper is never apparently named, it may be that this part of the story, and the ghost itself, are entirely fictional.

Aldwych is no longer a working station (although it is hired out as a party venue and for filming) and it too has a ghost legend associated with it. In this case, the ghost of an actress is said to appear on the tracks at night, startling engineers.

At Covent Garden station the ghost of a tall man wearing a frock coat and a top hat was reputedly seen in the 1950s and 1970s. The ghost has been identified as actor William Terriss, murdered by a rival actor in 1897 – he is also said to haunt the Adelphi Theatre. The ghost of a woman was reported at Aldgate in 1951, and the apparition was apparently accompanied by strange whistling sounds. Apparitions were also reported at Victoria during construction work in 1968.

However, in proportion to the size of the Underground network and the number of staff and passengers who use the Underground each day, the number of actual reports is tiny, and some have

The actor William Terriss, who was murdered in 1897. His ghost is said to haunt both the Adelphi Theatre and the London Underground. (© Mary Evans Picture Library)

wondered why these dark and often ominous places do not actually generate more 'ghost' experiences.

longevity, extreme *see* EXTREME LONGEVITY

lost cities

Once-thriving cities that experienced terminal decline.

History and folklore contain many accounts of cities that were once thriving and vibrant communities but which entered periods of decline leading not only to their abandonment but to being all but erased from human memory.

Some are known to have been destroyed in war, such as Troy or Carthage. Others succumbed to natural disaster, such as Pompeii, buried for centuries beneath the volcanic ash from an eruption of Vesuvius. Some were simply abandoned by their inhabitants when changes in such conditions as climate or water supply ended their viability.

A city in the last category was Ubar (also known as Iram of the Pillars), a legendary wealthy trading centre in the Rub' al Khali desert of the Arabian Peninsula. According to Muslim tradition, its decadence earned it divine punishment and it was buried in the sands. It was not known whether or not

The Loch Ness Monster

Prior to 1933, Loch Ness, a large expanse of fresh water – approximately 38.6 kilometres (24 miles) long, 1.61 kilometres (1 mile) wide and at least 297 metres (974 feet) deep – in the highlands of Scotland, was relatively secluded, but during the early part of that year a vast amount of earth and forest overlooking its northern shoreline was blasted away to provide a new motor road, the A82, which has since offered motorists driving along it some spectacular views of the loch – and its most celebrated inhabitant.

On the afternoon of 14 April 1933, Mr and Mrs John Mackay became the first two post-A82 eyewitnesses of a mysterious entity soon to become known world-wide as Nessie, the Loch Ness monster. Driving southwards alongside the loch, they were approaching Abriachan on its north-western shore when Mrs Mackay called out to her husband to look towards the centre of the loch. They later said that to their amazement, they saw an enormous animal rolling and diving amid a turbulent mass of water, and watched this extraordinary spectacle for several minutes before the creature in question finally plunged beneath the water. Their account was published in the local newspaper, the *Inverness Courier*. Other reports followed soon afterwards, and the great British monster story was up and running.

Since as far back as the 6th century, when St Columba supposedly repulsed an attack from a water monster at the mouth of the River Ness, there had been local reports of a giant creature inhabiting Loch Ness itself, but it was not until 1933 that it attracted international interest – an interest that shows no sign of waning more than 70 years later. During those years, countless sightings, photographs, films and other material allegedly substantiating the existence of such a creature have been obtained. Most have been discounted outright by sceptics, or damned plausibly or otherwise by claims of hoaxes – as with the classic Surgeon's photograph of 1934. However, there are some items of evidence that remain sufficiently compelling to merit serious attention.

A prime example of such evidence came from aeronautical engineer Tim Dinsdale's success in filming what appears to be a huge water creature in the loch on 23 April 1960. This was the final day of his six-day monster-hunting expedition, and Dinsdale claims that as he was driving along the Foyers Bay stretch of road in the morning he saw a hump-like object on the surface of the loch. He estimated that the object was approximately 1.2 kilometres (0.7 miles) away. Getting out of the car, he focused his binoculars upon the object, which was oval in shape and mahogany in colour with a dark blotch on the left side, but as he stood watching, it began to move.

Convinced that it was a huge living animal, Dinsdale started filming it with his tripod-mounted cine camera, and shot about four minutes of black and white film. It seemed to show something throwing up a conspicuous v-shaped wake as it swam towards the opposite shore, submerging slowly, but then changing direction and swimming south, parallel to the shore and almost lost beneath the water surface. This film was analysed by the Royal Air Force's Joint Air Reconnaissance Intelligence Centre (JARIC), which announced that the hump was 3.7–4.9

'Musical Nessies' on sale in the village of Drumnadrochit on the shores of Loch Ness. (© McPherson Colin/Corbis Sygma)

metres (12–16 feet) long, a cross-section through it would be no less than 1.53 metres (5 feet) high and 1.83 metres (6 feet) wide, and its speed was 11.3–16 kilometres per hour (7–10 miles per hour). Most significantly, JARIC deemed that rather than the hump being a surface craft or submarine, '… it probably is an animate object' – that is, part of a living creature.

In more recent times, sonar traces recording the presence of huge, seemingly solid, animate bodies under the water have been obtained by many expeditions, including those led by Dr Robert Rines from the Academy of Applied Science in Boston, Britain's own 'Operation Deepscan' of 1987 and investigators aboard the *MV Nessie Hunter* in July 2001. However, by far the most exciting sonar-related piece of evidence favouring the existence of Nessie was obtained in 1972. Indeed, it is still widely held that this is the most important evidence of any kind for the Loch Ness monster's reality.

In August 1972, Rines's team was using underwater cameras and sonar equipment positioned in Urquhart Bay. On the morning of 8 August the sonar detected a flurry of movement that appeared to be a shoal of fish swimming frantically away from something coming up behind. From the sonar readings obtained, this latter object seemed to be a very large solid body, moving purposefully through the water (rather than merely drifting), and measuring 6.1–9.2 metres (20–30 feet) long. At the same time that the sonar was recording the moving body, the cameras were taking photographs of it, and when their film was developed, some frames revealed an extraordinary flipper-like object, diamond in shape and estimated to be 1.22–1.83 metres (4–6 feet) long. Some believed that it resembled a diamond-shaped, paddle-like limb, attached to a much larger body.

What makes these results noteworthy is that whereas eyewitness reports are subjective (and thereby open to criticism and doubts concerning their precise interpretation and reliability), here were two independently obtained results that not only convincingly supported one another but, in addition, were obtained by wholly objective, disinterested witnesses – machines. Based upon the evidence of these photographs, Rines and British naturalist Sir Peter Scott formally christened the Loch Ness monster *Nessiteras rhombopteryx* – 'monster of Ness with diamond fin', in December 1975.

Even the most hardened Nessie sceptics were baffled by these 'flipper' photographs – especially as the creatures whose limbs most closely resemble such flippers are those long-necked aquatic reptiles of prehistoric times, the plesiosaurs, believed extinct for more than 65 million years. Even before the flipper photos were obtained, the numerous reports of a long-necked four-limbed monster with humped back had made the plesiosaur identity by far the most popular contender for the solution to the Nessie mystery. Moreover, as it is known that plesiosaurs used to swallow large stones for ballast purposes, this would even explain why dead Nessies do not float to the surface. Other cryptozoological identities proposed over the years include a highly specialized long-necked seal, a giant newt or salamander, a huge form of eel and even a massive worm, but none corresponds as closely and comprehensively with the Loch Ness monster's appearance (as described by those who believe they have seen it) as a plesiosaur (especially one of the long-necked elasmosaur forms). Sceptics favour such varied possibilities as diving birds, floating algal mats, swimming deer, stray seals, optical illusions, boats, sturgeons, otters and tree trunks or branches cast adrift on the loch surface.

In recent years, an additional but equally perplexing category of evidence has been forthcoming from the loch – unexplained animal sounds recorded by submerged microphones. These include a series of pig-like grunting noises recorded by a sonic survey of the loch in 2000, whose frequency (741–751 Hz) was comparable to sounds produced by various very big, known aquatic species such as killer whales, walruses and elephant seals.

Yet if sizeable animals of any kind do exist in the loch (and there would need to be at least 30 or so to sustain a viable breeding population), why have they not been discovered by now, after decades of intense investigation? The following claim is often made as an insight into the problems faced by Nessie seekers. It has been said that the volume of Loch Ness is such that if all of its peat-filled water could be removed, the chasm remaining would be so vast that the entire human population of the world could be fitted into it three times over. In short, some would say that a number of monsters could live concealed in Loch Ness with no more risk of being found than a moving needle in a visually impenetrable haystack. As for the oft-cited statement that there is insufficient food in the loch for any such creatures, it has been claimed that at any given time Loch Ness contains an estimated 27 tonnes of fish alone (mainly char, trout and salmon), not to mention all manner of smaller sources of nutrient, so should Nessie and her kin exist, they are certainly not going to starve!

this city had actually existed until modern scientific techniques were employed by expeditions searching the area. Ground-penetrating radar revealed a buried fortress and the remains of an underground water cistern, the destruction of which was thought to have caused the abandonment of the city.

Other lost cities are considered to be purely mythical, such as King Arthur's Camelot, or the city of Ys, portrayed in Breton legend as having been swallowed up by the sea in the Bay of Douarnenez. However, for centuries Troy was thought to exist only in the epic poems of the ancient Greeks until the German archaeologist Heinrich Schliemann (1822–90) excavated its site in 1871. Perhaps other legendary lost cities will in future years be shown to have a basis in fact.

lost continents

Continents believed to have sunk beneath the sea.
Many civilizations have traditional tales about continents that once existed but were said to have been swallowed up by the sea. By far the most famous of these is ATLANTIS, a name that inevitably appears whenever mysterious UNDERWATER RUINS are discovered in any part of the oceans. Other famous examples are LEMURIA and MU.

Some of these myths may have had a basis in reality as inundations by the sea are known to have happened throughout history. However, as life in these lost continents is inevitably portrayed as being as one of abundance and perfection, it may be that they simply reflect a deep human need to believe in a 'golden age' when society was more wonderful than in the world of today.

lost lands

Lands mentioned in history or fable and now unknown.
Like LOST CONTINENTS, lost lands form an element in many bodies of traditional folklore. One of the best-known is Lyonesse, a land said to have existed between the Scilly Isles and Land's End, reputed to be the birthplace of KING ARTHUR.

In South-East Asia, the Tamil tradition speaks of Kumari Kandam, a land to the south of India which was submerged in the sea by a great flood. It is not out of the question that such a place did exist, as the great tsunami of 2004 showed the destructive power of the seas of the region.

Ancient Greek geographers wrote of an island they called Thule, located somewhere north of the Orkney Islands. It is not known for certain whether or not this refers to an actual island (Shetland has been suggested), an island that is now under the sea or part of the mainland of Scandinavia. Unromantic as it may seem, it is likely that many supposedly lost lands were simply the creation of incomplete or misinformed geography.

lost time *see* TIME, MISSING

lost tribes *see* TEN LOST TRIBES OF ISRAEL

Loudon, nuns of

A 17th-century witchcraft case involving the alleged demonic possession of nuns at a convent in Loudon, France.
In 1634, Urbain Grandier, a young priest from Loudon, was found guilty of WITCHCRAFT and executed by burning at the stake. The trial was brought about through the accusations of a group of nuns from the local Ursuline convent.

Prior to these accusations, Grandier had already acquired a bad reputation through a number of adulterous relationships, and had made some powerful enemies, including Cardinal Richelieu, whom he had publicly criticized. It is suggested that the Mother Superior of the convent, Jeanne des Anges, was possibly complicit in a plot to bring about Grandier's downfall when in 1632 she accused him of being responsible for her demonic POSSESSION. This was quickly followed by similar accusations from many of the other nuns. They claimed that he had summoned the DEMONS Asmodeus and Zabulon against them. The nuns' 'possession' was characterized by shouting, speaking in tongues, pulling faces and fits during which their bodies were twisted into strange and often indecent postures. However, following the examination of the nuns by a doctor, on behalf of Archbishop Sourdis of Bordeaux, it was decided that the nuns were faking their possession and Grandier was acquitted.

Following the acquittal, the scandal surrounding the case was stirred up again by Richelieu for his own political reasons. He ordered the EXCORCISM of the nuns which revived the interest in their accusations and led to Grandier being arrested again. He was searched for the DEVIL'S MARK, of which four were found. The trial was carried out by a panel of judges which included Richelieu's own special envoy and, despite attempts on the part of some of the nuns to withdraw their accusations, he was found guilty. One of the more sensational elements of the trial was the production of the alleged DEVIL'S PACT signed by Grandier, a number of demons and THE DEVIL himself.

Despite brutal torture, Grandier never admitted to witchcraft. It is said that as a punishment for this, the rope with which he was to be strangled prior to burning was tied so that it would not tighten – thus ensuring that he was burnt alive.

The symptoms of the nuns' demonic possession continued for some time after the execution – the Mother Superior was only finally freed from them in 1638. Whether her symptoms were the result of mental illness or were simply fraudulent will never be known for certain. Some modern commentators have suggested that, whatever the cause of the original accusation, the behaviour and its spread through the convent was a case of MASS HYSTERIA or even, more specifically, MASS SOCIOGENIC ILLNESS.

loup garou
A species of werewolf of the North American bayou, whose legend was brought over by French settlers.

'Loup garou' is the French term for a werewolf (see LYCANTHROPY), and may have its origins in a shortened form of the phrase, '*Loup, gardez-vous!*' ('Wolf, watch out!'). French werewolf legends go back to the 6th century, and when French settlers came to North America, they brought these stories with them. Folklore held that a person could become a loup garou for failing to go to confession, and particularly missing Easter Mass, for seven years. It could also be the result of a curse by a WITCH, or a bite from an existing loup garou; in some accounts, simply meeting a loup garou and gazing into his blazing red eyes is all it takes to become one yourself. A loup garou is said to sometimes drink the blood of his victim like a vampire (see VAMPIRISM), as well as devouring his flesh. Once a loup garou has passed the curse on to another victim, this curse is lifted from the original werewolf. If injured or killed, he will instantly revert to human form, and it is believed that if he is sprinkled with salt, he will catch fire, and will shed his animal skin and become human again. However, to permanently return a loup garou to his human state, he has to be struck hard enough to draw three drops of blood. If a person has had the curse passed on to him by another werewolf, and can manage not to speak of it to anyone else for a year and a day, it is said that he will not only be freed of the curse himself, but will also free his original attacker.

Each loup garou is said to own a huge bat on the back of which he can fly to the houses of new victims. However, stories suggest that he can be distracted by a sieve or colander hung on the door of the house, because he will start obsessively counting the holes and will forget the purpose of his visit. A loup garou is also reputed to be terrified of frogs, and will flee if one is thrown at him. One belief associated with the loups garou of the Louisiana bayou is that they like to get together for wild dances.

Lourdes
A site in France of Marian visions.

Lourdes is a town in the Haute-Pyrénées department of France. In 1858, the 14-year-old Marie Bernarde Soubirous (now known as ST BERNADETTE) claimed to have received a series of visions of the Virgin Mary there, in a grotto at the Massabielle Rock. No one else shared her visions, even when, as with later occurrences, she was accompanied by groups of people. When asked to describe what she saw, the girl said:

> I saw a lady dressed in white. She wore a white dress, an equally white veil, a blue belt and a yellow rose on each foot.

According to Marie, the Virgin told her that she wanted a church to be built on the site, and in one of these MARIAN APPARITIONS she commanded the girl to drink from the nearby spring. Marie could not initially see such a spring, but she dug in muddy ground with her fingers until a spring appeared. A few weeks later a girl with a dislocated arm bathed it in the spring and was apparently immediately cured.

When Marie asked the lady in her visions to identify herself, she told her, 'I am the Immaculate Conception.'

Over the next few years, increasing numbers of pilgrims made their way to the spot and the waters of the spring began to be associated with 'miraculous' cures. There were, however, no further apparitions.

After four years of investigation by a commission of enquiry, in 1862 the Roman Catholic Church, in the person of the Bishop of Tarbes, officially acknowledged the visions as being both supernatural and divine, and true apparitions of the Virgin Mary. The Church also accepted that people had been cured by drinking or bathing in the waters of the Massabielle spring.

In 1864, a statue of the Madonna of Lourdes was erected in the grotto where the apparitions had taken place, and an impressive basilica was built nearby in 1872. This was by no means large enough to accommodate the millions of pilgrims, and in 1958 a massive concrete church was completed, with a capacity of 20,000 people. In 1983, Pope John Paul II was the first pope to go to Lourdes on a pilgrimage.

The Catholic Church has recognized over 60 MIRACLES as having occurred at Lourdes, while thousands of other cures effected there have been described as inexplicable. In 1954, the Lourdes International Medical Committee was set up to examine cases from a scientific medical viewpoint and continues to meet annually.

The sceptical approach to the miracles of Lourdes

tends to be that apparently inexplicable cures do take place, but that the fact that the current state of medical science is unable to explain them does not make them miracles. Like the PLACEBO EFFECT, it is often argued that strong faith and belief in the possibility of a miraculous cure can achieve wonderful results without medical intervention. For every person who is cured in this way, there must be thousands of afflicted believers who make a pilgrimage to Lourdes and are not cured. Is this because their faith is not strong enough or they are not truly repentant of their sins, or is it simply that they are not lucky enough to benefit from apparently random and spontaneous healing?

Irrespective of the answers to this kind of question, millions of pilgrims make their way to Lourdes every year, many of the sick choosing to bathe in pools fed by the waters of St Bernadette's spring, waters which, according to chemical analysis, contain no identifiable curative qualities.

love magic *see* MAGIC, LOVE

love potions *see* APHRODISIACS

Lovecraft, H(oward) P(hillips) (1890–1937)

US writer and poet; a highly influential author who fused the horror and science fiction genres, he created what came to be known as the Cthulhu Mythos.
H P Lovecraft was born in Providence, Rhode Island, where he lived almost all of his life. A sickly child, he was frequently kept out of school by his mother, but he read avidly, and from an early age he developed a taste for the works of horror writers such as Edgar Allan Poe and M R JAMES. His family life was a troubled one; his father died in an insane asylum when Lovecraft was only 5 years old, and his doting but eccentric mother told him he was a little girl and dressed him as one until he was 6. She would later die in the same asylum as had his father. In 1908, after two and a half years of high school, Lovecraft suffered a nervous collapse and left without graduating.

As a young man, he supported himself by editing and correcting the texts of other writers, and by ghost-writing, and continued to do so for the rest of his life. His first professionally published work was the short story *Dagon*, which appeared in the pulp magazine *Weird Tales* in 1923. From then on, he was a regular contributor to the magazine, and his body of work consists mainly of the 60 or so stories which were published in it. Although he was not a prolific writer, and had a limited readership during his lifetime, his work later earned him a cult following as a master of modern horror. He died in 1937, but in 1939, two young fans of his work, August Derleth and Donald Wandrei, established a publishing imprint called Arkham House (named after the fictional town of Arkham, based on Lovecraft's own home town of Providence, in which many of his tales are set) to publish a posthumous collection of his stories, *The Outsider and Others*.

In a unique fusion of horror and science fiction, Lovecraft created what came to be known as the 'Cthulhu Mythos' (the term was coined by Derleth after Lovecraft's death) in the short stories which he wrote mostly during the last decade of his life. In this pseudo-mythological framework, he postulates a powerful and ancient race of ALIEN and extra-dimensional beings called the Old Ones who inhabited the earth long before mankind; hideous and terrible beyond belief, these creatures are hinted at in age-old myths and legends, and are still worshipped by deranged human cults. They are led by the monstrous Cthulhu, who lives in hibernation in the sunken city of R'yleh, but who will awake and bring the Old Ones back 'when the stars are right' and wreak havoc on the Earth. Within these short stories, Lovecraft created one of the most influential plot devices in all of horror – THE NECRONOMICON, a secret book of magic supposedly written by a mad Arabian sorcerer called Abdul Alhazred.

Lovelock, James *see* GAIA HYPOTHESIS

low magic *see* MAGIC, LOW

Loys's Ape *see panel p399*

LSD

A hallucinogenic drug.
LSD (lysergic acid diethylamide) is a psychotropic hallucinogenic drug derived from lysergic acid, a substance found naturally in ergot and the seeds of the morning glory plant. It was first synthesized in the late 1930s and in the 1940s was hailed, because of its psychotropic effects, as a possible treatment for schizophrenia.

In the 1960s, the US psychologist Timothy Leary (1920–96) conducted experiments at Harvard University, testing the drug on volunteers in the attempt to evaluate its possible use in treating such conditions as alcoholism and criminal recidivism. However, he soon became more interested in the 'mind-expanding' and psychedelic effects of LSD and helped popularize the drug's illicit use.

Loys's Ape

It is nothing if not ironic that whereas many CRYPTIDS are represented only by the most blurry, ambiguous photographic evidence, one cryptid is highly controversial on account of the very fact that it is represented by a photograph of excellent, crystal-clear quality. Its story began in 1920, when Swiss geologist Dr François de Loys was leading an expedition through the jungles of the Río Tarra, at the south-western edge of Lake Maracaibo in Venezuela's Zulia State. Without warning, two strange ape-like creatures allegedly emerged from behind some bushes just ahead of the expedition members, walking upright on their hind legs, lacking tails and standing approximately 1.5 metres (5 feet) tall. It is said that they seemed greatly angered by the sight of the scientists, and moved closer, as if to attack them. It was also claimed that the creatures defecated into their hands and threw their excrement at the men. To protect themselves, the scientists said that they had to shoot and kill one of these animals, a female. The other, a male, fled back into the jungle and was not seen again.

As they were unable to identify the dead ape-like primate, and could not transport its heavy, decomposing carcase very far either, they propped it into a sitting posture on a wooden crate, and photographed it. Most of the photographs were later lost, but one excellent picture survived the team's return to Europe, where it astonished the scientific community.

In particular, Professor George Montandon, a French zoologist, believed that the creature it depicted was a bona fide, hitherto undescribed species of South American ape, which he named *Ameranthropoides loysi* ('Loys's American ape'), but others were more sceptical. As the creature bore certain resemblances to the familiar spider monkeys native to this continent, they concluded that this is all that it was, despite Loys's claims concerning its much greater size and various other peculiarities. They also challenged Loys's avowed statement that it was tailless, and suggested that

The controversial photograph of Loys's ape which was first published in 1920. (© Mary Evans Picture Library)

when photographing this animal he may have hidden or even deliberately cut off its tail, in order to give it a more ape-like appearance.

Yet some have suggested that it is odd that evolution has not fashioned a single ape-like species in a continent where numerous species of primate exist, and which would occupy an equivalent niche to that of the gorillas and chimpanzees in Africa as well as Asia's orang utans. Furthermore, other Western explorers have apparently seen creatures similar to Loys's ape in South America's rainforests – in 1987, for instance, a creature that was 1.5 metres (5 feet) tall and walked on its hind legs was observed by mycologist Gary Samuels at a distance of only 18 metres (59 feet) in the forests of Guyana – and many native tribes have special names for them. These include the 'didi' in Guyana, 'shiru' in Colombia, 'vasitri' ('big devil') in Venezuela, and 'mono grande' ('big monkey') of the region where Loys's ape was encountered. Also, palaeontologists have discovered in recent times the fossilized remains of giant spider monkeys, twice as large as any species known to exist today and no more than 10,000 years old. Could these be the ancestors of Loys's ape, or something very like it, inhabiting the dense jungles of South America?

Having said that, a hitherto unpublicized letter written in 1962 by Venezuelan tropical physician Dr Enrique Tejera, a field colleague of Loys, was recently reproduced in full within a scientific article. It states that the entire incident (including photograph) was a hoax that had got out of hand. It alleged that the photograph's enigmatic subject was nothing more than the body of an ordinary marimonda spider monkey that had been looked after by Loys during the expedition, and which, after its death, had indeed been modified, including having its tail removed, for this now-(in)famous photograph. Yet even if true (which now can never be confirmed or denied, as Tejera died in 1980), this only dismisses the photograph as evidence for the existence of a South American ape; the numerous eyewitness reports and local traditions of such creatures remain to be explained.

Informally known as 'acid', its effects include distortion of auditory and visual imagery and increased or distorted feelings of sensory awareness, thought processes outside the normal range as well as unpredictable behaviour. Among the hazards associated with abuse of the drug are paranoid delusions, possible long-term psychological damage and the recurrence of hallucinatory events without taking the drug (known as flashbacks).

The drug's effects give rise to the dismissal by some of many unexplained phenomena as the products of LSD-induced hallucinations.

Lucan, Lord (1934–)

English alleged murderer who famously disappeared.

Richard John Bingham, 7th Earl of Lucan, acquired the nickname 'Lucky Lucan' through his gambling exploits. It may be that his luck ran out on 7 November 1974.

Lord Lucan and his wife, Veronica, were estranged. In fact, he had sought to take custody of their children away from her. On the evening of 7 November, Lady Lucan claimed that he had attacked her in the basement of her London home after she had discovered him lurking there. When she fought him off, he told her he had killed their children's nanny, Sandra Rivett, having mistaken the unfortunate girl for his wife. Her corpse was later found in the house, stuffed into a large bag. Lady Lucan was able to escape from him and raise the alarm.

An extensive police search for the vanished aristocrat, who was also known to have large gambling debts, failed to locate him and he remains missing to this day. At an inquest in 1975 he was named as the murderer of Sandra Rivett.

Lord Lucan was officially proclaimed to be dead on 11 December 1992, but this is really only

The peer (and alleged murderer) Lord Lucan, who famously disappeared in 1974. (© TopFoto/UPP)

a legal formality necessary for inheritance purposes. Some believe that he took his own life on the night of the murder or shortly thereafter, while others are convinced that wealthy and influential friends smuggled him out of the country. Despite various 'sightings' of Lord Lucan in various parts of the world over the years, his continued existence (or otherwise) is a matter of speculation.

Lucifer

In Christian tradition, another name for Satan; it is most commonly used to refer to him before his fall from Heaven, when he was the most radiant of the angels ('Lucifer' being Latin for 'bringer of light').

In the Christian tradition, 'Lucifer' has, for centuries, been popularly used as another name for SATAN, the name given to the DEVIL, chief spirit of evil, adversary of God, tempter of mankind and ruler of Hell. 'Lucifer', which is Latin for 'bringer of light', is most commonly used as the proper name of Satan before his pride led him to rebel against God and be cast from Heaven, while he was still the most radiant of the angels and second in command only to God himself. But this convention is in fact based on a misreading of a passage in the Old Testament Book of Isaiah:

> How art thou fallen from heaven
> O day-star, son of the morning! [*Heilel ben Shahar*]

The Hebrew word *Heilel*, meaning 'bringer of light', was translated by the Church Father, St Jerome, as the Latin *Lucifer* in his 4th-century Vulgate version of the Septuagint Bible. This Latin word was also used by Roman astrologers and poets to refer to the planet Venus, also known as the Morning Star, and in the Isaiah verse, the word *Heilel* was actually an honorific title for the King of Babylon. However, Jerome followed earlier Christian writers in applying the name 'Lucifer' to Satan, a connection thought by some to have originated with the theologian Origen, and to have been reinforced by the similarity between the New Testament passages Luke 10:18 and Revelation 9:1 to the Isaiah scripture. Jerome's Vulgate translation thus established 'Lucifer' in the Christian tradition as Satan's name before his expulsion from Heaven, although it should be noted that the Vulgate version also uses the word 'Lucifer' to refer to 'the light of the morning', 'the signs of the ZODIAC' and 'the aurora', and that the name 'Lucifer' does not appear in most modern translations of the Christian Bible, since it means 'bearer of light', and in the New Testament, the bringer of light is Christ.

The story of Lucifer's rebellion and fall from

Heaven has no direct biblical source, and is never mentioned in the Old Testament; however, it became a part of the Christian tradition by about the 5th century onwards, and was developed and embellished in literary works such as Dante's *Divine Comedy* and Milton's *Paradise Lost*, which did much to popularize the identification of Lucifer with Satan.

Lucis Trust *see* BAILEY, ALICE

luck *see* FATE AND LUCK

Lughnasadh
One of the four major festivals, or sabbats, of the modern pagan calendar; celebrated around 1 August, the time of the beginning of the harvest.
The old Irish word *Lughnassadh* means 'Lugh's wedding' – Lugh being a Celtic sun god. It is a time of year traditionally associated with the first harvest and with weddings. Celebrations include fires, dancing and rituals to ensure the future fertility of the fields.

The Anglo-Saxon festival of Lammas (meaning 'loaf mass'), which was adopted by the Christian Church, occurs at the same time of the year. See also AUTUMNAL EQUINOX; BELTANE; IMBOLC; PAGANISM; SABBATS; SAMHAIN; SUMMER SOLSTICE; VERNAL EQUINOX; WINTER SOLSTICE.

luminous phenomena
Strange lights or glows seen in places or around people or objects.
For centuries, various types of luminous phenomena have been observed in nature and considered to be mysterious or paranormal. Some are now known to be produced by electrical or electromagnetic effects, and these include EARTH LIGHTS, quake lights (see EARTHQUAKES), BALL LIGHTNING, aurora (see AURORA BOREALIS) and ST ELMO'S FIRE. It is thought that certain of these effects are still responsible for many reported sightings of UFOs.

Another luminous phenomenon is the WILL-O'-THE-WISP. This is the common name for the *ignis fatuus* (Latin, 'foolish fire'), a glowing light produced through the combustion of marsh-gas over swampy areas, believed in the past to be created by FAIRIES or evil SPIRITS in order to lead travellers astray.

Foxfire is another form of naturally generated glow, in this case the phosphorescence generated by certain types of fungus on rotting wood. In the 19th century it was also discovered that the phosphorescence often seen by sailors in the wake of ships was caused by microscopic animals, such as *Noctiluca*, present in the water. See also AURAS and HALOES.

lunacy
A form of insanity once thought to come with the changes in the moon.
According to folklore, the rays of the moon can induce insanity, and this connection is shown by the word 'lunacy', which comes from the Latin *luna*, meaning 'moon'. This type of insanity is also known as 'moon madness', and a person affected used to be referred to as being 'moonstruck'. The lunar cycle has always been closely bound up with human experience, and the moon has an age-old association with the fairy world, contact with which might drive a mortal mad; there is a superstition that it is highly dangerous to sleep in direct moonlight, and sleepwalkers are sometimes believed to be more active during the full moon. It is also the influence of the full moon which is said to act as the catalyst for LYCANTHROPY. The link between the moon and insanity is mentioned by the 16th-century physician and occultist PARACELSUS, who wrote that the moon had:

> … the power to tear reason out of man's head by depriving him of humours and cerebral virtues.

He added that this influence was at its most potent when the moon was full. The Catholic Church, on the other hand, attacked the pagan notion of the moon's power over humans, seeing this insanity instead as the work of the DEVIL, who was himself influenced by the moon. The *MALLEUS MALEFICARUM* ('Hammer of Witches'), published in 1487, states:

> Certain men who are called Lunatics are molested by devils more at one time than at another; and the devils would not so behave, but would rather molest them at all times, unless they themselves were deeply affected by certain phases of the Moon.

The British Lunacy Act of 1842 defined a lunatic as a person who was lucid during the two weeks before a full moon, but was given to strange behaviour during the fortnight after it. As recently as 1940, an English soldier charged with the murder of a comrade pleaded 'moon madness' as his defence, saying that he was affected by this temporary insanity at every full moon. A number of studies have been carried out in an attempt to prove that there is an increase in violence and crime during the time of the full moon: in 1998 a study was carried out for three months on all 1,200 inmates in the maximum-security wing of Armley Jail in Leeds, and there seemed to be evidence that there was a definite rise in the number of violent incidents during the three days of the full moon. However, although modern science still has to prove conclusively the link between insanity and the full moon, the belief persists in folklore and popular culture.

lung-gom

A legendary art said to be practised by some Tibetan lamas, who, by means of psychic training, can travel non-stop for long periods of time very rapidly, covering great distances across rugged and inhospitable terrain.

Lung-gom is a legendary power attributed to certain Tibetan lamas who have undergone a lengthy training in MEDITATION and breath control. These lamas, known as *lung-gom-pa*, are thought to be able to cover great distances across rugged and inhospitable terrain for extended periods of time without food or rest. It has been claimed that a skilled *lung-gom-pa* is faster than a horse, and can travel non-stop for 48 hours or more, covering more than 322 kilometres (200 miles) in a day, appearing to fly when he runs.

Lung-gom training is not a physical regime, but a psychic one, and is said to involve living in complete darkness and seclusion for 39 months, during which the trainee has to master seated meditation, breath control and visualization techniques in which he imagines his body to be as light as a feather. He is also required to watch a single star in the sky intently for days at a time without allowing himself to become distracted. The word *lung* means 'vital energy' or 'psychic force', while *gom* means 'meditation' or 'concentration', and the *lung-gom-pa* is said to control his energy and focus it on his breathing and movement, always looking ahead and keeping his eyes fixed on a single object, usually a star.

In her book *Magic and Mystery in Tibet*, the French mystic scholar ALEXANDRA DAVID-NÉEL described an encounter with a lung-gom runner. She said that rather than running, he seemed to lift himself off the ground in leaps, as if made of elastic, and he passed her and her servants without being aware of their existence, in an apparent trance state. Her servants warned her not to speak to him, since if he broke his meditation while running, the god who was inside him would leave his body, shaking him so hard as it left that he would die.

lycanthropy

The power to transform magically into a wolf; also, a psychological condition in which the patient believes himself to be a wolf.

The word 'lycanthropy' comes from the Greek *lykos*, meaning 'wolf', and *anthrōpos*, meaning 'man'. The belief that under certain circumstances a human can transform into a wolf (or 'werewolf') has been found all over the world since ancient times. Possibly the first written reference to lycanthropy is in the Old Testament book of Daniel, in which King Nebuchadnezzar is described as displaying symptoms of werewolfism for several years. A Greek legend tells how Lycaon was transformed into a wolf by the god Zeus after serving him a dish of human flesh, and in the 5th century BC, the Greek historian Herodotus told of the Neuri, a strange people who became wolves for a short time each year. The Roman poet Virgil also wrote in the 1st century BC of a necromancer called Moeris who could transform himself into a wolf. During the Middle Ages, the rise of witch-hunting was accompanied by a rise in the number of accounts of werewolves, which were also attributed by the Church to demonic influence; in 1257, torture was officially sanctioned as a means of forcing werewolves to confess to their crimes, and alleged werewolves received the same punishment as those found guilty of WITCHCRAFT. The most notorious werewolf case of the 16th century was that of a French peasant called Gilles Garnier, accused of killing four children and devouring their flesh; he was said to have been seen in his half-man, half-beast state by many witnesses, and was burnt alive. One theory suggests that the explosion of werewolfism in the Middle Ages was caused by the contamination of rye bread with ergot, a fungal parasite which grew on the rye and was ingested with the bread made from it; ergot induces LSD-type HALLUCINATIONS, and may have caused people to think they were seeing werewolves.

However, since early times, lycanthropy has also been recognized as a medical or psychological disorder. The Greek physician Galen, in the 2nd century AD, considered it to be a melancholic state, and in the 7th century, Paulos of Aegina described the condition in detail and recommended treatments for it, which included massive bloodletting, baths of sweet water and milk whey, and purging with various herbs. And despite the links between werewolfism and demonic influence made by the INQUISITION, some 16th- and 17th-century writers maintained that it was a medical or mental affliction. The word 'lycanthropia', as used to describe this disorder, first appears in English in Reginald Scot's 1584 book *Discoverie of Witchcraft*, and Robert Burton's *The Anatomy of Melancholy* (1621) also describes the affliction of lycanthropia or wolf-madness, in which the sufferer runs howling about graves and fields at night and believes himself to be a wolf. During the Inquisition, the terms 'lycanthropy' and 'werewolfism' were used more or less interchangeably, but after then, the word 'lycanthropy' was generally restricted to the medical sense, rather than the supernatural one. With the emergence of psychology as a scientific field, the term almost disappeared from medical literature, the behaviour of the patient tending to be diagnosed as another condition such as schizophrenia, bipolar disorder, multiple personality disorder or necrophilia.

According to folklore, there are a number of ways in which an individual can become a werewolf: being bitten by a werewolf; being put under a curse; heredity; being conceived on the night of a full moon; being possessed by a demon; eating the flesh of a rabid wolf; or drinking water from a puddle formed in a wolf's footprint. A person can also voluntarily become a werewolf by putting on a wolf's skin, a special belt or a magical ointment. Signs that someone is a werewolf include hairy palms, eyebrows which meet in the middle, an index finger considerably longer than the middle finger and hair between the shoulder blades. It is said that a werewolf can be made to return to his human form by calling him by his human name, or by extracting three drops of blood while he is in his animal state. Also, if a werewolf can restrain himself from eating human flesh for nine years, he is said to be cured of the curse. The 1941 film *The Wolf Man*, starring Lon Chaney Jnr, introduced additional elements which have now become part of popular werewolf lore, although they were only created for this film: the vulnerability of werewolves to silver, the fact that a werewolf must transform at the full moon and the mark of the PENTAGRAM on the palm which identifies a werewolf or his next victim. See also LOUP GAROU; ROMASANTA, MANUEL BLANCO.

Lying Stones

A classic hoax from the 18th century which is often cited as an example of the triumph of scientific enlightenment.

The story of the 'lying stones' has achieved something of the status of a folk tale through the addition of numerous embellishments and moral messages in its various retellings. It often appears in academic textbooks as a cautionary tale or as a humorous example of the foolish notions that were once applied to fossils before the appearance of the current orthodox view.

In 1726, Professor Johann Bartholomew Adam Beringer, Dean of the Faculty of Medicine at the University of Würzburg in Germany, came by a remarkable collection of what appeared to be fossils, which he had been led to (or which had been found on his behalf, depending on the version of the story) on nearby Mount Eivelstadt. These stones had upon them three-dimensional images of lizards, birds, frogs and many other animals, apparently preserved with a level of detail that had never been seen in any ordinary fossil (and, on our current understanding, would not be possible). Further than this, some showed pictures of the sun and moon, and were inscribed with Hebrew lettering.

Although Beringer realized that these stones were not ordinary fossils, he dismissed the idea that they could have been produced by humans and went on to publish a book entitled *Lithographiae Wirceburgensis*

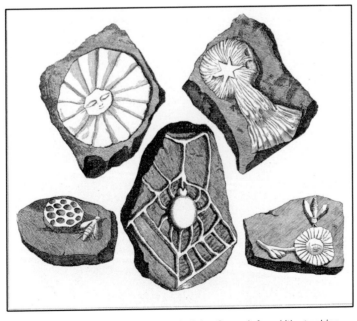

An engraving of Professor Beringer's 'Lying Stones', from *Lithographiae Wirceburgensis* (1726). (© Mary Evans Picture Library)

(1726, 'Wurzburg Lithography') to present his incredible finds to the scientific community for their consideration. It was only after publication that he realized that he had been tricked, and that the fossils were fakes, leading to an embarrassing withdrawal of his book. In some of the more sensationalized versions of the story, he only realized his mistake when one of the stones was found to have his own name written on it. It is also often claimed that he almost bankrupted himself trying to buy back copies of the book and that the disgrace and loss of reputation shortened his life. However, there is no basis for these claims – Beringer continued to work for many more years and published several further books. Likewise, the incident was not a simple prank, rather a malicious and carefully orchestrated attempt on the part of two academic colleagues to deceive him as a punishment for what they saw as his arrogance.

The incident occurred at a time when there was still much debate as to the exact nature and origin of fossils. Beringer held the view that they were not the product of prehistoric living organisms, which is often cited as the reason why he could be fooled by the juxtaposition of images of animals with pictures of astronomical bodies and writing. However, he was not alone in this view at the time, and in this instance he did not actually express an opinion as to the origin of the stones – other than the admittedly shortsighted assertion that they were not carved by humans. Although the story is often offered as an example of the way that the forward progress of science crushes foolish old-fashioned notions, the tale could equally be seen to show how scientists' preconceived ideas and beliefs, and the desire for glory, can sometimes lead them to take a less than careful approach when confronted by new evidence.

M

Mabon *see* AUTUMNAL EQUINOX

macrocosm and microcosm
The principle that there exists between man and the universe a correspondence in which the universe (macrocosm) is represented on a miniature scale by the individual (microcosm).

The ancient Greeks believed that there was a correspondence between the large and complex structure of the universe, which they called the macrocosm, and the individual human, or microcosm (literally, 'little world'). Man was regarded as a model or epitome of the universe, with each person mirroring, on a miniature scale, the structure and patterns of the cosmos. The idea that the same patterns are reproduced at all levels of reality may have begun with the philosopher Democritus in the 5th century BC, or with PYTHAGORAS, and this concept is the fundamental principle of Socratic and Platonic philosophy. Plato's *Republic* is based on the belief that the same qualities or characteristics are found in entities of many different sizes, from one man to the population of a whole city or culture. Plato, for example, describes three kinds of people, the appetitive, the irascible and the rational, and asserts that in the state, which may be regarded as a large human being, there are three classes of men who correspond to these three psychological types: the artisans (the appetitive), the military (the irascible) and the philosophers (the rational). The actual word 'microcosm' is thought to have been first used by Plato's pupil, Aristotle, who reasoned that if the human body, which represented the universe in miniature, possessed rationality, intelligence and a soul, so too must the universe. The principle of macrocosm and microcosm, as expressed in the axiom ascribed to Hermes Trismegistus (see HERMETICA), 'As above, so below', has also permeated the thinking of Hermetic philosophers and alchemists throughout the centuries.

Hindu cosmology similarly regards the body of man as a microcosm of the entire divine creation, and the outer world as a macrocosm of the inner one.

macro-PK
Large scale, observable demonstrations of psychokinesis.

The term macro-PK (short for macroscopic-PSYCHOKINESIS) is applied to psychokinesis involving effects which can be directly observed by the naked eye. Classic putative examples include the METAL-BENDING feats, and other demonstrations of the movement of inanimate objects apparently using the power of the mind, attributed to such people as URI GELLER and NINA KULAGINA.

Macro-PK is possibly the PSI phenomenon which figures the most prominently in the public imagination, and, if such effects could be clearly and unambiguously produced, the impact on the way we view the world would be enormous. However, there have still been no unchallenged examples of this skill offered, and no one has yet come forward with a display that satisfies the conditions laid down in JAMES RANDI's famous one-million-dollar challenge. See also MICRO-PK.

Macumba *see* CANDOMBLÉ

The Mad Gasser of Mattoon *see panel p409*

Magic

The belief in and practice of magic is probably as old as human history. Magic may be defined as the influencing of events and physical phenomena by humans using mystical, paranormal or supernatural means. The word ultimately derives from the Old Persian *magus* (plural *magi*), which referred to Zoroastrian priests and scholars of the Medes, credited by Classical commentators with mastery of ASTROLOGY and other OCCULT arts. The archaic spelling of MAGICK was repopularized by the 20th-century occultist ALEISTER CROWLEY, who used it to differentiate his mystical system from stage magic (see MAGIC, STAGE) and ILLUSION. Since his time, many other occult and spiritual traditions have adopted this spelling to refer to their practices.

In *The Golden Bough* (1890), anthropologist JAMES FRAZER argues that magic precedes religion as an attempt by man to understand, control and influence his external environment. In his opinion it involves an essentially animistic worldview, in which all natural objects and phenomena are regarded as being 'alive' and having a consciousness (see ANIMISM). Most cultures also have, or have had at one time in their history, some form of magical tradition which recognizes a shamanic interconnectedness of spirit. In many tribal societies, magic may only be practised by certain members of the group, such as the SHAMAN, MEDICINE MAN or WITCH DOCTOR, and is performed for social purposes – to help the tribe defeat its enemies, to bring rain, to increase the fertility of crops and livestock or for healing.

Common to many magical traditions is the belief that there is an inherent ENERGY radiating from the Earth and all living things, and it is this energy which magic, as a system, seeks to harness and channel. To the ancient Egyptians, it was known as *heka*; to the Yoruba of Africa, it is *ashé*; to the Polynesians, MANA. Magic is thus regarded as a source of power, neither good nor bad in itself, and whether it is used for good (see MAGIC, WHITE) or evil (see MAGIC, BLACK) depends on the MAGICIAN's intentions. Some practitioners of magic hold that magic does not break the laws of nature, but rather, obeys laws of nature which are simply not yet understood, and thus should not be called 'supernatural'.

Throughout the millennia, each culture has developed its own system of magic, reflecting its traditions and preoccupations. The belief in the power of magical names, SPELLS, figures, AMULETS, CHARMS and RITUALS was an important part of ancient Egyptian life, and magic also formed a common tradition in the Graeco-Roman world. Collections of magic spells rank among the world's earliest written documents, and, according to Egyptian mythology, the lunar god Thoth, credited as the inventor of both magic and writing, wrote the very first book – a revelation of spells and rituals, which was believed to hold the key to all the secrets of the universe. In Egypt, a large number of papyri were discovered which contain early examples of much of the magical lore later incorporated into Western ceremonial magic (see MAGIC, CEREMONIAL), and which describe the use of WANDS and other ritual tools, the MAGIC CIRCLE, and magical SYMBOLS and sigils. Modern Western practitioners have also drawn heavily upon the sacred magical texts of Hinduism, such as the *Atharva-Veda*, which discuss both white and black magic.

In Western history, the belief in and practice of magic has waxed and waned, either through pressure brought by the Christian Church (which has traditionally treated such things as WITCHCRAFT as sinful and forbidden) or through simple scepticism brought about by an increase in scientism. However, for many centuries most of Christian Europe maintained a reasonably tolerant view of magic, which formed a part of everyday life; ordinary people consulted the 'cunning men' and 'wise women' (see WISDOM) found in every village. These people were believed to be skilled not only in healing and herbalism, but in detecting and counteracting the practices of those who used magic for evil purposes. But in the Middle Ages, the Church ruled that all magic was brought about by evil SPIRITS manipulating nature on behalf of the SORCERER, who had entered into a pact with the DEVIL (see DEVIL'S PACT). Its practice was therefore forbidden, and was prosecuted with varying degrees of severity from the 15th to the 18th century. The Muslim faith has a similar relationship with magic, and its practice, known as *Sither*, is forbidden; it is written in the Koran that Allah permitted two angels to teach magic to mankind in order to test their obedience to the command not to use it. Magicians have always believed that by their arcane knowledge, and the power of their will, they can manipulate spiritual and natural forces and bend them to their own desires. It is perhaps this rejection of humility, and refusal to accept divine will, that has set magic in such opposition to the monotheistic religions of Judaism, Christianity and Islam.

Despite persecution, folk magic continued to be practised in secret, and the high-ranking and educated practitioners of high magic (see MAGIC, HIGH) generally escaped the censure of the Church and State. But by the 17th century, magic had come to be regarded as irrational in comparison with science, and those who practised ceremonial magic went underground; at this time, many SECRET SOCIETIES such as the ROSICRUCIANS and FREEMASONRY were formed. Toward the end of the 19th century, magic enjoyed a revival, as Romanticism fostered a renewed interest in exotic spiritualities, and European colonialism brought Westerners into contact with Indian and Egyptian beliefs. The late 19th century gave rise to many magical and OCCULT organizations, the peak of this wave of magic being represented by the HERMETIC ORDER OF THE GOLDEN DAWN. A further revival of interest in magic was heralded by the 1951 repeal of the last Witchcraft Act, followed by the publication of Gerald Gardner's book *Witchcraft Today*, which sparked off a resurgence in witchcraft in the form of the new magic-based religion of WICCA. The various branches of NEOPAGANISM and other earth-based religions which have since followed also combine the practices of magic and religion.

Practitioners of magic usually believe that it works on one or more of the following basic principles: the intervention of spirits; a mystical energy which exists in all things and can be manipulated by the magician; a mysterious interconnection in the cosmos which joins all things, with magic as the application of the magician's unity with the universe; the use of symbols, which can magically take on the physical quality of the phenomenon or object they represent, so that by manipulating the symbol, the magician can also manipulate the reality the symbol represents; the focus of the magician's will on the desired object; the power of the subconscious mind; and the principles of sympathetic magic, also known as contagious, homeopathic, or imitative magic, whereby a desired

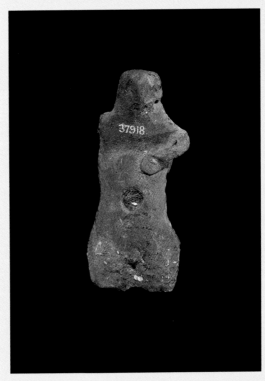

A 2nd-century Egyptian wax figure, with human hair pushed into its navel. The figure was probably used in a form of image magic. (© TopFoto/HIP)

effect is produced by imitating it, and whatever is done to a material object is believed to have the same effect on the person with whom it was once in contact, or of whom it was once a part (see MAGIC, CONTAGIOUS; MAGIC, HOMEOPATHIC; MAGIC, IMITATIVE; MAGIC, SYMPATHETIC).

The magical production of effects in the material world is usually achieved by SPELLS, which are believed to bring about the desired result either directly, or by summoning the relevant power for the purpose. The potent words of the spell are generally accompanied by a ritual which must be observed exactly to make the spell effective and to control its power. By CONJURATION, EVOCATION, INCANTATION or INVOCATION, spirits or powers may be summoned. Western ceremonial magic, Wicca and neopaganism focus strongly on the power of the four directions (see DIRECTIONS, FOUR) and their ELEMENTS of EARTH, AIR, FIRE and WATER, which are honoured and invoked during the casting of a MAGIC CIRCLE and represented on the altar and at each corner of the circle by ritual tools such as a CUP, CAULDRON, dagger, PENTAGRAM, SWORD or wand. These tools have no inherent power, but are magically charged by the magician. OILS, BELLS, ROBES and incense are also often used as part of the ritual.

Magic may be used for protection against harm or the malign influence of the EVIL EYE (see APOTROPAICS), and magically charged objects such as amulets, charms and TALISMANS are often worn or hung up to protect the bearer or their property. These protective objects sometimes incorporate a magical symbol such as an ANKH, pentagram, HEXAGRAM or LEMNISCATE, or a MAGIC SQUARE. Magic may also be used, in the form of a CURSE or hex, to cause harm, and image magic (see MAGIC, IMAGE) is sometimes employed for this purpose.

There are many types and traditions of magic. The simplest, sometimes known as low magic (see MAGIC, LOW), is the magic practised throughout the centuries by the village wise woman or cunning man. It does not involve long, complex rituals, and its aim is usually to change conditions or bring about events in the physical world, or for DIVINATION. It may involve love, plant or weather magic (see MAGIC, LOVE; MAGIC, PLANT; MAGIC, WEATHER), and is commonly used today by followers of various neopagan paths. The aim of high magic, ritual magic (see MAGIC, RITUAL) or ceremonial magic is usually to connect with the divine or to enable the magician to operate on a 'higher spiritual plane'. Sex magic seeks to harness and channel the energy of sexual intercourse (see MAGIC, SEX), while the practitioners of chaos magic (see MAGIC, CHAOS) are encouraged to adopt any belief or method which allows them to attain the altered state of consciousness necessary to bring about the desired magical effect.

At present, there is in general less persecution of practitioners of magic than at any time since the rise of Christianity, and magical tools and ingredients, together with books on magic, once rare or forbidden, can be bought in the high street and on the Internet. Magic features prominently in popular culture, with television series such as *Sabrina the Teenage Witch*, *Buffy the Vampire Slayer* and *Charmed*, and films and books such as the *Harry Potter* series, as well as countless computer and role-playing games and anime films. The idea of magic continues to capture and fascinate the imagination, as it has done since the dawn of mankind.

See also MAGIC, ENOCHIAN; MAGIC, HEALING.

Lorna Gilmour

The Mad Gasser of Mattoon

The Mad Gasser of Mattoon was one of the names given by the press to a mysterious prowler said to have plagued the US town of Mattoon, Illinois, in September 1944. He was also known as 'the phantom anaesthetist', and was said to spray unsuspecting victims with an incapacitating gas.

The first 'gassing' that was reported to the police came on the night of Friday 1 September, when a Mrs Kearney claimed that an unseen intruder had opened a window of her house and sprayed a gas into the building that had left her and her daughter feeling dizzy and sick. The police found nothing, but the next day the Mattoon *Daily Journal-Gazette* had a front-page report on the incident, with the headline, '"Anesthetic Prowler" on Loose: Mrs Kearney and daughter first victims'.

More reports followed. On 6 September, the *Daily Journal-Gazette* reported that Mrs C Cordes was 'overcome after picking up cloth found on porch' and by 9 September the *Charleston Daily Courier* reported that 25 people had fallen victim to the mad gasser and that:

Demands for a citizens' mass meeting to plot the capture of the 'Madman of Mattoon' grew today as an 11-year-old girl, three women and an eight-year-old boy reported to police that they were victims of the phantom prowler whose trail is marked by a sweet-smelling anesthetic that causes nausea and temporary paralysis.

The police were no nearer to apprehending the gasser, and the townspeople were awaiting further attacks when on 13 September the *Daily Journal-Gazette* carried the headline '"Gas Calls" at Vanishing Point'. Reports of the gasser ceased.

Various theories to explain the phenomenon of the mad gasser have been put forward over the years, with the most commonly accepted being that this was a classic case of MASS HYSTERIA, more than helped along by the sensationalist reporting of the time. It has been noted that the first headline in the *Daily Journal-Gazette* implied that there would be further incidents – 'Mrs Kearney and her daughter first victims' – and reports such at that in the *Chicago Herald-American* of 10 September were hardly objective:

A picture of the Mad Gasser of Mattoon, which appeared on a set of 'Myth or Real?' collector's cards. (© TopFoto/Fortean)

… bewildered citizens reeled today under the repeated attacks of a mad anesthetist who has sprayed a deadly nerve gas into 13 homes and has knocked out 27 known victims.

Mass hysteria has also been given as the explanation for a series of similar, although less well-known events in two counties of Virginia between December 1933 and January 1934, where reports of a figure spraying gas into homes at night also caused a sensation. As the *New York Times* reported on 22 January 1934:

Farmers' families of Botetourt County, terrified by a stealthy marauder who hurls gas into rooms, overcoming his victims or making them violently ill, are locking doors and windows securely these nights. Men keep their shotguns ready to guard their homes.

Less-well-regarded explanations for the Mad Gasser of Mattoon have included toxic pollution from nearby factories (although how the pollution affected individual homes rather than the whole town is not explained) and an actual assailant, who was even named as a disgruntled local chemistry student called Farley Llewellyn by the writer Scott Maruna in his *The Mad Gasser of Mattoon: Dispelling the Hysteria* (2003).

magi

In ancient Persia, members of the Zoroastrian priest-astrologer class; 'magi' is also used to refer to magicians or 'wise men'.

According to Herodotus, the original magi were the sacred caste of the Medes, who organized Persian society after the fall of Assyria and Babylon. Some of this Zoroastrian class of priest-astrologers are thought to have migrated west during the Classical era, settling first in Greece, then in Italy, and it is likely that they were instrumental in the rise of Mithraism, a belief system derived from Persia which at one point was the largest single religion in Rome. The best-known magi are the Three Wise Men, Zoroastrian astrologers whom the New Testament book of Matthew relates as travelling from the East to worship the infant Christ, bringing gifts of gold, frankincense and myrrh.

The New Testament book of Acts also tells of Simon Magus, a SORCERER of the 1st century AD who became influential in Samaria through his magic. He was converted to Christianity by the preaching of Philip the Deacon, and tried to buy from the apostles Peter and John the power of the Holy Spirit. In the apocryphal Acts of Peter, the rivalry between Simon Magus and Simon Peter is described, along with an account of his death; performing magic for the Roman Emperor Claudius in the forum to prove his powers, he was said to have flown into the air. The apostles Peter and Paul prayed to God to stop him, and he fell to his death.

In Greek, the Old Persian word *magus* became *magos*, and came to be used of any enchanter or wizard in general, later being applied especially to a charlatan or quack. The Latin plural form *magi* entered English around 1200, referring specifically to the Three Wise Men of Matthew 2:1; the singular form, *magus*, is not attested in English until the late 14th century, when it was borrowed from French with the more general meaning of 'magician'.

Magic see panel p406

magic, black

The use of magic with the intention of harming or destroying others, or for personal gain.

Practitioners of magic do not in general consider magic to be either black or white, but see it as a source of power which can be used for either positive or negative purposes. The conscious use of supernatural powers for evil – the perversion of the magical arts in order to destroy, harm or influence others against their will, or for selfish personal gain – is usually regarded as black magic. ALEISTER CROWLEY defined as 'black magic' any attempt to use the power of magic for purposes other than aiding one's mental or mystical development. While the black magician who has made a pact with the Devil to sell his soul for wealth and power is largely a creation of popular culture, magical texts are said to exist which detail procedures for invoking demons to serve the black magician, and for as long as people have practised magic, there have been accounts of those who have sought to use it for evil ends. See BLACK ARTS; DEVIL'S PACT.

magic, ceremonial

A form of magic which involves highly elaborate rituals guided by a complex set of correspondences.

In ancient times, ceremonial magic was the domain of the priesthood. During the Renaissance, MAGIC was one of the subjects which came to be studied by scholars whose interest in Classical knowledge had led them to rediscover the esoteric texts of ancient Greece and Rome, and at this time the KABBALAH also gained prominence as a philosophical and magical system. Ceremonial magic flourished in Europe between the Renaissance and the 18th century, when the cultural and intellectual atmosphere was highly conducive to the study of magic; it was often intertwined with medieval ALCHEMY, with the alchemists of the Middle Ages using arcane rituals as well as 'scientific' means in their quest for knowledge. Alchemists such as JOHN DEE, HENRICUS CORNELIUS AGRIPPA, and PARACELSUS were thought to have practised ceremonial magic. European Renaissance ceremonial magic was strongly Christian in its symbolism. Various secret societies such as FREEMASONRY and the ROSICRUCIANS, which flourished from the 17th century onwards, continued the spread of esoteric knowledge and the return to the West of 'ancient wisdom'. The 19th century saw an upsurge of interest in all aspects of the OCCULT, and the birth of modern ceremonial magic with the founding of the HERMETIC ORDER OF THE GOLDEN DAWN. ISRAEL REGARDIE, ALEISTER CROWLEY and DION FORTUNE were particularly influential in the development of modern ceremonial magic.

The tradition of ceremonial magic as practised today is still largely inspired by the Golden Dawn and the systems which were derived from it, and includes Goetic and Enochian magic (see MAGIC, ENOCHIAN), GRIMOIRE magic and Thelemic ritual (see THELEMA). It uses a combination of Graeco-Egyptian and Judaeo-Christian symbolism and spiritual thought, and tools such as the TAROT, ASTROLOGY and the kabbalah. It requires a group of people to work together, and is not practised by one person alone, and practitioners frequently organize themselves into societies such as the ORDO TEMPLI ORIENTIS and the Argenteum Astrum. Ceremonial magicians may be, but are not necessarily, pagan; Dion Fortune considered herself to be a Christian.

Ceremonial magic is usually held to be the most complex form of magic, utilizing elaborate magical theory and drawing from a large body of occult literature; it always involves ritual, usually highly intricate and taking a long time to perform, and following exact rules. A complicated set of magical correspondences guides the form of its rituals, with careful astrological calculations often being made to determine the best time to perform the work. Intricate sigils and symbols are used, which it is believed must be drawn perfectly in order to be effective, and the colours of the candles, altar cloths and robes of the participants are also governed by the aim of the magic. It is sometimes believed that the elaborate ceremonies will call up entities or demons from other realms, so the strict instructions for the ceremonies are not changed or deviated from, since it is thought that to do so may result in serious consequences. Also, a sacred space such as a triple MAGIC CIRCLE is used, as it is held that this confines the magical 'energies' raised and protects the magicians while they work.

This highly disciplined branch of magic is used by many of its practitioners with the aim of achieving enlightenment and self-knowledge and connecting to the Divine. It has greatly influenced the development of modern WICCA and NEOPAGANISM, which have adopted from it features such as the casting of the protective circle during magical work, and the use of ritual tools such as the wand, pentacle and ritual knife or athame. See also MAGIC, HIGH.

magic, chaos
A postmodern form of occultism which strives to reduce ritual magic to those techniques common to all magical systems; practitioners are encouraged to adopt any belief or method which allows them to attain the altered state of consciousness necessary to bring about the desired magical effect.

Chaos magic is a postmodern form of ritual magic (see MAGIC, RITUAL) which uses various methods to alter the magician's state of consciousness. Practitioners believe that only by achieving this altered state, which is referred to as 'gnosis', can magic be worked; once the person's mind is focused completely on a single point or thought to the total exclusion of all others, the reasoning, conscious mind shuts down, and any thought which is experienced in this gnostic state and is then immediately forgotten is sent to the subconscious mind, where it can be enacted through means unknown to the conscious. The theory is that when the mind stops thinking, the magician can direct the dynamic power built up and brought to the climax of gnosis, and direct it to shape reality. Each

chaos magician is encouraged to develop his or her own, sometimes extreme, ways of achieving this state, and MEDITATION, chanting, dancing, drugs, sex and sometimes pain may be used.

The term 'chaos magic' first appeared in print in 1978, in Peter J Carroll's book *Liber Null*, which he followed up with *Psychonaut* in 1981. In these two books, Carroll formulated concepts on magic which were radically different from those of preceding ritual magicians such as ALEISTER CROWLEY, and the teachings of the HERMETIC ORDER OF THE GOLDEN DAWN. His work was heavily influenced by the Zos Kia Cultus, the unorthodox magical system created by AUSTIN OSMAN SPARE, a 20th-century artist and sorcerer who developed the used of sigils and techniques involving states of ecstasy to empower them. Carroll's works are still important source books for chaos magicians, who variously refer to themselves as Chaotes, Chaoists and Chaosites. Together with Ray Sherwin, Carroll founded the Magical Pact of the Illuminates of Thanateros, an organization which continues to research and develop chaos magic to this day.

magic, contagious
A simple form of magic which depends on the belief that an item which was once in contact with, or part of, a person can be used to influence them.

Many anthropologists classify MAGIC according to the basic principles first set out by SIR JAMES FRAZER in *The Golden Bough* (1890). Frazer separated examples of sympathetic magic into two categories – homeopathic magic (see MAGIC, HOMEOPATHIC) and contagious magic. Contagious magic (in which the sympathetic link is one of physical proximity or contact) is based upon the belief that after a person has had contact with something, a permanent relationship is established, and that the object can continue to influence them. Similarly, anything which was once a part of a person or thing can supposedly be used to the same effect. As a result, people from cultures where there is a belief in contagious magic might make sure nothing they have worn or handled regularly is stolen, and take careful precautions when disposing of cut hair, nail clippings, teeth and even body waste. In practice, contagious magic is often combined with homeopathic magic – for example, a person's hair may be incorporated into an effigy (see EFFIGIES) representing them.

Damaging something which has been created by a person is also believed by some to have a harmful effect on them. It was once popularly believed that MAGICIANS were able to cripple an enemy by driving a sharp object (such as a nail) into the person's footprint. However, in some instances the effect can flow the other way – one of the folkloric beliefs relating to

LYCANTHROPY held that drinking water from a puddle formed by the footprint of a werewolf would cause the drinker to become a werewolf too.

However, contagious magic can reputedly also have positive applications. Pliny described the connection between a wounded person and the one who had given him the wound; he said that if one person had hurt another and wished to alleviate the pain, then he could do so by simply spitting on the hand which had inflicted the wound. In many parts of the world it is customary to put an extracted tooth in a place where it may be found by a mouse or rat in the hope that the remaining teeth may acquire the firmness and strength of a rodent's. There is a traditional belief among some aboriginal tribes in Western Australia to the effect that if a mother throws a child's umbilical cord into a river or pool, the child will grow to be a good swimmer; and among the Cherokee Native Americans, a boy's umbilical cord was once hung on a tree in the woods so that he would become a good hunter.

The folkloric belief in contagious magic also offers a historical precedent for the more recent concept of PSYCHOMETRY – the apparent ability to gain information about a person through touching an item belonging to them. However, reflecting a general move away from the magical in the modern age, this is now usually understood by believers to result from a PSYCHIC ability (an example of MIND OVER MATTER) on the part of the psychometrist.

magic, Enochian
A system of magic based on the work of John Dee and Edward Kelley.
When the Elizabethan occultists JOHN DEE and Edward Kelley allegedly communicated with the angels, they used a new language which they referred to as Enochian. As Kelley communicated with the angels, Dee would write the communications down. These texts and the complex Enochian language system were examined by the English occultist MACGREGOR MATHERS, who developed and incorporated the Enochian system of angelic magic into the system of the HERMETIC ORDER OF THE GOLDEN DAWN.

magic, healing
Magic used for physical, emotional or spiritual healing.
In almost every part of the world before the advance of the scientific age (and even today in those societies where institutionalized medicine has not yet become the norm) people have sought cures for their illnesses in the traditional methods of folk medicine and magical healing. Western 'rational' medicine is based upon the concept that the world works by means of observable (or potentially observable) physical causal processes. However, there are many alternatives to this paradigm which involve a magical or spiritual understanding of illness.

In some cultures, illness may be believed to result from the actions of evil SPIRITS or the effects of harmful SPELLS. Preventative measures, such as the careful observance of rules and TABOOS and the wearing of protective CHARMS or AMULETS, may be employed. If such precautions are not enough, a spiritual leader such as a SHAMAN or MEDICINE MAN, may be called in to fight the evil with his own magic, sometimes symbolically sucking the illness out of the body or exorcizing the evil spirit. Image magic (see MAGIC, IMAGE) may also be employed, with the evil spirit causing the illness being magically drawn from the afflicted person and transferred into a doll representing them, a process sometimes known as puppet healing. There are also shamanic traditions in which illness is believed to result from a part of the soul breaking off and being lost when someone is subjected to trauma. The shaman might then attempt 'soul retrieval' – engaging on a spirit quest to retrieve and reincorporate the missing part.

Plants and herbs have always been used for healing magic, whether drunk as infusions and potions, applied as a poultice, worn as an amulet or inhaled. Knowledge of the use of herbs for healing and magic was often passed down through generations of wise women (see WISDOM), 'cunning men' or WITCHES. The distinction between remedies and charms was also often blurred, since herbal remedies were generally administered with accompanying rituals and incantations. However, the physical mechanisms by which many herbal remedies work is now understood, and much herbal lore has made the transition from healing magic to modern medicine. See also ALTERNATIVE MEDICINE.

magic, high
A highly complex and disciplined form of magic in which power is said to be derived from the divine through the successful control of spirits, principally demons and angels; its ultimate aim is to advance the practitioners' spiritual enlightenment and to bring them into communication with their 'higher self'.
In the Middle Ages, the term 'high magic' was used to refer to esoteric magical disciplines such as ASTROLOGY, ALCHEMY and the TAROT, practised mostly by males of the educated upper classes. Its aim was to attain spiritual power over unseen forces. By contrast, low magic or folk magic (see MAGIC, LOW), as traditionally practised chiefly by uneducated village women, was much simpler and had strictly practical applications, such as healing a sick person or helping someone to gain wealth or love.

In the late 19th century, the HERMETIC ORDER OF THE GOLDEN DAWN was influential in the modern revival of high magic; its carefully compiled system of philosophy, rituals, magical incantations and symbols incorporated elements from the KABBALAH, Rosicrucianism (see ROSICRUCIANS), FREEMASONRY and THEOSOPHY, as well as material from the Egyptian BOOK OF THE DEAD, late medieval GRIMOIRES and the work of alchemists such as JOHN DEE. The stated purpose of the order was to test, purify and exalt the spiritual nature of the individual, and to further what it called 'the Great Work', which was to obtain control of the nature and power of one's being. A one-time member of the Golden Dawn, ALEISTER CROWLEY, went on to develop his own Thelemic (see THELEMA) system of high magic, and in more recent times, high magicians have expanded on what has gone before to create eclectic systems such as chaos magic (see MAGIC, CHAOS).

High magic makes use of ceremonial magic with its long and complicated rituals (see MAGIC, CEREMONIAL). Believed to be extremely powerful when successful, it involves many spiritual exercises and, unlike low magic, has little practical application. Power is said to be derived through the skilful control of spirits, usually DEMONS or ANGELS, and the high magician is, above all, a mystic who aims to change his or her consciousness while remaining in control; in a self-induced trance state, it is said that he or she can undergo an OUT-OF-BODY EXPERIENCE in which the astral planes can be manipulated. The ultimate goal of high magic is a transcendental experience which enables the magician to progress to and work in higher spiritual realms so that he or she can achieve communion with their 'higher self'.

magic, homeopathic

A simple form of magic which depends on the belief that an item which has some similarity to another can be used to influence it.

Homeopathic magic is based on the belief that like produces like, and that a symbolic action performed on one thing can affect another which it resembles in some respect. It can be classified as a form of sympathetic magic (see MAGIC, SYMPATHETIC). In practice, homeopathic magic is often combined with contagious magic (see MAGIC, CONTAGIOUS), which operates on the principle that anything which was once part of a person or thing, or with which they have had contact, retains a link to them; if an effigy of an enemy is harmed to injure them, this is homeopathic magic, but if the effigy incorporates the person's hair, it also becomes contagious magic. Homeopathic magic was used by the sorcerers of ancient India, Babylon, Egypt, Greece and Rome; it

is still used by some indigenous cultures. The specific use of a drawing, doll or other physical representation of the person whom the magician wishes to affect is known as image magic (see MAGIC, IMAGE), while the acting out of a desired event or outcome in the belief that it will bring it about is often called imitative magic (see MAGIC, IMITATIVE).

Many taboos are based on the concept of homeopathic magic. Something which is harmless in itself is avoided because it bears a resemblance to something harmful.

Homeopathic magic may be used to help as well as harm; in Sumatra, a barren woman might make a wooden image of a baby and hold it in her lap in the belief that it will bring her a real child. Rice is also sown in Sumatra by women with their long hair hanging down their backs to encourage the rice to grow luxuriantly and with long stalks. Drawing pictures of a desired event is also believed to make it come about, and this is a possible explanation for the many cave paintings which depict successful hunts.

Homeopathic magic is also used in an attempt to heal. A figure representing the sick person may be laid on an altar or in a MAGIC CIRCLE, sometimes with the afflicted area marked on it, and a white healing light is visualized as passing through the image to the person. The ancient Hindus used yellow flowers and birds to banish the yellow colour from a person suffering from jaundice to the yellow item, where it belonged. Some forms of ALTERNATIVE MEDICINE, such as Bach Flower Therapy (see EDWARD BACH), operate on the principle that emotional imbalances can be treated by taking an infusion to which the spiritual energy of certain flowers has been transferred. The plant's specific qualities are thus believed to pass to the person and help to balance them emotionally and spiritually.

magic, image

A simple form of magic which depends on the belief that something done to an image or representation of a person can bring about real effects in that person.

Image magic is often classified as a specific form of homeopathic magic in which a drawing, doll, or other physical representation of a person is acted upon in order to bring about a corresponding effect in that person (see MAGIC, HOMEOPATHIC).

The best-known form of image magic involves a doll or effigy (see EFFIGIES) made of cloth, wax or clay, which is used to symbolize the victim. The doll is specifically identified with the person, sometimes by naming it after them or baptizing it in their name, or, using the additional tool of contagious magic, incorporating scraps of their clothing, hair, nail clippings, or anything else which has come from them or been in close contact with them (see MAGIC,

CONTAGIOUS). This type of image magic has been in use for many thousands of years, and is said to have been practised in ancient Assyria and Egypt, as well as Greece and Rome; the Greek poet Theocritus is reputed to have disposed of his enemies by performing magical rites over their images. In Europe during the Middle Ages, witches made dolls known as 'poppets' and pierced them with thorns or pins in an attempt to cause similar injuries in the victims they represented.

The Native Americans are said to have drawn the figure of an enemy in sand or clay, and injured it to inflict a similar injury on that person. To kill them outright, the image was burned or buried. Peruvian Indians moulded an image of fat mixed with grain to represent the victim, and burned it on a road which they would pass along; this was called 'burning their soul'. In a similar Malay technique, a corpse was made of beeswax, which was transfixed from the head downward, wrapped in a shroud, prayed over as if dead and then buried in the middle of a path where the victim was sure to step over it. The use of dolls to affect those they represent is most commonly associated with popular notions of 'Voodoo' (see VOUDUN).

Image magic is also sometimes used in healing magic and love magic, or in attempts to help a person win a court case, for defence against a slanderer, or to return a curse to its sender (see MAGIC, HEALING; MAGIC, LOVE).

magic, imitative
A simple form of magic which depends on the belief that acting out a desired event or situation will cause it to happen.
Imitative magic is sometimes classified as a form of homeopathic magic (see MAGIC, HOMEOPATHIC). In imitative magic the acting out of a desired event or outcome is believed to bring it about. A magician who wishes to make rain fall may sprinkle water on the ground, imitating rain. Similarly, in some European folk dances, the dancers leap high into the air, reflecting a former belief that this would make the crops grow tall, and dances which include directional movement are performed at winter and summer solstices as it is thought that this will ensure that the seasons will turn in their proper cycle. In the past, some northern peoples lit fires during the winter solstice, the period when the sun seemed at it weakest, in an attempt to strengthen it.

It has been suggested that imitative magic has played a large part in the rituals formerly performed by hunters or fishermen in an attempt to secure a good catch. A fisherman might make a model of a fish and make it 'swim' into his net in imitation of the real fish which he hopes to catch. Traditional hunting dances include imitations of animals being respectfully killed by hunters. The earliest evidence of such a ritual appears to be shown in a painting on the wall of an inner cavern in the cave of the Trois Frères in Ariège, France, which dates from the Upper Palaeolithic era (around 10,000 BC). It depicts a man-like figure on whose head are the antlers of a stag; his body is covered with an animal's pelt and tail, and he has furry ears and owl-like eyes. Nicknamed 'The Dancing Sorcerer', this figure is taken by some to represent a shaman disguised as an animal, performing a ritual dance presumably designed to ensure successful hunts.

magic, love
The use of magic to make someone fall in love, attract a lover to oneself, foretell one's future husband or wife or make a union fruitful.
Throughout human history, love magic has been one of the most widespread forms of folk magic, and for thousands of years, folk magicians, witches and professional practitioners of magic in almost every society have dealt in APHRODISIACS. In ancient times, love and fertility were thought to be dependent on the goodwill of the gods, who could be appealed to by sacrifices and offerings. The Greeks used various types of love magic which included spells and incantations, some involving EFFIGIES of the loved one, and in the 2nd century AD, the writer Apuleius was accused of having won his wealthy wife by the use of a love potion.

Love magic may be used in an attempt to attract a lover for oneself, bring two people together or strengthen their love, bless their union, bring a straying lover back or end a relationship with affection and allow both parties to move on. A universally popular love spell is to gain an item which belongs to, or has come from, the loved one – perhaps an item of clothing, some fingernail clippings or hair – and charge it with a suitable incantation. Alternatively, the lover can do the same to some item of his or her own, and secretly put it into the possession of the loved one. An object in a symbolic form suggestive of the sexual organs of the opposite sex may be used in love magic; in medieval times, the mandrake, whose root often resembles the male form, was a highly prized aphrodisiac. Certain herbs and flowers are traditionally associated with love, and are used in potions, put in baths, worn as AMULETS, or placed inside sachets or cloth dolls: basil is said to attract and keep love; caraway seeds and cloves to be an aphrodisiac; and coriander is a popular ingredient of love sachets. The daisy is the most commonly used flower for the still-popular love magic divination of plucking one petal at a time while reciting, 'He/she loves me, he/she loves me not …'. A doll filled with rosemary is thought to attract lovers, and roses, the flower of Venus, are used in love rituals.

Love magic can also be used to try to find out the name of one's future husband or wife. In Europe, HALLOWE'EN is considered a good time for divination, particularly in matters of love. One method is to peel an apple while keeping the peel all in one piece, then throw it over your left shoulder; it is said that the shape it falls in will show the initial of your future spouse. The apple is an ancient symbol of enduring love, and the Hallowe'en custom of bobbing for apples is said to be a relic of an ancient Druidic marriage divination ceremony. To offer someone a pomander made from an apple studded with cloves is said to be a declaration of love, and a pomander hung in the centre of a room will allegedly attract a new lover.

magic, low
A simple form of magic which makes use of natural objects and whose aim is generally to make changes or to foretell events in the physical world.

Low magic is the oldest of all magical traditions, and exists within every culture. Also known as natural magic, folk magic or practical magic, low magic has been referred to as 'the magic of the common people'. In the Middle Ages, the term 'high magic' was used to refer to esoteric magical disciplines such as ASTROLOGY, ALCHEMY and the TAROT, practised mostly by males of the educated upper classes (see MAGIC, HIGH). Its aim was to attain power over unseen forces and to achieve a higher level of spirituality. By contrast, low magic, as traditionally practised chiefly by uneducated village women, was much simpler and less formal, and was directed toward more mundane aims, such as healing a sick person or helping someone to gain wealth or love. Based on the essential principles of nature, it is the magic practised throughout the centuries by the village wise woman or 'cunning man'. In Europe, low magic dates back to Celtic and Anglo-Saxon times, but different forms are found all over the world. It is strictly practical in application; unlike high magic, it makes use of objects which can be found in nature, does not involve long, complex ceremonies or rituals, and its aim is usually to change conditions or bring about events in the physical world, rather than to connect with the divine or to enable the magician to operate on a higher spiritual plane.

Low magic is commonly used today by followers of various neopagan paths, who may be solitary practitioners or members of traditional Wiccan covens; folk medicine, WITCHCRAFT, spell-casting, the making of CHARMS and TALISMANS, all types of sympathetic magic (see MAGIC, SYMPATHETIC), plant magic (see MAGIC, PLANT) and DIVINATION are forms of low magic. The connection with nature is still key, and natural objects such as feathers, stones, crystals and herbs are the tools of the low magician, although in more recent times, neopagans and Wiccans have also adopted some of the concepts and tools of ceremonial magic, such as the use of a MAGIC CIRCLE during magical work, and the ceremonial knife or athame (see MAGIC, CEREMONIAL). The sun and moon cycles are taken into account in the timing of low magic; for example, it is considered that a magical working intended to bring about growth and increase is best performed during the time of the month when the moon is waxing, while one designed to cleanse, purify or decrease is best performed when the moon is waning. Traditionally, those who practised low magic worked intuitively and used their innate skills for the benefit of their community, and most of their spells were created and performed in response to an immediate need; the curing of a fever, the love spell for the woman who wanted a husband, the protection of the house or livestock against malevolent spirits or the bringing of rain for the crops.

magic, natural *see* MAGIC, LOW

magic, plant
The use of plants, herbs, flowers or trees for magical purposes.

The use of plants, herbs, flowers and trees for magical purposes is as old as the history of magic itself. Many plants were known to have been used magically in ancient Egypt, and the first herbals – texts describing plants and their uses, magical as well as medical – were written in ancient Greece. During the Renaissance, the resurgence of interest in Classical knowledge led to such texts being rediscovered. However, plants have been used for magic and medicine in every culture since ancient times by folk magicians and SHAMANS. Knowledge of plant lore is frequently claimed to be a gift from the gods, and the use of plants in primitive societies is closely connected to magical practices, with many rituals requiring specific herbs to be used in healing magic (see MAGIC, HEALING), as incense or as an AMULET. The distinction between remedies and charms is often blurred in folk medicine, and herbal cures were often accompanied by magical rituals and incantations.

Plants can be burned as incense, stuffed inside herb sachets or dolls for use in image magic (see MAGIC, IMAGE), or added to ritual baths, brews or potions. Every flower, herb or tree is believed to have its own magical property or virtue which can be invoked by using it as part of a spell or ritual: the buttercup is associated with riches and self-esteem, the foxglove with fairy magic, the jasmine with passion and prophetic dreams and the dandelion with divination and wishes. Black cohosh may be carried to strengthen the courage, a piece of Devil's shoestring carried in the pocket for luck in work-related matters and angelica sprinkled in all four corners of the house or around its perimeter for protection against evil spirits. The holly protects against bad luck and harm, ivy defends against psychic attack and amulets made of rowan wood are believed to protect the wearer against death by drowning.

A common practice in herb gardens of the Renaissance and Middle Ages, especially those devoted to healing and magical herbs, was to set out plants in an arrangement based on their symbolic correspondences with the elements, planets or signs of the ZODIAC. In a planetary garden, for example, lavender and oregano might be planted in the segment assigned to Mercury, mugwort and lady's mantle for Venus and basil and garlic for Mars.

magic, ritual
Magic which involves the use of rituals to bring about the desired result.

Practically all magical traditions, ancient and modern, include some form of ritual magic. This may be extremely complex and incorporate almost all of the magical system, as in ceremonial magic (see MAGIC, CEREMONIAL) and high magic (see MAGIC, HIGH), or it may be merely a slightly more formalized aspect of intuitive magical traditions such as low magic (see MAGIC, LOW) and SHAMANISM. A ritual can be as simple as a single person lighting a candle to meditate, or a lengthy and highly structured and scripted ceremony involving a group of people, but the basic principles of ritual remain the same.

A magical working becomes a ritual when a fixed set of actions and words is employed, which has been designed to be repeated in the same sequence and manner every time; it is the cumulative repetition of the ritual which is believed to give it its power. Ritual is used to help create within the magician a mental state which allows him or her to send clear and direct instructions to their subconscious. It has also been suggested that any spiritual entities with which the magician may seek to make contact and interact learn, through the repetition of the ritual, to recognize it as a call to them; the use of ritual is thus thought to increase the likelihood and speed of their response.

With the exception of high magic, most rituals are fairly simple, and all rituals involve four stages. The first is preparation; the magician may take a bath to purify himself or herself of all negative energies and will often dress in a special garment, or put on a piece of jewellery with magical significance. In the second stage, the magician goes into the light trance state believed appropriate for magical work; this may be achieved by drumming, chanting, dancing, singing, rhythmic breathing or MEDITATION. The performance of a ritual often takes place within a deliberately circumscribed space such as a MAGIC CIRCLE, so next, the magician creates the ritual space. Any powers which are to be worked with are then invoked, and the magic is performed. Finally, the powers are thanked and dismissed, the ritual space or magic circle is closed and the participants spend some time in grounding themselves, often by eating or drinking, to allow them to return to a normal and everyday mental state.

Wiccans (see WICCA) and pagans (see PAGANISM) often use ritual magic to mark the passage of time throughout the cycle of the year, celebrating the full moon and the SABBATS.

magic, sex
The use of sexual energy for magical purposes.

The connection between sex, religion and magic has existed as an aspect of human spirituality for thousands of years. Sacred prostitution was practised in many ancient Mediterranean, North African and Middle Eastern civilizations; to have sex with one of the priestesses of a goddess's temple was to achieve union with the goddess herself, whether the purpose was to obtain wealth, luck or love or simply to worship the divine feminine. This practice did not formally end until Christianity became the predominant religion of the ancient world. Many spiritual traditions, such as Tantric yoga (see TANTRA), pagan mystery schools, TAOISM, Buddhism, ancient Egyptian magic and the Hebrew KABBALAH contain sexual teachings. Sometimes two 'paths' existed within a single broad religious culture, with most of the faithful being taught that the way to spiritual enlightenment was chastity and asceticism, while a small group believed that the conscious directing of sexual power was another road to illumination and spiritual insight. In such cases, the ascetic tradition was sometimes called the Right-Hand Path, while the sexual one was referred to as the LEFT-HAND PATH.

In modern times, sex magic is still fairly well integrated into Eastern spirituality, one of the oldest forms and still the best-known being Tantric sex. This is held to be an advanced form of spiritual communion – practitioners use sexual energy as a vehicle by which they can merge with the divine and achieve profound spiritual experiences. In the West, sex magic is mainly associated with OCCULT traditions and is thought by many to be the most powerful of all magical techniques. ALEISTER CROWLEY was probably the most famous sex magician of modern times, and wrote a number of books and articles on the subject. In sex magic, the energy created by the tension released in sexual orgasm is said to be harnessed and directed toward a magical goal.

Sex magic involving actual sexual intercourse is rare in formal ceremonies, and is generally performed in private, with the exception of the Great Rite, in which two participants invoke the powers of the god and goddess and unite sexually to re-enact their union. More frequently, though, this union is acted out symbolically, by placing a ritual knife or athame (which represents the male) inside a chalice (which represents the female); sometimes, a sword and a cauldron are also used. Sex magic is thought to be especially suitable for Beltane (May Eve) rituals, and its power is said to be increased if it is performed outdoors in a place of great magical significance, such as on an ancient hilltop burial mound, or on the flat stone which often lies at the foot of a Neolithic standing stone. The potency of the ceremony is also believed to be heightened if it takes place at the full moon, or high tide.

magic, stage

A form of entertainment usually performed for large audiences in theatres, in which illusions, sleight of hand and conjuring are performed to make the audience think they are seeing something which is apparently impossible; stage magic often makes use of elaborate, large-scale props and secret mechanisms.

Although the art which we recognize as modern stage magic is considered to be relatively new, its beginnings and many of the techniques still employed by stage magicians today are thousands of years old. An ancient Egyptian papyrus records how, around 2600 BC, Dedi, the favourite magician of King Cheops, decapitated various birds and restored their heads to their bodies to entertain the royal court, while the wandering magicians of India known as FAKIRS and the street conjurors of medieval Europe were entertaining audiences with illusions and sleight of hand in market places and fairs for many centuries before magicians had stages on which to operate. The profession of the stage magician flourished in the late 18th and early 19th centuries with the growth of the music hall and variety shows, when illusionists began to perform in halls and theatres. One of the first of these was the Scottish magician John Henry Anderson, the 'Great Wizard of the North', who enjoyed much popularity in the 1840s. Around the same time, the French magician Jean Eugene Robert-Houdin opened a theatre that was purpose-built for the presentation of magic on the stage, which lent itself to the use of hidden mechanisms and allowed the performer to control what was seen from the point of view of the audience. In 1873, the English

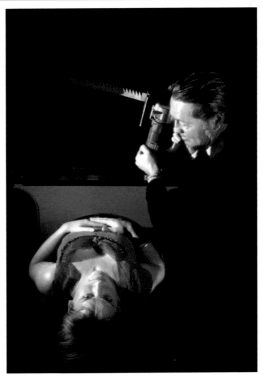

A woman about to be 'sawn in half' in a version of the popular stage magic illusion. (© TopFoto)

magicians JOHN NEVIL MASKELYNE and George A Cooke also established a magic theatre, the Egyptian Hall, in London, which similarly exploited the potential of the stage for magic.

The late 19th and early 20th centuries saw many magicians appearing in theatres and music halls all over America and Britain, and this period was the golden age of stage magic, giving rise to such internationally renowned performers as Chung Ling Soo and HARRY HOUDINI, possibly the most celebrated magician of all time, who developed a form of stage magic known as ESCAPOLOGY. In the mid-20th century, the popularity of stage magic declined, partly due to the advent of a new form of entertainment – television – but in the 1970s, there was a revival of interest in magic, largely thanks to a number of illusionists, such as Doug Henning, who successfully made the transition from the theatre to this new medium and re-established magic as a form of mass entertainment. Since then, magic has remained popular both on stage and on television, with each generation of magicians bringing new life to the art; in the early 1990s, British magician Simon Drake shocked and fascinated TV audiences with his use of gothic horror elements and gory effects, and his work continues to inspire many imitators. In 1994, US magician Franz

Harary, who specializes in illusions on a gigantic scale, made the US Space Shuttle 'vanish' before a live audience. Many internationally renowned stage magicians such as Lance Burton, Penn & Teller and David Copperfield regularly perform at the numerous theatres and casino-hotels in Las Vegas, where magic is a favourite form of entertainment.

Stage magic is typically performed for large audiences, and is often distinguished by the use of elaborate, large-scale props. It is understood that the effects are created by natural means – misdirection, secret mechanisms, mirrors, optical illusions, collaboration with assistants or members of the audience and other techniques – and are designed to instil a feeling of wonder, not to lay claim to any real magical or OCCULT powers on the part of the magician. However, it is still regarded as highly unprofessional for a magician to reveal to non-magicians how a trick or illusion is accomplished, and membership of most professional magicians' organizations, such as the MAGIC CIRCLE, usually requires the taking of an OATH not to divulge the secrets of their art.

magic, sympathetic

A simple form of magic which depends on the belief that one thing which resembles another in some way, or which was once in physical contact with it, can be used to influence it.

Sympathetic magic is one of the most common, and oldest, forms of magical belief, and depends on the perceived connection between two objects or operations; by performing some action on one, the magician seeks to influence the other. In *The Golden Bough* (1890), the anthropologist SIR JAMES FRAZER used the general term 'sympathetic magic' to cover both homeopathic magic (see MAGIC, HOMEOPATHIC) and contagious magic (see MAGIC, CONTAGIOUS). The principle of sympathetic magic is based on a belief in correspondences, and the hidden relationship between objects in the universe; things are thought to be able to act on one another at a distance through a secret 'sympathy' between them, and an impulse can be magically transmitted from one to the other via an invisible ether. It is this secret sympathy which is believed to transfer the magician's actions on a physical object to the person or thing which the magic is intended to influence.

Where the link between the objects is a similarity of some kind, the magic performed is usually known as homeopathic or sometimes imitative magic (see MAGIC, IMITATIVE), and where the sympathetic link is one of physical proximity or contact, it is known as contagious magic. Homeopathic magic is based on the belief that like produces like, and contagious magic on the belief that after a person has had contact with something, that thing can continue to influence him or her. The harming or destruction of a doll representing an enemy is thus homeopathic magic, while burning a lock of his or her hair would be contagious magic. In practice, both branches of sympathetic magic are often combined, for example if the effigy of the enemy incorporates some of his or her hair or fingernail clippings or a piece of his or her clothing.

Most forms of DIVINATION are based on the concept of sympathetic magic; the appearance of the entrails of the sacrificial animal, the patterns formed by the dice thrown, the cards selected during the tarot reading, and so on, are believed to have a sympathetic correspondence to the past, present and future of the empirical world, and this correspondence is interpreted by the diviner. See also MAGIC, IMAGE.

magic, weather

Magic performed in an attempt to control the weather.

Since the weather is a crucial factor in the success or failure of farming, it is hardly surprising that man's preoccupation with the weather is as old as society itself, and that magic seeking to control and regulate the weather has been a feature of almost every culture throughout history. Primitive weather magic was chiefly concerned with producing rain, which is vital to life as drinking water and for crops and animals.

The most common methods used in tribal societies to bring rain involved what the Scottish anthropologist SIR JAMES FRAZER described as sympathetic magic (see MAGIC, SYMPATHETIC), also known as imitative magic (see MAGIC, IMITATIVE), in which the rain-maker, shaman or magician performed a ritual which mimicked the effects of rainfall in the belief that 'like produces like', and that imitating the desired result would bring it about. Thus, water might be poured onto an altar or on the ground; a sacrificial animal or person might be beaten until the blood sprinkles the ground like rain; a fiery torch might be extinguished with water, or hot ashes or red-hot stones tossed into the air in the hope that the rain would come to put them out; or certain members of the tribe might be drenched or bathed in water. In some Russian villages, a small cask or kettle was drummed on to mimic the sound of thunder, while firebrands were knocked together to produce sparks in imitation of lightning and water was sprinkled from a vessel with a bundle of twigs. In New Guinea, a tree branch was dipped in water which was then scattered.

Some cultures held the belief that twin children had magical powers over nature, and particularly over the weather; in some Native American tribes, twins were thought to be able to produce rain by painting their faces black and then washing them, in imitation of rain dripping from black clouds, or by spilling water from a basket. In parts of Greece, a procession of children might visit every well or spring in the area, singing an invocation and led by a girl adorned with flowers, whom they sprinkled with water at each stop, while in a similar Romanian ritual called the *paparuda*, a girl wearing a skirt woven from vines and branches went from house to house, being drenched with water by the inhabitants. Bathing has also been used in some cultures as a rain-making technique, and ceremonial dances intended to bring rain are found in many cultures, from the ancient Egyptians to the Native Americans.

Since the gods and other supernatural forces were often held to be responsible for the weather, weather magic was frequently combined with a religious ritual in which the god was appealed to for the desired change. If there was still no result after the god had been petitioned and possibly offered a sacrifice, its image might be torn down and publicly ridiculed in the hope of shaming it into performing its divine duty.

It is also believed that wind can be summoned by whistling, and in Scotland, particularly in Shetland and Lewis, WITCHES were said to call up a wind by tying three knots in a cord and then undoing the knots; the more knots undone, the stronger the wind that would be released.

magic, white

The use of magic for positive purposes, such as healing or helping others or enabling the magician to achieve spiritual enlightenment.

Among occultists, magic is not generally considered to be in itself either good or evil, but a force which may be employed for positive or negative ends according to the intent of the MAGICIAN. It is the purpose of the magic which determines whether it is black or white. Some believe that a magician may summon demons and still remain a 'white' magician as long as his purpose in doing so is benevolent, and in occult lore, white magic is concerned with expanding consciousness and contributing to the common good, while any magic used to harm or coerce others is classified as black magic (see MAGIC, BLACK). Some magicians hold that magic which attempts to force spirits or entities to assist in its workings is black, regardless of its intent, and that the magician should instead seek to commune with them and prove himself worthy of their willing aid by his spiritual enlightenment and knowledge; indeed, for many high magicians (see MAGIC, HIGH) and ceremonial magicians (see MAGIC, CEREMONIAL), cosmic consciousness and the uniting of oneself with the divine or the higher self is the ultimate aim of white magic.

White magic is used to protect, bless, heal and help, and is intended to be positive and uplifting; it is characterized by those rituals and spells designed to produce beneficial effects for the community or the individual. Healing magic is one form of white magic (see MAGIC, HEALING); another is love magic, provided it is not used to force a person into a relationship against his or her will or to split up a marriage or romance (see MAGIC, LOVE). If a person is believed to have been cursed or hexed by means of black magic, or has an illness which is thought to be due to evil spirits, white magic may be used in an attempt to counteract the curse or drive out the spirit. Magic performed to destroy something negative, such as a bad habit or obsession, is not in itself negative, since it has a positive effect and causes no harm to any. White magic is used to bless a new venture or home, protect people or places from evil influences or bad luck, reverse unfavourable conditions and help people to achieve their goals, as long as doing so will not harm another. Similarly, magic done with the aim of helping oneself or improving one's own life is not considered selfish if it causes no harm to another in the process. See also THEURGY.

magical flight *see* FLIGHT

magical numbers
Numbers that are considered to be sacred or to possess magical significance.

Throughout history, people have been fascinated by numbers. Various types of NUMEROLOGY have been developed by those who believe they can find hidden meanings behind the numbers which make up our lives, and esoteric systems such as GEMATRIA have for centuries been used to determine numerical equivalencies for words. But some numbers figure more prominently than others as being magical in nature; THREE, FIVE, SEVEN and twenty-two are generally regarded as having particular significance.

Three is an especially magical number in many cultures, both ancient and modern. The Celtic gods and goddesses often had a triple aspect, and in Christianity, this number appears again in the Holy Trinity of Father, Son and Holy Spirit, while the Hindu Trinity consists of Brahma, Vishnu and Shiva. The moon goes through three phases, waxing, full and waning, and there is a magical belief that doing something three times will make it so – an idea which survives in the proverb 'third time lucky'.

Five has always held strong mystical associations, being considered in some beliefs as a number of grace, and is much revered in magical traditions as a number signifying spiritual communication and completion. The PENTAGRAM, or five-pointed star, is believed to be a powerful magical symbol which is said to link the human body to the heavens, and can be seen as representing the whole person, as made up by the four limbs and the head.

Seven has a long history as a lucky number. It is seen as symbolizing spiritual perfection, and in many cultures is sacred; there are seven days in the week, the world is said to have been created in seven phases, and in some versions of the KABBALAH, there are seven SEPHIROTH. In ancient times, astronomers could see seven moving heavenly bodies or 'planets' in the sky – the Sun, the Moon, Mercury, Venus, Mars, Jupiter and Saturn – and the astrological system which the Babylonians constructed around these is the basis of modern ASTROLOGY. In the TAROT, the significance of three and seven are seen again in the major ARCANA, which consists of 22 cards; leaving aside the first card, The Fool, which is assigned the number zero and is usually considered separately, the remaining cards, numbered from 1 to 21, fall naturally into three groups of seven.

Twenty-two is seen as a highly magical number which contains secret answers to many esoteric questions; there are 22 letters in the Hebrew alphabet, which correspond to the 22 paths linking the sephiroth in most versions of the kabbalah, and there are also 22 cards in the major arcana of the tarot.

Many ancient cultures also endowed perfect numbers with special magical and religious significance. A perfect number is one which is the sum of all its divisors, such as 6 (1 + 2 + 3) or 28 (1 + 2 + 4 + 7 + 14). Another magical use of numbers is in the MAGIC SQUARE, a grid of figures which total the same number whether they are added up horizontally, vertically or diagonally, for example a square made up of the rows 3, 7 and 6; 9, 5 and 1; and 4, 3 and 8. Such squares are often used in TALISMANS. In China, certain numbers are seen as being lucky or unlucky because their homophones have auspicious or inauspicious meanings. For example, the number six is thought to be lucky because it is sounds the same as the Chinese word meaning 'easy' or 'smooth'. See also ONE; TWO; FOUR; SIX; EIGHT; NINE; TEN; ELEVEN; TWELVE; THIRTEEN.

magic circle

In ceremonial magic, neopaganism and Wicca, a circle drawn or visualized as enclosing the space within which a ritual or other magical work is performed.

The creation of sacred space within which to perform rituals or other magical work is central to many belief systems (see MAGIC, CEREMONIAL; NEOPAGANISM; WICCA). This is done by casting a circle, visualized as a three-dimensional sphere of energy, in which the energies raised can be contained and focused for

magical use, and which also serves as a protective barrier against any unwanted energies or entities outside the sacred space. Every tradition has its own method of casting the magic circle, but in general, it will have an altar at its centre, and the FOUR DIRECTIONS, also known as the four corners or quarters, are invoked to assist in creating the circle, with each cardinal point being represented by a physical symbol of the ELEMENT with which it is associated – usually a candle for FIRE in the south, salt or a bowl of earth or sand for EARTH in the north, incense for AIR in the EAST, and a bowl of water in the west for WATER. The circle may be physically drawn or laid out with salt or a rope, or symbolically drawn, often with a ritual knife known as an athame, or a WAND or SWORD. Once the circle has been cast, it is symbolically sealed, and the chosen deity or spirit is invoked to join it and assist in the magical work.

If anyone has to leave the circle before the end of the ritual, a symbolic 'doorway' is sometimes drawn with an athame, and 'closed' behind the person to maintain the magical integrity of the circle, with the process being repeated when they wish to re-enter the circle. Once the magical work has been completed, the circle must be closed, with the deities or spirits and the four directions and elements being thanked and dismissed in turn.

Magic Circle, the

An organization dedicated to the art of stage and performance magic.

The Magic Circle was founded in London in 1905 by a group of 23 amateur and professional magicians (illusionists or performance magicians – see MAGIC, STAGE), including David Devant (often referred to as the greatest magician of the age), who became the organization's first president. The first official meeting was held at the Green Man public house in Soho, but later meetings took place in a room at St George's Hall in Langham Place, where Devant and JOHN NEVIL MASKELYNE regularly performed for the public. In 1906, Maskelyne edited the first issue of *The Magic Circular*, a magazine for Magic Circle members which is still published. The first issue's cover showed the signs of the ZODIAC arranged in a circular figure, and the Latin motto *Indocilis Privata Loqui* ('not apt to disclose secrets'). This phrase sums up the most important rule of the Magic Circle – the preservation of secrecy regarding the art of magic. Any member who reveals the secret of how a trick or illusion is performed to an outsider may be subject to expulsion from the organization.

To join the Magic Circle, applicants must be 18 or over, and be proposed and seconded by existing members who have known the candidate for at least a year. After being interviewed by one of the senior members and performing an audition to establish that they have the required skills and knowledge, applicants are elected by a ballot of the Council of the Magic Circle, and must study to pass an examination within one year. Full membership is restricted to those who have demonstrated a satisfactory practical ability in the art of magic, and higher degrees are awarded either by further examination, or through proven performance ability. The highest honour a member can receive is promotion to Member of the Inner Magic Circle with Gold Star, given for outstanding services to the Magic Circle, or to the art of magic in general. The organization stages annual competitions to showcase and encourage new talent. The Magic Circle's headquarters, still located in London, includes displays of priceless magical apparatus, posters and memorabilia, and its heritage centre houses lending and reference libraries which contain the largest collection of magical books in Europe.

Corresponding organizations dedicated to performance magic in other countries include the International Brotherhood of Magicians, and the Society of American Magicians.

magicians

Persons believed to have the ability to manipulate and control events by supernatural means.

The belief that some people have the ability to use supernatural means to bring about a desired result is as old as mankind. In every culture and age, the magician has been a powerful symbol of humanity's desire to influence its surroundings and take control over its life. Sometimes respected, and at other times feared and vilified, magicians appear at every stage in human history and legend.

In ancient Egypt, Greece and Rome, the main practitioners of magic were the priests, who were seen as guardians of secret knowledge given to humanity by the gods, and all forms of DIVINATION were their province. Rulers often employed personal magicians to advise them and to intercede with the gods on their behalf. After Christianity became the predominant religion in Europe in the 4th century, magic practised in systems outside the Church was seen as evil and identified with devil-worship; in the Middle Ages, magicians were condemned along with WITCHES, and were imprisoned and executed. The Renaissance saw a resurgence in hermeticism and other forms of ceremonial magic (see MAGIC, CEREMONIAL), along with ALCHEMY, and from then until the 18th century, the cultural and intellectual atmosphere was highly conducive to the study of MAGIC. Various secret societies (see, for example, FREEMASONRY and ROSICRUCIANS), which flourished from the 17th

century onwards, continued the spread of esoteric knowledge, and the 19th century saw a huge upsurge of interest in all aspects of the occult, and the birth of modern ceremonial magic with the founding of the HERMETIC ORDER OF THE GOLDEN DAWN. Today, many people in the West claim to practise various forms of magic using natural forces, spirits, spells and magical SYMBOLS, while in Eastern belief systems such as Hinduism, some ascetics are said to achieve, through penance and meditation, a state in which they attain supernatural powers.

Throughout history, many people have either claimed to be magicians, or have had their names linked with the practice of magic: examples include, from the ancient world, the philosophers PLATO and PYTHAGORAS, influential figures in occultism, and the magician Simon Magus, mentioned in the New Testament; in medieval Europe, ALBERTUS MAGNUS, and the alchemist Nicolas Flamel; in the Renaissance, AGRIPPA VON NETTESHEIM, JOHN DEE, NOSTRADAMUS and PARACELSUS; in the 19th century, ÉLIPHAS LÉVI, MADAME BLAVATSKY, MARIE LAVEAU and MACGREGOR MATHERS; and in the 20th century, ALEISTER CROWLEY, ANTON LAVEY, DION FORTUNE, GERALD GARDNER and ISRAEL REGARDIE. The romance and mystery of the magician is also personified in legend and literature by such characters as the Arthurian wizard MERLIN, Shakespeare's Prospero in *The Tempest* and Gandalf in J R R Tolkien's *Lord of the Rings*. See also MAGI; SORCERER; WIZARD.

magick

A spelling of 'magic' popularized by Aleister Crowley to distinguish magic as practised by occultists, witches and folk magicians from stage magic and sleight of hand.

'Magic' is found with the spelling 'magick' in works written in the Elizabethan era. The French author ÉLIPHAS LÉVI was the first to revive this archaic form to refer specifically to occult magic as opposed to STAGE MAGIC, and the occultist ALEISTER CROWLEY, who was influenced by Lévi, adopted the same distinction in his own work. In doing so, he popularized this spelling. Crowley chose the spelling 'magick' to distinguish between what he called 'the true science of the Magi' from 'counterfeits' such as sleight of hand, stage magic and illusions, and defined magick as 'the science and art of causing change to occur in conformity with the will'. In this broad definition, which encompasses any act designed to cause intentional change, he included ordinary acts of will as well as ritual magic, but 'magick' is now more commonly used in the more restricted sense of an act or ritual that is performed in the belief that it will bring about a change by supernatural means.

magic lamp

In Arabian folklore, an oil lamp to which a djinni (genie) has been magically bound. The djinni must grant the wishes of whoever possesses the lamp.

The idea of a magical object which is found underground, and which can fulfil wishes, is common throughout Asian and European folklore, and one of the most famous examples of this motif is the magic lamp in the story of Aladdin in *The Arabian Nights*. Aladdin, the son of a poor widow, retrieves a magic lamp from a cave on behalf of an evil magician and frees the djinni (genie, see DJINN) within it. With the help of the djinni's magic, Aladdin achieves great wealth and marries the daughter of a sultan. In Islamic mythology, djinn are often magically bound to an object, and must do the bidding of whoever possesses it. Traditionally, such magic lamps were the property of sheiks or potentates, and if they were stolen, an army would be called up to recover them. Since it was first introduced to the West in the 18th century, the story of Aladdin and his magic lamp has been a perennially popular one and has been used for a number of animated films, as well as being a staple of Christmas pantomimes, and the magic lamp has also become a powerful symbol of wish fulfilment.

magic square

Usually, a square filled with rows of numbers so arranged that the total is the same whether the figures are added up horizontally, vertically or diagonally; often used in talismans.

Magic squares have fascinated humans for thousands of years, and are found in a number of cultures. The most common type of magic square is a grid of figures which give the same total (known as the magic constant) whether they are added up horizontally, vertically or diagonally, for example a square made up of the rows 3, 7 and 6; 9, 5 and 1; and 4, 3 and 8, which all add up to 15. A magic square of the order 3 has three numbers in each row and column, one of the order 4 has four numbers in each row, and so on, and numerical magic squares can be constructed using a mathematical formula. Chinese literature from around 2800 BC tells the legend of the Lo Shu square, a magic square of the order 3 which was said to have appeared on the back of a turtle which came out of the River Lo, and a magic square from a Greek text was used by 9th-century Arab astrologers in drawing up horoscopes. The earliest magic square of the order 4 was found in an Indian inscription dating from the 11th or 12th century.

Such squares are often used for magical purposes, such as ensuring a long life and warding off disease, since they are believed to have astrological significance and divine qualities. Stone and metal TALISMANS

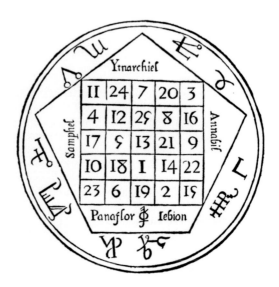

A magic square, from Cornelius Agrippa's *De occulta philosophia* ('On Occult Philosophy', 1533).
(© TopFoto/Fortean)

engraved with magic squares have been found in Egypt and India, and Cornelius Agrippa, the 16th-century alchemist and philosopher, constructed seven magic squares of the orders 3 to 9 inclusive, each of which he associated with one of the seven heavenly bodies or 'planets' then known, for talismanic purposes.

Another type of numeric magic square is the multiplicative magic square, in which it is the product of the numbers in each line which is constant, rather than the sum. There are also alphabetic magic squares, which consist of a series of letters arranged in a square to spell certain words which appear in the same order both horizontally and vertically, the best-known of which is made up of the Latin words SATOR, AREPO, TENET, OPERA, ROTAS.

magic symbols *see* SYMBOLS

magistery

In alchemy, a transmuting agent, especially the philosopher's stone.

The word 'magistery', which comes from the Latin *magister*, meaning 'master', was used in several different but nevertheless connected senses by alchemists. They referred to the concentrated essence of a substance as its magistery. The same word was also used to mean a sovereign remedy. But it appears to have been most commonly used of either the product of a TRANSMUTATION, or of any transmuting agent, and in particular, as another name for the most powerful sovereign remedy and transmuting agent of all – the PHILOSOPHER'S STONE (in which context it was sometimes also called the 'grand magistery').

magnetic anomalies
Areas where the earth's normal magnetic field is distorted.
The magnetic field of the earth follows a fixed and predictable pattern overall. However, in some areas this pattern is distorted, causing localized, untypical magnetic effects to be experienced. For centuries, sailors have reported the existence of regions where, for no apparent reason, their compasses become inaccurate. Such magnetic anomalies are believed to occur within the BERMUDA TRIANGLE, and regularly form part of the theories offered for the allegedly mysterious nature of the area.

In recent times it has been possible to identify and map these anomalies – particularly through the use of magnetometers and satellite detection. A number of suggestions have been offered as to their cause. It is now generally accepted that magnetic anomalies are the result of variations in the magnetic properties of the types of rock making up the earth's crust, with some rock strata being more magnetized than others. However, claims that there are some highly localized and incredibly strong magnetic anomalies have led to some slightly more controversial theories, ranging from the idea that they indicate the sites of giant meteorite strikes, through to the suggestion that they are evidence of the implantation by EXTRATERRESTRIALS of secret observatories or tracking stations.

magnetic hills
Places where objects appear to roll uphill.
A so-called 'magnetic hill' is a slope where the normal action of gravity appears to have been cancelled out by some mysterious force, leading objects to apparently roll uphill instead of down. If a motor vehicle is brought to a halt and placed in neutral on such a hill it will seem to roll uphill when its brakes are released.

In such instances, the apparent mystery is actually the result of an optical illusion brought about by the topography and other geographical features of the area. This is usually attributed to the human brain attempting to gain a sense of up and down, when there is no level horizon visible, by looking to things it expects to be vertical. If nearby trees are at an angle (perhaps having been affected by the prevailing wind), or if field walls and fences are not completely vertical, the brain can mistakenly interpret a slight downward slope as an uphill one. In many cases the illusion can be appreciated by moving away from the road, to a point where the broader configuration of the land can be seen.

Cases of this phenomenon are found all over the world – possibly the most famous being SPOOK HILL in Florida. Scotland is home to another well-known example – the 'Electric Brae' in Ayrshire (on the A719 between Dunure and Croy Bay), where local legend holds that an 'electric' force within the hill is responsible. The effect has become such a tourist attraction that a marker stone has been erected to explain the illusion.

magus *see* MAGI

Maharishi Mahesh Yogi (1911–)
Indian mystic, the developer of the simplified form of Hindu meditation known as transcendental meditation.
Little is known about Maharishi Mahesh Yogi's early life, but he was believed to have been born Mahesh Prasad Varma in Jabalapur, India. He graduated from Allahabad University with a degree in physics, but abandoned his scientific studies to work for 13 years as secretary to Swami Brahmananda Saraswati, known to his disciples as Guru Dev and renowned as the foremost exponent of the ancient Vedic science of consciousness. In 1955, after isolating himself for two years in the Himalayan foothills, Mahesh took the title of Maharishi Mahesh Yogi and began to teach a relaxation and meditation technique which was a simplified form of the Vedic science, organized by him into a complete system, and based on a literalist interpretation of yogic concepts and the use of MANTRAS. He dubbed this technique TRANSCENDENTAL MEDITATION. In 1957, he founded the Spiritual Regeneration Movement, the first of several organizations collectively known as the Transcendental Meditation Movement, whose aim he said was to save the world through meditation.

The Maharishi first introduced transcendental meditation to the West in 1958, and became one of the first Eastern gurus to gather a Western following, his most famous disciples being the Beatles, who travelled to India to meditate with him in 1968. The stated aim of the various programmes which he has implemented across the world is to create a 'Heaven on Earth', a society which is characterized by good everywhere, and which demands the reconstruction of the entire world, both inner and outer. His teachings are rooted in the belief that the basis of life is unbounded bliss, and that every individual can learn to experience this, without effort.

Of the two schools of AYURVEDA practised outside India, one, known as Maharishi Ayur-Veda, was introduced by him; it emphasizes meditation as the key to healing. It is a profit-making concern which

The mystic Maharishi Mahesh Yogi photographed in India in 1968. (© Nancy Cooke de Herrera/Corbis)

runs its own training programmes worldwide and sells an exclusive range of products. In 1971, he established the Maharishi International University, now the Maharishi University of Management, in Iowa, an accredited university which offers 'consciousness-based education' and degree programmes in the arts, sciences, business and humanities. He continues to establish educational institutions throughout the world, such as Maharishi Colleges of Vedic Medicine, and has written a number of books on Vedic wisdom. Using modern technology such as the online Maharishi Open University, weekly video press conferences and the transmission of his Maharishi Broadcasting via satellite and the Internet, his teachings have given rise to a worldwide network of over 1,200 meditation centres in a hundred countries, with an estimated five million practitioners.

Much controversy has surrounded the Maharishi's life, and he famously made an unsuccessful attempt to copyright the commonly known mental use of mantras for meditation as a technique exclusive to transcendental meditation.

Maitreya *see* BENJAMIN CREME

Majestic 12

The code name that it has been claimed was given to a top-secret committee created by the US government to protect, and carry out research into, proof that alien spacecraft had crashed on earth.

In 1982, the UFO researcher William Moore was working with Californian TV producer Jaime Shandera in an attempt to gain proof that there had been a massive GOVERNMENTAL COVER-UP of information relating to UFOs. They claimed that they had received intelligence, allegedly from inside sources, which indicated that a top-secret US government committee had been set up after the ROSWELL crash of July 1947.

Testimony from the scientist Dr Robert Sarbacher appeared to support this claim – he stated in writing that he had known since the 1950s about a high-level government team with access to both UFOs and their occupants. Indeed he had apparently been invited to participate, but had declined. He claimed further that autopsies had been carried out on recovered bodies (see ALIEN AUTOPSY), and that this had revealed that the beings had a form similar to that of insects.

In December 1984, Shandera received an anonymous package that contained undeveloped photographic film; when the film was developed the photographs showed a series of documents. These documents apparently related to a top-secret team, referred to as Majestic 12 (or MJ-12), and gave the names of its members. The list was composed of a mixture of (by then dead) intelligence and military personnel, who had been in high office 40 years earlier, together with a number of scientists believed to have been involved in secret research. The most surprising inclusion was Donald Menzel, a Harvard astronomer who had died in 1976 and had long been an outspoken debunker of UFO claims. The MJ-12 team was said to have been the brainchild of President Harry Truman.

During 1985 and 1986, Moore and Shandera apparently chose not to publicize this evidence in the hope that they might be able to establish its authenticity first. Unaware of this, in the UK, in late 1986, the BRITISH UFO RESEARCH ASSOCIATION (BUFORA) researcher and author Jenny Randles was approached by an ex-military man who claimed that he possessed documents that she would be interested in – it later became evident that the detailed description he gave was similar to that of the MJ-12 files. It was arranged that this man would meet covertly with Randles and her colleague Peter Hough. His story was that he had obtained the documents via a US military officer who had accidentally gained access to them while stationed at Wright Patterson Air Force Base. He agreed to hand over the files in a country park but later pulled out of the arranged transfer, claiming that he had been detained by intelligence personnel who had removed them from him. He may also have become wary as the suspicious researchers had begun to make discreet checks into his background.

A few weeks later another British researcher, Tim Good, made it known that he had come into the possession of copies of documents that turned out to be the MJ-12 files. Good expressed his intention to release them immediately – forcing the hand of Moore and Shandera, who also came forward with their story and released their MJ-12 files.

No independent evidence exists to suggest that MJ-12 was real. The documents have split opinion within the UFO community – a number of researchers think they are genuine, but others believe they are not and that they were created, possibly even by intelligence agents, in an attempt to muddy the waters surrounding the UFO phenomenon. Many critics are concerned by President Truman's signature as it appears on the purported memo authorizing the creation of the committee. The signature is absolutely identical to an authenticated signature on a non-UFO-related memo dated a week later. The level of correspondence is so exact that the only reasonable explanation, critics argue, is that somebody must have copied the definitely verified signature onto the fabricated MJ-12 files.

maleficia

A word formerly used as a general term for all evil magic practised by witches and sometimes also used to refer to a witch who performed such magic.

The word *maleficia* is Latin for 'evil doings'. It was carried over into the Middle Ages to refer both to evil magic worked by a WITCH, usually with the assistance of a DEMON, and to the witch who practised this demonic magic. In its narrowest sense, maleficia meant damage to crops and illness or death to animals, but it could be applied to any misfortune or calamity which was believed to have been caused by a witch or SORCERER out of revenge or malice. Witches were believed to bring about their maleficia through a variety of means, such as INCANTATIONS, powders, potions, ointments, herbs and EFFIGIES pierced with thorns and nails. In 1398, the University of Paris declared that maleficia, which it defined as the art of working with spirits, was a heresy if it involved the making of a pact with the DEVIL; a copy of a DEVIL'S PACT was not required as proof of its existence, which could be implied. In 1487, two Dominican inquisitors, Jacob Sprenger and Heinrich Kramer, compiled a bestselling book called *MALLEUS MALEFICARUM* ('The Hammer of Witches'), which details the maleficia practised by evil witches, and the word became so inextricably linked with the

idea of WITCHCRAFT that it also became a synonym for 'witch'.

Malkuth

In the kabbalah, the sephirah or emanation of God known as Kingdom, which is assigned the number 10; it represents the reality of physical existence, and the material world.

Malkuth is the tenth of the ten SEPHIROTH, or divine emanations, in the KABBALAH. It is called Kingdom, and represents the material world, and the physical plane of existence. Malkuth is the final emotive attribute of the sephiroth. It is assigned the number 10. On the kabbalistic TREE OF LIFE, it is positioned directly below YESOD, and is the fourth and lowest sphere on the middle axis, the Pillar of Equilibrium. It is given three paths on the Tree of Life, to HOD, Yesod and NETZACH, and is also linked with KETHER. It connects the three triangles formed by the other sephiroth – the Supernal Triangle, the Moral or Ethical Triangle and the Astral or Psychological Triangle – to the outer world. In its position at the base of the Tree of Life, it receives influences from the entire tree, and contains and expresses the descending powers on the central axis, the Pillar of Equilibrium, as well as the influences generated by the Pillar of Mercy and the Pillar of Severity. Malkuth is the only sephirah not to be part of the triangular structure of the tree, and is also the only one to be cross-quartered into four sections representing the four ELEMENTS. It is associated with the power of self-expression, and represents the end result of a process, the world of effect rather than of cause. It expresses force, form and consciousness in combination, and is the place of incarnation.

Malkuth is associated with the divine name *Adonai Ha Aretz* (Lord of the Earth), the archangel Sandalphon, the angelic order of the Ashim, the planetary force of the Four Elements and the Earth. In the TAROT, Malkuth corresponds to the four tens, and in the tarot Tree of Life spread, the card in the Malkuth position usually represents the world around the person, and the external influences of other people and situations. In some kabbalistic systems it is attributed with the magical image of a young woman crowned and throned, and is represented by various symbols: the Altar of the Double Cube, the Equal-Armed Cross, the Magic Circle and the Triangle of Evocation. It is often connected with the root or base CHAKRA. The word 'Malkuth' in kabbalistic GEMATRIA gives the number 496, which is the sum of all the numbers from 1 to 31. It is also a perfect number – one which equals the sum of all its divisors – and the ten sephiroth thus reach completion with this perfect number. Malkuth is also sometimes called by various other names such as The Gate, The Gate of Death, The Gate of Prayer, The Gate of the Garden of Eden and The Bride.

Malleus Maleficarum

The most widely used treatise on witchcraft during the 200-year peak period of witch prosecutions in the Middle Ages.

The *Malleus Maleficarum* (or 'Hammer of Witches') was published in Germany in 1487 (although there were possibly slightly earlier versions) by two Dominican inquisitors Heinrich Kramer and Jakob Sprenger. Its publication, they claimed, was as a result of a papal bull issued by Pope Innocent VIII in 1484. However, the Bull was issued as an instruction to prosecute witches in northern Germany, not as a specific endorsement of the methods they went on to employ. Kramer was an experienced WITCHFINDER, who had been expelled by the Bishop of Brixen for his over-zealous activities in the Tyrol, and Sprenger was a respected academic and Dean of Cologne University.

The book was submitted to the clergy at Cologne University, where it was roundly condemned. Shortly after this it was condemned by the INQUISITION and banned by the Church. None of this stopped the book from being republished several times, with false endorsements and the earlier papal Bull placed at the beginning. It became immensely popular, spreading throughout northern Europe, being used by Catholics and Protestants alike; it was reputedly the second biggest selling book after the Bible until the publication of John Bunyan's *Pilgrim's Progress* in 1678.

The book is split into three sections and most of the material contained in it is drawn from earlier works. It takes the form of a series of questions with arguments given in answer. Broadly speaking, the first section is concerned with proving and explaining the existence of WITCHCRAFT, the second gives a description of the various forms of witchcraft and the diabolical acts associated with it and the third lists the methods that should be employed in seeking out, trying and executing WITCHES.

The book reinforced many of the folkloric beliefs surrounding witchcraft, emphasized the direct association between witches and the DEVIL and offered counter arguments to those within the church who questioned the reality of witchcraft, or the seriousness of the threat it presented, arguing for the position that:

> … the belief that there are such beings as witches is so essential a part of the Catholic faith that obstinacy to maintain the opposite opinion manifestly savours of heresy.

The title page of the *Malleus Maleficarum* (or 'Hammer of Witches'), originally published in Germany in 1487. This edition was published in Lyon in 1669. (© Mary Evans Picture Library)

It also insisted that no mercy should be shown when trying accused witches and strongly endorsed the use of torture and a number of other dubious methods to secure a conviction. Its popularity probably stemmed from the fact that it appeared to validate many of the wild beliefs which drove those who sort to pursue campaigns against witchcraft. It also offered strong learned arguments to quell any unease that judges may have felt when it came to convicting those accused of witchcraft.

man-beasts

A diverse array of hairy humanoid cryptids reported from many regions of the world.

There is little doubt that the man-beasts constitute one of the most fascinating categories of CRYPTID on file, but what is so surprising (and little realized outside the cryptozoological community) is the extent of their diversity and geographical distribution. Also dubbed 'ape-men', especially by the media, these very hairy but generally humanoid entities come in a variety of shapes and sizes, and allegedly inhabit remote, little-explored terrain throughout much of the world.

Even among cryptozoologists (see CRYPTOZOOLOGY), let alone within the more sceptical, mainstream zoological community, there continues to be much dissension regarding the number of discrete man-beast types in existence, as well as their likely identities. For example, veteran BIGFOOT researcher Professor GROVER KRANTZ only accepted the existence of a single category of man-beast – a surviving species of the giant ape *Gigantopithecus* which, in his view, explained North America's bigfoot and also the YETI of Asia. American cryptozoologist Ivan T Sanderson, conversely, proposed four man-beast categories – Sub-Humans (Neanderthal-like beings); Proto-Pygmies (small man-beasts such as the AGOGWE and ORANG PENDEK); Neo-Giants (tall man-beasts including the bigfoot and dzu-teh or giant yeti); and Sub-Hominids (ape-like man-beasts such as the true yeti or meh-teh).

This classification was subsequently modified by fellow American cryptozoologist Mark A Hall, yielding six separate categories, including, most notably, True Giants (differentiated from Sanderson's Neo-Giants), to include man-beasts reportedly more than 3 metres (nearly 10 feet) tall. Even more recently, in their book *The Field Guide to Bigfoot, Yeti, and Other Mystery Primates Worldwide* (1999), veteran American cryptozoologist Loren Coleman and acclaimed science writer Patrick Huyghe proposed a radical, expanded version of Hall's classification system that contained no fewer than nine distinct categories of man-beast. These can be summarized as follows:

Category 1: Neo-Giants – Standing 1.8–2.8 metres (around 6–9 feet) tall, these man-beasts include such examples as the giant yeti and bigfoot, as previously proposed by Sanderson, with the most popular proposed identities including *Gigantopithecus* and *Paranthropus*.

Category 2: True Giants – Reputedly standing 3–6 metres (nearly 10–20 feet) in height, these gigantic man-beasts include the orang dalam or so-called 'Malay bigfoot' that hit international news headlines in late 2005 and 2006 following a spate of alleged sightings plus the discovery of giant footprints, with *Gigantopithecus* once again being hailed as the likeliest cryptozoological identity.

Category 3: Marked Hominids – Coleman and Huyghe distinguish these man-beasts from Neo-Giants, which they superficially resemble (although they are sometimes said to be more humanoid), by virtue of their characteristic piebald colouration; Coleman and Huyghe include as one such example the Siberian chuchunaa, which had previously been deemed by various other authors to be a Neanderthaloid man-beast.

Category 4: Neandert(h)aloids – As its name suggests, this category include man-beasts that may comprise relict modern-day Neanderthals, such as the WOODWUSE of Europe (although this may have died out in the past few centuries).

Category 5: Erectus Hominids – This category houses those man-beasts that may represent relict present-day versions of *Homo erectus*, including the Mongolian ALMAS (though classed by some other cryptozoologists as a surviving Neanderthaloid), Caucasus kaptar and various Oceanic man-beasts, as well as, in the opinion of Coleman and Huyghe, the Minnesota iceman (if it is genuine).

Category 6: Proto-Pygmies – As proposed originally by Sanderson, these are diminutive man-beasts, including such cryptozoologically famous examples as the Sumatran orang pendek and its Bornean counterpart the batutut, the Sri Lankan nittaewo, and Africa's AGOGWE and séhité, as well as South America's didi. However, it seems unlikely that these zoogeographically disparate examples all possess the same taxonomic identity – especially in view of the recent unexpected discovery in the Sundas of a hitherto unknown species of dwarf fossil human, *Homo floresiensis*, that may conceivably have direct, specific bearing upon the orang pendek's taxonomy.

Category 7: Unknown Pongids – These are man-beasts that Coleman and Huyghe consider to be unknown species of great ape, and they include in this category such examples as the Congolese muhalu, Japanese hibagon, North America's NAPE and skunk ape, the Chinese YEREN (alternatively deemed by others to be a relict *Homo erectus*), and the true yeti or meh-teh, as well as the Australian YOWIE (though other cryptozoologists have proposed a range of other identities for this last-named man-beast, including an ape-like marsupial, a regressed version of *Homo erectus* and even a giant wombat).

Category 8: Giant Monkeys – As distinct from giant apes, these cryptids, as their name suggests, are deemed to be extra-large, unidentified species of monkey, and include the South American ISNACHI, and the koddoelo version of NANDI BEAR from East Africa.

Category 9: Merbeings – Unquestionably the most controversial category in this classification system, these cryptids are deemed to be primates adapted for an aquatic existence, and include such examples as the traditional MERMAIDS and other mer-people, as well as STELLER'S SEA APE, and such decidedly bizarre entities as the North American lizardmen, as well as the CHUPACABRAS (not previously grouped within the man-beast division of cryptids).

The more conservative cryptozoologists, and certainly most non-cryptozoologists, may well have difficulty in accepting any proposition to the effect that so many different species of man-beast can exist, but remain undiscovered by science in the 21st century. Indeed, Dr BERNARD HEUVELMANS faced similar scepticism from some quarters regarding his multiple classification system for SEA SERPENTS. Moreover, there is no doubt whatsoever that eyewitnesses can be notoriously poor at providing accurate descriptions of what they have seen – yielding a variability of description far greater than is likely to be real. A good example of this is the astonishing variety of ALIEN BIG CATS reported in Great Britain, which, if genuine, would suggest the existence there of countless different species – a quite ridiculous scenario. Equally, the size and shape of footprints, another major source of evidence for man-beasts, as well as other cryptids (in particular alien big cats once again), can also vary considerably – it can depend upon the type of terrain in which they have been found, the speed at which the cryptid was moving when making them, atmospheric influences, the age and sex of the cryptid leaving them, and so on.

Any multiple-category classification system based primarily upon anecdotal evidence and footprints is vulnerable to the charge of having been influenced, or corrupted, by factors such as eyewitness unreliability, environmental conditions and intraspecific variation. Yet, even when all of this is taken into consideration, Coleman and Huyghe's study demonstrates beyond a doubt that certain well-defined man-beast categories can indeed be distinguished within the vast array of reports on file. However, until such time as any specimens or other items of conclusive physical evidence are procured and examined scientifically, the precise number and nature of these categories seem destined to remain purely the subject of on-going conjecture.

Man in the Moon

The supposed likeness of a man's face or figure seen on the surface of the full moon.

The various cultures of the world interpret the markings on the face of the full moon in different ways. In many countries, they are thought to represent a man's face, or the figure of a man. In Inuit legend, it is believed that the Man in the Moon is the keeper of the souls of men and animals. In Malaysia, he is seen as an old hunchback sitting under a banyan tree, plaiting bark into a fishing line to catch everything on earth. The moon markings are also said to show a rat which gnaws through the fishing line and a cat which chases the rat. As long as the equilibrium between the man, the rat and the cat continues, the world is safe, but if the man ever finishes making his fishing line, the world will end. On Florida Island in the Solomon Islands, the Man in the Moon is known as Ngava, and at the full moon people say, 'There is Ngava sitting.' In Europe, while many people see the markings as a friendly face, others see the figure of an old man carrying a bundle of sticks on his back and sometimes bearing a lantern and a forked stick; there are a number of legends explaining how he came to be there, one version of which relates how, instead of resting on the Sabbath like a good Christian, an old man once went to the woods to cut a bundle of sticks. On his way home he met a stranger who chided him for working on a Sunday, and he replied laughingly, 'Sunday on earth, or Monday in heaven, it's all the same to me'. The stranger replied, 'Since you do not value Sunday on earth, yours shall be a perpetual moon day in heaven; you shall bear your burden for ever and stand in the moon for eternity, as a warning to all Sabbath-breakers.' And the old man was banished from earth, to become the Man in the Moon.

mana

In the belief systems of Oceanic cultures such as those of Melanesia, Polynesia and Hawaii, a sacred impersonal force thought to pervade all living things and inanimate objects; in humans, mana is thought to be located in the head, and is associated with power, prestige and authority.

Oceanic cultures such as those of Melanesia, Polynesia, Micronesia and Hawaii use the word 'mana' to refer to a UNIVERSAL LIFE FORCE or power which they believe pervades all of creation – gods, nature, people, places and objects. Mana is seen as a universal power which is tapped into, controlled and directed in the practice of magic and religion. It is the source of all luck and success, and an object which possesses mana, such as a CHARM or AMULET, will confer this power on the person who has it. Animals, plants, inanimate objects and even places can have mana, which may be recognized by the sense of wonder and respect which they evoke in the observer. As a concentration of power, mana in a person resides in the head, manifesting as prestige, authority, skill and a dynamic personality, and individuals who are regarded as being descended from divine ancestors, such as Polynesian chiefs, are particularly charged with great mana. Dancing at religious festivals is designed to activate the mana of the gods and thus arouse their procreative power, on which the continuation of animal, plant and human life depends, and offerings are made to the gods accompanied by prayers or chants intended to transmit mana to the spirit world. The islanders of Easter Island have a legend that the famous giant statues situated on the coast were raised into position by the used of mana (see EASTER ISLAND STATUES).

In the Hawaiian HUNA belief, each person consists of three selves (low, middle and high), and these must be integrated before the higher self can manifest prayers for healing and magic. This is done by creating the prayer as a thought form, and then accumulating and directing mana to energize it.

The concept of mana has also entered popular culture, and has been adopted in fantasy novels, computer games and films, most notably in the *Star Wars* series, where it appears as 'the force'.

Manchurian Candidate

An individual brainwashed or programmed into performing a secret mission.

In 1959, the US writer Richard Condon (1915–96) published a novel, *The Manchurian Candidate*, in which a US soldier, captured by the enemy in the Korean War, returns home having been brainwashed by the Chinese so that he can later be triggered to carry out an assassination. The novel was soon made into a film, which was released in 1962, and a remake was released in 2004.

Whether such effects can be achieved through 'BRAINWASHING' (indeed, whether such a process is possible at all) remains highly controversial, but it is certainly true that research into the area of 'MIND CONTROL' has been carried out (see MKULTRA). Indeed, some people believe that the model CANDY JONES was really 'programmed' by the CIA to carry out secret missions at its bidding.

Various people in recent US history have been labelled 'the real Manchurian Candidate', the best known possibly being Sirhan Sirhan, the man convicted of assassinating Robert Kennedy in 1968. It has been suggested that Sirhan was brainwashed by the CIA into carrying out the killing. However, sceptics argue that, as Sirhan was a refugee from Palestine, his anger at Kennedy's apparently pro-Israeli stance offers a less fantastic explanation.

mandala

In Buddhism and Hinduism, a symbolic geometric design representing the universe, often constructed as a series of concentric circles within a square and incorporating a presiding deity or deities; the mandala is traditionally used as an aid to meditation.

Although mandalas originated in Hinduism, they are also prominent in Buddhism. The word *mandala* is Sanskrit for 'circle', and all mandalas, whether simple or highly complex in design, usually include a circle or a series of concentric circles. In Hindu cosmology, the earth's surface is represented as a square, and the mandala is therefore enclosed in a square which symbolizes the physical world, bound in four directions. The mandala is used in worship or as an aid to meditation, and the various aspects of its precise symbolic format represent objects of reverence or contemplation. It is often viewed as a symbolic representation of the universe, or, in Buddhism, the vision or land of the Buddha; it can also symbolize the qualities of the enlightened mind in harmonious relation with each other, or the path of spiritual development. The mandala frequently includes images of a presiding deity or deities, although these may be represented by a symbol such as a wheel, jewel or tree. The symmetrical geometrical shapes of the

An intricate sand mandala, made by gently tapping grains of coloured sand into place through a funnel. (© Sheldan Collins/Corbis)

mandala draw the eye in towards its centre as a focus for meditation.

Although mandalas are most commonly found on scrolls or as wall-paintings, they are also sometimes drawn in coloured sand on consecrated ground by Buddhist monks for important rituals. To symbolize the impermanence which is a fundamental teaching of Buddhism, the intricate sand mandala is erased after the ritual. The creation of a mandala is not only an artistic process, but also an act of worship, since the mandala is seen as imparting the teachings of the Buddha.

By meditating on the mandala while repeating MANTRAS, it is believed that one can not only attain enlightenment and union with the divine, but also invoke the mandala's presiding deity.

Manitou

An Algonquin word for supernatural power or a supernatural presence.

The word 'Manitou' is used by Algonquin-speaking Native American peoples as a general name for the world of the SUPERNATURAL or for SPIRIT beings. Such spirit beings were believed to reside in all natural things.

A medicine man would contact the Manitou during his rituals, and individuals would encounter them during VISION QUESTS. The Illinois people, for example, engaged on vision quests from the age of adolescence to attempt to encounter their own Manitou. These personal spirits took the form of an animal that would remain with them, helping them, among other things, to communicate with the Kitshi Manitou (or *Kitchesmanetoa)*, sometimes described as the Great Spirit or Supreme Being.

mantra

In Hinduism and Buddhism, a syllable, word or phrase believed to be of divine origin, repeated in religious ritual or meditation; mantras are now also used in a non-religious context.

The word 'mantra' comes from Sanskrit and translates as 'instrument of thought' or 'mind tool'. Mantras first appeared in the collection of Hindu Vedic hymns and chants known as the *Samhitas*, which date from around the 2nd millennium BC. A mantra is a syllable, word or phrase which is believed to be of divine origin, and which is repeated, either out loud or inwardly, in a religious or meditative context. Although mantras originated with Hinduism, and are particularly important in Tantrism, they were later also adopted as a central element of Buddhism and JAINISM.

In the Vedic tradition, sound is considered to be one of the most important principles of existence, being both the source of matter and the means of attaining freedom from it. A mantra is believed to be a manifestation of ultimate reality as a sound form, the repetition of which has the power to bring into being the reality it represents. Repeating a mantra produces a physical vibration which is thought to bring about in the subtle body of the speaker a powerful resonance, which corresponds to the specific spirit energy frequency and state of consciousness represented by and contained within the mantra. By chanting the mantra, the practitioner is said to be able to produce a spiritual effect which is associated with the physical sensation of the vibration the chant produces, eventually leading to its physical manifestation. The vibrations produced in the body by the repetition of the mantra are said to awaken the life force or *prana*, and even to stimulate the CHAKRAS. Repetition of mantras, known as mantra *japa*, is an established practice in all forms of Hinduism, and through *japa*, the devotee seeks to achieve complete focus on the chosen deity or idea expressed in the mantra, with the ultimate aim of attaining *moksha*, or enlightenment and release from the cycle of death and reincarnation. Mantras are repeated over and over in groups of auspicious numbers, 108 being especially popular, and Hindu necklaces called *malas*, containing 108 beads, are sometimes used to help the devotee keep track of the repetitions.

Some mantras have a linguistic meaning, for example the mantra *Nama sivaya*, which translates as 'homage to Siva'. Others, known as *bija*, or 'seed mantras', which are mainly used in Tantrism, have no semantic value, but are believed to contain the essence of particular deities or spiritual forces, and thus to have great power. The best known of these is the mantra *OM*. Use of *bija* mantras usually requires initiation by a guru. Other mantras, such as *Om mani padme hum*, contain a combination of both kinds. The most common type of mantra is associated with a particular deity, and is used as a form of praise, invocation or identification with that deity. Sometimes devotional phrases known as *mahamantra* are chanted, or, as in the mantras known as *nama japa*, the deity's name is saluted.

In Buddhism, the mantra as a meditational tool is seen as a complete way of enlightenment in itself, and in the branch of YOGA known as mantra yoga, meditation while chanting a mantra is said to allow the yogi to transcend the mind and emotions, and to experience the superconscious. In the West, TRANSCENDENTAL MEDITATION uses simple, two-syllable mantras as a meditational focus, and various NEW AGE groups and individuals have also enthusiastically adopted mantras, although usually without their original religious context.

map dowsing

A form of dowsing in which the dowsing tool, usually a pendulum, is held over a map to locate an object.

In map DOWSING, the dowser, instead of actually walking around a site to perform the search, holds the dowsing tool – usually a PENDULUM – over a map or simple sketch of the terrain or property. Many dowsers use this 'remote' map-dowsing technique to narrow down their search area before going out into it to dowse by the standard method. In map dowsing, distance is not a factor; the map used can represent any size of area, anywhere in the world, and for an extensive search, the dowser may start with a map showing the largest area, and work through maps covering an increasingly smaller and more detailed area. There are two main methods. In the first, the pendulum is held over the map, the dowser asks a question such as, 'Is this the way to…?' or 'Is X here?', and the dowser interprets the swing of the pendulum as a yes or no answer. Map dowsers claim that by a process of elimination, the location of the item being searched for will eventually be pinpointed. In the second method, a ruler or other straight-edged object is slid across the map from left to right, and the pendulum is asked to give a 'yes' answer when the straight edge reaches the target. The ruler is then moved from top to bottom, and the same question asked, and the point at which the two lines cross is said to show the target.

mapinguary

A cryptid from Brazil that may constitute a living species of prehistoric ground sloth.

One of the most bizarre 'monsters' of traditional Brazilian folklore is the mapinguary. Local tribes claim that it is a terrifying shaggy-furred reddish-coloured jungle beast, 1.5–1.8 metres (approximately 5–6 feet) tall when squatting upright, with a second mouth in the centre of its belly, backward-pointing footprints and body armour that renders it immune to bullets. It is said that its droppings resemble those of horses and that when it is threatened it discharges a hideous stench. Originally, cryptozoologists deemed it likely to be some form of mystery primate, perhaps akin to LOYS'S APE. However, Brazilian zoologist Dr David Oren, from the Goeldi Museum, who has been studying reports and local testimony concerning the mapinguary for many years, as well as seeking this elusive CRYPTID, has proposed a very different theory behind its identity – suggesting that it is a living species of prehistoric ground sloth, still undiscovered by science.

Oren bases his ideas on various key elements of the mapinguary's appearance and behaviour. Just like this cryptid, ground sloths of the genus *Mylodon* (which were similar in size to the mapinguary but officially died out several millennia ago) had shaggy red fur, were able to raise themselves onto their hind legs, produced horse-like droppings, sported backward-pointing claws and had bony plates in their skin that would have served as efficient body armour. He suggests that the 'second mouth' in the mapinguary's

A map dowser uses a pendulum and a map in an attempt to locate a missing person (whose photograph he holds in his left hand). (© Hekimian Julien/Corbis Sygma)

belly may in reality be nothing more than a large scent gland, secreting a foul-smelling discharge as a means of warding off would-be attackers in the same way that skunks utilize their infamously odoriferous anal gland secretions.

María de Agreda (1602–65)

Spanish mystic and nun who is said to have preached in the American Southwest without ever leaving Spain.

María de Agreda (also known as Sister María of Jesus) is said to have received VISIONS from her childhood. She and her mother became nuns when María was a teenager, and at the same time her father and brothers became Franciscan friars. María is said to have become abbess, against her wishes, at the age of 25. María wrote the *Mystical City of God* (published 1670), which is said to be based on the revelations she received in her visions from the Virgin Mary. However, María is best remembered for the claims that she preached Christianity in the American Southwest without ever leaving Spain.

Throughout the 1620s, María believed that she was transported, on 500 occasions, to a distant land where she preached to a non-Christian people. These alleged transportations (which have been interpreted as examples of either BILOCATION or TELEPORTATION) took her to New Mexico and Texas, where she contacted several native peoples, including the Jumanos. In the late 1620s, it is claimed that a number of Jumanos requested religious instruction at a Franciscan convent in New Mexico, and when they were asked where they had learnt their rudimentary knowledge of Christianity they replied that it had been from the 'lady in blue' – blue being the colour of María's outer habit. Legends of María's miraculous transportations persisted, and she became known in the American Southwest as the 'Blue Nun'.

Marian apparitions

Visions of the Virgin Mary experienced by various people throughout the ages.

From the early days of the Christian Church, various people around the world have experienced VISIONS of the Virgin Mary, the first recorded being her appearance in c.40 AD to the apostle James in Saragossa, Spain.

The apparitions have been experienced by individuals (as, for example, ST BERNADETTE at LOURDES) and by small or large groups (as at FÁTIMA or KNOCK). They have occurred not only in Europe but world-wide. In the New World, for example, a poor Aztec peasant (a convert to Christianity) called Juan Diego had visions in 1531 of a beautiful woman surrounded by light who said she should be called Our Lady of Guadaloupe, after the town near which

The plaque erected in San Sebastian de Garabandal, Spain, on the site of the first reported vision of the Virgin Mary to four local schoolgirls. (© Mary Evans Picture Library)

the visions were said to have taken place.

At La Salette, near Grenoble, France, in 1846, two shepherd children (Maximin Giraud and Melanie Calvat) experienced visions in which the Virgin urged the world to repent. It was also claimed that the Virgin confided a secret to the children which, according to some accounts, Pope Pius IX ordered not to be revealed. This case has striking parallels with the later events at Fátima.

Beginning in 1961, and lasting over the next four years, four schoolgirls in the mountain town of San Sebastian de Garabandal in Spain experienced visions of both the Virgin Mary and St Michael. While thousands attended during some of these visions, the Roman Catholic Church did not judge the phenomenon as 'worthy of belief', which is the usual formula used when it considers such events to be supernatural and divinely inspired.

Members of the Coptic Church of Egypt have also had Marian visions. In 1968, at the church of the Virgin Mary at Zeitun, thousands claimed to have witnessed the apparitions and brilliant displays of light. Many photographs were taken and miraculous cures were associated with the phenomenon.

At Kibeho in Rwanda, seven individuals, including one non-Christian, reported experiencing visions of the Virgin over a period of years from 1981. Among her messages was a warning of mass violence and anarchic slaughter that would follow if Rwanda did not 'come back to God'. The subsequent interracial massacres in Rwanda beginning in1994 were taken by many as confirmation of the truth of the prophecy; the Church, however, has not accepted the visions as genuine.

The visions of an American woman, Veronica Lueken, in Bayside, New York, lasted from 1970 until her death in 1995, but the Catholic Church has never recognized these as worthy of belief.

While the faithful may accept these manifestations as genuine divine events, what is the non-believer to make of them? It is easy for sceptics to dismiss visions appearing to single individuals as psychological or delusional, and even to attribute those experienced by small groups as being the products of MASS HYSTERIA or mass HYPNOSIS. Strong faith and eagerness to believe are well known to affect human beings both mentally and physically, as with the PLACEBO EFFECT or FAITH HEALING.

Another explanation that is advanced is that these apparitions are attributable to pareidolia (from Greek, meaning 'wrong appearance'), which essentially means that the mind interprets a random visual image as being something known and recognized, as when people staring into a fire seem to detect forms or even faces in the flames.

Some suspect hoaxes or 'publicity stunts' by the Church, designed to renew faith at times of political upheaval or decline in everyday religious belief. It has been pointed out that most of the documented apparitions are experienced by the very young or unsophisticated, who are most likely to be credulous. However, the response to this by religious believers would be that it is because in these people faith is at its strongest and most uncorrupted that they are chosen to communicate divine messages.

marine mysteries
Mysterious phenomena occurring as sea.
The seas of the world have always exercised a fascination for humankind, and their sheer size and power bring with them danger and a sense of isolation unparalleled elsewhere in human experience. In ancient times, the elemental force of the sea was worshipped as a god – for the ancient Greeks this was Poseidon and for the Romans, Neptune.

In addition to the terrifying physical phenomena that can be manifested by the waters themselves (such as GIANT WAVES and WHIRLPOOLS), seafaring lore is littered with accounts of the strange creatures to be found in the oceans of the world. One of the most famous of these sea monsters or SEA SERPENTS is the Kraken, which was once believed to haunt the shores of Norway and was said to be able to seize a ship in its tentacles and drag it beneath the water. It is now thought that the legend might have been inspired by a GIANT SQUID. Giant squid were rumoured to exist long before they became known to science, when badly decomposed specimens were washed up on beaches around the world (see also GLOBSTERS).

Legends dating back at least to ancient Greek times also tell of strange, part-human creatures such as SIRENS or MERMAIDS. Sirens were described as being half-woman and half-bird, and as singing seductive songs to lure sailors to shipwreck on the rocks. Mermaids were said to have the upper body of a woman, with the lower body being that of a fish, and were also said to lure sailors to their deaths – in this case, with their beauty.

Throughout the centuries there have been innumerable unexplained disappearances at sea. Whole areas, such as the BERMUDA TRIANGLE, have become associated with such mysterious happenings; and the stories of individual disappearances, such as that of the crew of the *MARY CELESTE*, or tales of GHOST SHIPS, such as the *FLYING DUTCHMAN*, have captured the public imagination.

The sea continues to tantalize the world of modern science. While humankind has ventured into space, much of the area beneath the world's oceans remains relatively unexplored. Creatures of strange shapes and colours, many of them bioluminescent, are known to exist at great depths. Scientists are also still searching for explanations of the behaviour of many sea animals, such as the annual migrations of whales or the fact that great masses of fish always assemble to spawn at the same places, year after year. Research and exploration regularly yield new wonders and will, perhaps, continue to offer further solutions to many long-standing mysteries of the deep.

marozi
A small maneless lion with spots reported from several mountainous regions of tropical Africa.
Kenya's Aberdares Mountains are believed by local hunters, as well as some Western naturalists, to harbour small maneless lions that retain their juvenile spots throughout their lives, instead of losing them when mature. Skins of this strange form of lion, referred to by native people as the marozi ('solitary lion' - it does not live in prides as savannah lions do), have occasionally been obtained. One pair of skins – a male and female – received favourable attention and interest from London's Natural History Museum, where they are still preserved.

Sceptics dismiss marozis as merely freak specimens of the normal lion, but it is interesting to note that they are only reported from shady mountain forests, where their mottled coat, smaller body size and near-absence in the male of a mane would all be favourable traits for a feline predator, aiding camouflage and movement in this particular terrain. Perhaps the lion has evolved a distinct montane version, specifically adapted for success in this particular habitat rather than the lion's more typical savannah home.

Supporting this possibility is the apparent existence of comparable mystery cats in other mountain ranges in East and Central Africa, where they are referred to as the ntarargo in Uganda, ikimizi in Rwanda, bung bung in Cameroon and abasambo in Ethiopia.

Mars, life on

The possibility that living organisms exist on Mars.

For centuries the inhabitants of the Earth, the third planet from the sun, have observed Mars, the fourth, and speculated on the possibility of life existing there.

In 1877, the Italian astronomer Giovanni Virginio Schiaparelli (1835–1910) surveyed the surface of the planet with the aim of producing a detailed map. He referred to the linear markings he detected as *canali* (channels, mistranslated as 'canals') and thought that their regularity mean that they must be artificial. The US astronomer Percival Lowell (1855–1916) later drew up maps of the planet's surface, showing these canals, which he believed must have been created by intelligent beings. However, later observation with more powerful telescopes showed these features to be an optical illusion.

Science fiction seized on the idea of 'Martians', particularly in THE WAR OF THE WORLDS (1898) by English novelist H G Wells (1866–1946), which featured a Martian invasion of Earth, and the novels of US author Edgar Rice Burroughs (1875–1950) about a Martian civilization which he called 'Barsoom'. In many contemporary science fiction novels and films, the idea of mankind settling Mars and 'terraforming' it (ie physically transforming it to be more like the Earth) continues to be popular.

However, what is the actual likelihood of the existence of life, now or in the past, on Mars? On the face of it, the Red Planet presents a rather inhospitable environment for life as we know it. The atmosphere is thin and mostly composed of carbon dioxide, which leaves it open to the sterilizing effect of unfiltered ultraviolet radiation from the sun, and the temperature can fall as low as −140°C. The surface and atmosphere contain very little water, but it may be possible that water deposits exist below the soil. Indeed, some of the planet's surface features have

been interpreted as having been formed by the action of water in the distant past, water which may still exist underground or in the polar icecaps (which consist of frozen carbon dioxide).

Many scientists believe that tiny micro-organisms may exist on Mars, just as they have been discovered to exist in environments on Earth that were previously thought to have been inimical to life, such as in the hydrothermal vents of volcanoes at extreme depths below the sea.

In 1996, there were claims that a meteorite discovered in Antarctica, identified by chemical analysis as consisting of rock from Mars, showed evidence of fossilized micro-organisms, proving that life did exist on Mars in the distant past at least; others, however, dismissed these traces as natural formations in the rock.

Space missions to achieve landings on Mars have been launched since the 1970s, and continue to use robot machines to explore the surface, analyse soil and send back pictures and data. The discovery by these 'rovers' of the types of mineral salts found in arid areas on Earth has fuelled speculation that microbial life may be present below ground. In 2004, a European Mars mission detected traces of methane in the atmosphere, leading to claims that this could be produced by microbes. The US space agency NASA plans to send a nuclear-powered rover to the planet by 2009 which may be able to substantiate this kind of theory.

Whatever the state of current scientific thinking, the idea of life on Mars continues to haunt the popular imagination, which is always ready to embrace the idea of 'little green men from Mars'. See also MARTIAN FACE.

martial arts feats

Feats of strength and endurance of pain carried out by martial artists.

To people who do not take part in martial arts, undoubtedly one of their most impressive and memorable aspects is the way in which practitioners seem able to perform feats of strength, pain endurance, balance and agility that seem almost superhuman, including breaking bricks with the bare hand, withstanding violent blows without flinching, licking hot metal, doing a handstand on a single finger and remaining unharmed by edged weapons. This leads to the question of how this could be done.

Martial arts have been studied, particularly in China and Japan, for centuries. The famous Shaolin Buddhist Temple in China, for example, was founded in the late 5th century AD. There, its monks practised techniques of MEDITATION and unarmed self-defence that gave rise to modern martial arts disciplines such as kung fu. To this day, Shaolin monks perform martial arts feats around the world, and there are Shaolin Temple teaching establishments in various countries.

The Shaolin monks ascribe much of their ability to QIGONG, a system of meditation and breath control that promotes physical and spiritual health. Essentially, they believe that by this method they can learn to channel the QI or 'life force' and direct it to a particular chosen part of the body, making it almost supernaturally strong and impervious to pain or injury.

In this way, the Shaolin channelling of qi, allied to mental discipline and prolonged training, allows them to carry out their martial arts feats. They also maintain a strict regular programme of exercises to strengthen the internal organs as well as the body in general, such as gradually increasing the hardness of the materials that they practise punching, and they claim that this gives them the power to withstand blows.

Many martial arts exponents claim that such feats as breaking bricks or thick planks with just the edge of a bare hand are a matter of concentration, of focusing the will narrowly on the task to be performed. Having mastered this ability, if a person has been trained properly, such seemingly impossible effects can be obtained. It is, according to this argument, something that is not confined to adepts or the initiated, but something that any person with the necessary mental discipline can learn. With the right attitude, technique and speed, if you believe that you can break a brick with your bare hand, then you can.

Scientifically speaking, the concentration of great force in a small point of impact, allied to the energy provided by the great speed of delivery, mean that a highly destructive blow can be struck, capable of breaking an extremely hard substance. In addition, the soft tissue of the hand acts as an efficient cushion, dissipating much of the force of the impact throughout the whole arm. Sceptics, however, maintain that demonstrations of breaking bricks and other materials involve elements of trickery known to stage magicians.

Martian face

The apparent image of a face on the surface of Mars.

In 1976, among the photographs taken of the surface of Mars by the Viking orbiter was one that appeared to show a giant three-dimensional human face rising up out of the ground. It was calculated that this feature was approximately 2.5 kilometres (1.6 miles) long, 2 kilometres (1.2 miles) wide and projected 940 metres (2600 feet) from the surface.

NASA scientists soon dismissed this as an optical illusion like the MAN IN THE MOON, produced by the play of shadows on a natural rock formation. However, some people believed it to be an artefact constructed by an unknown people, perhaps but not necessarily of Martian origin, and left on the planet for the human race to discover on venturing into space, as were the monoliths in *2001: A Space Odyssey*, filmed in 1968 by US director Stanley Kubrick (1928–99). It was further claimed that other structures, notably a pyramid, were also identifiable in these photographs and this was taken as proof of a (perhaps extinct) Martian civilization. Sceptics questioned the utility to its

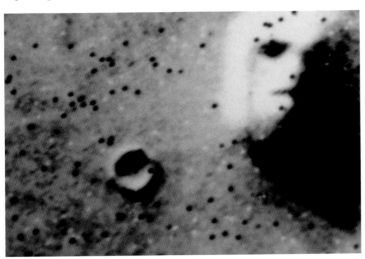

The 'Martian face', captured on film by the Viking orbiter in 1976. (© 1989 Roger Ressmeyer/NASA/Corbis)

creators of constructing an image of a human face. Would it not have been easier to build a linear feature that would be immediately recognized as artificial?

Subsequent, higher-definition, photographs of the same area taken by later orbiters, however, revealed nothing out of the ordinary but only natural geological formations. Those who prefer to believe in the reality of the face, however, maintain that in the intervening years the image had been destroyed by some kind of natural disaster.

Mary, Virgin *see* MARIAN APPARITIONS

The *Mary Celeste see panel p437*

Maskelyne, John Nevil (1839–1917)
A 19th-century English stage magician who famously exposed a number of fake psychics and mediums.
John Nevil Maskelyne, a descendent of the one-time Astronomer Royal Nevil Maskelyne (1732–1811), was a renowned Victorian magician and member of the MAGIC CIRCLE. Born in Cheltenham, he originally worked as a watchmaker, and later went on to design and manufacture many of his own mechanical magical effects. He is also credited with inventing a lock, activated with a penny, which was placed on the first pay toilets in London.

In 1865, he watched a performance by the famous 'MEDIUMS' Ira and William Davenport in his home town of Cheltenham. At the time, the Davenport brothers, from the USA, were performing at SÉANCES all over the world, and many believed that they were genuine mediums. A typical Davenport séance would be carried out in a theatre and would see the two brothers placed inside a cabinet, bound hand and foot. Then a number of items, such as musical instruments and tools, were placed in the cabinet with them. When the stage was plunged into darkness the instruments would be heard playing, and the sound of hammering would emanate from the cabinet – all apparently due to the actions of SPIRITS. When the lights came back up the brothers would be found to be still bound, exactly as they had been. Maskelyne quickly spotted how the trick was performed – in one version of the story, a small gap in the blackout curtains allowed him to actually see the Davenports escape from their ropes and performed the feats themselves, before retying their bonds and accepting the applause. He decided to set out on his own career as a professional magician and publicly exposed the Davenports by demonstrating their methods.

As a stage magician, Maskelyne was well placed to expose the tricks and sleight-of-hand employed by fraudulent mediums. On the back of his public exposure of the Davenports he toured the country for eight years with his partner, often performing some of the tricks fraudulent spiritualists employed at séances. As part of his act Maskelyne included an escape from a box in which he was tied with ropes, similar to that of the Davenports. In 1873, he and his partner took a permanent residency in a London theatre, The Egyptian Hall, Piccadilly.

Maskelyne was an eternal self-publicist and he engaged in constant exposures of mediums to gain publicity for his stage act in which he replicated the effects that mediums attributed to spirits. He billed himself as an 'anti-spiritualist', and, in 1914, he founded the Occult Committee, who aimed to 'investigate claims to supernatural power and to expose fraud'. The committee was heavily involved in attempts to prove that the INDIAN ROPE TRICK had never been performed. Maskelyne died in 1917. His grandson, Jasper Maskelyne, who was also a stage magician, famously went on to be involved in the use of STAGE MAGIC techniques to assist the Allied campaign during World War II.

Masons *see* FREEMASONRY

mass hypnosis
The apparent induction of a hypnosis-like trance state in a group of people.
As with the root term 'HYPNOSIS', the descriptive value of the phrase 'mass hypnosis' is the subject of debate. It is most commonly applied to situations in which crowds of people are apparently induced into a trance-like state during religious meetings or rituals. In these cases the group is driven by the leader, sometimes through the use of singing, chanting and music, into what might be described as an ecstatic state (see ECSTATIC PHENOMENA), in which they may appear to enter a trance (see TRANCE, HYPNOTIC) and apparently become highly suggestible.

Even in non-religious situations, the heavy beats of some types of music, coupled with repetitive notes and flashing lights, can induce an apparent trance in a crowd of dancers. It has been observed that the dancers 'lose themselves in the music' – there is a loss of sense of the individual self, and the crowd may start to act as a single entity. This effect is also often offered as an example of mass hypnosis.

Mass hypnosis is sometimes offered as an 'explanation' for multiple-witness reports of paranormal events, such as UFO sightings and MARIAN APPARITIONS.

The *Mary Celeste*

The story of the brigantine *Mary Celeste* (or the *Marie Celeste*, under which name it was portrayed in a fictional work by ARTHUR CONAN DOYLE) is perhaps one of the most widely known and enduring mysteries of the sea.

The legend surrounding the discovery of the *Mary Celeste* has been retold in a variety of forms. However, the common thread is that of the ship being found adrift with no sign of the crew and with every indication that they had vanished suddenly while going about their normal routine. The accounts include some intriguing 'facts' which give an eerie feel to the circumstances in which the vessel was found, such as the half-eaten breakfast on the table, the lack of damage to the structure of the ship and the fact that none of the crew's belongings had been taken. The theories propounded as to the reason for the disappearance of the crew over the years have included ALIEN ABDUCTION, pirates, sea monsters, mutiny, the involvement of the captain in an insurance scam and, more recently, that the ship was the victim of a sea spout or seaquake.

The story of the discovery of the abandoned *Mary Celeste* owes much of its legendary status (and many of the more colourful elements) to the Arthur Conan Doyle story, 'J Habakuk Jephson's Statement', first published in 1883, without which it may well have disappeared among the countless similar, lesser-known tales of disappearances at sea. Conan Doyle's story is a work of fiction built around some of the known facts of the case. It was written in such a way as to obscure its fictional status, and the confusion and controversy that followed its publication were said to have given its author some pleasure.

The records of the court proceedings and inquiries that followed the discovery of the *Mary Celeste* indicate that she had sailed from New York on 7 November 1872 bound for Genoa, carrying a cargo of barrels of alcohol. On the afternoon of 5 December the crew of the *Dei Gratia* came upon her drifting between the Azores and the coast of Portugal and, after watching for some time and receiving no response to their hails, they boarded her. Contrary to some of the popular versions of the legend, the boarding party did not find a half-eaten meal, or that the boat was intact. In fact, the galley was in a mess and the stove had been knocked out of place. There were open hatches and water had found its way in, only one of the two pumps was working and there were no lifeboats (although it was not known for certain if there had been any on board when she set sail). Some of the instruments were damaged and, among other things, the ship's chronometer, sextant and register were missing. The captain and crew of the *Dei Gratia* brought both boats back to Gibraltar. Although it was originally believed that the cargo was intact, on unloading in Genoa it was found that nine barrels were empty.

No trace of the captain of the *Mary Celeste*, his wife and daughter (who were known to be on board) or the crew of seven was ever found, and despite the many rational and plausible explanations put forward, their fate remains a mystery. The ship itself, considered unlucky by many sailors, changed hands several times over the following years and was eventually wrecked off the coast of Haiti in 1885.

mass hysteria

A term originating in the field of psychology that is popularly offered as an 'explanation' for a wide range of spontaneous mass panics or irrational group reactions (sometimes involving physical symptoms) based on an erroneous belief.

'Mass hysteria' (or 'collective hysteria') is used by psychologists to describe incidents involving groups of people suddenly appearing to display the physical symptoms of illness, without there being any apparent physical cause (see eg LOUDON, NUNS OF; MAD GASSER OF MATTOON; POKÉMON PANIC) — the implication being that in such cases the symptoms are wholly psychological in origin. 'Hysteria' is something of an old-fashioned idea, having unfortunate associations with Sigmund Freud's discredited notion of 'female hysteria' and so alternative phrases such as 'MASS SOCIOGENIC ILLNESS' are now often used in its place.

Other cases to which the label 'mass hysteria' has been applied include a wide range of incidents involving irrational beliefs or panic behaviour spreading rapidly and spontaneously through a group. These are often referred to in the fields of sociology or social psychology as 'collective delusions' and are further sub-divided into categories which relate to the specific type of behaviour and nature of its spread. Classic examples would be the LONDON MONSTER, the MONKEY MAN SCARE, the reaction to Orson Welles' famous WAR OF THE WORLDS radio broadcast and 'PENIS PANIC'. The concept of collective delusion might also be understood to include moral panics such as those surrounding claims of SATANIC RITUAL ABUSE and the European WITCH TRIALS of the Middle Ages. Sceptics often suggest that it is also at the heart of such things as WAVES of UFO sightings, MARIAN APPARITIONS and many other claims to group witnessing of a 'paranormal' event.

In practice an outbreak of a mass sociogenic illness will sometimes result in a collective delusion, and vice versa, and mass hysteria remains in widespread popular use as a catch-all term for incidents involving either or both of these phenomena.

mass sociogenic illness
An illness affecting members of a cohesive group, such as that found in a school or workplace, where the physical symptoms are believed to be the result of fear and anxiety rather than the effect of any pathogen.
The term 'mass sociogenic illness' (MSI) is used to describe an outbreak of illness where the physical symptoms are exhibited by a group of people with a shared social setting, such as that in a school or workplace. Symptoms often include dizziness, nausea and a rash, but no organic cause can be found for the illness and it is believed to be a result of anxiety – ie people subconsciously convert their stress into physical ailments.

MSI is most often reported in schools or similar institutions. For example, a case that is often cited as an example of MSI occurred in a day-care centre in Florida in 1989. Here, 63 out of the 150 children attending the centre suffered the symptoms of a gastrointestinal illness when no cause for such an illness was found. The children were eating a lunch provided at the centre when one child complained that her sandwich did not taste 'right', she left the dining area and when she returned said that she had vomited. Other children then started complaining of stomach ache, and also said that their sandwiches tasted strange. Other symptoms that were reported included nausea, headache and dizziness. A further number of children also reported vomiting. Amid concerns of food poisoning, the children were told to stop eating, and ambulances were called.

Within one to two hours all of the children who had reported the symptoms of illness had fully recovered, and on medical examination no cause for the illness was discovered. Food samples were also analysed but nothing untoward was detected. MSI was the diagnosis of a number of the physicians involved in examining the children and of the regional health department.

More commonly, cases of MSI have involved the rapid spread of symptoms after an unusual smell has been noticed – leading to dizziness and nausea in those who have experienced it and, occasionally, to buildings being evacuated while the 'noxious' odour is investigated. Some commentators have suggested that incidents of MSI are on the increase as anxiety about the use of chemical or biological warfare by terrorists is also increasing. Cases have been reported where innocuous paint fumes have been interpreted as a terrorist attack and led to classic MSI symptoms of dizziness and nausea. For a possible historical example of MSI see LOUDON, NUNS OF. See also MAD GASSER OF MATTOON; MASS HYSTERIA; POKÉMON PANIC.

mass telepathy
The term given to the hypothetical transmission of ideas to a group of people using the power of the mind alone.
Mass TELEPATHY experiments came to the fore with the advent of radio broadcasting. In 1927, the BBC carried out an experiment in conjunction with the SOCIETY FOR PSYCHICAL RESEARCH. Having announced in advance that the results would be inconclusive, they made an attempt to communicate images of a series of objects to their audience – this involved a group of people (agents) concentrating on five different objects for a period of three minutes each.

The public were told that two of the objects were playing cards (effectively making this part of the exercise a FORCED-CHOICE EXPERIMENT), and that one of the other objects was a picture. No information was offered regarding the last two objects. Listeners were invited to send in their impressions of the objects and details of any emotions that they felt had been 'transmitted' in relation to them. Approximately 25,000 people responded, but when the results were analysed the number of successful 'hits' was no more than would be expected by chance.

Since then, numerous similar mass telepathy experiments have been attempted, often using prominent self-proclaimed PSYCHICS; they proved particularly popular with newspapers for a time. However, none has produced any conclusive evidence for the existence of the phenomenon.

materialization
The manifestation of material objects apparently from nowhere.
Materializations are often claimed to have occurred during SÉANCES and also often feature in POLTERGEIST cases. Materializations take one of two forms: they can either involve something mysteriously transported from elsewhere within the real, physical world (usually referred to as an APPORT – see also TELEPORTATION), or they can involve the apparent spontaneous creation of an object (by spirits or other

supernatural means). ECTOPLASM is the name given to the hypothetical material from which such objects are said to be created.

Materializations that were claimed to have been produced by MEDIUMS include a vast range of (often bizarre) inanimate objects, as well as human figures – for example the materializations of Katie King by the medium FLORENCE COOK. In the stories of poltergeist cases the materializations are usually more mundane and include such things as stones, coins and water.

Although materializations were extremely fashionable during the heyday of Victorian SPIRITUALISM, the production of an apport or the manifestation of ectoplasm was never successfully demonstrated under laboratory conditions. Claims to have produced a materialization are now uncommon, although they do still occasionally appear – examples being the 'spiritual ash' and trinkets of SAI BABA.

Mather, Cotton (1662–1728)

A prominent Puritan minister in colonial New England famous for his strong views on witchcraft and for his involvement in the witchcraft trials at Salem.

Cotton Mather was the son of the strictly orthodox Puritan minister and scholar Increase Mather, who had argued that WITCHCRAFT and supernatural happenings were evidence of God's displeasure with the decline in religion in New England. Cotton was a brilliant student, who studied at Harvard University and went on to write 382 books on a wide range of subjects, including history and botany, and was a strong supporter of progressive ideas such as smallpox inoculation.

However, Cotton Mather is now remembered primarily for his writings and sermons on the evils of witchcraft. He developed his father's views, taking a firmer and less cautious approach. He argued and preached in favour of the WITCH TRIALS that had been taking place in New England since the 1640s and, in 1689, he published *Memorable Providences Relating to Witchcrafts and Possessions*, which stressed the reality of witchcraft and its relation to the activities of the DEVIL. He was approached for advice during the Salem witchcraft trials (see SALEM WITCHES) and, although he cautioned against reliance upon the 'spectral evidence' which featured in the trials he gave his support to those who were pursuing the investigation and convictions. He apparently believed that the trials brought to an end the Devil's campaign to destroy the Puritan communities of New England. It is reported that he attended the hanging of George Burroughs, who was convicted

The title page of Cotton Mather's *On Witchcraft: Being the Wonders of the Invisible World*.
(© Stapleton Collection/Corbis)

at the trials, and when the crowd appeared to be swayed by Burroughs' reciting the Lord's Prayer, he gave a speech which convinced them to continue with the execution.

In 1693, Mather wrote *On Witchcraft: Being the Wonders of the Invisible World*, which included:

> Some Accounts of the Grievous Molestations, by DAEMONS and WITCHCRAFTS, which have lately annoy'd the Countrey; and the Trials of some eminent *Malefactors* Executed upon occasion thereof: with several Remarkable *Curiosities* therein occurring.

However, public opinion was beginning to turn, and even his father spoke out against the methods employed in the trials. Mather now found that the tide was against him but continued to argue his case. Despite the undoubted value of his other works, his reputation suffered from attacks on his credulity, to the point that he was apparently repeatedly turned down for the presidency of Harvard.

Mathers, (Samuel Liddel) MacGregor (1854–1918)

Leading English occultist and co-founder of the Hermetic Order of the Golden Dawn.

Macgregor Mathers was born as Samuel Liddel in 1854, in London. He added MacGregor to his name, claiming Scottish ancestry, and later liked to wear full Highland dress when performing rituals involving the Celtic pantheon. He developed an early interest in MAGIC and the OCCULT, and became a Freemason in 1877, and a Master Mason in 1878. He also joined the Societas Rosicruciania in 1882, becoming a member of their High Council within four years.

In 1888, he and two fellow ROSICRUCIANS, Dr Wynn Westcott and Dr William R Woodman, founded the HERMETIC ORDER OF THE GOLDEN DAWN. The outer order of the Golden Dawn was controlled by an inner second order of which only Westcott, Woodman and Mathers were members and the self-appointed chiefs. Woodman controlled the day-to-day administration of the outer order, while Mathers concentrated on formulating its rituals and curricula. He claimed to receive instructions from a group of superhuman adepts called the SECRET CHIEFS who constituted a Third Order, and was the author of almost all of the important teachings and documents of the Golden Dawn. Since he was strongly influenced by the work of ÉLIPHAS LÉVI, the KABBALAH and the TAROT figured prominently in his system, and he created a new tarot deck, the Tarot of the Golden Dawn, which is believed to have been designed by him and painted by his wife, although he claimed to have produced it by himself while in a trance. He took the Enochian system of angelic magic formulated by the Elizabethan alchemist JOHN DEE, and developed and incorporated it into the Golden Dawn system, and was also responsible for introducing the Egyptian pantheon into its rituals. An early campaigner for women's rights, Mathers insisted that women not only be admitted to the Golden Dawn, but be given a completely equal footing as members. He was said to be able to read and translate a number of languages, such as Hebrew, Latin, French, Coptic and Greek, and his output included English translations of several important occult texts, in particular two ancient GRIMOIRES – *The Greater Key of Solomon* and *The Book of the Sacred Magic of Abramelin the Mage*.

Following Woodman's death in 1891, and the subsequent resignation of Westcott, Mathers was left in effective control of the Golden Dawn. Sponsored by Mathers, ALEISTER CROWLEY joined the society in 1898, but soon he and Mathers fell out and the antagonism between them is said to have led to a psychic war being waged between the two. Both were eventually expelled from the Order, which subsequently fragmented. Mathers moved to Paris, where he and his wife founded the Ahathoor Temple, in which they celebrated 'Egyptian Masses' honouring the goddess Isis, whose cult he tried to revive. His health declined, and he died in 1918; his widow is said to have blamed Crowley's prolonged psychic attacks, while interestingly, his death certificate apparently lists no cause of death.

Maya

Pre-Columbian people of South America.

Among the civilizations that existed in the Americas before Christopher Columbus (1451–1506) landed there in 1492, one of the most remarkable was that of the Maya people.

The Maya became dominant in the 4th century AD, ruling from their many cities over an area encompassing southern Mexico, Guatemala, northern Belize and western Honduras. Among their achievements were developments in astronomy, calendars and pictographs, but they are best known for their astonishing ceremonial architecture, in particular their pyramid temples.

These stepped pyramids were built from carved stones, ascending to a peak at which a shrine to a particular deity was placed. The material was local limestone, which they quarried and shaped using stone tools. Enormous amounts of manpower were necessary at all stages of construction, from quarrying the massive stones, to transporting them, to fitting them in place. Larger pyramids seem to have been built on top of smaller ones, such as the pyramid (known locally as 'El Castillo', the castle) supporting the temple of Kukulcan, the feathered serpent god, at Chichen Itzá in Yucatán.

The temples at the top of the pyramids would have been visible for miles, projecting above the surrounding jungle, and it is likely that they were intended to advertise Maya power. It is also thought that the Maya used their astronomical knowledge to ensure that the pyramids were built so as to be precisely aligned with heavenly bodies, particularly at equinoxes and solstices.

The Maya also built extensive palaces, many containing tombs, that were elaborately decorated with carvings, sculptures, pictographs and paintings. Ball-courts are also common at Maya sites, showing the importance of the ritual ball game, a violent and highly symbolic contest in which death might be the fate of the losing team. The city of Chichen Itzá had a particularly fine example of a Maya ball-court.

Maya cities were not laid out in strict grid patterns. A central axis was first laid down, aligning with the cardinal points of the compass, and further expansion seems to have taken place fairly organically, harmonizing with local natural features.

The city of Copán, in Honduras, is particularly rich in sculpture and stelae (upright stone tablets) decorated with portraits of rulers and pictographic records of their achievements, erected along ceremonial processional routes between its palaces, plazas and temples.

At Bonampak, in Mexico, the finest examples of Maya frescos have been preserved in the ruins of a temple. These masterfully painted images give an illuminating insight into Maya ceremonies and rituals, including the robing of nobles or priests, the playing of a band of musicians and the ritual bloodletting.

It is believed that Maya civilization began to decline in the 10th century, perhaps undermined by warfare, drought, climate change and over-exploitation of the environment. Their pictographic form of writing has yet to be completely deciphered, and it is hoped that one day it will reveal further clues as to the rationale, purposes and methods involved in creating their impressive architecture.

mazes
A network of paths laid out in such a way as to be confusing to those who attempt to pass through it.

Patterns for mazes are very ancient and have been found incised on rocks or tablets in many prehistoric cultures around the world, from Ireland to Greece. Perhaps the oldest myth connected with a maze is that of Theseus and the Minotaur, in which the hero has to penetrate the Cretan labyrinth, kill the monster at its heart and then find his way back out again. A maze seems to represent a puzzle to be solved and a goal to be reached.

In Britain, mazes were carved into turf as long ago as pre-Roman times and many of great antiquity have survived. It is not known for certain what function these had, but one suggestion is that they were laid out as the pattern for ritual dances. It has also been suggested that they were a means of entrapping evil spirits, by luring them into the centre from which they would be unable to escape.

Another idea is that they were used in worship, perhaps as a symbolic journey to spiritual purification. It has been claimed that medieval maze patterns near churches in Europe were walked (or followed on the knees) by penitents as a substitute for pilgrimage to Jerusalem.

By the time maze-makers in Britain began using hedges instead of patterns cut into turf the original motivations may have been lost, leaving an amusing pastime in the place of meaningful ritual.

McMinnville, Oregon
The location at which the first significant daylight UFO photographs were taken. They show a clearly defined object of apparently unknown origin.

Paul Trent and his wife, a farming couple in McMinnville, Oregon, claimed that, on the evening of 11 May 1950, a large, flattened metallic disc with a raised turret on top appeared over their house. Trent was able to get his camera and take two photographs as the object moved slowly above nearby hills. During the flight it supposedly turned slightly, revealing its underside – this appears on the second photograph.

The Trents were apparently unfamiliar with stories of UFOs (DONALD KEYHOE had produced the first book on the subject only a few weeks earlier). They assumed that the object was an experimental military plane and so thought it was only of modest interest. Indeed they did not develop the pictures until the film was finished – although they had already mentioned the sighting to friends. They showed the photographs to a local banker, who asked if he could put them on display in his window. It was there that they were seen by a local reporter, which led to their publication. The Trents never sought any money and did not even ask for the negatives back from the press. They appeared to have little concept of the potential importance of what they had photographed, even 17 years later when they were interviewed by members of the COLORADO UNIVERSITY STUDY.

The investigators who looked into this case were struck by the integrity of this unassuming couple and, unlike most other reported UFO photographs, there have been few charges of deception. The only significant attempt to criticize the photographs involved showing that shadows on the eaves of a building in the foreground of the shots indicated that the photographs were taken in the morning, not the evening. However, some claim that reflections of ambient light in the evening can create the same effect at that location.

The photographs are clear and contain much foreground and background detail, including the effects of distant mist on the object indicating that this is not a small model close to the camera. Modern computer analysis also suggests that the UFO is indeed a large object that is at least several hundred feet from the witnesses. However, it does not resemble any known aircraft from the period.

William Hartmann, the photographic specialist who investigated the case for the Colorado University study, reached a conclusion that was very close to a declaration that these pictures showed a real UFO:

This is one of the few UFO reports in which all factors investigated, geometric, psychological

One of the two UFO photographs taken by farmer Paul Trent on 11 May 1950. (© Bettmann/Corbis)

and physical, appear to be consistent with the assertion that an extraordinary flying object, silvery, metallic, disk-shaped, tens of metres in diameter, and evidently artificial, flew within sight of two witnesses.

medicine, alternative *see* ALTERNATIVE MEDICINE

medicine, behavioural *see* BEHAVIOURAL MEDICINE

medicine, Chinese *see* CHINESE MEDICINE

medicine, holistic *see* HOLISTIC MEDICINE

medicine bundles

Native American bags or pouches containing sacred objects.

Medicine bundles are widespread throughout Native American tribes. They consist of a bag made from an animal hide, which contains either objects that the owner has been guided to include by their personal spirit or MANITOU, or that have been included as part of the initiation into a medicine society. The types of objects contained within the bundle include feathers, bells, animal hooves and medicinal herbs. Bundles will also often have their own particular songs that are sung to accompany their opening.

Medicine bundles would be opened before important events such as long journeys, hunts or war. The opening would be accompanied by songs, dancing and ritual in an attempt to invoke the powers of the bundle to bring success.

Traditionally, medicine bundles were either buried with their owner or passed on to a relative. Those of important visionaries are sometimes kept among the possessions of a MEDICINE MAN or are owned collectively by MEDICINE SOCIETIES. The exchange or sale of personal medicine bundles (together with their songs) became common in the 18th and 19th centuries – a practice which was stimulated particularly by the fur trade.

medicine man

The term often used to describe a holy man, particularly in Native American cultures.

The word 'medicine' in this context comes from the

French word *médecin* meaning 'doctor'. Although the practice of 'medicine' (in its modern Western usage) is central to the medicine man's activities, their role is wider than simply that of a healer. The Native American medicine man is endowed with powers and knowledge, enabling him to see visions and to communicate (directly or indirectly) with the spirit world. Medicine men may also lead rituals and act as spiritual advisers.

Recourse to the healing practices of Native American medicine is currently enjoying something of a resurgence among the population as a whole, Native American and non-Native American alike. See also BLACK ELK; MEDICINE BUNDLES; MEDICINE SOCIETIES.

medicine societies
Mystical societies within Native American culture.
Medicine societies exist in many Native American cultures; however, they are particularly important among the Algonquin tribes of the Great Lakes area and the Pueblo people of the south-western USA. They tend to be closed and secretive organizations, dedicated to protecting and passing on tribal traditional lore, healing techniques, mythology and ritual.

One of the best-known societies is the Midewiwin, also known as the Great Medicine Society, which from historical evidence is known to have existed since before the beginning of the 18th century. This is a super-society which includes societies from many different Native American tribal groups, including the Ojibwa, Chippewa, Ottawa and Potawatomi. There are four grades of membership, with advancement through the grades sometimes involving years of teaching. Initiation at each level involves a ritual shooting with white clam shells, taken from a sacred MEDICINE BUNDLE made from otter skin, followed by a symbolic rebirth.

The term 'medicine lodge' is used to describe the buildings and associated ceremonies employed by the medicine societies.

medicine wheel
A circle of stones placed on the plains of North America by Native American tribes.
The term 'medicine wheel' was applied by white settlers in the 19th century to mysterious circular formations they found on the North American plains. The word 'medicine' refers to the supposed magical or mystical purposes for which they were thought to be used (see MEDICINE MAN; MEDICINE BUNDLES; MEDICINE SOCIETIES).

Medicine wheels are to be found at over 60 sites throughout the North American plains. Although many of them are of more recent origin than the STONE CIRCLES of Europe, the identity of their makers and the purposes they served still remain something of a mystery. The Plains Native Americans led a nomadic life, leaving behind them very little in the way of substantial archaeological evidence. They did, however, leave behind a

A modern medicine wheel at Sedona, Arizona, USA. (© George H. H. Huey/Corbis)

number of small rings of stones that have been identified as tepee rings (the stones being used to hold down the edges of the hide tepees) and the larger rings known as medicine wheels. Although they take many different forms, common elements of medicine wheels are a large central stone or cairn, surrounded by one or two concentric circles of stones or smaller cairns, often tens of metres in diameter. Many wheels also have lines of stones radiating out from the central point or from the outside of the circle. The stones are generally placed on the ground rather than erected in the manner of a STANDING STONE.

As with the stone circles of Europe, there are a number of different hypotheses relating to the exact purpose of medicine wheels, although it seems likely that different types of wheel may have been used for different ends. It is also possible that they had different meanings to different tribes, and there is evidence that they were altered and re-used over the centuries.

Archaeological excavations have revealed evidence of burials, within tepee rings, at the centre of some medicine wheels, including the Ellis medicine wheel near Medicine Hat in Alberta, Canada – an area associated with the Blackfoot people. This suggests that they may have been used among the Blackfoot as some form of honoured burial for important individuals.

Other theories include the ritual use of medicine wheels for ceremonies such as the SUN DANCE or (in common with those put forward for the stone circles of Stone Age cultures elsewhere) their use for purposes related to the seasonal movements of the sun, moon and stars. For example, the Bighorn medicine wheel at the top of Medicine Mountain in Wyoming has 28 radial spokes which may represent the days in a lunar month. There are six cairns around the circle, two of which are positioned to be in alignment with the sunrise and sunset on the summer solstice. Other cairns line up with the rise of the three bright stars, Aldebaran, Sirius and Rigel. Similar alignments are also found elsewhere.

It seems likely that medicine wheels were used for a diverse range of purposes and that they may have been used for some or all of the above at any given time. Their exact cultural significance remains beyond the reach of modern investigators. This is, unfortunately, due partly to the fact that at the very time that archaeologists and anthropologists were beginning to become interested in medicine wheels, the traditional culture that might have shed light on their secrets was being destroyed.

meditation

The achievement through thought control of a tranquil state and total relaxation of mind and body, usually as a religious or spiritual practice. Meditation is a common component of many Eastern belief systems, but is now also used in the West in a non-spiritual context as a relaxation technique.

The practice of meditation, which may be broadly defined as the quieting of the mind and focusing of the concentration, often formalized as a ritual, is recognized as a component of many religions and philosophies. The term 'meditation' has been used in a specifically Christian context since the 16th century to refer to a form of mental prayer, often a monastic practice, which involves thinking about a specific passage from scripture in order to gain a deeper understanding of it. However, since the late 19th century, when the theosophists (see THEOSOPHICAL SOCIETY) adopted the word to refer to spiritual practices drawn from Eastern systems such as Hinduism and Buddhism, it has generally been associated with a variety of techniques whose aim is to still the busy mind and free it from distractions so that it can be directed on a single object, as a means of spiritual growth.

As an Eastern spiritual technique, meditation is generally thought to have originated in Vedic Hinduism, although it also developed independently in Muslim SUFISM. Hinduism's raja YOGA involves several types of meditation, as does TAOISM. The KABBALAH and texts of Hassidic Judaism also refer explicitly to the concept of meditation. Meditation has always been a central feature of Buddhism as a means of spiritual enlightenment, and the Buddha is said to have become enlightened while meditating under a bodhi tree; Buddhism usually distinguishes between *samatha*, a calming meditation in which the practitioner focuses the attention on a single object or idea, and *vipassana* meditation, whose aim is to achieve insight and perceive the true nature of reality. In Japanese Mahayana Buddhist schools, concentration is cultivated through highly structured rituals, while in ZEN BUDDHISM, meditation is also considered necessary for enlightenment.

While each tradition has its own methods, they tend to share a number of common characteristics: the stilling of the mind; the focusing of the stilled mind on a single element, whether this is the action of the breath, a MANTRA, a MANDALA or a spiritual concept; the importance of a spiritual teacher; the use of preparatory RITUALS for cleansing oneself and the place where one meditates; and the necessity to integrate the mind, body and spirit so that the meditation leads to positive changes in one's daily life and outlook. Meditation is often performed seated in a cross-legged posture such as the lotus position;

a straight back is usually thought to maximize the flow of spiritual energy, vital breath or life force. A meditative state may also be induced by repetitive actions such as chanting or humming. However, meditation may also be a more active process. The Chinese martial art or bodywork system of T'AI CHI is often referred to as 'meditation in motion', while in Islam, the Sufi meditative ritual takes several forms, including the recitation of divine names, devotional music known as *qawwali* and the spinning dance of the whirling dervishes (see DERVISHES, WHIRLING).

Meditation may be practised for several reasons. The goal is traditionally a spiritual one – the opening up of the practitioner to the divine, the invocation of a higher power, a deeper understanding of one's religion or the attainment of insight into the nature of reality. But a number of modern forms of meditation, such as TRANSCENDENTAL MEDITATION, focus not on spiritual aims but on personal development, the release of creativity, the cultivation of mental discipline, physical wellbeing or relaxation.

The beneficial effects claimed for meditation are many: spiritual insight or enlightenment; increased compassion or patience; a feeling of deep peace or of great joy; or the experiencing of phenomena such as KUNDALINI awakening or spiritual visions. However, some studies have suggested that meditation can, if practised improperly or too intensely, have adverse effects, including psychological problems such as depression or disorientation.

meditation, transcendental *see*

TRANSCENDENTAL MEDITATION

medium

Someone who is allegedly able to communicate directly with the spirits of the dead or is able to allow such communication to take place through them.
The idea of the 'medium', or 'spirit medium', was popularized during the rise of the spiritualist movement in the 19th century (see SPIRITUALISM), although the concept of direct communication with SPIRITS has formed part of many religious and spiritual belief systems throughout history. Spirit mediums are attributed with the ability to be able to sense, hear or even see spirits (see CLAIRSENTIENCE, CLAIRAUDIENCE and CLAIRVOYANCE), and some are said to be able to bring about MATERIALIZATIONS of ECTOPLASM or APPORTS (see MEDIUM, PHYSICAL) – including on occasion physical manifestations of the spirits themselves. Such alleged abilities are usually demonstrated during a SÉANCE and may involve the medium having to go into a 'trance' (see MEDIUM, TRANCE and TRANCE, MEDIUMISTIC).

The medium and spiritualist Doris Stokes, photographed in 1986. (© TopFoto/UPP)

Some mediums claim to be able to manifest voices (see MEDIUM, DIRECT VOICE), others apparently allow the spirits to possess them so they can speak through them and a few even claim that they can effectively be transformed into the spirit (MEDIUM, TRANSFIGURATION). Processes such as this, where the spirit apparently communicates through the medium, are often described as forms of CHANNELLING. Channelling is also associated with the production of AUTOMATIC ART, AUTOMATIC SPEECH and AUTOMATIC WRITING. Other mediums claim that they experience the communication with the spirits themselves, and then pass on the messages to the other séance sitters (see MEDIUM, MENTAL).

Famous 19th-century mediums include the FOX SISTERS, DANIEL DUNGLAS HOME, EUSAPIA PALLADINO and HÉLÈNE SMITH, and those from the 20th century include STANISLAWA TOMCZYK, RUTH MONTGOMERY and DORIS STOKES. The activities of those who claim to be mediums have always been highly controversial, and the efforts on the part of such people as JOHN NEVIL MASKELYNE, HARRY HOUDINI and, more recently, members of organizations such as the COMMITTEE FOR THE SCIENTIFIC INVESTIGATION OF CLAIMS OF THE PARANORMAL have resulted in many mediums being exposed as frauds. Indeed, many of the feats originally associated with mediums are now standard features of stage magic acts (see MAGIC, STAGE), making it increasingly difficult for those who claim such powers to be taken seriously by the world at large.

medium, direct voice

A medium who can produce a voice which appears to have no physical source.

The voices produced by direct voice mediums appear to come out of 'thin air' and are supposedly those of SPIRITS.

One explanation offered by spiritualists for the mechanism by which this takes place is that ECTOPLASM is withdrawn from the medium and coalesces into a voicebox which is used by the spirit. If only a small amount of 'energy' is available then amplification (usually by means of a trumpet or loud hailer) is required. If a large amount of 'energy' is available (such as that which apparently comes from an accomplished medium) then the voice can be heard without assistance. Direct voice mediums were particularly popular during the late 19th and early 20th centuries, although the phenomenon has undergone something of a resurgence in recent years in the UK.

Some direct voice mediums have been shown to fake their abilities through the use of ventriloquism techniques or concealed tape recorders and record players.

medium, mental

A medium who apparently experiences contact with the spirits in his or her mind only.

Mental mediums claim that they effectively act as an interpreter for the other participants in a SÉANCE. They, themselves, apparently have a direct experience of contact with SPIRITS, through processes described as CLAIRVOYANCE, CLAIRSENTIENCE or CLAIRAUDIENCE – rather than producing direct, external communications from the spirits, or allowing the other séance participants to communicate with the spirits through them (see CHANNELLING). Modern PSYCHICS who claim to work in this way include the British mediums Derek Acorah and Gordon Smith – watching them perform can be likened to listening to a conversation take place while only being able to hear one of the people involved.

medium, physical

A medium who apparently manifests physical evidence of the existence of spirits.

Physical mediums claim to be able to produce (with the assistance of SPIRITS) MATERIALIZATIONS such as APPORTS or ECTOPLASM, or physical effects such as TABLE-TURNING or LEVITATION. During the heyday of SPIRITUALISM it was even claimed that some mediums were able to materialize spirits in full, human form – and photographs of such 'materializations' were very popular during the 19th century (see SPIRIT PHOTOGRAPHY). Performances involving physical effects and manifestations usually required darkness, or at least semi-darkness, leading to the obvious suggestion that this was a cover for trickery.

medium, trance

A medium who claims that he or she must enter a trance to contact the spirits of the dead.

The trance (see TRANCE, MEDIUMISTIC) entered into by a trance medium is described as being similar to those that can sometimes induced by HYPNOSIS. Some would argue that it is an example of an ALTERED STATE OF CONSCIOUSNESS.

Trance mediums will apparently enter a trance during a SÉANCE and, while they are in this state, communication with the spirits occurs. When they return from the trance at the end of the séance they are supposedly unaware of the details of what has taken place. A number of such mediums were involved in the investigation into life after death (see AFTERLIFE) undertaken by the SCOLE GROUP. The technique employed by trance mediums is sometimes described as mentally 'stepping aside' to allow the spirit to enter them. It can apparently be carried out only with the willing co-operation of both parties and requires a significant amount of training. However, those that claim that mediums are nothing more than stage magicians (see MAGIC, STAGE) would argue that the apparent entry into a trance is simply showmanship.

medium, transfiguration

A medium who supposedly takes on the physical characteristics of the dead person with whom he or she is in contact.

Transfiguration mediums claim that they can be possessed by the SPIRIT of a dead person, to the point that they will (usually very fleetingly) take on aspects of that person's appearance when they were alive. Such a change is an example of physical mediumship (see MEDIUM, PHYSICAL). Generally, it is said that no communication with the spirit is possible while the medium is taking on their appearance – this is supposedly due to the large amount of 'energy' required to achieve the change. It is claimed that the most advanced transfiguration mediums can even manifest the appearance of such things as facial hair – however, the few photographs in existence that allegedly show a transfiguration medium in action are remarkably similar to pictures of people simply pulling faces.

mediumistic trance *see* TRANCE, MEDIUMISTIC

Medjugorje

The site in Herzegovina of alleged Marian visions.
Medjugorje is a town in Herzegovina which became associated with MARIAN APPARITIONS.

On 24 June 1981, a group of six local youths (Ivanka Ivanković, Mirjana Dragićević, Vicka Ivanković, Ivan Dragićević, Jakov Čolo and Marija Pavlović) reported seeing a beautiful young woman carrying a child in her arms. They were too frightened to approach her, but the next day they saw her again, prayed with her and received various messages, mostly advocating peace, devotion, repentance and prayer. Since then the 'visionaries' claim to have received regular apparitions until the present day, even though some of them subsequently emigrated to other parts of the world.

The visions tend to follow a pattern of being received while the visionary is at prayer, reciting the rosary, no matter what the location. They last for a few minutes, during which the visionary appears to be in an ecstatic, trance-like state (see also ECSTATIC PHENOMENA). Different members of the group receive them with varying degrees of frequency, but all claim to receive a regular message on the 25th of each month.

The site of the original visions has become a place of pilgrimage, and various miraculous cures have been associated with visits there. However, unlike the visions that occurred at FÁTIMA or LOURDES, for example, the Roman Catholic Church has never recognized these apparitions as being supernatural, divinely inspired or 'worthy of belief'.

Critics from within the Church point out that, unlike ST BERNADETTE or Sister Lucia of the Fátima apparitions, none of the young people involved at Medjugorje went on to realize a religious vocation. Instead, they tended to marry and move abroad, often achieving comfortable lifestyles as a result of their fame among the faithful. This would imply that it is not a case of Medjugorje itself being a particularly holy place, but one of the visionaries themselves having been deemed particularly worthy of divine communication, which some would say they have not acted upon appropriately.

Some sceptics maintain that the visions were the hysterical product of a community under threat of civil war and seeking a source both of communal identity and strength, and that they were manipulated by the charismatic movement of the Catholic Church to affirm the resurgence of faith.

While many around the world believe in the truth of the Medjugorje apparitions, the Vatican maintains the position that they have not met the Church's criteria of authenticity and continues to investigate them.

Megaliths *see panel p448*

Meier, (Eduard Albert) 'Billy' (1937–)

One of the most prominent UFO 'contactees' of the late 20th century, whose stories of meetings with aliens, space philosophy and disputed photographs were the subject of much debate.
Billy Meier was born Eduard Albert Meier in Switzerland in 1937 and claimed to have had his first

A photograph said to show a UFO flying over the Swiss countryside, one of the hundreds of such photographs produced by 'contactee' Billy Meier. (© Mary Evans Picture Library)

Megaliths

The term 'megalith' is derived from the Greek words *mega*, large, and *lith*, stone, and is usually applied to prehistoric (literally Stone Age) monuments, whether in the form of STANDING STONES in groups (such as STONE CIRCLES or STONE ROWS), solitary pillars (monoliths or MENHIRS), or more complex structures built from large rocks. These constructions are of various types ranging from simple, box-like burial features (known as cists) made from stone slabs, or tombs made of upright stones topped by a large capstone (DOLMENS), to veritable Stone Age temples consisting of earth or rock mounds containing stone-lined passages and internal chambers. The general purpose of megaliths was usually of a funerary and ritual nature (they were much more than merely graves), but other functions also seem to have existed in some cases. Some megaliths have also been interpreted as acting as signposts, boundary markers or representations of ancestral figures or tribal and religious symbols, and sometimes a mix of these functions can be seen at one site. There are literally hundreds of thousands of surviving megalithic monuments worldwide built by diverse cultures throughout all the ages – some stones were used rough and ready, others dressed (that is, shaped and smoothed). It is possible here to give but a mere glimpse of the global extent of ancient megalithic culture.

Focusing solely on what 19th-century antiquarians called 'rude stone monuments', we find that various kinds occur in the Mediterranean area – in southern Italy and on islands such as Sicily, Sardinia, Corsica, Minorca (where there are megalithic sanctuaries containing giant T-shaped megalithic arrangements known as *taulas*), and, especially, Malta, where complex Stone Age temples abound (judging from the remnants of carved stone figures, these were apparently dedicated to a Mother Goddess).

In Africa, megaliths exist in Algeria and in Morocco (where the site of Msoura, comprising small stones surrounding a tall pillar stone, is the most notable). There are hundreds of stone circles in The Gambia on the west coast, sites in Ghana and Nigeria, tall standing stones and cists in central Africa, and hundreds of standing stones in Ethiopia, including a monstrous monolith that is 30.5 metres (100 feet) tall in the north of the country. There are also plain and engraved standing stones in the south, including the Soddo region, and dolmens in the east. In southern Egypt, a stone circle at Nabla appears to have astronomically orientated stone alignments associated with it.

In the Near East, stone monuments date back to the 4th and 3rd millennia BC and include simple dolmen structures. Far to the south, the Yemen can boast rows and rings of standing stones, and platforms surmounted by megalithic chambers, while Bahrain in the Persian Gulf has prehistoric tombs in the form of stone 'chests' up to 12 metres (40 feet) in height and divided internally into various areas.

Parts of the Himalayan region, Pakistan and India are scattered with megaliths. In the Deccan, southern India, there are thousands of mounds with holed stones covering the entrances of passages that lead to square or cruciform megalithic burial chambers. These sites appear to date to the first and second millennia BC – the age of the Vedas.

The Far East also has a share of megaliths, with rectangular megalithic chambers in some south-eastern regions of China. These can be substantial structures – the capstone of Che-pin-shan ('stone table mountain') in Manchuria weighs around 70 tonnes. In the latter centuries BC and the 1st millennium AD, megalithic building also took place in Japan, one of the best-known examples being the concentric circles of standing stones on the summit of the giant Tatetsuki mound at Okayama. Generally more recent megalithic sites occur in parts of South-East Asia and Oceania, including Malaysia, Borneo and certain Pacific islands. The *moai*, the giant sculpted stone figures of Easter Island, are the most famous of these (see EASTER ISLAND STATUES).

Although several civilizations in the Americas built in stone, megalithic features of the types we are considering are rare. One example, though, is the isolated group of megaliths in the San Augustin region of Columbia. There, sculpted stone uprights ('steles' or 'stelae') are accompanied by dolmen-like structures. Another example is found in the Yucatan, southern Mexico, where a cult existed that erected phallic-shaped stones ranging up to 2.1 metres (7 feet) in height. And in 2006, an isolated stone circle of over a hundred granite blocks, each weighing several tonnes and placed upright in the ground, was discovered in a remote part of north-eastern Brazil.

But it is western and northern Europe where probably the greatest concentration of megaliths is to be found – it is said over 5,000 survive in the Brittany area of France alone, primarily in extensive stone row complexes (see eg CARNAC). In Scandinavia, stone settings in the shapes of boats, and monoliths sporting runic engravings, date from the Viking era. A swathe of older megaliths (mainly dolmens) stretches from southern Denmark and northern Holland across northern Germany and into Poland. Lands around the Black Sea possess prehistoric stone monuments – such as the chambered burial mounds of Bulgaria and the rectangular slab-tombs of the Caucasus region – many with 'spirit holes' cut through their frontal stones. Some European megalithic sites are among the oldest known; material from megalithic tombs in southern Portugal yields radiocarbon dates of the 5th millennium BC, and some of the chambered mounds in Brittany have provided similarly ancient dates – two small chambered sites have been dated to c.5800 BC.

Ireland and the British Isles possess an exceptional megalithic heritage, with sites of world renown like England's STONEHENGE and AVEBURY, Scotland's CALLANISH and Maes Howe, and Ireland's Newgrange – older than Egypt's GREAT PYRAMID and possessing a stone-lined entrance passage over 18 metres (60 feet) long leading to a central chamber 6 metres (20 feet) high built of overlapping ('corbelled') stone slabs. But literally thousands of other megalithic sites grace these islands, including mysterious moorland stone rows, notably on Dartmoor.

Recent archaeological discoveries indicate that timber circles (see WOODHENGE) preceded the era of European megalith building, or at least overlapped with it, and there is evidence that stones were initially handled like timber. At Stonehenge, for instance, there are mortise and tenon joints fixing horizontal stone lintels on upright megaliths, and some of the bluestones in the monument, the first stones to be erected there, display tongue-and-groove work.

The first sacred sites were probably venerated natural locations (usually distinctive landmarks), and many megalithic monuments are built in sight of such topographical features – in some cases aligning to them. On Bodmin Moor in south-west England, for example, stone circles were so precisely placed that a shift of 90 metres (100 yards) would have put them out of sight of a prominent distant peak. There also seems to have been a Stone Age tradition of circulating 'pieces of places', similar to the way medieval monks circulated RELICS of saints; this may have been because the very rock of certain venerated spots was viewed as possessing magical power or *mana*. This might explain why quartz from the Wicklow Hills is found built into Newgrange 96.5 kilometres (60 miles) distant, and why the bluestones of Stonehenge came from the Welsh Preseli hills some 400 kilometres (250 miles) away. The stone circle of Gors Fawr is situated so that Carn Menyn, the rocky outcrop where most of the bluestones originated, is prominent on the local skyline.

Sometimes such topographical associations have astronomical dimensions. For example, on the island of Jura, off the west coast of Scotland, there is a range of mountains called the Paps ('breasts') of Jura, on account of two rounded peaks in their midst. The midsummer sun appears to set into the Paps when viewed from a major standing stone group at Ballochroy on the Kintyre peninsula on the mainland. A site near Loch Finlaggan on the island of Islay, immediately to the south of Jura, further confirms the symbolic importance of these breast-like mountains in prehistory. A standing stone there is the survivor of a stone row; looking along the axis of the former row the eye is directed to Jura's two rounded peaks, visible in dramatic isolation on the skyline. A slightly different example is offered by Callanish, an important group of stone circles on the island of Lewis (also off Scotland's west coast). From this group of standing stones the eastern skyline is formed by the Pairc Hills, which resemble the shape of a reclining woman. Sometimes called the 'Sleeping Beauty', her Gaelic name is *Cailleach na Mointeach*, 'the Old Woman of the Moors'. Every 18.61 years, the time in the complex lunar cycle known as the 'Major Standstill', the moon rises out of the hills as if the Earth Mother is giving birth to it. It skims the horizon to seemingly set among the standing stones of Callanish.

The old stones may be silent, but they still have much to tell us.

Paul Devereux

UFO contact at the age of 5. These contacts supposedly continued throughout his youth, during which time he also received communications from ALIENS in the form of telepathic messages (see TELEPATHY) beamed into his mind. The entities establishing contact apparently claimed to be from parallel universes and had names such as 'Asket'.

Meier led a colourful life, travelling the world, studying philosophy in the East and spending periods in the Foreign Legion and a detention centre. He claimed that he had taken many photographs of the UFOs that he saw, but for years was forbidden to release them by his alien contacts. His public profile began to grow when he married a teenage girl, lost an arm in an accident and moved back to Switzerland, where he gathered many acolytes around him. Money was raised for a grand house to act as the focal point of his crusade.

By now a new entity was apparently in contact with him, a beautiful blonde woman called Semjase, who came from the constellation of Lyra but whose race had originated in the Pleiades cluster. She expressed some disquiet about traditional earth religions, and this became a theme of Meier's teachings. He began using the nickname 'Billy' (drawn from his passion for the American 'Wild West') and was apparently given permission by his contacts to release his photographs, which he went on to do in a series of books. Eventually a dozen volumes of these colourful images were published, showing craft known as 'beamships' over the Swiss mountains and even images of Semjase herself, although these didn't appear to offer any direct proof that she was an alien.

The UFO community generally viewed Meier in much the same way as they had the earlier CONTACTEES (such as GEORGE ADAMSKI), and research published by the US investigator Karl Korff, who conducted extensive analyses of the photographs, suggested that the 'beamships' appeared to be suspiciously small. However, Meier also has many champions who have argued that his hundreds of photographs are the best ever taken – to these people Meier is akin to a spiritual prophet, suffering at the hands of a campaign to discredit his reputation.

memories, recovered

Forgotten memories apparently retrieved under psychoanalysis or hypnosis.

Many people receiving treatment through psychoanalysis or HYPNOSIS seem to discover memories of experiences of which they have previously had no conscious recollection. Some have suggested that these are hidden or repressed memories, buried by the unconscious mind because they are too traumatic to deal with (see MEMORIES, REPRESSED).

It is currently generally believed that there are two ways in which memories are stored in the brain – short-term and long-term. Short-term memories are continually renewed, with new ones replacing less recent ones (unless they are refreshed). Although a greater quantity of long-term memories are stored, they are not always easy to retrieve.

Beginning with the work of SIGMUND FREUD, it became a basic tenet of psychoanalysis that mental problems are often caused by the unconscious suppression of unpleasant memories, and that the act of bringing these to the surface of the mind, to be acknowledged by the patient, can remove the problems. The whole area later became highly controversial, however, when patients seemed to be 'recovering' memories of events that could not possibly have happened – particularly where these related to sexual or SATANIC RITUAL ABUSE. Critics of the technique argued that patients in a highly suggestible state were merely reacting to suggestions or cues given (unconsciously or deliberately) by the practitioner, and that false memories (see MEMORY, FALSE) were being created. In the field of UFOLOGY, for example, many people who are convinced that they were abducted by extraterrestrials (see ALIEN ABDUCTION) have been subjected to hypnotic regression by people who already believe that EXTRATERRESTRIALS exist and abduct human beings.

In addition to suggestion, it has also been argued that the process known as CONFABULATION (the replacement of gaps in the memory by invented recollections) might also sometimes play a part in recovered memories. Some psychologists also point out that subjects may construct memories from information absorbed from everyday contact with the culture all around them. In this way 'alien abductees' may be reflecting images from their experience of science fiction rather than their own lives (see CULTURAL TRACKING).

On the other hand, there are those who hold that the idea of false memory simply provides an easy 'get-out' for people who really are guilty of abuse and, likewise, there are many who still believe that recovered memories of alien contact cannot arise without a foundation in real experience.

memories, repressed

Unpleasant memories that it is claimed have been repressed by the unconscious mind.

One of the ideas championed by SIGMUND FREUD was that many types of neuroses or psychological problems were the result of the repression by the patient's unconscious mind of unpleasant or traumatic memories, and that retrieving these memories (see MEMORIES, RECOVERED) would be an important step towards resolving the problem.

Some people who are convinced that they have been abducted by ALIENS also believe that, under HYPNOSIS, they are recalling repressed memories of their terrifying and mentally scarring experiences.

Critics of the idea of repressed memories claim that, in many cases, what is being retrieved is not actual experience. This is not to say that the person involved is lying (indeed they may be utterly convinced of the truth of what they say) but rather that they are the victims of self-delusion.

memory *see* ART OF MEMORY; CELLULAR MEMORY; MEMORIES, RECOVERED; MEMORIES, REPRESSED; MEMORY, FALSE

memory, false
The apparent recollection of events that never happened.
A condition known as 'false memory syndrome' was recognized by medical science in the 1990s. This was partly as a result of cases in which a person undergoing psychoanalysis or HYPNOSIS seemed to recall previously hidden memories of traumatic events, especially childhood sexual abuse, ALIEN ABDUCTION or involvement in SATANIC RITUAL ABUSE. It was argued that what had been considered to be recovered memories (see MEMORIES, RECOVERED) were often simply the products of CONFABULATION or of suggestions made by the practitioner involved.

However, even prior to this it was understood that memories are not fixed and unchanging – they are regularly refreshed and reconstructed, sometimes incorporating new information from external sources. Such modified (or even entirely false) memories are indistinguishable from those that accurately represent real events, and we may remain utterly convinced of their veracity until confronted with clear evidence to the contrary. The human memory cannot, therefore, always be considered to be an entirely reliable source when it comes to claims that strange or unexplained phenomena have occurred. See also MEMORIES, REPRESSED.

menhirs
Individual megaliths.
A menhir is a single prehistoric MEGALITH or STANDING STONE. The word comes from Breton, meaning 'long stone', and was first used in the 19th century by French archaeologists studying such stones in Brittany. It is not known why early man conceived the idea of planting massive stones in the earth. Some suggest that they were used to mark routes, holy places or tribal boundaries, others that they commemorate dead heroes or significant events. Still others connect them with observation of the sun, moon and stars.

The Maen Llia menhir in the Brecon Beacons National Park, Wales. This diamond-shaped menhir is around 3.7 metres (12 feet) tall, 2.7 metres (9 feet) wide and 0.6 metres (2 feet) thick. (© Homer Sykes/Corbis)

Whether standing individually or in alignments, as part of DOLMENS or STONE CIRCLES, menhirs were usually simple dressed stones, but some have been found in central Mediterranean regions that were decorated by carvings of human features. Whether this means they are connected with a god, a particular tribe or a dead chieftain remains impossible to say.

men in black
The term used to describe visitors, of unknown origin, who are sometimes reported to have approached witnesses following a UFO sighting. They are often said to try to prevent the witnesses from revealing their story.
Tales of mysterious 'men in black' (often abbreviated to 'MIB') have been a feature of UFO cases since the earliest days. Even during the 1896 airship WAVE in the USA (see AIRSHIPS) there were claims that strangers had arrived in the town after a sighting to claim physical evidence connected with the incident. Whether such visitors are covert government investigators, seeking information as to what has occurred, or are a part of the phenomenon itself (perhaps trying to recover evidence and prevent the incident being made public) has been a popular theme for debate within the UFO COMMUNITY.

The link between these strangers and black suits dates from 1952, when American Albert Bender created one of the first open membership UFO societies, the Flying Saucer Bureau, in response to the huge popularity of the books and articles produced by DONALD KEYHOE. However, within a year the group suddenly folded, leading to suspicions that Bender had been silenced. Initially, Bender confirmed that three secret agents in dark suits had warned him that he was too close to the truth and must stop his work. In 1962, he wrote a book, *Flying Saucers and the Three Men*, in which the story had now changed – the suggestion being that the threats had come from shape-changing aliens.

Reports of men in black visiting witnesses have continued to be made; often the visits are said to be in the wake of an ALIEN ABDUCTION. A common feature of these reports is the assertion that the strangers behaved in an unusual way or looked slightly odd. For example, in a case from Cumbria in 1964, a witness who had photographed something strange claimed that he was questioned by two government agents, and that during their visit they had only referred to one another using numbers. In a 1976 case from Bolton, one of the two visitors apparently sat throughout the interrogation clutching a square box on his lap and, in a rare 'woman in black' case from the USA, the stranger was described as having lopsided breasts.

There is some evidence to suggest that intelligence agencies have occasionally sent officers to the scene of a UFO sighting. In the UK, documents released under the FREEDOM OF INFORMATION ACT revealed that a defence intelligence unit did this from time to time during the 1960s and 1970s. However, the Ministry of Defence deny that they ever threatened witnesses to silence them or behaved in any of the bizarre fashions associated with MIB stories.

MIBs are now an established feature of modern US folklore, and in recent years caricatured versions of the classic image of 'men in black' provided the theme for two blockbuster films *MIB: Men in Black* (1997) and *MIIB: Men in Black II* (2002).

mental medium *see* MEDIUM, MENTAL

mental photography *see* THOUGHTOGRAPHY

Mephistopheles

One of the chief demons of Christian mythology, said to have been the first angel to join with Lucifer in his rebellion against God; in the Faust legend, he is traditionally identified as the demon through whom Faust makes the pact to sell his soul to the Devil.

Mephistopheles, also referred to as Mephisto, Mephist and Mephistophilis, is the name given to one of the chief demons in Christian mythology. He

is not mentioned in the Bible and his name appears to have evolved during the Renaissance. However, he is traditionally said to have been the first angel who sided with LUCIFER in his rebellion against God, and was the second angel to be cast out of Heaven (see ANGELS, FALLEN). Satan rewarded him with power in Hell as his second-in-command, and his name, which is generally thought to derive from three Greek words meaning 'he who loves not the light', is often used synonymously with SATAN or the DEVIL.

While the origin of his conception and his name remains the subject of debate, Mephistopheles is best known for his central role in the 16th-century FAUST legend, in which he is identified as the demon through whom Faust makes his pact with the Devil to sell his soul for knowledge and power. Having secured Faust's soul, Mephistopheles remains with him as a familiar to grant his wishes, until Faust's allotted time runs out and Mephistopheles drags him down to Hell.

mercury

A heavy, silvery transition element, the only metal which is liquid at or near room temperature; of prime importance in alchemy throughout the ages.

Every civilization has its own legends about mercury, the silvery transition element which is the only metal to be a liquid at or near room temperature. Called quicksilver by the ancients, it has been used as a medicine by many cultures, in countries including China, India and Tibet, where it was thought to prolong life, and a great many of the elixirs consumed medicinally between the 6th and 12th centuries were made from a mercury base.

Mercury has always been of prime importance to alchemists throughout the ages, and was seen as one of the seven metals of ALCHEMY, along with GOLD, silver, copper, LEAD, IRON and tin. It was usually obtained alchemically by heating its solid red sulphide ore, cinnabar, and it readily vaporized in gentle heat to give a vapour called 'spirit mercury'. Since it transcended both the solid and liquid states, it was regarded as both fixed and volatile, suggesting that it was a 'divine principle' in the world, a hermaphroditic substance which united both male and female principles; to the alchemists, it symbolized the god Hermes, and was often personified as the Moon. The Sanskrit name for alchemy, *rasayana*, means literally 'knowledge of mercury'. One of the central ideas of European alchemy was the belief that all metals were essentially mercury, with different quantities and qualities of other substances producing different metals, and that the correct combination of mercury with these could produce gold. The striking reaction of mercury in nitric acid, in which bright red crystals precipitate to the bottom while a thick red vapour hangs over the surface, was seen by alchemists as a simultaneous separation into the Above and the Below, proving its 'divine' and hermaphroditic nature. See also PHILOSOPHER'S MERCURY.

mercury, red *see* RED MERCURY

meridians

In Chinese medicine, the channels through which vital energy, or qi, is believed to flow through the body.

CHINESE MEDICINE is based on the theory that a UNIVERSAL LIFE FORCE called QI flows through the body along channels known as meridians. In a healthy person, this energy flows freely through the body in a balanced and harmonious way, but if the flow becomes disrupted or unbalanced, it can result in illness. The qi is believed to circulate through the meridians along both internal and external pathways; there are twelve primary meridians, each named after the main organ or body function with which it is thought to connect, and each meridian enters its related organ by the internal pathway, while also passing close to the surface of the skin along an external pathway. On these external pathways there are hundreds of specific points called *hsueh* (hollows) which it is believed, if stimulated by massage (ACUPRESSURE) or the insertion of needles (ACUPUNCTURE), allow the practitioner to manipulate the flow of qi through a given meridian and its corresponding organ, opening up any blockages and restoring a healthy and harmonious balance of energy.

The twelve primary meridians are said to run vertically, bilaterally and symmetrically in the body; six are YIN and six are YANG, with three yin and three yang meridians situated on each arm, and three yin and three yang ones on each leg. The three yin meridians of the arm, which run from chest to hand, connect to the lungs, pericardium (the outer muscle of the heart) and the heart; the three yang meridians of the arm, which run from hand to face, connect to the large intestine, small intestine and 'Triple Burner', a special organ system thought to span the whole torso; the three yin meridians of the leg, which run from foot to chest, connect to the spleen, liver and kidney; and the three yang meridians of the leg, running from face to foot, connect to the stomach, gallbladder and bladder. The qi is said to flow from one meridian to the next in a continuous and fixed order – lung, large intestine, stomach, spleen, heart, small intestine, bladder, kidney, pericardium, 'Triple Burner', gallbladder, liver – travelling from meridian to meridian in a two-hour cycle, and making the complete circuit once a day. See also REFLEXOLOGY; SHIATSU.

Merlin

Legendary magician associated with King Arthur.

In the legends and medieval romances about KING ARTHUR, he is advised and aided by the famous magician Merlin.

According to the traditional tales, as well as being a wizard Merlin had the gift of prophecy and foretold the eventual defeat of the Britons by the Saxons. As he was the son of a mortal woman impregnated by an INCUBUS, tradition holds that he could not be killed. However, in different versions of the story, he met his end at the hands of his former pupil the enchantress Nimue, imprisoned by her magic beneath a great rock, or through the spells of Vivien, the Lady of the Lake, who entangled him in a thorn bush.

Among the magical feats associated with Merlin in Arthurian legend is the fixing of the sword into the stone, from which only the true king could withdraw it. His name was also connected with the construction of STONEHENGE, in which he was said to have used his magic to move and erect the great monoliths.

As to the possibility of there being a historical Merlin, there are references to him in the same chronicles that mention KING ARTHUR, most notably in the accounts of Nennius (fl.769), who describes his boyhood and youth under the name Ambrosius. The *Historia Regum Britanniae* (c.1136) of Geoffrey of Monmouth (c.1100–c.1154) contains a life of Merlin in which he is described as having been born in Carmarthen in Wales. One theory is that, rather than being King Arthur's wizard, Merlin was actually his bard, and several traditional poems have been attributed to him under the name Myrddin. In this version, Merlin is said to have died in battle beside his king. However, like King Arthur, it is most probable that the Merlin of legend is a composite figure, in this case partaking of elements of a traditional Welsh bard, a pre-Christian necromancer and a priest of the DRUIDS.

mermaid

A mythical sea-creature with the upper body of a woman and the tail of a fish.

Stories of mermaids, sea-dwelling creatures of human size with the upper body of a beautiful woman and the tail of a fish, are common in ancient mythology; they persisted in European folklore from medieval times up till the 18th century, with many reported sightings. Mermaids, from Old English *mere*, meaning 'sea', and *maegden*, meaning 'maiden', are usually portrayed as having long flowing hair, silvery blonde to light red in colour, either blue or green eyes and pearly white skin with a silver sheen. They live much longer than humans, and dwell in magnificent undersea palaces decorated with gold and jewels salvaged from wrecked ships, but they frequently come to the surface and sit on rocks, with a mirror in one hand and a comb in the other, grooming their long hair and singing with unbearable sweetness. Their beauty and their bewitching voices often lure sailors to their deaths. In some traditions they are more actively malevolent, dragging humans, especially young men, under the sea and keeping their souls in cages, or else drowning their victims and eating them. When angered, they can call up powerful winds and storms by dancing through the waves.

Mermaids have the ability to change their fish-tails into human legs so that they can come ashore and mix with people whenever they want, and although they have no souls, it is said that they can gain one if they marry a human and are baptized. Stories of mermaids marrying human husbands are common in British folklore, but sooner or later the mermaid will long to return to the sea again. She cannot do so as long as her husband keeps some magical possession of hers hidden, such as a sealskin, comb, belt, necklace or cap, but as soon as she finds the object, she will escape back to the sea. Mermaids are often credited with the ability to grant three wishes and to see into the future, and sometimes they are caught and held to ransom for these gifts. However, if pressed to grant wishes they will do their best to twist the words of the wish to the person's disadvantage.

In Ireland, mermaids are said to be female pagans banished from the island by St Patrick along with snakes. The legend of the mermaid probably developed from ancient mythological figures such as Aphrodite, the Greek goddess who was born from the sea, or the Syrian fish-tailed moon goddess Atargatis. It has been suggested that many of the recorded sightings of mermaids were in fact brief glimpses of marine mammals such as manatees.

mescal *see* PEYOTE

Mesmer, Franz Anton (1734–1815)

Inventor of a medical 'cure' known as mesmerism, which ultimately gave birth to hypnosis.

Franz (sometimes rendered as Friedrich) Anton Mesmer was born in Iznang, Swabia in Switzerland. After an uneventful early life he went to several universities; Dillingen, Ingolstadt and finally Vienna. Starting with philosophy Mesmer soon changed subjects to theology, then to law, finally settling on medicine. As part of his doctoral thesis in 1766 he published an overview of the influence of the planets on disease and, on the successful completion of his studies, he became a faculty member at the University of Vienna and began practising general medicine. In 1768, Mesmer married a wealthy widow, which allowed him to become a patron of the arts and gave

him the freedom to pursue his own areas of research. One such area was his belief in the presence of vital bodily fluids other than blood.

In 1774, Mesmer was attempting to induce an artificial tidal flow in a patient by first feeding her an iron solution and then attaching magnets to her. When she reported an easing of her pain, accompanied by the sensation of a liquid moving around her body, he felt that his research and his beliefs had been vindicated. After further investigations he came to the conclusion that the attached magnets were not necessary, it was in fact his own 'ANIMAL MAGNETISM' that had caused the temporary relief. He developed this idea and came to believe that the 'vital force of life' flowed through bodies, and that disease was a result of blockages in this flow. He thought that animal magnetism could be used to induce convulsions in patients which would, in turn, clear the blockages and effect a cure. After an initial period in which he received great acclaim, a highly publicized case in which he failed to cure a young musician of her blindness forced Mesmer to leave both Vienna and his wife.

In 1778, Mesmer set himself up in Paris where, despite many attempts, he failed to gain acceptance from the scientific elite of the city. In spite of this, he and his cures were enormously popular with the general population and, by 1780, he had more patients than he could deal with on a one-to-one basis. Loath to turn patients away, he introduced group treatments. These typically involved up to 20 people sitting in a circle around a covered container. Leading from this container were metal rods which were positioned on the affected areas of the patients. When they were all attached, Mesmer would move from patient to patient talking all the while and making complicated passes with his hands, and apparently effect a cure. The procedure became known as MESMERISM.

In 1784, King Louis XVI of France, prompted by concerns that mesmerism was actually harmful, set up a commission to investigate the work of Mesmer and his many protégés. The following year the commission reported that they could find no evidence for the existence of Mesmer's 'vital fluids'. Mesmer fled France and travelled extensively throughout Europe, eventually returning to general medicine when he lost his fortune in the French Revolution.

In 1814, the year before Mesmer died, a number of scientists carried out an investigation into his work. They concluded that he carried this out in good faith and that he believed everything he claimed. The investigating scientists thought that his apparent successes were largely brought about through the power of suggestion, and, ultimately, it is from Mesmer's methods, and the 27 principles of his system (including the ideas that animal magnetism can be communicated apparent 'cures' were probably just an example of the PLACEBO EFFECT.

Mesmer's techniques (without his accompanying theories) were later developed to form what we now know as hypnotism (see HYPNOSIS).

metal bending
A popular supposed demonstration of psychic abilities in which metal objects (usually items of cutlery) are bent using the power of the mind.

Metal bending, offered as a supposed example of PSYCHOKINESIS (more specifically MACRO-PK), became particularly popular in the 1970s when it was brought to world prominence by URI GELLER. Geller claims that he can make a spoon bend using the power of his mind, as at the same time he seems to gently stroke the object. Although his demonstrations have produced much excitement and many imitators, sceptics, such as JAMES RANDI, have always argued that the examples offered can be replicated by stage magicians and that its exponents can be observed using classic stage magic tricks (see MAGIC, STAGE).

'Spoon-bending' parties became popular during the 1970s and 1980s. They often featured groups of people, sitting in a circle, shouting at cutlery in an attempt to make it bend. However, attempts at testing the phenomenon under strictly controlled laboratory conditions have, so far, failed to produce any universally accepted positive results.

meteorites
Stones which 'fall from the sky', the very possibility of which made a dramatic transition from superstition, folklore and fragmentary scientific theories to accepted scientific fact at the end of the 18th century.

Meteors (from the Greek *meteōra*, meaning 'things on high') also known as 'aerolites', 'fireballs' or 'shooting stars', are small bodies of rock from space that are observed as they burn up on entering the earth's atmosphere. Any part of it that reaches the earth's surface (in the form of a lump of stone or metal) is described as a 'meteorite'.

Shooting stars have long been the subject of superstitious beliefs all over the world – wishing on a shooting star is one such superstition of which most of us are probably still aware. They have also been incorporated into many religious belief systems, in which, ironically, it was usually accepted that they fell from the sky, a fact that could be explained in terms of the actions of gods.

However, by the 18th century, scientific orthodoxy held that the idea that rocks could fall from the sky was nonsense. Although, with the benefit of hindsight, the connection between shooting stars and the lumps of rock and craters found on the ground seems obvious,

A portrait of Franz Anton Mesmer after a contemporary engraving. (© Bettmann/Corbis)

by sound, not all are equally susceptible and there are no associated dangers, such as those encountered with surgery), that hypnotism (see HYPNOSIS) arose.

mesmerism
A system of treatment invented by Franz Anton Mesmer, often cited as an early example of the use of hypnotism.

In the 18th century, FRANZ ANTON MESMER claimed to have discovered a method of treating medical patients by manipulating a magnetic fluid that he believed flowed through all living things. Initially, Mesmer carried out his treatments using magnets but, driven on by the idea that humans have an innate ANIMAL MAGNETISM, he soon spurned their use and instead passed his hands over and around the patient's body in order to effect a cure. The technique became known as MESMERISM.

Mesmer had a number of successes. However, although he put this down to his animal magnetism theory, some commentators have pointed out that his hand movements and constant talking during the treatment may have been inducing a heightened level of suggestibility in the patients. Others argue that any it must be remembered that to actually witness both the fall and the discovery on the ground of the still-hot rock is extremely rare. Even now, meteors remain unpredictable. Shooting stars were the subject of various competing theories along the lines that they were atmospheric or earthly in origin. Likewise meteorites, or 'thunderstones', were thought by many to be fossils, Stone Age tools or rocks that had been struck by lightning. Those who began to suggest the idea that the two were linked met with an entrenched mainstream scientific community, whose scepticism was bolstered by the fact that the eyewitness accounts offered in support of the theory were seen as just a small part of a wider collection of claims relating to FALLS from the sky.

The publication of a series of papers in the final years of the 18th century and the first years of the 19th century established that there were rocks drifting through space and that the composition of most meteorites found on the ground was similar. This was followed by the testimony of the French scientist Jean-Baptiste Biot, who witnessed a fall in Normandy in 1803. Although the exact origin of meteors and meteorites remained the subject of debate for many years to come, the idea that they fell from the sky had been firmly established.

Meteorite falls still attract much attention and are of great interest to scientists for the clues that they can give as to the nature and history of our solar system. However, human-interest stories of meteorites hitting cars or houses, and especially the occasional claims that they have struck people, are the firm favourites in the media. Likewise, observations that extremely large meteorites have collided with the earth in the past, causing enormous craters and dramatic climate change, regularly lead to the publication of predictions that such an event is likely to occur again in the near future.

Mexican UFO wave
Outbreak of UFO sightings following the best-documented UFO case in history, an incident was witnessed by thousands and filmed independently by dozens of different cameras.

On 11 July 1991, a total eclipse of the sun was visible from Mexico. Hundreds of astronomers converged to study the rare event, and thousands of citizens filled the streets in and around Mexico City. As they watched, just as the sky turned dark, many were amazed to see what appeared to be a dazzling UFO hovering beneath the blackened sun.

Over the next few days, Jaime Maussan, a local

The Ahnighito Meteorite at the American Museum of Natural History. It is the largest meteorite on display in a museum anywhere in the world. (© Jonathan Blair/Corbis)

TV reporter, received thousands of calls from people who had witnessed the event and, after publicizing the story, he was inundated with amateur video footage showing images of a bright blob of light with a slightly blurred edge. Curiously, however, none of the astronomers who had been intently observing that region of sky reported seeing anything unusual.

The story of the case rapidly spread through the world media, and the intense coverage was followed by a flood of further claimed UFO sightings, turning the incident into a WAVE. These new reports included a number of sightings in the vicinity of the Mexican volcano, Mount Popocatepetl, leading to it being dubbed a WINDOW AREA.

Many UFO researchers are convinced that the object originally seen below the sun was the planet Venus, which was definitely located in the right area potentially to be the object of the sightings and videos. Astronomers, of course, would have been aware of its presence during the eclipse, which explained why none of them had reported seeing a UFO. The mystery may also have been added to by a problem that was inherent in pre-digital camcorders – they often had difficulty focusing on point sources of light, such as stars or planets. This led to an apparent increase in the relative size of such lights when they were captured on video, an effect which produced many other seemingly mysterious pieces of video footage during the 1990s. However, some UFO enthusiasts still argue that this incident was significant and that it remains unexplained.

MIBs *see* MEN IN BLACK

microcosm *see* MACROCOSM AND MICROCOSM

micro-PK

Demonstrations of psychokinetic powers that produce weak or slight effects that cannot be observed with the naked eye and require statistical analysis for their evaluation.

The production of a measurable effect on the numbers produced by an electronic RANDOM NUMBER GENERATOR is a classic example of something that would be described as micro-PK (short for microscopic-PSYCHOKINESIS). In this instance the influence on the system (unless it is extremely dramatic) cannot be directly observed – it can only be assessed by carrying out a statistical analysis of the string of numbers produced.

Micro-PK phenomena are, for obvious reasons, less glamorous than those included under the heading of MACRO-PK. Consequently, they have generally

In this experiment into the existence of micro-PK, the subject attempts to influence the numbers selected by a random number generator. (© Mary Evans Picture Library)

attracted less public attention. They do, however, offer one advantage for academic study – they are less open to being fraudulently produced. But, so far, the slight effects apparently produced are unlikely to shake the foundations of mainstream science or convince the general public. Indeed, the statistical significance of the results achieved in such tests is still generally disputed.

millennium

The thousand-year period of peace foretold in certain biblical passages that it is believed will ensue after Christ has returned to earth.

For many Christians, the millennium is a literal period of a thousand years immediately following the return of Christ to earth; it will be an era of peace, when Christ will be the ruler of the world. That is, however, largely an evangelical Protestant belief, and there are many alternative versions.

The traditional view of mainstream Christianity (the historical denominations of Roman Catholicism, Orthodoxy and Anglicanism) follows the teaching of St Augustine (354–430 AD), that the millennium, like other passages about Christ's return, should be treated symbolically, not literally. This is known as a-millennialism; loosely speaking, if the millennium exists at all we are living through it now, because 'the kingdom of God is within you' (Luke 17:21). The RAPTURE, the Antichrist, the battle of Armageddon, even the return of Christ are seen as symbolic, not literal.

Post-millennialism teaches that Christians must bring about the millennium, the thousand years of peace, first, before Christ returns. This was a popular belief in the early 19th century, then went out of favour, but has recently returned among some ultra-conservative Christian groups in the USA. Known as Dominionists or Christian Reconstructionists, their stated aim is to impose their interpretation of Christian beliefs and moral practices onto the world; all other religions would be suppressed; adulterers, homosexuals and others who break their moral law would be executed. They hold that once the world has been converted, Christ will return.

The popular belief of most evangelical Christians is pre-millennialism: first Christ will return, then he will reign on earth for a thousand years of peace. This, in many different versions, is the predominant belief of evangelicals, particularly in the USA. The belief was promulgated in the Scofield Reference Bible, first published in 1909 (revised 1917), in which Cyrus I Scofield explained Christian doctrines alongside the text of the Bible itself.

Among the doctrines Scofield expounded was Dispensationalism, a controversial teaching by John Nelson Darby (1800–82), founder of the Exclusive Brethren (popularly known as the Plymouth Brethren). This taught that we are living in the sixth of seven Ages of Man; the seventh, the millennial reign of Christ, is still to come. Darby also set out the exact timetable for the End Times, including that Christians would be caught up to heaven in the Rapture, and so would be spared the seven-year tribulation which would be visited on the rest of mankind. Most US evangelical Christians now believe this pre-tribulationist version of pre-millennialism, as popularized in Hal Lindsay's book *The Late Great Planet Earth* (1970) and the 'Left Behind' series of novels by Tim LaHaye and Jerry B Jenkins.

The other main versions of pre-millennialism are post-tribulationism, in which Christians are only 'Raptured' *after* suffering the tribulation along with everyone else, and mid-tribulationism, in which the Rapture occurs half-way through the seven years.

There are several other permutations of millennialist belief, but the above are the main ones. The two main problems with all the various 'End Time' beliefs of both evangelicals and Christian sectarians (such as Seventh-day Adventists, Jehovah's Witnesses and Christadelphians) about the millennium and the return of Christ are: first, that they are pictures created from ill-matching jigsaw pieces scattered throughout the Bible – hence the many conflicting and mutually contradictory narratives; and second, that they take no account of the context of when and why and how these various biblical passages were written – a common problem with non-scholarly literalist interpretations of the Bible.

Most of the classic eschatological passages, for example in Daniel, Matthew 24 and Revelation, were written in times of great political turmoil, when the Jews were desperately hoping for the deliverance they believed God had promised them. The hoped-for Messiah of the intertestamental period and of the first century AD, a priest and king (many actually believed in two Messiahs), was to be both a religious and a political deliverer from the oppression of foreign rulers *at that time* – the New Testament writers clearly expected this imminently. It was only when this didn't happen that the Jewish Messiah became transmuted into the Christian Christ, a different figure altogether, with a completely different role. In the process, all the Jewish apocalyptic writings, including those about the millennium, were reinterpreted in the context of the return of Jesus Christ to earth. See also DOOMSDAY CULTS.

mind control
The hypothetical process of programming people to act in certain ways.

The central idea of mind control is that a person can be made to behave in ways that would normally be undesirable to them, and to carry out actions against their own will, at the behest of others who have somehow established power over their mental processes.

The controversial concept of BRAINWASHING, the systematic indoctrination of people to change their views or their normal behaviour, became a popular theme of the Cold War era. During the Korean War, it was claimed that the Chinese and North Korean captors of United Nations prisoners of war had subjected them to brainwashing in order to convert them to Communism and betray their own countries. Out of this alleged form of mind control sprang the idea of the MANCHURIAN CANDIDATE, or an assassin trained to obey orders implicitly when contacted with a codeword. However, although the use of such techniques as torture, sensory deprivation and suggestion can have a dramatic psychological effect, there is no evidence to suggest that the type of complete, permanent change of beliefs usually associated with the idea of brainwashing can actually be produced.

The US government MKULTRA project, which started in the 1950s, is believed to have involved experiments in mind control. These are said to have involved dosing human guinea pigs with drugs such as LSD and subjecting them to HYPNOSIS and autosuggestion in order to 'programme' them to carry out undercover activities on behalf of the CIA. It was later alleged that the model CANDY JONES (among others) had been treated in this way.

There is still a vocal minority, particularly in the USA, which believes that governments routinely exercise control over the minds of the population in order to minimize dissent and disguise secret activities. They offer a number of suggestions as to how this might be carried out – the use of infrasound transmitters, satellite broadcasts and subliminal messages in television and radio transmissions being among the most popular. Sceptics counter that, even if the idea that someone might wish to (and be able to) do this is accepted, it is not entirely clear how such methods are supposed to work. However, few would argue that we are all subjected to milder attempts at mind control on a daily basis – in the form of advertising, news reporting and political spin.

mind over matter

A phrase used to describe the supposed ability of the human mind to produce effects directly, without any form of physical intervention.

The popular phrase 'mind over matter' was originally used in the 1960s to refer in a general way to the areas of EXTRASENSORY PERCEPTION and PSYCHOKINESIS. Since then it has also been adopted by the NEW AGE movement, particularly in relation to the idea that positive thinking can be used as a method of self-help. The implication in all these instances is that the human mind is able to interact with the world, both internally and externally, in ways that are, as yet, not fully understood.

mind-reading

The supposedly direct mental accessing of thoughts within the minds of other individuals.

Mind-reading, a variation on TELEPATHY, is claimed to be a form of one-way direct mental interaction with another person – through which the mind-reader can access the thoughts, memories and perceptions of their chosen target.

Although many experiments into mind-reading have been carried out, they all suffer from criticism because 'mind-reading' is a long-established form of stage act, involving a number of very subtle (but entirely non-paranormal) techniques to draw information out of the subject. These techniques involve the careful observation and understanding of human reactions and behaviour, playing on an individual's natural tendency to look for significance in what they are told and sometimes pure 'cheating' (by acquiring in advance the information that will later be 'mind-read'). Thus any apparently successful experiment is open to the charge that the experimenters failed to exclude all possible means of fraud.

There are a vast number of very impressive performers who carry out such 'mind-reading' acts; prominent among them is Derren Brown, who belongs to a group of people who prefer to refer to themselves as 'mentalists' and who openly admit that they do not employ any PSYCHIC powers.

mindsight

The appearance of visual images in the minds of people who are unable to see by normal means.

The word 'mindsight' is sometimes used interchangeably with 'EXTRA-RETINAL VISION' or 'eyeless sight'. However, it is normally reserved for the apparent ability of some people who are visually impaired (specifically those who are totally blind from birth) to form 'visual' images in the mind. Such people commonly describe themselves as visualizing the place they are in, despite being unable to see it. There are also occasional claims from such people to have been able to see normally during an OUT-OF-BODY EXPERIENCE or NEAR-DEATH EXPERIENCE.

More recently, mindsight has been used by some psychologists to describe the apparent ability to discern differences which are not registered on a conscious level. This is a development of the idea of intuition or 'gut feeling' – a sensation that something has changed, or that something important has occurred, without consciously seeing exactly what it is.

mines

The natural habitat of mine spirits in European folklore. These creatures are often helpful to miners, directing them to rich seams or warning them of danger, and are treated with respect and left gifts of food and drink to win their goodwill.

Mine fairies or spirits are known throughout European folklore, and especially in Wales, Scotland, Cornwall, Germany, Yugoslavia, Romania and Austria. They are often thought to be the ghosts of miners who have died underground, and may either help or hinder miners, who therefore treat them with the utmost respect, frequently leaving them gifts of food and drink. They are described as being small in stature, between 45 and 90 centimetres (1.5–3 feet) tall, and are usually dressed as miners themselves in leather aprons, and carry small picks, lamps and hammers.

Some mine spirits, such as the German Kobold, are mischievous and enjoy frustrating the miners' work, and the Cutty Soams of the Scottish Borders are said to enjoy cutting the ropes that pull the coal trucks. If insulted, all mine spirits may, like the Polish Karzelek, cause rock showers or cave-ins. But they are in general disposed to be helpful to miners, as long as they are treated well. In south Germany, the Wichtlein warns of miners' deaths by tapping three times, and his presence indicates the proximity of rich seams of coal or ore. In Scotland, the Black Dwarfs perform a similar service, as do the Welsh Coblynau. The Coblynau are occasionally spotted on rock faces, apparently hard at work, but never actually achieving anything because they only pretend to mine.

The knockers who inhabit the tin mines of

Cornwall are perhaps the best known of the mine spirits. Benign in nature they are also known by a variety of other names including 'knackers', 'nickers' and 'spriggans', and 'blue caps' in the north of Cornwall. Their name reflects their penchant for making knocking sounds, again signalling when miners approached rich seams. Some Cornish miners maintain that they have also guided rescuers to the location of cave-ins by their tapping. Knockers are said to enjoy singing, particularly Christmas carols. They have a reputation for frightening miners by appearing suddenly and pulling faces, but miners are careful not to show anger if they do so, for fear of upsetting them. And no Cornish miner will ever whistle or swear while underground, because the knockers find both highly offensive. The tradition of knockers appears to have crossed the Atlantic to the USA where they have gained the prefix 'Tommy' to become 'Tommy-knockers'. Tommy-knockers, are said to be volatile in temperament, and sometimes malicious, and do not like to be seen by humans; one story tells of a coal miner whose co-workers wondered how he managed to produce so much more coal than they did every night, without ever getting tired. They followed him one night and found him sitting smoking in a shaft while a large team of Tommy-knockers did the work for him. On seeing his companions, the Tommy-knockers, thinking he had betrayed them to his fellow-miners, were furious, and in their rage they caused the entire mine to burst into flames.

minhocão

A giant subterreanean worm-like cryptid from South America said to be responsible for considerable subsidence caused by its underground activities.

For many years numerous native and Western inhabitants of southern Brazil and Uruguay have claimed that certain deep, furrow-like trenches that have suddenly appeared for no apparent reason – but often near to some sizeable lake or river – are the work of a mysterious serpentine creature called the minhocão.

Those who claim to have seen this beast state that it resembles a huge black armoured slug at least 4.5 metres (around 14.5 feet) long, with two mobile horn-like structures on its head and a pig-like snout. The channels allegedly excavated by the minhocão are so deep that the courses of entire rivers have been altered, roads and hillsides have collapsed and orchards have fallen to the ground.

Some zoologists have likened the minhocão to a giant lungfish, comparing its slender body and distinctive snout to those of the South American lungfish *Lepidosiren* – but this animal is very much smaller than the minhocão, attaining a total length of only 1.3 metres (4.26 feet). Others have speculated that it might be some form of peculiar snake, whose horns recall those of certain species already known to science, such as Africa's horned vipers.

Pioneering cryptozoologist Dr BERNARD HEUVELMANS even considered the possibility that the minhocão was a surviving, undiscovered species of glyptodont – a huge, armour-bearing relative of today's armadillos, with pointed ears and snout, which officially became extinct several millennia ago. However, glyptodonts had four large clawed feet and a long mace-like clubbed tail, features that have not been reported for the minhocão, therefore making this theory seem implausible. Conversely, British zoologist and cryptozoologist Dr Karl Shuker has suggested that the minhocão may be a giant species of caecilian – a superficially earthworm-like amphibian that spends much of its life underground, often near water sources, and has armour-like scales within its skin and a pair of horn-like sensory tentacles on its head.

miracle cures

Cures which are apparently supernatural in character, or which seem to defy conventional science.

Claims for miraculous cures which seem to be supernatural or to defy conventional science have been made since ancient times. The New Testament tells of various miracle cures effected by Jesus, and the Roman historians Tacitus and Suetonius both give accounts of the Emperor Vespasian healing people in Alexandria. It was once also believed that scrofula, known as the KING'S EVIL, could be cured by the touch of the monarch, and the waters of HOLY WELLS or springs (such as that at LOURDES) and the RELICS of SAINTS have, throughout history, been believed to have the miraculous power to heal (see also MIRACLES). Miracle cures are now also associated with modern American television evangelists, many of whom claim to cure afflicted people by FAITH HEALING.

For centuries, charlatans have sold products which promise a miraculous cure for a wide variety of ailments. The sellers of these miracle cures often mixed theatrics with their sales pitch, frequently accompanying travelling theatres and other entertainments from town to town so that they were safely gone by the time their customers discovered their wonder medicines contained little or no active ingredients and sometimes even included poisonous substances such as arsenic. Patent medicines offered as 'cure-alls' were particularly prominent in Britain and North America in the 17th and 18th centuries, and some of the sellers of these miracles cures, known in America as 'snake-oil peddlers', became wealthy men on the strength of their quack medicines, which they often marketed using pseudo-scientific claims and 'personal testimonials' as to the effectiveness of their products. Many people consider that similarly 'quack' products are still available through mail order and the Internet – including cures for baldness and instant weight-loss tablets.

miracles
A striking event which is contrary to the established laws of nature and which is attributed to a supernatural cause, usually divine intervention.

The word 'miracle' comes from the Latin *miraculum*, meaning 'something wonderful', and is applied to a striking event in which the established laws of nature are believed to be overruled, suspended or modified by a supernatural agency. Miracles appear in almost all religions, and are usually regarded as a sign of God's power, or as attesting to the spiritual authority of a prophet or holy person. Both the Hebrew Old Testament and the Christian New Testament describe a number of miracles, all of which are regarded as the intervention of God in the laws of nature, while the many miracles attributed to Jesus, such as the changing of water into wine, the feeding of the five thousand, MIRACLE CURES and walking on water, are central to Christian theology. Christian SAINTS, such as ST FRANCIS OF ASSISI and St Anthony of Padua, have been credited with miracles both during their lifetime and after their death, and holy RELICS of the saints are revered as instruments of their continuing power to perform miracles. Since the 19th century, the French town of LOURDES, where the Virgin Mary was said to have appeared, has been a place of pilgrimage for millions of Catholics every year, since the waters of the spring there are thought to have miraculous healing properties.

Miracles are also described in the Islamic tradition, and are particularly common in Eastern belief systems such as Hinduism, where they are thought to surround the birth of a teacher, holy man or individual regarded as a living manifestation of the divine, such as SAI BABA; miracles are also associated with the paranormal powers attributed to advanced yogis and Buddhists. See also PIOUS FRAUD.

missing time *see* TIME, MISSING

MJ-12 *see* MAJESTIC 12

MKULTRA
A mind-control research project run by the CIA.

A report appeared in the *New York Times* in December 1974 in which it was alleged that the CIA had conducted a number of illegal experiments on US citizens. After a series of congressional hearings

and reports by the Rockefeller Commission, it was brought to light that the CIA and the Department of Defense had been involved in a secret programme with the aim of investigating methods of controlling human behaviour. The most serious allegation was that the US Army biochemist Frank Olson had committed suicide following an experiment in which he was given LSD without his knowledge or consent.

The project had taken place under the code name MKULTRA and had started in April 1953. It was set up largely in response to claims that during the Korean War, United Nations prisoners of war had been subjected to BRAINWASHING by their North Korean and Chinese captors. The CIA was apparently interested in the possibilities of using similar techniques to interrogate its own prisoners. The project continued into the 1960s, and in 1964 it was renamed MKSEARCH.

Experiments were carried out on human guinea pigs, many of them US services personnel (not all of whom seem to have been volunteers), at various academic institutions across the USA. The experiments often involved the administration of mind-altering drugs (such as LSD and mescaline), partly in the search for an irresistible 'truth drug' which could be used during the interrogation of suspected spies. Among other things, HYPNOSIS, autosuggestion and sensory deprivation were also tested.

The revelations have spawned many conspiracy theories – among them being the suggestion that the CIA introduced LSD to the rising hippy movement in the 1960s as a means of subverting it, and the claim that MIND CONTROL was employed to achieve the assassination of President Kennedy.

Although a number of documents relating to the project were declassified in the 1970s, it is known that many more were destroyed beforehand. However, there is no evidence to suggest that any of the mind-control techniques employed ever worked consistently or effectively. See also JONES, CANDY; MANCHURIAN CANDIDATE.

moa, living
Mystifying 'giant kiwi' of New Zealand that some have suggested is a surviving species of dwarf moa.

New Zealand's ostrich-like giant moas, genus *Dinornis*, are among the most famous of all extinct birds. The last of these huge creatures are thought to have died out many centuries ago, but a much smaller, less conspicuous relative known as the upland or dwarf moa (*Megalapteryx didinus*) may have survived until as recently as the mid-1800s, and some consider it possible that it is still alive today.

There are Maori stories which relate to a

mysterious 'giant kiwi' with spurs on its feet, said to exist in New Zealand's South Island and to be as large as a turkey. None of the kiwis known to be living today is as large as this, and none has spurs. The giant kiwi's size corresponds with that of the dwarf moa, and the latter species had a well-developed claw-bearing hallux ('big toe') on each foot that might be mistaken for a spur. In addition, reconstructions of its likely appearance, based upon fossil evidence, indicate that it did resemble an extra-large kiwi in external appearance.

In 1978, a Japanese scientific expedition led by Gunma University biologist Dr Shoichi Hollie searched for dwarf moas in South Island's remote Fjordland region, equipped with a very unusual if sophisticated lure – the 'voice' of a moa. This had been created by closely examining fossil remains of the dwarf moa's throat, to discover from its structure the type of call that this bird could produce. During their search, they played the call many times through loudspeakers, hoping that they would attract the attention of a moa, if any did survive, but unfortunately their artificial moa voice was never answered.

In January 1993, three hikers in South Island's Craigieburn range claimed to have encountered and photographed a living specimen of giant moa, standing 2 metres (6.5 feet) tall. The photographs they provided were very fuzzy, and most scientists consider that they had simply seen a deer or some other ordinary species of large animal instead. The hikers, however, denied this, and one of them, hotelier Paddy Freaney, was planning to launch an expedition to seek out the enigmatic creature that he saw. Nothing further has emerged since then, however, so the mystery of just what they did see remains unresolved.

mokele-mbembe
An elusive long-necked Congolese cryptid said to resemble a living sauropod dinosaur.

The last dinosaurs are thought to have died out over 60 million years ago, by the end of the Cretaceous period – which is why a certain unidentified herbivorous animal reported from Central Africa has attracted so much cryptozoological interest in modern times. Known to the native pygmies as the mokele-mbembe ('one who stops the flow of rivers'), this CRYPTID supposedly inhabits the virtually unexplored Likouala swamps, including Lake Tele, in the People's Republic of the Congo.

The Likouala pygmies state that it measures approximately 9 metres (29.5 feet) in total length, has a heavy, elephant-sized body, is reddish-brown in colour, has a long slender tail and an even longer slender neck, a relatively small head, fairly short thick legs and three toes on each of its hind feet. This description is remarkably similar to reconstructions of the sauropod dinosaurs. When the pygmies have been shown pictures of animals by the several scientific expeditions that have been seeking the mokele-mbembe since the early 1980s, they have chosen pictures of *Diplodocus*, *Apatosaurus* (formerly called *Brontosaurus*), or some other sauropod as the animal closest in overall appearance to this mysterious creature.

The possibility that the mokele-mbembe is truly a living, modern-day species of sauropod is favoured by both of its principal seekers – now-retired Chicago University biochemist and veteran cryptozoologist Professor Roy Mackal and Scottish-born cryptozoological field researcher Bill Gibbons, both of whom have led major expeditions to the Congo's

An artist's impression of the mokele-mbembe fighting hippos in the swamps of the People's Republic of the Congo. (© TopFoto/Fortean)

swamplands in pursuit of this elusive aquatic cryptid. An alternative theory is that it is an exceedingly long-necked form of monitor lizard, but as the local people readily distinguish lizards from the mokele-mbembe, this might be thought unlikely.

Mongolian death worm
A deadly worm-like cryptid reported from the Gobi Desert, allegedly able to kill not only by spraying highly corrosive venom but also by electrocution.
Known to the nomadic camel-herders and others inhabiting Asia's Gobi Desert as the allghoi-khorkhoi ('intestine worm'), it first attracted cryptozoological attention little more than a decade ago. Since then, this greatly feared, potentially lethal CRYPTID has become widely known in the Western world as the Mongolian death worm. Its principal seeker is Czech explorer-writer Ivan Mackerle, who has led several expeditions to the Gobi in search of its elusive inhabitant. Much of what is claimed to be known about its appearance and behaviour is derived from his researches.

In appearance, the death worm resembles a bright red worm mottled with large darker blotches, or even an intestine (hence its local name); it measures up to 1.5 metres (5 feet) long and is as thick as a man's arm. Most people claim that it is rounded or blunted at both ends, but at least one local eyewitness has stated that its ends appeared pointed. It is said that it has no visible mouth, nostrils or eyes, that its body is smooth and that it moves via an odd rolling or sideways-squirming motion when above ground. During June and July, the two hottest months of the year in the Gobi, it has been claimed that it can sometimes be seen resting on the surface of sand dunes after a rainstorm, but otherwise it remains hidden, burrowing or resting beneath the desert's sandy surface. It seems to be associated underground with a desert plant known as the saxaul, whose roots are in turn parasitized by a poisonous cigar-shaped plant called the goyo.

If threatened, the death worm will raise half of its body upwards and can allegedly expel a stream of potent, acid-like venom that turns anything it touches yellow, and is highly corrosive, often resulting in death for anyone making contact with it. The local people believe that the death worm may derive its venom from the poisonous goyo plant. Even more alarming, and mysterious, however, is this cryptid's second, swifter method of dealing death. An entire herd of camels treading over a patch of sand concealing a death worm has allegedly dropped down dead en masse, caused by the camels having stepped on it. The same applies to anyone who touches a death worm – and not just via direct touch. Several decades ago, a

team of geologists working in the Gobi set up camp one night, and one of the team's members was using an iron rod to poke at the ashes of their camp fire when suddenly he fell to the ground, dead. It is said that at the same moment the sand where he had been idly prodding with the rod began to churn, and a death worm emerged. In other words, he had been killed not by touching the worm directly, but by touching it with a metal rod.

The only known method of death that could occur via conduction through such an implement is electrocution, which would also explain how a herd of camels could be felled simply by the beasts stepping on one of these worms. The problem with such a radical explanation is that all known electricity-generating animals that use their powers for killing or stunning prey are fishes, inhabiting water – a far more efficient conductor of electricity than sand. However, it is conceivable that the death worm may be able to generate electricity by way of friction (a phenomenon termed triboelectricity), via the rubbing of its body against the enveloping sand as it burrows beneath its surface – though whether it could generate sufficient electricity in this way to kill camels and people merely by touch is another matter. Perhaps this capability is an exaggeration on the part of local people who have experienced a non-lethal but nonetheless memorable electric shock when inadvertently touching a death worm, and this has duly entered traditional folklore and legend in embellished form.

As to the zoological identity of the death worm, if it does indeed exist, several candidates have been offered, including a giant amphisbaenian (worm-lizard) whose supposed lethal powers are merely legendary, rather than genuine; a highly specialized true worm with a water-retaining cuticle to assist its survival in its arid desert domain; a similarly adapted giant caecilian (limbless worm-like amphibian); and a venom-spitting snake allied to the death adders. Only a specimen made available for study, however, can conclusively resolve this mystery, and so far the death worm continues to evade all expeditions that go out in search of it.

Monkey Man scare
In April and May 2001 residents of New Delhi, India, claimed they were plagued by attacks by a strange creature which became known as the Monkey Man; many believe this was a case of mass delusion or mass hysteria.
The first known attacks by the Monkey Man were reported in April 2001. Residents of a village on the outskirts of New Delhi claimed that they had been bitten as they slept on their roofs at night, a

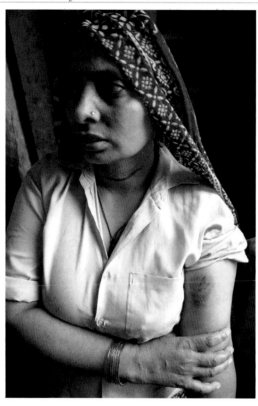

An Indian woman displays her injuries following an alleged attack by the 'Monkey Man' in May 2001.
(© Reuters/Corbis)

practice that is common at that time of year in order to escape the heat. Some of the injuries that were reported were consistent with monkey bites, and at first it was believed that one of the many monkeys that live in the area was to blame, but victims also described a man with a monkey face or a masked man as the assailant. Panic spread, as did the reported incidents of attacks by the creature. By mid-May, stories of a creature that scratched with long metal claws and that could leap across the rooftops before mysteriously vanishing were rife in the poorer areas of the Indian capital. Despite police orders, vigilante groups scoured the streets in search of the creature. On 17 May the police offered a reward of 50,000 rupees (£769) for information leading to the arrest of the Monkey Man (believing that it was indeed a man or several men rather than a supernatural creature) and it was reported that on 19 May they received 328 calls relating to the Monkey Man from different parts of New Delhi. It was at this time that the police also arrested a number of people they described as 'mischief-mongers' and reports of the Monkey Man dwindled.

The majority of commentators have since concluded that the Monkey Man scare was a case of mass delusion or MASS HYSTERIA rather than something arising from an actual attacker. Although a small number of deaths were claimed to be directly linked to the 'monster', there was no evidence of this, and the other fatalities (and the majority of serious injuries caused) came about when people fell from their roofs as they tried to flee what they perceived to be the threat of attack. Often the police were summoned simply because a shadow or sound was thought to be suspicious or there was a rumour that the attacker was in the area. It has been suggested that a number of the injuries presented to doctors were self-inflicted, or caused by dogs, cats or rats, and that as panic spread a number of copy-cat attacks may have been perpetrated (see OSTENTION). Some have noted that New Delhi was suffering from power shortages at the time, and that not only might the darkness have contributed to the fear, but some of the people who reported incidents may have believed that by doing so the police would ensure that the power was switched on in order that they could investigate. However, none of these observations prevented a number of theories as to the cause circulating among believers at the time, including a visiting alien and a remote-controlled robot.

Montgomery, Ruth (1913–2001)

A US journalist who after investigating mediumistic abilities apparently found that she had them herself.
Ruth Montgomery was a journalist whose career in the world of PSYCHIC phenomena began in 1965 when working on her book about the famous MEDIUM, JEANE DIXON (*A Gift of Prophecy: The Phenomenal Jeane Dixon*, 1965). Montgomery investigated the world of mediums further and apparently discovered she was able to produce AUTOMATIC WRITING, and soon found herself CHANNELLING information from her SPIRIT GUIDES. She wrote down the revelations she claimed to receive and published them in a series of eleven books (the first being *A World Beyond* in 1973). Among other things, the SPIRITS who communicated with Montgomery gave details of a karmic 'other life' involving REINCARNATION, existence on 'higher planes of being' and punishment for those who have committed wrong in the physical world (although with the potential eventually to earn redemption). Such spiritual notions were popular with many NEW AGE thinkers at the time. However, the books also contained a number of predictions, the accuracy of which has since proved to be somewhat disappointing.

Moon

The Earth's only natural satellite, which has long been the subject of speculation and has an important place in folkloric, religious, occult and esoteric traditions from around the world.

The Moon is second only to the SUN as a feature of the heavens. As the Sun is associated with the daytime, light, heat and the seasons, so the Moon is associated with the night and darkness. It also displays a shorter cycle of change than the Sun, going from the complete darkness of the new Moon, to the full glowing disc of the full Moon and back again in a period of approximately 29 days. This periodic cycle, which mirrors the menstrual cycle, may partly explain the fact that in many religious traditions it was seen as female, related to fertility and often associated with a goddess. This same cycle also led it to be the basis of many calendrical systems prior to the widespread adoption of the Roman calendar in the Western world.

Certainly within modern WITCHCRAFT practice (see NEOPAGANISM and WICCA), the Moon is associated with the GODDESS (see DRAWING DOWN THE MOON), an idea apparently taken from earlier European pagan traditions, including those of Classical Greece and Rome. In Chinese culture, the Moon is associated with the female principle, or YIN. However, historically the Moon has not always been seen as wholly feminine, as evidenced by the folklore surrounding the MAN IN THE MOON.

Another common folkloric association that is still occasionally the subject of debate is that between the cycle of the Moon and human psychology and physiology – particularly the phenomenon sometimes described as 'moon madness' or LUNACY. Some of the stories surrounding werewolves or LYCANTHROPY include more extreme examples of this supposed relationship between the cycle of the Moon and the human body.

As a prominent heavenly body, the Moon has, of course, always featured strongly in Western ASTROLOGY. Here it is perhaps second only to the Sun in importance, because, like the Sun, it also moves through all the signs of the ZODIAC and so is understood to have a significant effect on an individual's HOROSCOPE. Among other things, it is said to affect emotions and feelings, influencing such things as sensitivity and vulnerability. 'The Moon' is also the name of a TAROT card and is often associated with the element WATER.

The 1835 Moon Hoax *see panel p466*

Morgawr

Long-necked sea serpent reported from the waters off Cornwall, England.

For over a century, a mysterious sea creature, often described as having a long neck and varying numbers of dorsal humps, has been reported in the waters off Cornwall. Known locally as Morgawr ('sea giant'), the creature is also referred to as the Falmouth Bay SEA SERPENT.

In 1976, Morgawr was transformed from a local curiosity into an international cryptozoological celebrity. On 5 March that year, the *Falmouth Packet* newspaper published an article which included two apparent photographs of the creature, plus a handwritten note from the person who had sent them in. Naming herself only as 'Mary F', she claimed to have seen and photographed Morgawr from Trefusis, Falmouth, about three weeks earlier. Her photographs seemed to show a LOCH NESS MONSTER-like CRYPTID emerging above the surface of the sea. It was black or very dark grey in colour, with a long curving neck, tiny head and a large body. It also had three humps on its back. There were no background features to enable either the location to be identified or the creature's size to be gauged, only Mary F's claim that the portion of the creature visible above the water was 4.6–5.5 metres (15–18 feet) long, and that the reason why no background details were discernible was that the sun was shining into the camera and a haze was present on the water. These photographs engendered a certain amount of controversy within CRYPTOZOOLOGY, with some investigators supporting their validity, and others (notably Mark Chorvinsky, editor of *Strange Magazine* and an expert in cinematic and photographic special effects) dismissing them as a hoax.

Reports of sightings of Morgawr continued. Dorset writer Sheila Bird and her brother, scientist Dr Eric Bird, claim that they saw Morgawr at around 8pm on 10 July 1985. Apparently, they were relaxing on the clifftop west of Portscatho when Dr Bird observed (through his binoculars) a long-necked, small-headed, dorsal-humped sea beast with grey mottled skin. It was swimming smoothly but rapidly in an easterly direction just offshore. Estimated by the Birds to be 5.2–6.1 metres (17–20 feet) long, the monster was also seen to have a long muscular tail moving just beneath the surface of the sea. It swam along with its neck held high for several minutes before abruptly descending vertically into the water. It did not reappear. Long-necked sea serpents such as this one were deemed by cryptozoologist Dr BERNARD HEUVELMANS to constitute an unknown, highly specialized species of seal, but Morgawr is described as having a long tail, and seals do not have

The 1835 Moon Hoax

On 25 August 1835, the first of a series of six articles appeared in the *New York Sun* under the headline:

> GREAT ASTRONOMICAL DISCOVERIES Lately Made BY SIR JOHN HERSCHEL, L.L.D, F.R.S, &c. At The Cape of Good Hope. [From Supplement to the *Edinburgh Journal of Science*]

Purporting to relate to the amazing new astronomical discoveries of the English astronomer Sir John Herschel (1792–1871), the first article explains:

> To render our enthusiasm intelligible, we will state at once, that by means of a telescope of vast dimensions and entirely new principle, the younger Herschel, at his observatory in the Southern Hemisphere, has already made the most extraordinary discoveries in every planet of our solar system; has discovered planets in other solar systems; has obtained a distinct view of objects in the moon, fully equal to that which the naked eye commands of terrestrial objects at the distance of a hundred yards; has affirmatively settled the question whether this satellite be inhabited, and by what order of things; has firmly established a new theory of cometary phenomena; and has solved or corrected nearly every leading problem of mathematical astronomy.

The problems of mathematical astronomy aside, the most exciting sections of the articles related to the detailed descriptions of life on the moon, as apparently observed by Herschel. The moon was described as having vast forests and lush valleys and fantastic slender pyramids of lilac-coloured quartz. Herds of bison roamed the lunar plains, unicorns

of 'a bluish lead color' frolicked in the woodland glades, 38 species of trees had been identified and birds and mammals were to be seen everywhere. The third article described a creature that:

> … resembles the beaver of the earth in every other respect than in its destitution of a tail, and its invariable habit of walking upon only two feet. It carries its young in its arms like a human being, and moves with an easy gliding motion. Its huts are constructed better and higher than those of many tribes of human savages, and from the appearance of smoke in nearly all of them, there is no doubt of its being acquainted with the use of fire.

But perhaps even more elaborate claims appeared in the fourth article, which reported the discovery of winged human beings (which Herschel had supposedly named *Vespertilio-homo*, 'man-bat'):

> They averaged four feet in height, were covered, except on the face, with short and glossy copper-colored hair, and had wings composed of a thin membrane, without hair, lying snugly upon their backs, from the top of their shoulders to the calves of their legs.

In the fifth article, it was claimed that Herschel had discovered an exquisite temple:

> It was an equitriangular temple, built of polished sapphire, or of some resplendent blue stone, which, like it, displayed a myriad points of golden light twinkling and scintillating in the sunbeams.

And in the final article we hear of a further advanced species of 'man-bat':

tails. Others have suggested that should such long-necked sea serpents as Morgawr actually exist, they are similar morphologically to the plesiosaur of the dinosaur era.

Morton ghost

An apparition that was apparently witnessed repeatedly in a house in Cheltenham in the final quarter of the 19th century.

Often considered the best-attested example of an apparitional haunting, the Morton ghost was the

apparition of a woman which members of a family named Despard claimed they saw repeatedly between 1882 and 1889 in their house in Pittville Circus Road, Cheltenham, England. The family was given the pseudonym Morton in a report on the haunting published by the SOCIETY FOR PSYCHICAL RESEARCH in its *Proceedings*, under the title 'Record of a Haunted House'. It was claimed that the apparition was seen by 17 people and heard by 20. Rosina Despard described the figure as:

A lithograph depicting Herschel's 'flying moon animals', one of a series of
illustrations that accompanied the moon hoax articles in the *New York Sun*.
(© Bettmann/Corbis)

… and it was one of the noble valleys at the foot of this mountain that we found the very superior species of the *Vespertilio-homo*. In stature they did not exceed those last described, but they were of infinitely greater personal beauty, and appeared in our eyes scarcely less lovely than the general representations of angels by the more imaginative schools of painters. Their social economy seemed to be regulated by laws or ceremonies exactly like those prevailing in the Vale of the Triads, but their works of art were more numerous, and displayed a proficiency of skill quite incredible to all except actual observers. I shall, therefore, let the first detailed account of them appear in Dr. Herschel's authenticated natural history of this planet.

The articles were supposedly written by a Dr Andrew Grant, who it was claimed was a companion of Herschel, although no such person existed and authorship is generally attributed to a Cambridge-educated journalist called Richard Adams Locke – although some claim that he never publicly admitted involvement in the hoax. Indeed, even the *New York Sun* never fully admitted that the articles had been entirely fiction. Some say that the articles were satirical and that they were not meant to be believed, but at a time when many people expected intelligent life to be found on the moon, the articles were taken by some to be true, and a number of scientists of the time sought out the full reports in the *Edinburgh Journal of Science*, only to find that it had not actually been published since 1829.

… that of a tall lady, dressed in black of a soft woollen material, judging from the slight sound in moving. The face was hidden in a handkerchief held in the right hand … a portion of a widow's cuff was visible on both wrists, so that the whole impression was that of a lady in widow's weeds. There was no cap on the head, but the general effect of blackness suggests a bonnet with long veil or hood.

Some witnesses spoke of a cold wind that accompanied the figure, and said that dogs seemed to react adversely to its presence. The ghost was seen mostly at night but never when the family watched for it or when they were talking of it. Suggestions that the figure was that of a living woman secretly living in the house do not seem sustainable on account of its ability to pass through strings placed in its path, reports that it could simply vanish and its success in eluding pursuers trying to touch or catch it. The apparition was said to be that of Imogen

Swinhoe, second wife of Henry Swinhoe, a former resident who had died in 1878 and was buried at the Holy Trinity Church, close to the house. Apart from footsteps that were sometimes heard, the haunting seemed to cease in 1890. B Abdy Collins, who reviewed the evidence of the haunting in his book *The Cheltenham Ghost* (1948), considered the haunting as evidence of survival after death, but other researchers have been more cautious.

While some simply do not accept that the ghost ever appeared, later 20th-century reports suggest that the haunting did not cease as initially believed, and indicate that a similar figure continued to be seen in the area until the 1960s. Ghost researcher Andrew MacKenzie collected an account of a figure of a woman in black seen in Pittville Circus Road in 1985.

Mother Goddess *see* GODDESS, THE

Mothman

A mysterious bat-like humanoid, alleged sightings of which are particularly associated with the US town of Point Pleasant, West Virginia. Reported sightings were famously seen to be connected with other strange occurrences in the area, and later taken to be an omen of the Silver Bridge disaster.

In the 1960s in West Virginia, USA, numerous reports were made of sightings of UFOs and of a winged humanoid creature which came to be known as the Mothman. Witnesses who claimed to have seen Mothman generally described a large dark shape with glowing red eyes and bat-like wings. Mothman came to prominence with a number of widely reported sightings in November 1966, such as a sighting on 15 November, reported in the local newspaper, *The Athens Messenger*, under the headline 'Winged, Red-Eyed "Thing" Chases Point Couples Across Countryside':

> Point Pleasant – What stands six feet tall, has wings, two big red eyes six inches apart and glides along behind an auto at 100 miles an hour? Don't know? Well, neither do four Point Pleasant Residents who were chased by a weird 'man-like' thing Tuesday night.

When the journalist and fortean (see FORTEANA) John Keel (1930–) travelled to the area to investigate the claims, particularly in the town of Point Pleasant, he found that many of the witnesses said that since they had reported their sightings they had been visited by mysterious MEN IN BLACK, and told not to discuss their experiences with anyone. Keel also claimed that he was tormented over the phone by an entity called Indrid Cold, and he noted numerous other phenomena that

are usually associated with POLTERGEIST activity. The investigation was apparently characterized by intense fear on the part of the witnesses and the strange way that Keel, the investigator, was drawn further and further into the goings-on.

On 15 December 1967, the Silver Bridge at Point Pleasant, linking West Virginia and Ohio across the Ohio River, became backed up with traffic when traffic lights were stuck on red. The bridge collapsed, killing 46 people. Back in New York, John Keel heard about the bridge and put the UFO sightings, Mothman, DISEMBODIED VOICES and all the mysterious occurrences he had heard about together and developed the theory that these had been omens of the disaster. He published *The Mothman Prophecies* in 1975. The story was later adapted and released as a film, *The Mothman Prophecies*, in 2002. In the same year that the film was released, the town of Point Pleasant (which now boasts a statue of the Mothman) held the first annual Mothman Festival.

There have been many suggestions as to what occurred in the area of Point Pleasant during 1966 and 1967 – including ALIEN visitations, giant mutant birds or MIND CONTROL experiments. Some have also suggested that the bridge collapse and the Mothman visitations were the result of a Native American CURSE (known as 'the Cornstalk Curse') which was placed on the town by a chief of the Shawnee. Sceptics argue that the collapse of the bridge was due only to a terrible, coincidental combination of events and an inherent weakness in its structure. It has also been suggested that the Mothman reports might have been generated by misidentifications of one of the larger species of owl, among other things – with artificial connection, misinterpretation, distortion and exaggeration being encouraged by the media.

mountain tiger

An unidentified mystery cat of Chad, descriptions of which suggest it bears a resemblance to the long-extinct sabre-toothed tiger.

The Zagaoua tribe of Ennedi in northern Chad, West Africa, believe in the existence of a remarkable mystery cat known as the mountain tiger or *tigre de montagne*. According to their testimony, this unidentified animal is as large as a lion, with red fur and white stripes, no tail and a huge pair of fangs that project conspicuously from its mouth. When an elderly local game tracker was shown pictures of various animals, living and extinct, by Christian Le Noel, a French hunting guide, in the 1960s, he positively identified the mysterious mountain tiger as *Machairodus* – the African sabre-toothed tiger, officially believed to have died out over a million years ago. A creature similar to Chad's mountain tiger has also been reported from the Central African Republic, where it is referred to variously as the gassingram and vassoko. The mountain ranges of these countries are remote and little-explored, making it difficult to rule out the possibility that a large unknown species of cat does exist there.

Moving Coffins of Barbados
The repeated supernatural disturbance of coffins in a family vault, recounted in many books of 'true mysteries'.

Early in the 19th century, the coffins in the tomb of the Chase family at Christchurch, Barbados, were allegedly moved around by some mysterious force. The vault, partly carved from solid rock, was first used in 1807, although it was not owned by the Chase family at this time. The coffins of two young Chase daughters were placed in the vault in 1808 and 1812, at which times no disturbances were reported. However, when the vault was opened for a second time in 1812, the coffins of the Chase girls were apparently found to have been moved around – with one standing up on end. Further movement of coffins was apparently revealed in 1816 (twice) and in 1819 when the vault was again opened to admit new burials. Each time the coffins that had been moved were restored to their normal position, the floor was sprinkled with sand in an attempt to detect footprints, and the vault was carefully sealed. On 18 April 1820, the tomb was opened in the presence of the Governor Lord Combermere and a large crowd. The seals were intact, but once again the heavy coffins were found to have been moved and the sand on the floor showed no sign of human disturbance. At this time, all of the coffins were removed and buried elsewhere

Many different theories have been postulated for the movement of the coffins (all presupposing that the story is genuine). Psychical researcher Guy Lambert proposed in 1955 that tidal mechanisms might explain the movement of the coffins; similarly, localized earth tremors and strikes by lightning have been blamed. Other suggestions include movement caused by the growth of vegetation within the vault. Father Thurston, a Roman Catholic writer on psychic topics, speculated that the movements could have been the work of POLTERGEIST forces, and Harry Price also included a discussion of this and other cases of coffin movements in his book *Poltergeist Over England* (1945).

Mowing Devil, the
The case of a legendary 17th-century crop circle, said to have been created by the Devil.

In 1678, a woodcut pamphlet was published in England which purported to tell a story of devilish intervention in human affairs. The pamphlet's title was

The pamphlet which told the tale of the 17th-century crop circle created by 'the Mowing Devil'. (© TopFoto/ Fortean)

The Mowing-Devil: or, Strange News out of Hartford-shire, and the tale it told was of a farmer of that county who refused to pay the fee asked by a labourer to mow his field of oats. Somewhat rashly, the farmer swore that he would rather the DEVIL mowed it instead. That night, mysterious flames appeared among the crop and in the morning the farmer found it:

> … so neatly mow'd by the Devil or some Infernal Spirit, that no Mortal Man was able to do the like.

The woodcut illustration on the front page of the pamphlet shows a devilish figure, complete with horns and tail, working away with scythe in hand. What is arresting to those with an interest in CROP CIRCLES is that the cut cereal has been mown in concentric circles rather than, say, in parallel rows. The case of the Mowing Devil (even if one allows for exaggeration and embellishment on the part of the pamphleteer) indicates that crop circles may not be an entirely modern phenomenon. It also offers an interesting example of the way that explanations for unusual occurrences often reflect the cultural context in which they occur. See also CULTURAL TRACKING.

MSI *see* MASS SOCIOGENIC ILLNESS

Mu

Legendary lost land beneath the Pacific Ocean.

When the Jersey-born anthroplogist Augustus Le Plongeon (1826–1908) studied the ruins and ancient writings of the Maya civilization in Yucatan he claimed to have discovered that the Maya had originally come to America from a land that had sunk beneath the Pacific Ocean. He stated that this lost continent was called Mu.

This idea was further developed by the English soldier and writer James Churchward (1852–1936) in a number of books, beginning with *The Lost Continent of Mu* (1931). Churchward believed that the civilization of Mu was the same as that of Atlantis. Others have identified Mu with the equally legendary LEMURIA.

However, theories about the existence of Mu, as about the existence of any lost continent, are not generally accepted by current science.

MUFON *see* MUTUAL UFO NETWORK

mummification

The preservation of dead bodies, either through the application of deliberate embalming techniques or the chance natural occurrence of the necessary conditions.

The deliberate mummification of human bodies has formed part of the practice of many cultures throughout history. It is most commonly associated with the ancient Egyptians, who initially buried bodies in caskets and allowed them to dry in the heat, and went on to develop a complex process involving the removal of internal organs and the application of preparations to speed up the drying of the body, followed by wrapping it in cloth. However, there are a number of other notable historical examples of deliberate mummification – it was known to have been carried out by the Aztecs, Incas and ancient peoples of the Tarim Basin in China, among others. The word itself comes originally from the Persian word *mūm*, meaning 'wax', an allusion to the method of preservation they themselves employed.

Following the return of various archaeological expeditions to excavate Egyptian PYRAMIDS during the 19th and early 20th centuries, with tales of mysterious burial practices and curses (see TUTANKHAMEN, CURSE OF), a modern mythology has built up around mummification. The mummy has now entered film and comic-book folklore as an 'undead' creature to rival the ZOMBIE or the VAMPIRE. However, although the process of mummification appears macabre to many of us in the modern world, the horror associations probably have little basis in fact. It is likely that early civilizations stumbled upon the various physical processes by chance, and that mummification then became more ritualized as it was drawn into the sets of religious beliefs relating to the connection between the SOUL or SPIRIT and the physical body.

The natural mummification of human bodies occasionally produces remarkably preserved examples, which are of great interest to archaeologists. A famous example from recent years is Ötzi the Iceman, a 5,000-year-old body found in a glacier in the Ötztal Alps on the border between Austria and Italy in 1991. A number of others have been discovered across northern Europe preserved in the acidic environment of peat bogs. Such examples illustrate the possibility that chance environmental conditions can lead to the accidental preservation of bodies for a considerable period of time – something that may account for stories of INCORRUPTIBILITY.

mungoon-galli

A giant mystery lizard allegedly encountered in New South Wales, Australia.

Officially, the largest species of lizard inhabiting present-day Australia is the perentie (*Varanus giganteus*), a species of monitor lizard that can grow up to 2.5 metres (over 8 feet) in length. However, according to a number of eyewitness accounts, Australia is also home to a far bigger lizard, still unidentified and uncaptured by science, but well known to the Aboriginal people of New South Wales, who call it the mungoon-galli. One of the recent reports of a sighting of a mungoon-galli was made by the herpetologist Frank Gordon in 1979, in the Wattagan Mountains of New South Wales. Returning to his Land Rover after conducting some prolonged field research, he saw what he thought at first was a log lying on an embankment next to his vehicle. Suddenly the 'log' moved, revealing itself to be an enormous lizard that Gordon estimated to be 8.2–9.2 metres (27–30 feet) long, and which moved off into the nearby forest. As a comparison, the world's longest species of lizard, Salvadori's monitor (*Varanus salvadorii*), does not exceed 4.6 metres (15 feet); the famous Komodo dragon (*Varanus komodoensis*) is far heavier and bulkier but not so long. A similar beast to Gordon's had been reported in December 1975 by a farmer near Cessnock, New South Wales, who claimed to have seen it stalking across his land.

It is possible that such beasts are perenties that are either exceptionally large individuals or are normal-sized specimens whose dimensions have been exaggerated or over-estimated by their startled eyewitnesses. Intriguingly, however, until as recently (geologically speaking) as a million years ago, a species of giant monitor lizard did exist in Australia. Known as *Megalania prisca*, its fossils reveal that it was up to 8 metres (around 26 feet) long, and weighed around 1.3 tonnes (eight times as heavy as a Komodo dragon). Several cryptozoologists have suggested that mungoon-galli sightings are based upon living specimens of *Megalania*.

Murphy, Bridey

The name supposedly given by a 19th-century Irishwoman who it was claimed had either been reincarnated as, or whose spirit had possessed, a 20th-century woman from the USA.

Bridey Murphy supposedly lived in Cork, Ireland, roughly in the period between 1798 and 1864. In 1952, it was claimed that she paid a rather unexpected visit to Pueblo in Colorado, USA. When placed under HYPNOSIS by the amateur hypnotist Morey Bernstein, Virginia Tighe (1923–95) started to recount details of Murphy's life, in an Irish accent, complete with colourful tales of 19th-century Irish life and a few Irish songs for good measure. More hypnosis sessions followed, recordings were made,

An issue of *Fate Magazine*, from November 1956, which included an investigation of Bridey Murphy. (© Mary Evans Picture Library)

and after each session Tighe and Bernstein would listen to the tapes together. It was claimed that this case provided conclusive proof of the reality of either REINCARNATION or POSSESSION.

In 1956, Bernstein published a book, *The Search for Bridey Murphy*; a film version of the story was released and recordings from the original hypnosis sessions were made available to an eager public. Tighe was renamed Ruth Simmons in an attempt to protect her identity, but journalists rapidly tracked her down. Some researchers claimed that, as a child in Wisconsin, Tighe had lived opposite an emigrant from Ireland called Bridey Murphy Corkell. Corkell had entertained the young Tighe with stories of her early life in Ireland. It was suggested that Tighe was just recounting stories she had heard in her youth, a claim perhaps borne out by the fact that she had used slang that would not have been current during the early 19th century. However, none of this prevented a number of other people from coming forward with similar claims in the years that followed. See also BLOXHAM TAPES.

muti

South African traditional medicine using various natural products, many of which are derived from trees. In recent years, it has gained notoriety in the media for its associations with witchcraft, mutilation and murder.

The South African traditional medicine known as 'muti' takes its name from a Zulu word, *umuthi*, meaning 'tree'; the term is particularly used to refer to the herbal medicine practised by traditional healers called sangomas, which makes use of natural products, many of which are derived from trees. But the word is widespread in most indigenous South African languages, and in Afrikaans it is used informally to mean 'medicine' in general.

While most of the 70,000 traditional healers of South Africa provide herbal remedies, a darker side of muti has become prominent in the media in recent years. The basic principle of muti is that energy can be taken from another living thing and absorbed into the practitioner's own body to bring about healing, power or good fortune. This energy can be taken from plants or animals, but humans are believed by many to have more energy than plants and animals, and children to have the most energy of all. Some sangomas therefore use human body parts, blood and vital organs as magical ingredients, and there have been many documented instances of apparent 'medicine killings' or 'muti murders' carried out in order to obtain these ingredients. These are not, in a strict religious sense, human SACRIFICES, since their purpose is to obtain the body parts from the victim. The parts are often consumed: genitals being thought to cure infertility; brains to improve knowledge and intelligence; eyes farsightedness; and the healthy heart or kidneys of another to cure heart and kidney ailments in the person who consumes them. The hand of a victim is sometimes buried in front of a shop to draw in customers. The potency of the body parts is thought to be increased if the victim is still alive when they are removed.

The discovery of a young boy's torso in the River Thames in London in 2001 brought the subject of muti murders to the attention of the British public, when it was shown that the nature of his mutilations was consistent with this practice. Conservative estimates put the number of muti murders in South Africa in the last decade at 300 or more, and they are believed to be on the increase, and to be spreading to European countries. However, with so few of the victims' bodies ever being recovered, the full extent of this crime is difficult to judge.

Mutual UFO Network
The largest general-membership UFO group operating in the USA.
The Mutual UFO Network was originally founded in 1969 as the 'Midwest UFO Network'. The name was changed to its current form in 1973, to reflect its wider membership, while still allowing the continued use of the acronym MUFON.

MUFON is an open membership group, the stated aim of which is:

> The scientific study of UFOs for the benefit of humanity.

The organization works to investigate UFO sightings and promote research into the UFO phenomenon, concentrating primarily on the possibility that they are aerial craft operating with an unknown method of propulsion. It has many scientists and engineers working for it and was one of the first groups to produce its own training manual giving instructions on the correct procedures to adopt when researching cases.

Although the network has overseas liaison officers, it operates primarily in the USA, with each state having its own separate administration. States vie for the right to host the themed annual conferences, and these have become the major event in the UFO calendar. A book-length report usually follows these conferences, containing all the papers that are presented.

MUFON has resisted the problems that the rise of the Internet has created for many other UFO organizations, and it continues to publish a monthly magazine, the *MUFON UFO Journal*.

mysterious falls *see* FALLS

mystery animals *see* CRYPTID

mystery birds
A general description for the wide range of cryptozoological birds that have been recorded, few of which have attracted extensive attention.
With only a small number of exceptions – for example THUNDERBIRDS and suspected living moas (see MOA, LIVING) – mystery birds have attracted far less attention than many other categories of CRYPTID. Yet there is a surprising diversity of examples on file, as demonstrated by the following selection.

In New Guinea, for instance, several very unusual types of bird of paradise have been reported, and even occasionally collected over the years, that do not correspond with any species described and named by science. In the past, they have all been dismissed as hybrids of various known species. However, at least six of these supposed hybrid types are now believed by a number of authorities to constitute valid species in their own right – however, as no living specimen of any of them has been recorded for many years, they may well be extinct and have therefore been dubbed 'the lost birds of paradise'. In addition to these, a large black long-tailed mystery bird spasmodically observed on Goodenough Island (just north of New Guinea's eastern tip) and known for its explosive rattle-like cry, may also be an undescribed bird of paradise species.

Africa's checklist of avian cryptids includes an unidentified green touraco spied by at least three renowned ornithologists within Uganda's Impenetrable Forest; a very large all-black swift sighted on Kenya's Marsabit Mountain; a long-tailed greyish mystery bird with reddish-chestnut under-tail-coverts observed in Kenya's Matthews Range; an unidentified gallinule frequenting the Sudd; and a glossy-black red-billed red-clawed fowl-like bird, with identical sexes and lacking a cry, that has long been reported from South Africa's Zululand, where it is known locally as the kondlo. Strangest of all is an exceedingly large bird from Zanzibar, resembling a giant secretary bird, which was reported during the 19th century. It was said by the local people to make a loud crashing sound when it clapped its wings together, earning it the name of makalala ('noisy'), but it is no longer referred to and therefore may have died out – assuming that it ever existed at all.

Asia's mystery birds include the infamous devil bird of Sri Lanka, which earns its name from its hideous cry that is said to resemble the shrieks of a boy being slowly strangled. Suggestions as to its identity range from an owl or a nightjar to an eagle or even a rail. Equally elusive is the chicken-like alovot of Sumatra, which has dark plumage mottled with lighter spots, and sometimes a comb-like crest. This may be an undescribed species of peacock-pheasant, of the genus *Polyplectron*. An even more mysterious pheasant, the double-banded argus pheasant, is known only from a single uniquely patterned feather, whose form has suggested to some experts that it may actually have been flightless. The feather's provenance is unknown, but the Malaysian island of Tioman is a favoured possibility, although if that is indeed the correct locality the bird is almost certainly extinct as searches have been conducted there to no avail.

While visiting Far Eastern Russia's Bering Island during the 1740s, the renowned explorer-naturalist Georg Wilhelm Steller spied a mysterious white bird that became known as Steller's sea raven, although it has never been recorded since. Identities proffered include a young or even albino specimen of Steller's cormorant, *Phalacrocorax perspicillatus*, (now itself extinct) or perhaps some species that is now known to science but was unfamiliar to Steller, such as the surfbird *Aphriza virgata*.

The Marquesas island of Hiva Oe in the Pacific is allegedly home to a bizarre flightless bird, known to locals as the koao, that runs through burrows in the island's long grass in a manner more like that of a rodent. The eminent explorer Thor Heyerdahl claimed to have seen a koao while visiting the island in 1937, but was unable to catch it. There is also a tantalizing possibility that a painting by Gauguin contains a depiction of this mystery bird, as it includes an unidentified bird that matches the description given by locals – chicken-sized, with purple-blue plumage, and yellow beak and tail. This description resembles that of a moorhen-like bird known as a gallinule, as does Gauguin's painting. Intriguingly, a supposedly extinct species of gallinule did exist there until relatively recently, as confirmed by fossil remains, leading some cryptozoologists to suggest that the koao and this fossil gallinule may be one and the same species.

In South America, an unknown fourth species of flamingo has been reported by Chilean natives, who refer to it as the jetete, whereas in Peru's Yanachaga National Park a mystifying wattle-lacking guan with black plumage has been observed but has not yet been captured for identification and study purposes.

In addition, unconfirmed sightings of several officially extinct species are reported from time to time – including the Asian pink-headed duck, *Rhodonessa caryophyllacea*, and North America's Carolina parakeet, *Conuropsis carolinensis*. Most recently, what appears to be a bona fide specimen of the ivory-billed woodpecker, *Campephilus principalis*, was observed and videoed by a team of ornithologists during 2005 in Arkansas – resurrecting the species from 60-odd years of extinction.

mystic

A person who seeks or attains a direct, personal experience of the divine, or the absolute, through intuition or insight.

The word 'mystic' derives from the Greek *mystes*, meaning 'a person initiated into sacred rites'. Elements of MYSTICISM exist in most religions and also in many non-religious philosophies and metaphysical systems, and the aim of all mystics is knowledge of the divine, or direct consciousness of the absolute or ultimate reality. The mystic seeks to attain this knowledge by a direct, personal experience which he or she achieves not through rational thought or discourse, but through intuition and insight. Mystics claim to reach a transcendent state in which they see, hear or feel things which are beyond conventional perception; VISIONS, DREAMS, revelations, prophecies, the hearing of supernatural voices and ecstatic trance states have been described by religious and non-religious mystics alike. The primary means by which mystics pursue their goal are the disciplines of PRAYER, MEDITATION or contemplation, along with fasting, abstinence and self-denial. However, mystics of some cultures and traditions, such as Native American mystics, may also use mind-altering, psychotropic substances as catalysts to facilitate the transcendent experience, as well as spirit journeying, trance dancing, chanting and ritual.

The tradition of Christian mysticism is as old as Christianity itself. The two major aims of the Christian mystic are to achieve unity between the human spirit and that of God, and the perfect experience of God in which the mystic seeks to understand God 'as He is'. In the Middle Ages, mysticism was often associated with monasticism, with its emphasis on prayer and contemplation, and some of the most celebrated Christian mystics are found among the monks of both the Eastern and the Western Church of this time, notably St John of the Cross and ST FRANCIS OF ASSISI, who remains an important figure in mysticism.

The aim of mystics in monistic belief systems such as Hinduism and TAOISM is to seek unity and identity with a universal principle. Thus, in Hindu philosophy, the self, or *atman*, in man is identified with the supreme self, or *Brahman*, of the universe. The apparent individuality or separateness of beings is believed to be an illusion, which can be dispelled by the mystic through his or her realization of the essential oneness of *atman* and *Brahman*. Mystics of the contemporary Goddess religion, which includes NEOPAGANISM and WICCA, seek a direct mystical experience of Nature in which all boundaries or separation between the person and Nature disappear – in other words, the mystic becomes 'one with Nature'.

Notable mystics include: the Hindu mystics Adi Shankara, Gopi Krishna, Ramana Maharshi and the female mystic poet Mirabai; the Chinese Taoist mystic LAO TZU; the Jewish mystic Isaac Luria, considered by many to be the founder of the KABBALAH in its modern form; the Sufi mystics Abdul Qadir Jilana and Mahmud Shabistari; the Christian contemplative mystics St Thomas Aquinas, JOAN OF ARC, Juliana of Norwich, St Theresa of Lisieux and JOHANNES ECKHART; and the occult mystic ALEISTER CROWLEY.

mysticism

A conscious and intuitive awareness of God, the divine or ultimate reality, achieved through direct personal experience.

The word 'mysticism' derives from the Greek *mystes*, meaning 'a person initiated into sacred rites'. Elements of mysticism exist in most religions, both Christian and non-Christian, with their quest for knowledge of the divine, and also characterize many non-religious philosophies and metaphysical systems in which the goal is a direct consciousness of the absolute, or ultimate reality. Wide variations have been described in both the form and the intensity of mystical experiences, but it is generally thought that what determines the authenticity of the experience is the quality of life which follows it; the mystical life is typically characterized by vitality, serenity and joy, and a sense of having been touched by some higher or greater truth or power.

Mysticism involves a direct, personal experience achieved through intuition or insight, rather that by rational thought or discourse. Central to mysticism is a belief in the existence of transcendent dimensions beyond the material world as a genuine and important source of knowledge. The MYSTIC sees, hears or feels things which are beyond conventional perception, and for this reason, mysticism is often associated with the OCCULT, and with paranormal phenomena such as TELEPATHY and LEVITATION. The word 'mysticism' is also sometimes used very broadly to refer to MAGIC, occultism or the esoteric. VISIONS, DREAMS, revelations, prophecies, the hearing of supernatural voices and ecstatic trance states have been described by religious and non-religious mystics alike, but because of the essentially personal nature of the mystical experience, firsthand objective studies of it are virtually impossible.

Mystics usually subscribe to one of two theories of God, or the supreme reality, either regarding this higher power as being outside the soul, which rises to it by successive stages, or else dwelling inside the soul, and able to be found by the mystic's going deep within his or her own consciousness in meditative self-exploration. Theistic mysticism, as characterized by Christianity, Judaism (in the KABBALAH), and Islam (in SUFISM), seeks unity, but not identity, with God, while the object of monistic mysticism, as found, for example, in the *Upanishads* of India, and in TAOISM, is to seek unity and identity with a universal principle.

Since elements of mysticism are found all over the world in such a wide range of belief systems, some mystics claim to be able to trace a common thread of influence back to a shared source, and believe that true unity of religion and philosophy can be found in mystical experience. The Vedic tradition is inherently mystical, as are ZEN BUDDHISM and the doctrines of Sufism, and Muslims believe that that the angel Gabriel inspired the Koran in a mystical manner. Taoism, as expounded by its traditional founder, the Chinese philosopher LAO TZU, also has a strong mystical emphasis. The Bible's Old Testament Song of Songs, St Paul's New Testament letters and the apocalyptic book of Revelation are all of a deeply mystical nature, and Christian GNOSTICISM, Mormonism (founded, as it is, on visions, revelations and angelic ordination), Anabaptism and the theology of Quakerism (which regards God as dwelling within the soul), also display strong elements of mysticism.

In the Middle Ages, mysticism was often associated with monasticism, with its emphasis on prayer, MEDITATION and contemplation. Some of the most celebrated mystics are found among the monks of both the Eastern and the Western Church of this time. In the 17th and 18th centuries, the metaphysical poets, such as John Donne and George Herbert, and the artist and poet WILLIAM BLAKE, wrote a great deal of mystically inspired literature on the contemplative life, and the late 19th century saw a marked increase of interest in mysticism, occultism and Eastern philosophy, with MADAME BLAVATSKY and the THEOSOPHY movement doing much to popularize these subjects. The 20th century saw a revival of interest in both Christian and non-Christian mysticism, and in the last half of the 20th century there was a resurgence in the study of Eastern mysticism.

Mythology *see panel p475*

Mythology

The word 'mythology' comes from the Greek words *mythos*, a story or legend, and *logos*, a discourse. It is used to describe bodies of traditional stories about gods and superhuman beings, although many also include human heroes. However, it is extremely difficult to give a hard and fast definition; the boundaries between mythology, LEGEND and FOLKLORE are blurred, and in many instances the words are used interchangeably – as can be seen in the body of modern folk tales that are known (among other things) as both 'URBAN LEGENDS' and 'urban myths'.

Humankind has always demonstrated a need to create such stories, whether as the basis of religion or simply to try to explain in human terms phenomena or events that seemed mysterious. In pre-literate societies these myths would be communicated orally and passed down from generation to generation, often being elaborated on and expanded as the need for more comprehensive accounts and explanations developed. Perhaps the earliest known examples of myths come from the worship of the Moon and the Sun by early cultures. The Sun and Moon were seen as possessing power, for good or evil, over human lives, while being changeable and largely unpredictable. CREATION MYTHS explain how life began and how the world and its inhabitants came to be – this is usually attributed to a deliberate act by a supreme being (or beings). Such myths often include an account of the first human beings, the progenitors of a whole race.

Often, what is called mythology by one culture, or a subsequent generation within a culture, should more properly be described as the elements of religious belief that have been superseded, discredited or are just considered not to describe the 'true' faith. This is the case, for example, with Classical mythology, perhaps the most familiar body of such stories within Western societies and passed down through centuries of literature and scholarship.

The ancient Greeks believed in immortal gods that emerged from the primeval chaos to control aspects of their daily lives, characterizing them as human-like beings whose capriciousness went a long way towards explaining seemingly random incidents. These gods included Zeus, the 'father of the gods', Athene, goddess of wisdom, Ares, god of war, Poseidon, god of the sea and of earthquakes, and Aeolus, god of the winds. They inhabited a different world or 'heaven' (Olympus), from which they could look down on human affairs and interfere at will. They had to be honoured or propitiated with sacrifices and other offerings to ensure that they would look favourably on terrestrial endeavours. Their control even continued beyond the mortal lifespan, with Hades, god of the underworld, ruling over the spirits of the dead.

Below the rank of these Olympian gods was ranged a cast of thousands of lesser, but still superhuman, usually immortal, creatures such as NYMPHS, OREADS and DRYADS, spirits such as the genius loci (literally, 'spirit of the place'), or monsters such as SIRENS. The existence of human beings who seemed to be possessed of extraordinary powers, such as strength, wisdom or musical ability was often explained in terms of their being the offspring of an immortal and a mortal. This was the case with great heroes, often known as demigods, such as Heracles (or Hercules as the Romans knew him).

Heroes in myths were often obliged to undertake dangerous quests, such as Jason's epic voyage in search of the Golden Fleece, or to carry out seemingly impossible tasks, such as the Twelve Labours of Hercules. These feats have been interpreted as allegories of the passage from boyhood to manhood, using ARCHETYPES who embodied exaggerated levels of recognizable human qualities. The retelling of such traditional tales was thought to demonstrate important lessons in what it is to be an adult, encouraging the virtues of strength and resourcefulness in the young men of a tribe or people.

Often, cities or societies would seek to establish their legitimacy or ancient lineage by attributing their origin to some mythical figure. Examples of this include the story of the founding of Rome by the wolf-suckled twin brothers Romulus and Remus. Similarly, in the mythology of Japan, Japanese emperors were said to have had a common ancestor who was the offspring of the sun goddess Amaterasu.

The 'national myth' by which a nation or state

sought to affirm its particular identity or right to independent existence typically featured heroes fighting to win freedom from tyrants or monsters and victoriously founding their own societies. Examples of this are to be found all over the world, not all of them being essentially ancient. A relatively recent national myth is that of the Swiss hero William Tell. Stories are told of his struggle for Swiss freedom from the Austrian oppressors, locating the events in the 14th century. Everyone knows the tale of Tell being forced to shoot an arrow through an apple placed on his son's head, even if they are unsure of the specific circumstances surrounding this feat of skill and courage. However, there is no evidence that William Tell ever existed in real life. His supposed deeds are echoed in myths found in other European countries, and it seems that he was actually a 15th-century product of a need to create a legitimizing mythical hero around whom a glorious tradition of fighting for freedom could be constructed. Such stories may not have any religious content and could, perhaps, be considered to be better categorized as legend.

Many of the gods of the Greek pantheon were taken up by ancient Rome, sometimes differing only by a change of name – Jupiter for Zeus, Neptune for Poseidon, Mars for Ares and so on. Many elements of Greek religion were also believed in by the Romans, such as the ELEUSINIAN MYSTERIES or the gift of PROPHECY attributed to the SIBYLS and the ORACLE OF DELPHI.

In Britain the various peoples who invaded the country after the decline of the Romans brought their own brands of mythology. In particular, Norse mythology had many echoes of its Classical counterpart, with a pantheon of gods installed in a kind of heaven (Asgard) under a father-figure (Odin). Heroes who died bravely in battle would be carried off by the Valkyries to the great hall in heaven (Valhalla) where they could continue to feast and brawl to their hearts' content. The Norse peoples, however, did not believe that this arrangement would last forever. The world would come to an end in a great, mutually destructive, conflict between good and evil gods (known as Ragnarok) – a better world would then emerge. In German myth this was called Götterdämmerung ('Twilight of the Gods').

The older Celtic mythology survived in those parts of the British Isles that were not overrun by these invaders. The Gaelic-speaking peoples of Ireland and Scotland shared many myths and tales of heroes such as Finn MacCool (also known in Scotland as Fingal), Cuchulain and the warrior-poet Ossian (or, in Irish myth, Oisin). The strangely regular, almost geometric, basaltic rock formations seen in the Giant's Causeway and Fingal's Cave on the coastlands of the Gaels (now known to be the product of ancient volcanic activity) were explained by them as being the work of such mythical giants.

There was a Celtic heaven, of course, known as Tir nan Og ('the land of youth'), where the dead remained eternally young. In one tale this was visited by Ossian, who thought he had spent only a short time there but who, on his return to Ireland, was immediately transformed into an aged man (having actually been away for over a hundred years). The fame of Ossian was revived as late as the 18th century when the Scottish poet James Macpherson (1736–96) achieved Europe-wide literary fame with poems based on Celtic mythology, which he claimed he had translated from Ossianic originals.

Welsh myths were collected in the medieval period in a group of tales known as the *Mabinogion* and an English translation was published in the 19th century. These stories of pre-Norman heroes, with their connection to a centuries-old oral tradition, played an important role in the development of the modern Welsh nationalist movement.

Enduring traces of many mythologies remain in modern society. We still talk of an uncertain outcome as being 'in the lap of the gods'. We continue to divide our week into days named after ancient gods: Sunday (from Sun), Monday (from Moon), Tuesday (from Tiw, Norse god of war), Wednesday (from Woden, a form of Odin), Thursday (from Thor, Norse thunder god), Friday (from Freyja, Norse goddess of married love) and Saturday (from Saturn, Roman god of agriculture). Similarly, in an increasingly secular age, many strands of mythology, which are unconnected with mainstream modern religion, continue to exercise a hold on believers.

Some myths go further than simply involving supernatural beings and human heroes; as well as numerous mythical beasts, mythical places also feature in many cultures. These often take the form of LOST LANDS or LOST CONTINENTS. Such stories show extraordinary persistence, the story of ATLANTIS, for example, having been current since the Classical period. To this day explorers make new claims to have discovered its submerged ruins.

Why does humankind still feel the need for mythology? Perhaps it fulfils a desire for larger-than-life heroes and feats, or helps satisfy a yearning towards the magical or mysterious that forms a fundamental, albeit unconscious, characteristic of the human psyche – or maybe we all just enjoy a good story.

Michael Munro

names of power *see* WORDS OF POWER

Namibian flying snake

An alleged African winged snake, said to emit a light from its head.

The Namaqua people of southern Namibia's Namib Desert have long spoken of an extraordinary serpent that is believed by them to inhabit high rock ledges. It is described as being 2.75–7.6 metres (9–25 feet) long, and brown or yellow in colour, speckled with dark spots. It is also said to have an inflated neck, and a very large head bearing a short pair of recurved horns – but the most startling characteristic of this reptilian CRYPTID is the pair of large membranous bat-like wings that reputedly spring from the region of its mouth or upper neck. According to local eyewitnesses, it will leap from a rock ledge, expand its wings, and soar down to the ground, landing with a loud thump before slithering away, leaving a clear scaly track in the sand. This mystery snake is also said to have a bright light-emitting torch in the centre of its brow. The latter could conceivably be explained as a patch of very shiny, light-reflecting scales, but the wings are much more mystifying. In Asia, there is a species of gliding snake that flattens its body before leaping from trees and gliding through the air, but no known snake has any structure approaching wings. Coelacanth discoverer Dr Marjorie Courtenay-Latimer observed a track allegedly made by a Namibian flying snake after landing, and confirmed that it was definitely a snake trail. Perhaps this unidentified species merely has expandable lateral flaps near its mouth, which have been mistaken for wings or elaborated into wings during generations of orally preserved folklore, and which may also have subsequently been coloured by imported Germanic myths of airborne lightning snakes.

Nandi bear

A ferocious man-eating African cryptid that in reality may be a composite beast, 'created' by the erroneous piecing together of reports describing several totally separate animals, both known and unknown.

The pioneering cryptozoologist Dr BERNARD HEUVELMANS called it 'an East African Proteus', because few (if any) other terrestrial CRYPTIDS have been likened to so many different animals as the infamous man-devouring Nandi bear of Kenya's Nandi district. Some who claim to have seen it liken this bloodthirsty creature to a bear, even though there are no known species of bear in sub-Saharan Africa. Others have favoured a hyena, albeit an extra-large, exceptionally hairy and ferocious version. There are those who describe it as a giant baboon, and one observer claims to have seen a weird anteater (possibly based upon an unexpected night-time encounter with an aardvark).

A depiction of the Namibian flying snake.
(© TopFoto/Fortean)

Not surprisingly, therefore, when attempting to disentangle these diverse strands in his book *On the Track of Unknown Animals* (1958), Heuvelmans proposed that the most likely explanation for such dramatic variation in descriptions of the Nandi bear is that it is actually a non-existent composite, 'created' by the erroneous grouping together of descriptions of several totally separate, and very different, animals.

The descriptions of the Nandi bear that most closely resemble those of a bear (a version sometimes referred to as the 'chemosit', meaning 'devil') are, in Heuvelmans' view based upon sightings of very large, old, all-black specimens of the ratel or honey badger, *Mellivora capensis*. Despite being a member of the weasel family, the ratel is remarkably ursine in overall appearance, especially when, in advanced years, its silver dorsal colouration darkens to black (and thus matches the rest of its coat). It can also be exceedingly aggressive – so much so that not even a lion will dare attack it.

Another version, known in Kenya's Lower and Middle Tana River regions as the koddoelo, is much more baboon-like, but is considerably larger than any known species living today – it allegedly stands 1.08 metres (3.5 feet) high at the shoulder. It is said to be extremely savage, attacking humans on sight, and to have very large canine teeth and powerful forelegs. As recently as 650,000 years ago, a gorilla-sized baboon, *Theropithecus oswaldi*, did exist in Kenya, which, combining the gorilla's stature with the ferocity of a baboon, would have indeed been a terrifying beast for any human to encounter. If it has survived to the present day, it would make an exceedingly convincing candidate for the koddoelo.

As for the giant hyena-like version of the Nandi bear (often termed the 'kerit' or 'gadett', meaning 'brain-eater', but also sometimes 'chemosit'), several separate candidates have been suggested. Some shot specimens have proven to be abnormally red-furred individuals of the spotted hyena, *Crocuta crocuta*. Unexpected encounters with the rare, heavily-maned brown hyena, *Hyaena brunnea*, which is capable of putting on a frighteningly belligerent display if threatened, have also been offered to explain Nandi bear reports. However, neither of these proposed solutions can explain the discovery of 'Nandi bear' footprints that are apparently hyena-shaped but as large as those of lions, or the shooting of two still-unidentified dark-furred beasts in the Nandi district during the late 1950s – these were later dismissed as 'giant forest hyenas' (even though science does not officially recognize any such species). A similar beast that was twice the size of a spotted hyena, with a lion-sized head, rearward-sloping back and long shaggy brown hair was shot in 1962. Again it was referred to as a giant forest hyena, but its body was not preserved for examination.

In recent (geologically speaking) prehistoric times, Kenya was home to a species that, if it were still alive today, would correspond perfectly with a hyena-like version of the Nandi bear. Known as the short-faced hyena, *Pachycrocuta brevirostris*, it sported the typical sloping hyena-like outline but was the size of a lion, with enormous canine teeth, and was a more active hunter than its smaller, predominantly scavenging modern-day relatives. This possible solution was proposed by the British cryptozoologist Dr Karl Shuker in his book *In Search of Prehistoric Survivors* (1995). Shuker argued that such a creature could readily carry out the horrific attacks claimed for the Nandi bear by local people, and would certainly resemble the mysterious 'giant forest hyenas'.

A second postulated prehistoric survivor, a form of chalicothere, has been considered by various authors in relation to the Nandi bear reports. These bizarre ungulates (hoofed mammals) had longer forelegs than hind legs, yielding a rearward-sloping back that gave them a surprisingly hyena-like outline and, in spite of their ungulate affinities, they possessed claws which they used for digging up roots. A living chalicothere would certainly fit the description given by a number of Nandi bear eyewitnesses, and pictures of chalicothere reconstructions have been identified by local tribespeople as the chemosit. Rinderpest disease seriously depleted the numbers of many ungulate species in Africa during the late 19th century and, according to native tribes, numbers of the once-common Nandi bear also plummeted at this time – a potentially interesting observation because rinderpest normally kills only ungulates rather than also harming any known carnivorous species. Because the harmless chalicothere is superficially hyena-like, it may have been erroneously blamed for kills that were actually the work of hyenas.

However, with virtually no Nandi bear reports in recent years, it is possible that this most feared, yet elusive, of African cryptids may have already died out – effectively lost to science before the nature of its controversial, confused identity was ever resolved.

nape

An unidentified ape-like cryptid from North America, smaller than, and reputedly totally distinct from, the bigfoot.

'Nape' is a contraction of 'North American ape', a name coined by the US cryptozoologist Loren Coleman and applied to a lesser-known tailless primate CRYPTID of the New World that is often confused with the much more famous BIGFOOT. Yet whereas the latter mystery primate is said to stand over 1.8 metres (6 feet) tall and is habitually bipedal, the nape is generally described as being no more than gorilla-sized or even chimpanzee-sized, and although it is sometimes seen standing or walking on its hind legs, it has also often been encountered moving on all fours, sometimes knuckle-walking like Africa's anthropoid apes.

Napes are usually sighted in the swamplands or deciduous and mixed forests of the Mississippi Valley and its tributaries. Sightings have been recorded since the 19th century, and the animal seen has often been described as a 'gorilla' or a 'chimp' by the local people. Moreover, tracks of napes tend to exhibit an opposable big toe, which is typical of apes but not of hominids (nor of the bigfoot). The most straightforward explanation for these creatures is that they are escaped or released African apes that have adapted to living in the North American terrain. However, Loren Coleman has suggested that they comprise a relict species of *Dryopithecus*, an early ape-like primate from the Miocene epoch of Europe, which is currently understood to have died out approximately nine million years ago. As yet, however, there is no fossil evidence to suggest that *Dryopithecus* ever reached North America.

Some cryptozoologists categorize reports of an odorous, ape-like cryptid from Florida (usually referred to as the 'skunk ape') as nape sightings – particularly because it is frequently described as employing a quadrupedal mode of locomotion, leaving behind knuckle-walking tracks. It is also often (but not invariably) said to be of modest size. In contrast, others point to their sometimes bipedal locomotion, and the fact that they apparently occasionally appear to be of relatively large size (especially when standing upright), as indications that skunk apes should be classed as examples of bigfoot.

NASA

The organization which directs the US space programme.

NASA (the National Aeronautics and Space Administration) has long been associated with UFOs. A number of its space missions have reported sightings – these include video footage of unusual white lights darting across the earth's upper atmosphere taken by the Space Shuttle *Discovery* on 15 September 1991. Members of the public often write to NASA with questions about UFOs, assuming that it must have investigated the phenomenon. In fact, it has gone to great lengths to avoid doing so.

When President Jimmy Carter was elected to office in 1976, he had made a public pledge to reveal all that was known about UFOs. Carter had a personal motive; he had reported his own sighting in Leary, Georgia, when he was the state governor. On 6 January 1969, he had seen a very bright light that he considered unusual – although many UFO investigators now believe that it was probably the planet Venus shining through layers of ice in the atmosphere. Nevertheless, the event had impressed Carter, and he chose to fulfil his promise by asking NASA to officially investigate UFOs. At the time there was no official government UFO research in the country, the US Air Force having closed PROJECT BLUE BOOK eight years earlier on the recommendation of the COLORADO UNIVERSITY STUDY.

In July 1977, as letters released under the FREEDOM OF INFORMATION ACT have since revealed, NASA was asked to carry out an in-depth inquiry into the UFO phenomenon, and it apparently considered this for several months. Carter's plans had brought protests from some scientists, who warned NASA that it would face problems if it took on this project.

Evidence relating to this plan originally came to light in 1981, during the investigation of the RENDLESHAM FOREST INCIDENT, which involved a US Air Force base in the UK. One of the witnesses in this case, seeking to prove his credentials to UFO investigators, leaked a copy of a letter held by the base Public Affairs Office. It had been sent by Colonel Charles Senn of the US Air Force to a retired Lt General, Duward Crow, who was working for NASA at the time. The letter was dated 1 September 1977 (shortly after Carter had made his request) and it was an attempt to dissuade NASA from becoming involved. It included the line:

> I sincerely hope you are successful in preventing a reopening of UFO investigations.

On 21 December 1977, Dr Robert Frosch of NASA wrote to the President's science adviser to reject even the less-onerous UFO study that had been proposed as a compromise. NASA cited as its reason the lack of any physical evidence for UFOs, making it impossible to devise meaningful scientific protocols. This was almost the same motive cited by the US Air Force when rejecting the ESTIMATE OF THE SITUATION REPORT three decades earlier.

National Investigations Committee on Aerial Phenomena

An early civilian UFO investigation group in the USA – the first to attempt to treat the subject as one with scientific importance.

Created in late 1956 in Washington, DC, by a naval scientist and a number of other professionals, the National Investigations Committee on Aerial Phenomena (NICAP), sought to counter the waning

Executive Director of the National Investigations Committee on Aerial Phenomena, Stuart Nixon, photographed in 1971. The UFO photograph he is holding was later proved to be a hoax. (© Bettmann/Corbis)

interest in UFOs that followed the downgrading of the US Air Force UFO team, PROJECT BLUE BOOK. In January 1957, NICAP placed the outspoken UFO writer Major DONALD KEYHOE at its head. His conviction that the US government had proof of the truth of the EXTRATERRESTRIAL HYPOTHESIS, but was engaged in a GOVERNMENTAL COVER-UP, was to become a central theme of the organization. NICAP set out to persuade Congress that it was not being told the full truth about UFOs and gathered together an impressive team of scientists and military figures. However, it had difficulty combating the image that the subject had already gained through the actions of some members of the now-flourishing private UFO COMMUNITY.

During the 1960s, NICAP was a major player on the world UFO stage and had over 10,000 members. It regularly bombarded politicians with information in an attempt to change their stance and alter public attitudes. It was influential in the protests that arose within the US Congress, eventually leading to the instigation of the COLORADO UNIVERSITY STUDY. However, NICAP publicly dissociated itself from the study when it became convinced that its leader, DR E U CONDON, was heavily biased against the reality of UFOs.

In 1964, NICAP published *The UFO Evidence*, a mammoth report written by the UFO researcher Richard Hall, which detailed the evidence for what the group considered to be the strongest UFO cases then on record. The book is considered to be one of the most influential in the field, particularly because NICAP paid for a copy to be sent to every

member of Congress and to all of the major media companies.

NICAP membership went into a severe decline following the ending of official US Air Force investigations in 1968, and Keyhoe was removed from office in 1970. Although NICAP tried to survive in a new era, it remained tied to the UFO themes of the 1950s and started to appear old-fashioned in its reluctance to embrace new trends. For example, it considered the increasingly common ALIEN contact cases (reports of which were almost entirely absent in *The UFO Evidence*) to be too bizarre for Congress members to take seriously.

The organization eventually folded in 1980, having only existed as a shadow of its former self during its latter years. Its extensive files were taken over by its less politically orientated successor, CUFOS.

nats
Spirits worshipped in Myanmar (formerly Burma). Nats are grouped into the Thirty-Seven (the spirits of specific warriors and heroes) and generic nature spirits.
'Nat' is a term which encompasses two groups of spirits worshipped in Myanmar (formerly Burma). It is used principally of the Thirty-Seven – the officially recognized spirits of 37 specific individuals, warriors and heroes, male and female, who have become supernatural beings and function both as beneficent guardians and vengeful spirits. Their images are displayed in the Shwezigon pagoda in Bagan, and their tales are collected in the *Mahagita Medanigyan*. The other group of spirits known as nats are the nature spirits who inhabit trees and groves; these are

generally considered to be of an evil disposition, and are believed to cause ague or malaria. Nats have power over the weather, crops and the health of humans and animals, and are propitiated with gifts of fruit and flowers. They belong to the indigenous pre-Buddhist religion of Myanmar, and the worship of nats has been incorporated into Myanmar Buddhism; many Buddhist pagodas include a special house or shrine to the nats, called a *natsin*, and verses from the *Mahagita Medanigyan* are read aloud at festivals to honour the Thirty-Seven. The most important nat is Tha Gya Min, who is identified with the Hindu god Indra. He is shown standing in a lotus supported by three elephants, and is associated with the coming of the new year. The biggest nat pilgrimage site in Myanmar is at Mount Popa, an extinct volcano near Bagan.

natural

A person who allegedly displays psychic abilities without having had to undergo any form of training.

Some believers suggest that most people have some form of PSYCHIC ability and that they can learn to use it if they undergo suitable training (there are schools that say that they can teach people how to undertake REMOTE VIEWING, for example). Others say that only a few people have such abilities. However, they would all agree that some people, referred to as 'naturals', are apparently born with, or naturally develop, an ability to use psychic powers. It is said that a natural will always out-perform someone who has simply been trained.

It is often claimed that training, or attempts to change the way in which they perform, can actually reduce the effectiveness of a natural's ability. Sceptics argue that this appears to be a poor excuse for the fact that such naturals are often unable to demonstrate their abilities under strictly controlled conditions.

nature spirits

Spirits which represent trees, streams, vegetation, the weather and other natural forces.

In earlier times, human beings were at the mercy of all the forces of nature. Our Neolithic ancestors, who were farmers, were dependent upon the yearly cycle, and ancient religions were largely concerned with entreating the gods and spirits of nature to provide the conditions for the crops and livestock to flourish. ANIMISM, the belief that everything has a spirit, pervaded the old religions, and continues to be the basis for many native belief systems to this day, as well as a feature of modern WICCA and NEOPAGANISM. Every aspect of nature was seen to have its spirit, and since humans coexisted with these spirits and were dependent on their goodwill, they had to be understood, treated with respect, worshipped and appeased. The rich lore of FAIRIES and mythical creatures found all over the world since ancient times is a result of this animistic view of nature.

Vegetation spirits such as the Russian polevik and the GREEN MAN of European lore were believed to nurture the crops and cause them to grow and ripen, and the Green Man also represents the regenerative power of Spring. One aspect of the Celtic hag-fairy, the cailleach, is as a corn-spirit embodied in the last sheaf to be gathered from the fields, and the German Kornbocke and kornwolf are similar spirits. A whole host of nature spirits controlled the weather, which was all-important for the survival of crops, beasts and humans alike; there were spirits who represented the winds, storms, rain, lightning and sunshine, and others who brought about changes in the seasons, such as the Russian Father Frost and another aspect of the cailleach, who both personified Winter. Myths of tree spirits are common in folklore all over the world, including the DRYADS of Greek mythology, the NATS of Myanmar, the moss maidens of Germany, who spin the moss for the trees, and the tree FAIRIES of Celtic and Druid lore. Humans must be very careful not to offend such spirits by harming their trees, and in Britain it is particularly unwise to damage or cut down a hawthorn, oak, birch or rowan, since these are most closely associated with the fairy folk. Water, with its power to sustain life, was once considered to be a living thing, and every society honoured its rivers, WELLS and springs as sacred. The ancient Celts often sacrificed treasure to propitiate the river and lake spirits, and the mythology of almost every culture in the world has a wide range of water spirits, who are frequently described as being temperamental and dangerous, as prepared to call up storms and drown humans as they are to show them favour by granting them wishes, healing or treasure. Such river spirits include the Greek naiads of rivers and streams and nereids and undines of the seas; the kappas of Japan; the Scottish kelpies; the German NIXIES; and the beautiful but sometimes deadly MERMAIDS. In addition, there were also the guardian spirits of specific locations, such as groves, meadows, mountains and valleys. See also NYMPHS.

Nazca lines

A series of straight lines and animal drawings on the ground in Peru.

The Nazca lines is the name given to a series of ground markings discovered in the Nazca Desert, a high, arid plain in coastal Peru. They were first detected in the 1920s by aircraft pilots beginning to make commercial flights over the area. Over 300 patterns have been identified, including many straight lines, drawings of animals such as spiders, birds and monkeys, and more

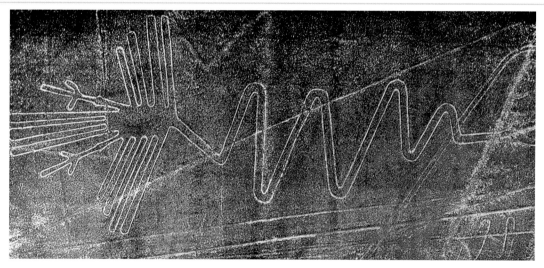

An aerial view of an image of a bird, one of the many animals represented in the Nazca lines in Peru.
(© TopFoto)

abstract shapes. The markings were made by clearing away the stones on the arid surface, exposing the sand beneath, which is a much lighter colour. It is believed that they were created by the Nazca people, whose culture flourished in the region between c.200 BC and c.600 AD. The Nazca are known to have decorated pottery with stylized drawings of people and animals, but the marking out of such gigantic shapes must have taken many years and much communal labour. The lines' survival through the centuries testifies to the lack of rainfall or any other form of erosion in the region.

Why, then, was this done? One theory was that they formed some kind of astronomical chart and that the animal shapes represented constellations, but the drawings do not tally with the appearance of the stars in the night sky over the area. Another idea was that they were tracks used for ceremonial running races. While this might explain some of the markings, others would have made for rather tortuous races, some involving climbing from the plain into the surrounding hills.

The idea that the Nazca lines represented landing strips for extraterrestrial craft was popularized by the Swiss writer ERICH VON DÄNIKEN in his book *Chariots of Fire* (1968). However, while this theory might be used to explain the straight lines, it does not account for the animal figures and abstract shapes, which must have been somewhat distracting for the alien pilots. Also, it might be expected that any such take-offs and landings would have disturbed the markings as well as the surrounding ground and no such traces have been found.

Some theorists connect the lines with shamanic

religion, interpreting them as images and guiding lines to be seen by those undertaking 'spirit flight', an OUT-OF-BODY EXPERIENCE created by the ingestion of HALLUCINOGENS. The most likely explanation is indeed a religious one: that the markings are intended to be seen by gods or ancestral spirits, whether depicting these beings themselves or presenting images as symbolic offerings. The Nazca were a settled agricultural people and would have been likely to associate weather with deities who would have to be propitiated. However, all theories are essentially speculation, and the true origins and purposes of the Nazca lines remain mysterious.

near-death experience
A dream-like narrative supposedly experienced by some people when their physical body is at the point of death – successful resuscitation then allows them to relate the details. Such experiences are often interpreted as a journey of the self, or spirit, towards the afterlife.
Near-death experiences (often abbreviated to NDEs) are regularly reported by people who recover from being very close to death, or in some cases from being clinically dead for a short period. NDEs became a popular area of study after 1975 when the originator of the term, Dr Raymond Moody, published a book called *Life After Life*, listing a number of cases he had recorded. However, records exist of earlier reports of what would later be described as NDEs, such as, famously, that of the psychologist CARL JUNG, after he suffered a heart attack in 1944.

The stories related by those who report NDEs vary, but there are a number of commonly occurring elements.

Typically the experience may begin with a buzzing or ringing sound followed by a sense of peace and the sensation of 'leaving the body'– some even report being aware of floating around the room in which the physical body is lying (see OUT-OF-BODY EXPERIENCE). This is often followed by the impression of moving through a tunnel towards a light, and, as they approach the light they may 'meet' dead relatives, friends or other spiritual beings. Another commonly reported feature is that of the 'life review'. Essentially, this means the person has a vision of the whole of their life or of the key events in it; this may include being 'shown' things that they did that they can identify as being morally good or bad, and the consequences of these actions. While the 'review' covers the person's whole life, they feel that it passes very quickly. The NDE usually ends with the person being told to return to their body because their time for death has not yet come.

A 1992 Gallup poll reported that nearly eight million Americans claimed to have had an NDE, and a Dutch report published in *The Lancet* in 2001 stated that in a sample of 344 patients who had been successfully resuscitated after a heart attack, 18 per cent reported a classic NDE. When questioned about their NDE many people say they believe that they have seen a glimpse of the AFTERLIFE. Most report that it was a positive experience, although approximately 15 per cent report a negative experience of a 'hellish' place. A large number even say that they were disappointed when they 'returned', because there was such a feeling of calm and love around them during the NDE.

Some people regard NDEs as positive proof of life after death, while others argue that there is a fundamental philosophical (or even theological) problem with this, in that the patient was not really dying during the experience, as they did 'come back'. Some researchers have offered non-supernatural explanations for the experience. They believe that the NDEs result from normal, chemical processes in the brain which may even occur as a natural result of the brain 'closing down', releasing endorphin-like chemicals to reduce pain and preparing to die. The images may well be akin to HALLUCINATIONS resulting from the expectations many people have relating to what will happen when they die – it has, for example, been observed that certain drugs produce hallucinations which bear all the hallmarks of a classic NDE.

It has been claimed that some surgeons have placed a card bearing a message in such a way that the message can only be read from the top of the operating theatre. They have then asked patients who have reported an NDE to tell them what the message

was. Apparently this has not produced any success.

Spiritual interpretations of NDEs remain extremely popular, and a fictional depiction of attempts to induce them deliberately formed the central theme of the 1990 film *Flatliners*.

necromancy
The art or practice of revealing future events by calling up and questioning the spirits of the dead; also, another name for sorcery or black magic.

The word 'necromancy' is often used synonymously with black magic (see MAGIC, BLACK), but strictly speaking, necromancy is defined as divination by calling up and questioning the spirits of the dead (from the Greek *necros*, dead body, and *manteiā*, divination). The belief is that spirits, being no longer bound by physical bodies, are not limited to the earthly plane, and therefore have access to knowledge of the past and future which the living do not. Necromancy has been used in attempts to find buried or sunken treasure, and to try to determine whether a person died by natural means or was murdered.

Necromancy dates back to the times of the ancient Persians, Greeks and Romans. There are many references to necromancy in the Bible. The book of Deuteronomy warns the Israelites against the Canaanite practice of divination from the dead, and in the book of Samuel, King Saul asks the Witch of Endor to invoke the spirit of the dead prophet Samuel. In the Middle Ages, necromancy was thought to be widely practised by magicians, sorcerers and witches, and in Jacobean England, it was outlawed by the Witchcraft Act of 1604. It is not generally held to include spirit communication involving MEDIUMS, as in SPIRITUALISM, nor encounters with the souls of the departed during shamanic spirit journeys nor ghostly APPARITIONS.

Necronomicon, The
A fictional book of magic referred to in the works of H P Lovecraft; although Lovecraft insisted it was purely an invention on his part, it has inspired the publication of a number of texts claiming to be the 'real' Necronomicon.

As part of the 'Cthulhu Mythos' he created in his horror stories, US writer H P LOVECRAFT introduced the idea of a GRIMOIRE or book of magic called *The Necronomicon*. This book is first explicitly mentioned in his 1923 short story *The Hound*, and is also referred to in a number of his other stories. It is described as having been written around AD 730 by Abdul Alhazred, a mad Arab poet who had spent ten years alone in the vast southern desert of Arabia, a place believed to be inhabited by evil spirits and monsters. Alhazred is said to have found, beneath the ruins of a nameless desert town, the shocking annals of a race much older than mankind – the Old Ones – and to have written the book, originally titled *The Al Azif*, as an account of the Old Ones and their history, with instructions on how to summon them. According to Lovecraft's stories, the book was translated into Greek as *The Necronomicon* in AD 950, and suppressed in 1232 by the Pope, but a few copies are said to have survived, with the Elizabethan magician JOHN DEE acquiring one and translating it into English. Lovecraft claimed that the title of the book came to him in a dream, but that its etymology was valid, deriving from the Greek words *necros*, a corpse, *nomos*, law, and *eikon*, an image – thus, 'an image of the law of the dead'.

Although Lovecraft insisted that the book was pure imagination on his part, such was the resonance and power of his invention that many people believed he referred to a real text, and during his lifetime he received many letters from fans asking about its authenticity. The issue was further confused in 1970 with the publication of a book by 'Simon', whose author claimed it was a translation of the 'real' *Necronomicon*, and attempted to connect Lovecraft's mythos with historical Sumerian mythology. Later, the paranormal researcher and writer Colin Wilson produced a blatant hoax version which even incorporated quotes from Lovecraft's stories in its passages.

Lovecraft's fictitious text has inspired many books by later writers, as well as several horror films, the most famous being the *Evil Dead* trilogy, and a 1993 Lovecraft anthology film titled *Necronomicon*. His work also inspired two books of paintings by the Swiss artist H R Giger, *Necronomicon* and *Necronomicon II*, and features in a number of video and computer games.

neopaganism

A catch-all term for a wide variety of religious and spiritual movements which are connected by being based upon or resembling pre-Christian pagan religious practices.

The word 'neopaganism' is often used in preference to 'PAGANISM' to emphasize the fact that it is generally considered that modern PAGAN practice is a reconstruction rather than a continuation of pre-Christian pagan practice. Some would still prefer that the 'neo' prefix be dropped, although claims to underground continuity, such as those associated with Charles Godfrey Leland (see *ARADIA, OR THE GOSPEL OF THE WITCHES*), GERALD GARDNER and the British anthropologist Margaret Murray are now largely discredited.

In the minds of the population as a whole, neopaganism is primarily associated with the modern practice of what might be described as religious WITCHCRAFT, particularly the movement that refers to itself as WICCA. However, the range of religious and spiritual belief systems that might be described as neopagan is vast. There are many that are based around pre-Christian or even pre-Judaic European and Asian spiritual practices, although many also take, adopt or are based around religious and magical practices from elsewhere, including ancient and modern shamanic traditions (see SHAMANISM). Some are even completely new constructions along 'pagan' lines, without making any claim to a historical source. Neopagan religions are often characterized by being pantheistic or polytheistic, they may contain animistic elements and are usually earth- or nature-centred with a calendar of festivals that is connected with the changing seasons. Many bring together aspects of a range of diverse spiritual beliefs and rituals (a practice known as SYNCRETISM). See also CHURCH AND SCHOOL OF WICCA; CHURCH OF ALL WORLDS; CULTS, NEW RELIGIOUS MOVEMENTS AND ALTERNATIVE RELIGIONS; DRUIDS; ECO-PAGANISM.

Nessie *see* LOCH NESS MONSTER

Netzach

In the kabbalah, the sephirah or emanation of God known as Victory or Eternity, which is assigned the number 7; it represents the formless energy which can overcome obstacles, great strength and force of personality.

Netzach is the seventh of the ten SEPHIROTH, or divine emanations, in the KABBALAH. It is called Victory or Eternity, and is the fourth of the emotive attributes of the sephiroth. It is the first of the sephiroth to be emanated by TIPHARETH, and represents the formless energy which can overcome obstacles, and the tendency of life to flourish despite difficult conditions. It is assigned the number 7. On the kabbalistic TREE OF LIFE, it is positioned directly below CHESED, and directly opposite HOD, with which it has a polarized relationship, and is the third and lowest sphere of the right-hand axis, the Pillar of Mercy. It is also the first point on the lowest of the three triangles formed by the sephiroth, the Astral or Psychological Triangle, which it makes up with Hod and YESOD. It is given five paths on the Tree of Life – to Chesed, Tiphareth, Hod, Yesod and MALKUTH. Netzach and Hod achieve balance in Yesod, and taken together, these two sephiroth constitute the powers of Force and Form within the Astral Triangle; in *THE ZOHAR* they are referred to as 'the scales of justice'. Netzach is associated with the divine name *Jehovah Tzabaoth* (the Lord of Hosts), the archangel Haniel, the angelic order of the Elohim and the planetary force of Venus.

In the TAROT, Netzach corresponds to the four sevens, and in the tarot Tree of Life spread, the card in the Netzach position usually represents discipline, risk-taking, experimentation and the ways in which a person can put their imagination to work. In some kabbalistic systems it is attributed with the magical image of a beautiful naked woman, and is represented by various symbols such as a lamp, a girdle and a rose. It is often connected with the solar plexus CHAKRA. The word 'Netzach' in kabbalistic GEMATRIA gives the number 148.

neurolinguistic programming
A form of alternative therapy aimed at improving self-awareness.

One of the forms of therapy associated with the NEW AGE movement of the 1980s is neurolinguistic programming (NLP). The initial ideas from which it was born appeared in the early 1970s, and are attributed to the US author Richard Bandler and the US linguist John Grinder. The methods were derived primarily from observing successful psychotherapists, and studying the way in which they behaved and influenced their patients (as opposed to the theories that lay behind their techniques).

The aim of NLP is to 'program' the human brain to heighten self-awareness, and to encourage the ability to set goals and actively pursue them. It has been

Richard Bandler, regarded by some as the father of neurolinguistic programming. (© Peter Dench/Corbis)

widely used as a motivational tool, both for individuals and organizations. Its original advocates argued that it should involve a purely practical approach, based upon observing and applying methods that work, rather than being overly concerned with theory. However, since then, many of its practitioners have incorporated a variety of theories of their own.

One of its central themes is the importance of the unconscious mind in influencing everyday behaviour. In order to bring about positive changes in the unconscious, a form of self-HYPNOSIS is often advocated. NLP is also very much concerned with communication, aiming to teach people how to put their views across more effectively and how better to understand what others are trying to communicate both overtly and through unconscious body language. However, while its name suggests that it is a scientific discipline, sceptics believe that there is little (if any) scientific basis for the claims and methods advocated.

New Age
The name particularly associated with a cultural and spiritual trend which became prominent in the late 1980s. It is concerned with the integration of mind, body and spirit, and is characterized by an eclectic interest in a variety of beliefs and practices, including astrology, meditation, mysticism and holistic medicine.

The term 'New Age' was popularized by the American mass media in the late 1980s to refer to an alternative spiritual subculture which became prominent around that time. This broad, free-flowing movement has no single external source of authority, no official leaders or formal clergy and no headquarters, membership list, single external source of authority or holy book. It is a loose network of spiritual teachers, healers and seekers rather than a unified cult system, and is characterized by an individual and eclectic approach to spiritual exploration. 'New Agers' typically construct their own spiritual path, sampling many different beliefs and practices taken from the mystical traditions of many world religions and systems, including shamanism, PAGANISM and occultism. It should be noted that many people who are labelled 'New Age' object to the term.

Typical areas of interest to many members of the New Age movement include MEDITATION, CHANNELLING, HOLISTIC MEDICINE, environmentalism, psychic phenomena and 'unsolved mysteries' such as UFOs. Many frequently make use of healers, spiritual counsellors, astrologers and psychics, and may use CRYSTALS for a number of purposes, such as healing, and practise various forms of DIVINATION, for example TAROT, SCRYING and RUNES.

New Age thinking is syncretic in nature,

seeking to merge elements from different belief systems and practices. Its emphasis is on subjective knowledge and experience, and it is mysticism-based. Common to many New Agers are the belief in the law of KARMA and in REINCARNATION; the belief in the existence of spiritual beings, such as ANGELS, who can guide humans in their spiritual path; the reverence of ancient sites, such as STONEHENGE, as centres of special power or energy; the belief that all life in the universe is spiritually interconnected, and that all religions are one in God's eyes; a respect for and interest in the mystical traditions of world religions such as Tibetan Buddhism, ZEN BUDDHISM, TAOISM, SHAMANISM, KABBALAH, and GNOSTICISM; the use of alternative and holistic medicine, such as ACUPUNCTURE, HOMEOPATHY and CHAKRA healing with crystals; and an appreciation of the need for ecological responsibility.

As a loose network of like-minded groups, the New Age movement's roots can be traced back to the counterculture of the 1960s – the Findhorn Foundation, founded in northern Scotland in 1962, was an early New Age community – but some of its elements are identifiable in 19th-century THEOSOPHY and SPIRITUALISM, which in turn had adopted ideas and practices from Western esoteric and occult traditions such as ASTROLOGY, ALCHEMY and MAGIC, as well as Eastern mysticism. RUDOLF STEINER and his ANTHROPOSOPHY movement were also a major influence on the New Age.

Critics of the New Age movement include some evangelical Christian groups who reject all forms of occultism and regard New Age as embracing and propagating this; scientists and sceptics who reject its paranormal claims; and traditional adherents of disciplines from cultures such as India and China, who sometimes see New Agers as having misunderstood or trivialized their teachings. Some Native Americans, in particular, have objected to the eclecticism of those whom they see as profiting from tribal beliefs without understanding or respecting all their aspects. In addition, some spiritual movements, such as PAGANISM, may distance themselves from the term 'New Age' because of the negative connotations occasionally associated with it, such as commercialism, media sensationalism and its potential openness to charlatanism. See also AGE OF AQUARIUS.

new religious movements *see* CULTS, NEW RELIGIOUS MOVEMENTS AND ALTERNATIVE RELIGIONS

Newton, Florence *see panel p488*

Newton, Sir Isaac (1642–1727)
English scientist and mathematician who devoted much of his life to alchemy and biblical prophecy.

Some biographies of Isaac Newton, 'the father of modern science', mention briefly in passing that, as well as being a brilliant mathematician who was responsible for major scientific work on gravity and light, Newton had an interest in ALCHEMY and other esoteric subjects. In fact he spent far more time studying, and wrote immeasurably more, on spiritual matters than he did on science.

Newton was President of the Royal Society for 24 years from 1703 to his death. The Royal Society, founded in 1661, was initially a reification of the famed 'invisible college' of Rosicrucianism (see ROSICRUCIANS); it was the successor to the Gresham College meetings which brought together the brightest minds in Britain at the time – scientists who were also Hermetic philosophers (see HERMETICA), Rosicrucians, Freemasons (see FREEMASONRY), alchemists and astrologers (see ASTROLOGY).

Whether he could be called a Rosicrucian or not, Newton was one of the last of the natural philosophers – scientists driven by a thirst for knowledge, who saw no contradiction between religion and magic and science. Newton actively pursued practical alchemical research, performing experiments and writing over a million words on the subject. He was also utterly absorbed by biblical prophecy, writing, among many other works, *Observations upon the Prophecies of Daniel and the Apocalypse of St John* (an incomplete version of which was published posthumously in 1733). Despite several conservative Protestant organizations claiming Newton for their own, he was in fact anti-Trinitarian; although deeply religious, in terms of mainstream Christianity he was a heretic.

In 1998, a group of academics at Imperial College, London, and the University of Cambridge, began the Newton Project, aiming to make every word Newton wrote, including his alchemical and biblical work, publicly available.

NICAP *see* NATIONAL INVESTIGATIONS COMMITTEE ON AERIAL PHENOMENA

nimbus *see* HALOES

nine
The ninth whole number, represented by the digit 9; considered significant in numerology.

Nine is the ninth whole number. It is seen as the number of judgement, and of spiritual and mental achievement, and represents change, invention and growth. It was considered a sacred number by the ancients, being 3 times 3, and was held to be the number of wisdom, spiritual power and mastery. It has also always been considered significant because pregnancy lasts for nine calendar months. In Classical mythology, there are nine Muses, and many Maya and Egyptian pyramids were constructed to have nine levels. It is an important number in FENG SHUI, where it is the number of perfection. In the minor ARCANA of the TAROT, the nines represent completion of a cycle, and conclusion. In the major arcana, 9 is the number associated with the Hermit card. In Hebrew GEMATRIA, 9 corresponds to the Hebrew letter Tet, and in the KABBALAH, it is the number assigned to the sephirah YESOD. In NUMEROLOGY, it is considered to be a YANG number; it is the numerical value of the letters I and R, and a person with 9 in their numerological profile is believed to be intuitive, fortunate, artistic and compassionate. A nine personality may also display the more negative traits of emotional extremes, intolerance and a tendency to be unforgiving. In Chinese culture, 9 is considered to be a lucky number, especially when used with reference to friendships and marriage, because the Chinese word for 'nine' sounds the same as the word for 'everlasting'. See also ONE; TWO; THREE; FOUR; FIVE; SIX; SEVEN; EIGHT; TEN; ELEVEN; TWELVE.

Nine, the (Council of)

An alleged group of godlike beings that maintains the balance of the universe.

People who believe in their existence describe the Nine (or Council of Nine) as a group of highly evolved beings who are charged with maintaining the balance of the universe. They are said to communicate with humankind by the process of CHANNELLING, that is, speaking through a sensitive person in much the same way as the dead are said to speak to the living through a MEDIUM.

The main source of this channelling, described as the principal 'spokesman' for the Nine, is known as Tom, identified with Atum, the father of the ancient Egyptian gods. This has led to the Nine being identified with the Ennead or nine major Egyptian gods. Through this means the messages of the Nine, mostly advocating peace, love and understanding, are given to the world. There have been various channellers, some of whom have produced books setting out the wisdom of the Nine for our edification, and believers are said to be found at all levels of society around the world, including some highly influential figures.

Among the revelations vouchsafed by the Nine is that human beings were 'planted' on earth

US doctor and psychical researcher Andrija Puharich, who is believed to have done much to spread belief in 'the Nine'. (© Mary Evans Picture Library)

by extraterrestrials, who continue to watch over mankind and are full of concern for the fate of the planet. Sightings of UFOs and ALIENS are therefore explained as part of an on-going benevolent process of observing human life.

While belief in the Nine spread rapidly in the late 1980s and early 1990s, it has been traced back to the 1950s and the career of Andrija Puharich (1918–95), US doctor and psychical researcher. It was Puharich who introduced the Indian mystic D G Vinod, the first known 'channel' for the Nine, to the West.

At the same time, Puharich was apparently involved with the CIA, especially in connection with the MKULTRA project on MIND CONTROL. He was engaged in research on the use of conscious-altering drugs, BRAINWASHING and HYPNOSIS and continued to work for the CIA until the 1970s. It has been suggested that the whole idea of the Nine was a creation of the CIA, whose motivation in doing so, although obviously connected with the field of mind control, remains unclear.

Florence Newton (c. mid-17th century)

Florence Newton, also known as the 'Witch of Youghal', was tried for WITCHCRAFT at the Cork assizes in 1661. The details of the trial have been handed down to us in the form of an account contained within Joseph Glanvill's *Saducismus Triumphatus: or, Full and plain evidence concerning witches and apparitions* (first published in 1681), which allegedly retells the story from notes taken by the trial judge.

Newton had been charged with bewitching Mary Longdon, who was a maid in Youghal in Cork, Ireland. It seems that Longdon had refused to give Newton a piece of her master's beef, at which Newton had said 'Thou had'st as good have given it me' and had left 'grumbling'. Following this, when the pair met in the road about a week later, Newton grabbed Longdon and violently kissed her, saying, 'Mary, I pray thee let thee and I be Friends; for I bear thee no ill will, and I pray thee do thou bear me none.' A few days later Longdon woke in the night to find a woman with a veil and a little old man in silk clothes, whom she took to be a spirit, standing beside her bed. The spirit lifted the veil, revealing the face of Florence Newton, and promised that if she followed his advice she would have 'all things after her own Heart' to which she replied that she would have nothing to do with him 'for her trust was in the Lord'.

The account goes on:

… within a month after the said Florence had kiss'd her, she this Defendant fell very ill of Fits or Trances, which would take her on the sudden, in that violence that three or four men could not hold her. And in her Fits she would be taken with Vomitings, and would Vomit up Needles, Pins, Horsenails, Stubbs, Wooll, and Straw, and that very often. And being asked whether she perceived at these times what she vomited? She said she did. For then she was not in so great distraction as in other parts of her Fits she was. And that a little before the first beginning of her Fits several (and very many) small stones would fall upon her as she went up and down, and would follow her from place to place, and from one room to another, and would hit her on the head, shoulders, and arms, and fall to the ground and vanish away. And that she and several others would see them both fall upon her, and on the ground, but could never take them, save only some few, which she and her Master caught in their hands. Amongst which one that had a hole in it she tied (as she was advised) with a Leather thong to her Purse, but it was vanish'd immediately, though the Leather continu'd tied on a fast Knot.

The symptoms of the bewitching described in the account are similar to those that appear in many other stories of POLTERGEISTS or demonic POSSESSION. The allegation that they were due to

nirvana

In Hinduism, Buddhism and Jainism, a higher state of being in which all worldly desires and attachments are extinguished and the individual is liberated from the cycle of reincarnation.

In Hinduism, Buddhism and JAINISM, the ultimate goal of existence is the realization of nirvana. This Sanskrit word, which means 'extinction', refers to the final release from the cycle of REINCARNATION known as *samsara* and the cessation of individual existence. It is believed that nirvana can be achieved by transcending all worldly desires and attachments. An individual who realizes nirvana is freed from the KARMA which keeps us bound in the cycle of death and rebirth; such a person ceases to accumulate any further karma from that incarnation onward, and once they have worked through all their remaining karma, they are not reborn again. In the Hindu tradition, it is thought that after the final incarnation, the soul of the enlightened person who has achieved nirvana reunites with Brahman, their ego being extinguished in a blissful reunion with the universal God or Absolute.

Buddhism does not subscribe to the notion of an individual soul or self, or to a divine being with which such a soul can be reunited, and the Buddhist view of nirvana is as the realization of this ultimate truth; nirvana is not a subjective state of consciousness, has no origin or end and has always existed. It cannot be described, only experienced. Life, and the cycle of death and rebirth, is suffering, and this suffering is caused by ignorance of the true nature of reality, and by a selfish craving for worldly things. When one has transcended earthly attachments, one attains a perfect knowledge of reality, and a state of absolute blessedness.

nixies

Female freshwater fairies of Germanic folklore.

Nixies are freshwater FAIRIES in the folklore of Germany and Switzerland. These female water spirits are said to

Newton was apparently supported by the fact that Longdon's fits became worse when Newton was in her presence and subsided when Newton was restrained in 'bolts'.

The case is interesting because it did not appear to involve the use of torture, due legal process was followed and the evidence was apparently carefully weighed. In addition to the witness testimony, Newton was tested by being asked to recite the Lord's Prayer accurately and in full (which she consistently failed to do, despite teaching) and she was also subjected to 'pricking' by a group of men who included the Irish healer VALENTINE GREATRAKES:

And so they sent for the Witch, and set her on a Stool, and a Shoemaker with a strong Awl endeavoured to stick it in the Stool, but could not till the third time. And then they bad her come off the Stool, but she said she was very weary and could not stir. Then two of them pulled her off, and the Man went to pull out his Awl, and it dropped into his hand with half an Inch broke off the blade of it, and they all looked to have found where it had been stuck, but could find no place where any entry had been made by it. Then they took another Awl, and put it into the Maid's hand, and one of them took the Maid's hand, and ran violently at the Witch's hand with it, but could not enter it, though the Awl was so bent that none of them could put it straight again. Then Mr.

Blackwall took a Launce, and launc'd one of her hands an Inch and a half long, and a quarter of an Inch deep, but it bled not at all. Then he launc'd the other hands, and then they bled.

The account contains a number of other interesting insights into the beliefs relating to witchcraft at the time. Early on in the proceedings, Newton had apparently admitted to casting the EVIL EYE over Longdon but not to 'bewitching' her which, it seems, would have been a greater crime. She also tried to implicate two others as the source of Longdon's suffering, at which point the Mayor of Youghal had suggested subjecting all three to the 'water experiment' (also known as 'ducking', 'swimming' or 'trial by water', whereby the accused would be tied and thrown into water which, being the medium of holy baptism, would 'reject' her if she was guilty). It was also alleged that, during their testing, Greatrakes and others had heard noises in the prison which Newton confessed were due to a SPIRIT (in the shape of a greyhound) that was her FAMILIAR. Finally, the account includes testimony to the effect that Newton cast a spell on David Jones, one of the prison sentries, by kissing his hand – supposedly resulting in pain in his arm and his eventual death two weeks later.

There is no record of the outcome of the trial or of what eventually happened to Florence Newton. See also WITCH TRIALS.

seduce handsome young men, visiting village dances disguised as beautiful women or appearing in the water as lovely girls with long golden hair and blue eyes – although according to some accounts, in their natural state they are completely green, including their skin, hair and teeth. If they manage to lure a young man into the water with them, he will never be seen again. It has been suggested that in some areas it was thought that if the river nixies were not given a life a year, they would take one for themselves, and so an annual human sacrifice was made. Later, although the sacrifices no longer took place, it was still considered unlucky to rescue a drowning person and deprive the nixies of what they considered to be their due. Nixies are reputedly able to call up storms and are said to trap sailors' souls in lobster pots to prevent their reaching heaven. Unlike MERMAIDS, nixies always stay close to human communities, often living in mill ponds, and they like to go shopping in markets, where they may sometimes be detected by the glimpse of a fish tail peeping out from under the hem of their long skirts, or by the trail of fresh water they

are said to leave behind them. In some accounts they have no fish tails, but give their true nature away by their webbed hands and feet. They are said to be able to live on land for long periods of time, and often marry human men and raise families with them, but there is always the danger that their original water spirit families will come to claim them back. They are particularly associated with the River Rhine.

Nordics
Humanoid entities of a type frequently reported during the early years of the modern UFO phenomenon.
'Nordics' were the most common form of ALIEN reported in Europe during the 1950s. The name refers to the fact that their appearance was said to be similar to that popularly associated with people of Scandinavian origin.

Britain's first well-documented alleged alien encounter took place during the major European WAVE of 1954. A young mother, Jessie Roestenberg, and her two young children claimed that they had been involved in a scary encounter in an isolated farmhouse at Ranton, Staffordshire, on 21 October of that year. They were apparently forced to hide under a table as a lens-shaped craft circled over the roof of the house. Roestenberg said that behind a window set into a dome on the UFO were two Nordic entities staring down on the scene with a 'wistful' expression, as if they tourists. The beings were very human in appearance, with long blond hair and blue eyes – distinguishing features of this alien type. This type of alien was significantly different to the GREYS that now dominate ALIEN ABDUCTION cases and, when Roestenberg was asked about greys 30 years after her own encounter, she reportedly said: 'I do not believe in little men – not after what I have seen.'

During the 1950s one-fifth of all reported sightings of aliens were Nordics, and the proportion was higher still in Europe. They were rarely reported to engage in any kind of hostile act or carry out medical tests on witnesses – they were usually said to be just observing or communicating using telepathic powers (see TELEPATHY). Mrs Roestenberg, like many other people who claimed to have met Nordics, apparently found herself receiving PSYCHIC messages after the sighting. Other 'magical' aspects of the behaviour attributed to Nordics include an ability to materialize and dematerialize inside rooms. The messages conveyed to witnesses often reportedly involved ecological warnings or the expression of a desire for peace. There were also some intriguing cases in which Nordics were said to be aware of the presence on earth of their rivals, the greys, and had apparently given warnings that humans should avoid them.

Reports involving Nordics fell steadily from the 1960s onwards, holding on longest in Europe, and they now very rarely feature in UFO claims.

north *see* DIRECTIONS, FOUR

North Berwick witches

An alleged coven of witches from the 16th century, the 'exposure' of which resulted in what is probably the most famous Scottish witchcraft trial and even involved King James VI (James I of England).

The story of the North Berwick witches began in 1590 when a maid called Gillis Duncan who worked for David Seaton in Tranent, near Edinburgh, was accused by him of WITCHCRAFT. Seaton had apparently become suspicious of her new-found healing gifts and habit of sneaking out of the house at night. Duncan was tortured on the instruction of Seaton, a horrific process involving the used of 'pilliwinks' (thumbscrews) and 'thrawing' (twisting and jerking the head using a rope). She was then searched for the

A contemporary illustration of James VI and I examining the North Berwick Witches, which appeared in 'Newes from Scotland'. (© Mary Evans Picture Library)

DEVIL'S MARK, which was apparently found on her throat, and eventually confessed.

While in prison, Duncan supposedly provided a long list of the other WITCHES in the area with whom she had been involved. These included four who were then brought to trial: Agnes Sampson, an elderly woman from Haddington; a schoolmaster from Saltpans called John Fian; and two gentlewomen, Euphemia Maclean and Barbara Napier. JAMES VI AND I and a number of noblemen became involved in the interrogations (possibly because of the high standing of some of those accused and, more particularly, because of Maclean's association with the Earl of Bothwell who was a pretender to the throne). Agnes Sampson was shaved and the Devil's mark apparently found on her genitals. She was then tortured and deprived of sleep until she too gave in. In a long and colourful confession she admitted that the accused witches had attended SABBATS on HALLOWE'EN in the company of scores of others, entered into a pact with the devil (see DEVIL'S PACT) at North Berwick church, sailed on the sea in a sieve and, crucially, plotted to kill the king. There had been a number of attempts to kill the king by means of magic, the most famous being the alleged attempt to raise a storm to drown him while he was sailing to Denmark (see CATS).

James VI and I was apparently highly sceptical when presented with these wild 'confessions'. However, according to his own account, it was at this point that Agnes Sampson gave proof of her powers by whispering to him the exact words that had passed between him and his new bride on their wedding night. This convinced him of their guilt and, despite reservations on the part of others involved in the trial, he ensured that all four were found guilty. They were condemned to death, although it is believed that Barbara Napier's execution was delayed because she was pregnant, and that she was later set free. The Earl of Bothwell was arrested and imprisoned in Edinburgh, but later escaped. It is not known how many of the others accused of witchcraft and treason were finally tried and convicted.

The circumstances of this trial – its development from a single allegation, to the involvement of a number of noble families and the apparent uncovering of a plot against the king – would strongly suggest that the motives of those who prosecuted it were wholly political. It is especially interesting to note that, although James VI and I went on to gain something of a reputation as a demonologist, in trials other than that of the North Berwick witches he took a more sober approach and often acted to try to curb some of the judicial excesses of the time.

Northern Lights *see* AURORA BOREALIS

Nostradamus (1503–66)

French physician and astrologer, also known as Michel de Nostredame. His enigmatic predictions, written in rhymed quatrains, have established him as one of the most famous prophets in history.

Michel de Notredame, better known as Nostradamus, was born in Provence, France. He was Jewish by birth, but his family had converted to the Roman Catholic faith. From his youth, he showed an aptitude for mathematics, astronomy and ASTROLOGY, and studied medicine at the University of Montpellier, becoming a doctor of medicine in 1529. A skilled apothecary, he travelled around France helping to treat victims of the plague, and during these travels, he is said to have met and exchanged information with a number of underground alchemists, kabbalists and mystics. In 1537, after the death of his first wife and children, he resumed his travels all over France and Italy, exploring more mystical teachings and moving away from medicine to the OCCULT. He remarried and settled down again in 1547, and rumours about his powers as a prophet began to circulate.

He then began on the body of work for which he would become famous – *Les Propheties*. This was a set of almost a thousand four-line rhymed poems, called quatrains, grouped into sets called 'centuries' because each group contained around a hundred poems. Nostradamus used a form of SCRYING in order to achieve the meditative state in which he composed these prophetic verses; this usually involved his gazing into a brass bowl filled with water. The first edition of his *Propheties* was published in 1555, and contained over 300 poems; the second edition, published 1557, contained an additional 300 or so quatrains, and the third edition, published in 1568, two years after his death, included another 300 new poems. Each of the ten centuries is usually referred to by a Roman numeral from I to X. Most of these poems deal with the prediction of some sort of disaster, such as plagues, earthquakes, wars, fires, floods and droughts, although the prophecies do not appear to have been written sequentially by date. The quatrains are in general written in a very obscure and ambiguous style, using cryptic language and a mixture of Provençal, Greek, Latin, Italian and even Hebrew and Arabic. It is generally held that he wrote in such an enigmatic way in order to avoid persecution by the INQUISITION. When the first edition was published, it had a mixed reception; some people believed him to be an agent of evil, some a fraud, some a madman, and others a divinely inspired prophet. Soon he was being sought by the nobility for his HOROSCOPES and predictions, and Catherine de Medici, queen consort of King Henry II of France, had him made the royal Counsellor and Physician-in-Ordinary.

Nostradamus has been credited with predicting many world events, such as the French Revolution, the rise of Hitler and the assassination of John F Kennedy. However, sceptics say that his reputation as a prophet is largely the result of modern-day supporters 'shoehorning' his highly obscure and metaphorical words to make them fit an event which as already happened – known as 'retroactive clairvoyance' – or of selective thinking. His writings have been frequently misquoted or altered by his believers to link them retrospectively to an event, and a number of quatrains have even been completely fabricated. But since his death in 1566, over 400 books and essays have been published about his writings, and today, more than four centuries later, people everywhere still puzzle over and debate the meanings of his quatrains.

numbers

Abstract entities used to describe quantity. The most familiar type of numbers, and the most significant in various occult and esoteric contexts, are the natural numbers (0, 1, 2, 3, 4, 5, etc) which are used for counting.

A number is an abstract entity used to describe quantity. The most basic and familiar type of number is the natural number, used in counting for thousands of years; natural numbers are usually represented by the Arabic numerals 0, 1, 2, 3, 4, 5 and so on, although these numerals were only introduced to Europe in the Middle Ages. Before the 13th century, Roman numerals (I, II, III, IV, V, etc) were still in use in Europe, but then the Italian mathematician Leonardo

Fibonacci, realizing that Arabic numerals would be much easier to use in arithmetic that Roman ones, played a major role in introducing the modern Arabic positional decimal system to the West. The numeral 0, or zero, was the last one to be created in most number systems, since it is not a counting number.

Some numbers have special mathematical and arithmetical qualities. Prime numbers are natural numbers greater than 1, whose only positive divisors are 1 and themselves: 2, 3, 5, 7, 11, 13, 19, 23 and so on, with 2 being the only even prime number. Perfect numbers are natural numbers which are the sum of all their divisors, such as 6 (1 + 2 + 3) or 28 (1 + 2 + 4 + 7 + 14). Many ancient cultures endowed perfect numbers with special magical and religious significance (see MAGICAL NUMBERS). Triangular numbers are natural numbers which can be formed by adding consecutive integers: 1, (1 + 2 =) 3, (1 + 2 + 3 =) 6, (1 + 2 + 3 + 4 =) 10, (1 + 2 + 3 + 4 + 5 =) 15, and so on; all perfect numbers are also triangular numbers. The Fibonacci sequence (0, 1, 1, 2, 3, 5, 8, 13 …), in which each number is the sum of the previous two, is sometimes referred to as 'nature's numbering system', because its numbers are found so frequently in living things, such as the arrangement of leaves and the number of petals in plants and flowers, the shape and curve of a spiral shell and the number of bracts in a pine cone.

Alchemists, magicians and occultists have been fascinated by numbers throughout the centuries, and the study of the mystical significance of numbers can be traced back to the ancient Babylonians. PYTHAGORAS taught that each number represented an eternal truth, with certain combinations of numbers representing the interactions between humanity and the divine. Various types of NUMEROLOGY have been developed all over the world by those seeking the hidden meanings behind numbers, and numbers are of particular importance in Hebrew spirituality and the KABBALAH, especially in its use of GEMATRIA, in which Hebrew letters are replaced by corresponding numbers, with the result that every Hebrew word has a numerical equivalent and numbers can thus be used in an attempt to discover hidden links between scripture and ideas. Another magical use of numbers is in the MAGIC SQUARE, a grid of figures which total the same number whether they are added up horizontally, vertically or diagonally. Such squares are often used in TALISMANS.

In China, certain numbers are seen as being lucky or unlucky because their homophones have auspicious or inauspicious meanings. THREE is an especially magical number in many cultures, and features prominently in folklore and mythology, with the threefold repetition of an action being one of the

most characteristic motifs in many fairy tales; the first two attempts usually fail, but the third brings success. Many fairy tales feature two older sisters or brothers and a younger one, or three tasks to be performed. SEVEN also has a long history as a lucky and magical number. See also ONE; TWO; FOUR; FIVE; SIX; EIGHT; NINE; TEN; ELEVEN; TWELVE; THIRTEEN.

numbers, magical *see* MAGICAL NUMBERS

numerology
The study of the occult meanings of numbers and their supposed influence on human beings and events.
Numerology, the study of names and numbers for character analysis and DIVINATION, was a popular practice among early mathematicians, and the Greek mathematician and mystic PYTHAGORAS is considered to have been the father of Western numerology. He stated that 'The world is built upon the power of numbers' and that all of nature is systematically ordered and consists of a set of numerical relationships; numbers are the measure of form and energy in the world, and everything can be computed and understood through the study of these numbers. The belief that dates and times have a numerological significance is based on the idea that the underlying vibrations of the universe happen in regular cycles, and that anything created or altered at a given point in a cycle will demonstrate the properties created by the vibrations at that point.

Historians believe that modern numerology is a combination of teachings from various sources: the ancient Babylonians; Pythagoras and his followers; Graeco-Egyptian astrological philosophy; early Christian mysticism; and the Jewish system of the KABBALAH known as GEMATRIA. Following the First Council of Nicaea in AD 325, numerology was, along with divination and MAGIC, condemned as an unapproved practice, but although it was suppressed by the official Church, its many adherents kept it alive in secret. In the early 1900s, Mrs L Dow Balliett pioneered a system of spiritual teachings based in Pythagorean theory, and is generally credited with the westernization of numerology; she greatly influenced another scholar, Dr Juno Jordan, who founded the Californian Institute of Numerical Research and made a comprehensive study of numerology for 25 years.

As with Pythagoras's system, the numbers 1 to 9 are the basis of modern numerology. Any numbers which total more than 9 have their digits added together repeatedly until they give a single digit. The numbers of a person's birth date and time, and the numerical equivalencies of their name, are used to analyse their character and predict upcoming events and trends in their life. There are generally held to be four core numbers in a subject's numerological profile: the Life Path Number, which is calculated from the birth date numbers; the Destiny Number, calculated from the numerical values of the birth name – A to I and J to R being numbered 1 to 9, and S to Z being numbered 1 to 8; the Soul Number, derived from the vowels in the birth name; and the Personality Number, taken from the consonants in the birth name. Some systems include a fifth core number, the Maturity Number, which is worked out by adding the Life Path Number and the Destiny Number, but the full impact of this number is not thought to become operational until after the age of 35. Using these core numbers it is believed that a character analysis can be determined, and the subject can map out his or her life so as to avoid negative influences and find the best way to fulfil their potential. Numerologists hold that life operates on a repeated nine-year cycle, and that each year has a number which has a particular meaning. The number 0 is also significant; it is thought to represent unformed energy which is filled with potential, and it intensifies the qualities of any number which it follows.

The numbers 11, 22, 33, and any other double-digit number in which a single number repeats itself, are considered particularly significant in numerology, and are known as master numbers. A master number appearing in a person's numerological profile is thought to reveal a particular kind of potential, and is said to indicate spiritual gifts which make the person highly intuitive and in touch with their own spirituality; numerologists believe that those with a master number in their profile have a special responsibility to help mankind. See also ONE; TWO; THREE; FOUR; FIVE; SIX; SEVEN; EIGHT; NINE; TEN; ELEVEN; TWELVE.

nunda

A ferocious mystery cat reported from the coastal forest regions of Tanzania.

Judging from an appreciable amount of intriguing anecdotal evidence currently on record, Africa may house several types of large cat still eluding scientific detection. The most formidable of these is the nunda ('fierce animal') or mngwa ('strange one' in Swahili), reported from Tanzania's coastal forests. It is described by native hunters as a huge, terrifying man-eating cat, with tabby-striped fur and great claw-bearing paws that leave behind tracks resembling a leopard's in shape, but comparable in size to those of large lions.

Victims of alleged attacks by nundas, as well as nunda fur and tracks, have been examined by animal experts, who are convinced that such a creature does exist. It has been suggested by some cryptozoologists that the ferocious nunda, which has occasionally been heard to purr but never roar, may be a gigantic version of the African golden cat *Felis auratus*. This is a medium-sized species with a considerably variable coat, which inhabits many parts of tropical Africa and is greatly feared by its human neighbours, but is very elusive and rarely seen.

nymphs

Female nature spirits of Greek mythology, often regarded as minor goddesses.

In ancient Greece, nymphs were female spirits who were believed to inhabit and guard rivers, woods and other natural features. They were all beautiful, and personified youth and fertility (their name comes from the Greek word for a bride) and were often the objects of desire of lustful satyrs. Nymphs were classified into various types, according to their habitat, and were usually bound to a particular location. Land nymphs were divided into alseids, nymphs of groves; auloniads, nymphs of pastures; leimakids, who inhabited meadows; orestiads or OREADS, nymphs of mountains, caves and grottoes; DRYADS and hamadryads, nymphs of trees; and napaeae, who were found in mountain valleys and glens. Water nymphs were classified into naiads, the nymphs of streams; crinaeae, the nymphs of fountains; limnades, nymphs of lakes; pegageae, who lived in springs; potameides, found in rivers; the eleionamae, the nymphs of marshes; and the nereids or oceanides, the sea nymphs. Nymphs were the traditional companions of Artemis, the goddess of the Moon and of hunting, and in Greek mythology they often acted as foster-mothers to the heroes and infant gods.

oaths

Solemn promises or statements of fact in which the oath-taker calls on something he or she considers sacred, usually a deity, to witness the binding nature of the promise or the truth of the statement.

Oaths exist in various forms all over the world. It is probable that the earliest oaths were specifically religious in nature, with a divinity being invoked directly to witness the solemnity of the oath. Oath-taking was common in ancient Israel; the Scroll of the Law was held and the oath was sworn by God or one of his attributes, and involved a kind of self-curse which would be activated if the conditions of the oath were broken by the one swearing it. This calling on something which the oath-taker regards as sacred, such as a deity, to witness the binding nature of a promise or the truth of a statement, appears in almost all cultures. In India, the water of the holy river, the Ganges, may be sworn on, while in Christian societies, the Bible is traditionally used. In the majority of oaths, the implication is that divine retribution is being invited if the oath is not kept. Many folk tales are based on the motif of the perjured oath, in which the penalty invited by the oath-taker befalls him because he has sworn falsely.

Oaths of secrecy are often sworn by initiates to SECRET SOCIETIES such as the Freemasons (see FREEMASONRY), or various occult groups, to preserve the privacy of the other members and the mysteries of the society, while newly appointed government officials also frequently swear oaths before taking office. Witnesses in court trials are required to take an oath to tell the truth, traditionally swearing on a book of scripture, while physicians still take the Hippocratic oath which binds them to the code of medical ethics contained in it. Certain religious groups, such as the Quakers and the Mennonites, object to the taking of oaths, citing the words of Jesus in Matthew 5, where he warns against elaborate formal promises and advises simply, 'Let your "yes" be "yes", and your "no", "no"'.

OBE *see* OUT-OF-BODY EXPERIENCE

Obeah

A Jamaican form of shamanistic magic.

Obeah, or Obi, is a form of Afro-Caribbean SHAMANISM, found particularly in Jamaica. Rather than a popular religion like VOUDUN, CANDOMBLÉ and SANTERÍA, Obeah is closer to MAGIC, and is sometimes thought of as a form of WITCHCRAFT – the word 'Obeah' means 'sorcery' in Ashanti. As quite often happens with a religion, the name was originally imposed by its opponents, the West Africans (Ashanti) in Jamaica being antagonistic to the Central African (Congo) practitioners of Obeah.

Despite some interpretations of Obeah as 'dark occult', partly because of the origin of its name, it is really more a form of folk magic, employed for healing, love charms, wealth and good luck – magic being inherently practical and results-orientated. People go to the SHAMAN for spells or for advice, and are often given TALISMANS or AMULETS, which themselves are also known as Obeah or Obi.

Obeah is actually closer to Hoodoo than to VOUDUN, Hoodoo being a form of folk magic with Central African origins and incorporating Native American practices, found in the USA.

obelisks

Tall, four-sided tapering stone pillars of ancient Egypt.

The ancient Egyptian stone pillars known as obelisks were originally erected in pairs outside the portals of temples. They were four-sided and tapered to a pyramidal point which was usually sheathed in copper. Each side was carved with hieroglyphics, usually recording the life and deeds of the pharaoh who commissioned the monument. It is thought that their purpose was both to commemorate a great king and to direct the immortal record of his life upwards to where he was enjoying the AFTERLIFE. Many have been removed from their original Egyptian locations, whether as the trophies of conquering armies or given as gifts by modern Egyptian governments. It is estimated that at present there are more intact obelisks outside Egypt than in it.

Perhaps the best known of these is 'Cleopatra's Needle', which was originally erected at Heliopolis c.1500 BC by the Pharaoh Thutmose III. The Roman Emperor Augustus had it moved to Alexandria c.14 BC, whence it was moved in turn to London in 1878. Its original partner column is in New York City. The tallest known obelisk, at almost 33.5 metres (110 feet), is in Rome, where it was brought from Heliopolis by the Emperor Caligula c.37 AD.

Most obelisks are of granite and seem to have been quarried at Aswan and then floated down the Nile. Nothing is known for certain, however, of the methods used to erect them.

Occult *see panel p496*

occult symbols *see* SYMBOLS

odour of sanctity
A sweet smell associated with the body of a saint.
One of the phenomena taken throughout the Christian era as evidence of sainthood is the odour of sanctity: a pleasant fragrance (most often described as the scent of flowers) detected when a holy person dies. If an individual is described as dying in the odour of sanctity, this means that he or she dies a saint. This was taken as proof of sanctity even in the case of people whose lives appeared to have been less than holy.

A similar odour is said to replace the stench of putrefaction when the body of such a person is exhumed for reburial or as part of the beatification process. According to Pope Benedict XIV (1675–1758):

> That the human body may by nature not have an overtly unpleasant odour is possible, but that it should actually have a pleasing smell – that is beyond nature. If such an agreeable odour exists, whether there does or does not exist a natural cause capable of producing it, it must be owing

to some higher course and thus deemed to be miraculous.

The odour of sanctity is particularly associated with saints whose bodies are incorruptible (see INCORRUPTIBILITY). The idea of a pleasant fragrance being associated with the divine predates Christianity, however. For example, Classical poets often describe the perfumes sensed whenever a deity appears.

ogham
An ancient alphabet used in Celtic and Pictish inscriptions; also, a modern form of divination based on this alphabet.
The ogham is an alphabet which was used by the ancient Celts and Picts. It appears on inscriptions cut on the edges of rough standing gravestones found throughout the British Isles, principally in southern Ireland and Wales, and dating between around 300 and AD 500. It has 20 main characters, which consist of one to five perpendicular or angular strokes either meeting or crossing a single, vertical line; their form allows them to be carved easily on wood or stone. An Irish medieval manuscript, *The Book of Ballymote*, provided an overview of the alphabet's characters and explained their meanings, suggesting that each character could be related to a tree or plant such as ash, oak, vine or reed. Then in the 20th century, the ogham came to prominence with Robert Graves's 1948 book *The White Goddess: A Historical Grammar of Poetic Myth*, which included two chapters on the spiritual meaning of the ogham. While most modern critics consider this work as imaginative rather than strictly factual, it helped to spark off a new interest in the ogham.

Although there is no historical evidence that

Stones showing letters of the ogham alphabet; such stones are used as a divination tool. (© TopFoto)

Occult

The word 'occult' comes from the Latin *occultus*, meaning hidden, secret or unknown, and occultism may be defined as the doctrine or study of mysterious or hidden things. The term 'occult' is commonly used to refer to knowledge meant only for certain people, or knowledge that must be kept hidden, but is often misused as being almost synonymous with 'evil' or 'satanic'. Strictly speaking, the word has no moral connotations; for most of its practitioners, occultism is simply the study of a deeper reality that cannot be understood using pure reason or the physical sciences, and nowadays, information on the beliefs and practices of occultists is, far from being hidden or secret, readily accessible in print and on the Internet.

What exactly constitutes the occult has always been something of a grey area, although it is generally associated with MAGIC in some way. Some people's use of the term encompasses all forms of magic, WITCHCRAFT and SORCERY, while many would also include fields such as ASTROLOGY, NUMEROLOGY and all forms of DIVINATION. Others consider all aspects of the PARANORMAL to be occult. The major monotheistic religions such as Christianity, Judaism and Islam officially proscribe occult practices. However, although Islam forbids the practice of sorcery, known as *Sither*, the occult sciences, which include divination, astrology and PROPHECY, are regarded as celestial rather than infernal knowledge, and some forms of Islam permit the spirits known as DJINN to be commanded in the name of Allah to do righteous works. Similarly, the Jewish mystical system of the KABBALAH, while not conforming to mainstream Jewish ritual, has always been a permitted area of study for rabbis and chosen students, and many GRIMOIRES of the late medieval period demonstrate a form of Christianized magic, in which the MAGICIAN is advised to strengthen himself with fasting, prayers and sacraments before invoking divine power to summon DEMONS and coerce them into serving his (usually worldly) magical goals.

The dividing line between the occult and science has also, until relatively recently, been somewhat indistinct; astronomy and astrology were for many centuries closely intertwined, and astrology and ALCHEMY (which might be considered the forerunner of chemistry) were popularly practised among the educated upper classes between the 14th and 17th centuries in an attempt to gain an understanding of the workings of the universe. Many notable scientists and philosophers, such as PLATO, PYTHAGORAS, ALBERTUS MAGNUS, AGRIPPA VON NETTESHEIM, PARACELSUS and Francis Bacon, have had a deep and lasting influence on occult studies and practices; and ISAAC NEWTON, often credited with being the father of modern science, worked extensively outside the strict bounds of science and mathematics, and wrote a number of largely unpublished works which included what would now be regarded as occult studies – particularly alchemy.

Modern occult ideas were born in the Renaissance, when the focus was on uniting the individual soul with God. The work which most influenced Renaissance occultists was the group of Greek writings collectively known as the HERMETICA. Almost as significant was the kabbalah, since this group of Jewish mystical texts was interpreted by Christian Renaissance scholars and many of its rituals were adopted for occult magic. The spiritual philosophy of Neoplatonism, which held that the universe was full of powers whose secrets could be unlocked by those who sought knowledge of them, was widely popular among educated people, as was the study of alchemy, on whose principles entire occult systems have been built. The traditional initiatory movement of Rosicrucianism (see ROSICRUCIANS), one of Christianity's best-known mystical branches, has influenced most Christian-based occultism since the 17th century, and the visionary writings of the 17th-century theosophist and MYSTIC, JACOB BÖHME, influenced occultists in Germany, Holland and England.

During the 17th century, the rise of two schools of thought – scientific rationalism and Protestantism (which sought to remove from religious practice what it regarded as 'magical' ritual elements) – drove occultism underground. Those who practised it were attracted to the numerous SECRET SOCIETIES which were established at this time, such as the Rosicrucians and FREEMASONRY. In the 19th century, occultism and magic made a remarkable comeback. It was an age when established religions were declining, and many people sought other keys to the mysteries of the universe. The THEOSOPHICAL SOCIETY, founded by MADAME BLAVATSKY, played a major part in spreading occult ideas at the turn of the century, and was responsible for introducing Eastern ideas about REINCARNATION to Western occultists. It greatly influenced the modern Western magical tradition, and its roots were deeply intertwined with those of the magical fraternity of the HERMETIC ORDER OF THE GOLDEN DAWN, founded in the 1880s by MACGREGOR MATHERS, among others. The Golden Dawn assembled the work of earlier occultists such as ÉLIPHAS LÉVI, and focused on the ceremonial magic form (see MAGIC, CEREMONIAL), with its disciplined practice of ritual INVOCATION and EVOCATION for the working of high magic (see MAGIC, HIGH).

When a one-time member of the Golden Dawn, ALEISTER CROWLEY, the self-styled GREAT BEAST and the most notorious occultist of the 20th century, published most of the order's material (and added his own voluminous writings) he provided the occult community with a coherent body of magical thought and practice to which most ceremonial magic groups still owe a great debt. His ideas remain influential to this day, and helped to shape modern WITCHCRAFT. Another former member of the Golden Dawn, DION FORTUNE, rejected the Eastern influence in THEOSOPHY and turned instead to a mystical Christianity and to the mythology of Britain, particularly Arthurian legend. She was one of the first occult writers to approach magic using the principles of psychology, and her writings are valued as a rich source of ritual; the practices and ceremonial aspects of contemporary witchcraft again owe much to her works.

Throughout the 20th century, occultism continued to grow and diversify. In its search for a new order based on spiritual enlightenment, the NEW AGE movement, which originated in the 1960s, introduced many people to the principles of SHAMANISM and Eastern spiritual systems such as ZEN BUDDHISM, YOGA and TANTRA, and many other practices commonly regarded as occult, such as the use of the TAROT. The late 1960s also saw the rise of SATANISM, a religious or philosophical movement based on the recognition or worship of SATAN, either in a literal form or, more commonly, as a symbol of man's carnal nature. Satanists focus on the spiritual advancement of the SELF, rather than on submission to a deity or set of moral codes, and of the several traditions of Satanism, the best-known is the CHURCH OF SATAN, founded by ANTON LA VEY in 1966.

From the various forms of modern witchcraft, or WICCA, to the wide variety of Western magical traditions, such as Egyptian magic, the northern tradition of Odinism, Celtic magic and modern Druidism (see DRUIDS), most Western occultism is based on some form of spirituality and the idea of an otherworld, or realm of spiritual beings. In the form of ritual magic (see MAGIC, RITUAL) known as THEURGY, benevolent deities or other supernatural powers are invoked with the aim of uniting the magician with the divine, or raising him to a higher spiritual level. However, unlike most other magical paths, chaos magic (see MAGIC, CHAOS), which originated in the late 1970s and was inspired by the magical philosophy developed by AUSTIN OSMAN SPARE (a pupil of Aleister Crowley) is not a spiritual one, but takes a highly pragmatic approach to the occult; its practitioners are encouraged to use whatever technique, belief system or SYMBOL works for a given purpose, and then discard it. It may even use material from fiction and popular culture, such as the 'Cthulhu mythos' from the writings of H P LOVECRAFT.

Divination, whether by SCRYING, RUNES, astrology or other means, is an occult practice which is almost as old as history. Rulers, particularly powerful ones, have historically made use of diviners and fortune-tellers (see FORTUNE-TELLING). Elizabeth I's astrologer royal and personal adviser, JOHN DEE, believed he could contact the angels through scrying. MacGregor Mathers later developed Dee's system (see MAGIC, ENOCHIAN), and Enochian magic was incorporated into the Golden Dawn, influencing the work of Aleister Crowley. PALMISTRY has always been another popular form of divination, and one of the most colourful occult figures of the 20th century, CHEIRO, enjoyed a highly successful lifelong career practising this art. Also central to many magical practices is the tarot, which is regarded by occultists as much more than simply a means of divination (CARTOMANCY); in the 19th century, Éliphas Lévi linked it to the kabbalah and the 22 letters of the Hebrew alphabet, and his theories were further developed by the Golden Dawn and Crowley.

Horror films and novels have popularized a sensational image of the occult in which SORCERERS, WITCHES and WARLOCKS practise black magic (see MAGIC, BLACK) and NECROMANCY, call up demons, harm their enemies with CURSES and make DEVIL's PACTS in which they sell their SOULS for earthly gain, like FAUST. However, this bears little or no resemblance to historical fact. Since ancient times, humans have always sought spiritual knowledge and an understanding of the mysteries of the universe, and this is, as it has been throughout history, the true nature of occultism.

Lorna Gilmour

the ancient Druids used it for anything other than communication, the ogham has, in recent years, been studied and developed as a divination tool which operates in a similar way to RUNES. Each of the 20 characters, known as *fid*, is named after the sacred tree or plant to which it corresponds, and each of these trees or plants has a meaning associated with it. From a set of 20 sticks or cards, each with a *fid* inscribed on it, the diviner thinks of a question and then draws one without looking. Its meaning is interpreted. Alternatively, three *fid* may be drawn, the first representing the past, the second the present, and the third the future.

Ogopogo *see* LAKE OKANAGAN MONSTER

ogre
An ugly man-eating creature of roughly human form, larger than a man but smaller than a giant, most commonly encountered in northern European folklore.
Ogre-type figures appear all over the world, in the folklore of such countries as India, Japan and Scandinavia, but are most commonly encountered in the folklore and fairy tales of northern Europe. The word 'ogre' is French in origin, and appears to have entered the language with the publication of Charles Perrault's *Fairy Tales* in 1687. Ogres are described as being human in form but taller and broader than a man, though smaller than giants. They are extremely ugly, with big round heads, deformed faces, very hairy bodies, huge bellies and often a hump on their backs, but they can change their shape at will to become any animal or object. They can see in dim light and like to live in caves, or magnificent underground palaces. The ogres of Norse mythology caused storms and earthquakes by hitting the ground with their iron clubs. Ogres smell like rotting meat, which is not surprising since their favourite food is human flesh, and they are hostile, aggressive and fearless. However, they are also slow-moving, clumsy and stupid, and can often be outrun or outwitted. Ogres appear frequently in children's fairy tales, and the witch in the story of Hansel and Gretel is a female ogre (ogress). The way in which she is tricked into getting inside her own oven to be roasted alive is typical of the gullibility traditionally attributed to ogres.

oils
Viscous substances obtained from animals or plants. Oils have been used for religious, magical and healing purposes since ancient times, and are an essential component in aromatherapy.
Oils are viscous substances obtained from animals and plants, and the practice of anointing with oils for a number of purposes has been a common feature of almost every religion and culture since ancient times. Ritual anointing with oil is generally performed to banish negative influences, such as evil spirits thought to cause disease, or to introduce a sacramental or divine spirit or power.

The practice is frequently mentioned in the scriptures; high priests and kings are sometimes referred to as 'the anointed', as also are prophets. In Christian Europe, the Frankish Merovingian dynasty is said to have been the first to incorporate anointing into the coronation ceremony to represent the conferring on the king of the Church's religious sanction of his divine right to rule, a practice still found in many coronation rituals to this day. For the Greeks and Hebrews, anointing was also an act performed on a guest or oneself to refresh and invigorate the body, and the custom is still practised in some parts of the Middle East.

Oils have also, for many centuries, been used for healing purposes – originally as an actual healing agent, and later as a symbol of God's healing power – and the bodies of the dead are anointed in some religions and cultures. The Anointing of the Sick with consecrated oil, known as chrism, is one of the sacraments of the Catholic Church, also referred to as Extreme Unction.

Most magical groups anoint members during their initiation, and magical tools are anointed as part of their consecration. Essential oils are used to anoint candles for spells, burned as incense or worn for magical purposes. They are also used in AROMATHERAPY and aromatherapy massage.

Oimelc *see* IMBOLC

ointment, flying *see* FLYING OINTMENT

Old Moore
English astrologer.
Francis Moore (1657–1715) was born in Bridgnorth, Shropshire, and practised medicine at the court of Charles II in London. He was also an astrologer (see ASTROLOGY), and between 1698 and 1713 he published the annual 'Francis Moore's Almanac' containing predictions for the year ahead, particularly for the weather, and also medical and herbal remedies.

So successful was this that it was continued by others after his death, beginning with the London Liveried Stationers Company, becoming known as 'Old Moore's Almanac' and being published annually to this day.

The publication contains predictions on a range of topics, from politics and international affairs to horseracing and the love lives of celebrities. It also gives details of high and low tides and lighting-up times.

Oliver

A highly controversial ape capable of walking erect on his hind legs and claimed by some to be a crossbreed between a chimpanzee and a human.

Sometimes dubbed 'the humanzee', Oliver is one of the most discussed and most controversial mystery apes of all time. He first came to public attention during the mid-1970s, when he was exhibited at various conventions and learned society meetings by his owner, a New York attorney called Michael Miller, and as a result was filmed for several television news reports. What was so astonishing about Oliver was not just his appearance – superficially resembling a chimpanzee but with a bald head, prominent jaws and virtually no body scent – but his extraordinary ability to walk totally erect in an apparently habitual manner.

Oliver the 'humanzee', photographed at a press conference in New York in March 1976. (© Bettmann/ Corbis)

As a result, speculation as to Oliver's true identity became rife, with suggestions ranging from a mutant chimpanzee, or a hybrid between the common chimpanzee and the pygmy chimpanzee or bonobo, to an unknown species of ape, and, most sensational of all, a genuine crossbreed between a human and a chimpanzee. However, this fascinating riddle seemed destined never to be solved, because after a few years in the limelight, Oliver vanished. Miller had apparently sold him, and there were rumours that after changing ownership several times Oliver had eventually been purchased by a scientific research laboratory.

Then in the late 1990s, news of Oliver's whereabouts finally emerged. He had been living at a Texan animal sanctuary called Primarily Primates since 1996, and during his previous years at the research laboratory had never been used as a test specimen, although he was arthritic through having been confined in a small cage there for long periods of time. In 1998, a team of US geneticists who had been intrigued by Oliver's mysterious taxonomic status published the results of their sequence analysis of samples of his mitochondrial DNA – an analysis that would finally determine his true identity beyond any shadow of doubt. Their study revealed that Oliver's chromosomes' appearance, number and arrangement were totally consistent with those of the common chimpanzee *Pan troglodytes*, and that genetically he compared most closely with West African chimps – suggesting that this is where he had originated from all those years ago. Oliver's upright walking stance was probably nothing more than a learned ability, acquired by training – just as he had also learnt how to drink from a cup and smoke cigars – and his jaws looked strange simply because teeth had been removed.

Om

The most sacred syllable in Hinduism, which is believed to be the primal sound from which all things were created; it is placed at the beginning and end of most Hindu sacred writings and is used as a mantra.

Om, or Aum, is the most sacred and representative sound in Hinduism, in which it is regarded as the syllable of supreme reality. It first appears in the Vedic scriptures, and is placed at the beginning and end of most Hindu sacred writings. It is often regarded as the *bija*, or seed, of all MANTRAS, and many other mantras begin with it. In Hindu philosophy, all things, ideas and entities have a name and form, and the most basic of these is the primordial vibration of Om, which is believed to be the first manifested name-form of Brahman, or Absolute Reality. According to Hindu cosmology, the whole universe stemmed from its sound; before the beginning, Brahman was one and non-dual, but caused a vibration which eventually became the Om sound, and this sound set creation in motion.

It symbolizes, in its three sounds, the Hindu triad of Brahma, Vishnu and Shiva: the A sound, represents creation, when all existence issued from Brahma, the creator; the U sound corresponds to Vishnu, the god of maintenance; and the M sound represents Shiva, the destroyer. Its written symbol consists of three curves, which represent the three states of waking, sleeping and dreaming; a dot, representing the absolute state of consciousness, which illuminates the other three states; and a semicircle, which represents *maya*, the illusion that the physical world is the only reality. The symbol thus represents the infinite Brahman and the entire cosmos.

It is sometimes referred to as the *Pranava* mantra, and the vibration produced by chanting it is thought to correspond to the original vibration of creation. Its sounds are said to operate on the energy centres or CHAKRAS of the body, and chanting it is believed to drive out worldly thoughts and fill the chanter with vigour and strength.

Sikhs, Jains and Buddhists also attach great significance to it as a mantra and it is widely used in YOGA; in Buddhism, the syllable is nearly always transliterated as Om, rather than Aum.

omens

Phenomena or occurrences seen as a sign of some future event, either good or bad.

Since ancient times people of all cultures have believed that future events, both good and bad, cast a shadow before them, which can be read by those who have the wisdom to recognize it. The interpretation of omens is a form of DIVINATION, and in most ancient and shamanic cultures, this function was performed professionally by the recognized holy man. ORNITHOMANCY, the interpretation of the flight and behaviour of birds, is a form of omen-reading found all over the world, the most famous example being the AUGURY practised by the priests of ancient Rome. Omens were also read by Roman priests from the entrails of sacrificed animals.

Almost any natural phenomenon can be interpreted as an omen. Of particular significance in all cultures are astronomical occurrences such as solar and lunar ECLIPSES and COMETS. An eclipse is almost always regarded as an evil omen, and many cultures developed elaborate rituals such as sacrifices, drumming and incantations to preserve the sun or moon during this disruption of the natural order. Even today, when the scientific cause for eclipses is known, some people regard them as omens of significant births and deaths. Throughout history, comets have been interpreted as omens of social unrest, collapses in government and other calamities, and the ancient

Greeks and Romans regarded them as sure signs of warfare and disaster; they were also believed to herald the births and deaths of kings, and to carry their souls to heaven, and seven days after the death of Julius Caesar, a comet which appeared in the sky was taken as a sign that he had become immortal.

Many omens have survived in modern times as SUPERSTITIONS, with a large number of people still believing that to break a mirror brings seven years of bad luck, that a white Christmas is an omen of a good year ahead while an overcast or stormy Christmas day warns of sickness in the coming year, and that a ladybird landing on a person's clothes or hand is a lucky sign. The folklore of almost every country in the world also tells of certain supernatural creatures whose appearance is believed to be an omen of death, such as the BLACK DOG and the BANSHEE. Many people who would not consider themselves superstitious continue to regard certain events as warnings or signs caused by SYNCHRONICITY, a term coined by psychologist and researcher CARL JUNG to describe a 'meaningful coincidence' of two or more events where something other than the probability of chance is taken to be involved. See also PORTENTS.

one

The first and smallest whole number, represented by the digit 1; considered significant in numerology.

The number one is the smallest whole number. It is the first number used in counting, and is considered to have great power; without it there would be no numbering system as we know it, and every known numerical system has 1 as its initial starting point. Since it is the common factor of all other whole numbers, it is often viewed as being the origin of all things, and is taken to represent unity and creation. It symbolizes perfection, the absolute and, in monotheistic religions, deity.

In geometry, 1 represents a point – the first emergence of existence. In the TAROT, the ones or aces of the minor ARCANA signify singularity, and represent the basic quality of the suit, while in the major arcana, 1 is the number associated with the Magician card. In Hebrew GEMATRIA, 1 corresponds to the Hebrew letter Aleph, and in the KABBALAH, it is the number assigned to the sephirah KETHER. In NUMEROLOGY it is considered to be a YANG number; it is the numerical equivalent of the letters A, J and S, and signifies an independent and headstrong personality, ambition, determination and innovativeness. On the negative side, it indicates a person who can be self-conscious, egotistical and critical of others. It is seen as the number of beginnings, signalling new opportunities. See also TWO; THREE; FOUR; FIVE; SIX; SEVEN; EIGHT; NINE; TEN; ELEVEN; TWELVE.

oneiromancy

Divination by the interpretation of dreams.

Oneiromancy (from Greek *oneiros*, a dream, and *manteiā*, divination) has been practised in almost every culture since ancient times. For thousands of years, DREAMS were seen as messages from the gods, and, since these messages were cloaked in cryptic imagery, they required a professional interpreter. The dream reader was thus a highly regarded figure in most cultures, and the holy man of the community usually performed this service. In ancient Greece, sick people often visited the temple of Asclepius, the god of medicine and healing, to bathe, pray and sleep there in the hope that the god would visit them in a dream and either prescribe a remedy or effect the cure. The Bible refers to many prophetic dreams; for example, in the book of Genesis the Pharaoh of Egypt dreams of seven fat cattle being eaten by seven thin ones, and seven plump ears of corn being consumed by seven withered ones – Joseph interpreted this as foretelling seven years of plenty followed by seven of famine.

Oneiromancers continued to enjoy a privileged position in most societies for centuries, but with the advent of printing and the rise in literacy dream manuals began to be produced which allowed people to interpret their own dreams. In the 20th century, psychologists put forward other theories about the function of dreams; SIGMUND FREUD, in his 1900 book *The Interpretation of Dreams*, stated that they were merely the product of the unconscious mind, while CARL JUNG held that dreams were a storehouse for memories, reflection and impressions, and a manifestation of the spiritual archetypes which come from the COLLECTIVE UNCONSCIOUS. Since Freud, theological scholars and philosophers have suggested that the divine makes contact with the material world by means of the unconscious, and that through dreams, we receive messages which our conscious mind might ignore or fail to understand. To this day, dream interpretation is still popular, and many books are available which aim to help people to decipher the symbols contained in their dreams.

onza

A controversial and elusive Mexican big cat.

On the evening of 1 January 1986, Andres Rodriguez encountered a very large cat near his home in Sinaloa, Mexico. Fearing that it was about to attack him, Rodriguez shot it dead. He expected it to be either a puma or a jaguar, Mexico's two largest species of cat, but was surprised to discover that it differed from both of them.

Although it resembled a puma in colour, the creature's legs were longer and its body was much slimmer than a puma, so that in basic outline it seemed more like a cheetah. When a local naturalist examined it, he announced that it was an onza – Mexico's legendary, third type of big cat.

For over three centuries, there had been reported sightings in Mexico of a very distinctive form of long-limbed, tan-furred cat that was referred to as an onza, but scientists had always assumed that such accounts were based upon poorly observed pumas. Now that a complete onza specimen had finally been obtained, however, it seemed that the eyewitnesses had been correct after all. But what is the onza? Several theories have been suggested, including a starved puma, a crossbreed of puma and jaguar, a new puma subspecies and a completely new species in its own right. Perhaps the most intriguing suggestion was that it is a living fossil. Twelve thousand years ago, the New World was still home to a native species of puma-like cheetah (sometimes considered, conversely, to be a cheetah-like puma), so perhaps the onza was a direct descendant of this species.

The cat shot by Rodriguez was transported to a scientific laboratory in Mexico, where it became the subject of detailed research. Early studies showed that it contained adequate amounts of body fat, proving that it was not merely an emaciated puma, and further research ruled out the crossbreed option and also the living fossil possibility. Indeed, when the full studies were eventually published in the late 1990s, they revealed that no genetic differences had been found between this specimen and specimens of the puma, suggesting that despite its distinctive appearance the Rodriguez onza was nothing more than a puma after all. This corresponded with the predictions made in 1998 by British cryptozoologist Dr Karl Shuker, who suggested that the onza as a whole was most probably no more than a somewhat gracile (long-limbed) mutant version of the puma (and hence would be extremely similar genetically to normal pumas), and that the Rodriguez specimen may not even be a genuine onza, but merely an infirm, malformed puma. The mystery of the onza's identity has yet to be satisfactorily resolved.

OOPs *see* OUT-OF-PLACE ANIMALS

oracle

A shrine or temple dedicated to the worship and consultation of a prophetic god; a person through whom the god is believed to transmit prophecies; the prophecy itself.

The use of oracles as a means of DIVINATION is found in many civilizations throughout history. In ancient Egypt, Alexander the Great is said to have consulted an oracle in a temple dedicated to Ammon, and in

Norse mythology, Odin was said to have used the severed head of the god Mimir as an oracle. In Tibet, where prophetic spirits are said to enter MEDIUMS known as *kuten*, oracles still play an important part in religion and government. However, oracles are most closely associated with ancient Greece, throughout whose history they played a crucial role, with most important decisions being made only after consultation with an oracle.

The word 'oracle', which comes from the Latin word *ōrāre* to speak, is used to refer to a shrine or temple dedicated to the worship of a prophetic god, to the person through whom the god is believed to transmit prophecies and to the prophecy itself. Oracles were usually associated with a sacred place; in the ancient Mediterranean world, certain locations, such as caves, springs and hills, were believed to possess a special sanctity. One of three techniques was used at oracular shrines. In lot oracles, divination was performed by random selection in the casting of lots. In incubation oracles, such as the one at Epidaurus, dedicated to Asclepius, the Greek god of medicine, the afflicted person slept near the temple in the hope of receiving either a DREAM in which the remedy was revealed to them by the god or a healing from the god himself. But the best-known type of oracle was the inspired oracle, in which a priest or priestess acted as an intermediary of the god and transmitted his responses to questions put to him.

Most, but not all, of the ancient Greek inspired oracles were dedicated to Apollo. The most famous of these was the ORACLE OF DELPHI, where the god was believed to speak through a priestess known as the Pythia. Her influence was considerable; she was consulted before all major undertakings, such as wars or the founding of colonies, and even outside Greek culture, she was widely known and respected. However, the responses given by most oracles were ambiguous, and the Delphic oracle in particular. The gods were not expected to give straightforward answers, and although the inquirer was usually allowed to be there when the question was put to the medium, the actual answer was made only in the presence of a priest, who then shaped the medium's confused utterances into an official response, often in the form of a cryptic or allegorical verse which was open to more than one interpretation. Another important oracle sacred to Apollo, on the island of Crete, was said to be one of the most accurate in Greece.

The oldest and the second most important oracle in ancient Greece was the one at Dodona. It was dedicated to Zeus and was the oracle most often consulted by private individuals for advice on personal matters. The client scratched a question on a lead tablet, and the oracle's priestesses would interpret the rustling of the leaves in the surrounding oak trees as a 'yes' or 'no' answer to the question.

oracle of Delphi, the

A shrine in ancient Greece where prophecies were made.
Delphi in ancient Greece was the site of an ORACLE sacred to Apollo, the prophecies of which became famous throughout the ancient world from the 9th century BC onwards. It was consulted by both individuals and cities and gave advice mainly on matters of religion but also on personal, political and legal issues. It was said to have been consulted by many famous figures, including Alexander the Great and Socrates, as well as in myth by such characters as Orestes and Oedipus. Many cities constructed treasuries on the site to house the rich gifts offered by them to Apollo in gratitude for prophecies, and the ruins of the Athenian treasury are still standing.

Built on a plateau on the side of Mount Parnassus, in the central sanctuary of the oracle was the *omphalos*, a stone which purportedly marked the centre of the entire world. The person consulting the oracle would make a sacrifice (later reduced to a monetary payment) and undergo ritual purification before being taken into the presence of the Pythia or priestess, who, possessed by Apollo, would make prophecies by divine inspiration. The office of Pythia was not a hereditary one, but rather any woman could assume the role as long as she was a virgin, or, if already married, lived a chaste life.

The prophecies given were intended as indications or suggestions rather than simple instructions. They were notoriously opaque or ambiguous, often taking the form of riddles, and it was up to the interpreters who accompanied the priestess to give them a recognizable meaning. For example, Croesus, the 6th-century king of Lydia, is said to have consulted the oracle as to whether or not he should go to war against the Persians. He was told that if he did he would destroy a great empire and took this as an omen of victory. Instead, it was his own realm that was destroyed in the ensuing war.

A more fortunate outcome resulted when the Athenian leader Themistocles (c.523–c.458 BC) was advised, during the war with Xerxes of Persia, to trust in the city's wooden walls. He interpreted this as meaning that it was her ships that would save Athens, and was vindicated when the Athenian fleet defeated the Persians at the battle of Salamis (480 BC).

While prophesying, the Pythia sat on a tripod over the opening of a chasm into which Apollo was said to have hurled the giant snake Python. Greek historian Plutarch (c.46–c.120 AD) suggested that the Pythia achieved a state of trance through inhalation of intoxicating vapours such as carbon dioxide rising naturally from this chasm out of the depths of the earth. This has been disputed by some, but given that Greece is prone to earthquakes it is not out of the question that gases could have been released and accumulated in the sanctuary. Another explanation is that the waters of the sacred spring that ran through the sanctuary may have picked up naturally occurring mildly toxic chemicals such as ethylene. Other accounts suggest that it was the vapours of burning laurel leaves that the Pythia inhaled to achieve her trance.

The oracle continued to be consulted throughout the Hellenistic and Graeco-Roman periods but was banned as a work of the DEVIL by later Christian Roman emperors. The ruins of a 4th-century BC temple still stand on the site.

orang pendek

A short, hairy man-beast reported from Sumatra, believed by many to be the cryptid that is most likely to be formally discovered in the near future.

There are many classic CRYPTIDS – world-famous mystery beasts whose reality and likely identity have been discussed extensively for a very long time. Nevertheless, most of these seem no nearer than ever to being formally discovered. However, there is at least one very notable exception – the orang pendek ('short man') or sedapa, Sumatra's relatively diminutive and famously elusive MAN-BEAST.

Reported in both Sumatra and Borneo (where it is called the 'batutut') for centuries, the orang pendek is often said to stand no more than 1 metre (approximately 3 feet) tall. It is bipedal and tailless, and its body is covered in short yellow-orange, or dark reddish-brown, hair (it has been suggested that the sexes might have different hair colour). It has short legs but relatively long arms, a large pot-belly, jet-black hair that falls over its broad thick shoulders in a mane, a pointed head, a high brow with bushy eyebrows, a broad nose, prominent ears, human-like eyes and long canine teeth. The orang pendek is a forest-dweller, and is most commonly reported walking on its hind legs, although it can readily take to the trees if necessary.

For many years, the orang pendek, like the majority of cryptids, was known only from native reports and travellers' tales. A supposed specimen was found to be a hoax (created from the body of a monkey) and during the 1940s two allegedly genuine orang pendek bodies were 'lost' – another all-too-familiar occurrence with cryptids. The same misfortune befell a cast of supposed orang pendek tracks, when in 1989 British explorer-journalist Debbie Martyr sent them to the Indonesian National Parks Department. Undeterred, however, Martyr continued seeking

A depiction of orang pendek, a short and hairy Sumatran man-beast, the existence of which some believe will soon be confirmed by science. (© TopFoto/Fortean)

this elusive creature, and on 30 September 1994 she finally spied an orang pendek, walking bipedally in the Mount Kerinci area of western Sumatra's Kerinci Seblat National Park. It paused to look at her, from a distance of only 180 metres (590 feet), then it disappeared into the jungle. She has since made at least two further sightings, and several more footprints have been found, some of which seem to exhibit a semi-opposable big toe, readily distinguishing them from *homo sapiens* prints.

The next momentous event took place in 2001, when a three-man team of British adventurers, led by Adam Davies, happened upon some strands of long yellow-orange hair hanging from a bush right next to a fresh footprint – again in the Mount Kerinci vicinity. On their return home, they consulted with British cryptozoologist Dr Karl Shuker, who advised them to send the hairs to Melbourne's Deakin University for DNA analysis, and to contact the renowned primatologist Dr Colin Groves in Canberra for his opinion regarding the footprint. All of this they did, and in 2003 they announced that the DNA analysis had been unable to provide a match between these hairs and those of humans or of a range of known Sumatran animals that had seemed plausible contenders.

This was followed by a second announcement later that year, in which Dr Hans Brunner, who had been investigating the hairs, stated publicly that they did not match those of any animal currently known to science. A comparable statement was released in 2003 from Dr Groves concerning the footprint, revealing that it possessed several features that distinguished it from the prints of humans and was, in Groves' opinion, 'unique'. In short, it looked increasingly likely that the orang pendek was indeed a species of higher primate totally unknown to science.

This dramatic likelihood gained remarkable support in 2004 with the news that, in 2003, a team of Australian anthropologists led by Dr Peter Brown had uncovered a series of diminutive humanoid remains – skulls, skull fragments and limb bones, dating from around 16,000 BC – in a cave on the Lesser Sundas island of Flores. The entities had only been 1 metre (3 feet) tall, and so had been duly dubbed 'hobbits'. The scientists believed that the hobbits' species may well have continued to exist long after the specimens that had been uncovered in the cave had died.

This discovery attracted particular scientific interest because, after having studied the hobbits' remains meticulously, Brown and his colleagues decided that they constituted a hitherto unknown but valid dwarf species of human, which they formally named *Homo floresiensis*. The announcement attracted considerable scepticism from various other scientists, who considered that the hobbits were nothing more than stunted specimens of our own species, *Homo sapiens*, who had suffered from a condition known as microcephaly. However, it seemed highly unlikely that all of the specimens in the cave could have been microcephalic. The Australian team listed a series of distinctive features exhibited by the hobbits that not only argued against the microcephaly theory, but also argued for their sufficient distinction from *Homo sapiens* to warrant classification as a separate human species. It was also apparently quite an advanced species too – hundreds of tiny stone tools were found alongside the skeletons, together with charred elephant bones, indicating that the hobbits knew how to use fire.

Inevitably, the discovery of the fossil hobbits on Flores led to considerable discussion within the cryptozoological community as to whether they could be the same as, or at least ancestors of, the living orang pendek on Sumatra. Moreover, native people on Flores have long claimed that tiny humans known as the 'ebu gogo' existed there until quite recently. Could these have been modern-day hobbits, and might there still be some surviving today in Flores' more remote, inaccessible regions? Scientists are currently seriously reflecting on the plausibility of such possibilities

– especially after hearing some remarkable local testimony, such as that of Flores fisherman Abdul Wani. He claimed that in 1979 he had encountered some long-haired, child-sized little people standing around a mound of earth, from which they fled away screaming when they saw him. He apparently then dug into the mound, where he allegedly discovered the body of a tiny naked woman with the face of a monkey. Wani preserved the body by binding it in linen like a mummy, and many villagers subsequently viewed it until it was eventually discarded several years later. All of this occurred well before the discovery by scientists of the first hobbit remains, and the publicity that this subsequently generated.

Suddenly, the whole orang pendek saga has gained a new significance, and the orang pendek itself is enjoying a major renaissance in the scientific as well as the cryptozoological world – a rare feat indeed for any cryptid.

orbs

'Ghostly' spheres which have appeared on photographs taken by many digital and compact cameras since the 1990s.

Since the advent of digital photography in the 1990s, and the changing design of compact cameras at this time, many photographs have been taken which show small globular luminous patches or smudges, apparently not visible to observers at the time the picture was taken. Such blemishes have been dubbed 'orbs' and were virtually unknown before this time. Various extraordinary claims have been made for orbs – some have said that they represent packages of psychic energy invisible to the naked eye, while others have suggested that they are the spirits or souls of the deceased. Some even claim to see structures, faces or messages within orbs. The orb phenomenon became a hugely popular topic on the Internet, and in the USA, the first orb photography courses have been offered.

However, the perception of orbs is very much in the eye of the beholder; it appears that only individuals predisposed to a belief in the supernatural are convinced of the reality of orbs as a psychic phenomenon. The major objection to a paranormal explanation for orbs is that the air is constantly filled with minute specks of moisture, smoke or dust and these may be recorded on sensitive cameras, particularly where the flash is situated close to the lens, as with most modern cameras. Research conducted by British photographer Philip Carr and incorporated into a short film, *The Riddle of the Orbs* (2004), demonstrates that such photographs can be easily obtained or created anywhere by taking flash photographs of mundane airborne particles, the resultant images being indistinguishable from alleged orb pictures. Certainly, the frequent appearance of orbs in photographs obtained using flash photography in dusty and damp environments such as ruined castles and ancient manor houses – sites often selected for ghost hunting – is consistent with them being nothing more than mundane airborne particles. Nonetheless, advocates of a paranormal explanation for orbs often stridently reject this solution. As with other GHOST PHOTOGRAPHS, the will to believe sometimes overrides a more rational assessment of the images.

Order of the Knights Templar *see*

KNIGHTS TEMPLAR

Ordo Templi Orientis

An esoteric order associated with the teaching of sex magic.

The Ordo Templi Orientis (OTO) is usually associated with ALEISTER CROWLEY, his Book of the Law, and his esoteric spiritual philosophy of THELEMA. In fact the OTO had been in existence for six years before Crowley was invited to become its UK head – not its world-wide head, as often believed.

The OTO was founded by Theodor Reuss (1855–1923) and Carl Kellner (1851–1905) around 1902. Its rituals were based on those of the esoteric Masonic order, the Rite of Memphis and Misraim; Reuss and Kellner were also involved in the German branch of the THEOSOPHICAL SOCIETY. They believed that the hidden secret at the heart of both FREEMASONRY and Rosicrucianism (see ROSICRUCIANS) was sex magic (see MAGIC, SEX). On Kellner's death in 1905 Reuss became the sole leader. In 1912, Reuss appointed Crowley as UK head, Crowley assuming the title of 'Supreme and Holy King of Ireland, Iona and all the Britains in the Sanctuary of the Gnosis'. It appears that Reuss expelled Crowley from the OTO in 1921. Reuss died in 1923, Crowley appointed himself Reuss's heir, and in 1925 claimed authority over the whole German Rosicrucian movement, causing the assorted German esoteric orders to split into pro- and anti-Crowley factions.

Similarly, there are divisions in today's OTO. Most OTO books and websites give the impression that theirs is *the* OTO, the only one, or at least the only valid one. The largest, the US-based Caliphate OTO, follows the succession of Grady Louis McMurtry. McMurtry had been a member of an OTO lodge in the USA, and had been given some sort of instructions by Crowley that he could take over the lodge at a time of emergency. McMurtry and his followers set up the Caliphate OTO in 1977. The other major claimant to being 'the' OTO is the Typhonian OTO led by English occultist Kenneth Grant, author on Crowley and the artist AUSTIN OSMAN SPARE. There are also groups called Society (or Societas) OTO, separate from either of the two main groups.

The OTO (in its various manifestations) is routinely attacked by evangelical anti-occultists as being satanic (see SATANISM); it is also criticized for the sex-magic element of its teachings.

oreads

Mountain nymphs in Greek mythology.

In Greek mythology an oread was a type of NYMPH, a kind of local divinity usually personified as a young woman, that lived in mountains or grottoes. In some versions of the myths they were free to roam the mountainsides; in others they were particularly associated with mountain oaks and pines, and it was said that when one of these trees died an oread died with it. In most accounts they lived for much longer than the human lifespan but were not themselves immortal. Oreads were associated with Aphrodite and considered to be part of her retinue.

Perhaps the most famous oread was Echo, who inhabited Mount Helicon. Her unrequited love for the self-obsessed Narcissus led her to pine away until nothing but the sound of her voice remained.

orgone energy *see* REICH, WILHELM

ornithomancy

Divination by observing the flight and behaviour of birds.

In ornithomancy, from Greek *ornis, ornithos*, a bird, and *manteiā*, divination, the flight, behaviour and songs or cries of birds are studied and their meanings interpreted. Ornithomancy has been used since ancient times, by cultures as diverse as the Tibetans, the Aztecs, the Hittites and the ancient Greeks, and became a principal branch of AUGURY for the ancient Romans, and an important part of their religion.

One ritual involved the augur sitting on a hill, circumscribing a particular area of the sky with a special divining staff, and then watching this area for birds in order to obtain a 'yes/no' answer to a question. If one or two birds appeared in the area while the augur was watching, this was usually taken to be a good omen, but more than two birds was an ill omen; alternatively, an odd number of birds might be taken as a 'no' answer, while an even number signified 'yes'.

Of particular significance to the Romans were the flights of eagles and vultures, the calls of crows, the hoots of owls and the cries of ravens, while the number of birds seen, the direction of their flight and whether or not they shed feathers as they flew were all also highly significant. In the system practised by the ancient Celts, the crow, the eagle and the wren were the most important birds.

Vestiges of this ancient form of divination can still be seen today in a number of superstitions regarding birds: a bird flying in and out of a room or window is almost universally taken to be an omen of an imminent death; to hear a crow cawing on your right side is a warning to be cautious in all you do that day; and an owl hooting in the daytime is bad luck. An interpretation of the number of magpies seen together also survives to this day in a nursery rhyme, one common variation of which begins:

> One for sorrow, two for joy,
> Three for a girl, four for a boy,
> Five for silver, six for gold,
> Seven for a secret never to be told.

osculum infame

An obscenity supposedly performed by witches and Devil-worshippers at black masses, in which they kiss the Devil's buttocks or anus as an act of submission and devotion.

The belief that WITCHES and Devil-worshippers celebrated the BLACK MASS as a parody of the Roman Catholic Mass goes back to the Middle Ages, and during the WITCH TRIALS of those times, people charged with witchcraft were routinely accused of participating in such ceremonies. As part of the black mass or witches' SABBATS, witches and Devil-worshippers were said to perform the *osculum infame*, a Latin phrase which means 'kiss of shame' or 'infamous kiss'. It was claimed that as a ritual greeting, they kissed the buttocks or anus of the DEVIL, who was present in the form of the coven leader or an animal such as a black billygoat, a feathered toad or a tomcat. This kiss was not only seen as an act of adoration and submission to the Devil, but also as an obscene perversion of the kiss of peace performed in the Roman Catholic Mass. In addition, it was a parody of the feudal practice, common at the time, whereby the bond between a lord and vassal was affirmed in a ceremony of homage in which the vassal took an oath of fealty and his lord bestowed on him a ceremonial kiss. Medieval paintings and woodcuts of black masses and similar heretical rituals are dominated by depictions of the *osculum infame*, with both men and women queuing up to kiss the Devil's rump.

In the 14th century, the KNIGHTS TEMPLAR were also accused of heresies which included the conducting of black masses and the worship of a figure called BAPHOMET in a debauched form of Muslim idolatry; under torture, some of them confessed to the charges and attested that as part of their initiation rites, they had been required to bestow the *osculum infame* on the officiating prior, or on the idol itself.

Witches queue to perform the *osculum infame*. From the *Compendium Maleficarum* (1626) by Francesco Maria Guazzo. (© Mary Evans Picture Library)

ostention

The occurrence in real life of incidents or behaviour that has been guided by the content of fictional folk tales or urban legends.

The word 'ostention' was originally (and still is) used to describe the use of gestures to replace words in conversation, a coinage that is attributed to the Italian novelist and semiotician Umberto Eco. However, ostention developed an additional meaning when it was first used in connection with actions driven by fictitious folk tales and URBAN LEGENDS by the US folklorists Professor Linda Degh and Andrew Vazsonyi in a 1983 paper entitled 'Does the Word Dog Bite? Ostensive Action as a Means of Legend-Telling'.

The concept of ostention when used in this context is fairly wide in its scope. It can cover situations where people actually carry out actions which mirror those that are reported in fictional stories, or cases where the authorities follow a course of action through the mistaken belief that modern legends are based on truth (tales of devil worship and SATANIC RITUAL ABUSE have produced examples of both). It can also include the mistaken acceptance of unrelated occurrences as proof of the reality of an urban legend – such as the disappearance of a cat reinforcing the belief in claims that gangs are roaming the area stealing cats for use in the fur trade, or, where sightings in Central Park in New York appeared to confirm the ALLIGATORS IN SEWERS story. Some people also include instances where individuals claim, for whatever reason, that an incident that forms the basis of a fictional modern folk tale has actually happened to them.

ouija board

An item of equipment employed during séances, through which messages can allegedly be received from spirits of the dead.

A ouija board (also known as a 'talking board' or 'spirit board') consists of a board upon which the letters of the alphabet and the words 'yes' and 'no' are written. Some boards also have a few additional words, or numbers, on them. A PLANCHETTE sits on top of the board. The participants in a SÉANCE each place a finger on the planchette. Questions are then asked and the planchette moves over the board, supposedly under the guidance of the SPIRITS, spelling out their answers.

The ouija board was invented in the 1890s and originally sold in the USA. The final version employing the planchette (which had previously been used as a system for producing AUTOMATIC WRITING) developed from an early version which used letters placed on a table over which a PENDULUM would be swung to spell out the message. The name was originally claimed to be the Egyptian for 'good luck', but when this was rapidly discredited it was then said that it was in fact derived from a combination of the French and German words for 'yes'. The use of ouija boards went on to become a very popular parlour game during the early 20th century, and many examples are still available today – some are sold as games by well-known manufacturers, while others are marketed as specialist items specifically for séances.

Although believers hold that the movement of the planchette is wholly down to the actions of the spirits, sceptics argue it is unconscious (or even conscious)

Two people use a ouija board in an attempt to communicate with the spirits.
(© Bettmann/Corbis)

movement by the participants that causes the messages to be spelt out – pointing to observations which indicate that when the participants are blindfolded the result is usually nonsense.

out-of-body experience

An experience in which an individual allegedly has the sensation of the self leaving the body – usually claimed to involve being able to observe the physical body from elsewhere.

Out-of-body experiences (OBEs) are commonly reported to occur as part of NEAR-DEATH EXPERIENCES (NDEs). They can also apparently be brought on by a traumatic experience, and are sometimes said to occur to people while they are in comas, under anaesthetic or under the influence of certain drugs. Some even claim to be able consciously to induce them – for example, the supposed ability to engage in ASTRAL PROJECTION allegedly involves a form of out-of-body-experience; in this instance it is interpreted as being due to the SPIRIT being deliberately allowed to leave the physical body.

A common feature of OBEs is the apparent sensation of looking down on one's own body. The period during which the experience is said to have occurred is often very short (typically only minutes); however, the subject often reports feeling that a longer period of time has elapsed. At the end of the OBE the subject may report the sensation of 'snapping back into' their body. Some research carried out in the area has indicated that as many as one in ten people report experiencing an OBE at some point in their lives.

Proposed explanations include the suggestion that they are experiences manufactured within the brain when it is cut off from external stimuli, and that they resemble DREAMS or HALLUCINATIONS, although a significant number of people accept the objective reality of NDEs and offer spiritual explanations involving the SOUL leaving the body. The very nature of the experiences ensures that evidence for their existence is mostly anecdotal, and those who claim to be able to induce them at will have so far failed to demonstrate satisfactorily that they can use OBEs to obtain information which could not have been gained via other means.

out-of-place animals

Creatures of an already-known species that are sighted in an unexpected geographical location.

Out-of-place animals, or OOPs for short, constitute a very unusual category of mystery animal which straddles the border between mainstream zoology and CRYPTOZOOLOGY. Although there are several instances in which OOPs have been clearly identified as known species, and their existence in a non-native locality has been confirmed, there are many other cases where the identity (and even presence) of OOPs remains a matter of conjecture.

Examples of the former, non-controversial subcategory of OOP include such exotica as North American prairie dogs thriving on the Isle of Wight, a colony of baboons well established in the Spanish province of Cadiz, herds of dromedaries (one-humped camels) in many parts of Australia, flocks of ring-necked parakeets in London and other English cities and towns, pythons and monitor lizards in Florida's Everglades and a wide diversity of other animal species that have become naturalized in geographical regions far from their native homelands. Such populations are clearly the result of escapes (or even deliberate releases) from captivity and, because there is no longer any doubt concerning their identity or existence, they cannot be considered to be CRYPTIDS.

Conversely, there are also a significant number of cryptozoological examples of OOPs, whose identity and existence remain the subject of debate. Probably the most famous of these are the ALIEN BIG CATS (or ABCs) – very large feline cryptids reportedly sighted in areas where creatures of this type are definitely not native, such as the UK, continental Europe, Australia, New Zealand and (in the case of black panther-like beasts and maned leonine creatures) North America. If these are indeed what they seem to be, they too have escaped from captivity or have been purposely released. However, in the absence of conclusive physical evidence, the identity of these creatures is much disputed; sceptics offer a number of more mundane options for their true identity – such as big dogs.

Perhaps even more interesting are the cases in which an animal that is clearly a bona fide cryptid for another reason can also acquire a secondary classification as an OOP. The THYLACINE is a good example. Accounts of alleged sightings of living thylacines in Tasmania and mainland Australia, occurring long after their respective extinction dates in those locations, clearly fall within the realm of cryptozoology. However, for quite some time, there were also reports of sightings in New Guinea – a location in which thylacines were not known ever to have occurred and in which it would therefore also be considered to be an OOP. This changed in 1963 when a scientific paper was published formally documenting the discovery of the first fossil thylacine remains in New Guinea.

There are many other cryptids on record for which there are proposed identities that, if they are correct, would also lend them the status of an OOP. Notable among these is the BIGFOOT, for which the two most popular suggested identities are the giant ape *Gigantopithecus* and the hominid *Paranthropus*.

Both of these are not only currently understood to be long-since extinct but are also not known ever to have existed in North America.

out-of-place objects
Objects allegedly discovered in chronologically anomalous places.

Traditional archaeology is occasionally challenged by the alleged discovery of objects or artefacts in places where they do not seem to fit, whether in terms of the geological strata in which they are embedded, or in relation to the culture in which they are found. The ICA STONES are a well-known example of this, as is the work of MICHAEL CREMO.

In 1991, gold prospectors working along the River Narada in the Ural Mountains of Russia claimed to have found a number of strange, very small, unusually shaped metal objects. Some of the items were apparently buried as deep in the soil as 12 metres (40 feet). The objects, many of which were spiral in shape, were composed of metals such as copper and tungsten and were obviously manufactured rather than natural formations.

Many of these items were so small that they could only have been the products of nanotechnology, but the depths at which they were unearthed would indicate that they had been in the ground for thousands of years. It was argued that they must have been left there either by a long-vanished superior civilization or by EXTRATERRESTRIALS visiting earth.

For over 30 years, it is claimed that miners in the Transvaal, South Africa, have been coming across nickel-steel spheroids in strata that are millions of years old. Again, these seem to be manufactured rather than natural, and so regular as to rule out being debris from meteorites.

Sceptics claim that these 'discoveries' are simply hoaxes or even ignorant misinterpretation of our own industrial waste. However, if such reports are true they have tremendous significance for the history of life on earth.

owlman
A bizarre winged creature spasmodically reported in Cornwall since the mid-1970s.

The Cornish owlman is one of several baffling, truly bizarre CRYPTIDS that exist on the fringes of cryptozoology. The owlman first came to prominence in 1976, following various sightings near Mawnan church in south Cornwall. The first took place on 17 April, when two young sisters, June and Vicky Melling, holidaying in Cornwall with their parents, claimed to have seen a sizeable 'bird-man' hovering in the air near the church tower. A similar sighting was reported in this same location on 3 July by two more

Barbara Perry's drawing of the 'owlman', as she claimed she saw it on 3 July 1976. (© TopFoto/Fortean)

girls – 14-year-old teenagers Barbara Perry and Sally Chapman. They likened the creature to a big owl covered in grey feathers, with pointed ears, red eyes, an owl-like face and pincer-like feet with black claws. Rather more macabre was the description given by a third pair of girls, Jane Greenwood and her sister, who sighted the owlman the next day, claiming to have seen it standing in the trees 'like a full-grown man, but the legs bent backwards like a bird's'. It had silver-grey feathers, and its body and legs were the same colour. Its mouth was very large, its feet were black and crab-like and its slanting eyes were red. In 1978, various additional sightings, all by girls, were reported at or near the Mawnan church, but nothing further was heard of the owlman until the late 1980s when a male teenager revealed, albeit anonymously, that while walking through woodlands near Mawnan one evening, he and his girlfriend had encountered the owlman standing on a thick branch of a conifer tree with its wings raised. Brown and grey in colour, with glowing eyes, it appeared to be approximately 1.25 metres (4 feet) tall, and they could pick out two large toes on each foot.

There has been much speculation that at least some of the 1970s owlman reports may have been hoaxes. If, however, they are genuine, then, based upon all of the descriptions, as well as a good sketch of this creature prepared by Sally Chapman the day after her sighting, the most reasonable explanation is that the Cornish owlman was merely an escapee European eagle owl *Bubo bubo* – the world's largest species of owl, standing 1.2 metres (almost 4 feet) tall, with a 1.85 metre (6 feet) wingspan. Although not native to Britain, this species is commonly exhibited in public and private animal collections, and often escapes. Indeed, so frequent are such escapes, and so infrequent are any reports of subsequent recapture, that several years ago it was suggested that this species may well become established in the UK – a prediction perhaps confirmed in 2005 when it was reported that at least one breeding pair of eagle owls now exists in Britain; photographs of the adults and chicks have been released but their exact location has been withheld to preserve them from possible harm and egg-collectors.

Oz factor

A set of psychological and physiological symptoms described by many people who claim to have been involved in UFO close encounter incidents. These are said by some to indicate that the experience involved, or was even due to, entry into an altered state of consciousness.

The term 'Oz factor' was coined by the British UFO researcher Jenny Randles, and popularized in her 1983 book *UFO Reality*. It refers to the parallels between the experiences reported by people claiming to have been involved in CLOSE ENCOUNTERS and those in the Frank L Baum story, *The Wonderful Wizard of Oz* (1900), in which a young girl enters an 'alternative reality' following a strange encounter. The phrase is now often used as a shorthand label for the whole set of unusual sensations that often appear in stories of UFO encounters.

A classic example appears in a report made by four people from the Calder Valley area of the Pennines in 1995. On 15 July they were holding an evening barbecue when they suddenly noticed that the garden seemed to be enveloped in a strange aura. The air had become very heavy and there was a tingling, electrical feel to it. At the same time all the usual ambient sounds disappeared, including birdsong and noises from the surrounding houses; they said that it felt like the garden had been encased in a bubble, separating it from the rest of the universe. Time began to 'stretch out' and lose all meaning – it became impossible for them to estimate whether a second or an hour elapsed. A dark grey mass then appeared overhead, projecting a beam of light to the ground. This was followed by an apparent jump in continuity, with the subjects coming round from this disorientating experience several hours later, suffering PHYSIOLOGICAL EFFECTS – including extreme tiredness and nausea.

Although the physical after-effects in this case might suggest that there was a 'real' component to this close encounter experience, the Oz factor symptoms raise further questions. Are such symptoms (in this and other similar cases) induced in the subject by the occupants of a real, external UFO, or do they indicate that the whole sighting is a subjective experience connected with entry into an ALTERED STATE OF CONSCIOUSNESS (either generated internally or triggered by something external, but of earthly origin)? An important clue might be found in the fact that such sensations are not exclusive to reports of UFO close encounters – they are also sometimes feature in claims of other paranormal phenomena, notably TIME SLIPS and NEAR-DEATH EXPERIENCES.

P

pacts

Binding agreements or bargains between two parties; a recurring motif in religion, folklore and mythology.

The pact, an agreement between two parties which is considered to be binding whether written or merely spoken, is a recurring motif in RELIGION, FOLKLORE and MYTHOLOGY. In the Old Testament, God promises Abraham that he will become the father of a large people through his son, Isaac, and that kings will be descended from his kin. The symbol of this pact between Abraham and God is the circumcision of all Jewish male children at eight days old. In Norse mythology, the Swedish king Aun makes a pact with Odin to have his life prolonged in exchange for sacrificing his sons. Many folk tales involve a pact made between supernatural creatures and humans, and traditionally, the breaking of such a pact brings dire consequences. One of the best-known folk tales, 'Rumpelstiltskin', centres around a pact made between a miller's daughter and the dwarf Rumpelstiltskin, that in exchange for his spinning straw into gold for her, she will give him her first child. When he comes to claim payment, her tears move him to make a second pact, that if she can find out his name in three days, she can keep her child, which she does.

The most notorious and enduring of pacts in folklore and the occult is the DEVIL'S PACT, said to be made between a human being and the DEVIL, in which the person promises the Evil One their soul, either for diabolical favours such as wealth, power, knowledge or youth, or as a sign of recognition of the Devil as their master. The best-known devil's pact is that made by FAUST in German legend. Although Faust loses his soul in accordance with the terms of his agreement, in many folk tales the hero tricks the Devil by finding a loophole in the contract, and escapes the consequences of the pact.

paganism

A form of spirituality generally characterized by a reverence for nature and a belief in the female divine principle in the form of a Goddess, as well as a God. Paganism can be understood to include a wide range of spiritual practices including Wicca, Druidism and shamanism.

The word 'pagan' comes from the Latin *paganus*, which originally meant 'a country-dweller or rustic'. As Christianity spread throughout the Roman Empire, people in the rural communities of the empire tended to hold on to their traditional earth- and season-centred spiritual practices, rather than embracing the new belief of Christianity – the word 'pagan' came to be used synonymously with 'non-Christian'. In later centuries it took on the additional and more negative sense of 'primitive and savage'.

The word 'paganism' came into the English language during the 17th century. Until the spread of freedom of religion in the Western world, the term 'paganism' was almost exclusively used in a disparaging way of any religion outside Christianity, Judaism or Islam. However, with 19th-century Romanticism came a resurgence of interest in pre-Christian religions. The occultism and THEOSOPHY which characterized the beginning of the 20th century also played a part in the re-awakening of interest in old beliefs. Consequently, attempts at a restoration of indigenous religions, especially those of ancient Europe, have become increasingly popular over the last hundred years, and the word 'paganism' is no longer simply used as a negative term.

'Paganism' is now used as a descriptive term for

a broad range of belief systems, including WICCA, druidism (see DRUIDS) and SHAMANISM. The spiritual paths that might be included under the banner of paganism are generally characterized by being earth-centred, with a reverence for nature and the sanctity of the planet. Many pagan religions or spiritual systems also incorporate the idea of a female divine principle in the form of a GODDESS, as well as (or in a few traditions, instead of) a male God (see HORNED GOD). Pagan practice usually involves living in harmony with the earth and observing and celebrating its cycles – these are represented by the pagan 'wheel of the year', a calendar of festivals which honour the changes in the seasons. The eight major pagan festivals, or SABBATS, mark the WINTER SOLSTICE, SUMMER SOLSTICE, the VERNAL EQUINOX, AUTUMNAL EQUINOX, and four ancient Celtic festivals known as SAMHAIN, IMBOLC, BELTANE and LUGHNASADH (many of which were later absorbed into the Christian calendar and renamed). The cycles of the moon are also often honoured.

Modern pagan practice is frequently characterized by polytheism and ANIMISM, and the use of ancient mythologies. Spiritualism is seen as a matter of personal experience, and while some pagans regard 'Spirit' as a single, unified and universal deity, others see it as something with male–female polarity, with a God and Goddess, whose many aspects and facets are represented by the gods and goddesses of different religions. Some pagan groups draw on only one tradition, such as Egyptian, Celtic or Norse, while others incorporate elements from more than one tradition and merge various religious practices, customs and rituals (see SYNCRETISM). Many, but by no means all, pagan movements include a belief in MAGIC and occultism. Most groups do not have temples as such, but perform their rituals at home or at outdoor locations. It is not necessary to belong to a pagan community in order to practise paganism, and many people follow their faith as solitary practitioners.

While some modern pagan traditions try to claim a direct continuity between the old, original forms of paganism and their own practice, other pagans accept or even prefer the alternative 'neopagan' (see NEOPAGANISM), holding that theirs is a new spiritual system based upon and adapted from what we know of the true, pre-Christian pagans.

pain endurance
The ability to tolerate pain.

Very few people have true INSENSITIVITY to pain, but enduring it is often seen as a worthwhile achievement. Pain endurance is a quality that has been prized in many primitive societies, particularly among warriors or hunters. The stoical toleration of wounds or ritual

A 1935 poster for 'The Pain Proof Man', presumably an exponent of pain endurance. (© Swim Ink 2, LLC/Corbis)

piercing, circumcision or scarring would be taken as a sign of courage or manhood, demonstrating worthiness to belong to the society.

To some extent, this would be achieved by the use of mental techniques to control or block out the pain altogether, and this type of activity would also have been engaged in by religious mystics, such as FAKIRS, as a demonstration of the power of their faith.

In MARTIAL ARTS FEATS, practitioners who have mastered special techniques of breathing and channelling their QI (or life force) to specific areas of the body often demonstrate their ability to suffer pain and tolerate blows unflinchingly. Entertainers have also used techniques of mental discipline, repeatedly piercing themselves in so-called 'human pincushion' acts.

palindromes
Words, phrases, sentences or numbers that read the same backwards and forwards; often used in magical writing and spoken charms, talismans and magic squares.

A palindrome (from the Greek word meaning 'running back') is a word, phrase, sentence or number which reads the same backwards and forwards. Palindrome symmetry is usually by character or letter, although it can also be symmetrical by word, and palindromes are particularly common in English. They are known to have been popular for at least 2,000 years; fountains in ancient Greece often bore the inscription *Nipson anomēmata mē monan opsin* ('Wash the sin as well as the face'), which is palindromic in Greek characters, and the Romans also enjoyed palindromes, such as the one which described the behaviour of moths – *In girum imus nocte et consumimur igni* ('We enter the circle at night and are consumed by fire').

Palindromes are often used in magical writing, spoken charms and AMULETS, since the repetitive nature of the word or sentence is thought to create a kind of magical loop in which power is built up until released by a magician. During the late Roman Empire, Gnostics used the word *ablanathanalba* (a palindrome when written in Greek characters) meaning 'the Father hath given to us', as a magical word on amulets.

The most remarkable and possibly best-known of all magical palindromes is the Latin phrase SATOR AREPO TENET OPERA ROTAS (which can be translated as 'the sower Arepo holds the wheels with effort', although its meaning is not important); this also reproduces itself if words are formed from the first letter of each word in the phrase, then the second letters of each, and so on. It is thus often arranged into a MAGIC SQUARE which reads horizontally or vertically from both the top left to the bottom right, and from the bottom right to the top left.

Palladino, Eusapia *see panel p514*

palmistry
Fortune-telling by inspecting and interpreting the features of the subject's hands.
Palmistry, a form of FORTUNE-TELLING in which the hands are inspected and their shape, lines and other features are interpreted, is believed to have been practised as much as 5,000 years ago in places such as India, China and Egypt. The Greek physicians Hippocrates and Galen are also both said to have used palmistry as a clinical aid. While many of the oldest writings on palmistry originate from India, one of the first works on the subject in the English language is thought to be a manuscript from the 1440s called the *Digby Roll*, which contains a basic treatise on palmistry.

The practice is thought to have been brought to Europe in the 12th century by Arab traders who had learnt of it on their travels. In the 14th century, the Roma also came to Europe, bringing with them a version of palmistry which combined the system they had learned in India with their own alleged gifts for CLAIRVOYANCE, and palmistry has since then continued to be associated strongly with Roma fortune-telling. In the 18th century, a famous French fortune-teller

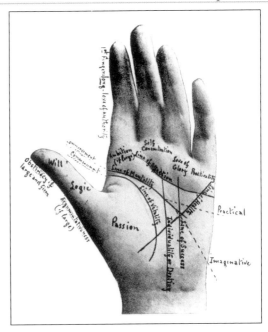

A chart of the hand by famous Irish palmist Cheiro, drawn in 1900. (© Mary Evans Picture Library)

called Marie-Anne le Normand made predictions for Napoleon and Josephine, and created a great deal of new interest in this form of divination, and two 19th-century Frenchmen, Casimir D'Arpentigny and Adrien Desbarolles, wrote books based on their respective studies of palmistry – D'Arpentigny focusing on hand shapes and Desbarolles on the lines of the palm – which established them as the co-founders of modern hand analysis. Famous palm-readers, or palmists, such as CHEIRO, also did much to popularize palmistry.

Palmistry is divided into three main subsets: CHIROGNOMY, in which a person's character is read from the size, shape and appearance of the hands and fingers; CHIROMANCY, which involves studying the lines and markings on a person's hands; and dermatoglyphics, the study and interpretation of the fingerprints. Both hands are studied, the hand used for writing (the dominant hand) being taken to reflect the subject's personality and the changes and experiences they have undergone, and the other hand (the destiny hand) being read as representing the subject's potential, their subconscious self and their future.

Papus (1865–1916)
A French esotericist best known for his work on the tarot.
Papus was the pseudonym of the Spanish-born French esotericist Gérard Encausse. Although

Eusapia Palladino (1854–1918)

Eusapia Palladino is widely regarded as one of the most remarkable mediums in history. Born in a small Italian village, she was orphaned at an early age, and moved to Naples. Her psychic abilities apparently manifested when she was still very young, and she became a successful medium. She came to the attention of Dr Ercole Chiaia, who had an interest in the occult, and in 1888 he wrote to the eminent Italian psychiatrist and criminologist Cesare Lombroso to alert him to her amazing abilities:

The case I allude to is that of an invalid woman who belongs to the humblest class of society. She is … very ignorant; her appearance is neither fascinating nor endowed with the power which modern criminologists call irresistible; but when she wishes, be it by day or by night, she can divert a curious group for an hour or so with the most surprising phenomena. Either bound to a seat, or firmly held by the hands of the curious, she attracts to her the articles of furniture which surround her, lifts them up, holds them suspended in the air … and makes them come down again with undulatory movements, as if they were obeying her will … If you place in the corner of the room a vessel containing a layer of soft clay, you find after some moments the imprint in it of a small or a large hand, the image of a face (front view or profile) from which a plaster cast can be taken … This woman rises in the air, no matter what bands tie her down … she plays on musical instruments – organs, bells, tambourines – as if they had been touched by her hands or moved by the breath of invisible gnomes.

When Lombroso attended one of Palladino's SÉANCES some two years later, he too was impressed by her apparent gift of PSYCHOKINESIS:

Eusapia's feet and hands were held by Professor Tamburini and by Lombroso. A handbell placed on a small table more than a yard distant from Eusapia sounded in the air above the heads of the sitters and then descended on the table, thence going two yards to a bed. While the bell was ringing we struck a match and saw the bell up in the air.

Members of the SOCIETY FOR PSYCHICAL RESEARCH (SPR) took Palladino to Cambridge in 1895 to test her abilities for themselves. In a series of 20 sittings, the researchers deliberately allowed Palladino to cheat – which she did, constantly. The SPR concluded that she was nothing but a fraud, but this did not deter her supporters, who claimed that she only cheated when her powers were weak or when the SPIRITS were not communicating, and this was done merely to prevent disappointment. Others said that her deception was the result of a mischievous temperament. She toured widely and successfully, despite further exposures for fraud at her séances, and while many dismissed her she retained some supporters until the end. While there is absolutely no doubt that Palladino frequently employed trickery, there are some who still claim that this was mixed with genuine psychic ability.

generally known only for his work on the TAROT (he published *le Tarot des bohémians* in 1889), he also wrote extensively on the KABBALAH and other areas of esoteric religion, and was highly influential in a number of esoteric organizations. He was greatly influenced by the work of ÉLIPHAS LÉVI.

A practising doctor and homeopathist, Encausse took the name 'Papus' from the genius associated with physicians in a work by Apollonius of Tyana (c.3–c.97 AD), *Nuctemeron*, which was quoted in Lévi's works.

Encausse was briefly a member of the THEOSOPHICAL SOCIETY (1884–5), but disliked its Eastern focus. In 1888, the same year the HERMETIC ORDER OF THE GOLDEN DAWN was founded, Encausse and several other major esotericists including Joséphin Péladin and Oswald Wirth founded the kabbalistic Order of the Rose-Croix. In 1891 he founded a Martinist masonic order, *l'Ordre des Supérieurs Inconnus*; Martinism is still a small but significant masonic branch today. In 1895 he joined the Paris temple of the Golden Dawn.

He was also an early member of the Gnostic Catholic Church (founded by Jules Doinel in 1890 as a revival of the Cathar religion), becoming Bishop of Toulouse with the title Tau Vincent. In 1908 Encausse was invited to join the ORDO TEMPLI ORIENTIS by one of its founders, Theodor Reuss, and in turn consecrated Reuss a bishop in the Gnostic Catholic Church; the two organizations are still closely associated. Encausse was also a member of the esoteric masonic Order of Memphis-Misraim, becoming its leader in 1913.

Although some of his later pseudonymous writings were anti-Semitic, Encausse was not, as some have claimed, the author of the PROTOCOLS OF THE LEARNED ELDERS OF ZION.

Paracelsus (1493–1541)

Swiss physician, alchemist and astrologer.

Theophrastus Phillippus Aureolus Bombastus von Hohenheim was born in Einsiedeln, Switzerland, the son of a German physician and chemist, from whom he received his early instruction in practical medicine. As a youth, he worked in the nearby mines as an analyst, acquiring a knowledge of metallurgical practices that provided him with the background for his future work in chemistry and ALCHEMY. He graduated with a baccalaureate in medicine from the University of Vienna at the age of 17. Some writers say that he was then forced to leave Basle after trouble with the authorities over his studies in NECROMANCY, and for a time led a nomadic life, supporting himself by astrological predictions and various occult practices. What is known is that he embarked on extensive travels for many years after his graduation, journeying to Egypt, Arabia, the Holy Land and Constantinople, seeking out the best practitioners of alchemy in an attempt to learn from them their most effective medical treatments. He also worked as a military surgeon, during which time he gained a reputation as a healer who successfully used unconventional methods where conventional ones had failed.

On his return to Basle in 1526, at the age of 32, he took a professorship in physics, medicine and surgery at the University, and was appointed as city physician. But he did not retain his chair of medicine for long; he adopted the name Paracelsus, meaning 'superior to Celsus' (an early Roman physician) and gained a reputation for arrogance, antagonizing his more conservative colleagues by pouring scorn on their beliefs, and even publicly burning the works of such revered medical authorities as Galen and Hippocrates. It was possibly this behaviour that earned him the nickname 'the Luther of Medicine'. In any case, he was forced to leave Basle in haste shortly after this and take up a wanderer's life once again, writing prolifically but seldom finding anyone to publish his iconoclastic works, and finally died in Salzburg in 1541, at the age of 48.

The scientific debates of the late 16th century often centred on the innovations of Paracelsus. He pioneered the use of chemicals and minerals in medicine, and is credited with the introduction of opium and mercury as medical treatments. Many regard him as the first homeopath in Western Europe.

An engraving of Paracelsus which appeared in the 1567 edition of his book *Astronomica et Astrologica Pouscula*.
(© Stapleton Collection/Corbis)

He was a firm believer in the power of the mind to determine the success of a patient's recovery, and although he was contemptuous of those who called themselves magicians, and did not consider himself to be one, ASTROLOGY was a very important factor in his medicine, since he believed strongly in the astral influences on human health. He contributed significantly to modern medicine, particularly with regard to diagnosis and chemical treatment, and his works laid the foundations for modern chemical physiology.

paranormal

Something that cannot be explained in terms of the laws of nature and reason as we currently understand them.

The word 'paranormal' is used to mean something that is beside, or parallel to, the 'normal'. The term has proved more acceptable and durable than the alternative 'supernormal' which was coined by the spiritualist F W H Myers. It has become more widely used in recent times in the fields of PARAPSYCHOLOGY, ANOMALISTICS and FORTEANA, where it is felt to imply that further research into the phenomenon in question may result in an alteration of our understanding of the laws of nature, bringing it into the scientific mainstream. See also SUPERNATURAL.

Parapsychology *see panel p516*

Parapsychology

Parapsychology is concerned with what appear to be paranormal experiences, ie interactions between individuals, or between an individual and the environment, which seem to be inexplicable in terms of current scientific understanding. While popular representations of parapsychology often include such phenomena as HAUNTINGS, POLTERGEISTS and UFOS, most parapsychological research is rather less exotic.

Parapsychology might be defined as the scientific study of 'anomalous cognition' (normally referred to as EXTRASENSORY PERCEPTION, or ESP), and 'anomalous influence' (PSYCHOKINESIS, or PK). ESP typically includes CLAIRVOYANCE (discerning information that is beyond the normal range of sense or perception), TELEPATHY (sharing thoughts and images with another individual through mind-to-mind contact) and PRECOGNITION (gaining prior knowledge of future events). PK is typically divided into MACRO-PK (large-scale, observable demonstrations of PK, such as the movement of objects using the power of the mind) and MICRO-PK (small-scale demonstrations of PK, unobservable but measurable via statistical analysis, such as influencing a RANDOM NUMBER GENERATOR). The term PSI (the Greek letter ψ) is a blanket term used to refer to any paranormal phenomenon or process. Thus, the PSI HYPOTHESIS in parapsychology is that some of these experiences at least are indeed paranormal, the result of ESP or PK. However, research in parapsychology has always included the pseudo-psi hypothesis, ie that most, perhaps all, such experiences are misattributed 'normal' experiences, the result of self-deception and deception. Research into ostensibly paranormal experiences and paranormal belief, therefore, overlaps with the interests of 'normal' or mainstream psychology.

The origins of parapsychology can be found in Victorian SPIRITUALISM, when many scientifically minded individuals took an interest in the phenomena of the SÉANCE room. The first serious experiments were those of William Crookes in 1870–1, who began testing the 'physical phenomena' (similar to what is now called PK) of the medium DANIEL DUNGLAS HOME. The following year, in the *Quarterly Journal of Science*, Crookes announced that, as a result of these experiments, he had discovered the existence of a new 'psychic' force. The response of the scientific community was largely negative, however, and subsequent exposures of fraudulent mediums did not help. In 1882, the SOCIETY FOR PSYCHICAL RESEARCH (SPR) was founded, and focused less on physical phenomena than on mental phenomena (similar to what is now called ESP), the word 'telepathy' being coined in 1892, though the SPR retained a significant interest in the question of survival after death. Thus, in Britain at least, psychical research has tended to be broader than parapsychology, including non-experimental research into case studies of, for example, REINCARNATION. Such an approach is unavoidable with spontaneous phenomena (such as poltergeists), but invariably relies upon eyewitness testimony, the problems of which make strong conclusions difficult.

Experimental parapsychology is generally regarded as having been established by J B RHINE. Rhine adopted the term *parapsychology* (first coined by the psychologist Max Dessoir), and helped found the Duke University Parapsychology Laboratory in 1935. Rhine sought to study the paranormal through controlled experiments that would eliminate not only fraud but also the influence of known sensory processes. By introducing a programme of experimental research based upon robust methodologies and statistical analysis, by setting up recruitment and training for members, and by creating a new vehicle of communication (the *Journal of Parapsychology*), Rhine hoped to gain scientific legitimacy for parapsychology. Unlike prior investigations into gifted individual psychic claimants and mediums, Rhine's approach involved experiments with the general population, based on his belief that paranormal abilities were common. These included ESP tests (Rhine introduced the term 'extrasensory perception') that employed ZENER CARDS (designed by Rhine's colleague, Karl Zener), each of which showed one of five symbols (a circle, a cross, wavy lines, a square or a star). Rhine found that participants in experiments often scored well above the 20 per cent hit rate that one would expect by chance. Later, in PK tests (Rhine also popularized the term 'psychokinesis'), participants attempted to influence the roll of DICE in controlled conditions, though results were less successful. Nevertheless, Rhine came to believe that ESP and PK were part of a single process, one that came to be termed 'psi'. After leaving Duke, Rhine set up an independent institute, though its reputation was tarnished as a result of a subsequent scandal in 1974 associated with its Director of Research, Walter Levy, who was caught tampering with data in order to produce erroneous positive results (see RHINE RESEARCH CENTER).

Elsewhere, experimental parapsychology began to explore other ways of studying ESP and PK. In New York, the Maimonides Dream Laboratory tested the ability of individuals to obtain information through ESP while they were in a dream state. At the Stanford Research Institute (founded by the trustees of Stanford University, California, and later fully independent), REMOTE VIEWING experiments were conducted in which individuals were asked to describe and draw a location that had been randomly selected, and to which one of the experimenters had travelled. In both cases, the best results were obtained with a few 'gifted' individuals. Of the various 'free-response' approaches to ESP (ie participants are free to select any possible target, rather than being limited to a range of targets, such as the Zener cards; see FREE-RESPONSE EXPERIMENTS), the most successful has been the 'Ganzfeld' (German for 'whole field'). The GANZFELD EXPERIMENT uses SENSORY DEPRIVATION to enhance mental imagery. In a typical experiment, the participant sits in a comfortable chair listening to white noise through earphones. The eyes are covered with half ping-pong balls, and a light is shone upon them. A target has been randomly selected from a range of visual images, and the participant is asked to describe their mental imagery while in this relaxed state. Afterwards, she or he is shown four randomly selected images (one of which is the target), and asked to rate each in terms of how well it corresponds with the images experienced. In many experiments, participants identified the target image significantly more than 25 per cent of the time (ie what one would expect by chance).

Meanwhile, experimental work on micro-PK began to use random-event generators (REGs), machines that used the emission of electrons randomly to produce one of two outcomes. Participants were asked to attempt to influence the outcomes, and small but significant deviations from chance were obtained. More recent research at the PRINCETON ENGINEERING ANOMALIES RESEARCH (PEAR) laboratory has used both mechanical and electronic REGs, the latter involving enormous numbers of trials and again obtaining small but significant results. PK research has also studied the possibility that individuals can affect other living systems, as is often claimed in reports of PSYCHIC HEALING. A variety of experiments have been carried out with plants, animals and humans in order to test so-called BIO-PK and, more recently, DIRECT MENTAL INTERACTION WITH LIVING SYSTEMS (DMILS). This latter approach draws in part upon the widely held view that one can sense when one is being stared at. Experiments typically involve a receiver and an agent in separate rooms, the former being observable on a video screen by the latter. The receiver may try to guess when she or he is being stared at, or the agent may try to influence the physiology of the receiver.

In both ESP and PK experiments, ongoing criticisms about possible flaws in procedure have led to increasingly rigorous experimental controls which attempt to rule out sensory leakage and other possible 'normal' explanations for results. Meanwhile, as academics have largely focused on experimental work with the general population, the testing of 'gifted' individuals and psychic claimants such as Ted Serios (see THOUGHTOGRAPHY) and URI GELLER has remained a part of parapsychology. For many people, the abilities of such individuals are not only highly implausible, but also similar to the equally puzzling feats of conjurors. Indeed, the case of PROJECT ALPHA, in which magicians posed as psychics and were tested at the McDonnell Laboratory for Psychical Research, led to the claim that parapsychologists were not competent to detect trickery. Subsequently, parapsychologists have worked more closely with open-minded stage magicians (see MAGIC, STAGE), and a significant amount of work has been done within parapsychology on the pseudo-psi hypothesis in general, and the techniques of pseudo-psychics in particular. Alas, this has not prevented some unqualified amateur investigators from being taken in by clever, and sometimes not so clever, trickery.

One of the ongoing criticisms of the psi hypothesis is that, despite some success, parapsychologists have failed to replicate successful experimental results. To date, no standardized procedure can reliably produce positive evidence for psi. Meta-analyses have been carried out, which have analysed the data from large bodies of work, and have suggested that the overall evidence points to an anomalous effect in need of explanation. In 1999, however, the data from all Ganzfeld experiments since 1986 (when improved procedures were established) were analysed, and the conclusion was that there was no overall significant difference from chance. This paper provoked something of a debate within parapsychology about whether all the relevant experiments had been included, but the evidence that Ganzfeld provides a replicable method of obtaining psi in the laboratory has yet to convince the scientific community as a whole. A more recent meta-analysis of REG data has come to similarly disappointing conclusions, though it remains to be seen what the implications of this will be.

While there remains widespread scepticism within the scientific community about the existence of psi, parapsychological research is being carried out in several universities in the UK and elsewhere, with Chairs having been established at Edinburgh, Northampton and Lund. Given that ostensibly paranormal experiences are common, and belief in the paranormal is widespread, a better understanding of what is going on would seem to be highly desirable, even if the scientific community is unconvinced that such experiences might be explained in terms of psi. Meanwhile, regardless of what happens in academia, the media and the public will no doubt continue to be fascinated by the possibility, and the inevitable mixture of enthusiastic investigators, sincere believers and outright frauds will ensure that the mystery never entirely goes away.

Peter Lamont

passing caller

The term used to refer to a discarnate entity that manifests only once to deliver a message.

Those who consider GHOSTS to be a spiritual manifestation indicative of survival after death may embrace the idea of the 'passing caller' – a DISCARNATE ENTITY that appears only once to deliver a message, typically a warning or a farewell. Many CRISIS APPARITIONS might fall into the category of passing callers, although psychical researchers since the 1880s have preferred to account for them in terms of TELEPATHY rather than visitation of a spirit. Spiritualists link the idea of passing callers with 'drop-in communicators' at SÉANCES who appear in place of invited or regular communicators.

past-life regression

The apparent recovery under hypnosis of details relating to individuals' 'previous lives', taken by some to be evidence of reincarnation.

The use of past-life regression became popular following the BRIDEY MURPHY case in 1952, and the subsequent publication of Morey Bernstein's book, *The Search for Bridey Murphy*, in 1956. The procedure involves the use of HYPNOSIS, under the effect of which a suitable subject will appear to recall details of a former life (or lives). Some have even claimed that the process can be used for therapeutic purposes – the suggestion being that problems in our current life may result from events in our past lives.

Hypnosis itself is a notoriously controversial process, and it is widely known that a number of bizarre effects can apparently be produced through its application. Indeed, it has been shown that subjects (whether it is through a desire to please the hypnotist, the use of leading questions or suggestion or for other reasons) can be made to apparently recall all sorts of strange information. In practice, it can often be demonstrated that the past-life regression subject has, or certainly could have, previously encountered most of the information in books or through other 'ordinary' sources. The difficulty for the believer lies in demonstrating that the subject is not simply consciously, or unconsciously, recalling this. See also the BLOXHAM TAPES.

Patterson, Roger *see* BIGFOOT

PEAR *see* PRINCETON ENGINEERING ANOMALIES RESEARCH

pedestrians, spectral *see* SPECTRAL PEDESTRIANS

pendulum

A weight suspended from a thread or string so that it can swing freely, used for divination or dowsing.

One of the tools most widely used for DOWSING is the pendulum – a weight suspended from a thread or string so that it can swing freely. Any material can be used for the weight, but wood and crystal are believed by some to give the most accurate results. The weight may also be hollow, to allow a small sample of any material being dowsed for to be placed inside.

The pendulum can swing in one of four ways:

A pendulum being employed by the dowser Jean Louis Crozier. (© Hekimian Julien/ Corbis Sygma)

clockwise, anticlockwise, forward and backward, or from side to side, and to dowse with a pendulum, the diviner first needs to decide which movement the pendulum will give for a 'yes' and which for a 'no'. This is done by asking a question to which the answer is known to be 'yes' and then asking the pendulum for its response, then asking a question with a known answer of 'no', and again watching the movement of the pendulum. Many dowsers believe that these directions remain constant for any future questions.

Pendulums are thought to be particularly suitable for MAP DOWSING, in which the pendulum is held over a map of the search area. In recent years, pendulums have also come to be used in ALTERNATIVE MEDICINE, particularly in France; the body is dowsed in an attempt to diagnose physical weaknesses or blockages in energy, the AURA is scanned with the pendulum for imbalances or other damage, and some believe that a pendulum can even be used to check for food allergies.

Those who believe that pendulum dowsing works offer a number of theories as to how this might be possible, the most popular being that the pendulum is a means of accessing the dowser's subconscious sensitivity to the electromagnetic field given off by the object, which produces tiny, involuntary muscle movements that are amplified by the pendulum into a visible movement. For this reason, pendulum dowsing is sometimes also known as RADIESTHESIA, from Latin *radius*, meaning ray, and *esthesia*, meaning feeling.

penis panic
The popular name for incidents of mass hysteria involving claims that malicious individuals are using magic to shrink, or even steal, men's genitals.
Penis panics are related to a condition sometimes known as 'genital retraction syndrome', which is most common in south-east Asia (where, among other things, it is known as 'Koro') and parts of Africa. This condition is often described as 'culture-bound' (it only appears among certain cultures and is not recognized in all populations), and involves the sufferer believing (erroneously) that his penis is shrinking back into his body. The supposed causes of this are many and varied.

Penis panics have been reported in many countries in central and western Africa over recent years. They often involve an accusation of WITCHCRAFT against a particular individual, or a claim that an unspecified 'penis snatcher' is in the area. This results in a rapid spread of panic with men claiming, and believing, that black magic has been used to steal their penises. Many of these incidents of MASS HYSTERIA have ended with deaths at the hands of lynch mobs. A representative example of this occurred in Cotonou in Benin in November 2001 when five people were killed (four of them burned to death) following such accusations. The victims of the mob are usually strangers who become the subjects of suspicion as the panic spreads. However, the accusers generally appear to have a real belief that their penises have been stolen, a belief that stems from a set of cultural conditions that can be difficult for the outside observer to fully understand.

These incidents are often dismissed as resulting from superstition, lack of education and a fear of strangers in isolated areas. However, outbreaks of mass hysteria or MASS SOCIOGENIC ILLNESS are certainly not restricted to the developing world – for examples see *WAR OF THE WORLDS*, MAD GASSER OF MATOON and POKÉMON PANIC.

pentacle *see* PENTAGRAM

pentacles, suit of
One of the four suits into which the cards of the tarot's minor arcana are divided.
The suit of pentacles in the tarot is also known as the suit of coins. It contains 14 cards: numbered 'pip' cards going from one to ten, plus four 'court' cards – the Page, the Knight, the King and the Queen. Some people believe that the four suit emblems may originally have symbolized the four main social classes in medieval Europe, with the pentacles or coins representing the merchants. Astrologically, this suit is associated with the element of EARTH, and the three earth signs, TAURUS, CAPRICORN and VIRGO. Corresponding to the suit of diamonds in a modern deck of playing cards, the suit of pentacles is identified principally with the material aspects of life, and with wealth, possessions and finances. It is also believed to represent issues connected with the subject's value, status and sense of self-worth, and to symbolize our connection to the earth and to nature. See also CUPS, SUIT OF; SWORDS, SUIT OF; WANDS, SUIT OF.

pentagram
A five-pointed star drawn with five straight lines whose intersection forms a pentagon; a powerful symbol in neopaganism, Wicca and ceremonial magic.
The pentagram, also known as the pentangle, pentalpha and pentacle, is probably the most widely revered of all esoteric symbols. This five-pointed star, drawn with five straight lines whose intersections form a pentagon, has been a magical sign for thousands of years, and is first found in Mesopotamian writings of around 3000 BC. It has been seen as a sacred symbol of Isis, and is thought by many to represent the Triple Goddess. In ancient times, it symbolized life or health, and was used symbolically in ancient Greece and

A pentagram from the 1896 edition of *Transcendental Magic* by Éliphas Lévi. (© TopFoto/Fortean)

Babylonia. At one time Christians commonly used it to represent the five wounds of Christ; however, in more recent times it has come to be associated with MAGIC, NEOPAGANISM and SATANISM. It is much used by Wiccans and ceremonial magicians, and by extension, it has become part of the symbolism of neopaganism in general.

In the Western magical tradition, WICCA and neopaganism, its five points are thought to represent the five elements – EARTH, AIR, FIRE, WATER and spirit or quintessence; the elements' points are all connected by the unbroken 'eternal' line which runs between them, and traditionally, the pentagram is drawn with a single point at the top, representing spirit, the most important element. The next two points down represent air on the left and water on the right, and the bottom two points represent earth on the left and fire on the right; the pentagram thus symbolizes the elements in ideal balance, and the perfected human being in whom the qualities of the elements are similarly balanced. Some writers refer to it as the endless knot, others as the Seal of Solomon, although the latter term is more commonly used of the HEXAGRAM.

The pentagram, as a figure which can be drawn with a single unbroken line, is believed to be a powerfully protective magical symbol, and depending on the starting point and the direction in which the lines are drawn, can be used as either an invoking or a banishing symbol. Satanists use the symbol of the pentacle inverted so that it has two points at the top, like horns, drawn inside a double circle, with a goat's head – the head of BAPHOMET – depicted inside the pentagram.

A physical representation of the pentagram, called a pentacle, is one of the ritual tools used in neopaganism, Wicca and ceremonial magic. A flat disk with a pentagram drawn or engraved inside a circle, the pentacle is seen as a female tool symbolizing the element of earth, and all that this element signifies – stability, practicality, abundance, structure and humility. It is usually placed in the north of the altar during rituals, the north being the direction associated with the element of earth. A dish with a pentacle on it is sometimes also used to hold the cakes which are shared by the participants after a magical ritual. The pentacle's importance as a magical symbol is demonstrated by the fact that one of the suits of the TAROT is the suit of pentacles (see PENTACLES, SUIT OF). See also MAGIC, CEREMONIAL.

perpetual motion

The hypothetical motion of a machine that performs work indefinitely without an external source of energy.

The concept of a machine that will perform work indefinitely without a constant input of energy is one that has had an attraction for human thought since the days of the alchemists. Such a phenomenon would, however, contravene Newton's laws of thermodynamics, particularly in that energy is conserved and cannot be created from nothing.

Leonardo da Vinci (1452–1519) was interested in the concept and made various drawings of possible machines that might achieve it, but in the end he concluded that it was impossible and that those who pursued it were no better than alchemists seeking to make themselves rich by finding the PHILOSOPHER'S STONE. Indeed, the English alchemist JOHN DEE claimed to have witnessed a perpetual motion machine invented by someone else, but he was unable to examine it closely.

In 1630, Robert Fludd (1574–1637), the English physician, mystic and pantheistic theosophist, proposed a machine that would operate by the constant recirculation of water. It would not have worked, but the idea behind it continues to inspire variations on his original design.

Other scientists who are well known for their work in other fields have spent time and thought on the quest for perpetual motion, but without any practical success. Among them are Edward Somerset, Earl of Worcester (1601–67), inventor of a steam water pump, Jean (or Johann) Bernoulli (1667–1748), the Swiss mathematician, Sir William Congreve (1772–1828), inventor of the Congreve rocket, and NIKOLA TESLA, the US physicist and electrical engineer.

Throughout the centuries, and up to the present day, many inventors have claimed to have produced a perpetual motion, or 'free energy', machine. However, without exception, none of their designs has been shown to be viable. In a large number of cases, their projects have simply been hoaxes, or elaborate confidence tricks aimed at defrauding would-be investors of large sums of money. Prototypes that have been convincing enough to impress the non-scientific witness have inevitably been shown to be bogus, appearing to run without the input of energy but in reality powered by hidden springs, unseen air pressure tubes or concealed connections to external power sources.

Many patents for perpetual motion machines have been issued in the United Kingdom, the USA and many other countries, and some take this as proof that these devices are genuine. However, these patents refer to the designs and do not in themselves indicate that the patented machine will actually work when built and none so far has been satisfactorily demonstrated in action to an unrestricted objective audience.

The idea of a machine running without input of energy, and the savings in power costs that it would represent, is perhaps more attractive to scientists than the 'holy grail' of perpetual motion for its own sake. Science continually breaks new ground and finds explanations for phenomena that have puzzled preceding generations. However, while scientists accept that the current knowledge of physics may yet be superseded by future discoveries, no work in the field of perpetual motion has yet produced evidence that Newton's laws of thermodynamics can safely be set aside.

Persinger, Dr Michael (1945–   )
Canadian neuroscientist who has conducted experiments in an attempt to find evidence to support the idea that UFO close encounters are visionary in nature.
In 1977, Michael Persinger, a professor at the Laurentian State University in Ontario, Canada, published a study of the locations of hundreds of mysterious phenomena. These included APPARITIONS and other visionary reports (see VISIONS), but also featured many UFO sightings. He found statistical evidence to indicate that these events clustered in certain geographical locations and he suggested that environmental factors were making these places 'hot spots' for strange phenomena – details were published in his report, *Space-Time Transients*. His ideas tied in with the WINDOW AREA concept that UFO researchers had independently recognized from a study of their own case files.

Persinger developed a theory that, at these hot spots, a locally strong electrical field could trigger the strange phenomena. He suggested that these fields might generate ionization and produce a visible glow, seen by a witness as a UFO. They might even remain entirely invisible, being only indirectly recognized by the effects that they had on a witness. He labelled these hypothetical fields 'transients' because they would only exist for a short period, but be prone to recurring in these hot-spot areas as a result of specific geological or atmospheric conditions.

In order to prove the viability of his theory Persinger began a series of experiments in which university students were subjected to artificially created transients and asked to report on their experiences. The results were published in a long series of reports in professional journals. The participants reported a wide range of unusual symptoms, including feelings of dissociation, isolation and dreaminess. Many of the feelings were similar to those described as the OZ FACTOR, already identified by UFO researchers as a commonly reported set of symptoms that were experienced by witnesses to CLOSE ENCOUNTERS.

As Persinger developed his experiments he also found that extraordinary visionary experiences were reported by some of his subjects; although by a smaller number of them than reported vague alterations to their state of consciousness. While these experiences had a 'mystical' feel, they were not as specific or consistent as those reported in ALIEN ABDUCTION cases.

Further research has suggested that the electrical field can stimulate the temporal lobe of the brain and that this effect is responsible for the Oz-factor-like sensations. The depth and quality of a visionary experience may depend on existing psychological factors, including how prone to fantasy the subject is. Expectation may also play a part. Witnessing a strange light (whether it is one generated by a transient or whether it is a misperception while under the influence of a transient) could cause some people to report a UFO of the type referred to as LIGHTS IN THE SKY. Others might develop a more vivid visionary experience and think they had encountered ALIENS. The same trigger within a different context, perhaps inside a dark old house at night, might produce a reported sighting of a GHOST.

The theory remains controversial, and the exact link between changes in brain chemistry and the sensations of seeing a physically real UFO is still unclear. However, many UFO researchers (particularly in Europe and Australia, where psychosocial theories have gained more attention – see PSYCHOSOCIAL HYPOTHESIS) consider Persinger's work to be potentially significant.

Petit Trianon, Ghosts of the *see panel p524*

petrifaction

The process of organic tissue turning to stone.

Petrifaction is the process by which organic tissue is turned into stone, with the original molecules being replaced over time by molecules of such chemicals as calcium carbonate or silica. It is this process that produces fossils of once-living animals and plants, immortalizing their remains in rock.

The Petrified Forest in Calistoga, California, is a famous example of a forest that has undergone petrifaction. The redwoods there have been dated back to the Pliocene epoch, over two million years ago, when they are believed to have been covered in volcanic ash. They were gradually exposed as the softer rocks around them eroded.

Discovery of petrified plants and animals may have given rise to the accounts in mythology of creatures with the power of magical petrifaction. In ancient Greek legend, anyone who looked on the face of the Gorgon Medusa was instantly turned to stone. The hero Perseus was able to avoid this fate and kill her by only looking at her reflection in a polished shield.

Myths connected with many STONE CIRCLES in the British Isles and elsewhere often claim that the monoliths represent giants or legendary warriors that have been turned to stone, usually by a curse or through having earned the displeasure of a deity. On Dartmoor, for example, the Nine Maidens stone circle is said to represent maidens who were turned to stone for dancing on a Sunday, and in Cornwall, The Blind Fiddler and the Two Sisters are also said to be people turned to stone for acting in an unchristian manner on the Sabbath – the Blind Fiddler played his instrument and the Two Sisters did not attend church.

petroglyphs

Pictures carved on stone by prehistoric peoples.

A petroglyph is an image either carved or otherwise marked into the surface of a stone. The word comes from the Greek *petra*, meaning stone, and *glyphein*, to carve. Petroglyphs have been found in various parts of the world, from Europe to Asia, the Americas and Australia, and most of them date from 10 000 BC to 5000 BC. After this period they tended to be replaced by more sophisticated methods of art or communication such as cave painting, although some more isolated cultures such as the Australian Aborigines and Native Americans continued to make them for longer periods.

Various methods were used, including scoring, hammering and chipping away the surface levels of stone, depending on the hardness or sophistication of the tools available. The images tend to be stylized forms of human beings or animals such as deer or other creatures that were the usual prey of hunter-gatherer

societies, but in many cases it remains unknown what is represented. Some may have been a primitive form of pictorial writing, and markings found in Russia have been compared to RUNES, although it has not been possible to establish any firm connection.

It is thought that most petroglyphs had religious or cult significance, or show tribal or personal markings which established the ownership of territories or particularly significant sites.

Some analysts have claimed that they have detected similarities between petroglyphs in different parts of the world, and have used these to postulate cultural contacts in the prehistoric world. However, given that the images tend to represent the lives of the primitive peoples that created them, including the animals they hunted, it is hardly surprising that petroglyphs from different parts of the world should display common themes.

Particularly impressive petroglyphs are found, for example, at the megalithic passage tomb at Newgrange in Ireland, where stones have been decorated with intricate spiral patterns whose meaning is unclear. At Dampier in Western Australia, the ancestors of the Aboriginal people created perhaps the world's largest number of petroglyphs in a single site. The ICA STONES of Peru constitute one of the more controversial collections of petroglyphs.

In the British Isles, one of the more common types of petroglyph is the cup and ring mark. This is the name given to the characteristic pattern of a round hollow made in the surface of a rock and usually surrounded by concentric circles. The method for creating these seems to have been one of 'pecking' (chipping stone away using a sharp-pointed instrument) followed by grinding. Examples have been found marked on both megaliths and natural rock outcrops. There are fine examples of cup and ring marks on Ilkley Moor in Yorkshire, at Lordenshaw in Northumberland and at various sites in Argyll, Scotland. These designs are not unique to Britain, however, and examples have also been found in Brittany. It is not known what these patterns represent, but the fact that they are fairly widespread would suggest that they had some kind of cultural significance. They seem to have become less popular during the Bronze Age.

peyote

The peyote cactus, Lophophora williamsii, *found in Mexico and the south-western USA, whose dried tubercles, known as mescal buttons, are chewed or drunk in infusion either as part of a religious ceremony, for healing, or as a recreational drug.*

Peyote (*Lophophora williamsii*) is a spineless cactus that grows in the south-western USA and in Mexico. Its buttons are either chewed or drunk in infusion and produce a trance state accompanied by powerful

Ghosts of the Petit Trianon

On 10 August 1901, two English women, Miss Annie Moberly and Miss Eleanor Jourdain, were visiting the 17th-century palace at Versailles, near Paris. As they walked in the grounds of the palace, near the small chateau of Petit Trianon, they wondered at the quaint old-fashioned costume of the staff working in the gardens and also noticed that a fellow tourist, who sat sketching, was wearing a peculiarly outdated form of dress. The two women were impressed by their visit, although they had experienced a sense of oppression, which they felt was caused by the August heat.

On looking into the history of the palace after their visit, the two women came to a startling conclusion – that they had witnessed a series of apparitions and a wholesale transformation of scenery back to the 18th century. They claimed that they discovered that the grounds as they had seen them, and the buildings contained in them, had been those of the 18th century, not the early 20th century (by which time numerous alterations had been made). They also claimed that they could date the scenes they had witnessed more specifically – they believed that the tourist they had seen sketching was Marie Antoinette, who had last been at Versailles in 1789.

Each woman wrote a detailed account of her experiences, and their story was eventually published as *An Adventure* in 1911. The book included very precise details of the former garden design and architectural features at Petit Trianon, and of the costumes of the late 18th century. However, from its initial appearance

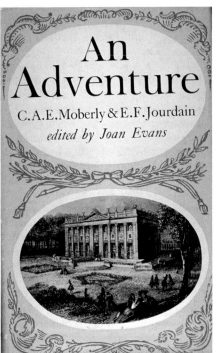

The cover of the 1955 edition of *An Adventure* by C A E Moberley and E F Jourdain, in which they related the details of their alleged encounter with a time slip at Petit Trianon, Versailles. (© TopFoto/Fortean)

An Adventure was criticized by many psychical researchers, although the work remained popular and was reprinted five times in the next 45 years. The case has continued to be the subject of much discussion since the last edition of *An Adventure* in 1955. Some credence was given to the account by the researcher Guy Lambert, who argued in 1958 that there were some 20 distinguishing features to their experiences inconsistent with 1901, and suggested that the two women had witnessed the Petit Trianon as it had appeared in around 1770.

One theory proposing a natural explanation of the events is that the two women inadvertently observed a costume masquerade – although this would not account for the architectural discrepancies they described. Others have suggested that Moberly and Jourdain simply imagined their experiences, or built them up from subconscious recollections of books or pictures they had seen relating to the history of Versailles. Supporters of a paranormal explanation claim that the case of Petit Trianon is a genuine example of a TIME SLIP, and that the women really did witness 18th-century Versailles. Others have pointed out that Jourdain and Moberly were not the only people to see strange things there – in 1908 there were reports of a 'sketching tourist' near Petit Trianon, and a number of visitors reported seeing other figures in old-fashioned dress over the next few decades. However, hopes that there might be a repetition of phenomena in 2001, on the hundredth anniversary of the famous Petit Trianon experience, were not fulfilled.

hallucinogenic visions, due to the active substance, mescaline, which they contain.

Peyote, or mescal, was originally used for religious and medicinal purposes among the native tribes of Mexico and among the Navajo. Its use spread northwards during the late 19th century, particularly with the foundation of the Native American Church movement (sometimes also known as the Peyote religion or Peyotism) which incorporates both Native American and Christian tradition. The group use of peyote is believed to help church members commune with God (or the Great Spirit – see MANITOU), the ancestors, and the spiritual world (see VISION QUEST), although the beliefs associated with the use of peyote vary from tribe to tribe.

The harvesting and use of peyote is strictly controlled by both federal and state laws in the United States, its legal use being restricted solely to bona fide Native American religious practice.

Phaistos Disc
A stone disc found in Crete that is inscribed with an as-yet-undeciphered set of symbols, said by some to represent an alien language.
Phaistos, near the Kashi Hills of Crete, was an important city during the Minoan civilization – a highly educated society that thrived for many centuries, more than 4,000 years ago. The region is considered by some to be a strong contender for the

The Phaistos Disc, believed by some to be engraved with writing in an alien language. (© Gianni Dagli Orti/Corbis)

origin of the ATLANTIS legend – the Minoans possessed artistic and scientific skills before suffering a major earthquake that caused massive destruction.

In 1903 the Phaistos Disc was unearthed from a small room at the site of the palace in this ancient city. It was alongside pottery that was dated to c.1700 BC. The plate-sized disc carries glyphs or symbols in a spiral. They have not been decoded but are thought by many archaeologists to represent something mundane, such as a military record.

However, some supporters of the theory of ANCIENT ASTRONAUTS propose that the inscriptions on the disc may be written in an alien language, placed there by highly advanced extraterrestrial visitors that they argue lived on earth thousands of years ago. These beings are said to have inspired or guided both scientific discovery and enigmatic artwork across the world. Possibly owing to the similarity in shape to a modern computer disc, some theorists have suggested that the Phaistos Disc might be a technological device, perhaps used to measure distances through space.

phantasm
The term used by early psychical researchers for visual apparitions, or ghosts.
During the early years of the Committee on Haunted Houses – organized by the SOCIETY FOR PSYCHICAL RESEARCH – it was felt that the traditional word 'GHOST' was an inappropriate term to describe the phenomena which the Society was engaged in studying. Noting that many apparitions appeared to be hallucinatory in nature and showed little or no awareness of observers and that the forms of living people were as frequently encountered as those of the dead, it was felt an alternative terminology was needed. Furthermore, the word 'ghost' was felt to have spiritual and superstitious connotations which the fledgling society was keen to be dissociated from, considering itself to be engaged upon a scientific exercise. As a result a number of leading members of the Society adopted the term 'phantasm' to describe an apparitional appearance. Phantasm was used by Edmund Gurney, Frederic Myers and Frank Podmore in the title of their monumental two-volume work *Phantasms of the Living* (1886), detailing hundreds of contemporary reports of CRISIS APPARITIONS. However, while psychical researchers and parapsychologists still remain wary of the term 'ghost', the word 'phantasm' failed to catch on outside a limited circle.

phantom aeroplanes
The manifestation of ghost aeroplanes, either seen or heard.
Reports of phantom aeroplanes have emerged

sporadically since the 1930s in different parts of the world. In some cases they have come in WAVES, as with reports of unidentified ghost planes in the skies over Scandinavia during the 1930s, and have been considered as an aspect of wider UFO phenomena. In other reports the phantom is identifiable as a specific aircraft which is known to have crashed or a military aircraft dating from World War II.

The first British case appears to have been a ghostly biplane seen by local residents over Shepperton, Surrey, during 1931. It was believed to be the spectral form of a Vickers Vanguard test aircraft which had crashed in the area two years earlier killing its pilot. Former World War II aerodromes have also produced reports of phantom aeroplanes, including an account of a phantom plane seen landing at Barkston Heath, Lincolnshire, witnessed by a 17-year-old girl in the late 1960s. There are also reports of a phantom bomber plane seen in the 1990s over Bleaklow Hill in Derbyshire, in the vicinity of a number of known bomber crash sites.

In other cases the phantom aeroplane may be heard rather than seen; a ghostly spitfire is said to have been heard over Biggin Hill in Kent, and the sound of a World War II phantom plane was allegedly captured on tape at the former Bircham Newton Aerodrome in Norfolk in 1972. See also FOO FIGHTERS.

phantom armies *see* SPECTRAL ARMIES

phantom coaches
Apparitions of horse-drawn carriages.
Stories of phantom coaches are common in English folklore, but some consider that there are a small number of reports that suggest that they may also constitute a genuine apparitional experience. With most examples the phantom coach is a horse-drawn private carriage but in other cases the vehicle may be a funeral hearse. In many traditional tales both the occupants of the coach and the horses pulling it appear headless, but no reliable first-hand sightings are known.

Tales of phantom coaches were particularly common in the English county of Norfolk in the 19th century. Tradition frequently links phantom coaches with the aristocracy (who were among the few who could afford the luxury of a private coach), with particular landed families or with executed criminals (usually noblemen, rarely commoners). In some folktales driving a phantom coach is a form of punishment for the soul of someone who has committed heinous sins in life, such as Tobias Gill at Blythburgh, Suffolk, who was hanged for murder in 1750 and who is said to be seen thundering past in a phantom coach pulled by four black chargers.

Similarly, a phantom coach is said to carry Sir Thomas Boleyn, father of Anne Boleyn (the second wife of Henry VIII), from his home of Blickling Hall around a circuit of twelve Norfolk bridges. The story goes that Sir Thomas is atoning for his part in his daughter's execution, and that if anyone speaks to him they will be carried away.

Some phantom coaches are said to have a prophetic function, acting as an OMEN of death for particular families, while others are said to be dangerous to encounter and capable of causing injury or of stealing the lives or souls of witnesses (as with that of Sir Thomas Boleyn). Folklorists have detected within this tradition both echoes of the belief in the WILD HUNT of Odin and also the abduction motif common in supernatural folklore and UFO mythology (see ALIEN ABDUCTION).

Sightings of phantom coaches that some researchers believe may be more than simple tradition include examples reported at Enfield, London, in December 1961; a phantom coach seen to plunge into the moat at the Old Court House, Shelsey Wash in Worcestershire on Christmas Eve 1965; and a coach and horses reputedly seen by a motorist at Lion's Grave near Ditchingham, Norfolk, in the early 1970s.

phantom dogs *see* GHOST DOGS

phantom funerals
Apparitions of funerals, thought to herald the death of a local person.
In Celtic tradition, apparitions are often considered to be warnings of future events, particularly an impending death in the locality. In many such stories the warning takes the form of a sensory perception of a funeral some days or weeks before the real burial ceremony occurs. In Scotland such impressions are taken as examples of SECOND SIGHT. An extensive tradition of phantom funerals as a warning was also known in Wales, examples having been documented since the 18th century. It is often thought that the experience is limited to a vision of a funeral cortege or procession, almost invariably encountered on an empty highway at night. However, analysis of traditional and contemporary reports suggests that the predictive vision may in fact be conveyed by a much wider range of visual or auditory hallucinations. The vision may be of acts preparatory to the funeral (such as sounds of coffins being made) or forming part of the ceremony itself (the sound of psalms being sung). A study conducted into modern Scottish second sight experiences by Edinburgh-based researcher Dr Shari Cohn in the mid 1990s showed a decline

in sightings of phantom funeral processions but this might be accounted for by the fact that people no longer travel long distances on foot at night. Nonetheless, the survey of 140 women and 68 men who claimed second sight experiences indicated phantom funeral processions were reported by 10 per cent of the women and 4.8 per cent of the men. The study also confirmed the continuing role of auditory hallucinations with accounts of noises variously interpreted as symbolizing a forthcoming funeral, such as the clink of glasses used at a wake. Fragmentary accounts of ghostly funeral processions in other parts of the UK may suggest that the belief was once more widespread.

phantom hitch-hikers

Ghostly hitch-hikers, the subject of ubiquitous folktales in which a hitch-hiker is picked up by a driver only to vanish during the journey.

One of the most widespread of ghost motifs is the story of the phantom hitch-hiker (or vanishing hitch-hiker, as they are known in the USA). The basic story involves a motorist picking up a hitch-hiker, usually a young woman, at night. The hitch-hiker travels some distance only to vanish inexplicably from the vehicle. On reporting the disappearance to the authorities (or going to an address mentioned by the hitch-hiker in the course of the journey), the motorist often learns that she was killed in a road accident in the recent past. In some accounts the driver lends the phantom hitch-hiker an item of clothing which is later found on top of the girl's grave; in other versions it is the hitch-hiker who leaves a garment, such as a book or a purse, that is apparently later identified as belonging to the deceased person. Versions of the story have been recorded in every state of the USA and in many British counties. Examples are also known from other countries including Italy, Pakistan and Colombia. Alternative versions of the story from the late 1960s have the phantom hitch-hiker as a hippy who utters prophecies to the driver of disasters or the Second Coming. A study of over 100 different variants of the story, carried out in 1984 by the folklorist Michael Goss, concluded that such stories have been in circulation for many years and long pre-date the motor car: in a Swedish case from 1602 the vehicle was a sleigh.

Although tales of phantom hitch-hikers are widespread, the stories invariably lack any hard facts capable of corroboration. Also, reliable first-hand accounts for any such phenomena are virtually non-existent, as most tales seem to relate to 'a friend of a friend who picked up a hitch-hiker', giving them the status of URBAN LEGEND. One of the few British cases in which a named witness is cited is the story of Roy Fulton. Fulton claimed that he picked up a silent male hitch-hiker on 12 October 1979, along a road at Standbridge, near Dunstable, Bedfordshire. The passenger then vanished without explanation during the journey; subsequent investigation revealed that Fulton had reported the case to the police but no similar encounters were known in the area. Reviewing such stories Goss concluded that the phantom hitch-hiker is a 'classic fabrication', though some would argue that it is likely that occasional genuine apparitional encounters, particularly with SPECTRAL PEDESTRIANS, may have contributed to its propagation and survival as a story. See also RESURRECTION MARY.

phantom pedestrians *see* SPECTRAL PEDESTRIANS

phantom phone calls

Telephone calls purportedly made by discarnate entities.

The first account of a phantom telephone call was detailed in the spiritualist journal *Borderland* in the autumn of 1896. A correspondent claimed that the psychic message 'Go to your father's house poor Nellie is dead' was heard over the telephone at the moment of his sister's death. Since then, occasional reports of telephone calls purportedly from discarnate entities (see DISCARNATE ENTITY) have appeared in the literature of SPIRITUALISM, and phantom phone calls are also a feature of many popular ghost stories, but research in this area reveals that the testimony relating to allegedly true cases rarely reaches evidential significance.

Telephone interference has been reported in a number of POLTERGEIST cases, most notably in the ROSENHEIM POLTERGEIST case in Germany in 1968. Alleged UFO witnesses in the USA have also claimed that they have received mysterious phone calls – typically menacing voices – but if such incidents are true, human pranksters cannot be eliminated.

Some believe that phantom phone calls represent a form of ELECTRONIC VOICE PHENOMENA, and that they are essentially messages from the spirit world. Indeed, the US journalist and parapsychologist D Scott Rogo published a number of claims of phone calls from deceased persons in his 1979 book, *Phone Calls from the Dead*. However, the claims were met with widespread scepticism and were ridiculed by Robert A Baker (a sceptical psychologist) in a chapter entitled 'Calling All Corpses: Dial D for Dead' in his book *Hidden Voices* (1990), and little has been heard of the phenomenon since.

phantoms, aerial *see* AERIAL PHANTOMS

phantom ships *see* GHOST SHIPS

phantom trains

In British folklore, apparitions of trains, particularly associated with the sites of earlier rail accidents.

While stories of apparitional vehicles such as PHANTOM COACHES are occasionally reported as fact, ghost researchers suggest that there appear to be only folkloric accounts of phantom trains. A phantom train is said to be heard running along the route of the former mineral line near Washford in Somerset that closed in 1917, and is associated with a train collision of 1857. A ghostly train is said to cross the River Tay at Wormit, near Dundee, on the anniversary of the Tay Bridge disaster – when the rail bridge collapsed on 28 December 1879 and 75 lives were lost. A phantom train is also said to run along the old Highland line at Dunphail, Grampian, appearing a few feet above the ground. At Soham, Cambridgeshire, a ghostly train is said to appear at the site of the now closed station on the anniversary of the destruction of an ammunition train in 1942 when two people were killed. First-hand accounts of these phantom trains are largely lacking (hence they are labelled as folklore) but phantom trains still regularly feature in fiction, and 'ghost trains' are a popular entertainment at fairgrounds and theme parks.

Philadelphia Experiment

An alleged US Navy experiment resulting in teleportation.

One of the more unusual stories to emerge from the USA's involvement in World War II is that of the Philadelphia Experiment. According to the story, in the autumn of 1943 the US Navy conducted an experiment that went wrong in unexpected and bizarre ways, resulting in the accidental teleporting of the destroyer USS *Eldridge* from Philadelphia, Pennsylvania to Norfolk, Virginia.

Apparently, the experiment, codenamed 'Project Rainbow', was intended to investigate the possibility of making a warship invisible using degaussing technology. The danger of magnetic mines, triggered by the magnetic field of a ship rather than needing actual physical contact, had been found to be lessened by neutralizing a vessel's magnetic field by encircling it with an electric current, a technique known as degaussing. It was suggested that if a ship could be made 'invisible' to magnetic mines, it might then be possible to make it invisible to human sight.

Details of the technology and methods supposed to have been used in the experiment are, somewhat predictably, rather sketchy, but the result is said to have been that the *Eldridge* disappeared from sight for a few moments, to appear briefly and mysteriously in its other location, before rematerializing at its moorings in Philadelphia. The apparition at Norfolk was said to have been witnessed there by members of the crew of the merchant ship SS *Andrew Furuseth*.

Apart from the astonishing main result, the experiment is also said to have had alarming side-effects, including the vanishing of personnel, some of whom rematerialized partially embedded in the fabric of the ship, and some of whom never reappeared at all. Other crew members apparently caught fire or became insane. Horrified by these developments, the Navy is said to have abandoned the experimental programme and discharged all of the service personnel involved, even brainwashing many of them to remove their memories of their experience.

Much of this information is dependent on the testimony of a single witness, apparently called Carlos Allende (see ALLENDE LETTERS), a US sailor who claimed to have been on board the SS *Andrew Furuseth*. He was later dismissed by sceptics as a fantasist and hoaxer.

The US Navy has always denied the existence of 'Project Rainbow' and claims that its records show exactly where the USS *Eldridge* was at all times during its service and that no such anomalous events took place. It also maintains that the master of the *Andrew Furuseth* denied in writing that he or any of his crew saw anything extraordinary while they were in Norfolk. The official explanation is that confusion arose between making a ship 'invisible to magnetic mines' and making it actually invisible, and that the story grew out of all proportion from gossip based on a simple misunderstanding.

Conspiracy theorists are quick to allege, of course, that this is merely part of an official cover-up being put into place, both to protect military secrets and to avoid the Navy being sued by the dependants of the experiment's 'casualties'. This ignores the fact that the technology necessary to perform TELEPORTATION was simply not available at the time (and is still not available) and that the effect was beyond the laws of physics, even in theory.

Philip experiment

A parapsychological experiment in Toronto in the 1970s in which a 'ghost' was created.

In September 1972 members of the Toronto Society for Psychical Research, led by Iris Owen, engaged in an experiment to create an artificial ghost. Known as the Philip experiment, it drew inspiration from 19th-century accounts of TABLE-TURNING and the work of Kenneth Batcheldor in Great Britain in the 1960s, who tried to create physical manifestations of ghosts on demand. Members of the group invented an imaginary 17th-century character named Philip. They created a wholly fictitious biography for Philip: born in 1624, he was an aristocrat, married to a beautiful woman called Dorothea, but he kept a mistress named Margo in a gatehouse on his estate – when Dorothea discovered his infidelity she had Margo burnt as a witch, and the broken-hearted Philip committed suicide in 1654.

Initially the group tried to make an apparition of their imaginary ghost materialize through meditation and visualization, but for some months little happened at their weekly meetings. Eventually they took a different approach, and they attempted to communicate with Philip through verbal questions while the members of the group were seated around a card table. Within a few sessions the group were rewarded by rapping sounds in response to these questions – answers which sometimes confirmed, but sometimes contradicted elements of Philip's fictitious biography. 'Philip' was also apparently able to apply force to the table, causing it to levitate, and the group also claimed he could produce cool breezes. The story of Philip was first published in *New Horizons* magazine in 1974 and a short factual film, *Philip, The Imaginary Ghost*, was made the same year; on one occasion the table movement was captured on film by a local television station. Further experiments by the Philip group were also conducted at Kent State University in March 1975, allowing physicists to test the processes involved. Iris Owen also wrote a book, *Conjuring Up Philip: An Adventure in Psychokinesis* (1976), describing the experiment.

As Philip was wholly invented, it appears that the phenomena attributed to the ghost were the product of PSYCHOKINESIS (coming from the unconscious minds of the sitters) rather than from any form of DISCARNATE ENTITY. However, having established a limited range of phenomena, interest in the project waned and the group ceased their sittings in 1978.

Despite its success, there have been few attempts to recreate the Philip experiment, although a number of other Canadian groups have produced similar results with other fictional 'ghosts'.

philosopher's mercury
One of the three basic 'principles' that alchemists believed to be present in all material substances; also used as another name for the philosopher's stone.
Mercury, called quicksilver by the ancients, has always been of prime importance to alchemists. But they also sought to acquire a substance they called philosopher's mercury, which is not to be confused with the common mercury they used in their experiments.

Alchemists believed that all physical substances could be divided, via alchemical processes, into the 'three principles' of which they were ultimately composed – SALT, SULPHUR and mercury. Also known as the *tria prima*, these three principles were thought to be present in all base matter, and were said to be in perfect balance in gold. Sulphur and mercury, combined, were considered to be the 'parents' of all metals. The sulphur to which alchemists referred in this context was perceived as an oily form which adhered to the mercury of a substance, and which was separable from it by alchemical means. This notion of the three 'heavenly substances' was central to the scheme of Nature proposed by PARACELSUS, who held that mercury represented the principle of fusibility and volatility, and that it corresponded to the spirit. It was personified as Luna (the Moon), and was thought to represent the female, or YIN, principle.

Without philosopher's mercury, it was said, no alchemical work could begin or be brought to its perfect end. In its most elementary state it was perceived as pure energy, and was believed to be the source of all activity in the universe. Philosopher's mercury was known by many other names, such as Celestial Water, Aqua Vitae, Water of Chaos, Water of the Wise, Dew of May, Alkahest and AZOTH. It was also used as another term for the universal remedy theorized by Paracelsus, which contained the virtues of all other medicines, and hence, for the PHILOSOPHER'S STONE.

philosopher's stone
An imaginary stone or compound sought by alchemists as a universal remedy and a means of transforming other metals into gold.
The Magnum Opus or 'Great Work' often referred to by alchemists was their quest for the philosopher's stone, a mythical substance which could transmute inexpensive metals into gold and create an elixir that could prolong life indefinitely.

> Our Stone is nothing but gold digested to the highest degree of purity and subtle fixation … Our gold, no longer vulgar, is the ultimate goal of Nature.

The making of the philosopher's stone, also called by various other names, such as AZOTH, the Grand Catholicon, quintessence, philosophical powder, and PHILOSOPHER'S MERCURY, was thought to confer upon the alchemist a type of initiation, which was held by many to be the proper culmination of the Great Work – not the mere turning of lead into gold, or the production of an elixir to gain immortality, but the purification and perfection of the self. It was often said that in order to be able to create the philosopher's stone, the alchemist had to have already succeeded in the 'inner work' of attaining spiritual purity. Alchemists, it should be remembered, often used highly symbolic language, and it may be that the stone was in fact used as a symbol of man himself, and that the transformation of lead into gold was an analogy for spiritual progress; many modern writers believe that the goals of ALCHEMY as symbolized by the philosopher's stone were really a metaphor for the transformation of the alchemist himself, his attainment of spiritual perfection, from a base state to one of purity, refinement and incorruptibility.

phone calls from the dead *see* PHANTOM PHONE CALLS

photographs, ghost *see* GHOST PHOTOGRAPHS

photographs, UFO *see* UFO PHOTOGRAPHS

photography, spirit *see* SPIRIT PHOTOGRAPHY

phrenology
The investigation of mental faculties by feeling bumps on the head.
We tend to think now of phrenology as essentially a Victorian enthusiasm. The pioneer of this would-be science was the Viennese physician Franz Joseph Gall (1758–1828). While in medical practice, he gradually evolved the theories by which he traced talents and other qualities in human beings to the functions of particular areas of the brain and the shape of the skull.

He believed that the surface of the skull could be 'read' by passing the fingers over it, and that the results could be used to indicate psychological tendencies because, in his opinion, it was the size and shape of the brain that determined the shape of the skull. For example, a protuberance near the forehead was considered to be the seat of the 'organ' of benevolence.

From Austria phrenology spread to Britain, where a phrenological society was established in Edinburgh in 1820, soon followed by many more throughout the UK and USA. The 'science' was highly popular for a while, with many setting themselves up as practitioners and hundreds of enthusiastic amateurs taking it up as a hobby. After a decline in interest, it was an American, Lorenzo Niles Fowler (1811–96), who reinvigorated phrenology in Britain in the 1860s, with his series of lecture tours. Fowler also made money by performing personal readings for a fee.

By the end of the 19th century, however, phrenology was largely discredited. Above all, medical science had established that individual faculties or personality traits had no relation to the size of the so-called 'organs' in the brain.

physical medium *see* MEDIUM, PHYSICAL

physiognomy
The judging of character by the appearance of the face.
The word 'physiognomy' derives from Greek words meaning 'interpretation of nature' and it was in ancient Greece that the practice seems to have begun. The philosopher and scientist Aristotle (384–322 BC) believed that the operation of passions and desires

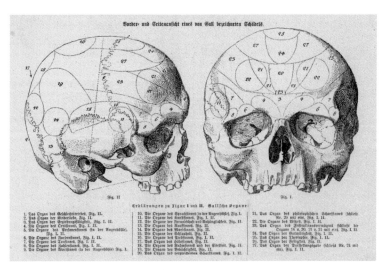

A diagram of Gall's phrenological system from a 19th-century German treatise.
(© Mary Evans Picture Library)

could affect both the soul and the body, including the face. The Romans also believed in the validity of physiognomy and through the dissemination of Roman learning it became well accepted throughout medieval Europe.

Physical traits of the face, such as the length of the nose, the width of the space between the eyes, the shape of the ears and the angle of the forehead or cheeks, were variously interpreted by different analysts as indicating the fundamental nature of the person involved. Treatises were written on how to make judgements of character simply by close observation of individual faces. The whole body was also involved, with various characteristics being assigned to such indicators as height, the length of the limbs, the fullness (or otherwise) of the belly, and the hair of both the head and body.

Along with its use in interpreting character, physiognomy was considered a useful tool in ASTROLOGY and taken as a physical manifestation of planetary influences on the human character. Like PALMISTRY, it was used by practitioners as a means of telling fortunes or predicting the future.

Physiognomy was popular in the Renaissance and, among others, the Italian natural philosopher Giovanni Battista Della Porta (1535–1615) wrote on the subject.

One of the chief proponents of physiognomy in modern times was the Swiss theologian and poet Johann Kaspar Lavater (1741–1801). In an attempt to elevate the subject into a recognized science he wrote five volumes of essays on it, published in English (1789–98) as *Essays on Physiognomy, designed to promote the knowledge and the love of mankind.*

Many 19th-century novelists, such as Honoré de Balzac (1799–1850) and Charles Dickens (1812–70), were believers in physiognomy and this is reflected in their extensive descriptions of the faces and physical appearances of their characters. At this time criminologists attempted to use physiognomy in determining or predicting criminal tendencies and in identifying social undesirables.

Critics characterized physiognomy as merely a justification of natural human tendencies to judge people solely on their appearance, to be attracted by the physically beautiful and repelled by the ugly. Racists also used it to explain differences between races and to justify the alleged superiority of one race over another. In particular, the Nazis systematized these kinds of ideas into a pseudoscience in their persecution of the Jews. Such objectionable uses helped to discredit the practice and undermine its would-be scientific status in the 20th century.

Physiognomy, sometimes referred to as face reading, continues to have its adherents; computer programs are available that claim to give the user access to 'digital physiognomy'. However, the practice is now firmly confined to the non-scientific sphere.

physiological effects

Unusual physiological sensations reported in some UFO cases that have caused a number of researchers to speculate about radiation emissions during reported encounters.

Physiological effects are heavily associated with CLOSE ENCOUNTER cases. While they feature in less than 1 per cent of LIGHTS IN THE SKY reports, they are a factor in over 20 per cent of close-proximity sightings.

What is possibly the earliest example of such a report dates from 1645, when a Cornish woman at St Teath described what is taken by some to be the first known ALIEN ABDUCTION case. She apparently encountered what she described as pixie-like entities that took her to a strange realm, but many of the elements of her story tally with modern reports of alien contact – including MISSING TIME and the OZ FACTOR. She also described some of the physiological sensations common to today's UFO sightings – including a sense of disorientation.

Physiological sensations that are often reported include a tingling feeling on the skin, watering eyes, sunburn effects, body hair standing on end and pounding headaches. Many of these have been taken to suggest the presence of electromagnetic radiation – indeed there are a number of cases where witnesses claim that their body and clothing were so electrically charged in the immediate aftermath of a sighting that sparks were emitted when they brushed themselves down.

Very serious physical effects are extremely unusual. Such severe medical traumas (ranging from skin burns to terminal cancer) as were reported following the CASH–LANDRUM incident are found in only a handful of cases worldwide, and it is often impossible to prove a direct link with the incident that was reported as a UFO sighting.

pig-faced ladies

Women said to have the facial features of a pig.

Stories of pig-faced ladies are common in several European countries. The traditional pattern involves a lady of rank being cursed by a beggar woman for having refused her alms and calling her baby a pig. The outcome of the curse is that the lady will bear a child that really does look like a pig, specifically, a girl who is perfectly formed other than having the face of a swine and, later, manners to match.

In 1640 a book was published in London called *A Certain Relation of the Hog-faced Gentlewoman called Mistris Tannakin Skinker.* This purported to tell the story of the lady of the title who, being cursed in her

The pig-faced lady, from Henry Wilson and James Caulfield's early 19th-century *The Book of Wonderful Characters*. (© Mary Evans Picture Library)

mother's womb, was born on the Rhine in 1618 with a nose like that of a pig. She is described as having come to London seeking a husband, without success. Despite being more courteous and kind than other similarly afflicted women, she was said to be unable to speak, making only pig-like sounds.

Another pig-faced lady was identified as living in Manchester Square, London, in the early 19th century, having been born in Ireland. Again, she is described as being attractive and well made, apart from her face. Having come from a wealthy family, she was reputed to be an heiress. Whether or not such a person existed in reality, rumours that her family was in need of someone to look after her gave rise to the following personal notice in *The Times* on 9 February, 1815:

FOR THE ATTENTION OF GENTLEMEN AND LADIES.—A young gentlewoman having heard of an advertisement for a person to undertake the care of a lady, who is heavily afflicted in the face, whose friends have offered a handsome income yearly, and a premium for residing with her for seven years, would do all in her power to render her life most comfortable;

an undeniable character can be obtained from a respectable circle of friends; an answer to this advertisement is requested, as the advertiser will keep herself disengaged. Address, post paid, to X. Y., at Mr. Ford's, Baker, 12 Judd. Street, Brunswick Square.

The young Charles Dickens (1812–70) had undoubtedly heard of the pig-faced lady of Manchester Square, referring to her in a magazine piece written in the 1830s (collected and published in *The Mudfog Papers* in 1880):

The President wished to know whether any Member of the section had ever seen or conversed with the pig-faced lady, who was reported to have worn a black velvet mask, and to have taken her meals from a golden trough.

After some hesitation a Member replied that the pig-faced lady was his mother-in-law, and that he trusted the President would not violate the sanctity of private life.

Pig-faced ladies became a standard feature in FREAK SHOWS throughout Europe and America, but these seem to have been merely deformed or particularly ugly women, men in frocks, or even bears with their faces shaved, dressed up in women's clothing and strapped into a chair.

Was there ever really a pig-faced lady? In less politically correct times than our own, women born with shocking facial deformities would be labelled as such and considered as objects of ridicule or fear rather than pity. If the deformity also extended to the mouth and palate, the inability to communicate other than in unintelligible sounds would have been seen as adding to the comparison. Perhaps even a markedly upturned nose would be enough to invite comparisons with a pig's snout, and the human fascination for oddity would do the rest.

Pio of Pietrelcina, St *see panel p533*

pious fraud
A fraud motivated by misguided religious zeal rather than by a desire for profit.
According to some historians, pious frauds, or deceptions motivated by misguided religious zeal in an attempt to win converts or strengthen the faith of believers, have been practised since the earliest days of the Christian Church. Hundreds of 'alternative gospels' and epistles purporting to be first-person accounts are believed to have been written by early Christian missionaries during the first century or so of

St Pio of Pietrelcina (1887–1968)

Francesco Forgione was born of a simple farming family in Pietrelcina, southern Italy. He claimed to have heavenly visions and to experience ECSTATIC PHENOMENA from an early age, and even as a child he was said to have been exceptionally pious. In 1903, at the age of 16, he entered the novitiate of the Capuchin Friars at Morcone, and took the Franciscan habit and the name of Brother Pio. In 1910, aged 23, he was ordained as a priest at Benvenuto.

He served in the Italian medical corps between 1917 and 1918, and on his return he was assigned to the friary of San Giovanni Rotondo. He was referred to affectionately as Padre Pio, and gained a reputation not just for his piety, but as a worker of MIRACLES; he was said to have the ability to levitate, to appear in two or more locations simultaneously (known as BILOCATION), to make prophecies, to heal at a touch, and to be able to see into men's hearts. This latter gift was said to be particularly useful to him in the confessional, where he was said to be able to read the consciences of those who were holding back, thus allowing him to reconcile countless sinners with God. In 1918, while kneeling in front of a large crucifix giving thanks after Mass, he received for the first time the STIGMATA, or wounds of Christ, which would recur for the rest of his long life; he claimed to have experienced a VISION of Christ, his hands, feet and side dripping with blood, and found that the five open wounds had appeared on his own body, making him the first stigmatized priest in the history of the Catholic Church. The blood which flowed from his wounds was said to have smelled of flowers or perfume, similar to the ODOUR OF SANCTITY, and these stigmata, which disappeared on his death, were regarded by many as further proof of his holiness.

Even during his lifetime, miracles were attributed to Padre Pio. In 1962, Karol Wojtyla, who later became Pope John Paul II, wrote and asked Pio to pray for a friend of his in Poland who was suffering from cancer; the cancer then inexplicably regressed. It was said that at this time, Padre Pio also predicted that Wojtyla would one day become Pope.

In the 1920s, Pio started a series of prayer groups which continue to this day, with many thousands of members all over the world, and in 1956, he opened a hospital called Casa Sollievo della Sofferenza ('Home to Relieve Suffering'), which is today considered one of the most efficient in Europe, serving some 60,000 patients a year.

In 1982, only 14 years after his death at the age of 81 in San Giovanni Rotondo, the Holy See began investigations to consider whether Pio should be made a saint. In 1990, he was declared a Servant of God, the first step toward canonization; in 1997, he was declared venerable; in 1999, a beatus; and following consideration of several healings attributed to his intercession after his death, the Pope canonized him as a saint in 2002. A statue of him in Messina, Sicily, allegedly wept tears of blood in that same year. His canonization miracle, which took place in 2000, involved the cure of a seven-year-old boy suffering from meningitis; during a night-time prayer vigil at the child's bedside, attended by his mother and several Capuchin monks of Padre Pio's order, his condition dramatically improved, and when he came out of his coma, he described an old man with a white beard and a long brown habit, who had told him that he was going to be healed.

Tens of thousands of pilgrims visit his tomb and the friary where he spent most of his life each year, and in 2004, the Padre Pio Pilgrimage Church in San Giovanni Rotondo was dedicated to his memory.

the Church's existence, when the aim was to convert as many people as possible to the new religion of Christianity by any means, in order to save their souls. Some historians have even called the authenticity of the four New Testament gospels of Matthew, Mark, Luke and John into question, citing as evidence the fact that these four texts were apparently unknown to the early Church Fathers, since they are not mentioned by any Christian writers until around AD 150; they have therefore suggested that the gospels are not eyewitness accounts written by the apostles themselves, but later forgeries written with the good intention of winning converts. The 18th-century historian Edward Gibbon, in his controversial work *The History of the Decline and Fall of the Roman Empire*, also frequently uses the phrase 'pious fraud' with reference to the miracles and martyrs of the early Christian Church.

Many stigmatics (see STIGMATA) are regarded by some as classic examples of pious fraud. The wounds which are displayed by stigmatics, generally on the hands and feet, duplicate those of Christ's crucifixion, and their sufferers claim that they appear miraculously; however, sceptics assert that these wounds are self-inflicted; ST FRANCIS OF ASSISI is said by some to have inflicted stigmatic wounds on himself in his desire to imitate Christ in all ways, and a modern stigmatic frequently accused of pious fraud is Catalina Rivas, who also claims to receive messages from Christ, Mary, and the angels, although critics maintain that these messages are in fact plagiarized from existing books.

Many believe that the TURIN SHROUD is an example of pious fraud. This strip of linen, allegedly bearing the miraculous image of Christ, is venerated as a holy RELIC by many, but some claim that it is a 13th- or 14th-century fake. Claims to the gift of INEDIA, the ability to survive without food and to be sustained only by the Eucharist, such as that made by Therese Neumann of Bavaria (also a stigmatic), are also regarded by sceptics as pious frauds, as are many alleged MARIAN APPARITIONS. For a further example of a potential pious fraud, see CHRONOVISOR.

Pisces
In astrology, the twelfth sign of the zodiac, between Aquarius and Aries.

In Western ASTROLOGY, Capricorn is the sign of the ZODIAC for those who are born between 20 February and 20 March. The symbol for Pisces is the fishes, and the sign is ruled by Jupiter and Neptune. Pisceans are said to be artistic and sensitive, although they may seem impractical. Pisces is believed to be a water sign, having an affinity with the element WATER.

pixies
In folklore, small fairy-like spirits of the English West Country, who are fond of leading travellers astray and playing tricks on humans.

In folktales, the pixies of the English West Country are generally said to be similar to FAIRIES, but of a different race, although they share a number of fairy characteristics. They are diminutive in stature and are usually described as having a homely appearance, often red-headed, with pointed ears and upward-slanting eyes, and dressing in green. They are not actively malicious but they like to play pranks on humans, and their favourite trick is to lead travellers astray; a person who has been rendered lost and confused by pixies is described as being 'pixie-led', a term which is sometimes extended to apply to anyone in a bewildered state. It is said that the pixies' confusing magic can be dispelled by turning one's coat or jacket inside out, as this is said to confuse the pixies in their turn. Like fairies, pixies are repelled by iron, and crosses are another means of protection against them. Pixies love to dance in the moonlight, and to ride horses, and will frequently steal horses at night to ride round

and round in circles known as gallitraps, bringing them back in the morning exhausted and confused and with their manes twisted into knots. Anyone who puts both feet inside one of these circles will be taken prisoner, but if he puts only one foot inside, he will be able to see the pixies but can still escape. Some say pixies ride around on snails, and that they can transform themselves into hedgehogs at will, and it is believed that they leave behind footprints of silver or gold 'pixie dust'. However, those who deliberately follow their trail to try and find them often vanish without trace.

Pixies, like BROWNIES, will sometimes help with household chores and appreciate a gift of food or milk as thanks, but will vanish at once if new clothes are offered to them. They will also sometimes indulge in disruptive behaviour, pinching lazy people – pixies deplore human laziness – knocking on walls and blowing out candles. They are particularly prevalent in Cornwall, where they are known as piskies, and a number of places are named after them.

The origin of their name is obscure, but many people believe pixies to be the souls of unbaptized children, while others hold that they are the souls of those prehistoric dwellers of Britain who died before the coming of Christ; not fit for heaven but not bad enough to go to hell, they were sentenced by God to wander the earth forever, condemned to grow smaller and smaller until they accept Christianity. One theory based on this account of their origin suggests that the word 'pixies' is derived from 'Picts', although there is no firm evidence to corroborate this idea.

PK *see* PSYCHOKINESIS

PK, time-displaced
The supposed affecting, by psychokinesis, of the results of an experiment after *it has been run.*

Time-displaced PK (also known as retroactive or retro-PK) is an apparent effect on a PARAPSYCHOLOGY experiment after it has been completed. It is claimed that in some instances where an electronic RANDOM NUMBER GENERATOR has been used, a PSYCHIC can still affect the outcome in the time between the results being gathered and being fully played back.

The idea was first put forward in 1971 by the researcher Helmut Schmidt. He went on to test his hypothesis with a series of experiments using a binary output random number generator. The output of ones and zeroes was recorded and then played back, with each number being represented by either a red or a blue light. The psychic under test, working at the point of playback, had to get one of the lights to appear at a frequency greater than that which would be expected by chance alone. Schmidt concluded that individuals could influence previously recorded but unobserved results and that the level of success was the same as he found with real-time experimentation. Other researchers reported similar effects, even when the second part of the experiment (the delayed influence) took place a day or more after the initial results were recorded.

Subsequent research has even involved attempts at time-displaced PK on living systems (see DIRECT MENTAL INTERACTION WITH LIVING SYSTEMS) ranging from attempts to influence the point at which a gerbil gets off its exercise wheel in a previously filmed sequence, to influencing previously recorded brain activity data. The argument in these instances is not that the agent (see AGENCY) is changing the film or recorded data as it is played back, but rather that the agent is making a retrospective attempt to control events in the past.

Leaving aside the philosophical problems of this idea, sceptics would argue that such apparently positive results are equally exposed to the same criticisms levelled at the statistical analysis of the results of experiments into 'ordinary' PSYCHOKINESIS.

placebo effect

The beneficial effect of a treatment that contains no real medicine.

A 'placebo' (from a Latin root meaning 'to please') is a 'medicine' given to a patient ostensibly as a treatment, but which contains no real curative substances. The placebo effect is the name given to the phenomenon of a patient's illness being alleviated or cured by such a treatment. Studies have shown that this does indeed happen, albeit in a relatively small number of cases.

Some say that the effect is a biochemical one. This theory suggests that the administering of a placebo gives patients the satisfaction of being treated, hope for eventual cure and a general lifting of the spirits. This in turn acts on the body's neuro-chemical system, triggering the release of beneficial substances, such as hormones, which help bring about a physical improvement in the patient's condition.

Others believe that the effect is purely psychological. According to this line of thought, there is no real physical improvement but the perception of being treated makes a patient 'feel better'. Some medical practitioners believe that patients treated with placebos often are simply recovering naturally, as they would have done with or without the treatment, but argue that the placebo is still useful in reassuring the patient that they are receiving help.

Sceptics argue that there is no such thing as the placebo effect, and all that is happening is that patients merely say they are feeling better in order to please the doctor. However, the fact that there is a substantial body of evidence of the real effect of placebos tends to contradict this argument.

It may be that each of the possible explanations of the placebo effect plays a part in it, but it is true to say that the effect is not completely understood.

planchette

A device purported to assist the user to communicate with the spirits of the dead.

The name 'planchette' is sometimes said to be derived from the name of its inventor. However, it is equally possible that it is simply taken from the French for 'small board'. Planchettes, or 'automatic writers', first appeared in the early 19th century. They originally took the form of a small, flat, vaguely oval-shaped piece of wood supported on two or three wheels, with a pencil held in the centre. This device would be used (usually during a SÉANCE) for the production of AUTOMATIC WRITING – the planchette is placed on a piece of paper and (if the process has been successful) it will begin to write, apparently without the conscious control of the person holding it. When it is used by MEDIUMS, the messages produced by the planchette are said to come from the spirits of the dead.

Planchettes are now more commonly encountered in combination with an OUIJA BOARD, where they are still used as a means for alleged spirit communication. A writing implement is not required when the planchette is used in this way – participants in the séance place their fingers on the planchette, which

A picture of a planchette in use during a séance, from an 1885 issue of *The Scientific American*. (© TopFoto/HIP)

moves across the board (supposedly under the guidance of the spirits) to point at letters and spell out words.

planetary consciousness
Awareness of the earth as a single entity.
Planetary consciousness is essentially an awareness of the earth as a single living ecosystem, together with a belief that all human beings are responsible for helping to nurture it. The roots of the idea have been traced back to the first photographs taken by astronauts on space missions in the 1960s showing the planet suspended against the blackness of space.

Added to this were the theories of the Canadian writer Marshall McLuhan (1911–80), who coined the term 'global village' to describe the 20th-century world. McLuhan believed that modern mass communications had the effect of making the world seem smaller and making it more interconnected. The phrase 'spaceship earth' was used by the American engineer and architect Buckminster Fuller (1895–1983) to describe the modern world, seeing it as a fragile closed system. Fuller believed that in the 1970s the world was entering a new age in which wars and competition for the earth's resources must be replaced by cooperation and conservation to ensure the survival of the planet.

In the later 20th century the 'green' movement grew in strength, championing the causes of environmentalism, conservationism and recycling, and much of this thinking became absorbed into the mainstream.

It was from this range of influences that the idea of planetary consciousness developed. Its advocates believe that the earth can only survive if all of its inhabitants change their mindsets from selfish or nationalistic modes to thinking about the planet as one community, or even as a single living entity. They see all life on earth as interconnected and interdependent. Because of this, every individual is able to take action that will benefit the world as a whole, even at the level of the goods they buy. They urge people to espouse green consumerism: to buy products that do not harm the environment and buy them locally if possible, thus cutting down on the pollution and consumption of fossil fuels necessitated by transporting goods around the world. In this way, we can all help to sustain the planet.

For them, a post-industrial, information-based, harmonious and peaceful world, in which the spiritual, artistic and compassionate sides of our natures are paramount, represents the next stage in the evolution of the human race. Planetary consciousness is achieved by an individual when he or she automatically thinks in terms of humankind as a whole and acts responsibly in ways that will help transform society to the planetary way of thinking.

Some advocates of planetary consciousness see this as inextricably linked with one particular aspect of the future of mankind: that of space travel. Those who believe that other forms of life exist in the universe argue that we can only hope to contact and interact with them if the earth is a united and homogeneous whole, with all knowledge and resources held in common. See also GAIA HYPOTHESIS.

plant magic *see* MAGIC, PLANT

plasma vortex
A suggested cause of crop circles.
Plasma is the scientific term for a very hot, highly conductive form of ionized gas. This is formed in the earth's atmosphere by electrical discharge, such as that found in lightning. One explanation for the apparently overnight formation of CROP CIRCLES is that the patterns are created instantly by vortices of plasma forming and discharging in the air above the affected fields. The plasma vortices themselves are said to be created by mini-vortices in the magnetic field in the earth's ionosphere. This theory maintains that plasma vortices strike the ground and heat the stalks of cereal to a point at which they wilt. The fact that often complex patterns are created is also apparently explained – nature is full of examples of such complex, yet random, patterning, such as in individual snowflakes.

Those who accept that plasma vortices are the source of crop circles do not necessarily agree on their causes. Some say they are entirely natural, others that they are the engine blasts of UFOs. Yet others believe that plasma vortices are being created or harnessed by secret military weapons technology.

Plato (c.428–c.348 BC)
Greek philosopher who influenced the development of esoteric and mystical thought.
Little is known of Plato's early life, but he is believed to have been born in Athens around 428 BC. While still young, he became a pupil of the philosopher Socrates, and after his teacher's death, Plato travelled widely; in southern Italy, he encountered the Pythagoreans (see PYTHAGORAS), whose notions of numerical harmony later deeply influenced his 'Theory of Forms'. He returned to Athens around 357 BC, where he founded the Academy – named after the grove of the hero Academus, where it was situated – and presided over it for the rest of his life. Among his pupils were Aristotle and Theophrastus. The Academy became a famous centre for philosophy, scientific research and

mathematics, and operated until AD 529, when it was closed down by the Byzantine Emperor Justinian I, who saw it as a pagan threat to the spread of Christianity.

The most important writings in the body of work credited to Plato are his philosophical dialogues, of which there are about 30. It is generally agreed that the earlier dialogues are the most closely based on Socrates' thought, with the later writings increasingly breaking away from the views of Plato's former teacher and reappraising his earlier metaphysical and logical assumptions. The dialogues are usually in the form of a series of questions and answers in which Plato and his companions examine the validity of assumed ideas on such matters as moral virtue, and discuss varied topics including the philosophy of mathematics, political philosophy, religious philosophy, atheism and pantheism. In his most famous dialogue, *The Republic*, Plato begins by describing a political utopia ruled by philosopher-kings. From there, he proceeds to set forth the doctrines at the heart of his philosophy, the most central of which is his Theory of Forms or Ideas.

Traditionally seen as a form of metaphysical dualism, Platonism is based on the belief that there is another world beyond the one we live in; the world we perceive with our senses is transient, changeable and deceptive, and everything in it consists of imperfect copies of a world of Forms or Ideas, which are perfect, unchanging, eternal, and comprehensible only by the use of intellect and understanding – not by sense perception or imagination. All we see and feel in this perceptual world are only dim reflections of these Forms or Ideas; the true objects of knowledge are therefore the Forms themselves. Plato suggests that there is something called the Form of the Good, often interpreted as God, which sheds light on all other Forms, and from which all Forms emanate. It is this Form of the Good that is the ultimate object of knowledge. Plato's distinction between an 'Ideal' and an actual world also lends itself to an interpretation that the soul or mind is a non-material and immortal entity which can exist apart from the body.

Platonism would later inspire thinkers such as Plotinus, who founded Neoplatonism around the 3rd century, the Gnostics, and many other metaphysical realists. During the Renaissance, with its general rediscovery of classical works, Plato's philosophy became once more widespread in the West, and many of the greatest early modern scientists and artists of this period saw Platonism as the basis for progress in arts and sciences. Notable Western philosophers continue to be influenced by his thinking, particularly in the areas of science and mathematics.

Point Pleasant *see* MOTHMAN

Pokémon panic

An incident from Japan that involved fainting and seizures among thousands of children, allegedly brought on by watching a television cartoon. It is sometimes cited as a modern incident of 'mass sociogenic illness'.

The incident that has become popularly known as the 'Pokémon panic' occurred on the night of 16 December 1997, during and immediately following the showing of the 38th episode of the Pokémon cartoon series on Japanese television. It resulted in several thousand children reporting effects including nausea, fainting and seizures.

The cartoon series (derived from a computer game) was immensely popular and was watched by millions of Japanese children. The cartoon, computer games, toys, collectors' cards and other merchandising became a huge worldwide phenomenon. The episode in question contained a scene in which rapidly flashing lights were used to depict an 'electric attack' by the central character Pikachu. It was reported that, within half an hour of the broadcast, over 600 children had been taken to hospitals complaining of a range of effects. The news of this spread rapidly, and when the scene was shown again as part of news reports later the same evening, further children fell ill. A number of sensationalized reports were made including descriptions of children vomiting and suffering from temporary paralysis, convulsions and blurred vision.

The incident became headline news over the next few days. TV Tokyo issued an apology and the series was temporarily taken off the air in the face of public outrage. The government and the police conducted investigations. A number of explanations were offered, some based around the suggestion that seizures had been induced by the flashing lights and the combination of colours used in the cartoon (similar to the effect that can occur in some sufferers from epilepsy). However, such sequences had been included in most of the other episodes, and appear in many other cartoons. The numbers of children apparently involved were also several times higher than would be expected from our current understanding of the incidence of epilepsy. The range of symptoms reported were also not consistent with this diagnosis.

Commentators began to suggest that, while it was possible that a few children had indeed suffered seizures brought on by the cartoon, overall this was actually an instance of MASS HYSTERIA or, more correctly, MASS SOCIOGENIC ILLNESS. Others have pointed out that mass sociogenic illness usually involves groups of people within a closed situation such as a school or hospital – the Pokémon panic apparently involved thousands of children sitting separately in their own homes. However, initial reports indicated that fewer

A balloon in the shape of the Pokémon character Pikachu on Broadway during the 2002 Macy's Thanksgiving Day Parade in New York. (© Reuters/Corbis)

than 700 children were affected – the higher figures began to appear over the next few days, following widespread reporting of the incident. The exact cause is still a matter of debate.

Pollock twins

A pair of British twins who appeared to show a number of signs that they were the reincarnations of their two dead sisters.

The British twins Gillian and Jennifer Pollock were born in 1958. Two years earlier their elder sisters, Jacqueline (aged 6) and Joanna (aged 11) had been killed in a car accident. Jennifer was born with similar birth marks to Jacqueline and when the twins began to speak they seemed to be able to recall events that had happened to their dead sisters. They were also apparently able to identify toys previously owned by their sisters, and it was even claimed that they had identified a house that the family had previously lived in. Gillian seemed to remember the life of Joanna and Jennifer that of Jacqueline.

The case received a great deal of publicity at the time and was offered as evidence for REINCARNATION. However, sceptics pointed out that although the twins' mother, Florence, was not a strong believer in reincarnation, their father, John, was – this, it is suggested, is likely to have led to even the slightest correspondences being noted, and to have shaped his interpretation. Conversely, believers argued that there were a number of specific recognitions of places and objects that proved that the twins remembered their past lives, and that the twins were overheard discussing the accident on at least one occasion – and these are possibly difficult to dismiss as simple 'wishful thinking' or 'cognitive bias' (see CHANCE AND COINCIDENCE). Ultimately, it seems likely that the tragic events surrounding the crash, and the lives of the elder sisters, would have been talked about in front of the twins – making it very difficult to establish that this case offers conclusive proof of anything out of the ordinary.

poltergeist

A mysterious invisible force asserted to cause a number of phenomena, most commonly noises (bangs, thuds and rappings) and object movements (from the hurling of smaller items, to the lifting and upsetting of large pieces of furniture).

The word 'poltergeist' comes from the German *poltern*, to make a racket, and *Geist*, ghost. However, alleged poltergeist activity includes a broad spectrum of phenomena, not necessarily covered by the literal translation of the word, 'noisy spirit'. Poltergeist-related phenomena can involve objects seeming to move with no cause, including heavy items such as furniture as well as smaller items; bangs, knocking and rapping noises; thrown objects, which sometimes follow an unusual trajectory, or seem to be aimed at a specific person; rains of small objects such as stones or coins, sometimes falling inside a house or building; foul smells; spontaneous fires, sometimes breaking out on walls or ceilings; electrical disturbances, including the switching on and off of lights and appliances; telephone disruption; the levitation of either objects or people; and the manifestation of liquids such as blood, water or oil. Some poltergeists are said to physically assault their victims, although this is usually in the form of pinching and scratching rather than serious physical harm. Apparitions are only rarely reported in poltergeist cases.

Poltergeist incidents have been reported around the world since ancient times, and have exhibited many commonalities, with object movements the most consistent feature. It has been suggested that these commonalities lend weight to the existence of the phenomena, as reports were independent of each other. The activity usually starts and stops very abruptly, and occurs over anything from several hours to several months, although disturbances over longer periods have been reported. Generally, one individual seems to be at the focus of the activity. Until the 19th century poltergeist events were attributed to the DEVIL, WITCHCRAFT or the GHOSTS of the dead. After this time, and with the development of psychical research in the late 19th century, a more scientific explanation was sought. In the 1930s the psychologist Nandor Fodor brought psychoanalytical analysis to his research of poltergeist cases and developed a theory that some poltergeist occurrences were caused by living individuals who were suffering from intense repression, anger or sexual tension. More recently William Roll of the Psychical Research Foundation in Durham, North Carolina, identified in his research what he termed RECURRENT SPONTANEOUS PSYCHOKINESIS (RSPK). His work suggested that the poltergeist focus (or poltergeist agent) was most commonly a child or teenager who was unknowingly using PSYCHOKINESIS (PK) to express their hostility or unhappiness. Further, the focus was usually unaware that they were causing the chaos of poltergeist activity but was pleased with the disturbances.

Most parapsychologists have adopted the explanation of the psychokinetic abilities of a living person as the source of poltergeist activity. Many of the recorded cases (both historical and modern) revolve around one individual (frequently female and under the age of 20) to the extent that phenomena only occur when that individual is present. There have also been recorded incidents of the poltergeist phenomena 'following' the focus to another location.

During some of the high-profile investigations of poltergeist activity, the focus has been seen (and sometimes recorded on film) deliberately causing the movement of objects. Some cases are revealed to be entirely hoaxed, whereas in other instances – for example, the TINA RESCH case, and the ENFIELD POLTERGEIST – an example of hoaxing has been observed which does not necessarily invalidate all of the phenomena, but can be attributed to the effect of the pressure to perform during the intense and disruptive involvement of investigators and particularly the media. See also BELL WITCH; DRUMMER OF TEDWORTH; EPWORTH PARSONAGE POLTERGEIST; GEF THE TALKING MONGOOSE; HUMPTY DOO POLTERGEIST; LAMB INN; ROSENHEIM POLTERGEIST.

pooka *see* PUCK

portents
Signs foretelling future events, especially calamitous ones.

In every culture in the world, since primitive times, man has interpreted certain events as being portents, or signs of things to come. Anything which seemed to run contrary to the natural order was likely to be taken as a portent of disaster; ECLIPSES, particularly total solar eclipses, were almost always believed to be an evil OMEN, and in certain parts of Africa they are still thought to be a sign of a future drought. COMETS were also generally interpreted as a portent of doom, and the appearance in 1066 of the comet which later became known as Halley's Comet was thought to have foreshadowed the defeat of the Saxons at the Battle of Hastings. So significant was this heavenly sign that it is thought that it was incorporated into the Bayeux Tapestry. In more superstitious times, the birth of a deformed child or animal was also taken as a sure sign of coming disaster.

There are many smaller-scale portents which foretell death or misfortune to an individual, and which have been retained in modern culture as SUPERSTITIONS. If a bird, especially a robin, flies into a house, it is taken to be a sign of a death in the family. Some other signs of impending death are seeing a butterfly at night; a bat flying round a house three times; hearing an owl hooting in the daytime; a jackdaw settling on a house, or a single magpie circling it; the sudden chiming of a clock which has not been working; and the sound of a deathwatch beetle. There are a number of supernatural creatures that are also portents of death. Apart from the many local ghosts which every area or castle lays claim to as its own particular harbinger of death, the sighting of a spectral BLACK DOG such as the barghest of Yorkshire or the trash or skriker of Lancashire, even from a distance, is a sign of doom for the one who sees it. To meet your own double, or DOPPELGÄNGER, is sometimes taken as a portent of your death. The WILD HUNT is also an omen of death to the person who sees it. A mysterious human-like creature with moth wings called MOTHMAN is a more recent portent of doom; sightings of this creature in Point Pleasant, West Virginia, were later taken to be a portent of the Silver Bridge disaster, when 46 people were killed.

Another relatively modern death portent is the dead man's hand in poker. This hand, consisting of two aces and two eights, was the hand which Wild Bill Hickok is said to have been holding when he was shot in the back and killed in 1876, and it is mentioned as a sign of doom to the player holding in it a number of popular songs and books.

possession

The apparent state of being dominated or controlled by a spirit.

Many religions include the concept that a person, and sometimes a thing or place, can be possessed by a supernatural spirit. These spirits are usually evil and possess their victims against their will, for malicious purposes, and most religions hold that they can only be expelled by a ritual of EXORCISM. The idea of spirit possession is an ancient one; Sumerian and Chaldean inscriptions and cuneiform tablets have been found which describe procedures for expelling demons, and the New Testament contains numerous accounts of Jesus casting out evil spirits from afflicted people. During the Middle Ages, many people who would nowadays be diagnosed as mentally or physically ill were believed to be possessed, because they exhibited one or more of the symptoms which were ascribed to demonic possession: sudden and dramatic personality changes; the ability to speak one or more unknown languages; abnormal physical strength; a fear and hatred of religious objects such as crosses and holy water, and the inability to say the name of Christ; fits and convulsions; obscene and blasphemous speech, often in a rasping or guttural voice totally unlike the person's normal one; the making of animal noises; and the emission of a foul smell. Possession is usually thought to be involuntary, with the victim not being held responsible either for the possession or for their actions while possessed. Islam, Judaism and Hinduism also subscribe to the idea of involuntary possession of people by evil spirits.

However, possession may also be voluntary, as in the case of someone who allows themselves to become the host of a demon as part of an occult ritual, or in the religious practices of some shamanic societies. Voluntary spirit possession is also a feature of SPIRITUALISM, in the apparent process of CHANNELLING.

powder of projection

A powder that was said to assist alchemists in the transmutation of base metal into gold; another name for the philosopher's stone.

A number of ancient writings describe a mysterious powder, usually said to be white, which was claimed to have extraordinary powers such as the ability to transmute base metal into gold, assist in LEVITATION and TELEPORTATION, produce brilliant light and deadly rays and prolong physical life. The ancient Mesopotamian name for this powder was *shem-an-na*, and the Egyptians called it *mfkzt*. It was revered by the Alexandrians as a gift from Paradise, and later alchemists referred to it as the powder of projection, because in projection (the final stage in the alchemical process of turning base metal into gold), the powder was tossed upon the base metal to transmute it. It is often used as another name for the PHILOSOPHER'S STONE. See also ALCHEMY; TRANSMUTATION.

prayer

A personal form of communication with a deity or spiritual power, especially in the form of supplication, adoration, praise, contrition or thanksgiving; also a specific form of words used when praying.

The word 'prayer' comes from the Latin *precare*, meaning 'to beg or entreat', and refers to a variety of practices in many religions and belief systems which are intended to bring about personal communication between the devotee and a deity or other spiritual power. It is thought that some form of prayer has been practised by mankind for at least 5,000 years. The most common types of prayer are in the form of supplication, adoration, praise, contrition or thanksgiving, but each religion has its own way of praying. Prayer may be performed individually or as part of a group; spoken, chanted or sung out loud, or inwardly, in silence; recited from memory, read from a prayer book, or composed spontaneously; it may be accompanied by music, or by various outward ritual acts, such as the ringing of a bell, the lighting of a candle, or the burning of incense; and it may be performed with the eyes open or closed, or by specific physical postures or actions. Many Christians pray with heads bowed and hands folded, often kneeling, and may make the sign of the cross, while Muslims pray facing Mecca, Sufis whirl, and Orthodox Jews move their heads back and forth. Prayer is often preceded by some form of ritual cleansing, and most religions have specific forms of prayer for particular occasions, as well as for days of special religious significance.

The model for Christian prayer is the Lord's Prayer, given by Jesus to his disciples, which begins with adoration of God and moves through surrender to his will, and a petition for sustenance, to a recognition of the need for forgiveness and an entreaty for deliverance from the world's evils. The major prayer book of the Anglican Church is the Book of Common Prayer, while in Roman Catholicism, the prayer cycle of the rosary is a prominent feature, with its repeated recitation of the 'Hail Mary'.

Muslim prayer has three major forms: *salat*, the obligatory prayer performed five times a day (before dawn, just after noon, mid-afternoon, just after sunset and in the evening) while kneeling on a prayer mat called a *sajjada*; *dhikr*, or remembrance of God, which has been particularly developed in SUFISM; and *du'a*, a more personal calling upon God. Muslim prayer may be performed in a mosque, but

A Buddhist prayer wheel in use in Lhasa, Tibet.
(© Rob Howard/Corbis)

is considered valid in other settings, although more virtue is attached to prayers offered as part of a group than those offered individually. Those engaging in prayer must first perform a ritual cleansing known as the *wudhu* on their hands, feet, face and mouth, to symbolize spiritual purification, and Islamic prayer involves repeated sequences of bowing and standing postures, each of which is preceded by a recital of the first Surah of the Koran.

Prayer also permeates Hindu daily life, and great merit is accumulated from the recital of prayers, many of which are derived from Vedic hymns and which often merge into MANTRAS.

Jews pray three times a day, and more often on special days. The Jewish prayer book known as the *Siddur* contains a set order of regular prayers, which are recited while wearing a fringed prayer shawl called a *tallit*. The most important prayers in Judaism are the *Shema Yisrael* ('Hear, O Israel') and the *Amidah*, or 'standing prayer'. In Buddhism, prayer is generally regarded as a practice secondary to meditation and scriptural study, but Tibetan Buddhists use a cylindrical device known as a prayer wheel. This is inscribed with a mantra, usually *Om Manipadme Hum* (see OM), and contains scrolls with other mantras or sacred texts. Turning the wheel clockwise repeatedly is believed to release the inherent power of the texts and prayers.

precognition
Prior knowledge of future events gained by psychic means.

The word 'precognition' comes from the Latin *praecognitio*, which literally means 'prior knowledge'. In the past, the ability to 'see into the future' was sometimes referred to SECOND SIGHT and its exponents as SEERS, and various forms of DIVINATION were employed for the purpose of achieving such powers of PREDICTION. Belief in the possible precognitive nature of DREAMS has also been a feature of many societies throughout history.

Precognition is one of the areas into which research is carried out by modern parapsychologists (see PARAPSYCHOLOGY). Whereas in the past it was often considered to involve GODS, SPIRITS or other supernatural forces, the ability is now usually thought of as a potential natural feature of the human mind. In some of the experiments into TELEPATHY carried out by J B RHINE, it was noted that the results could be interpreted as showing evidence of precognition. For example, receivers participating in CARD-GUESSING EXPERIMENTS sometimes appeared to be consistently giving the answer for the next card, rather than that which was being 'sent' to them at the time. However, sceptics would argue that this is simply a 'favourable' reinterpretation of what were, effectively, negative results. Further, more specific research has been carried out, although no widely accepted, significant results have so far been produced.

Famous dramatic examples of claimed precognition include foreknowledge of the R101 AIRSHIP DISASTER, the CINCINNATI PREMONITION and JEANNE DIXON's supposed prediction of the death of John F Kennedy. See also PROPHECY and PREMONITION.

predestination
The theological doctrine that whatever is to happen has been unalterably fixed by God from the beginning of time, especially with regard to which souls will be saved and which will not.

The doctrine of predestination has been the subject of much controversy in Christianity for centuries. Predestination is the belief that since the beginning of time, God has not only had foreknowledge of, but has also preordained, all that is to happen. Judaism generally rejects the idea of predestination outright, while Islam's belief in *qadar*, or the decree of Allah, which is said to determine all eventualities, is one of predestination. In Christianity, this doctrine is applied especially with regard to eternal salvation, and the debate which has occupied Christian theologians throughout history concerns the question of to what extent a soul's salvation or damnation is preordained by God, and how far the individual is responsible for their own salvation or condemnation – that is, how to reconcile the concept of an omnipotent and omniscient God with that of free will.

The Christian doctrine of predestination became particularly associated with St Augustine of Hippo, who held that humans are so corrupted by sin that they have the capacity neither to seek nor to find salvation, and cannot produce works which will make them worthy of salvation in the sight of God; thus, it is God alone who chooses who will be saved by his grace, and who will not. The theologian Pelagius, on the other hand, believed that the free will granted to humans by God allowed them to choose or deny him, and that they could therefore come to salvation by their works. The doctrine of semi-Pelagianism steers a middle course between these two diametrically opposed views, and holds that God's grace is a necessary precondition for a man's decision to choose or deny him, but that thereafter, his works count toward his salvation.

prediction
The act or art of foretelling an event or outcome that will take place in the future, usually arrived at by paranormal or supernatural means; something so foretold.

The word 'prediction' (from Latin *prae-*, before, and *dicere*, to say) is used to apply both to informed guesswork based on prior knowledge of the subject, such as scientific predictions about the weather, and to the foretelling of an event or outcome arrived at by supernatural or paranormal means. Predictions made using ASTROLOGY, or any form of DIVINATION, fall into the latter category, as does PROPHECY, which is held to be divinely inspired, and which plays an important part in many religions; of the 39 books of the Bible's Old Testament, 18 are ascribed to prophets.

Possibly the most famous collection of predictions in history is the work of the French physician and astrologer NOSTRADAMUS, whose *Les Propheties* – almost a thousand four-line rhymed poems, called quatrains, written between 1555 and 1558 – have remained in print since their first publication. The cryptic and obscure language of these predictions means that their interpretations are still debated to this day. See also DIVINATION; MOTHER SHIPTON; PROPHECY.

premonitions
Intuitions or forebodings of a future, and usually unpleasant or disastrous, event.

The word 'premonition' (from Latin *prae-*, before, and *monēre*, to warn) is used to refer to the foretelling of an event, usually calamitous in nature, by means of a psychic experience. The premonition often comes in a dream, although it may also be experienced as a strong sense of foreboding or uneasiness, or as a psychic vision taking place in a state of full consciousness.

Almost every major disaster is accompanied by accounts of premonitions which predicted it. The American president Abraham Lincoln is said to have had a prophetic dream in which he foresaw his own death by assassination. Other events are said to have been predicted by mass premonitions. One such was the disaster at the Morfa Colliery in Port Talbot in Wales in 1890, when such a feeling of foreboding is reported to have fallen on the entire village on the morning of the disaster that half of the miners stayed away from work that day; of the 87 who did not, all were later killed in a huge explosion at the mine.

Probably one of the most famous mass premonitions of disaster concerned the tragedy which took place in another Welsh village, Aberfan, in 1966, when a massive tip of coal waste slid on to the village, crushing the local school and resulting in the deaths of 116 children and 28 adults. After the disaster, accounts of premonitions began to flood in, including one reported by the mother of a girl who had later died in the accident. Because of the large number of premonitions reported after this event, three separate independent organizations conducted a study whose results seemed to point to more than 24 individual precognitive episodes foretelling the disaster.

The wreck of the *TITANIC* in 1912, in which the ship struck an iceberg and sank in the North Atlantic, taking with her more than 1,500 lives, was also followed by mass claims of premonitions of disaster; several people claimed to have gone so far as to act on their premonitions by cancelling their passage or leaving the ship before it sailed. See also CINCINNATI PREMONITION; DREAMS.

Presley, Elvis Aron (1935–77)
Famous entertainer believed to have been sighted alive after his reported death.

According to the official record, Elvis Presley, the celebrated US popular entertainer, was born in Tupelo, Mississippi, in 1935 and died in 1977 in his Graceland mansion, in Memphis, Tennessee.

In his heyday Presley, known as 'the King', was the world's most popular singer, its biggest-selling recording artist and an object of devotion to his millions of fans. His relatively early death produced widespread and intense mourning and his home became a shrine. However, not long after his official

Elvis Presley's grave at Graceland, Memphis, Tennessee. Despite the fact that his burial was witnessed by thousands of mourners in 1977, claims that he has been seen alive since then regularly appear in the popular press.
(© Walter Bibikow/JAI/Corbis)

demise rumours began to circulate that he had never really died at all and that his 'death' was simply a stunt that would allow him to escape the pressures of being continually in the public eye.

Reported sightings of Elvis began to appear in the media and have not ceased to this day. In various places around the world, from all over the USA to Germany and Japan, people claim not only to have seen the King but to have spoken to him. He is said to have been spotted doing the most mundane things, including driving along suburban streets in unremarkable cars, fishing in remote rivers, going to the cinema or, unsurprisingly, given his notorious junk-food habits, eating in small-town fast-food restaurants.

The obvious explanation for many of these reports is that the world is full of Elvis impersonators and that those who prefer not to accept that he ever died will not go short of opportunities to shore up their belief.

In some ways, the Elvis sightings phenomenon is an echo of traditional myths of the dead king who will one day return to save his people, such as the idea of King Arthur as the 'Once and Future King'. It taps into a desire, even a need, for devotees to feel that

their hero has not disappeared for good.

It may be that some of this is fuelled by the fact that Presley famously turned his back on live performances for seven years, only to return in triumph with a live television special in 1968, which, to his fans, showed the world that he still had the old magic. To followers of the Presley cult it is perhaps not such a great leap of faith to imagine fondly another miraculous comeback.

preternatural *see* SUPERNATURAL

Princeton Engineering Anomalies Research

A laboratory at Princeton University, established to research the interaction of consciousness and reality, mind and machine.

The Princeton Engineering Anomalies Research (PEAR) laboratory was established at Princeton University in 1979, by physicist Robert G Jahn, then Dean of the School of Engineering and Applied Science. Its declared purpose was to pursue scientific study of the interaction of human consciousness with sensitive physical devices, systems and processes and to establish practical devices and procedures in accordance with contemporary engineering practice.

Since 1979, an interdisciplinary staff of engineers, physicists, psychologists and humanists has been conducting experiments in the 'mental' control of machines and probability. Thousands of experiments, involving millions of trials, have been performed by several hundred operators. The observed effects have been small, but are regarded as 'highly significant statistical deviations from chance expectations'.

The largest of the programmes, 'Engineering and Consciousness', concerned ANOMALIES arising during human-machine interactions. PEAR developed and improved custom 'random mechanical cascades' to reduce any 'operator bias' or known physical influences as human operators attempt to influence the output of a variety of mechanical, electronic, optical, acoustical and fluid devices. They found significant differences between 'unattended' states producing random data and the human experiments, possibly hinting at some sort of PSYCHOKINESIS effect.

In the field of 'Remote Perception' (see also REMOTE VIEWING) PEAR conducted over 650 remote perception trials, concluding that the phenomenon is inconsistent but valid. Both of these programmes have contributed to a third, the development of 'Theoretical Models' that may aid in the understanding of the role of consciousness in the operation of physical reality.

Their conclusion is that the contemporary scientific approach needs to change to facilitate better research and to understand its results:

> Science as we know it either must exclude itself from study of such phenomena, even when they precipitate objectively observable physical effects, or broaden its methodology and conceptual vocabulary to embrace subjective experience in some systematic way.

In 2006, PEAR decided that, after nearly three decades of data accumulation, 'many of the salient correlates of these intriguing anomalies have now been identified' and 'further accumulation of comparable data … no longer seems to be the best investment of our intellectual and financial resources'. They plan to 'migrate' from their Princeton laboratory to privately funded research programmes while archiving their research data 'for future scholars'; encouraging their network of scholars, volunteers and interns; and developing 'beneficial applications' in partnership with entrepreneurs and venture capitalists.

Process, The

A psychoanalytic group that became a controversial religion.

The Process was founded by Robert de Grimston (born Robert Moore) and his wife Mary Anne Maclean. They met when they were both members of the Church of SCIENTOLOGY. Both were interested in the psychoanalytic teachings of Alfred Adler; both were disillusioned with Scientology and its founder L RON HUBBARD. They left Scientology in 1963 and set up a therapy group called Compulsions Analysis in London. This group was in some ways similar to Scientology's DIANETICS.

In 1966, now known as The Process, they moved to the Bahamas. They later moved to Mexico, before returning to the fashionable Mayfair area of London. By now they were more of a religion than a therapy group. In the late 1960s the leaders encouraged members to go out in pairs to spread the religion and to solicit donations.

The Process was also known as The Process Church of the Final Judgement. It held that there were three great Gods of the Universe – Jehovah, Lucifer and Satan. Jehovah was the wrathful God of the Old Testament; Lucifer, the Light Bearer, was kind and fun-loving; Satan was a God of extremes, both rising above and delving beneath normal human needs and values. Christ was the link between these Gods and mankind. The combination of this theology and the movement's increasing emphasis on extreme sexual activities (an entire issue of *Process* magazine was devoted to sex) led to them being labelled Satanists.

In 1970 The Process moved to the USA and set up successful centres (called Chapters) in New York, Boston, Chicago and New Orleans. These had a strong emphasis on social care, feeding the homeless, visiting the elderly and handicapped, and working alongside the Salvation Army and Red Cross.

Robert and Mary Anne de Grimston referred to themselves as the Omega, and became increasingly separated from the rest of the movement. Tensions between Robert and Mary Anne, and between Omega and the senior members of the movement, led to Robert's removal from the leadership in 1974. Mary Anne and the other leaders changed the focus and some of the beliefs of the movement, and changed its name yet again to the Foundation Faith of God, which eventually became the well-respected Utah-based animal welfare charity, Best Friends Animal Society. Robert de Grimston is thought to have become a business consultant in New York.

In the 1980s The Process was revived under new leadership as the Society of the Processeans, but without its unconventional spiritual beliefs; these were declared obsolete in 1993, and the Church's archives were destroyed. The emphasis now appears to be completely on social welfare.

The popular belief that the convicted murderer Charles Manson was a member of The Process, as claimed in early editions of Ed Sanders's book *The Family*, is untrue.

Project Alpha
A hoax perpetrated to expose weaknesses in the experimental methods employed by some parapsychologists.
In 1979, Washington University of St Louis established the McDonnell Laboratory for Psychical Research (after receiving a gift of half a million dollars from the chairman of McDonnell-Douglas Aircraft). The magician, and famous sceptic, JAMES RANDI believed that the apparently positive results obtained by researchers in the field of parapsychology at the time were purely due to lax controls and poor experimental protocols, rather than any real PSYCHIC ability. He believed that many experimenters could be fooled by fraudsters employing simple STAGE MAGIC techniques (he had already argued that this had happened during the investigation of URI GELLER). In an effort to publicly demonstrate this he embarked on a secret hoax, under the name 'Project Alpha'. The deception continued for four years until it was eventually exposed in 1983.

Out of 300 potential test subjects attending the newly established laboratory in 1979, only two were chosen by researchers as being worthy of serious investigation – Steve Shaw and Mike Edwards. However, in truth, Shaw and Edwards were two teenagers who had been trained in a number of techniques by Randi. The primary area of research at the laboratory was to be METAL BENDING. Randi helpfully offered his services to the researchers, suggesting that he could help them to spot trickery and subterfuge. He also suggested a number of possible improvements to the experimental protocols. His offers were turned down – the experimenters were apparently happy that they could spot cheating without his help.

After some remarkable results were achieved, film footage of the investigations was shown at a PARAPSYCHOLOGY conference, following which a number of faults in the experimental technique were pointed out by audience members. Back at the laboratory changes were made, and Shaw and Edwards appeared to suddenly lose their psychic powers. It was at this point that Randi publicly admitted to his hoax. Both participants had been instructed by Randi to tell the truth at all times, including admitting to being hoaxers if they were directly asked – however, they claim that throughout the whole period of the project they were never asked this question.

Randi's stated rationale was to expose poor scientific technique and to show how well-meaning people could easily be fooled. By his exposure he hoped to force a tightening-up of research protocols, although some argue that, in truth, he takes a hard-line position on the non-existence of psychic abilities, and so the whole thing was engineered to publicly ridicule those involved in parapsychology. Lessons were certainly learned within the field, but public confidence in parapsychological research was seriously damaged and a number of research projects were abandoned as a direct result.

Mike Edwards is no longer professionally involved in stage magic, but Steve Shaw is now a magician, performing under the stage name Banachek. Metal bending is still a mainstay of his act.

Project Blue Book
The principal US Air Force team charged with investigating UFOs during the 1950s and 1960s, the work of which was dramatized in the short-lived 1970s television series Project UFO.
After the failure of the first two US Air Force UFO projects, PROJECT SIGN (1948) and PROJECT GRUDGE (1949), the longevity of Blue Book, the last in the sequence, was something of a surprise.

Despite the downgrading of Grudge at the end of 1949, UFO sightings (including some involving military personnel) continued to be reported. Following the massive increase in public interest after the publishing of articles and books by Major DONALD KEYHOE, the Pentagon was forced to react to low public confidence in their handling of the matter. They invited a respected investigative officer, Captain EDWARD J RUPPELT, to take over the moribund Grudge in October 1951. He laid down his requirements, which included more staff and an increase in sober investigation. He apparently thought this essential in the face of the existing Pentagon requirement to explain cases away by coming up with any vaguely credible solution.

The US Air Force met many of Ruppelt's requests, including his suggestion of a change in code name, and Project Blue Book began in March 1952. The name was taken from a tough college exam paper, supposedly to reflect the hard questions that were to be asked. While Ruppelt was not then a 'believer', he was felt to be a man who would not avoid the truth. He won support from all quarters – many in the Pentagon thought that he would finally rid them of the entire problem, whereas those who believed that UFOs were real considered him such a thorough investigator that he could be swayed by the evidence.

Blue Book adopted the term 'UFO', to replace

A photograph of Hector Quintanilla and other members of the Project Blue Book team from the mid 1950s. (© Mary Evans Picture Library)

the outdated 'FLYING SAUCER', and presided over a contract with the prestigious Battelle Memorial Institute to conduct a massive statistical analysis of the available evidence. The figures produced by this study were taken to strongly suggest that something more than the misperception of known phenomena was occurring. DR J ALLEN HYNEK continued to act as scientific advisor to the new project, and the files that were released in 1976, when the US FREEDOM OF INFORMATION ACT came into force, indicate that the quality of the investigations carried out in the early 1950s was consistently high.

However, the US government was apparently uncomfortable with the findings and, by this time, the CIA had also become involved in the UFO mystery – a situation of which the staff at Blue Book were unaware. The project continued under a range of new leaders, none of whom are felt by those with an interest in the phenomenon to have matched Ruppelt's objective approach. Throughout the late 1950s and 1960s case work was much more low-key and the US Air Force appeared to be uncomfortable with what had become something of a public relations headache. When the UNIVERSITY OF COLORADO STUDY was set up in 1967 many within the organization hoped that it would provide the excuse to close the Blue Book project. The team leader of the study, EDWARD CONDON, made that recommendation in January 1969 and the Pentagon acted on it immediately. However, the news was only made public at the end of the year, to coincide with the staging of a public debate on the UFO question staged by the American Association for the Advancement of Science – a move seen by many to be a cynical attempt to demean the event.

Although the end of Project Blue Book officially marked the end of US Air Force interest in UFOs, the files were retained. When they were released seven years later, the difficult dilemma faced by the US government became apparent. Many UFO cases could be explained but some apparently defied all investigation. At the time, at the height of the cold war, it had not been considered politically expedient to admit anything that implied that the Pentagon was not in complete control. In the end, objective scientific analysis appears to have taken a back seat to politics when it came to handling a delicate subject for which there was little desire to take responsibility.

Project Grudge

The second, short-lived, US Air Force UFO project, that ran for just six months during 1949. It operated under a new brief to explain away UFO sightings.
Following the rejection of the ESTIMATE OF THE SITUATION report in the summer of 1948, the staff at Wright Field in Dayton, where PROJECT SIGN was based, were largely demoralized. Several attempted, unsuccessfully, to persuade the Chief of Staff, General Vandenberg, to change his mind. Instead, all those who had backed the report were transferred away.

Those that remained were much less open to the EXTRATERRESTRIAL HYPOTHESIS, believing that even the most remarkable cases could probably be resolved. By February 1949 they had produced a final report explaining that 80 per cent of the 237 sightings that they had studied had now been explained. They added that, if the Pentagon increased funding and put UFO officers onto every air base, this would rise towards 100 per cent.

It was argued that the name 'Sign' had been compromised – the decision was taken to refocus the project and give it a new name – Grudge. Officially there was no significance to the word used; although some US Air Force personnel thought that it reflected the new attitude at high level, where UFOs were beginning to be seen as something of a nuisance. The new orders were specific – to explain away as many sightings as possible, even if the explanations offered were far from proven. Grudge officers were to be allowed to work with 'friendly' journalists who were willing to write dismissive articles in exchange for access to secret files. However, many of the writers who studied the evidence were not easily persuaded to toe the line. The policy was not entirely successful – it effectively produced the leaks that inspired Major DONALD KEYHOE to raise the public profile of UFOs, and the perceived GOVERNMENTAL COVER-UP.

Unaware that research was also being conducted elsewhere, at a higher level (see PROJECT TWINKLE), the Grudge team published a final report in August 1949. Ironically, despite the new orders, they had failed to resolve 23 per cent of their cases, a worse performance than Project Sign. The report also warned that UFOs might be used by Communists to encourage insurrection – an idea that was to resurface several years later when the CIA began to infiltrate UFO investigations in an atmosphere of increasing cold war tension.

After the report was released, it was announced to the public that the project was closed. In reality, it had been downgraded to the point where it involved just a single officer acting as a filing clerk for incoming cases. It remained that way until Captain EDWARD J RUPPELT was charged with reviving the department in October 1951 – see PROJECT BLUE BOOK.

projection *see* ASTRAL PROJECTION

Project Sign
The codename of the first official UFO investigation team operated by the US Air Force. It was created in response to the sightings reported during the summer of 1947.

In the summer of 1947 a WAVE of UFO sightings was reported from across the western USA. The KENNETH ARNOLD sighting was the most influential of these, inspiring the familiar term 'FLYING SAUCER'. On 30 July 1947, Lieutenant Colonel Donald Springer published an investigation into 16 of the key cases in that period, most of which involved trained observers, such as pilots. They ranged from LIGHTS IN THE SKY to the sighting of a 'giant wagon wheel', but only one of them was actually saucer shaped. Springer concluded that:

> This 'flyig saucer' situation is not all imaginary or seeing too much in some natural phenomenon. Something is really flying around.

The report led to a call for action by the head of Air Material Command (AMC), Lieutenant General Nathan Twining. He wrote to intelligence chief, Brigadier General George Schulgen, on 23 September 1947, stressing that UFOs were 'something real and not visionary or fictitious'. On 30 December 1947 an approval order came through to set up Project Sign, under the control of the AMC, and operated from Wright Field in Dayton, Ohio – the base to which wreckage from ROSWELL had been flown for study some five months earlier.

The existence of the project was leaked but its code name remained a secret. After the official launch on 22 January 1948, the media nicknamed it 'Project Saucer'. It faced an immediate crisis when Captain Thomas Mantell died while chasing a bright daylight UFO above Kentucky. He had been asked to investigate after a number of civilians had seen a glowing object. When he crashed, the wreckage of his plane could not be hidden. The press also learned that the pilot's final words had been about seeing a huge UFO overhead as he climbed towards it, leading to speculation that his plane had been shot down by something unknown.

The young local astronomer, DR J ALLEN HYNEK, was appointed scientific advisor to the project. At the time he was a sceptic and was charged with the task of explaining as many sightings as possible to reassure the public. Unfortunately, Hynek could not solve the Mantell case. He tried to stop Sign proposing that the UFO report had been generated by a sighting of the planet Venus. Hynek pointed out that it was almost impossible to see Venus in the daylight and that it certainly would not fit the description of a large metallic craft. However, he could not persuade them to alter their official explanation, adding to a growing suspicion among the public that there was a GOVERNMENTAL COVER-UP obscuring the fact that a pilot had been killed by ALIENS. The truth did not emerge until decades later, when it was revealed that a top-secret experiment (of which members of Project Sign were unaware) had taken place using a high-altitude balloon. Captain Mantell had tried to fly too high, without suitable oxygen equipment, causing him to black out in the increasingly thin air.

Reports of sightings continued to flood in during 1948, notably the incident on 24 July when an Eastern Airlines DC-3 was 'buzzed' by a UFO over Alabama – the crew were adamant that the object was just like a 'Flash Gordon rocket ship'. Hynek thought it might have been a meteor but could not find sufficient evidence. By now, several members of the Sign team were becoming convinced that the best explanation lay with the EXTRATERRESTRIAL HYPOTHESIS. On 8 August 1948, Project Sign produced an ESTIMATE OF THE SITUATION REPORT putting forward this view. It was rejected by the Pentagon on the grounds that there was a lack of physical evidence. Many members of Sign expressed their dismay, only to find themselves reassigned. Left behind were those team members (including Hynek) who hoped to find a mundane explanation for these frightening CLOSE ENCOUNTERS.

In February 1949 the remainder of the team put together a report summarizing the first year of the project. Some 237 cases had been investigated and 20 per cent of them remained unexplained. Dissatisfied with this track record, the Pentagon decided to close Project Sign and replace it with a team dedicated to explaining away the UFO phenomenon – see PROJECT GRUDGE.

Project Stargate

A US government project that involved attempts to train and use remote viewers for military purposes.

During the cold war the US government believed that the USSR was carrying out experiments into PSYCHIC abilities, with some apparent successes (for example, see NINA KULAGINA). Even if these apparent successes were unconvincing, the concern was that the USSR seemed to feel that this was an area into which investigation was worthwhile. The USA apparently decided that it needed to 'keep pace' just in case there was a genuine effect.

Project Stargate was one of a number of code names for experiments which formed part of a US-government-funded REMOTE-VIEWING programme. After initial trials were conducted at the Stanford Research Institute during the 1970s (see BAY AREA REMOTE-VIEWING EXPERIMENTS), Project Stargate was born.

Project Stargate, and the related projects, allegedly involved further experiments into remote viewing, including attempts to gain information about security measures in particular locations. In its later years the experiments are believed to have even included attempts to read specific documents which were locked inside a safe. The project employed a mixture of NATURALS and subjects who underwent training. A number of people have since made public claims to have been involved in Project Stargate, both to relate their experiences and to offer remote-viewing courses for a fee.

Research continued in various forms until 1995 – the official reason for the project's demise being the lack of sufficient evidence for the validity of the results. It is believed that, by the time the research came to an end, some 20 million dollars had been spent on it.

Project Twinkle

A covert project involving leading scientists, with sophisticated equipment, in a search for physical evidence relating to a type of UFO persistently reported near secret US military bases.

During late 1948, and early 1949, a series of reports were made in the area around Los Alamos, New Mexico – the secret scientific research facility where many of America's top scientists were developing rocket propulsion and nuclear weapons technology – of a particular type of UFO. They were given the name 'green fireballs', and the following description, by a pilot from Sante Fe, is typical:

> Take a soft ball and paint it with some kind of fluorescent paint that will glow a bright green in the dark. Then have someone take the ball 100 feet out in front of you and about 10 feet above you. Have him throw the ball at your face as hard as he can. That's what a green fireball looks like.

Soon many scientists working at Los Alamos were among the hundreds of witnesses. Dr Lincoln La Paz, one of the world's leading experts on meteors, was brought in from the University of Albuquerque to solve the riddle. He soon witnessed a fireball himself and was able to estimate the wavelength of light emitted. The results implied a high copper content, and the discovery of copper dust scattered on the ground supported his theory. Copper is extremely rare in meteors, just one of several reasons why that particular theory was rejected by La Paz.

In February 1949 La Paz told a secret meeting at Los Alamos, convened by the intelligence agencies, that the green fireballs were very strange. He thought that they were not a natural phenomenon. However, Edward Teller, one of the physicists who had designed the atom bomb, who was also part of the research project, argued otherwise. He felt that these UFOs might be some new kind of atmospheric phenomenon, possibly associated with the sudden creation of plasma. It was unclear whether they were linked to any experiments taking place in New Mexico at the time, but the Pentagon was adamant that the US government was not deliberately responsible for their creation.

One result of the meeting was the creation of the world's first scientific UFO investigation. It was given the codename Twinkle and placed in the hands of Dr Joseph Kaplan, a leading geophysicist. Its research was top secret – even members of the ongoing US

Air Force UFO projects, PROJECT SIGN and PROJECT GRUDGE, were not privy to the work. Kaplan was given until October 1949 to formulate plans. The team then went on to work with a government contractor, Land-Air, to develop automatic twin-camera systems and spectrographs to record the green fireballs and obtain data relating to them. Much of this work was similar to that carried out by UFO researchers at the site of recurrent UFO activity in HESSDALEN, Norway, 30 years later.

Although the equipment was in place for 18 months, until late 1951, the project was not a success. The Korean War intervened, taking away many of the personnel who had been trained to use the sophisticated devices. The WAVE was also beginning to peter out by the time the operation commenced. Sightings became more sporadic. When the team set up in one spot, the fireballs appeared elsewhere, and when they moved the equipment, sightings were reported from the location they had just vacated. A few images were captured, and some readings were taken, but these were often spoiled by operator errors or technical difficulties. Overall, the results were inconclusive and the project was abandoned.

None of those who saw the fireballs, or took part in the project, doubted that the phenomenon was real. Opinions as to the cause were split, but none thought there was a simple explanation.

Sudden bursts of similar 'green fireball' activity have been recorded elsewhere since 1951. Reports are often linked with locations at which atmospheric research is thought to be taking place – particularly high-energy radar systems. The region around Rendlesham Forest in the UK, scene of Britain's most famous close encounters (see RENDLESHAM FOREST INCIDENT), was one such location during the 1970s and 1980s. At that time 'Over the Horizon' radar experiments were underway at installations on nearby Orford Ness. Similar claims were made in relation to experimental radar facilities in Pine Gap, Australia.

prophecy
A prediction of the future that is generally held to be divinely inspired; the gift of being able to make prophecies.
In the broadest sense, a prophecy, which comes from a Greek word meaning 'speaking before' or 'foretelling', is any PREDICTION of future events. But prophecy is generally held to be divinely inspired, and throughout history, people have sought knowledge of the future from individuals or groups believed to have the gift of prophecy, such as ORACLES, who were said to receive their predictions either through direct communication with a deity, or through some form of DIVINATION. Prophecy as a revelation of divine

will plays an important part in many religions and cultures.

The Bible contains hundreds of prophecies, and of the 39 books of the Bible's Old Testament, 18 are ascribed to Hebrew prophets. The Bible refers to many prophetic dreams, the most famous of which appears in the Book of Genesis – in it, the Pharaoh of Egypt dreams of seven fat cattle being eaten by seven thin ones, and seven plump ears of corn being consumed by seven withered ones, which Joseph interprets as foretelling seven years of plenty followed by seven of famine. Some prophecies in the Bible involve the coming of the Messiah, while other 'end time' prophecies refer to a time of war, famine and pestilence to come, after which the Messiah will reign over the world in justice; Christians believe that Jesus was the Messiah foretold in the Messianic prophecies, and the New Testament Book of Revelation is thought by many to be a prophecy of Armageddon.

Muhammad, the prophet of Islam, claimed to have had a spiritual awakening in a cave, from which point he spoke teachings received directly from Allah.

Sceptics argue that the power of prophecy will never be scientifically proven, and that many prophecies, such as those of NOSTRADAMUS, are so vaguely worded that they can be made to fit many events after they have happened.

Protocols of the Learned Elders of Zion, The
An anti-Semitic forgery claiming to be evidence of a Jewish world-takeover conspiracy.
More than 80 years after *The Protocols of the Learned Elders of Zion* were proved to be an anti-Semitic forgery, there are still conspiracy theorists and right-wing Christian books, magazines and websites promoting them as true. A long document entitled *The Protocols of the Learned Elders of Zion* was first published in Russia by Sergei Nilus in 1905, having been privately circulated since 1897. The document claimed to be a detailed explanation by Jewish elders of how they planned to take over the world by controlling each country's media and finances, and by destroying both the Christian religion and democracy, as summed up in Protocol 5:

> By all these means we shall so wear down the *goyim* [Gentiles or non-Jews] that they will be compelled to offer us international power of a nature that by its position will enable us without any violence gradually to absorb all the State forces of the world and to form a Super-Government.

It is a long and repetitive work; there are 24 protocols, some of them several pages long.

In 1920 the *Protocols* were first proved to be a forgery; this was publicized in *The Times* the following year. However, by then the *Protocols* had already been translated into English, and were published in a Michigan newspaper used by the US car manufacturer Henry Ford to publish his anti-Semitic and anti-Communist views. The *Protocols* were later taken up by Adolf Hitler as part of his justification for the Holocaust.

In fact the *Protocols* originated in a novel by Hermann Goedsche, *Biarritz* (1868), itself inspired by a plot to take over the world in a pamphlet of political satire by Maurice Joly, *Dialogue in Hell between Machiavelli and Montesquieu* (1864); Goedsche changed the conspirators to Jews. There are conflicting theories about who rewrote the relevant chapter of Goedsche's novel to become the *Protocols*.

The *Protocols* include the assumption that FREEMASONRY is already in the process of taking over the world, saying that this is on behalf of Jews. Any late 20th-century or early 21st-century conspiracy theory that includes phrases such as 'the Jewish-masonic cover-up' is ultimately based on this century-old anti-Semitic faked document.

psi

A general term covering all areas of extrasensory perception and psychokinesis.

The term 'psi' (from ψ, the 23rd letter of the Greek alphabet) was proposed by psychologists B P Wiesner and Robert Thouless in 1942. It was originally intended to be used in relation to EXTRASENSORY PERCEPTION only but, in 1948, J B RHINE extended the definition to include PSYCHOKINESIS. The term is now often used to include all psychic abilities and any paranormal process or phenomenon. Some claim that psi is an abbreviation for 'paranormal sensory information'. See also PARAPSYCHOLOGY and PSI HYPOTHESIS.

psi, animal *see* ANIMAL PSI

psi hypothesis

The contention that certain apparently paranormal events and psychological phenomena result from the conscious or unconscious use of psi.

Strictly speaking (as with the root term 'PSI') the phrase 'psi hypothesis' should only be used in connection with EXTRASENSORY PERCEPTION and PSYCHOKINESIS – however, it is now often used much more loosely. Much modern parapsychological research involves testing the psi hypothesis by taking on the working assumption that psi abilities exist, and attempting to find experimental evidence of their use. Those

who give credence to the hypothesis effectively accept that it is possible that the human mind is able to produce effects, or receive information 'at a distance' via mechanisms that we do not currently understand. The alternative position to the psi hypothesis is the 'non-psi hypothesis', which holds that apparent evidence of the use of psi is the result of mistake, misinterpretation, trickery or fraud. See also PARAPSYCHOLOGY.

psyche

The human mind or soul.

The word 'psyche' comes from a Greek original meaning 'soul' and is usually taken to mean the human mind or soul. The ancient Greeks personified the psyche as a young woman with the wings of a butterfly who was the beloved of Eros.

In terms of the modern science of psychology, the psyche is usually seen as being made up of both the conscious and the UNCONSCIOUS. Speaking more broadly, it can be said to represent everything about a human individual that is not physical, including thoughts, ideals, dreams and memories. There are, however, those who maintain that the idea of a separation between mind and body is an artificial one at best.

SIGMUND FREUD and the psychoanalysts who followed him believed that the key to the psyche was the unconscious and that bringing to light the repressed secrets stored there would provide the cure for mental disorders. The Swiss psychiatrist CARL JUNG believed in a more spiritual, less mechanistic, approach to the psyche and that there existed both a personal and a collective (common to all human beings) element. The split between the purely scientific and the more metaphysical view of the psyche continues to this day.

psychedelic drugs

Drugs that heighten perception and increase mental powers.

The word 'psychedelic' (from Greek terms meaning 'soul' and 'visible or clear') is usually applied to drugs that heighten perception and increase mental powers. Their use in 'altering consciousness' has been known in many cultures around the world and throughout history. In Europe, plants with both poisonous and psychedelic properties, such as deadly nightshade, henbane and mandrake, were traditionally used in medicine as well as in religious practices but came to be associated with WITCHCRAFT in the late Middle Ages.

In ancient Egypt, the blue lotus was used to induce a state of blissful indolence and forgetfulness, and this was reflected in Greek myth with the encounter between Odysseus and the Lotus-eaters. It is thought that some kind of psychedelic drug may have been used as part of the ELEUSINIAN MYSTERIES.

In Asia, the native peoples of Siberia evolved a religion based on the SHAMAN, who was believed to heal by magic, communicate with the dead and travel vast distances mentally. It is thought that ingesting the hallucinogenic fly agaric toadstool was important in these practices.

Similar beliefs and ceremonial use of psychedelics arose in the Americas, with such plants as the PEYOTE cactus, morning glory and psilocybin mushrooms (popularly known today as 'magic mushrooms') providing the ingredients. In addition, the roots of the ayahuasco vine of South America were used to make a hallucinogenic drink, and this practice continues among certain indigenous peoples. In fact, the US government permits traditional medicinal uses of psychedelics among some Native American peoples, while, certainly in many states, the medicinal use of cannabis is illegal.

In the 20th century, psychedelic drugs were developed for medicinal use. LSD, for example, was thought to have beneficial effects in the treatment of mental disorders such as schizophrenia. Similarly, methylene-dioxymethamphetamine (MDMA or, as it is popularly known, 'ecstasy') was synthesized in laboratories but experiments and trials revealed no apparent medical applications. It was only after its psychedelic properties had been discovered by illicit users that it became widely known. So-called 'designer drugs' came to be created simply for the recreational use of their psychedelic effects.

Some of the stronger forms of cannabis are now known to have psychedelic properties, and followers of Rastafarianism claim that use of the drug is a part of their religious practice, holding it to be both a sacrament and an aid to meditation. They are able to quote excerpts from the Bible which, referring to 'herbs', they say endorses such use.

Some claim that the use of psychedelic drugs has been responsible throughout the ages for VISIONS and other supernatural spiritual experiences. One theory that has been suggested to account for the MASS HYSTERIA of the Salem witch trials (see SALEM WITCHES) in 17th-century North America is that several of those involved may have been poisoned by eating rye infected with the ergot fungus, which is now known to have psychedelic and hallucinatory effects. Similarly, the recreational use of LSD and other psychedelic drugs has been linked with reports of UFOS, ALIEN ABDUCTIONS and other anomalous experiences of the post-war era.

psychic
A term describing both paranormal powers and the possessor of such powers.

When someone claims to be a psychic, they are now normally understood to be claiming that they possess certain powers above and beyond the normal physical abilities and senses of the human body – these would include such things as EXTRASENSORY PERCEPTION, PSYCHOKINESIS and PRECOGNITION.

Many people also use the word 'psychic' interchangeably with 'MEDIUM' or 'clairvoyant' (see CLAIRVOYANCE). However, while it is true that some self-proclaimed mediums or clairvoyants do also say that they have psychic powers, it is usually the case that they are actually making a separate and distinct claim to be communicating with SPIRITS, rather than exercising any innate power of their own. Equally, however, it might be argued that the ability to communicate with spirits could be understood to be a psychic power in itself – indeed, the term was first used by the scientist William Crookes in 1870, in reference to the medium DANIEL DUNGLAS HOME. See also PSI.

psychical research
The scientific investigation of claims of psychic powers and paranormal events.

Interest in PSYCHIC phenomena was stimulated during the 19th century, particularly by the rise of the SPIRITUALISM movement. This coincided with the development of 'scientism' and a growing belief that science could provide the answers to questions about the nature of the world around us. Although many people of a scientific bent began to dismiss the idea of the supernatural and paranormal, others felt that a scientific approach could be applied in these areas for the purposes of proving (or disproving) the multitude of claims that were being made. In the UK the SOCIETY FOR PSYCHICAL RESEARCH was founded in 1882 and very soon an American offshoot, the AMERICAN SOCIETY FOR PSYCHICAL RESEARCH, was formed. During this time many fraudulent MEDIUMS were exposed as the results of research, much GHOST HUNTING was carried out and there were investigations into the emerging areas of SPIRIT PHOTOGRAPHY and GHOST PHOTOGRAPHY. Unfortunately, a lack of conclusive evidence, and some high-profile mistakes made by some of the more credulous 'researchers', led to psychical research attracting something of a 'crackpot' image among much of the general public. However, research continued.

In the 1920s and 1930s EXTRASENSORY PERCEPTION became a popular area of psychical research and a new laboratory-based approach developed. The term 'PARAPSYCHOLOGY' was introduced in an attempt to move away from some of the negative connotations associated with the original name for the discipline. Prominent among the new investigators was J B RHINE who set up a research unit at Duke University in North Carolina and provided a means of statistically analysing the results of experiments into TELEPATHY with the introduction of CARD-GUESSING EXPERIMENTS. Since then, research and investigation has continued, into a wide range of phenomena, from GHOSTS, POLTERGEISTS and HAUNTINGS through to CLAIRVOYANCE, REMOTE VIEWING, METAL BENDING and other examples of alleged PSYCHOKINESIS.

The whole area of psychical research remains highly controversial. In 1976 a group of sceptics in the USA set up the COMMITTEE FOR THE SCIENTIFIC INVESTIGATION OF CLAIMS OF THE PARANORMAL (CSICOP) in response to what they perceived to be poor experimental procedure, and biased consideration of data, resulting from research being carried out by 'believers'. Many with an interest in the area countered that CSICOP's own approach was equally flawed – they argued that its members had already dismissed the possibility that any paranormal phenomena exist and so brought their own bias to the interpretation of evidence.

The terms 'psychical research' and 'parapsychology' are now generally used interchangeably. However, it is important to note that the word 'psychical' is preferred in this context to 'psychic' – the latter implying the existence and use of psychic powers for research purposes rather than the impartial and unbiased investigation of claims of the paranormal.

psychic archaeology

The alleged use of psychic powers to locate historical artefacts and to discover information relating to them.

The process of using psychic means in an attempt to find an archaeological site might involve the employment of techniques such as REMOTE VIEWING or DOWSING. Once a site has been found, and items have been recovered, attempts at contact with the SPIRITS of the dead or PSYCHOMETRY may be employed to try to obtain further information. Some psychic archaeologists claim that they do not even need to be present at the site in order to exercise their powers, although in many instances they do apparently require a map of the area under consideration (see MAP DOWSING).

When psychic archaeologists appear to achieve successes, sceptics usually argue that their results are merely a product of common sense and prior knowledge – for example, there are a number of patterns and features that can be used to predict the probable locations of settlements, without recourse

to the paranormal. In addition to this, the personal details provided in relation to the owners of artefacts and inhabitants of dwellings are, by their very nature, usually extremely difficult (if not impossible) to check.

psychic art

The production of works of art without conscious control.

The phrase 'psychic art' is used in relation to three distinct areas. The first two are SPIRIT DRAWING, in which a MEDIUM produces an image of a SPIRIT with whom they claim they are in contact, and AUTOMATIC ART, in which the medium claims that they are possessed or guided by the spirit of a dead person – often an artist – to produce a work in that person's style.

The third area to which the term is applied does not involve any form of alleged contact with the spirit world – rather it involves a subject apparently entering an ALTERED STATE OF CONSCIOUSNESS, during which they produce works of art. These pictures are said to be created without the conscious control of the artist. As well as being a way to produce free-form artwork, it is often claimed that the process is a means for tapping into the artist's subconscious, possibly to obtain spiritual insight or answers to troubling questions. See also AUSTIN OSMAN SPARE.

psychic attack

An alleged form of 'mental attack' supposedly carried out using psychic powers.

There are two ways in which the term 'psychic attack' is used. Firstly, it is applied to attempts at DIRECT MENTAL INTERACTION WITH LIVING SYSTEMS by human agents, to bring about harm to other humans or animals by affecting the physical function of their bodies. Experiments in this area were allegedly carried out by the CIA during the cold war, in response to leaked films of Russian psychics, such as NINA KULAGINA, which appeared to show them influencing the beating of a frog's heart. The experiments carried out in the USA were also said to have included attempts to affect the heart rates of animals – the ultimate aim was believed to be the creation of a group of psychic assassins who could kill at a distance, using the power of the mind alone. URI GELLER claims to have been approached to participate in such experiments but apparently he declined.

The concept of psychic attack also features in some NEW AGE philosophies, where the term refers to situations in which a subject is plagued by a range of less specific symptoms, including bad DREAMS, a feeling of a crushing weight on the chest, nervous exhaustion leading to physical collapse and visualizations of SPIRITS. Such attacks are said to result variously from the actions of malevolent supernatural beings, POLTERGEIST activity or the efforts of a human PSYCHIC or practitioner of MAGIC (among other things). However, it has been pointed out that the symptoms interpreted as resulting from a psychic attack in such circumstances bear a striking resemblance to those commonly understood to result from stress. See also PSYCHIC WARFARE.

psychic detectives
Individuals who attempt to aid the police by use of their self-proclaimed psychic talents.
Psychic detectives often offer their services for the location of missing persons or dead bodies. The means through which they apparently achieve this are various forms of EXTRASENSORY PERCEPTION – particularly REMOTE VIEWING and PSYCHOMETRY.

Although there have been several apparent successes over the years (notably those of GERARD CROISET), sceptics would point out that there are a number of reasons to suspect that these are simply chance occurrences, or the result of selective interpretation after the event. In most instances psychic detectives either give information that is so vague as to be useless, and then try to claim success when the person turns up, or they provide so much information that there is a significant chance that at least some of it will be correct – the correct information is remembered and the large number of incorrect guesses are quietly forgotten (a process sometimes referred to as 'cognitive bias' – see CHANCE AND COINCIDENCE).

psychic energy
The claimed underlying driving force for all psychic phenomena.
The term 'psychic energy' is freely used within much NEW AGE literature. It is often offered as an 'explanation' for how PSYCHIC or paranormal phenomena are brought about. It is variously said to be an all-enveloping force which interlinks everything, the 'life force' and a form of 'mental energy' which can be manipulated by someone with the appropriate powers. However, to the uninitiated, it is very difficult to understand what any of these descriptions actually mean. As with much New Age thought, the concept of psychic energy appears to have been drawn partly from Western interpretations of Eastern philosophies (for example, see QI) and, indeed, it is often claimed that MEDITATION and YOGA can help people to access and control it.

psychic healing
The healing of one person by another by psychic means, without the use of any conventional curative agents such as drugs.
Psychic healing is claimed to help or cure patients by the use of psychic energy; it complements conventional medicine and is believed to aid the body in its own self-healing process. It is based on the theory that illness is characterized by a deficiency or imbalance of vital energy in the body; the psychic healer therefore channels and transfers healing energy to the patient in order to restore the balance. When performed in a religious context, it is usually referred to as FAITH HEALING, or the LAYING ON OF HANDS, and Christian psychic healers believe that God's healing power is transferred to them through the Holy Spirit. Many spiritualist psychic healers believe that the spirits of physicians heal through them, while some healers claim to be helped by spirit guides or angels, and others describe themselves as channelling a force variously known as cosmic energy, UNIVERSAL LIFE FORCE or bioenergy. A few healers claim to work by channelling the collective healing energy from a group of spiritual healers. In 'absent healing' or 'distant healing', the patient is not even present, but healing energy is sent to them from a distance. Creative visualization, in which the patient is visualized as being well, is often combined with prayer and ritual.

Some psychic healers touch the patient, while others manipulate their 'energy field', as in REIKI, THERAPEUTIC TOUCH and AURA therapy. They may also combine their healing techniques with massage,

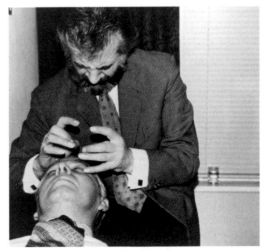

The psychic healer George Chapman at work during the 1950s, apparently under the guidance of the spirit of Dr William Lang who died in 1937. (© Mary Evans Picture Library)

or use CRYSTALS. Several sessions may be required, and treatment often includes a HOLISTIC approach in which the patient's underlying emotional problems are also examined, since it is believed by many healers that disease begins in the emotions, and that if healing is done on the emotional level, this will manifest on a physical level. Psychic healers are therefore encouraged to train in counselling techniques, and part of the treatment many include teaching the patient how to integrate their 'shadow' – that part of themselves which for some reason they have disowned, and which they need to embrace in order to heal. For example, if a patient is suffering from depression caused by an unhappy childhood, the healer may work to heal the 'inner child' on the spiritual plane.

However, if an inept psychic healer overdoes the healing process or does not ensure that they psychically disconnect from the patient afterwards, there is said to be a danger that the healer will suffer a drain in their own energies; similarly, they should only operate when they themselves are in good health, so as not to accidentally transfer their own illness to the patient.

Psychic healing is regarded with scepticism by many physicians and scientists, who dismiss any beneficial effects as being due to suggestion; however, its supporters claim that it has been seen to help babies, animals and even plants, which are not open to such influences. It is said to be especially effective in alleviating the symptoms of chronic illnesses and musculoskeletal problems, as well as stress and depression. Psychic healing should not be confused with PSYCHIC SURGERY.

psychic photography *see*

THOUGHTOGRAPHY

psychic questing

The alleged use of psychic powers to find objects, information or enlightenment.
Psychic questing is a popular NEW AGE pastime. The phrase is used to describe the apparent use of PSYCHIC powers or intuition to find hidden information about historical happenings, to locate artefacts, to find the answers to questions or even to gain spiritual enlightenment. Psychic quests are said to begin with an event such as a message in a DREAM, a vision or simply an overwhelming desire to begin looking. The process may involve MEDITATION, ritual magical practices and alleged communication with the SPIRITS.

psychic spying

Attempts to access secret information by psychic means.
Experiments into the use of REMOTE VIEWING and MIND-READING for the purposes of spying were allegedly carried out by both sides during the cold war. Such experiments took place in the USA with CIA funding, starting with the BAY AREA REMOTE VIEWING EXPERIMENTS, which were followed by PROJECT STARGATE and other similar initiatives over a period of 20 years and more. However, despite the many claims that the experiments achieved some success (and occasional suggestions that they still continue in secret), no conclusive evidence has ever been produced, leading, at least officially, to the withdrawal of all government funding in this area.

psychic surgery

A technique in which psychic abilities are allegedly employed to assist in the removal of tissue from the body without resort to conventional means.
Psychic surgeons have claimed over the years to be able to conduct operations in a non-invasive manner, without using tools, anaesthetics or antiseptics. The procedures carried out have supposedly included major surgery, such as the removal of cancerous tumours and kidney stones. The process often involves much in the way of elaborate hand movements, and may include calling on divine or spiritual help. An incision is apparently made in the patient (often appearing to produce copious amounts of blood) and damaging tissue is then supposedly removed before the entry hole is sealed, leaving no scar.

Psychic surgery first came to prominence in the Philippines in the 1940s, firstly through Eleuterio Terte and later through his student Tony Agpaoa, who were associated with the Christian Spiritist Movement of the Philippines. By the 1950s it was also becoming popular in Brazil, where it is thought that it may have been derived from CANDOMBLÉ rituals and similar spiritual practice.

Many famous personalities have used psychic surgeons or have supported their work. In 1984 the US comedian Andy Kaufman underwent an extensive course of treatment in the Philippines, two months before dying of metastatic carcinoma. In 2005, the psychic surgeon Alex Orbito (famous in the US through his association with the actor Shirley MacLaine) was charged in Canada with fraud and living off the proceeds of crime.

It is often claimed psychic surgery works by the surgeon entering a new 'vibrational state' (although it is not clear what this is actually supposed to mean), allowing them to enter the body and remove the problem. However, on investigation, tissue that has allegedly been removed from a human body during psychic surgery has been found to include such things as chicken livers and pieces of animal flesh; and a number of magicians (notably JAMES RANDI) have demonstrated the types of fraudulent

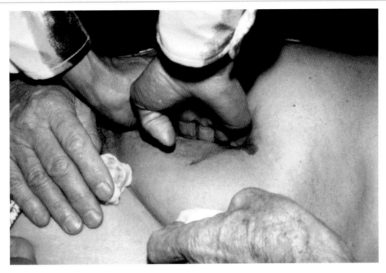

The Filipino psychic surgeon Feliciano Omilles working in Mexico in the early 1970s. (© TopFoto/Fortean)

techniques that can be used to make psychic surgery appear 'real'.

Psychic surgery is still carried out worldwide (particularly in the Philippines and Brazil), despite the US Federal Trade Commission declaring it a hoax in 1975.

psychic warfare
The potential use of psychic powers for military applications.

During the latter part of the 20th century (particularly during the cold war period) there were a number of attempts by the major world powers at investigation into the possibility of using PSYCHIC powers for military purposes. The potential applications were seen as ranging from passive attempts at gathering information (see PSYCHIC SPYING) through to the active use of PSYCHOKINESIS and DIRECT MENTAL INTERACTION WITH LIVING SYSTEMS to produce physical effects or cause direct harm.

Intelligence leaked to the West from the Soviet Union, such as the film of NINA KULAGINA apparently performing a range of psychic feats, prompted a response from the USA – the US government instigated a range of research programmes, predominantly under the control of the CIA. These apparently included a number of REMOTE VIEWING and DISTANT-INFLUENCE EXPERIMENTS (see PROJECT STARGATE and BAY AREA REMOTE-VIEWING EXPERIMENTS).

Despite admitting to spending a significant amount of money over a number of years, the US government appear (at least officially) to have ended up with nothing to show for their projects. The

Russian government continue to be secretive about how much research was conducted during the Soviet era, and how much success was achieved. However, it is widely believed that their apparently impressive evidence of success was faked and deliberately leaked to spread disinformation, prompting the US to carry out expensive and fruitless research. Whatever the official position, there are still a number of people who claim that research into psychic warfare continues as part of covert 'black ops'.

psychokinesis
The movement of material objects, or the influencing of mechanical systems, using only the power of the mind.

Psychokinesis (constructed from the Greek *psyche*, meaning 'soul', and *kinesis*, meaning 'movement'), often abbreviated to 'PK', is the term given by parapsychologists to the range of effects previously known as MIND OVER MATTER or TELEKINESIS. It is one of the main areas of research in modern PARAPSYCHOLOGY, where the phenomena are now usually sub-divided into the two categories of MACRO-PK and MICRO-PK, depending upon the scale of the effect under consideration. METAL BENDING is one of the most widely known supposed manifestations of the former. The latter would include attempts to influence the output of an electronic RANDOM NUMBER GENERATOR.

The idea of psychokinesis first appeared during the 19th century (although the term was not coined until the 20th century) as a suggested explanation for a number of SÉANCE phenomena – this was in opposition to the popular belief at the time that spirits

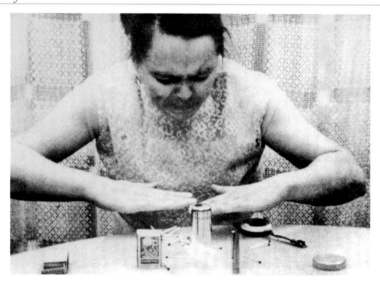

Russian psychic Nina Kulagina attempting to raise objects from a table using psychokinesis, c.1970. (© Mary Evans Picture Library)

were interacting with the physical world (possibly by the production of ECTOPLASM). The concept that many phenomena previously attributed to ghosts or spirits of the dead actually have their roots in a (currently unproven) capability of the human mind has since been developed further – a prime example being the RECURRENT SPONTANEOUS PSYCHOKINESIS theory of the origin of POLTERGEIST phenomena.

Over the years, many individuals have claimed to be able to use the power of psychokinesis. Among the most famous are URI GELLER and NINA KULAGINA.

psychometry
The supposed employment of psychic powers to gain information about an object's previous owner or its history by handling it.

The idea that inanimate objects can pick up and store memories, thoughts and feelings from those who have handled them, and that these 'recordings' can then be accessed by a suitable PSYCHIC, is associated with the 19th-century US physiologist Joseph Rhodes Buchanan. He coined the term psychometry (from the Greek *psyche*, meaning 'soul', and *metron*, meaning 'measure') in 1842 and conducted a number of experiments in the area using his students.

Psychometry is the skill supposedly employed in PSYCHIC ARCHAEOLOGY and by PSYCHIC DETECTIVES. One major difficulty with psychometry is the fact that most of the historical information produced cannot be checked and, in the cases where it can, it is perfectly feasible that the psychometrist has actually obtained the information by normal means. Sceptics also point out that its proponents employ

techniques which take advantage of chance and our natural tendency to attribute significance to events – they make so many claims that there will inevitably be some apparent successes, or they make vague and general claims that are favourably interpreted as successes in hindsight. The vast numbers of failures are conveniently forgotten.

Despite this, psychometry remains popular in NEW AGE circles and a number of 'scientific' explanations for the mechanism by which it works continue to be offered. These range from the interaction of human AURAS with objects in close proximity to references to quantum theory and the vibration of sub-atomic particles.

psychosocial hypothesis
A theory which suggests that reports of UFOs can be explained as psychological experiences, moulded by sociological influences.

The most simplistic view of UFO sightings is that the witnesses' stories are either true or false. However, even sceptics agree that relatively few are deliberate hoaxes and that the majority are sincerely described events – only the cause is in doubt. Most UFO reports are framed in terms of EXTRATERRESTRIAL craft, leading to the popularity of the EXTRATERRESTRIAL HYPOTHESIS among some researchers. However, in recent years, particularly in Europe, psychosocial theories have grown in strength. Initially, these were inspired by the Swiss psychiatrist, CARL JUNG, who wrote one of the earliest UFO books, *Flying Saucers: A modern myth*, published in 1959.

Jung took no position as to whether there were

real UFOs causing some sightings. However, he was intrigued by the clear evidence that many reports were heavily influenced both by the psychology of the reporter and the social circumstances that surrounded that person. In loose terms, he felt that we 'see' what we expect to see, and what we are conditioned by our lifelong experience to accept.

As UFO researchers gathered more and more reports, the lack of solid proof for the physical reality of alien contacts began to appear more problematic. There were no good photographs of ALIENS or landed spacecraft, no other-worldly metal alloys and no tissue samples from which DNA could be recovered. It was also noted that the aliens encountered apparently exhibited very human behaviour and did not attempt to communicate concepts or ideas that were apart from human reasoning.

Jung drew comparisons between the types of entity reported and deep-rooted folkloric beliefs that prevailed in the regions from which the reports came (see ARCHETYPES). The UFO researcher JACQUES VALLÉE also found parallels between alien contact cases and the various folk tales from around the world relating to LITTLE PEOPLE. Other researchers have categorized the types of aliens reported by witnesses, and have drawn comparisons with older folk beliefs. For example, the NORDICS were the wise magicians, (typified by the legendary MERLIN) and the GREYS were the GOBLINS that appear in myths and legends all over the world. This developed into the theory that all CLOSE ENCOUNTER imagery was a reflection of our inner selves, rather than being generated by the observation of beings with a physical existence external to us. There was no physical evidence, because there was nothing physically real to be left behind.

Psychosocial thinkers point to the OZ FACTOR as an indication that many cases involve the witness slipping into an ALTERED STATE OF CONSCIOUSNESS. HYPNOSIS is used to dredge up memories (see MEMORIES, RECOVERED), but it can bring out fantasies or other inherited themes from within the UNCONSCIOUS. The phenomenon of CULTURAL TRACKING has also been recognized – the nature of the phenomena reported often mirrors the contemporary state of human knowledge, prevailing social attitudes and references from popular culture. In 1896, when airships were state-of-the-art technology, the crews of UFOs were reported to be human inventors. Now that space travel lies at the forefront of human endeavour, they are aliens.

There are a number of different working theories that fall under the broad umbrella of psychosocial thinking. Some researchers have investigated 'fantasy-proneness' – an idea introduced by psychologists in the 1980s. This is based around the observation that a small percentage of the population appear to have such vivid imaginations that they can find it hard to distinguish between reality and illusion. Other researchers believe that close encounters may be a form of 'waking dream' (see DREAMS, WAKING) and note the comparisons with a rare psychological phenomenon known as 'false awakening' – where a particularly vivid dream is falsely assumed to occur after waking. These are just two among many, but all share the common position that some form of wholly psychological experience lies at the heart of all unexplained UFO cases.

psychosomatic

A word used to describe illnesses that are psychological rather than physical in origin.

The word 'psychosomatic' comes from Greek roots (*psyche*, meaning 'soul', and *soma*, meaning 'body') and is used to describe illnesses that are considered to be produced in the mind of the sufferer rather than by a physical cause.

In medical terms, it is thought that some conditions, such as high blood pressure, allergies, asthma or duodenal ulcers, may well be largely produced, or at least exacerbated, by particular mental or emotional states. Eating disorders, such as bulimia nervosa or anorexia nervosa, are often considered to have a purely psychological cause, with the sufferer's mental image of their own body being the trigger.

The medical explanation tends to focus on the autonomic nervous system, the network of nerve fibres, glands and muscles involved in controlling the body's involuntary functions, such as the heartbeat or the secretion of substances by the glands. The theory is that overactivity in these nerves can produce a physical reaction, such as inflammation, which in turn leads to the destruction of cells. This is thought to be capable of producing disorders such as skin rashes and bowel problems.

At the heart of the debate about psychosomatic illnesses is the question of whether or not the mind and the body can really be regarded as separate. A 'holistic' approach to medicine, which looks at the whole person, both physically and psychologically, became increasingly popular in Western medical thinking in the later 20th century.

It is a common belief that emotional distress can lead to illness and even death, the classic example being when someone is said to have died 'of a broken heart' after a crushing emotional setback such as the end of a romance or the ultimate failure of a cherished ambition. Many instances exist of an elderly spouse dying soon after the death of their life-partner, as if, lacking the desire to go on, they simply will themselves to die.

Many people believe that thinking you are ill, or worrying about your health, will actually make you ill. The opposite belief, of course, is thought to be involved in the PLACEBO EFFECT, in which people treated with inactive substances often recover as well as patients who have been given actual drugs.

The paranormal comes into play when psychics claim to detect an unsuspected illness in individuals. It is sometimes argued that such a 'diagnosis' plants the idea of being ill in the subject's mind and turns out to be a self-fulfilling prophecy. Sceptics would argue that this is no more likely than the old belief that witches and curses could magically cause people to decline and die.

It has also been suggested that some phenomena such as the apparent witnessing of ghosts may be psychosomatic in origin. The argument is that if a person has been told, for example, that a particular place is haunted then that person will believe they are experiencing a haunting when they visit it.

puca *see* PUCK

puck
A mischievous English woodland spirit, made famous as a character in Shakespeare's A Midsummer Night's Dream.

The English woodland spirit known as puck was, in medieval times, considered to be a malicious goblin or worse; in Langland's *Piers Plowman*, Hell is called 'Pouk's Pinfold', and 'Pouk' was used as a nickname for the DEVIL. However, in later times, he came to be identified with the mischievous but good-natured Robin Goodfellow, Jack Robinson, and even sometimes Robin Hood in his capacity as the lord of the forest. His close cousins are the Irish puca or pooka, and the Welsh pwca. He is often described as having a form like that of the god Pan, with the top half of a young man and the legs of a goat, pointed ears and small horns, and like Pan, he has a lusty nature, plays a set of pipes, and is a guardian to the plants and creatures of the forest. He is adept at bird and animal calls, and is usually followed by a host of animals dancing to his music. He may be a fairy remnant of the ancient horned gods and nature spirits; earlier accounts tell of a race of pucks. In *A Midsummer Night's Dream*, Shakespeare gave puck an individual character synonymous with Robin Goodfellow, which has stayed with him to this day. Some Welsh writers believe that Shakespeare based his Puck on stories told to him by his friend Richard Price of Brecon, who lived near Cwm Pwca, one of the pwcas' favourite haunts.

Puck is never seen between Hallowe'en and the Spring Equinox. He has shapeshifting powers and will sometimes assume the form of a horse and fool a human into riding him, vanishing when they are halfway across a river to dump his victim in the water. But his most well-known trick is to lead travellers astray, taking them into ditches and bogs and then abandoning them with a loud laugh. In the Midlands, someone led astray in this way used to be described as 'pouk-ledden'. He loves to ridicule human folly, but dislikes and sometimes persecutes those who scorn their lovers. Like BROWNIES, he has been known to perform household chores, although he does not become closely attached to a specific house.

pwca *see* PUCK

pyramids
Huge constructions built in ancient Egypt as monuments.

The pyramids of Egypt were built around 2000 BC as royal tombs on a gigantic scale – it has been calculated that the largest of them, the GREAT PYRAMID, was originally 147 metres (481 feet) high.

Earlier Egyptian kings were buried under stone mastabas, which had sloping sides but a flat roof, and the first pyramid was that of King Zoser, built at Saqqara c.2700 BC, which had stepped sides. The classic, smooth-sided pyramid evolved later, when a stepped pyramid at Meydum had its steps filled in to give a uniform slope (c.2600 BC). The name 'pyramid' comes from the Greek, and some have claimed it derives, humorously, from 'wheat cake', but this has not been established. Over a hundred pyramids have been identified in Egypt, but it is the three great pyramids at Giza, those of Cheops, his son Chephren, and Menkaure, that are most famous.

It has been estimated that a workforce of at least 20,000 would have been necessary to build any of the three largest pyramids at Giza. This represents an enormous communal effort, and given the technology available at the time, it is an amazing feat. No one knows for certain how the pyramids were built but the most likely method would involve the use of ropes and pulleys, and great lubricated ramps of earth and bricks to allow the massive blocks of stone to be hauled or pushed into position. It has sometimes been assumed that those who laboured on these monuments must have been slaves, but graffiti and other inscriptions discovered more recently seem to indicate that at least some of the work was done by ordinary people, perhaps carrying out a period of obligatory service to their overlords. Despite the claims of the Jewish historian Josephus (37–c.100 AD) that the enslaved Jews were made to

The pyramids at Giza. (© David Sutherland/Corbis)

work at pyramid-building, the pyramids were built long before the Jews arrived in Egypt.

The pyramid shape itself is believed to symbolize the ancient Egyptian belief in the emergence of new life from the ground. In this way the deceased monarch entombed inside would be given new life in the next world, where he would make use of the many artefacts buried with him.

In several excavated pyramids inscriptions known as pyramid texts have been found, written in an old form of hieroglyphics. These appear to be religious incantations, perhaps uttered by priests when the dead Pharaoh was being entombed, intended to secure him power and protection in the AFTERLIFE.

Down through the ages, the pyramids have always inspired awe and wonder, with many people being unwilling to accept that ordinary human beings could have built them. The word 'pyramidology' is used to describe the body of theories that have been suggested as to their origins. Such ideas include those of occultists who believed that the pyramids must embody great secrets of magic power, and those who saw in them the remnants of a greater civilization, now lost, perhaps linked to the legendary lost continent of ATLANTIS. The space age spawned its own myths, with ERICH VON DÄNIKEN leading the ranks of those who contended that the pyramids must have been created by extraterrestrial beings.

However, the more that is discovered about the pyramids, the more they must be seen as the remarkable achievements of a gifted and resourceful human society with no need for divine or alien assistance.

pyromancy
Divination by fire.

Pyromancy (from Greek *pyr*, meaning fire, and *manteiā*, meaning divination) was perhaps one of the earliest forms of divination. In ancient Greece, the virgins of the temple of Athena were said to have practised pyromancy by studying the sacred flame which burned perpetually there.

In the most basic form of pyromancy, the observer studied the flames of a sacrificial fire; if the fire burned vigorously and consumed the sacrifice quickly, this was a good sign, but if the fire was slow to kindle and burned fitfully, it was a bad OMEN. Specific materials may also be burned: alomancy is a variation of pyromancy in which salt is tossed into the fire, and the nature and behaviour of the flames, and the shapes formed by them, are interpreted; in botanomancy, certain plants are burned; in daphnomancy, laurel leaves are burned; and in capnomancy, it is the smoke rising from the fire which is interpreted. In another form of pyromancy, the diviner supposedly observes the activities of the fire elementals, SALAMANDERS, which are said to inhabit the flames. See also LAMPADOMANCY.

Pythagoras (c.580–c.500 BC)
Greek philosopher, mathematician and mystic.

The life and works of Pythagoras are shrouded in myth and legend, and very few details are known for certain. It is believed that he was born around 580 BC in Samos, but left his native city as a young man, possibly to escape the government of the tyrannical ruler Polycrates. He is thought to have spent some time in Egypt, where he gained much of his knowledge, and returned to settle in Croton, where he attracted a group of followers and established a community which was half religious and half scientific. This community was open to men and women alike, and as well as following a structured programme of religious teaching, reading, philosophical study and music, its members practised moral asceticism and vegetarianism, observed rituals of abstinence and purification, and held all their property in common. Pythagoras believed in the transmigration of souls, and taught that the soul was immortal, and imprisoned in the body, and that by leading a pure life it was possible to allow the soul to eventually become free of the body. Some have credited Pythagoras with the first use of the term 'philosophy', which he considered to be the highest purification of the soul, and he is said to have regarded himself as a mystic.

Because of the essentially oral nature of his teaching, Pythagoras left no written record of his works. It is therefore impossible to be sure which views and discoveries were taught by him, and which were later added by his followers, especially since in ancient times it was a common practice to credit great teachers with the discoveries of their students. But Pythagoras, and the Pythagoreans, are principally regarded as philosophical mathematicians. They held the belief, formulated from Pythagoras' observations on music, mathematics and astronomy, that 'all is number'; all things have a numerical attribute which uniquely describes them, and numbers constitute their essential nature. All relationships can be expressed numerically, and the laws of the universe can be entirely understood and represented through mathematics. For this reason, Pythagoras is often described as being the first pure mathematician. The most famous mathematical discovery credited to him is the one bearing his name, the Pythagorean theorem, which states that in a right-angled triangle, the square on the hypotenuse is equal to the sum of the squares of the other two sides.

Pythagoras is also credited with the discovery of the musical scale. He found that if a string which vibrates at a certain musical note has its length halved, it will produce a note which is a whole tone up from the first note, and if the length of the vibrating string continues to be halved, seven distinct whole-tone notes are produced before the eighth note brings a return to the original note, one level higher. Esotericists believe that these seven notes of the musical scale, do, re, mi, fa, so, la, and ti – the eighth returning note being referred to as the 'octave' of the first one – carry a special magical meaning and power. Pythagoreans also believed that the celestial spheres of the planets produced a harmony which they called 'the music of the spheres'.

Pythagoreanism was the prime source of inspiration for PLATO and Aristotle, and had a profound influence on many later philosophers, astronomers and mathematicians; this influence transcended the field of mathematics, and is also found in visual art and music, particularly during the Renaissance and Baroque periods.

qabalah *see* KABBALAH

qi

In Chinese medicine, a universal life force which is believed to exist in all things, and is thought to circulate in the human body via channels called meridians; the free flow of qi in the body is believed to be necessary for physical and spiritual health.

The idea of qi, also spelled *chi*, *ch'i*, and *ki*, is at the basis of CHINESE MEDICINE, and the philosophical concept of qi dates back to the earliest recorded Chinese texts. This Chinese word for 'air' or 'breath' is used to denote the UNIVERSAL LIFE FORCE, spiritual energy, or life essence which is thought to be part of everything which exists. References to this energy, under various names, are found in many Eastern philosophies, and AYURVEDA is based on a similar belief. Qi is said to enter and leave the body, and to circulate through it, via channels called MERIDIANS, and to maintain and nourish the mind, body and spirit. Practitioners of Chinese medicine believe that a free flow of qi in the body is needed for physical and spiritual health, and that illness is due to disruptions, imbalances or deficiencies in this flow. Chinese medicine therefore seeks to correct the balance or to clear blockages using a variety of therapeutic techniques, such as ACUPRESSURE, ACUPUNCTURE, meditation, herbal medicine, or T'AI CHI. Many Oriental martial arts include some concept of qi in their philosophies.

The nature of qi is still the subject of much controversy. In the West, it is often seen as an esoteric and spiritual force rather than a primarily physical one, and is frequently associated with NEW AGE spiritualism; the idea of qi as a mystical power which can be controlled by a master to the point where he or she can use it to influence other people, or the forces

of nature, has become a common notion in the West through the depiction of such characters in martial arts films. See also QIGONG; REFLEXOLOGY; SHIATSU.

qigong

A Chinese therapeutic system of gentle exercise combined with meditation and breathing techniques which is said to promote physical and spiritual wellbeing.

The Mandarin word 'qigong' translates roughly as 'breath work' or 'energy work'. Qigong, also spelled *chi kung*, is an increasingly popular aspect of CHINESE MEDICINE in which deep breathing and MEDITATION are combined with gentle physical postures and movements to promote physical and spiritual wellbeing. In China it is also sometimes taught as a means of treating specific health problems. It is based on the principle that the practitioner can learn to feel and move the energy which flows through the body, known as QI, through the use of slow, choreographed physical exercises performed while breathing slowly and deeply, and visualizing the qi flowing smoothly through the body. This is believed to develop great inner power, enabling the person to control and conserve their qi and integrate mind and body.

Qigong is referred to, by various names, in written Chinese records dating back over 3,000 years. In ancient China a traditional form was practised in Taoist and Buddhist monasteries as part of martial arts training, but over time, many new forms have been developed and passed down through numerous schools, such as Taoist, Buddhist, Confucian, Chinese medicine and traditional martial arts. Banned in China as a superstitious practice during the Cultural Revolution, qigong was later studied scientifically by the Chinese government and in 1989 was officially recognized as a standard medical technique and added to the range of treatments offered in traditional Chinese medicine hospitals. It is now included in the curricula of various medical universities, and is practised daily by millions of people in China and all over the world. It is known to promote relaxation and flexibility, and is also said to combat stress, boost the immune system, and alleviate conditions caused by aging. Some believe that the expert practitioner can even use it to generate and direct qi so as to influence the physical world outside their own body.

quake lights *see* EARTHQUAKES

Quarouble

Site of one of the first significant UFO cases in which it was claimed that there was physical evidence left behind (in the form of landing marks) and injury to the witness.

Until 1954, reported sightings of ALIENS were relatively few in number. At that time the stories about wise 'space brothers' paying friendly visits to our world, spread by members of the new CONTACTEE movement in the USA, were not taken seriously by the wider UFO COMMUNITY. Meanwhile, Hollywood had begun to embrace the idea of the UFO mystery, producing a series of films that featured monsters bent on destruction or global invasion. In the autumn of 1954 the first significant WAVE of reports of contact with aliens appeared. These occurred mainly in Europe and differed substantially in detail from the film monsters and contactee claims. Some were considered so credible that even sceptical UFO investigators began to take the idea more seriously.

The earliest reported example in France occurred on 10 September 1954, in the small village of Quarouble close to the Belgian border. The primary witness was Marius Dewilde, a 34-year-old steel worker who lived with his wife and family beside a freight railway line. He claimed that, late that night, as he was reading, his dog started to bark. Fearing that there was a prowler, Dewilde went outside with his torch to investigate. In the gloom ahead he could see something on the tracks. He assumed that it was a single wagon and, as this was a crossing point, he became concerned that there might have been an accident. He walked towards it to check.

Suddenly his dog emerged from the darkness crawling on its belly, yelping in distress. At the same time the sound of footsteps came from the railway lines. Dewilde shone his torch to illuminate the culprit and was surprised to see two small figures, the size of five-year-old children, wearing what resembled diving suits. They had helmets that seemed to be too large for their small bodies. As he continued to walk in their direction a 'magnesium flare' of light emerged from the object on the tracks, immobilizing him.

An article describing the UFO close encounter at Quarouble from *Radar* (26 September 1954).
(© Mary Evans Picture Library)

For some moments the beam of light remained in place, as the scuttling footsteps indicated that the entities were entering the 'wagon'. The beam was then extinguished, immediately releasing the witness from his temporary paralysis. Dewilde stumbled forward again, but in seconds the object on the track climbed skyward, making a whistling sound, with steam emerging from beneath it. It vanished at great speed across the sky, turning into a red glow as it departed. Several other locals reported witnessing this as it flew over nearby fields.

Dewilde staggered back home apparently disoriented, not speaking coherently and suffering other PHYSIOLOGICAL EFFECTS. His wife, thinking he had been assaulted, called the police, but Dewilde was incapable of explaining what had happened. However, both he and the dog soon recovered, and a while later he went to see the local police chief and asked him to investigate. The police chief was so convinced by the story that he called in an army unit.

The next day, indents were discovered in the railway sleepers – tests later indicated that these must have been caused by an object weighing 30 tonnes. The army also took away some stones from beside the line that apparently crumbled to a powder when touched. The police chief reportedly told Dewilde some time later that these rocks appeared to have been heated to an extreme temperature.

quasars

Star-like bodies, conventionally thought to be extremely bright and billions of light years away.

In the early days of radio astronomy, very powerful radio sources were detected where there were no known stars. Eventually very faint sources of light were found which coincided with the radio sources, and these were termed quasars, or *quasi*-stell*ar* objects. These objects had some puzzling characteristics. The light from quasars is red shifted – it appears redder than would be expected – which appears to be caused by their moving away from us at extremely high speed, more than a third of the speed of light. This high speed implies that they are very distant, and so they must be very bright. One quasar in Virgo is estimated to be a trillion times brighter than our sun, or about a hundred times more luminous than our entire Milky Way.

The physics behind quasars is still unclear, but it is believed that they are small galaxies, each with a gigantic black hole at the centre consuming matter at a tremendous rate and turning it into energy. It is the means by which matter is converted into energy that astronomers find hardest to explain.

An alternative view has been put forward by US astronomer Halton Arp (1927–). During the 1960s Arp built up a collection of anomalous observations which he published as the *Atlas of Peculiar Galaxies* (1967). This included images which appeared to show that rather than being billions of light years away, quasars are actually interacting with much closer objects. Arp argues that the red shift is not caused by quasars receding at high speed but by another, so far unproven effect. In this view quasars are fairly small objects in our cosmic neighbourhood and not the galaxy-devouring monsters that conventional astronomy depicts. Arp has put forward a theory to explain that quasars are actually an early state of matter, and that they gradually evolve and expand into normal galaxies. He believes that the high red shift is a property of new matter, and that this wears off as quasars age.

Arp's work has been rejected by the mainstream as FRINGE SCIENCE, and as a result his reputation has suffered, and he has been blocked from using the Mount Palomar telescope and other facilities. The heated arguments and allegations of dirty tricks against Arp and his supporters in what should be a field of pure intellectual inquiry reveal that even when dealing with very solid scientific data, human factors can be overwhelmingly important.

Queensland tiger

A striped feline cryptid long reported from the forested regions of Queensland but still undescribed by science.

Since the mid-1800s, reports by Aborigines and Western settlers have regularly emerged from the forested areas of northern Queensland, Australia, of confrontations with a large, tiger-like creature. Reportedly the size and shape of a leopard, but with black/dark grey and white bands around its body, a distinctly cat-like head and very prominent, peculiarly tusk-like teeth at the front of its mouth, this unidentified feline animal has become known as the Queensland tiger or yarri (an Aboriginal name for it, meaning 'attack' or 'threaten').

Its extremely aggressive nature means that this cryptid is usually avoided by eyewitnesses who encounter it, but specimens have occasionally been shot and killed. However, the carcases have always been discarded, rather then made available for scientific study, as those who have shot them have not realized the creature's significance. In one instance the carcase was simply left outside, where its head and body were devoured by wild pigs and its pelt rotted away.

As almost all of Australia's native mammals are marsupials (pouched mammals), this mysterious beast is probably a marsupial too, but it does not resemble any living species discovered by science so far. A mere 10,000 years ago, however, many more Australian marsupials existed, including a sizeable cat-like species known as the marsupial lion (*Thylacoleo carnifex*), whose fossil remains have been found in Queensland. Reconstructions of the marsupial lion's likely appearance, based upon studies of these remains, portray a creature that closely resembles eyewitness descriptions of the Queensland tiger, sharing its size, shape and even its tusk-like teeth. As the marsupial lion is believed to have been a tree-climbing, forest-dwelling species, it may also have been striped for effective camouflage.

Accordingly, some cryptozoologists, including Dr BERNARD HEUVELMANS, have postulated that the Queensland tiger may be a modern descendant of the marsupial lion. Whether it proves to be a living species, conversely, is another matter; there have been very few reports of Queensland tigers in recent years, leading to speculation that this remarkable beast may have died out before science was able to confirm its existence, let alone its identity.

quicksilver *see* MERCURY

quoit *see* DOLMEN

radiesthesia

The practice of dowsing using an instrument such as a pendulum; also, dowsing used specifically for medical purposes.

In its general sense, the term 'radiesthesia' is used more or less synonymously with DOWSING. The term is the anglicized form of the French *radiesthésie*, which was coined in the early 19th century by the French dowser, Abbé Bouly. Before then, dowsing had been known in France as *la sourcerie* ('sourcing'), but with the discovery of X-rays, Bouly formed the theory that the phenomenon of dowsing might be caused by the unconscious sensitivity of the dowser to rays of some kind which were emitted by the object being dowsed, and invented a new word to reflect this, from the Latin *radius*, meaning ray, and *esthesia*, meaning feeling.

The word is often used in a more restricted sense to denote the use of dowsing specifically for medical purposes, also known as clairvoyant healing or medical dowsing. Medical dowsing was pioneered in France by Abbé Mermet in 1920, but today many natural therapists in other countries also use the technique to help in assessments of a patient's condition. Practitioners believe that every object has a characteristic electromagnetic field which can be detected by a sensitive person using an instrument such as a PENDULUM. It is generally thought that the instrument itself serves purely to amplify the vibrations picked up by the dowser. Sometimes the pendulum is held over a healthy and an unhealthy part of the body in turn, so that its movement over each can be compared. It may also be held over a sample of tissue or body fluid, a photograph of the patient or one of their belongings, and a diagnosis is based on the nature of the pendulum's swing, or the direction in which it rotates. Some therapists suspend a pendulum over each of the patient's 'energy centres' or CHAKRAS in turn, to detect the strengths and weaknesses of each by means of the pendulum's movement. Dowsing is also used where yes/no questions are applicable, for example when attempting to check for food allergies or intolerances in the patient, or to select the appropriate remedy from a range of options. See also RADIONICS.

radionics

A form of remote diagnosis and treatment based on the principles of radiesthesia. Radiations from the patient's energy field are said to be tuned in to using something such as a sample of hair or blood, in conjunction with a special instrument to make the diagnosis, and healing radiation is then thought to be transmitted to the patient from a distance using another device.

The form of remote diagnosis and treatment known as radionics was invented in the 1920s by the US neurologist, Dr Albert Adams. Based on the same principles as RADIESTHESIA, radionics holds that all life forms have an electromagnetic energy field; Dr Adams claimed to have discovered that diseases also had a specific energy, and he devised an instrument which he said enabled him to identify diseases in a patient at a distance. Using a sample such as hair, nail clippings or blood from the patient, he believed his device could pick up their energy field vibrations; the sample, which he called a 'witness', acted as a link between the practitioner, the device and the patient. Once the patient's condition had been analysed, he then used another radionic instrument which he believed could direct healing or corrective 'energy patterns' to them, again from a distance.

Although it has been in use for decades, radionics is still highly controversial and is banned in the USA. It is considered by many to be a combination of clairvoyant or remote diagnosis and PSYCHIC HEALING in which the instruments function as a focus for the practitioner to establish a psychic link with the patient. It is HOLISTIC in nature, and is intended to complement conventional medicine; the analysis of the 'witness' is supplemented by a detailed questionnaire regarding the patient's diet, lifestyle, mental and emotional state, and so on, and the practitioner may then also recommend HOMEOPATHIC remedies, lifestyle changes or nutritional therapy, or conventional medical treatments. It is claimed to help conditions such as asthma, eczema, allergies, chronic pain and migraine, and is even said to have been used to increase crop yields, control pests and improve the health of livestock.

Raelian Movement

A UFO religion that sponsors research into human cloning and teaches sexual freedom.

The Raelian Movement was founded by Claude Vorilhon (1946–   ), a French sports journalist. In his books *Le Livre qui dit la verité* (1974) and *Les Extra-terrestres m'ont emmené sur leur planète* (1975), Vorilhon described his alleged encounters with aliens – from his first meeting with them in December 1973 to his journey with them to their planet in October 1975. His first two books, in one volume, have been translated into English under a variety of titles: *Space Aliens Took Me To Their Planet* (1978), *The Message Given To Me By Extra-terrestrials: They Took Me To Their Planet* (1986) and *The Final Message* (1998).

In these and later books Vorilhon sets out what he claims to have learned from the aliens. He says that they came to earth thousands of years ago, and were mistranslated in the Bible as 'Elohim' – which they told him actually means 'those who come from the sky'. They are not God or gods, just a much more advanced civilization who created mankind in their own image, not by divine *fiat* but scientifically, by DNA manipulation. They gave Vorilhon the name Raël, apparently meaning 'the messenger of those who come from the sky'.

The Elohim had revealed themselves to Raël because they believed that mankind was now ready for them to return to earth – though the Elohim would only do this when we had prepared a welcome for them by building an embassy, preferably on a piece of land given to the Raelian Movement by the State of Israel. Part of the income of the movement goes towards a fund for building this embassy.

Claude Vorilhon, spiritual leader of the Raelian Movement. (© Christopher J Morris/Corbis)

Mankind is also now scientifically capable of manipulating DNA, and the Raelian Movement caused a worldwide stir in December 2002 by announcing that their related company, Clonaid, had successfully created the world's first cloned human baby, with four more on their way. However, they have offered no proof to back up their claims.

The Raelian Movement teaches that the Judaeo-Christian emphasis on guilt is harmful. Instead their aim is:

> … to create a world of leisure, love and fulfilment where we have rid ourselves of the moralistic social inhibitions which paralyse our joy for life, so that everyone has the courage to act as they wish, as long as this action does not harm others.

As part of this the movement encourages sexual freedom and teaches 'Sensual Meditation', which they believe can lead to a 'Cosmic Orgasm'.

rains, mystery *see* FALLS

Rajneesh, Bhagwan Shree (1931–90)
Indian mystic, founder of the Osho-Rajneesh movement.

Bhagwan Shree Rajneesh, later known as Osho, was born Rajneesh Chandra Mohan, in Kuchwada, central India, in 1931. Although he was of Jain parents, he never subscribed to any religious faith. He claimed to have attained enlightenment at the age of 21, and received a Master's degree in Philosophy at Saugar University, thereafter teaching at the Sanskrit college of Raipur and occupying the post of Professor of Philosophy at Jabalpur University during the 1960s. In 1966, a group of his disciples established a foundation to support his work and allow him to give up his university work, and he began a speaking career, adopting the name Bhagwan Shree Rajneesh, and set up an ashram for religious study and teaching in Bombay. He moved from Bombay to Poona in 1974, where his teachings attracted many thousands of Westerners throughout the 1970s.

Rajneesh claimed that the greatest values in life are love, meditation and laughter, and that the sole goal of human life is to attain spiritual enlightenment. He taught a form of Monism, which saw God as in everything and everyone, and all people as divine. He encouraged the exploration of all religions, which he said were valid as having been founded by enlightened masters, although later corrupted by their official churches. He taught a syncretistic path (see SYNCRETISM) which combined elements from Hinduism, JAINISM, ZEN BUDDHISM, TAOISM, Christianity, ancient Greek philosophy and many other traditions, as well as humanistic psychotherapy. He insisted that enlightenment meant simply being in a meditative state, a condition which came naturally to anyone, and developed new forms of meditation, the best-known of which was Dynamic Meditation, in which meditation was preceded by exercises found in Western gestalt therapy, such as jumping around, laughing and crying, hyperventilation, and the use of gibberish. He also reintroduced a minimalist version of several traditional meditation methods in which the ritual and tradition were stripped away.

In 1981, he transferred his base to the USA, establishing a new ashram on a ranch near Antelope, Oregon, which had been bought by his followers, and which was renamed Rajneeshpuram (City of Rajneesh). However, the movement became the centre of much controversy; in the 1980s, it achieved notoriety amid reports of financial misconduct and the abuse and manipulation of political power. Until 1985, his disciples, who were known as Sannyasins, Rajneeshees or Followers of Bhagwan, wore red robes, which were later changed to orange, resulting in the nickname 'The Orange People'. Although his followers lived a frugal lifestyle, Rajneesh lived in luxury, famously amassing a collection of 93 Rolls-Royces. His advocacy of free sexual expression as a form of therapy met with increasing opposition, and when he took a vow of silence until 1984, the foundation was run by his personal assistant, Ma Anand Sheela, who, along with some of his other aides, was charged with a number of crimes, including a bioterrorist attack in which the salad bars of several restaurants in Oregon were contaminated with salmonella. Sheela and another of Rajneesh's close advisers confessed to the crime, and were removed from their posts. They absconded, but were arrested in 1985. Rajneesh was also arrested and charged with immigration fraud, but was given a suspended sentence on condition that he leave the country.

Rajneesh returned to Poona in 1987, adopting the new name of Osho. His health began to fail, and he died in Poona in 1990, after claiming that he had been poisoned by the US authorities during his imprisonment. Although he had frequently stated that he would not appoint a successor, since he saw each of his disciples as a successor, he appointed an inner circle to look after the ashram in Poona, now known as the Osho International Resort, and to carry on his work after his death. This group now operates a number of meditation centres worldwide, and his main influence nowadays is through his many writings.

Randi, James (1928–   )
Possibly the most famous 'sceptic' and debunker of claims of the paranormal.

James Randi was born Randall James Hamilton Zwinge in Toronto, Canada. Following an illustrious career as a stage magician (see MAGIC, STAGE) and escapologist (see ESCAPOLOGY), he became famous worldwide as a sceptic and debunker of pseudoscience and claims of the paranormal.

Randi's stage magic career began in 1946. He appeared on numerous television programmes and toured the world with his live show – initially under his own name and later as 'The Amazing Randi'. However, he rose to world prominence in the early 1970s when he publicly challenged the claims of URI GELLER. He accused Geller of using standard stage magic tricks to perform his feats of apparent METAL BENDING, and he even published a book in which he detailed exactly how he believed the effects were produced.

In 1976 Randi was a founder member of the COMMITTEE FOR THE SCIENTIFIC INVESTIGATION OF CLAIMS OF THE PARANORMAL (CSICOP). He later resigned from CSICOP when the organization asked him to stop commenting on Geller – they were concerned at the potential for them to be drawn into the frequent legal battles between the two individuals. Randi and CSICOP maintained an amicable relationship. The James Randi Educational Foundation (JREF) was formed in 1996 and the two organizations continue to work closely together.

Randi has been responsible for a number of hoaxes which he claims he has perpetrated to expose the gullibility of believers in many NEW AGE ideas or the shortcomings of research in the area of PARAPSYCHOLOGY. Possibly the most widely known of these was PROJECT ALPHA, when two people with some stage-magic training were used to show up poorly designed experimental procedures.

The JREF offers a $1 million prize to anyone who can conclusively demonstrate a paranormal event under agreed test conditions. This challenge was initially instigated by Randi in 1964 as a $1,000 challenge. As a condition of the challenge, both parties must agree beforehand on what will constitute a success or a failure. However, Randi's critics claim that the full terms of the challenge are framed in such a way that nothing will be accepted as conclusive proof.

Randi has written a number of books exposing various self-proclaimed PSYCHICS and has received a number of awards for his work. However, his confrontational style (something which he says is a product of his frustration at having to repeatedly act to protect the public from charlatans and fraudsters) antagonizes many who might otherwise be in agreement with much of what he has to say.

random number generator
Any device which is used to produce a series of random numbers in tests for psychic ability.
Random number generators (RNGs) can take a variety of forms – from something as simple as tossing a coin or rolling a dice, through to electronic random number generators (ERNGs), the most complex of which rely on radioactive decay.

In theory, any RNG can potentially be used to test for PSYCHIC powers. A tossed coin is a binary RNG (producing one of two unpredictable possible outcomes with equal probability) and a rolled dice (assuming it is fair) can randomly produce any number from one to six. Experiments take the form of either tests for MICRO-PK, where the subject attempts to impose order on the string of random outcomes, or tests for PRECOGNITION, in which the subject tries to predict the numbers generated.

RNG tests are popular within the field of PARAPSYCHOLOGY because they are FORCED-CHOICE EXPERIMENTS which lend themselves to statistical analysis. An inevitable development in the use of such tests was the introduction of electronic and computer-based systems – they can rapidly produce long strings of random numbers, with far less possibility for fraud and human error. However, most electronic systems are not truly random, a fact which led to a further development – systems dependent on the chance decay of atoms within a sample of a radioactive element.

ERNGs generally only produce a string of binary numbers (a series of ones and zeros), and most can do so at rates of many thousands per second. They have now been used extensively over a number of years in tests for psychic powers. In the classic test the generator is attached to a visual display device and the output is displayed as a line or series of dots. The task of the agent (see AGENCY) is then to impose a pattern on the display, or to skew the output towards one or other of the potential random outcomes – for example to try to make the system produce more ones than zeros. If the output is truly random and the test is run for long enough, there should be no significant deviation from the production of an equal number of each of the two outcomes. The theory is that if, when the results are analysed, a significantly larger number of one outcome has occurred then there is evidence of influence over the system. Such research has been carried out since the 1960s but no uncontroversial positive proof of psychic ability has yet been forthcoming.

Rapture, the
A belief that the faithful will be caught up to be with Christ in the End Time.
The Rapture is the belief of many Millenarian Evangelical Christians that, at some point in the End Time (that is, the time preceding the coming of a Messiah figure), true believers will be 'caught up in the air', rising up to be with Christ at his Second Coming. The belief is based on I Thessalonians 4:16–17:

> For the Lord himself shall descend from heaven with a shout, with the voice of the archangel, and with the trump of God, and the dead in Christ shall rise first. Then we which are alive and remain shall be caught up together with them in the clouds, to meet the Lord in the air. And so shall we ever be with the Lord.

The general belief is that this will occur before the seven-year Tribulation (the period in which believers will suffer for their sins before being purified) begins, or perhaps halfway through it, though some believe that it will occur immediately after the Tribulation.

Belief in the Rapture is not shared by all

Millenarian Christian sects (see MILLENNIUM), but it became an essential part of (particularly American) Evangelical beliefs as one of the Dispensationalist Millenarian teachings set out in the influential Scofield Reference Bible, first published in 1909. Roman Catholics, Orthodox and Non-Evangelical Protestants, following the guidelines of St Augustine, tend to view such Eschatological ideas symbolically rather than literally.

On Millenarianism in general, within both Evangelical Christianity and sectarian movements, it is worth noting that there are a huge number of conflicting and mutually contradictory belief systems, and those who accept any one of them tend to believe adamantly that theirs is the *only* possible correct interpretation.

Rasputin, Grigori Efimovich (1871–1916)

Russian peasant and religious mystic.
Although Grigori Efimovich Rasputin was sometimes nicknamed 'the Mad Monk', he spent only a matter of months in a monastery at the age of 18. Apparently born to a Siberian peasant family, it is known that he married and fathered children before joining a sect of flagellants known as *Khlysty*. He travelled widely as a pilgrim before ending up in St Petersburg in 1903, calling himself a *starets* or holy man.

Taking advantage of the current fashionability of mystic religion, he brought himself to the attention to the royal household of Tsar Nicholas II (1868–1918) and the Empress Alexandra (1872–1918), suggesting that he could use prayer and hypnotism to treat the haemophilia that afflicted their son, the Tsarevich Alexei. Whether or not he had any real healing ability, the Empress in particular was convinced that Rasputin had helped her son, and placed great trust in him.

He soon became notorious for his alcoholic excesses and sexual debauchery, apparently convincing women that intercourse with him was spiritually purifying. The more scurrilous rumours even hinted at a sexual relationship between Rasputin and the Empress. Whatever its nature, his hold over the royal family was deeply resented, especially his alleged ability to influence government appointments.

Rasputin's unpopularity grew when Russia entered World War I against Germany. He was closely identified with the Empress, who had been born a German princess, and it was even rumoured that he was a German spy. To many at the Imperial court, Rasputin was seen not only as a source of scandal but also as dangerously undermining the standing of the monarchy at a time of great political unrest. His enemies were not only powerful but ruthless,

A photograph of Grigori Rasputin from 1908.
(© Mary Evans Picture Library)

and a group of aristocrats led by Prince Felix Yusupov (1887–1967) determined to do away with him.

Rasputin's murder became a focus of legend in modern folklore, as it was claimed that it showed Rasputin as miraculously immune to a series of attempts that would surely have killed any normal man. According to Yusupov's account, Rasputin was first poisoned, being given food and drink laced with large amounts of cyanide. When this failed to kill him, Yusupov took out a revolver and shot him. Again Rasputin refused to die. He attacked Yusupov and staggered out into the snow to make his escape. Here he was shot again, beaten and stabbed by Yusupov and several accomplices until, apparently unconscious, he was thrown into the partly frozen Neva River. When his body was recovered a few days later, it was decided that he had died by drowning.

While Yusupov may have been interested in creating a legend and glorifying his own part in the story, the truth seems to have been more prosaic. The actual report of the autopsy carried out on Rasputin apparently recorded no trace of poison. The mystic had indeed been beaten but the cause of death was identified as a bullet in the head.

In 2004 a BBC investigative documentary suggested that the fatal shot had not been fired by Yusupov but by a British intelligence agent attached to the Imperial court. It was, of course, vital to British interests that Russia continue to wage war against Germany, and Rasputin's activities were seen as a threat to this.

recovered memories *see* MEMORIES, RECOVERED

recurrent apparitions
Ghosts that are seen or experienced on a series of different occasions.
'Recurrent apparition' is the term used to refer to a ghost that is seen or experienced repeatedly, on a number of different occasions. Such apparitions are often reported in HAUNTED HOUSE cases, and a classic example of a recurrent apparition is the MORTON GHOST. Many recurrent apparitions are reported always to appear in the same location and always to perform the same actions with no awareness of the observers and little or no variation in routine (see RE-ENACTMENT GHOSTS), which has led some ghost investigators to suggest that they may be a form of recording (see STONE TAPE THEORY). It has been put forward that such phenomena represent an emotional imprint left on a place or building, arising from a tragedy (such as a suicide or murder). It has also been suggested that a routine pattern of life by a living person might leave a trace on a building which can be picked up on after their death.

recurrent spontaneous psychokinesis
The production of repeated physical effects over a period of time by psychic means, without conscious control. It forms the basis of a theory for the cause of poltergeist phenomena.
The term 'recurrent spontaneous psychokinesis' (RSPK) was coined by the parapsychologist William Roll, of the Psychical Research Foundation, in Durham, North Carolina. Roll studied 116 POLTERGEIST cases from around the world and observed that there were patterns in the phenomena exhibited – particularly noting that the activity often appeared to be centred upon a single child or teenager within the household. He developed the idea that the effects might be being unknowingly produced by the human 'focus' (as opposed to an external supernatural entity) and that they might be outward, physical manifestations of their internal psychological state through a process of PSYCHOKINESIS.

The idea that RSPK lies behind the majority of poltergeist cases has all but replaced supernatural, SPIRIT theories among researchers into the paranormal. The argument now tends to be between supporters of RSPK and sceptics who feel that no paranormal explanation is required.

red mercury
Alleged radioactive compound used in bombs.
In the 1970s the story emerged in the West that Soviet Russian scientists had developed a new radioactive compound that could offer tremendous explosive power when used as a weapon. At the height of the cold war, this information was of vital importance. Spies reported that this substance was called red mercury, but it was not clear if this was actually a military code name for standard or modified weapons-grade nuclear material or in fact a newly manufactured compound.

The story was officially denied by the Soviet government and it disappeared from the public eye for 30 years before re-emerging in connection with terrorism. It was reported that red mercury had in fact been developed in Russia and made available in the post-Soviet era to terrorists, who, it was claimed, could use it to manufacture a small, 'dirty' bomb of enormous destructive potential or use it as a trigger for a fusion bomb. It was even suggested that red mercury was one of the weapons of mass destruction possessed by Iraq under Saddam Hussein.

However it might be used, one important property of red mercury was that because of its highly explosive nature only very small quantities would be needed and thus it would be easy for terrorists to transport or smuggle into target countries.

In September 2004 the story broke in the UK that terrorists had been arrested for trying to buy a quantity of red mercury. However, doubts soon emerged, and it was argued that a hoax had been going on, perpetrated either on the newspaper that ran the story or on the hapless would-be buyers of the material by Russian gangsters, who in reality possessed nothing more threatening than cinnabar (mercury sulphide, an ore of mercury which is also used as vermilion pigment) or indeed ordinary mercury dyed red with nail varnish. Another theory was that the hoax originated with the Russian government, and was designed as an elaborate 'sting' engineered in order to bring weapons dealers to light.

Some scientists believe that red mercury is real, having been created by bombarding mercury with mercury antimony oxide under extremely high pressure inside a nuclear reactor. However, the judgment of the International Atomic Energy Agency is that the substance does not exist:

> The whole thing is a bunch of malarkey.

This is the position accepted by the mainstream science community.

In the absence of actual samples of this material being made available for impartial analysis, as far as the lay person is concerned, as with most highly technical scientific disputes, it becomes a question of whom one chooses to believe.

re-enactment ghosts

Ghostly apparitions that appear to be re-enactments of events from the past.

Certain apparitions appear to be re-enactments of events from the historic past. Ghosts of this type are often referred to as 'place memories', the idea being that certain locations seem to retain images which can be re-activated and replayed in the present. The ghosts described do not recognize or react to the presence of observers, and simply perform some action. Some have suggested that such re-enactment ghosts are a form of recording, like video clips being replayed (see STONE TAPE THEORY). Should this be true, re-enactment ghosts may be established as a result of one emotional incident (for example, a suicide or a murder) or a pattern of life where the sight or sounds of a once regularly performed activity have been imprinted on the environment. See also RECURRENT APPARITIONS.

reflexology

A form of therapy which is based on the theory that certain areas of the feet, hands and ears correspond to specific organs and parts of the body, and that massaging the appropriate area on the foot, hand or ear can help treat ailments in the corresponding body part.

Although it is believed that foot massage was practised in ancient Egypt, China and India, the Western form of reflexology used today was developed in the first half of the 20th century. In 1913, Dr William Fitzgerald observed that pressure on specific parts of the feet and hands seemed to have an anaesthetic effect on other, apparently unrelated, parts of the body. In the 1930s, physical therapist Eunice Ingham believed that manipulation of these areas provided other health benefits, and she expanded and refined Fitzgerald's research, mapping out the specific 'reflex zones' on the feet, hands and ears which are still used by reflexologists today.

Also known as zone therapy, or reflex zone therapy, reflexology has its roots in CHINESE MEDICINE'S principle that life energy, or QI, flows through the body along channels called MERIDIANS. It is thought that these channels of energy converge at many points, known as microsystems – areas on the feet, hands and ears which are in effect small, local representations of various other parts of the body. For example, the brain reflexes are said to be located in the tips of the toes, those of the eyes and ears underneath the toes, and those of the shoulders and lungs on the ball of the foot. If the circulation of energy is blocked in a certain part of the body, the corresponding zone in the foot is thought to reflect this blockage. After a HOLISTIC diagnosis based on a detailed consultation which takes into account the patient's medical history and lifestyle, the reflexologist massages the relevant reflex zone, which is usually located in the foot, but may be on the hand or ear, for between 5 and 20 minutes. This is thought to prompt the nervous system to speed up the body's healing response in the afflicted area by stimulating the flushing of toxins from that part; some practitioners claim that an energy blockage in a body part causes a deposit of crystals in the corresponding reflex zone, and that this deposit is broken down by massage.

Reflexology is said to be effective in promoting relaxation, reducing stress and anxiety, and relieving migraines and chronic pain.

Regardie, Israel (1907–85)

English-born esoteric writer who preserved and revealed the teachings of the Hermetic Order of the Golden Dawn.

Israel Regardie was born Francis Israel Regudy in London, the son of poor Jewish immigrants. He moved with his family to the USA in 1921. He is best known as the most important figure in disseminating and thus preserving the teachings of the HERMETIC ORDER OF THE GOLDEN DAWN, despite being born after the Golden Dawn had fragmented.

In 1926 Regardie joined the Societas Rosicruciana in America, a non-masonic offshoot of a US version of the British masonic order, Societas Rosicruciana in Anglia, three of whose members had founded the Hermetic Order of the Golden Dawn in 1888. Around the same time he read a book by ALEISTER CROWLEY and contacted him. Crowley invited him to Paris to be his secretary, a post he held from 1928 to 1930. He co-authored a very favourable book, *The Legend of Aleister Crowley*, in 1930, but some time after that Crowley (always a mercurial figure) fell out with him.

In 1932 Regardie wrote *A Garden of Pomegranates* and *The Tree of Life*, the first about KABBALAH and the second on the teachings of the Golden Dawn. As a result of these he was approached by DION FORTUNE in 1933 and invited to join Stella Matutina, the offshoot from the Golden Dawn which still followed its magical teachings and practices. He rapidly rose through the grades to Adeptus Minor, the first grade in the second Order, but became disillusioned with the leadership of the order and left a declining Stella Matutina in 1934. Through Dion Fortune, Stella Matutina spawned the Society of the Inner Light; two members of this, W E Butler and Gareth Knight, later founded the Servants of the Light. Both organizations have been hugely influential in the continuation of esoteric teaching in Britain and elsewhere.

In 1937 Regardie committed what some saw as an act of treachery: he published most of the teachings of the Golden Dawn in four volumes, simply entitled *The Golden Dawn*. His defence for breaking his oath of secrecy was that the teachings must not be lost; there had already been 'partial and irresponsible disclosures' and he believed there should be a proper presentation of the teachings: 'Only thus may the widespread misconceptions as to Magic be removed.'

Although Regardie went on to write over a dozen well-received books on esoteric subjects, including *The Eye in the Triangle: An Interpretation of Aleister Crowley* (1970), *The Golden Dawn* has had the greatest impact. By putting the teachings into the public domain he effectively became not the father but certainly the midwife of most esoteric and many pagan organizations of the next half century or more.

Reich, Wilhelm (1897–1957)

Austrian psychoanalyst.

Wilhelm Reich was born in Galicia, in the then Austro-Hungarian Empire. He studied medicine in Vienna, but became a follower of SIGMUND FREUD and a practising psychoanalyst before completing his medical training.

He developed a particular interest in sexuality, and formed the belief that regular orgasms were necessary for mental stability in both men and women. He set out his theories in *The Function of the Orgasm* (1927; English translation 1942), *The Sexual Revolution* (1936–45) and other writings.

Reich believed that there was a vital force that permeated the universe, and he labelled this *orgone* or *orgone energy* (from *orgasm* and the chemical suffix *-one*). He theorized that this energy consisted of massless particles which, when collected and concentrated in his invention the 'orgone accumulator', could be used to treat disease and enhance sexual satisfaction. He thought that diseases were essentially caused by the blockage of orgone energy within the sufferer, and that a person sitting inside the machine, which was the size of a telephone booth, would have these levels restored by exposure to concentrated energy.

Among his other concerns was a wish to synthesize psychoanalysis with Marxism, stigmatizing the bourgeois family as responsible for producing both the Oedipus complex and unfulfilled sexual satisfaction in adults. He became an advocate of free contraception and abortion on demand.

Reich's ideas were not widely accepted and he was considered a crank or charlatan by many in Europe. Expelled from both the German Communist Party (in 1933) and the International Psychoanalytical Association (1934), he eventually emigrated to

Wilhelm Reich with his 'cloudbuster' c.1954.
(© Mary Evans Picture Library)

the USA in 1939. He set up an Orgone Institute, and invented another orgone-linked device: the 'cloudbuster'. This was a machine intended to harness orgone energy in order to force clouds to yield rain.

Reich was investigated by the FBI on the grounds of having been a communist. He was not considered a political threat, but his orgone therapy was denounced by the Food and Drug Administration as a fraudulent treatment, and he was forbidden to practise it. He disregarded this injunction and was jailed for two years. While in prison he suffered heart failure and died.

Interest in Reich's theories revived in the 1960s as much of what he said seemed to chime with the ongoing movement towards sexual liberation. Many of his books were reprinted and his influence on 'counterculture' was widespread. In 1985, the English singer and songwriter Kate Bush (1958–) released a song inspired by Reich's son Peter's account of his father's life in *A Book of Dreams* (1973). In the video accompanying 'Cloudbusting', one of Reich's cloudbusting machines can be seen.

REICHIAN THERAPY, designed to release inhibited or disturbed energies by the use of massage and

A reiki practitioner holds her hands above her patient's forehead in the belief that this will transmit healing energy. (© Luca Tettoni/Corbis)

controlled breathing, also underwent a revival in the 1980s and 1990s and is still practised.

Reichian therapy

A form of alternative therapy based on the theories of the Austrian-born psychoanalyst Wilhelm Reich, who believed that a universal life force in the body called 'orgone' could become blocked as a result of the tensing of the muscles in response to emotional or psychological pain, causing neuroses and physical disorders.

Techniques including massage and controlled breathing are used to dissolve the blockages, which are referred to as 'body armour'.

During the 1930s and 1940s, the Austrian-born psychiatrist and psychoanalyst WILHELM REICH developed the concept of a primordial cosmic energy which he called 'orgone'; in living beings, this energy, which was frequently sexually generated, sometimes became blocked, giving rise to neuroses and most physical disorders. He believed that these blockages were caused by the body's natural response to unendurable mental or psychological pain, which was to protect itself by tensing the muscles; in particular, these muscular contractions were said to be triggered by the fear of losing love by displaying unacceptable emotions. The contractions produced physical blocks within the muscles and organs, which acted as what he called 'body armour', and prevented the release of orgone. According to Reich, a healthy sex life was necessary for overall physical and psychological wellbeing, since orgasm was one way to release this energy.

Reich devised a psychoanalytical form of BODYWORK called Reichian therapy, which was intended to 'dissolve' the body armour and release the inhibited or disturbed energies. This therapy includes deep breathing, exercises in which the patient is encouraged to cry, kick and scream, and especially massage; practitioners of neo-Reichian massage, a technique developed from Reich's theories, claim to locate and dissolve the 'holding patterns' of the body armour by manipulating the physical body. See also BIOENERGETICS.

reiki

A form of energy-balancing therapy in which it is claimed that the practitioner channels healing 'reiki', or universal life energy, through his or her hands to the patient, correcting any imbalances in their body's energy flow to promote physical, emotional and spiritual wellbeing.

Reiki is a Japanese word which means 'UNIVERSAL LIFE FORCE'. This unseen energy is said to permeate all living things, and reiki practitioners claim to be able to tap into this energy and channel it, usually through their hands, into a patient. Illness is believed to be caused by imbalances in the body's energy flow, and the reiki practitioner is thought to correct these imbalances.

Reiki is thought to have originated as a branch of Tibetan Buddhism whose secrets were lost over the centuries, but were rediscovered in the late 19th century by a Japanese minister, Dr Mikao Usui. Dr

Usui claimed that he found the knowledge of reiki in a sacred Indian text. He also claimed that after a long period of meditation, prayer and fasting, he had a vision of four symbols and that by attuning himself with these symbols he achieved the ability to channel the healing energy of reiki. He then passed on the secrets of reiki to a group of pupils, one of whom, Dr Chujiro Hayashi, codified its techniques – particularly a series of 15 fixed hand positions designed to cover all the body's 'systems'. Many different forms of reiki are popular today, especially in the West. It is not taught, in the strict sense of the word, but transferred from teacher to pupil through a series of 'degrees' involving initiations by the reiki master.

The principle on which reiki is based is that illness is caused by a lack of balance and harmony in the energy flow of the body. The patient lies down fully clothed while the practitioner taps into the universal source of reiki energy. This energy then flows, either via the crown CHAKRA or base chakra, into the practitioner's hands, which are placed on or over the patient's body, to transmit this energy into the patient. Most schools of reiki teach that the energy is 'intelligent' and knows, without being directed, where it needs to go. It is then said to rebalance and harmonize the body's energy flow, healing at all levels of mind, body and spirit.

reincarnation
The rebirth of a spirit, or soul, to live a new life within a new physical body.

Reincarnation (literally 'being made flesh again') is a central tenet of many religions and philosophical systems, including Hinduism, SPIRITISM, THEOSOPHY and SCIENTOLOGY. It has appeared among the religious beliefs of human societies throughout history – certainly as far back as the ancient Egyptians – and is a popular theme in much NEW AGE philosophy.

Belief in reincarnation is often combined with a belief that there may be a period of waiting following death, before the spirit is reborn (this may be described as a period of learning, punishment, time spent simply in a state of 'non-existence' or a wait for the right body to be available). In some philosophies it is held that the soul will not necessarily be reborn in human form – it may be transferred to the body of an animal, depending on how virtuous the previous life has been (see KARMA and NIRVANA).

During the 20th century a number of people claimed that they had recovered memories of previous lives while undergoing HYPNOSIS (see PAST-LIFE REGRESSION). Famous examples include BRIDEY MURPHY and the BLOXHAM TAPES. In the case of the POLLOCK TWINS the apparent recall appeared to be spontaneous, and the occultist ALEISTER CROWLEY claimed that he was the reincarnation of ÉLIPHAS LÉVI (among others) without recourse to any form of memory recovery.

It is sometimes claimed that apparent examples of CHANNELLING by MEDIUMS are, in fact, remembrances of past lives and, despite the various psychological and neurological explanations offered, there is still a popular belief that reincarnation lies at the heart of the sensation of DÉJÀ VU. See also AFTERLIFE; DEATH.

relics
The material remains of a religious figure such as a saint, or an item which belonged to them, venerated after their death as possessing spiritual virtue or miraculous powers.

The preservation and veneration of relics – the material remains of a religious figure after their death, for example hair, bones or a body part, or items which were associated with them during life – is found in many spiritual and religious systems. Parts of Buddha's body, such as the Sacred Relic of the Tooth of Buddha at Sri Lanka, and trees believed to be grown from the seeds or cuttings of the original bodhi tree under which he attained enlightenment, are objects of veneration to Buddhists to this day. Relics are traditionally believed to possess great spiritual virtue or the power to perform MIRACLES.

However, it is Christianity, and particularly Roman Catholicism, that is most often associated with the veneration of holy relics – traditionally kept in churches in decorated receptacles called reliquaries. In the early centuries of Christianity, the tales of miracles attributed to relics helped to foster the cult of SAINTS which developed in the Middle Ages, and during the times of the Crusades, many questionable relics were brought back to Europe, some even purporting to be of Christ himself. One of the most famous relics of Christ is the TURIN SHROUD, said to be the linen strip in which Jesus's body was wrapped as it lay in the tomb, which appeared in Europe in the 14th century. A number of churches also claim to house the crown of thorns, or a piece of the True Cross, one of the most highly sought-after relics in the Middle Ages.

The Catholic Church classifies relics in three degrees: first class relics are items believed to be directly associated with events in Christ's life, or the physical remains of saints, with those of martyrs being prized above relics of other saints; second class relics are items worn by a saint, or a personal possession such as a crucifix or book; and third class relics are pieces of cloth which were touched to a saint's body after their death, or have been brought to their shrine. See also PIOUS FRAUD.

Religion *see panel p575*

remote viewing

A process involving attempts at 'seeing' places from a distance, using psychic powers.

'Remote viewing' (or RV) is a title that was originally applied to experiments in the early 1970s involving a particular type of EXTRASENSORY PERCEPTION. Its first use in this context is usually attributed to the US artist Ingo Swann, the most famous subject of the early experiments. The concept was then popularized through the work of Harold Puthoff and Russell Targ at the Stanford Research Institute (see BAY AREA REMOTE-VIEWING EXPERIMENTS).

There is no generally agreed definition of the phrase 'remote viewing' – although it was originally used only in relation to scientific experiments, and the set of agreed protocols attaching to them, it is now used much more freely. It might be most usefully understood as a process of gaining information from a location that the 'viewer' is unable to perceive using the normal five senses, without recourse to any currently understood means of communicating such information. In general terms, such a process might be described as a type of CLAIRVOYANCE – claims to be able to use PSYCHIC powers in this way existed long before the modern term came into use.

The approach to scientific research in the area involves FREE-RESPONSE EXPERIMENTS in which the 'viewer' attempts to give details of impressions, images and feelings about the location in question. Early versions of the experiments involved two people – the viewer remained at the laboratory and the 'target' was sent out to a randomly selected location. The viewer then attempted to describe the target's location. However, they were developed to include a range of other experiments in which only a viewer was required – in such experiments the viewer may be given a set of coordinates, for a location of which they have no prior knowledge, and asked to describe what is there.

Those who claim to be able to use remote viewing offer a wide variety of descriptions of the mechanism by which it occurs. Ingo Swann described the process as a type of psychic 'projecting out of body'; others have described it as akin to seeing with all of the intermediate matter removed or as involving a form of ASTRAL PROJECTION.

Official government-funded experimentation in the area of remote viewing was carried out in the USA for a period of over 20 years (see PROJECT STARGATE). These experiments included attempts at training individuals to improve their remote-viewing ability, following on from Puthoff and Targ's suggestion that it is an innate, natural ability of all humans. However, although research is still being carried out by parapsychologists elsewhere, the direct link between the phrase 'remote viewing' and organized scientific investigation has broken down somewhat in recent years – a number of people now offer their services as remote viewers and claim to be able to teach the techniques, for a fee.

As with all other areas of PARAPSYCHOLOGY, there have been a number of anecdotal claims of successes over the years, all of which are disputed by sceptics on the grounds of chance, selective interpretation and poor experimental method. The cause has not been helped by some of the more bizarre claims associated with the technique – for example, during the US experiments of the 1970s and 1980s, among other things, attempts were made at viewing the planets Mercury and Jupiter, and the MARTIAN FACE, with some entertaining, but fairly unconvincing, results.

Rémy, Nicholas (c.1534–c.1600)

French magistrate and witch hunter who claimed he had been responsible for the executions of 900 witches.

Nicholas Rémy was born in Charmes and studied law at the University of Toulouse. It has been claimed that his crusade against witches was inspired by the death of his son a few days after he was cursed in the street by a beggar. It is said that Rémy concluded that the beggar was a witch, and subsequently had her charged and prosecuted. In a ten-year period from the early 1580s to the early 1590s Rémy claimed that he had been responsible for the executions of 900 witches. Like his contemporary JEAN BODIN, Rémy believed that witches entered a pact with the DEVIL. He also believed the most fantastic descriptions of DEMONS and SABBATS and held that the Devil could appear in the shape of a man or an animal. His *Demonolatreiae libri tres* (Demonolatry) was published in 1595. Including details from his trials, descriptions of the alleged escapades of witches (from satanic pacts to sexual orgies) and suggestions as to how the Devil first drew people into his service, Rémy backed up his claims with the 'evidence' from the confessions of witches that he had prosecuted:

> The truth is that, when Satan cannot move a man by fair words, he compels him by fear and threats of danger. When Claude Morèle, who was convicted of witchcraft at Serre (5th Dec.,1586), was asked what was the chief inducement that had first led him to give himself to the Demon, he answered that he had withstood the temptation of all the Demon's fair words, and had only yielded when Satan had threatened to kill his wife and children. At Guermingen, 19th Dec., 1589, Antoine Welch no longer dared to oppose

Religion

So far as archaeologists and anthropologists can tell, for as long as there have been humans there has been religion – at least in the sense that some of the earliest burials found show evidence of ritual associated with the dead continuing in another life. As to exactly how or why religion originated, and how it developed in pre-history, we can only make educated guesses.

Religion is surprisingly difficult to define. Socio-anthropological definitions tend to be either substantive (what religion *is*) or functional (what religion *does*). Both are useful, but both have problems. Substantive definitions are often too exclusive; any definition that includes 'God', for example, will miss out most forms of Buddhism. Functional definitions suffer from the opposite problem: they are often too inclusive. By some functional definitions, Marxism would be a religion. If the definition is broadened enough to include, for example, NEW AGE beliefs and practices, it can also be argued that football crowds, rock concerts and science-fiction fandom have characteristics of religion.

For general purposes, a working definition of religion could be: 'A social construct encompassing beliefs and practices which enable people, individually and collectively, to make some sense of the Great Questions of life and death.' This leaves open what the Great Questions are – they might include, among others: Is there any purpose to life? Do we continue to exist in any way after death? Is there a Higher Being, and if so, how should I relate to him, her or it?

Émile Durkheim suggested that the main purpose of religion was to be the glue that held society together. Karl Marx, coming from a different direction, described religion as 'the opiate of the people'. Nineteenth-century anthropologists believed that religion evolved from MAGIC, and was itself being out-evolved by science, a theory which time has discredited. Indeed, with the late 20th-century rise of New Age movements and NEOPAGANISM in its many forms, magic has seen a resurgence in our high-tech age.

One of the main preoccupations of sociologists of religion in the second half of the 20th century was

'secularization', ie the decreasing influence of religion on society in Europe (the USA didn't follow the same trend). However, while mainstream Christian denominations (again in Europe) were having to close church buildings, more and more people seemed to flock to new religious movements (see CULTS, NEW RELIGIOUS MOVEMENTS AND ALTERNATIVE RELIGIONS). Perhaps, in the late 20th and early 21st centuries, religion has become not so much secularized as individualized; certainly in the Western world, people now feel free to pick and choose what to believe from the wares laid out before them, instead of being constrained to accept what they are told by authority figures. Beliefs are no longer set in stone. Despite all this there are countless millions who still follow the major world religions.

The term 'ANIMISM', basically meaning 'belief in the spirits of nature or the physical environment', is loosely and incorrectly applied to the religious beliefs of many tribal cultures. The 19th-century anthropologist Edward B Tylor's theory that animism was the earliest form of religion is no longer generally accepted.

Pantheism is the belief that God is present in all of the world – indeed, the entire universe. The world-affirming or cosmic version equates the world with God; the world-denying or a-cosmic version denies the ultimate reality of the world – the divine is real, but our sense experience is illusory. Pantheism underlies Hinduism and some schools of Buddhism.

Polytheism is the belief in many gods. Historically the great pantheons of the Sumerian, Egyptian, Greek, Roman and Norse mythologies (among others) each have families of GODS who are effectively men and women writ large. They are superheroes with all the virtues and flaws of real people: they love, they hate, they get jealous, they fight and they trick each other. In one way or another they intervene in the world of mankind, both helping out and involving humans in their squabbles. The gods could be good exemplars to follow, but their fickle nature made them useful 'fall guys' to be blamed when things went wrong.

The largest polytheistic religion today, with around

800 million adherents, is Hinduism – though strictly speaking, Hinduism is a group of inter-related religions from 'the land beyond the Indus river' (ie India). It is also arguable whether it is actually polytheistic, because some schools of Hinduism believe that there is one God, Brahma, above and beyond all the others, who are effectively attributes of the godhead rather than actually being gods themselves. But, at the level of grassroots believers, there are three main gods: Brahma the Creator, Vishnu the Sustainer (often better known through his avatar Krishna) and Shiva the Destroyer. However, because what we know as Hinduism incorporates all the local gods of small communities throughout the Indian subcontinent and elsewhere in Asia, it has been calculated that there is a total of some 33 million gods. Perhaps Hinduism's most distinctive characteristic, in contrast with the monotheistic religions of the Middle East, is its inclusivity.

Above all Hinduism emphasizes the right way of living (*dharma*), rather than any specific set of doctrines. Under one broad, tolerant umbrella are numerous very different schools: some, such as *Advaita Vedanta*, which teaches the essential oneness of God and man, are deeply philosophical; others are very down to earth. Most teach some form of REINCARNATION, with the quality of the next life determined by one's KARMA, the consequences of one's actions in this life. The ultimate aim is *moksha*, to step off the circle of repeated incarnations (*samsara*). Hinduism has a wealth of scriptures, including the Vedas which go back to 1200–500 BC, and the great mythological epics, the *Ramayana* and the *Mahabharata*, which includes the *Bhagavad Gita*, the famous discourse between Krishna and Arjuna.

The other great Eastern religious tradition is Buddhism, dating back to the Buddha Siddhartha Gautama, c.500 BC. As in Hinduism, the ultimate aim is to step off the cycle of reincarnations, and so to achieve NIRVANA or *nibbana*; this is often described as blissful nothingness in union with God, but as most versions of Buddhism don't acknowledge the existence of gods, this is not correct. The root verb of *nibbana* means to cool something by blowing on it, and *nirvana* is the cooling of all passions such as hate, greed and delusion, and being set free into a state of tranquillity, purity and non-attachment. Buddhism teaches the Four Noble Truths: life is full of suffering; at the heart of suffering lies craving; we can avoid suffering by losing craving through achieving nirvana; we can achieve this by following the Eightfold Path. This path involves: right knowledge or understanding, right thought or intentions, right speech, right action, right livelihood, right effort, right mindfulness and right composure or concentration.

The two main strands of Buddhism are Theravada, found mainly in Burma, Sri Lanka and Thailand, and Mahayana, found mainly in China, Japan and Korea. Each of these contains many different traditions; for example, the Tibetan Buddhism of the Dalai Lama stems from Mahayana Buddhism. There are 300–400 million Buddhists in the world.

Monotheism is the belief that there is only one god. Deism and theism are also both beliefs in One Creator God; the main difference, briefly, is that in deism God does not get actively involved in the world, and in theism he does. Deism generally accepts natural theology as opposed to revealed religion, in which God makes himself known through revelations and miracles. Theism, in contrast, asserts a personal God who intervenes in his creation; thus it is the basis of Judaism, Christianity and Islam.

Many Christians today assume that Christianity emerged fully fledged almost immediately after the death of Jesus, and that the religion it grew out of, Judaism, was also fully developed from the beginning. Neither is true. Biblical scholars have long rejected the concept of 'revealed religion' in the face of the clear historical and theological development of the Religions of the Book.

Judaism, the religion of a small Middle-Eastern tribe, absorbed influences from surrounding tribes with whom the Israelites fought or traded or, often controversially, intermarried. From the time of Abraham, and then Moses' encounter with the burning bush, it is clear that one of the major early influences on Judaism, and thus later on Christianity and Islam, was Zoroastrianism. This was arguably the first monotheistic religion, with the concept also of a powerful opponent to God (Angra Mainyu or Ohriman, SATAN, the DEVIL); Zoroastrianism also had a major influence on Jewish, Christian and Muslim beliefs about good and evil and about the afterlife, including resurrection, heaven and hell. Most scholars today accept that when Israel was in captivity in Babylon in the 6th century BC it took on many Sumerian beliefs and myths, including the Creation and Flood stories.

By the time of Jesus the main factions within Judaism were the Pharisees and the Sadducees, with the Essenes and Zealots providing the spiritual and political radical edge. Today's Judaism, with around 15 million members, developed mainly from the rabbinical Pharisees.

Many scholars believe that Jesus was seen as, and probably saw himself as, a messianic figure within the context of his time and place (see MILLENNIUM), but by half a century after his death the Jewish concept of the messiah had developed into the Christian concept of the Christ. The new religion of Christianity was universal (catholic); it taught salvation through faith in Jesus's atoning death on the cross, a sacrifice for the sins of all mankind. It also taught the complex doctrine of the Trinity, that Jesus and the Holy Spirit are equal with the Father: three distinct persons within one godhead (see HERETICAL SECTS). The teaching that Jesus is God is fundamental to orthodox Christian belief, but is anathema to Jews and Muslims, who are united in one thing: their belief that God is One, not three-in-one.

The crucial factor in the success of Christianity was its adoption by Emperor Constantine, leading to its spread throughout the Roman Empire. Over a thousand years Europe was entirely Christianized, followed by the New World, north and south, and the British Empire. Christianity is now the largest world religion, with around 2,000 million adherents, half of those Roman Catholic; there are roughly 300 million Orthodox, and the remainder are made up of Anglican/Episcopalians, Methodists, Baptists, Pentecostals and other varieties of Protestantism.

Islam developed from the same roots as Judaism and Christianity; indeed, the Koran devotes much time to Adam, Abraham, Moses, and even Jesus. They were all prophets of the one God, but Muhammad (c.570–c.632) was the greatest prophet with the final revelation from God. The teachings he was given by the angel Gabriel were written down in what became the Koran. Very early on Islam split into two major divisions, Sunni (roughly four-fifths of the total) and Shiite (one-fifth), and there are numerous sects within both. There are around 1,000 million Muslims worldwide, including around 1.5 million in the UK and perhaps 5 million in North America.

The essence of Islam, which in Arabic means 'submission' or 'surrender' to the will of God, is: 'There is no God but God (Allah), and Muhammad is his prophet.' Islam is not just a religion but an entire structure of living, of behaviour, of morality. The Five Pillars of Islam, essential religious duties, are the profession of faith; formal prayer five times a day facing Mecca; alms-giving; fasting during the month of Ramadan; and the *hajj*, pilgrimage to Mecca at least once in every Muslim's lifetime, if possible.

Three religions in one way or another connected with Islam are SUFISM, Sikhism and the Bahai Faith. Sufism is actually the mystical side of Islam rather than a separate religion, though in the West it is often seen as a universal religion, especially in its influences on some New Age and ESOTERIC movements. Sufism focuses on the individual's personal loving relationship with God through poetry, music and dance; the famous WHIRLING DERVISHES belong to the Mevlevis, a Sufi order (or *tariqa*, meaning 'way') founded by the poet Rumi in the 13th century.

Sikhism originated in the Punjab, on the borders of what are now India and Pakistan, so inevitably absorbed elements of both Islam (particularly Sufism) and Hinduism (particularly Bhakti Hinduism – devotion to God rather than to ritual – and Advaita), though its founder Guru Nanak (1469–1539) wrote: 'There is neither Hindu nor Muslim, so whose path shall I follow? I shall follow God's path. God is neither Hindu nor Muslim and the path which I follow is God's.' Guru Nanak taught meditation, devotion and worship of the one God; the word *sikh* means 'student' or disciple'.

Sikhs have a strong veneration for their ten gurus, and most especially for their sacred text the *Guru Granth Sahib* (*Granth* means 'the Book') which is regarded as the immortal guru. Guru Nanak came from the Sant spiritual tradition of northern India and, as well as his hymns, those of other Sant leaders are included in the *Granth* (see SANT MAT TRADITION). Most Sikhs are still of Punjabi descent; there are around 20–25 million Sikhs worldwide.

The Bahai Faith regards itself as the next world religion in order after Judaism, Christianity and Islam. Like them it is monotheistic. It was founded by Bahaullah (1817–92), and developed from the teachings of the Báb (1819–50), a religious teacher in Iran who claimed to be either the long-awaited return of the twelfth imam of 'Twelver' Shi'a Islam, or the gateway (*báb*) to the twelfth imam; before he was executed for blasphemy he spoke of a successor, 'He whom God would make manifest'; this was Bahaullah ('the glory of God').

Bahais have a huge number of authoritative texts written by the Báb, Bahaullah and his successors as leaders of the Bahai Faith; they also include the Bible and the Koran. There have been at least 14 Manifestations of God, people who received divine revelation and guidance; these include Abraham, Moses, Jesus, Muhammad, Zoroaster, the Buddha, Krishna – and the Báb and Bahaullah. They believe in One God who is unknowable except through his attributes, such as love, mercy, justice, patience, etc. They teach the unity of God, the unity of religion and the unity of humankind. The Bahai Faith has no priests; all people, men and women, are equal before God. The movement lays great emphasis on the education of women, especially in societies where this is found wanting. Bahais express their faith practically through working to improve the community around them at all levels from their immediate environment to the United Nations, where the religion is a non-governmental organization. The Bahai Faith has expanded rapidly in the last few decades, now having perhaps seven million members.

David V Barrett

the Demon in anything after he had threatened to twist his neck unless he obeyed his commands, for he seemed on the very point of fulfilling his threat … Therefore we may … conclude that it is no mere fable that witches meet and converse with Demons in very person.

Rémy's claim to have sent 900 witches to their executions cannot be substantiated from the records of the time, and he cites fewer than 150 witchcraft cases in his book. However, the *Demonolatry* became an influential handbook for other witch hunters of the time.

The Rendlesham Forest Incident *see*

panel p580

Rennes-le-Château

A medieval castle village in southern France. A 19th-century priest, Bérenger Saunière, was rumoured to have found a mysterious treasure in the church, and from the 1950s onward, the location became the focus of various conspiracy theories linking Saunière's discovery to the Knights Templar, the Priory of Sion, the Holy Grail and the alleged bloodline of Christ and Mary Magdalene.

The medieval castle village of Rennes-le-Château is situated in the Aude département of the Languedoc area in southern France. In the late 19th century, rumours began to surround the local priest, Bérenger Saunière, who was said to have mysteriously acquired a great deal of sudden wealth; although poor when he took up his position there, he began to spend lavishly, renovating the church, decorating it elaborately with statues, and building a villa with a formal garden, a belvedere and a neo-Gothic tower dedicated to Mary Magdalene. It is thought that most of the money he spent came from the practice of trafficking masses, which eventually led to his suspension and prosecution by the ecclesiastical courts, and by the time of his death at the age of 65 in 1917, he was apparently penniless again.

In the 1950s, a local businessman, Noel Corbu, opened a restaurant on Saunière's estate, and to attract business, he suggested that Saunière had in fact amassed his wealth after uncovering something mysterious in the church; according to one version, he had discovered certain parchments in an ancient pillar, and, following the clues in these documents, had been led to a great treasure hidden there by Saint Blanche of Castille in the 13th century. This idea was taken up by a man called Pierre Plantard, who was at that time propagating the story of a mysterious organization he called the Priory of Sion. According to Plantard,

Jesus had not died on the cross, but had founded a bloodline with Mary Magdalene – the Merovingian dynasty of France – whose descendants the Priory of Sion were charged with protecting. Plantard sought to prove that he was not only the current Grand Master of the Priory of Sion, but also the last descendant of the Merovingians, and therefore the legitimate heir to the throne of France, and he claimed that Saunière's 'treasure' included parchments that substantiated his story. To this end, in the 1960s either he or an accomplice anonymously deposited a collection of documents in the Bibliothèque Nationale in Paris, which allegedly linked Saunière's secrets to the Priory and its sacred charge.

Although the documents were quickly dismissed as forgeries, they sparked off a national interest in the village of Rennes-le-Château, which became inundated by treasure hunters, and fuelled a number of increasingly sensationalist conspiracy theories which suggested that whatever Saunière had found threatened the very foundations of Catholicism: some artefact or document of spiritual significance hidden by the KNIGHTS TEMPLAR, or by the Cathars in that region in the 13th century before their final defeat; proof that Jesus and Mary Magdalene had descendants; maps showing the location of Jesus's burial place, or documents proving that he was not resurrected; or scriptures challenging the legitimacy of the Church. These theories greatly influenced the authors of the popular 1982 book *Holy Blood, Holy Grail*, Umberto Eco's novel *Foucault's Pendulum* (1989), and Dan Brown's 2003 bestselling novel THE DA VINCI CODE. As a result, the village still attracts visitors from all over the world, looking for evidence of conspiracy, or for hidden treasure.

repressed memories *see* MEMORIES, REPRESSED

Resch, Tina

A US teenager who was the focus for apparent poltergeist activity in 1984, one of the most widely known cases of modern times.

In 1984, Tina Resch was a 14-year-old girl living with her adoptive parents in Columbus, Ohio, when she became the centre of one of the most famous modern POLTERGEIST cases. Apparently, electrical items would malfunction, and objects would fly through the air (sometimes directed at Resch herself) whenever she was present. Following coverage of the phenomena in the local press, parapsychologist William Roll, who had spent a number of years at Duke University, working under J B RHINE, became one of the chief investigators of the case, studying Resch for the next eight years.

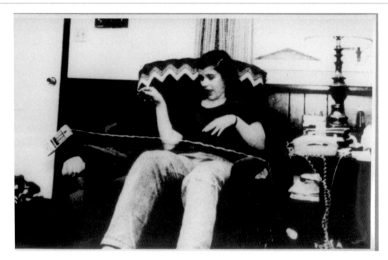

A telephone flies past Tina Resch, apparently without human intervention.
(© TopFoto/Fortean)

Numerous incidents of the apparently paranormal movement of objects in the house were noted, including cups that flew through the air, and lights that switched themselves on. One of the most spectacular pieces of evidence in the case is a set of photographs captured by a local newspaper photographer. The photographs show the extended cord and handset of a telephone in flight past Tina Resch as she is seated in a chair. Roll believed that the various phenomena constituted a genuine case of PSYCHOKINESIS, and Resch was tested in the laboratory for such powers. Although the case was criticized by sceptics (who claimed that Resch was simply a disturbed teenager who knowingly and deliberately caused the disturbances), Roll strongly believed that paranormal forces were at work, and that Resch had the ability to affect the physical world through the power of her mind. Opportunities for further research with Resch were curtailed in 1992, when she was convicted for the murder of her three-year-old daughter, and she was subsequently sentenced to life imprisonment with no prospect of parole.

resurrection

The supposed instance of a dead person's coming back to life; the religious concept of the rising of all mankind from the dead at the Last Judgement.

The motif of gods dying and being resurrected is a common one in the mythology of ancient cultures: Osiris in Egyptian myth is killed and rises again, as does Tammuz in Babylonian myth and the god Mithras in the ancient Roman mystery tradition. However, it is thought that it was in the Hebrew culture that the first expression of a belief in personal resurrection came, and the permanent reunion of the physical body and soul on the Day of Judgement; at the time of Jesus, there was much debate between the Jewish sect of the Pharisees, who believed in a future resurrection, and the Saducees, who did not, although nowadays, mainstream Judaic doctrine regards the resurrection of the dead as one of the cardinal principles of the Jewish faith.

The resurrection of the dead is a fundamental tenet of Christianity, which is based on the belief that Jesus was brought back to life by God three days after his crucifixion, and his teachings that the dead will be resurrected for judgement along with the living at his Second Coming. According to Christian belief, the souls of the departed will be reunited with their bodies, and those which are saved will live forever in Heaven in a reformed body adapted to the soul in its glorified state.

In Islam, the day of resurrection of the dead, and the union of their flesh and spirit, is called *Yaum al-Qiyama*, and is referred to frequently in the Koran, and on the *Yaum al-Din*, or Day of Judgement, each person's deeds will be weighed and the righteous shall enter Paradise.

There are also stories in the Old Testament of prophets such as Elijah and Elisha raising people from the dead, and Jesus is described in the New Testament as having brought several people back to life, but these are generally referred to by theologians as 'resuscitations' rather than 'resurrections'.

Resurrection Mary

A phantom hitch-hiker associated with the Resurrection Cemetery in Chicago, USA.

It is rare in stories of PHANTOM HITCH-HIKERS for the ghost to have any recognizable identity, but one

The Rendlesham Forest Incident

Rendlesham Forest, on the Suffolk coast, is in a strategic defence location that has several military facilities. During the cold war, secret technological development took place in this area – including the testing of radar, electromagnetic detection equipment, nuclear weapon components and atmospheric energy beams. In 1956 BENTWATERS AIR FORCE BASE in these woods was at the focus of a major radar and visual UFO encounter. In December 1980 this same base and its satellite unit at Woodbridge were home to a large number of US Air Force personnel. Tensions were high in the light of cold war developments in Poland. Bentwaters held a secret nuclear arsenal, potentially placing it in the firing line.

In the early hours of 26 December 1980, a two-man security patrol at the east gate of Woodbridge observed a light in the sky which appeared to come down into the woods between the base and the coastal spit of Orford Ness. The patrol called for assistance, and three officers went to investigate the light. They apparently encountered a strange semi-transparent shape in a clearing. What was described as a wave of energy poured from it, making their skin tingle and their hair stand on end. Moments later the object climbed through the trees and disappeared, leaving the airmen standing in the woods feeling disoriented.

At dawn an aircraft flew over the forest and identified the landing spot as emitting heat energy. Inside the woods, at this location, a circular area was found that showed signs of an impact. There was also a hole punched through the tree canopy, some shallow holes in the ground and score marks on surrounding trees.

On the evening of the following day light was again seen inside the forest by airmen at the base. Surrounded by mist, the light was described as splitting into rainbow colours. The deputy base commander, Colonel Charles Halt, was ordered to take a team of men into the woods to investigate. The team included a photographer and a 'disaster-preparedness' officer, who carried a Geiger counter. Halt had a tape recorder that made a live record as they studied the landing site using gas-powered floodlights in the early hours of 28 December. The tape captured the conversations of the men as they took samples and recorded high readings on the Geiger counter, before being startled as a huge eye-like glow appeared, winking through the trees. After chasing this through the forest and out towards the coast over a period of two hours, the men saw various star-like lights that remained visible as they retraced their steps at dawn. At one point a pencil beam of light was apparently projected from one of the objects onto the ground, just a few feet from them. The tape records their cries of 'this is unreal' as the events unfold.

Halt reported these incidents to the government in mid-January. Despite the fact that the events were supposed to be kept secret, however, the British UFO researcher Jenny Randles had been put in contact with a radar operator in Norfolk who claimed that US Air Force

that has achieved at least recognition by nickname is 'Resurrection Mary', or 'Rez Mary', associated with the area around the Roman Catholic 'Resurrection Cemetery' in Chicago.

Stories concerning Resurrection Mary seem to date back to the 1930s. One frequently related tale tells of a young man named Jerry Palus who allegedly met a woman in a white dress at the now demolished Liberty Grove Hall Ballroom. Her skin was said to be cold and clammy when he kissed her. After a night of dancing, she asked for a lift home and to be dropped by the Resurrection Cemetery. Palus obliged and she ran to the gates of the cemetery and vanished. Stories have circulated ever since of motorists picking up a young blonde woman near the cemetery late at night (or alternatively from a dance hall) who later vanishes without explanation during the journey or when getting out of the vehicle. Such reports continued through to the 1980s but seemed to dwindle during in the 1990s.

Various candidates have been put forward for the identity of the 'ghost' known as Resurrection Mary, including a number of teenage girls or young women killed in road accidents in the area between 1927 and 1936. However, in many respects she fits an archetypal WHITE LADY ghost as much as a phantom hitch-hiker.

resurrection men

Men who stole bodies from the grave for dissection.

In the 18th and early 19th centuries schools of medicine and surgery found that their demand for human corpses – on which to practise anatomical research and dissection – far exceeded legitimate supply. It became a common practice for these institutions to pay for recently deceased cadavers with intelligence officers had come to him, with RAF personnel, to take film for analysis. During this visit, just days after Halt's report went to London, the officers apparently advised him that they were looking for evidence to confirm the claims of the US Air Force staff at Bentwaters. Meanwhile, two local UFO investigators had received reports from local residents around the forest who had seen strange lights above the trees. The UFO group, BUFORA, approached the Ministry of Defence (MoD) for answers but the existence of the case was denied for two years. It wasn't until April 1983 that the government wrote to Randles confirming the story, but adding that 'no explanation was forthcoming'.

UFO researchers in the USA then used the US FREEDOM OF INFORMATION ACT to obtain the report that had been filed with the British MoD. There was no similar act in place in Britain at the time, so the BUFORA researchers had been denied their own copy. They obtained one from their US colleagues and took it to Whitehall, unannounced, explaining that they intended to release it to the UFO COMMUNITY. The story hit the news headlines in the British media during October 1983.

Since 1983 a number of other witnesses have come forward with the details of what they claim they saw on those nights. The full MoD file was released in 2002, following the arrival of the Freedom of Information Act in Britain. The file reveals some confusion, and delays at the hands of the government, but offers no real answers. However, it was decided that the radiation levels were not significant and that the tree marks were not connected to the reported incident.

As the years have passed a number of other elements of this case do seem to have been resolved. Some of the lights were almost certainly just stars. A lighthouse on Orford Ness is thought to have been the source of some of the observations, given its odd appearance when viewed through the trees at night. The presence of mist which possibly produced an optical mirage, distorting the bright glow, might also offer a partial explanation. It has also been pointed out that, at the time when the first sighting occurred, a bright fireball meteor crossed eastern England and broke up over the North Sea. Foresters also say that holes in the ground, of the type seen by the witnesses, can be caused by local wildlife.

Some parts of the case remain unexplained. The PHYSIOLOGICAL EFFECTS reported during the CLOSE ENCOUNTER phase are mysterious. Opinions of the case now vary – some UFO researchers refer to the case as Britain's ROSWELL, whereas an astronomer has described it as a 'ghastly embarrassment' because obvious solutions were missed for so long. Most UFO investigators take a middle view, recognizing that there are unresolved aspects but acknowledging that it is a good example of how a case can require years of study to bring together a variety of seemingly unconnected explanations. At least six books have been devoted to the Rendlesham Forest Incident – easily the record for a British UFO sighting, and second only to Roswell worldwide.

---

no questions asked, and this encouraged the activities of those familiarly known as body snatchers or grave robbers. Grim humour, with a nod towards the idea of an unlooked-for rising from the grave, also dubbed them 'resurrection men'.

Originally, only bodies of the poor and friendless were taken (and in America, those of black slaves), but in time even the remains of the respectable became the prey of these unscrupulous individuals. Typically, they would watch graveyards and note when funerals were taking place. Then, in the dead of night, they would disinter the coffin, remove the body and quickly and secretly transport it to the buyer.

Some resurrectionists were careful to strip the corpse of any burial clothes and take it away naked. This was done because taking clothes would make the crime into a felony, while stealing a body was merely a misdemeanour!

So prevalent did this activity become that various precautions were adopted by the bereaved to avoid violation of the loved one's last resting place. These included mounting a guard over the burial place for a few nights after the funeral until decomposition had begun to make the body useless for the purpose, burying the deceased in a metal coffin and the installation over the grave of a heavy iron grating or set of bars known as a mortsafe.

Medical practitioners involved in dissection ran the risk of unpopularity among a public that preferred not to consider how valuable medical knowledge was sometimes obtained. In New York City in 1788 there was a serious riot, known as the Doctors Mob, in which the anatomy laboratory of the New York Hospital was ransacked and the homes of several medical men were attacked.

Two of the most famous resurrection men were

Burke and Hare, who plied their trade in Edinburgh, supplying corpses to the anatomist Robert Knox (1791–1862). William Burke (1792–1829) was an Irish immigrant who worked in partnership with William Hare (1790–1860). These two took their disreputable activities a step further when they began to ensure a ready supply of bodies by killing people themselves. Hare eventually turned king's evidence against Burke, who was hanged, but not before giving his name to a method of murder by smothering (leaving no marks on the body): to burke someone.

The trade of the resurrection men in Britain was brought to an end by the Anatomy Act 1832, which laid down that anyone wishing to practise anatomy had to be licensed by the government. The Act also made the legitimate supply of corpses easier by stipulating that any unclaimed body could be used for dissection.

revenant

A person who returns from the dead; a ghost.

The word 'revenant' (from the French *revenir*, meaning 'to come back') is generally used to refer to a person who returns from the dead to visit the living, particularly those who were known or loved in life. Not surprisingly, the theme of revenants has been a popular one in folklore and literature, where the deceased may manifest at their own initiative or as a result of being summoned by a sorcerer.

Revenants rarely seem to convey messages of much overt significance, seemingly being motivated more by a desire to glimpse their loved ones or revisit the scenes of their earthly activities. In cases documented since 1700, little ever happens beyond an exchange of recognition and tacit greetings between the living and the dead. However, prior to 1700 revenants often returned to deliver important personal messages or to confirm or rebuke complex theological and doctrinal beliefs. They also returned to exact revenge or right a wrong they committed in life.

The term 'revenant' is also often used to describe malign forms of ghosts from medieval folklore. These were frequently more physically solid in nature than apparitions in later historical accounts. Capable of inflicting physical harm and even jousting or fighting with the living, medieval revenants are more reminiscent of ZOMBIES than ghosts proper. Changes in theology, burial practice and attitudes to the spiritual status of the corpse in popular culture seem to have put paid to physical revenants in Western Europe but the traditions continued in parts of Eastern Europe until well into the 20th century.

reverse engineering

An unproven belief that some advances in modern technology have arisen from the study of captured UFOs.

It is often stated that science advances in two ways – evolution and revolution. As we accumulate knowledge, we gradually develop new ways of doing things by building upon our existing technology. For example, computers double their storage capacity every couple of years as manufacturers learn how to squeeze more memory into smaller components. Major events sometimes appear to act as catalysts for sudden surges in scientific development. World War II saw rapid advances in military technology, such as radar and the atomic bomb, as well as in computer technology. Likewise, it is often claimed that the cold war driven space race resulted in the accelerated development of new kinds of plastics, foodstuffs and other unexpected benefits for the households of the world that might have taken decades to appear without this impetus.

Some UFO researchers claim that modern aviation may owe a similar debt to the alleged recovery of crashed UFOs, beginning with the ROSWELL case in 1947. Such claims are extremely contentious, even among the UFO COMMUNITY – there is no conclusive proof that any EXTRATERRESTRIAL craft has ever fallen to Earth, let alone been studied at a top-secret location. However, the stories about MAJESTIC 12 include the claim that ALIEN technology has been recovered from several crash sites – this has supposedly been intensively studied by top scientists. The level of secrecy successfully maintained is apparently way beyond that which accompanied the development of the first nuclear weapons during the 1940s.

It is argued by some that this work still continues, decades later, because the alien technology was so far ahead of our own knowledge that thus far only small elements have been understood. Much of this analysis is said to have taken place at the real, highly secret US military base which is often referred to as AREA 51. It has certainly been admitted that advanced aircraft propulsion systems, some of them highly experimental, have been tested here (see BLACK AIRCRAFT).

Some people have approached UFO researchers, claiming that they have worked on such projects, stating that some highly advanced modern aircraft incorporate technology taken from alien spacecraft. They use the term 'reverse engineering' to describe the process of 'working backwards' from the captured item of equipment in an attempt to understand the basic principles by which it operates.

rhabdomancy *see* DOWSING

Rhine, J(oseph) B(anks) (1895–1980)

An important and influential US parapsychologist who helped found the first university department devoted to research in this area.

J B Rhine originally trained as a botanist but later moved to the psychology department at Harvard University to study with Professor William McDougall, a leading social psychologist with an interest in PARAPSYCHOLOGY. When McDougall moved to Duke University, North Carolina, Rhine moved there to work under him. At Duke, Rhine started his pioneering work on parapsychology (a subject he apparently became interested in after attending a lecture by ARTHUR CONAN DOYLE). Rhine popularized the term 'parapsychology', and attempted to put research in this area onto a systematic, scientific basis, and he is regarded by many as the 'father of experimental parapsychology'.

Rhine conducted experiments in TELEPATHY, CLAIRVOYANCE, PRECOGNITION and PSYCHOKINESIS. In his CARD-GUESSING EXPERIMENTS, he used ZENER CARDS to test for EXTRASENSORY PERCEPTION (a term introduced by Rhine). Rhine discovered that participants in these experiments often scored significantly above chance. Between 1934 and 1941 Rhine conducted 651,216 experimental DICE throws, in an attempt to establish whether psychokinesis could be used to influence the outcome of a roll of a dice. Again, Rhine felt that his results pointed toward a genuine psychic phenomenon, although the results are generally regarded as inconclusive.

Unlike earlier researchers in this field, Rhine used not only 'gifted' individuals in his experiments (ie self-proclaimed PSYCHICS and MEDIUMS), but also members of the general population. He attempted to introduce robust methodologies for testing psychic ability, and applied statistical analysis to his results, aiming to legitimize parapsychology as a scientific field. With the help of McDougall, Rhine founded the Duke University Parapsychology Laboratory, the first university department devoted to research in this area, in 1935. In 1937 he established the *Journal of Parapsychology* and his proposal led to the formation of the Parapsychological Association in 1957. After leaving Duke, Rhine established an independent institution, the Foundation for Research on the Nature of Man, in 1962. This organization was renamed the RHINE RESEARCH CENTER in 1995 to celebrate the centenary of his birth.

It has been shown that Rhine was, at various times, the victim of hoaxes and fraud (sceptics claim that early in his career he was taken in by claims of a telepathic horse called Lady Wonder). Some of Rhine's co-workers were caught altering their results (some were

Dr J B Rhine, founder of the first university department devoted to parapsychology. (© Bettmann/Corbis)

exposed by Rhine himself) but there is no evidence that Rhine acted in an inappropriate manner. Some of his experimental procedures have been criticized and many of his results remain controversial, and have never been reproduced, but Rhine was a pioneer of parapsychological research and the work he started continues. He authored many influential books in the field, including *Extra-Sensory Perception* (1934), *New Frontiers of the Mind* (1937) and *Parpasychology, Frontier Science of the Mind* (1957, with J G Pratt).

Rhine Research Center

A parapsychology research institute which continues the work of J B Rhine and the Duke University Parapsychology Laboratory.

In 1962 the PARAPSYCHOLOGY researcher J B RHINE set up the Foundation for Research on the Nature of Man, in response to the withdrawal of formal funding for the Duke University Parapsychology Laboratory (which he had founded in 1935). The Foundation was to be an independent and privately funded sponsor of research into parapsychology – the original donors included Chester Carlson, the founder of Xerox. The intention was that the foundation would continue Rhine's earlier work. It would also continue to operate the Institute for Parapsychology and Parapsychology Press from the premises at Duke University. Rhine felt that an independent institute would have the freedom to pursue any areas of research interest and would not come under any undue pressure to find either positive or negative results – he wanted to ensure that scientific methods and principles were followed at all times. However, the reputation of the Foundation was somewhat tarnished in the 1970s, when it became apparent that its Director of Research, Walter Levy, had faked the results of an experiment in order to show positive results.

In 1995 the foundation was renamed the Rhine Research Center, to celebrate the centenary of Rhine's birth. The organization still continues the work of its founder, and is now based at new premises in Durham, North Carolina. The Research Center describes itself as 'an institute for the study of consciousness'; it offers a number of resources for the public and the media, and continues to publish the twice-yearly *Journal of Parapsychology*.

rhinoceros dolphin

A mystery dolphin named after the horn-like extra dorsal fin on its head.

In October 1819, a shoal of very odd-looking dolphins was observed in the Pacific Ocean by Jean Quoy and Joseph Gaimard, leaders of the *Uranie* and *Physicienne* expedition that was sailing between the Hawaiian Islands and New South Wales, Australia. Dark in colour, with white dappling on the anterior region of their bodies, what made these dolphins so distinctive and unusual is that each one of them bore not one dorsal fin but two – with the extra one positioned on the dolphin's head, curving backwards in a similar way to the horn of a rhinoceros. Subsequently dubbed the rhinoceros dolphin, this species has received an official scientific name – *Oxypterus mongitori* – and is well known among dolphin researchers, but no specimen has ever been obtained for formal study and classification.

Right-Hand Path *see* LEFT-HAND PATH

ritual magic *see* MAGIC, RITUAL

rituals

A ritual is a set of actions performed, mainly for their symbolic value, in a prescribed form. Rituals generally fulfil a religious or social purpose.

The use of ritual is a feature of almost all societies, both past and present. Ritual may be used to serve many purposes, chiefly either religious or social, but the essential feature of any ritual is that its actions and their symbolism are not spontaneous or arbitrary, but are prescribed beforehand; they are formalized

to a greater or lesser degree, and have usually been established by custom. Rituals may be performed at regular intervals, such as the Catholic mass; on a specific occasion, such as a wedding or funeral; or at specific dates in the religious calendar, such as the Christian rituals of Palm Sunday and Good Friday, and the Jewish ritual of Yom Kippur. They may be conducted by an individual, a group or the whole community, and may be performed in a place specially reserved for them, such as an altar, church or sacred grove, or in any place which is appropriate under the circumstances. Rituals may involve the use of special music, song or dance, the wearing of special clothing, or special food, drink or incense, and they may also include SACRIFICES, human or animal. They may even, as in the Japanese practice of seppuku or hara-kiri, involve suicide.

Religious rituals are usually performed for purposes of worship, purification, atonement or penance, or dedication. Ritual is also an important element of MAGIC, WITCHCRAFT and the OCCULT; for example, the effectiveness of a charm or TALISMAN is believed to be increased by the use of ritual in its making. Social rituals generally express and reinforce the shared beliefs of a given society, and may, as in rituals of INITIATION, mark the passage of an individual from childhood to adulthood, or their acceptance as a full member of a group or community. Rituals performed for life events such as birth, marriage and death often contain both religious and social elements. Ritual also features in the inauguration of officials to government posts, the coronation of monarchs, and the acceptance of new members into SECRET SOCIETIES or college fraternities.

RNG *see* RANDOM NUMBER GENERATOR

road ghosts *see* HAUNTED HIGHWAYS

robes

Loose-fitting outer garments, traditionally worn as part of the dress of priests, monks and other officials of various religions. They are also ritually worn by practitioners of many magical traditions.

Robes, loose-fitting outer garments usually distinguished from cloaks by their having sleeves, are worn by priests, monks and officials of many religions, as well as by some practitioners of magical traditions such as WITCHCRAFT. The wearing of special clothes as part of a religious or magical ritual is an ancient practice. Some hold that the putting on of an article of clothing specifically reserved for religious ceremonies or magical rituals sends the subconscious mind a signal which prepares it for the required state of consciousness for those rites; the robes help to focus the mind and enhance spiritual energy. In some religions and magical groups, the person officiating may wear differently coloured robes according to the season or time of year, or for performing specific ceremonies, such as initiations or marriages, and in some Wiccan covens, the colour of the cord tied around the robe of the practitioner indicates the magical degree which they have achieved. On the other hand, some traditions of witchcraft prefer to practise their rituals naked, or 'skyclad'.

According to the New Testament's Gospel of John, the robe worn by Jesus until shortly before his crucifixion was not divided up between the Roman soldiers, but kept intact because it was woven in one piece, without seams; instead, they cast lots for it. The Roman Catholic tradition holds that this robe was found in the Holy Land by Helena, the mother of Constantine the Great, and is now housed in the German Cathedral of Trier, although many scholars believe it to be a medieval forgery. The robe is not on view to the general public, but on rare occasions it is exhibited, the last such exhibition being in 1996.

rods, suit of *see* WANDS, SUIT OF

Roff, Mary *see* WATSEKA WONDER

Rollright Stones
A stone circle formation in Oxfordshire connected with witchcraft.
The Rollright Stones are a megalithic STONE CIRCLE formation near the Oxfordshire villages of Little and Great Rollright. There are upwards of 70 standing stones in the main circle, known as the King's Men, which has a diameter of around 30 metres (100 feet). Nearby stands a smaller group, now thought to be the remains of a DOLMEN, called the Whispering Knights (so called because they appear to be leaning their heads together in confabulation), as well as a solitary stone known as the King Stone. The stones are all made of a local limestone, but it has been shown that the three separate groupings were not erected at the same time.

The stones are on a much smaller scale than those of STONEHENGE or AVEBURY and many have weathered into grotesque and pitted forms. Most of them had fallen over by the 18th century, and as many were re-erected in the late 19th century it may be that the original arrangement was quite different.

According to legend the Rollright Stones are the petrified bodies of a king and his invading army, turned to stone by the spells of MOTHER SHIPTON, a

The main stone circle of the Rollright Stones in Oxfordshire, known as the King's Men. (© TopFoto/Fortean)

famous local witch, who is said to have accosted the invaders with the following words:

> Seven long strides shalt thou take,
> If Long Compton thou canst see
> King of England thou shalt be.

To this the king is said to have replied:

> Stick, stock, stone,
> As King of England I shall be known.

The King thereupon paced out his seven strides but found that an ancient mound called the Archdruid's Barrow blocked his view of Long Compton (a nearby village). Mother Shipton then completed the spell with the following:

> As Long Compton thou canst not see,
> King of England thou shalt not be,
> Rise up stick and stand still stone,
> For King of England thou shalt be none.
> Thou and thy men hoar stones shall be
> And myself an eldern tree.

Quite why the triumphant witch felt obliged to turn herself into an elder tree remains unclear.

The area has long been associated with the OCCULT and for centuries WITCHES have been said to hold gatherings there. The stones have been associated with FAIRIES and fertility rituals and are said, at times, to move about, whether to dance or to go for a drink at a spring at midnight on New Year's Eve. On

Midsummer Eve, if a nearby elder tree is cut, its sap is said to run like blood. It is said to be impossible to count all of the stones with any accuracy, and that a local baker who tried to do this by placing a loaf on top of each stone simply ran out of loaves.

Romasanta, Manuel Blanco (b.c.1809)

Nineteenth-century Spanish serial killer who claimed to be a werewolf.

In the 1850s a Spanish man called Manuel Blanco Romasanta confessed to the murders of 15 people, claiming that he was a werewolf and that he had been assisted in the killings by two werewolf accomplices. A native of the northern Spanish village of Reguiero, Romasanta was a peddler who often visited the neighbouring village of Rebordechao to sell his wares. He befriended a woman and her daughter in Rebordechao and suggested he might arrange jobs in service for them both in the house of a priest who lived in Santander. They agreed, and he offered to accompany them to their new home. It was the last anyone ever saw of the women, although several weeks later, Romasanta returned to the village with letters which he said had been written by the women, telling their relatives how happy they were in their new positions. He did the same for several other villagers, claiming to have found them work in the towns he visited on his travels and offering himself as a chaperon on the journey. Eventually the villagers began to suspect that Romasanta was in fact murdering the people he had lured away, killing them in the mountains and either using their body fat to make the soap he sold, or selling it to WITCHES, since in those days it was believed that witches would pay large sums of money for human fat to use in their spells and potions. Either way, the rumours grew so strong that Romasanta left the area and went to live in Castile, where he changed his name to Antonio Gomez and took up a new trade as a nail maker, later moving to Verin to work as a farm hand.

But in 1852, three villagers from Rebordechao happened to be visiting Verin and spotted Romasanta. Recognizing him at once, they reported his real identity and their suspicions to the mayor, who had him arrested and imprisoned in the nearby town of Allariz. Romasanta then confessed to the murders of 15 people, but claimed that he was a werewolf, and had committed the crimes with the help of other werewolves. He said he had become a werewolf after having a curse placed on him, and said he had gone into the mountains, where he had met two men who were also werewolves; they would run as a pack for several days before transforming back into humans, and they had helped him to kill his victims.

Romasanta then announced that he had felt the curse lift while he was in custody, and said that the blood lust no longer possessed him, but he was nevertheless condemned to death in April 1853. However, in Spain, a death sentence had to be confirmed by a special court, and a new defence lawyer for his case dismissed the notion of werewolves as a medieval superstition and argued that Romasanta was clearly insane; he was suffering from a specific mental disorder known as LYCANTHROPY, in which the victim believes himself to be a werewolf, and was thus not responsible for his actions. The case divided public opinion. The superstitious and fearful villagers believed he was indeed a werewolf, while the educated upper-class citizens, who subscribed to the new 19th-century scientific theory, saw him instead as a fascinating psychological study. The court accepted the case for his defence and commuted his death sentence to one of life imprisonment, but pressure from the newspapers caused the sentence to be changed back to death. Finally, Queen Isabella II overruled the death sentence and it was once again changed to life imprisonment. Romasanta died in prison a few years later, some say under mysterious circumstances.

R101 airship disaster

The R101 was an airship that crashed in 1930, with the loss of 46 lives. A few days after the incident, it was claimed that the spirit of the deceased airship captain appeared at a séance, through a medium some believe had also had a premonition of the disaster.

Irish (later US) MEDIUM Eileen Garrett (1893–1970) is perhaps most famous for her work following the R101 airship disaster. However, some claim that her first experience of the R101 came in the years prior to the accident, when she apparently had visions of a large airship crashing in flames.

On 4 October 1930 the British dirigible R101 took off for India. Among the passengers for the flight was the then head of civil aviation, Sir Sefton Brancker. The airship crashed in the early hours of the following day, having travelled no further than France, and killing 46 people on board, including Brancker, and the airship's commander, Flight Lieutenant H Carmichael Irwin.

On 7 October a SÉANCE was held at psychical researcher Harry Price's National Laboratory of Psychical Research in London. Attendant at this séance was self-professed trance medium (see MEDIUM, TRANCE) Eileen Garrett. Garrett had been asked to attend at the behest of one of Price's friends, a Mr Coster, who wished to know if it would be possible for her to communicate with ARTHUR CONAN DOYLE, who had died some months previously. It has been claimed that Garrett was not aware of this request.

As soon as Garret fell into her usual trance, her SPIRIT GUIDE or 'control', 'Uvani', apparently spoke through her, and after some standard greetings, said:

> I see for the moment I-R-V-I-N-G or I-R-W-I-N. He say he must do something about it … apologizes for coming … for interfering … speaks of Dora, Dorothy, Gladys … for heaven's sake, give this to them … the whole bulk of the dirigible was entirely and absolutely too much for her engine capacity.

The medium's voice then changed, and this 'different' voice claimed to be that of Flight Lieutenant Irwin. This voice went on to describe, in an agitated and broken manner, the apparent details of the crash, including a great deal of technical information relating to problems with the airship. The 'testimony' was recorded by Ethel Bennham, secretary at the Laboratory, and included such fragments as:

> … not sufficient feed – leakage. Pressure and heat produced explosion … Weather bad for long flight. Fabric all water-logged and ship's nose is down. Impossible to rise. Cannot trim. You will understand that I *had* to tell you … At inquiry to be held later it will be found that the superstructure of the envelope contained no resilience and had far too much weight in envelope. This was not so until March of this year, when no security was made by adding of super-steel structure. I knew then that this was not a dream but a nightmare. The added middle section was entirely wrong – it made strong but took resilience away and entirely impossible too heavy and too much over-weighted for the capacity of engines. From beginning of trouble I knew we had not a chance – knew it to be the feed, and we could never rise.

Was it possible that Irwin was communicating from the grave, giving evidence as to why the R101 had crashed? Garrett's supporters claimed that it was. They believed that Garrett simply did not have enough technical knowledge of flight and airships to have made the statements fraudulently. However, sceptics would point out that she had had two days to prepare, and although some of the suggestions made at the séance were borne out by the later crash investigation, this was down to little more than chance or educated guesswork.

Following 'Irwin's' communication at the séance, the medium lapsed into silence, until an entity called 'Doyle' appeared.

ropen

A winged pterosaur-like cryptid reported from Rambutyo, an island off Papua New Guinea.

The caves on the island of Rambutyo (also spelled Rambunzo), sited off the eastern coast of Papua New Guinea, are reportedly home to a modest-sized but highly intriguing winged CRYPTID known as the ropen ('demon flyer'). With a wingspan of 0.9–1.2 metres (3–4 feet), and sporting a long toothy beak and an even longer tail terminating in a diamond-shaped flange, the ropen, according to descriptions collected from the local people, strongly recalls an early fossil pterosaur known as *Rhamphorhynchus*. Also claimed to exist on the island of Umboi, situated between eastern Papua New Guinea and the large island of New Britain, it is greatly feared despite its relatively modest dimensions, as it is said to be attracted from its cave by the smell of rotting flesh – stories are told of the ropen attacking funeral parties and digging up newly buried corpses.

The ropen should not be (but very frequently is) confused with a much bigger mystery beast known correctly as the duah. Although it too is superficially pterosaurian, it has a long neck, a bony crest and enormous leathery wings said to span up to 6.1 metres (20 feet), making it more similar in overall appearance to later, more advanced pterosaurs like *Pteranodon*. The duah was reported from mainland Papua New Guinea during the 1990s by various missionaries as well as the local people there, and some claim that its underside glows when it flies overhead at night.

rope trick *see* INDIAN ROPE TRICK

Rosenheim poltergeist

A well-attested German poltergeist case from 1967.

In November 1967 a law office in the Bavarian town of Rosenheim, Germany, was the scene of an outbreak of POLTERGEIST disturbances. Light bulbs on hanging fittings would swing wildly before exploding, fluorescent lights went out repeatedly for no apparent reason and the office's electrical fuses would blow again and again. The telephone lines were particularly badly affected – sometimes the four office telephones would all ring when there were no callers on the line, and at other times phone calls would be interrupted or cut off. The telephone bills also revealed hundreds of calls that were never made, particularly numerous calls to the speaking clock, sometimes as many as six calls a minute. Initially, the lawyer Sigmund Adam suspected that the electrical supply was to blame for the alarming disturbances, and engineers were called in. They set up monitoring equipment to detect unusual fluctuations in the power supply, and these were duly recorded, often coinciding with physical disturbances in the office. However, when the office was equipped with its own power unit, which should have been immune to such fluctuations, they continued, as did the other phenomena.

Following press coverage of the unexplained occurrences at the office, a research team, led by Professor Hans Bender of the University of Freiburg, began an investigation of the phenomena. This team was later joined by members of the Max Planck Institute for Plasma Physics. Bender's team noted that the phenomena only occurred during office hours, and further, they concluded that the phenomena were linked to the presence of Annemarie Schneider, an employee in her late teens. Lights were observed and filmed swinging above her head as she walked down a corridor, and often the first power fluctuation of the day coincided with her arrival at the office. The investigations seemed to stimulate new phenomena, as pictures fell from the walls or rotated, and drawers opened and filing cabinets moved without physical intervention. When Schneider left the office to find employment elsewhere, the phenomena ceased, leaving many to conclude that that disturbances had been caused by RECURRENT SPONTANEOUS PSYCHOKINESIS, with Schneider as the focus. The case remains one of the most highly attested poltergeist incidents, with around 40 witnesses, including members of the research teams, police officers, engineers and journalists.

Rosicrucians

An occult secret society which was alleged to have been founded in the 15th century by Christian Rosencreuz and then rediscovered in the 17th century; any of various modern societies based on this tradition.

The history of Rosicrucianism is a much-debated one. In the 17th century, the existence of a secret brotherhood of alchemists and sages called the 'Order of the Rosy Cross' was proclaimed with the publication of three German texts known as the *Fama Fraternitatis Rosae Crucis* (1614), the *Confessio Fraternitatis* (1615) and *The Chemical Marriage of Christian Rosencreuz* (1616) – also collectively known as the Rosicrucian Manifestos. The first two works describe the foundation and aims of the Order, and tell the story of a poor but noble 15th-century German who went on a pilgrimage to the Holy Land, and while there, learned Arabic and studied with several Arabic alchemists. His occult studies led him to conceive of a form of Christianity united with theosophy as being an ideal religion, and he devised a plan for a universal and simultaneous reform of religion, philosophy, science, politics and art; to this end, on his return to Germany, he took the mystical name Christian Rosencreuz (Christian

Rose-Cross) and in 1407 he founded an order called The European Fraternity of the Rosy Cross, whose aim was 'to study Nature in her hidden forces' and to make its discoveries and inventions available for the benefit of mankind. Its eight members travelled incognito, healing the sick, and each had to find himself a successor so that the Order could continue its secret work. After Rosencreuz's death, so the story went, the Order carried on, but nothing was known of its existence for nearly 200 years, until its founder's perfectly preserved body was discovered in a crypt, one hand clasping a parchment scroll in which the Fraternity offered its secrets to the world. The publication of these three texts caused great excitement and sparked off many literary works, some arguing for Rosicrucianism, others against; some people eagerly sought admission to the Order, while others claimed to actually be Rosicrucians, and everyone wanted to know who its members were. But all attempts to find out anything more about the Order were unsuccessful.

Research seems to point to a Lutheran theologian called Johann Valentin Andrea as being the author of all three works (although some have argued that he in turn based them on the writings and philosophy of JOHN DEE). He was believed to have chosen the Rosy Cross as the symbol of his fictitious Order because it was an ancient symbol of occultism. Some commentators think he wrote the documents as a hoax to show how eager the people of the age were to believe in the notion of such a secret organization, but most are of the opinion that he had a vision of an enlightened and reformed society, and had created the legend of the 15th-century Order and its 17th-century 'rediscovery' and published his works in order to catalyse others into initiating Rosicrucianism as a reality. And it did in fact spread throughout Europe during the 17th century, with the formation of a number of Rosicrucian groups that combined a vision of social transformation with the study of ALCHEMY, MYSTICISM and Christian theology. Little was heard of Rosicrucian activity in Europe again until the end of the 18th century, when some of its teachings were revived by Alessandro di Cagliostro (founder of EGYPTIAN RITE FREEMASONRY) and SAINT GERMAIN, and there was considerable diffusion of ideas between Rosicrucianism and Freemasonry in England. During the late 19th century and the early 20th century, various modern groups were formed which styled themselves as Rosicrucian and claimed to be the authentic heirs to a historical tradition; among these were the Ancient Mystical Order Rosae Crucis, the Fraternitas Rosae Crucis, the Rosicrucian Fellowship and the Societas Rosicruciana. See also SECRET SOCIETIES.

Roslyn Chapel

Fifteenth-century chapel south of Edinburgh in Scotland; it is noted for its ornate interior carvings, which display links with the Knights Templar and elements of Freemasonry. There is much speculation as to the contents of its vault, which has been unopened since the 17th century, and one popular theory is that the Holy Grail is hidden somewhere in the chapel.

Roslyn Chapel (also sometimes spelled Rosslyn or Roslin) is a 15th-century building situated a few miles south of Edinburgh in Scotland. It was founded in 1446 by Sir William St Clair, who had originally planned a much larger structure in a cruciform shape with a tower at its centre. However, he died in 1484 and was buried in the unfinished chapel. Even in its incomplete state, it is a remarkable and unique construction, but during the Reformation its many statues were smashed and the original altar was destroyed, and the chapel fell into ruin. It remained abandoned until 1736, when Sir William's descendants began to repair and restore it, and it was rededicated in 1862. Restoration work continues on it to this day.

The building is most remarkable for its exquisite interior stone carvings, which fortunately have survived relatively undamaged; these are among the finest in Europe, and display imagery not found in any other 15th-century chapel. They show both Christian and pagan themes, with the GREEN MAN motif appearing many times, and much of their symbolism, along with the geometry and architecture of the building itself, links the chapel unmistakably with the KNIGHTS TEMPLAR and FREEMASONRY. It is said that after their Order was suppressed in 1314, some Knights Templar went to Scotland. Sir William St Clair is believed to have befriended some Templars, or perhaps even to have become one himself, and to have built the chapel as a lasting tribute to the Order and its mysteries; it has been suggested that his intention had been to construct it as a representation of the Temple of Solomon, and that this can be seen from its original foundations. Such is the richness of symbolism in its carvings that the chapel has been described as a 'tapestry in stone', a repository of arcane knowledge with its secrets hidden in plain sight – recorded on its very walls, ceilings and pillars, and only to be understood by those with the knowledge to decode it.

Outstanding among the chapel's carvings are the two pillars at its East end – the Mason's Pillar and the Apprentice Pillar. The latter is entwined by stone coils snaking up its length from the bottom to the top, thought to symbolize the Tree of Life, and a legend tells of how a stonemason began work on it and went to Rome to seek inspiration. While he was gone, his ambitious apprentice completed it, and when his master returned, he was so consumed by jealousy at the beauty of his work that he killed the apprentice with a blow to the head. A stone head halfway up

The Green Man in the Lady Chapel at Roslyn Chapel, one of the many ornate carvings that adorn the stonework of the building. (© Sandro Vannini/Corbis)

a wall in the south-west of the chapel is thought to represent the murdered apprentice, while two carved heads elsewhere in the chapel are said to depict his killer and his grieving mother.

The building has always attracted visitors from all over the world, but it has been the focus of increased interest since the publication of Dan Brown's 2003 novel *THE DA VINCI CODE*, in which the Holy Grail is said to be hidden in Roslyn Chapel. Brown's book is not the first to have made this suggestion; the contents of the chapel's vaults, which have been sealed up since the last burial there in the 17th century, have been the subject of much speculation over the years, and a number of books have been published suggesting that along with the remains of the St Clair family's ancestors the vaults house the Holy Grail, the Ark of the Covenant, the mummified head of Christ, a piece of the true cross of Christ, or scrolls bearing the lost gospels of Jesus. These various sacred relics are supposed to have been discovered by the Knights Templar while they were excavating in the Holy Land, and after their order was disbanded, they are said to have brought them to Scotland and hidden them in the chapel. One theory claims that the Holy Grail is built into the Apprentice Pillar.

Roswell

Site of the most famous UFO case in the world, around which many myths and legends have grown. The story includes the discovery of unexplained debris by a rancher in 1947 – the debate as to whether this came from an alien spacecraft or something more mundane continues to this day.

William 'Mac' Brazel was foreman on a ranch around 130 kilometres (80 miles) north of the town of Roswell, New Mexico. On the stormy night of 2 July 1947 he heard a mysterious explosion somewhere over the desert scrub. The next day he set out to investigate, concerned that his stock might have been injured by what he presumed was a lightning strike. Instead he found a mass of debris scattered over a wide area – including silvery foil, thin pieces of a balsa-like wood and parchment with what seemed to be stained marks or writing on it. There was also a gouged mark on the ground. It looked as if something had been dragged along the desert floor before breaking up.

Just a few days earlier the KENNETH ARNOLD sighting had occurred, the 1947 WAVE of UFO sightings was entering full swing and UFOs were big news. Brazel was not sure what he had found but, thinking that it might be connected with the military, he picked up some of the smaller pieces and decided to take them to the large Army and Air Force base at Roswell when he next visited the town. This was the area where the early US experiments into rocket technology and nuclear weapons were underway – much of the activity naturally being subject to secrecy.

Brazel did not visit Roswell until 6 July. The debris found its way from the Sheriff to the Air Base, where Major Jesse Marcel took charge of the recovery of the rest. He spent the night on Brazel's land filling a pick-up truck with the material. It seems that there was general puzzlement as to what this debris might be – speculation was rife to the effect that it came from one of the FLYING SAUCERS being discussed in the media. Once Marcel was back in town, the base decided to issue a press release – the results of which seem to have taken them by surprise.

The local paper, the *Roswell Daily Record*, featured the story under the headline 'RAAF captures flying saucer on ranch in Roswell region' on 8 July. This told how:

> … the intelligence office of the 509th bombardment group at Roswell Army Air Field (RAAF) announced at noon today that the field has come into possession of a flying saucer.

It quoted Major Marcel and added that the 'instrument' had been found near the town. The actual press release, made available only 30 years later via the FREEDOM OF INFORMATION ACT, calls the wreckage a 'flying object' and a 'disc'; however, in hindsight, the use of the word 'instrument' in the newspaper report may be telling.

Within hours the press story was distributed via the news wires. It created a sensation. The Pentagon reacted in horror and put pressure on radio station owners and newspaper editors to drop the story. Meanwhile, the wreckage was being ferried 'by special plane' to Wright Field in Dayton, Ohio (see AREA 51), soon to become the home of the US government UFO study, PROJECT SIGN. Some of the crew of that flight claimed, many years later, that they were told that they were ferrying something that just might be an ALIEN device.

As the plane was heading to Wright Field it stopped off at regional headquarters in Carswell, Texas, where Marcel disembarked to pose for an invited press photographer. Here some of the debris was displayed and filmed. A new press release was issued by the Air Force saying that the material had now been identified as the wreckage of a weather balloon. Several of those present, Marcel included, later insisted that this was a cover story, hastily concocted to stem the tide of publicity while experts searched for the truth.

The media accepted the explanation and the story was rapidly forgotten, only to be rediscovered by the UFO COMMUNITY some 30 years later. By this time, many of the original witnesses had died. However, others had now retired from the military and were willing to talk. It was at this stage that the story that was to become the Roswell legend was pieced together – yet none of the principal witnesses ever described seeing a spacecraft, let alone any aliens. The stories that link the case with claims relating to bodies and a crashed spaceship all appeared after the case was promoted by UFO researchers in the late 1970s.

Since its 'rediscovery' the Roswell story has assumed a prominence way beyond any other case in UFO history. Real people, such as the long-dead Jesse Marcel, have featured as characters in television series built around the case – such as UFO cover-up drama, *Dark Skies* (1996–7). In 1994 a film called *Roswell* told a fairly sober version of the story, but countless others have featured it in more fanciful terms. It has spawned comedy episodes of both the television drama series *Star Trek*, and the cartoon series *Futurama*. There has even been a TV serial, called *Roswell High*, based around the fictional adventures of aliens stranded in the town after the crash and forced to attend the local high school in disguise.

As to what was really found on Brazel's ranch in 1947, what is probably the most likely explanation surfaced in 1995, after an independent investigation into government records conducted by the General

Viking runes engraved on a stone at Maes Howe near Stromness in the Orkney Islands. (© Homer Sykes/Corbis)

Accounting Office. According to their findings, the debris was indeed from a balloon, but not the ordinary weather balloon that was put on show at Carswell. It was a complex instrument package attached to a new type of high-altitude balloon that was being used in an experiment. The covert project was looking for signs that the Soviet Union had detonated their first atomic weapons. None of the staff at Roswell Air Base knew about it, and it is very likely that they were genuinely mystified. Once the Pentagon discovered the truth they had genuine reasons, totally unconnected with UFOs, to stop the media from investigating.

RSPK *see* RECURRENT SPONTANEOUS

PSYCHOKINESIS

runes

A set of letters forming an ancient Germanic or Anglo-Saxon alphabet, in use from around the 2nd century AD to the end of the Middle Ages for writing, magic and divination; a set of tiles or stones inscribed with runes, used for divination.

Runes were used as the writing system of various North European countries, mainly Scandinavia and the British Isles, from about the 2nd century AD onward. Each culture which used them adapted them to accommodate changes in their languages, creating new runes, rearranging or renaming the ones they retained, and dropping any which became obsolete for their purposes. The three best-known runic alphabets are the Elder or Germanic Futhark, consisting of 24 runic letters; the Anglo-Saxon Futhorc, with 29 or 33 runes; and the Younger Futhark, a reduced form of the Elder Futhark with only 16 runes, several of which represent multiple sounds. Their names are derived from the first six letters in each alphabet – F, U, Th, A or O, R, and K or C.

According to myth, runes were invented by the Norse god Odin, who hung upside down from Yggdrasil, the World Tree, for nine days and nights to discover them. At the end of this self-inflicted torment, he had a blinding flash of insight which allowed him to realize their full potential for human use.

Runes are believed to have been first used for magical purposes – the Old English and Old Norse word *rūn* means 'a secret or mystery' – then for everyday writing. As a writing system, runes were generally replaced by the Latin alphabet with the growth of Christianity, but they continued to be used in magic, where they were often employed in spells, for healing, as TALISMANS and as a DIVINATION tool. Each rune, as well as having a literal meaning which relates to its name and the speech sound it represents, also has a precise concept in its own right, which encapsulates a symbolic meaning. The main source of information on these meanings is an Anglo-Saxon rune poem translated by monks from Old English into Latin. This poem names each rune in turn and gives its associations, and was presumably used as an aid in memorizing and passing on their lore. For example, the rune whose sound is F has the name Feoh or Fehu, which literally means 'cattle', but it also represents wealth, and thus the power needed to gain and hold on to wealth, making it a rune of power and control. These symbolic meanings make the runes an appropriate tool for both magic and divination.

There are a number of ways of using runes for divination. The natural world can be studied for runic patterns, for example in the branches of trees, markings on stones, and so on. Rune sticks can be used; nine sticks are cut from a tree, preferably a birch or rowan, and held loosely in both hands before being thrown on to a casting cloth. Any sticks which do not fall completely on to the cloth do not count and are put aside, and the overlapping patterns of the remaining sticks are examined for rune shapes. A set of stones or pieces of wood can be used, inscribed with a different rune on each. A single rune may be selected from this set at random and its meaning interpreted, or in a method sometimes called 'The Three Fates', or 'The Three Norns', three runes are selected, representing the past, the present and the future, or the present state, the possible action and the outcome of this action. Alternatively, all the stones or pieces of wood can be cast; those which fall face down are discarded, and from the remaining ones, those closest to the reader are interpreted. The stones or pieces of wood can also be selected at random and set out in a specific pattern like a tarot spread, and rune cards can be used in a similar way. Special sets of dice with a rune on each face are sometimes cast instead of rune stones.

Ruppelt, Edward J (1922–59)

The first head of the US Air Force UFO study, Project Blue Book, who briefly succeeded in making the investigation of the phenomenon objective and scientific.
When Captain Edward J Ruppelt was invited to take charge of PROJECT GRUDGE in 1951, the US Air Force UFO study was in a state of stagnation. It involved a single filing clerk, based at Wright Patterson Air Force Base in Ohio. The aim was to maintain the impression that the Pentagon was taking UFOs seriously but, in reality, no real investigation was being carried out.

However, public interest in UFOs had been heightened following the publication of a number of successful magazine articles and a book by Major DONALD KEYHOE. He argued that the US government knew that aliens were visiting but was afraid to admit this to the public. Ruppelt was seen as the ideal man to counter

this – he was known to be a thorough investigator, with no prior interest in UFOs. The hope was that his appointment would appease the general public.

Ruppelt took to his new job with great enthusiasm. He revitalized the investigation procedure, often flying hundreds of miles to get evidence, and he designed a new approach employing objective scientific methods. He was behind the change of name to PROJECT BLUE BOOK, and he also pioneered the use of the term 'UFO', which was seen as a much more restrained description than emotive phrases such as 'FLYING SAUCER'.

Unfortunately, his tenacity brought unexpected problems. When Ruppelt could not solve a case he was willing to entertain the possibility of a real UFO. During his tenure there was huge controversy when a major WAVE of sightings occurred in restricted air space over WASHINGTON. So much publicity surrounded these events that US government policy was changed – the CIA were given a direct role in UFO investigations. Ruppelt found that when he attempted to investigate sightings he met with resistance from his superiors. At one stage he was even apparently threatened with a charge of going AWOL if he did not stop investigating the incidents.

Ruppelt began to wonder if he was being manipulated and, during 1953, he decided to leave the Air Force. In 1956 he published a book, the first by a professional UFO investigator, in which he revealed details of the forensic study of several dramatic cases. This book – *The Report on Unidentified Flying Objects* – is still regarded by many as one of the most persuasive documents in support of the existence of a genuine scientific anomaly.

However, Ruppelt made a sudden and dramatic U-turn. Three years after the publication of the book he added extra chapters and denounced his previous leanings towards the alien origin of some UFOs. He also withdrew his speculation with regard to a GOVERNMENTAL COVER-UP. He argued that UFOs were easy to explain and was less than complimentary about the thriving UFO COMMUNITY. Ruppelt implied that this change of heart was due to the fanciful stories coming from members of the CONTACTEE movement at the time – he found them so absurd that they had destroyed his previous faith. An alternative theory became popular among UFO enthusiasts – they claimed that he had been 'persuaded' to change his tune because of the influence of his book. However, while it is possible to see how the CIA might have been worried by Ruppelt's book, at a time when it is suspected they were involved in secret attempts to ridicule UFO research, there is no evidence to support this idea. Sadly, Ruppelt was never able to answer the claim – shortly after the new edition of his book appeared he died from a heart attack, at the age of 37.

sabbats

In modern paganism and witchcraft, eight seasonal festivals that are celebrated each year; historically, the word 'sabbat' was used to refer to meetings of witches, where they allegedly took part in devil-worship and obscene behaviour.

Many modern pagans and practitioners of WITCHCRAFT celebrate eight festivals in the year, known as the major sabbats and the minor sabbats. The four minor sabbats are the AUTUMNAL EQUINOX, SUMMER SOLSTICE, VERNAL EQUINOX and WINTER SOLSTICE, and the four major sabbats are BELTANE, IMBOLC, LUGHNASADH and SAMHAIN. Not all modern traditions celebrate all of the sabbats, but generally the sabbats are times of rejoicing, feasting and dancing, honouring THE GODDESS, HORNED GOD and Nature.

Historically, the word 'sabbat' was used to refer to the alleged meetings of witches where they were said to form pacts with the DEVIL, hold orgies and copulate with DEMONS. At a time when witches were persecuted, they were said to fly to sabbats on

Witches feast at the sabbat and are waited on by demons. From the *Compendium Maleficarum* (1626) by Francesco Maria Guazzo. (© Mary Evans Picture Library)

BROOMSTICKS, accompanied by their FAMILIARS, where they would perform the *OSCULUM INFAME* and take part in other unspeakable acts. While many people accused of witchcraft admitted that they had attended sabbats, and named others who had done so, it is likely that such confessions were simply the result of torture, and that the historical witches' sabbat was an invention of the WITCHFINDERS and others who campaigned against witches.

sacrifices

The ritual practice of offering food, or the lives of animals or humans, to the gods as an act of worship, propitiation or supplication.

The word 'sacrifice' comes from the Latin *sacrificium*, meaning 'to make sacred'. The RITUAL practice of offering food or sacrificial animal or human victims to the gods is an ancient one, and is found in many religions. The sacrifice may be made because it is believed that the gods, like humans, require sustenance, and will diminish without it; to atone for the sins of the individual or community, in the hope that the gods will give something in return for the offering; or in an attempt to appease the gods' anger.

The sacrifice may be of fruit, vegetables, bread or grain, but the practice of animal or human sacrifice is also found in many ancient cultures, such as those of the Hebrews, Greeks and Romans, and the pre-Columbian civilizations of Mesoamerica, most notably the Incas, Mayans and Aztecs. The life or blood of the victim may have been thought to contain some vital force which was pleasing to the gods. In modern times, Muslims, some Hindu sects and practitioners of syncretic religions such as CANDOMBLÉ still perform animal sacrifices, usually as part of a religious ritual or festival in which the meat from the sacrifices is shared among the participants after the ritual. In ancient Judaism, the sacrifice of animals, as well as of grain and wine, was regarded as part of serving God; however, after the destruction of the Second Temple in AD 70, animal sacrifice ceased to be practised among the Jewish people.

A number of ancient civilizations practised human sacrifice. Sometimes this was done to dedicate a new temple, or on the death of a king, high priest or great leader, with the intention that the victims would accompany and serve the dead person in the afterlife. Also, natural disasters such as floods, droughts, earthquakes and volcanic eruptions were seen by many ancient peoples as signs of the gods' displeasure, which could only be propitiated by human sacrifice. The Incas are believed to have sacrificed children, especially those of their nobles, presumably offering the most precious thing they had to the gods; these victims were mainly killed by being drugged and buried alive in high mountain shrines, where their mummified bodies have been found, richly dressed and startlingly well preserved, hundreds of years later. The Aztecs, on the other hand, preferred to sacrifice the hearts of human victims in bloody rituals, particularly to the plumed serpent god Quetzalcoatl, and it is thought that they performed a human sacrifice every day to help the sun to rise, while the dedication of the great temple at Tenochtitlán was marked by the sacrifice of thousands of victims. It is thought that these victims were usually prisoners or conquered peoples, and during the wars of the Spanish Conquest in Mexico in the 16th century, captured Spanish Conquistadores were reported to have been sacrificed in this way.

sages

Old men revered for their profound wisdom; the sage is a classic figure in legend and literature, and is an archetype as described by Carl Jung.

The word 'sage' comes from the Latin verb *sapere*, meaning 'to be wise'. The figure of the old man revered for his profound wisdom is an ancient and powerful one in mythology and legend, and is a classic figure in literature; CARL JUNG described the ARCHETYPE of the Wise Old Man, or 'Senex', as a father-like being who uses his knowledge to help the hero, or mankind, by offering guidance. He is often represented as being in some way 'alien', coming from a different culture or country to that of the people he advises. Tiresias in Greek mythology, Odin, the principal god of Norse myth, and the pagan wizard of Arthurian legend, Merlin, are all examples of the archetypal sage. In more recent times, the wizard Gandalf in J R R Tolkien's *Lord of the Rings* trilogy, and Professor Albus Dumbledore in J K Rowling's *Harry Potter* series, carry on the literary tradition of the sage.

The word 'sage' is also used historically to refer to the scholars and biblical interpreters, known as the *Hazal*, who were the active leaders and teachers of the Jewish religion from the beginning of the second Temple period until the Arabian conquest of the East. In Hinduism, sages are known as *rishis*, and are regarded as a combination of patriarch, priest, saint, ascetic and hermit. In the Vedas, the term *rishi* is also used specifically to denote the authors of the *Rig-Veda*, who were said to have 'heard' the Vedic hymns from the Supreme Being, Brahman, while in deep meditation; according to legend, these Hindu sages possessed extraordinary magical powers, such as the ability to fly, and much of Sanskrit literature is devoted to their superhuman exploits. The most famous of the many Chinese sages who have influenced Oriental religion and philosophy for many centuries are Confucius and LAO TZU, the founders of Confucianism and TAOISM respectively.

Sagittarius

In astrology, the ninth sign of the zodiac, between Scorpio and Capricorn.

In Western ASTROLOGY, Sagittarius is the sign of the ZODIAC for those who are born between 23 November and 22 December. The symbol for Sagittarius is the archer, and the sign is ruled by Jupiter. Sagittarians are said to be strong-willed and idealistic, although they can be rebellious. Sagittarius is believed to be a fire sign, having an affinity with the element FIRE.

Sai Baba (c.1838–1918)

Indian spiritual guide, regarded by millions of followers as a saint and as an incarnation of Shiva and Dattatreya.

Little is known for certain about the birth and early life of Sai Baba of Shirdi. A number of people believe that he was born to Brahmin parents in the village of Pathri, in the Parabhani district of the Indian state of Marathwada, around 1838, and that after being abandoned, he was adopted by a FAKIR and later put in the care of a guru with whom he stayed for twelve years. He is said to have arrived in the village of Shirdi in the state of Maharashtra at the age of about 16, initially staying on the outskirts, then sleeping on the floor of a Khandoba temple, and finally moving into a dilapidated mosque, where he spent the rest of his days, living a simple, ascetic life as a mendicant monk. His given name is not known; a villager called Mahalsapathi who came to worship at the temple first addressed him as 'Sai' ('saint'), and he soon attracted followers who called him 'Baba' ('father').

By example, and by his teachings, Sai Baba tried to embrace and reconcile the two apparently disparate faiths of Hinduism and Islam, encouraging tolerance between them, regularly reciting both Hindu and Muslim prayers, worshipping at both Hindu temples and Muslim mosques, and teaching using figures and words from both traditions. Numerous MIRACLES were attributed to him, such as the healing of the sick, clairvoyance and controlling the elements, and crowds of pilgrims came to be blessed by him. He left no written records, but in his teachings, which were typically short, pithy sayings, he advocated simplicity, charity and compassion. He died in 1908, and his shrine, the Samadhi Mandir, is visited by many pilgrims every day. With millions of devotees in India and other parts of the world, Sai Baba is regarded by his Hindu and Muslim followers as a saint, and many of his Hindu devotees believe him to be an incarnation of Shiva and Dattatreya.

Several gurus have, since his death, claimed to be the reincarnation of Sai Baba of Shirdi, the best-known of whom is Sathyta Sai Baba, born in 1926.

Saint Germain, Comte de (?–c.1784)

Eighteenth-century French courtier, adventurer and alleged occultist. His date of birth is unknown, but he was rumoured to possess the secret of eternal life and to have lived for centuries. Although he is thought to have died in the 1780s, many occultists believe that he is engaged in the spiritual development of the West as an Ascended Master.

The Comte de St Germain as a historical figure is known to have lived in Europe in the 18th century.

Sathyta Sai Baba with his followers at Puttaparti Ashram. Sathyta Sai Baba claims he is the reincarnation of Sai Baba. (© Christophe Boisvieux/Corbis)

A mysterious and enigmatic man, he never revealed details of his background or identity, and his date of birth is unknown. There has been much speculation as to his ancestry, but the most plausible theories are that he was the son of the exiled Transylvanian Prince Ferenc Rakoczy II, or the illegitimate son of Marie-Anne de Neuborg, widow of Charles II of Spain. Either would put his date of birth at some time around 1700, since at the time of his first chronicled appearance in Europe in 1743, he was described as being a man in his mid-forties. However, part of his legend is that he is supposed to have retained this appearance until his death in the 1780s, never seeming to get any older, and he frequently hinted that he was hundreds of years old.

He was said to be fluent in many languages, and to be an accomplished violinist. He was reputed to be a student of the OCCULT, particularly ALCHEMY; it was rumoured that he could transmute base metals to gold, had a secret technique for removing flaws from diamonds, and possessed the ELIXIR OF LIFE. He was also an astute politician, and a friend and confidential adviser to Louis XV of France. He was considered by many to be a spy, and to be working for Frederick the Great of Prussia as well as for the King of France, and Henry Walpole wrote that he had been arrested in London for spying in 1743. In 1760 he travelled through England, the Netherlands and Russia, where later conspiracy theories would credit him with having helped the Russian army to put Catherine the Great on the throne in 1762. He then apparently vanished for over a decade, reappearing in France in 1774, where he was said to have tried to warn Louis XVI and Marie Antoinette through PROPHECY, some 15 years before the event, of the French Revolution and its consequences for them both, although his warning was unheeded. He is generally thought to have died in 1784, although according to some accounts he was seen in Paris in 1789, with other people claiming to have sighted him in Paris in 1835 and in Milan in 1867.

In the centuries since his death, many stories and legends have grown around this mysterious figure. According to some, he was immortal, an alchemist who had discovered the secret of eternal life. Others said he was a reincarnation of the prophet Samuel; of Joseph, stepfather of Jesus; of Merlin; of Christopher Columbus; and of Sir Francis Bacon. Some hold that he was a member of the ROSICRUCIANS, or the Freemasons (see FREEMASONRY), or the KNIGHTS TEMPLAR, and others that he was a reincarnation of Christian Rosencreuz, the mythical founder of the Rosicrucian Order. Napoleon III compiled a huge dossier on him, which was later destroyed in a fire. Many esoteric movements recognize him as an ASCENDED MASTER and a great adept, part of the Great White Brotherhood which is said to protect the wisdom of the ages. ALEISTER CROWLEY identified with him, and MADAME BLAVATSKY said that he was one of her Masters of Wisdom, declaring that he was still alive and engaged in the spiritual development of the West, living in a lamasery in an inaccessible part of the Himalayas in Tibet. The theosophist CHARLES W LEADBEATER claimed to have met him in Rome in 1926, and GUY W BALLARD, founder of the I Am Religious Activity (see I AM MOVEMENT) said he met Saint Germain in California in 1929 or 1930.

saints

People who, after death, are recognized as having been particularly holy and worthy of veneration. In the Christian and Orthodox Church, sainthood is conferred by a formal process of canonization, but in other religious traditions, such as Islam and Hinduism, there is no such process. Saints are generally regarded as having powers of intercession with God and the ability to perform miracles.

The word 'saint' comes from the Latin *sanctus*, meaning holy, and the term 'saint' may be applied to a person of any religion who, after their death, is recognized as having lived a holy life and thus being worthy of veneration. Saints of almost all belief systems are thought to have special powers of intercession with God, so they are appealed to for help by believers, and they are also thought to be able to perform MIRACLES, often through their RELICS. The most well-known saints are those of the Christian, and in particular the Roman Catholic, tradition. Early Christian saints were recognized as such by public acclaim, and were generally martyrs – those who had died for their faith – but gradually, as the persecution of Christians ceased, many individuals who were not martyrs but who had lived exemplary lives of holiness, asceticism or chastity also came to be acknowledged as saints. From the 10th century onward, the conferring of sainthood was the province of the Catholic Church, and was done by a formal process of canonization; from the 13th century onward, only the Pope could canonize a person as a saint. For full sainthood, particular importance is placed on miracles attributed to the person after their death. The Orthodox Church also has a formal process of canonization, carried out by synods of bishops. Sometimes a Christian saint is recognized or chosen as a patron saint, or special protector of a place or trade, or appealed to in specific circumstances; for example, St Anthony of Padua is prayed to for help in finding lost objects.

Islam also venerates holy people, and particularly their tombs; while there is no formal canonization process, the traditions of the prophets and the sayings of Islamic scholars describe the qualities of true saints, or *awliya* (literally 'Friends of God'). Similarly, saints are recognized in Hinduism, but no formal process is required. One of the most famous of Hindu saints, Raghavendra Swami, is said to have performed miracles in his own lifetime, and SAI BABA is also regarded by his followers as a saint. In Buddhism, a fully enlightened person, or Holy One, such as Gautama Buddha, is also considered worthy of reverence, and may be regarded as a saint.

salamanders

Elemental spirits believed to live in fire.
Alchemists believed that just as visible Nature is inhabited by living creatures, so the four ELEMENTS (FIRE, WATER, EARTH and AIR) were populated by a host of beings known as ELEMENTALS – beings with bodies and spirits but no soul, which inhabited the intermediate world between the material and the immaterial. The concept of elementals still survives among some modern magicians, who claim that they call on their help as part of their magical workings.

The spirits which lived in fire were known as salamanders, and it was thought that without their assistance, material fire could not be created. Salamanders were said to be the strongest and most powerful of the elementals, and were ruled by a magnificent and terrible flaming spirit called Djinn. They were divided into several types; those of the most common form (the Urodela) were said to be lizard-like in shape and a foot or more in length, and it was held that they could be seen twisting and moving in the heart of a fire. Others (the Acthnici) were visible as small indistinct balls of light which floated over water at night and sometimes appeared as tongues of flame on the rigging and masts of ships (now usually explained as the electrical phenomenon called ST ELMO'S FIRE). Members of the third group were described as flaming giants in flowing robes, clad in sheets of fiery armour. Salamanders were thought to have an affinity for the south, since this was the cardinal direction which the ancients associated with heat and fire, and to exert a particular influence over people of a fiery or tempestuous nature.

The Salem Witches *see panel p598*

salt

One of the three basic 'principles' that alchemists believed to be present in all material substances.
Alchemists believed that all physical substances could be divided, via alchemical processes, into the 'three principles' of which they were ultimately composed – salt, SULPHUR and MERCURY. Also known as the

tria prima, these three principles were present in all base matter, and were said to be in perfect balance in gold. The salt to which alchemists referred in this context was not common sodium chloride, but the physical body of the substance; after the sulphur and mercury had been extracted alchemically, they believed the remaining material could be burned in a process of purification and reduced to ash, then reduced further to a fine powder, and this remaining powder was the substance's salt. This notion of the three 'heavenly substances' was central to the scheme of Nature proposed by PARACELSUS, who held that salt represented the principle of incombustibility and non-volatility, and that in a spiritual sense, it corresponded to the body.

samadhi

A state of super-awareness which is said to be brought about by profound yogic meditation, in which the yogi becomes one with the object of meditation.
The Sanskrit word *samadhi* is used in YOGA and Buddhist meditation to refer to an apparent state in which all mental functions except for consciousness have ceased. In this state of pure awareness, the yogi (ie the practitioner) is aware of his or her own existence, but without thinking; the object of meditation is consciousness itself, and the practitioner attains a sense of oneness and identification with his or her 'Atman', or true soul.

Sometimes referred to as 'one-pointedness of mind', samadhi is understood to have three levels or intensities. In the first, Laja Samadhi ('latent' samadhi), a feeling of joy, wellbeing and peace is experienced. In the second stage, Savikalpa Samadhi, bliss and 'Beingness' begin to be experienced, but the mind is still present; the yogi remains aware of and identifies with his or her body, and is still in a subject–object relationship with the world. With the third intensity, Nirvikalpa Samadhi, pure awareness and a sense of oneness with the Atman is achieved – a non-dual union with one's own consciousness.

Samadhi is said to be attained through the advanced and prolonged practice of yoga, and is held to be the only unchanging reality. All else, being constantly changing, cannot bring lasting peace or happiness. In samadhi, all awareness of and attachment to the material world, and all KARMA, is dissolved. During the process, breathing and heartbeat are both said to cease. Unless the practitioner eventually returns from samadhi, NIRVANA, also known as Maha Samadhi or Great Samadhi, is reached; this is the realized yogi's conscious departure from the physical body, or death, when the personal soul is surrendered to God and is dissolved into the Divine. However, it is believed that the truly enlightened can remain in Nirvikalpa

The Salem Witches

In January 1692, in the village of Salem, Massachusetts, both the daughter and the niece of Reverend Samuel Parris became ill. Nine-year-old Betty Parris began to have fits and make strange noises, and when she and her cousin, 11-year-old Abigail Williams, were examined by the local doctor, William Griggs, he diagnosed bewitchment. This diagnosis started a chain of events, now claimed by many to be an example of MASS HYSTERIA, that led to the execution of 20 people as WITCHES and ensured that the Salem WITCH TRIALS became the most famous witch trials of all.

In the 1690s the New England community of Salem Village was beset by troubles. A recent smallpox epidemic, land disputes with nearby Salem Town, the threat of attack by Native American tribes, and a strong belief in the DEVIL all added to the fear and suspicion of the villagers. The two 'afflicted' girls (Betty and Abigail) were the first to level accusations of WITCHCRAFT, by crying out the names of those that possessed them and caused their afflictions – they accused Tituba (the Parris's Caribbean slave, who had been known to tell the girls stories of her native folklore and VOUDUN) and the local women Sarah Good (a homeless beggar) and Sarah Osborne (known to have lived with her hired hand before marrying him, and thought immoral). Several other Salem girls also began to exhibit strange behaviour, and as time went on, other witnesses made accusations – Ann Putnam and Mary Warren also had fits and cried out names, and when Sarah Churchill refused to testify against her master, it is believed that these two forced her to change her mind. While many of those accused were perhaps 'easy' targets – those who did not attend church regularly or were regarded with suspicion by the community – less-likely witches were also named. Ann Putnam and other girls claimed that the spectre of Rebecca Nurse – a 71-year old woman

Children accuse adults of witchcraft in a 19th-century illustration of the Salem witch trials.
(© Bettmann/Corbis)

who was well-liked in Salem – came to their rooms at night, pinching and torturing them. Nurse was later hanged.

Witchcraft was punishable by death in New England, and eventually more than 150 men and women were in prison awaiting trial. In June 1692, a special Court of Oyer (to hear) and Terminer (to decide) sat in Salem to hear the cases. The first person tried was Bridget Bishop, who by Puritan standards led a somewhat outrageous lifestyle – she was found guilty and hanged. The court held three 'hanging days', executing a total of 14 women and 5 men in this manner. One further man, an elderly farmer called Giles Corey, refused to enter a plea at his trial, and was crushed to death with large stones. The Court of Oyer and Terminer was disbanded in October 1692, and replaced with a Superior Court of Judicature. This court did not allow 'spectral evidence' – that is, it did not accept the belief of the earlier court that the accused could use spectres to attack their victims. The new court released those who had not been tried and pardoned those awaiting execution. The witch trials were over.

A number of theories have been put forward to explain the tragic events in Salem. Many say that mass hysteria was responsible – the young girls who made the first accusations were suffering from adolescent hysteria, and the involvement of clerics such as COTTON MATHER did much to fuel panic in a community that was already full of fear and suspicion. When George Burroughs recited the Lord's Prayer at his execution, many doubted his guilt, but Mather persuaded the crowd that he was guilty all the same, and the execution went ahead. Some believe that some of the accusations were motivated by a desire to appropriate the land of certain elderly spinsters. Another theory holds that several of those involved may have been poisoned by eating rye infected with the ergot fungus – now known to have psychedelic and hallucinatory effects – but there is no definitive answer to explain the girls' behaviour.

Samadhi indefinitely while also fully functioning in this world.

Samhain
One of the four major sabbats of modern paganism, celebrated on or around 31 October.

The word 'samhain' comes from the Irish and Scots Gaelic and loosely means 'end of summer'. In pagan tradition it is associated with the final harvest and the beginning of winter and in the ancient Celtic calendar it marked the beginning of the new year (see PAGANISM).

As with many of the other SABBATS recognized by modern pagans, celebrations traditionally involved fire and the slaughter of animals. Some of the traditions associated with the festival survive into modern times in the form of the practices associated with HALLOWE'EN. See also AUTUMNAL EQUINOX; BELTANE; IMBOLC; LUGHNASADH; SUMMER SOLSTICE; VERNAL EQUINOX; WICCA; WINTER SOLSTICE.

Sanders, Alex(ander) (1926–88)
English occultist and self-styled 'King of the Witches'; founder of the Alexandrian tradition in modern witchcraft.

Alex Sanders was born Orell Alexander Carter in Birkenhead near Liverpool, and was the son of a music-hall entertainer. He said that he was initiated into 'the Craft' (ie WITCHCRAFT) at the age of seven by his grandmother, Mary Bibby. He claimed his grandmother was a hereditary WITCH, and also claimed that when he discovered her standing naked in a circle drawn on the kitchen floor she revealed her secrets to him, and gave him her 'book of shadows' (her personal collection of SPELLS and witch lore). She also apparently taught him a number of magical rites. He went on to discover his own PSYCHIC powers.

After many years in a number of minor jobs, and a first marriage that lasted only five years, he decided to take the LEFT-HAND PATH, experimenting with a variety of OCCULT practices, before settling on WICCA and forming his first coven in the early 1960s. It was at this point that he began to rise to public fame, courting publicity and media attention, starting with a front-page article in the *Manchester Evening News* in 1962.

During the 1960s he made extravagant claims about the number of his followers, and said that they had persuaded him to be elected 'King of the Witches'. He allegedly carried out many magical feats, sometimes with the help of his spirit FAMILIARS, and was particularly known for his magical 'cures'. He met and married his 'high priestess', Maxine Morris, and together they ran a coven and taught many people the Craft. Towards the end of the decade he managed

Alex Sanders with his 'high priestess' Maxine Morris, photographed in 1966. (© TopFoto)

to attract much media publicity, regularly appearing in newspapers and on television programmes, and in 1969 he became the subject of a biographical book, *King of the Witches* by June Johns, and a film, *Legend of the Witches*.

Sanders's media antics upset many of his contemporary Wiccans, particularly as it became clear that many of his writings and teachings were simply copied from those of GERALD GARDNER and ÉLIPHAS LÉVI (among others). However, he remains one of the most prominent (if controversial) figures of modern witchcraft and continues to have a following in many countries to this day.

Sanderson, Ivan T *see* SOCIETY FOR THE INVESTIGATION OF THE UNEXPLAINED

Santería
A Caribbean religion combining African beliefs and Roman Catholicism.

Broadly speaking, Santería is the Caribbean equivalent of the Brazilian religion CANDOMBLÉ and the Haitian religion VOUDUN.

Like other African-American religions, Santería combines African beliefs, especially Yoruban beliefs from West Africa, with elements of Roman Catholicism. The name 'Santería' was originally pejorative; it was coined by whites, and referred to the religion's great emphasis on the saints. Practitioners usually call their religion *Regla de Ocha* or 'Reign of the Orishas', Orishas being approachable African deities below the remote High God, Olorun. Some revered ancestors have achieved the status of Orishas, and these are often identified with images of Catholic saints.

Santería is spread throughout the Spanish Caribbean, and is particularly strong in Puerto Rico and Cuba. Its leaders are called *santeros* or *Babalochas* (male) and *santeras* or *Iyalochas* (female).

As with similar syncretic (see SYNCRETISM) religions, dance and music are an important part of the rituals of Santería. Particular drum rhythms are used to invoke certain Orishas, who possess the priests or priestesses, speaking through them. Animal sacrifice is also often part of the ritual. The animals, generally chickens, are killed humanely and are normally later eaten. Complaints about the animal sacrifices have led to a number of court cases in the USA, culminating in a ruling of the US Supreme Court that the practice was permissible under the First Amendment on freedom of religion.

Santilli film

Reels of what were apparently old film of an autopsy carried out on an alien body recovered from the Roswell crash.

In the autumn of 1993 the British UFO COMMUNITY learned that an 82-year-old man in the USA claimed to be in possession of film footage taken during an ALIEN AUTOPSY carried out in 1947 near ROSWELL, New Mexico. He had allegedly held this film in his attic for 46 years without the Pentagon knowing, but was now endeavouring to sell it. The price quoted to the BRITISH UFO RESEARCH ASSOCIATION (BUFORA) was well beyond their means, and buyers were not to be allowed an opportunity to have the film analysed before concluding a deal.

The man claimed that he had been taken to the desert a day after the Roswell crash and shown what he thought were 'circus freaks' amid the wreckage. These small humanoids were alive but under attack by US servicemen, who hit them with rifle butts, tied them up and dragged them away. He had apparently been asked to film one of the now-dead beings inside a nearby tent. Then, some time later, he was taken to a secret base and asked to film the autopsy carried out on one of the bodies in a clean, white room.

The source of most of this information (as supplied to BUFORA) was a London video entrepreneur called Ray Santilli, who said that he had heard the story when purchasing old Elvis Presley footage from this man. He took some time to agree to pay the asking price for the Roswell film but, realizing its potential value, he completed the deal in late 1994. He showed brief snatches of what was said to be the tent footage to several people, including a BUFORA officer, but

it was dimly lit and did not impress those who saw it. Interestingly, this footage was not subsequently released.

In the spring of 1995 Santilli invited a number of guests to a London preview. The much clearer shots he showed do appear to show figures in white gowns fussing about a human-like body and taking indistinct organs from the open chest cavity. However, there is nothing unmistakably ALIEN about the subject of the apparent autopsy.

BUFORA was granted an exclusive full presentation of the footage, under strict security, at a conference in Sheffield four months later. This screening was in advance of its release on video and formed part of a major marketing exercise. Many UFO researchers were wary of the footage, since it did not match what was known about the Roswell case, and some expressed disenchantment with BUFORA over their plans. Moreover, the Roswell incident had recently been explained as resulting from a top-secret balloon project, and a number of UFO researchers had accepted this. By now, some experts in film technology had also raised doubts about the antiquity of the footage, although it also had some supporters.

After 1995, UFO researchers made a number of attempts to track down the supposed source of the footage. However, the story was not widely regarded to be of great importance and largely disappeared. Then, in April 2006, a big-budget film of the story was released under the title *Alien Autopsy*. Popular television stars, Ant and Dec, played Ray Santilli and a work partner. Statements made by Santilli, tying in with the theme of the new film, revealed what he claimed was the true story. He said that he had bought cans of film from the man claiming to have filmed the Roswell autopsy but, on his return to London, he found that these had deteriorated and that nothing was salvageable. In order to protect his investment he had been forced to recreate the autopsy scenes, using crude techniques, resulting in the footage that was shown to BUFORA and the world. It was, he insisted, not exactly a hoax – just a remake of the real autopsy film that he would have shown if he could have done so.

Sant Mat tradition

An Indian spiritual tradition that has inspired several modern Western movements.

Like THEOSOPHY and the HERMETIC ORDER OF THE GOLDEN DAWN, the Sant Mat tradition is probably more important, at least in the West, for the movements it has spawned than just for itself. Historically it comes from a spiritual movement in northern India dating back as far as the 13th century, but it came to prominence in the late 19th century in the form of the Radhasoami movement. The original *Sants*, like the later Sufis (see SUFISM), were known for their spiritual poetry; they focused on the indwelling nature of God, and on the equality of all people. *Sant* does not mean 'saint', but 'one who has experienced Truth and Reality'.

Radhasoami was founded in 1861 by Siv Dayal Singh. He taught that focusing on the sound of God's name could bring self-realization; this is part of Surat Shabd Yoga, or the yoga of the celestial sound. On his death his movement split into several offshoots, the most prominent of which was Radha Soami Satsang Beas (RSSB), founded by Baba Jaimal Singh in 1891. One of his former followers, Kirpal Singh (1894–1974), was most responsible for the late-20th century development of these beliefs in the West, partly though his prominence as president of the World Fellowship of Religions for many years. He founded Ruhani Satsang when he lost the leadership succession of RSSB in 1951. Although Kirpal Singh is not seen as part of the succession of RSSB, he is the most significant forerunner of modern Western movements with a grounding in Sant Mat.

As the beliefs developed in the West they sharpened into a focus on 'divine light and sound'. Three of the best-known Western religious movements stemming from Sant Mat teachings are Eckankar, founded by Paul Twitchell in 1965, Elan Vital, since 1983 the name of the former Divine Light Mission founded by Maharaji in 1966, and the Movement of Spiritual Inner Awareness (MSIA), founded by John-Roger in 1971. All these teach MEDITATION techniques to experience the 'Inner Light and Sound of God', such as pressing on the eye-balls and the ears; these are two of four techniques taught as 'the Knowledge' in Elan Vital.

sasquatch *see* BIGFOOT

Satan

In Christian, Islamic and Jewish tradition, the chief enemy of God and personification of evil, who seeks to tempt mankind to sin.

In the Christian, Islamic and Jewish traditions, Satan, also known as the DEVIL, is the archfiend, the personification of evil and the chief adversary of God, who seeks to tempt mankind to sin in the hopes of condemning him to hell. The word 'devil', which comes from the Greek *diabolos*, is not found in the Old Testament, which is written in Hebrew; it uses the word *sātān*, meaning 'adversary', and in the older books of the Hebrew Bible, this is a common noun which refers to a human enemy. In the later Book of Job comes the most well-known reference to Satan in the Old Testament, as a figure who tests Job's patience

by afflicting him with misfortunes. However, in this story, although Satan is described as a definite character, he acts only under God's instruction, and is thought by most scholars to be a device traditionally used in Jewish aggadic, or allegorical, tales, to illustrate a concept; he fulfils the necessary role of the Adversary to advance the point of the story.

Satan figures much more prominently in the New Testament, and the Christian tradition in general, where he is also referred to as the Devil. In the gospel of Mark, Satan's temptation of Jesus in the wilderness is only touched upon briefly, and is described in similar terms to his role in the Book of Job, as merely testing Jesus. However, in the gospel of Matthew, written perhaps a generation later, he does more than test; he offers Jesus untold wealth and power if he will worship him, thus setting himself up as a rival to God. Many scholars regard this as showing the influence of the Zoroastrian tradition, which had a dualistic belief in one god and a supremely evil spirit in direct opposition to him. In the Book of Revelation, Satan becomes identified with the fallen angel, LUCIFER, whose pride caused him to rebel against God and be cast down from Heaven, and he is depicted as an aggressive and malevolent spirit bent on the corruption and ultimate destruction of man. The belief that Satan is in Hell derives more from Christian literature than from biblical sources; a number of passages in the Bible state that he roams heaven and earth, seeking to tempt humans to sin and separate them from God for ever. According to most Christian traditions, Satan will wage a final war against Christ before being defeated and cast into Hell.

In Islam, too, Satan is described as the personification of evil and corrupter of mankind. The Koran uses the Arabic term *Al-Shaitan*, which translates as 'the adversary', in reference to Iblis, the chief of all the DJINN, who refused to bow down to Adam as instructed by Allah, rebelled against him and was thereafter known as Shaitan. Allah condemned him to Hell for all eternity, but at his request, his sentence was postponed until the Day of Judgement. Shaitan then swore that he would spend the time left to him to subvert and tempt humans so that they, too, would be condemned to Hell.

There is no description of Satan's appearance in the Bible, but in Christian folklore he is traditionally pictured as a red, human-like figure with horns, a pointed tail and cloven hooves, features which may be the result of the demonization by early Christian missionaries of pagan horned gods such as Pan and Dionysus. In the Middle Ages, Satan was believed to be the master of WITCHES and warlocks, who were thought to hold BLACK MASSES in his honour. Those who have a superstitious fear of referring to him by name may call him by such euphemistic titles as Old Nick, Old Clootie, Scratch and The Dark One.

In the 20th century, Satan became the focus of several modern movements of religious SATANISM – most notably the CHURCH OF SATAN, founded in 1966 by ANTON LAVEY – which recognize or worship him, either in a literal form or, more commonly, as a symbol of man's carnal and earthly nature.

satanic ritual abuse

A practice that it was once suggested was widespread, involving the repeated, ritualized violent abuse of children by groups of adults in the name of Satan. It produced a number of panics and overreactions among some professionals, but is now widely regarded to be nothing more than an urban legend.

In the 1980s and early 1990s, particularly in the USA and Britain, there were a number of cases in which allegations of 'satanic ritual abuse' (SRA) were made. The claim in these cases was that children were being sexually abused by their parents, teachers and others in positions of responsibility, during rituals that were supposedly born out of the practice of SATANISM. Serious accusations were made, wild stories appeared in the popular press and those accused became the subject of suspicion and criminal investigations. Homes were raided by the authorities and large numbers of children were taken away from their parents.

The whole scare seems to have stemmed from work carried out by psychiatrists in the USA using HYPNOSIS to 'recover' patients' memories of childhood abuse (a process that is now largely discredited – see MEMORIES, RECOVERED). This took place against a backdrop of popular, media-driven images of the practice of Satanism and stories promulgated by religious extremists, all of which then coloured the interpretations and actions of psychiatrists and social workers on both sides of the Atlantic.

In 1980 a book called *Michelle Remembers* was produced by Dr Lawrence Pazder and Michelle Smith – Pazder was Michelle's psychiatrist, and later married her. The book purported to tell the story of Michelle's childhood in which, from the age of five in 1955, she was allegedly subjected to terrifying ordeals of 'Satanic abuse'. These, she said, included being kept in a cage with snakes, being put in a car with a woman's corpse before the car was then deliberately crashed, witnessing the mutilation of kittens and the sacrifice of babies, and being forced to drink blood at the altar of Satan. It was later shown that Pazder's methods, which included the use of hypnotic regression, had encouraged his patient to believe and embroider her darkest fantasies. However, other books followed, including *Satan's Underground* by Lauren Stratford

(1988) – a book which was later withdrawn by its original publisher.

In Britain social workers responded to accusations made in several places, including Rochdale, Nottingham and the Orkneys, making headline news by taking children away from their parents in a series of dramatic raids. The accusations were not supported by any evidence and no one was found guilty of abuse in any of the cases – however, it was often a considerable time before the children were allowed to return to their families. In the USA the owners and staff at the McMartin Pre-School in Manhattan Beach, Los Angeles, spent several years in prison awaiting trials and retrials on accusations of abusing the children in their care – they were also eventually acquitted.

There were a number of similar SRA scares in the Netherlands, Scandinavia, Australia and New Zealand. In each case it was observed that these followed visits by 'SRA experts', causing some to draw parallels with the witch hunts of the middle ages – as the 16th-century Spanish explorer Alonso de Salazar wrote:

> I have observed that there were neither witches nor bewitched in a village until they were talked and written about.

Eventually it was realized that rumour was feeding off rumour, and that there really was no evidence for SRA. The State of Virginia in the USA, and the British and Dutch governments commissioned official reports. These concluded that SRA did not exist. In addition, anthropologists and folklore specialists have since traced the geographical progression of the SRA story, and the recurring themes within it, and have drawn comparisons with other forms of URBAN LEGEND.

There have been two positive outcomes of the SRA scare. Firstly, the guidelines for interviewing children have been extensively redrawn to try to avoid the possibility of either intimidating or leading those involved. Secondly, attention has been drawn to 'False Memory Syndrome' (see MEMORY, FALSE), in which people can be led, through hypnotic regression, group therapy or other forms of counselling, to 'remember' in great detail events in their lives which never occurred.

Satanism

A religious or philosophical movement based on the recognition or worship of Satan, either in a literal form or, more commonly, as a symbol of man's carnal and earthly nature; Satanism focuses on the spiritual advancement of the self, rather than on submission to a deity or set of moral codes.

Satanism, as a modern religious or philosophical

concept, has no connection with the devil worship, blood sacrifice and blasphemous rituals depicted in horror films and alleged by the Church in the late Middle Ages to have been perpetrated by WITCHES and heretics. A wide variety of belief systems such as SANTERÍA, Druidism (see DRUIDS) and WICCA are also sometimes mistakenly identified with Satanism, but these are completely separate religions with no connection at all between them.

There are four essentially unrelated types of 'Satanism', and it is important to stress the differences between them. Religious Satanism, as it is often known, regards Satan as a deity or a principle, and while a small proportion of Satanists may believe in and worship Satan as a spiritual entity, this is rare; he is generally recognized and revered as a pre-Christian archetype, an aspect of human carnal nature, and a pagan image of power, virility and sexuality, and has little or nothing to do with the Christian DEVIL. Religious Satanism is opposed to the concept of a deity who answers the prayers of believers and punishes sinners and unbelievers, and instead of submission to divine laws or externally imposed moral codes, it teaches individualism, materialism and personal spiritual enrichment through self-development. It sees everyone as being responsible for their own actions and life, and its adherents often refer to it as a LEFT-HAND PATH. It has three main traditions, although since the primary focus is on the individual, they all acknowledge that it is not necessary to join any organization in order to become a Satanist: the CHURCH OF SATAN, the Temple of Set, and the Church of Satanic Liberation. Modern Satanism began in 1966 with the Church of Satan, which was founded by ANTON LAVEY as an alternative to organized Western religion and the cultural repression of man's natural instincts and desires, and LaVey's 1969 book *The Satanic Bible* formed the bedrock of modern Satanism. His design of the 'Sigil of BAPHOMET' – a goat's head inside an inverted PENTAGRAM, circled with the Hebrew word 'Leviathan' – has become a symbol of Satanism all over the world.

There is no real evidence for the historical existence of organized cults such as those which the Christian Church claimed to have existed in the late Middle Ages, although the idea of such cults has survived to this day. This type of Satanism, often referred to as 'Gothic' Satanism, with its ritual sacrifice of victims, blasphemous ceremonies, and pacts with the Devil, is a popular theme in horror fiction and films, but while it provided the Church with a theological foundation for executing alleged witches and heretics in the 'burning times' of the Middle Ages, it is not generally thought to be practised today, and has no connection with Religious Satanism.

Satanic 'dabbling', as typically practised by rebellious teenagers and disaffected young adults, usually combines elements from Religious Satanism and Gothic Satanism with some ceremonial magic. Dabblers may occasionally engage in minor criminal acts such as vandalizing cemeteries or graffiti involving Satanic symbols, and in rare cases may go as far as performing animal sacrifices. Impressionable individuals may also be influenced by rock bands which claim to be associated with Satanism, although such claims are generally motivated by the band's desire to increase its notoriety rather than having any spiritual basis.

Occasionally, serial killers or child abusers may claim to be Satanists in order to justify their crimes, but investigations usually reveal that these individuals have little or no knowledge of real Satanism. Religious Satanism in fact holds life as precious, condemns the harming of children under any circumstances, and is against the killing of animals except for food or in self-defence.

Scepticism *see panel p604*

sceptres, suit of *see* WANDS, SUIT OF

Scientific and Medical Network

A British-based organization of medical anomalists.
The Scientific and Medical Network (SMN) is a cross-disciplinary forum for the exploration of subjects such as MEDITATION and consciousness, alternative healing, EXTRASENSORY PERCEPTION and PSI, and NEAR-DEATH EXPERIENCES. It was founded in 1973 by George Blaker, Dr Patrick Shackleton and Sir Kelvin Spencer, based on their collective desire to reconcile scientific investigation and scientific models of reality with the spiritual dimension of life. Their aim was to stimulate a holistic approach to research including a dialogue between scientists and MYSTICS of all backgrounds. The founders believed that neither orthodox religion nor conventional science were, in their current forms, sufficient to answer pressing questions about human existence, including the possibility of its continuance after bodily death.

The mysteries of existence, they believed, demanded new ways of thinking and new interdisciplinary approaches that drew across all relevant areas. In their mission statement, they say:

> … 30 years on from our birth as an organisation, scientific and medical orthodoxy is still compartmentalised, reductionist, atomistic, and still dismissive of spiritual or non-material dimensions to human experience or cosmic

Scepticism

The earliest identifiable philosophy of scepticism can be found among the Hellenist schools, where it was first systematized by Pyrrho (d.275 BC). The word is derived from the ancient Greek *skeptomai*, meaning 'to look about', 'to consider', via the Latin *skepsis*, meaning 'inquiry', or 'doubt', with the added implication that any absolute judgement is premature. Generally, philosophical scepticism has been epistemological, more concerned, as Bertrand Russell put it, with 'how we know rather than the attempt to acquire fresh knowledge'. Modern usage, however, especially when applied to the PARANORMAL, varies according to the context.

Sceptics (or skeptics, US spelling) have sometimes been accused of denying the existence of absolute 'truth' and maintaining the impossibility of any certainty about defining what is true, but this position is more properly attributed to the Stoics. For the ancient Greek Sceptics, logical argument was flawed because it relies upon propositions which, in turn, rely on other propositions for their validity and, thus, may lead to errors of circular reasoning. Instead of saying 'We can't know', they simply said 'We don't know.' This agnosticism was expressed in a modern form by CHARLES FORT. He brought his empirical scepticism to the consideration of scientific and other ANOMALIES, independently reaching the same conclusions about circular reasoning and the 'relative' nature of definitions as the ancient Sceptics – see FORTEANISM.

When applied to most subjects, scepticism (in its original sense) can be a positive factor, driving curiosity, discovery, innovation and, ultimately, understanding – this is particularly true in the areas of science, technology and the arts. One of the most significant developments in the application of scepticism in modern times occurred in the USA in 1976 with the foundation of the COMMITTEE FOR THE SCIENTIFIC INVESTIGATION OF CLAIMS OF THE PARANORMAL (CSICOP). It lived up to its name by challenging 'extraordinary' claims in nearly every area of the paranormal. Its brand of 'scientific scepticism' was effectively an extension of atheism, a traditional

sceptical position in relation to the existence of GOD, to include other supernatural entities (including SPIRITS, FAIRIES, GHOSTS, POLTERGEISTS and even ALIENS) on the grounds of their being scientifically unlikely.

The declared aims of CSICOP include critical scrutiny of claims of the paranormal, with careful consideration and without *a priori* rejection. Where members of CSICOP depart considerably from the sceptics of old is in their political activism; for example, as well as seeking to improve scientific literacy, CSICOP executive Lee Nisbet stated, in the 25th anniversary issue of *Skeptical Inquirer*, that 'CSICOP originated … to fight mass-media exploitation of supposedly "occult" and "paranormal" phenomena'. Similarly, the Skeptics Society (founded in 1992) includes among its aims 'resisting the spread of pseudo-science, SUPERSTITION, and irrational beliefs'.

It has been argued that many scientific sceptics confuse rational doubt with wilful disbelief – an issue that concerned US sociologist Marcello Truzzi (1935–2003). In 1979, a few years after resigning from CSICOP, Truzzi warned his former colleagues about the dangers of being too rigid in their approach to the paranormal. 'Absence of evidence does not constitute evidence of absence', he wrote. 'If science is to remain an open system capable of modification with new evidence, ANOMALISTICS must keep the door ajar even for the most radical claimants willing to engage in scientific discourse.' Consequently, he advised, sceptics must avoid both 'Type I' errors ('thinking something special is happening when it really is not'), and 'Type II' errors ('thinking nothing special is happening when something special, perhaps rare, is actually occurring').

A decade later, Truzzi ventured an analysis of modern scepticism in relation to the paranormal. He identified four major types of sceptics: proponents, anomalists, scoffers and mystery-mongers, each with their own approach to anomalies:

Proponents can come from any background, but have in common a desire for 'scientific legitimacy'.

Truzzi calls them 'protoscientific' and notes that, unlike anomalists, their interests may be narrowly confined to the subject for which they proselytize.

Anomalists are primarily concerned with protoscientific claims, which they test according to the rules of evidence commonly approved by the scientific community. Truzzi stated that it is only proper for anomalists to 'engage in legitimate debunking' and explore many different subjects better suited to accommodate the data under investigation. Anomalists are, perhaps, the closest to empirical scepticism.

Scoffers loath a mystery and seem more interested in discrediting an anomaly and its proponents than properly investigating it or acquiring solid disproof. 'In their most extreme form, scoffers represent a form of quasi-religious Scientism that treats minority or deviant viewpoints in science as heresies', noted Truzzi. With the more extreme of his former colleagues in mind, Truzzi wrote, 'Although many in this category, who dismiss and ridicule anomaly claims, call themselves "sceptics", they often are really "pseudo-skeptics" because they deny rather than doubt anomaly claims.' Scoffers – well represented in CSICOP – are characterized by their *a priori* conviction in the non-existence or impossibility (not just improbability) of the paranormal, and their dogmatic defence of contemporary science which, in their view, is 'beleaguered' and threatened by (in Freud's phrase) 'the black tide of occultism'. They have also been called 'militant' or 'aggressive' sceptics as their attacks on pseudo-scientific 'nonsense', superstition and hoaxing take on a tone of intolerant fervour. In this they are sometimes indistinguishable from the 'believers' and cranks they attack.

Activists of this type have been known to challenge claimants directly and even perpetrate hoaxes to prove their point. In the 1990s, Truzzi coined the terms *pathological scepticism* and *pseudo-scepticism* to define these extreme forms of scepticism. Pathological scepticism refers to the determined bigot who says 'I won't believe it!' Pseudo-scepticism is a form of argument in which a person pretends to be or thinks

they are a knowledgeable sceptic, but is, instead, merely clouding the issue. There are also scoffers, of all types, outside of science who aim their direct anger or scorn at science itself, many of them convinced that a conspiracy of some sort opposes them.

Truzzi's fourth type of sceptic – the *mystery-monger* – tends to seek out the extraordinary, taking pleasure in data that defies conventional explanation, partly for its contrary nature, and partly because it indicates some limitation of scientific knowledge. Many mystery-mongers are fundamentally anti-scientific, but not as extreme as the scoffers, and less interested in the impartial investigation that distinguishes the anomalists. However, Truzzi is wrong to number Charles Fort among the mystery-mongers, as Fort advocated the improvement of science (not its overthrow or undermining) through the study of anomalies, and only discoursed on the fallibility of scientists when they themselves traded on their superiority or made pronouncements that were unjustifiably *ex cathedra* or based on personal belief. On the other hand, Truzzi is quite correct to include many self-proclaimed forteans as mystery-mongers. In his *Fads and Fallacies in the Name of Science* (1952), Martin Gardner (1914–), a scourge of crackpots, acknowledged that Fort 'had a firm grasp of the subject matter' but was often let down by the quality of his followers. Fort himself anticipated the problem of scoffers and mystery-mongers, five years before the founding of the FORTEAN SOCIETY. In a 1926 letter to science-fiction author Edmund Hamilton (1904–77), Fort responded to the suggestion that a 'fortean society' would be a 'good thing' with words that ring true today:

> The great trouble is that the majority of persons who are attracted are the ones we do not want ... persons who are revolting against science, not in the least because they are affronted by the myth-stuff of the sciences, but because scientists either oppose or do not encourage them.

Bob Rickard

reality. And as yet there has developed no meta-subject in which all disciplines in science, medicine, theology and spirituality may be brought together. In this context, the SMN still has a unique and an important role to play in providing a truly trans-disciplinary, truly progressive, place to discuss, dialogue and learn about the universe in which we live and which gives us our being.

The SMN began as a small, invitation-only club but steadily expanded as the quality of debate in its forums attracted scientists and medics to pose questions considered taboo in orthodox departments, and to share ideas and research on topics such as non-local consciousness, alternative forms of healing and PARANORMAL phenomena, and the philosophy of science and spirituality. Initially British, the SMN has now developed into an internationally recognized organization with members in over 50 countries providing incisive conferences, lectures and publications. They also run online discussion groups for members, and an extensive educational programme. For example, in 2006, they ran a special event at the 2006 British Association for the Advancement of Science's annual Festival of Science, at which the SMN's Dr Peter Fenwick, a distinguished neuropsychiatrist, presented a 'new model of dying'; while Perrot-Warrick Fellow Dr RUPERT SHELDRAKE and parapsychologist Dr Deborah Delanoy of the University of Northampton, presented research on two different forms of 'remote cognition'.

Scientology

A controversial 20th-century religion that aims at improving individuals and humanity as a whole.

Of all the new religions of the 20th century, Scientology is perhaps the most controversial. Its founder, its history, its beliefs and its practices have all come under intense scrutiny both from critics and in the courts. In this entry, 'Scientology' refers to both the religion itself and the organization the Church of Scientology.

The first Church of Scientology was founded in Los Angeles in 1954. Originally it was based on the psychoanalytic system of DIANETICS developed by L RON HUBBARD in 1950, but during the 1950s Hubbard greatly expanded its teachings. The essence of Scientology is its practicality, as *The Scientology Handbook* says:

> Scientology is an applied religious philosophy which contains workable answers to the problems people face in their lives. The subject matter of Scientology is *all* life. It contains practical means

Tom Cruise gives a speech at the opening of a Scientology church in Madrid in 2004. (© Paul Hanna/Reuters/Corbis)

> through which predictable improvement can be obtained in any area to which it is applied.

This includes drug rehabilitation and criminal rehabilitation through the sister organizations Narconon and Criminon, and also techniques for health, education and administration.

Scientology refers to its practical teachings as 'technology' or 'Tech'. Every procedure must be followed precisely, with no variation from the way that Hubbard wrote it. Two organizations, the

Religious Technology Center and Author Services Incorporated, were set up to protect the Tech and to preserve Hubbard's writings – in the Church's words, 'to prevent attempts to alloy or subvert the purity of the religious teachings of Scientology'.

Scientologists are encouraged to progress up 'The Bridge to Total Freedom', a long and complex graded system of auditing up to Clear (see DIANETICS) and then beyond to what are called Operating Thetan levels, with a parallel progression of training to be an auditor at progressively advanced levels. The word 'thetan' refers to the individual's inner spiritual being.

Most religions have CREATION MYTHS. At the heart of Scientology's belief system is the story of a galactic dictator called Xenu who, 76 million years ago, imprisoned the billions of people of the 75 planets of the Galactic Federation in volcanoes on Earth and dropped H-bombs on them. This traumatic event separated the thetans from their bodies. These deeply troubled thetans attach themselves in their millions to humans today, and are responsible for illness, perversion and many of the other problems of the human race. Advanced levels of auditing can help Scientologists to rid themselves of these 'body thetans'.

Scientology has the reputation of being a litigious religion, frequently taking legal action against ex-members and other critics, some of whom have accused it of being authoritarian. In recent years it has attempted to stop discussion of the religion's beliefs on the Internet on the grounds that quoting its beliefs is a 'violation of copyright laws'.

From the outset, Scientology has fought in countries around the world to be recognized as a religion. After many years of battling, the US Internal Revenue Service finally recognized Scientology as a tax-exempt religion in 1993. The British Home Office accepted that it is a religion in 1996, but the UK Charity Commissioners have so far rejected Scientology's application to be registered as a charity.

Scole group, the

A five-year research programme to find evidence for life after death through communication with spirits.

The Scole group set out to investigate evidence for life after death in an experiment which ran from 1993 to 1998. They took their name from the Norfolk village of Scole where their SÉANCES took place. Initially the project was run with seven members, two of whom were TRANCE MEDIUMS – however, the last three years of the project were carried out with the two mediums and only two others (although at various times there were outside visitors in attendance). It was claimed that the group produced over 200 different physical

effects during the 500 or so séances, including APPORTS, LEVITATIONS, spirit lights, ELECTRONIC VOICE PHENOMENA, AUTOMATIC WRITING and 'psychic photographs' (see THOUGHTOGRAPHY).

During the later years of the project, the SOCIETY FOR PSYCHICAL RESEARCH carried out an investigation of it and sent members to attend the séances as impartial observers. In a 300-page report, they confirmed that none of their investigators could find any evidence of fraud in the sessions they observed. However, as had been the problem with such investigations during the heyday of SPIRITUALISM, the séances took place in the dark and the MEDIUMS had the final say on the conditions and controls in place – the results, as far as sceptics are concerned, were therefore inconclusive.

Scorpio

In astrology, the eighth sign of the zodiac, between Libra and Sagittarius.

In Western ASTROLOGY, Scorpio is the sign of the ZODIAC for those who are born between 23 October and 22 November. The symbol for Scorpio is the scorpion, and the sign is ruled by Mars and Pluto. Scorpians are said to be intense, resourceful and passionate, although they can be secretive. Scorpio is believed to be a water sign, having an affinity with the element WATER.

Scott, Sir Walter (1771–1832)

Scottish historical novelist and poet.

Walter Scott, the historical novelist and poet, was born in Edinburgh. Contracting polio at the age of eight, he was sent to recuperate at his grandfather's farm at Sandyknowe in the Scottish Borders, where he gained the knowledge of traditional Scottish ballads, tales and legends which characterized much of his literary work. He studied at Edinburgh University and entered his father's law office, but at the age of 25 he began to dabble in writing, first translating German ballads and then collecting ballads from the Western Borders, publishing the latter between 1802 and 1803 as his first major work, the three-volume *The Minstrelsy of the Scottish Border*. In 1805 followed his first great narrative poem, *The Lay of the Last Minstrel*. He founded a printing press with James and John Ballantyne, and published a few more romantic poems such as *Marmion* (1808) and *The Lady of the Lake* (1810). But by the early 1810s, his printing press was in financial difficulties, and Scott set out to write a novel to make money – *Waverley*, a tale of the Jacobite rising. Published in 1814, it was an instant success, and Scott followed it up over the next five years with a prodigious output of further historical novels. But careful of his reputation as a poet, he did not put his name to these, publishing them anonymously as 'the Author of Waverley'.

Eventually, after the printing press suffered further financial disasters, he acknowledged authorship of his historical novels, which he continued to write at an astonishing rate. Producing 27 novels in all by the time he died in 1832, Sir Walter Scott was essentially the father of the modern historical novel. But it is perhaps less well known that he was also the author of a work titled *Letters on Demonology and Witchcraft*, written in 1830 at the request of John Murray, publisher of a series called *The Family Library*, to which he asked Scott to contribute a volume on DEMONOLOGY. Although by this time in poor health, Scott accepted the commission; he had been fascinated by the subject since childhood, and had proposed to collaborate on a study of demonology as early as 1809. He had a large collection of books on the topic, and many students of the OCCULT also sent him source material for his book, which was written in the form of ten letters addressed to his son-in-law, J G Lockhart.

In the *Letters*, Scott examines opinions on demonology and WITCHCRAFT from Old Testament times to his own day, taking a strictly rational view of the subject and ascribing phenomena such as supernatural visions to physical illness and superstitious credulity. Although it is generally agreed that the book is inferior in quality to his other work, it is nevertheless of interest to students of the occult, since it is illustrated with traditional tales and anecdotes, and his accounts of demonology in France and Sweden have been particularly noted. The book received a mixed critical reaction on its publication in 1830, but has been acknowledged by later scholars as one of the first attempts by an author to approach magic and demonology from a scientific angle, anticipating much of the late 19th-century research by scholars of FOLKLORE, religion and ethnology.

Scratching Fanny *see* COCK LANE GHOST

screaming skulls

Ancient skulls that are said to scream or generate psychic manifestations if removed from their dwelling-place.

Screaming skull superstitions are associated with at least 20 different buildings in England, including Burton Agnes Hall, Yorkshire; Calgarth Hall, Cumbria; Chilton Cantelo, Somerset; Warbleton Priory, Sussex; and Wardley Hall near Manchester. In each case the skull has been preserved in the dwelling for hundreds of years and its origin is often uncertain – although screaming skulls are traditionally linked to former residents from between the 15th and 17th centuries. The skull must not under any circumstances be removed – otherwise psychic disturbances including screams, POLTERGEIST phenomena and bad luck are said to follow.

The screaming skull of Bettiscombe Manor.
(© Robert Estall/Corbis)

Most famous of all screaming skulls is the specimen still preserved at Bettiscombe Manor in Dorset, said to be that of a black male servant of the Pinney family. Legend tells that this servant had come to England from the West Indies in the 17th or 18th century, and that on his deathbed he asked that his body be returned there for interment. This wish was disregarded, and the servant was buried in the local churchyard. It is said that almost immediately screams and moans were heard coming from the grave. Pinney was forced to have the body disinterred and (for reasons that are unclear) the skull was preserved in the house. Traditionally, attempts to bury or otherwise dispose of the skull have led to psychic disturbances and ill fortune. It is said that one resident of the Manor threw the skull into a pond, but constant screams and moans forced him to retrieve the skull and return it to the house. On another occasion, it is claimed that the skull was buried in a deep hole, but within a few days it was found inexplicably sitting on top of the ground.

Apparently, an examination of the Bettiscombe skull carried out in 1963 indicated that it was that of a European female and that it might be 2,000 or more years old. This has led some to believe that the skull was originally venerated at a Celtic shrine. In a number of ancient traditions the skull had a protective function, and skulls were said to preserve the fertility and prosperity of farmland. In 1995, researchers David Clarke and Andy Roberts undertook a study of screaming skulls, and speculated that the majority of surviving skulls could have similarly ancient origins. Others have suggested that most date to the

16th and 17th centuries and are either Catholic relics or examples of the Elizabethan and Jacobean cult of memento mori. Whatever their origins, legends relating to screaming skulls remain popular.

scrying
Divination by gazing into a reflective surface, such as a crystal ball, mirror or bowl of water.

The form of divination known as scrying is believed to have been practised since ancient Babylonian times, and its use is documented in ancient Egyptian texts. Almost any reflective surface is suitable as a scrying medium, although the best known scrying tool is undoubtedly the CRYSTAL BALL. However, a bowl of water, INK or oil may also be used, as can any clear crystal, or a mirror – either a conventional mirror, or a black mirror, made of a material such as obsidian. The size of the scrying tool is of no importance, as is demonstrated by one technique said to have been used by the Babylonians. In this method, the scryer's thumbnail was anointed with olive oil, and the shiny nail acted like a magic mirror in which the scryer was thought to see spirits, known as the 'Princes of the Thumb'.

Whichever scrying tool is used, the principle is the same; it is thought that scrying is best done in near or total darkness, to minimize the possibility of distracting reflections, and if a candle is used for illumination, it should preferably be placed behind the scryer so that it is not reflected in the scrying object. When scrying, the gaze is focused not on the surface of the object but in its centre, as if the object is a window on the 'astral world', and images are thought to appear to the scryer, who then interprets them.

The most famous historical practitioners of scrying are JOHN DEE, Queen Elizabeth I's court astrologer, who used a crystal ball and a black mirror to receive communications which he claimed to be of angelic origin, and the French astrologer NOSTRADAMUS, whose water scrying was the claimed source of his famous predictions.

Seahenge
An ancient circle of wooden stumps found on a beach in Norfolk, England.

In 1998 high tides washed away a layer of peat near the shore on the north coast of Norfolk, exposing an obviously man-made circle of over 50 oak stumps. A similar formation had been uncovered in the 1970s but it had been washed away, leaving no traces. It was discovered that the stumps revealed in 1998 were actually upturned tree trunks and that a larger object in the centre of the circle was a large upside-down oak tree. Carbon dating has shown the trees to be over 4,000 years old.

Who put them there and why? It is important to bear in mind that the 'sea henge' was not originally so close to the sea; rather, the sea encroached on the land, which was salt marsh, to 'claim' it. Nothing can be known for certain about the site's purpose, but it has been conjectured that it had religious significance to the Bronze Age culture that constructed it. It may have had a funerary role, with a dead body being placed on the central upturned tree to decompose, or it may have simply been a shrine. Trees, particularly the oak, were certainly sacred to the much later Celtic inhabitants; perhaps Seahenge is an earlier manifestation of this.

The timbers were removed for preservation and further study, the fear being that without their peat covering they would quickly decompose, and it was discovered that many of them bore the impressions of the tools that had been used to cut and shape them.

séance
A meeting of psychical researchers or spiritualists for the purpose of trying to communicate with the spirits of the dead.

The word 'séance' (from the French for a 'sitting' or a 'meeting') was first recorded in English in 1845 – however, the activity itself had been taking place long before that date. Early séances often took the form of social gatherings (see TABLE-TURNING) and, later in the 19th century, they even became something of a parlour game – the OUIJA BOARD allowing people to conduct their own séances (often as nothing more than light-hearted entertainment) without the help of an established MEDIUM.

Séances were the cornerstone of the SPIRITUALISM movement and were particularly popular from the middle of the 19th century. There was a massive boom in attendance at private séances or public demonstrations at theatres, fuelled by the fantastic claims of the supporters of famous mediums such as the FOX SISTERS and DANIEL DUNGLAS HOME. A wide variety of phenomena were claimed to occur during sittings, including APPORTS, SPIRIT RAPPING, table-turning, LEVITATION, MATERIALIZATIONS (such as the production of ECTOPLASM), AUTOMATIC WRITING, AUTOMATIC ART and disembodied voices.

Séances still take place today, although the range of phenomena manifested is much reduced. They are still usually held in complete darkness, or low light conditions, and often involve a group of people sitting around a table, their hands in contact. However, the exact approach to setting up, and the form that the following events take, varies depending on the type of medium involved (see TRANCE MEDIUM, DIRECT VOICE MEDIUM, PHYSICAL MEDIUM, MENTAL MEDIUM

A 19th-century newspaper illustration of a séance. The drawing includes a spirit hand writing a message and the apport of a guitar. (© Corbis)

and TRANSFIGURATION MEDIUM). In most instances it is held that the medium is CHANNELLING some form of communication from the spirit world.

Sceptics argue that the conditions under which séances normally take place make fraud all the more easy, and people such as HARRY HOUDINI and JOHN NEVIL MASKELYNE spent many years exposing the mediums' tricks. Likewise, since the 19th century, organizations such as the SOCIETY FOR PSYCHICAL RESEARCH have been involved in attempts to investigate and possibly validate the claims made.

Search for Extraterrestrial Intelligence

The quest to find evidence for intelligent beings living on a planet other than our own.

The title 'Search for Extraterrestrial Intelligence' (or SETI) has been applied to a number of projects since 1960 when Dr Frank Drake, one of the new breed of radio astronomers working at Green Bank, West Virginia, began the search for signs that there might be technologically advanced civilizations elsewhere in the universe. In April of that year his team set up Project Ozma, named after the princess of the far-off Land of Oz in the stories by L Frank Baum. The aim of this pioneering project was to scour relatively nearby stars to look for signals that might be emerging from powerful alien transmitters.

Ozma surveyed two stars roughly 11 light years from Earth. At that stage the only hope was that pre-existing ALIEN signals would be picked up – because radio waves travel at the speed of light, it would be the mid-1980s before a reply to any message sent from earth could be expected.

In the early years of such projects there were great hopes of success, and a number of strange signals were picked up. However, one by one they all proved to have prosaic explanations. Green Bank received intelligent messages – but these turned out to have come from a secret military radar base on earth. At Cambridge in England, regular pulses of energy coming from deep space were detected – initially thought by some to be potential evidence for an advanced race using unknown power sources, they were later interpreted as evidence for a then-unknown natural cosmic phenomenon.

Perhaps the most famous signal that could potentially show evidence of extraterrestrial intelligence was the 'Wow!' signal picked up by the Ohio State University SETI project on 15 August 1977. It lasted for 72 seconds, and gained its name from the note that Professor Jerry Ehman wrote beside it on the computer printout. Whether the signal was significant is still a matter of debate. However, the fact that it has never been picked up again, despite repeated attempts, tends to count against an intelligent EXTRATERRESTRIAL origin.

The money expended on SETI projects has proven difficult to justify in the light of a continued lack of success, although there are still a number of ongoing projects in place. A very popular development occurred in 1999 with the advent of the 'SETI@ home' project based at the University of California, Berkeley. The project invites home computer users to donate processing time on their personal computers to assist in analysing data received by the Aricebo radio telescope in Puerto Rico. So far, it has not produced any conclusive evidence, but has apparently identified a number of potentially interesting signals for further investigation. The search goes on.

sea serpents

Huge, often elongate or long-necked marine cryptids of worldwide occurrence that may constitute several different species of scientifically unrecognized animal.

Since time immemorial, sailors and other maritime travellers have reported sightings of mysterious, often exceedingly large and superficially serpentine creatures that came to be referred to collectively as the great sea serpent. Nevertheless, for centuries these were resolutely dismissed by scientists as legends and superstition. However, a serious scientific analysis of sea serpent sightings was conducted during the late 1800s by eminent Dutch zoologist Dr Anthonie Cornelis Oudemans, who announced in his seminal book, *The Great Sea-Serpent* (1892), that this controversial beast was actually an unknown species of giant long-necked, long-tailed seal, which he formally christened *Megophias megophias*. No animal fitting this description, however, is known either from the present day or from the fossil record, and other researchers realized that Oudemans's theory was fatally flawed by his attempt to explain all sea serpent reports, featuring as they do a very diverse array of animal forms, by way of just a single species.

In the 1960s, cryptozoologist Dr BERNARD HEUVELMANS published *Le Grand Serpent-de-Mer* ('Large Sea Serpents'), the result of analysis of almost 600 sea serpent sightings reported between 1639 and 1965. From his study, he concluded that as many as nine different categories of sea serpent existed, five of which he considered to be sufficiently well-defined to warrant receiving an official zoological name. Heuvelmans's sea serpent categories are as follows:

Category 1: The super-otter *Hyperhydra egedei* – a long, four-limbed, web-footed, otter-like mammal with a distinct head, rough-skinned body and long tapering tail, measuring 20–30 metres (66–98 feet) long. Confined to the Arctic Ocean, no sightings of this once-familiar sea serpent appear to have been reported since the mid-1800s. Heuvelmans proposed that the super-otter was actually an exceedingly primitive whale that had retained its full set of four limbs, and that it was the identity of the famous Scandinavian 'soe-orm' ('sea worm'). Heuvelmans

named it after Protestant missionary Hans Egede, whose sighting of such a creature on 6 July 1734 off Nuuk, Greenland, was utilized by Heuvelmans as the principal report supporting the existence of the super-otter category of sea serpent.

Category 2: The many-humped sea serpent *Plurigibbosus novaeangliae* – a long marine CRYPTID characterized by a row of humps running along its back, a whale-like tail, and a total length of 18–35 metres (59–115 feet). Most familiar to cryptozoologists from an abundance of reports from the east coast of America, in reality it is apparently distributed throughout the cold temperate waters of the North Atlantic, and is the suggested identity of such well known cryptids as CADDY from the waters off Vancouver Island. Heuvelmans proposed that it was a surviving zeuglodont – a very elongate, primitive prehistoric whale.

Category 3: The many-finned sea serpent *Cetioscolopendra aeliani* – perhaps the most bizarre of all sea serpents, as it sports numerous lateral fins running down the sides of its body, and is encased within a segmented, jointed armour of bony plates. Measuring 9–30 metres (30–98 feet) long, this very strange cryptid has only been reported from tropical and subtropical waters, and was deemed by Heuvelmans to be the identity of a multi-limbed sea monster from Vietnam known as the 'con rit' or 'sea millipede', as well as a shrimp-tailed marine cryptid from Madagascar called the 'tompondrano' ('lord of the sea'). Heuvelmans considered this category of sea serpent to be a highly specialized, armoured species of living zeuglodont, basing this upon the discovery of zeuglodont fossils with associated scales.

Category 4: The long-necked sea serpent (or longneck for short) *Megalotaria longicollis* – the most common sea serpent of all, deemed by Heuvelmans to be a gigantic, highly specialized species of seal measuring 4.6–20 metres (15–66 feet) in total length, and characterized by its very long neck and a pair of small horns that may be external ears. It is sighted in temperate waters throughout the world, close to the coast in colder waters and mid-ocean in warmer ones, living near the water surface. In the past it has also occasionally become trapped in lakes and fjords, giving rise to sightings of long-necked freshwater cryptids like the LOCH NESS MONSTER, which during the course of time and geographical isolation may have subsequently evolved into separate species from their marine ancestor. According to Heuvelmans, *Megalotaria* is the cryptid responsible for the numerous reports of long-necked sea serpents on file – such as MORGAWR of Cornwall's Falmouth Bay, and possibly the famous cryptid reported on 6 August 1848 by several eyewitnesses aboard HMS *Daedalus*, travelling between South Africa's Cape of Good Hope and the island of St Helena, as it approached and then swam past the vessel. A number of long-necked, four-limbed 'sea monster' carcases have been examined from time to time, which have borne a striking resemblance to prehistory's plesiosaurs, but, oddly, have been covered in hair. In reality, however, they have invariably been shown to be the decomposed remains of sharks, their appearance having become distorted by what is known as the pseudoplesiosaur effect – whereby during decomposition the backbone is exposed and is mistaken for a long slender neck, the dried fins are mistaken for limbs, and exposed fibres of connective tissue are taken to be hair.

Category 5: The merhorse *Halshippus olaimagni* – an even more specialized seal than the longneck, measuring 5–30 metres (16–98 feet) long, and characterized by a horse-like head, long floating mane, well-developed whiskers and, in particular, a pair of enormous eyes, presumably adapted to very dim light and thus to deep water. Virtually cosmopolitan in distribution, the merhorse is apparently absent only from the Arctic and Indian oceans, and may well have been the original inspiration for ancient Greek legends of a bona fide sea-horse, half horse and half fish, known as the hippocampus.

Category 6: The marine saurian – this is a very large ocean-going reptile shaped like a lizard or crocodile, 15–18 metres (49–59 feet) long, which Heuvelmans considered may be a surviving mosasaur (a huge prehistoric sea lizard), or a living thalattosuchian (a highly specialized prehistoric crocodile modified for an exclusively marine existence by possessing web-footed flippers and a finned tail). One of the most famous sightings of a sea monster matching this description allegedly occurred on 30 July 1915, when a German submarine, the *U-28*, torpedoed the British steamer *Iberian* off Fastnet Rock, Ireland. After the *Iberian* had sunk there was a huge underwater explosion that is said to have blasted a sea-beast straight out of the water. It was crocodilian in form, 18 metre (59 feet) long and had webbed feet. The creature dropped back into the water, and was not seen again.

Category 7: The super-eel – one or more species of at least superficially eel-like fishes but of enormous length. This category of sea serpent was partly inspired by the collection of what appeared to be a super-eel larva in waters off southern South Africa by the Danish research vessel *Dana* on 31 January 1930. For although only a juvenile specimen, it was 1.8 metres (6 feet) long – normal eel larvae only measure approximately 8 centimetres (around 3 inches) – leading to speculation that the still-undiscovered adult form of this species may grow to anything from 33–55 metres (108–180 feet). Further, albeit

somewhat smaller, specimens were later obtained, and during the 1970s these were re-examined, but were found to be larval swamp eels or notacanthids, not true eels after all. This was very significant, because swamp eels acquire most of their total length while still larvae (the exact reverse of what occurs with true eels), meaning that adult swamp eels are not much longer than their larvae. Consequently, had it lived to adulthood, the *Dana* eel would not have grown much longer than it already was as a larva. In short, there may conceivably be undiscovered giant eels in the oceans, but the *Dana* specimen is not evidence for them.

Category 8: The Father-of-All-the-Turtles – a truly colossal species of marine turtle, with enormous flippers, and large scales on its back. One relatively recent sighting took place in June 1956 when the cargo steamer *Rhapsody*, journeying south of Nova Scotia, Canada, encountered a white-shelled giant turtle. Crew members claimed that it was 13.8 metres (45 feet) long, with flippers of 4.6 metres (15 feet), and a lengthy neck that raised its head 2.4 metres (8 feet) above the water surface.

Category 9: The yellow-belly – this is the least-defined sea serpent category, referring to a rarely reported tropical marine cryptid resembling a giant flat-headed tadpole, 18–30 metres (59–98 feet) long, and pale yellow in colour, adorned with black transverse stripes plus a black dorsal stripe. One such beast was apparently observed for 30 minutes on 11 September 1876 in Malaysia's Strait of Malacca by the captain and surgeon of the steamer *Nestor*. Heuvelmans himself was unclear as to what kind of creature the yellow-belly could be, but suggested a shark or an amphibian as two plausible candidates.

Although Heuvelmans's multiple-category classification system for sea serpents attracted some degree of criticism from sceptics who doubted that so many different species of giant sea creature could still exist unknown to science, his system was largely accepted for many years by cryptozoologists, although some did adapt it to create alternative or extended versions. More recently, however, continuing research has revealed a number of faults and imperfections in relation to various of his categories. For example, some modern-day longneck sightings include specific mention of the creature having a long tail, which would rule out a seal identity, but continue to support that of an evolved plesiosaur capable of surviving in cool waters. Heuvelmans's identification of the many-finned sea serpent as a modern-day armoured zeuglodont is no longer tenable, because the fossils which inspired this identity are now known to be artefacts – their scales were not their own but from an entirely different animal, inadvertently associated with zeuglodont remains during the fossilization process. A giant species of crustacean has been suggested as a more reasonable alternative identity for the many-finned sea serpent. And the super-otter category has suffered greatly from the fact that its most important sighting, made by Egede, appears to have been of something far removed from the super-otter as envisaged by Heuvelmans, because Egede's original description (only lately made public for the first time) does not match the latter beast. In a recent paper, two scientific authors have seriously contemplated the startling prospect that the object spied by Egede was nothing more than a whale exhibiting sexual arousal.

second sight

The supposed ability to be able to 'see' into the future.
Second sight is a form of PRECOGNITION in which the future is apparently literally 'seen' in the form of a vision. As such, it might also be described as a type of CLAIRVOYANCE.

Second sight is a PSYCHIC ability which is particularly associated with the SEERS of the Highlands of Scotland. The most famous of these was the BRAHAN SEER. Historically, in many rural areas, second sight was accepted as a fact of life, and it was usually regarded as something of a curse rather than a blessing – this was particularly due to the fact that many of the visions associated with second sight apparently related to the forthcoming deaths of individuals close to the seer. See also PHANTOM FUNERALS.

Secret Chiefs

One of the terms used to designate to a group of entities of superhuman intelligence and power referred to in several schools of the occult, and believed to be immortal transmitters of secret knowledge.
Several schools of the occult have made claims to having been given secret knowledge by a mysterious group of entities of superhuman intelligence and power. These beings are variously believed to be discarnate spirits of the great Magi of the past, living Magi who can astrally project themselves, angels or discarnate ethereal spirits, and are thought by some to inhabit the unpopulated regions of Tibet. MACGREGOR MATHERS, one of the founders of the HERMETIC ORDER OF THE GOLDEN DAWN, claimed to be in contact with them, and to be directly responsible to them; he called them the Secret Chiefs, and said that the ritual magic which he set down for the Golden Dawn was transmitted to him by them. The Golden Dawn consisted of an Outer and an Inner Order, and a third Order which Mathers said consisted solely of Secret Chiefs.

When some members of the organization rebelled against him, he is said to have threatened them with a 'Punitive Current' generated by these all-powerful entities. ALEISTER CROWLEY also claimed to have direct contact with them, and discussed them in detail in a chapter of his book *Magick Without Tears*, although the term appears in many of his writings. He stated that they may or may not be in human form depending on their own needs at the time, and are utterly unknown to the rest of humanity except on the very rare occasions when they find it part of their plan to reveal themselves to one person. MADAME BLAVATSKY, co-founder of the THEOSOPHICAL SOCIETY, referred to a similar group of beings as the ASCENDED MASTERS, Mahatmas or Masters of Wisdom, claiming to have received secret knowledge from them.

Secret Doctrine, The

The principal source book for students of theosophy, published in 1888 by Madame Blavatsky, co-founder of the Theosophical Society.
MADAME BLAVATSKY, co-founder of the THEOSOPHICAL SOCIETY, published her magnum opus *The Secret Doctrine: The Synthesis of Science, Religion and Philosophy* in 1888 as an expansion, clarification and refinement of her earlier major work, *Isis Unveiled* (1877). *The Secret Doctrine* was originally published in two volumes: *Cosmogenesis*, a study of the origins and development of the universe, and *Anthropogenesis*, which dealt with the origins and development of mankind. In this seminal book Blavatsky outlined the fundamental tenets of her 'Secret Doctrine of the Archaic Ages', bringing together religion and science within the context of THEOSOPHY. She claimed that it was largely based on an archaic manuscript called the *Book of Dyzan*, which she had interpreted, and that other parts had been communicated to her by a group of entities of superhuman intelligence and power she called the Mahatmas or the Masters of Wisdom (and later known as the ASCENDED MASTERS), who advised and directed her, although some critics argue that she in fact copied the ideas in it from earlier, original works. *The Secret Doctrine* became the principal source book for students of theosophy. Blavatsky had intended to publish a third and fourth volume of *The Secret Doctrine*, and after her death a controversial third volume was compiled from the writings found in her desk and published by the theosophist Annie Besant.

Secret Societies *see panel p614*

sects, heretical *see HERETICAL SECTS*

Secret Societies

Secret societies can be divided into three broad categories – spiritual, criminal and political – though these may overlap (in the case of some terrorist groups they could be all three). Whichever type they might be, secret societies tend to share some of the same characteristics. They are exclusive rather than inclusive (they are often difficult to join and, therefore, elitist) and they are generally concerned with the acquisition of knowledge and/or power (the first often leading to the second). Some, like the Freemasons (see FREEMASONRY), are secret in full view – their existence is open and public, with identifiable buildings, but what goes on in their ceremonies and rituals is secret; indeed, they have described themselves as 'not a secret society but a society with secrets'. Others are known about, but don't advertise their presence (the Mafia, for example). Others might have a public face but a very different private purpose; conspiracy theorists would point to various international political bodies such as the Bilderberg Group. With some, their existence and purpose are suspected but unproven, and we can assume that there are others so secret that even their existence isn't guessed at.

Of the spiritually based secret societies the best known are the ROSICRUCIANS and the Freemasons – and whatever protestations there might be, they are indisputably close relatives in ideas and ideals, even if the latter might not be directly descended from the former. However, this is the story with most esoteric societies, secret or not (see WESTERN MYSTERY TRADITION).

In the days of classical Greece and Rome there were numerous mystery cults dedicated to various gods and goddesses, including Mithraism (men only) and the ELEUSINIAN MYSTERIES (men and women). These were initiatory societies to which people of different ranks in the outside world could belong equally; in Mithraism, for example, a grizzled common soldier might be at a higher initiatory level than a young noble officer. The same principle holds true in Freemasonry today. There is a bond in their normal lives between members who go through the same secret rituals together; Freemasonry is sometimes called 'the Brotherhood'.

Although today Freemasonry might be considered by many to be akin to a charitable social club (albeit with some unusual rituals), it has at its symbolic heart a deep mystical spirituality which can be seen in the writings of A E WAITE, W L Wilmshurst and others. This was inherited from the Rosicrucians and Hermetic Philosophers of the 17th century.

Rosicrucianism almost certainly didn't exist, at least not under that name, before the publication in Germany in 1614, 1615 and 1616 of the three Rosicrucian Manifestoes. These told of a secret Brotherhood dedicated to spiritual self-improvement for the betterment of the whole of mankind. Such people did exist, dedicated to the same ideal of a search for spiritual knowledge and power, and engaged in the same practices: ALCHEMY, ASTROLOGY, astronomy, mathematics, medicine, scientific enquiry and so on. Because many of their activities (from raising DEMONS to scientific experimentation) would get them into serious trouble with the Church, secrecy was essential – the esotericist Giordano Bruno was burned at the stake in 1600 for teaching his beliefs (see ART OF MEMORY). Alchemical treatises, for example, were written in symbolic language sometimes several layers deep.

The Rosicrucian Manifestoes didn't include an address or a membership form. For years radical thinkers, both spiritual and scientific, searched Europe for a Rosicrucian society they could join – in the end some of them founded their own. Early Rosicrucians spoke, perhaps as a joke, of an Invisible College, but there were meetings of 'natural philosophers' at Gresham College in London during the Protectorate, which transmuted into the Royal Society when Charles II came to the throne. The Invisible College had been reified, and was to become one of the most important scientific institutions in the world (while demonstrating that secret societies do not always have to remain secret). But the links between spiritual and scientific exploration were not completely severed; many of the early Fellows of the Royal Society were Freemasons, and some of them (including ISAAC NEWTON, their president from 1703 to 1727), were engaged in alchemical research and other spiritual quests. Science and spirituality did separate during the 18th century, 'the Age of Reason', but not in a single move.

In the 18th and 19th centuries numerous Rosicrucian-related societies were formed in Europe, and later in the USA – many of them laying dubious claim to be direct descendants of an original secret order. The HERMETIC ORDER OF THE GOLDEN DAWN, founded by three members of the masonic order *Societas Rosicruciana in Anglia*, even had forged letters from a non-existent German order granting it 'legitimacy'. It is paradoxical that organizations pledged to the improvement of self and society often have deception in their origins. The *Prieuré de Sion*, first brought to prominence by Baigent, Leigh and Lincoln in *The Holy Blood and the Holy Grail* (1982), was not founded in the Middle Ages to protect the bloodline of Jesus, or for any other esoteric purpose; it was the creation of a few eccentric Frenchmen in the mid-1950s, and everything about it, including its much-vaunted list of Grand Masters, is a fake.

Although most of today's many esoteric or occult societies are open about their existence (some, such as the Ancient Mystical Order Rosae Crucis, even advertise themselves in magazines), the majority can still be called secret societies because they have graded levels of knowledge which are only revealed as members rise up the initiatory ladder. However, the same applies to the Church of SCIENTOLOGY, with its 'Bridge to Total Freedom', blurring the lines between secret societies and religion even more.

Criminal and political secret societies overlap considerably (leaving out, for the moment, government secret societies). Italy was shocked in 1981 to discover that it had been harbouring perhaps the ultimate real-life secret society. Founded in the mid-1960s, *Propaganda Due*, or P2, was an illegal masonic lodge whose members (somewhere between 1,000 and 2,400 in Italy alone) included senior politicians, businessmen, financiers, generals, admirals and the head of the Italian Secret Service. It also had close links with the Mafia and with some senior figures in the Vatican. It was organized, with a cell-like structure, so that only its head, Licio Gelli, knew all the members. Gelli had impeccable right-wing credentials: he fought for Franco in the Spanish Civil War, and had worked as a liaison officer between the Nazis and the Italian Fascists. Through intelligence gained from members, often induced to join through blackmail and corruption, Gelli was able to influence major decisions in politics and finance – and when he required money-laundering services, or muscle, he could call on the Mafia. P2 was closely involved in the scandal of the Vatican Bank under Archbishop Paul

Marcinkus, and the death of Roberto Calvi, head of the Banco Ambrosiano, who was found hanging under Blackfriars Bridge in London in June 1982.

The best-known criminal organization in the world, the Mafia, is generally thought to have begun as an armed movement to protect the people of Sicily from one set of invading overlords after another. But men with guns learn to like power for itself, and when the Mafia, along with hundreds of thousands of poor Sicilians, moved to the USA in the late 19th and early 20th centuries, it quickly became synonymous with extortion, protection rackets, organized gambling and prostitution. It was also wealthy enough and well-enough connected in some cities, such as Chicago and New York, to be able to exert influence on the police and (at least local) politicians. Despite being a criminal organization, the Mafia, in common with many secret societies, has a high sense of internal honour, in looking after its own – its name for itself, *Cosa Nostra*, means 'our affair'. It also has an inviolable code of silence, the *Omertà*, which has been compared to the oaths of secrecy of other secret societies.

The Triads or Tongs are in some ways the Chinese equivalent of the Mafia. It is thought that they began as a form of organized resistance to the Manchu dynasty in China in the 1760s. One story has it that five Buddhist monks founded five monasteries and five secret societies to protect the oppressed. The secret societies of the 19th century included the White Lotus Society, the Red Fists and the Illustrious Worthies. The Boxer Rebellion in Beijing in 1900 was promoted by several secret societies including the Fist for Righteous Harmony Society. Today they have degenerated into well-organized criminal gangs, operating protection rackets and controlling crime within the Chinese communities of major cities in the West.

Other criminal societies are motivated by racial or religious hatred. There have been several versions of the Ku Klux Klan (KKK). The first, founded at the end of the American Civil War, had Confederate political motivations – it was not just anti-black, but anti Northern Republicans and anti corrupt Northern businessmen (carpetbaggers). It soon became a vehicle for Southern whites to commit robbery, rape and murder, to the extent that its founder, Nathan Bedford Forrest, having failed to close it down, disowned it completely. The KKK faded in the late 19th century, but was revived in 1915 in Alabama as a fraternal secret society along similar lines to Freemasonry. Within a few years two internal coups changed it once more into an openly racist and violent society, against blacks, Jews, Catholics, communists and others. It flourished for some years, with its membership peaking at around four million, before its own reputation for violence sickened not just non-members but many members as well. The KKK as such may now be a spent force, but ultra-right-wing 'redneck' views are still espoused by some Christian white-supremacist movements in the USA and elsewhere, and by 'survivalist' militia groups – armed secret societies. Timothy McVeigh, who killed 168 people in the Oklahoma bombing in 1995, had connections with such groups.

The Republican protest movement in Northern Ireland sprang up in the 1960s to demand rights for the oppressed Catholic minority. The Provisional Irish Republican Army, founded in 1969, was always a proscribed organization and so, in a sense, a secret society – as were the various Protestant Loyalist paramilitary groups which sprang up in opposition to it. Both militant sides in 'the Troubles' were motivated by political ideologies that had roots firmly set in religious difference. Other European terrorist organizations with political motivations include the Basque nationalist group, ETA, which began in the 1960s and is still active, and the Baader-Meinhof gang (or the Red Army Faction), a militant anarchist group which was active in Germany from 1968 to 1977, and killed 34 people.

The terrorist organization al-Qaeda should correctly be called an Islamist rather than a Muslim group – its motivations are political rather than spiritual, and the vast majority of Muslims are opposed to its actions. It is unclear how much al-Qaeda itself is responsible for all the outrages attributed to it, or how much the name has become an umbrella term for a number of loosely connected, but separate, small terrorist groups. When Osama bin Laden founded al-Qaeda in 1989 he was following the ideology of other Islamist groups – the aim being to remove Western cultural and political influence from Muslim countries and restore pure Islamic rule. The USA's move into Kuwait in the Gulf War, and the presence of its troops in Saudi Arabia, birthplace of Islam and home to two of its most important holy places, fuelled bin Laden's anger, and he joined forces with the Taliban in Afghanistan, calling for a 'jihad against Jews and Crusaders' (ie the USA and her allies) while they have any presence or influence in the Middle East, 'the lands of Islam'. Any Muslims who do not support this cause are labelled apostates and can be killed, as can Shia Muslims; this form of jihadism stems from a fundamentalist Sunni sect called Wahhabism, which rejects all developments of teachings since the death of Muhammad. Like many other terrorist groups, its operational units are small autonomous cells, in which each member often only knows the identity of a small number of other members, thus maintaining security.

All countries have government secret services. For example, Britain has the Security Service (MI5) for internal intelligence on terrorism, counter-intelligence, etc, the Secret Intelligence Service (MI6) for overseas intelligence, and Government Communications Headquarters (GCHQ) for signals intelligence – plus security and intelligence sections of the police and military. In the USA the equivalents are the Department of Homeland Security, and to some extent the Federal Bureau of Investigation (FBI), the Central Intelligence Agency (CIA) and the National Security Agency (NSA), the initials of which are popularly said to stand for 'Never Say Anything'. These organizations are well known, though their operations are secret.

According to some commentators there is a host of other, far more secretive groups drawn from politics, international finance and big business – a world-government-level equivalent of P2. Some of these organizations do exist, but the Trilateral Commission, the Council on Foreign Relations, the Bilderberg Group and others are spuriously linked to American college fraternal societies, such as Skull and Bones, and to the ILLUMINATI, a short-lived society founded in Bavaria in 1776. These groups, with their alleged controlling influence on the world, are actually linked only in the claims of a number of conspiracy theorists, many of whom are from ultra-conservative fundamentalist Christian groups. Their claims revolve around a supposed Jewish-masonic conspiracy and an anti-Semitic forgery, the PROTOCOLS OF THE LEARNED ELDERS OF ZION.

Prostitution and the priesthood (along with espionage) vie for the title of 'the world's oldest profession'. Unlikely as it may seem, they are linked by an ancient symbol of secrecy and a Latin phrase. Traditionally a prostitute would have a rose carved into her bed head; it signified that anything said to her in pillow talk would go no further. The grill between priest and penitent in a Catholic confessional often shows a rose; 'the seal of the confessional' is inviolable. Freemasons use the phrase 'under the rose' or *sub rosa*; a rose on or above the dining table guarantees that anything said incautiously after too much wine will not be repeated outside. The rose is a symbol of the HOLY GRAIL and it lies at the heart of Rosicrucianism. The perfection of the rose symbolizes purity and virginity, and hence the Virgin Mary; but the opening rosebud, surrounded by thorns, symbolizes female sexuality. The rose, beauty surrounded by suffering (its thorns), also symbolizes a very different passion, the passion of Christ. With all these hidden meanings, some of them contradictory, there is perhaps no more suitable symbol for secret societies.

David V Barrett

seers

People who have the psychic ability to see into the future.

'Seer' is the name given to someone who has the psychic ability to see into the future. Seers appear very frequently in Greek mythology and legend; a true seer was believed to be an instrument of the gods, who possessed and spoke through the seer. Many Greek seers claimed to have received their gift from Apollo. One famous Trojan seeress was Cassandra, to whom Apollo was said to have granted the power of SECOND SIGHT in an attempt to win her love. When she rejected him, he could not take back his gift, but he deprived her of the ability to persuade others of the truth of her prophesies, so that although they were always true, they were never believed. She warned the Trojans against bringing the Wooden Horse inside the city, but was disastrously ignored. Another legendary Greek seer was Tiresias, who was given his powers by Zeus; it was he who revealed to Oedipus the terrible truth that he had killed his own father and married his mother.

Seers sometimes use a tool of DIVINATION to assist them in seeing the future. In the 16th century, NOSTRADAMUS, the most famous seer in history, employed a form of SCRYING – he would gaze into a brass bowl filled with water in order to achieve the meditative state in which he achieved his alleged visions of the future.

The Scottish Highlands have produced many people known for the gift of second sight, the most well-known of whom is Coinneach Odhar, the 17th-century psychic known as the BRAHAN SEER, who was said to have received his powers after coming into possession of a mysterious stone.

The most famous seer of the 20th century was the American psychic EDGAR CAYCE, who apparently channelled answers to questions while in a trance.

self

In philosophy, the distinct identity of a person, which is essential to them as a unique individual and is the agent responsible for their thoughts and actions. In mysticism and religion, the self is often identified with the soul and is regarded as a spark of the divine consciousness.

In philosophy, the self is the distinct identity of a person that is the agent responsible for their thoughts and actions. It is the self that makes each person an individual and is often identified with the mind as opposed to the body, as a permanent subject of successive and varying state of consciousness. The particular characteristics of the self determine its identity, and self-awareness is the knowledge that one exists as a unique entity. Identity is the term used throughout the social sciences to denote an individual's comprehension of himself or herself as a discrete and separate being, and the psychological concept of identity in humans is related to a person's view or mental model of himself or herself, known as the self-image.

Many philosophies hold that to truly know oneself is the most difficult thing of all to achieve. The temple of Apollo at Delphi was inscribed with the words 'To Know Thyself', and in the *TAO TE CHING* it is written that:

> Knowing others is wisdom; knowing the self is enlightenment.
> Mastering others requires force; mastering the self is strength.

According to many religious and philosophical traditions, especially mysticism, the self incorporates the innermost essence of each living being, and is the basis of true sentience, being regarded as the source of pure consciousness. The 'embodied self' or 'individual self' is often thought to be able to exist independently of or after the death of the physical body, and to contain a spark of the divine consciousness; in this sense, 'self' is used synonymously with SOUL. It is this truth, that the self is a minute part of God, which is realized in the enlightenment or 'self-realization' that is the goal of many spiritual paths, including YOGA, which refers to this 'true self' as the *atma*.

In psychology, the 'self' generally refers to the sentient, reflective personality of the individual, or the conscious mind which perceives both its environment and itself in, but distinct from, this environment. PARAPSYCHOLOGY, the scientific study of the properties of the mind which are believed to lie beyond those accepted by conventional science, seeks to prove the existence of mental powers such as EXTRASENSORY PERCEPTION and PSYCHOKINESIS; if such abilities are real, this would support the theory that consciousness, or the self, has a power of its own, which it can exert on its environment independently of its physical body.

Seljordsvatnet Monster *see* LAKE

SELJORDSVATNET MONSTER

Selma *see* LAKE SELJORDSVATNET MONSTER

sensory deprivation

In parapsychology, the removal of external stimuli in an attempt to heighten psychic powers.

Sensory deprivation began to be employed in a number of experiments in the area of PARAPSYCHOLOGY in the latter half of the 20th century. Researchers worked with the idea that the ability to focus the mind on the task in hand would be improved if the amount of 'background noise' from sense data received through the usual five senses were cut down or, ideally, removed entirely.

Such attempts at sensory deprivation are central to GANZFELD EXPERIMENTS. The methods used have developed from the simple placing of half ping-pong balls over the eyes, and the playing of white noise through headphones, to immersion in flotation tanks filled with warm water.

Sensory deprivation is also employed by some as a means of attaining a state of deep relaxation or to attempt to enter an ALTERED STATE OF CONSCIOUSNESS.

sephiroth

In the kabbalah, one of the ten emanations of God, through which he created the universe, and by the medium of which he interacts with the physical and spiritual world.

In the Jewish mystical tradition of the KABBALAH, God is seen as being neither matter nor spirit, but the Creator of both, and has two complementary aspects: the unknowable God himself, and the revealed aspect of God, who created and preserves the universe, and who interacts with mankind. The first, unknowable aspect of God is spoken of as *Ein Sof*, 'the infinite', while his second aspect, as seen by the universe, is represented by ten emanations known as the sephiroth, through which he is said to have created all things, and which mediate the interaction of the ultimate and unknowable God with the physical and spiritual world.

God is believed to have created the universe in stages, so that there is not one level of creation or reality, but four – the lowest being the physical world we experience in our ordinary lives, and the highest the world of pure light closest to God himself. These four worlds are, in descending order, Atziluth (the archetypal world, or world of deity); Briah or Beriah (the world of creation); Yetzirah (the world of formation); and Assiah or Asiyah (the world of matter or actions). God is said to have created the universe through ten channels of divine energy known as the sephiroth (the plural of the singular Hebrew word *sephirah*, meaning enumeration); in the process of creation, these ten attributes or emanations of God are thought to have formed an intermediate stage between his infinite light and the creation of the finite reality which humans experience. They each have their own unique quality, and manifest in each of the four worlds with the same name and quality but with a different energy according to which world they are in.

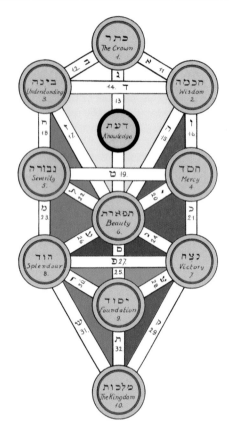

The kabbalistic Tree of Life, a visual representation of the interrelationship between the ten sephiroth. (© Mary Evans Picture Library)

In the kabbalah, each of the sephiroth is assigned a name and number, and is associated with a name of God, an archangel, an angelic order and a planetary force. Taken sequentially, the sephiroth represent the various stages of the creative process by which God generated, from the core of his infinite being, the progression of realms which culminated in the physical universe. They are sometimes called Vessels of Light, and each sephirah, or sphere, is seen as proceeding from the previous one. The first sephirah, which represents the highest attainable understanding of God by man, is KETHER, the Crown, whose number is 1. All the remaining sephiroth partake of its nature, although each has its own separate identity and function. Kether is followed by, in descending order: CHOKMAH or Wisdom (2); BINAH or Understanding (3); CHESED, Mercy or Love (4); GEBURAH, Severity or Judgement (5); TIPHARETH, Beauty or Harmony (6); NETZACH or Victory (7); HOD, Splendour or Glory (8); YESOD or Foundation (9); and MALKUTH or Kingdom (10). The ten sephiroth can be considered as concentric circles with Malkuth, which represents the physical world, as the innermost and Kether as the outermost. Some kabbalistic schools teach of an eleventh, 'hidden' sephirah called Daath, but the first kabbalists did not include such a sphere, and its existence as a full sephirah is a much debated point.

THE ZOHAR and other early kabbalistic works focus primarily on the sephiroth, and as an aid to MEDITATION, Jewish mystics created various visual structures of the sephiroth to show the interrelationship between them, the most popular of which is the TREE OF LIFE.

Serios, Ted *see* THOUGHTOGRAPHY

serpent *see* SNAKES

SETI *see* SEARCH FOR EXTRATERRESTRIAL INTELLIGENCE

seven
The seventh whole number, represented by the digit 7; considered significant in numerology.
Seven is the seventh whole number. In the minor ARCANA of the TAROT, the sevens represent risk-taking, experimentation, courage and victory. In the major arcana, 7 is the number associated with the Chariot card. In Hebrew GEMATRIA, 7 corresponds to the Hebrew letter Zayin, and in the KABBALAH, it is the number assigned to the sephirah NETZACH. In NUMEROLOGY it is considered to be a YANG number; it is the numerical value of the letters G, P and Y, and a person with 7 in their numerological profile is believed to be analytical, observant and insightful; they are often spiritual and sometimes psychic, and they greatly value privacy, to the point of being a loner. It is also believed that a 7 personality may also display the more negative traits of unsociability, eccentricity, scepticism and insincerity.

Seven has a long history as a lucky and magical number. It is seen as symbolizing spiritual perfection, and in many cultures is sacred; it is a recurring number in folklore, mythology and nature. There are seven days in the week, the world is said to have been created in seven phases, and in some versions of the kabbalah, there are seven SEPHIROTH. Man's life is said to have seven stages, and the Bible lists seven deadly sins and seven virtues. There are seven visible colours in the spectrum and in a rainbow – red, orange, yellow, green, blue, indigo and violet – seven seas, and seven wonders of the ancient world. In ancient times, astronomers could see seven moving heavenly bodies or 'planets' in the sky – the Sun, the Moon, Mercury, Venus, Mars, Jupiter and Saturn

– and the Babylonian astrological system constructed around these is the basis of modern ASTROLOGY. The seventh son of a seventh son is said to possess mystical powers. In Buddhism, there are seven stages in the journey toward the spiritual centre, and in Egyptian mythology, the number 7 is sacred to Osiris, while in classical mythology, 7 is sacred to Apollo and Pan. In the tarot, the significance of 7 is seen in the major arcana, which consists of 22 cards; leaving aside the first card, The Fool, which is assigned the number zero and is usually considered separately, the remaining cards, numbered from 1 to 21, fall naturally into 3 groups of 7.

The ancient Greek philosopher and mystic PYTHAGORAS discovered that if a string which vibrates at a certain musical note has its length halved, it will produce a note which is a whole tone up from the first note, and if the length of the vibrating string continues to be halved, seven distinct whole-tone notes are produced before the eighth note brings a return to the original note, one level higher. Esotericists believe that these seven notes of the musical scale, do, re, mi, fa, so, la and ti – the eighth returning note being referred to as the 'octave' of the first one – carry a special magical meaning and power. See also ONE; TWO; THREE; FOUR; FIVE; SIX; EIGHT; NINE; TEN; ELEVEN; TWELVE.

sex magic *see* MAGIC, SEX

shaman
Traditionally, a shaman is an intermediary between the people of his community and the spirit world.
In most instances the word 'shaman' has replaced the use of the 19th-century phrases 'WITCH DOCTOR' or 'MEDICINE MAN' as it avoids the potentially pejorative interpretations that can be applied to these terms (although 'medicine man' is still often used specifically in the context of Native American holy men). In recent years the use of the word shaman as a generic term has itself become increasingly controversial – many people feel that it has been misappropriated by the Western NEW AGE movement, and that it is sometimes incorrectly applied by Western academics to figures within tribal societies when they do not fully appreciate the beliefs held by those within the culture.

Etymologically, 'shaman' comes from Tungusic Siberian roots, probably meaning 'he or she who knows' (the word is gender-neutral). A shaman is usually understood to be someone who is both separated from normal society and holds a position of honour in a community, who works for the good of the people alone rather than as a part of a religious hierarchy. More colourfully, shamans are sometimes described as 'walkers between worlds'. The idea of the spiritual journey undertaken while in a trance state, sometimes called the shamanic flight, is central to the concept of shamanism. This process might involve the use of HALLUCINOGENS derived from local plants and the use of rhythmic drumming and dance (see SHAMANIC VISUALIZATION).

Shamans are believed to be able to speak to the SPIRITS to bring back knowledge or invoke their assistance in processes of healing. In some cultures they take the role of accompanying the souls of the dead, guiding them safely away from the world of the living.

The shaman is a solitary figure, and in many societies his status as such will be established when he is young – for example, he might have survived a serious illness or accident as a child, or he may be separated from the rest of his community by his appearance or behaviour. He will be singled out by an existing shaman, for one of these reasons, and given training before going through an initiation. If he passes this trial he will go through further training, perhaps for many years, before he is ready to take over from his predecessor, or to branch out on his own.

In recent years 'shamanism' has gained in popularity in the West. In this instance, devotees make their own adult choice to follow a shamanic path, either by learning from an established shaman or by making their own way.

shamanic visualization
The subjective reality of the shaman's journeys while in a trance state.

The religious scholar Mircea Eliade has described SHAMANISM as 'techniques of ecstasy' and 'ecstatic' experiences (see ECSTATIC PHENOMENA) that lie at the very heart of shamanic practice. To carry out their work a SHAMAN will work him- or herself into a trance state, perhaps through the use of fasting, HALLUCINOGENS, dancing or rhythmic drum beats – entering such a state is the beginning of the process of shamanic visualization.

Once in this condition the shaman is often described as going on a journey, or shamanic flight. For the shaman, this is experienced as a real journey, perhaps soaring as an eagle, or hunting as a jaguar. He may fly up into the 'sky world' above, or he may descend into the underworld. These may be the worlds of the SPIRITS, or the worlds of the dead, or they may be 'other worlds' (in the form of 'alternative realities'). While there, the shaman is believed to be able to speak to the spirits of plants, birds, animals, aspects of the landscape such as rivers and mountains, or the souls of the dead. He seeks answers to the questions he has been asked; sometimes he is acting

in a role that might be described as similar to that of an ORACLE, SEER, PSYCHIC or CLAIRVOYANT. Often a shaman will conduct the journey to find a cure for an illness at the request of someone who has approached him for help – it was for this reason that many who might better be described as shamans were previously given the labels WITCH DOCTOR or MEDICINE MAN.

shamanism
The practice of being an intermediary between people and the spirit world.

There are many different forms of shamanism. Some argue that the term should be limited to beliefs which exist within a very specific set of cultures. However, it has become common to apply it to a wide range of spiritual practices found in non-literate societies – both historically and in the modern world – particularly in Siberia, South America, Indonesia and Australasia.

The central theme of shamanism is the idea of the journey of an individual, the SHAMAN, into the worlds of the SPIRITS, on behalf of others. This usually involves entering a trance state through the use of HALLUCINOGENS, drumming or dance.

In the last few decades shamanism has also developed as a spiritual practice in the Western world, alongside other NEW AGE religions and belief systems – there are now probably more 'urban shamans' in London or New York than there are traditional shamans in Siberia.

Shaver Mystery
The theories of Richard Shaver, who, following the publication of his stories relating to an ancient civilization and their descendants who still live beneath the earth's surface, claimed that his stories were true.

The American writer Richard Sharpe Shaver (1907–75) became famous in science-fiction circles in the late 1940s, particularly through pieces written for the *Amazing Stories* magazine, which was edited by Ray Palmer (1910–77). The stories described a superhuman race who had inhabited great cities inside the earth in prehistoric times, and who had eventually left the planet for another world.

According to these stories, this people had left behind not only the physical remains of their civilization but their degenerate and diseased descendants, still living in an underworld beneath the earth's surface. Shaver called these creatures 'Dero' (short for detrimental robots) and portrayed them as kidnapping humans from the surface for food and sadistically projecting disturbing thoughts to the surface dwellers using telepathic rays.

Shaver and Palmer caused controversy when they began to declare that the stories were not purely the products of a sci-fi writer's imagination but represented fictionalized accounts of real beings and events. Shaver went on to claim that he had visited these underground cities and communicated with their inhabitants. These claims, their subsequent elaboration and the literature that grew up around them became known as the Shaver Mystery.

This had obvious echoes of existing HOLLOW EARTH THEORIES, although how far Shaver was influenced by these remains unclear. Many people were convinced by Shaver's claims and numbers of 'Shaver Mystery Clubs' were set up around the USA. Some even asserted that they too had journeyed to the underworld and met the Deros. Shaver spent many years gathering physical evidence to back up his claims, especially samples of rocks which he believed contained writings and pictures created by the vanished prehistoric race. He also interpreted SPONTANEOUS IMAGES such as rock formations or polished sections of stone as being evidence of his ancient civilization. However, apart from his band of believers, few gave any credence to these ideas.

The Shaver Mystery, with its stories of interplanetary travel, is often credited with setting in motion the UFO 'industry' that arose, particularly in the USA, from the 1950s onwards. In some ways it was a casualty of the FLYING SAUCER craze, which was much more exciting and open to participation than searching for creatures living under the earth. This did not prevent some of Shaver's followers from trying to explore caverns in the search for man-made constructions or artefacts as well as an entrance to the subterranean world. Some even claimed to have found them, but satisfactory evidence of their discoveries was never forthcoming.

Interest in the Shaver Mystery declined after the deaths of both Shaver and Palmer in the 1970s but it continues to have its followers and there is a magazine (*Shavertron*) dedicated to Shaver's work and its subsequent developments and interpretations.

SHC *see* SPONTANEOUS HUMAN COMBUSTION

Sheldrake, Rupert (1942–)
Controversial English biologist and philosopher.
Rupert Sheldrake began his academic career as a biochemist and plant physiologist at Cambridge University (with philosophy research at Harvard). From 1974 to 1985 he worked as a plant physiologist at the International Crops Research Institute for the Semi-Arid Tropics in Hyderabad, India, and he is currently the Perrott-Warwick Scholar for parapsychology, a scholarship administered by Trinity College, Cambridge.

Sheldrake's best-known book, *A New Science of Life*, was published in 1981. In it, he put forward his hypothesis of 'formative causation' and his theory of 'morphic resonance'. He proposes that 'memory is inherent in nature' and that 'most of the so-called laws of nature are more like habits'. He holds that the previous behaviours and forms of organisms influence the behaviours and forms of present organisms (the process of morphic resonance). He believes that the 'living memory within nature' is an underlying law of science and gives us an answer to how everything happens. While Sheldrake's theories are regarded as pseudoscientific at best by much of the mainstream scientific community, his work is popular, and since *A New Science of Life* was first published many people have participated in experiments that have attempted to prove his theories.

As part of Sheldrake's ideas, EXTRASENSORY PERCEPTION is a normal occurrence. His most famous experiments in this area include those into the existence of ANIMAL PSI, and also staring experiments. In *Dogs that Know When Their Owners are Coming Home* (1999), Sheldrake claimed that many pets possess psychic ability and 'know' when their owners are on their way home. Sheldrake has been carrying out research into the sense of being stared at (see also DIRECT MENTAL INTERACTION WITH LIVING SYSTEMS) since the 1980s. He claims that statistical analysis of the results of thousands of experiments show significant evidence that the sense of being stared at is real. In tests where the 'starer' randomly stares at the back of the 'staree', he claims that the 'staree' can consistently predict with 55 per cent accuracy when they are being stared at.

Sheldrake's theories remain controversial, and he is frequently criticized by mainstream scientists. His other works include *Seven Experiments that Could Change the World: A Do-It-Yourself Guide to Revolutionary Science* (1994) and *The Sense of Being Stared At* (2003).

shiatsu
A form of therapy in which pressure is applied to acupuncture points in order to balance and restore the free flow of energy in the body. Body stretches and gentle manipulation of the joints are also part of the treatment.
Shiatsu (in Japanese, literally 'finger pressure') is a contemporary form of BODYWORK which has its roots in traditional Japanese massage but also incorporates elements from Western techniques such as physiotherapy and osteopathy. Its origins date back thousands of years to the massage systems of ancient China, which were brought to Japan and eventually developed into separate therapies. Sometimes described as Japanese physiotherapy, shiatsu is a

Japanese adaptation of ACUPRESSURE. Shiatsu seeks to identify imbalances and deficiencies in the body's flow of ENERGY or QI ('ki' in Japanese). Such imbalances are thought to be the cause of most illnesses, and a diagnosis is made by questioning the patient as well as carrying out a physical examination – such as palpating the abdomen to detect strengths and weaknesses in the MERIDIANS and internal organs.

Treatment is HOLISTIC, with the aim of balancing the body as a whole rather than focusing on specific symptoms. It is usually performed on a mat on the floor, with the patient fully clothed. Deep finger pressure is applied to certain points (known as *tsubos* in Japanese) along the meridian lines, to clear energy blockages and restore a balanced flow of ki. In general, this pressure is sustained and stationary, lasting for about 30 seconds at a time, and as well as the fingertips, the thumbs, knuckles, elbows, knees and even feet are used in some styles of shiatsu. In addition to massage, the joints are gently rotated and manipulated, and body stretches are used.

Shiatsu is practised widely in Japan, and is also becoming increasingly popular in the West. It is claimed to reduce stress, calm the nervous system, boost stamina, improve the digestion, promote better posture, and relieve neck and back pain.

ships, ghost *see* GHOST SHIPS

Shipton, Mother *see panel p623*

shrines
Originally, containers for sacred relics, or the tombs of saints or other holy people. Now also applied to a place of worship hallowed by its association with a religious figure, or a structure for public or private worship dedicated to a particular deity or holy person.
The word 'shrine' comes from the Latin *scrinium*, meaning 'a box or case for papers', and in its original sense, a shrine was a container, usually made of precious materials, for a holy relic, such as that of a saint. The word also came to be used of the tomb of a saint or other religious figure, or a place of worship that was considered particularly holy because of its association with a sacred person, object or event. Such sites became the destination for pilgrimages, and many shrines continue to be visited for that purpose to this day. A shrine may be an elaborate place of public worship, or a simple altar in a home or workplace, a room, an alcove, or a shelf furnished with religious symbols or images, but what generally distinguishes a shrine from a temple is that it is dedicated to the veneration of one particular deity or religious figure. In ancient Greece and Rome, domestic shrines were usually dedicated to ancestral or tutelary spirits.

Shrines are a feature of a number of religious traditions, including Hinduism, Buddhism, Anglicanism, Orthodox Christianity, and Roman Catholicism, whose long tradition of the veneration of saints has produced a large number of internationally renowned shrines, such as the minor basilica of Our Lady of LOURDES in France, the Shrine of the Three Kings in Cologne Cathedral, Germany, and the Shrine of the Blessed Virgin Mary in Walsingham, England.

The principle worship in Shinto, the indigenous nature-focused religion of Japan, is carried out at large public shrines which are made of wood and are usually situated near sacred trees and flowing water. Each Shinto shrine is dedicated to a particular divine spirit, or *kami*. Small portable shrines are also carried in processions, and home worship is performed at private shrines that may consist of no more than a shelf holding a few ritual objects.

Shroud of Turin *see* TURIN SHROUD

Siberian Hell Hole *see panel p624*

sibyls
Female prophets or oracles of the ancient world.
A 'sibyl' was the name given in classical times to a female prophet or ORACLE and famous examples were found in such regions as Greece, Rome, Babylon and Egypt. They were each believed to be inspired by a particular deity.

The Pythia of Delphi is sometimes described as being a sibyl (see ORACLE OF DELPHI, THE). Next to her, probably the most famous sibyl is the one who inhabited a cave at Cumae, near Naples (the Cumaean Sibyl), and who was greatly venerated by the Romans.

In the *Aeneid* Aeneas is described as meeting the Cumaean Sibyl, who was inspired by Apollo and whose prophecies were written on leaves. She was supposed to have written the Sibylline Books, collections of oracles and prophecies kept at Rome and consulted by the Senate in emergencies until they were destroyed in a fire in 83 BC.

The Emperor Augustus is said to have consulted a sibyl, perhaps but not certainly the Cumaean Sibyl, as to whether or not he should be worshipped as a god.

When Christianity became the dominant religion of the Roman world the sibyls were banned along with all other elements of pagan belief. Later, however, the sibyls were adopted into the Christian tradition as prophets and the Cumaean Sibyl is traditionally believed to have prophesied the coming of Christ.

Mother Shipton (1488–c.1560)

The English witch and seer known as Mother Shipton (originally Ursula Southeil) was reputedly born near Knaresborough, Yorkshire, in 1488. She is generally held to have married a builder called Tony Shipton at the age of 24, and to have lived for more than 70 years. Said either to be a child of the DEVIL, or to have inherited powers of clairvoyance from her mother, Shipton made a series of prophesies that rival those of NOSTRADAMUS, both in popularity and in alleged accuracy.

In a series of incredible prophecies written in crude rhyme, Mother Shipton is said to have foreseen the development of many scientific inventions – including the telegraph, the automobile, aeroplanes, submarines, iron-clad boats and Crystal Palace – as well as making predictions of wars and political upheavals:

> Chariots without horses shall go,
> And accidents fill the world with woe.
> Around the world thoughts shall fly
> In the twinkling of an eye …
> Under water men shall walk,
> Shall ride, shall sleep, shall talk;
> In the air men shall be seen,
> In white, in black, and in green …
> Iron in water shall float,
> As easy as a wooden boat;
> A house of glass shall come to pass,
> In England, but alas!

Sadly, however, it is thought likely that Mother Shipton never actually existed. The first book of Shipton's 'works' was published in 1641, but it contained no biographical information and omitted the most famous of the prophecies. In 1684 Richard Head published *The Life and Death of Mother Shipton … strangely preserved amongst other writings belonging to an old Monastery in York-shire, and now published for the information of posterity, etc.* This did contain biographical information, and although written many years after Shipton's supposed death, it contained a detailed description of her appearance:

> … with very great goggling, but sharp and fiery eyes; her nose of incredible and unproportionable

Mother Shipton, the English witch and seer, depicted with a familiar. (© Mary Evans Picture Library)

length, having in it many crooks and turnings, adorned with many strange pimples of divers colours, as red and blue mixed …

In 1862, Charles Hindley published a collection of Shipton prophecies which he claimed he had copied from a manuscript in the British Museum. It is in this version that the famous rhyming prophecies such as those quoted above can be found. Hindley later admitted that he had concocted these predictions himself, and by the time he wrote them, many of the 'prophecies' had already been fulfilled – for example, Crystal Palace was built for the Great Exhibition of 1851, and a practical telegraph system had been invented by the 1830s. However, some of Hindley's prophecies related to future events, including the famously inaccurate:

> The world to an end shall come
> In eighteen hundred and eighty one.

Siberian Hell Hole

In the 1990s, a story began to circulate in the media that a team of Russian geologists conducting an extremely deep drilling operation in Siberia had actually opened a hole into Hell. According to the story the drill had penetrated over 14 kilometres (8.5 miles) into the earth when it broke though into empty space.

The geologists were said to have measured the temperature in this cavity as greater than 1,100°C, leading them to believe that they had reached the hollow centre of the planet. Not content with such an astonishing reading, the intrepid Russians felt moved to lower a microphone into the hole. When this picked up sounds identified as the agonized cries of a multitude of human beings in intolerable pain, the only conclusion to be reached was that a window had been opened into Hell itself.

According to some versions of the story, this diabolical outcome was further emphasized by the brief emergence from the hole of a luminous gaseous bat-like being that could only be the DEVIL.

Believe it or not, how did such a story originate? According to *Scientific American* it seems that in 1984 a Russian geological expedition in the Kola Peninsula (in north-west Russia, not Siberia) did carry out drilling to the extreme depth of 12 kilometres (7.5 miles), encountering temperatures of around 180°C as well as discovering gas. Some have suggested that this inspired various accounts, published in Christian fundamentalist publications, in which Hell began to feature – seen as a blow against atheism and proof of the existence of eternal punishment for sin. Perhaps sensing the mileage in this story, a Norwegian citizen claimed to have been inspired to perpetrate it as a deliberate hoax on such publications and radio shows after having been exposed to some of their more extravagant excesses on a visit to the USA.

The story acquired the status of an URBAN LEGEND, spreading rapidly via the Internet, where recordings of the alleged cries of damned souls in agony could be downloaded by the curious. Sceptics would point out that drilling equipment or microphones would have to be made of stern stuff indeed to function undamaged at such extraordinary temperatures. Questions could also be asked as to why no further exploration of this fortuitously discovered underworld has ever taken place. Conspiracy theorists might reply that this would have been covered up by those involved, but they must have had the devil of a time keeping it quiet.

Michelangelo included representations of twelve sibyls in his frescoes for the Sistine Chapel.

Silbury Hill

A Neolithic earthwork near Avebury in Wiltshire, England.

Silbury Hill, near AVEBURY in Wiltshire, is one of the greatest prehistoric earthworks in Europe. It is around 40 metres (130 feet) high at its flat summit and is ringed by a ditch that is 6 metres (20 feet) deep in places. Its base is round, and has a diameter of 168 metres (550 feet). This great mound, made from the earth and chalk dug out of the ditch, is believed to have been created c.2600 BC and would probably have been much higher at that point. It was built in terraces that were filled in to give a smooth conical shape when it was completed, although visible remnants of these remain. It has been estimated that it would take ten years for 700 men to construct it.

The reason for building Silbury is not known. The obvious purpose would be as a burial mound, and local folklore has it that it marks the grave of the legendary King Sil, who was said to have been interred astride a golden horse. While the antiquary William Stukeley (1687–1765) claimed to have unearthed bones and artefacts on the site, subsequent excavations, most recently in the 1960s, have failed to uncover any important finds. In another folk tale the DEVIL was preparing to drop an apronful of earth on the nearby town of Marlborough (just for devilment?) when priests from Avebury forced him to dump it elsewhere.

One theory links Silbury Hill with LEYS, maintaining that it is a kind of way-marker connecting, among other places, Avebury and STONEHENGE. Certainly, the area has so many Neolithic sites that the obvious inference is that it was of particular religious significance.

simulacra

Spontaneously occurring forms, faces and figures.

The word 'simulacra' comes from the Latin, usually meaning devotional objects in the likeness of sacred objects. In earlier times, the term would have applied to a cult statue of a deity, having the sense of being a

The simulacrum of a giant's profile at a rocky outcrop on Dartmoor known as Bowerman's Nose. (© TopFoto/Fortean)

vessel for the spirit or essence of that deity; something more than a mere lifeless effigy. While most simulacra of this type would have been crafted by artisans for ritual purposes, some images were believed to have been created by divine power as expressions of that divinity – for example, the TURIN SHROUD and the Veil of Veronica. In the Catholic Church, historians called these magical images 'acheropites', from the old Greek meaning an image not made by human hands. Other religions also have their acheropites and simulacra; Buddhists venerate designs in the shape of the idealized footprint of Buddha, especially if they have occurred naturally; and animists the world over hold sacred rock formations that resemble GODS and heroes.

By Victorian times, the meaning of simulacra had shifted toward implying a relatively valueless copy or imitation. In modern usage – especially in FORTEANA – simulacra are a genre of spontaneous images (see IMAGES, SPONTANEOUS), especially natural formations of figures or faces. Typical types of modern simulacra would include the shapes of animals perceived in clouds, faces in the bark of trees or rock formations, and marks in vegetables that resemble the Arabic script for

'Allah' (see HOLY VEGETABLES). More specific examples would include the Japanese crab 'Heikegani' (*Dorippe japonica*), whose carapace bears the distinct form of a samurai warrior mask, found mainly at the location where, legend tells, the remnant of the Heike clan committed suicide by jumping into the sea; the image of the Virgin of the Hermits found imprinted on hailstones that fell in Remiremont, France, on 26 May 1907; and the complete sequence of numerals and alphabet found in the scale patterns of butterfly wings.

sirens
Mythological creatures whose song lured sailors to shipwreck.
In classical mythology the sirens were sea NYMPHS, daughters of the river-god Achelous. Part woman and part bird, they lived on a rocky island and used their seductive songs to lure sailors toward them, to wreck their ships on the rocks.

In the story of Jason and the Argonauts, the crew of the *Argo* escaped the sirens through being sung to by their fellow crew-member, the poet Orpheus, whose song was even lovelier than theirs. Faced with the same trial, Odysseus instructed his crew to plug their ears with wax, while he, eager to hear the sirens' song, had himself tied to the mast of his ship. He was said to have been driven to the point of madness, begging his unheeding crew to release him. In some versions of the myth, the sirens, despairing at their failure, drowned themselves after this episode.

Their name survived in everyday language, however, coming to mean any woman who is seen as both highly alluring and highly dangerous to men.

Those who look for rational explanations for myths have suggested that the sirens are symbolic of a narrow strait at sea where the sound of water rushing between cliffs sounds melodious but represents great danger.

SIS *see* SOCIETY FOR INTERDISCIPLINARY STUDIES

SITU *see* SOCIETY FOR THE INVESTIGATION OF THE UNEXPLAINED

six
The sixth whole number, represented by the digit 6; considered significant in numerology.
Six is the sixth whole number. It is the first perfect number, that is, a number which is the sum of all its divisors (1 + 2 + 3), and it is therefore endowed with special magical significance in many cultures, and symbolizes perfection and balance; as the double of 3, it also implies generation. Spiritually, 6 is the essence of love. In the minor ARCANA of the TAROT,

the sixes represent harmony and communication. In the major arcana, 6 is the number associated with the Lovers card. In Hebrew GEMATRIA, 6 corresponds to the Hebrew letter Vav, and in the KABBALAH, it is the number assigned to the sephirah TIPHARETH. In NUMEROLOGY it is considered to be a YIN number; it is the numerical value of the letters F, O and X, and a person with 6 in their numerological profile is believed to be dutiful, responsible, humanitarian and highly family-oriented. They are said to greatly prize beauty, harmony and balance. It is also believed that a 6 personality may also display the more negative traits of jealousy, bitterness and vengefulness, and a tendency to make a martyr of themselves. In the Chinese culture, 6 is thought to be a lucky number because it sounds the same as the Chinese word meaning 'easy' or 'smooth'. See also ONE; TWO; THREE; FOUR; FIVE; SEVEN; EIGHT; NINE; TEN; ELEVEN; TWELVE.

666

The number given in the New Testament's Book of Revelation as the number of the Beast, traditionally identified with the Antichrist.

The New Testament's apocalyptic Book of Revelation describes a series of visions in which a beast, traditionally identified with the Antichrist, or with an entity controlled by the Antichrist, is ascribed the number 666:

> He also forced everyone, small and great, rich and poor, free and slave, to receive a mark on his right hand or on his forehead, so that no one could buy or sell unless he had the mark, which is the name of the beast or the number of his name. This calls for wisdom. If anyone has insight, let him calculate the number of the beast, for it is man's number. His number is 666.

Scholars have long debated the meaning of this passage and the number, which in the King James version of the Bible is given as 'six hundred three score and six'. A common idea is that 666 is a coded reference to the letters of a specific person's name, and through ingenious interpretations of the number, various candidates have been identified as the Beast, including Hitler and Ronald Reagan. Such theories are discounted by many people, but some scholars, using the Hebrew form of NUMEROLOGY known as GEMATRIA, in which each Hebrew letter has a numerical value, hold that the number represents the name of the Roman emperor Nero (*Neron Caesar* in Greek, which becomes *Nrwn Qsr* in Hebrew). Others, who believe that the prophecies refer to future events, have suggested that the mark may be a reference to

the Universal Product Code barcode, whose three sets of 'guard bars' seem to be arranged in the pattern of a 6.

Some early texts of the Book of Revelation give the number of the Beast as 616, which has been interpreted by scholars as a coded reference to the emperor Caligula, and many versions of the Bible give a footnote to say that the number, as translated from the Greek, could be 616, although Irenaeus, a Church father from the 2nd century AD, considered and rejected it in favour of 666.

In Western societies, the number is regarded with superstitious fear and avoided by many; for example, the US Highway 666, nicknamed 'the Devil's Highway' or 'the Highway of the Beast', was renumbered as US Route 491 in 2003.

sixth sense

A term popularly used to refer to extrasensory perception – the idea being that the human mind has a faculty for gaining and transmitting information which lies beyond the usual five senses.

The term 'sixth sense' was coined by the German researcher Rudolph Tischner in his 1920 book, translated into English in 1925 as *Telepathy and Clairvoyance*. He used the term to describe the receiving and sending of information by PSYCHIC means – among other things this was taken to include TELEPATHY, CLAIRVOYANCE, PRECOGNITION and PSYCHOMETRY. It has since become a popular term for all things psychic, and regularly appears in books, films and other areas of the media.

skepticism *see* SCEPTICISM

skunk ape *see* NAPE

skywatching

Deliberate observation of the sky, usually at night, in order to look for UFOs or to familiarize oneself with sources of misperception.

The most common image of a UFO researcher portrayed by the media is of someone wearing an anorak, sporting a pair of binoculars and staring heavenward, in the hope of seeing a spaceship from Mars on its way to Earth.

However, 'skywatching', as this practice is known, does have a valuable contribution to make. While the likelihood of seeing a UFO by randomly scanning the horizon is low, the technique does help newcomers to become aware of what is normally visible in the sky. This is especially true at night, when the majority of UFOs reports are generated. Many people, particularly those who live in our larger towns and cities, have little familiarity with bright meteors, satellites, the way that the underbellies of birds can reflect the light from street lamps, luminous clouds and the many other natural phenomena that regularly produce 'UFO' sightings. The first step towards solving a case is an awareness of possible explanations and most UFO groups recommend that their new investigators skywatch to see these things for themselves.

In the past there were a number of co-ordinated skywatch exercises, operated for example by the BRITISH UFO RESEARCH ASSOCIATION, across the British Isles. These major projects were curtailed because of perceived media ridicule. As a result, the relatively few experiments to occur after the 1970s were carried out without media involvement and were set up to serve a specific purpose. For instance, the Manchester UFO Research Association mounted a carefully planned skywatch following repeated sightings of a bright orange light over the Lancashire hills at night. In order to test their possible explanation they set up teams at various locations, and negotiated with a large radar facility to allow a team member to monitor air traffic. This skywatch solved the case, proving that the UFO was actually a cargo aircraft switching down its engines, turning off most of its lights and gliding for a few minutes over the rural terrain.

A similar joint operation was mounted by the Belgian UFO group, SOBEPS, and the military authorities during the BELGIAN WAVE – skywatch sites were manned by UFO researchers, while jet fighters were placed on standby to react immediately if anything strange appeared. Needless to say, skywatches of such sophistication are rare, particularly given the light-hearted way that the pursuit is often viewed.

PROJECT TWINKLE, set up by the US government in 1950 to obtain evidence for widespread sightings of green fireballs in New Mexico, was possibly the first known organized skywatch (although it was never promoted as such). Project HESSDALEN, in which scientists and UFO researchers joined forces to obtain instrumental readings relating to the regular sightings in a very active Norwegian WINDOW AREA, was, perhaps, the best example so far of a well-organized and successful skywatch. Many UFO researchers feel that by 'staking out' active locations for UFO reports, with the proper automatic equipment, real progress could be made.

slate-writing
A technique employed for the alleged production of written messages from the spirit world.
Slate-writing, a variation on AUTOMATIC WRITING, was a staple of many 19th-century MEDIUMS. It was first used by Henry Slade (1840–1905), who travelled the world demonstrating his messages. However,

although a number of prominent people, including respected scientists, attested to his genuine abilities, he was charged with fraud in London in 1876. The magician JOHN NEVIL MASKELYNE exposed his trickery and demonstrated to the court how slate-writing could be easily replicated. But although Slade disappeared from the SPIRITUALISM circuit, slate-writing did not.

To produce the effect, a medium would take a piece of slate, wash it and seal it in a container (or wrap it up) with a slate pencil. The slate would then be left alone and writing would appear on it, apparently without human intervention. Variations included wrapping two slates together with a pencil sealed between them, laying a single slate face down over the pencil or holding a slate under a table at a SÉANCE.

Those of a more sceptical bent pointed out that it would be expected that a spirit's writing should match the writing of that individual in life – strangely, in practice, it usually bore no resemblance at all.

sleep
The regular period of reduced consciousness experienced by most animals.
Sleep is a regularly experienced state of immobility and reduced consciousness. Most animals sleep during a particular period of the day, with the duration of the period of immobility varying by species. It is influenced by circadian rhythms, which are cyclical variations in the intensity of metabolic or physiological processes of approximately 24 hours.

Sleep is not the same as unconsciousness, but is rather a state of modified or reduced consciousness in which the sleeper is still aware of and influenced by their surroundings.

Scientists studying sleep often use an electroencephalograph (EEG) to detect and record the small electrical impulses produced by the brain. Such techniques allow them to identify different phases during a period of sleep.

The first phase is a transition between being awake and falling asleep, known as the HYPNAGOGIC STATE, during which hallucinations may occur. Dreaming is thought to take place in the period known as REM (rapid eye movement) sleep: in this state the eyes of the sleeper move almost constantly. Towards the end of a period of sleep the HYPNOPOMPIC STATE is reached, which again is productive of hallucinations.

People who are, for whatever reason, deprived of sleep tend to suffer from a range of effects such as inability to concentrate, loss of memory, exhaustion, depression, hallucination, irritability and reduction in the ability to solve problems. It is thought that this is caused by a reduction in the body's ability to metabolize glucose, which then affects the frontal cortex of the brain.

Some aspects of sleep are not fully understood, but it is clearly necessary for its restorative effects, as shown by the consequences of being deprived of it. See also DREAMS; SLEEP STATES; SLEEPWALKING.

Sleeping Preacher, the

The name given to Rachel Baker, a young girl who apparently preached the word of God while asleep.

In the early 1800s, an American teenager called Rachel Baker started to talk in her sleep. She would fall into a trance state, and apparently start preaching sermons, although when she awoke she claimed she had no recollection of what had occurred. Occasionally the sermons would be interspersed with original poetry and musical compositions, but it was for her preaching that she became known, earning the nickname 'the Sleeping Preacher'. Baker was examined by a number of physicians in New York, all of whom were puzzled by her symptoms. Dr Samuel L Mitchell, who investigated her case, remarked:

> The latter of these remarkable affections of the human mind, *somnium cum religione*, belongs to Miss Rachel Baker, who for several years has been seized with somnium of a religious nature … Her face being turned to the heavens, she performs her nightly devotions with a consistency and fervor, wholly unexampled in a human being, in a state of somnium. Her body and limbs are motionless … the only motion the spectator perceives, is that of her organs of speech, and an oratorical inclination of the head and neck … According to the tenor and solemnity of the address, the attendants are affected with seriousness.

It would seem that a course of medical treatment, including doses of opium, eventually cured the Sleeping Preacher of what some described as divine inspiration, and others either hysteria or hoax.

sleep paralysis

A form of paralysis experienced on waking up or going to sleep.

Some people find that for a few seconds as they are awaking from sleep, or about to fall asleep, they have a sensation of being unable to move or speak. This can also occur during the night, with the sleeper then going back to sleep again.

Associated with this phenomenon are hypnagogic or hypnopompic hallucinations (see HYPNAGOGIC STATE and HYPNOPOMPIC STATE), feelings of fear or great anxiety, difficulty in breathing, a sensation of pressure on the chest and the sense of someone or something else being present. The person may also experience AUDITORY HALLUCINATIONS, such as buzzing or rushing noises, animal sounds and indistinct or garbled voices.

The 'presence' that people sense is usually vague and indefinable, but it is generally characterized as being evil or menacing and produces intense fear. People often describe it as being invisible, or at least unseen, but at the same time they feel that if they turn around quickly enough they will be able to see whatever it is. Many report a feeling of being watched, with the self-consciousness that this inevitably brings. While most people have experienced an inexplicable sense of not being alone, while no one else is visibly present, this is most marked during sleep paralysis.

Some people also report a feeling of floating, which can sometimes be pleasurable or produce a sensation of calm, and this can develop into a full OUT-OF-BODY EXPERIENCE in which the person is able to look down on their own sleeping body.

The phenomenon of sleep paralysis seems to begin most often in adolescence, with some people continuing to experience it regularly and throughout their lives, and others undergoing it only rarely and sometimes appearing to outgrow it.

Some scientists say that sleep paralysis is an anomalous form of the state of REM sleep, in which most DREAMS are experienced. According to this theory, the phenomenon results from a mechanism in the brain that acts to immobilize the body during dreaming, as an automatic safeguard against physically acting out the events of the dream. The sleeper, for some reason, is awoken suddenly from the REM state, not giving the body enough time to fully recover from the immobilized condition and thus producing a feeling of being paralysed.

It is thought that many people who report mysterious or supernatural experiences, such as having been abducted by aliens (see ALIEN ABDUCTION) or being visited by SPIRITS, have actually undergone a form of sleep paralysis, with accompanying hallucinations. Some consider that the legends of the INCUBUS or SUCCUBUS (respectively male and female demons believed to have sexual intercourse with sleeping people) are also explained by this phenomenon.

Sleep paralysis is often thought to be related to narcolepsy, a condition in which a person suffers short attacks of irresistible drowsiness at any time of day. However, not everyone who suffers from narcolepsy also suffers from sleep paralysis, and not everyone who experiences sleep paralysis is narcoleptic.

sleep states

Different stages passed through by someone sleeping.

We may think of SLEEP as a uniform period of being immobile and at rest, but in fact time spent sleeping can be divided up into several different states, during each of which the body and brain are undergoing various kinds of activity that are still very much unexplained.

Sleep usually begins with what is known as the HYPNAGOGIC STATE, when the sleeper is going through a transitional phase between wakefulness and falling asleep. It is well known that some people are prey to hallucinations at this stage. This is followed by various periods of relatively light sleep, and a sleeper may oscillate between different levels of this.

At some point most people will enter a stage of REM (rapid eye movement), during which it is believed dreaming takes place. An automatic mechanism in the brain comes into play during dreaming which ensures that the body remains immobile and cannot physically act out the events of the dream. Because this phase is characterized by increased brain activity with simultaneous immobility it is often known as paradoxical sleep. This may be followed by further periods of lighter sleep.

The period of transition between sleeping and being awake is called the HYPNOPOMPIC STATE, and again this can be productive of hallucinations.

sleepwalking
The act of walking around while asleep.
Sleepwalking, also known as somnambulism or noctambulism, is a form of behaviour in which a person who has been sleeping gets up and walks around while not becoming fully conscious. It is fairly common in children and less so in adults. With children the episodes last only a few minutes and, as long as the child is prevented from coming to accidental harm and gently guided back to bed, the medical view is that it is not important. In most cases the person involved remembers nothing of the incident.

People sleepwalking will have their eyes open (not closed as in popular belief), and this is one of the elements of the behaviour that have led it to be seen as frightening, eerie and unnatural by witnesses to it throughout the ages. In some cultures sleepwalking was thought to be caused by the influence of the moon, or the result of the person being possessed by SPIRITS.

The fact that children usually grow out of it suggests that in them the behaviour is triggered by changes in the natural sleep patterns between childhood and adolescence. Sleepwalking often runs in families, and this lends weight to the argument that physiological factors are important.

In adults, however, sleepwalking can involve longer periods of time and may lead the person to leave the bedroom, or even the house, where they are sleeping. Contrary to the received wisdom about never waking a sleepwalker, in fact it can often be more dangerous not to wake them. Sleepwalking, or as it is often called in legal contexts, AUTOMATISM, has been used as a defence in criminal trials, even in murder cases, with defendants claiming to remember nothing of the actions of which they are accused.

What is happening seems to be that the states of waking and sleeping become dissociated, with activity going on in the brain that is typical of deep sleep (but not REM sleep, in which DREAMS occur), and at the same time brain activity that is associated with being awake. This, apparently, is why a sufferer can move about while simultaneously being in a trancelike state of unawareness. Similarly, a sleepwalker's brain is thought to be in a state in which memory is not functioning and events are not recorded, and this explains the failure to remember the actions that have taken place.

Sleepwalking in adults is often described as being hysterical, triggered by ongoing worries or stress. One of its most famous portrayals in literature is in Shakespeare's *Macbeth*, in which Lady Macbeth sleepwalks, tormented by the guilt of her murderous actions, and tries to wash imaginary blood from her hands. In her case, the end result is madness.

The causes of sleepwalking are also thought to include sleep deprivation, sleep apnoea, extreme fatigue, abuse of alcohol or drugs, the effects of an illness that includes fever and the taking of certain medicines. Measures used against it include psychological treatment, hypnosis and the teaching of relaxation techniques to counter stress. In some cases antidepressant drugs have been shown to have good effects.

Smith, Hélène (c.1861–1929)
Swiss medium who apparently channelled messages from Mars.
Born Catherine Elise Muller in Geneva, Switzerland, the MEDIUM Hélène Smith specialized in AUTOMATIC WRITING, although she was also said to display CLAIRVOYANCE and CLAIRAUDIENCE. She believed herself to be the REINCARNATION of both Marie Antoinette and an Indian princess.

Smith became interested in SPIRITUALISM in the early 1890s, and began attending SÉANCES at which her mediumistic abilities were revealed. She claimed that two of her early 'controls' (spirits through whom she communicated with the spirit world – see SPIRIT GUIDE) were the French poet and writer Victor Hugo (1802–85) and 'Leopold' (alias the Italian adventurer and founder of EGYPTIAN RITE FREEMASONRY, Count Alessandro di Cagliostro). Perhaps inspired by a comment from fellow spiritualist Auguste Lemaître,

An example of Hélène Smith's 'Martian' writing.
(© TopFoto/Fortean)

that humans might soon make contact with life forms from other planets, Smith soon fell into a trance and reported on life on the planet Mars. She went on to produce a large body of work on the subject, apparently able to both speak and write in the Martian language. Her 'Martian' revelations included detailed descriptions of the landscape of Mars and its inhabitants.

Smith's apparent paranormal abilities were studied by the Swiss psychologist Théodore Flournoy (1854–1920), and his book *From India to the Planet Mars* (1900) popularized her claims. Flournoy believed that Smith's amazing Martian experiences resulted from a highly developed imagination and 'repressed' but familiar memories (see CRYPTOMNESIA). He did not accept her mediumistic abilities, although he did conclude that she may have been able to use TELEPATHY. As to the Martian language that Smith used in her automatic writing, while it was apparently written in unknown characters, the translations provided by Smith led language experts to find remarkable similarities to Smith's native French.

snakes
Recurring symbolic creatures in myth and religion.
The snake has been an important symbol in many mythologies and religions around the world for thousands of years. There is quite a variety, however, in terms of what the snake represents.

In Christianity, snakes tend to be associated with evil, treachery and mendacity, often with the DEVIL himself. In the Bible, for example, it is in the form of a serpent that the Devil tempts Adam and Eve to taste the forbidden fruit from the Tree of Knowledge, leading to their expulsion from the Garden of Eden. One of the miracles associated with St Patrick is that he drove all of the snakes out of Ireland, which is unequivocally and unthinkingly presented as a good thing. Among certain fundamentalist Christian believers in the USA, the ritual handling of poisonous snakes is still practised as a sign of adherence to their faith, as derived from biblical references.

In ancient Egypt, a rearing cobra known as the uraeus was often depicted on the heads of Pharaohs, symbolizing many things including the god Re, the sun, and dominion over Lower Egypt.

The ancient Minoans worshipped a snake goddess, portrayed as a woman holding a living snake in each hand, but nothing much is known about the beliefs involved. In Greek mythology, when Apollo killed a giant snake called Python at Delphi he established an oracle on the spot, and gave prophecies through the medium of a priestess known as the Pythia (see ORACLE OF DELPHI, THE). In another myth, the Hydra was a monstrous water snake with many heads which was killed by Hercules as one of his twelve labours. The Gorgon Medusa was said to have snakes growing out of her head instead of hair. The basilisk was a serpent believed to have the power of killing by its glance alone.

The Roman god Mercury was said to have stopped a fight between two snakes by separating them with his staff. The image of the snakes entwining themselves around the staff became a symbol of peace and this was represented in the staff (caduceus) carried by Roman heralds. This image also became associated with Aesculapius, the god of healing, and is still recognizable as a symbol of the medical profession.

It was the Greeks who gave the name *ouroboros* (tail-devouring) to the already ancient image of a snake forming its body into a circle by biting its own tail. This was a symbol of totality, completeness or eternity known to both the Egyptians and Phoenicians. The Midgard Serpent (also known as Jormungand) of Norse mythology is often portrayed in the same way, having grown so monstrously large that it could encircle the earth. In the Norse myth of the end of the world (Ragnarök) the thunder-god Thor fights with the Midgard Serpent until he kills it but dies himself from its venomous bite.

The Aztecs worshipped a deity called Quetzalcoatl,

whose name means 'feathered serpent'. He was seen as a benefactor of the human race who, among other things, discovered maize and gave fire to mankind.

The most widespread idea associated with snakes in mythology is that of immortality or constant renewal. This is based on observation of snakes regularly shedding their skin, which was taken as an act of surviving death and being reborn in a new body.

Society for Interdisciplinary Studies

An international group that investigates 'catastrophic anomalies'.

The Society for Interdisciplinary Studies (SIS) was founded in 1974 to explore the suggestion that catastrophes of a global and cosmic nature may have played a part in the history of mankind, and may have been recorded by many cultures worldwide in their oral and written traditions. Because the SIS acknowledges that these investigations and discussions necessarily include the effect such catastrophes have on other disciplines – such as biology, cosmology, geology, psychology, archaeo-astronomy, astrophysics, linguistics, history and RELIGION – it is truly interdisciplinary and properly a branch of ANOMALISTICS. The Society's main publication (*Chronology & Catastrophism Review*) appears twice a year, and they organize occasional conferences.

Topics discussed in recent years have included: the 'stability' of the solar system; the origins and history of religion; rock art and mythology as a historic record; the role of plasma in the universe; the long-term trauma of catastrophes; linguistics and the origin of words; the cause of evolution and its rate of change; revisions of historical chronologies and dating methods; meteorite impacts and other catastrophes affecting climate change and extinctions; and astronomical anomalies that indicate major catastrophes.

Society for Psychical Research

The oldest organization still in existence that is dedicated to the scientific investigation of claims of the paranormal.

The Society for Psychical Research (SPR) was founded in 1882 with the aim of investigating, in a scientific and unbiased manner, claims of the PARANORMAL. It was initiated by three researchers at Trinity College, Cambridge – Edmund Gurney, Frederick Myers and Henry Sidgwick – all of whom had an interest in SPIRITUALISM. They set up headquarters in London shortly afterwards but still continued to maintain library facilities in Cambridge. In its early years there was some conflict between the spiritualist members and those (led by Sidgwick) who wished to pursue a more rigorous, academic line of investigation. A large number of spiritualists left the organization before the end of its first decade. In 1885 an American branch of the SPR was formed and they eventually became an affiliate organization in 1890 (see AMERICAN SOCIETY FOR PSYCHICAL RESEARCH).

Throughout its history the SPR has produced many reports into cases that they have investigated; in some instances they debunk and in others they support, depending upon the evidence they find. The society takes an interest in all areas of PSYCHICAL RESEARCH such as spiritualism and mediumship, GHOSTS and APPARITIONS, PSYCHOKINESIS and EXTRASENSORY PERCEPTION. Famous investigations of HAUNTINGS have included those of the ENFIELD POLTERGEIST, BALLECHIN HOUSE, the BROWN LADY OF RAYNHAM HALL and the MORTON GHOST.

The SPR currently publishes the quarterly *Journal of the Society for Psychical Research* and an infrequent *Proceedings of the Society for Psychical Research*. It continues to hold an annual conference and its stated aim is:

> … understanding events and abilities commonly described as 'psychic' or 'paranormal' by promoting and supporting important research in this area.

Society for Research in Rapport and Telekinesis

A society which aims to investigate parapsychology and spirit communication as they were experienced during the Victorian era of séances.

The Society for Research in Rapport and Telekinesis (SORRAT) was founded in Missouri in 1961 by John G Neihardt. The intention was to conduct PSYCHICAL RESEARCH by attempting to employ many of the techniques used in the SÉANCE rooms during the heyday of SPIRITUALISM. Members believed that the key to TELEKINESIS taking place was an initial rapport with the SPIRITS or other external 'communicators'. John Thomas Richards wrote a history of SORRAT in 1982 and eventually took over the leadership of the organization.

From the earliest sittings SORRAT recorded a range of phenomena from TABLE-TURNING and 'spirit' messages, through to whole rooms shaking. Sittings of the group resembled the traditional séance with members seated in a circle with their hands loosely placed on a table. Messages were said to be spelt out using a system of raps. The organization became particularly well known for an experimental procedure which involves placing objects in a glass container with a lockable lid, where they can be observed but apparently not touched. This arrangement is called a 'minilab' and is now used extensively in PARAPSYCHOLOGY research elsewhere. SORRAT reported successes with this set-up, including such effects as rings linking and unlinking, balloons inflating and METAL BENDING. However, the process often involved the somewhat dubious technique of leaving the box alone and unobserved for a period, and the results have never been independently verified.

The organization now keeps largely to itself after being the subject of much criticism from members of the mainstream PARAPSYCHOLOGY community. As a consequence, there is little external appraisal of their investigations.

Society for Scientific Exploration
An international group of scientists investigating anomalous phenomena.
The Society for Scientific Exploration (SSE), was founded by physicist Peter Sturrock of Stanford University in 1982, when a group of 14 scientists and scholars agreed on the need for a new type of scientific organization that would investigate anomalous phenomena (see ANOMALIES) that are amenable to scientific investigation without restriction. Today, they have nearly a thousand 'anomalists' in 45 countries worldwide. Their annual meetings, held in the USA and in Europe, and their peer-reviewed journal (*Journal of Scientific Exploration*), provide a forum for the presentation and criticism of relevant research.

Topics under investigation cover a wide spectrum: from 'apparent anomalies in well-established disciplines to paradoxical phenomena that belong to no established discipline and therefore may offer the greatest potential for scientific advance and the expansion of human knowledge'. Major anomaly topics often involve deep philosophical questions, says Sturrock:

> Is the mind a machine or an entity that is in some sense independent of the body? Is there credible evidence that intelligent life exists on other planets … or that our solar system has ever been visited by EXTRATERRESTRIAL beings? Do some human beings have the capability of locating water and other life-giving resources? Are there sources of energy available to mankind other than sunlight, fossil fuels, and nuclear energy?

In its mission statement, the SSE outlines its parish:

> To the research scientist, we commend the intellectual challenge of explaining away an apparent anomaly or seizing the new knowledge presented by a real one. To the student scientist,

we point out that science does not begin with textbooks: it begins with the unknown and ends with textbooks. To the non-scientist, we acknowledge that deep public interest in some of these topics calls for unprejudiced evaluation based on objective research. To the policy-maker, we point out that today's anomaly may become tomorrow's technology.

Society for the Investigation of the Unexplained
US fortean society founded by Ivan T Sanderson in 1965.
Ivan T Sanderson was born in Edinburgh in 1911. His father was a whisky distiller and owned an estate in Kenya, where the young Sanderson grew up. During the 1920s, he was schooled at Eton and went on to obtain degrees in zoology, botany and geology. Then, joining numerous scientific expeditions to remote regions, he gained a reputation as a brilliant specimen collector. After serving in British Naval Intelligence during World War II, Sanderson spent several more years working for the government as a press agent in New York.

In 1947, Sanderson turned his hand to writing and lecturing, exploiting his wealth of experience as a well-travelled naturalist in Africa and the Caribbean. His books, including *Animal Treasure* (1937), *Living Mammals of the World* (1958), *The Dynasty of Abu* (1962), *Book of Great Jungles* (1965) and *Caribbean Treasure* (1965) were bestsellers of their day. Together with his informative articles in popular magazines such as *Argosy*, *Fate* and the *Saturday Evening Post*, Sanderson's skill as a raconteur made him welcome on radio and television as a celebrity expert on everything from pets and ZOOS to UFOS, living dinosaurs and MAN-BEASTS.

Inevitably for someone filled with curiosity, Sanderson's interest in the ANOMALIES of natural history grew. He claimed that, in his youth, he had attended a lecture given by CHARLES FORT, and, while crossing a river in the Cameroons in 1932, had a close encounter with a huge unidentified creature that he was later told was MOKELE-MBEMBE, a dinosaur-like swamp-dweller. He published a paper in 1948 on the possibility of dinosaurs surviving in remote jungles and, in 1954, was one of the founders of Civilian Saucer Intelligence, an American group that attempted a more scientific approach to UFO investigation.

At some point, Sanderson established the Ivan Sanderson Foundation to formalize his diverse interests and projects in the field of natural history. Cryptozoologist Loren Coleman – who corresponded with Sanderson from 1961 until his death – remembers encouraging Sanderson 'to start a society to study FORTEANA and CRYPTOZOOLOGY'. It seems likely that Sanderson received legal advice to drop the personal identification in the title of his Foundation in order to qualify for tax-exempt status as a non-profit organization. All of this came together in 1965 with the creation of the Society for the Investigation of the Unexplained (SITU).

SITU flourished under Sanderson's leadership, and he gathered a dynamic group of acolytes – including Loren Coleman, Mark A. Hall, Bob Warth and Bob Durrant – who helped with his investigations and published a journal called *Pursuit*. Some of them lived with him and his wife Sabina in a compound at Columbia, New Jersey, where they built a library and archive. However, things began to fall apart in the mid-1970s – vital helpers left the organization and Sanderson died in 1973. For a few years, *Pursuit*, with a succession of editors, was published from Warth's home in Little Silver, New Jersey. With the last issue, in 1975, SITU effectively ceased.

Sanderson's legacy cannot be over-estimated; he probably ranks with John Keel (see MOTHMAN) as having directly inspired most of today's leading forteans, cryptozoologists and ufologists, with his writings and exploits. His 1961 book, *Abominable Snowmen: Legend Come to Life*, not only brought BIGFOOT and the YETI to the attention of the modern world but broadened the discussion to suggest the survival of 'sub-humans' from the Ice Age to today. His two books on UFOs were typically eccentric, taking unexpected but valuable and fresh views: *Uninvited Visitors* (1967), which speculated on whether UFOs might be protozoic space-creatures; and *Invisible Residents* (1970), which brought together a plethora of material associating UFOs with oceans, rivers and lakes.

Of Sanderson's fortean writing, we have, chiefly, three anthologies of essays: *Things* (1962), *More Things* (1969) and *Investigating the Unexplained* (1972). These cover many anomalistic subjects including teleporting ant-queens; mysterious ocean vortices, the forerunners of the BERMUDA TRIANGLE hypothesis; unusual FALLS; giant bats; SPONTANEOUS HUMAN COMBUSTION; the LOCH NESS MONSTER; and ancient gold trinkets that resemble modern aeroplanes. Sanderson also had a productive friendship with Dr BERNARD HEUVELMANS. In October 1968, Sanderson invited Heuvelmans to join him in investigating the 'Minnesota Ice man', as recorded in Heuvelmans' *L'Homme Néanderthal est toujours vivant* (1974). The object of their attention was a convincing 'frozen Neanderthal' exhibit owned by showman Frank Hansen, who claimed it had been recovered from a block of ice floating in the sea off Siberia. Heuvelmans and Sanderson both pronounced it genuine, pending

Ivan T Sanderson, founder of the Society for the Investigation of the Unexplained. (© TopFoto/Fortean)

further investigation. This Hansen would not allow, and since then, suspicion has grown that it was a HOAX.

Sanderson advocated a 'hands on' approach that encouraged his followers to get out there and investigate, and he led by example. He was, for example, credited with re-examining the 1909 evidence for the JERSEY DEVIL. It was also Sanderson's initial researches into the famous THUNDERBIRD sighting by two cowboys in the Arizona desert, as reported in the *Tombstone Epitaph*, that sparked today's hunt for a legendary lost photograph of a pterodactyl. Sanderson, however, was not always able to bring investigations to a successful conclusion, as demonstrated by one of his most famous investigations. It concerned the discovery, in 1948, of giant three-toed footprints on a part of the Florida coast. After interviewing witnesses and studying the prints, Sanderson concluded, publicly, that a previously unknown type of giant penguin had wandered too far north. It was not until 1988 that the perpetrator of this hoax came forward and confessed that it was all done using specially made cement shoes.

solid light *see* LIGHT, SOLID

solstice *see* SUMMER SOLSTICE; WINTER SOLSTICE

Soma

An intoxicating plant-juice drink offered to the gods and drunk as a sacrament in Hindu Vedic rituals. The plant and the drink made from it are personified as a god, although the identity of the plant originally used, as described in the Rig-Veda, *is unknown.*

The drink known as Soma was an important sacrament both to the early Indo-Iranians, and to the Hindu Vedic and Iranian cultures into which this group split around 4,000 years ago. Soma is frequently mentioned in the Hindu *Rig-Veda*, the Ninth Mandala of which consists entirely of 114 hymns which praise its energizing and intoxicating qualities, and describe the ways of preparing and drinking it. Both the plant and the drink made from it are personified as a god, and the three are inseparable from one another, forming a mythological trinity.

The god Soma is depicted in Hindu art as a bull, bird or embryo, and evolved into a lunar deity who protects herbs and rides in a chariot drawn by white horse or antelopes; he is associated with the underworld, and is identified with the moon god Chandra. The moon is the cup of Soma, and the waxing moon is sometimes seen as Soma regenerating himself ready to be drunk again. According to the *Rig-Veda*, drinking Soma gives one the eight powers of the god. The Iranian people call it Haoma, and the *Avesta*, the holy book of Zoroastrianism, makes a reference to the god Haoma and his ritual, giving us a clue as to its importance in the early Aryan religion of Persia. Soma is also associated with the warrior god Indra, and Haoma was apparently drunk before battle. In addition, several Hindu texts, such as the *Atharva Veda*, refer to Soma's medicinal properties, calling it 'the king of medicinal herbs'.

Soma is said to have been made by pressing the juice from the stalks of a certain mountain plant, the identity of which is now unknown but which has been the subject of much debate by scholars, who have variously identified it as cannabis, an asclepiad, a hallucinogenic mushroom and ephedra. Nowadays, non-psychoactive plants are used for the drink, which is mixed with other ingredients such as milk and honey before being offered to the gods and ingested by brahmans and other participants in sacrificial rituals.

soothsayers

People who foretell the future, often using means of divination such as astrology or augury.

The first element of the word 'soothsayer' comes from the Old English *sōth*, meaning 'truth' or 'true'; a soothsayer is thus literally a 'speaker of truth'. In ancient times, rulers and generals of armies employed soothsayers to interpret their dreams and use means of DIVINATION, such as AUGURY and ASTROLOGY, to advise them. In 44 BC, a soothsayer was famously said to have warned Julius Caesar to beware the Ides of March, the day on which he was assassinated.

Soothsaying, along with astrology and all other attempts to divine the future by a spiritual or supernatural medium, is explicitly condemned in both the Old Testament and the New Testament, and in his epic poem *Divina Commedia*, the 14th-century Italian poet Dante Alighieri describes the eighth circle of Hell, which is reserved for 'Diviners and the Fraudulent'; in the fourth ditch of this circle are the soothsayers. Since they have tried to look too far into the future, their punishment is to have their heads turned backward for eternity.

sorcerers

People who practise sorcery; magicians who use supernatural powers, usually for evil purposes.

While WIZARDS have throughout the ages generally been portrayed as benevolent magicians, sorcerers have almost universally been seen as harnessing supernatural powers for evil purposes. The word 'SORCERY' was, in the Middle Ages, used synonymously with 'WITCHCRAFT', and sorcerers, like WITCHES, were believed to call up DEMONS, to have spirit FAMILIARS in the form of animals who assisted them in their practice of black magic (see MAGIC, BLACK), and to attend SABBATS in order to worship their god, SATAN.

The New Testament tells of Simon Magus, a sorcerer who converted to Christianity but tried to buy from the apostles the power to convey the Holy Spirit. The apocryphal Acts of Peter describes the legend of his death; performing magic for the Roman Emperor Claudius in the forum to prove his powers, he was said to have flown into the air. The apostles Peter and Paul prayed to God to stop him, and he fell to his death. In Russian folklore, a sorcerer was thought to have the power to take over the body of a person who was dying or had died, and become a type of vampire. In the 16th century, a German called Peter Stubb was accused of being a sorcerer, and in his confession, he claimed that he had practised the 'wicked arts' from the age of 12, and that the DEVIL had given him a magic girdle which enabled him to transform into a wolf; under its influence, he had murdered 15 people. One of the most famous so-called sorcerers of recent times was ALEISTER CROWLEY.

sorcery

The practice of magic, usually for evil purposes.

The word 'sorcery' comes to us via the 13th-century French *sorcerie*, probably from Latin *sortiarius* meaning 'one who influences fate'. Sorcery is broadly defined as the human harnessing of supernatural powers in order to bring about a desired effect, and is thus often used synonymously with 'magic', but historically, it has specifically negative associations and is more often used to refer to black magic (see MAGIC, BLACK). It has long been held that sorcery involves the calling up of evil spirits for malevolent purposes, and in medieval Europe, 'sorcery' was used as another name for WITCHCRAFT, and had the same connotations – the employment of magic for evil, the invocation of demons and evil spirits, NECROMANCY, and the worship of the DEVIL. Sorcerers were believed to be priests of SATAN and it was assumed that, like WITCHES, they attended SABBATS and had spirit FAMILIARS. In the Middle Ages, anyone who studied science or had a laboratory might be accused by his more superstitious neighbours of sorcery, just as the village wise woman ran the risk of being branded a witch.

SORRAT *see* SOCIETY FOR RESEARCH IN RAPPORT AND TELEKINESIS

sortes
Divination by opening a book at random and interpreting the passage thus revealed.
The ancient Romans practised a form of divination by the drawing of lots; small tablets or counters of wood or other material, called *sortes*, were selected at random to determine the will of the gods, and various inscriptions were often written on these, according to the circumstances. It became popular to write the verses of illustrious poets on the *sortes*, the verse selected being then taken to apply to the person who had drawn it. But later, an actual book of poetry came to be used, the book being opened at random and the first passage which met the eye being interpreted and applied to the question being asked. The works of Virgil were most commonly used in this way, and this form of divination came to be known as the Sortes Virgilianae. Similarly, the poetry of Homer was used in the Sortes Homericae. Early Christians adopted this method, substituting the Bible for Virgil, although many church councils condemned this practice, which was called Sortes Sanctorum. Nowadays, the name sortes may be applied to divination using any book. See also BIBLIOMANCY.

sortilege
Divination by drawing lots; also another name for magic or sorcery.
Sortilege (from Latin *sortilegus*, a diviner, from *sors*, fate or lot, and *legere*, to read) is a form of divination by the casting or drawing of lots. Any of a number of objects may be used, such as DICE, slips of paper,

knucklebones, stones or pieces of wood. A method in which small tablets or counters of wood were thrown into an urn filled with water and then drawn at random, or tossed like dice, was much employed by the ancient Romans, and RUNES, which were popularly used as sortilege tools in Viking and Anglo-Saxon times, are still in use today. The fortune cookies served in many modern Chinese restaurants are also, essentially, a form of sortilege!

The word sortilege is also sometimes used in a less specific sense, to mean magic or sorcery, presumably because of the occult associations it holds for some people.

soul
The inner essence of a living being, thought in many religions and belief systems to be immortal. The soul is thought to be self-aware and to be the true basis for sentience in living beings. It is widely held that the soul can exist separately from the physical body and survives after death. In some belief systems, the soul is thought to be reincarnated into a new body after death, while in others, the person's actions during life are judged and their soul is rewarded by admission to Heaven, or punished by being condemned to Hell.
The belief that living beings have an inner essence called a soul is widespread in most religions and belief systems. This inner essence is generally described as being immortal, pre-existing its incarnation in the flesh and surviving the death of the physical body, and the concept of the soul has strong links with a belief in the AFTERLIFE, although ideas as to the nature of the soul and what happens to it after physical death vary widely from culture to culture. As the soul is thought to be self-aware, it is seen as the true basis for sentience in living beings, which has led some people to assert that only humans, and not animals, have souls.

Some shamanic cultures believe that the body and soul are divisible and can operate, at least for a limited time, independently; the soul is thought to leave the body during sleep, and dreams are seen as adventures experienced by the soul. It is therefore thought dangerous to wake or disturb a person suddenly while they are asleep, in case the soul has no time to find its way back, and both physical and mental illness are regarded as a symptom that the soul, or part of it, has been lost. The shaman thus needs to retrieve or call back the soul or its lost part by spirit journeys, rituals or invocations.

In some belief systems a person's shadow or reflection is thought to be the soul made visible, and it is occasionally believed that taking someone's photograph will steal their soul. The idea that the soul may be contained in a concrete object is found in a number of primitive religions, and folk tales all over the world include the motif of the soul-object's being hidden away, with its owner being invulnerable so long as it is not found or destroyed. In some parts of West Africa it is believed that the soul of each individual human dwells in a wild animal, often said to be one born at the same moment as the human, and their fates are inextricably linked. Some people, especially tribal chiefs, have more than one such soul, which is known as a 'bush soul'.

A number of philosophies and religions view the soul as being made up of two or more parts. Plato described three parts – the reason or mind, also known as the logos; the appetite, body or passion; and the spirits, or emotions – each of which had a function in the balanced and harmonious soul. Hinduism also regards the *Atman*, that is, the portion of God or Brahman which corresponds to the soul, as being made up of the three elements of eternity, knowledge and bliss. In Hinduism, the soul is reincarnated and undergoes many physical lives before it achieves union with Brahman (see REINCARNATION).

The Hebrew Bible gives no systematic definition of the soul, but *THE ZOHAR*, one of the classical works of the mystical Jewish tradition of the KABBALAH, also describes three divisions of the soul: the *Nefesh*, or lower animal part, which enters the body at birth and is linked to the instincts and physical cravings; the *Ruach*, or middle soul, which corresponds to the psyche or ego; and the *Neshamah*, or higher self, which relates to intellect, and distinguishes man from other living beings. The *Ruach* and *Neshamah* are thought to fully exist only in those who have become spiritually awakened. After death, the *Nefesh* disintegrates, while the *Ruach* passes to an intermediate place where it is purified, and the *Neshamah* returns to its source; after RESURRECTION, the *Ruach* and *Neshamah* will be permanently reunited in a transmuted state.

Islam and Christianity both regard the soul as the immortal part of a person which after death is judged on their actions during life, to be either rewarded by admission to Heaven or punished by being sent to Hell. See also SPIRIT.

south *see* DIRECTIONS, FOUR

Spanish Inquisition *see* INQUISITION, THE

Spare, Austin Osman (1886–1956)
English artist, writer and magician.
Austin Osman Spare was born in London. He demonstrated artistic talent from an early age, and briefly attended art school. In his teenage years he also became fascinated by the occult, and this heavily

'Blood on the Moon' by Austin Osman Spare. (© TopFoto)

influenced the works he produced. Sometimes compared with the art of Aubrey Beardsley and WILLIAM BLAKE, his drawings and paintings were full of grotesque, sexualized human figures, semi-human spirit forms and magical symbols. He claimed that he produced much of his work while in a trance state, and felt himself to be guided by SPIRITS and familiars.

Spare came to the attention of ALEISTER CROWLEY, and in 1909 he became a probationer of Crowley's Order, the Argenteum Astrum, but he was never initiated as a member; Crowley disapproved of the goals of Spare's magical philosophy, which was very free-form, psychically orientated and personal, focusing on the magician's individual universe and the influence of his will upon it. Spare's magical methods were encapsulated in *The Book of Pleasure (Self Love): The Psychology of Ecstasy* (1913), which contains the core of his philosophy. His other publications include *Earth Inferno* (1905) and *The Focus of Life* (1920). He developed an occult method using sigils – ideograms composed of words – and was working on a GRIMOIRE of his iconoclastic magical system, known as the Zos Kia Cultus, when he died in 1956. Spare's art works remain popular, and he is acknowledged as the inspiration for the practice of what is now known as CHAOS MAGIC.

speaking in tongues *see* XENOGLOSSY

spectral armies

Apparitions of armies, generally either appearing in the sky or re-enacting previous battles.

The earliest report of a spectral army dates from in c.160 AD, in an account given in Pausanias's *Description of Greece* describing ghostly sounds heard on the site of the Battle of Marathon. Much later, stories of spectral armies appearing the sky were a common theme in 17th-century pamphlet literature (see AERIAL PHANTOMS). Unfortunately, the best-known British cases (including stories of phantom Civil War armies at Edgehill and spectral soldiers seen at Souter Fell, Cumbria, in the mid-18th century) seem to be merely ghost stories, which collapse under critical scrutiny of the historical sources.

Nonetheless, some investigators feel that there are a small number of plausible first-hand accounts of spectral armies collected by psychical researchers. Generally, witnesses believe that they have experienced the sights or sounds of a battle from the historic past. Shortly after the end of World War I, for example, author James Wentworth Day claimed to have seen a spectral skirmish between phantom French and German cavalry in woods near Neuve Église, Flanders, at a site known for cavalry battles in 1870 and 1914. Researcher Peter McCue also considered that there was some evidence of a spectral battle being witnessed near Loch Aishie, Scotland, at various times during the 20th century.

For an example of phantom Roman soldiers, see TREASURER'S HOUSE.

spectral pedestrians

Ghostly human figures that appear on highways in the path of on-coming traffic.

One of the frequently reported forms of modern apparitional experience is the spectral pedestrian. Unlike the lore of PHANTOM HITCH-HIKERS, there are many well-attested examples of spectral pedestrians as a type of road ghost. Realistic human apparitions are seen crossing or standing in a road in the path of on-coming motorists. Frequently drivers believe they have struck or killed a living person until an immediate search of the area reveals no trace of a body. It is surely no coincidence that spectral pedestrians have emerged in parallel with the growth of motorized traffic. Persons travelling by foot have become a rarer sight on modern roads and are more likely to be noticed by a driver. Furthermore, reports come largely from quiet, rural roads where an individual pedestrian stands out more than on a crowded highway in more populous and urban areas. Certain country locations seem particularly prone to reports, such as the A23 near Brighton, Sussex, and most notably Blue Bell Hill in Kent – where the Ghost of Blue Bell Hill is said to be the phantasm of a young woman killed in an accident there in the 1960s.

Spectral pedestrians are usually solitary figures and may appear in modern dress or clothing from another era; some appear to be manifestations of a WHITE LADY. Occasionally a more complex apparition will appear – in 1972, a lorry driver on a road near Blythburgh, Suffolk, reported seeing the phantoms of a man and woman leading a horse. Notably, spectral pedestrians always appear to be adults; phantom children do not seem to be reported in these incidents although fatalities among children on roads are far from uncommon.

spectre

An apparition, ghost or phantom; also used of a naturally occurring phenomenon known as the Brocken spectre.

The word 'spectre' (from the Latin *spectrum*, meaning 'an appearance') is generally used to refer to any apparition or ghost of the dead, and to various classes of supernatural being. It is also famously used to refer to a type of illusory ghost, known as a Brocken spectre, that can be explained as a natural phenomenon. Named after the Brocken, the highest peak in the Harz Mountains in Germany, where it is said to occur frequently, a Brocken spectre is the shadow cast on clouds or fog by an observer standing on a high mountain ridge or peak. The effect is caused when a low sun is shining from behind a climber who is looking down on clouds or fog, and can range from a simple shadow pattern to figures resembling vast, distorted giants moving across the clouds while surrounded by rings of light.

spells

Magic formulae performed by a witch, wizard or magician, and said to have tangible outcomes.

A spell is a set of words believed to have magical force, so that when a spell is performed by a WITCH, WIZARD or MAGICIAN, it will have a tangible outcome. A spell can be an INCANTATION or INVOCATION, and famous books of spell, or GRIMOIRES, include *The Book of the Sacred Magic of Abramelin the Mage* and *The Greater Key of Solomon*.

It is believed that spells can be cast for either good or evil purposes, and the belief in and use of spells is common in all forms of magical practice. In its original sense, the word 'spell' (from the Old English, *spellian*, meaning to speak) referred to a spoken formula, but it has long been associated with not only spoken words but also written forms, as well as the actions or rituals associated with them.

SPIRICOM

A series of machines designed to enable direct and immediate communication with the spirits of the dead.
During the 1970s, while carrying out research into ELECTRONIC VOICE PHENOMENA, George W Meek and William J O'Neil (of the Metascience Organisation) claimed to have invented a machine which allowed direct, real-time conversations to take place with the spirits of the dead.

Unlike the processes used until then, SPIRICOM (short for 'spirit communication') machines apparently removed the necessity to wait and play back tape recordings to hear replies. From 1972 to 1982 five different versions of the SPIRICOM machine were made; all were based around the idea that spirits would be able to manipulate an electromagnetic field, ultimately producing a voice through a loudspeaker. Various shielding was employed to eliminate extraneous interference and a number of other modifications were made, supposedly in response to a range of suggestions made (via SPIRICOM) by Dr George Jeffries Mueller, a physicist who had died in 1967.

Voices produced by SPIRICOM had a monotonal electronic sound to them, with no pauses for breathing. In addition to Mueller, it was alleged that a number of other entities (representatives of a research group composed of dead scientists) communicated via the machine. Among other things they predicted the ultimate demise of the project in 1982. The machine was never patented (to encourage others to take the principles of SPIRICOM and expand and improve them), and a number of similar devices have been subsequently produced, including Otto Koenig's 'Generator' and Klaus Schrieber's 'Vidicom'.

spirit

Discarnate portion of a human being, animal or natural object or of 'nature' itself which is capable of independent existence
The word 'spirit', used to describe a discarnate being, essence or SUPERNATURAL 'force', comes from the Latin *spiritus* meaning 'breath'. Within the major monotheistic faiths the spirit is understood to be the non-physical component of a human being (the word is sometimes used interchangeably with SOUL), and many other religions also recognize the existence of spirits in animals, plants and the natural world in general. Certain cultures and OCCULT belief systems also admit the idea of spirits of non-human entities such as ELEMENTALS, FAIRIES and DEMONS and do not necessarily draw hard and fast boundaries between the material spirit worlds.

Belief in spirits in various forms is still strong even within urbanized, developed societies although now it is often separated from the framework of organized religious practice. Human spirits are considered by many to be capable of surviving death – GHOSTS and HAUNTINGS are often attributed to their presence. Many psychical researchers have also been prepared to consider the existence of spirits as a possible explanation for many other PSYCHIC phenomena. In his book *Human Personality and Its Survival of Bodily Death* (1901), Frederic Myers described the spirit as 'that unknown fraction of a man's personality … which we discern as operating before or after death in the metetherial environment', and the spirit hypothesis has been variously proposed as the explanation for mediumistic communications (see MEDIUMS and SPIRITUALISM), the apparent evidence for past lives (see REINCARNATION and PAST LIFE REGRESSION), OUT-OF-BODY EXPERIENCES, NEAR-DEATH EXPERIENCES and apparent instances of POSSESSION.

spirit drawing

The sketching of images of spirits by a medium.
A number of MENTAL MEDIUMS, who claim that they can see SPIRITS, attempt to communicate their impressions to others. Usually, this takes the form of a verbal description – however, a small number choose to draw the spirit they say that they are able to see. Rita Berkowitz of Boston is one of the best-known mediums currently using this technique.

As well as producing drawings of spirits from a SÉANCE, such mediums sometimes also claim to be able to draw people's GUARDIAN SPIRITS or GHOSTS that are responsible for HAUNTINGS.

The term 'spirit drawing' is also sometimes used to refer to AUTOMATIC ART, although in these cases the drawing is supposedly produced by a medium under the direct control of a spirit.

spirit guide

A spirit helper who supposedly assists a medium to communicate with the dead.
Many MEDIUMS claim that they use a 'spirit guide', also known as a 'control', as a go-between for their communications within the realm of the dead. These guides are also sometimes referred to as 'spirit helpers', and they supposedly ensure a safe passage within the world of the spirits (see ASTRAL PLANE) and pass messages or 'fetch' other spirits to speak to the medium.

In the 19th century Native American SPIRITS regularly featured as spirit guides at SÉANCES, and the spirit Katie King (sometimes together with her father, John King, said to be the pirate Henry Morgan) supposedly assisted countless mediums throughout London – the most famous being FLORENCE COOK. Even today, the popular British television medium Derek Acorah claims to use a spirit guide called Sam.

DIRECT VOICE MEDIUMS sometimes speak in what is allegedly the voice of their spirit guide, whereas MENTAL MEDIUMS appear to hold conversations with their spirit guide, with the audience only being able to hear the medium's contribution.

Some people claim that everyone has a spirit guide, and the term is often used interchangeably with 'GUARDIAN SPIRIT'.

spiritism

The belief that the human spirit or soul survives the death of the physical body and may communicate with the world of the living.

Spiritism – essentially the belief that the spirits of the dead survive and are able to communicate with the living – is a feature of many religious and spiritual belief systems throughout the world, although the word is now often used more specifically as a collective term for a wide variety of syncretist (see SYNCRETISM) religious practices found in Brazil (for example, CANDOMBLÉ). Followers of such religions, or holders of the basic belief, are called spiritists.

'Spiritism' also formed the name of a movement founded in France in the mid-19th century (sometimes described as Kardecist Spiritism for the sake of clarity). The set of beliefs and ideals held by its members were similar to those of SPIRITUALISM, but there were some differences, particularly in the prominence given to the idea of progressive REINCARNATION. The movement was founded by Hippolyte Léon Denizard Rivail, working under the pseudonym of Allan Kardec. In the mid-1850s Kardec apparently felt that religion was an ineffective guide for humanity, although from his spiritual research he was convinced of the continued existence of the human soul after death. Spiritism was to offer a way for people to commune with the world of the dead, and to come to terms with it and the process of reincarnation, without the need to turn to the traditional organized religions. The official books of spiritism were allegedly CHANNELLED by Kardec. He claimed that they included the words of Jesus Christ and that spiritism was the successor to Christianity.

This particular brand of spiritism fell out of favour in Europe in the first half of the 20th century. However, the group of Brazilian religions collectively referred to as spriritism, within which SÉANCES, mediumship and spirit possession are central, continue to draw millions of followers.

spirit medium *see* MEDIUM

spirit photography
A once-popular pastime involving the alleged photographing of spirits.

In 1861, in Boston, William H Mumler was developing some glass-plate photographs he had taken, when he found something strange. There were images of people on the photograph – but they had not been present when it was taken. The images were semi-transparent, looking like the classic description of a GHOST. Recognizing an opportunity, he went into business as a spirit photographer. This worked well – until someone recognized some of his 'ghosts' as living people from the area around his Boston studio. Mumler moved to New York and continued in business until he was finally convicted of fraud in 1869.

Prior to Mumler, GHOST PHOTOGRAPHS had been sold as novelties, but he was the first to claim they were the real thing. The growing interest in SPIRITUALISM proved to be fertile ground for the new art of 'spirit photography'. Photographs were produced at SÉANCES, allegedly depicting the SPIRITS materialized by the MEDIUM. Interest increased during and after World War I when photographs were produced claiming to show soldiers who had died – SIR ARTHUR CONAN DOYLE famously attempted to obtain such a photograph of his deceased son. In the case of these séance photographs, it was usually stated that ECTOPLASM had come together to produce the spirit form. However, many of the early photographs are now regarded as laughable – they often clearly involve very crude attempts at deception, such as a 'spirit' that can be clearly seen to be a piece of cloth with a cardboard cut-out face attached.

Other spirit photographs (such as Mumler's) were produced using the standard photographic technique of double-exposure. Glass plates would be pre-exposed, with a slightly underexposed image of a person posing as the 'ghost', before being used to photograph the customer. When the plate was developed, both images would be present.

As early as 1875, even the accomplished medium William Stainton Moses declared in an article in *Human Nature* that:

> Some people would recognise anything [as a ghost]. A broom and a sheet are quite enough for some wild enthusiasts who go with the figure in their eye and see what they wish to see … I have had pictures that might be anything in this or any other world sent to me and gravely claimed as recognised portraits.

Part of the explanation lies in the fact that such

One of William H Mumler's spirit photographs.
(© Mary Evans Picture Library)

photographs reached a less visually sophisticated audience. However, a more powerful factor was the will to believe, even in cases of explicit fraud. This was illustrated during the prosecution in Paris, in June 1875, of an infamous spirit photographer, Jean Buguet. Despite his confession, and the discovery by the police of his large stock of fake heads, there remained bereaved relatives who were prepared to testify for the defence at his trial and to insist his pictures were genuine. Buguet was fined and jailed for a year but continued to have his supporters.

In the 20th century the introduction of infrared photography into the séance room, and the increasing sophistication of the public, led to a marked decline in the popularity of spirit photographs. However, although such photographs have largely fallen out of fashion, the related areas of THOUGHTOGRAPHY and photographs of ORBS continue to attract a following.

spirit rapping

Apparent communication from spirits in the form of tapping, knocking and banging noises – supposedly produced by the interaction of spirits with physical objects.

Since the Victorian heyday of the SPIRITUALISM movement, spirit rapping has been an important ingredient of many SÉANCES. Rapping is supposedly a spirit communicating by hitting a solid object to make a sharp noise – sometimes explained as occurring through the means of a brief MATERIALIZATION of ECTOPLASM, allowing the spirit to affect the physical world.

The spirit-rapping craze began with the FOX SISTERS in 1848, after they allegedly used this method to establish communication with a spirit for the first time. Initially a method was used in which the number of raps corresponded with the position of the appropriate letter in the alphabet, so that communications could be spelt out. Eventually this gave way to the much less cumbersome (and now much parodied) 'once for yes, twice for no' system.

This form of spirit communication became very popular and still continues, to a lesser extent, today – despite the Fox sisters' admission that they obtained their results fraudulently, by cracking their toe joints.

spirits, nature *see* NATURE SPIRITS

spirits of the dead *see* SPIRIT

spiritual healing *see* FAITH HEALING

Spiritualism *see panel p641*

spirit writing

Writing allegedly produced by spirits.

Spirit writing, within the context of a SÉANCE, can take one of two distinct forms: AUTOMATIC WRITING, in which the MEDIUM is in direct contact with the writing implement (or in some cases a PLANCHETTE) but their hand is supposedly guided by a SPIRIT, or versions in which the writing implement and media are isolated from human contact (for example SLATE WRITING). In both instances, the medium is considered to be CHANNELLING the messages from the spirits.

Spirit writing also features in some cases of alleged hauntings or poltergeist activity. Such writing appears without its production being witnessed, often on walls, and supposedly without the involvement of a living person. There have even been cases where it is alleged that it was possible to attempt to communicate with the spirit producing the writing, by adding written questions or responses. Spirit writing of

Spiritualism

Spiritualism started as a 19th-century religious movement the central belief of which was that the SPIRITS of the dead could be contacted directly by the living. This was usually accomplished through a MEDIUM during a SÉANCE. The spirits were believed to exist on a different 'plane' and it was thought that they could offer help and advice to overcome earthbound problems.

Modern spiritualism is often said to have begun on 31 March 1848 with the FOX SISTERS of Hydesville, New York. From 1849, they gave demonstrations of their table-rapping communications with spirits; it was from here that the traditional code of 'one knock for yes and two for no' arose. In 1852, the first public demonstrations were carried out in the United Kingdom. From 1856 to 1869, French scholar Allan Kardec wrote a series of books which looked at the philosophy and practice of spiritualism, and these became the basis of another religious movement called SPIRITISM.

A key year for spiritualism was 1861 – it brought the first recorded instance of SPIRIT PHOTOGRAPHY. William H Mumler took photographs in his studio which, upon development, appeared to show spirits next to the sitter. Frequently the sitter would claim to recognize the individuals. Photographs of spirits had been produced prior to this but they had been deliberately faked and sold as such. Mumler was the first to claim his apparitions were genuine, although he was convicted of fraud in New York in 1869. Despite this apparent setback spirit photography thrived, and it was not until the 1920s that it ultimately fell out of fashion.

From 1865, the Brooklyn Enigma, MOLLIE FANCHER, was confined to bed and apparently CHANNELLING five different spirits. The messages mostly appeared in the form of AUTOMATIC WRITING – she produced some 10,000 different pieces of writing, ranging from poems to long letters.

Almost as soon as public performances by mediums started to appear, people began exposing the methods they used. One of the most famous debunkers was JOHN NEVIL MASKELYNE who, in 1865, saw a performance by the US mediums the Davenport brothers. Due to a chance opening of a curtain Maskelyne was able to see how they produced their effects. He publicly exposed them in British newspapers and set himself up as a magician, replicating many of their effects on stage (see STAGE MAGIC). Maskelyne promoted himself as an 'anti-spiritualist'.

Magicians were not the only ones who were keen to find out how mediums performed. In 1872, FLORENCE COOK claimed that she had produced a MATERIALIZATION of her 'spirit guide' Katie King for the first time. A number of séance appearances followed until Katie put in her final appearance with Florence in 1875. Throughout most of this time Cook was investigated by eminent chemist Sir William Crookes. At the same time Crookes was also carrying out investigations on DANIEL DUNGLAS HOME. Crookes was satisfied that both were genuine and he even delivered a paper on the subject to the prestigious Royal Society. In 1882, several prominent scientists from Cambridge University formed the SOCIETY FOR PSYCHICAL RESEARCH (SPR). The SPR investigated all forms of psychic ability but they also took (and still do) a special interest in the claims of mediums.

In 1877, one case of channelling was so extreme it nearly led to incarceration in an asylum. Lurancy Vennum of Watseka, Illinois became possessed (see POSSESSION), apparently channelling a number of spirits. She was told to try to connect with one who seemed to be less troublesome than the rest. She claimed that she settled on the spirit of a girl the same age, giving the name of a dead girl whose father was so convinced that his daughter had taken possession of her that he took Vennum to live with her. Vennum spent several weeks every year living with her new family and she earned herself the name of the WATSEKA WONDER.

In 1888, the Fox sisters demonstrated on stage how they had faked their 'spirit' rappings by the cracking of toe joints. Although they later tried to retract the confession, spiritualism had suffered a severe blow. However, in the 1890s, a new device was to make communication with the spirit world available in every home – the OUIJA BOARD, or spirit writer, was invented. This was an aid to automatic writing, a development of the PLANCHETTE, which did not seem to need to have an established medium present to produce results. But, although it seemed to make spirit communication available to the masses, the real stars were still the mediums, and in 1893 one of the most impressive took the world by storm. EUSAPIA PALLADINO, from Italy, alternately amazed and confused – it was claimed that she was the greatest medium who had ever lived, despite the fact that she was frequently caught cheating. Palladino argued that it was easier to cheat and that she did not want to disappoint an audience so, if the spirits were not performing, she would fake it.

Channelling of messages from the dead took a bizarre turn in 1900 when the medium HÉLÈNE SMITH claimed to be receiving messages from dead Martians – although the automatic writing she produced, supposedly in Martian, looked remarkably like her native French. Another allegedly powerful medium of this time was the Pole STANISLAWA TOMCZYK – she claimed that her psychic powers came from her spirit guide, Little Stasia. Tomczyk was scientifically tested up to 1910 and never performed publicly.

From 1913 to 1922, a series of books, supposedly written by PATIENCE WORTH, were published. Patience had actually died two centuries earlier and it was claimed that the books had been channelled by Pearl Lenore Curran. However, in 1922 Worth and Curran apparently fell out and no more work was produced.

Interest in spiritualism had been declining for a number of years until the huge loss of life associated World War I temporarily reversed the trend. ARTHUR CONAN DOYLE, creator of Sherlock Holmes, had been lecturing and writing on spiritualism for many years, and his second wife was a medium. Like many, he turned to spirit photography and the séance room for comfort after losing his son in the war. This put him in conflict with his friend the arch-debunker HARRY HOUDINI, who made a show of publicly exposing fraudulent mediums.

After the 1920s spiritualism lost many of its converts, although belief in it as a religion and interest in attempts to communicate with the dead have never vanished entirely. In 1959, the Swede Freidrich Jurgenson opened a new chapter. While recording bird song he picked up voices which he believed were the spirits of the dead communicating with him – the study of ELECTRONIC VOICE PHENOMENA (EVP) was born. Between 1972 and 1982, George W Meek and William J O'Neill created the SPIRICOM machine which supposedly allowed real-time communication with the dead.

Technology has not, however, replaced the medium and the séance. From 1993 to 1998, a series of scientifically designed séances were held by the SCOLE GROUP. Observation by the SPR yielded a 300-page report, covering 500 séances which included a number of APPORTS, a phenomenon which had been popular during the Victorian era.

Spiritualism is still practised today but on nothing like the scale that it was during the Victorian era. For the majority of those who attend séances, use ouija boards or call on the services of mediums, they are merely fun distractions – relatively few would now consider themselves to be involved in serious attempts to communicate with the afterlife. However, there are still a number of popular mediums, who appear in television programmes in which there are apparently attempts to communicate with the dead, helping to promote a continued interest in the subject. Whether this will be sustained remains to be seen.

Gordon Rutter

this type famously featured in the HAUNTING of BORLEY RECTORY and the case of the HUMPTY DOO POLTERGEIST.

spodomancy
Divination by means of ashes.
In spodomancy (from the Greek *spodos*, ashes, and *manteiā*, divination), the ashes, soot, or cinders from a fire are examined and interpreted. In ancient times, the ashes from burnt offerings made to the gods were used for this form of divination. In the Middle Ages, the shapes of cinders were considered to be significant: hollow, oblong cinders, known as coffins, were believed to mean a coming death in the family; oval cinders, known as cradles, foretold the birth of a child; round cinders, called purses, signified wealth; and heart-shaped cinders indicated a lover. One Scottish superstition held that if a clot of soot fell down the chimney during a wedding breakfast, this was a bad omen for the marriage.

In one method of spodomancy, a quantity of wood is burned, and the ashes spread thickly over an area out of doors. The diviner then traces words or symbols representing his or her question in the ashes, and leaves them overnight. Any changes wrought by the elements, or passing animals, are inspected and interpreted the next morning.

spontaneous combustion
The ignition of something without flame being applied.
Spontaneous combustion is not an unfamiliar phenomenon in science. Its causes include a slow process of oxidation in a substance or material. Rags soaked in flammable liquids such as petrol can also spontaneously combust when the surrounding temperature reaches a particular height (the spontaneous ignition point of the liquid).

However, some cases of apparently spontaneous combustion are not so easily explained. In 2004, in the village of Canneto Di Caronia, Sicily, a series of spontaneous fires erupted in several houses. Local police were quick to ascertain that arson or pyromania were not involved, and demonic activity was soon ruled out by representatives of the Catholic Church.

As the fires seemed to be associated with electrical appliances, some mysterious electrical phenomenon was suspected but even when the power was disconnected the fires continued. Sicily is home to an active volcano, Mount Etna, and vulcanologists were called in to determine if volcanic effects were playing a part in the phenomenon. No obvious connection was found, but one theory is that methane gas emanating from volcanic channels in the ground beneath the village was being ignited by electrical discharges.

No definitive explanation, however, has been universally accepted. See also SPONTANEOUS HUMAN COMBUSTION.

spontaneous human combustion
The apparent sudden incineration of a human body.
Accounts of spontaneous human combustion (SHC) have been known for centuries, one of the most famous being that of the COUNTESS BANDI OF CESENA, a case that inspired Charles Dickens to include a fictional example in his novel *Bleak House* (1853).

Typically, the victim's body, or most of it (often legs or other extremities remain unburnt) is completely consumed while furniture or other fittings around the body are not damaged at all – merely coated with a glutinous ashy deposit. Reported incidents tend to have taken place in a closed room in which the victim was alone. For this reason, it is thought that there has never been a case of the phenomenon that was witnessed while it was actually in progress. Instead, SHC is usually suggested as an explanation for a death by fire that has mysterious aspects to it.

Another celebrated instance of SHC is the death of a Frenchwoman, Nicole Millet, who in 1725 was found burnt to death in a room at her inn in Rheims. Her husband was accused of her murder but was acquitted when the court was convinced that she had died from SHC. Apparently, the court's verdict was that she had died 'by a visitation of God'.

In 1763 the French writer Jonas Dupont published *De Incendiis Corporis Humani Spontaneis*, a collection of accounts of alleged SHC. This was far from scientific and included cases purportedly brought about by excessive drinking of alcohol, no longer considered to be a possible cause.

The modern scientific consensus on the idea of a human being bursting into flames without the presence of an external fire source is that it is impossible, and that in well-documented cases there is always a logical explanation. The human body contains too much water to burn readily, and extremely high temperatures are needed in crematoria to reduce a corpse to ashes. However, there are scientists who believe that the phenomenon does exist, suggesting such theories as the action of localized static electrical discharges or an unexplained molecular effect within bodily tissue.

One of the most commonly suggested theories to explain SHC is known as the wick effect. According to this idea, victims are unconscious at the start of the fire, whether through intoxication or illness – such as through the effects of a stroke or heart attack. In some cases, the victim is thought to have been already dead before being burnt. This means that the person will not have been aware of, or able to move away from, the source of the flame, which may be a lit cigarette, an open fire or an oil-burning lamp. As the

The remains of Dr John Irving Bentley of Coudersport, Pennsylvania. Many believe that he was a victim of spontaneous human combustion. (© Mary Evans Picture Library)

flame begins to ignite the victim's clothes, the flesh also begins to burn. The natural water content of the body tissue is gradually evaporated by the heat. As subcutaneous fat is then exposed and liquefied this too burns with a slow but intense heat until the tissue is completely burned, leaving only ashes.

Attempts have been made to reproduce the wick effect in a controlled environment using the remains of animals such as pigs, but the results have been inconclusive. In the absence of a reliably witnessed instance of SHC, the phenomenon, if it truly exists, has yet to be satisfactorily explained.

spontaneous images *see* IMAGES, SPONTANEOUS

Spook Hill
A hill in Florida, USA, where vehicles appear to coast uphill.
Spook Hill, in Lake Wales, Florida, is an example of a MAGNETIC HILL. In these locations, objects appear to roll uphill rather than down, and a vehicle with its engine switched off will begin to move in what looks like an upwards direction.

In local legend, the site is the burial place of a great chief of the Seminole people who killed a giant alligator in a nearby lake. Years later, when the Seminoles had been displaced by white settlers, mail riders began to notice that their horses were labouring hard on what looked like an easy downward trail and the place soon garnered its superstitious nickname.

However, this local tourist attraction has nothing to do with the paranormal, the effect being an optical illusion produced by a deceptive land configuration. In the absence of a clear horizon the mind is tricked into mistaking a downward slope for an upward one.

spoon bending *see* METAL BENDING

SPR *see* SOCIETY FOR PSYCHICAL RESEARCH

Sprenger, Jakob *see MALLEUS MALEFICARUM*

spring equinox *see* VERNAL EQUINOX

Spring-Heeled Jack *see panel p645*

sprites
A general name for fairies, especially of the more ethereal realms of air and water.
A sprite is a generic term for FAIRIES and other spirits of air and water; it is not generally used for the earthier members of the fairy realm. Sprites are said to be found only where the atmosphere is serene and cool. The word comes from the Old French *esprit*, from the Latin *spiritus*, meaning spirit. In popular folklore, sprites change the colour of the leaves in autumn. The variant form 'spright' gives us the word 'sprightly', meaning lively or energetic.

SSE *see* SOCIETY FOR SCIENTIFIC EXPLORATION

stage magic *see* MAGIC, STAGE

standing stones
Large stones set erect in the ground by prehistoric people.
Standing stones, or large stones set on end in the ground, have been found in various places all over the world, but the most famous examples occur in Western Europe, particularly in France (for example at CARNAC, in Brittany) and the British Isles. However, little can be known for certain about the purposes of these monuments. Standing stones occur in four main forms: individual stones (known as MENHIRS), DOLMENS, STONE ROWS or alignments and STONE CIRCLES.

Spring-Heeled Jack

Spring-Heeled Jack was the popular name of a mysterious male phantom who supposedly haunted many parts of England between 1837 and 1904. Numerous crimes and assaults (particularly against young women) were reputedly perpetrated by Spring-Heeled Jack, although most of his victims seem to have suffered shock rather than serious injury. That Spring-Heeled Jack was no ordinary mortal was shown by his reputed ability to jump great distances, breathe blue flames and appear and disappear seemingly without trace.

The first reported sightings of Spring-Heeled Jack were noted in the London press in 1837, with witnesses describing a mysterious figure who could jump over high railings and who had bulging, glowing eyes. A report of a physical assault by this strange creature soon followed, and news of the phantom spread, but some of the best-known accounts date from the following year. In February 1838, Jane Alsop (the teenage daughter of an East End family) apparently opened the door in response to a policeman's cries of 'For God's sake, bring me a light, for we have caught Spring-Heeled Jack here in the lane.' When she ventured outside, the 'policeman' attacked her, and after her screams roused help from within the house, Spring-Heeled Jack leapt high into the air and disappeared. Alsop described her attacker as having long metallic talons and eyes like fire, and said that he wore some sort of helmet and a tight garment of white oilskin. She also said that he vomited blue and white flames.

During the winter of 1838–9 rumours of his attacks in central London were taken so seriously that special patrols led by the Duke of Wellington were organized to calm public fears. Incidents such as the widely reported alleged attack on Jane Alsop had done much to fuel such fears, and Spring-Heeled Jack's fame spread. Although reports of him were less frequent in the subsequent decades, they did become widespread – he was apparently seen in many different parts of England, and a number of crimes were attributed to him, including murders. In 1888, the name 'Jack' lent itself easily to the far more real and deadly Jack the Ripper, the unidentified murderer of six prostitutes in the East End of London.

The last reported manifestation of Spring-Heeled Jack was in Liverpool in 1904, but after this he was seen no more. Various explanations postulated for Spring-Heeled Jack include a ghost, a bear, a human prankster (particularly the Marquess of Waterford, a well-known practical joker) or even an alien humanoid originating from a high-gravity planet and capable of performing great leaps in the lower gravity of Earth. However, for modern folklorists Spring-Heeled Jack provides an example of a powerful URBAN LEGEND.

The most basic of these forms is, of course, the single standing stone. There are various theories as to why, in different cultures around the world, prehistoric humans were impelled to erect these monuments. Some say that they are simply markers of some kind, perhaps to indicate the boundary of the territory under the control of a particular tribe or chief, or to guide travellers from place to place in a hazardous landscape in much the same way as later Christian crosses were set up to guide pilgrims on the route to a shrine.

Others believe that the significance of these stones must have been religious, that their erection was a form of religious duty or demonstration of faith. The fact that their very form gives them phallic overtones leads some to interpret them as belonging to the worship of a fertility deity or as offerings to ensure the continuing fertility of the tribe itself. Or perhaps they were intended as commemorations of important events or colossal gravestones to mark forever the last resting place of some hero or great leader.

Another idea is that they played an astrological or astronomical role. Study of some of the more complex megalithic structures have led to the conjecture that the early peoples who erected them had fairly sophisticated knowledge of the movements of the stars and planets. It may be, then, that standing stones were used to mark the position of the moon, the sun or some other conspicuous heavenly body at times of the year that were particularly vital, such as the solstices or equinoxes, times when the seasons were changing and primitive peoples would have to know which elements of their agricultural year should be in progress.

That they were considered of great importance is beyond doubt. We can only theorize about the physical methods used, but the immense labour needed to carve, transport and erect these massive stones would have been no small sacrifice in an age when life was relatively short and spent, by the majority at least, in daily work just to ensure that everyone had enough to eat. Also, having been made of the most durable material available, they can only have been meant to last, long beyond a human lifetime or even the collective memory of the people to whom they were obviously so significant.

At least in this way, their creators have achieved a kind of immortality, even though their motives and beliefs must remain mysterious. See also MEGALITHS.

Stargate Project *see* PROJECT STARGATE

Steiner, Rudolf (1861–1925)
Austrian social philosopher, founder of anthroposophy.
Rudolf Steiner was born in Kraljevic, Croatia. He studied science and mathematics, and edited Goethe's scientific papers in Weimar, gaining his doctorate in philosophy at Rostock University in Germany in 1891 with his thesis *Truth and Knowledge*. During this period he also collaborated on a complete edition of Schopenhauer's work. He had a keen interest in the OCCULT, and was involved in the THEOSOPHICAL SOCIETY for a time, becoming head of its German section (1902–12), but he came to disagree with a number of its aspects, and left in 1912 to found his own Anthroposophical Society, taking most of the German Theosophical Society members with him. In Dornach, Switzerland, he then built his first Goetheanum, a cultural centre which included activities in mathematics, medicine and schools of art; Steiner himself was also an architect, playwright and sculptor. This centre was burnt down by arsonists in 1922, but Steiner immediately began to build another on the same site, and it was still under construction when he died in 1925.

Steiner conceived of ANTHROPOSOPHY as a 'Spiritual Science'. He was convinced that reality was essentially spiritual, and his aim was to teach people how to restore their capacity for spiritual perception, which he believed had been blunted by the material preoccupations of the modern world. He taught that this spiritual perception operates independently of the body and bodily senses, and that it was by its means that he had gained his knowledge of the occult. He claimed to be able to access the AKASHIC RECORDS, a collection of mystical knowledge said to be stored in the ether and to contain the entire history of the evolution of man and of the world. Steiner saw history as being essentially shaped by changes formed through the progressive development of human consciousness, and advocated the possibility that humans could become spiritually free beings through the conscious activity of thought and the integration of the psychological and practical aspects of life.

At the end of the 19th century, all of the sciences were developing rapidly, and Steiner was determined that they should be based on spiritual rather than material truths. He was instrumental in founding a company which promoted and manufactured homeopathic and herbal medicines and products, and his teachings were the basis for a medical movement which gives particular importance to homeopathy, and which now has its own hospitals and medical schools. He also laid the groundwork for a system of biodynamic agriculture, in which only organic materials are used for fertilization, and his work led to the founding of a group of centres (Camphill Villages) dedicated to community building for people with developmental or learning disabilities. But the most significant influence of Steiner is probably in the field of education; while pursuing his academic studies, Steiner also worked as a private tutor, and he formed his own ideas about the best methods for teaching children. He believed education should be designed to meet the changing needs of children as they develop physically, mentally and emotionally, and that its purpose is to help them to realize their full potential, rather than to push them blindly to achieve goals which adults or society consider desirable. He founded a school with teaching methods based on these principles in 1919, for the children of the Waldorf Astoria factory workers. Steiner or Waldorf Schools are now found in many countries, and are still based on his holistic educational theories, with a strong emphasis on the arts, social skills and spiritual values.

Steller's sea ape
An unidentified marine mammal sighted by Arctic explorer and naturalist Georg Steller during the 18th century.
On 10 August 1741, while exploring the Arctic waters of what is now called the Bering Sea, separating Russia's Kamchatka Peninsula from Alaska, the explorer and naturalist Georg Wilhelm Steller claimed he saw a bizarre sea creature. He said he had observed it for over two hours as it frolicked in the sea ahead of his ship, and, according to his detailed description, it was approximately 1.5 metres (around 5 feet) long, with a dog-like head and a pair of pointed erect ears. He said that it had long whiskers hanging down from both its upper and lower lips, that in Steller's opinion made the creature look almost like a Chinese man. It had large eyes, and its body was longish, round and thick. Its skin seemed very hairy, grey above and reddish-white underneath. Its tail was divided into two fins, which in Steller's view made it seem shark-like, because the upper fin was twice as large as the

lower. Most surprising of all was that it did not appear to possess any front limbs, as evinced when it raised as much as a third of its total length up out of the water, just like a human, a position that it could maintain for several minutes at a time. Steller had a considerable knowledge of the area's wildlife, and during his voyage discovered several major new species of animal, some of which were duly named after him. Yet he was wholly unable to identify this creature, which eventually became known as Steller's sea ape or sea monkey.

One further sighting of this creature has been claimed – from 1965, when renowned British yachtsman-adventurer Brigadier Miles Smeeton and his wife reported seeing a similar creature in the same area, complete with drooping mandarin-like whiskers. Attempts to liken it to various species of seal, or even a sea otter, have proven far from satisfactory, especially if Steller's description of its shark-like tail and absence of front limbs is correct. To date, therefore, all that can be said is that this chilling stretch of Arctic water may still be home to a species of marine CRYPTID that was first reported over 250 years ago.

St Elmo's fire

An electrical discharge from isolated points above ground, associated with thunderstorms.

From the time of the ancient Greeks and Romans there have been reports of an eerie glow seen to form before or during THUNDERSTORMS around prominent isolated points above ground, particularly the masts of sailing ships and latterly church steeples. The Greeks gave the phenomenon names, referring to a single flame as 'Helena' and a double one as 'Castor and Pollux'.

The modern name comes from St Elmo (also known as Erasmus of Formia; died c.300), the patron saint of sailors, who interpreted the phenomenon as a sign of divine blessing. This belief is reflected in another name for it: 'corposant', which comes from the Portuguese, meaning 'holy body'. Superstitious sailors would greet its appearance as a propitious sign. Descriptions appear in many accounts of sea voyages, from Magellan (c.1480–1521) to Charles Darwin (1809–82). It is usually described as a bluish light resembling flames rising upward from the tips of sharp objects.

The American statesman and scientist Benjamin Franklin (1706–90) was the first to identify the phenomenon as electrical in nature. While described as 'fire', this is technically a corona or point electrical discharge of ionized particles; it is at a relatively low temperature and does not burn the objects that it forms around.

stigmata

Marks corresponding to the wounds received by Christ during the crucifixion, which are said to appear spontaneously on the bodies of certain Christian individuals, usually on the hands, feet or side.

The word 'stigmata' is the plural of *stigma*, a Greek word which means 'tattoo' or 'brand'. It is applied to marks corresponding to the wounds received by Christ during the crucifixion, which are believed to appear on the bodies of certain individuals. Sufferers, known as stigmatics, often experience extreme pain, and in some cases, known as invisible stigmata, the pain is felt but there are no external marks. The 14th-century stigmatic, St Catherine of Siena, was said to have initially displayed visible wounds, but in her humility, she prayed that they might be made invisible, and her prayer was granted.

The most commonly demonstrated stigmata correspond to the 'Five Holy Wounds of Christ' – one on each hand and foot, and one in the side, where Christ was said to have been pierced by a Roman soldier's lance. However, cases have also been reported of stigmatics displaying wounds on the forehead like those that might be produced by a crown of thorns, weeping tears of blood, showing marks on the back like those caused by scourging or wounds on the shoulder, as from carrying a heavy cross.

In some stigmatics, the blood from the wounds does not appear to clot, and the wounds stay fresh and open; the blood is believed by many to be that of Christ, and is often described as having a pleasant, flower-like smell, similar to the ODOUR OF SANCTITY. The wounds are generally unresponsive to medical treatment, and once the phenomenon stops, they heal very quickly, with no scars. They may be multiple slashes, small slits, crosses or mere dots, and range from superficial to deep. Wounds in the side may appear on the left or right side, and may have various forms, from slits to crosses. Some stigmatics claim to manifest their wounds continually, while in others the wounds recur periodically, most typically at Easter, on Holy Friday.

The phenomenon of stigmata is primarily associated with the Roman Catholic faith, the majority of reported stigmatics being members of religious orders, especially contemplative ones, and about 90 per cent of reported stigmatics have been female. Around one fifth of all stigmatics have been beatified or canonized, including 62 Catholic saints. The first well-documented case of stigmata, and the first which was accepted by the Church as authentic, was that of ST FRANCIS OF ASSISI in 1224. In the century after his death, more than 20 further cases of stigmata were reported, and by the end of the 19th century, this figure had risen to 300 or more, of which over

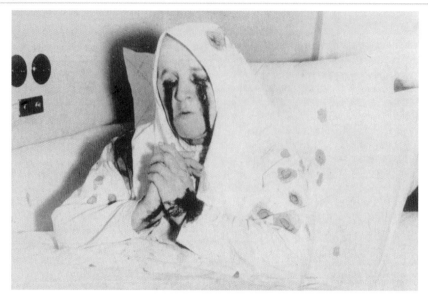

Therese Neumann (1898–1962), of Konnersreuth, Germany, showing the stigmata that she claimed appeared on her body each year during Holy Week. (© Mary Evans Picture Library)

a third were in Italy, the remainder being in France, Spain and Portugal. In the 20th century, the number of cases of alleged stigmata rose dramatically, and now stands at over 500. Interestingly, in more recent years, an increasing number of reported stigmatics have been ordinary people, rather than members of religious orders or mystics, and some have been non-Catholics. The most famous 20th-century stigmatic was ST PIO OF PIETRELCINA.

Stigmata are often accompanied by VISIONS, for example of the Passion of Christ, and other ECSTATIC PHENOMENA. A large number of stigmatics are said to have had powers of LEVITATION, BILOCATION, PROPHECY or INEDIA, and many have suffered from ill-health, or have claimed to be subjected to demonic attacks.

Sceptics dismiss stigmata as PIOUS FRAUD, an attention-seeking ploy, or the psychosomatic result of an extreme desire to identify with the sufferings of Christ.

Stokes, Doris (May Fisher) (c.1920–1987)

English medium who did much to revive the popularity of spiritualism during the late 20th century.

Born Doris Sutton in Grantham, Lincolnshire, Doris Stokes was a noted MEDIUM during the latter part of her life. She claimed that her mediumistic abilities became apparent when she was a young child, when she both saw and heard SPIRITS, and she later became involved in SPIRITUALISM, joining a spiritualist church where she was encouraged to develop her 'talents'. In the mid-1970s Stokes became popular as a psychic medium in Britain, and following an appearance on Australian television, she began to tour widely in Australia and the UK, performing to sell-out audiences at the Sydney Opera House and the London Palladium. Allegedly using her powers of CLAIRAUDIENCE, Stokes would apparently deliver messages from deceased friends and family to members of the audience.

Sceptics claimed that Stokes' alleged paranormal abilities could be quite easily explained as trickery. Some claimed that those members of the audience that received messages from the spirit world were plants – ie people who Stokes already knew a great deal about. Others suggested that she used techniques such as 'cold reading': for example, fishing for information then repeating it back as though it was something the performer had been told by the spirits; bombarding someone with lots of information and watching to see which they react to before elaborating on these elements; and making very general statements which could actually apply to most people while appearing to make them specific – this latter form of cold reading could be compared to the information given in newspaper horoscopes, where at least some of the details given will seem relevant to a lot of the population at any one time.

Stokes always claimed that her mediumistic talents were genuine, and wrote a series of very popular books outlining her life and work. Her frequent television appearances, and her notoriety in the press, led to an increased interest in spiritualism, and while many would dismiss her as a clever stage performer, others still believe that she genuinely communicated with the dead.

stone circles
Great circular patterns of megaliths erected by prehistoric cultures.

When people think about the stone monuments erected by prehistoric cultures, most tend to visualize the great stone circles such as at STONEHENGE or AVEBURY. Perhaps this is because it is evident to all that they are the product of great feats of engineering, or that they show the artistic impulse present in humankind even in primitive times, much more so than individual STANDING STONES or DOLMENS can do.

The earliest known stone circles appeared in the British Isles in the Neolithic period and their construction seems to have died out during the Bronze Age. Some are more extensive than others; some use greater individual megaliths; some have stones with lintels, while others are composed of rough undressed stones; some are more complex, with concentric circles, 'avenues' and deep ditches, but in every case the reasons for their construction remain in the province of conjecture.

Do they show evidence of astronomical sophistication in the cultures responsible? Some of those who have studied stone circles believe that they are colossal calendars or observatories, erected by agricultural peoples as a guide to the changing seasons of the year. At Stonehenge, for example, it has been shown that the axis of the circle is aligned with the position in which the sun rises on the longest day (21 June) and that in which it sets on the shortest (21 December).

It is also argued that this kind of astronomical alignment was not an end in itself but more probably an aspect of their true purpose, which was as centres of worship of the sun or moon. In other words, the positioning of the stones was a symbolic homage to these heavenly bodies rather than an attempt to track or mark their progress with any degree of accuracy.

Graves have been excavated within some stone circles, but the very size of the circles tends to argue against the idea that their sole purpose was as elaborate funerary monuments. Some argue that it seems inconceivable that any one individual (or even family) could have been so important as to justify such elaborate commemoration.

Different circles show different standards of preservation. Depending on the actual stone used, long centuries of weathering have played their part in eroding stones, and toppling or burying others.

Human interaction has also played a part, with generations of inhabitants removing stones, whether to clear fields for cultivation or to supply materials for buildings of their own. Sometimes, antiquarians have caused fallen stones to be re-erected. This means that many circles are far from complete and others may not reflect the original design, which means that their intended purposes are even more obscured.

Whatever the aims of the builders, it cannot be denied that astonishing amounts of cooperative work were necessary to carry them out, in hewing the stones, transporting them from their quarries (often at some distance) and erecting them in position. There must have been a purpose of overriding concern to the whole tribe for these great labours, sometimes carried on over many generations. This might indicate that religion must have played a major part in the motivation of those who built these enigmatic structures. See also MEGALITHS.

Stonehenge
A colossal stone circle on Salisbury Plain in Wiltshire, England.

On Salisbury Plain, an upland chalk moor in Wiltshire, stands Stonehenge, probably the most famous STONE CIRCLE in the British Isles, if not the world. The name itself essentially means 'stone gallows', deriving from the comparison made by Old English speakers between a gallows and a trilithon (a pair of MEGALITHS topped by a lintel stone). The site is a complex one, with a surrounding ditch and at least three concentric circles, and work seems to have gone on there over a period of almost 1,500 years, beginning before 3000 BC, that is, before the building of the PYRAMIDS. However, the instantly recognizable element is that of the main inner circle of trilithons.

This circle is built of dolerite, the source having been identified as the Preseli Mountains in Wales. Exactly how these massive stones were transported to the site remains unexplained, but the circle seems to have been built c.2500 BC. The outer circle consists of sarsen stones, quarried from Marlborough Downs. The English antiquarian John Aubrey (1626–97) noted the existence of over 50 shallow pits within the surrounding ditch, and these are known as the 'Aubrey Holes'. The construction of the site undoubtedly called for an enormous communal effort over many years, a fact which alone points to its importance to those who built it.

The purpose of Stonehenge is open to conjecture. It has been shown that the axis of the circle is aligned with the position in which the sun rises on the longest day (21 June) and that in which it sets on the shortest (21 December), when sighted against the free-standing Heel Stone outside the entrance. Some have

An aerial view of Stonehenge. (© Adam Woolfitt/Corbis)

deduced from this that the site is some kind of giant astronomical calendar perpetualized in stone so that its builders could track the movements of sun and moon and mark the changing of the seasons. Others, however, maintain that this is to ascribe too great a sophistication to the builders and that the alignment is simply a reflection of the site's true purpose: as a centre of worship of the sun. To support this theory it has been pointed out that the shadow of the Heel Stone casts a phallic shadow into the circle, perhaps symbolizing the mating of the sun and the earth.

Nothing is known for certain about the eventual abandonment of Stonehenge. Changes in religious belief probably played a part, and it has been suggested that climate change turned what had been a lush and fertile area into a bleak and unwelcoming one, with cloudy skies tending to obscure the heavens, making consistent observation impossible.

The site was not lost to history, however, and the medieval chronicler Geoffrey of Monmouth (c.1100–c.1154) identified it as the burial place of the Dark Age King Constantine. Early antiquarians connected the site with the rituals of the DRUIDS, and modern-day druidic devotees took their cue to mark the SUMMER SOLSTICE there. While it can be shown that Stonehenge had fallen into disuse long before the cult of the Druids arose this does not discourage periodic revivals of interest in it, from the hippies of the 1960s and 1970s to the NEW AGE travellers of the 1980s and 1990s.

stone rows
Linear arrangements of standing stones.

When a number of STANDING STONES can be seen to have been arranged in a particular straight line, this is known as a stone row, or alignment.

The great prehistoric site at CARNAC in Brittany has some of the most extensive surviving stone rows, comprising well over two thousand individual standing stones. These are grouped into the Alignments of Kerlescan, with 555 stones in thirteen rows, the Alignments of Kermario, with 1,029 stones in ten rows, and, largest of all, the Alignments of Menec, with 1,169 stones in eleven rows.

There are different theories as to why such alignments were constructed. Many believe that they have some kind of astronomical significance, whether as a form of grid on which to plot the movements of heavenly bodies, or as elaborate pointers indicating the place at which the sun or moon is seen to rise or set on particular important days of the year. Others argue that it is more likely that alignments had a more symbolic role for the people who erected them, perhaps as tribal or territorial markers or as monuments to the power and importance of those who ordered them to be built.

It may be that these massive constructions will never be satisfactorily explained, as many of them are so incomplete (stones having been quarried over the centuries for other uses) or partially and not always accurately restored, that their current appearance may be greatly different from their original arrangement. See also MEGALITHS.

stones, standing *see* STANDING STONES

stone tape theory
A theory that suggests that recurrent hauntings are a form of recording on the material environment analogous to video or audio tapes.

The stone tape theory (or rather hypothesis) explains recurrent HAUNTINGS as recordings of scenes or events that are imprinted in the fabric of buildings and rocks, which are then played at intervals in the form of ghostly manifestations. If you accept this suggestion, ghostly manifestations have no consciousness and cannot interact with human observers – they are rather more like video clips.

It is thought that the term 'stone tape theory' comes from Nigel Kneale's television play, *The Stone Tape*, broadcast on the BBC in 1972. In this play, the fabric of a room 'records' or 'stores' tragic or emotional events which are then replayed. Although a popular theory with many ghost researchers, proponents are unable to suggest any physical mechanism by which such effects might operate.

Some suggest that the term is best considered as a metaphor or analogy for certain aspects of place- or object- centred PSYCHIC experiences, including hauntings.

St Winefride's Well

A holy well and noted landmark in Wales, located in Holywell, Flintshire. Its waters are said to have sprung forth from the place where the severed head of St Winefride came to rest after she was beheaded by the son of a local chieftain for refusing to marry him, and they have been attributed with miraculous healing powers since the 7th century.

The Welsh town of Holywell in Flintshire gets its name from the HOLY WELL of St Winefride which has, since the 7th century, been a place of pilgrimage for people who seek miraculous healing by bathing in its waters. It is known as the 'Lourdes of Wales', and is commemorated in the traditional list of notable Welsh landmarks, the anonymous rhyme *The Seven Wonders of Wales*:

> Pistyll Rhaeadr and Wrexham steeple,
> Snowdon's mountain without its people,
> Overton yew trees, St Winefride wells,
> Llangollen bridge and Gresford bells.

The legend of St Winefride was not written down until some 500 years after the events which are said to have led to the holy well's creation. The story goes that some time around the year 660, a young woman, Winefride, refused to marry Caradoc, the son of an Armorian prince, and fled to take sanctuary in the church. However, Caradoc caught up with her before she reached it, and in his fury, beheaded her. Where her severed head came to rest, a spring of water arose. This wonder was followed by another; when Winefride's uncle, St Beuno, placed her head next to her body and prayed over it, it became miraculously reconnected and Winefride rose, alive once more. She became a nun, and eventually, abbess of a convent. The place where the spring rose had previously been known as Sechnant, or 'The Dry Valley', but its name was subsequently changed, first to St Winefride's Well and then to Holywell. A shrine was established in Shrewsbury around 1138, and both it and the well were subsequently visited by thousands of pilgrims. Two 12th-century documents, preserved in the British Museum, relate the story of the saint and include the earliest written records of the MIRACLE CURES effected by the spring's waters, including the healing of dropsy, gout, sciatica, cancer, chronic pain, bowel flux and melancholia, as well as deliverance from evil spirits.

Henry V, who asked for St Winefride's aid at the

St Winefride's Well in Holywell, Wales. (© Homer Sykes/ Corbis)

Battle of Agincourt in 1415, made a 72-kilometre (45-mile) pilgrimage of thanksgiving from Shrewsbury to Holywell on foot the year after his victory. St Winefride's Well is the only shrine in Britain to have survived the 16th-century Reformation with an unbroken record of pilgrimage, apparent healing and prayer; even during those years of religious persecution, when Henry VIII had the shrine and its saintly relics destroyed, both Catholic and non-Catholic pilgrims continued to visit it, and it became a centre of Catholic resistance. James II visited the well with his wife, Mary of Modena, in 1686, after a number of failed attempts to produce an heir to the throne. Shortly after their visit, Mary became pregnant with a son.

Thousands of people continue to make pilgrimages to the well today. Its cold, pale bluish water is said to be so clear that a pin can be seen at the bottom of the basin, some distance below the surface, and the stones at the bottom are stained deep crimson and purple; according to Catholic tradition, these stains are the blood of the saint, although scientists have attributed them to a kind of moss. Those seeking a cure pass through the pool, traditionally three times, kneel in the water, and kiss the ancient cross carved in the stonework. On emerging from the pool, they throw themselves on their knees before a statue of the saint and pray for her intercession. Carvings of St Winefride's legend adorn the stone of the arched crypt above the spring, and in the ceiling, she is depicted seated with a staff in her hand and wearing a crown.

succubus

A female night-demon of medieval Christian legend, believed to seduce men in their sleep.

The succubus is the female counterpart of the INCUBUS. A night-demon who is said to seduce men while they sleep, the succubus (whose name comes from a Latin word meaning 'to lie beneath') appears prominently in medieval Christian lore, her favourite prey being monks. She is usually described as taking on the appearance of an alluring woman of unearthly beauty, often with demonic bat-like wings, and is believed to drain her victims of their energy to the point of exhaustion or death, or to steal their semen in order to produce demonic offspring. According to legend, incubi are nine times more numerous than succubi, and the 15th-century *MALLEUS MALEFICARUM* relates that succubi collect semen and pass it on to incubi, who then use it to impregnate sleeping women. The semi-human children begotten in this way (known as cambions) are thought to be particularly susceptible to the influence of DEMONS. In later times, the succubus and incubus were seen as the same being in different forms.

Lilith, identified in rabbinic lore as the first wife of Adam, was said to have been ejected from Eden for refusing to acknowledge her husband's sexual dominance, and to have become a succubus in order to avenge herself on Adam's descendants. Succubi are therefore often referred to as Daughters of Lilith. Nahema is said to be the queen of all succubi.

From the 16th century onwards, the carving of a succubus on the outside of an inn indicated that it also functioned as a brothel. In the Middle Ages, nocturnal emissions were always attributed to the attentions of a succubus, and the prevalence of such claims, especially among monks, have led some to suggest that the origins of the medieval succubus lie in the extreme repression of sexual urges dictated by the Church at that time.

sucuriju gigante

A colossal form of anaconda, far longer than any confirmed by science, reputedly existing in remote Brazilian swamplands.

No snake of any species measuring 9.15 metres (30 feet) or more has ever been formally confirmed by science. Yet explorers and local tribes inhabiting the jungle swamplands of South America, particularly Brazil, claim that truly monstrous anacondas measuring at least double this size, and sometimes even longer than that, exist in these regions' more remote, inaccessible areas. When swimming through their aquatic domain these giant reptiles are said to be readily revealed by virtue of their huge eyes – which glow an eerie green, like ghostly lanterns. Such super-snakes even have their own special name – the sucuriju gigante ('giant anaconda'). Perhaps the best-known example is a stupendous specimen spied and shot dead by the famous lost explorer Colonel Percy Fawcett in January 1907 on the Rio Abuna, near Brazil's border with Peru. According to his account, this serpentine colossus, part of which lay out of the water with the remainder still submerged, measured 18.91 metres (62 feet) in total length. Sometimes giant anacondas are reported with small horns over their eyes, as in the specimen allegedly encountered by Amarilho Vincente de Oliveira on a tributary of Brazil's Rio Purus in 1977.

Many outsized anaconda skins have been recorded and measured, but these are unreliable because snake skins can be readily stretched – unlike living specimens! Equally, it is not always easy to provide an accurate length estimate of a living snake, especially if the eyewitness has no experience of snakes or does not have a detailed sighting, often leading to exaggeration. So it is likely that many sucuriju gigante reports are mistaken. However, bearing in mind that the anaconda is an amphibious species, spending much of its time semi-submerged in water, the occurrence of extra-large specimens is not as unlikely as it might otherwise seem, because their watery abode would readily buoy their weight – thus enabling anacondas to attain far greater lengths, and weights, than would be possible for an exclusively terrestrial species.

sudden unexplained death syndrome

A condition in which sudden death occurs from unknown causes.

In the 1980s reports began to accumulate in various parts of the world, particularly the USA, of mysterious sudden deaths among young men of South-East Asian origin. These men had apparently been in good health and had not contracted any identifiable illness before dying, often in their sleep.

The condition was soon labelled as sudden unexplained death syndrome (SUDS). It has been suggested that the most likely cause was cardiac arrest, perhaps arising from a hereditary and previously undiagnosed heart disease. Also, as most of the cases in the USA occurred among refugees from Cambodia, Laos, Vietnam and other South-East Asian countries, the stress of fleeing one's home country and having to adapt to an unknown new society may have played a part. A definitive identification of the cause, however, remains to be found.

SUDS *see* SUDDEN UNEXPLAINED DEATH SYNDROME

Sufism

A mystical tradition of Islam the adherents of which aspire to a direct, personal experience of and union with God. Sufism began in the late 7th century and is now made up of a number of different orders which encompass a wide diversity of thought and practices.

According to Sufi historians, Sufism originated in the esoteric teachings of the Prophet Muhammad. Known as *Tasawwuf* in the Muslim world, Sufism developed in the late 7th and 8th centuries as a mystical dimension of Islam, and its rejection of the worldliness of Muslim life at that time did much to reinvigorate the Muslim faith. The Sufi emphasis on intuitive knowledge and the love of God, and its flexibility with regard to local tradition and custom, increased its appeal to non-Muslims and played an important role in extending Islam to new parts of the world. During the 9th century, Sufism developed into a mystical doctrine, and in the 10th to 12th centuries, it became a complex movement, the popularity and influence of which led to its being organized into formal orders with varying approaches to Islamic orthodoxy. The classical period of Sufism is considered to be around 1200–1500, when it enjoyed a period of intense activity in many parts of the world, propagating from its centre in Baghdad, Iraq, to Persia, India, North Africa and Muslim Spain.

Sufism is not a sect of Islam, but rather, an aspect of it; Sufi orders can be found in Sunni, Shi'a and other Islamic groups. It emphasizes a direct, personal experience of God through mystical contemplation, asceticism and prayer. It calls for a life of love and pure devotion to God, and involves a spiritual path consisting of a series of stages of piety and Gnostic psychological states through which each Sufi has to pass. This spiritual development in general involves the awakening, in a certain order, of the 'Six Subtleties' (*Lataif-e-Sitta*), spiritual centres of perception believed to be dormant in everyone. These six 'organs' or faculties are named *Nafs, Qalb, Sirr, Ruh, Khafi* and *Akhfa*. After undergoing this process of awakening, the Sufi adherent, known as a dervish, fakir or marabout, reaches a state of 'completion'. By a combination of meditation, the purification of oneself from negative patterns of thinking, emotions

and practices, the use of techniques which bring about ecstatic trance states, and the love of God and, by extension, of all humanity, without seeking any reward, the Sufi aims to become one with God.

Sufi leaders are known as *shaykhs*. Sufis teach in personal groups, making wide use of parables, allegory and metaphors. The central concept in Sufism is love, which its initiates believe is a projection of the essence of God to the Universe. The main Sufi doctrine, known as *Wahdat* (Unity), is that all phenomena are manifestations of a single reality, which is Truth, or God, and the goal of the Sufi is to transcend all ideas of duality and of the individual self, and to perceive and join with this Divine Unity.

The Sufi tradition within Islam is noted for its distinctive practices. While other branches of Islam generally frown on the use of music in religious rituals, many Sufi orders, or *turuq*, use a wide variety of rituals which include song, music and dance. Over time, each order developed its own distinctive ritual observance, called a *dhikr* or 'remembrance of God'. The best known of these is seen in the spinning dance performed by the Mevlevi order, popularly called the whirling dervishes (see DERVISHES, WHIRLING). The Chishtiyya order also makes music central to its *dhikr*, and has given rise to the *qawwali* singers, whose songs of love and devotion to God are a feature of festivals and holidays.

Although Sufism has sometimes come into conflict with the Muslim religious authorities over the centuries, it has mostly developed within the lines of orthodox Islamic practice, and has made significant theological and literary contributions to Islam. A large part of Muslim literature, especially poetry, comes from the Sufis, the best-known work in the West being *The Rubaiyat of Omar Khayyam*, and Sufism has played an important part in the development of Persian, Turkish and Urdu literature. In recent decades in the West there has also been a growth in non-traditional Sufi movements, which do not exist within the framework of Islam.

Sullivan, Roy Cleveland (1912–83)

A man who was struck by lightning several times.

Popular wisdom has it that lightning never strikes in the same place twice. The experience of Roy Sullivan supplied a vivid refutation of the old adage. Sullivan was a US Forest Ranger in Shenandoah National Park, Virginia, who claimed to have been struck by lightning no less than seven times between 1942 and 1983. Becoming known as the 'Human Lightning Rod', he suffered various minor injuries in these events, ranging from losing a toenail, through having his hair set alight, to burns on his body.

These strikes mostly occurred when he was outdoors but on one occasion lightning sought him out indoors, standing in the office of a Ranger station. There was also one near-miss when Sullivan and his wife were hanging out washing; his wife was struck instead.

While this earned him a place in the record books as the world's most lightning-struck person, Sullivan himself could not explain his apparent attraction to lightning. It has been suggested that working permanently among trees may have increased the risk, but whether this holds true or not, the odds against these repeated occurrences are immense.

Sullivan committed suicide by shooting himself, apparently over a romantic disappointment.

sulphur

One of the three basic 'principles' that alchemists believed to be present in all material substances.

Alchemists believed that all physical substances could be divided, via alchemical processes, into the 'three principles' of which they were ultimately composed – SALT, sulphur and mercury. Also known as the *tria prima*, these three principles were present in all base matter, and were said to be in perfect balance in gold. Sulphur and mercury, combined, were considered to be the 'parents' of all metals. The sulphur to which alchemists referred in this context was not common brimstone, but an oily form adhering to the mercury of a substance, and separable from it by alchemical means. This notion of the three 'heavenly substances' was central to the scheme of Nature proposed by PARACELSUS, who held that sulphur represented the principle of combustibility, and that in a spiritual sense it corresponded to the soul. Sulphur was associated with passion and will, and was thought by alchemists to be the cause of colour, taste and odour in matter. It was personified as Sol (the Sun).

summer solstice

The day in the year on which the sun is above the horizon for the longest period. It is of importance in both historical and modern pagan spiritual practice.

The summer solstice generally falls on 21 June in the northern hemisphere. The associated festival of midsummer has traditionally been celebrated on 24 June in many parts of the United Kingdom. It is one of the four minor SABBATS recognized by modern pagans and practitioners of WITCHCRAFT and has historically had great significance in the folklore of Europe where the night before midsummer's day, Midsummer's Eve, has long been associated with

Celebrants of the summer solstice at Stonehenge.
(© Patrick Ward/Corbis)

magic, FAIRIES and WITCHES.

The importance of the summer solstice to people who lived by working the land is obvious, as with the other festivals linked to the changing seasons. It is a time when crops are growing and livestock is thriving, but is also the point from which the days begin to grow shorter. It has been seen in religious practices throughout the world as the point at which the sun god's power is at its greatest (see SUN and HORNED GOD).

In Europe, as with BELTANE, celebrations often involved great bonfires and dancing through the night. Modern pagans, DRUIDS and other followers of spiritual practices tied to nature and the seasons converge on sites associated with ancient religious practice at this time of year – most famously STONEHENGE.

The midsummer festival is also known by neopagans as Litha or Alban Hefin and was adopted by the Christian Church as the feast day of St John the Baptist. See also AUTUMNAL EQUINOX; IMBOLC; LUGHNASADH; SAMHAIN; SUMMER SOLSTICE; VERNAL EQUINOX; WICCA; WINTER SOLSTICE.

Sun

Our nearest star, the most obvious feature in the sky and provider of the energy needed for life. Throughout history, and prehistory, it has had an important place in folkloric, religious, occult and esoteric traditions from around the world

The Sun has long been recognized as the provider of light, heat and life. It so controls the annual cycle of summer and winter, birth and death, growth and decay. As such, it was central to much ancient religious practice, and the archaeological record suggests that many ancient religions were built around sun worship or recognized a sun god. In Chinese culture it is associated with the male principle, or YANG, and in modern WITCHCRAFT practice it is associated with the HORNED GOD.

Within ASTROLOGY the Sun is considered to be the planetary ruler of LEO. It travels through the twelve signs of the ZODIAC during the year and its position in the zodiac at the time of a person's birth determines what is popularly known as someone's 'star sign' (more correctly, their Sun sign). It is believed to represent the 'life force' and the self. The Sun is also the name of a TAROT card and is associated with the element FIRE. See also HOROSCOPE.

Sun Dance

A sacred ritual observed by many plains Native American tribes.

The Sun Dance is traditionally performed annually in the summer at the time of a full moon. It takes many different forms and has many different names, including names which translate as 'the dance looking at the sun', 'the new life dance' and 'the thirst dance' – the name Sun Dance comes from the Dakota.

The dance may have originated as a ritual to give thanks for the plants and animals (particularly the buffalo) with which the people fed, housed and clothed themselves. It incorporates a number of other spiritual and communal elements which vary from tribe to tribe.

Commonly the various versions of the dance include the building of a lodge with a central pole which both represents and, for the period of the ritual, becomes the centre of the universe. The dancers taking part in the ritual undergo a period of fasting and purification, followed by the dance itself, which takes place around the pole. Dancers often stare into the sun and dance, sometimes for several days, without food or drink. In some versions of the dance, young male dancers volunteer to have the flesh of their breast or back pierced with a skewer, and they dance while being hung from the skewer, by a rope attached to the central pole, until they are pulled free.

The Sun Dance was outlawed by the US government in 1904 and remained so for several decades. Even when it was again permitted, the elements involving the piercing and cutting of flesh remained banned until the passing of the Native American Religious Freedoms Act in 1978.

sunwise *see* DEOSIL

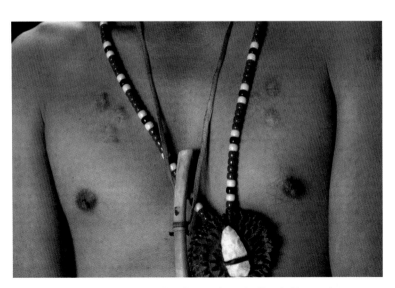

Steven Benally, Jnr, an apprentice shaman from the Navajo Reservation near Window Rock, Arizona, shows the scars he has received from four Sun Dances.
(© Kevin Fleming/Corbis)

super-ESP

A term used to describe a possible explanation for supposed communication with the spirits of the dead.

In 1959 the US parapsychologist Hornell Hart coined the phrases 'super-ESP' and 'super-psi' to cover descriptions of possible mechanisms by which MEDIUMS can appear to be communicating with SPIRITS. Such descriptions were based on the theory that, rather than contacting some element of the self which has survived death, mediums might be inadvertently using EXTRASENSORY PERCEPTION to access information from the minds of the sitters.

The hypothesis introduces an additional difficulty for spiritists: even if obtaining information by normal means can be eliminated from an investigation, if that information is known to anyone present at a SÉANCE (consciously or otherwise) then it is still not necessary to admit the idea that it was provided to the medium by the spirits. In fact, the theories offered by a number of researchers went further, suggesting that the information could be gained from further afield than the séance room – mediums might effectively be creating 'pseudo spirit personalities' by unconsciously gathering information using a wide range of PSYCHIC faculties over long distances. The idea is related to similar theories based upon the idea that a whole host of paranormal phenomena, popularly attributed to spirits of the dead are, in fact, generated through supposed powers of the minds of the living (for example, see RECURRENT SPONTANEOUS PSYCHOKINESIS).

Sceptics would, of course, contend that super-ESP can only serve as a useful theory if and when uncontroversial evidence is produced to the effect that the pronouncements of any medium actually require a paranormal explanation.

supernatural

Something that is above or beyond nature and any naturalistic explanation or understanding.

The word 'supernatural' is typically applied to an action that violates or disrupts natural laws, such as a MIRACLE or other form of divine intervention. By extension, the word also applies generally to the realm of non-human entities (such as ANGELS, DEMONS, FAIRIES, SPIRITS etc), and their modes of action. The word differs in use from PARANORMAL in that it is often understood to mean that the phenomenon concerned is beyond or not amenable to the scientific mind or approach.

'Preternatural' is a similar term (now considered somewhat archaic) meaning something beyond and different from the natural. In old metaphysical rhetoric, this usually meant something that was outside or which violated 'God's natural order' and was therefore beyond 'normal' understanding. See also PARANORMAL.

super-psi *see* SUPER-ESP

superstition

A deep-rooted but irrational belief in the supernatural, and especially in omens and luck; a rite or practice based on such a belief.

Since ancient times, people of every culture all over the world have subscribed to superstitions and have indulged in rites or practices based on these. A superstition is generally defined as an irrational and erroneous belief in a supernatural agency or in a connection between two unrelated events; a superstitious person may see OMENS and PORTENTS everywhere, and believes that a future event or outcome can be caused or influenced by some unrelated occurrence or act – for example, that putting new shoes on a table will bring bad luck or even death. Superstitions are not based on reason, and may be a result of unenlightened fears, or the misinterpretation of some correlation as cause and effect, or they may have a basis in some fact which has long since been forgotten, leaving only the superstition. Most superstitions involve omens or causes of good or bad luck, many of them regarding the most important phases of human life – birth, marriage and death – and some professions, such as the theatre and sailing, are particularly given to superstitions. Certain times of year, such as Christmas, May Day and Hallowe'en have many superstitions connected with them. Sometimes there is a way to increase one's chances of good luck in an undertaking, or to counteract the bad luck which an omen indicates, for example crossing one's fingers or knocking on wood.

Many people have their own individual superstitions: for example, they might insist on always keeping a particular talisman or charm with them to ensure no bad luck befalls them. However, other superstitions are so widespread and deep-rooted in popular culture that even the most cynical individual may still feel uneasy about disregarding them: that breaking a mirror brings seven years' bad luck, that misfortunes come in threes, that FRIDAY THE 13TH, and the number THIRTEEN in general are unlucky, and that it is bad luck to walk under a ladder, open an umbrella indoors or spill salt, unless, after doing the last, you immediately throw a pinch over your left shoulder. And many people still consider it lucky to find a four-leaf clover, have a black cat cross their path, find a pin on the ground or see a shooting star (which entitles them to make a WISH). Brides today still try to wear 'something old, something new, something borrowed, something blue' on their wedding day, and are given representations of HORSESHOES for good luck, while May is still traditionally considered an unlucky month for a wedding. A baby born on Hallowe'en is believed to have SECOND SIGHT, while one born with a caul will enjoy good fortune and will never die of drowning. There are countless superstitions involving omens of death, such as a bird flying into the house or an owl hooting in daytime, and a funeral on a Friday is thought to portend another death in the family during the year.

Even those who are not involved in the theatre know that Shakespeare's *Macbeth* is considered to be an unlucky play, so much so that actors do not mention it by name, but refer to it indirectly as 'the Scottish play', and will not quote lines from it while in the theatre, except when on stage. It is thought unlucky to quote the last line of any play until its first-night performance, whistle in the theatre or have real flowers on stage, while no actor ever wishes another 'good luck' before a performance, but instead urges them to 'break a leg'. Sailors are equally given to superstitions, the best known of which is that it is disastrous to kill an albatross, as Coleridge's Ancient Mariner found to his cost. Whistling on board ship is also unlucky because it is thought to call up a wind, especially if it is done by a woman – although a woman on a ship is considered to be unlucky in any case, and a whistling woman is just as bad luck on dry land as she is at sea.

supreme beings

Postulated supernatural beings, usually regarded as having considerable power, and revered or worshipped in many religions and belief systems. Almost all creation myths include the agency of a supreme being or beings.

Nearly every religion and culture throughout history has included the concept of supreme beings, also known as GODS or DEITIES. These postulated beings are usually regarded as possessing IMMORTALITY and having considerable power, often controlling the forces of nature, or human fate, and are consequently revered or worshipped; nearly all CREATION MYTHS include some kind of supreme being whose deliberate actions bring about the creation of the universe, the world and mankind. Some cultures and faiths subscribe to the concept of a pantheon of many supreme beings, while monotheistic religions, such as Christianity, Judaism and Islam, believe in a single supreme being – God or Allah.

In the 18th century, the leader of the French Revolution, Robespierre, rejected atheism and tried to institute a new, official state-sponsored religion called the Cult of the Supreme Being, based on the worship of a Deist-style creator god who prized liberty and opposed tyranny. The festival of this new god was set for 8 June 1794, but it was not a success, and the 'religion' sank without a trace.

Candidates for FREEMASONRY are required to declare their belief in a 'Supreme Being', this term being a generic one which allows the individual to adhere to his own concept of a deity. In Masonic ritual, the Supreme Being is often referred to as the 'Great Architect of the Universe'.

surgery, ancient *see* ANCIENT SURGERY

surgery, psychic *see* PSYCHIC SURGERY

Surrey Puma *see* ALIEN BIG CATS

suspended animation
A state in which the body's functions slow down to a minimum.

Suspended animation is defined as a state in which the body's principal functions are slowed down temporarily to an absolute minimum. The most common form of this is the hibernation of some animals in winter, in which they relapse into a state of partial or complete torpor, thus conserving energy until the weather becomes warmer. Animals in this state have a much reduced need for oxygen or sustenance.

It has been claimed that people in extreme situations can achieve a similar type of metabolic reduction. For example, stranded explorers in desert or arctic conditions have been seen to have survived longer than might be expected with insufficient food and water and to have recovered from this.

Scientists have conducted experiments on animals in which creatures such as mice (which do not hibernate in nature) have been put into a state of artificial hibernation by lacing their air with hydrogen sulphide. This has been shown to reduce the animals' metabolic rate, rate of breathing and body temperature.

If this type of artificial suspended animation could be induced in humans, it could have various desirable uses, such as allowing astronauts to make long space journeys without having to load the spacecraft with food and water, as has already been imagined in science fiction. It might also allow people with terminal illnesses to be kept alive while awaiting transplant, or undergo radiation treatment without damaging healthy cells. Science fiction again has already imagined a process of 'freezing' ill or dying people until a time when medical science will be able to cure them. However, whether this can be applied in real life remains to be seen.

swastika

A good luck symbol found in many traditions, which has now become tainted following its use as the emblem of the Nazi Party.

The swastika, a cross with its arms bent at right angles, is a symbol that has been found on prehistorical and historical items throughout the world, including those from Iron Age cultures in Europe and Asia and among Native American artefacts in Mexico and southwestern USA. The word itself comes from the Sanskrit 'svastika' and can loosely be translated as 'good to be', although it also has deeper meanings within the Hindu tradition.

Although the swastika is still very common in Indian artwork and architecture, in the West it is still strongly associated with the National Socialist German Workers (Nazi) Party of the 1930s. They adopted it as a symbol of the Aryan master race, which they supposed to have originated in India, and of which they believed the German people were the cultural descendants.

Swedenborg, Emanuel (1688–1772)

Swedish mystic, theologian and scientist.

Born in Stockholm, Emanuel Swedenborg studied at Uppsala University and travelled widely in Europe before returning to Sweden in 1715. He enjoyed a highly successful career as a scientist and inventor for the next 20 years, being appointed as assessor at the Royal Board of Mines (1716–47), beginning and contributing greatly to the country's first scientific journal, *Daedalus Hyperboreus*, and writing prolifically on topics such as mathematics and astronomy as well as technical subjects such as docks and navigation. His long treatise, *Philosophical and Logical Works* (1734) was a mixture of metallurgy and metaphysical speculation on the creation of the world, and included the earliest version of the hypothesis that the solar system originated as a single stellar mass. In the 1730s he became increasingly interested in spiritual matters, and sought to find a theory to explain how matter relates to spirit.

In 1743 or 1744, at the age of 56, Swedenborg underwent a severe religious crisis in which he claimed to experience angelic and demonic dreams, trances and visions in which the spiritual world underlying the natural sphere was revealed to him. His visions of this world, in which he said that he met and talked with angels and spirits – including St Paul, Moses, Abraham, PLATO, Cicero and St Augustine – made him turn his attention to religious matters. When he also had a vision of Christ, he felt that his crisis had been resolved and he had been given clear instructions to abandon his scientific career and devote himself to sharing the view of the order of the universe which he had been granted, and which was radically different from the teachings of the Christian Church. He recorded his dreams and visions in his *Journal of Dreams*, published posthumously, and in 1747, he resigned his scientific post in order to expound his spiritual experiences and the mystical doctrines which he formulated from them. He produced some 30 volumes of religious revelations in Latin, the best known of which were his eight-volume *Heavenly Arcana* (1749–56), *On Heaven and Its Wonders and On Hell* (1758) and his last work, a summary of his religious views, *The True Christian Religion* (1771). Because of the restrictions on the freedom of the press in Sweden, he published all of his religious works in England or Holland, at first anonymously, although in 1768 he made their authorship public.

According to Swedenborg, and Swedenborgianism, God opened his sight to the spirit world so that he might teach the doctrines of the New Church; he claimed that Jesus had revealed Himself to him and told him that He would dictate what Swedenborg was to write. Swedenborg was strongly opposed to the Christian doctrine of the Trinity, holding that Father, Son and Holy Spirit were three different aspects of the One God. He also opposed the Lutheran doctrine that Man is saved by grace alone through faith alone, and wrote that there is no inherent goodness in Man, that selfishness and worldliness create the world's evils and that all love comes from God, if Man uses his free will to accept it. Unlike many mystics, Swedenborg proposed an approach to spiritual reality and God through material nature, rather than in rejection of it, in a unique synthesis between science and religion. He saw God as the origin of the basic life principles of love and wisdom, which manifested themselves as three spheres of reality, the Divine mind, the spirit world and the natural world, with each sphere corresponding to the next.

Swedenborg died in London in 1772, and his followers, who regarded him as a prophet, founded the Church of the New Jerusalem (in 1778 in London and in 1792 in the USA). Many of his views were adopted by 19th-century SPIRITUALISM.

sword

A weapon consisting of a long, two-edged blade with a handle; used as a ritual tool in Wiccan and pagan traditions and in ceremonial magic.

The sword, with its smaller counterpart, the ritual knife or athame, is an important ritual tool in WICCA, NEOPAGANISM and ceremonial magic (see MAGIC, CEREMONIAL). It usually symbolizes the element of AIR, and all that this element signifies – learning, discernment, intelligence and communication – although in some traditions it is seen as the tool of FIRE and is interchangeable with the WAND. The sword is usually placed in the east of the altar during rituals, the east being the direction associated with the element of air. In recent years, the sword has become a very popular magical tool which can be used in place of, or in addition to, the athame; however, while every member of the magical group will usually have their own personal athame, most groups usually have one sword, used by the Priest or Priestess, to represent the whole group.

The double-edged blade symbolizes the dual powers of positive and negative, male and female, life and death, and it is believed that its use focuses and directs psychic energy in order to set up ritual space, and dismantles this energy after the ritual. Since the sword is considered to be a male tool, it is also sometimes used in male/female sacred rites along with the CAULDRON, being thrust into it to symbolize the union between the God and the Goddess. Neither the sword nor the athame is ever used to cut physical objects, but only to 'cut' energy in a spiritual or magical way; in fact, in some traditions, a blade which has come into contact with blood is no longer considered fit to be used as a magical tool.

The sword's importance as a magical symbol is demonstrated by the fact that one of the suits of the TAROT is the suit of swords (see SWORDS, SUIT OF).

swords, suit of
One of the four suits into which the cards of the tarot's minor arcana are divided.
The suit of swords in the tarot contains 14 cards: numbered 'pip' cards going from one to ten, plus four 'court' cards – the Page, the Knight, the King and the Queen. Some people believe that the four suit emblems may originally have symbolized the four main social classes in medieval Europe, with the swords representing the nobility. Astrologically, this suit is associated with the element of AIR, and the three air signs, GEMINI, LIBRA and AQUARIUS. Corresponding to the suit of spades in a modern deck of playing cards, the suit of swords is identified with the intellectual and rational faculties. Characteristics associated with this suit are strength, reason, ambition, will, courage and above all a desire to seek the truth, but also, on the negative side, aggression, anger and conflict. See also CUPS, SUIT OF; PENTACLES, SUIT OF; WANDS, SUIT OF.

sword swallowing
The temporary passing of a sword down the throat.
Sword swallowing seems to have originated in ancient India, where it was one of the feats used by FAKIRS to demonstrate the power of their faith and their command over the body.

A street performer swallowing a sword in Washington Square Park, Manhattan. (© Bob Krist/Corbis)

The practice spread both East (notably to China and Japan) and West (to ancient Greece and Rome). In these regions it lost its religious connotations and became a performance art associated with magic displays. Sword-swallowing acts became a staple item on the bill at fairs and circuses as well as in theatrical variety shows.

To distinguish themselves from competitors, practitioners began to vary their acts to include swallowing either a number of swords, or a diverse range of other items such as bayonets, saws and even (from the 1930s onwards) illuminated neon tubes.

Throughout the ages, many sceptics have suspected trickery of some kind, such as the sword-blade folding up inside the handle. With the advent of X-ray photography, however, exponents were able to show beyond doubt that the swords were indeed passing down inside their bodies.

How is it possible? The term 'swallowing' is rather misleading, as the sword is not swallowed at all but only temporarily passed down the throat and oesophagus into the upper stomach. It is vital for a performer to learn the knack of suppressing the 'gag reflex', the automatic reflex contraction of the soft palate that is the body's guard against swallowing something undesirable. Then they must master the skill of forming a relatively straight line from the pharynx to the stomach, beginning by tilting the head well back.

Sword swallowing is, therefore, an art, with nothing magical about it, but not one to be tried at home.

symbols
Signs or objects used to represent something else by association, resemblance or convention.

A symbol (from the Greek *symbolon*, a token) is a sign or object which is used to represent something else, either by association, resemblance or convention. The use of symbols is as old as mankind; it has been said that infants think in symbols before they learn to think in words, and this essential preverbal 'language' remains with us throughout life as the language of our dreams and unconscious. Graphic symbols have been used in every culture throughout history, and all number and alphabet systems – indeed, language itself – are symbols which we use to represent objects or ideas.

For as long as humans have practised MAGIC, they have used magic or occult symbols as tools; symbols speak to our subconscious, and the human subconscious is a vital element in magic. In order to perform an act of magic, it is said that the magician raises energy from within himself or herself, and taps into his or her subconscious mind to communicate their magical purpose to it. The subconscious then increases the energy raised and sends it into the universe so that it can bring about the desired result. Magical symbols are considered to be a physical representation of a transcendent reality, and by manipulating them, the magician is said to be able to manipulate the reality the symbol represents. The oldest form of magic, sympathetic magic (see MAGIC, SYMPATHETIC), is based on one thing being used as a symbol of another; it is the perceived correspondence, and thus relationship between, two objects in the universe which allows the magician's actions on one to influence the other. All types of DIVINATION, for example the *I CHING*, RUNES, the TAROT and dream interpretation, also make use of symbolism. A magical tool such as a SWORD, or a physical object such as a bowl of salt, may symbolize an ELEMENT on an altar or in a MAGIC CIRCLE.

But magic also uses abstract 'alphabets' or symbol systems, often highly complex and with layers of correspondences which are ordered in a deliberate and scientific way. Thus, the traditional Western magical symbol system includes the occult ideas of the four elements, the seven 'planets' or

heavenly bodies, the twelve signs of the ZODIAC and the 22 letters of the Hebrew alphabet from the magical symbol system of the KABBALAH. The magical symbol usually contains something of the character of that which it symbolizes, thus linking the two by some similarity or pattern, and typically, each symbol in a magical system might be associated with a sign, image or pictograph; a letter or speech sound; a number; a colour; a geometric form; a part of the body; a species of animal or plant; a gemstone or mineral; and a time of day or month. Through such a system of magical symbols, everything in the universe is linked by a set of correspondences which connect all orders of being, and most, if not all, spells have some symbolic element, whether it is an action, a word or, as in the case of AMULETS and TALISMANS, a physical representation of a symbol.

Certain magical symbols are so commonly found in almost all cultures as to be universal. One such symbol is the CIRCLE; it is the symbol of the sun, and, since it has no beginning or end, and no divisions, it also symbolizes completeness and eternity, and the soul. The equal-armed cross is another universal symbol, which represents the four elements, the four cardinal directions and the conflict between matter and spirit. The ancient Egyptian ANKH is a worldwide symbol of life, and the serpent, which sheds its skin and renews itself, plays an important role in most cultures as a symbol of rebirth. The symbol of the cosmic egg – the egg as a container for the universe – appears in many ancient religions, such as Hinduism, and in many folk legends, and is also found in alchemy.

sympathetic magic *see* MAGIC, SYMPATHETIC

synchronicity
A theory of COINCIDENCE, *and a state in which seemingly unrelated events occur simultaneously, and which gain a significant relationship through an observer's interpretation.*

The idea of synchronicity evolved during correspondence between psychologist CARL JUNG and physicist Wolfgang Pauli, from 1932 to 1958, and is defined in Jung's *The Interpretation of Nature and the Psyche* (1955) as 'an a-causal connecting principle' that seems to operate in some events as distinct from the usual and natural cause-and-effect processes. Later, in his *Synchronicity: An Acausal Connecting Principle* (1972), Jung expanded the theory to help explain EXTRASENSORY PERCEPTION, suggesting it operated in the realm of the ARCHETYPES in the COLLECTIVE UNCONSCIOUS, from where it intruded into everyday life creating significant associations between events which had no other observable connection. The chief objections to the theory are that its manifestations seem opportunistic and its interpretations subjective and arbitrary.

See also CHANCE AND COINCIDENCE.

syncretism

The reconciliation of, or an attempt to reconcile, different systems of belief; an amalgamation of the beliefs and practices of various religions.

The word 'syncretism' first appears as *sunkrētismos*, in an essay by the Greek historian Plutarch, who used it to describe the alliance of the Cretan communities, habitually at odds, when confronted by a common enemy. But its first appearance in English is in the early 17th century, where it refers to an attempt to reconcile disparate or even opposing schools of thought. It is nowadays used especially in a religious context to denote a fusion or blending of spiritual beliefs and practices, but religious syncretism is much older than the term itself. The ancient Egyptians often combined different deities, both Egyptian and non-Egyptian, into a single one, the most famous being Serapis, a syncretization of Osiris and Apis with the Greek gods Zeus and Helios. Greek paganism was essentially a syncretic religion,

merging Persian, Egyptian and later Etruscan and Roman elements within its Hellenistic framework, and the Romans, too, adopted syncretic gods such as Serapis, Isis, Mithras and Cybele; when they encountered Celts and Teutons, they similarly merged some of the Celtic and Teutonic gods with their own.

Early Christianity incorporated many European pagan elements. The rededication of pagan HOLY WELLS to Christian saints is a prime example of Christian syncretization, a later one being the adoption of pagan festivals into the Christian calendar. VOUDUN and SANTERÍA both combine African beliefs and Roman Catholicism, and Rastafarianism is another highly syncretic religion which combines elements from the Bible with Marcus Garvey's Back-to-Africa movement and Caribbean culture.

Although the term 'syncretism' is sometimes used in a pejorative sense with implications of illogical compromise or the abandoning of one's historic faith, it can be argued that all religions are to some degree syncretistic, and that syncretism tends to promote a coexistence and constructive interaction between disparate cultures.

table-turning

The supposedly unexplained, sometimes violent, movement of a table during a séance.

Table-turning or 'table-tipping' is one of the wide range of physical phenomena that are said to occur during SÉANCES. To achieve the effect, the participants sit around a table, with their hands gently resting on it. If they are successful, the table will begin to move without any apparent human intervention – the movement is then usually ascribed to the actions of the SPIRITS. In some séances the table moved very energetically – for example, the séances of EUSAPIA PALLADINO were usually characterized by quite violent movements of this sort.

Table-turning was a common feature of séances from the very early days of the SPIRITUALISM movement. By the mid-1850s it had become a popular pastime in the homes of Victorian Britain. Many were happy to accept that the movement was produced by the spirits, but a number of scientists and sceptics investigated further. Michael Faraday devised a system of two table tops, one sitting on rollers above the other. If even a small amount of pressure were applied to the top table, the rollers would move, telegraphing the fact that the movement had been produced by a push or a pull from one of the sitters.

The popularity of table-turning started to wane at the start of the 20th century and, while it is still reported in some séances, it is now more likely to be encountered as part of a stage magician's act.

In its broadest sense the phrase 'table-turning' can be used to refer to any movement of objects during a séance.

taboo

A strong religious or social prohibition relating to any area of human activity that has been declared sacred or forbidden.

The word 'taboo' comes from the Tongan *tabu* or *tapu*, meaning 'marked off', and was adopted into English in the 18th century by Captain Cook, who found it among many Polynesian cultures. However, the concept of the taboo, a strong religious or social prohibition against any form of human behaviour that has been declared forbidden, has been a feature of almost all societies and cultures since primitive times. The taboo object or activity is generally forbidden either because it is regarded as sacred, or because it is considered unclean. Thus, it may be taboo to say the name of a god out loud or to touch a dead body. The origins of taboos seem to predate religion, and to be rooted in primitive magic, when certain objects were thought to contain a power which could harm or defile the one who touched them. With the development of religion, taboos were seen as divine prohibitions, the breaking of which would be punished by the gods themselves. In modern Western societies, taboos have for the most part become socially restrictive rules of behaviour, the infringement of which may lead to severe legal penalties, or may simply bring about social ostracism or embarrassment.

The taboos of each individual culture reveal its preoccupations, and while no taboo is known to be universal, certain taboos, such as those involving incest and cannibalism, are found in most cultures. The most fundamental taboos in all societies are connected with the basic human experiences of death and sex, as is seen in such widespread prohibitions as those against adult–child sex, necrophilia and bestiality. Certain foods and drinks are taboo in some cultures;

only the flesh of animals slaughtered in a prescribed way (*halal*) may be eaten by Muslims, while pork is forbidden to Jews, and Hindus and Jainists typically practise religious vegetarianism. The public exposure of the genitals is taboo in most cultures, but exposing other parts of the body may also be taboo: in Victorian England, it was taboo for a woman's ankles to be seen in public; in Saudi Arabia, there is a taboo against women showing their faces. Sexual or blasphemous language, and in some cases, the discussion of sexual topics, is generally considered taboo, leading to the use of euphemism or 'taboo deformation' to allow the speaker to refer to the forbidden subject without breaking the prohibition.

t'ai chi

A Chinese system of exercise in which a series of slow, continuous movements are performed with synchronized breathing while the practitioner meditates on the flow of energy or 'qi' through the body.

T'ai chi ch'uan, usually referred to simply as *t'ai chi*, is a Chinese phrase which translates literally as 'greatest extreme fist'. T'ai chi was originally developed a few centuries ago as a 'soft combat' martial art in which the opponent's aggressive energy is absorbed and used against him. However, nowadays it is mainly practised as a health discipline. T'ai chi is believed to have developed from traditional QIGONG practices; it is now one of the most popular Oriental movement arts in the West, and is practised daily by millions of people.

Students learn a sequence of slow, continuous movements which are circular in nature. Each movement has a specific name which generally describes what it looks like, such as 'playing with the waves' or 'the snow goose spreads its wings'. The set of movements may take from five minutes to an hour or more to complete, depending on the length of the sequence, and the emphasis is on balance and co-ordination; breathing is synchronized with the movements, while at the same time, the practitioner learns to sense and 'flow with' the UNIVERSAL LIFE FORCE, known as QI, as it moves in and around the body. The combination of movement, breathing and meditation is believed to produce a build-up of inner power, which the student later learns to direct to specific areas of the body which need it; t'ai chi masters are said to have developed this ability to such an extent that they can direct this qi to others.

There are numerous t'ai chi styles, mostly named after their founders, for example Chen style, Sun style and Wu style. T'ai chi is thought physically to balance the body's YIN and YANG principles, and is claimed by some to provide the same cardiovascular benefits as more strenuous exercise, but without putting strain on the heart. It is thought to be particularly beneficial in lowering high blood pressure, relieving stress, spinal problems and arthritis and improving balance.

talismans

Object which have been magically charged with a specific energy to bring about a desired effect, such as attracting health, wealth or luck; usually worn or carried about the person.

Talismans have been used since ancient times in an attempt magically to bring about a desired effect. While AMULETS are designed to protect the wearer or bearer by warding off evil or disease, talismans are

A group of t'ai chi practitioners in Beijing. (© Wolfgang Kaehler/Corbis)

generally intended actively to draw magical energy into them and connect it to the earth plane in order to attract what is wanted – health, money, luck, love or success – and they are seen as possessing power in themselves. The word 'talisman' comes via the Arabic *tilsam* from medieval Greek *telesma*, meaning ritual or consecrated object, and talismans were traditionally made and sold by specialists who produced and dedicated them for their purpose through ritual acts. They were an important part of the burial rites of ancient Egypt, and were common in Greek and Roman times. In the Middle Ages, the cult of saints gave rise to the popularity of Christian talismans, with miracles being attributed to bones and other RELICS of saints, and pilgrimages were made to churches which contained these; one of the most sought-after of Christian talismans at this time was a piece of the True Cross, on which Christ was said to have been crucified.

The Jews turned the making of talismans into a scientific art. Jewish talismans, which were usually metal disks or pieces of paper or parchment, gained their potency from the fact that they incorporated Hebrew letters, phrases from the Scriptures and WORDS OF POWER – the names of God or of angels. During the Renaissance, AGRIPPA OF NETTESHEIM's *De occulta philosophia* included a great deal of information on the making and charging of talismans. Later GRIMOIRES also frequently gave instructions on how to make talismans. But any object which is regularly carried or worn for luck is, in effect, a talisman; it is the belief of the carrier in its power which gives it its magical significance.

tantra

Any of a number of Hindu and Buddhist texts concerned with the ritual use of symbolic speech and images, meditation on the union of the male and female divine principles, and the ritualized use of sexual intercourse to achieve heightened spiritual awareness; a system of Hindu yoga based on these texts.
The word 'tantra', which is Sanskrit for 'woven together', refers to a body of Hindu and Buddhist literature which focuses primarily on the use of symbolic speech, or MANTRAS, and symbolic diagrams, or MANDALAS; the meditation on and worship of the union of the male and female divine principles; and the ritual use of sexual intercourse to achieve heightened consciousness. The term is also applied to the esoteric tradition of ritual and YOGA based on this. Tantra derives from the pre-Hindu religions of Shaktiism and Shivaism.

Classic tantra yoga is composed of several strands, including the physical postures and breath control of *Hatha* yoga, the study of sacred writings and rituals, the chanting of mantras and meditation on iconographic symbols, but the aspect for which it is best known, particularly in the West, is the use of sexual pleasure, awakened and sustained through ritualized intercourse, as a path to experience of the divine. In this strand of tantric yoga, the object is to awaken KUNDALINI, the subtle energy which is believed to rest like a coiled serpent in the root CHAKRA, at the base of the spine. Consciousness is seen as consisting of two parts which correspond to the male and female divine principles of the static, formless Shiva and the dynamic, creative Shakti. Tantra yoga identifies Kundalini with Shakti, the female divine aspect, and by awakening this energy and raising it through the chakras to the crown, yogis believe that they can merge it with the Shiva, or godhead, and experience them in their state of union, bringing spiritual enlightenment.

While sexual intercourse is not part of every form of tantric practice, tantra has become so closely identified with this feature that the term 'tantric' has also come to be loosely applied to other, primarily Western, religious or spiritual practices which use ritualized sex as a path to spiritual ecstasy.

Taoism

A philosophical system set out principally in the Tao Te Ching, *a text ascribed to the legendary Chinese sage Lao Tzu; also, a pantheistic religious system which combines Taoist philosophy with Chinese folk religion and magic.*
The term 'Taoism' is used to refer to both a philosophical system and a religious one. Taoism's most famous and important source text is the *TAO TE CHING*, or 'Book of the Tao', which is ascribed to the legendary Chinese sage, LAO TZU. The Tao, which is usually translated as 'The Way of Life' or simply 'The Way', is regarded as the first cause of the universe, a force which flows through all life, and the source of harmony throughout nature. It is sometimes referred to as the way the universe functions, and the path taken by natural events, although it is also said that the Tao cannot truly be described, but only understood instinctively, and that 'the Tao that can be put into words is not the Everlasting Tao'.

Taoism teaches that everything is forever changing, and that time is a never-ending cycle, not a linear process. The physical and the spiritual are seen as indivisible aspects of the same reality, while reality itself is not regarded as fixed, but as subject to constant change. Nothing is permanent, everything is part of everything else, and spiritual liberation comes from a consciousness of one's own ever-changing nature; the unique and unchanging 'self' is seen as a myth. In Taoism, all things in nature are said to have a complementary or opposite component, represented by the opposing but interdependent attributes of YIN and YANG, and harmony is established through a balance of these two principles. The yin-yang symbol, which represents the ideal balance of opposites in the universe, is the most common graphic representation of Taoist philosophy.

The Taoist's ultimate goal is to become one with the Tao, and it is believed that a person who could live their life in full accordance with it would achieve a perfect balance of yin and yang, and thus complete physical, emotional and spiritual wellbeing. Taoism advocates a doctrine called *Wu Wei*, or 'non-action'; this does not mean passivity, but rather, observing nature and acting only in accordance with its laws – for example, not building a dam that would interfere with the flow of a river, but allowing it to follow its natural course. Another Taoist doctrine is that of the 'Uncarved Block', which refers to the pristine state of existence in which all humans are born, before the influences of family, education, environment and society condition them to become tainted with negative qualities like greed and bigotry. To attain spiritual fulfilment and inner peace, one must become once again like an uncarved block, and this simplicity and freedom from desire can only be achieved by a mystical contemplation of nature and the inner harmonies of the universe.

Although Taoism began as a philosophy, it had, by the 5th century, also evolved into a fully developed pantheistic religious system which combined Taoist philosophy with practices such as Chinese alchemy, folk magic and divination. It was adopted as a state religion with an organized doctrine and monastic orders and flourished, along with Confucianism and Buddhism, as one of the major belief systems of pre-Communist China, but it was officially proscribed in the 1950s after the establishment of the Communist regime. Many techniques of CHINESE MEDICINE are ultimately based on Taoist principles, as are martial arts and exercise systems, such as T'AI CHI and QIGONG, and FENG SHUI.

Tao Te Ching

An ancient Chinese text, the authorship of which is traditionally attributed to the sage and philosopher Lao Tzu in the 6th century BC. It is one of the most important works of Chinese philosophy and religion, and its teachings form the basis of Taoism.

The *Tao Te Ching* is one of the most important texts in Chinese philosophy and religion, and is regarded as the seminal work which forms the basis of TAOISM. Its authorship is traditionally ascribed to the legendary Chinese sage and philosopher LAO TZU in the 6th century BC, although its date of composition and origins are the subject of much debate; some hold that Lao Tzu never existed, and that the *Tao Te Ching* is the work of several Taoist scholars, or that the first part may have been written by Lao Tzu and the second by later writers.

The *Tao Te Ching*, or 'The Book of Tao ('the Way') and Its Power', is the shortest of the world's great scriptures; in its original Chinese version, it only uses around 5,000 characters, and consists of 81 maxims in two sections. The first section, the *Book of Tao*, contains chapters 1–37, and the second section, the *Book of Te*, contains chapters 38–81. Each chapter is short, expressing its frequently deep and complex ideas poetically in only a few characters, and many chapters are open to several interpretations. It teaches that all things in the universe are manifestations of one interconnected and inseparable whole, which maintains balance and harmony; everything arises from this essentially unexplainable source, known as the Tao. Although the book's core topic is the Tao, it does not specifically define it – indeed, its first line states that 'the Tao that can be put into words is not the Everlasting Tao'. But its ever-changing cosmic nature underlies everything that happens; all thing come from it and return to it, and it represents the highest form of truth. To become one with the Tao is the goal of Taoism, and this can only be attained by discovering and living according to it, rather than trying to bend the universe to our will. The *Tao Te Ching* can be seen as advocating mostly 'feminine', or YIN values, such as fluidity, softness and mystery – 'controlling without ruling', or 'having without possessing'. This challenges the 'male' or YANG values of clarity, stability, action and domination of nature which characterize the teachings of Confucius.

According to the *Tao Te Ching*, humility is the highest virtue, and it is essential to know oneself, and to be flexible. The more one acts in harmony with the universe, the more one will achieve, with less effort. Materialism, envy, overindulgence, self-absorption and force are to be avoided. One must achieve emptiness (*Wu*) and simplicity, and practise *Wu Wei*, or 'non-action'; this is not to be confused with mere passivity, but rather, means observing nature and acting only in accordance with its laws.

Despite its brevity, the *Tao Te Ching* expresses doctrines of such depth that it has been the subject of many commentaries and treatises throughout the centuries, and is the world's most translated classic after the Bible; many believe it contains universal truths which have since been recognized independently by other religious and secular philosophies. It has been used as a source of inspiration by many Chinese poets and artists, and its influence has also spread widely outside the East.

tarot

A set of cards, traditionally 78 in number, used mainly for divination.

The traditional tarot deck is made up of 78 cards, which are divided into two main groups – 22 trump cards, known as the major ARCANA, which depict highly allegorical images, and 56 numbered 'pip' cards, known as the minor arcana, which are grouped into four suits of 14 cards – the suits of CUPS, PENTACLES, SWORDS and WANDS.

For a long time, students of the tarot believed that modern playing cards were descended from the tarot deck, but historical evidence suggests that both types of deck – playing cards and tarot – originated at around the same time, and developed alongside each other. Playing cards first appeared in Europe in the second half of the 14th century, and some historians believe they were brought back from Palestine by the Crusaders. Islamic playing cards had four suit emblems – polo-sticks, cups, swords and coins – which probably inspired those used in the European decks.

The earliest surviving tarot deck dates from around 1450, and was hand-painted by the artist Bonifacio Bembo for the Duke of Milan. It was used for an Italian card game called *tarocchi* (from which the word 'tarot' derives), and consisted, like the modern tarot, of four suits of 14 cards, plus a fifth suit of 22 cards showing various allegorical scenes. Most of the 15th-century tarots were, like the Bembo deck, hand-painted and expensive works of art created for wealthy patrons, but in the 16th century, Marseilles became a major centre for the manufacture of tarot cards, and the *Tarot de Marseilles* soon enjoyed great popularity. It is still considered to show the classic set of images for the major ARCANA, and later occult decks have almost all based their pictures and symbolism on this French one.

Playing cards were being used for DIVINATION by around 1540, and inevitably, tarot cards soon came to be used for the same purpose. By the end of the 18th century, the tarot was being used almost exclusively as a means of divination, rather than for card games. The Roma were particularly instrumental in popularizing the tarot as a FORTUNE-TELLING device, introducing the cards to new areas as they travelled all over Europe. Occultists were quick to recognize the cards' esoteric nature, and began to speculate on their origins, making various claims for them as sources of ancient and secret knowledge. One popular notion was that the cards originated in Egypt, and that their symbols were in fact fragments of the ancient Egyptian text, the *Book of Thoth*. Another theory was that the tarot had been handed down through the centuries by kabbalists (see KABBALAH) who had disguised their knowledge within the cards to preserve it in the face of persecution by the Christian Church – with the 22 cards of the major arcana corresponding to the 22 letters of the Hebrew alphabet, and to the 22 pathways that connect the ten SEPHIROTH in the kabbalah's TREE OF LIFE. However, it is generally agreed that there is little or no hard historical evidence to support such theories.

The cards of the major arcana have always been the main focus of theory and speculation, because of their allegorical imagery, but in 1910 a new deck was created by A E WAITE, a member of the HERMETIC ORDER OF THE GOLDEN DAWN, and published by Rider & Company. The Golden Dawn taught that in addition to divination, the images of the tarot could be used for meditation and as gateways for ASTRAL PROJECTION. Waite designed his own interpretation of the tarot, which he had painted by a fellow-Golden Dawn member, Pamela Colman Smith, using what he considered to be the original mystical meanings of the major arcana cards; although Waite did not believe that the tarot itself was ancient, he believed that it used ancient symbols, and his designs drew on his knowledge of the Hermetic (Western) Kabbalah, and of ALCHEMY, including also symbols taken directly from FREEMASONRY. However, the most striking difference between this deck and previous ones was that it included a pictorial scene on all of its cards – those of the minor as well as the major arcana – whereas most decks before it, and many since, merely show the suit emblems of the minor arcana arranged in simple geometric patterns. The Rider-Waite tarot, as it is usually known, is still a classic standard today.

Because the cards of the major arcana depict archetypes, they lend themselves to many interpretations, as can be seen by the enormous variety of modern tarot decks available; for example, the *Mythological Tarot*, in which characters from Greek myths are used to fill the archetypal roles; the *Arthurian Tarot*, which shows the many characters and storylines of the Grail legend; the *Tarot of the Orishas*, which uses the gods and goddesses of Western Africa; the *Motherpeace Tarot*, which shows female goddesses and is based on a female-centred spirituality; and the Japanese-inspired *Ukiyoë Tarot*.

Tasmanian tiger *see* THYLACINE

Tasmanian wolf *see* THYLACINE

tasseography

Fortune-telling by means of tea leaves or coffee grounds.
Divination by reading tea leaves left in a cup, known as tasseography (from French *tasse*, a cup, and Greek

A fortune-teller predicts the future by reading tea leaves, a practice known as tasseography. The photograph was taken in 1855. (© Hulton-Deutsch Collection/Corbis)

graphein, to write) or tasseomancy, has been used for hundreds of years in many parts of the world. Although commonly associated with Roma fortune-tellers, the tradition is thought by some to have been practised in ancient Greece as well as in Asia and the Middle East. Tea-leaf reading became a popular parlour game in Victorian times, and is still traditionally practised in Scotland, Ireland and several cultures throughout Eastern Europe. Coffee grounds may also be used instead of tea leaves.

A cup of tea made with loose tea leaves is poured without using a tea strainer (practitioners advise against simply opening a tea bag, since bagged tea leaves are thought to be too small and cut too uniformly to create sufficiently varied patterns), the tea is drunk or poured away and the cup shaken well; the diviner then examines the shapes formed by the leaves, and interprets them either intuitively, or by a fairly standard system of symbolism. For example, a typical interpretation of a shape which suggests an acorn is good health; a bell is taken to signify good news; a cross indicates suffering; a tree, success; and an umbrella, annoyances. The handle of the cup is usually seen as representing the person for whom the reading is being done, so that the further away

from the handle the symbol is, the more distant its connection is with the person. The proximity of the symbol to the rim of the cup is also relevant, with those closest to the rim being thought to indicate the immediate future.

tatzelworm

Elusive worm-like reptilian cryptid reported since antiquity from the European Alps.

During June 1997 Czech-born explorer Ivan Mackerle led a week-long expedition to the Austrian Alps in search of a mysterious creature known to the inhabitants of the Austrian, Swiss and Bavarian Alps since the earliest times, yet which remains unidentified and uncaptured by science.

Generally referred to as the tatzelworm ('clawed worm'), stollenworm ('hole-dwelling worm') or springworm ('jumping worm' – on account of its alleged ability to jump aggressively at anyone who approaches too closely), it is described by most eyewitnesses as a very large, lizard-like creature, measuring up to 1 metre (around 3 feet) in length. It is said to have a somewhat stumpy body, sturdy head (sometimes described as feline in appearance) and blunt snout, large eyes and brownish skin (covered in scales, according to certain reports). One major discrepancy between different eyewitness accounts concerns its legs – because whereas some observers have stated that it has two pairs (both very small), others have said that it has only one pair, at the front.

Several lizards already documented by science do have just a single, front pair of legs (though none of these is currently known to exist in Europe). Alternatively, it may be that the tatzelworm does have hind legs too, but of such inconspicuous appearance that they were not noticed by some observers.

If officially discovered one day, the tatzelworm would constitute one of Europe's biggest reptiles. One theory is that it may be a distant, currently undescribed relative of a large legless European lizard known, confusingly, as the glass snake. Another possibility is that it is allied to the skinks – lizards often possessing only the smallest of legs. It has also been suggested that the tatzelworm may be an Old World version of the famous Gila monster from Arizona in the USA, or conceivably not even a reptile at all but instead a form of siren – a newt-related amphibian again from the USA that only possesses a pair of front legs, lacking hind legs completely. Until a specimen can finally be obtained, however, the tatzelworm's true identity – always assuming, of course, that this animal does exist – is destined to remain as cryptic as the creature itself.

Taurus

In astrology, the second sign of the zodiac, between Aries and Gemini.

In Western ASTROLOGY, Taurus is the sign of ZODIAC for those who are born between 21 April and 20 May. The symbol for Taurus is the bull, and the sign is ruled by Venus. Taureans are said to be obstinate, practical, loyal and reliable, although they can also seem lazy. Taurus is believed to be an earth sign, having an affinity with the element EARTH.

tea leaves, divination by *see* TASSEOGRAPHY

Tedworth, Drummer of *see* DRUMMER OF

TEDWORTH

Tehran

The site of a significant 1970s UFO case, during which an Air Force jet attempted to fire a missile at an object that was deemed to be an imminent threat.

In September 1976 Iran was undergoing a WAVE of UFO sightings which included one of its few known ALIEN ABDUCTION claims. In that particular case the witness said they were lifted into a UFO and taken on what they described as a 'magic carpet ride', making this an unusual blend of modern CLOSE ENCOUNTER and Arabian folklore.

Just a few hours before this alleged abduction, at 12.30am on 19 September, a bright light was seen over the mountains in the Shemiran region. There were countless witnesses, including a number of military personnel on the ground. Deputy Operations Commander B G Yousefi assumed that these people had just observed stars. However, when he looked out and saw the UFO for himself, he decided to order the launch of an Iranian Air Force Phantom jet to investigate. The pilot closed in on the bright object and reported a dramatic close-range contact with the UFO, describing the light it emitted as pulsing orange and violet. As he locked his instruments onto the object, radio contact was temporarily lost.

By now the Air Force had placed a high-level general in charge of the intercept mission. Pilot Lieutenant Jafari was directed towards the UFO and established a radar lock at around 43 kilometres (27 miles), the data showing that his plane was closing on the object at a relative speed of around 240kph (150mph). Suddenly, the UFO appeared to accelerate and rushed away. Jafari accelerated in an attempt to keep pace, passing through the sound barrier. His radar officer reported that the target was equivalent in size to a Boeing 707.

At this point a smaller glowing object detached from the UFO and appeared to fly straight towards the jet. Jafari was apparently convinced that they were under alien attack and attempted to fire a Sidewinder missile – becoming the first person to try to make such an attack on a UFO. However, just as he pressed the button, all of the jet's electronics and communication systems failed, stopping the launch. Jafari said that he believed that the UFO had acted in direct response to his attempt at a retaliatory strike.

Jafari took emergency evasive action, placing the jet into a twisting dive. The projectile, meanwhile, appeared to cut inside the jet's path and returned to the UFO. As soon as this happened the jet regained full power, but Jafari abandoned any thoughts of a second attempt to fire on the UFO. Instead he watched as a new bright object fell from the UFO toward the ground. He braced himself for an explosion but there was none – only a blinding flash of light that lit up a large area.

Jafari now flew down toward the desert floor to mark the spot where the object had landed, hoping to secure physical evidence later. His radar officer noted a pulse of electromagnetic interference at the spot – a similar effect was also reported by a civilian aircraft flying into Tehran at the same time. The brilliance of the flash of light impaired Jafari's vision – he had to be guided back towards Shahrokhi Air Force base, and made several circuits before his eyes recovered sufficiently to attempt a landing.

At dawn the crew were flown by helicopter to the dry lake where the object had apparently landed, but there was no evidence to be found. They visited the only house in the area – the occupants reported hearing a roaring noise (presumably the jet) and seeing a blinding flash of light that they assumed to be lightning.

The details of this case come from a Defence Intelligence Agency report sent from Tehran to the Pentagon by the Iranian Defence Attaché. In 1976 the US government had closed PROJECT BLUE BOOK and ended official UFO investigation. However, they still collected details of dramatic cases such as this. The file was later released under the US FREEDOM OF INFORMATION ACT, without the accompanying evaluation report. This was only released some time later – possibly because it rated the case as 'outstanding' and insisted that 'the credibility of many of the witnesses was high'. It also noted that the case met 'all the criteria necessary for a valid study of the UFO phenomenon'. Such observations may not have been popular with the US government at a time when they were arguing for the closure of their own investigation into the subject of UFOs.

telekinesis

The movement of objects through paranormal or psychic powers.

Telekinesis (meaning 'distant movement') is the original term for what is now generally called PSYCHOKINESIS or PK. It was coined by the British psychical researcher Frederick Myers (see SOCIETY FOR PSYCHICAL RESEARCH) in 1890. The more modern term carries with it the implication that such effects are brought about through a power of the human mind; although the earlier term is also usually used in this context, it was first used at a time when it was also very popular to invoke the SPIRITS of the dead in explanations for supposed paranormal events.

telepathy

Direct mind-to-mind contact with another individual so that thoughts and images can be shared.

Telepathy literally means 'distant feeling' (from the Greek) and it is a shortened form of the phrase 'mental telepathy'. The term was coined by Frederick Myers (see SOCIETY FOR PSYCHICAL RESEARCH) in 1882. He used the term in place of such phrases as MIND-READING and 'thought transference'.

Experiments into the possible existence of telepathy as a form of EXTRASENSORY PERCEPTION have been one of the main themes of research in the area of PARAPSYCHOLOGY since the 1920s. Classic examples include the CARD-GUESSING EXPERIMENTS introduced by J B RHINE – ZENER CARDS becoming the cards of choice for such tests.

Some argue that the apparent successes of some MEDIUMS are actually examples of telepathy (see SUPER-ESP). Telepathy also forms the basis of a proposed explanation for certain supposed cases of REMOTE VIEWING (those where the target is a person at a remote location and the agent attempts to ascertain what they are seeing). However, despite well over one hundred years of research into telepathy, and claims that a substantial proportion of the population believe in its existence, there have been no conclusive demonstrations of the effect.

telepathy, mass *see* MASS TELEPATHY

telepathy, twin *see* TWIN TELEPATHY

teleportation

A hypothetical mode of instantaneous travel or transport.

Teleportation is the apparently instantaneous transportation of an object or living entity from one point directly to another, seemingly without going through the intervening space or around physical obstacles. The word was coined by CHARLES FORT and first used in the second chapter of his third book, *Lo!* (1931), in a discussion of things observed to appear or disappear.

Fort was aware of the APPORT phenomena of SÉANCES, but wanted a word that was not restricted to the then current beliefs of SPIRITUALISM. He suggested the existence of a hypothetical force that distributed objects, creatures and people around a young universe – for example, stocking new areas with wildlife – but the efforts of which became increasingly erratic as the universe aged. This unpredictable nature of vestigial teleportation might account, for example, for the sightings of OUT-OF-PLACE ANIMALS, FALLS of frogs and stones, the outbreak of wounds on stigmatics (see STIGMATA), of fluids on weeping images (see IMAGES, WEEPING), and the reported APPEARANCES or DISAPPEARANCES of people under unusual circumstances. In *Wild Talents* (1932), Fort suggested that:

> It seems to me … that there is a force, distributive of forms of life and other phenomena that could switch an animal, say from a jungle in Madagascar to a back yard somewhere in Nebraska.

He went on to speculate that the force or ability might be manipulated, consciously or unconsciously, by girls who were apparently the focus of POLTERGEISTS, or by WITCHES, or that it might be triggered by a crisis of some sort:

> Girls at the front – and they are discussing their usual not very profound subjects. The alarm – the enemy is advancing. Command to the poltergeist girls to concentrate – and under their chairs they stick their wads of chewing gum. … A regiment bursts into flames, and the soldiers are torches. Horses snort smoke from the combustion of their entrails. Re-enforcements are smashed under cliffs that are teleported from the Rocky Mountains. The snatch of Niagara Falls – it pours upon the battle field. The little poltergeist girls reach for their wads of chewing gum.

In the 1950s, John W Campbell, then editor of *Astounding* science-fiction magazine, encouraged his stable of authors – such as Robert Heinlein, Theodore Sturgeon and Alfred Bester – to read Fort's books for inspiration. Several of them seized upon the idea of human teleportation – notably Bester whose *The Stars My Destination* (1956), featured a character called

The crew of the starship *Enterprise* await teleportation in an episode of the 1960s US television series *Star Trek*.
(© Paramount TV/Album/AKG)

Charles Hoy Jaunt who discovers how to teleport at will. More recently, technology-based teleportation devices have been a feature of the *Star Trek* canon of stories and in many computer games.

Teleportation, if it exists at all, would have extensive implications for science; however, those physicists who have ventured an opinion on it are convinced that *Star Trek*-like teleporters would be beyond today's technology. A study for the US Air Force, in 2004, by Dr Eric W Davis, concluded that it would take the energy equivalent of hundreds of nuclear bombs to 'dematerialize' just one human body and several thousand times the present age of the universe to 'encode' the resulting 10^{28} kilobytes of data. Other physicists are investigating the idea that some type of teleportation may work on a quantum level. According to astrophysicist Phil Schewe, of the American Institute of Physics, it may be more applicable to data encryption than to 'beaming' people across space.

Templars *see* KNIGHTS TEMPLAR

ten
The tenth whole number, represented by the digits 10.
Ten is the tenth whole number. It is a higher octave of the number 1; the intuitive counting system for humans is based on 10, because we have ten fingers. In the minor ARCANA of the TAROT, the tens represent the end of one cycle and the beginning of another, a double-edged condition which may generate extreme states. In the major arcana, ten is the number associated with the Wheel of Fortune card. In Hebrew GEMATRIA, 10 corresponds to the Hebrew letter Yod, and in the KABBALAH, it is the number assigned to the sephirah MALKUTH; there are ten SEPHIROTH altogether in the traditional kabbalah. In numerology, 10 is regarded as a Karmic Number (see KARMA); if it appears in a person's numerological profile, it is thought to be auspicious, since it represents karmic completion and indicates that the person has paid off whatever karmic debts they had brought from previous lives and that in this lifetime they have the opportunity to make a new beginning. In Hinduism, there are ten documented instances of incarnation of the god

Vishnu, which are termed the *avatars* of Vishnu. See also ONE; TWO; THREE; FOUR; FIVE; SIX; SEVEN; EIGHT; NINE; ELEVEN; TWELVE.

Ten Lost Tribes of Israel

Tribes of Israel that never returned after deportation in 721 BC.

According to the Old Testament, the conquering king of Assyria took ten tribes of Israel away into Assyria as captives. History ascribes this act of mass deportation to Sargon II (died 705 BC) and dates it as happening in 721 BC. These ten tribes were those of Asher, Dan, Ephraim, Gad, Issachar, Manasseh, Naphtali, Reuben, Simeon and Zebulun and they are traditionally believed never to have returned to their homes.

Throughout history, various theories have arisen to account for the fate of these tribes. The Spanish rabbi Benjamin of Tudela (died 1173) was the first European traveller to describe the Far East. In an account of his travels he claimed to have found the descendants of some of the lost tribes, still worshipping as Jews, in Persia and Arabia.

When the Americas were discovered by Europeans, it became a fairly popular theory that the Native American peoples must be descended from the lost tribes – some travellers claimed that they detected Jewish influences in the speech and religious observances of some Native American tribes.

The idea that the lost tribes were the progenitors of the English people took hold in Britain, especially in the 17th century. Part of the driving force behind this concept was the belief in the Old Testament prophecy that Israel would be restored and that this would mark the coming of the Millennium. Puritan extremists at the time of the English Civil War seized on this as proof that the second coming of Christ was at hand. While this did not happen, the idea of Anglo-Israelites persisted, and in 1793 the English religious fanatic Richard Brothers declared himself Prince of the Hebrews and Nephew of the Almighty. In fact, this theory still has its adherents in Britain and the USA today.

Descendants of the lost tribes were identified by others as living as far from Israel as Ireland, Africa, Australia, Siberia, China, Japan and Afghanistan, where the Pathan people were said to have customs similar to those of the Jews. Other candidates included the black Jewish people of Ethiopia, known as Falashas, many of whom were welcomed into Israel in the late 20th century.

Were the tribes really lost? Some maintain that when the Persian Emperor Cyrus the Great (c.600–529 BC) conquered the Babylonian captors of the Jews and allowed them to return to their homeland the 'lost' tribes simply went back with them.

There is very little real evidence for the survival of the lost tribes of Israel as a separate ethnic group. It would take a superhuman will to maintain a collective identity over a period of thousands of years. Also, if they were able to travel, as some of the more outlandish theories suggest, to the very ends of the earth, why could they not have reversed their direction and returned to Israel? Much more likely is the idea that, assuming they did not in fact make their way back to their ancestral homeland, these people would simply have become assimilated over the generations into the communities in which they found themselves.

Tesla, Nikola (1856–1943)

US inventor, physicist and electrical engineer, dubbed by one journalist as the 'New Wizard of the West'.

Nikola Tesla was born of Swerbian descent in what is now Croatia and studied at the universities of Graz, Prague and Paris before emigrating to the USA in 1884.

He worked for US inventor Thomas Edison (1847–1931) at his Menlo Park laboratory but left after a disagreement to concentrate on his own inventions. In 1888 he invented the alternating current electric motor; in 1900 he discussed the theory of radar (not practically demonstrated until 1930). He also made improved dynamos, transformers and electric light bulbs, demonstrated a radio-controlled boat and invented the high-frequency Tesla coil.

Tesla went on to promote the use of AC supply in competition with direct current supply, in 1893 using it to illuminate the Chicago World Columbian Exposition. He predicted wireless communication, although Marconi was first to demonstrate it, and experimented with a transmission system using the Earth as a conducting medium. He demonstrated artificial lightning with discharges of enormous power and length of arc.

In his experiments with radio communication he claimed to have detected and recorded regular signals from space, leading him to believe that intelligent life existed on other planets, and he spent a great deal of time trying to reply to these signals. His claims were met with derision within the scientific community.

In 1900 Tesla began constructing a world broadcasting tower, the Wardenclyffe Tower, in New York. He hoped to be able to use it to send radio communications, as well as pictures, and broadcast music all around the world. However, the project had to be abandoned when he lost his financial backing and the construction was demolished.

Arising from his work on lightning and plasma, in the 1930s Tesla claimed to have invented a destructive ray that could be used as a weapon, particularly against aircraft. It was designed to send beams of highly charged particles over great distances, and Tesla envisioned it as making future wars impossible. What the press labelled a 'death beam', Tesla preferred to call a 'peace beam'. While this device was never made, it undoubtedly influenced later particle-beam weapon research.

One of his last patents was for a flying vehicle that would be able to rise from the ground vertically, a forerunner of the VTOL aircraft developed later in the 20th century.

He was a tireless worker, subsisting on little food and sleep, and few colleagues or employees could keep pace with him. Not the most sociable of men (although he counted Mark Twain as a friend), Tesla never married and he lived alone in a series of hotels, nursing sick pigeons back to health, his fastidious but eccentric dress giving ammunition to those who labelled him the typical 'mad scientist'. Despite his many patents, he died in debt, particularly owing large sums in unpaid taxes, apparently suffering from a variety of obsessive compulsive disorders and a phobia about germs. He claimed to have been working on a Unified Field Theory but this was never published.

The tesla, a unit of magnetic flux density, was named after him.

thanatology

The study of death and deathbed experiences.

Thanatology (from the Greek *thanatos*, meaning death) is the scientific study of death and the customs and practices associated with it. One particular aspect of this is the study of deathbed visions and experiences.

It is not uncommon for people on the point of death to relate to those nearby that they can see a person or people who are not seen by anyone else. Often, this apparition will involve deceased members of the dying person's family (even, according to some reports, people that the dying person does not know to be dead), and their presence always seems to offer reassurance and comfort. The dying person will often assert that the others have come to escort or assist them to 'the other side'.

Other individuals perceive figures of religious significance, such as angels or the Virgin Mary. In some cases, no individual person is seen, but radiant forms of light or a vision of another place. The function of these phenomena remains the same: to lend an air of peace and rightness to the process of dying and to allow the dying person to see that they are in fact ready to let go of their life.

Witnesses report such events as the dying person focusing their gaze on an area where nothing is to be seen and addressing someone who is not present. Another common experience is of a person who had been unconscious, even in a coma, suddenly sitting up and speaking before relapsing into unconsciousness. The affected person often says that what they see is beautiful, and that they want to see it again or go to where it springs from.

The other side of this type of experience is that it also eases the transition for those who witness it. People who have seen a loved one go through a deathbed vision often report feeling calmer and more resigned, more able to see that death is not to be feared but accepted as fitting.

Sceptics would say that such visions are merely the hallucinations generated by the dying brain, the product of a mind under the influence of medication, subject to fever or the lack of oxygen caused by imperfect breathing. Others would argue that they represent a kind of desperate wishful thinking by someone who is afraid to die and has a fundamental need to believe that it will not be traumatic or mean the end of existence. It can hardly be unexpected that at the end of one's life, one's thoughts turn to those whom one has loved but has not seen for some time.

To counter this, it can be argued that deathbed visions have been reported as having happened to people who were not drugged or in great pain but were already calm and composed. See also NEAR-DEATH EXPERIENCE.

theatre ghosts

Apparitions associated with theatres.

Stories of haunted theatres are very common in Britain, the USA and elsewhere. London has many reputedly haunted theatres, possibly the most famous being the Theatre Royal in Drury Lane. Here the 'Man in Grey', described as wearing a tricorn hat, riding cloak and boots, is said to appear in the auditorium during the day rather than at night. Some say that he is the ghost of a man who was murdered in the theatre, whose remains were found in the wall of a passageway in the mid-19th century. It is also claimed that a sighting of the 'Man in Grey' is a good omen, and that if he is seen during rehearsals the play will have a successful run. Other Theatre Royal apparitions include the ghosts of past performers – the actor Charles Macklin is said to appear backstage on the spot where he killed a fellow actor in 1735 during an argument over a wig, and some claim that the comedian Dan Leno (1860–1904) sometimes appears in his dressing room.

The Adelphi Theatre in the Strand is said to be haunted by the actor William Terriss who was murdered in 1897 – Terriss is also said to haunt the London Underground (see LONDON UNDERGROUND GHOSTS); it is claimed that the Haymarket Theatre is haunted by the former actor manager John Buckstone; some say that the Sadler's Wells Theatre is haunted by 19th-century clown Joseph Grimaldi; and tales tell that the Old Vic is haunted by a woman playing the part of Lady Macbeth. Many English provincial theatres are also reputedly haunted, notably those in Bath, Brighton, Bury St Edmunds, Farnham, Margate, Portsmouth and Whitby. The haunting is not normally experienced when shows are taking place but rather when the building is quiet either before or after performances. Examples of haunted theatres are also found in other parts of Europe, the USA and Latin America.

Thelema
The religious magical philosophy taught by Aleister Crowley.

Thelema, the Greek for 'will', is the name that ALEISTER CROWLEY gave to his religious philosophy, summed up in the Law of Thelema: 'Do what thou wilt shall be the whole of the Law. Love is the Law, Love under Will.'

Crowley took both the name Thelema and the 'Do what thou wilt' aphorism from the satirical works *Pantagruel* (1532) and *Gargantua* (1534) by the 16th-century French monk François Rabelais; the 'law' was carved above the entrance to Rabelais' fictional Abbey of Thélème, where monks were encouraged to live just as they wanted, without rules. Christians who attack Crowley for the supposedly selfish attitude of 'Do what thou wilt' are usually unaware of the qualifier about 'Love' and 'Will', and also that the concept originated with St Augustine, who wrote 'Love, and do what thou wilt.' It was never intended to be an invitation to licence or self-indulgence.

Crowley used 'Do what thou wilt' in one of his most important works, *The Book of the Law* or *Liber Legis*, which he claimed was dictated to him by the spirit Aiwass in 1904, but which was not published until some years later. He established his own Abbey of Thelema at Cefalu in Sicily in 1920, but was expelled from Italy in 1923 after various scandals.

Most Thelemites today use rituals formulated by Crowley in their magical work. Many work alone, but some are members of organizations including (among others) the several competing versions of the ORDO TEMPLI ORIENTIS and recreations of Argentium Astrum, the order Crowley founded after he left the HERMETIC ORDER OF THE GOLDEN DAWN.

theories of origin
The collective title given to the wide range of theories that have been offered to explain the cause of UFO sightings. Most commentators agree that any single theory cannot offer the solution for every sighting.

At least one hundred theories have been suggested for the ultimate cause of UFO sightings, ranging from the scientifically absurd to the very down to earth. However, the term 'UFO' is applied to such a wide range of phenomena that it is clear that no individual suggestion is ever going to resolve the entire mystery.

All researchers agree that the most likely outcome of any individual sighting is that it will prove to have been of an IDENTIFIED FLYING OBJECT. The explanations range from commonplace things, such as aircraft lights or meteors, to rarer (but scientifically recognized) phenomena like BALL LIGHTNING and atmospheric mirages. Since over nine out of ten UFO cases are eventually found to involve IFOs, there is a strong argument for the case that the remainder could also be solved in this way, given enough resources. This is the conclusion that has been reached by most government UFO studies and, at least officially, by the team of scientists involved in the COLORADO UNIVERSITY STUDY. There are now very few ongoing official projects of this type – GEPAN in France being one of the exceptions.

GEPAN investigates UNIDENTIFIED ATMOSPHERIC PHENOMENA (UAP), and this is now deemed by many to be a way in which some unsolved cases may be explained. Some reports suggest that rare natural phenomena may lie at the heart of a small number of UFO reports. Further investigation might reveal new data relating to ionized gases, plasmas and optical distortions within the air. Studies into recurrent or WINDOW AREA UFO events, such as those at HESSDALEN, and some reports of PHYSIOLOGICAL EFFECTS and VEHICLE INTERFERENCE might support this theory. There may well be a wide range of UAP that are reported by witnesses as UFOs. Ball lightning, for example, may be much more unusual in its behaviour than atmospheric physicists currently realize because important sightings bypass science and are misreported as UFOs.

CLOSE ENCOUNTER cases, especially those involving ALIENS, add another layer to the problem. These cases inspire a further group of rational theories, under the broad heading of the PSYCHOSOCIAL HYPOTHESIS. Supporters of these theories propose that the events are sincerely reported but not physically real. Instead they are visionary in nature and may occur while the witness is experiencing an ALTERED STATE OF CONSCIOUSNESS – reports are often characterized by witnesses describing peculiar effects, known as the OZ FACTOR. There are many working theories in this area; psychologists have investigated ideas relating to 'fantasy proneness', false awakenings (see DREAMS, WAKING), epilepsy and various other potential explanations for sudden visionary experiences involving UFOs.

There have also been attempts to build a bridge between UAP and psychosocial theories – working along the lines that the former might sometimes induce visionary experiences (see MICHAEL PERSINGER).

Finally, there are the exotic suggestions of the origins for UFO sightings. These all share one defining characteristic – they all depend upon ideas currently regarded by the scientific community as hypothetical at best. Most UFO researchers agree that such ideas are a last resort, only to be considered when all other possibilities have been rejected. These theories will, therefore, only potentially apply to a very small fraction of reported cases.

The EXTRATERRESTRIAL HYPOTHESIS (ETH) is the best known of these exotic theories. Indeed it is widely presumed among the general public to be the only theory of origin for UFOs – other than the simple assertion that they don't exist and all reports are hoaxes. Many UFO researchers support the hypothesis because it neatly explains the way that the phenomenon apparently presents itself to some witnesses. It is also a scientifically credible idea – the idea that it is likely that there are intelligent, technologically advanced alien species elsewhere in the universe (see SEARCH FOR EXTRATERRESTRIAL INTELLIGENCE) would not be dismissed out of hand by most people. However, the aliens reported in UFO cases have suspiciously human characteristics, and no convincing physical evidence (such as samples of alien technology or DNA) has ever been produced.

Other ideas for possible sources of visitations by humanoid entities have support within the UFO COMMUNITY but, like the ETH, they are extremely difficult to argue for in the absence of evidence. The suggestion that the beings are time travellers from our own future overcomes the problem of their reportedly human appearance and behaviour – the alien imagery might be a disguise designed to obscure their true identity. Some researchers, such as JACQUES VALLÉE, have also been intrigued by the way in which modern close encounters resemble stories from folklore, concluding that the FAIRIES of past centuries might be the same beings that are now reported as aliens. Observations such as this have inspired an 'ultraterrestrial theory' – the idea that these beings co-exist with us on this world but in another dimension, beyond the spatial realm in which we live. Modern physicists takes the multi-dimensional nature of the universe seriously and many ideas currently popular in mainstream science are compatible with the suggestion that higher dimensions exist around us without our being able to perceive them. The theory is that we only interact with the beings occasionally when they intrude into our restricted three-dimensional space (the means by which they make such intrusions remains unexplained). However, theoretical arguments of this nature certainly do not constitute proof that UFOs come from such a realm.

For the time being, UFO research remains rich in theories but poor in evidence to support them.

Theosophical Society

An organization co-founded in 1895 by Madame Blavatsky, Henry Steel Olcott and William Quan Judge, dedicated to advancing the doctrine of theosophy; its aims were to study and make known the ancient religions, philosophies and sciences and to investigate man's psychic and spiritual powers.

In 1875, the Russian-born US writer MADAME

A bust of Henry Steel Olcott, one of the founders of the Theosophical Society, in the garden of the Library of the Theosophical Society in Adyar, near Madras. (© TopFoto)

BLAVATSKY founded the Theosophical Society with a lawyer, writer and journalist called Henry Steel Olcott, and William Quan Judge. The concept of THEOSOPHY was not invented by the Society, nor was the term 'theosophy' itself, but it is with the Society that theosophy is nowadays chiefly identified. Its initial objective was the study and explanation of mediumistic phenomena, but it expanded into a modern-day Gnostic movement that took its inspiration from Hinduism and Buddhism, and did much to spread Eastern religious, philosophical and occult concepts throughout the Western world. In formulating the doctrines and teachings of the Society, Blavatsky claimed to be directed and guided by a group of spiritual teachers variously called the Mahatmas, Masters of Wisdom, or ASCENDED MASTERS, and her major work *THE SECRET DOCTRINE* (1888), an eclectic combination of Hindu, Egyptian, Gnostic and other exotic scriptures and teachings, along with Neoplatonism and stories such as the Atlantis myth, became the principal source book for modern students of theosophy.

The Society expressed its aims as being to study and make known the ancient religions, philosophies and sciences; to form a universal brotherhood of man; and to investigate the laws of nature and the divine powers latent in man. It was dedicated to the practical realization of the oneness of all life and the independent spiritual search, and was non-sectarian, non-political and open to all races, nationalities, classes and creeds.

After Blavatsky's death in 1891, arguments and schisms developed in the Society. Judge was accused by Olcott and another Society member, Annie Besant, of forging letters from the Mahatmas, and he ended his association with them in 1895, taking most of the Society's American section with him. The faction led by Olcott and Besant became the Indian-based 'Theosophical Society – Adyar', while the faction led by Judge continued to be known simply as the 'Theosophical Society'. A third group, the United Lodge of the Theosophical Society, split away from the latter in 1909.

theosophy

Any of various philosophical or religious systems which claim to be based on intuitive insight into the divine nature.

The word 'theosophy' comes from the Greek *theos*, meaning 'god' or 'divinity', and *sophia*, meaning 'wisdom', and literally means 'divine wisdom'. It has affinities with MYSTICISM, in that it claims to derive direct knowledge of the divine through inspiration, philosophical speculation or some physical process, but while mysticism generally confines itself to the soul's relation to the divine, theosophy aims to use this knowledge to formulate a complete philosophy of humanity and nature.

Neoplatonism, GNOSTICISM and the KABBALAH are generally considered to be types of theosophy, and the philosophies and theologies of Asia, and particularly of India, contain a vast body of theosophical doctrine; modern theosophy derives much of its vocabulary from Indian sources. Jakob Böhme developed a theosophical system in which he attempted to reconcile the existence of an all-powerful and loving God with the presence of evil in the world. The THEOSOPHICAL SOCIETY, with which theosophy is nowadays generally identified, was founded in 1875 by MADAME BLAVATSKY, Henry Steel Olcott and William Quan Judge. The name of the Society was suggested by Charles Sotheran, who found the word 'theosophy' in a dictionary, and it was unanimously accepted because the definition of theosophy seemed to combine the concepts of both esoteric truth and occult research which were the goals of the Society.

therapeutic touch

A method of touch-free healing developed in the 1970s. Practitioners claim to use their hands to manipulate the patient's energy field or aura in order to correct imbalances and deficiencies caused by illness, to restore its integrity and harmony and to assist the body's natural self-healing process.

Therapeutic touch, often referred to as TT, is a type of BODYWORK sometimes described as a secular form of FAITH HEALING. It was developed in the 1970s by a US nursing professor, Dolores Krieger, and her mentor, Dora Kunz, who believed she had various psychic abilities. Therapeutic touch is based on the belief that all living things possess an energy field or AURA which extends beyond the body, and that physical or mental illness, pain or injury is reflected in this energy field as imbalances, deficiencies or blocked areas. Since all living things are seen to exist as part of a UNIVERSAL LIFE FORCE, and are thus all interconnected, it is thought that the energy field of the healer can be made to interact with that of the patient and direct the flow of the patient's energy to restore its integrity, balance and harmony, which will assist the body's natural self-healing abilities.

The healer therefore holds his or her hands together, palms down, a few inches over the patient's body and passes them over it, claiming that in this way they can assess the condition of the patient's energy field and identify any weak or unbalanced spots. The practitioner is then said to manipulate the patient's energy field by making flowing movements similar to massage over the affected areas, without physical contact, while feeling compassion for the patient. The process is sometimes visualized as the untangling of knots, the warming of cool areas or the smoothing of rough spots in the energy field, or as a stream of energizing colour flowing through the patient's aura. Some healers may combine therapeutic touch with other therapies, such as massage and ACUPRESSURE.

Therapeutic touch is frequently practised by nurses as well as by alternative healers, and it is mainly used for relaxation and pain relief, although its critics attribute any perceived benefits to the placebo effect.

theurgy

Magic performed by invoking the aid of beneficent spirits or gods; miraculous divine action or intervention.
The word 'theurgy' comes from the Greek *theourgiā*, from *theos*, meaning 'god', and *ergon*, meaning 'work', and is taken to mean 'divine magic' or white magic (see MAGIC, WHITE). Theurgy is defined as both divine intervention – the miraculous action of good spirits or gods – and as a form of ritual magic (see MAGIC, RITUAL) in which benevolent gods or other supernatural powers are invoked with the goal of uniting the magician with the divine, or helping him to progress to a higher spiritual level.

The source of Western theurgy is found in the philosophy of the late Neoplatonists, and especially in the teachings of the 3rd-century Greek Neoplatonist Iamblichus of Syria, who popularized the term 'theurgy' to denote his method of achieving individual union with the gods and bringing a person into conscious communion with their higher self. The late Neoplatonists regarded the universe as a series of emanations from the Godhead, and held that matter was merely the lowest of these emanations, so that it was not, in essence, different from the divine; most also believed that all gods represented different aspects of one reality. The ultimate goal was to reunite with this divine reality, but Iamblichus believed that mystical contemplation and philosophy alone were not enough to unite the philosopher with the gods, and that the appropriate religious and magical actions, or theurgy, were also needed. He therefore formulated a system which apparently involved INVOCATION and religious, as well as magical, ritual. By means of such ritualized methods, he believed that the gods could be requested to confer power and divine grace on the theurgist, purifying him so that he could be raised to a higher spiritual state. The gods could not be summoned by theurgy, since a lower spiritual being could not command a higher one, but by invocation, they could be called upon to commune and work with the theurgist and bring him into contact with his higher self – thereby raising the theurgist to their own divine world.

The Jewish system of mysticism called the KABBALAH displays many Neoplatonic elements, and the practices of the Western magical tradition, such as those of hermeticism and the HERMETIC ORDER OF THE GOLDEN DAWN, borrow heavily from both Neoplatonism and the kabbalah, and share their ultimate aim, which is not the attainment of material goals such as worldly power, but union with the divine through ritual and contemplation. The occultist ALEISTER CROWLEY, who felt that the term 'theurgy' was inadequate, chose to rename it as 'high magick'.

thiotimoline

An imaginary chemical compound supposed to enable time travel.
In 1948, the US novelist, critic and popular scientist Isaac Asimov (1920–92) published a spoof scientific research paper called 'The Endochronic Properties of Resublimated Thiotimoline'. In this he described the fictitious chemical compound of his title.

He was inspired by an earlier experiment in which he had to dissolve catechol crystals in water and was struck by the almost instantaneous nature of the reaction. This led him to imagine a substance so ready to dissolve that it would do so even before it came into contact with the water.

In subsequent articles he explored the properties of this imaginary substance, explaining its behaviour in terms of its chemical bonds being so closely compacted that they were forced out of the dimension of space and into the dimension of time. This led to the idea that thiotimoline crystals could be used in a device to anticipate events slightly in the future, a rudimentary form of TIME TRAVEL.

third eye

The organ of spiritual perception, believed to be located in the centre of the forehead; one of the higher chakras, known as the Ajna *chakra, it is also identified with the pineal gland.*
The concept of the third eye, or spiritual eye, is a very old one. In Hindu spiritual traditions, it refers to the brow CHAKRA, or *Ajna* chakra, situated between and a little above the eyes, and it is seen as the organ of spiritual perception. In Hinduism and Buddhism, the third eye is a symbol of enlightenment, and Lord Shiva, the Buddha and many yogis and BODHISATTVAS are depicted with a dot or eye on their forehead to represent the third eye. The third eye is also known in Hinduism as the Eye of Shiva, and it is believed that the opening of Shiva's third eye will bring about the end of the universe.

As one of the main chakras, the third eye is part of the main MERIDIAN which separates the left and right hemispheres of the body. When opened, it is said

A Hindu monk wears a mask of Mahakala, an aspect of the god Shiva, showing the third eye. (© Charles & Josette Lenars/Corbis)

to become a line of communication, via the crown chakra, with the higher planes, and is associated with EXTRASENSORY PERCEPTION and spiritual insight. It is often equated with the pineal gland, which is connected to the visual cortex of the brain; while this gland's physiological function was unknown until recent times, mystical traditions and esoteric schools have for many centuries regarded this area in the middle of the brain to be a link between the physical and spiritual worlds, and the development of psychic abilities has long been associated with the activation of this organ. The third eye and its powers are said to be stimulated by MEDITATION, by the practice of visualization, by total darkness and, sometimes, by a head injury.

thirteen
A number traditionally considered unlucky, especially in Christian societies.
Thirteen has for centuries been considered an unlucky number, particularly in Christian societies. This superstition, which probably originated in medieval times, is usually thought to have come about because

there were thirteen people at the Last Supper – Jesus and his twelve disciples, including Judas Iscariot – although there may also be a connection with the fact that the lunisolar calendar sometimes has thirteen months in a year, while the solar Gregorian and Islamic calendars always have twelve. Norse mythology tells of another evil thirteenth guest at a feast; twelve of the gods were feasting in Valhalla when Loki arrived uninvited, and tricked Hod, the blind brother of Balder, god of joy, into firing a sprig of mistletoe at his brother. Mistletoe was the only thing which could kill Balder, and at his death, the world was plunged into darkness and sorrow. Satan is also sometimes referred to as the thirteenth angel. No doubt influenced by the number who attended the Last Supper, there is a very common superstition that thirteen people should never sit down to dine at a table, or one of their number will die before the year is out.

The fear of the number thirteen is a very real one to many people, so much so that many tall buildings will not number a floor as the thirteenth, but will get round the problem by numbering the floors straight from twelve to fourteen, by calling the floor above the twelfth one 12a or 12b, by leaving the thirteenth floor unoccupied or using it for storing equipment. House numbers and aeroplane seats may also skip from twelve to fourteen to avoid distressing those who fear the number thirteen. The extreme fear of the number thirteen is known as triskaidekaphobia, and the composer Schoenberg is said to have been triskaidekaphobic.

However, the number thirteen holds great positive significance in the Jewish tradition and the KABBALAH. It is both the age of maturity and (by some calculations) the number of tribes of Israel; God is said to have revealed himself to Moses by thirteen Attributes of Mercy, and the orthodox Jewish prayer book holds the Thirteen Principles of Faith. Also, according to the kabbalah, the number thirteen indicates the ability to rise above the influence of the twelve signs of the ZODIAC, and thus not be bound by the influences of the cosmos. The number thirteen is held to be lucky by a small minority of left-handed people, and modern-day witches have adopted thirteen as a lucky and significant number, with thirteen being the maximum size for a COVEN, and in some traditions the ideal number. See also FRIDAY THE 13TH.

thoughtography
A claimed means of producing photographs by the power of the mind alone.
Claims that people had successfully produced images by thoughtography (sometimes also known as 'psychic

photography' or 'mental photography') first appeared among the spiritualist (see SPIRITUALISM) movement in the 1870s. It was alleged that certain people could produce photographs using only the power of the mind, and such images were initially referred to as 'psychographs'.

However, the subject was not particularly popular until the publication in 1967 of psychiatrist Jule Eisenbud's *The World of Ted Serios*, a book about an apparently remarkable man. Serios, a Chicago hotel worker, claimed to be able to project images from his mind onto unexposed Polaroid instant film while it was contained within a camera. The process apparently required him to maintain sufficient contact with the camera, which he did by placing a cardboard tube, which he called his 'gizmo', over the lens. Eisenbud claimed the resultant photographs were 'thoughtographs' and that they were produced by PSYCHOKINESIS. Sceptics suggested that the low-quality, blurred images were more likely to have been produced by whatever he put inside the 'gizmo' than by an image projected from his mind.

Ted Serios remains the most famous producer of thoughtographs, despite being notoriously difficult to work with, having repeated his performances in laboratories and on many television shows. Other self-

Ted Serios with his 'gizmo', the device he placed over the lens of his camera when taking thoughtographs.
(© Mary Evans Picture Library)

proclaimed PSYCHICS have also offered demonstrations of the production of thoughtographs – notably URI GELLER. Sceptics remain unconvinced, pointing to a range of possible ways in which the effects can be fraudulently produced using optical devices and previously exposed film.

thought photography *see*
THOUGHTOGRAPHY

thought transference *see* TELEPATHY

three
The third whole number, represented by the digit 3; considered significant in numerology.
Three is the third whole number. In geometry, 3 represents a plane or surface with both length and breadth, and thus, the second dimension. In the minor ARCANA of the TAROT, the threes represent the resolution of the tension brought about by the polarity of two, resulting in integration and wholeness; it is the number relating to expansiveness and learning through life experiences, and signifies communication and expression. In the major arcana, 3 is the number associated with the Empress card. In Hebrew GEMATRIA, 3 corresponds to the Hebrew letter Gimel, and in the KABBALAH, it is the number assigned to the sephirah BINAH. In NUMEROLOGY, it is considered to be a YANG number; it is the numerical value of the letters C, L and U, and signifies power and the generative force. A person with 3 in their numerological profile is believed to possess wisdom, understanding and knowledge, and to be creative, optimistic, emotional and joyful, but may also display the more negative traits of pessimism, foolhardiness and recklessness.

The number 3 is considered to be lucky, and it has a particular prominence in magic and mysticism; the basic symbol for plurality among the ancient Egyptians was the number 3, and the hieroglyph for 'plurality' consisted of 3 vertical marks. Triads of deities are commonly referred to in religion to signify a complete system; in Egyptian mythology, the god Atum is said to have become three when he gave birth to Shu and Tefnut, and Horus, Osiris, and Isis formed another group of three deities. The divine triad is again seen in Christianity in the Holy Trinity of Father, Son and Holy Ghost, and in Hinduism by the trinity of Brahma the Creator, Vishnu the Preserver and Shiva the Destroyer. The moon has three stages – waxing, full and waning – and the Celtic gods and goddesses often had a triple aspect, while in Greek mythology, there were Three Fates. In the tarot, the significance of 3 is seen in the major ARCANA, which consists of 22 cards; leaving aside the first card, The Fool, which is assigned the number zero and is usually considered separately, the remaining cards, numbered from 1 to 21, fall naturally into 3 groups of 7. See also ONE; TWO, FOUR; FIVE; SIX; SEVEN; EIGHT; NINE; TEN; ELEVEN; TWELVE.

thunderbird

The name given to a famous mythical bird and also to allegedly real-life counterparts spied in the skies over North America.

According to the mythology of many Native American tribes, the thunderbird was a huge bird of prey that soared through the skies on enormous wings, bringing thunder and rainstorms to the lands below. It was once assumed that this creature was completely imaginary, but cryptozoologists are no longer quite so sure.

Numerous people all over North America (but particularly in southern USA) claim to have observed extraordinarily large, vulture-like birds with wingspans of 3.0–3.6 metres (around 10–12 feet). For example, on 10 April 1948, Clyde Smith, his wife and a third person, Les Bacon, were at Overland, Illinois, when they saw a dark-grey object flying overhead that was so huge they assumed it to be a pursuit plane – until it flapped its wings. Of course, it is not always easy to judge accurately the size of an airborne object. However, the thunderbird allegedly spied around 1940 by naturalist Robert Lyman in the Black Forest region of Pennsylvania was much easier to size – he claimed that it was resting on the ground, with its wings spanning the entire width of a road. Brown in colour, and resembling a very large vulture, he described it as at least 1 metre (around 3 feet) tall, and said that it flew away as he approached it. However, he was able to measure the width of the road that its wings had spanned, and found that it measured just over 6.1 metres (20 feet) – more than twice the wingspan of the Andean condor, which possesses the greatest wingspan of any known modern-day bird of prey.

The similarity between such reports and the supposedly fictitious thunderbird is certainly intriguing, but even more interesting is that until only a few thousand years ago birds almost precisely fitting these descriptions and exhibiting truly enormous wingspans did exist in southern USA. Gigantic relatives of the American vultures and condors, they are known as teratorns ('monster birds') on account of their formidable appearance. Not surprisingly, the coincidence of teratorn-like birds currently being reported from the very same areas that were once inhabited by teratorns have led some cryptozoologists to suggest that perhaps the mysterious modern-day 'big birds' (as they are popularly termed in newspaper stories) are living teratorns.

In the late 1800s, an Arizona newspaper called the *Tombstone Epitaph* is said to have published a report and photograph of an alleged dead 'big bird' with its wings stretched out to reveal a wingspan of 10.8 metres (around 35.5 feet). If this photograph could be verified as genuine and studied, it might disclose whether the bird was really a teratorn, but it has apparently been lost, and the accompanying newspaper report cannot be traced either. Although numerous people claim to have seen this photograph over the years (either reproduced in magazines or even on television) there are many who believe that the story of the article is in itself a hoax.

thunderstorms

Storms of heavy rain, thunder and lightning during which strange phenomena can appear.

A thunderstorm, with its attendant torrential rain and lightning, can be dramatic enough in itself, but thunderstorms are sometimes accompanied by strange weather phenomena. One such phenomenon involves FALLS of bizarre objects, including living fish, blocks of ice and showers of stones. Another is BALL LIGHTNING, in which glowing balls of light are seen moving along the ground or through the air.

Among the more spectacular effects seen during particularly powerful thunderstorms are those known as sprites and elves. Sprites are great plumes of light, often bluish or reddish in colour, that flash up into the sky for miles above a storm. Records exist of them being seen from the ground for over a hundred years, but in more recent times weather satellites have produced images of sprites in very complex shapes, sometimes being compared to the limbs of an octopus.

Elves are a similar phenomenon, consisting of huge cones or discs of light spreading out for many miles above the top of a storm, but they are so brief as to be instantaneous. It is thought that, along with sprites, they are produced by electromagnetic impulses moving up through the electrically charged air of the ionosphere.

thylacine

An officially extinct wolf-like marsupial still reported from three totally separate geographical locations.

Also known as the Tasmanian wolf (on account of its strikingly lupine outward form) and the Tasmanian tiger (due to the series of distinctive stripes running across its back and haunches), the thylacine, *Thylacinus cynocephalus*, is, perhaps uniquely, three separate CRYPTIDS in one. It formerly existed in three totally separate localities – the island of Tasmania, mainland Australia and the island of New Guinea.

The last recognized thylacine, pictured at Hobart Zoo before its death in 1936. (© TopFoto/Fortean)

Officially, it is now extinct everywhere, but sightings of tantalizingly thylacine-like mystery beasts continue to be made in all three of its erstwhile haunts.

The thylacine survived longest in Tasmania, where, after suffering sustained persecution by farmers during the 1800s, numbers rapidly dwindled, until the last recognized specimen died at Hobart Zoo in 1936. However, since then so many sightings of alleged thylacines have been made here that the Tasmanian thylacine is popularly dubbed 'the world's most common extinct animal'. True, 70 years have now passed without a single piece of verified physical evidence for its survival having been obtained, and there is little doubt that a fair proportion of eyewitness reports feature misidentified feral dogs. Nevertheless, a compelling core of sightings remains unexplained by such mundane solutions. Of these, perhaps the most convincing post-1936 thylacine encounter occurred on 9 March 1982, and featured no less reliable and experienced an eyewitness than Hans Naarding – one of Tasmania's National Parks and Wildlife Service rangers.

Naarding had been taking a nap inside his Land Rover, parked in a remote forested area of north-west Tasmania. Picking up his spotlight after waking, he scanned the area around his vehicle to see if anything had approached it, and to his great surprise the beam revealed a large wolf-like creature that sported twelve clearly visible black stripes, standing to one side of the Land Rover. Apart from opening its mouth, revealing its teeth, the animal remained quite still for several minutes, enabling Naarding to observe it closely, but when he reached for his camera his movements disturbed the animal, which swiftly vanished into the undergrowth. In his subsequent report, Naarding had no qualms about referring to what he had seen as a large adult male thylacine. And in 1995, a second National Parks ranger, Charlie Beasley, had a two-minute sighting of just such another creature in some light forest near St Helen's, in north-east Tasmania.

On mainland Australia, the thylacine died out much earlier, approximately 2,300 years ago, when competition with the introduced dingo is believed to have brought about its extinction. Notwithstanding this, reports of striped canine cryptids regularly emerge, and occasionally something more – such as the beautifully preserved hairy thylacine carcase discovered in a cave at Mundrabilla Station in

Western Australia during 1966. Attempts at dating it have proven controversial, with some alleging that it is ancient but exceptionally well preserved, and others claiming that it is very recent. Muddying the waters further are unconfirmed statements that genuine Tasmanian thylacines were released in parts of mainland Australia prior to the 1930s.

Perhaps most exciting of all are reports of thylacines in Irian Jaya – the western, Indonesian half of New Guinea, which remains one of the least-explored jungle lands on the planet. Here, native tribes speak of an elusive, nocturnal, cave-dwelling cryptid termed the dobsegna, which they describe as having the head and shoulders of a dog, a powerful mouth with huge jaws, light brown fur marked with dark stripes towards the rear end of its body and a long thin tail. A better description of a thylacine could hardly be imagined – and until a few millennia ago, the thylacine did indeed exist in New Guinea, as confirmed by fossil evidence. Ned Terry investigated dobsegna sightings in the Baliem Valley during 1993, and found that locals identified pictures of thylacines as the creature they had seen. Of the thylacine's three former territories, New Guinea is the likeliest to harbour present-day survival of this species by virtue of its remote, inaccessible mountain terrain.

Tighe, Virginia *see* MURPHY, BRIDEY

time, missing
A period of time not accounted for in the memory of a witness during, or immediately following, a UFO close encounter.
The concept of 'missing time' emerged from a study of CLOSE ENCOUNTER cases during the 1960s, in the wake of the BETTY AND BARNEY HILL abduction case in 1961. The Hills reported that they had seen a UFO carrying ALIENS and had then undergone peculiar 'jumps' in their recall of the journey home. The trip appeared to have taken much longer than it should have done, as if part of their memory of that night was missing.

The Hills then began to experience nightmares in which they were given medical examinations by the aliens. The 'memory block' then appeared to be removed as they pieced together the story of their apparent encounter during later sessions with a psychiatrist. UFO researchers developed the idea that an experience of missing time, in cases such as this, might suggest that what appeared to be a simple sighting actually included an abduction phase, of which the witness had retained no conscious memory.

Examination of close encounter cases then revealed many with apparent periods of missing time – ranging from 15 minutes, as in the ALAN GODFREY encounter, to the five days in the TRAVIS WALTON affair. Most periods of missing time reported fall in the range of one to two hours.

From the late 1960s, UFO researchers applied the technique used in the Hill case – regression HYPNOSIS – with specialists coaxing the witness to try to recover memories (see MEMORIES, RECOVERED) from the blank 'period'. This is the method by which a large percentage of the apparent evidence for ALIEN ABDUCTION cases has emerged. However, in some instances, similar memories have allegedly been retrieved without using hypnosis – coming through dreams or sudden conscious recall, sometimes months or even years after the original incident (as happened in the KELLY CAHILL abduction case).

The use of regression hypnosis as a tool to retrieve missing-time memories is highly controversial – the technique is still not fully understood, is open to abuse and is known to stimulate fantasy and even produce 'false memories' (see MEMORY, FALSE). This is why evidence obtained in this way is admitted in very few legal systems. As the facts of any reported alien abduction cannot be independently verified, the true status of testimonies obtained under hypnosis is extremely uncertain. A few UFO groups, such as the BRITISH UFO RESEARCH ASSOCIATION, were concerned enough to ban the use of regression. However, hypnosis remains in widespread use for this purpose elsewhere, particularly in the USA, where, as a consequence, the highest proportion of missing-time cases are known.

Some researchers have observed that in many reports, the last memory of a witness prior to a period of missing time often involves being struck by a beam of light. The search for a memory from the resulting time gap may be misguided if, in fact, the witness is actually simply unconscious or in another altered state, such as sleep.

time-displaced PK *see* PK, TIME-DISPLACED

time slips
Experiences in which a person seems to be physically present in a different time.
A small number of APPARITIONS involve an apparent wholesale transformation in scenery and environment to that of an earlier time. Such incidents have been dubbed 'time slips'. In addition to percipients seeing detailed physical features which belong to an earlier age they also have a strong sensation of being physically present in the past. In a small minority of cases witnesses also claim to interact with human characters. The classic example of a time-slip experience is the case of the ghosts of the PETIT TRIANON – in 1901, two Englishwomen walking near the chateau

of Petit Trianon in the grounds at Versailles believed they witnessed scenes from the 18th century. Another example dates from 1957, and involved three young naval cadets – as they walked towards the village of Kersey, Suffolk, the season seemed to change from autumn to spring, church bells stopped ringing and everything became very still. The men apparently saw the village as it would have been hundreds of years earlier, before becoming afraid and running away.

Time slips have been the subject of relatively little study. Although a number of cases involving the apparent perception of historic buildings that are no longer extant have turned out simply to be cases of mistaken location, a small residue of cases remain where no obvious explanation is available. Despite the intensity of time-slip experiences it seems likely that they occur only on a subjective level, involving perhaps either powerful hallucinations or an altered state of consciousness. Furthermore, cases are known where individuals encounter scenery which could never have existed in that location in the historic past. For example, in his book *More Things* (1967), the cryptozoologist Ivan T Sanderson described an experience shared with his wife while walking near the isolated Lake Azuey in Haiti. The couple suddenly became aware of houses on either side of the road and felt as if they were walking in Paris as it would have appeared some 500 years earlier, an experience which persisted until a companion raised a flame from a cigarette lighter, bringing their shared vision to an end.

A small number of reported time slips seem to relate to the future, and these are usually classed as VISIONS (often of an apocalyptic nature) or examples of SECOND SIGHT or PRECOGNITION.

time travel

The supposed capability to travel backwards and forwards in time.

The human mind has long been fascinated by the possibility of travelling backwards and forwards in time, and scientific opinion is still divided on whether or not such a thing is even theoretically possible.

One element in the dispute is the so-called 'grandfather paradox'. Essentially, this concerns a scenario in which a person travels back in time to a period in which their grandfather is alive but has not yet fathered any children. If the time-traveller kills their grandfather, what would be the result: would the person then be immediately snuffed out of existence as having never been born, or would the person be responsible for creating a fork in the path of time, on one side of which they exist and on the other (in a 'parallel universe') they do not? Some argue that the paradox would be avoided by nature

somehow contriving that the act of killing one's own grandfather in the past could not be accomplished.

One theory of time travel involves the use of wormholes. These are hypothetical 'tunnels' in space-time, acting as shortcuts between widely distant parts of the fabric of space-time itself in the same way as the hole made in an apple by a worm connects two different surfaces while leaving both ends open. If a craft could enter one end of a wormhole it might very well come out in a different era of time.

Some scientists theorize that time travel might be accomplished through travelling at close to the speed of light. The special theory of relativity formulated by the mathematical physicist Albert Einstein (1879–1955) states that time slows as speed reaches that of light. In this way, one of two twins who travels in space at light speed for a period of years will age less than the twin who remains on earth. If time is thus relative, and if it is possible to exceed the speed of light (considered by many to be impossible) it should be theoretically possible to go forwards or backwards in time, but the technology for accomplishing this is, at the moment, only the stuff of science fiction.

Science fiction has, of course, often taken time travel as its theme, from *The Time Machine* (1895) by English novelist H G Wells (1866–1946), to the phenomenally popular BBC television series *Dr Who* (first made in 1963 and periodically revived to the present day) and the *Back to the Future* series of Hollywood films (beginning in 1985). The bestselling novel *The Time Traveller's Wife* (2003) by US writer Audrey Niffenegger (1964–   ) has as its hero a man who cannot control his spontaneous 'leaps' back and forth in time.

The English theoretical physicist Stephen Hawking (1942–   ) has argued that the laws of physics make time travel impossible, citing as proof the fact that no time-travellers seem to be around in the here and now. Those who disagree argue that the laws of physics as we now know them may one day have to be adjusted by as-yet undiscovered knowledge. Some even suggest that the presence of time-travellers and their craft would explain accounts throughout the ages of such mysterious phenomena as ghostly apparitions, visions of angels and, especially more recently, UFOS. What if reported sightings of 'aliens' are really sightings of our own descendants who have evolved the technology to travel back from the future?

Tiphareth

In the kabbalah, the sephirah or emanation of God known as Beauty or Harmony, which is assigned the number 6; it represents the ideal balance of justice and mercy necessary for the proper running of the universe.

Tiphareth is the sixth of the ten SEPHIROTH, or divine

emanations, in the KABBALAH. It is called Beauty or Harmony, and is the third of the emotive attributes of the sephiroth. It represents the ideal balance of justice and mercy needed for the proper running of the universe, and is associated with the power to reconcile the conflicting inclinations of CHESED and GEBURAH in order to allow for focused compassion. It is assigned the number 6. On the kabbalistic TREE OF LIFE, it is positioned directly below KETHER, and is sometimes called the Lesser Countenance because it is seen as the place where Kether, the Great Countenance, is reflected. It is the central sephirah of the Tree of Life, and holds the qualities of all the other sephiroth together; it may be considered as the pivotal point on which the entire tree is balanced. It is a place of balance and transformation, where the ascending and descending powers meet. Tiphareth is the third point of the middle triangle on the Tree of Life, the Moral or Ethical Triangle, which it forms with Chesed and Geburah, and it is also the central sphere on the middle axis, the Pillar of Equilibrium. Uniquely, it is given eight paths on the Tree of Life – to Kether, CHOKMAH, BINAH, Chesed, Geburah, NETZACH, HOD and YESOD – and unites these eight surrounding sephiroth. It is associated with the Divine name *Jehovah Aloah va Daath* (Lord God of Knowledge), the archangel Raphael, the angelic order of the Malachim and the planetary force of the Sun. In the TAROT, Tiphareth corresponds to the four sixes, and in the tarot Tree of Life spread, the card in the Tiphareth position usually represents health. In some kabbalistic systems it is attributed with the magical image of a child, a king or a sacrificed god, and is represented by various symbols such as a Rose Cross, a Calvary Cross and a cube. It is often connected with the heart CHAKRA. The word Tiphareth in kabbalistic GEMATRIA gives the number 1081, the sum of all the numbers from 1 to 46, and adding together the numbers of the three sephiroth which represent the primary emotions of the heart – Chesed (72), Geburah (216) and Tiphareth (1081) – produces 1369, the square of 37; in the kabbalah, square numbers are highly significant. It is also sometimes called Zoar Anpin, Adam, Melech and the King.

The *Titanic* see panel p684

Toft, Mary (c.1701–1763)
A woman who claimed she gave birth to rabbits.
In September 1726, something of a medical sensation occurred in England when the surgeon John Howard was summoned to the bedside of Mary Toft, a 25-year-old married woman of Godalming in Surrey. She had had a miscarriage a few months before but had claimed to be still pregnant. However, more amazing than this, Howard apparently assisted her to give birth to several rabbits.

To be accurate, they were actually parts of rabbits, all dead. Howard was convinced that something unknown to science was happening and wrote to various eminent men about his experience. The story became a national sensation and the king sent his surgeon-anatomist Nathanael St André and Samuel Molyneux, secretary to the Prince of Wales, to look into the matter. Mary explained that before her miscarriage she had experienced cravings for rabbit meat, dreamt about rabbits and had tried to catch some. Meanwhile, in the presence of these illustrious witnesses, she continued to deliver stillborn and dismembered rabbits.

In November, Mary was taken to London for further investigation, to the intense curiosity of the public. In the house where she was lodged, she was to be observed round the clock, and, disappointingly, the phenomenon ceased. Stories began to circulate that, while they were still in Godalming, Mary's husband had been taking delivery of unusually large numbers of rabbits. When it was suggested that a surgical operation should be carried out to examine Mary's womb, she suddenly confessed that the whole thing had been a hoax.

Apparently, she had inserted the rabbit parts into her vagina in private to be 'delivered' later, for no more compelling reason than to achieve fame and make some money. She was accused of fraud, arrested and confined to the Bridewell prison. However, after a few months she was released without being put on trial. Some suggested that this was a cover-up and that something out of the ordinary really had been going on, but in reality it was probably done to save blushes all round. If that was indeed the motivation, the plan failed.

The main effect of the hoax was to attract ridicule to the medical profession in general and to John Howard and Nathanael St André in particular, whose careers never recovered. The famous English painter William Hogarth (1697–1764) created a satirical print 'The Wise Men of Godalming', showing the esteemed medicos reacting with astonishment as a line of rabbits is seen escaping from beneath Mary's skirts.

How could experienced medical practitioners have been so easily conned? In a way, they were merely reflecting contemporary misconceptions. Folk wisdom had long held to the belief that if something made a deep impression on a pregnant woman, this would be shown somehow in the child. For example, it was believed that an expectant mother frightened by a dog would give birth to an exceptionally hairy baby. The famous English 'Elephant Man', Joseph

The *Titanic*

When the British passenger liner *Titanic* was launched in Belfast in 1912 she was considered to be unsinkable. However, on her maiden transatlantic voyage she struck an iceberg and sank on 14 April 1912. More than 1,500 of her passengers died through drowning or hypothermia.

The fact that an 'unsinkable' vessel so quickly ended up at the bottom of the sea led people to search for reasons beyond those commonly accepted for her demise. Among the most fantastic was that the sinking was a gigantic insurance scam by the ship's owners, the White Star Line, in order to rid themselves of the already damaged sister ship, the *Olympic*. Having switched the ships' identities, it was alleged, the conspiracy went catastrophically wrong, leading to the unintentional loss of many lives.

Another popular idea was that the ship was cursed. Many believed that a series of coincidences that took place before the disaster show that the ship was 'fated' to sink and that nothing could have saved her. These include the fact that the ship's 'unsinkability' was based on the series of watertight compartments beneath her decks. If the ship had struck the iceberg head-on, damage would have probably been limited to the first of these and the ship was designed to remain afloat even if more than one of these compartments was flooded. As it was, after the iceberg was spotted the ship was turned in an unsuccessful attempt to avoid a collision, resulting in the side of the vessel being gashed open, allowing too many of the compartments to fill with water.

Also, various other ships had sent radio messages to the *Titanic* warning of icebergs in her path, but these seem to have been ignored or discounted by her captain, who did not allow her speed to be slackened.

PREMONITIONS were also said to have forecast the fate of the *Titanic*. In particular, the US writer, and avowed psychic, Morgan Robertson (1861–1915) had in 1898 published a novel, *Futility*, in which a gigantic liner called the *Titan* collides with an iceberg and sinks in mid-Atlantic. Some say that the real and fictional vessels shared so many features in common that surely the work predicted the *Titanic*'s demise, although others argue that Robertson was simply very knowledgeable about ships, and iceberg collisions did happen.

The English journalist and reformer William Thomas Stead (1849–1912), who was drowned in the sinking, was reputed to have secretly had the mummy of an Egyptian priestess of Amon-Ra carried aboard, which was supposed to be cursed. He is said to have discussed the 'mummy's curse' over dinner on the night of the sinking. Some even said that the mummy appeared on deck after the iceberg was struck. However, the truth is that this mummy had never left the British Museum. Intriguingly, however, Stead had published a short story in 1892 entitled 'From the Old World to the New', in which an ocean liner picks up survivors from an iceberg collision in the Atlantic. The fictitious captain is named E J Smith, the same name as the captain on the *Titanic*, and neither the fictional nor the real vessel was carrying enough lifeboats.

Others claimed that they had premonitions of the sinking of the *Titanic*. The second engineer, Colin McDonald, refused on a number of occasions to sign on as crew, later claiming that he knew that something terrible would happen. Passengers who decided not to travel also claimed that they had hunches that something would go wrong, and some claim that a small English boy witnessed a vision of the sinking as it took place.

The *Titanic* disaster was very productive of legends, one of the most popular and enduring being that the ship's band continued to play as the vessel went down, famously ending with the well-known hymn 'Nearer, My God, to Thee'. It is undoubtedly true that the band members sacrificed their own lives in order to keep frightened passengers calm. However, some survivors remembered the last tune played, not as a fittingly solemn and spiritual piece, but as a chirpy ragtime dance.

Carey Merrick (1862–90), was convinced that his deformity was caused when his pregnant mother was trampled by an elephant. The surgeons involved in Mary's case were perhaps the last men of science to give this idea any credence.

Tomczyk, Stanislawa (Early 20th century)

Polish medium who claimed to be able to use psychokinesis to move objects and stop clocks.

Stanislawa Tomczyk was a Polish MEDIUM who was involved in a number of experiments into alleged paranormal abilities in the early part of the 20th century. Tomczyk claimed to be able to levitate objects without touching them, stop a clock within a glass case and influence the turning of a roulette wheel. In the early 1900s, her abilities were investigated by the psychologist Julien Ochorowicz of the University of Lemberg. While under HYPNOSIS Tomczyk revealed an alternative personality called 'Little Stasia'. Those who believed in Tomczyck's powers later took Little Stasia to be Tomczyk's SPIRIT GUIDE, and claimed that it was through her spirit guide that Tomczyk was able to perform her amazing feats. Ochorowicz believed that solid rays could emanate from Tomczyk's fingertips and it was these that caused objects to move, apparently by PSYCHOKINESIS. Sceptics counter that the 'solid rays' were fine threads that Tomczyk used to suspend items in an attempt to deceive people about her powers.

Tomczyk's abilities were also tested by members of the SOCIETY FOR PSYCHICAL RESEARCH. In these experiments it was suggested that the medium was

The Polish medium Stanislawa Tomczyk apparently using psychokinesis to cause a pair of scissors to levitate.
(© Mary Evans Picture Library)

better able to control the movement of objects when under hypnosis. Tested again in 1910 by a group of scientists in Warsaw, Tomczyk was apparently able to produce remarkable phenomena under laboratory conditions. Although claimed by some to display the greatest proof ever of mediumistic ability, Tomczyk later took no further part in public life.

tongues, speaking in *see* XENOGLOSSY

totem

In some societies, especially those of the Native Americans, a species of animal or plant regarded as having an intimate mystical relationship with an individual, family or clan, and often venerated as a progenitor and protector.

Although the term 'totem' comes from a Canadian Ojibwa word meaning 'he is a relative of mine', and the concept of the totem is most typically associated with Native Americans, the belief system of totemism is found all over the world – in Africa, Australia, India, central Asia, North and South America, Eastern and Western Europe and the Arctic polar regions. Totemism is an ancient practice largely associated with shamanic societies, and is based on the central principle of an intimate mystical bond between humans and nature, and is not, strictly, a religion or magic, although it often exists alongside religion or magic in many societies.

In totemism in its most common form, a species of animal, such as wolf, eagle or bear, or more rarely, a plant, is regarded as the supernatural ancestor of an individual, family or clan; it is thus adopted as their emblem or symbol, and revered as their progenitor, protector and sustainer. It is frequently taboo for a person or clan to touch, kill or eat their totem animal except in a ritual sacrificial ceremony, when the animal is praised, thanked and mourned. In systems of individual totemism, which are found especially among Australian Aborigines, each person is thought to have such a close mystical relationship with a particular animal that the death of one will bring about the death of the other. Some have suggested this is the original form of totemism, and that the clan system subsequently developed among people who shared a common totem.

In modern times, many people, particularly those in the NEW AGE movement, have adopted animals as personal totems or 'power animals', some regarding them as literal spirit guides or as ARCHETYPES. This practice is viewed with disapproval by some Native Americans and other practitioners of tribal religions, who argue that totemism cannot be fully understood outside its tribal context.

touching for the evil *see* KING'S EVIL

Tower of London

The historic medieval fortress in London that is reputedly the most haunted spot in the British Isles.

Often dubbed the most haunted spot in Great Britain, the historic Tower of London is traditionally haunted by a wide-ranging collection of ghosts – apparently arising from its blood-soaked history as a fortress, prison and execution site. The first ghost reported in the Tower's history was that of Archbishop Thomas Becket in 1241, an apparition that was blamed for knocking down walls (even though Becket was murdered some distance away in Canterbury Cathedral). Other reputed ghosts include those of Queen Anne Boleyn, said to walk headless at Tower Green; Lady Jane Grey seen in 1957; King Henry VIII; Margaret Countess of Salisbury; Sir Walter Raleigh; and Edward V and his brother Prince Richard, who were imprisoned in the Tower in 1483 and most likely murdered.

Another famous sighting of an altogether more unusual apparition reportedly occurred in the early 1800s, when the 'Keeper of the Jewels', Edmund Lenthal Swifte (or similar), and his wife, claimed that they witnessed a phantom object resembling a glass cylinder hovering in the air in their dining room in the Jewel House. According to Swifte his sighting occurred within a few days of a sentry seeing a ghostly bear, an experience which induced a shock which allegedly proved fatal.

Over the last 50 years, clearly identifiable sightings of the historic ghosts seem few and far between, but reports continue of other more anonymous apparitions, and cold spots and strange noises in different parts of the Tower. In keeping with a number of historic haunted properties (see also HAMPTON COURT PALACE) efforts are now being made to record the ghostly experiences reported by staff and visitors.

traditional Chinese medicine *see*

CHINESE MEDICINE

trains, phantom *see* PHANTOM TRAINS

trance, hypnotic

A (real or apparent) state of deep relaxation characterized by a high level of suggestibility.

The idea that those undergoing HYPNOSIS enter an 'ALTERED STATE OF CONSCIOUSNESS' described as a 'hypnotic trance' is central to 'state' theories of hypnosis – that is, theories which hold that hypnosis involves a specific (and unique) mental state, which may be induced in a subject by a hypnotist. However, despite a significant amount of research in the area, it has not been conclusively shown that there is a consistent set of neurological conditions that can be isolated as the particular brain state associated with hypnosis.

The exact mechanism by which hypnotic suggestion is achieved remains an area of complex debate amongst the academic community. In recent years 'non-state' theories (ranging from explanations based upon a narrowing of attention and expectation, through to the suggestion that the effects are a result of social conditioning) have gained in popularity. However, there are still a number of psychologists who argue that there is a particular set of outward behaviours and subjective sensations, common to the experience of undergoing hypnosis, which might usefully be referred to as a hypnotic trance.

trance, mediumistic

A trance state apparently entered into by certain mediums as part of the process through which they claim that they communicate with the spirit world.

A TRANCE MEDIUM appears to be able to fall into a trance state at will, and once in this state they are apparently able to begin CHANNELLING messages from the spirits. The process often involves the MEDIUM appearing to fall into a deep sleep, during which they become possessed by a spirit which temporarily takes over control of their body. Such displays were particularly popular during the heyday of the SPIRITUALISM movement.

It has been suggested that entering into a mediumistic trance simply involves a form of self-HYPNOSIS, during which the medium recalls knowledge they have gained by ordinary means but do not have conscious access (see CRYPTOMNESIA). Some sceptics go further and suggest that mediumistic trances are nothing more than a stage act employed by mediums to lend authenticity to their fraudulent claims.

trance medium *see* MEDIUM, TRANCE

transcendental meditation

A meditation technique developed in the 1950s by Maharishi Mahesh Yogi. Based on the repetition in the mind of words or sounds known as mantras, it is said to allow the practitioner to naturally and effortlessly attain a heightened state of awareness known as cosmic consciousness. It is also the name of the worldwide organization which promotes his teachings.

In 1955, Mahesh Prasad Varma, an Indian exponent of the ancient Vedic science of consciousness, took the title of MAHARISHI MAHESH YOGI and began to

The audience at a 1967 lecture on transcendental meditation in Bangor, Wales, includes John Lennon and George Harrison. (© TopFoto)

teach a simplified form of this science, which he had developed and organized into a complete system designed to make the ancient practice of meditation more accessible for Westerners. He dubbed this system 'transcendental meditation', and in 1957 he founded the Spiritual Regeneration Movement, the first of several organizations collectively known as the Transcendental Meditation Movement, which now promote his teachings world-wide. He first introduced transcendental meditation to the West in 1958, and became one of the first Eastern gurus to gather a Western following.

Transcendental meditation is simple and easy to learn. Rather than attempting to concentrate and control the mind, the practitioner is given a word or sound called a MANTRA to repeat over and over in the mind while sitting in a comfortable position. Each student's mantra is unique to them, and is selected on the basis of their temperament and occupation, and is communicated to them at their initiation. Students are encouraged to keep their mantra private and never to repeat it aloud. The mental repetition of the mantra is said to prevent distracting thoughts, but if these enter the mind, the person is taught simply to notice them and then resume focus on the mantra. It is claimed that this technique allows the practitioner to drift naturally and effortlessly into a heightened level of awareness called 'cosmic consciousness', a state of 'restful alertness' in which the person is said to transcend thinking and reach the source of thought – the mind's store of energy and creative intelligence. The person's consciousness

is then said to grasp its connection to everything in the universe and understand its infinite potential, an experience described as at once relaxing and blissful. It is recommended that this mantra-focused meditation should be practised for 20 minutes or more, once or twice a day.

Transcendental meditation, often referred to as TM, is now a trademarked and highly successful commercial enterprise with teaching centres all over the world; the movement stresses that the procedure for using the mantra can only be learnt from a trained teacher. The TM organization has an accredited university in Iowa, the Maharishi University of Management (formerly the Maharishi International University), and in 1992, it founded a political party, the Natural Law Party, to support candidates dedicated to promoting TM and the Maharishi's teachings. The Natural Law Party was also, in the 1990s, associated with the practice of YOGIC FLYING, in which it was claimed that advanced practitioners of TM could perform a kind of LEVITATION while sitting cross-legged. The organization also markets a trademarked range of Indian health and beauty products, *Maharishi Ayur-Veda*, which are said to be manufactured from formulas in strict accordance with traditional AYURVEDIC principles.

TM has been the subject of controversy throughout its history. Its advocates claim that it promotes physical and mental health, and is especially effective in curing insomnia, reducing stress, anxiety and depression and improving intelligence and memory; however, its critics hold that, since the only studies done so far to support these claims have been made by its followers, the integrity of their findings is questionable. While its techniques are generally agreed to aid relaxation, some people maintain that other methods, such as the repetition of prayers performed in saying the rosary, achieve the same results. It has also been suggested that it can produce negative side effects, such as panic, depression and loss of motivation. TM has been linked with a number of prominent practitioners, including the Beatles, actress Mia Farrow and film director David Lynch.

transfiguration medium *see* MEDIUM, TRANSFIGURATION

transmigration

The apparent movement of the immortal part of a human being from one 'host' to another after the death of the physical body.

Those who believe in the possibility of transmigration hold that the human SOUL or SPIRIT may be transferred from one body to another after death. The new host may be human or animal, and in some cases it is even claimed that it can be vegetable or mineral. The use of the word 'transmigration' differs slightly from that of REINCARNATION in that it describes only the process of the movement of the soul – it does not include the wider concept of progression or regression based upon the quality of, and actions during, the previous life, or the idea of an ultimate goal. Transmigration is sometimes also referred to as 'metempsychosis', which literally means 'change of soul'.

transmutation

The changing of one form, nature or substance into another, especially the transformation of a base metal into gold through alchemy.

The term 'transmutation' comes to us from ALCHEMY. Although it is most commonly associated with attempts to change base metals into gold, the word was in fact used by alchemists in a broader sense. They believed that any form, nature or substance could be transmuted into any other by alchemy, and this applied not just to metals, but to any element. It applied also to the body, which could be transmuted from a sick one to a healthy one, and to the soul, which could be transmuted from an earthly existence to an eternal one. The goal was to transmute the impure into a state of perfection.

However, the most celebrated transmutation attempted by alchemists was undoubtedly that of turning base metals into gold. This was believed to be possible either by subjecting the base metal to a lengthy sequence of procedures such as heating, mixing with other substances, and distillation, or by using a mythical substance called the PHILOSOPHER'S STONE, which, if discovered, would facilitate transmutation. Through the ages, a number of alchemists claimed to have successfully performed this feat: the 9th-century Arab alchemist Rhazes was said to have become famous for his practical displays of changing base metal to gold, and in the 1350s the French alchemist Nicolas Flamel recorded his successful transmutation of mercury into gold.

Using nuclear radiation, modern physicists can in fact change the atoms of one element into those of another, and the old alchemists' term of transmutation is also applied to this technique. By this means, physicists have successfully transmuted lead into gold, but the expense of the procedure far outweighs the value of the gold thus produced.

transvection *see* FLIGHT

tratratratra

A Madagascan mystery beast resembling an enormous lemur, far larger than any species known to be alive today.

In 1658, French traveller Admiral Étienne de Flacourt described an extraordinary beast of solitary lifestyle that had allegedly been observed near the Lipomani lagoon in Madagascar. According to his account, this mysterious creature, known locally as the tratratratra, and said to be very frightened of humans, was as big as a two-year-old calf, with a round head, a man's face and ears, ape-like feet, frizzy hair and a short tail. More recently, during the 1930s, a comparable Madagascan cryptid was reputedly encountered at close range by a French forester, who stated that it sat 1.2 metres (almost 4 feet) high, resembled a gorilla, lacked a muzzle, and sported 'the face of one of my ancestors'.

Although such descriptions do not correspond with any modern-day species of Madagascan animal, they do recall an officially extinct giant lemur known as *Palaeopropithecus*, which was as large as a chimpanzee, had a flattened face, was probably at least partly terrestrial due to its extremely large size and is known to have still existed in Madagascar as recently as a thousand years ago. Scientists believe that *Palaeopropithecus* went extinct due to hunting and habitat loss, but perhaps, in view of the above accounts, small numbers lingered amid Madagascar's more remote forests and swamplands into more recent times.

Treasurer's House

A famous haunted house in the city of York, England, where phantom Roman soldiers were allegedly seen in 1953.

The Treasurer's House, close to the Minster in York, England, was the scene of one of the UK's most famous ghost sightings when, in 1953, Harry Martindale, a 17-year-old apprentice carpenter, claimed he saw a procession of Roman soldiers travelling through the cellars where he was working. Some noted that his description of the figures did not correspond to the image of Roman soldiers popularly portrayed in books and films – they were bedraggled and appeared to have little armour, although their weapons included spears and short swords and at least one round shield. They walked rather than marched and appeared to be extremely tired and dishevelled. The figures appeared thigh deep in the floor, indicating that the ground level had risen since Roman times. The unusual detail of round rather than rectangular shields was found to be appropriate to auxiliary soldiers who were garrisoned in York during Roman times. Harry Martindale later became a police officer and also a guide on ghost walks organized in the city; all who interviewed him were convinced of his sincerity. Other sightings of the Roman soldiers are reported to have occurred in the 1930s and at least one other witness, a former curator-caretaker at the Treasurer's House, reported similar experiences in the cellars there after Harry Martindale's experience was made public in 1974. See also SPECTRAL ARMIES.

Tree of Life

In the kabbalah, a symbolic structure which links the ten sephiroth and the 22 letters of the Hebrew alphabet.

The earliest texts of the KABBALAH which describe the Tree of Life are the *Bahir, Sefer Yetzirah, Sefer Raziel* and, most importantly, THE ZOHAR. Jewish mystics developed various visual structures of the ten emanations of God, or SEPHIROTH, to show the interrelationship between them, and the vertical representation known as the Tree of Life became the most popular kabbalistic symbolic aid to meditation on the sephiroth. It shows the ten sephiroth as circles or spheres arranged and linked by lines in a pattern which forms an inverted 'tree' with its roots in the heavens and its branches extending downward toward the earth. (Some kabbalistic schools speak of a 'hidden' eleventh sphere, Daath, in the middle of the tree, but the first kabbalists did not include such a sphere, and it is not generally considered to be a full sephirah.) The Tree of Life is seen as a deeper way of understanding the nature of God, and over the centuries has been elaborated by kabbalists into a 'map' of creation.

It has a number of clearly defined internal structures, each with its own significance. Between the ten sephiroth are 22 connecting 'paths', each of which carries a specific meaning, and which corresponds to a letter of the Hebrew alphabet, whose symbolism is a key concept in the kabbalah. The journey through the ten sephiroth and the 22 paths which link them

The Treasurer's House in York where the ghosts of a Roman legion are said to march through the cellars. (© Mary Evans Picture Library)

on the Tree of Life make up the 32 Paths of Wisdom of the kabbalah. In this symbolic structure, the sephiroth are arranged in a pattern which establishes the interrelationships between them as pairs of opposites, as trinities, and in relation to each other as parts of a whole. The first or top sephirah, KETHER, which comes closest to the original divine light which created it, gives rise to the rest of the Tree of Life, with all of the remaining sephiroth partaking of its nature in some way. The light is seen as descending from Kether through the other sephiroth in numerical order in a pattern known variously as the Lightning Flash, the Descent of Power, the Path of the Flaming Sword or the Lightning Bolt of God, and with the tenth sephirah of MALKUTH, it becomes contained within the physical world.

The Tree of Life has two main patterns. The first consists of three triangles, the top one being formed by the three sephiroth Kether, CHOKMAH and BINAH; this represents the higher consciousness, and is sometimes known as the Supernal or Archetypal Triangle. The middle one, formed by the sephiroth CHESED, GEBURAH and TIPHARETH, represents the unconscious, and is sometimes called the Moral or Ethical Triangle. The third and lowest is formed by the sephiroth NETZACH, HOD and YESOD, and represents the conscious or action; it is also called the Astral or Psychological Triangle. The tenth sephirah, Malkuth, representing the physical world and outer reality, forms the entry point to these ascending triangles.

The arrangement of the sephiroth on the Tree of Life can also be seen as forming three vertical columns which derive from the concept of polarity, or opposing forces. The right and left columns are known as the Pillars of Manifestation, and in kabbalah they signify the way in which God directs existence. The right-hand pillar, known as the Pillar of Grace or Mercy, contains the sephiroth Chokmah, Chesed and Netzach, whose qualities tend toward expansion, while the left-hand pillar, known as the Pillar of Severity, contains the sephiroth Binah, Geburah and Hod, which stress qualities that restrict. The middle pillar represents Equilibrium or Reconciliation, the blending and harmonizing of the principles of the two opposing pillars, which, if they existed alone, would pull so strongly against each other that they would tear the universe apart. This middle pillar contains the sephiroth Kether, Tiphareth, Yesod and at the bottom, MALKUTH, which symbolizes physical existence.

By means of the Tree of Life, medieval kabbalists thus managed to encode and translate their whole sacred and mystical philosophy into a single, complex symbol.

trees, bleeding
Trees that ooze red resin.

Many varieties of tree have a sap or resin that is naturally red in colour, and in various parts of the world this has given rise to accounts of trees miraculously 'bleeding'.

The dragon tree, varieties of which are found from the Canary Islands to the Middle East, has such a resin, which exudes from its bark if it is scored. The resin is popularly known as dragon's blood, and has been put to various uses throughout history, from ointment for the wounds of Roman soldiers to artists' pigment or varnish.

Legend has it that the Christ's-thorn jujube tree of Mediterranean regions was the source of the crown of thorns used in Christ's crucifixion. The red sap that oozes from it is considered to have healing properties by many peoples.

In the Iranian city of Qazween there is a famous tree that Shi'a Muslims believe exudes warm blood on Ashura, a fast-day observed on the tenth day of Moharram, in commemoration of the death of Imam Hosain.

Sometimes, however, the phenomenon of bleeding trees is neither natural nor welcome. In 1995, oak trees on the west coast of the USA began to develop bloodlike cankers which oozed dark red sap. Affected trees died rapidly, and the blight was christened Sudden Oak Death. It later spread across America and trees were infected in the United Kingdom. Scientists attributed the disease to infection with the fungus *Phytophthora ramorum*. Some environmentalists, however, believed that the trees were succumbing to an over-polluted atmosphere, as well as the use of toxic pesticides and chemical fertilizers.

Trindade Island
The site of a famous UFO case in which the witnesses were the crew of a scientific survey vessel.

On 16 January 1958, a converted Brazilian navy vessel, the *Almirante Saldanha*, was moored off an uninhabited island 966 kilometres (600 miles) out into the Atlantic. It carried a crew of around 200 naval personnel and scientists who were establishing a weather station on this remote outpost. The project was part of an international venture, known as the IGY (International Geophysical Year), which involved a number of nations co-operating in geological and atmospheric research.

Most of the task had been completed, and the crew was preparing to return to Rio. Shortly after midday, a strange object appeared from over the island, came towards the ship and then circled back and away over the choppy waters. Many of the sailors who were on deck at the time reported seeing something that looked a bit like the planet Saturn – it had a solid, lens-shaped central part surrounded by edges that appeared to be formed out of a fuzzy cloud. One witness said that the object appeared to be contained within a greenish haze. As the crew stared at the spectacle, Almiro Barauna, who was present as the official photographer for the voyage, took four black and white still photographs of the object. These included the rocky crags of the island in the background to give perspective and add dimensions to the image of the UFO. The crew also reported that, as the object passed them, the power to the electric winch, which was being used to bring aboard a small boat, failed. The power then returned after the UFO departed. Other reports suggest that there was interference recorded by other on-board equipment, including the radar.

Barauna developed the photographs almost immediately – leading some to speculate that he altered the images or employed double-exposure techniques. Suspicion increased when it became known that the cameraman had previously produced a number of trick photographs (superimposing treasure chests on pictures of the sea, for example). He had also admitted to an interest in UFOs. On arrival in Rio, Barauna was made to hand over the negatives to the Brazilian government for thorough investigation at the hands of their naval photo reconnaissance unit. The investigation produced no evidence of fraud, and subsequent studies, using modern computer techniques, have added support to this view. See also UFO PHOTOGRAPHS.

trolls

Originally, giants of Scandinavian origin, who are powerful, ugly and extremely antagonistic toward humans, animals and other fairies; in later lore, particularly in southern Scandinavia, conceived of as small or dwarf-like beings.

In older Norse lore, the word 'troll' is synonymous with 'giant', and these Scandinavian monsters were originally described as huge, thick-set, powerful, ugly and hairy. In later folklore they are conceived of as being smaller and more dwarf-like, but are still strong. The males often have humps on their backs. Trolls are extremely ill-disposed toward humans, animals and other fairies, and live in remote, rocky regions, in underground hills or mounds, or sometimes under bridges, where they will demand a heavy toll – sometimes their life – from anyone who crosses. Their favourite sport is throwing rocks at other creatures, and in general, they behave like neighbourhood bullies, going around in gangs, but they have no loyalty to one another and will frequently fight among themselves. However, they are slow-witted, and if they can be tricked into staying above ground until daylight, they will turn to stone. They hoard treasure, but unlike some FAIRIES, they do not like to enter human dwellings because they think humans smell terrible, although in some traditions, troll children are not born with hearts or eyes, and these must be stolen from human children.

Trunko *see panel p692*

tsomgomby

A very large cow-like amphibious cryptid of south-western Madagascan swamplands, bearing a close resemblance to Madagascar's extinct dwarf hippopotamuses.

In 1976, a man called Constant, living with his wife near the fishing village of Belo-sur-Mer, in south-western Madagascar, were woken up one night by the loud grunting cry of an animal whose existence is not recognized by science – the tsomgomby ('not cow'), also known, due to its very large pendant ears, as the kilopilopitsofy ('floppy ears'). Native Madagascans claim that this swamp-dwelling CRYPTID is the size and general shape of a hornless cow, but that it is not a cow. It is described as having dark skin and areas of pink around its eyes and mouth. It is also said to be swift-moving and amphibious, and to give voice to very loud deep grunts. Intriguingly, it is also said that it sprays urine at people who approach it, and if threatened will attack and even kill people. In 1876, an unidentified antelope-like skin said to be from a tsomgomby was examined by German zoologist Josef-Peter Audebert.

Madagascar has never been home to antelopes, but until as recently as a thousand years ago it did harbour at least two different species of dwarf hippopotamus, one of which, *Hippopotamus lemerlei*, was amphibious, roughly the size quoted for the tsomgomby and also bore more than a passing resemblance to the mystery beast. In addition, it is known that hippos will spray urine at opponents or would-be aggressors, will kill humans if threatened and emit extremely loud grunting cries. Only the huge floppy ears of the tsomgomby offer a problem when attempting to match its morphology to that of hippos, but perhaps Madagascar's dwarf hippos did have larger ears than their bigger, mainland African relatives. Certainly, it seems plausible on all other counts that should it truly exist as described, the tsomgomby may indeed represent a relict species of native dwarf hippopotamus persisting into modern times in south-western Madagascar.

Trunko

One of the most baffling cryptozoological episodes of all time took place on the morning of 1 November 1922, when a crowd of bemused onlookers was drawn to the beach at Margate, South Africa, by a truly titanic battle out at sea. The participants were a pair of whales attacking an astonishing sea CRYPTID unlike anything ever previously reported. The creature was covered in eye-catching snow-white fur like that of a polar bear, but was instantly distinguished from this familiar species by its lengthy elephantine trunk. After a time the marine monster was presumably weakened from the fray, and three hours later its dead body was discovered washed ashore, where eyewitnesses were able to observe it in detail.

Befitting its monstrous form, the creature – since nicknamed 'Trunko' – measured more than 14 metres (46 feet) long, including the baffling trunk of 1.5 metres (5 feet) that took the place of a distinct head, and also a tail of 3 metres (10 feet). Its luxuriant white fur was 20 centimetres (around 8 inches) long. Perhaps most amazing, not to say ironic, of all, however, was that during the ten days that this anomalous carcase lay beached, not a single scientist came to examine it, let alone make any attempt to preserve any part of it for study. Eventually, the sea carried it back out, and Margate's enigmatic 'marine elephant' was not seen again.

It is well known that beached shark and whale carcases become exceedingly distorted once they begin to decompose, and shark carcases can even acquire a covering of 'fur', due to connective tissue fibres becoming exposed. However, such explanations are not tenable in relation to Trunko, because its fur was readily visible while this cryptid was still alive, fighting the whales. Nothing like Trunko is known either from modern-day zoology or from the fossil record, which makes the lack of interest shown by the scientific world in its washed-up carcase all the more frustrating and mystifying.

tumo

A Tibetan Buddhist technique in which, through meditation and breathing exercises, an intense body heat is said to be generated, allowing the practitioner to survive in freezing temperatures.

Tumo, also spelt tummo, is the Tibetan term for an advanced type of meditation taught as one of the six yogas of Naropa, which were passed down from the Tibetan Buddhist Naropa (1016–1100) to Marpa Lotsawa, the founder of the Kagyu school of Tibetan Buddhism. Tumo is best known for the intense body heat generated as a side-effect of this religiously oriented meditational practice. Variously translated as 'fierce woman', 'brave female' and 'full of power', the word 'tumo' is also regarded as the Tibetan equivalent of KUNDALINI, and the 'mystic fire' of tumo is related to Kundalini heat; Kundalini yogis describe similar experiences to those of tumo practitioners. The heat, which is generated in the navel or solar plexus CHAKRA and sent to the veins, arteries and nerve channels of the entire body, is understood to be the outward manifestation of an inward state of religious ecstasy or enlightenment achieved through meditation and breathing techniques.

There are many stories of tumo practitioners being able to generate enough heat to dry wet sheets wrapped around their naked bodies, even while sitting outside in freezing temperatures, and the French mystic scholar, ALEXANDRA DAVID-NÉEL, witnessed a demonstration of the practice. One of the most famous practitioners of tumo was the Tibetan Buddhist saint Milarepa (1043–1123). Scientific attempts to study the physiological effects of tumo have shown that individuals have the ability to increase the temperature of their fingers and toes by as much as 8.3° C.

In recent years, a form of REIKI has been developed, based on a syncretization of Japanese reiki with Tibetan tumo techniques, which claims to awaken Kundalini in a safe and controlled manner.

tumulus

A prehistoric burial mound.

A tumulus is a prehistoric burial mound, examples of which have been found in many countries around the world, particularly dating from the Neolithic and Bronze Ages but often belonging to more recent cultures. Some of these mounds are made of earth, others of mixed earth and stones, and some completely of stones (in which case they are usually known as CAIRNS). One of the largest known tumuli is that heaped above the tomb of Alyattes, king of Lydia, which was completed near Sardis c.560 BC. It is around 61 metres (200 feet) in height and 360 metres (1,180 feet) in diameter.

In the British Isles, a type of tumulus known as the long barrow often covered a chambered tomb or DOLMEN built from huge megaliths, a fine example

The Maes Howe tumulus on the Orkney Islands. (© Adam Woolfitt/Corbis)

being that of Maes Howe in Orkney. Burial mounds have also been excavated in central Asia (where they are known as kurgans) to reveal the rich tombs of Scythian royalty and nobility. The Vikings also often buried their rulers beneath mounds, sometimes large enough to contain a whole ship. Extensive mounds have also been identified in North America, particularly along the Mississippi, where at the site of the ancient Native American city of Cahokia some have been shown to contain richly furnished tombs.

Little is known about the methods of construction used but in each culture a tremendous co-operative effort must have been required. This, along with the sheer scale of these monuments, constitutes a testimony to the importance to their peoples of the great personages buried within.

The Tunguska Event *see panel p695*

Turin Shroud

A shroud claimed to be that used for Christ.

In the Cathedral of St John the Baptist in Turin, a length of linen cloth is kept which many believe to be the shroud in which Jesus Christ was wrapped after the crucifixion. Imprinted on the fibres is an image of the naked body (front and back) of a bearded man, hands crossed over the groin, who appears to bear the marks of a victim of beating and crucifixion. Dark brown stains, which some have identified as blood, are also present on the cloth.

The authenticity of the shroud is still a matter of debate. Some accept it as a genuine and divinely created image, known as an *acheiropoietos* (from the Greek, and meaning 'made without hands'). Others

claim it is a medieval fake (and an example of PIOUS FRAUD).

While there were previous reports of items claimed to be the shroud of Jesus in various parts of the Christian world, it is only possible positively to trace the provenance of the Turin Shroud to the 14th century. In 1357, it was displayed in a church in France, and it was subsequently displayed on several other occasions throughout the century. Even at that time there were clerics who denied its authenticity, claiming that it had been painted by an artist.

During the 15th and 16th centuries it passed through various hands and was stored or displayed in several European cities, until it eventually arrived at its present location in 1578.

Leaving aside any supernatural explanation, scientific opinion is divided as to how the image was produced. Some claim that it was painted on with a pigment intended to suggest blood; others maintain that the image has three-dimensional characteristics and must have been formed by contact with a body (not necessarily that of the crucified Christ).

In 1988, with the agreement of the Vatican (its owner), a piece of one corner of the material, not containing any of the imprinted image, was detached and divided into three parts, each of which was subjected to radiocarbon dating by a different academic institution, including the Oxford Research Laboratory for Archaeology. The results of the analysis showed that the cloth must have been made between 1260 and 1390.

While some scientists have questioned these findings, arguing that the method is not infallible and the fibres analysed may have been contaminated by

An enlargement of the face of the Turin Shroud is examined by visitors to an exhibition in Turin, Italy.
(© David Lees/Corbis)

much later handling or repairs to the cloth, the general scientific consensus is that the dating is probably not far out. Further, and hopefully finally conclusive, radiocarbon dating tests on an area of the cloth impregnated with the image have been ruled out by the Vatican. It is argued that damaging the image, if it is authentic, would be sacrilegious. Sceptics, however, maintain that fear of its being definitively revealed as a fake are behind this.

The Roman Catholic Church has never made any pronouncement on whether or not it considers the shroud to be a genuine relic, declaring that it is a matter of faith.

Tutankhamen, curse of
The legend that the discoverers of the tomb of Tutankhamen were cursed.

The tomb of Tutankhamen (died c.1340 BC), an Eighteenth-Dynasty king of Egypt, was discovered and excavated in the Valley of the Kings in 1922 by the English Egyptologists LORD CARNARVON and HOWARD CARTER. Unlike any previously discovered tombs it was virtually intact, having been hidden by the debris created when a later tomb was built nearby, and it contained many rich and informative artefacts.

It was perhaps the idea that the tomb had been largely undisturbed for so many years that led to the belief that those who desecrated it would call down punishment on themselves. It was rumoured that an inscription had been found inside the tomb warning that anyone entering it would be cursed, but this has never been produced. Those who believe in the curse maintain that Lord Carnarvon removed and hid it so as not to alarm the workers. In any case, Carnarvon died a few months later, as the tomb was still being excavated. It was said that at the moment of his death all of the electric lights in Cairo went out. At the same time, back in England, it is claimed that his faithful dog began to howl before dropping dead.

British newspapers were quick to pick up on these events and sensationalize them, probably influenced by popular horror stories featuring mummies that mysteriously became reanimated to terrorize the living. The story of the 'curse' was too appealing to be allowed to drop and it was duly trotted out every time a member of the expedition happened to die, especially over the following ten years. How much could this be substantiated by the facts?

Lord Carnarvon was already an elderly man by the time the tomb was discovered and not in the best of health. His cause of death was pneumonia, contracted after his system had been weakened by an infection arising from the bite of a humble mosquito. Such was the state of the contemporary electricity system of Cairo that sudden blackouts were by no means uncommon. As to the wider group of people involved in the expedition, those who died in the years immediately following the discovery tended to be the older members; the younger members mostly lived out their natural terms. As for Carnarvon's dog, perhaps it had a particularly empathetic connection with its master, or its death was simply a coincidence.

Scientists have looked at possible causes for any assumed fatal effects of opening a tomb that had been sealed for generations. The most common theory is that the inrush of fresh air into the previously confined spaces could have disturbed moulds whose spores could then have been breathed in by the excavators, possibly causing adverse medical reactions. Whether this actually caused any premature deaths cannot be established; it is certainly the case that modern Egyptologists tend to wear masks when working with mummies, but this is as much to prevent them introducing contamination as to protect them against it.

The Tunguska Event

On 30 June 1908, an enormous explosion occurred over the Tunguska region of Siberia. Locals reported a huge fireball in the sky, followed by a blinding flash and a shock wave that flattened trees and shattered windows. The resulting seismic wave was detected in various locations throughout Europe and Asia, where, in addition, abnormal light effects at twilight had been reported in the days before the event.

The explosion seems not to have been immediately investigated, probably through a combination of circumstances: the site was in a remote area, and the political and societal turmoil that preceded the Russian Revolution of 1917, and the subsequent civil war, might have hampered any attempts at investigation for some years. It was only in the late 1920s and 1930s that the Russians are recorded as mounting expeditions to the area. It was believed that they might find a large meteorite containing valuable minerals. However, no such meteorite was found and there was no crater on the ground to indicate the point of impact. The only apparent explanation was that the explosion had taken place in the air and not on the ground.

Subsequent Russian expeditions concluded that a meteorite had been involved, exploding before it hit the earth. As with other known meteorite strikes, they found minerals and glass particles in the soil. The post-war development of atomic bombs and observation of their effects during weapons tests influenced some lines of inquiry, but the fact that scientists on these expeditions detected no unnatural levels of radiation led them to conclude that it was certainly not a nuclear explosion. The most common scientific explanation remains that of a meteor exploding in the air several kilometres above the ground.

There are other theories, however. It has been suggested that an asteroid rather than a meteor was responsible, or perhaps rocky detritus from a comet trail. Most scientists, however, discount these ideas as unlikely. The area was once the site of an active volcano and some have suggested that the explosion was caused by the ignition of massive amounts of methane gas emerging from the earth. More imaginative ideas include the arrival from space of a body of antimatter, or even of a black hole, although current science does not recognize these explanations as physically possible.

Believers in extraterrestrial life claim that the explosion was caused by the firing, intentional or otherwise, of an alien weapon of unimaginably destructive power. Others say that an interstellar craft crash-landed on the site, even going so far as to suggest that the Russians (in an echo of the American ROSWELL stories) actually recovered wreckage and alien technology. This kind of theory has generated numerous science-fiction interpretations.

Whatever the origin of the explosion, it has been shown that the forest was extremely quick to regenerate afterwards, and some have claimed this as evidence of something not quite natural going on. However, while controversy continues as to the exact scientific explanation of the event, extraterrestrial interpretations remain on the outer fringes of the debate.

twelve

The twelfth whole number, represented by the digits 12.
Twelve is the twelfth whole number. It is a higher octave of the number 3 and is thought to symbolize great understanding and wisdom gained from life experiences. It is a number which recurs in many cultures and belief systems; in Greek mythology there were twelve gods and goddesses of Olympus, and Hercules was given twelve seemingly impossible labours to perform. In the Bible, Jesus had twelve disciples, and by some calculations there were twelve tribes of Israel. There are twelve signs of the ZODIAC in Western ASTROLOGY, the year is divided into twelve months, and analogue (non-digital) clocks divide the day into two groups of twelve hours.

Twelve is considered to be the number of completion, signalling the end of childhood and the beginning of adulthood. Many older numbering and measuring systems are based on twelve, as can still be seen in the concepts of a dozen (12) and a gross (12 × 12), the pre-decimal British monetary unit of a shilling (made up of twelve pennies) and the pre-decimal unit of measure, the foot (consisting of 12 inches). In numerology, 12 is reduced to the single digit 3 by the addition of its two component digits, 1 + 2, and symbolizes perfection.

twins

Pairs of children born from the same pregnancy.
The birth of twins is not uncommon in human experience. They are recorded in history throughout the ages and around the world. In ancient Greek

mythology, Castor and Pollux (or the Dioscuri) were the twin sons of Zeus whose names were given to stars, while the ancient Romans believed their city to have been founded by the twins Romulus and Remus.

Essentially there are two types of twins: those born from the same egg which divides into two after fertilization (thus producing identical or monozygotic twins), and those born from two eggs fertilized at the same time (non-identical or dizygotic twins). A further sub-category of identical twins is that of 'mirror' twins. In this case the twins appear to be reflections of one another, one being left-handed and the other right-handed, and so on. Medical opinion is undecided on how this comes about.

A very rare form of twinning is known as conjoined or Siamese. These twins are physically joined, usually at the trunk or the head, and the phenomenon occurs when the fertilized egg fails to divide completely. With modern surgical techniques conjoined twins can often be separated and lead healthy lives, but in the past they were often shut away or exhibited in FREAK SHOWS. They were originally called Siamese twins after Chang and Eng Bunker (1811–74), born joined at the waist in Siam (modern Thailand).

Many people believe that twins, particularly identical ones, share extraordinary empathy, even to the point of being able to feel each other's pain or communicate telepathically (see TWIN TELEPATHY).

Twins who have been separated at birth, for example having been given up for adoption by different families, provide a very fruitful area of study for various scientific disciplines. When twins who have been raised in different homes, even in different countries, eventually meet in later life they often seem to discover an uncanny amount of experiences and preferences in common, such as the name of their spouses, the career they follow, their favourite foods or hobbies and usually the types of ailments that they have suffered.

Some twins, especially those who suffer from a speech impairment, seem to develop a private language (or idioglossia) when they are children, using it to communicate freely while remaining unintelligible to others, only abandoning it when they are eventually sent to school.

The scientific consensus on the seeming empathy and shared thought processes of twins is that it can be explained by genetic factors. Since the genetic structure of twins is so similar, it is argued, they are predisposed to thinking and reacting in similar ways, to having the same tastes, making similar decisions and so on. They are simply genetically 'programmed' to live their lives along the same lines.

However, many continue to believe that this is not the whole story and that twins do indeed share a mysterious link that science as yet cannot fully explain.

twin telepathy
A supposed special 'mind link' shared by two closely related individuals.

Stories of incidents which apparently indicate that there is some form of telepathic link between TWINS (particularly identical twins) feature regularly in the popular press. Typically, stories involve one twin suffering an accident or traumatic experience. The other twin, geographically removed from the first, suddenly thinks of their sibling or experiences discomfort in the area of their body corresponding with their injury. Upon checking with each other, they find that the injury and the sensations all occurred at exactly the same time – the conclusion is that some form of TELEPATHY produced the effect. Often the stories are extremely compelling. One twin will often report a feeling that the other is in trouble or needing help, only to find later that this was in fact the case.

Twelve-year-old twins take part in an experiment to test twin telepathy at Mississippi State University in 1961. The twin in the background is trying to telepathically 'tell' her sister what is on the card she is holding.
(© Bettmann/Corbis)

Twins whose sibling dies, whether at birth or in early childhood, often report a feeling of loneliness or being incomplete that accompanies them throughout their lives.

Theories offered to explain these stories, and the many other types of supposed examples of this phenomenon, include the idea that there is some form of PSYCHIC bond due to the twins' 'closeness of being'.

However, when twins have undergone laboratory testing for telepathic powers they have generally scored no better or worse than unrelated individuals. Many sceptics argue that the anecdotal evidence for twin telepathy is an example of 'cognitive bias' (see CHANCE AND COINCIDENCE) – significant coincidences are remembered, while instances where twins suffer accidents without their sibling feeling a related sensation at a similar time are forgotten.

two

The second whole number, represented by the digit 2; considered significant in numerology.

Two is the second smallest whole number. It has many different meanings, with its duality representing partnerships and interaction with others, but also disunion and polarities such as black and white, good and evil, male and female, and left and right. One pole cannot exist without the other, so 2 can represent a complementary relationship such as YIN and YANG, but such polarity can also create strife and discord. In geometry, 2 represents a line connecting two points, which creates the first dimension. In the TAROT, the twos of the minor ARCANA indicate duality, unions, dialogue and the possibility of opposition, while in the major arcana, 2 is the number associated with the High Priestess card. In Hebrew GEMATRIA, 2 corresponds to the Hebrew letter Beth, and in the KABBALAH, it is the number assigned to the sephirah CHOKMAH. In NUMEROLOGY it is considered to be a yin number; it is the numerical equivalent of the letters B, K and T, and indicates a sensitive, receptive and patient person who loves beauty, likes living in peace and is gifted at finding harmonious solutions. On the negative side, such a person's co-operative nature can become passivity. See also ONE; THREE; FOUR; FIVE; SIX; SEVEN; EIGHT; NINE; TEN; ELEVEN; TWELVE.

tzuchinoko

A squat Japanese mystery snake said to have a unique triangular cross-sectional shape when viewed head- or tail-on.

Even by cryptozoological standards, the tzuchinoko, one of Japan's most famous mystery beasts, is truly extraordinary. Said to be short and squat, measuring no more than 0.6–0.9 metres (2–3 feet) in total length and bearing noticeably large body scales and ten or so big black blotches dorsally, the most striking morphological feature of the tzuchinoko is its cross-sectional shape. It is claimed that, when viewed head- or tail-on this curious snake is virtually triangular, with a distinct ridge running down the centre of its back. Adding to its memorable appearance are a pair of short horns above its eyes, a pair of clearly visible facial pits and a well-delineated neck.

Overall, the tzuchinoko is most similar in superficial form to the pit viper *Agkistrodon halys*, and prominent tzuchinoko investigators Michel Dethier and Ayako Dethier-Sakamoto believe that it may either be a mutant version of this species or a closely related but currently undescribed, separate species.

UAP *see* UNIDENTIFIED ATMOSPHERIC PHENOMENA

Uffington White Horse

The figure of a horse cut into the chalk of an escarpment near Uffington in Oxfordshire, the earliest and largest of the 'Wessex' white horses.

The Vale of White Horse in Oxfordshire is named after the great stylized figure of a horse that has been carved there on a north-facing chalk hill. The elongated figure measures more than 106 metres (350 feet) in length and is now believed to have been cut into the turf during the Bronze Age, contrary to the traditional theory that it was made to celebrate the defeat in battle of the Danes by Alfred the Great at nearby Edington in 878.

The Uffington White Horse, near Uffington in Oxfordshire.
(© Skyscan/Corbis)

Stylized it may be, but does it actually represent a horse? Some, notably the English archaeologist Jacquetta Hawkes (1910–96), believe that the figure is actually meant to suggest the dragon killed by St George. According to local legend, the dragon's blood was spilt onto the nearby Dragon Hill, where it is said that no grass will grow. Most archaeologists, however, believe that it may be a symbol of a horse goddess of a local Celtic tribe or some kind of tribal symbol stamping ownership of territory on the land itself.

Whatever its provenance, the Uffington White Horse is an amazing feat of artistry as on the ground it would have been impossible for those actually cutting the turf to make out the overall design. The full form can only be appreciated from far across the vale or from the air, where in the days of its creation only the gods would be looking down.

UFO

The acronym for 'unidentified flying object', in simple terms it applies to any strange object seen in the sky which cannot immediately be identified by the witness.

Throughout history, strange objects have been seen in the sky and subjected to various interpretations, often reflecting the cultural beliefs and current social themes of the time. Likewise, the terms applied to such objects have changed over the years, often being shaped by the context of the sighting – for example, during the 1890s there were reports of mystery AIRSHIPS, and during the 1940s there were GHOST ROCKETS.

In 1947, the phrase FLYING SAUCER was first used in connection with the new WAVE of reports that appeared in the media. This, and similar phrases, such as 'flying disc', are still occasionally used. However, in the early 1950s the US Air Force investigation team,

PROJECT BLUE BOOK, needed a less emotive term that did not imply a specific shape – particularly because only a few reports included discs or saucers – and that was not associated with an alien invasion because of its use in Hollywood B movies. Captain EDWARD J RUPPELT, then the chief investigator, settled on the use of 'unidentified flying object' (UFO) because this described the content of the reports without implying any particular cause.

The acronym UFO is now in everyday use in the English-speaking world and has been translated into several other languages – the most widely used alternative being 'OVNI' (short for *objet volant non-identifié* in French, *objeto volador no identificado* in Spanish, *objecto voador não identificado* in Portuguese and *oggetto volante non identificato* in Italian). Several other new words have also been produced from the root 'ufo', such as UFOLOGY, meaning the study of UFOs, and 'ufologist', to describe someone who conducts such study.

Most ufologists agree that only between one and five per cent of reported sightings should really be considered to be UFOs. After investigation, the remainder are generally found to be IDENTIFIED FLYING OBJECTS (IFOs).

In popular culture, the word UFO is often understood to be synonymous with 'alien spacecraft' – this is based upon the (media-driven) mistaken belief that the EXTRATERRESTRIAL HYPOTHESIS (ETH) is the only proposed explanation for the phenomenon. The accompanying claims that someone believes in, or doesn't believe in, UFOs technically makes little sense – unless these are taken to be expressions of opinions as to the validity of the ETH. Of course, if the hypothesis proves to be correct, the objects that are then identified as alien spacecraft will cease to be described as UFOs. There are, in fact, a large number of proposed THEORIES OF ORIGIN for UFO sightings, with no single theory appearing to offer an adequate explanation for the vast range of forms that they take – it is for this reason that the term UFO continues to serve a useful purpose.

UFO community
A generic term for the diverse group of people involved in UFO study.
'UFO community' is used loosely to describe the vast range of people with an interest in UFOS. Members of the 'community' have such an interest for a widely divergent set of reasons.

Witnesses to a UFO comprise the largest single group. An estimated 50 million people worldwide have reported seeing something strange in the sky. While most go on to give little further thought to the phenomenon as a whole, approximately one in ten pursue the matter further by reading published literature or joining UFO groups or internet discussion forums.

Ufologists are those people who are so interested in the subject that they devote further time to research. Many have a personal interest driven by their own UFO sighting. Ufologists of this type have been investigating sightings since KENNETH ARNOLD began to explore other reports following his encounter in June 1947. Ufologists have been producing books on the subject since 1950 (several thousand are currently in print in the English language alone). Since 1951 they have also been joining forces to form UFO groups that carry out investigations, publish magazines, stage lectures and hold conferences. Groups such as the BRITISH UFO RESEARCH ASSOCIATION, CUFOS and MUTUAL UFO NETWORK have remained active for decades. However, such 'traditional' groups have been on the wane since the 1990s – UFO-related websites have now become the centre for the majority of activity in this area – there are countless discussion forums, databases, case-related information centres and even real-time images sent from webcams set up in WINDOW AREAS, to allow 'virtual' SKYWATCHING from home. It is estimated that, world-wide, approximately 100,000 people are involved in UFO groups at some level, although the number who devote large amounts of time to investigating and reporting on cases is probably less than 5,000.

There are a number of sceptics who consider that UFO sightings are something to be explained away, and there have been a number of organizations created with the express purpose of attacking what they regard to be a pseudoscience at best and, at worst, the realm of credulous fanatics. Such sceptics are, however, far fewer in number than ufologists and possibly the most useful criticisms of their primary concern, the EXTRATERRESTRIAL HYPOTHESIS, have come from within the UFO community. A relatively small, but dedicated, band of UFO researchers accept that there is a possibility that something 'exotic' lies behind a few cases and consider it vital to resolve as many sightings as possible in order to focus on these truly strange reports.

Mainstream scientific interest in UFOs is limited, possibly because an open association with the subject generates potentially career-damaging stories in the popular press. Over the years there have also been a number of prominent ufologists who have publicly expressed some fairly bizarre-sounding ideas, increasing the tendency for the media to treat the subject with a certain amount of derision. Consequently, those scientists who are interested in UFOs generally prefer not to be publicly named in connection with the UFO community.

Ufology *see panel p701*

UFO photographs
Photographs which purportedly contain images of UFOs.

The first known UFO photograph was taken by an astronomer in 1882 at ZACATECAS, Mexico. Since then an estimated 20,000 cases of apparent UFO photographs have been studied; although the true number of such photographs is thought to be considerably higher as many are never made public. Still photographs were by far the most common until the 1990s, and there were a number of impressive examples, including the MCMINNVILLE, OREGON photographs from 1950 that have defied several scientific analyses.

Cameras have been involved in a number of cases of misperception, and the vast majority of photographs turn out to be of IDENTIFIED FLYING OBJECTS (IFOs). The subjects include such things as aircraft, satellites and weather balloons, but there are some sources that are unique to the camera lens. Hundreds of UFO photographs apparently involve objects not seen by the witness while taking the picture, only appearing when the film is developed. Almost without exception, such cases are regarded as very likely to have a mundane explanation – they commonly turn out to result from light reflecting as flares inside the lens system, marks caused by the film-processing chemicals or even birds frozen into UFO-like poses by the fast shutter speed of the camera.

There were a few cases of apparent UFOs being captured on cine film from the 1950s through to the 1980s, but the vast majority were explained away as resulting from such things as high-flying birds reflecting sunlight. Only rarely was professional footage obtained, such as the KAIKOURA films captured in 1978 by a TV camera crew aboard a cargo plane. Unfortunately, both still and motion pictures of UFOs are far more likely to be taken at night, greatly increasing the problems of evaluating the cause.

The massive expansion in the use of video cameras from the late 1980s onwards has produced a huge rise in the number of UFOs recorded by this method. Most of these are again just LIGHTS IN THE SKY, seen at night – this has created problems for the focus systems of many cameras. Images of stars, or the planet Venus, have taken on UFO-like dimensions as the auto focus systems struggle to resolve a point source of light.

Each new type of photography produces its own set of explanations for the images produced. Even security camera systems occasionally record UFOs, and modern mobile phones with cameras attached have been used to snap pictures during unexpected sightings, although the poor resolution makes them of limited value. No case has provided the definitive evidence and there are thought to be fewer than 500 truly significant pieces of photographic evidence for the reality of UFOs. These rarely reveal structured craft, landed UFOs or their alien occupants (although BILLY MEIER has been a prolific producer of highly controversial photographs of this type over a number of years). Most of the best UFO photographs show anomalous light phenomena, such as those filmed over HESSDALEN in Norway.

Hoaxes using photography represent less than 5 per cent of all reported UFO photographs, but as cameras and photographic techniques have become more sophisticated the options for trickery have increased. There is some evidence that hoaxed photograph numbers are on the rise, but they remain heavily outweighed by sincere (but generally mistaken) reports. See also ORBS.

Ummo
The name given to an affair which involved a long-running series of communications from allegedly alien senders who claimed to come from a planet called Ummo.

Starting in 1966, a series of over 8,000 letters, documents and even phone calls were received by a diverse group of European (particularly French and Spanish) ufologists, scientists and professionals over a period of more than two decades. Initially these originated from a variety of towns in France and Spain but later communications also came from Asia and North America. No contact addresses were ever given.

The documents that were received contain philosophical messages and purport to describe the life of beings on a planet called Ummo, which supposedly orbits the star Wolf 424. They paint a detailed picture of a spiritual race, who use TELEPATHY and have a strong belief in religion, God and the soul. These entities apparently visit Earth but choose not to interfere with the lives of humans. Many of the messages are stamped with an insignia (the astrological symbol for the planet Uranus), and the contents show some evidence of good scientific knowledge on the part of the senders.

In 1967, photographs were sent to UFO researchers based in a suburb of Madrid. They showed a large disc-shaped craft bearing the Ummo symbol on the base. Pieces of metal tubing with the mark embossed on them were also submitted. They contained a rare chemical which it is believed would probably have had to come from a military source at the time. Careful study of this 'evidence' strongly indicated that the case was a hoax, and later analysis of the photographs revealed traces of string holding up what appeared to be a small model.

Ufology

Ufology, or the study of UFOs, dates from the aftermath of World War II, but in many respects the pursuit is as old as mankind.

A member of an early civilization would have viewed the sudden appearance of a rainbow as something awesome and mysterious. It was often considered to be a sign from the gods, and stories or legends built up around visions of this arc of coloured light in the sky. It was only in relatively recent times that we began to understand the physical processes within the atmosphere that produce such a spectacle – what is now readily explained was, for millennia, an unidentified supernatural event.

During the period in which their origin was unknown, a rainbow was a simple form of UFO (unidentified flying object). Further human understanding was required to turn such a mysterious event into an IDENTIFIED FLYING OBJECT, or IFO – this is the same process that is at the core of modern UFO research. Members of the UFO COMMUNITY (which includes people who study UFOs from a wide variety of perspectives) seek to explore sightings of unexplained phenomena in the skies in an attempt to find the most probable explanation.

There are records of sightings of what we would now call UFOs from far back into history. Examples exist in the annals of Greek and Roman scholars, in medieval manuscripts and on Renaissance tapestries and etchings. Few of these things were properly investigated at the time but they were widely interpreted according to the prevailing cultural beliefs. Retrospectively we can see that many of these reports describe phenomena we now understand – such as aurora (see AURORA BOREALIS), fireball meteors or unusual cloud formations. At the time they were just unidentified LIGHTS IN THE SKY.

Among records from more recent times we can identify WAVES of further UFO sightings, such as the mystery AIRSHIPS that appeared across the Midwest of the USA during the 1890s, or the glowing lights, nicknamed FOO FIGHTERS, that chased aircraft during World War II. The most significant reason why there were suddenly large numbers of such sightings was

the rise of the mass media – newspapers in the 19th century, radio and television in the 20th and the Internet during the 21st – ensuring that UFO stories are rapidly spread far and wide. Those in the media also soon realized that the more extraordinary the suggested interpretation the more people would be interested by the story. As the 20th century went on, the UFO phenomenon began to adapt into a form of space age mythology.

From the 1940s, these apparent spates of UFO activity were afforded the same level of awe that was once attached to the rainbow. However, instead of being regarded as supernatural signs or wonders, these modern UFOs started to be attributed to the actions of visitors from outer space. This interpretation became dominant – it was culturally appropriate now that humanity had conquered the heavens, sending rockets to the Moon and beyond.

The major wave of June and July 1947 was centred on the western states of the USA – this time the press had dubbed the objects FLYING SAUCERS. Coming as it did in the aftermath of World War II, at the dawn of the Cold War, it gave the US government cause for concern – their fear was that the glowing discs and other strange objects being reported, often by trustworthy witnesses, might be weapons or spy craft used by the Soviet Union. It was for this reason that the first government UFO studies (see PROJECT SIGN, PROJECT GRUDGE and PROJECT BLUE BOOK) were all put in the hands of the US Air Force, and the heavy hand of security services like the FBI and CIA was felt from the outset. Secrecy was the order of the day, and politically motivated attempts were made to explain away UFO sightings.

During the early 1950s, the CIA manipulated the evidence in order to defuse rising public interest. Their concern was that an enemy might fake UFO reports in order to take advantage of public hysteria – this was only revealed in the 1980s. The secret services were worried by the growing public membership of UFO groups, set up amid claims of an official cover-up (see GOVERNMENTAL COVER-UP). Leaders of the new community, such as ex-Marine DONALD KEYHOE, believed that this cover-up was hiding the astounding fact that the US government had proof that UFOs were ALIEN spacecraft. Some went further and suggested that they had captured the remains of crashed UFOs, putting them into secret facilities such as AREA 51, and had even conducted autopsies on recovered alien bodies (see ALIEN AUTOPSY). However, such claims of conspiracy were short on actual evidence.

As a result of these claims, UFOs began to be portrayed in the media almost entirely in terms of one particular, extreme belief about their nature – that is, that they were alien spacecraft. Meanwhile nations all over the world, who had followed the US lead and created their own military study projects, found that many of the sightings were simply the result of misperceptions of aircraft, balloons or many other everyday things. They certainly found no evidence of an alien invasion. These highly polarized positions on the question of what were, at heart, sightings of a few strange lights in the sky, laid the way for a war of rival ideologies. For several decades ufology was dominated by this obsession with the EXTRATERRESTRIAL HYPOTHESIS. Governments really did keep information secret, for political reasons – which played into the hands of those who charged them with duplicity. Silence was taken to imply that there were guilty secrets and dark truths – whereas, in fact, it only hid a lack of answers. Many researchers in the UFO groups that sprang up around the world made it their aim to bring to an end a cover-up of evidence that almost certainly never existed.

During the 1960s, the sightings continued and even more extraordinary types of case emerged – including claims of ALIEN ABDUCTION. The mythology grew, fuelled by sensationalist books, television series and films. This rising level of oddity among the claims associated with UFOs inspired a new generation of thinkers, of which the psychiatrist CARL JUNG was the first. This group approached UFOs as a psychosocial phenomenon (see PSYCHOSOCIAL HYPOTHESIS), observing how the nature of sightings changed in line with prevailing beliefs and other cultural trends – something that came to be called CULTURAL TRACKING.

During this period a few UFO groups began to operate in a more objective way – seeking to investigate and explain as many sightings as possible without presupposing any particular cause. Organizations such as the BRITISH UFO RESEARCH ASSOCIATION, and CUFOS in the USA, attempted to apply scientific thinking to the subject. The latter arose out of an informal team of interested academics brought together by the former US Air Force science consultant DR J ALLEN HYNEK and the scientist and writer DR JACQUES VALLÉE. These bodies established teams of investigators and

codes of ethics. They accepted that 95 per cent of all sightings were misperceptions and looked for possible explanations for the remainder. The extraterrestrial hypothesis was only regarded as one unproven possibility among many, and the number of possibilities investigated increased considerably: ALTERED STATES OF CONSCIOUSNESS, potential links with PARAPSYCHOLOGY, 'fantasy proneness', unusual atmospheric processes such as BALL LIGHTNING and other ideas that had not been considered by earlier UFO groups. The term 'UNIDENTIFIED ATMOSPHERIC PHENOMENA' (UAP) emerged out of attempts to classify the data gathered – the term was felt to be a more appropriate way to describe many of the unsolved cases, while avoiding the alien imagery attaching to the acronym 'UFO' in the minds of the public. Studies began to be carried out at locations around the world at which there were concentrations of UFO sightings. These were named WINDOW AREAS, and it was suggested that they might be focal points for natural phenomena that might trigger certain types of UAP. Such areas exist on all continents and research projects have been mounted at several of them, including HESSDALEN in Norway. Specialist equipment has been used to monitor and film the unusual light activity at these points, and a number of theories have been offered (see EARTH LIGHTS).

During the latter years of the 20th century, FREEDOM OF INFORMATION ACTS all over the world resulted in the release of documents describing government UFO investigations since the 1940s. The files indicate that the official investigators reached very similar conclusions to the scientifically minded members of the UFO community – most sightings could be explained, but a few hundred cases per year remained puzzling. However, although these could not be explained in terms of mundane occurrences, there was no physical evidence that they involved any exotic alien technology. For this reason most countries eventually closed their UFO projects, satisfied that there were no defence implications – although some continued to monitor new reports as they came in.

In May 2006, the British government provoked some surprise by publishing an in-depth report, known as Project Condign, detailing the outcome of a process of secret scientific analysis of UFO evidence that had been set in motion during the late 1990s. It concluded that the unsolved cases were likely to have resulted from sightings of various forms of unidentified natural atmospheric phenomena – a finding that closely matched the conclusions of some UFO groups. Indeed the British Ministry of Defence had even adopted the preferred terminology of those UFO researchers, using UAP to refer to these unsolved cases.

By the beginning of the 21st century many UFO groups had closed down. Physical evidence of visits by aliens had failed to materialize and it appeared that there were no government X-FILES. Media coverage and publication of UFO books and magazines had dwindled as the public accepted that the truth was more likely to be of interest to physicists than science-fiction enthusiasts. However, there remains a hard core of people who support the extraterrestrial hypothesis (particularly in the USA) and the Internet has provided the perfect forum for their style of ufology, in which the search for that elusive proof continues.

UFO investigators tackling the decreasing levels of UFO sightings operate in small teams, working on interesting cases as they emerge. Most now act with more realistic expectations – appearing to be more in tune with the sceptics than with the believers in visitors from outer space that were once their compatriots. Opinions within the mainstream UFO community vary. Some think that there might still be a few UFO sightings that will add to scientific knowledge. Others suspect that the UFO phenomenon might turn out to be nothing more than a short-term fad that thrived when the social and cultural conditions were right.

As for those who continue to support the extraterrestrial hypothesis, they see this change of heart by many of their colleagues to be further evidence for the great conspiracy – they believe that doubting members of the UFO community have just become part of the cover-up. In turn, the doubters point out that this attitude is part of the reason why they have turned away from conspiracy theories. And so the battle goes on.

Jenny Randles

A letter received by UFO researcher Hilary Evans, which purportedly came from aliens originating on the planet 'Ummo' – one of thousands sent to a variety of recipients.
(© Mary Evans Picture Library)

The sending of the Ummo messages slowed down after the 1970s. Most UFO researchers believe that the whole affair was a complex hoax, co-ordinated for reasons as yet unknown. JACQUES VALLÉE suggested that it might have been an attempt by military intelligence to use the UFO COMMUNITY for an experiment in social conditioning. Others suggest that the communications were made by a group of intelligent tricksters who were merely playing a highly evolved practical joke.

Unarius

A UFO religious group with New Age beliefs.

The Unarius Academy of Science, generally referred to as Unarius, was one of the first 'flying saucer cults' or UFO religions. Ernest Norman (1904–71) and his wife Ruth Norman (1900–93) met at a psychics' convention in 1954 and shortly afterwards founded the Unarius Educational Foundation. The name Unarius is an acronym for the *Uni*versal *Art*iculate *I*nterdimensional *U*nderstanding of *S*cience.

In terms of UFO religions, Unarius is closer to the AETHERIUS SOCIETY than to the RAELIAN MOVEMENT. It includes New Age elements related to the many ALICE BAILEY-influenced offshoots of THEOSOPHY, including a belief in REINCARNATION. Both Ernest and Ruth Norman claimed a number of past lives: for example, Ernest (or Raphiel) was the pharaoh Amenhotep, and Ruth (or Uriel) his mother. They also claimed that later, Ernest was Jesus, and Ruth was Jesus' betrothed, Mary of Bethany. In another incarnation Ruth apparently sat as the model for Leonard da Vinci's *Mona Lisa*, but she wasn't always a woman – she also said that she had reincarnated as Confucius, Socrates, King Arthur, Charlemagne, Henry VIII and Benjamin Franklin.

The couple wrote around 20 books, but after Ernest's death Ruth revamped the organization and its teachings. She wrote a further 80 books, claiming that she channelled (see CHANNELLING) most of these from beings on Venus, Mars and lesser-known planets including Hermes, Eros, Orion and Muse.

Ruth Norman predicted that the 'Pleiadeans' and other 'Space Brothers' would come to Earth in 1974; when this didn't happen she changed the date to 1975, then 1976 and then to 2001. After her death in 1993, Unarius was led by a long-term member, Charles Spiegel (known as Antares) until his own death in 1999; both were thus spared the difficulty of explaining away the failed prophecy. In predicting alien landings with specific dates Unarius is similar to the UFO group of Mrs Marion Keech (Dorothy Martin), whose claims prompted the classic sociological study *When Prophecy Fails* (1956) and inspired Alison Lurie's novel *Imaginary Friends* (1967). Such predictions can also be seen as a modern equivalent of earlier failed prophecies relating to the return of Christ on a specific date, made by various religious groups.

unconscious, collective *see* COLLECTIVE UNCONSCIOUS

unconscious, the
The deepest level of the human mind.

While various philosophers had long discussed the idea that the human mind retains ideas and perceptions without necessarily being consciously and constantly aware of them, it was SIGMUND FREUD who developed the theory that the unconscious was a level of the PSYCHE characterized by memories and desires that were inaccessible because they were repressed.

He devised a threefold division of the unconscious into the id (the source of desires), the ego (the rational self) and the superego (the controlling mechanism preventing the ego from being dominated by the id).

Freud thought that it was in the unconscious that the keys to various forms of neurosis and mental illness were hidden, and that by identifying these, through HYPNOSIS or psychoanalysis, the disorders they caused would be cured. Certain memories and desires, he believed, were suppressed by the unsconscious because they were too distressing for the mind to deal with on a conscious level. He believed that DREAMS were an indication of some of the contents of the unconscious and that their analysis led to the discovery of significant insights.

The Swiss psychiatrist CARL JUNG was initially a disciple of Freud but split with him over the Freudian idea that neuroses must have psychosexual origins. Jung developed his own theory of the unconscious, envisaging it as a valuable counterbalance to the conscious mind, as well as proposing the concept of a COLLECTIVE UNCONSCIOUS. According to this theory, part of the unconscious mind incorporates ARCHETYPES of basic human nature that are shared by us all. These include collective memories and instincts that we inherit from the experiences of our forebears and which influence both our dreams and our behaviour.

Many of the ideas of Freud and Jung about the unconscious are now thought to have little basis in science, but they are difficult either to prove or disprove and they continue to be influential. It is a generally accepted belief that the unconscious affects our behaviour and the decisions we make in our everyday lives.

The world of advertising exploits the unconscious in using images, colours and sounds intended to appeal to us on a level below conscious awareness. The most extreme form of this is subliminal advertising, in which images are inserted in a film or television programme that appear so briefly as to go unnoticed by the conscious mind. The theory is that the images will register on the unconscious and influence buying behaviour without our being aware of this.

Believers in the OCCULT ascribe great powers to the unconscious, thinking of it as a way of tapping into different levels of reality or gaining access to powers, such as TELEPATHY, communication with SPIRITS or PROPHECY. Many artists and writers believe that the unconscious is the source of creativity and that by establishing a connection with it, perhaps through drugs or the act of dreaming, they will achieve inspiration or be shown images and ideas from which they can mould their art.

undead, the
A collective term for various types of supernatural entities which are dead, but which behave as if still alive; applied especially to vampires and zombies.

The term 'undead' was first used by the Irish writer Bram Stoker in 1897 as the original title for his classic vampire novel, *DRACULA*, but the concept of the undead – supernatural entities that are dead but behave as if still alive – features in various forms in the folklore of most cultures. An undead being may be incorporeal, having no physical body, such as a GHOST, POLTERGEIST or wraith, but the term is more commonly applied to corporeal beings, such as ghouls, vampires and ZOMBIES.

In the folklore of many European countries, it was believed that unless the proper funerary precautions were taken to prevent such an occurrence, a deceased person could return from the dead as a vampire, to drink the blood of the living. Any unexplained death was likely to give rise to suspicions of undead activity, and exhumation was sometimes performed to check whether a buried body had started to decompose. If, as occasionally happened, the corpse had not begun to rot, and had fresh blood around its mouth, this was taken as a sign that it was undead. This is now known to be a common and natural stage in the decomposition of a body, but for many centuries such a corpse would routinely be decapitated, staked through the heart or burned to release its spirit. Vampires are generally thought to be vulnerable only to holy objects such as crosses, sunlight and, sometimes, fire.

In popular culture, zombies are unreasoning and implacable corpses which feed on the flesh of the living and can only be killed by destroying their heads. In modern times the undead feature prominently in fantasy and horror films and fiction, and are popular adversaries in role-playing games and computer games.

underwater objects
Strange objects sighted under the surface of seas and lakes.

For centuries there have been stories of strange objects or organisms sighted by sailors and fishermen under the surface of the world's seas or lakes, from undersea lights to giant creatures (see LAKE MONSTERS and SEA

SERPENTS). As science progressed and mankind began to use submarines to explore the deep waters of the planet, many of these phenomena could be observed and accounted for (for example, undersea lights often turned out to be volcanic activity), but some continue to resist explanation even in the modern era.

Ships belonging to various navies around the world, including those of the USA and Russia, have reported instances of the detection by sonar of metallic objects under the sea that appeared to move under their own power. While encountering submarines belonging to other countries is not unusual, these strange craft would flee speedily if pursued, at much greater velocities than their pursuers could attain.

Even stranger, some reports speak of such craft attaining high speeds while underwater before rising suddenly, perhaps hovering briefly above the waves, then disappearing up into the air. The obvious comparison with UFOs led to these sightings being labelled as USOs, or Unidentified Submersible Objects. These phenomena were not confined to the open oceans but were also detected in large lakes and the fjords of Norway. However, a particular 'hot spot' for such sightings is the waters off Puerto Rico.

Northwest of the island lies the Puerto Rico Trench, one of the deepest regions of the world's oceans, and apparently a large number of sightings of USOs have occurred here. Is it a coincidence that the Arecibo radio telescope, which as part of the SEARCH FOR EXTRATERRESTRIAL INTELLIGENCE (SETI) programme has sent radio-wave messages into space hoping to receive an answer, is sited on Puerto Rico? Many ufologists think not, preferring to believe that the area is a hotbed of alien activity and that extraterrestrial craft are visiting long-established underwater bases at depths in the oceans at which no human submarines could withstand the pressure.

Some attribute much of this activity to the testing of experimental craft and weapons by the US military, perhaps using technology borrowed from aliens. Others dismiss such modes of thinking, explaining the sightings as freak weather or electromagnetic phenomena created naturally from within the earth by effects that are not yet completely understood.

One strain of thought connects this underwater activity with the enduring legends of ATLANTIS, the 'lost' civilization said to have vanished beneath the sea. According to such theories, the Atlanteans, whether originating from another planet or indigenous to ours, have been coexisting with humankind for thousands of years and it is only the advances of earthly science that have revealed more of their activities over the last hundred or so years. However, belief in USOs is largely dependent on whether or not an individual has experienced the phenomenon personally.

underwater ruins
Undersea stone structures that appear to be submerged buildings.

At various sites around the world, structures have been found beneath the sea which have been interpreted not as natural features but as the remains of buildings.

For example, in Japan in 1995, divers swimming at around 15 metres (50 feet) off the coast of the island of Okinawa discovered what appeared to be massive, coral-encrusted ruins. The 'buildings' were thought to resemble traditional Japanese temples but they appeared to be solid, composed of great monolithic blocks of stone, with no rooms or passageways within them. Some of those who later studied the formations detected similarities to stone temples found in Hawaii and other Pacific islands, leading to postulations of an ancient, extinct trans-Pacific culture. It is thought that the buildings were submerged when sea levels rose or land masses sank, but their age has not been established.

Further formations were found in 2004, off the coast of Atami on Honshu, the main island of Japan, including what appeared to be stone walls, paving stones, platforms and carved steps. It is speculated that these are the remains of a city thought to have sunk into the sea in the 13th century, although some believe they may be much older than that.

One by-product of the highly destructive Asian tsunami in 2005 was the exposure of a submerged temple off the coast of Tamil Nadu in southern India. Local observers watched as the sea receded prior to the onslaught of the tidal wave, revealing hitherto undetected buildings offshore, including the ruins of both the temple and a house as well as fragments of giant statues. This seemed to confirm legends of temples being engulfed by the sea as divine punishment.

Perhaps the best-known underwater structure is the 'Bimini Road', a row of parallel stones discovered in shallow water off the Bahamian island of Bimini by a low-flying pilot in 1968. The apparent regularity of the stones and the way in which they were closely fitted together led to claims that they were the remains of a submerged 'cyclopean megalith roadway', created by unknown hands. Speculation was fuelled by the fact that the American psychic EDGAR CAYCE had predicted that the lost civilization of ATLANTIS would be discovered near Bimini. However, sceptical archaeologists who have made detailed analyses of the composition of the stones claim that they represent a natural formation known as beach rock. This type of rock is formed by tidal action beneath the sand, precipitating calcium carbonate that accretes into large solid masses. The fact that this rock forms quickly is shown by the examples that have been found in which World War II artefacts have already become embedded. The formations become covered by any rise in the level of the sea. Another submerged site in the Bahamas, the so-called Andros Platform, was discovered in 2003 and has been similarly explained.

Any discovery of underwater ruins inevitably gives rise to speculation connecting them with the legendary Atlantis. Whether or not such a place ever existed has yet to be established, but, obviously, not every submerged site around the world belongs to the same civilization. Some have origins that remain unexplained, while others are simply ruins belonging to identifiable cultures that have become inundated by natural rises in sea level, landslips or earthquakes.

unicorn

A fabulous beast resembling a horse, but with one long spiral horn growing from its forehead; often used as a symbol of strength and purity and in heraldry.

Travellers throughout the centuries have made claims of sightings of the fabulous unicorn and have given conflicting descriptions of this beast. There have been accounts of unicorns in China, Mongolia, the Middle East, Egypt, North Africa, India, Japan, Europe and America. The Indian unicorn, it was said, was like a horse in form, but was a much swifter beast, and had a white body, a red or purple head, blue eyes and a long horn about 45 centimetres (18 inches) long

growing in the centre of its forehead. This horn was white at the base, black in the middle, and red at the tip. The European version of the unicorn is usually depicted as being pure white and having the head and body of a horse, the hind legs of an antelope or stag, the whiskers of a goat, the tail of a lion and a white or pearly spiral horn.

In folklore, unicorns are said to be very aggressive toward their own kind, except at mating season, when they become gentle. The colts are born without horns, and stay with their mothers until their horns are fully grown. All the medieval bestiaries which give accounts of unicorns agree that they are attracted to virgins, and that the only sure way to capture a unicorn is to use a virgin as bait, when the unicorn will come and lay its head in her lap. It therefore became a symbol of purity, and came to be depicted with various female saints and the Virgin Mary, and in its role as a willing sacrificial victim, it was also used as a symbol of Christ. The horn, called an alicorn, was highly prized in the Middle Ages for its properties; it was said that it could purify water and protect against poison and disease. For this reason, prudent monarchs drank from a supposed unicorn horn, which was said to sweat in the presence of poison and neutralize or reduce its effects, and the poor would beg to be given water into which a unicorn horn had been dipped, as this was believed to cure all maladies. The horns were much sought after in the 16th and 17th centuries and were a popular ingredient for sale in apothecaries'

The Maiden and the Unicorn by Domenichino (c.1602). (© Alinari Archives/Corbis)

shops, where it may be assumed that many narwhal and rhinoceros horns were passed off as unicorn horns. In addition, a magical ruby or carbuncle was said to grow at the base of the horn, and this also had powerful healing properties, especially against the plague.

Because they are seen as a symbol of strength and nobility as well as purity, unicorns frequently appear as heraldic beasts, and when James VI of Scotland became James I of England in 1603, he chose one lion and one unicorn as the supporters of his royal shields.

See also UNICORN, LIVING.

unicorn, living
An actual rather than folkloric unicorn, certain early reports of which may be explained by the survival into historical times of a supposedly prehistoric rhinoceros.

There is little doubt that some historical reports of living unicorns were based upon sightings and second-hand descriptions of various real-life scientifically known animals, such as the Asiatic wild ass, Arabian oryx, great Indian rhinoceros, European wild ox, Tibetan antelope and even specially modified sheep. It has also been suggested that certain reports of living unicorns may have been inspired by encounters with a spectacular species of rhinoceros officially believed to have died out during prehistoric times.

For instance, as noted in the *Nordosk Familjebok*, a major Swedish encyclopedia, the legends of the Evenk (Tungus) people from Russia's Siberian taiga recall the former existence of a huge black bull instantly distinguished from normal cattle not only on account of its size but also by virtue of the large single horn that it bore on its brow. The 10th-century writer and traveller Ibn Fadlan provided a detailed account of a comparable unicorn from the Russian steppes, which was greatly feared by local riders, as it would pursue any rider that it encountered, hook him from his saddle, and toss him up into the air with its great horn, over and over, until the rider was dead. This formidable beast was said to be taller than a bull though smaller than a camel, with a thick, round, pointed horn in the centre of its head, bovine hooves and tail, a ram-like head and a mule-like body. Its horn was very substantial, growing 3–5 ells (3.45–5.71 metres) in length. Sometimes, the locals got revenge by hiding in trees and shooting poisoned arrows into the unicorn when it passed by underneath. While staying in Russia, Ibn Fadlan saw three large bowls shaped like Yemeni seashells that the locals claimed were made from the horn of this creature.

During the Pleistocene epoch (2 million to 10,000 years ago), the steppes of southern Russia and Siberia were home to a truly enormous and extremely distinctive species of rhinoceros, *Elasmotherium sibiricum*. Approximately 6 metres (20 feet) long, standing 2 metres (6.5 feet) high, and weighing up to 5 tonnes, this huge beast was almost the size of a present-day elephant, and is sometimes known as the giant unicorn. This is due to its single colossal horn, measuring up to 2 metres (6.5 feet) long and with an extremely broad base – which instead of being borne on the creature's nose (like the principal or only horn of all modern-day rhino species), arose from the centre of its brow, exactly like that of the fabled unicorn.

Such a beast might well have appeared reminiscent of a monstrous unicorn bull if it had been encountered by humans, which led to speculation that in the remote Russian tundra *Elasmotherium* may have lingered longer than its fossil record would suggest, persisting into historical times and giving rise to the legends of giant black bull-like unicorns in this region. Perhaps the distinctly bovine Persian unicorn known as the 'karkadann' and renowned for its highly aggressive, belligerent nature may also have been based upon reports of *Elasmotherium* – though in this instance by way of second-hand stories brought back to the Middle East by travellers who had visited Russia and heard tell of this mighty beast.

Unicorn of the Harz, the
Alleged unicorn skeleton found in Germany.

In 1663, a number of fossil bones were discovered in a cave in the Harz Mountains in Germany. Among them was a skull that seemed to have a single central horn protruding from it. A skeleton was reconstructed and claimed as that of a unicorn.

A scientific investigation into the discovery was undertaken by the German engineer and physicist Otto von Guericke (1602–86). He later published a volume called *Protogaea* (1663), which included a drawing of the reconstructed skeleton, showing a creature that was obviously a mishmash of bones that did not really belong together. The find, however, was enough to convince the previously sceptical German philosopher Leibniz (1646–1716) of the existence of unicorns.

In 1991, the same region of Germany saw a further account of a unicorn. The Austrian naturalist Antal Festetics (1937–) claimed to have seen a unicorn while filming a documentary of the wildlife of the Harz Mountains. Not only had he seen the beast, he asserted, he had also shot video footage of the encounter. As this has never been seen it is assumed to be a hoax.

unidentified atmospheric phenomena

A term applied by many modern UFO researchers to unsolved UFO cases that are believed to have natural, terrestrial phenomena at their heart which are, as yet, unexplained.

For many years a number of UFO researchers have been uncomfortable with the terms commonly applied to the phenomenon they study, the most widely known being 'UFO' and 'FLYING SAUCER', because the majority of public and the media believe these to be synonymous with 'alien spacecraft'. Most researchers accept that at least 90 per cent of 'UFO' sightings are simple misperceptions, and the alternative term IFO (IDENTIFIED FLYING OBJECT) can be used to distinguish these reports. However, the remainder still present a problem. While the concept of ALIEN visitors remains prominent among the various THEORIES OF ORIGIN, there are many UFO researchers who do not feel that this is a viable explanation, despite believing that there is a real phenomenon to investigate. There are even a number of supporters of the EXTRATERRESTRIAL HYPOTHESIS who agree that some UFO sightings probably involve natural, earthly phenomena which lie outside our current scientific knowledge.

The term 'unidentified atmospheric phenomena', usually abbreviated to UAP, has gained wider use in recent years because it does not imply that the source of a sighting has any particular attributes or cause – other than that it is something currently unidentified which appears within the atmosphere. It is frequently applied to cases where the cause is thought likely to be one of a range of unusual natural phenomena that are not yet fully understood – such as plasmas, ionized gases, EARTH LIGHTS, prismatic mirages or BALL LIGHTNING. The use of the term UAP has grown in line with an increasing acceptance that unexplained UFO cases may fall into these categories, and a general decrease in the popularity of the extraterrestrial hypothesis, within the UFO COMMUNITY.

unidentified flying object *see* UFO

universal life force

An invisible and subtle energy which is believed to surround and permeate all living beings, integrate mind, body and spirit, and connect all things. Many traditional healing systems are based on the principle that a balanced and harmonious flow of this energy is necessary for physical, mental and spiritual well-being.

The concept of the universal life force is fundamental to many traditional healing practices, including CHINESE MEDICINE, AYURVEDA, shamanic healing and Native American medicine. For thousands of years, healers in many cultures have insisted that each person is more than just a physical body, and that a subtle and invisible ENERGY surrounds and permeates all living beings. This force is thought to integrate mind, body and spirit, and to connect all things, and is recognized as the source of life and the driving force in healing; a balanced and harmonious flow of this life force, both in the body and between the individual and their environment, is held to be necessary for mental, physical and spiritual well-being. Illness is seen as a manifestation of imbalances, blockages or disharmony in the universal life force, and the role of the healer is to help restore the optimum flow of energy in order to enable the body's natural self-healing capacity to function.

The universal life force is known by many names. In Chinese medicine it is called QI, in Japanese medicine ki, in HUNA mana and in Indian systems such as Ayurveda it is called prana. The ancient Greeks knew it as *pneuma*, and in the West it is referred to variously as bioenergy, vital energy, vital force and life force. In the mid-19th century, the chemist Baron Carl von Reichenbach postulated a similar vital energy which he called 'Odic force', after the Norse god Odin, and which he associated principally with electromagnetic properties. Most traditional healing systems share the belief that the universal life force flows around the body in a complex network of channels, and also extends beyond the physical body to create an energy field, usually called the AURA or biofield. Energy centres in the body control the energy flow around, in and out of the body, and in a healthy individual, this energy circulates smoothly, feeding the organs and cells and supporting their functions. When this flow is disturbed, it affects the operation of the organs and tissues. The energy is also believed to be responsive to emotions, and to be disrupted by negative thoughts and feelings; this can lead to symptoms of emotional and physical distress, which may ultimately manifest as disease. Thus, mind, body and spirit are interconnected by the individual's energy centres and field, and the healer's task is to treat the patient holistically – that is, to work on the person as a whole, adjusting and balancing their energy, rather than focusing only on their symptoms.

There are many types of BODYWORK which aim to restore the equilibrium of the individual's energy. In Oriental medicine, the qi or ki is thought to circulate through channels called MERIDIANS. Techniques such as ACUPUNCTURE, ACUPRESSURE and SHIATSU work on the principle that the meridians come close to the surface of the body at many points, and that the flow of energy can be unblocked or adjusted by the manipulation of these points. In Hindu medicine, the body is believed to have seven major energy centres called CHAKRAS through which prana enters and leaves the body. The chakras regulate the energy system, and when they are in balance, they maintain a healthy mind, body and spirit. Massage, breathing exercises or CRYSTALS may be used to rebalance the chakras. Some energy-balancing therapies, such as REIKI (which literally translates as 'universal life force') and THERAPEUTIC TOUCH, do not even require physical contact between the patient and the healer. A number of exercise systems, such as YOGA, T'AI CHI and QIGONG, are designed to regulate the flow of life force in the body, which the practitioner feels and directs as the movements and postures are performed, while FENG SHUI uses design, placement and the arrangement of space to achieve harmony within an environment so as to create a free flow of qi.

urban legends

Modern popular stories of dubious veracity, often viewed as something distinct from historical folk tales but probably simply a continuation of the same cultural phenomenon.

Urban legends (sometimes also referred to as 'urban myths' or 'contemporary legends') are so called to distinguish them from older folk tales – 'urban' in this instance does not describe their setting. The term was popularized during the 1980s by the US professor of English Jan Harald Brunvand, who is perhaps the best-known researcher in this area. They are often passed on as true stories by those that tell them, and frequently begin with the assertion that they happened to a 'friend of a friend' (or FOAF), which has led to their other popular names – 'foaftales' and 'foaflore'.

Although describing a story as an urban legend is usually taken to imply that it is completely untrue, this does not have to be the case. However, they are generally at the very least exaggerated, sensationalized, misattributed or corrupted and are characterized by their repeated retelling by a narrator who implies that they are wholly true and happened to someone not too far removed from them. Many are believed by those who hear them and they are occasionally mistakenly reported as fact in newspapers or on news broadcasts. In recent years the growth of the Internet, and widespread access to email, has created something of a boom in such stories, allowing new ones (or, more frequently, recycled old ones) to be disseminated throughout the world in minutes. As with the older traditional forms of FOLKLORE, the stories vary and change with each telling, although the same basic forms reappear over and over again.

It is very difficult to produce a fixed definition of what constitutes an urban legend. In a similar way to many classic folk tales, urban legends often contain elements of horror, sensation, humour and a moral message. They are generally compelling and entertaining, which is perhaps why they remain popular and are retold. They can take a wide variety of forms – from the tales of ALLIGATORS IN SEWERS in New York to the story of the PHANTOM HITCH-HIKER, which regularly reappears in a variety of forms throughout the world.

In an interesting twist, it has been observed that some urban legends can appear to generate occurrences that render them (at least partly) true – a phenomenon referred to as OSTENTION.

urban myths *see* URBAN LEGENDS

V

Valensole

The site of one of the best-documented UFO cases from France. It allegedly involved the landing of a craft which left behind physical traces and produced physiological effects in the witness. There was also the hint of an alien abduction claim, something which is rare in cases from France.

Maurice Masse, a 41-year-old farmer in the Basse-Alpes region of southern France, claimed that, just after dawn on 1 July 1965, while he was sitting in his tractor preparing to start work, he heard a strange whistling noise. He looked around and saw what, at first, he thought was a helicopter – military crews did occasionally land in his fields, so he did not think it was odd. However, he was concerned that they might damage his plants so he left his tractor and headed towards the aircraft. As he got closer it apparently became clear to him that the object was not a helicopter – it was a giant egg-shaped craft resting on six legs in the middle of his lavender crop.

As Masse neared the object he could see two figures about the size of young teenagers. At first he thought that they were local youths – he had previously had trouble with his crop being vandalized. However, as he moved towards them, and gestured at them to leave the farm, he realized that they did not appear to be human. He described them later as ALIENS with white skins, cat-like eyes and pumpkin-shaped heads with notably pointed chins. They were both wearing greenish-grey overalls. One of the beings then pulled a small tube from a belt around its midriff, pointed it at Masse, and a beam of light shot out. He was stopped in his tracks, just a few feet away from the entities, unable to move forwards or backwards.

The two figures entered the egg-shaped object via a door that slid open and then closed behind them. The

craft then shot upwards with a whooshing noise and seemed to suddenly disappear. The PHYSIOLOGICAL EFFECTS suffered by Masse apparently persisted for

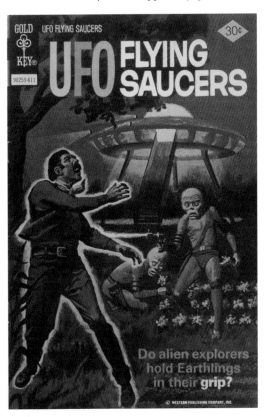

Maurice Masse, the French lavender farmer from Valensole who claimed to have encountered aliens in his field, from the cover of *UFO Flying Saucers* magazine (November 1976). (© Mary Evans Picture Library)

several minutes and he had poor muscle co-ordination for some time afterwards. He was also said to have collapsed with exhaustion two days later and slept for most of a day.

There were indent marks within the field of lavender, presumably left by the legs of the craft, and it was claimed that the soil became liquid in the centre of the landing area, before solidifying later the same day. An investigation was carried out by a group of UFO researchers led by Aime Michel. They apparently discovered that there were high levels of calcium in this area after the event. For a number of years lavender could not be grown on this one small circular patch of the field.

Masse did not make any direct attempt to make the story public – it was reported by a friend to whom he had told it. Even then he avoided publicity, but he did agree to work with Michel. However, the farmer went on to hint to researchers that his experience may have even included an ALIEN ABDUCTION – one of the earliest claims of this type in France – although he declined to discuss the suggestion in more detail, saying only:

> These people do not force anyone. If you say 'I do not want to go' then they would leave you in peace … I have not told all, but I have already said too much. It would have been better if I had kept it all to myself. You have to have undergone it to understand it.

Valentich, Frederick (c.1958–   )

An Australian pilot who apparently vanished in midair while being pursued by a UFO.

On the evening of 21 October 1978, trainee pilot Frederick Valentich was flying solo in a Cessna 182 across the Bass Strait, from Melbourne to King Island, to buy some crayfish for friends. The journey would add to his limited night-flight experience and increase his hours flying over water – both were necessary for him to obtain his full licence.

For some unknown reason he had changed his flight plans at the last minute, meaning that both legs of the 257-kilometre (160-mile) trip would have to be completed in the dark. He crossed the coast just after 7pm and began to descend towards the island. This placed him below radar cover – a normal state of affairs for the final 20 minutes of the journey. However, a few minutes later, at 7.06pm, he radioed air traffic control back in Melbourne, telling them that something was flying very near to him – he described a dark mass showing four landing lights. Melbourne assured him that there was no other traffic in the area, and even checked military sources to confirm this.

Six minutes into the CLOSE ENCOUNTER, at 7.12pm, Valentich explained that the UFO was 'orbiting' directly overhead. He described it as metallic with a green light attached, adding that the engine of his aircraft was 'rough idling' and failing. He indicated that he was going to try to make it the last few miles to King Island before finally saying, 'It's not an aircraft it's …' before his voice tailed off and the transmission was interrupted by scraping noises, followed by a static hiss and then silence.

Despite an extensive aerial search, and a four-year aviation accident enquiry, no trace of the pilot or aircraft was ever found. The enquiry report, published in May 1982, included the consideration of a number of theories but concluded that the reason for the disappearance remained a mystery.

Many suggested that the plane had crashed as a result of its proximity to the reported UFO or because the pilot had been distracted by its presence. Valentich's father believed for many years that his son had been the victim of an ALIEN ABDUCTION, and that he may be returned one day.

Other theories explored the idea that the pilot had fallen foul of smugglers (they were known to operate in the area, towing their loads in large nets attached to planes) or that a meteor had struck and destroyed the aircraft, although the protracted length of the sighting counted against this. It was even suggested that Valentich had faked his own disappearance by inventing the UFO story; at the time Australia was in the middle of a major WAVE of UFO sightings, and this was something of which Valentich was well aware – he had a scrapbook containing a number of press cuttings of the stories. However, no reasons for him wishing to 'disappear', or explanations as to what he would have done with the aeroplane, were ever offered. The case remains unsolved.

Vallée, Dr Jacques (1939–   )

French-born US scientist who has been one of the most prolific writers on the UFO phenomenon since the early 1960s.

Jacques Vallée was born in Pontoise, France, and gained a mathematics degree from the Sorbonne and a masters in astrophysics from the University of Lille. In the early 1960s, he worked as an astronomer at the Paris Observatory before moving to the USA where he specialized in computer science, obtaining his doctorate at Northwestern University in Chicago in 1967.

His decision to settle in the USA was formed partly because of his interest in UFOS. J ALLEN HYNEK, who was a professor at Northwestern University, was impressed by Vallée's scientific mind and saw him as someone who could help him in his aim of making UFO research credible. Vallée worked with Hynek in his 'invisible college' of scientists in the late 1960s, but was not centrally involved in the UFO group,

CUFOS, that followed. Instead he moved to California to pursue his computer studies and, while he never lost his interest in UFOs, he only participated in the debate within the UFO COMMUNITY when he felt that he had something new to say.

Vallée had also been a celebrated writer from his early twenties. His first books were science fiction novels – for which he received the prestigious Jules Verne prize. However, in 1965, he became the first working space scientist to produce a serious, scientific analysis of UFO evidence when he published *Anatomy of a Phenomenon*. The book's objective overview of the evidence inspired many other scientists to take a fresh look at the subject.

Vallée's thinking on the UFO phenomenon is much more in line with European (as opposed to North American) trends. In his 1969 book, *Passport to Magonia: From Folklore to Flying Saucers* (the first to assess the connections between historical folklore and modern UFO reports), he suggested that UFO encounters might be part of a longer-term interaction that changes through a process of CULTURAL TRACKING, and offered some theories on the links between the phenomenon and human consciousness. In 1979, he produced *Messengers of Deception: UFO Contacts and Cults*. In this book he began to develop a complex idea in which the UFO mystery is seen as something akin to a thermostat, modifying its behaviour and appearance through time to balance out and harmonize conditions within the human psyche. A decade later he went on to explore how UFOs were perceived within remote tribal communities in South America where there was no direct contact with the UFO imagery present in the USA. In the 1990s, he returned to writing UFO-inspired science fiction.

Vallée's interests have also taken him away from the central areas of UFO research. He was fascinated by URI GELLER's less well-known adventures with UFOs, and his CONTACTEE messages, which led to a study of the role that contact legends have played in the moulding and shaping of patterns within society. He has also inspired a fictional film character. Steven Spielberg was apparently so impressed by Vallée's work while he was carrying out the research for the 1977 film *CLOSE ENCOUNTERS OF THE THIRD KIND* that he modelled his lead character on him. In the film the mysterious government UFO investigator Lacombe is the head of the secret UFO project and expounds ideas linking UFOs with sociological phenomena.

vampire *see* VAMPIRISM

Vampire of Croglin Grange *see* CROGLIN GRANGE VAMPIRE

vampirism

In folklore, the action of drinking the blood of the living, as thought to be practised by the returning dead, known as vampires; also a clinical condition in which the sufferer believes he or she is a vampire and must drink the blood of the living to survive.

The vampire legend is universal, and bloodsucking demons appear in the folklore of Haiti, Indonesia, the Native Americans, the Inuit and many Arab tribes. All cultures, however ancient or primitive, have long understood that blood is the essential fluid of life, so it is natural that legends of monsters who drain the living of blood would have become a prevalent feature of worldwide folklore. Most of the European myths of vampires are of Slavic or Romanian descent; the etymology of the actual word 'vampire', which first appeared in French and English literature and correspondence in the late 17th century, is still debated, but most contemporary scholars favour the theory that it is of Slavic origin. The European vampire is usually a dead person who has returned to feed on the blood of the living. According to Slavic lore, there are many ways in which a person can become a vampire: if they were born with a caul, teeth or a tail; if they were conceived on certain days; if they were excommunicated in life, or died a violent, sudden death or committed suicide; if they died before being baptized; if, after their death, an animal, especially a cat, walked over the corpse; and the best-known method, if they were bitten by a vampire and the curse has been passed on to them. Werewolves also become vampires after their death. From the early-19th century, the word and the concept were firmly established in English literature, and the first real English vampire story, called *The Vampyre*, was published in 1819. Its success was partly due to the erroneous belief that it had been written by Lord Byron, although it was in fact written by Byron's one-time physician, John Polidori.

Until the 19th century, vampires were still depicted as repulsive monsters, but when Bram Stoker's 1897 novel DRACULA was adapted into a highly successful stage play in 1924, and then into a classic film starring Bela Lugosi (1931), the Count was portrayed as a handsome, seductive figure, and since then, popular culture has tended to represent the vampire as being evil but irresistibly attractive. The *Vampire Chronicles* series of novels written by Anne Rice have also done much to foster the image of the vampire as a romantic and enthralling character.

The vampire has hypnotic powers, and the strength of many men. He can shapeshift into a cat, a dog, a bat and especially a wolf, and has the power to command various animals, such as rats. He can also turn into mist and enter a room through the keyhole or under the

Bela Lugosi plays a handsome vampire in the 1931 film version of *Dracula*. Prior to Bram Stoker's novel *Dracula* (1897), vampires were portrayed as repulsive monsters.
(© TopFoto/Arenapal)

door. He has a pallid complexion and long, pointed incisors with which he bites his victims, and having no soul, he casts no shadow or reflection in a mirror. He is reluctant to enter or cross a body of running water, and cannot enter a house unless he is invited in the first time. Contemporary lore states that a vampire is destroyed by sunlight and has to return to his native soil to rest during daylight hours, although there is no basis in folklore for either of these beliefs. Vampires are repulsed by garlic and iron, although their aversion to crosses is a relatively recent imposition of Christian influences on a much older pagan folklore tradition. Old customs to prevent and destroy a vampire include filling the coffin with small seeds such as poppy or millet, which the vampire will spend all his waking hours counting obsessively; decapitating the body, pinning it to the coffin with a stake, or burning it to ashes; and EXORCISM. If a person is suspected of being a vampire, the body may be exhumed for the telltale signs – an undecomposed corpse with a healthy, lifelike bloom and fresh blood on its lips.

There exists a pathological condition known as clinical vampirism, also known as Renfield's syndrome after the character in *Dracula*, in which the sufferer believes he needs to drink the blood of the living to survive. Among the magical community there is also a strong belief in psychic vampirism, in which instead of blood, the 'vampire' either deliberately or unknowingly drains others of energy and vitality.

See also CROGLIN GRANGE VAMPIRE.

vehicle interference cases

Cases in which it is claimed that the close proximity of a UFO appears to affect the running of motorized vehicles.
There are approximately 1,500 cases on record in which a CLOSE ENCOUNTER with a UFO is said to have resulted in some type of interference with a motor vehicle. The most common type is the CAR STOP case – examples include the LOCH RAVEN, MARYLAND sighting and the intriguing case at LEVELLAND, TEXAS, where it was reported that several cars were affected at the same time. However, motor cars are not the only vehicles that have apparently been subject to such effects.

There are a few cases in which it has been said that motorcycles have suffered similar interference, and some reports have included claims of a tugging sensation apparently pulling both bike and rider forward, as if in the grip of some unseen 'energy beam'.

Reports of interference on ships are extremely rare, but there have been a handful of cases in which it was said that there were problems with sonar or other equipment during UFO sightings. In the TRINDADE ISLAND case an electric winch used to haul lifeboats onto the deck was also said to have stopped operating when a UFO passed overhead.

Aircraft occasionally report problems, although claims of a complete failure of critical systems, resulting in a crash, are almost unknown – the mysterious VALENTICH affair is possibly unique in this respect. Certainly, elsewhere, a direct link between a crash and an apparently hostile act on the part of a UFO has never been alleged. Even in the Mantell case, investigated by PROJECT SIGN, the crash that killed the pilot occurred only because he chased a UFO to an altitude that his aircraft was not designed for.

Claims of effects on an aircraft's electronic systems, leading in loss of radio contact or navigation systems, are more common. In the TEHRAN case the effects were even said to have extended to the blocking of the launch of an air-to-air missile after the pilot had set the procedure in motion.

No clear theory as to the exact nature of the cause of such vehicle interference has been offered. However, there have been some intriguing cases in which it is claimed that the diesel engines in vehicles have continued to run, while the electrical systems have failed, and petrol engines in close proximity to the same sighting have been stopped.

Vennum, Lurancy *see* WATSEKA WONDER

veo

A very large, scaly cryptid reported from the Lesser Sundas in Indonesia.

Rintja is a small isle in Indonesia's Lesser Sundas island group, but it is apparently home to a very sizeable, highly distinctive CRYPTID known as the veo. It is said to be as big as a horse, with large overlapping scales on its back, flanks and long tail, hair on its underparts, huge claws on its feet and a long head. During the day it apparently remains hidden away in the mountains, but it comes down to the coast at night to feed upon ants, termites and any small stranded marine creatures that it discovers. The island's native hunters avoid it whenever possible, because if threatened the veo will allegedly rear up onto its haunches and slash out with its front claws.

This physical description is very reminiscent of a pangolin or scaly anteater, but there is no modern-day species that is anywhere near as big as the size claimed for the veo. However, during the Pleistocene epoch (2 million to 10,000 years ago), a gigantic species of pangolin, *Manis palaeojavanicus*, measuring over 2.5 metres (over 8 feet) long, existed on nearby Java and also Borneo, leading to cryptozoological speculation that perhaps a relict population still survives on remote Rintja.

vernal equinox

The day in the spring when the sun is above the horizon for the same period as it is below the horizon. It is of importance in both ancient and modern pagan spiritual practice.

The vernal equinox, or spring equinox, which generally falls on 21 March in the northern hemisphere, is one of the four minor SABBATS recognized and celebrated as a festival by many modern practitioners of PAGANISM and WITCHCRAFT.

Also known as Ostara and Lady Day, the rituals performed at the vernal equinox often relate to the fertility of the coming crops. Wiccans see it as a time of balance between dark and light, as also experienced at the AUTUMNAL EQUINOX. See also BELTANE; IMBOLC; LUGHNASADH; SAMHAIN; SUMMER SOLSTICE; WICCA; WINTER SOLSTICE.

Virgo

In astrology, the sixth sign of the zodiac, between Leo and Libra.

In Western ASTROLOGY, Virgo is the sign of ZODIAC for those who are born between 24 August and 23 September. The symbol for Virgo is the virgin, and the sign is ruled by Mercury. Virgoans are said to be methodical and analytical, although they may seem cool and reserved. Virgo is believed to be an earth sign, having an affinity with the element EARTH.

vision quest

A Native American ritual that is performed for the purpose of seeing visions, obtaining guidance from the spirit world or finding a guardian spirit.

The vision quest is a traditional rite that was once common throughout the native tribes of North America.

The quest generally involves a period of purification and prayer, followed by an ordeal involving a solitary journey into the wilderness to fast, smoke tobacco and pray. The quest may last for several days – it is hoped by the participant that at the end of this time they will fall into a trance and see visions. Although a vision quest may be made for a number of reasons, they were traditionally particularly important as a rite of passage for adolescent males. During their quest they hoped to find their GUARDIAN SPIRIT (who usually took the form of an animal), to learn the powers that their guardian spirit would give them (and the rules they must follow to keep them) and to receive instructions for putting together a MEDICINE BUNDLE.

Vision quests can be entered into at any time and provide a way for an ordinary individual (as opposed to a MEDICINE MAN) to commune with the spirit world (see MANITOU). Some people, such as BLACK ELK, undertake several vision quests during their lives.

It is believed that similar contact with the spirit world – through trance and visions – may be achieved communally by the participants in rites such as the SUN DANCE.

visions

Mystical or religious experiences of seeing some supernatural being or event.

The mystical or religious experience of visions – the seeing of some supernatural being or event – is common to many cultures, and has been documented since ancient times. In almost all religions, visions are regarded as proceeding from a deity, and are typically inspirational or revelatory. The prophets of the Old and New Testaments were accorded visions from God which were often disclosures of hidden things or of the future, and Jewish and Christian texts which describe visions of the end of the world and the Last Judgement are collectively referred to as apocalypse literature.

Visions are usually described as having more clarity and impression of reality than DREAMS, and frequently accompany other ECSTATIC PHENOMENA. Many people who claim to have experienced STIGMATA also report having visions; the 20th-century stigmatic, St PIO OF PIETRELCINA, was said to have had many religious visions as a youth, and the 16th-century Carmelite mystic, St Teresa of Avila, described one recurring vision she had of Christ being present to her in a physical, though invisible, form, and another in which an angel drove a lance though her heart.

The Spanish mystic St Teresa of Avila claimed to witness many visions in her life. Here, in a stained glass window in a church in Avila, she is depicted with the child Jesus.
(© Mary Evans Picture Library)

There are numerous accounts of one or more people, typically Roman Catholics, receiving visions of the Virgin Mary, which sometimes recur at a particular site over an extended period of time; such sites often become places of pilgrimage at which it is said that MIRACLES such as healing may occur. The most famous locations of MARIAN APPARITIONS include LOURDES and FÁTIMA. It has also been claimed that a number of popes have received visions of the Virgin Mary.

In some Native American cultures, the VISION QUEST is a rite of passage for adolescent males, who fast before journeying alone into the wilderness in the hope of receiving visions.

Some sceptics claim that PSYCHEDELIC DRUGS (including naturally hallucinogenic substances) are responsible for many apparently spiritual visions.

Vissarion (1961–)

The leader of a Siberian messianic movement.
Born Sergei Torop in 1961, Vissarion is the founder and leader of the Church of the Last Testament (also called the Community of Unified Faith), a new religious movement based in southern Siberia. Formerly a metalworker, then a traffic policeman, Vissarion started preaching in 1991, apparently having received a revelation in 1990.

Soft-spoken, smiling, wearing a robe and with a beard and long hair, Vissarion looks like many classic images of Jesus. It has been suggested that this is deliberate, as he claims to be the reincarnation of Jesus and the Messiah for the present day; he claims that he is the living word of God, though he is not God.

He sees Christianity as divided, and that his mission is to finish the job he started 2,000 years ago, a living teacher being necessary in order to unite the people.

In some ways his Church is not so much a religion as a way of life – a social experiment including both communal living and strict vegetarianism. Members eat only what they can grow or find growing: such as potatoes, cabbage, berries, nuts and mushrooms. Members are not allowed to drink alcohol or to smoke. Despite these and many other restrictions, and the harshness of their daily life, the Church has attracted many thousands of followers, largely middle-class professionals, not just from Russia but also from Western Europe.

Voodoo *see* VOUDUN

Voodoo Science

A pejorative term applied to 'scientific' research that it is argued is unscientifc.
In the 1990s, the US physicist Robert L Parks coined the term 'Voodoo Science' to describe the various types of pseudoscience that he encountered daily. In 2000 he published a book called *Voodoo Science: the Road from Foolishness to Fraud* in which he further analysed the phenomenon, showing the danger of scientists travelling the path from self-delusion through deluding others to cynical deception of the ignorant, non-expert public.

According to Parks, Voodoo Science covers a wide spectrum, including 'science' that depends on supernatural explanations, groundless speculation, deliberate fraud and mere mistaken thinking. People promoting pseudoscience tend to give themselves away by characteristically announcing their discoveries directly to the media rather than submitting their work to peer review. They will back up their claims with anecdotal rather than documentary evidence and often protest that there is a conspiracy to suppress their work. They repackage old myths as 'ancient wisdom'. Results reveal effects which are barely detectable, and photos or videos are always blurred and ambiguous. However, the greatest giveaway for Voodoo Science is that its 'findings' contravene the fundamental laws of science as we know it.

Parks castigates pseudoscientists for formulating a theory first and only then looking for evidence to support it. Their experiments are self-fulfilling prophecies and they see only what they want to see. In an article in the US periodical *The Chronicle of Higher Education*, in 2003, Parks said:

> There is, alas, no scientific claim so preposterous that a scientist cannot be found to vouch for it.

Areas in which Parks claims Voodoo Science predominates include TELEPATHY, PARAPSYCHOLOGY, CRYPTOZOOLOGY, ASTROLOGY, NEUROLINGUISTIC PROGRAMMING and any number of NEW AGE beliefs and practices. Parks also condemns UFOLOGY, ALTERNATIVE MEDICINE, EXTRASENSORY PERCEPTION and COLD FUSION, and he believes that manned space travel has no future.

According to Parks, the media, more interested in offering entertainment than information, are much to be blamed for publicizing Voodoo Science. The more fantastic or sensational a 'discovery' is, the more likely it is to generate uncritical column inches and credulously eager television exposure.

Crtics accuse Parks of arrogance, especially in the assumption that the fundamental laws of science cannot be wrong or at least open to revision, and also of being selective in his presentation of evidence. In this way they turn one of his own criticisms back on himself: that he ignores any evidence that does not fit in with his theory. They maintain that it is unscientific to operate with a mind closed to the new and challenging.

Vorilhon, Claude *see* RAELIAN MOVEMENT

Voronezh

The site of a dramatic UFO case from the USSR, which was officially supported by the TASS news agency, included a number of witnesses and featured claims of landing traces and alien encounters.

On 9 October 1989, in the latter days of Communism, a remarkable report was issued by the official news agency of the Soviet Union. The report stated that a UFO landing had occurred in the industrial city of Voronezh, around 480 kilometres (300 miles) south-east of Moscow, and that there were many sightings of the ALIENS that had emerged from the craft. Such was the impact of this statement that the story appeared in heavyweight newspapers and television news broadcasts across the world. TASS were asked to confirm that the report was serious – a spokesman replied, as if offended, 'TASS never jokes!'

The initial claim was that a UFO shaped like a banana had landed in a park and that dozens of local citizens had seen it and witnessed the peculiar entities that emerged. The beings were apparently approximately 3 metres (10 feet) tall but had disproportionately tiny heads. This description was unlike any found in reports of previous CLOSE ENCOUNTER cases outside the USSR. The TASS report went on to say that LANDING TRACES had been discovered, and that odd rocks found in the park were being studied by scientists.

The case prompted an editorial in the *New York Times* in which it was speculated that this might be 'the story of the century', adding that scepticism, while understandable, might just be the easy way out. However, as is so often the case, the story faded away, becoming old news, before UFO researchers eventually discovered the truth.

It transpired that the story had reached TASS via a Russian UFO investigator – a fact that might have produced a much more muted response had it been known from the start by the Western media. The Soviets had a long history of treating UFO evidence with more interest than governments in the UK or USA – teams of scientists and astronauts had been engaged in research since the 1960s. They were also believed to use UFO reports as a 'smokescreen' for military rocket launches – allowing the observation of covert space missions by their own citizens to be misreported as UFO sightings.

The true story behind the Voronezh incident was indeed odd. There was a major WAVE of UFO sightings centred on the city during September and October, leading to local skywatches (see SKYWATCHING) attracting over 300 people. Many of the witnesses were local schoolchildren, who gave vivid descriptions of various robots and assorted monsters that appeared from hovering balls of light.

The most useful account from the time came from Dr Henry Silanov, a spectrum analyst at the geophysical laboratory attached to the local university. He investigated the landings and said:

> In the period between 21 September and 28 October 1989, in the Western Park of Voronezh, six landings and one sighting (hovering) were registered, with the appearance of walking beings … We have no doubts that they (the children) are telling the truth in their accounts, because details of the landings and other signs are recounted by the children, who could otherwise have only got this information from specialist UFO literature which is not publicized in our country.

The incident that formed the basis of the TASS report appears to be one of the first sightings, which occurred on 21 September. A group of children playing football apparently saw a pink mist, out of which emerged a red ball of fire. By now all of the people nearby were watching as the spherical object shot from the mist into the air and landed in the top of a tree, causing it to bend beneath the weight. Many of the observers fled at this point, but several youngsters hid in bushes and later claimed that they had seen a tall, silvery figure emerge from a door that appeared in the side of the UFO. The entity started to climb down from the tree and fired a beam of light from a small tube at a man who was hurrying past in the road outside the park. The beam struck him and he vanished. The entity then scrambled back into the UFO before it took off at speed. As soon as the UFO had gone the man in the street reappeared, in mid-stride, and carried on walking as if nothing had happened in the intervening minutes.

An interesting feature of two of the sightings during this wave is that witnesses described seeing a symbol on the underside of the UFO. This symbol was the astrological symbol for the planet Uranus – a mark associated with the long-running UMMO saga, widely believed to be a hoax.

What about the rocks found at the landing site and studied by Silanov? TASS stated that the mineralogical analysis had revealed that the specimens were of non-terrestrial origin. However, Silanov told British UFO researchers that the rocks were ordinary iron-rich ore. This would also offer an explanation for the magnetic anomaly noted at the site. TASS also reported claims that abnormal levels of radiation had been recorded in Western Park after the landings, but studies had actually found that this was concentrated in indentations in the ground. In the wake of the massive radiation leak at Chernobyl in April 1986 similar effects were being detected all over Europe – radioactive material was gradually accumulating in such indentations partly due to the effect of rainfall.

Once investigated, this apparently remarkable case became much less clear-cut. The story ended in a manner that epitomized the transition from Communism to capitalism within the USSR – the public were offered tours of the UFO landing site, complete with lectures by experts, for a fee of 59 roubles.

vortices

Hypothetical conduits of 'energy' at points on the earth's surface.

Among the NEW AGE beliefs that have arisen around interpretations of the concept of LEYS is the idea that 'energy' is transmitted along them, coming to focal points on the earth's surface called 'vortices'. Energy is said to flow either into or out of the earth in these places: a point at which energy is leaving the earth is called a 'masculine vortex', and one where it is said to be entering the earth is called a 'feminine vortex'. The word 'vortex' describes the whirlwind or whirlpool-like flow of energy that is believed to occur.

Believers ascribe a variety of different properties to such vortices – some are said to promote healing or meditation and others are credited with giving energy to pursue one's goals or take action. It is claimed that buildings erected over vortices fall victim to 'negative energy', and this has been offered as an explanation for so-called 'sick building syndrome'. It has even been suggested that vortices may be connections between different areas in space-time, or even different dimensions and that if they are harnessed they may make space travel much easier.

Needless to say, sceptics would argue that we still await convincing evidence of the very existence of vortices of this type before we can even begin to consider such extravagant claims.

Voudun

The Haitian Africa-American religion usually incorrectly called Voodoo.

It has often been said that Voodoo does not exist outside of Hollywood, either in its name or in many of its supposed practices. The spelling has many variants, but Vodou, Vodun, Vodoun and Voudun are generally accepted as the most accurate.

Broadly speaking, Voudun is the Haitian equivalent of the Caribbean religion SANTERÍA and the Brazilian religion CANDOMBLÉ. Because of its popular corruption in films as Voodoo it has become the best known, and some people use it wrongly as a generic term for all Central or South American religions that blend African beliefs with Roman Catholicism.

Voudun originally emerged in the plantations of the French colony of Saint-Domingue, partly as a protest against the brutal treatment of slaves. Because it was illegal to practise it, Voudun has always had an anti-establishment nature, with more than a tinge of political resistance – and, inevitably, of secrecy.

The African elements of the religion are largely from Yoruba, Fon and Kongo origins, and include ancestor veneration and dealing with spirits. There is a single creator God, Bondyé, and many spiritual beings; the Dahoman word *voduns* means 'lesser deities, spirits'. Roman Catholicism is a religion rich with imagery, particularly of Mary and the other saints; these were readily co-opted into Voudun as powerful spiritual beings who could be approached and asked to intervene in earthly matters.

Trained practitioners (not strictly speaking priests, and certainly not witch doctors) are called *oungan* or *hungan* (male) and *manbo* or *mambo* (female). They use divination or spirit possession to communicate with the dead (*lemo*) or with powerful protective spirits (*lwas* or *loas*). During a ritual loas will possess or 'mount' participants or 'horses', either speaking through them or causing them to behave in unusual ways – laughing, joking, dancing, singing – specific to each loa.

Voudun magic is usually used for protection, for healing or for love potions, though harmful magic is also sometimes attempted. Magical charms, herbs and other ingredients are kept in a mojo bag or *gris-gris*. So-called voodoo dolls are part of the popular misperception of the religion, and have nothing to do with genuine Voudun.

Voudun is widely practised throughout Haiti; it has also spread to the Dominican Republic, Cuba, and parts of the USA, particularly New Orleans.

waheela

A huge snow-white wolf-like cryptid reported from northern Alaska and Canada.

Also known as the great white wolf, the waheela is said to inhabit the snowy tundra regions of Canada's Northwest Territories, northern Alaska and northern Michigan. As its English name suggests, it is said that superficially it resembles a giant burly wolf, but its pure-white shaggy fur is extremely dense, its limbs are proportionately shorter than those of a wolf (with its front limbs long in comparison to its hind legs), its head is noticeably large and broad though its ears are very small, its tail is very thick, and its feet are markedly splayed, yielding tracks that are lupine but up to 20.3 centimetres (8 inches) across. Apparently, one of these CRYPTIDS was encountered and shot at twice by a hunter friend of cryptozoologist Ivan T Sanderson, while he was tracking along a tributary of the Nahanni Valley in the Northwest Territories during the 1940s or 1950s, but the creature merely moved off, apparently unharmed. Moreover, whereas normal wolves are pack-hunters, waheelas are said to be solitary hunters.

If not based upon sightings of exceptionally large, totally white male wolves adrift from their packs, it has been suggested that the waheela may actually be a surviving species of bear-dog or *Amphicyonid*. Very large bear-like carnivores but with wolf-like heads, they supposedly died out several million years ago in North America, but in the inhospitable tundra terrain rarely explored or traversed by humans, perhaps a relict species, adapted for existence in this bleak habitat, has survived, and is still occasionally spied by the more intrepid Inuit or Western tracker.

Waite, A(rthur) E(dward) (1857–1942)

Important writer on Rosicrucianism, Freemasonry, kabbalah and the tarot.

A E Waite was born in the USA but lived most of his life in England. His name is most widely known in connection with the Rider-Waite TAROT, published by the London publisher Rider & Company, designed by Waite, and painted by Pamela Colman Smith. Within esoteric circles, however, he is known mainly as a writer on and historian of esoteric organizations.

Waite joined the magical teaching order the HERMETIC ORDER OF THE GOLDEN DAWN in 1891; he left shortly afterwards, but rejoined in 1896, and entered the inner Second Order in 1899. He became a Freemason in 1901, and joined the Golden Dawn's 'parent' organization within FREEMASONRY, the *Societas Rosicruciana in Anglia*, in 1902.

When the Golden Dawn fragmented between 1900 and 1903 three main splinter groups formed. A few members loyal to MACGREGOR MATHERS became the Alpha et Omega Temple; more significantly, those continuing the magical research and teaching of the Golden Dawn formed the Order of the Stella Matutina, led initially by the poet W B Yeats (see ISRAEL REGARDIE and WESTERN MYSTERY TRADITION). Waite and a large group of similarly minded members managed to retain ownership of the Golden Dawn's Isis-Urania Temple and vault in London, and formed the Independent and Rectified Rite of the Golden Dawn (also known as the Holy Order of the Golden Dawn), and later the Fellowship of the Rosy Cross. Led by Waite, these groups abandoned magical work, changing the emphasis to mystical Christianity. Among the members of Waite's order were the mystic

Four cards from the Rider-Waite tarot. (© TopFoto)

Evelyn Underhill and the occult fiction writers Arthur Machen and Charles Williams.

Waite wrote several significant works on ROSICRUCIANISM, Freemasonry and the KABBALAH, as well as his more popular books on the tarot, and translated books by the French occultist ÉLIPHAS LÉVI. Some readers criticize him for his heavy, pedantic writing style, but this disguises a very dry humour, seen most clearly in the ultra-polite but utterly devastating way he puts down many other writers in the field for their poor scholarship; Waite did not suffer fools gladly.

One of Waite's shortest but most important contributions to esoteric scholarship was *Devil-Worship in France* (1896), in which he disproved the supposed revelations by 'Leo Taxil' (Gabriel Jogand), of Palladism or Palladian Freemasonry, involving sexual and Satanic rites. (Despite this, and Jogand's subsequent confession, some Christian anti-masonic writers today still quote Taxil's fiction as fact.)

waitoreke

A mystifying four-footed, allegedly native mammal reported from New Zealand.

Long before the evolution of most of the major types of mammal known to science from fossils or from living forms, New Zealand separated from all other land. Except for two species of bat, New Zealand consequently has no native mammals – which makes the waitoreke a particularly puzzling creature.

According to Maori lore, the waitoreke is an otter-like beast that is 1 metre (around 3 feet) long, has brown fur and a flattened tail, and has been present in New Zealand since well before the arrival of the first European explorers and settlers (who brought with them many European mammals that have since become established there). While the ancestors of New Zealand's native bats were able to reach the country by air, it would have been very difficult for any early flightless mammal to have arrived from elsewhere, as the only means of doing so would have been to swim across a considerable expanse of ocean, containing all manner of predatory, carnivorous animals. Assuming that even some of the numerous eyewitness accounts of waitorekes are indeed genuine, and that this beast is not some introduced species of European mammal, what could it be? Some believe that recent fossil evidence shows that one group of mammals may have evolved early enough to have reached New Zealand on foot, before it broke away from the other land masses.

These mammals are the egg-laying monotremes, represented today by Australia's famous duck-billed platypus and the spiny anteaters or echidnas of Australia and New Guinea. Perhaps the monotremes invaded New Zealand too, and the waitoreke is a modern-day descendant. Intriguingly, the male platypus possesses a pair of distinctive spurs on its hind feet, and one translation of the name 'waitoreke' is 'spurred water-diver', which may allude to this cryptid's tendency to dive underwater when observed and also to it having spurred feet.

waking dreams *see* DREAMS, WAKING

waking impressions

Things perceived while awake that later reappear in dreams.

The interpretation of DREAMS has been of interest to humankind for thousands of years. One idea that constantly recurs is that in dreams we are replaying waking impressions, things that we have seen, heard, tasted or otherwise perceived while awake. While we may not have consciously seized on these experiences as particularly remarkable, they have been absorbed on a deeper level of consciousness that releases them when we are dreaming. Such impressions are also said to be brought to the surface of the mind by HYPNOSIS.

The term 'waking impression' is also sometimes applied to a flash of intuition or a 'hunch'. We have all experienced occasions when we seem to know something instinctively, or become convinced of the truth of something without thinking deeply or analysing it. Some say that this phenomenon is a relatively minor form of EXTRASENSORY PERCEPTION. On the other hand, it has been explained in the same way as dreams, in that we are simply dredging up and connecting ideas or thoughts that we have stored at a subconscious level.

Walpurgisnacht

A festival celebrated on 30 April (the eve of May Day) in the Germanic countries of Northern Europe. Since the Middle Ages it has been associated with magic, witchcraft and evil.

Walpurgisnacht (or Walpurgis Night) takes its name from St Walburga, an 8th-century nun from the Anglo-Saxon kingdom of Wessex who died in Franconia in Germany in 779. The connection with her is coincidental: 30 April happens to be the eve of the day in 870 when her remains were transferred to Eichstätt, to a new church built in her honour. There may also be some confusion with Waldborg, a pagan fertility goddess. The name was attached to a much older festival of pagan origins, associated with fertility and the spring (see BELTANE).

Within Germanic cultures the festival has similar associations to those of HALLOWE'EN. In the Middle Ages it was considered to be a night when WITCHES flew on their BROOMSTICKS to SABBATS where they feasted and danced with the DEVIL. The most famous annual meeting of witches was said to occur on the Brocken in the Hartz mountains in Germany – indeed, in Germany Walpurgisnacht is also known as Hexennacht (Witches' Night).

Walton, Travis

US forestry worker who disappeared for five days after seeing a UFO. On his return he claimed that he had been held captive by aliens.

Travis Walton was a member of a seven-man team of forestry workers who were logging in the Sitgreave National Forest near the small town of Snowflake, Arizona, on 5 November 1975. At around 6.10pm they were returning home by truck when they apparently saw a strange object in the sky through the forest. They described it as 'two pie cans stuck together', glowing a yellowish white. The leader of the team, Mike Rogers, pulled the truck to a halt in

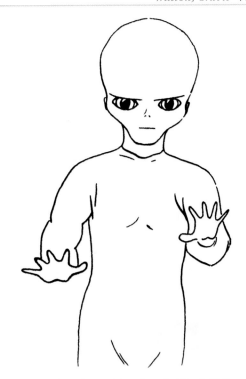

A depiction of one of the aliens that Travis Walton claimed had abducted him, drawn from his descriptions.
(© TopFoto/Fortean)

a clearing so that they could watch the object. The UFO emitted beeping sounds and then a beam of blue LIGHT shot out and hit Travis Walton, who had left the truck to go into the trees for a closer look. Walton was thrown into the air and fell backwards to the ground, as if hit by lightning.

Apparently thinking that Walton was dead, his workmates drove away but then felt that they should go back to help him. On their return they found that he had vanished, as had the UFO. They drove to the nearest town to report the incident. The local sheriff was not convinced and ordered them to take a lie detector test. Five agreed, and all passed, upon which a massive search for the missing woodsman began. No trace of him was discovered and, for a brief period, there was suspicion that his fellow workers had been involved in his disappearance, or even his murder.

However, after five days, Walton telephoned his family from a phone booth in the nearby town of Heber. He said that he was back but that he had only a hazy recall of what had happened after he was struck by the beam of light from the UFO. Over the days that followed further details apparently returned to him. He claimed that he had been in the presence of small beings who were 'like a crowd of well-developed foetuses' and one man of human appearance. He said that he had been shown a room like a planetarium and a space where a landed UFO was situated. The beings had then performed a medical examination, put a mask over his face and he could remember nothing more until he awoke on the road in Heber.

This case divided opinion among both the UFO COMMUNITY and the media. Some people supported Walton and his six colleagues, who all stood by the story, noting that it had similarities with other ALIEN ABDUCTION cases. Walton also later passed a lie detector test and many people who have met him have found him to be convincing. Others pointed to the fact that a television movie of the BETTY AND BARNEY HILL abduction case had been broadcast shortly before the alleged sighting, and that the film included features, such as the beeping noise, reported by the loggers. There were also claims that the men were running late on a logging contract and faced major penalty clauses – a suggestion that they strongly denied.

In 1993, the case became the subject of a Hollywood dramatization in the film *Fire in the Sky*.

wand

A rod used as a ritual tool in Wicca, neopaganism and ceremonial magic.

The wand is one of the best-known symbols associated with the witch or wizard in folklore. It is an important ritual tool in WICCA, NEOPAGANISM and ceremonial magic (see MAGIC, CEREMONIAL). The wand is traditionally handcrafted, if possible by the person who is going to use it. It is usually made from the living branch of a tree which has been ceremonially cut after asking the tree's permission, although long, clear quartz crystals which are pointed at one end are also popularly used as wands. Different trees are said to have different powers, so the choice of wood from which the wand is made may depend on the qualities which the magician wishes the wand to have; for example, holly is thought to be protective, and oak is associated with wisdom. The wand may also have a small crystal attached to the tip, or be personalized and decorated with runes, feathers and other items of symbolic significance to the magician.

The wand usually symbolizes the element of FIRE, and all that this element signifies – passion, vigour, sexual energy and enterprising spirit – although in some traditions, it is thought to be the ritual tool of AIR, and is interchangeable with the athame or ritual knife, and the SWORD. It is usually placed in the south of the altar during rituals, the south being the direction associated with the element of fire. It is used to direct energies, to draw magic circles and to trace PENTAGRAMS in the air, and is thought especially appropriate for rites involving love, healing, fertility, prosperity and abundance.

The wand's importance as a magical symbol is demonstrated by the fact that one of the suits of the TAROT is the suit of wands (see WANDS, SUIT OF).

wandering bishops

Self-styled 'bishops', some members of small denominations, some effectively solo, outside the recognized episcopal Christian denominations.

'Wandering bishops' and its Latin equivalent, *episcopi vagantes*, are slightly pejorative terms applied to people who have been consecrated as bishops outside the established denominations of the Roman Catholic, Orthodox and Anglican/Episcopalian Churches. Wandering bishops claim to have the full rights and powers of 'established' bishops, through the apostolic succession.

The apostolic succession is the derivation of holy orders by unbroken chain of transmission from the Apostles through bishops. In most cases, the line is thought to go back to Peter, supposedly the first Bishop of Rome and hence counted as the first pope, but there are ancient Churches around the Mediterranean and elsewhere that trace their line back to other apostles. (Whether such an unbroken link actually exists in reality is uncertain, but the symbolism of the apostolic succession is very powerful.)

Once someone has been consecrated a bishop that cannot be taken away from them, even if they leave or are expelled from their Church. Over the centuries there have been several schisms in the Roman Catholic Church, when bishops have left, taking their powers with them, and thus able to pass on the apostolic succession to others. So far as the Roman Catholic Church is concerned, such ordinations and consecrations are 'valid but illegal', hence another term for those consecrated in this way, 'bishops irregular'.

Today's wandering bishops, whether they are in organized denominations or effectively one-man-bands, trace their apostolic succession through several lines. Many, like the LIBERAL CATHOLIC CHURCH and its offshoots, go back through Bishop Arnold Harris Mathew (1852–1919) to the Old Catholic Church of Utrecht which split from Rome in 1870 in protest against the new doctrine of papal infallibility; they had no bishops themselves, but gained episcopal orders from a Dutch Jansenist bishop; the Jansenists, named after Cornelius Jansen (1585–1638), Bishop of Ypres, had separated from Rome in the mid-17th century. In the Netherlands, the Old Catholic Church is a significant and respected denomination, and does not itself usually come under the label of *episcopi vagantes*. However, its many offshoots, including a variety of Old Catholic Churches in the USA, do.

Two other major lines come through Bishop Jules Ferrette (1828–1904), who claimed a consecration from the Jacobite or Syrian Orthodox Church; and Joseph Villatte (1854–1929), who was consecrated by the Independent Catholic Church of Ceylon. Villatte's line lies behind many independent Episcopal Churches in the USA.

Ferrette's consecration is in some considerable doubt – he never provided proof of it – but it points up another complication in both the origins of lines and the multiplicity of independent episcopal Churches today: the Orthodox connection. Although we generally think of only the Greek Orthodox Church and the Russian Orthodox Church, both of these have produced offshoots, and there are also Orthodox Churches, some very ancient, with little or no historical connection with either of them. Some of these have been less than careful in whom they have consecrated over the years. Today, as well as the many Old Catholic, Liberal Catholic, Independent Catholic (etc) Churches, there is also a multiplicity of independent Orthodox Churches – Britain alone has several – many of them with as many bishops as priests, and more priests than members. With Catholic, Orthodox, Independent, Old, New, Liberal, Apostolic, and so on, the permutations of names are almost endless.

The names are no indication of the nature of the Churches. Some, like the Liberal Catholic Church, have esoteric beliefs; others are liberal in the sense of welcoming gay clergy and female bishops. Some, like the original Old Catholics, are more traditionalist than the Roman Catholic Church. In recent years in Britain and the USA, traditionalist clergy have left the Anglican Church in protest against new liturgy or women priests; some are currently seeking an independent alliance with the Roman Catholic Church.

And there are other individuals, with few if any followers, who collect consecrations from wherever they may find them, and who will consecrate whoever asks them. These are the true wandering bishops.

Wandering Jew

A Jew who according to Christian legend mocked Jesus on his way to Calvary, and as a punishment is condemned to wander the earth until the Second Coming.

The earliest written reference to the legend of the Wandering Jew is in the medieval English chronicler Roger of Wendover's *Flores Historiarum* (1228). In this version of the story, which was said to have come from an Armenian archbishop who claimed to have seen him in person, the Wandering Jew was a shoemaker called Cartaphilus who taunted and struck Jesus on his way to the Crucifixion and urged him to keep moving when he stopped for a rest. Jesus cursed him, saying, 'I will stand and rest, but you will go on until the last day', thus condemning him to travel the earth without hope of rest until the Second Coming. In 1602, the legend was published in a German pamphlet which brought it to the attention of the general public, and with its figure of a doomed sinner forced to wander without respite, it captured the popular imagination, spreading quickly through Germany and on to the rest of Europe. In this version the Jew is called Ahasuerus, the name by which he subsequently became best known, and the pamphlet quotes the line from Matthew 16:28 which some people believe is the origin of the story:

> Verily I say unto you, there be some standing here, which shall not taste of death, till they see the Son of Man coming in his kingdom.

The anti-Semitism prevalent in the Middle Ages helped to increase the popularity of the legend, and in most tellings of the story, the Wandering Jew is baptized as a Christian in the hope of receiving salvation. In the Italian version he is known as Giovanni Buttadeus ('strike God'), and to the Spanish he is Juan Espera en Dios ('John Hope-for-God'). He became a staple figure of the Christian oral and literary tradition, and sightings of him have been claimed throughout the centuries, most frequently during the Middle Ages, when he was said to have been seen in Armenia, Poland, Moscow and virtually every western European city including London. His legend has been the subject of many poems, short stories and books, including science fiction and graphic novels, as well as several films.

wands, suit of

One of the four suits into which the cards of the tarot's minor arcana are divided.

The suit of wands in the tarot is also known as the suit of batons, suit of rods or suit of sceptres. It contains 14 cards: numbered 'pip' cards going from one to ten, plus four 'court' cards – the Page, the Knight, the King and the Queen. Some people believe that the four suit emblems may originally have symbolized the four main social classes in medieval Europe, with the wands representing the peasants, who worked in the fields and woods. Astrologically, this suit is associated with the element of FIRE, and the three fire signs, ARIES, LEO and SAGITTARIUS. Corresponding to the suit of clubs in a modern deck of playing cards, the suit of wands is identified with career or work-related matters, enterprise and ambition. Characteristics associated with this suit are creativity, energy, enthusiasm and optimism. See also CUPS, SUIT OF; PENTACLES, SUIT OF; SWORDS, SUIT OF.

warlocks

Men who practise black magic, sorcerers; often also used of a male witch.

The word 'warlock' has been used in various senses throughout the centuries, most of them pejorative. In its original Old English form, *waerloga*, it referred to an oath-breaker or traitor, and from about 1000 to 1500 it was a general term for any wicked person or scoundrel. However, during this time it was also used to refer to the DEVIL, or a demon or spirit of Hell, and by extension, to any savage or monstrous creature, such as a giant or cannibal. From the 14th century onwards it had taken on the more familiar sense of a person who was in league with the Devil and was possessed of occult and evil powers – a SORCERER or WIZARD. In this context, it was used as the male equivalent of 'witch', and like 'witch', it had highly negative connotations in the Middle Ages. In medieval times, warlocks were thought to ride pitchforks or cats in the same way that WITCHES were said to ride BROOMSTICKS. The use of 'warlock' to mean 'male witch' or 'sorcerer' persists to this day, but the word has never been used in this way by modern Wiccans, for whom 'witch' refers to both male and female practitioners; to Wiccans, the word has a meaning very close to its original Old English one, and is used of a person who has broken his oath of trust to his COVEN, and has as a result been ostracized by his magical community. The term is considered offensive by most male witches.

Another theory for the etymology of the word is that it derived from the Norse *vardlokkur*, meaning a man who had the power to bind spirits by means of runes and knot magic.

War of the Worlds, The

Fictional tale of a Martian invasion of earth.

In 1898, the English writer H G Wells (1866–1946) published his science-fiction novel *The War of the Worlds*. It tells the story of a Martian invasion, with rockets landing on earth to unleash fearsomely destructive war machines that quickly overcome human resistance and destroy major cities including London. Survivors living in hiding dream of fighting back but in the end the Martians are killed off by bacteria, to which they have no natural resistance.

The novel became the archetype for many more 'alien invasion' stories in science fiction, but one of its more interesting offshoots was the radio adaptation of it broadcast on 30 October 1938 by the US film director and actor Orson Welles (1915–85). The action was transposed from England to the USA

Orson Welles performing in the famous 1938 broadcast of *The War of the Worlds*. (© TopFoto/Fortean)

(New Jersey), and updated to the current year, and the use of mock news bulletins within the broadcast was so convincingly real that a major panic was caused among listeners who thought the invasion was actually happening. Many people took to the roads in their cars, heading away from cities; others wrapped wet towels around their heads as protection against gas attacks or barricaded themselves in basements to await the end of the world.

Welles had not intend to deceive the audience and had prefaced the performance with an announcement that it was a radio play by the Mercury Theatre, but those tuning in part of the way through would not have been aware of this or his final out-of-character speech in which he reminded listeners that the next night would be HALLOWE'EN. Over the next few days Welles was pilloried in the press and received death threats from members of the public who had recovered enough from their fright to become angry. He felt obliged to apologize, albeit with incomplete repentance, in a newsreel broadcast.

The USA was the setting for the next major adaptation of the novel, this time in a film made in 1953, directed by Byron Haskin (1899–1984) and starring Gene Barry (1919–). In this case the aliens landed in the Midwest. Their spacecraft took the classic FLYING SAUCER shape, perhaps tapping into the contemporary UFO craze. The movie was not an unqualified success, being praised for its spectacular scenes of battle, including an unsuccessful nuclear attack on the Martians, less so for the acting performances.

Another film version was released in 2005, this time directed by Steven Spielberg (1946–) and starring Tom Cruise (1962–), with a cameo appearance by Gene Barry. Again set in the USA, it followed Welles in locating the action in New Jersey, and its use of computer-generated imaging allowed its portrayal of Martians and their deadly weapons to be more impressive than ever. The film was a great box-office, but not a critical, success.

Washington DC wave

Possibly the most influential flurry of UFO sightings ever, in which incidents were reported from the heart of the US capital, including apparent invasions of restricted air space, causing a stir at government level.

By the summer of 1952 it was beginning to be recognized that UFO sightings sometimes come in WAVES. However, no spate of sightings had as much impact as the one that occurred that year in Washington DC. It had a dramatic effect on the official study of the UFO phenomenon on both sides of the Atlantic.

The wave began in May when a top CIA operative was holding a garden party at his home in Langley, Virginia. A strange light apparently appeared in the sky, flew directly over the assembled influential guests and then treated them to an air display. At this time Captain EDWARD J RUPPELT had just taken over the newly renamed PROJECT BLUE BOOK, and he flew straight to Washington to investigate the case. He could find no explanation, but was astonished to discover that CIA analysts thought the sighting was only the precursor of a coming wave. Ruppelt was not told why they thought this, but the statement proved correct. By early July the rise in sightings was noticeable, and by the middle of the month the floodgates appeared to have opened.

On 14 July, a Pan American flight passing over Washington on its way to Miami encountered a series of lights that danced about the sky with a peculiar motion. Within a few days the radar systems at both civilian and military facilities controlling this high-security air space started to pick up unusual targets. On the night of 19 July, three separate systems recorded these objects, often at the same time, moving slowly. They then began to speed across the sky at incredible speeds. Experienced air traffic controllers were horrified when the targets began to appear over the White House and the Capitol buildings – an area in which air traffic was banned. Various lights were seen by aircraft passing through the area in the early

hours of that morning, but the Pentagon responded only slowly to repeated calls for an interceptor aircraft to be sent up to investigate. By the time one fighter did get there, three hours later, the UFOs had gone – the last one apparently vanished from the radar only moments before the jet arrived.

By chance, Ruppelt was in Washington the next day. He attempted to investigate after discovering the reports in the press but received no help from the Pentagon. They declined his request for transport to interview witnesses and later ordered him to return to his home base with crucial interviews still to be conducted. He was not to know at the time that the Washington wave was being investigated at a higher level – the CIA had been involved in the situation, amid fears that the wave might be used as a camouflage tactic for a Soviet invasion.

A week later there were further sightings and radar traces. However, Ruppelt only found out about these new incidents when reporters started calling asking him what Project Blue Book was doing. 'Probably nothing' was his frustrated reply. Nevertheless Ruppelt ensured that one of his team went straight to the air traffic control tower at Washington airport, where he saw the targets for himself. As jet interceptors arrived (this time more promptly) all non-military personnel were removed from the airport. The Project Blue Book officer felt sure that this would be the night when the alien nature of UFOs would finally be proven. The jet fighters played cat-and-mouse with the radar targets and occasional lights darting about the sky for a number of hours. It seemed that as soon as they were sent towards a UFO it vanished, then reappeared somewhere else. One interceptor got a radar lock and a close visual sighting of a light but it apparently shot away at an incredible speed as he gave chase.

Two days later what was then the largest ever peacetime press conference was held. The official line was that the radar targets and UFOs were all caused by the weather creating an effect known as a temperature inversion. This can distort the image of stars to make them appear to move across the sky and can produce the strange effects on radar screens known to operatives as 'angels'. However, the radar experts involved in this case were not convinced by this theory, as became clear 15 years later when they were interviewed by the team from the COLORADO UNIVERSITY STUDY. Nevertheless there have been other cases since 1952 where similar UFO incidents have been known to have been produced by temperature inversions and, at the time of the Washington wave, radar was more prone such effects than it is now.

Whatever the cause, the fact that a series of sightings of this type could occur in a highly sensitive location changed official US policy with regard to

UFOs and precipitated Ruppelt's exit from Project Blue Book. It also alerted the British prime minister WINSTON CHURCHILL to the significance of the UFO phenomenon and led to the imposition of restrictions on the publication of UFO sightings made by military witnesses in the UK. See also GOVERNMENTAL COVER-UP.

water

One of the four elements believed in ancient and medieval cosmology to be the fundamental components of all things; of prime importance in magic and the occult.

In ancient and medieval philosophy and alchemy, all things were believed to be composed of a blend of four classical ELEMENTS: AIR, FIRE, EARTH and water. These four elements are central to magical and occult thought. Water is seen as the realm of the emotions, the subconscious, psychic powers, dreams, visions and constant change. The power of water may be called on for assistance in spells or rituals involving emotional healing, friendships, love, marriage and purification. It is associated with the west, the season of Autumn, middle age, dusk and the colour blue, and is thought to be a feminine element, since it is cold, wet and passive. Water governs the zodiacal signs of CANCER, SCORPIO and PISCES, and is connected with the Moon and the planet Neptune. In the TAROT, it is represented by the suit of cups (see CUPS, SUIT OF). In the casting of a MAGIC CIRCLE, it is frequently symbolized in physical form by a bowl of water, and is associated with the magical tools of the CUP or chalice, and the CAULDRON. Its position in the five-pointed star or PENTAGRAM is the upper right point. The four fluids known as humours, which were once popularly believed to permeate the human body and determine the temperament, were each associated with an element, and water was associated with the humour of phlegm. Water is said to be governed by the archangel Gabriel, and its specific animating spirit or ELEMENTAL is the Undine. Water is the element of rivers, oceans, lakes, wells, fog and rain. See also WATER, CURIOUS PROPERTIES OF.

water, cars running on

Many inventors claim to have made a technological breakthrough that allows cars to be run on water instead of petrol.

An early example of someone who claimed to have discovered the technology that would allow a car to be run on water was the Dallas inventor C H Garrett, who gave a demonstration in 1935. A gallon of water was drawn from a lake and poured into his car. The car was then driven around the lake, apparently using only the lake water for fuel. Like many subsequent inventors, Garrett claimed his invention worked by electrolysing the water – using electricity to split it into hydrogen and oxygen – and then burning the hydrogen instead of petrol vapour in the engine.

The problem with this type of invention is that the energy required to split a water molecule is exactly the same as that released when the hydrogen and oxygen join together to form it. Even if the device were 100 per cent efficient, which is impossible in practice, the net output of energy would be zero. It is a form of PERPETUAL MOTION and thus impossible according to the laws of thermodynamics.

This has not stopped many inventors from attempting to create an engine which runs on water, and there have been many rumours about such engines. According to popular mythology, the invention always disappears because the patent is bought up or suppressed by powerful oil companies protecting their business.

More recently, research into alternative fuels has focused on cars powered by fuel cells which burn hydrogen and oxygen, and these are sometimes described as 'running on water'. However, it is freely acknowledged that a power source is needed to produce the hydrogen in the first place, and the fuel cell is simply a highly efficient battery.

water, curious properties of

Properties ascribed to different varieties of water.

Water makes up a large proportion of the earth's surface. Essential for life as we know it, it is present in all living organisms. Apart from the water we drink, wash with or sail over, there are different varieties of water to which curious properties are ascribed.

One of these is polywater, a supposed polymer of water said to behave in ways markedly different from that of ordinary water. In the late 1960s, scientists working in the Soviet Union claimed to have produced a condensed, viscous form of water with a higher boiling point and lower freezing point than plain water. However, when attempts were made in the West to reproduce this substance none were successful. The scientific consensus was that this water was not anomalous at all but simply contaminated with enough traces of other substances to affect its behaviour.

Some believe that water has 'memory', specifically the power to retain a memory of substances that were once dissolved in it. This belief is found in HOMEOPATHY, which treats patients with highly diluted forms of remedies. The French immunologist Jacques Benveniste (1935–2004) claimed in 1988 that he had scientifically identified the phenomenon of the memory of water, but subsequent attempts to duplicate his experiments failed and his work was discredited. Most scientists continue to assert

Holy water has long been associated with religious practices. Here a Russian orthodox priest sprays holy water onto a group of schoolchildren. (© Reuters/Corbis)

that purified water is pure, no matter what it once contained.

Holy water is water that has been blessed by a priest for religious uses. As the natural agent of cleansing, water has been associated with religious practices throughout recorded history. According to the Roman Catholic Church, water has been used for purification and expiation since the earliest days of Christianity, especially in the rite of baptism. Fonts of holy water were introduced into Christian churches so that worshippers could be blessed with it as they entered. It is used in various sacraments, from benedictions to services for the dead. Many Catholics keep small quantities of consecrated water at home, using it primarily in blessing themselves.

In some faiths, water associated with holy places or people is credited with miraculous powers. Water from HOLY WELLS, or from the Catholic shrine at LOURDES, for example, is believed by the faithful to have healing powers. The concept of 'miracle water' which can cure various ills is one that has long been used by evangelists, revivalists, faith healers and downright quacks.

Water is, of course, along with AIR, FIRE and EARTH, one of the four ELEMENTS believed from ancient times to be the foundation of everything in the world, including the makeup of the human body. In the medieval theory of the humours, water is associated with phlegm. In ASTROLOGY, there are three signs of the ZODIAC that are believed to have an affinity with water (water signs): CANCER, SCORPIO and PISCES. People born under these signs are supposed to be particularly sensitive and intuitive.

water monsters *see* LAKE MONSTERS; SEA SERPENTS

Watkins, Alfred *see* LEYS

Watseka Wonder, the

The name by which Lurancy Vennum, an American teenager who was allegedly possessed by a series of spirits, came to be known.

Lurancy Vennum lived in the town of Watseka, Illinois. From July 1877, when she was 13 years old, she apparently fell into a series of trances and suffered from a complete change of personality. At times she was quiet and sullen, and on other occasions she reported ecstatic visions. She was heard to speak in a variety of voices and to converse with 'angels' or the SPIRITS of the dead. Within a few months her parents were considering having her committed to an asylum. In January 1878, Vennum was visited by Dr E W Stevens, a medical practitioner and spiritualist, at the suggestion of one Mr Roff. Roff had heard of Vennum's condition, and believed that she did indeed communicate with the spirits, as he believed his own dead daughter, Mary, had done. Vennum was initially quite violent towards Dr Stevens and warned him to stay away from her, but she later revealed to him that she was actually several different people. It was claimed that Vennum was possessed by, among others, a 63-year-old woman called Katrina Hogan and a young man called Willie Canning.

Under HYPNOSIS Vennum apparently revealed that a further spirit wished to come into her, and when asked for a name she revealed that it was Mary Roff. Soon after this incident, Vennum began to act as if she was the dead Mary Roff, begging her parents to be allowed to leave their house and 'go home'. The Roffs agreed and for over three months Vennum lived as Mary in the Roffs' house, allegedly able to recognize Mary's friends and relations and to recall many incidents of Mary's life. After this period of time Vennum's own personality returned and she moved home, although Mary would periodically 'return'. Some commentators believed that the level of detail that Vennum provided regarding the life and habits of Mary Roff proved that she had indeed been possessed, or even that Mary had temporarily been reincarnated in the body of Vennum. Others suggested that a psychological explanation was more likely, and that Vennum perpetrated a hoax simply because the idea of living as a guest in the Roffs' home was an attractive one. In either case, Vennum became known as the Watseka Wonder, and had either successfully carried off an elaborate deception, or had truly been possessed.

wave

A term used to describe a significant concentration of UFO reports in a particular geographical region over a short period of time.

Reports of UFO sightings often appear to follow patterns. There is a general 'background' level of activity that remains constant year in, year out, and at least short periods of UFO activity have been reported from nearly every country on earth. However, it has been observed over a period of several decades that there are times when the number of UFO reports increases dramatically. If such bursts of activity last for just a few days, and are quite localized, then they tend to be known within the UFO COMMUNITY as 'flaps'. However, if such flaps occur over a wider geographical area (sometimes as much as an entire country or even continent) and involve a significant increase in sightings, they are known as waves. Such waves will often include as many sightings within a few weeks as might normally be expected to occur over the period of a year.

Waves are frequently not recognized until some time after they have finished. Establishing that a wave has occurred often requires the collation of tens or hundreds of reports received through a variety of channels – including the media, UFO groups and the police or military (whose official records are usually not released immediately).

The AIRSHIP waves of 1896 and 1897 occurred in North America and lasted for a month or so in each instance. The numbers of reports being made were swelled by the extent of the newspaper coverage – something that has certainly been an important factor in the propagation of waves ever since. The recognition and growth of some waves has also been helped by active members of local UFO groups collecting evidence.

One of the longest US waves occurred in the western states during the summer of 1947. This included important historical cases such as the ROSWELL incident and KENNETH ARNOLD's seminal FLYING SAUCER sighting. The first major spate of ALIEN sightings accompanied Europe's first big wave during the autumn of 1954.

Sometimes an occurrence that many might consider to be little more than a flap has gained the status of a wave because it contained individual cases that have had a significant impact. The WASHINGTON DC WAVE of 1952 falls into that category. Although it lasted only a couple of weeks, and was confined to a small region, it had a dramatic effect on the study of UFOs by the US government (see PROJECT BLUE BOOK).

Although attempts have been made to find a mathematical pattern underlying the 50 major waves that have been identified from around the world, nobody has been able to make accurate predictions of future occurrences. One suggestion involves the idea that some types of UNIDENTIFIED ATMOSPHERIC PHENOMENA might occur more readily as a result of ionization within the atmosphere during periods of increased sunspot activity. Other potential natural explanations have also been offered, as have a number of more unusual theories – it has been observed, for example, that numbers of UFO sightings increase when the planet Mars is closest to Earth. However, the evidence to support many of these theories is limited.

It is not clear whether waves are a feature of the 'real' phenomenon (or phenomena) which underlie UFO sightings (extraterrestrial, terrestrial, psychological or otherwise), or whether they simply result from social factors such as periodic, media-driven increases in public interest.

weather forecasting

The apparent ability of some people to foretell weather.

In the age of television and radio, regular weather forecasts are ubiquitous, whether or not we believe in their reliability. However, human beings throughout history have always attempted to predict weather in advance. To civilizations dependent on agriculture, it was vital to know if conditions were going to be right for planting or if a harvest might be threatened by drought or unseasonably heavy rainfall. Sailors taking to the seas in fragile wooden vessels were at the mercy of weather and had to know when to stay on shore or run for port.

Ancient weather forecasters depended for much of their knowledge on observing the behaviour of animals and plants. The pine cone, for example, is traditionally a weather indicator. If the cone is open, this is supposed to indicate dry weather; if damp weather is on the way the cone will close to protect the seeds inside it. The mistle-thrush is traditionally called the 'stormcock' because it is believed that it sings when a thunderstorm is on the way.

Similarly, in folk belief a severe winter is to be expected if there are large crops of berries on the autumn trees and if squirrels are seen to accumulate especially large stores of nuts.

Forecasters would also study weather over long periods and learn to detect typical patterns and signs of what could be expected. 'Red sky at night; shepherd's delight. Red sky in the morning; shepherd's warning' is a proverbial piece of weather lore, versions of which are as old as the Bible. How reliable is this? The redness of the sky depends on the quantity of dust particles in the air. In Britain, most of the weather approaches from the west, with the prevailing winds. If the sky is red in the evening, this indicates that dry weather is coming from the direction of the sunset, that is, the west. Whereas, if the morning sky is red the dry weather has already passed over, heading towards the east.

Similarly, the old adage about St Swithin's Day (15 July)

St Swithin's Day, if it does rain
Full forty days, it will remain
St Swithin's Day, if it be fair
For forty days, t'will rain no more

Various folk methods have been employed for weather forecasting. In this picture from Georg Buschan's *Die Sitten der Völker* ('Customs of the People', 1884) a man predicts the weather by watching the behaviour of his captive frog. (© Mary Evans Picture Library)

seems to reflect a basic truth about the way in which weather patterns become established at that time of year and is often accurate.

Many people claim to be able to tell if it is going to rain by a physical sensation in a part of their body, usually a dull pain in a limb that has been injured or affected by a disorder such as rheumatism, arthritis or gout. Some people seem to be unusually sensitive to differences in atmospheric pressure, and this tells them when the weather is about to change. They 'feel it in their bones' or 'in their water' in much the same way as people become convinced that something is likely to happen.

Believers in ASTROLOGY often assert that the weather is as affected by planetary influences as the fortunes of individuals. Publications like OLD MOORE's Almanac would often contain weather predictions for the whole year in advance, derived from astrological observations.

Meteorological science made great strides in the 18th and 19th centuries, largely usurping the place of traditional weather forecasting, but is modern weather prediction any more accurate than the methods of the past? Probably, but people like to remember occasions when it goes spectacularly wrong as when in 1987 weathermen failed to predict the path of the 'Great Storm' that devastated much of Britain.

weather magic *see* MAGIC, WEATHER

weeping icons *see* IMAGES, WEEPING

weeping images *see* IMAGES, WEEPING

wells
Springs of fresh water flowing naturally from the earth, often venerated in pagan times as places of healing sacred to goddesses; many were later Christianized and rededicated to female saints as holy wells throughout Europe.

In pagan times, wells were thought to be magical places associated with goddesses of fertility and healing, especially in England, Ireland and Norway. In all cultures, the emergence of fresh, life-giving water from the earth was seen as a symbol of generation and purification; springs, fountains and wells were traditionally female symbols in ancient religions, and wells in the Celtic tradition were viewed as leading to the womb of the earth mother herself. They were places of healing and fertility, and offerings of small statues, coins or other treasures were made to the goddesses who presided over them in the hopes that petitioners would be cured or granted their prayers. In later times the treasures were replaced by flowers, pins or small pieces of rag tied to the branches of a tree growing near the well, a tradition which is practised to this day, as is seen by the number of 'clootie trees' or 'rag trees' still found near wells. The belief was that by the time the rag had rotted off the branch, the request would be granted. People would make pilgrimages to the wells, traditionally at May Day and Midsummer, to either drink or bathe in the water to seek relief from various ailments, such as scurvy, rheumatism and leprosy, and to cure infertility. Dreaming at sacred wells was a popular form of divination.

With the coming of Christianity, the early Church tried to stamp out the pagan practice of 'well worshipping', but it continued nonetheless, so instead, they Christianized the pagan goddesses as female saints and adopted the sacred wells as holy places. Churches were often built near these sacred wells, and a number of them contained a crypt or grotto which opened onto a subterranean spring. The many wells sacred to the goddess Brigit were rededicated to St Brigid or the Virgin Mary – hence the frequency in England and Ireland of holy wells

and districts called Bridewell or Ladywell – while other wells were renamed for St Anne, St Margaret and other Christian saints. Almost every old English town had a well dedicated to a saint which would originally have been sacred to a pagan goddess, and the veneration of such wells persists to modern times; in Ireland, pilgrimages to holy wells are an important part of the Christian calendar, and many of these take place on St Brigid's Day, which falls on the old Celtic festival of Imbolc on 1 February. In some places in England and Norway, wells are still 'dressed' between the end of May and early September, decorated with pictures made of flowers, seeds and crystals. The pictures may nowadays be Christian in nature, and services may be held at the well, but the principle is the same as it was in pagan days – to honour and placate the resident spirits.

The goddesses of ancient times may also have been preserved by local lore in the form of well guardians or fairies. These shapeshifting spirits may take the form of a salmon, trout, snake, frog, toad or a beautiful nymph, and can be dangerous, since, if they grab an unwary mortal, they will drag him down into the well and force him to live forever with the fairies. These well spirits are most often sighted at May Day and Midsummer, and must be propitiated with gifts such as pins or coins. The modern custom of throwing a coin into a WISHING WELL recalls the offerings once made to well spirits. See also HOLY WELLS.

werewolf *see* LYCANTHROPY

west *see* DIRECTIONS, FOUR

Western Mystery Tradition
A loose collection of esoteric beliefs and practices, which grew particularly during the medieval and Renaissance periods in Europe. Many of the teachings have been drawn upon by more modern spiritual, esoteric and occult organizations.

The Western Mystery Tradition, or Western Esoteric Tradition, incorporates a variety of individuals, teachings and movements which might not always have a continuity of lineage, but which share many of the same spiritual ideas and ideals. The words 'mystery' and 'ESOTERIC' indicate that, until recent years, these teachings were not openly available to everyone – they were only revealed to those within inner circles of initiates. They are heterodox rather than orthodox, and are regarded as heretical by mainstream religions – in the face of the vilification (and even persecution) that this attracted, secrecy on the part of followers was often born out of a regard for their own safety.

Many of the beliefs of the Western Mystery

Tradition go back to the teachings of non-Christian Greek and Egyptian initiatory groups from shortly before, and the first few centuries after, the time of Jesus. The main sources of hidden wisdom from that time are GNOSTICISM, neo-Pythagoreanism, Neoplatonism and the teachings of Hermes Trismegistus ('Thrice-Great Hermes' – see HERMETICA), once thought to be a mythical semi-divine teacher contemporary with Moses, but now known to be a composite name for several esoteric writers of the first few centuries AD. The emphasis of all of these, expressed in different ways, was on the individual's personal relationship with the divine.

In the 11th to 13th centuries there was a huge growth in the following of non-orthodox spiritual beliefs in what are now southern France (the Languedoc), northern Spain and northern Italy. Early Christian Gnostic beliefs, which had previously appeared in the Manichaeans and the Bogomils, now resurfaced very strongly with the Cathars, who were seen as such a threat to the Roman Catholic Church that they were brutally wiped out in the Albigensian Crusade beginning in 1209. At around the same time, and in roughly the same place, non-mainstream and mystical beliefs also developed within Judaism (KABBALAH).

Many heterodox beliefs continued to grow within this small geographical area. King Alfonso X (the Wise) of Castile and León (now northern Spain), a poet, astronomer and law-maker, encouraged Jews and Moors to his court (1252–84). He also encouraged troubadours, whose songs often contained a mixture of sex and spirituality. Around 1285 the kabbalist text *THE ZOHAR*, or 'Book of Splendour', was published by Moses de León in northern Spain – it became extremely influential among both Jewish and non-Jewish mystical thinkers. In southern France, in the late 12th century, the powerful spiritual allegory of the Grail quest (see HOLY GRAIL) had been added to the Arthurian myth (see KING ARTHUR), and in northern Italy, in the early 15th century, came the TAROT. Kabbalah, Grail and tarot all became important parts of the Western Mystery Tradition – an individual spiritual path outside the control of the Church.

In 1471 in Florence, Cosimo de Medici, a great patron of learning, commissioned Marsilio Ficino to translate the recently rediscovered *Corpus Hermeticum* into Latin. This collection of esoteric writings included the aphorism usually rendered 'As above, so below', which became the heart of the philosophical underpinning of ASTROLOGY, ALCHEMY and the hermetic philosophies of the 16th, 17th and 18th centuries. In 1614, 1615 and 1616 the three Rosicrucian Manifestos appeared – if ROSICRUCIANS had not existed before that date, they certainly

did after it. From Giovanni Pico della Mirandola, HENRICUS CORNELIUS AGRIPPA VON NETTESHEIM, PARACELSUS and JOHN DEE, via a host of other esoteric scholars, up to ISAAC NEWTON, the study of astrology, alchemy, kabbalah and much else occupied the minds of the greatest thinkers of their times.

One group of these natural philosophers (as those with scientific interests were called at this time) met regularly in Gresham College in London, and sometimes at Oxford University, during the early 17th century. At the Restoration of the monarchy in 1660 they petitioned Charles II for his patronage, and established the Royal Society (still the premier independent scientific academy in the world) – the Invisible College had become visible. Early presidents included Sir Christopher Wren (1680–2) and Sir Isaac Newton (1703–27). Although the focus was now on practical science, the esoteric links were still strong – in the early years of formally established FREEMASONRY, in the 1720s, around 90 of the first 250 Fellows of the Royal Society were Freemasons. Freemasonry has, at its spiritual heart, similar aims to those of the Rosicrucians.

In the 18th and 19th centuries it was largely through masonic and Rosicrucian organizations that the Western Mystery Tradition developed. The French occultist ÉLIPHAS LÉVI published *Transcendental Magic: Its Doctrine and Ritual* in 1855, which was widely influential. In England three members of the masonic order Societas Rosicruciana in Anglia founded the HERMETIC ORDER OF THE GOLDEN DAWN; in Germany there were links between the masonic order of Memphis and Misraim and the formation of the *ORDO TEMPLI ORIENTIS* and the Gnostic Catholic Church. PAPUS, who was involved in these, wrote hugely influential works on the tarot.

Through ALEISTER CROWLEY, elements of the Western Mystery Tradition continued in Thelemic groups (see THELEMA); through GERALD GARDNER, it continued into WICCA. When the Golden Dawn split, the magical emphasis continued in Stella Matutina; through DION FORTUNE this spawned the Society of the Inner Light, which in turn, through W E Butler and Gareth Knight, spawned the Servants of the Light, one of the largest and most respected schools of occult science in the early 21st century.

Some writers say that the Western Mystery Tradition has split into two strands today – one stemming from the THEOSOPHICAL SOCIETY and resulting in the many NEW AGE movements, and the other, with the Rosicrucian and Golden Dawn heritage, resulting in NEOPAGANISM. Although there is some validity in this distinction, THEOSOPHY is considered by many to be a somewhat artificial combination of Eastern and Western philosophies and, as such, not really a part of the Western Mystery Tradition. Conversely, it can also be argued that both the 'New Age' and 'neopaganism' labels include such a vast range of diverse groups that the value of attempting to draw such a distinction is questionable – indeed many movements and practices that might be described as 'New Age' emphasize the tarot, the Grail Quest, kabbalism and inner transformation through esoteric techniques, thereby making their own direct connections. The complex evolution of the Western Mystery Tradition continues.

wheel of fortune

The tenth card in the major arcana of the tarot. It depicts a wheel, usually inscribed with the letters TARO, the four Hebrew letters YHWH and the alchemical symbols for mercury, sulphur, water and salt. It usually represents the introduction of random forces which will bring unexpected and uncontrollable change in the subject's circumstances.

The tenth card in the major ARCANA of the TAROT is known as the wheel of fortune. In traditional decks this card shows a wheel floating in the sky, usually inscribed with several sets of characters. Four winged creatures are also often shown at each corner of the card. The four letters TARO appear round the rim of the wheel at the compass points north, east, south and west, and may be read as ROTA (Latin for 'wheel'), TARO ('tarot'), ORAT (Latin for 'speaks'), TORA ('Torah', the Hebrew law) and ATOR (the Egyptian goddess of eternal life), which are taken together to mean, 'The wheel of the Tarot speaks the Law of Ator' (that is, of eternal life). Interspersed between these letters on the wheel's rim are the four Hebrew letters Yod, Heh, Vav and Heh, which spell YHWH – the unpronounceable 'true' name of God as represented in the Torah. This name has been regarded as magical by occultists for over 2,000 years, and to scholars of the KABBALAH, it symbolizes all the mysteries of the world.

The four alchemical symbols for MERCURY, SULPHUR, WATER and SALT are also traditionally shown inside the wheel, and are a reference to the alchemical goal of TRANSMUTATION. These symbols also represent the four elements which underlie the four suits of the tarot: fire (WANDS), water (CUPS or chalices), earth (PENTACLES or coins) and air (SWORDS). The card's astrological ruling planet is Jupiter, and the four winged creatures holding open books, which are often shown at the corners of the card – a man, an eagle, a bull and a ram – are thought to have originally represented the four 'fixed' signs in Babylonian ASTROLOGY, namely LEO, SCORPIO, AQUARIUS and TAURUS. In different traditions these figures are variously interpreted as symbolizing the four seasons, the four evangelists,

or the four horsemen of the apocalypse. Some tarot decks also include Egyptian imagery, with a sphinx above the wheel, representing Horus, the god of resurrection, and also the mystery of life.

The wheel of fortune is generally taken to signify an unexpected and catalytic change in the circumstances of the subject, which is outside their control, and which will bring about the end of one cycle in their life and the beginning of another. It is said to signal the introduction of random forces, and may suggest that the person needs to accept coming events and learn from them. Appearing upright in a reading, the card represents positive change, and its position in relation to other cards in the spread may indicate the areas of life where this change is likely to take place. In a reversed position, the card signals the approach of negative change, but also reminds us that the wheel is constantly in motion, and that this negative cycle will also end and a new one will begin.

Negative aspects associated with the wheel of fortune card are over-optimism, overindulgence, a lack of attention to detail, a failure to keep one's word and the recurrence of difficulties. It is variously interpreted to indicate that the subject should appreciate their good fortune, cultivate faith in the future, exercise moderation, be patient or refrain from making unfulfillable promises.

wheels of light

Patterns of light seen in the sea.

For centuries, sailors, particularly those travelling in the Persian Gulf and the Indian Ocean, have reported seeing anomalous 'wheels of light' below the surface of the water. It is believed that sightings are most common in these regions as the sea water there is particularly clear.

These light displays have been described as having dimensions ranging from several feet to several miles across. The wheels often appear in a group of three and are not stationary, but usually have rotating spokes, which are often compared to the shape of a flattened letter S, with the direction of rotation apparently changing at random. Overlapping between wheels has been reported, as well as some examples of their being concentric.

Sometimes the light displays are affected by the passage of the ship from which they are observed, changing in pattern or even following the vessel for distances of miles. Occasionally, a swishing or boiling sound is heard in the water. A few accounts even speak of the light wheels appearing to rise out of the water and be visible in the air.

In 1879, a report was published of such a sighting, attributed to the hydrographer of HMS *Vulture*, a Royal Navy gunboat cruising in the Persian Gulf:

On looking towards the east, the appearance was that of a revolving wheel with centre on that bearing, and whose spokes were illuminated, and looking towards the west a similar wheel appeared to be revolving, but in the opposite direction.

Various explanations have been offered for this phenomenon. One theory is that the lights are produced by a kind of natural electromagnetic discharge, or 'earth energy' from LEYS, being transmitted through particles or microscopic life-forms in the water.

Some have suggested that such a large and bright amount of light must be produced by mechanical means, and as no human activities are known to be involved the source must be extraterrestrial. Comparisons have been made between the wheel shapes and patterns and some of the formations and whorls seen in CROP CIRCLES, giving rise to speculation that similar, unexplained, forms of energy may be involved in creating them.

If there is alien activity under these waters, what is it that they are doing? One idea is that unidentified submarine craft are being used to generate the lights and that some kind of trawling for fish is going on. Observers have reported seeing large numbers of fish swimming away from the light wheels in alarm. Perhaps they are being herded to a place where they may be easily captured. It remains to be explained whether the purported alien interest in the planet's fish population is driven by a purely scientific quest for knowledge or by appetite.

Another theory is that the lights are caused by the natural phosphorescence of microscopic animals in the water, such as *Noctiluca*. Such phosphorescent effects have been known to science since the 19th century. However, this does not account for the peculiar wheel-shaped form that it takes in this particular instance, or for the fact that these displays are most common in a particular region of the earth's oceans.

whirling dervishes *see* DERVISHES, WHIRLING

whirlpools
Circular currents in water.
Whirlpools are circular currents in seas, lakes or rivers, thought to be produced by opposing tides, winds or currents, especially where the water is relatively shallow and concentrated in a narrow strait. Essentially, a vortex is formed in the water, with a circular depression at the top and spiralling currents narrowing towards the bottom. A similar effect, albeit on a much smaller scale, is produced by water emptying down the plughole of a sink or bath.

For centuries powerful whirlpools have been ascribed the power of sucking ships or swimmers down to the bottom of the sea. In Greek tradition Charybdis was the name of a whirlpool on the Sicilian coast, well known as a danger to shipping and often personified as a monster.

The strongest whirlpool is believed to be the Moskstraumen, located in the Lofoten Islands off the coast of Norway. The Vikings knew it as the Maelstrom, and it has been recorded in writing since the 16th century. This whirlpool forms twice a day, between high and low tide, when the prevailing current changes direction.

Other famous whirlpools include the Corryvreckan, formed in the strait between the western Scottish islands of Jura and Scarba, and that known as the Old Sow, which occurs between Deer Island, New Brunswick, Canada, and Moose Island, Maine, USA.

whirlwinds
Small rotating windstorms.
Whirlwinds are tornadoes on a smaller scale, rotating windstorms that may extend hundreds of feet into the air. They are believed to be caused by clashing currents of air producing a vortex effect with spiralling winds narrowing from a circular top down to the bottom, which may be in contact with the ground.

Depending on their force, they can be highly destructive, albeit on a smaller scale than tornadoes. It has been suggested that small localized whirlwinds may be responsible for the creation of CROP CIRCLES.

In many ancient cultures whirlwinds were attributed to the actions of evil spirits or gods. For example, in Greek mythology they were often associated with the Harpies. In the Bible, the whirlwind was used as a symbol of the punishment to come for transgressors against God:

> For they have sown the wind, and they shall reap the whirlwind. (Hosea 8.7)

To this day small whirlwinds that whip up a column of dust in dry regions are known as dust devils.

white horses *see* CHALK FIGURES

White Lady
Archetypal phantom of a woman clad in white.
White Lady apparitions are common throughout Great Britain, the term coming from the colour of their attire; variants include Grey Ladies, and particularly in Scotland, Green Ladies. Many ancient manor houses, castles, monastic ruins, roads and

A 19th-century etching of an apparition of a White Lady.
(© Mary Evans Picture Library)

open spaces are said to be haunted by White Ladies and there are many well-attested sightings outside folklore. The costume of White Ladies is usually historical but of no particular period; occasionally they manifest in modern apparel. While many White Ladies are identified by folklore as historical characters such attributions are often dubious; the majority seem wholly anonymous. PHANTOM HITCH-HIKERS and many SPECTRAL PEDESTRIANS may also be seen as an aspect of the tradition.

Outside the British Isles, White Ladies are said to haunt rural crossroads and bridges in France; castles in Germany (where they are often taken to be an omen of death); a number of sites in Switzerland; and they are also known in Eastern Europe and Latvia. White Lady apparitions are also common to both North and South America with many Latin American countries having a screaming White Lady apparition known as 'La Llorona'. The ubiquitous nature of sightings encourages the view that White Ladies represent an archetypal feminine figure emanating from the unconscious mind, or that they are a form of 'genus loci' or 'spirit of place' manifestation, linked with certain landscapes. A number of theorists link them with female gods and spirits from classical or Celtic mythology and even with MARIAN APPARITIONS.

white magic *see* MAGIC, WHITE

Wicca
A modern nature-based religion with strong links to mainly European mythologies.

Although Wicca lays claim to some continuity of beliefs and practices with pagans of the past (see PAGANISM), it is actually a new religion, a major part of the neopagan and counter-cultural movement of the late 20th century (see NEOPAGANISM). The word 'wicca' is usually traced back to a Saxon root meaning 'to bend', though some link it to a word meaning 'wit' (as in knowledge or understanding); interestingly, the Saxon word would have been pronounced 'witcha' rather than 'wikka'.

Wicca was founded by former colonial customs official GERALD GARDNER, who published his influential books *Witchcraft Today* (1954) and *The Meaning of Witchcraft* (1959) in the wake of the abolition of British legislation against witchcraft in 1951. Gardner claimed that he discovered a group of hereditary witches in the New Forest in 1939, and was initiated into their COVEN. Debate continues as to whether this actually happened or not, mainly because there is no evidence of any sort of continuing witch tradition, hereditary or not. That idea had been put forward in *The Witch Cult in Western Europe* (1921) by anthropologist Dr Margaret Murray; although her books were taken as a scholarly underpinning of history for the fledgling movement in the 1960s, they are now considered to be of very dubious scholarship.

Gardner was interested in the OCCULT, and he was also a naturist, a sado-masochist and apparently a voyeur. For his new religion he borrowed large elements of ritual from ALEISTER CROWLEY'S ORDO TEMPLI ORIENTIS (which itself had borrowed from, among others, the HERMETIC ORDER OF THE GOLDEN DAWN and FREEMASONRY); he mixed these in with nudity, ritualized sexual intercourse and flagellation. Perhaps fortunately for the future of the movement, an early initiate, Doreen Valiente (1922–99), rewrote much of the ritual, dropping much of Crowley's input and downplaying the sexual elements. The workings of the coven became the *Book of Shadows*, which each initiated witch has to copy by hand.

By the time of his death in 1964 Gardner's initiates had set up a number of covens around Britain, and modern witchcraft was taken to the USA by Raymond and Rosemary Buckland. Gardnerian groups continued, but there was a major schism in the movement with the development of Alexandrian witchcraft, led by Alex and Maxine Sanders. This was more flamboyant; ALEX SANDERS was a great self-publicist, and brought modern witchcraft to the attention of the popular press, much to the disapproval of traditional Gardnerians.

Although there are still both Gardnerian and Alexandrian covens today, many Wiccans have developed the rituals to suit their own needs and preferences. Some Wiccans still perform some of their rituals naked (skyclad), but it is more usual for them to wear robes. The Great Rite, or ritual sexual intercourse between the High Priest and High Priestess of a coven, today is almost always replaced by the symbolic act of the plunging of a knife (athame), representing the male principle, into a chalice, representing the female.

Today the term 'Wicca' is generally seen as applying to coven-based witchcraft. Both male and female Wiccans refer to themselves as witches. Many witches prefer to work as 'solitaries', sometimes called 'hedge-witches'. Many also prefer the term 'the Craft', and some avoid the word 'witch' because of its historical negative connotations.

Wicca, or modern witchcraft, is a nature-based religion. Its ritual life centres on the eight-fold wheel of the year: the solstices (SUMMER SOLSTICE; WINTER SOLSTICE), the equinoxes (AUTUMNAL EQUINOX; VERNAL EQUINOX) and the four festivals of BELTANE (spring), LUGHNASADH (summer), SAMHAIN (autumn) and IMBOLC (winter). Wiccans honour the divine in all things, including both nature and themselves. The divine is both immanent and transcendent. The divine can be perceived in many ways: as the Goddess and the God; as the triple Goddess (Maid, Mother and Crone); as any number of deities from any number of mythologies. Modern witchcraft is eclectic and syncretic; if a witch wishes to conceptualize the Goddess as Ishtar or Inanna rather than Diana or Brighde, he or she is free to do so. One of the most powerful rituals in the religion is called DRAWING DOWN THE MOON in which the spirit of the Goddess (by whatever name) is invoked into the body of the High Priestess of a coven.

Magic is a fundamental part of witchcraft: not black magic (see MAGIC, BLACK), but the magic of healing and making whole. Because of Wicca's historical roots in Crowley's Ordo Templi Orientis, correspondences of spirits, the planets, colours, scents, precious stones, etc are used in working magic; and so, in a genuine link to the 'wise women' of the past, are herbs and natural oils. 'Witches' potions' are likely to include lavender for its calming effects, witch-hazel for the skin, or fennel for stomach problems.

There is no connection between Wicca (or any other neopagan movement) and SATANISM or Devil worship. Pagan religions are nature-based, and although they may have numerous gods and goddesses, SATAN is not one of them. See also CHURCH AND SCHOOL OF WICCA; CHURCH OF ALL WORLDS.

widdershins

The word used to describe circular movement in witchcraft and magical practice that goes against the direction of the movement of the sun around the sky.

The word 'widdershins', or 'withershins', comes from the Low German *weddersins*, from *wider*, meaning against, and *sin*, meaning direction. Circular movement in this direction, the opposite direction to that in which the sun moves around the sky (the movement of the sun being clockwise in the northern hemisphere), is associated with the unnatural and is believed to produce negative magic. In the northern hemisphere, for example, a witch or sorcerer may walk anticlockwise, or widdershins, in casting a black magic spell (see MAGIC, BLACK).

Movement in the opposite direction, following the movement of the sun (ie clockwise in the northern hemisphere) is referred to as DEOSIL.

Wild Hunt

A spectral hunt which appears in folk myths across Northern Europe and Britain; anyone who sees it is said to be doomed to die.

The folk myth of the Wild Hunt is prevalent all over Northern Europe and Britain. This noisy and riotous band of spirits is accompanied by a pack of ghostly hounds, and is said to ride out most commonly at HALLOWE'EN, Yule and New Year's Eve, when the souls of the dead are traditionally allowed to return to earth, thundering across the sky amid raging winds and striking terror into any below. To hear the sound of the Wild Hunt is taken to be an OMEN of strife and disaster, and those who are unlucky enough to see it will either die, or be caught up by the hunters and swept away. In Norse mythology, the Wild Hunt's leader is Odin, or Wotan to give him his Teutonic name, and he rides his eight-legged steed, Sleipnir, with his pack of black dogs, hunting the spirits of the dead. In Celtic countries, the hunt was sometimes thought to consist of a fairy host, whose leader was variously identified as Gwydion, Nuada, King Arthur, Cernunnos or HERNE THE HUNTER; the quarry was said to be a boar, a wild horse, the damned, a ghostly deer or female FAIRIES. In some areas the hunt leader was a goddess, and the riders were female, and were known as the 'Hag Riders'. The hounds were often believed to be the souls of unbaptized children. In Wales and the West Country, the leader of the hunt was said to be Gwyn ap Nudd, the fairy 'Lord of the Dead', accompanied by white hounds with blood-red ears. In the Middle Ages, the Wild Hunt became more and more associated with WITCHCRAFT, and it was believed that WITCHES participated in the hunt, gathering the souls of sinners and unbaptized infants, led by a demonic spirit and sometimes by the DEVIL

The Norwegian myth of the Wild Hunt, as depicted by the painter P N Arbo in the *Asgaardsreiden* (1873). (© Mary Evans Picture Library)

himself; this was one of the main charges made in witch trials during the Middle Ages. But in later times, the Wild Hunt lost its associations with evil and witchcraft and became a popular literary and artistic device, featuring in many paintings, poems and books. See also AERIAL PHANTOMS.

wild men *see* WOODWUSES

Wild Wood
Wild, uncultivated woodland, in folklore believed to be the realm of fairies.
Areas of wild, uncultivated woodland have, since ancient times, been seen as strange and marginal places. The Wild Wood in folklore is a magical and primal forest where one may encounter NATURE SPIRITS or FAIRIES, and is a powerful metaphor for the unknown, and also for the shadowy aspects of the self. In Greek mythology, it was under the protection of Artemis, the goddess of the hunt, and in Norse folklore, it was protected by Freyja. In fairy tales such as 'Little Red Riding Hood' and 'Hansel and Gretel', the Wild Wood is a dangerous realm inhabited by monsters. In other stories, such as the legend of Merlin or the tale of Sir Orfeo, a character may go mad with love or grief and retreat into the Wild Wood to live like a beast for a period of time. Arthurian knights rode into the Wild Wood in quest of adventure, and it became a place of safety for Robin Hood, who, along with HERNE THE HUNTER (whose spiritual son Robin Hood is said to be in some traditions), is often identified in British folklore as its protector, and is called the lord of the greenwood. In earlier times the HORNED

GOD, or Cernunnos, was also named as its protective spirit. It is the natural habitat of the WOODWUSE. Solitary witches who practise magic which focuses on the power of nature sometimes refer to themselves as wildwood mystics, and pagans have for centuries traditionally gone into the forest to celebrate festivals such as May Eve, or BELTANE, returning with branches of greenery to bring the vitality and life force of the Wild Wood in Spring into their own homes.

Williams, Rhynwick *see* LONDON MONSTER

will-o'-the-wisp
An elusive moving light sometimes seen over marshes or bogs at night, thought in folklore to be a mischievous fairy or a restless spirit.
The will-o'-the-wisp is a natural phenomenon which occurs all over the world, and every region has its own name for this mysterious moving light which is sometimes seen hovering over marshes or bogs at night. Scientists generally agree that the light is caused by the spontaneous ignition, by traces of hydrogen phosphide, of the methane produced by the decaying organic matter found in marshes. It has also been suggested that the little-understood phenomenon of BALL LIGHTNING may be the cause. However, in folklore, the will-o'-the-wisp is feared as an ill OMEN which foretells the death of the person who sees it, or of someone close to them. When seen near a graveyard it may be called a corpse light or corpse candle, and is believed to light the way from the victim's house to the grave, and in Ireland, it is often thought to lead a spectral funeral procession.

It is also popularly believed to be a wandering soul rejected by both heaven and hell, or in some places, the spirit of an unbaptized child. In Northern Europe it is sometimes seen hovering over burial mounds, when it is said to be the souls of the dead, guarding the treasure buried in their graves. In German and Swedish folklore it may also be the soul of a person who, in life, disregarded boundary markers and stole a neighbour's land.

When approached, the will-o'-the-wisp vanishes, often reappearing just out of reach, so that in many parts of the world it is seen as a mischievous spirit which delights in leading travellers astray, a fairy which either appears as a ball of light or carries a lantern to lure the unwary over cliff-tops or into a bog. However, these spirits have occasionally been known to help rather than hinder, showing travellers the way to safety.

The will-o'-the-wisp is known by many other names, such as ignis fatuus ('foolish light'), jack o'lantern, friar's light, fairy light and fox fire, and the word is also used figuratively to refer to any elusive or deceptive person or idea which leads people astray.

Wilmington, Long Man of

A chalk figure of a man on a hillside near Wilmington in East Sussex.

On Windover Hill, near Wilmington in East Sussex, the figure of a naked man, holding a staff or pole in each hand, is cut into the turf. The image is some 70 metres (229 feet) in height. Various theories have existed as to who created the figure and why. Some connect it with the same Bronze Age culture responsible for the UFFINGTON WHITE HORSE; some ascribe it to the Romans on the strength of similar figures found on coins; and some to the Anglo-Saxons, who are known to have carved helmeted figures as decorations. It has also been suggested that it could be the work of Phoenician traders, echoing a figure from their culture shown holding two pillars of a temple.

Whatever its age, the figure is known to have been changed over the centuries. A drawing made by the English surveyor John Rowley in 1710 shows facial features and a helmet that are no longer visible. Such details may have been removed when the figure was extensively restored in the Victorian era. The staffs or poles have not been satisfactorily explained, with some claiming that they once represented a scythe and a rake and others conjecturing that they were spears. In local legend the Long Man is the outline of a giant, traced around him where he fell dead on the hillside.

The true age of the Long Man may never be known, but research by environmental archaeologists in 2003 established that a great deal of chalk debris was produced on the site in the 16th century, leading them to the conclusion that the figure may only be 400 years old.

window area

A geographical location from which UFO sightings are reported far more frequently than would be expected.

Across the world approximately 40 window areas have been identified by members of the UFO COMMUNITY. They are each small geographical regions that have been isolated and marked out as unusual following analysis of UFO sighting report totals. The window phenomenon manifests itself in two distinct ways: some areas have a long track record of sightings (dating back decades or even centuries) whereas others have more brief periods of activity that can often be explained in terms of social factors.

BONNYBRIDGE in Scotland had no evident history of high levels of UFO sightings until a WAVE occurred during the early 1990s. The wave resulted in a considerable amount of attention being focused on the region – UFO researchers set up phone lines to receive reports, the world media promoted the region as a UFO hotspot and some local politicians gave the matter serious attention. The result was a big rise in the number of reports being filed with UFO groups, although it was not clear whether the actual level of sightings had increased. Media coverage in cases such as this often persuades witnesses to come forward, boosting the apparent level of UFO sightings.

In GULF BREEZE, Florida, a case in which a number of UFO PHOTOGRAPHS were taken brought the media and other sightseers to the area, resulting in frequent skywatches (see SKYWATCHING). This tempted hoaxers to create sightings for the assembled enthusiasts, helping to boost artificially the town's window-area status.

Window areas of a more durable nature exist in places such as Marfa, Texas, where strange lights have been reported since the area was first settled and lookout points have been set up for travellers to watch what seems to be a rare natural phenomenon. Similar glowing lights have been reported from parts of Queensland in Australia, and sightings appear to have been made here over hundreds (or even thousands) of years – the 'UFOs' here appear in Aboriginal folklore as the 'min min' lights.

In Britain, the Pennine Hills between Manchester, Sheffield and Leeds have produced sightings of LIGHTS IN THE SKY for many years. These have been interpreted in different ways during different eras. Once they were regarded as the product of DEMONS, or of WITCHCRAFT, and some local place names, such as the Devil's Elbow in Derbyshire, reflect the fact that strange phenomena (including lights and buzzing sounds emerging from the ground) were reported there. With the arrival of the modern UFO phenomenon a 'space-age' spin has been applied to the same events. The Longdendale Peaks near Sheffield have a spooky reputation as a result of similar sightings, and many locals know the area as 'the haunted valley'. In recent years it became the first window area to set up a live webcam link to allow armchair skywatchers to look for UFOs without leaving their homes.

One famous window area that has been subjected to extensive scientific study is that in the HESSDALEN valley of Norway, where the reports of sightings come in short, concentrated bursts, followed by years during which the lights are apparently dormant. Evidence from this and some of the other long-term window areas suggests that the sightings may result from UNIDENTIFIED ATMOSPHERIC PHENOMENA, which are related to particular geological factors in the areas concerned.

Winged Cats *see panel p739*

winter solstice
The day in the year on which the Sun is above the horizon for the shortest period. It is of importance in both historical and modern pagan spiritual practice.
The winter solstice normally falls on 21 December in the northern hemisphere and has historically been important in religious practices throughout the world. It is the point in the year when the sun is lowest in the sky, when the Sun God's powers are weakest (see SUN and HORNED GOD), but is also a turning point from which the days begin to lengthen. It is one of the four minor SABBATS recognized by modern pagans and is sometimes known by the alternative name Alban Arthan.

The English version of the name by which the midwinter celebration is known through much of Europe is 'Yule', a word of Germanic origin possibly derived from the same root as words meaning 'yellow', 'gold' or 'shining', and may refer to the use of fires and shining decorations to encourage the Sun to return. Many religions and spiritual traditions have celebrations involving light at this time of the year, and it is widely believed that the early Christian church adopted the existing festival for the celebration of Christmas. See also AUTUMNAL EQUINOX; BELTANE; IMBOLC; LUGHNASADH; SAMHAIN; SUMMER SOLSTICE; VERNAL EQUINOX; WICCA.

wisdom
The quality of being wise; learning or knowledge, especially the sum of learning throughout the ages; wise teachings or writings.
Wisdom is defined in various ways: as the quality of being wise, as learning or knowledge, as wise teachings or writings, and as the ability to make the right use of one's knowledge. Wisdom is often associated with the idea of secret knowledge made available to only a few; it is sometimes thought to be divinely inspired, and the various pantheons throughout the ancient world each had their own god or goddess of wisdom – the god Thoth of the ancient Egyptians, the Greek goddess Athena and her Roman counterpart Minerva, the Hindu goddess Sarasvati, and the Norse goddess Freyja. Most villages used to have a 'wise woman' or 'cunning man' skilled in the use of herbs and wild plants for medicinal and other purposes; such people were often accused of WITCHCRAFT in the Renaissance and Middle Ages and were persecuted accordingly.

The word 'WIZARD' has as its first element the Middle English word for 'wise'; wisdom is thus closely linked with the idea of occult or magical knowledge. The word 'wisdom' is often also used to refer to the sum of learning and knowledge of a particular belief system or magical tradition, such as 'Celtic wisdom' or 'Native American wisdom'.

wish
A supernatural gift granting the recipient whatever they ask for.
In myths and folk stories all over the world, wishes may be granted by gods, goddesses or other supernatural beings, and sometimes, by an inanimate object such as a magic ring. MERMAIDS and LEPRECHAUNS are said to be compelled to grant wishes if they are captured, and MAGIC LAMPS in stories such as that of Aladdin contain a genie or djinni (see DJINN) who will grant the wishes of the lamp's possessor. The number of wishes granted by magic is variable, but is traditionally three. Leprechauns are notorious for trying to trick the recipient into making a fourth wish, whereupon all they have gained with their first three wishes will immediately be lost, and FAIRIES and mermaids will often try to twist the meaning of the words used to make the wishes, or interpret them over-literally, in order to avoid giving the wishers what they actually want.

The consequence of making foolish or poorly expressed wishes is frequently the subject of a tale with the clear moral, 'be careful what you wish for'. In these stories, it is not the malice of the wish-granter which causes distress to the wisher, but their own folly or thoughtlessness. Greek myth tells of Eos, goddess of the dawn, who fell in love with

Winged Cats

The concept of domestic cats with wings would normally be confined to fantasy books and 'silly season' tabloid stories, were it not for the remarkable fact that such creatures are unquestionably real. British cryptozoologist Dr Karl Shuker is a leading investigator of winged cats, and has documented dozens of verified cases from around the world. One of the earliest cases, and still among the most famous, was that of a kitten from Wiveliscombe in Somerset, which was photographed for the *Strand Magazine* in November 1899. The photograph clearly revealed a pair of large fluffy wing-like extensions arising from the cat's back.

Other noteworthy examples include: a black-and-white cat with a very sizeable pair of 'flappable' furry dorsal 'wings' that was captured in some stables near Oxford in 1933 and later photographed for news reports and exhibited at the local zoo; a record-breaking Swedish example from 1949 with a wingspan of almost 30 centimetres (12 inches); a beautiful winged Angora cat called Angolina, owned by a porter living near Spain's parliament buildings, which entranced Madrid's media in 1959; also in 1959, a specimen of confused sex from Pineville, West Virginia, known in press reports as Thomas-Mitzi, that was the subject of a legal ownership case but shed its wings while being exhibited in court; another densely furred winged cat photographed sometime prior to the 1970s that made a home for itself in a Manchester builder's yard; a fluffy-winged tabby spied in April 1995 in Backbarrow, Cumbria, and owned by the village's retired postman; a Japanese specimen stroked by Rebecca Hough while staying in Kumamoto, Kyushu, on 23 May 1998; and even a historical report of a winged cat encountered in some woods at Walden, in Concord, Massachusetts, by writer Henry David Thoreau and later documented by him in his book *Walden; Or Life in the Woods* (1854).

Yet despite the relative abundance of winged cat reports and photographs, any explanation for these extraordinary animals remained conspicuous only by its absence, until in the early 1990s Dr Shuker uncovered the long-awaited answer while searching for clues in various obscure tracts of veterinary literature. He discovered that winged cats exhibit a rare, little-known genetic disorder known as feline cutaneous asthenia (FCA), in which the skin is extremely stretchable, especially on the back, haunches and shoulders – so much so that if a cat with FCA merely rubs itself against something, or grooms itself with its paws, this can be enough to stretch its skin outwards in long, furry, wing-like extensions. And because these extensions often contain muscle fibres, they can sometimes even be gently raised or lowered, exactly as reported by certain winged-cat eyewitnesses. Moreover, because the skin of FCA cats is so fragile, occasionally the wings are stretched out too far, and they will then simply peel away from the rest of the cat's skin, falling off as if moulted and without any blood loss, which might explain Thomas-Mitzi's dramatic loss of wings in the courtroom. After countless years of baffling their startled observers, the mystery of the winged cats would seem to have been solved.

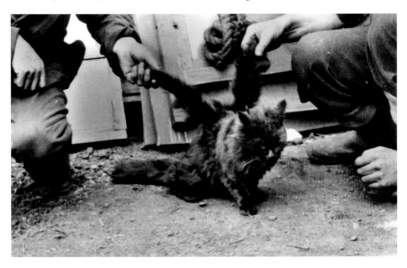

The winged cat that made its home in a Manchester builder's yard. (© TopFoto/Fortean)

a mortal prince called Tithonus. She wished that Tithonus might have eternal life so that they could be together forever, and Zeus granted her wish – but she forgot to ask that he also have eternal youth, and he grew older and older, unable to die, until she turned him into a cricket to be rid of his complaining voice. Similarly, the avaricious King Midas soon came to regret his wish that everything he touched would turn to gold. Alternatively, hasty wishes may cancel each other out and leave the recipients no better off than they were; in one humorous folk tale, a poor farmer and his wife are given three wishes. One of them immediately wishes for a fine sausage, whereupon the other scolds them for wasting a wish and wishes the sausage would become attached to the end of their spouse's nose as a punishment. The third wish then has to be used to get rid of the sausage, leaving the foolish couple back where they started. In a much darker modern version of this tale, the 1902 short story 'The Monkey's Paw' by W W Jacobs, an old couple are given the mummified paw of a dead monkey which grants the possessor three wishes. The father wishes for £200, and the next morning, their son is killed in a factory accident; his company pays the couple £200 as compensation. After the funeral, the distraught mother uses the second wish to wish her son alive again. Something begins to hammer on the front door, and the father, realizing that it is the mangled corpse of his son, just manages to wish him gone before the mother opens the door to the horror on the other side.

There are many superstitions of circumstances in which wishes may be granted, such as pulling a WISHBONE with someone else and breaking off the longer part, blowing out all the candles on your birthday cake with one breath and blowing off all the white seeds on a dandelion head with one breath. You can also make a wish on the first star you see on a given night, on a shooting star or on a rainbow – provided you can manage not to look at the rainbow again after doing so. Throwing a coin in a WISHING WELL also entitles you to a wish, as does entering a church for the first time. In most cases, the wish must not be revealed to anyone until after it has been granted.

wishbone

The V-shaped bone between the neck and breast of a fowl, traditionally pulled apart in order to grant a wish to whoever breaks off the longer piece.

The custom of pulling apart the wishbone of a cooked fowl, usually a chicken or a turkey, to grant a wish to whoever breaks off the longer piece is an ancient one. It is thought to have originated with the Etruscans, and to have been adopted by the Romans, who

Two people pull a wishbone – it has long been popularly believed that whoever is left holding the longer piece will be granted a wish. (© Philip James Corwin/Corbis)

brought the superstition over to Britain when they invaded in the 1st century BC. It is customary to keep the bone intact when carving the bird at dinner and to dry it until it is brittle. Then two people each crook a little finger round one end of the 'V', thinking of a wish, and pull. It is generally believed that they must neither speak nor laugh while doing so. The person who breaks off the longer piece will have their wish fulfilled, although they must not reveal what they wished for until after it has been granted. This is thought to be the origin of the expression 'to get a lucky break'. In the unlikely event that the wishbone breaks evenly, both parties will be granted their wishes.

An earlier name for the wishbone is the merrythought, referring to the older version of the custom in which it was believed that the recipient of the longer piece would marry first. The word 'wishbone' seems to have appeared in the mid-19th century, and soon became the more commonly used term. Small gold or silver charms in the form of wishbones are often worn or carried for good luck.

wishing well

A well which is supposed to have the power to grant the wishes made at it.

In pagan Europe, many WELLS were thought to be mystical places sacred to goddesses of fertility and healing, and people would make pilgrimages to them to bathe in or drink the water in the hope of being cured of their ailments. They would also make requests and leave the well's goddess offerings such as coins, small statues or other treasures. The site of the main spring at Bath was dedicated by the Celts to the goddess Sulis, and when the Romans occupied the area in the 1st century AD, they identified it with their own goddess Minerva; its popularity as a focus for petitions and votive offerings can be gauged from the fact that some 16,000 coins and other items were found in the spring. Around 50 curses were also found, hand-written on sheets of lead and then rolled up and cast into the water, demonstrating that the wishes made at ancient wells were not always for health, wealth or happiness. With the coming of Christianity the goddesses were either replaced by female saints or the Virgin Mary, but the notion of the well as a magical place at which offerings were made and wishes granted was not so easily suppressed, and has persisted in folklore in the form of the wishing well. A coin is usually dropped into the well after a wish has been made, a relic of the votive offerings originally made to the presiding spirits of ancient wells. Such is the power of the wishing well in popular imagination that almost any shallow pool of water, such as a fountain, may be treated like one, and have coins thrown into it; many parks and even shopping precincts and malls include a wishing well, the money thrown into them usually being collected for charity, and nowadays wishing wells are a popular garden feature. See also HOLY WELLS.

witch balls

Hollow spheres of glass, often hung in a window to ward off evil spirits, ill fortune or the spells of witches.

Witch balls are hollow spheres of glass that became popular in England in the 18th century, although their origin is possibly older. Often green or blue in colour, witch balls were traditionally hung in the windows of a house, and were believed to be APOTROPAICS – that is, objects that have the power to turn away evil. Witch balls were believed to avert the harmful influences of evil spirits, ill fortune and the spells of WITCHES, and this function has led some to suggest that the name 'witch ball' is a corruption of 'watch ball', as the ball was intended to watch over and protect the household.

witch bottles

Bottle or flasks, often containing items such as bent pins, human hair and urine, that were believed to counteract the spells of witches or to protect a household against evil spirits.

The use of witch bottles is believed to date back to the 16th century, and they were most commonly in use in Britain in the 1600s, at the height of the WITCH TRIALS. Often made from a small stoneware flask, the witch bottle would be filled with items that represented a person who believed that they had been the victim of a witch's spell – such as their hair, nail clippings or urine – plus other items such as bent pins. The bottle would then be buried, traditionally either in the farthest corner of the house or under the hearth. It was believed that these actions caused the spell placed on the victim to be nullified. Some have suggested that the inclusion of urine and pins caused the witch that had cast the spell to feel the discomfort of passing pins each time she urinated, while others believe that the bent pins were included to catch evil, and the urine may have been a counter-charm which caused a witch to be unable to urinate. In some instances the witch bottle would have been thrown onto a fire rather than buried, and it was believed that the spell would be broken and the witch who cast it killed when the bottle exploded. It is thought that part of the popularity of witch bottles lay in the fact that a supposed victim could rid him- or herself from the malevolent attentions of a witch without needing to know who the witch was.

Witch bottles that date from as late as the 18th century have been discovered hidden in houses in Britain, although only rarely are the contents of historical witch bottles still intact.

Witchcraft *see panel p742*

witch doctor

A term in popular use to describe traditional healers in certain societies, especially in Africa, who are thought to possess magical powers which are used to cure sickness.

In many societies individuals widely referred to as 'witch doctors' are highly respected and sometimes even feared figures. They are often believed to act as mediums between the visible world and the invisible SPIRIT world, and to practise magic for the purposes of healing, DIVINATION and control over natural events. The alternative title SHAMAN is now also often used in an attempt to avoid the pejorative connotations associated with what is considered to be the old-fashioned use of the term 'witch doctor'. However, it has been argued that although this alternative is accurate in some situations, its use in others is equally

Witchcraft

A belief in witchcraft, whereby certain people are believed to possess magical powers which allow them to influence human affairs and the environment, is found in nearly every society throughout history. The belief in witchcraft is part of a magical worldview common to many cultures, in which it is thought that the unseen powers inherent in the universe may be directed by skilled practitioners. It is referred to in ancient Egyptian, Indian and Babylonian texts, and is frequently mentioned in the Bible, which strongly condemns its practice. However, the precise definition given to the term 'witchcraft' varies from society to society. In cultures such as African and Native American tribal societies, which accept MAGIC when practised for beneficial ends, witchcraft is the specific use of magic for selfish or malicious purposes. In such societies, it is the role of the WITCH DOCTOR, SHAMAN, MEDICINE MAN or other legitimate practitioner of magic to detect and expose the actions of WITCHES, and to counteract this black magic (see MAGIC, BLACK) with their own powers.

Witchcraft is the subject of folklore in many countries, and ideas about witchcraft are deeply embedded in European culture. With the advent of Christianity in Europe around the 4th century, the early Church adopted a pragmatic approach to the worship of the old pagan deities, acknowledging that it was easier to superimpose Christian festivals on the existing festivals of the pagan calendar (see AUTUMNAL EQUINOX; BELTANE; HALLOWE'EN; IMBOLC; LUGHNASADH; SAMHAIN; SUMMER SOLSTICE; VERNAL EQUINOX; WINTER EQUINOX) than to try to stamp out PAGANISM altogether. Pope Gregory I (pope 590–604) had churches built on the sites of pagan temples, while HOLY WELLS, once sacred to pagan goddesses, were rededicated to Christian SAINTS. For centuries, the two belief systems co-existed, and most of Christian Europe maintained a reasonably tolerant view of magic, which remained a part of everyday life; ordinary people still relied on the services of the 'cunning men' and 'wise women' (see WISDOM) found in every village, who were skilled not only in healing and herbalism, but in detecting and counteracting the practices of witches – those who used magic for evil purposes.

However, by the 15th century, the figure of the witch in Europe had begun to take on a particularly Christian interpretation. The powers of the witch were generally thought to be innate, or to be bestowed by a supernatural agent, rather than being acquired through learned magical techniques and INVOCATIONS, as in high magic or ritual magic (see MAGIC, HIGH and MAGIC, RITUAL). The Church began to foster a belief that it was the DEVIL who conferred these powers, and to promote an image of the witch as a follower of SATAN. The distinction between healers and witches became blurred, and the practitioners of folk magic found themselves being accused of witchcraft, although high-ranking and educated practitioners of high magic generally escaped censure.

The medieval concept of witchcraft focused on Devil worship, with perversions of Christian rites in the form of the BLACK MASS, the celebration of witches' SABBATS in which the Devil was greeted with the obscene kiss under the tail known as the OSCULUM INFAME, the SACRIFICE of human babies and orgies. It was believed that one became a witch by selling one's SOUL to the Devil in a DEVIL'S PACT, and received in return Satanic powers; witches had the power of FLIGHT using BROOMSTICKS or FLYING OINTMENT, and could change their forms or become invisible, invoke spirits, harm their victims or influence them using SPELLS, HEXES, CURSES, potions or EFFIGIES, damage property and livestock, perform DIVINATION and conjure the dead. They were thought to be aided by a FAMILIAR or spirit helper in the form of an animal, and any old woman who lived alone and kept a pet, especially a black CAT, was likely to be accused of witchcraft – particularly if she was also skilled in herbalism. Shakespeare's portrayal of the three witches in *Macbeth*, written at the beginning of the 17th century, reflects the stereotypical view of witches held by most Europeans of the time; isolated from society, working at dead of night and mixing gruesome ingredients in a huge CAULDRON to bring about evil magic.

The great witch hysteria of the late Middle Ages began around 1450, as legal sanctions were introduced in Europe which made it a crime against the Church to be a witch. In 1484, Pope Innocent VIII appointed two clerics, Heinrich Kramer and Jakob Sprenger, as inquisitors against witchcraft and heresy, and in 1486 they published the MALLEUS MALEFICARUM, a hugely influential work which was regarded for several centuries as the authoritative manual for inquisitors and WITCHFINDERS. For the next 300 years, and particularly during the time of the Reformation (1520–1650), Protestant and Catholic churches alike pursued WITCH TRIALS ferociously throughout Europe and Scandinavia, with the hysteria spreading to the American colonies in the 17th century. Superstition, rivalries and tensions within communities, and the fear of being accused oneself if one did not join in the witch hunt, all helped to fan the flames.

Torture was officially condemned as a means of extracting confessions of witchcraft, but in practice it was widely used, as were trials by ordeal such as 'swimming the witch', in which the accused was tied up and thrown into water; if they drowned, this was taken as proof of innocence, but if they floated, they were found guilty. In Scotland, the commonest ordeal was pricking for the DEVIL'S MARK or WITCH'S MARK. The worst period for executions was between the mid-15th and late 17th centuries, an era sometimes known as 'the Burning Times', which reached its peak in the early 17th century. About three-quarters of those killed as witches in England and Scotland were female, mostly lower-class, older women, but anyone who was in any way different – eccentric, deformed or living alone – might be accused, with the Church and State not only legalizing but, at times, encouraging persecution. It is sometimes claimed that, in the 17th century, MATTHEW HOPKINS, the self-styled 'Witchfinder General' brought about the executions of over 100 accused witches in England.

The vigorous and widespread persecution of witches was in part a by-product of the campaign against heretics by the Church, which regarded witchcraft as an organized heretical sect opposed to Christianity. But witch-hunting was also motivated by greed. England's Witchcraft Act, passed by Elizabeth I in 1563 and added to in 1604 by her successor, JAMES I, decreed witchcraft to be a felony punishable by death, with the convicted witch's property being forfeited to the Crown. Accusations of witchcraft became a convenient way of evicting those such as elderly peasant widows or spinsters who refused to give up their land rights, and the desire to appropriate land appears to have been the motive for at least some of the mass accusations of witchcraft which were made in the trials of the SALEM WITCHES in Massachusetts, in 1693, and which resulted in the hanging of 19 people. Not everyone joined in the hysteria, however; in his 1584 book *The Discoverie of Witchcraft*, Reginald Scot sought to demonstrate that the fear of witchcraft was largely unfounded, and that the apparent magic of village witches could be accomplished by trickery.

By the 18th century, with the Enlightenment and the development of rationalism, a belief in magic had come to be regarded as superstition based on ignorance, although some witch trials continued to be prosecuted under the Witchcraft Act. The last execution for witchcraft in England took place in 1712. In 1736, George II introduced a new Witchcraft Act which marked a complete reversal in attitude to witchcraft, since it decreed that a person who *claimed* to have occult powers was to be punished, not as a witch, but as a vagrant and fraud, with fines and imprisonment. In 1951, this Witchcraft Act was finally repealed and replaced with the Fraudulent Mediums Act (see HELEN DUNCAN).

During the centuries of persecution, the practice of folk magic survived in secret, especially in the countryside, with traditions being passed down mainly by word of mouth. In 1954, Gerald Gardner published *Witchcraft Today*, in which he described the existence of the craft in the 20th century. Gardner researched and rewrote many rituals and chants in an attempt to reclaim the lost knowledge of the 'old ways', and developed a neopagan form of nature-based spirituality (see NEOPAGANISM). He is regarded by many as the founder of modern-day witchcraft, or WICCA, which has been growing in popularity since the 1950s. Wicca venerates the forces inherent in nature, as personified in the GODDESS and the HORNED GOD, celebrates the cycle of the seasons and the moon in sabbats and ESBATS, offers a spirituality which is in tune with the natural world, and, unlike many orthodox faiths, views women and sexuality as sacred. It therefore appeals to many who are disenchanted with mainstream religions. Recognized by the American Supreme Court in 1986 as a legal religion, it has been claimed that Wicca is the fastest-growing religion in the USA today and, as well as Gardnerian witchcraft, a number of other traditions have developed, such as Alexandrian Wicca, founded by ALEX SANDERS; Celtic Wicca; Norse Wicca; Faery Wicca; and the feminist Dianic Wicca. Solitary witchcraft, a less formal method which may or may not use elements from various traditions, is also becoming increasingly popular among those who do not wish to work in the traditional witches' COVENS.

Contemporary witchcraft in all its forms is a modern construct, a revival rather than a survival of pre-Christian pagan practices. However, it is inspired by and draws on the past, and many modern witches thus regard themselves as carrying on an ancient tradition.

Lorna Gilmour

based upon a misunderstanding of the cultural beliefs involved.

In most instances of its modern usage the term 'witch doctor' is not intended to signify simply a doctor who uses WITCHCRAFT to heal, rather a traditional healer who detects ailments thought to be caused by magical means and who uses his or her own abilities to remove the problem. However, it is also often believed that a witch doctor, can, if he or she chooses, use their own magic to harm as well as to heal. In South Africa, such traditional healers may be referred to as either an 'inyanga' or a 'sangoma' (both words of Zulu origin) – terms which distinguish whether they primarily use herbalism or DIVINATION to produce healing. Healers who might be described as witch doctors continue to practise throughout much of Africa in both rural and urban areas. See also MEDICINE MAN; MUTI.

witches

Practitioners of witchcraft.

A witch is a practitioner of WITCHCRAFT. While most commonly associated with women, the term can also be used to refer to male practitioners of witchcraft; the majority of male practitioners of modern witchcraft (see WICCA) prefer the name 'witch' to WARLOCK, which is also sometimes used, finding the latter offensive. While witches are often associated with COVENS, many modern witches prefer to work alone, as 'solitaries'.

During the witch hunts of the 15th to late 17th centuries, witches were thought to enter pacts with the DEVIL and to engage in abominable practices. The persecution of witches had largely ended by the start of the 18th century, and in 1951 witchcraft ceased to be a crime in Britain.

witchfinder

In the past, a person employed to detect witches and bring them to trial.

Historically, witchfinders were professionals employed to detect witches and bring them to trial (see WITCH TRIALS). Witches were often first accused by other members of their community, but once someone had been denounced as a witch, the witchfinder would perform a number of tests to establish his or her guilt or innocence. Famous witchfinders include MATTHEW HOPKINS, the self-styled 'witchfinder-general' who carried out witch hunts between 1644 and 1647 in East Anglia, and Heinrich Kramer, co-author of the *MALLEUS MALEFICARUM*, which became a popular tool of witchfinders. Witchfinders were known to use extreme interrogation and torture to gain confessions from those accused of witchcraft, and a great many innocent people were executed on account of their actions.

Witch of Youghal *see* NEWTON, FLORENCE

witch's hat

A tall, black, pointed hat with a wide brim that appears in stereotypical images of witches.

The tall, black, pointed hat so often associated with WITCHES is generally thought to be a fairly modern artistic invention. Medieval woodcuts of witches show them wearing a variety of headgear, reflecting the fashions of the time, or going bare-headed. It has been suggested that the hat associated with witches today could be an exaggeration of the tall but flat-topped hats of traditional Welsh costume. Others have suggested that the witch's hat does have earlier origins, citing ancient Etruscan coins which appear to show the goddess Diana wearing a brimless conical hat. For a more recent invention of the stereotypical witch's hat Victorian illustrators have been suggested.

witch's mark

A protuberance or mark on the skin that was once considered to be proof that an accused person was a witch.

Traditionally taken to be an extra nipple through which a FAMILIAR or IMP would suckle blood, in medieval WITCH TRIALS an accused WITCH would be searched for any marks or irregularities that would be taken as physical proof of their WITCHCRAFT. Although the term 'witch's mark' is sometimes used interchangeably with DEVIL'S MARK, which was considered proof that a witch had entered a covenant with the Devil, the two are distinct. However, many witchfinders, including MATTHEW HOPKINS, did not distinguish between the two, and as they also believed that these marks were impervious to pain, they used a process called pricking to discover them. The accused would be jabbed with a sharp implement until an insensitive area was found and their guilt proclaimed. In his *The Discovery of Witches*, Hopkins explained how a witch's mark could be distinguished from a natural blemish:

> The reasons in breefe are three, which for the present he judgeth to differ from naturall marks which are:

> 1. He judgeth by the unusualnes of the place where he findeth the teats in or on their bodies being farre distant from any usuall place, from whence such naturall markes proceed …

> 2. They are most commonly insensible, and feele neither pin, needle, aule, &c. thrust through them.

3. The often variations and mutations of these marks into severall formes, confirmes the matter; as if a Witch hear a month or two before that the 'Witch-finder' (as they call him) is comming they will, and have put out their Imps to others to suckle them, even to their owne young and tender children; these upon search are found to have dry skinnes and filmes only, and be close to the flesh, keepe her 24. houres with a diligent eye, that none of her Spirits come in any visible shape to suck her; the women have seen the next day after her Teats extended out to their former filling length, full of corruption ready to burst, and leaving her alone then one quarter of an houre, and let the women go up againe and shee will have them drawn by her Imps close againe.

Witchfinders often claimed that witches displayed a number of these marks on various parts of their bodies.

witch trials

A witch trial was the examination by a court of someone accused of witchcraft to determine his or her guilt or innocence; witch trials were particularly common from the late Middle Ages to the late 17th century.

Witch trials had already begun before the publication of the MALLEUS MELEFICARUM in the late 1480s, but its appearance, and the papal bull issued by Pope Innocent VIII in 1484 that was an instruction to prosecute WITCHES in northern Germany, indicates how seriously the Church took the threat of WITCHCRAFT at that time.

Witches were generally found out by accusation – when a person was denounced as a witch, a series of tests could be made by a WITCHFINDER to determine their innocence or guilt. These included the searching for a WITCH'S MARK or a DEVIL'S MARK, or the water test – the accused would be thrown into a body of water with his or her hands tied, and if they sank they were assumed innocent, but if they floated they were assumed guilty and executed. Under extreme interrogation or torture, those accused of witchcraft were encouraged to confess to their crimes, and admit to the pacts they had entered into with the DEVIL, accept that they had FAMILIARS and name others who had allegedly attended SABBATS with them. In these circumstances, many named names and so witch hunts and witch trials grew in size.

Famous witch trials include those of the BAMBERG WITCHES in the early 1600s, and most famous of all (and the last major outbreak of widespread suspected witchcraft), the trials of the SALEM WITCHES. While it is clear that thousands of innocent people died as a result of the persecution of witches, there is no clear way of estimating the exact numbers involved, and many exaggerated figures are commonly referred to. During the early 18th century, both the belief in witchcraft and attempts to suppress it waned. The last execution for witchcraft in England took place in 1716, and the last person in Britain to be tried under the Witchcraft Act was HELEN DUNCAN in 1944 – the Act was repealed in 1951.

A witch is tried by ducking in the mill-stream, from a 17th-century woodcut. (© Mary Evans Picture Library)

withershins *see* WIDDERSHINS

wizards

Male practitioners of magic, popular figures in folklore and literature.

The word 'wizard' comes to us from medieval times. It is formed from the Middle English *wys*, meaning 'wise', plus the noun suffix *–ard*, as in 'drunkard', and in the 15th century it was used to refer to a philosopher or SAGE. By the 16th century it had come to denote a helpful male folk magician or 'cunning man', and soon it had taken on the sense we know today, of a master practitioner of MAGIC. Unlike 'witch' or 'SORCERER', however, the word 'wizard' has historically not had negative associations with black magic (see MAGIC, BLACK), and wizards have not in general been identified with malignant purposes; they are traditionally portrayed as elderly, learned individuals, helpful and benevolent, and wizardry is represented as a scholarly craft. Wizards are often thought to have been born with a natural talent for magic, and tend to work alone. Although sometimes feared or regarded with suspicion on account of their knowledge and powers, wizards throughout history and folklore have mostly escaped the persecution suffered by their female counterparts.

The most famous wizard of folklore and mythology is MERLIN, who as KING ARTHUR's adviser is a key figure in Arthurian legend. The historical Merlin is thought to have been the last great British pagan, a Druid shaman of the 6th century. Several men throughout history have been described as wizards, or have claimed this title, most notably HENRICUS CORNELIUS AGRIPPA VON NETTESHEIM, JOHN DEE, Nicolas Flamel and ALEISTER CROWLEY. The wizard is also an archetypal figure in literature and fiction, appearing as Prospero in Shakespeare's play *The Tempest*, Gandalf and Saruman in J R R Tolkien's *Lord of the Rings*, and in more recent years, Professor Albus Dumbledore in J K Rowling's *Harry Potter* series.

Woodhenge

Concentric circles of Neolithic wooden posts in Wiltshire.

Pilots flying over Wiltshire in the early 1920s identified strange circular markings on the ground near Amesbury. Aerial photographs were taken and archaeologists excavated the area later in the decade to discover a Neolithic site consisting of six concentric circles of wooden stumps. Like other HENGES, its central area was enclosed by an earthen bank and ditch, and as this was only 32 kilometres (20 miles) from STONEHENGE the find was quickly christened Woodhenge. The structure has been dated to c.2300 BC but its purpose has not been satisfactorily established.

Some have interpreted the wooden stumps as the remains of supporting pillars for the roof of an extensive wooden building. Others maintain that the posts are too numerous and too close together to serve this purpose, and that the wooden pillars would have been free-standing, as in a STONE CIRCLE. As at Stonehenge, there was an entrance at the northeast, and a general alignment in the direction of the midsummer sunrise. This led to theories that the original construction must have had religious purposes, and this interpretation was further supported by the discovery at the centre of the remains of a 3-year-old child whose split skull suggested ritual sacrifice. Another theory is that the structure may have been a tribal meeting-place, built of wood rather than stone precisely because it was *not* a religious site. However, the truth may never be known.

The wooden stumps have been replaced by concrete posts to mark out the site.

Woodhenge in Wiltshire – the six concentric circles of wooden stumps are now marked with concrete posts. (© Macduff Everton/Corbis)

woodwuses

Hairy wild men of the woods, mentioned occasionally in literature of the 16th and 17th centuries and sometimes appearing as heraldic figures and in church carvings.

The woodwuse is a powerful pre-Christian forest guardian who appears in the folk traditions of Europe, particularly in Gaul and Britain. Also known as the woodhouse, woodwose, wodewose, wodwo and Wild Man of the Woods, he is a link between the civilized human world and the dangerous nature spirits of the WILD WOOD, and is described as being naked but thickly covered in hair all over his body. He bears a leafy oaken club, perhaps a phallic symbol since he is sometimes seen as an aspect of the HORNED GOD, who is the lord of fertility. He has connections with the GREEN MAN, and like the Green Man, appears in church carvings, for example in Canterbury Cathedral; in medieval times his features were used on masks, and he appears as a supporting heraldic figure on coats of arms. There are scattered references to him throughout the literature of the 16th and 17th centuries. Merlin is said to have been driven mad with grief after a bloody battle and to have gone into the woods and become a woodwuse for a time. The word comes from the Anglo-Saxon *wuduwāsa*; the second element is unexplained, but while *wudu* is frequently taken to mean 'wood', it may in fact be derived from the Old Saxon *wod* meaning 'wild or ecstatic'.

words of power

The use of a word of power, often the name of a god, angel or demon, is believed to grant magical power to the person who speaks or writes it.

While objects are often used either directly or symbolically for magical purposes, the use of words, both written and spoken, has also been a prominent feature of ritual and MAGIC throughout the centuries. Sounds are believed to contain power, and in most cultures, repeated chanting is known to have an auto-hypnotic effect; Hindu mantras are believed to create spiritual energy, and many Graeco-Egyptian magical papyri contain strings of vowel sounds which may have been believed to transport the chanter to an altered level of consciousness, or to impart power to a ritual or spell. The concept of words of power appears to have originated with the ancient Egyptians and Greeks, and the Hebrews believed that power could be unleashed by the vibrations of spoken words; the Jewish mysticism which preceded the KABBALAH emphasized the importance of names of power, such as the names of angels and the secret names of God.

In magic it is generally held that knowledge of the true name of something gives knowledge of, and thus power over, the thing itself. The names of gods, angels and demons are thought to be particularly effective tools in ritual and magic, because it is believed that they contain and transmit the power of the entity itself. Various medieval GRIMOIRES give words or names of power to be used during incantations or the construction of a MAGIC CIRCLE. By using their names it is believed that spirits can be invoked and made to obey the magician's commands, whether for help in working magic, or to exorcise and dispel demonic forces. The speaking of such a name is said automatically to bring the power of the being into operation, and repeated chanting of the name taps into this power. By naming, one controls what is named, and angels and demons are thought to be particularly susceptible to this kind of control; however, caution must be exercised in doing so, since it is believed that naming a spirit also gives it power and reality, bringing it into existence and strengthening it. For this reason, a Norse/Germanic magical principle known as *kenning* is sometimes employed in order not to attract an entity's attention when this is not wanted; the entity is referred to by some form of circumlocution or euphemism, or by describing it in detail, without using its actual name.

Some languages have long been considered magical by their very nature, particularly dead or ancient ones such as Egyptian, Hebrew, classical Greek and Latin, and the names of foreign deities are frequently found in spells of the Graeco-Roman period in Egypt, as well as in later mystical and magical traditions. The proper names of angels have always been thought to have great power. Most angelic names in Judaic and Christian lore are Hebrew names; only three angels are named in Christian scripture – Michael, Gabriel and Raphael – but ex-canonical works such as the Apocrypha give many more angelic names. The power of these names is determined through GEMATRIA, a kabbalistic system for discovering the hidden meanings behind words through numbers. Numerical values are assigned to each letter of the Hebrew alphabet, and the numbers of each letter in the name are added up, and the total is interpreted in terms of other words with the same numerical value. In this way, names can be related to other names, or to passages in scripture.

The most powerful magical word imaginable is thought to be the true name of God, often referred to as the Tetragrammaton, since in the Old Testament it is written in Hebrew as four letters: YHVH. Its exact pronunciation is not known, but it is commonly pronounced as Yahweh or Jehovah. Practising Jews are forbidden to speak it aloud, but the numerical values of its Hebrew letters Yod, He, Vav and He add up to 10, which in Hebrew gematria represents the basic organizing principle in the universe.

Worth, Patience

The pseudonym of US writer Pearl Lenore Curran, who claimed that she not responsible for her written works, but that she channelled them from Worth, a 17th-century Englishwoman.

Born Pearl Lenore Pollard in Illinois in 1883, Curran showed little interest in writing in her early life. Although she had demonstrated an aptitude for music, she had shown little interest in other subjects and had not done particularly well at school. In 1913, Curran was shown a OUIJA BOARD by a neighbour, and although she was apparently sceptical, thinking that such parlour games were silly, and her first attempts at using it were not successful, she persisted and eventually claimed that she received the following message:

> Many moons ago I lived. Again I come. Patience Worth my name … If thou shalt live, then so shall I.

Following this message, Curran began to ask specific questions of the spirit of Patience Worth, and claimed that she received coherent answers. Worth had supposedly been a 17th-century Englishwoman who had lived in Dorset before travelling to America where she had been murdered by Native Americans. Soon Curran felt that the ouija board was no longer needed for her communications with Worth, as Curran could anticipate Worth's responses. Curran claimed that whole sentences from Worth would form in her mind – and a series of books were published setting out Curran's claims. Curran went on to publish a great many works – novels, poems and a play – which she claimed were composed by Worth. Sceptics pointed out that one of the novels supposedly by 17th-century Worth was set in the Victorian era, but the books were very popular, and many were fascinated by Curran's claims. Her supporters insisted that Curran could not have written the books herself as she had not received enough education to enable her to do so, and a 'ghost' truly was responsible for them.

By 1922 it seems that Curran and Worth had apparently fallen out, and by the time of Curran's death in 1937 she no longer claimed further communication.

wraith

An apparitional double; also a general term for a ghost of the dead.

In Celtic folklore, a wraith is an apparitional double or ghost of the living (a DOPPELGÄNGER or FETCH), that is said to herald death. The appearance of a wraith is generally taken to indicate that the person it represents has either just died or is about to do so. The word 'wraith' (originally Scottish, and perhaps from the Old Norse *vörthr*, 'a guardian') is also used more generally to refer to an APPARITION or GHOST of any kind.

Wright, Elsie *see* COTTINGLEY FAIRIES

xenoglossy

A phenomenon in which a person is said to speak or write spontaneously in a foreign language that is unknown to them, and which they could not have acquired by natural means; because it is superficially similar to the phenomenon of glossolalia, it is sometimes used as if synonymous with it.

Xenoglossy, also known as xenoglossia or xeno-glossolalia (from Greek *xeno-*, meaning strange, and *glossa*, meaning language) is an apparently miraculous phenomenon in which a person demonstrates the ability spontaneously to speak or write in a foreign language that is unknown to them, and which they could not have acquired by natural means. This ability is sometimes said to be demonstrated by MEDIUMS and clairvoyants who claim to channel spirits who speak or write in a language that is unfamiliar to the channeller. Xenoglossy has also been cited by some as proof of REINCARNATION, the argument being that the only way a person can speak a language unknown to them is if they have retained knowledge of it from a past life. Some people who have undergone the controversial process of PAST-LIFE REGRESSION are said, while under hypnosis, to have spoken in languages which they no longer know when they are awake.

There has, however, been no scientifically proven case of xenoglossy. Sceptics hold that in most, if not all, alleged cases, the knowledge of the 'unknown' language displayed is minimal, and could have been learned by casual exposure – as, for instance, in the case of the subject whose ability to speak Russian was the result of his having overheard, as a child, a language tutor teaching students Russian phrases in the next room, and having unconsciously memorized some of what he heard.

Since xenoglossy superficially resembles a religious ECSTATIC PHENOMENON called glossolalia, in which language-like but unintelligible sounds are uttered, the term is often used synonymously with it. Glossolalia, or 'speaking in tongues', has a long historical precedent, and is found in many religions, including pagan and shamanic ones. At the Greek ORACLE OF DELPHI, the god Apollo was said to have spoken through his priestess, the SIBYL, in strange utterances, which were interpreted by a priest, and the Coptic Gospel of the Egyptians contains a hymn of largely nonsense syllables which are believed to be an early example of Christian glossolalia.

'The gift of tongues' is most commonly associated with, and is a major feature of, charismatic and Pentecostal Christian groups, being linked to an individual's salvation and their subsequent 'Baptism of the Holy Spirit'. Subjects may have convulsions or fall into a trance, and often claim later to have no memory of having spoken in tongues, but they believe that they have been possessed by the Holy Spirit and that their utterances are meaningful; however, only one with faith and the gift of interpretation can translate these utterances. Speaking in tongues is one of the signs listed in the New Testament, in Mark 16: 16–18, which may be manifested by those who believe in Christ, and there is debate among Christians and scholars as to the exact nature of the MIRACLE described in chapter 2 of Acts of the Apostles, where it is said that on the day of Pentecost, tongues of fire alighted on the apostles, filling them with the Holy Spirit so that they 'spoke in the language of their hearers'. The primary function of this miracle was as a sign to convince unbelievers of the power of the Holy Spirit, and to spread the message of the gospel. An impressive list of the many languages heard by the listeners is included and some interpret this passage as describing an instance of true religious xenoglossy.

x-files

A popular colloquial term applied by the media, and some UFO researchers, to official records of UFO activity.

The popular 1990s fictional US television series, *The X-Files*, was based loosely on the many conspiracy theories surrounding ALIEN ABDUCTIONS and UFOS. The plots leant heavily towards the idea that there was a GOVERNMENTAL COVER-UP of details relating to an alien presence on earth and to secret experiments being conducted on hapless victims.

At the height of its popularity the series led to thousands of people being attracted to UFO research. However, it also led them to enter the field with unrealistic expectations. Many hoped to find evidence for major conspiracies and exciting real-life UFO incidents; instead they found confusion as to the nature of the phenomenon, large numbers of cases involving little more than reports of LIGHTS IN THE SKY and an admission by UFO researchers that most cases resulted from misperceptions of ordinary things. They found few signs of the type of hard evidence for alien contact that appeared in episodes of *The X-Files*.

At the time when the television series was first being shown, many nations were in the process of introducing FREEDOM OF INFORMATION ACTS. These began to allow public access to records relating to government interest in UFOs since 1947. Most countries had launched some kind of investigation into the phenomenon and had gathered together the reports received through official channels such as the military or the police force. Such records became known to a new, younger generation of UFO enthusiasts as a nation's 'x-files', and the term began to appear in newspaper headlines and television documentaries. However, many seasoned members of the UFO COMMUNITY were less inclined to use the phrase because they were concerned that it inspired images that were never likely to be matched by the evidence.

yang

One of two opposing and complementary principles of Chinese philosophy, religion and medicine, seen as the positive, masculine, light, warm or active element; opposite of yin.

The ancient Chinese philosophers believed that before the universe was created, there existed a void called *Wu Chi*. Out of this emptiness there separated two opposing but complementary principles: activity or motion, known as yang, and its opposite aspect, inactivity or stillness, known as YIN. These two forces exist in a creative relationship in which they constantly interact and change, and it is this constant interaction of yin and yang which create the changes that keep the universe in motion, and which are said to have given rise to the five basic Chinese elements of fire, wood, earth, metal and water, of which all things are said to be composed.

Yang (Chinese for 'bright') is seen as masculine, symbolizing positive polarity, and is associated with the qualities of activity, heat, hardness, light and movement. Yin and yang cannot exist without one another, and each is believed to contain the seed of its opposite, and to be able to transform into it; day ultimately changes into night, life into death, heat into cold and so on. This interdependence is shown in the symbol of yin and yang called the *Taijitu*, a circle divided into a light yang half with a small dark yin spot in its centre, and a dark yin half which contains a small light yang spot.

Everything in nature is said to have a complementary and opposite component which is represented by these two attributes, and harmony is thought to be established by a balance of yin and yang. This balance is a central concept in CHINESE MEDICINE, which holds that yin and yang regulate the

body's vital energy, or QI. A state of health requires a perfect balance of yin and yang as they interact in the body, and if these become imbalanced it causes a disruption in the flow of qi, which can lead to illness. An excess of yang energy is thought to be characterized by nervousness, hyperactivity or high

The *Taijitu*, the symbol which represents yin and yang. The circle is divided into a light yang half with a dark yin spot, and a dark yin half with a light yang spot.
(© TopFoto)

blood pressure, and the gallbladder, small intestine, stomach, large intestine and bladder are considered to be yang organs.

The concept of yin and yang is found in a number of Chinese philosophies, but is particularly prominent in TAOISM.

yeren

A hairy man-beast reported from China that apparently constitutes two totally separate creatures.

Also known as the Chinese wild man and commonly reported from central China's Shennongjia Mountains, the yeren appears to comprise two very different species. The smaller version, frequently seen running on all fours, is nowadays believed to be an unusually large type of macaque monkey. Conclusive evidence for its existence has existed for some time, in the form of a pair of preserved hands – taken from the body of one such animal when it was killed on a Zhejiang mountain in May 1957. In 1985, a specimen was actually captured alive, near Anhui Province's Huangshan Mountain, and was exhibited at Hefei Zoo.

However, some eyewitness accounts, such as that of forestry worker Xiao Xingyang, who claimed that he encountered a yeren in a Shennongjia wood during August 1977, describe a very different creature – a shaggy humanoid entity with reddish hair, standing 1.5–1.8 metres (5–6 feet) tall, and walking on its hind legs. One was apparently shot dead in 1940, and was closely observed afterwards by biologist Wang Zelin, who likened its head to that of a Chinese version of the ancestral human species *Homo erectus*, called Peking Man, with protruding jaws, high cheekbones and sunken eye sockets. Unfortunately, no record exists regarding the fate of this scientifically invaluable corpse.

In recent years, hair samples left behind by this form of yeren – on trees and in vegetation – have been meticulously studied by a method of analysis termed particle-induced x-ray emission (PIXE), which reveals the relative proportions of the various chemical elements contained within the hairs. The ratios obtained do not correspond with those of any known animal recorded from China, and contain an exceptionally yet consistently high ratio of iron to zinc.

Yeren investigators have variously identified the larger version as a specialized orang-utan (a species officially extinct in China), or as a relict version of *Homo erectus*, or even as a surviving species of *Gigantopithecus* – a huge ape believed to have died out 100,000 years ago. This latter possibility is particularly interesting, and potentially significant, because *Gigantopithecus* is also a much-favoured identity for North America's BIGFOOT, as well as for the giant version of the YETI. See also MAN-BEASTS.

Yesod

In the kabbalah, the sephirah or emanation of God known as Foundation, which is assigned the number 9; it represents the unconscious and the imagination.

Yesod is the ninth of the ten SEPHIROTH, or divine emanations, in the KABBALAH. It is called Foundation, and is the sixth of the emotive attributes of the sephiroth. Yesod is a place of force and energy, and represents the dream world above earthly human consciousness. It is assigned the number 9. On the kabbalistic TREE OF LIFE, it is positioned directly below TIPHARETH, and directly above MALKUTH, and is the third sphere on the middle axis, the Pillar of Equilibrium. It is also the bottom point on the lowest of the three triangles formed by the sephiroth, the Astral or Psychological Triangle, which it makes up with NETZACH and HOD, and as such, it reaches down into the unconscious, and underpins the physical universe. It is given four paths on the Tree of Life – to Hod, Tiphareth, Netzach and Malkuth. Netzach and Hod achieve balance in Yesod. Yesod is seen as the source of images and symbols which make up mythology, and relates to the power to contact, connect to and communicate with outer reality, as represented by Malkuth. It is associated with the divine name *Shaddai El Chai* (the Almighty Living God), the archangel Gabriel, the angelic order of the Holy Cherubs and the planetary force of the Moon. In the TAROT, Yesod corresponds to the four nines, and in the tarot Tree of Life spread, the card in the Yesod position usually represents the imagination, and the shape and mood of the person's unconscious. In some kabbalistic systems it is attributed with the magical image of a very strong, naked man, and is represented by the symbol of perfume or sandals. It is often connected with the sacral CHAKRA. The word Yesod in kabbalistic GEMATRIA gives the number 80. It is also sometimes called the Treasure House of Images.

yeti

The name given to the famous 'abominable snowman' said to inhabit the Himalayan mountain range, but which may describe more than one cryptid.

For well over a century, mountaineers scaling the Himalayan peaks that straddle the borders of southern Tibet and Nepal have reported seeing man-sized, shaggy-haired, ape-like creatures, sometimes walking on their hind legs and leaving footprints in the snow that are up to 33 centimetres (12 inches) long. Referred to as yetis by the Nepalese people, and also known as the 'meh-the' ('man-beast'), in the West they have become known as abominable snowmen, and their identity remains one of the greatest cryptozoological mysteries of modern times.

According to many eyewitnesses the yeti appears to be some form of predominantly terrestrial, fruit-eating ape, standing about 2 metres (6.5 feet) tall when bipedal, with long reddish-brown fur, a very powerful well-muscled body, noticeably lengthy arms, a generally hairless face and a large head with a prominent crest running along the top of its dome-shaped skull. Some have suggested that it may be a type of ground-living orang-utan, spending much of its time in the rhododendron forests on the mountains' lower reaches, only ascending to the snow-covered higher regions when food is scarce. However, some sceptics would dismiss all the reports of yetis as misinterpreted sightings of bears, while others would say that it is a non-existent creature of traditional local folklore.

Nevertheless, a number of alleged yeti relics have come to light over the years. Perhaps the most controversial are several reputed yeti scalps, displaying this cryptid's familiar crest of hair. When examined, however, these items were found not to be scalps at all, but pieces of pelt taken from the shoulders of a species of mountain-dwelling goat-antelope called the serow. However, the lamas whose monasteries loaned these relics for examination responded that they were never claimed to be genuine yeti scalps, but merely costume items representing yeti scalps which are worn by participants taking the role of the yeti in ceremonies. More intriguing was the skeleton of an alleged yeti hand formerly owned by the Pangboche monastery in Nepal. When examined by Western scientists, the consensus was that it had come from an unknown species of primate, but, tragically, this vital piece of evidence was mysteriously stolen from the monastery in May 1991, and its current whereabouts remain unknown, though photographs of it still exist. Possibly most significant of all was a sample of supposed yeti hair collected in 2001 by British zoologist Rob McCall from a hollow cedar tree in Bhutan. When this hair sample's DNA was analysed at the Oxford Institute of Molecular Medicine, it could not be identified as that of any species of animal currently known to science.

The yeti is very commonly confused with a much bigger, flatter-headed mystery primate, usually reported from eastern Tibet, Sikkim, Bangladesh and other mountainous regions outside the Himalayas, and known locally as the dzu-teh ('hulking beast') or giant yeti. Unlike the true yeti, which often runs on all fours, the dzu-teh is habitually bipedal, and stands at least 2.7 metres (8.9 feet) tall. Its fur is said to be blackish-brown, and it apparently includes meat in its diet.

Some zoologists have speculated that the dzu-teh may be a surviving descendant of *Gigantopithecus* – a huge ape that is now known to have lived in Asia until at least 100,000 years ago. Others believe it to be a very large, possibly still-unknown species of bear. In 1953, a Tibetan lama called Chemed Rigdzin Dorje Lopu claimed to have examined two giant mummified dzu-tehs, which resembled enormous apes. One was housed in the monastery at Riwoche in Tibet's Kham Province, the other at Sakya monastery. Many Tibetan relics and monasteries were destroyed following China's annexation of Tibet a few years later, so whether these remarkable specimens still exist somewhere is unknown. See also MAN-BEASTS.

yin

One of two opposing and complementary principles of Chinese philosophy, religion and medicine, seen as the negative, feminine, dark, cold or passive element; opposite of yang.

Ancient Chinese philosophers believed that before the creation of the universe there was a state of emptiness. Out of this void came the separation of two opposing but complementary principles: inactivity or stillness, known as yin, and its opposite aspect, activity or motion, known as YANG. The union and interplay of the forces of yin and yang are said to have given rise to the five basic elements of which all things are thought to be composed – fire, wood, earth, metal and water – and it is the constant interaction of yin and yang which is believed to create the changes that keep the universe in motion.

Yin (Chinese for 'dark') is seen as feminine, symbolizing negative polarity, and is associated with the qualities of passivity, cold, softness, darkness and stillness. Yin cannot exist without yang, or yang without yin, and each principle is believed to be able to transform into its opposite, and to hold its seed; night eventually becomes day, cold water can be transformed into hot steam and so on. This interconnectedness is represented graphically in the *Taijitu*, the symbol of ying and yang which shows a circle divided into a dark yin half which contains a small light yang spot, and a light yang half with a small dark yin spot.

All things in nature are believed to have a complementary and opposite component represented by these dual and inseparable forces, and the balance of yin and yang brings harmony. CHINESE MEDICINE is based on the concept that yin and yang regulate the body's vital energy, or QI, and that a perfect balance of yin and yang is required for health; if these become imbalanced, it causes a disruption in the flow of qi, which in turn leads to illness. A person who is sluggish, emotionally sensitive or slightly overweight, or who has a tendency to catch cold easily, may be diagnosed by a practitioner of Chinese medicine as having an excess of yin, and the liver, heart, spleen, pancreas, lungs and kidneys are considered to be yin organs.

The concept of yin and yang appears in several Chinese philosophies, and is especially prominent in TAOISM.

yoga

Any of a number of physical and mental disciplines designed to promote physical and spiritual well-being, based on an ancient Hindu system.

It is thought that yoga may be as much as 5,000 years old. As a means to spiritual enlightenment, this ancient system is central to Hinduism, Buddhism, Sikhism and JAINISM. It is designed to produce in its practitioners a state of perfect physical well-being and an advanced meditative state known as SAMADHI. Throughout India it is still used mainly as a spiritual path, but in the West, it is often practised purely for its perceived health benefits. The name 'yoga' comes from a Sanskrit word meaning 'union', and yoga is based on the Hindu philosophy that mind, body and spirit are all united and interconnected. It is held that a UNIVERSAL LIFE FORCE, known as prana, surrounds and permeates the body, its flow being controlled by energy centres called CHAKRAS. When the balance and harmony of this flow is disrupted, illness may result; many yoga postures, breathing exercises and meditation techniques are therefore designed to maintain the optimum balance of energy in the body, and to correct any weaknesses or blockages which impair its flow.

The classic description of yoga, which helped to define and shape its modern practice, can be found in the Yoga Sutras, written by the Indian sage Patanjali some time between 200 BC and AD 200. Other important texts include the *Bhagavad Gita* and the *Hatha Yoga Pradipika*. Although it was developed from Hinduism, classical yoga is not a religion, but a way of life which includes ethical modes of behaviour and incorporates eight paths to self-realization, each believed to contribute to the practitioner's personal development. These paths consist of *Yama*, or abstinence (which includes non-violence and truthfulness); *Niyama*, or personal discipline (which includes study and austerity); *Asana* (physical postures); *Pranayama* (control of prana, or vital breath); *Pratyahara*, or detachment; *Dharana*, or concentration; and *Dhyana*, or meditation. These seven 'paths', when practised together, lead to the experience of samadhi, an advanced meditative state of bliss in which the yogi's consciousness unites mystically with the universe, or the supreme being, to become 'mind without thought'.

In the West, yoga classes tend to emphasize the physical aspects of the discipline. (© Ronnie Kaufman/Corbis)

During its long history, a number of different yoga traditions have emerged, each focusing on certain aspects of this eightfold path. In the East, the four main forms are considered to be *Karma* yoga, which stresses service to all beings as a path to enlightenment; *Bhakti*, which emphasizes devotion to the divine; *Inana* or *Jnana*, knowledge of the self and direct experience of the divine; and *Raja* yoga, which primarily involves the control of the intellect by meditation and concentration. Other important yoga forms include *Mantra*, the yoga of sacred sounds; KUNDALINI, which focuses on raising the 'serpent' of dormant energy thought to coil at the base of the spine and moving it up the spine to the head, activating each chakra in turn as it does so, to bring about enlightenment; and *Tantra* yoga, which includes the study of sacred writings and rituals, but is best known as a means of sustaining sexual pleasure through ritualized intercourse to heighten consciousness (see TANTRA).

However, it is the physical forms of yoga which are most commonly practised in the West. The best known of these is *Hatha* yoga, which focuses on the control of the physical body and emphasizes the use of physical postures known as *asanas* and breath-control techniques known as *pranayama*. Like Chinese QIGONG, *pranayama* promotes the ability to control the flow of energy in the body. The most strenuous form, *Ashtanga* yoga, also known as eight-step yoga, combines elements of *Hatha* and *Raja* yoga, and links *Hatha* postures in a flowing, almost continuous movement while combining them with *pranayama* and meditation. Although traditional *Hatha* yoga is a complete system which includes mental disciplines, it is often practised in the West purely as a therapeutic aid to fitness and health, rather than as a path to spiritual enlightenment. See also AYURVEDA.

yogic flying
The purported ability to levitate, which is claimed to be gained through the practice of transcendental meditation.

The tradition of yogic flying is said to have originated with the Vedic *rishi*, or seer, Avatsara, and the power to levitate by means of yogic techniques is described, in varying degrees of detail, in a number of yogic texts. The Yoga Sutras of Patanjali describe three stages of yogic flying: the first is that of 'hopping like a frog', the second is that of flying through the air for a short time, and the third is complete mastery of the sky. A system of yogic flying also exists within the tantras of Tibetan Buddhism as a means of attaining enlightenment.

In recent times, however, yogic flying has been mainly associated with TRANSCENDENTAL MEDITATION (TM), and, for a period during the 1990s, with the Natural Law Party. A programme which included yogic flying was introduced by the founder of transcendental meditation, MAHARISHI MAHESH YOGI, in 1976, as an extension of his TM technique, and in 1992, his organization founded a political party, the Natural Law Party, to support candidates dedicated to promoting TM and the Maharishi's teachings. One of the most memorable platforms of the Natural Law Party in the early 1990s was that of yogic flying, in which it was claimed that advanced practitioners of TM could perform a kind of levitation while sitting cross-legged in the lotus position.

Although no TM practitioners of yogic flying have been known to have progressed beyond the first stage of 'hopping', it is claimed to induce a state of restful alertness and to bring about increased activity and coherence in the brain waves. When yogic flying is practised in large groups, these positive influences are said to spread throughout the environment, resulting in a drop in the crime rate, sickness and accidents (referred to as 'the Extended Maharishi Effect'). There are current plans by the TM movement to create permanent groups of 8,000 yogic flyers, which it is claimed would generate sufficient positivity and harmony to bring about world peace.

yowie
A gorilla-like cryptid reported from Australia, an island continent where the native mammals are predominantly marsupials.

Ever since Westerners first settled in Australia, there have been sightings reported by them of a tailless gorilla-like MAN-BEAST. Usually said to stand around 1.5–2.1 metres (5–7 feet) tall, but sometimes much taller, and generally bipedal, it is said to have a small dome-shaped head, little or no neck, a very broad chest, broad back and very powerful shoulders, long dark brown hair on black skin, long arms, relatively thin legs and large feet up to 45.8 centimetres (16 inches) long, including their proportionately lengthy toes. Well known to the aboriginal people, who have given this unexpected CRYPTID many names throughout its range, it first became known to Western pioneers as the yahoo (a name probably derived from the human savages featured in Jonathan Swift's classic satirical fantasy, *Gulliver's Travels*). However, more recently, certainly from the 1970s onwards, this name has been largely supplanted by yowie ('dream spirit').

Out of the numerous eyewitness accounts on record, there are some that are quite outstanding. Perhaps the most remarkable of all featured a Queensland National Parks and Wildlife ranger, who claimed he had been extremely sceptical of yowie reports – until the day when he encountered one of these mystery man-beasts at close range. One sunny afternoon in March 1978 in south-eastern Queensland's Springbrook region, the ranger claims that he heard what he believed to be a wild pig, rooting among some trees. He moved towards the creature – only to discover when he finally caught sight of it, just 3.5 metres (11.5 feet) away, that it was definitely not a pig. Instead it was a bipedal gorilla-like entity, 2.3 metres (7.5 feet) tall covered in black hair, with big yellow eyes, a flat shiny-black face, a hole-like mouth, a very short thick neck and human-like fingers. Perhaps the yowie sensed him, because without warning it emitted an absolutely foul stench, so rank that the ranger vomited, and while he did so the yowie swiftly moved away through the trees, vanishing from view. The ranger reported what he had seen to his boss, who told him not to publicize his sighting (which is why the ranger has never released his name), in case it attracted hunters to the area. Nevertheless, the ranger is now totally convinced that yowies are real. Interestingly, the stench-producing trait he described is frequently reported for the BIGFOOT of North America.

The problem with the yowie is that by all the

laws of zoogeography, it should not exist at all. Australia became an island continent when the ruling mammals were marsupials. Although they largely died out elsewhere in the world (South America, which was also an island continent for millions of years before eventually rejoining North America via the Isthmus of Panama, is the only other major present-day marsupial stronghold), marsupials remained unchallenged in Australia by advanced (placental) mammals until historical times, when the latter were introduced here by man (except for bats, which could fly here, and certain swimming mammals). So if the yowie is truly native to Australia, it is most likely to be a marsupial, a morphological counterpart of bona fide apes found in Africa and Asia, engineered by convergent evolution. Some cryptozoologists have even nominated a remarkably ape-like herbivorous marsupial called *Hulitherium* as a possible candidate, even though it is currently known only from fossils found in New Guinea, not Australia. An alternative marsupial identity that has been put forward by some investigators is that the yowie is actually a giant species of wombat, but such a creature would surely appear much more bear-like than gorilla-like in form.

If the yowie is a true man-beast rather than a marsupial, conversely, the principal options on offer include: a representative of the extinct giant Asian ape *Gigantopithecus*, though how a species of ape could have reached Australia without a land-bridge is difficult to say; a relict, regressed version of our own species' ancestor, *Homo erectus*, which may have reached Australia from Asia on floating rafts; a surviving population of a highly distinctive, early Australian form of *Homo sapiens* known as Kow Swamp Man and inhabiting Victoria, whose fossils suggest that it shared certain primitive features with *Homo erectus*; or even a particularly hairy race of modern-day human. Whatever it is, however, there is no doubt that the yowie is the most enigmatic and perplexing of all man-beasts.

Z

Zacatecas

The location for the first recorded photograph of a UFO, which was taken by a professional astronomer.

In 1883, Jose Bonilla was an astronomer working as the director of the observatory situated 3,350 metres (11,000 feet) up a mountain in Zacatecas, Mexico. On 12 August he was using a large reflector to view the sun – projecting an image onto a screen to protect his eyesight. He was looking for phenomena, such as sunspots, on the surface of the sun.

According to Bonilla's testimony, he discovered that there were strange objects moving across the face of the sun, leaving luminous trails as they travelled. They appeared dark when in front of the sun – in the same way that sunspots (which are really very bright) appear black in contrast to the greater brilliance surrounding them. The astronomer was able to take some photographs of the incident, thus producing the first surviving UFO pictures.

Bonilla described what he saw as follows:

> I was able to fix their trajectory across the solar disc … some appeared round or spherical, but one notes in the photographs that the bodies are not spherical but irregular in form. Before crossing the solar disc these bodies threw out brilliant trains of light but in crossing the sun they seemed to become opaque.

It was speculated that these objects were either birds or, more likely, insects that happened to cross the field of view of the telescope. If so they would have been much closer than Bonilla assumed – he believed, from the measurements he had taken, that they were in space but inside the orbit of the moon. If they were actually closer than his estimate then they would have

been out of focus – this would also account for the apparent trails.

Bonilla was an experienced observer and argued that these explanations did not fit the facts of the sighting. He provided no explanation for the phenomenon. The 'UFO' interpretation, with its modern connotations, has, of course, been applied by others in hindsight.

Zen Buddhism

A Japanese school of Buddhism that teaches that enlightenment is not to be found in the study of texts and scriptures, but in meditation and the contemplation of one's own essential nature.

Zen is the Japanese name for a school of Buddhism which was said to have been brought from India to China by Bodhidharma, a legendary practitioner of Mahayana Buddhism, near the end of the 5th century. In China, Zen was known as Ch'an. According to tradition, Bodhidharma meditated for nine years in his quest for insight into the ways of enlightenment, and began to teach a group of disciples, passing on his teaching to his successor, Hui-k'o, known as the Second Patriarch. Under the Third Patriarch, Seng-ts'an, Zen came under the influence of TAOISM, and to a lesser extent, Confucianism, and the Sixth Patriarch, Hui-Neng, added emphasis to the discovery of one's own 'original mind' and true nature. In the 8th and 9th centuries, Zen grew and developed its traditions of one-to-one instruction and its focus on the direct experience of enlightenment, or *satori*, as opposed to the study of texts; Bodhidharma was said to have described Zen as 'a special transmission' outside the scriptures.

Although Zen gradually declined in China, it flourished in Japan, particularly among the medieval military classes, and had a strong influence on Japanese art and literature. Two main schools of Zen developed, with different approaches to the attainment of enlightenment. The Southern school, which came to be known as Soto, focused on 'sudden enlightenment' through the use of tools such as *koans* – paradoxical teaching riddles like 'What is the sound of one hand clapping?' Meditating on the *koan* is said to allow the student to 'short-circuit' the logical and conceptual way in which we usually think, and trigger an altered mindset which facilitates enlightenment. This school developed further into many independent schools, often related to other forms of Buddhism. The Northern school, brought to Japan in 1191, was known as Rinzai, and encouraged cross-legged meditation, or *zazen*, with no expectation of sudden enlightenment; its masters taught by constant questioning, and sometimes even physical violence.

As developed in China, Korea and Japan, the Zen way of life was very different from that of Indian Buddhism, which had a tradition of mendicants, or holy beggars. The cultural and social conditions in China meant that Zen evolved as a temple and training-centre system in which the monks performed mundane tasks and lived in a community. This perhaps influenced Zen's emphasis on an enlightenment which has a relevance to the demands of everyday life; not only are scriptures and dogma regarded with suspicion, but Zen teaches that direct personal experience of meditation and an actual, engaged presence on a moment-to-moment basis are of prime importance. Zen is not seen primarily as an intellectual philosophy or a solitary pursuit, nor as a state of consciousness, but as a way of life characterized by humility, labour, service, prayer and gratitude. The purpose of meditation is not to become withdrawn or self-absorbed, but to discover the authentic self, capable of participating fully in the world and of becoming totally involved with whatever one is doing, without distraction.

As a branch of Buddhism, Zen is based on and deeply rooted in the Buddha's teachings, and all Zen schools are versed in Buddhist doctrine and philosophy. Like other Mahayana Buddhist traditions, Zen emphasizes cultivation of the virtues known as the *pāramitās*, or 'Six Perfections': generosity, morality or ethics, patience, energy or effort, concentration and wisdom, which is seen as the sum of the other five. The aim of Zen is the realization of the true Buddha-nature which underlies all appearances, and the discovery of one's own Buddha-nature.

The history of Zen has been closely connected to the development of several martial art forms, such as Aiki jujutsu, Judo, and in particular, Aikido in Japan and Kung Fu in China. Since the mid-20th century,

it has become popular in the West, albeit sometimes in a diluted form.

Zener cards

A standard set of cards used in parapsychology experiments.

Zener cards were developed by J B RHINE (in consultation with the psychologist Karl Zener) in the late 1920s, for use in research in the area of EXTRASENSORY PERCEPTION (ESP). A set of Zener cards uses only five different designs, a circle, a cross, three wavy lines, a square and a five-pointed star – each design appears five times in a full pack. At the time they were created Rhine was engaged in a series of CARD-GUESSING EXPERIMENTS, using a standard deck of playing cards. This alternative set of cards made the statistical analysis of the results of such experiments easier, and eliminated ambiguity when it came to 'sending' and 'receiving' the images on the cards.

In a classic card-guessing experiment using Zener cards, an agent (see AGENCY), or sender, tries to use TELEPATHY to transmit a randomly chosen card to a recipient. Statistically there is a 20 per cent chance of getting a single card correct by guesswork. If more than 20 per cent of the 'guesses' are correct over an

The five designs found in a set of Zener cards.

(© Mary Evans Picture Library)

extended trial this is taken to support the existence of some form of ESP. Some researchers also regard scores significantly lower than 20 per cent as evidence of negative ESP. Initial experiments appeared to yield positive results, but it was subsequently recognized that the way that the cards had been manufactured, and the results of their handling, could give clues to the receiver – as could the fact that the recipient was able to see the agent in some versions of the experiment. The cards were redesigned and experimenters now usually place the two participants in separate rooms.

zodiac

In astrology, the collection of twelve signs through which the sun passes in a year.

The zodiac (derived from the ancient Greek for a small figure of an animal) is an imaginary belt in the heavens, about 18° wide, through which the ecliptic (the apparent path of the SUN's annual motion among the fixed stars) passes centrally, and which forms the background of the motions of the sun, MOON and planets. It is divided into twelve equal parts of 30° called signs of the zodiac, named from the constellations that once corresponded to them (they now no longer do so due to an effect called the precession of the equinoxes). The constellations, with the symbols of the corresponding signs, and the approximate times during which the sun is said to pass through them, are as follows:

> ARIES (*Ram*) ♈ 21 March–20 April
> TAURUS (*Bull*) ♉ 21 April–20 May
> GEMINI (*Twins*) ♊ 21 May–21 June
> CANCER (*Crab*) ♋ 22 June–23 July
> LEO (*Lion*) ♌ 24 July–23 August
> VIRGO (*Virgin*) ♍ 24 August–23 September
> LIBRA (*Balance*) ♎ 24 September–22 October
> SCORPIO (*Scorpion*) ♏ 23 October–22 November
> SAGITTARIUS (*Archer*) ♐ 23 November–22 December
> CAPRICORN (*Goat*) ♑ 23 December–20 January
> AQUARIUS (*Water Bearer*) ♒ 21 January–19 February
> PISCES (*Fishes*) ♓ 20 February–20 March

The understanding of the signs of the zodiac in modern ASTROLOGY has its roots in the astronomy of the ancient Greeks. The marking of the seasons by some of the constellations that appear within it can be traced back further to the ancient Egyptians and early civilizations of the Middle East.

Zohar, The

The most influential text of the kabbalah, published in the 13th century.

The Zohar, or 'Book of Splendour', is the most important text of the KABBALAH. Its name derives

from the Hebrew word for splendour, radiance or illumination. Originally written in Aramaic, the language spoken by the Jews 2,000 years ago, it was published in the 13th century by a Spanish Jew called Moses de León (c.1240–1305). He claimed to have discovered the text, and attributed it to the 2nd-century rabbi Shimon bar Yohai, who was said to have escaped the Romans and hidden in a cave for 13 years, during which time he was inspired by God to write this vast work. However, a number of rabbis later held that it was written by de León himself; it was a common practice at that time to attribute authorship of a document to an ancient rabbi in order to give it more weight, and some scholars believe there are Spanish terms and even Spanish grammatical errors in the text that indicate that de León was the real author of *The Zohar*. Whatever its origins, it spread among the Jews in a remarkably short period of time, and within 50 years of its publication, it was being cited by many kabbalists; even representatives of Judaism who were not mystically orientated began to regard it as a sacred book. The concepts of what came to be known as the Classical Kabbalah were developed extensively by Spanish Hebrews in the 13th century, and were based largely on *The Zohar*, which remains the most important kabbalistic book in the Jewish tradition.

The book is a mystical commentary on the Torah, or Pentateuch, and discusses the nature of God, the origin and structure of the universe, the nature of souls and the mystical aspects of the Hebrew alphabet. It elaborates on much of the material found in the *Sepher Yetzirah* – the first kabbalistic text, a short work written sometime between the 3rd and 6th centuries – and focuses primarily on the SEPHIROTH. It is virtually impossible to understand without a great deal of training, since it does not present a clear, concise account of the creation; instead, it is highly symbolic in its language, and its lack of clarity makes it impenetrable for many people. Traditional practitioners of Judaism rarely attempt to study it because of its abstruse and esoteric nature, and even many Jewish scholars feel themselves unqualified to tackle its complexities.

zombie

More fiction than fact, zombies are said to be the mindless 'undead'.

The word 'zombie', like 'voodoo' (see VOUDUN), has two quite different meanings: the Hollywood B-movie usage, and the reality. The reality has nothing to do with the shambling hulks seen on screen, or with fearless, mindless and utterly obedient armies of the UNDEAD.

A zombie is supposedly someone who has died

and been brought back to life by arcane means, and is now a body without a mind (or a soul), completely subject to the will of his controller. But stories of encounters with real-life zombies, usually associated with voodoo, tend to fall apart on investigation.

However, in the 1980s a Canadian anthropologist and ethnobotanist, Wade Davis, claimed that people could be put into a zombie-like state by being given a drug, tetrodotoxin, found in species of fish related to the highly toxic puffer fish – a Japanese culinary delicacy when correctly prepared, but otherwise lethal. This drug apparently slows heartbeat and respiration to the extent that people are declared dead, even by doctors. The idea is that after the victim is buried, he is dug up again and partially revived, his zombie characteristics no doubt stemming from the trauma he has suffered.

This intriguing theory is often popularly stated as a factual explanation for zombies, but it has met with considerable scepticism in the scientific world.

Zugun, Eleonore (1913–late 1990s)
Romanian girl who was the focus of a biting poltergeist and believed she was possessed by the Devil.
Born in the northern Romanian village of Talpa, Eleonore Zugun became famous as the Romanian peasant girl who was the centre of attention by a so-called biting POLTERGEIST between 1925 and 1927. In 1925, Eleonore found a coin by the road when she was on her way to visit her grandmother. It was a folk belief in that area that such coins were the property of the Devil, and when her grandmother discovered that Eleonore had bought sweets with the money and eaten them she told her granddaughter that she had swallowed the Devil. That night Eleonore became the focus of poltergeist disturbances including stone throwing and object movements. These incidents were attributed to an invisible entity dubbed *Dracu*, or Devil in Romanian. Eleonore was placed first in a convent and then in some form of institution. Her case attracted attention, and she was investigated by psychical researchers including Fritz Grünwalde of Germany, who made an extensive record of the apparent poltergeist incidents surrounding her, although he died before he could complete his observations.

Another interested investigator was the Countess Zoe Wassilko-Serecki. In September 1925, she arranged for Eleonore to be taken to Vienna. In the months that followed, hundreds of strange events occurred, and it became clear that Eleonore believed

Eleonore Zugun was the focus of poltergeist disturbances and believed she was possessed by 'Dracu', the Devil. The marks on her face were said to appear when Dracu was angry. (© Mary Evans Picture Library)

she was possessed by Dracu. In 1926, the Countess published a short book on the case, *Der Spuk von Talpa*. In April of that year, Eleonore was taken to London, to be studied by Harry Price at his National Laboratory of Psychical Research. Price observed the mysterious movement of objects in Eleonore's presence, and by this stage it became apparent that if Dracu was insulted or made angry, scratches, weals and bite marks would appear on Eleonore's arms, hands and face.

Although there was some evidence that in the latter stages of the investigations Eleonore resorted to fraud, many of the incidents surrounding her remain difficult to explain. All phenomena ceased entirely on Eleonore reaching puberty and she grew to adulthood without any further repetition of the manifestations. She was traced by Harry Price after World War II and reported to be running a hairdressing salon; she lived on in Romania into her eighties and died in the late 1990s.